Exchange 2000 Server

On Site

Göran Husman

President and CEO
Roland Elgey

Publisher
Steve Sayre

Associate Publisher
Katherine R. Hartlove

Acquisitions Editor
Charlotte Carpentier

Development Editor
Jessica Choi

Product Marketing Manager
Tracy Rooney

Project Editors
Dan Young
Stephanie Palenque

Technical Reviewer
Andre Paree-Huff

Production Coordinator
Marcos Uzueta

Cover Designer
Jody Winkler

Layout Designer
April E. Nielsen

CD-ROM Developer
Chris Nusbaum

Exchange 2000 Server On Site

The Coriolis Group, LLC
14455 N. Hayden Road
Suite 220
Scottsdale, Arizona 85260
www.coriolis.com

Library of Congress Cataloging-in-Publication Data
Husman, Göran
Exchange 2000 Server On Site / by Göran Husman.
p. cm.
Includes index.
ISBN 1-57610-969-0
1. Client/server computing. 2. Microsoft Exchange server. I. Title.
QA76.9.C55 H88 2001
005.7'13769--dc21 2001042231

Printed in the United States of America
10 9 8 7 6 5 4 3 2 1

The Coriolis Group, LLC • 14455 North Hayden Road, Suite 220 • Scottsdale, Arizona 85260

A Note from Coriolis

Coriolis Technology Press was founded to create a very elite group of books: the ones you keep closest to your machine. In the real world, you have to choose the books you rely on every day *very* carefully, and we understand that.

To win a place for our books on that coveted shelf beside your PC, we guarantee several important qualities in every book we publish. These qualities are:

- *Technical accuracy*—It's no good if it doesn't work. Every Coriolis Technology Press book is reviewed by technical experts in the topic field, and is sent through several editing and proofreading passes in order to create the piece of work you now hold in your hands.
- *Innovative editorial design*—We've put years of research and refinement into the ways we present information in our books. Our books' editorial approach is uniquely designed to reflect the way people learn new technologies and search for solutions to technology problems.
- *Practical focus*—We put only pertinent information into our books and avoid any fluff. Every fact included between these two covers must serve the mission of the book as a whole.
- *Accessibility*—The information in a book is worthless unless you can find it quickly when you need it. We put a lot of effort into our indexes, and heavily cross-reference our chapters, to make it easy for you to move right to the information you need.

Here at The Coriolis Group we have been publishing and packaging books, technical journals, and training materials since 1989. We have put a lot of thought into our books; please write to us at **ctp@coriolis.com** and let us know what you think. We hope that you're happy with the book in your hands, and that in the future, when you reach for software development and networking information, you'll turn to one of our books first.

Coriolis Technology Press
The Coriolis Group
14455 N. Hayden Road
Suite 220
Scottsdale, Arizona
85260

Email: ctp@coriolis.com
Phone: (480) 483-0192
Toll free: (800) 410-0192

Look for these related books from The Coriolis Group:

Exchange 2000 .NET Black Book
by Phillip Schein, Evan Benjamin, and Cherry Beado

MCSE Exchange 2000 Design Exam Prep
by Michael Shannon and Dennis Suhanovs

MCSE Exchange 2000 Administration Exam Prep
by Phillip Schein and Evan Benjamin

MCSE Exchange 2000 Administration Exam Cram
by David Watts and Will Willis

Also published by Coriolis Technology Press:

Windows 2000 Server On Site
by Joli Ballew

Windows 2000 Professional On Site
by Erik Eckel and Brian Alderman

Active Directory On Site
by Mark Wilkins

IIS 5 On Site
by Scott Reeves and Kalinda Reeves

SQL Server 2000 On Site
by Anthony Sequeira

Windows 2000 Group Policy Little Black Book
by Sean Stecker

I dedicate this book to all my kids—you are the true joy in my life!

❧

About the Author

Göran Husman started his career as a computer programmer and administrator for a medical research institute in 1977, specializing in statistical analysis. Later, he was responsible for developing graphical editors for medical researchers. Göran has been working extensively with Unix-based workstations, such as Sun Microsystems and Apollo/HP.

Göran has been a trainer for more than 20 years and in 1993, became one of Sweden's first Microsoft Certified Trainers (MCTs); he is certified to give training in all MS Mail and MS Exchange versions, plus TCP/IP, IIS, and Active Directory.

Acknowledgments

This book is the result of my fascination with electronic messaging in general, and MS Exchange 2000 Server in particular. I truly love working with this product, and solving all of the challenges and problems that always seem to show up in a complex product like this.

First I want to thank all the great people at The Coriolis Group that helped me develop this book; a special thanks goes to Charlotte Carpentier for giving me the opportunity to write this book and for her trust in me—I will always be grateful to you. Thanks to Jessica Choi for all her encouragement and faith—it really meant a lot to me! I also want to thank my project editor, Stephanie Palenque, for her guidance and hard work through the development of the book—and a special thanks to her newborn daughter Sophia! I want to thank Dan Young for his professional support and guidance in completing this book. Finally, I want to thank Jennifer H. Mario for all her hard work proofreading my manuscripts; and to my technical reviewer, Andre Paree-Huff, for all of your tips and corrections.

This book could not have been written without some assistance; I am grateful for the Exchange 2000 tips from Paul Bowden and Johan Huss, both at Microsoft; a special thanks to my colleagues and friends for all their tips and comments: Lasse Pettersson, Jonas Borelius, Magnus Björk, and Henrik Rehnmark. I am also deeply grateful to my co-worker at Human Data, Suzan Andersson, for all her encouragement and understanding during the extremely intensive five months it took to write this book.

Finally, I want to thank my family and my wife Marina for her support and understanding during this writing period. She had a tough time, especially since she also gave birth to our lovely daughter Anna during this time; And to my daughter I want to say "Anna! Daddy is coming home at last."

—Göran Husman

Contents at a Glance

Table of Contents

Chapter 3
Routing and Monitoring in Exchange 2000 75

Chapter 4
SMTP in Exchange 2000 119

Introduction

Thanks for buying *Exchange 2000 Server On Site*! In this book you will find detailed descriptions of Microsoft Exchange 2000 Server, including MS Exchange 2000 Conferencing Server, Microsoft Chat Server, and Microsoft Instant Messaging Server. You will also find a description of the new Microsoft .NET strategy and how it relates to Exchange 2000. This book is written to give you the knowledge needed to design, implement, and troubleshoot all sizes of Exchange 2000 organizations. It also describes how to handle non-U.S. character sets, such as Swedish and French characters in SMTP addresses and object names. In this book, you will find the following features:

- Step-by-step instructions on how to install and configure each feature
- Troubleshooting tips for Exchange 2000, SMTP, and DNS
- A detailed description of how and why all features work
- The background and history of various applicable topics
- A summary at the end of each chapter, to give you a quick repetition of the most important features

Is This Book for You?

Exchange 2000 Server On Site was written with the intermediate or advanced user in mind. Among the topics covered are:

- SMTP and DNS
- Windows 2000 and Active Directory
- All features of Exchange 2000 Enterprise Server
- Exchange Conferencing Server, Chat Server, and Instant Messaging
- Designing and migrating to Exchange 2000

The new Exchange 2000 Server is very different compared to the previous Exchange versions. Even if you are an experienced Exchange 5.5 administrator today, you will need the information in this book to fully understand how to install, migrate, and design an optimized Exchange 2000 organization.

How to Use This Book

This book is written so that you can read only the chapters you are interested in. However, for the most complete understanding of Exchange 2000 and what you can do with it, I recommend that you read the entire book from start to finish. Use this book when you want to understand how Exchange 2000 works, and its dependencies on SMTP, DNS, and Windows 2000. You can also use this book as a guide on how to install every feature of Exchange 2000, including optional parts such as the Chat Server, Instant Messaging Server, and MS Exchange Conferencing Server. The information in this book is built on real-life experiences with Exchange 2000.

The *On Site* Philosophy

Written by experienced professionals, books in The Coriolis Group's *On Site* series guide you through typical, day-to-day needs assessment, planning, deployment, configuration, and troubleshooting challenges. The *On Site* series uses real-world scenarios and indispensable illustrations to help you move flawlessly through system setup and any problems you may encounter along the way. The illustrations, including concise flowcharts with clear and logical steps, help professionals diagnose problems and assess needs to reduce total cost of ownership.

I welcome your feedback on this book. You can either email The Coriolis Group at **ctp@coriolis.com** or email me directly at **goran@humandata.se**. Errata, updates, and more are available at **www.humandata.se**.

Chapter 1

Introduction to MS Exchange 2000

Email has a relatively long and interesting history. The first mail systems were restricted to local use, allowing you to send messages only to other people on the same server. When Ray Tomlison developed the first email program in 1971, it could send mail between servers on a network. A year later, he modified the program so it could be used on the ARPANET (the predecessor of the Internet) and also decided that email addresses should use the @ sign. This version of the program quickly became a big hit, and in 1973 about 75 percent of all ARPANET traffic was made up of email. When Steve Walker created the first mailing list in 1975, the email community quickly adopted it, the most popular unofficial mailing list being Science Fiction (SF)-Lovers. It had caught on so well that soon after, in 1976, even Queen Elizabeth II sent out her first email message. And in 1979 a guy named Kevin MacKenzie changed email as we knew it, introducing the concept of "smileys" to express emotions in email. :-)

I remember when I got my first email account in 1982. It was a Unix-based program, and the instructions I got were brief: "Start the mail program; type l to get a list of all mail and r for reply...well, you can probably guess the rest. Good luck!" I spent the rest of that day using the Unix help system, called man, until I finally got the information that I needed in order to use the mail system. An amazing world had opened up for me; I could send messages to my colleagues next door, to other people in the university (I was working as a computer programmer at the Karolinska Institute, a medical school, in Stockholm), and even to people at other Swedish universities. But the real kick came when I found out that I could send mail to people all over the world. I remember when I read a book, found an error, and sent a message to the writer—he replied to me within 3 hours. At that moment I understood that email would forever change the way people communicated.

However, it took much longer for organizations and companies outside the university setting to adopt email. At the end of the 1980s, only a few companies in the "real world" had installed mail systems that could actually send email outside the organization. And most of those that had mail systems used the systems for internal use and keeping contact with friends, rather than for business needs. Most email products of that time were built upon proprietary techniques—there were simply no standards that the computer business had accepted at that time, not even any de facto standards. And that meant that it was hard or impossible to exchange mail between different mail systems. So mail was used mostly for internal matters. If you really needed to send mail to other mail systems, you needed a gateway program, a translator between different mail systems that was expensive and hard to administer. Only if you were lucky could you send attachments between the mail systems. And since most email products were from U.S. vendors, they seldom could cope with the national characters that most European countries had—I remember computer nerds in Sweden strongly arguing that it would be simpler if we could just skip all the extra characters instead of trying to make the programs handle them.

Today it may seem strange that no standard seemed to exist, but let's be honest. There actually was a mail standard—the X.400 E-mail standard, released in 1984 and developed by the CCITT standard committee, was basically controlled by a bunch of European telecommunication companies. Their standard was complex and hard to implement, built to run on the network transport protocols TP4 and TP0 (X.25). And at this time the United States couldn't have cared less about it. A European email standard? Ha! Not invented here? Sorry, guys! Most U.S. universities at that time were using an email protocol called Simple Mail Transfer Protocol, or SMTP. It was developed for the Unix environment in 1982 by Jonathan Postel (RFC821) and David Crocker (RFC822), and it was based on the TCP/IP protocol. In fact, most of the universities in Europe also used the SMTP protocol. But a majority of the corporations that were using any PC LAN at all were using Novell or possibly IBM's DOS-based PC Network, and none of them were based on TCP/IP. So SMTP was never really a choice for them.

Note: *ITU, International TeleUnion, founded in 1865, is one of the United Nation's special groups and one of the oldest international organizations. One of the most well-known ITU suborganizations is CCITT—"Comité Consultatif International Télegraphique et Télephonique," usually translated as "International Telegraph and Telephone Consultative Committee." It publishes a number of "recommendations" that are in fact standards. Some of the most well-known standards are X.400 and X.500. In 1993, CCITT was renamed ITU-TS, Telecommunication Standardization.*

Microsoft's Email History

Microsoft didn't have its own email product, so in 1988 it bought a product called Courier Mail and renamed it MS Mail. Microsoft worked to develop the MS Mail product and was surprisingly successful with it. It was really meant for organizations up to maybe a few thousand users, but several large companies ended up using MS Mail; I remember one company with 60,000 clients. You can still find MS Mail installations running today.

MS Exchange Server Is Born

Soon more and more organizations started to treat email as important or even critical to their operations. They wanted more than MS Mail could deliver, like being able to send mail attachments to other mail systems, handle national characters correctly, and send SMTP mail. So in 1991, Microsoft started to develop the next generation of email, a very ambitious project first called "Touchdown" and later renamed "Hermes." It needed to be built on standards, it needed to be able to communicate with other email systems, and it needed to be suitable even for very large organizations. The project was to be completed in about one year. But it would be delayed. Much more delayed. In fact, its first release wasn't until March of 1996. One of the reasons that this project was so delayed was because of a competing product called Lotus Notes, which not only handled email but also had lots of features for sharing information between groups. Microsoft wanted to have a competing product—not only did Touchdown need to be the best email system ever seen, it also needed to be able to share all sorts of information between users, like calendars, addresses, and any type of files. And that took time. Lots of time.

Microsoft built its new product on the X.400 email standard. Why? Well, for several reasons. For one thing, corporate America was not using TCP/IP networks to any extent at that time. SMTP was really nothing more than a research project. And the U.S. government had decided that email programs should be based on X.400. So Microsoft did the only right thing. At least that's what they and all others believed at that time. But there was one disturbing cloud in the then sunny sky. In 1995, the Internet was exploding. Everyone wanted to start surfing the World Wide Web, every organization wanted to have its own Web site, and it turned out that everyone (except Novell sites) had started to use TCP/IP. Now SMTP quickly became the Esperanto of the email world, while at the same time, interest in X.400 quickly decreased. So when the new MS Exchange 4 was released, it was based on an email standard that no one wanted. Too bad. Microsoft, though, quickly adapted by adding an SMTP gateway to Exchange called the Internet Mail Connector, which made the new program fully SMTP-enabled. And most of the X.400 features were so well hidden behind nice graphical interfaces and wizards that sometimes Exchange administrators did not even know that it was based on X.400.

Have you ever wondered why the first release was 4 and not 1? Well, Microsoft made the decision to simply continue the release number from the last MS Mail version, 3.5. And the marketing people at Microsoft probably thought that customers would be more receptive to a 4 version than they would be to a 1 version. To be fair, though, not just Microsoft has tried this trick; others in the Internet world have done it, too. The new Internet mail client protocol IMAP, for example, got version number 4 because it replaced the old POP 3 protocol.

New Features—And New Drawbacks

In November of 1997, Microsoft released MS Exchange Server 5. Some of its most interesting new features were that the SMTP was much better integrated than before, and for the first time it was possible to use a Web browser to read your mail, calendar, contacts, and more. It was great news for people on the move; if they could just find a browser, even a Netscape browser, they could read their mail and check their calendar. But it was painfully slow. In 1998, Exchange 5.5 was released; it was faster, more stable, and had a database for storing mail that could now be as large as 16TB, as compared to the 16GB of space in Exchange 5. Companies, though, had to make sure they purchased the Exchange

5.5 Enterprise version rather than the Standard version, which was still limited to 16GB. But the increase meant that you could now run thousands of users on the same Exchange server without hitting the limit. This was very good because Exchange Server, built on the principle of "single instance store," would only have to store a message going to 25 people belonging to the same server once.

But there was a drawback, too. This new database with greater capacity would take time to back up. And it would be even harder to restore—because Exchange Server stored all its users' mail in one database, you simply could not do a restore of a single mailbox or message; you had to restore the entire database. This posed a problem because you more than likely did not want to restore a complete database just because you needed to restore a single message, especially when to do this, you needed a spare server. This, obviously, took time. And if you had not done this before, it probably took even more time. But several vendors of backup programs did find a way to back up each mailbox separately. "Brick-level backups," as they were called because they treated each mailbox as a separate object, managed to solve the problem for small organizations but unfortunately, not for large organizations. It simply took too long to first take a normal backup of the database and then do a brick-level backup. The problems that came with having a large database, as a result, were usually avoided by simply installing a new Exchange server and moving some mailboxes to that server.

The Goal with MS Exchange 2000

Microsoft had lots of goals for its new version of Exchange. It needed to solve the problems of large databases. It needed to be faster and have more features. It needed to be suitable not only for small organizations with just a few users, but also very large organizations with hundreds of thousands of users. And it needed to be based on the only email standard left, the SMTP standard. But also important, it needed to be able to communicate seamlessly with all old X.400-based Exchange systems and be built to run on MS Windows 2000 Server, with its Active Directory, which was new at the time.

Additionally, customers demanded that it be easier to develop third-party programs that utilized Exchange as a transport vehicle and a storage mechanism, i.e., document handling systems, help desk systems, and groupware applications. And Microsoft wanted to create a "Notes Killer," a new version of Exchange, fully Internet and Web aware, that would outperform Lotus Notes in every way. It also needed to be able to use the new clustering features of the Windows 2000 Server family. With all that, you can see that this was indeed not an easy task for the Exchange team. And again, it took much more time than originally planned.

The Project Platinum

Microsoft called the new version Platinum. The Platinum team was large, at one point about 600 people. One of the great challenges for the team involved working with the new Active Directory in Windows 2000 Server instead of the old built-in directory from

Exchange 5.5. And since the Platinum team had developed its code at the same time that the Windows 2000 team had developed its code, this was an even greater task than you first may think. Every night, the Windows 2000 team rebuilt its code, so the Platinum team decided to stay with certain builds of Windows 2000 in order to have a chance to test its builds. And for a long time, you needed a special build of Windows 2000 in order to run a special build of Platinum. But in April of 2000, Microsoft finally released Beta 3 of Platinum to the public, made to run on the newly released Windows 2000 Server.

Part of the Platinum team came from the MCIS group and from people working with the Web-based mail system, Hotmail. Its task was to give input on how to run mail systems with millions of users. MCIS, or MS Commercial Internet Service, is Microsoft's POP3/IMAP4-based email system, targeting the ISP market. The Hotmail system is a specially developed Unix-based application. One unofficial goal for Platinum was to replace the Unix application, something previously unthinkable with the old Exchange architecture, but hopefully achievable this time around. I believe that the whole idea behind Microsoft's purchase of Hotmail in 1997 was to get the experience it needed in order to design a mail system capable of scaling to millions of users. As of today, Hotmail has over 60 million users and adds more than 150,000 new users every day.

The Goals for Platinum

Since MS Exchange 5.5 has more than 50 million clients installed, with several hundred thousand servers, one extremely important goal for Platinum was to be able to coexist and upgrade from previous Exchange versions. Due to the technical differences in previous versions, the team decided that the only version that Platinum could coexist with and be upgraded from was Exchange 5.5 with Service Pack 3 or later.

The Exchange 5.5 version came with lots of connectors, or gateways, that made it possible to communicate with many other email systems. Platinum also needed to be able to communicate with them. But since customer interest in some of them was low, especially in mainframe computer based email systems, the Platinum team decided not to implement connectors to them. That is why you will not find Exchange 2000 connectors to SNADS and PROFS; if you really need these, you should keep an Exchange 5.5 server with this connector in your site. Table 1.1 shows a list of the most important goals of Platinum.

Table 1.1 Some important goals of Platinum.

Goal	Description
SMTP-based	Change the architecture from X.400-based to SMTP-based and get rid of the Remote Procedure Call (RPC) traffic
Smarter routing	Overcome the problems with the MTA routing that sometimes could result in looping mail
More stable and intelligent	Make it full of new and enhanced features but make it rock solid
Easier to program	Make it easier to build groupware applications
Web centric	Make every possible feature accessible from Web clients

(continued)

Table 1.1 Some important goals of Platinum *(continued)*.

Goal	Description
Web store	Make the Exchange information reachable, even from the ordinary file system
Scalable	Make it possible to have more than 10,000 users on one server without getting into serious problems due to a large database
Killer application	Make Platinum the killer application for Windows 2000
Cluster support	Make Platinum run on the advanced cluster techniques that are available in the Windows 2000 Server family
Active Directory	Make Platinum integrated with the Active Directory in Windows 2000

Normally, when a software program is being developed, a team sits by itself and thinks hard about what features should be included. The Platinum team, however, took a different approach, instead involving key customers during very early stages of development, explaining to them what it planned to do. The customer's input from those many sessions, in turn, helped the team make decisions about what to do and how to do it.

Eating Your Own Dog Food

Microsoft has a policy that is usually referred to as "Eating your own dog food." That means that you use your own products in your daily work, even in very early stages of the program. This was true for Windows 2000 and certainly also for Platinum. The best way to quickly discover any bugs or strange behavior, Microsoft believes, is to run it in a production environment. So most Microsoft employees were using all the Platinum Beta versions, and every week there was a new Platinum version built with new and interesting bugs to discover. You can imagine that it must have been hard sometimes to work under such conditions. As the Release Manager for Exchange, Larry LeSueur once said: "Some weeks it's wonderful and we feel like we're close to RTMing the product. Other weeks it doesn't go quite as well, and we realize we still have a lot of work ahead of us before we're ready to sign off."

***Note:** Microsoft has different release levels for its software products. First is the Alfa release, only for internal use. When it becomes reasonably stable, it enters the Beta level. At this point, it is released to selected key customers for evaluation and testing. In this level, the product has all the features that the development team has planned for. Not all features will make it to the final product, due to technical problems or marketing decisions. When the product is almost done, it enters the RC, or Release Candidate, level. It is normal to have two or three RC versions. This is the time for "feature stripping," to remove features that will not be in the final product. And finally, the program enters the RTM, Release to Manufacturing, level. This is the version that will be distributed to all customers.*

Versions of Exchange 2000

Finally, in October of 2000, Microsoft released the Exchange 2000 Server family. Table 1.2 below summarizes the most important differences between the versions, followed by a more detailed description of each.

Exchange 2000 Server

This is the basic version of Exchange 2000. It has most of the features that a small organization would need, like full SMTP connectivity, support for all Outlook and Outlook Web Access clients, the Web Store, integration with Windows 2000 Active Directory, and the Microsoft Management Console (MMC) administrative tools. It is limited in the number of connectors that are included, so, for example, the Lotus Notes Connector is not included. It also can't be used in front-end/back-end scenarios and is limited in the number of stores, i.e., the databases, and the maximum size of each store. This version allows only one PRIV store, but up to four PUB stores. Each store can be a max of 16GB. This means that if you have 1,000 users on one server, they would each only be allowed to have a 16MB mailbox. This book will describe features and properties beyond what's included in this basic Exchange version.

Exchange 2000 Enterprise Server

This is the full product. It has all the features you'll see described in this book with all connectors available from Microsoft for Exchange 2000 included. You can have up to four storage groups, with up to five stores each. Every store is practically unlimited; the max size is 16TB, a thousand times larger than 16GB, so you can build one server with up to $4 \times 5 \times 16$TB = 320TB. You can also build extremely large Exchange organizations by utilizing the new front-end/back-end server features. This is the first Exchange version that can utilize Windows 2000's new active-active clustering technique. You will learn more about this later in Chapter 2.

Table 1.2 Differences between Exchange 2000 versions.

Version	Equivalent to	Description
Exchange 2000 Server	Exchange 5.5 Standard	Full SMTP functionality, but limited to one PRIV database with max 16GB. Targeted at single-server installations.
Exchange 2000 Enterprise Server	Exchange 5.5 Enterprise	All the features in Exchange 2000 Server, but with up to four storage groups of up to five stores each and max 16TB per store. Full connectivity to most other popular mail systems.
Exchange 2000 Conferencing Server	No equivalent	An add-on to any Exchange 2000 version. Adds functionality to do data, audio, and video conferencing in realtime.

Exchange 2000 Conferencing Server

This is not a complete Exchange Server. In order to use its functionality, you will need any of the previous versions installed in your Exchange 2000 environment, but not necessarily on the same machine. With this, you can add functionality for data, voice, and video conferencing in realtime. You have a simple form of conferencing already today with the NetMeeting client, but that is limited to peer-to-peer communication. With the Exchange 2000 Conferencing Server, you can organize a meeting by inviting attendees with Outlook calendars and control exactly what they can do. You can distribute audio and video streams with the TCP/IP's Multicast technique and make sure it will look good for the recipient by using Quality of Service settings. So this version really makes it possible to use the network for conferencing without disturbing other network traffic. For example, you can send your new video file to 150 recipients simultaneously, or just send an audio file. You could demonstrate a new program for all recipients, or share an electronic white board. There are many possibilities. Microsoft likes to call this feature "Meetings without walls," which is indeed accurate.

New Features in Exchange 2000

Many new features in Exchange 2000 make it faster, more resilient, and easier to manage. Both small and very large organizations will find enhancements that will make their use of email easier and more reliable. The next section will describe some of them, but they all will be covered in detail in the following chapters.

Enhanced Messaging and Collaboration

The new SMTP-based Exchange 2000 Server is not just a simple upgrade from the previous Exchange 5.5 version. Most of the code is rewritten and optimized in order to increase the overall speed and stability. Most of the features from Exchange 5.5 are still there, but some have changed radically. For example, the new routing engine in Exchange 2000 is now much smarter, and actually very similar to the way intelligent routers talk to each other. If a message link goes down, this information will be propagated to all Exchange 2000 servers in the organization, even if it is a far away link, and Exchange 2000 will not try to send messages over that link. In Exchange 5.5, every server had to discover broken links by itself, and there was no way to learn about link problems in remote sites, so in some situations you could end up with lots of messages looping between sites.

It was hard to develop programs that could utilize the Exchange 5.x transport and storage. True, you could add programs that did things with messages as they arrived in a mailbox folder or public folder, but not while they were being transported inside Exchange. That is one reason Microsoft had to release a special Anti Virus-API, AVAPI, to give antivirus programs a way of catching viruses during the transport before they landed in a user's mailbox. All this is now history. The new Exchange 2000 is much easier to use for the developer. Now you have lots of places inside the transport and routing engines where your program can hook in and interact with the messages. This will probably give rise to a number of new applications, like smarter antivirus programs, programs that check whether messages follow the company's mail policies, and of course document management programs, help desk programs, and more. It will be very interesting to see all the applications built for Exchange 2000 one year from its release.

The Web Store

Exchange has always had the possibility to store any kind of file in its databases—for example, Word files, AVI movies, and MP3 music; it is not merely limited to messages, contacts, or calendar appointments. But the only way to access those files was through a mail client, like Outlook. Let's say you stored a Word document in a public folder. That meant that this file was now protected by the transaction log system in Exchange. You could then access this file with the Outlook Web Access client wherever you were in the world. That was a good thing. The bad thing was that you could not open the file with Word's File|Open command; you had to open the file from the Outlook client, and since it was a DOC file, it would automatically open the Word program. That was a slow and clumsy way to go about it.

Windows 2000 has a feature called IFS, installable file systems. With IFS, you can read and write to whatever the file system is connected to. When you install Exchange 2000 Server, you will also get the ExIFS, Exchange Installable File System installed. With this, you can read and write to the Exchange stores directly from a DOS prompt or the File Explorer. Just use the standard File|Open command in Word or any other program to access the Exchange Server's stores, like with any normal file system. Of course, all the access controls are still in place; you can only access those parts of Exchange that you can also access with your normal Outlook client. Even if you have 10 different stores on one Exchange server, it will still look like one file system. It is the ExIFS that does this trick. Nice, isn't it? Microsoft calls this new feature the Web Store.

The Storage Group

One of the problems with earlier versions of Exchange was that each server was limited to one database, the Priv.edb file, for all users, and another database, the Pub.edb, for public folder data. Depending on what version of Exchange you had, they were limited to 16GB or 16TB each. Having just one database made it possible to use the single-store feature (i.e., one message to 15 people was only stored once). It was also possible to make the system more fail-proof by using an advanced transaction log system, previously only seen in large database applications in mini and mainframe computers. But the bad thing with all this was:

- To restore a singe item, like a mailbox or a message, you needed to restore the complete database. That meant that you needed a spare server since you didn't want to overwrite the production server's database.
- Since all mailboxes were stored in one database, this would grow to the point where you had problems making backups, forcing you, therefore, to install a new server and move some users to the original one.

- You had to treat all mailbox users alike. In some situations, you may have wanted to have different service level agreements (SLAs) affecting, for instance, the time it takes to do a restore of data. Your management may have demanded an SLA of four hours, but the normal users accepted eight hours. To solve this, you had to put these two groups on two different servers.

In Exchange 2000 Enterprise Server, on the other hand, you can have up to four different storage groups, each with up to five stores and each store with a limit of 16TB. One such store is almost the same as an Exchange 5.5 database and may be either a mailbox store or a public store. For example, let's say you need to solve the different SLA needs described in the previous bullet; instead of having to use two computers, you can now use two different priv stores, one for the management and one for the normal users. So, some of the good things involved with this are:

- To avoid the problem of having your databases grow to a point where it is hard to do backups and restores, you can simply create new stores as you need them. Remember that you can have up to 20 stores total in one server.
- Small stores are faster to back up and easier to restore.
- If one store crashes, it does not have any effect on the others. They can each continue to run without any problem.
- You can do a restore of one store without stopping the whole Exchange server. The others will still be able to run, and those users won't be affected.

Please note that only the Exchange 2000 Enterprise Server has this feature built-in. With the Exchange 2000 Server, you will only be able to use one storage group with one mailbox store limited to 16GB, making this version equivalent to the previous Exchange 5.5 Standard Edition.

Warning! *If you have done a test installation with the evaluation version of Exchange 2000 and then decide to upgrade this to the full Exchange 2000 Server product, you will have a problem. Since the evaluation version is based on the Exchange 2000 Enterprise Server version, you cannot demote it to the Exchange 2000 Server version. You must remove the evaluation version before installing Exchange 2000 Server.*

Indexing Your Databases

Previous Exchange versions did not have any intelligent indexing, which meant that if you wanted to search your mailbox or a public folder for a particular item, it could take a long time. The search feature in Exchange 5.5 and earlier versions simply opened every item to look for whatever you were searching for. I have a public folder with more than 10,000 messages; if I had to search that folder for a message containing a certain word, it would take at least 5 minutes to complete. And if you were to do this regularly, then it could, of course, get very annoying.

Exchange 2000 (both versions) has a built-in index engine called MS Search. It's not activated by default, since the index file will be large, about 10 to 30 percent of the data you are indexing. When this index is activated, you will be able to search for words and certain attributes, like a sender's name, in both messages and their attachments; regardless of how large the store is, you will have an answer within a few seconds. If it's not activated, you will have the same linear text searching as in previous Exchange versions.

New Things to Expect

Due to the new features and architecture in Exchange 2000, as compared to previous versions, you must be prepared to think differently than before. Even if you were an Exchange 5.5 expert, you will have lots of things to learn. Many features are the same but they are handled differently, which means that you install and administrate them completely differently. I strongly recommend that before installing your first Exchange 2000 Server in a production environment, you do at least two test installations in a separate Windows 2000 forest that mirrors your upcoming production system. You should also read one or two books about Exchange 2000 and Windows 2000, and if possible attend the Microsoft TechEd Conference or the MS Exchange Conference, both running once a year.

The reason I stress this so much is that in previous versions of Exchange, you could install a test server, play with it, and then simply uninstall it if you did not want to keep it. But since Exchange 2000 is built on Windows 2000 and its Active Directory, you simply cannot do this anymore. If you add a test server to your Windows 2000 production domain now, you will update the schema on all Windows 2000 domain controllers. And if you uninstall your Exchange 2000 test server, the AD will still remember many Exchange configurations, such as the name of the Exchange organization and administrative groups. You could remove these names by using the ADSI Edit utility, but the updates to the AD schema will be impossible to remove unless you first reinstall all domain controllers.

Tip: *If you need to remove Exchange 2000 completely from a Windows 2000 domain, follow the instructions in this MS Knowledge Base article: Q27 3478, "How to Completely Remove Exchange 2000 from Active Directory." This article suggests that you use the LDP utility—I recommend you use the ADSI Edit utility instead, since it is easier to work with. You will find this utility in the Windows 2000 Tools on the Windows 2000 Server CD. Run \support\tools\setup.exe to install it.*

All Windows 2000 domain controllers replicate the Active Directory schema between them. This is true even between AD domains that belong to the same Windows 2000 forest. That means that you can have only one Exchange 2000 organization per forest. That is completely different from previous Exchange versions. Then it was perfectly acceptable to have two or more Exchange organizations even in the same Windows NT 4 domain. So you should realize that before you can install your first Exchange 2000 Server now, you should have at least a fair amount of knowledge about Windows 2000 and Active Directory, even if it's just one single Exchange server.

Changes in the Site Concept

In Exchange 5.5 and earlier, you designed your Exchange environment based on two things:

- How good a network connection you had between your upcoming Exchange servers
- How the administration should be controlled

All servers belonging to the same site needed to have at least 64kbps of free bandwidth. To administer a particular server, you needed administrative rights to the complete site, even if there were five servers in that site. That meant that you could administrate all five servers, not just the single one you wanted. If that was unacceptable, you had to divide your site in two. I have designed many Exchange 5.5 organizations, and this was always a problem for large corporations. You had to strike a balance between the technical side (considering what network speed you were working on and trying to keep down the number of sites) and the administrative side (making the site contain only servers that the administrator should be able to configure). It usually ended with a compromise. In Figure 1.1, you see two Exchange sites with two Exchange 5.5 servers each. The design was based on technical reasons, so the administration had to be separated even though the company really wanted to have only one enterprise-wide administrator.

In Exchange 2000, you do not have to worry about that anymore. The old site concept has been divided into two new groups:

- the routing group
- the administrative group

A routing group is equivalent to the old site concept regarding the network connectivity. Exchange 2000 servers belonging to the same routing group are expected to have a permanent and reliable network connectivity between them, with at least 32kbps of available bandwidth. In the old site concept, all servers were using RPC to communicate with each other, whereas in a routing group, SMTP is used instead. It is faster and more tolerant to bad network connections.

All permissions are now stored in the Active Directory. That means that you can now create a group of servers and define who will have administrative rights to this group, regardless of what routing group they belong to. This group is called the Administrative Group.

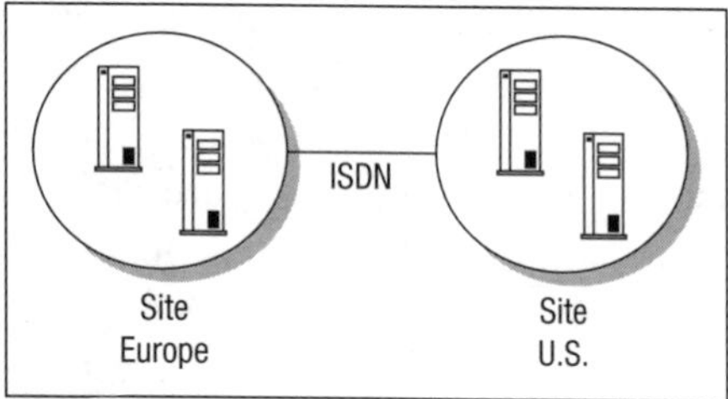

Figure 1.1
The Exchange 5.5 site.

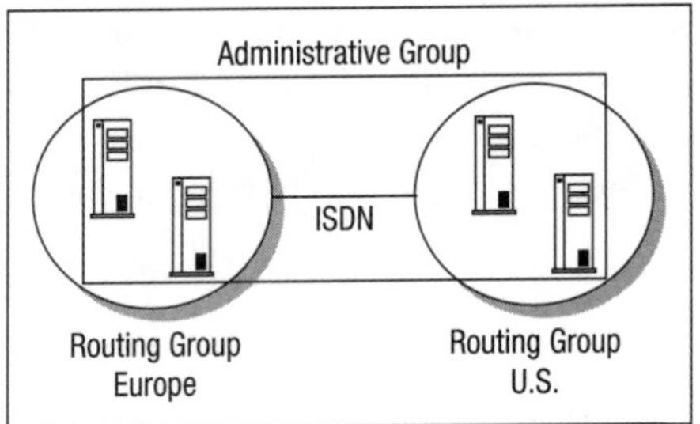

Figure 1.2
Routing groups and administrative groups in Exchange 2000.

If you were to have two routing groups with three servers each and needed to move one of the servers to another routing group, the task is easy—just drag the computer to the other routing group, regardless of what administrative group it belongs to. In Figure 1.2, you see the same environment from Figure 1.1 but this time built on Exchange 2000. There are two routing groups, designated by the ovals, due to the slow ISDN link between Europe and the United States. In Exchange 2000, we can define an administrative group, designated by the square, regardless of the communication links, so now we can have one enterprise-wide administrator, managing both of these two routing groups.

These two new concepts give you freedom to design your Exchange 2000 organization based on both technical decisions and administrative need without dependencies between them. And although it is, therefore, much easier to design the organization now, you must be prepared to think differently, and that can be harder than you had first believed. It takes a while to get used to your new freedom, but it is worth it.

Note: *Please observe that these new features are only possible when you are running Exchange 2000 in native mode. When you first install Exchange 2000, it will be in mixed mode. This makes Exchange 2000 treat the administrative group and routing group exactly as an old site. The reason for this is that otherwise you cannot connect the Exchange 2000 server with an Exchange 5.5 site. When you are absolutely sure you will use only Exchange 2000, you can switch to native mode—but then you can never change back to mixed mode again.*

New Routing Connectors

Previously, you used the Site Connector or X.400 Connector to enable traffic between two Exchange sites. Both of them are based on the X.400 protocol and are actually a special configuration of the MTA service in Exchange. Since Exchange 2000 is SMTP based, they are not as interesting anymore. A new connector called the Routing Group Connector is based on SMTP. It has the best of all features from the old Site Connector and X.400 Connector. For example, now you can set up a limit for the maximum size that will be transported, declare that mail over a certain size should be transported during the night, and also say how often the Routing Group Connector will connect to the other site.

The Site Connector is now gone, but the X.400 Connector is still there. Its main purpose is to be able to communicate to external X.400-based mail systems and to Exchange 5.5 systems using the X.400 Connector. This version of the X.400 Connector has one change; it is not able to use the TP4 protocol anymore (who would miss it?); instead, you have the possibility of using the RAS protocol.

New Administrative Tools

In previous versions of Exchange, you used the Exchange Administrative program to do almost everything from managing your mailbox users to configuring your Exchange servers. Now this has changed. Not only has the Exchange Administrative program been replaced by the Microsoft Management Console (MMC); you must now use several administrative programs (or MMC snap-ins) to do what you did before. Below are the two tools that you will work with most of the time as an Exchange administrator, the AD Users and Computers tool (shown in Figure 1.3) and the Exchange System Manager (shown in Figure 1.4).

Exchange 5.5 and earlier versions had their own directory, the Dir.edb database, where all mailbox accounts, address lists, and server configurations were stored. Each mailbox account in Exchange was connected to a Windows NT account, so if you had to create a new user, you would do two things:

- Create an NT account with User Manager for Domains
- Create a mailbox account with the Exchange Administrative program

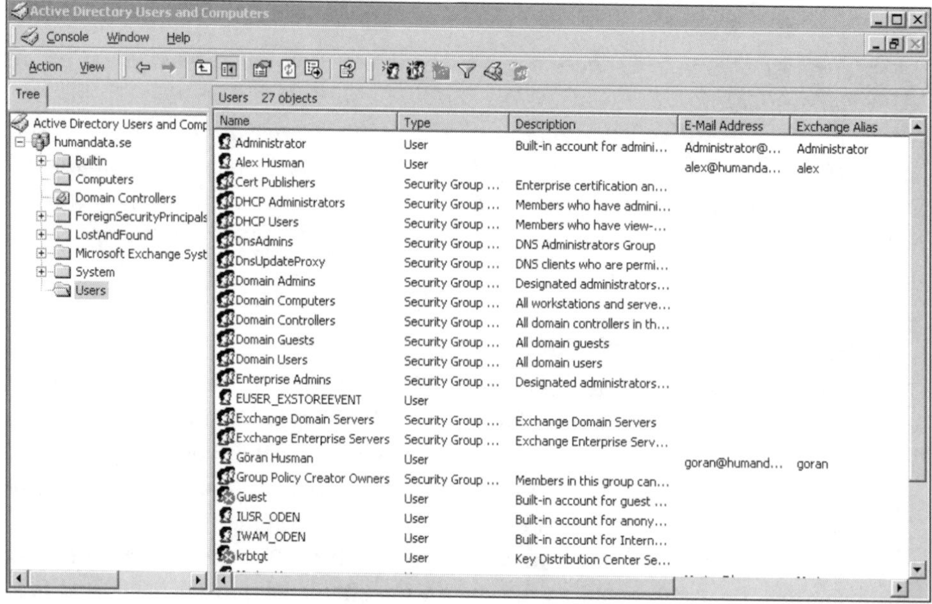

Figure 1.3
The AD Users and Computers tool.

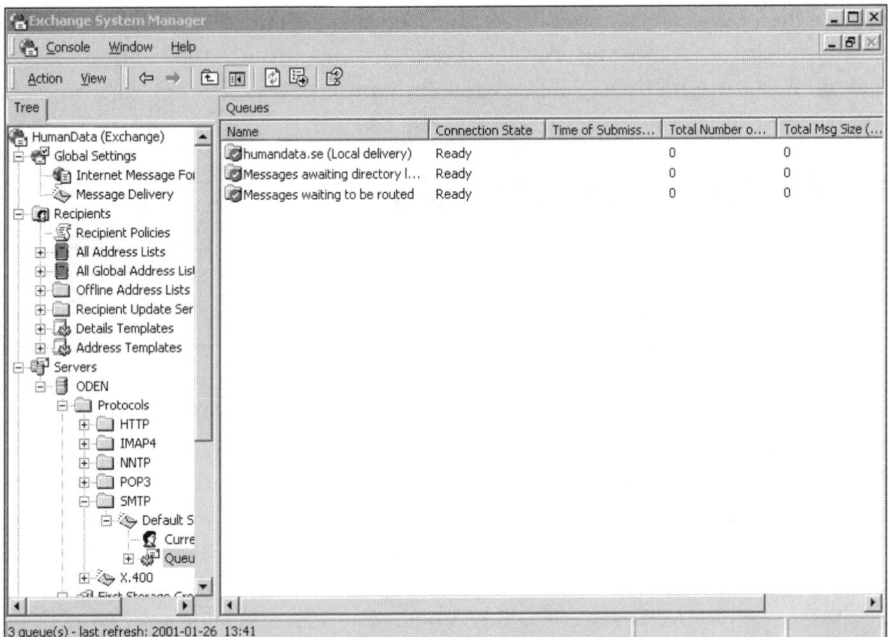

Figure 1.4
The Exchange System Manager.

Windows 2000 has taken the 5.5 directory, expanded it to handle all sorts of objects, like user accounts and server configurations, and calls this the Active Directory. Since Exchange 2000 does not have its own directory anymore, it relies completely on the Active Directory in Windows 2000. This has several consequences:

- You must now use the AD Users and Computers utility in Windows 2000 in order to configure all properties of users' accounts, including properties related to Exchange, like email addresses and mailbox limits.
- Exchange 2000 does not store any address lists anymore. It needs access to a Windows 2000 domain controller and its AD database to see all address lists and server configurations, etc.
- Each Exchange 2000 server does not have to keep a local directory anymore; this decreases the load on the server since no directory replication is necessary.

You have a new administrative tool for configuring the Exchange 2000 server, the Exchange System Manager (ESM). With this, you do almost the same things as the old Admin.exe program, except mailbox management. Beware though, because many features that you are used to configuring in previous Exchange versions have now been moved or must be accessed in a different way. This is especially true for SMTP-related tasks that were previously found in the Internet Mail Service; these configuration settings have now been spread out on several objects. For example, to define a mail domain that you accept as in-bound, you use the Recipient Policies object, and to look at the queues, you use the virtual SMTP server under the Protocol container. Be prepared to take some time and learn what all objects are used for. Remember that it took you some time to find your way around the old Exchange Admin program, so now you have to make a similar journey in order to familiarize yourself again.

The Site Service Account Is Gone

If you have ever worked as an administrator for an Exchange 5.5 system, then you are aware of the special NT user account, the Exchange Site Server account. This account was the owner of all Exchange services, and was also used for validation in RPC communication between servers in a site. The password of this account was stored both in the local Exchange directory and in the NT account database. All servers in a site shared the same Site Service account; the recommendation from Microsoft was to create a separate account for this, but many inexperienced administrators used the default suggestion, usually the Administrator account used during the installation of the first server in the site. The reason why Exchange 5.5 did not use the system account was simply because there was no replication of account information between the NT account database and the Exchange directory; since Windows NT automatically changes the system account password every 14 days, it would give Exchange an invalid password error whenever it tried to use this account because it wouldn't know about this new password.

In Exchange 2000, you won't run into that problem, since all accounts are stored in the AD. Exchange 2000 can now use the local system account, so there is no need for a special Site Service account any more.

***Tip:** When you install your first Exchange 2000 server, you will be asked about the administrator account—do not misinterpret this as the Site Service account; the installation program simply asks you who the first Exchange 2000 Administrator should be. The only time you will use a Site Service account in Exchange 2000 is when you have a mixture of Exchange 2000 and Exchange 5.5 belonging to the same site.*

New Dependency on DNS

As a result of the switch from X.400 to SMTP architecture and Exchange 2000's use of the AD, we are now completely dependent on the DNS system. I know of many Exchange 5.5 administrators who have little or no knowledge of DNS, but now must get at least a basic level of understanding in order to install and administer Exchange 2000. An excellent resource to refer to for help is the book *DNS and BIND*, by Paul Albitz and Cricket Liu.

DNS, or the Domain Naming Service, was first described in RFC 882 and 883 and was released in 1984. It was then updated in RFC 1034 and 1035; this is the version that has been used ever since. DNS normally stores information about names and their corresponding 32-bit IP numbers in an ordinary file that is manually updated whenever a change occurs. For example, you store the name of your network server and traditional Internet services like www, FTP, and mail service in the DNS. The Active Directory in Windows 2000 Server uses the DNS server to store information about Windows 2000 specific services, like what servers operate as domain controllers (for logon purposes, etc.), global catalogs (storing the global address list, etc.), and ldap servers. These are new types of DNS services, called service records (SRV); such service records have names beginning with an under-score, like "_gc" or "_ldap."

But this was problematic because many previous DNS versions did not accept names beginning with an underscore, as first described in RFC 2052. Another problem was that these service records had to be added whenever a new server was connected to the network. And each domain controller in a Windows 2000 domain needed to register a number of service records. It was simply impractical to update the DNS manually, so a new RFC that described a DNS that could be dynamically updated was needed. In 1997, RFC 2136 was released, describing exactly this. The DNS server included in Windows 2000 (see Figure 1.5) is based on both RFC 2136 and 2052, but this DNS server is not the only version that has support for these RFCs; others exist too. The most used DNS implementation in Internet history is called BIND (Berkeley Internet Name Domain). Versions 8.2.1 and later of BIND have support for RFC 2136 and 2052.

For Exchange 2000, I recommend you use the DNS server that is built into Windows 2000 Server. This information can be stored in the AD and will be replicated to all other domain controllers. If your DNS is not working properly, you will have all sorts of problems, like clients who are unable to see the address list, Exchange servers that can't route mail, or an AD service that may complain about RPC problems when it tries to replicate with other domain controllers.

Tip: *Every time Windows 2000 Netlogon service is restarted on a domain server, it will register itself and its resource records in the DNS. If you suspect that your DNS server is not updated regarding the resource records, like if your clients don't see an updated global address list, you can try to restart the Netlogon service on the domain controller.*

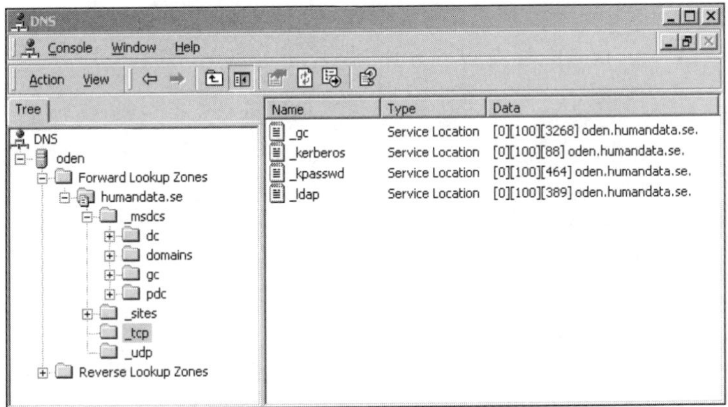

Figure 1.5
The DNS in Windows 2000.

Some people tell me that for whatever reason, they can't replace their existing DNS servers, most often Unix-based BIND versions. My advice to them is that it is no problem to keep their servers as they are, as long as people make sure that they also use the DNS in Windows 2000 for AD and Exchange 2000 registrations. If this happens to you, don't switch completely to an external DNS outside Windows 2000 without first doing a lot of testing.

Changes in Security

In previous versions of Exchange, you had RPC traffic between the client and the Exchange server, and also between servers within one site. This RPC traffic was default encrypted between servers, but not between the client and server. Should you need to, you can configure your Outlook client to use encrypted RPC by applying the following steps (see Figure 1.6):

1. Select the Outlook menu Tools|Service.
2. Open the properties for the Exchange Server.
3. Switch to the Advanced tab.
4. Put a checkmark next to Encrypt Information When Using The Network.

Still in the Exchange 2000 environment you have RPC traffic between MAPI clients like MS Outlook and the Exchange server, and the situation regarding encryption is the same; it is default off, but can be enabled as described above. Please note that encryptions slow down the traffic and are rather CPU-intensive for both the client and the server. It could affect the overall performance of the Exchange server if lots of users have activated the encryption feature in Outlook.

The traffic between Exchange 2000 servers is based on SMTP, not RPC. While normally this would mean that the information is transported in clear text, this is not the case now.

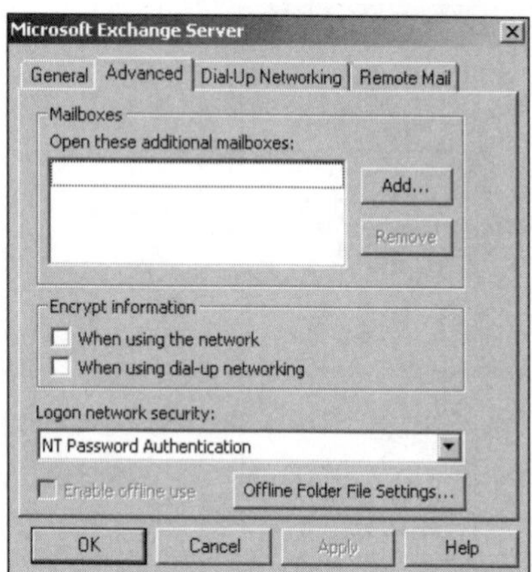

Figure 1.6
Enabling encrypted RPC traffic between the Outlook client and the Exchange server.

Exchange 2000 uses a rather unusual SMTP 8-bit format, so that it can send binary information without any need to convert it to MIME attachments. The result is a very fast SMTP-based transport in binary 8-bit mode. This makes it harder to read the transferred data, even if you are using a network sniffer, but it is important to understand that the information is not encrypted. If you really need to encrypt the traffic, you can use IPSec or TLS; both of them encrypt the complete session between the servers. The price is again performance; it takes time to encrypt and decrypt the traffic. You need to design your Exchange environment with this in mind.

Note: *TLS, or Transport Layer Security, is a way of encrypting an SMTP session between two computers. It is described in RFC 2487 and is based on Secure Socket Layer (SSL), which is popular for encrypted HTTP traffic. To use it, you need an X.509 certificate; use the MS Certificate Server in Windows 2000 Server to create the certificate or buy it from a certificate vendor like VeriSign, Entrust, or others.*

Do not confuse this encryption with S/MIME or PGP-based email encryption. These two techniques are used to encrypt (and electronically sign) messages transferred between clients. This is a much more secure transport, since the message will be completely protected all the way, including between servers regardless of what type of communication they may have. If you want to activate your client for using PGP, you can download a free version from this Web site: **http://web.mit.edu/network/pgp.html**. Most corporations and governments are using S/MIME instead, and Exchange 2000 has a built-in feature called Key Management Server, which makes it rather easy to implement S/MIME for all users (or just some) in your Exchange organization. You can find more information about this in the Exchange 2000 online help file, "Configuring Security", and in Chapter 14.

Summary

Below is a list of some of the most important topics mentioned in this chapter. Use it as a quick way to refresh your memory:

- The project name for Exchange 2000 was Platinum.
- Exchange 2000 is now SMTP based instead of X.400 based. It has a completely new architecture compared to previous Exchange versions.
- The routing engine is much smarter and faster than before. A very disturbing problem regarding looping mail has now been eliminated.
- The SMTP traffic is also more tolerant to bad or slow network connections.
- Exchange 2000 does not have its own directory anymore—it now relies completely on the Active Directory in Windows 2000 Server.
- No more directory also means no more directory replication, resulting in a significant reduction of the CPU load and network traffic.

- Although it seems there are three different Exchange 2000 versions, there are really only two, Exchange 2000 Server and Exchange 2000 Enterprise. The third, Exchange 2000 Conferencing Server, is just an add-on to either of the first two.
- The new name for the message databases is "stores."
- You still have a limit of 16GB databases in Exchange 2000 Server. Only the Exchange 2000 Enterprise version has 16TB limits.
- In Exchange 2000 Enterprise, you can have up to four different storage groups with up to five stores in each, giving you a total of 20 stores (each up to 16TB).
- It is easier to add code to Exchange 2000; expect to see lots of new third-party applications.
- Exchange 2000 Enterprise has support for active-active cluster solutions.
- You can use front-end/back-end solutions to handle a very large number of Internet clients (but not with Outlook 2000 or earlier versions of it).
- The Exchange 2000 Conferencing Server makes it possible to organize data and video and audio conferences in realtime, without too much load on the network.
- The new Web Store makes it possible to use the stores in Exchange as a normal file system.
- You get much faster search capabilities by using the new MS Index feature.
- You should be prepared to learn a lot about Windows 2000, Active Directory, and DNS.
- The new concept in Exchange 2000 makes it possible to design the communication layout based on technical decisions and the administration layout based on administrative needs.
- Use the new Routing Group Connector between routing groups rather than the X.400 Connector, unless you're communicating with X.400 systems.
- Two new administrative programs have replaced the old Exchange Administrator. Use the AD Users and Computers tool to manage users and groups, and use the Exchange System Manager to administrate your Exchange servers.
- There is no more Site Service Account like in Exchange 5.5.
- You should use the built-in Dynamic DNS in Windows 2000. Only use an external DNS if you are very sure it will support Windows 2000, Active Directory, and Exchange 2000.
- No built-in encryption exists between servers anymore, due to the fact that RPC has been abandoned for SMTP. But traffic can be encrypted by IPSec or TLS.
- You'll want to use the Key Management Server feature built into Exchange 2000 if you need to enable S/MIME for your clients.

Chapter 2

The Storage Architecture

One of the most fundamental parts of Exchange 2000 is the storage architecture. This chapter will describe all the files you may find in Exchange that are related to the storage system. Before you install an Exchange organization or even a single server within an organization, it is of paramount importance that you understand how these files work. In this chapter, you will find not only lots of step-by-step instructions for installing and configuring these files, but also some tips and notes that can help you avoid some of the usual traps.

The History of ESE

Ever since the first version of MS Exchange, the program has been using advanced database architecture with features like transaction-based log files, online backups, and online optimizing. The first database engine was built on an enhanced version of the JET Red engine, the same one MS Access used. Many people have wondered why Microsoft did not build the Exchange database on the MS SQL Server engine, the reason being that SQL Server was not as effective as the JET engine at handling *Binary Large Objects (BLOBs)*. And that is very important for a mail system, since such a system must be able to handle all sizes of objects very quickly. One message might be only 1K, but the next could be 10MB. The SQL Engine was built more for structured data, not to handle the chaos that a mail server can sometimes expect. A database expert once told me that "using SQL Server to store BLOBs is like trying to park your car in a garage with a very small door; you need to disassemble the car first, move all parts inside the garage, and then assemble it again. And when you want to go out, you need to do the reverse."

Have you ever wondered why the default directory for the mailbox and public store is called \mdbdata? It is because the first JET Red engine databases had the file type MDB (check some old MS Access files). As described above, JET Red was fast and could handle BLOBs without any problems. But the JET Red database did not have the transaction features that SQL Server had. So the development team had to enhance the database engine. Microsoft did apply for more than 60 software patents directly related to the enhanced version before releasing the JET Blue engine. To separate these enhanced database files from ordinary

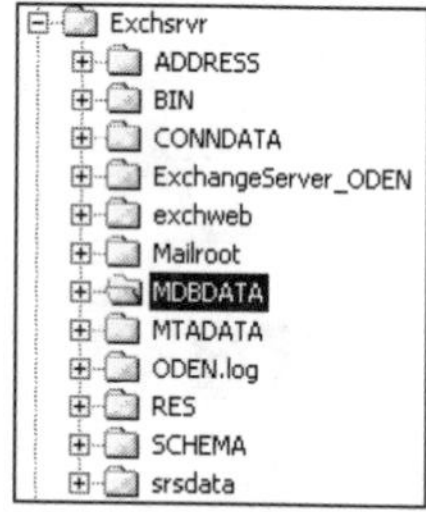

Figure 2.1
The default directory for the first storage group.

JET Red databases, Microsoft decided to change the file type to EDB, but it left the directory name unchanged, so the MDBDATA directory name is a historical remnant left over from its development. And still, in Exchange 2000, you will find this name for the default first storage group, as you can see in Figure 2.1.

Every new version of Exchange and almost all service packs have included an upgraded version of the database engine. Version 5.5 had a completely new database structure built on JET97, also known as the Extensible Storage Engine (ESE). This version allowed up to 16TB large databases, which was 1,000 times larger than previous databases. Microsoft called this "the unlimited database" because it was not possible to build a server capable of storing this much data, at least not at that time. It was only the Exchange 5.5 Enterprise edition that had the unlimited storage capacity, whereas the Exchange 5.5 Standard edition was still limited to 16GB even though it was also built on the ESE engine. Exchange 2000 is built on JET98, which basically has the same ESE engine as Exchange 5.5 but also several enhancements that make it more stable and fault-tolerant.

***Tip:** It is hard to see whether an Exchange 2000 or 5.5 server has the unlimited database (16TB) or the limited (16GB) version just by looking in the Exchange admin tools. You need to check the Event log to find that. Look in the Application event log for EventID 1217. This is written to the log every time the Information Store service is started. If this event id has the text "unlimited storage capacity enabled," then you know this server is an enterprise version.*

ACID Transactions

In database theory, you will often come across the term *ACID*. It is an abbreviation for Atomic, Consistent, Isolated, and Durable. A database must be reliable, and it must be able to cope with catastrophic situations like a disk crash or unexpected power down. To do this, your database must treat your modifications in the database as a series of operations. For example, if you want to move a message from one folder to another, all steps must be fully completed or not performed at all. You do not want to perform only half of the steps, since this would leave your database in what is called an inconsistent state, causing you to lose data or even crash the database.

Table 2.1 The ACID transactions.

Transaction	Description
Atomic	All steps performed in a transaction must be completely successful or else none will perform; this is known as *all or nothing*.
Consistent	A transaction must take the database from one consistent state to another.
Isolated	No modification will be visible until the complete transaction is completed.
Durable	Completed transactions will persist even if the system goes down or crashes.

Your ESE engine will therefore use a transaction log file to register all transactions or steps before they are written to the store itself. If some problem happens before all steps are taken, then ESE will roll back all steps taken up to that moment, restoring the store to the last known consistent state. In Table 2.1, you will see a more detailed description of each ACID transaction.

The Dynamic Memory Allocation

All pages are temporarily stored in the memory. In versions before Exchange 5.5, you had to manually allocate buffers, but now it is done automatically. This means that Exchange 2000 can use as much memory as is available—and that means better performance for the server and all its users.

When another program requests memory from the system, ESE will release part of its allocated buffers. If you use the Task Manager to look at the memory allocation, you can see that the Information Store service will dynamically grow and shrink, depending on how much other programs need memory. So don't get nervous when your Information Store service is allocating 90 percent of the memory; this is by design, and is not any kind of memory leak.

Exchange 2000 will manage to work, even with very little memory. But the more memory you have, the better the performance will be. I have a lab server with only 96MB of memory that is configured as a Windows 2000 domain controller and an Exchange 2000 Enterprise server, and it works, even if it is slow.

Design Goals for the Store

The problem with previous versions of Exchange was that all your mailbox users had to share the same database. That often resulted in very large databases, and consequently, both long backup times and very long restore times. Since all users shared the same database, it also meant that all users would be shut off from the Exchange server if you needed to do a restore or some offline maintenance on a database. So one important design goal for the new store in Exchange 2000 was to overcome this problem.

The result was a new version of the Information Store service, capable of handling multiple stores at the same time. The system design allows for more than 90 stores, whereas the current version of Exchange 2000 is limited to only 20, due to its high demand on system resources, like memory and the CPU. With the new Information Store, you can create up to four separate storage groups, with up to five stores each. Every storage group has its own set of transaction log files, regardless of how many stores are in the storage group.

Another very important goal was to make it possible to run the server 24 hours per day, 7 days per week, designing it so that a single disaster in a file or a disk would not stop the server from running as long as there were other disks and stores that still worked. By enabling a disk layout where the stores and transaction log files are placed on different physical disk sets, you can minimize the risk of a total stop due to disk failure. If you install Exchange 2000 in a cluster environment, you can even handle a situation in which a total server goes down, and the users won't ever notice.

With this new design, you can have an Exchange server with thousands of users but still have control over how large the stores will be. It will also make the impact of restore procedures much smaller than before; only the store in question will be taken offline. No other store will be affected, even if you replace the faulty store during office hours. The restore procedure will also be faster since the store is smaller. When you make your design, you should take this into account. It may result in fewer Exchange servers and less network traffic.

Understanding the Store

This section describes how data is stored in the files, explains how the Information Store governs all access to files, and offers a detailed description of the EDB and STM files.

How Data Is Stored

The process that controls all database activities is the IS, or the Information Store, service (Store.exe). All data in the Exchange server is stored in three different places:

- In the IS memory buffers
- In a transaction file
- In a store file

In Figure 2.2, you can see how incoming data is first received in the memory, immediately written to the transaction log, and then shortly after that is also written to the database file. The data is accepted as received when it is stored in the transaction log, i.e., before it's written to the database.

If the transmission of new data is aborted before it is completely stored in the transaction log, the data will be discarded, and Exchange will try to send an error message back to the sender.

When you modify existing data in the store, the procedure works a little differently (see Figure 2.3). First, the page containing the data is copied from the store to the memory,

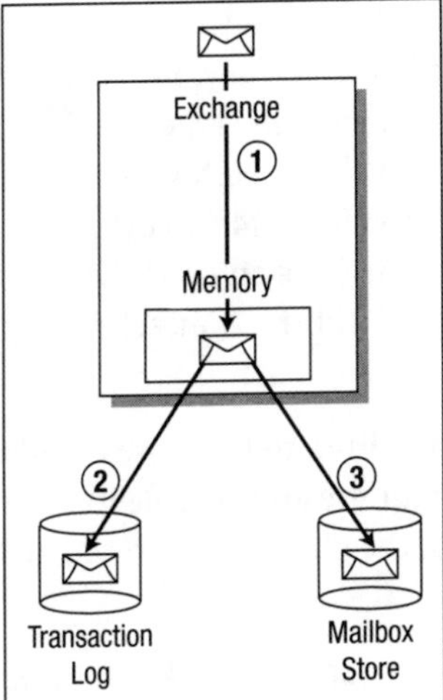

Figure 2.2
How Exchange treats incoming data.

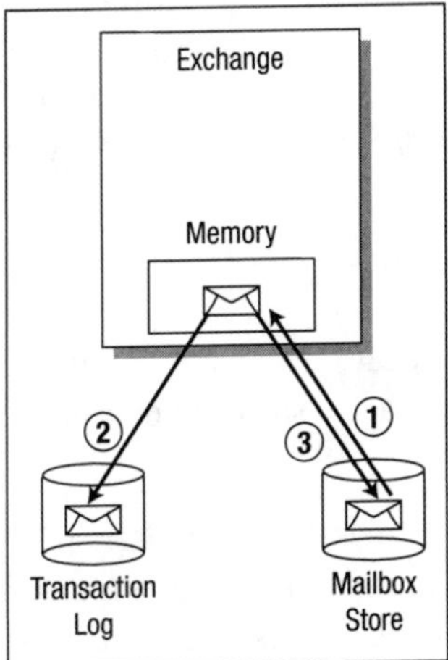

Figure 2.3
Modification of existing data.

then it is modified in memory. Although this increases the performance of the ESE operation, it also means that the page in the store is different from the page in the memory. If your server were to go down at that point, you would lose the modification. The next step is to write the modified page to the transaction log. When this is successfully completed, the final step is to write the page back from memory to the store. If the server goes down before the data is written to the store, this is not a problem. When you reboot the server, Exchange compares the transaction logs with the stores and replays all missing transactions.

Each ESE store is organized as a file based on the B+ Tree structure. This is a very common structure for databases because of its high performance and efficiency. You can find more information about B+ Tree in books about database concepts. This type of structure is logically organized as a number of pages, in this case 4K each. The total number of pages is 2^32 or 4,292,967,296, which is a total of 16TB, or 17,586,994,044,416 bytes to be exact. Even the memory buffer is organized as 4K pages so you will have an exact match between the store and the memory, except for the number of pages. But the transaction log file is not organized in pages. You'll read more about transaction logs later.

Before each page is saved, a checksum is calculated and written to the store together with the data. This will be used later when the Information Store reads the page to ensure that no corruption has occurred; every time the page is read, the checksum is recalculated and compared with the stored checksum value.

Note: *If the recalculated checksum value does not match the stored checksum value, you will get an EventID: 1018 Error in the Event log. This can be a sign that the disk or disk controller is not working properly. Some old disk controllers would get this error several times and then suddenly start to work again. Microsoft added a fix in Service Pack 2 for Exchange 5.5 (also included in Exchange 2000) that makes the Information Store try to read the data 16 times before generating a 1018 error. So if you get this error, you know the Information Store has tried 16 times and still did not manage to read the page correctly. You can use the utility ESEFILE, included with SP3, to test the checksum on the faulty page, as reported in the 1018 error message.*

The Single-Instance Message Store

Exchange has always had support for SIS, Single-Instance Message Store, and in Exchange 2000 it is still there. But, since there can now be as many as 20 stores in one single server, it works a bit differently than before.

The SIS feature, illustrated in Figure 2.4, means that one message to 10 users belonging to the same Exchange server and the same store is stored just once. Each mailbox will have a link to that single instance. If one of these 10 users deletes this mail, he will only remove the link, not the message itself. Only when the last user has deleted the mail will the message really be deleted.

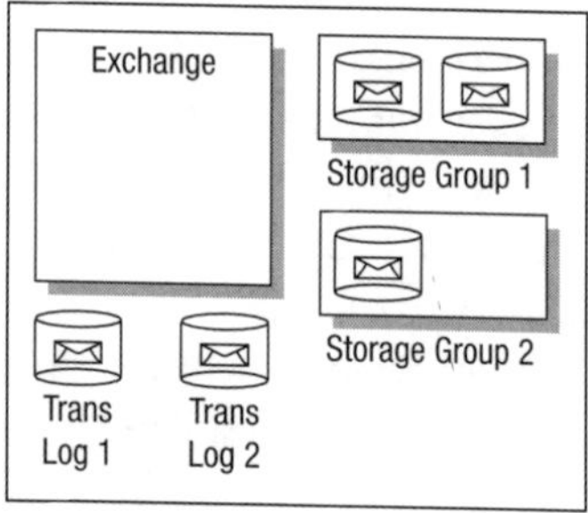

Figure 2.4
Example of the Single-Instance Message Store.

If the 10 users belong to different stores, it does not matter if they are in the same storage group or not; each store must have its own copy of the message. But still, this is much better than not using an SIS-enabled ESE engine.

***Note:** The complete message size will be included in the calculation of each user's total mailbox size. This will of course be a bit misleading, since the messages will be counted 10 times in the example above. But to do it any other way would be impractical. For example, assuming we have a 50K message, each of the 10 users would account for 5K, and when one of these users deletes his mail, his 5K shares are spread out among the other nine users—not really practical.*

Let's say you have an Exchange 2000 server with two storage groups. The first storage group has two mailbox stores and one public store; the other storage group has one mailbox store and one public store. You are sending mail with a 2MB attachment to 50 people in this server. Forty of these users belong to the first storage group, with 20 users in each store; 10 belong to the second storage group and its single store. Remember that each storage group has its own set of transaction log files. That would bring the total number of copies to: 1 + 1 (first storage group) + 1 (second storage group) + 2 (one for each transaction log) = 5, with a total disk space of 5 × 2MB = 10MB. Without the SIS feature, you would instead have 50 × 2 = 100MB in utilized disk space. And that is only one message. You can easily see that SIS makes a large difference.

The File Structure

It is clear that Microsoft is moving away from the present MAPI-centric world and its way of storing rich text messages. Don't be surprised if the support for MAPI files will be gone two or three releases from now. Microsoft is switching to Internet-related protocols as fast as it can, but it needs to be compatible with the "old" world for a few more years.

One example of this ongoing process is the new feature that makes the server able to store Internet-formatted information in native mode without first converting it to the format used in EDB files, MDBEF, or MS Database Encapsulated Format. The Exchange server can in fact use both formats simultaneously with its new ESE engine. Even though a store is treated as a single database, each store will in reality be a combination of two files—one EDB file and one STM file. Depending on the source format of the data, ESE will select either the EDB or the STM file for storage. Both files will have the same name, except for the file type (see Figure 2.5). They are, by default, stored together in the same directory, but can be moved to different directories or even different disks for increased performance and recoverability.

Name	Size
priv1.edb	226 312 KB
pub1.edb	10 248 KB
priv1.stm	90 120 KB
pub1.stm	2 056 KB

Figure 2.5
A PRIV1 and PUB1 store, each with an EDB file and an STM file.

These two files have the following characteristics:

- The EDB file is exactly like the old EDB database in previous Exchange versions; it stores information in Microsoft's proprietary RTF format, which is used by MAPI clients like Outlook 2000 and all previous Outlook versions. It also stores all the message headers.
- The new STM, or STreaM, file stores information in native Internet format, like MIME or UUencode. Internet clients like POP3, IMAP4, and Outlook Web Access 2000 use this format. No message headers are stored in the STM file.

They work like this: If a message is created with a MAPI client, like Outlook 2000 for example, the message will be stored in the EDB file. However, if a message is received from the Internet or created on an Internet client, like POP3 or IMAP4, the message will be stored in the STM file in its raw format exactly as it was received. Since a mail organization may have a mix of both client types, ESE must make sure that whatever file type the clients are using, it must see all mail regardless of where it is stored. This is done by letting all clients, regardless of type, access the header information in the EDB. Every time a new message is stored in the STM file, a corresponding message header is stored in the EDB file.

In-Memory Content Conversion

When a client opens a message that is in the "wrong" format, like, for example, if Outlook 2000 opens a message stored in the STM file, an automatic content conversion is performed. Microsoft calls this *deferred content conversion* or *in-memory content conversion*, since the operation is done in memory only. The stored message is not changed in any way, but rather is still stored in the same file as before.

For example, let's say that user Anna uses an Outlook 2000 client in her office; therefore, she is working with the EDB file. At home, Anna uses an IMAP4 client and connects to the office network. Now she will use the EDB file to see the headers of all messages, including headers for the sender, recipients, and subject. If she opens a message stored in the STM file, then information is sent to her client without any conversion since it is already in a MIME format that IMAP4 understands.

Later, Anna opens a message that is actually stored in the EDB file, it must now be converted before Anna's IMAP4 client can read it. This is done automatically in the Exchange server's memory. Microsoft calls this *in-memory content conversion* (shown in Figure 2.6). No permanent conversion of the EDB data is done. Every time Anna uses her IMAP4 client and opens up the same message, the same in-memory content conversion will take place. And the same thing happens when Anna uses her MAPI-based Outlook 2000, opening up a message that is really stored in the STM file—in-memory content conversion.

Permanent Content Conversion

If a client modifies a message that was converted in memory, then the message will be moved to the new file and the old message will be deleted, except for the mail header.

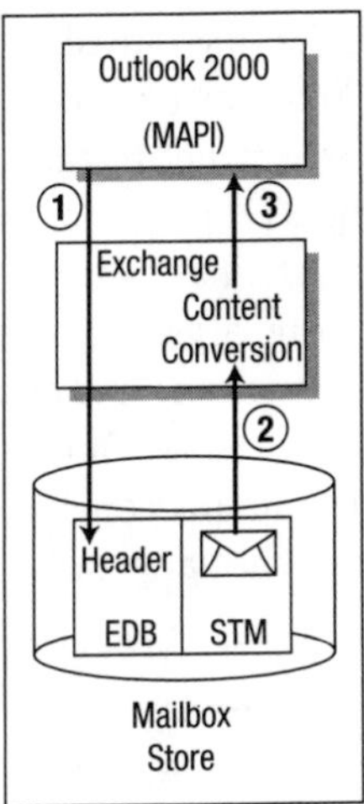

Figure 2.6
In-memory content conversion when a MAPI client opens a message that is stored in the STM file.

For example, if Anna used her Outlook 2000 to modify a mail stored in the STM file, this is what would happen:

1. The ESE engine would get the mail from the STM file.
2. The mail would be converted from MIME to RTF format in memory.
3. Anna would modify the mail and save the change.
4. ESE would see that the modified mail is in RTF format and store it in the EDB file.
5. The original mail, stored in the STM file, would be deleted, unless some clients have a pointer to the message in the STM file.

If later on an Internet client modified the same mail, the reverse would happen—the mail would once again be stored in the STM file and removed from the EDB. Note that Exchange does not shrink the size of a store when a message is deleted; both the STM and the EDB file may therefore continue to increase whenever this permanent conversion happens, up to the point when the STM and EDB files are almost equal in size.

The Stream File

This new file is used to increase the performance for handling Internet-based information. The number of messages per day is increasing, and each message often includes very large file attachments that can be in the form of MP3 music, video clips, and other multimedia. We are seeing that the nature of what people are sending by mail is changing since just a few years ago, when it was mostly text messages, sometimes with an MS Word document or some other attachment. It is clear to everyone working with email that we must prepare our messaging systems, both the mail servers and the network, to be able to handle all this information.

Microsoft's solution in Exchange 2000 is the streaming file, STM. This file is used whenever a message is received into Exchange in an Internet format. It can be any type of MIME- or UUENCODE-formatted message. The EDB file is based on B+ Tree structure, and that is not really suitable for storing really large messages. However, the STM file is not based on B+ Tree, but instead organized much like the NTFS file system, as a flat data structure grouping information together in clusters. It is much faster to write large files to the STM file instead of the EDB file, since it does not have the overhead of re-indexing any B+Tree, like the EBD structure has to. If you are using Internet clients like Outlook Web Access, they can read the STM information as a data stream without any conversion. This offers a dramatic improvement to the overall performance, especially for large messages with video and audio attachments.

It is important to understand that the STM file does not work alone. You should look at it as a complement to the EDB file. For example, all header properties like sender, subject, and size are still stored only in the EDB file. Data pages, checksums, and information about page usages are also stored in the EDB file. All clients use the EDB file, but the STM files are used only if the message is stored there.

Note: *When a client reads a message in the STM file, no recalculation of the checksum occurs again. This is for performance reasons. It is a trade-off since it would take too long to get the checksum for each page from the EDB file.*

You can actually open the STM file with a text editor or Internet Explorer (see Figure 2.7). But first you must stop the Information Store service or dismount the store;

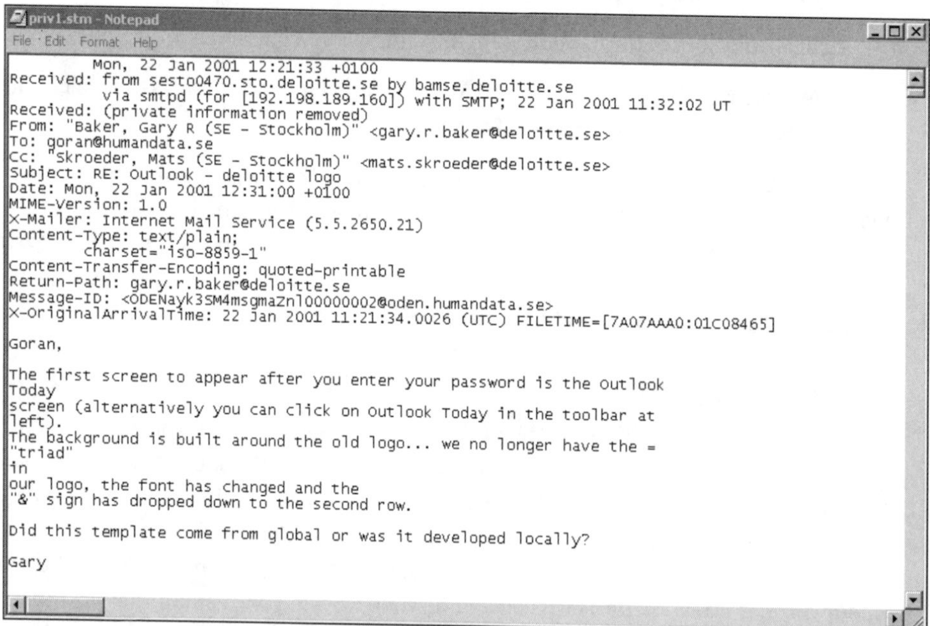

Figure 2.7

Information in the STM is stored in native MIME format.

otherwise, you will find the file locked. The STM file is organized in 4K pages—the first two pages will be header info and after that, you will find all the data pages. Each page in the STM file will be in one of four possible states:

- *Free*—This page is free to use.
- *Reserved*—The ESE engine has reserved this page for incoming messages.
- *Committed*—This page is already storing data.
- *Deleted*—The data on this page is now deleted. It will later be changed to the Free status when online defragmentation process occurs (usually each night).

The fact that you can read the STM file and its messages in clear text sounds like a security threat. But you must not forget that only the administrator is able to dismount a store and access the STM files. Be sure no one except trusted personnel is able to access these files at any time.

The STM File in Action

Now you know most of the details about the new STM file. Let's see how it works in more detail by assuming that our user, Anna, is using an IMAP4 client. When she opens a message that is stored in the STM file, here's what will happen (see Figure 2.8):

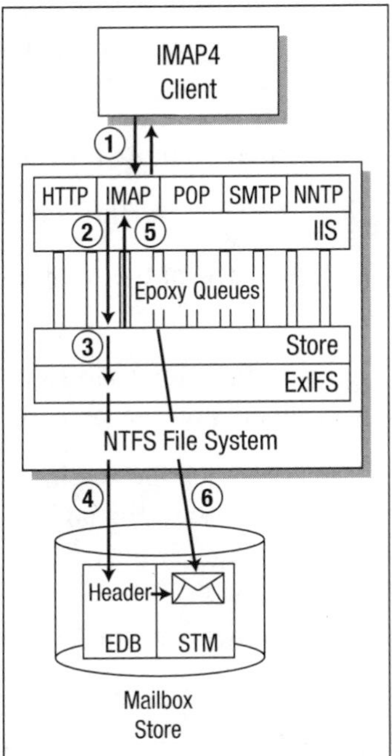

Figure 2.8
How the STM file is accessed.

1. The IMAP4 client connects to the IMAP4 server in IIS and sends its request.
2. The IIS server contacts the Information Store process (Store.exe) and asks for a handle to the message inside the STM file.
3. The store asks the ExIFS for this handle.
4. ExIFS locates the message inside the STM, creates the handle, and sends it back to the store process.
5. The store sends the received handle back to the IMAP4 server.
6. The IMAP4 server now issues a **TRANSMITFILE** command that uses the handle to load the message; the handle has a list of all pages that belong to the message.

Even though this seems to be a lot of steps, it is actually a very fast operation. Most commands and operations are performed in kernel mode only.

Understanding the Transaction Logs

The transaction system is the foundation for the high recoverability of the ESE file system. With this system, you can have a complete disk crash, losing all your EDB and STM files, and still manage to get it all back. Sounds like magic, doesn't it? Like all good magic it needs to have the right conditions and preparations; otherwise it will not work as expected and can even make things worse. We have talked about transaction logs before, but let me just remind you of how Exchange treats any incoming messages (take a look back at Figure 2.2 also):

1. The data is received into the memory buffers in the Information Store process.
2. The data is immediately written to the transaction log—for example, the E00.LOG file.
3. When all data is written to the transaction log, the IS will accept the message as received.
4. As soon as the CPU has some idle time, maybe a few seconds later, then IS will write the same data but now to the EDB file (or STM file, depending on the format).

Now we have the same message in two places—in the transaction log file and in the store (EDB or STM). If a store file gets corrupted, we simply replace it with the latest backup, and Exchange will reply to all transactions that have occurred since the last backup. If the transaction log file gets corrupted, then it's not a problem yet—as long as the store is working, we are safe. But if this ever happens, you should immediately make a backup of your store to make sure you have one more copy.

There are some things that you need to do before this magic works. The most important thing is to store the transaction log file and the stores on different physical disks. The reason for this is simply so that one disk failure will not affect both copies of the data. I have seen lots of installations in which the Exchange administrator has not followed this advice. These administrators usually do one of these two things, both leading to bad configurations:

- Storing both the EDB and the STM files and the corresponding transaction log files on the same disk.
- Separate the disk into two partitions—for example, C: and D:, and then storing the transaction logs in C and all the stores in D.

The problem with the first bad choice is that when (not if) the disk breaks down, it will destroy everything on it. True, a mirrored disk set or a RAID5 disk set is more reliable than a single disk. But still I have seen several of these "100% foolproof" RAID5 systems get corrupted. The sense morale is that you simply cannot rely on one single disk system alone, even if it's a fault tolerant system; you should always stores transaction logs on one disk, and stores on another . . . .

It is interesting to see how much faith an inexperienced administrator places on computer hardware. Maybe I am a bit too cynical, due to the number of computer catastrophes I have seen during my 24 years in the computer business, but I still think that you should be very careful with data, especially if it's not your data. I've found that you are able to live more of a relaxed life if you are taking the necessary precautions in the computer world. I used to tell my Exchange students that they should view themselves as doctors working in a hospital. At any moment, one of their patients could become seriously ill. As a doctor, your first priority should be to make sure the patients have a stable and controlled situation. If something critical happens, you must be prepared to deal with the situation very quickly; you must have the routines figured out and equipment ready to be used. And on the flip side, if you were this sick patient, you wouldn't exactly want to see your doctor picking up a manual, looking as if this is the first time he's ever seen your condition, and starting to fumble with some tools that he obviously has never used before. You probably also wouldn't want to notice that these tools your doctor's wielding in his hands look suspiciously similar to the things you saw in a second-hand shop the other day.

As an Exchange "doctor," you must be prepared for the most common failure—disk crashes. You do this by using high-quality equipment, establishing well-proven daily routines, and regularly practicing what to do during emergency situations. This has always been important, of course, but in Exchange 2000 you may have a very complex database setup, with up to four different storage groups, each using its own set of transaction log files. Microsoft recommends that you put the Windows 2000 files on one mirrored disk, each set of transaction log files on separate mirrored disks, and the storage groups on a separate RAID5 set (see Figure 2.9). It's an expensive solution, but it provides maximum security.

Some companies are not prepared to pay that much money for a server. The cheap but in many cases acceptable solution is to store all the storage groups in one RAID5 disk set and all transaction log files in a mirrored disk, like you'll see illustrated in Figure 2.10. Of course, you need to be very careful then, making sure that all disks are working fine since

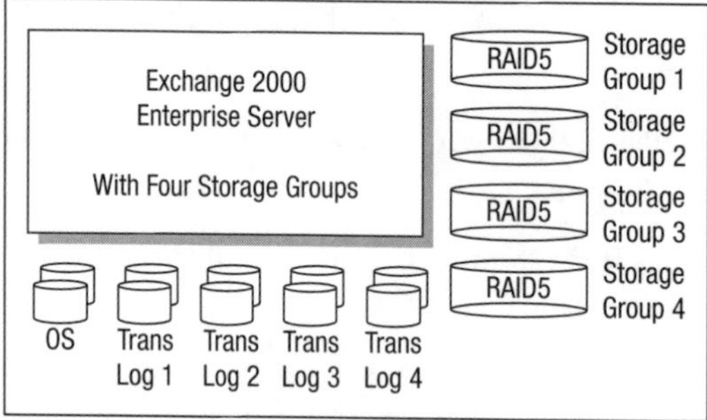

Figure 2.9
Recommended disk layouts with four storage groups.

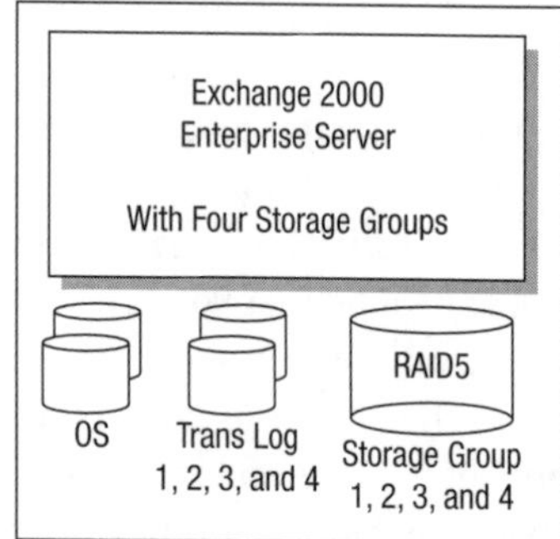

Figure 2.10
The cheap disk layout with four storage groups.

you've now placed all your eggs in just two baskets instead of eight. You should also be aware of the differences in read and write performance between mirrored disks (RAID1 and RAID5). The mirrored set is much faster for writing than RAID5, due to the fact that RAID5 must update its rather complex indexes and checksum for every written page. That makes RAID5 a bad choice for transaction log files.

Finally, let me offer some words about disks and their controllers. You should build your system on SCSI disks instead of IDE disks; they are much faster. You should also use the fastest SCSI type that you can afford, since the performance of the disk will affect the overall performance of the server. Remember that Exchange is a disk-intensive system that reads and writes all the time. If possible, use separate disk controllers; that will increase the speed up to 40 percent since Exchange is a multithreaded application (meaning it can read and write to separate disks simultaneously if given the possibility). And avoid write-ahead caches. Even if the hardware vendor tells you that it has battery backup for its cache, it can fail. I have personally seen at least two really bad cases in which this occurred. The big problem with a write cache is that Exchange thinks it has safely stored the data, when in reality, the data is still stored on the controller; if that breaks down, your database will be corrupted. Definitely do everything you can to avoid that at all costs.

The Transaction Files

In previous Exchange releases, there was just one set of transaction log files, named EDB.LOG for the current log file, and EDBxxxxxx.LOG for the previous log files where "xxxxxx" stands for a hexadecimal number. Now that Exchange 2000 can have up to four different transaction file sets, one for each storage group, they have a new name standard:

- E00.LOG is the current log file for the first storage group, E01.LOG is the current log for the second storage group, E02 is for the third group, and so on.
- Old log files are given names with a hexadecimal numbering scheme, added to the name of the current log file, like E001120A.LOG for the first storage group and E0100249.LOG for the second storage group.

Each log file will be 5MB in size (or exactly 5,242,880 bytes). If it's not, you have a problem—immediately take a backup and then start to solve the problem. When a 10MB message is received, it clearly can't be stored in just one log file; Exchange will solve this by creating a new log file when needed and renaming the old current log file as described above. The log file with the highest number, after the current one, is the latest log file.

A log file has two parts, the header and the data. The header has information about what storage group it belongs to and what its identity is. Every storage group has a unique identity, called a signature. By storing the signature in the header, Exchange will prevent you from using the file with the wrong store, even if the store should have exactly the same name. You can look at the header information by using the **ESEutil /ML** command. You will then see the generation number, the path to the storage group, the signature, and other features. Take a look at Listing 2.1 and the description in Table 2.2.

Table 2.2 Some of the information in the transaction log header.

Parameter	Description
Base name	e.g., E00. The name that prefixes all files, both log files and store files.
Log file	The name of this log file.
LGeneration	This is the log generation number (in decimal).
Checkpoint	First value: the next available log number (hex).
Creation time	When this file was created.
Signature	The unique id for this log file.
Env LogFilePath	The path to storage groups (not the log file directory).

Listing 2.1 A dump of a transaction log file.

```
F:\Exchsrvr\Second Storage Group>c:eseutil /ml e0100001.log

Microsoft(R) Exchange Server(TM) Database Utilities
Version 6.0
Copyright (C) Microsoft Corporation 1991-2000.  All Rights Reserved.

Initiating FILE DUMP mode...

      Base name: e01
      Log file: e0100001.log
      lGeneration: 1 (0x1)
      Checkpoint NOT AVAILABLE
      creation time: 02/02/2001 10:56:31
      prev gen time: 00/00/1900 00:00:00
      Format LGVersion: (7.3704.2)
      Engine LGVersion: (7.3704.2)
      Signature: Create time:02/02/2001 10:56:31 Rand:921104327 Computer:
      Env SystemPath: C:\Program Files\Exchsrvr\Second Storage Group\
      Env LogFilePath: C:\Program Files\Exchsrvr\Second Storage Group\
      Env Log Sec size: 512
      Env (CircLog, Session, Opentbl, VerPage, Cursors, LogBufs, LogFile, Buffers)
          (    off,     202,   30300,    1365,   10100,      84,   10240,   65356)
      Last Lgpos: (0x1,27FF,0)

Integrity check passed for log file: e0100001.log

Operation completed successfully in 3.255 seconds.
```

You can also dump the header info of both EDB and the STM file with the **ESEutil / MH <file>** command (see Listing 2.2). It gives you a lot of information. Note that you need to dismount the store before you can dump the header; otherwise, the file is locked by the IS. Some of the more interesting information you will find is described in Table 2.3.

Listing 2.2 A dump of the EDB header.

```
G:\Program Files\Exchsrvr\Second Storage Group>c:eseutil /mh store1.edb

Microsoft(R) Exchange Server(TM) Database Utilities
Version 6.0
Copyright (C) Microsoft Corporation 1991-2000.  All Rights Reserved.

Initiating FILE DUMP mode...
      Database: store1.edb

        File Type: Database
   Format ulMagic: 0x89abcdef
```

```
   Engine ulMagic: 0x89abcdef
 Format ulVersion: 0x620,9
 Engine ulVersion: 0x620,9
     DB Signature: Create time:02/02/2001 10:56:36 Rand:921118520 Computer:
         cbDbPage: 4096
           dbtime: 27519 (0-27519)
            State: Consistent
     Log Required: 0-0
   Streaming File: Yes
         Shadowed: Yes
       Last Objid: 123
     Scrub Dbtime: 0 (0-0)
       Scrub Date: 00/00/1900 00:00:00
     Repair Count: 0
      Repair Date: 00/00/1900 00:00:00
  Last Consistent: (0x3,E64,1E)  02/02/2001 17:41:22
      Last Attach: (0x1,12B9,C8)  02/02/2001 17:28:49
      Last Detach: (0x3,E64,1E)  02/02/2001 17:41:22
             Dbid: 1
    Log Signature: Create time:02/02/2001 10:56:31 Rand:921104327 Computer:
       OS Version: (5.0.2195 SP 1)

Previous Full Backup:
        Log Gen: 0-0 (0x0-0x0)
           Mark: (0x0,0,0)
           Mark: 00/00/1900 00:00:00

Current Incremental Backup:
        Log Gen: 0-0 (0x0-0x0)
           Mark: (0x0,0,0)
           Mark: 00/00/1900 00:00:00

Current Full Backup:
        Log Gen: 0-0 (0x0-0x0)
           Mark: (0x0,0,0)
           Mark: 00/00/1900 00:00:00

Current snapshot backup:
        Log Gen: 0-0 (0x0-0x0)
           Mark: (0x0,0,0)
           Mark: 00/00/1900 00:00:00

     cpgUpgrade55Format: 0
    cpgUpgradeFreePages: 0
cpgUpgradeSpaceMapPages: 0

Operation completed successfully in 0.631 seconds.
```

Table 2.3 Some of the information in the store header.

Parameter	Description
File type	Streaming (STM) or Database (EDB).
DB signature	The unique name of this store—should be the same for both the STM and the EDB file.
State	Should be consistent.
Streaming file	(EDB only) Yes means that it has a corresponding STM file.
Repair date	When it was last repaired by IS or a utility like ESEutil.
Log signature	The identity of the corresponding log files—must match the signature in the log files.
Previous full backup	Time and date of the last full backup.

Since the log file is storing the actual file directory for the stores, you must never try to move the stores manually to another place. This would make it impossible to do a recover from the transaction logs. Exchange will give you a warning when you try to mount the moved database, since it now cannot find the EDB and/or STM file. The warning reads, "At least one of this store's database files is missing. Mounting this store will force the creation of an empty database. Do not take this action if you intend to restore an earlier backup." If you need to move a store file, you must use the Exchange System Admin tool, select the properties for the store, and use the *Database* tab.

The Checkpoint File

As previously stated, information is first written to the log file and then to the store file so most of the time the log file is one step ahead of the store file. Exchange uses a checkpoint file named E00.CHK for the first storage group, E01.CHK for the second group, and so on, to keep track of what data in the log file has been written to the store file. There is one checkpoint file for each transaction log set, i.e., for each storage group. The checkpoint file makes the recovery process faster by pointing to the first transaction in the log file that has not yet been written to the store file. This means that IS doesn't have to look for transactions before this point. If the checkpoint file is missing, IS needs to scan all available log files since it now does not know where to begin its recovery process.

Note: *In Exchange 2000, the checkpoint file will always be stored together with the store files, like the EDB and STM files, not with the transaction log files as you might expect. That is different from previous Exchange versions in which the checkpoint file was always stored together with the transaction log files. Do not try to move this file manually.*

This checkpoint file is small, only 8K. Besides storing a pointer to the log file, it also stores both a list of transaction log files and the sequential order needed to restore the store to a consistent state. If the recovery process fails to find all log files needed to restore, it will abort and write the error code 543 to the Event log. If you want, you can force Exchange to write, or flush, all messages to the store by stopping the Information Store process (but of course this is never needed in normal situations). You can use the

ESEutil /MK command to dump the information in the checkpoint file. And you can see things like the checkpoint value, telling you what the name will be for the next "old" log file, when the last full and incremental backup was performed, whether circular logging has been enabled or not, and more. In Listing 2.3, you can see that this database has never been backed up, and that the next log file name will be E000004C.LOG (look at the first value in the checkpoint record).

Listing 2.3 A dump of the checkpoint file header.

```
G:\Program Files\Exchsrvr\Second Storage Group>c:eseutil /Mk E01.chk

Microsoft(R) Exchange Server(TM) Database Utilities
Version 6.0
Copyright (C) Microsoft Corporation 1991-2000.  All Rights Reserved.

Initiating FILE DUMP mode...
      Checkpoint file: E01.chk

      LastFullBackupCheckpoint: (0x0,0,0)
      Checkpoint: (0x3,1CBC,DD)
      FullBackup: (0x0,0,0)
      FullBackup time: 00/00/1900 00:00:00
      IncBackup: (0x0,0,0)
      IncBackup time: 00/00/1900 00:00:00
      Signature: Create time:02/02/2001 10:56:31 Rand:921104327 Computer:
      Env (CircLog, Session, Opentbl, VerPage, Cursors, LogBufs, LogFile, Buffers)
          (     off,     202,   30300,    1365,   10100,      84,   10240,   65356)

Operation completed successfully in 0.140 seconds.
```

The transaction system in Exchange is excellent and can really help you with disk failures and crashed databases, but it is also complex and won't accept things like your trying to move files without Exchange knowing it or deleting transaction files. The last operation is especially dangerous. Let's say that you need more disk space on the transaction log disk; you notice that many log files are there and Exchange seems to work fine, so you decide to delete some of them, including the checkpoint file. Two hours after that, you restart the Exchange server for some other reason and suddenly you get error messages saying that your Exchange store is corrupt. Not good.

What happened? Well, since you restarted the server, Exchange also restarted the Information Store service. As always, when this happens, IS does a soft recovery, checking to see that all is okay. This time, it does not find any checkpoint file, so it simply has to scan all available log files. Now let's assume that in log file 35, there was a new page added to a store, and in log file 36, the same page was deleted. The problem is due to the fact that you deleted log file 35 but not 36, so when the recovery process logs file 36, it sees a delete instruction and will remove whatever is in that page.

How the Replay of Transactions Is Performed

If a store gets corrupted and you need to restore it from the backup, your store will actually go back in time to the moment when the backup process occurred, for example, to 4 A.M. All messages received after that time are lost, since they aren't stored on the backup; however, since you still have a copy of each of them in the transaction logs they can be re-created, thanks to what is known as a *hard recovery*. This is how the Information Store process replays these transactions during the hard recovery:

1. First, the corrupted store is dismounted.
2. Next, the store file is restored from the backup.
3. When you mount the new store, the Information Store will enter the first phase, the recovery phase. Exchange will indicate this by creating a file called "restore.env" and start comparing the transaction logs with the store file. This phase can take a long time.
4. IS will now look for the first transaction log file to be used.
5. For each page in this log file, it compares the timestamp on this page with the timestamp on the corresponding store page; if the log page is newer, the information is written to the store. If the time stamp on the store page is equal or higher, then IS will not update the store.
6. When all transactions are checked in this log file, open the next log file and repeat Step 5.
7. After all log files have been replayed, IS enters the second phase, checking for transactions that were started but not committed. So mail that was moved but had failed is now going to be unmoved; this is called *physical redo, logical undo*.

Note that every time you stop and start the Information Store process, it will automatically enter the recovery phase just to make sure it has everything updated. This is called *soft recovery*, since you are not restoring any database. You can also start the recovery phase using ESEutil and the ISInteg utilities found in the exchsrvr\bin directory.

It is absolutely vital that all transaction log files are readable to be able to restore a database completely. Remember that they are all in sequence and if even one single log file is missing, the restore process will terminate. Please do not try to be "smart," taking an old log file and renaming it to the missing file; this will only make the situation worse.

Circular Logging

Exchange 2000 is the first version that has circular logging disabled by default; previous versions always had it enabled. There are lots of existing Exchange installations that are still using the circular logging simply because they don't know about this. That is a serious problem, since enabling circular logging means that your transaction system will keep only four old log files besides the current one, making it a total of five; since each log file is 5MB, you will only have 25MB for logging. Because the log files are so important, a limit of 25MB is really not much at all. And if you take a backup each night, any old information that exceeds 25MB of transaction will be overwritten. The circular logging setting is done on the storage group level; you cannot have individual settings for each store in this regard, since all stores in a storage group share the same transaction log files.

There are situations in which circular logging can still be useful. If, for example, you have a storage group dedicated for a large volume of data that changes all the time, like a Usenet News feed or a stock market folder, you may not need the full transaction system. In this case, you are best off with circular logging enabled. Otherwise, you'll find that you will quickly get a large number of log files and maybe even fill the disk, since the Usenet News feed can send up to 25GB per day. You probably don't want to save these transactions or even take a backup of this, since you can ask for a retransmission in case of a disk failure. When you set up a test environment, you can also use the circular logging to avoid storing a lot of log files.

The Reserved Log Files

What should Exchange do if the disks get full and there are transactions stored in the IS memory but no available transaction log file? Exchange solves this dilemma by simply reserving two extra log files to be used just for this particular scenario. These files, 5MB in size, are just like normal transaction log files, but their names are Res1.log and Res2.log. If the disk fills up, Exchange will first rename the Res1.log to E00.log, (or E01 for second storage group, and so on), and use that for storing the data in the memory. If this is not enough, Exchange will also use the Res2.log after renaming it first. And if that is still not enough, you may have a problem because Exchange will lose any remaining data that it doesn't have space to store.

Normally, you will get a warning from the Windows 2000 Server that the disk is almost full, long before the 10MB that Exchange has reserved. But don't wait until you see this message before you act. The disk may be filled during off-hours, or when mail traffic is so intensive that you don't even have time to react. The best practice is to monitor daily all disks that Exchange uses, both for transaction logs and for storage groups. After monitoring your system for a while, you'll know on average how much space you need each day; make sure your disks for storage groups are at least double the size you are using now and that the disks for transaction log files are at least five times the daily load.

Storage Groups

We have discussed the concept of storage groups several times now, but exactly what are they and how can you use them to optimize your Exchange environment? In this section, I will try to answer that question for you. Today, many Exchange 5.5 servers have databases that are up to 20GB or even larger. The large size makes the databases harder to maintain and administer. And today, even though fast backup hardware is available, making it possible to back up 5 to 10 or even more megabytes per hour, a large database can still take four hours or more to back up, which is sort of a practical limit. Either you should make sure your databases aren't growing beyond that limit or you should get a faster backup solution. The situation, though, can be even worse when you need to do a restore, especially with Exchange 5.5, because first you have to stop the complete server, then restore the database, and then start all Exchange services again, making the Information Store service go into hard recovery mode, and replay the transaction logs. If you are lucky, the system can be up and running again after about five hours. During that time all mailbox users on this Exchange 5.5 server will have been without mail functionality.

Exchange 2000 has a solution to this problem—multiple stores (or databases) grouped together in storage groups, also known as SGs. Now, instead of using just one database for your users, you can divide them among several, making the size of each store smaller and more manageable. The Information Store process is responsible for handling all storage groups and their stores. It is now possible to manage each store individually regarding backup and restore procedures. For example, you can split your 20GB store into four stores, making each store about 5GB in size. This provides several benefits:

- You can have more users per server
- You can do an individual backup and restore of each store
- You can use a store for special needs

More Users Per Server

The most important reason why administrators set a limit on how many users they allow on one single Exchange server is because of the size of the store. Since you can now have multiple stores, you can add many more users to the server. Exchange 5.5 previously had a limit of 3,000 users, based on practical experience and tests done with the excellent Loadsim tool (you can find it on the Exchange resource kit or download it from Microsoft's Web site at **www.microsoft.com/exchange**). With the new features in Exchange 2000, tests are done that now set the upper limit to about 30,000 simultaneous MAPI users for a server with eight CPUs—that's a lot of users on one single server.

Currently, you can have up to four different storage groups per server with up to five different stores for each of these storage groups. Each individual store is limited to 16TB in size, as with the databases in the previous Exchange 5.5 Enterprise version. That makes a total of 20 stores per server. How many users could you have on such a server? Well, assuming you don't want stores larger than 20GB, and with a max mailbox size of 100MB (rather normal today, in my experience), you would have 20GB / 100MB = 200 users per store. You could then have up to 3,800 users (200 × 19) if you used all available stores. Keep in mind that each server needs to have at least one store for public folders, so you can actually have only 19 mailbox stores as compared to the total 20. But you can still have 3,800 users as compared to 200 users. And no store will be larger than 20GB, which is great, isn't it?

You must not forget that you need to back up all stores too. And if it takes four hours to take a backup of one 20GB store, it would take about 80 hours to back up all 20 stores, including the public store, which really is something to think about, isn't it? Eighty hours really seems like an unacceptable number of hours. But you can help solve this both by using faster backup solutions and by running several backups simultaneously. So you see, it's not necessarily the number of stores that solves every problem; you must still remember to plan the backup solution very carefully.

Individual Backup and Restore

The Information Store process controls all storage groups and their storage files. Although previous versions of the IS process let you take online backups, if you needed to do a restore, you had to stop the IS process and in doing that, stop all user access to the server. In this version, the IS has been enhanced not only to handle the multiple storage groups and stores, but also to make it possible to do a restore of one single store without affecting the other. And, of course, you can still take online backups just as you did before.

It is important to understand that each storage group shares the same set of transaction log files. So regardless of whether you have only one or up to five stores in your storage group, they all share the same log files. That means that you normally won't take backups of a single store even if it is possible; you will take a backup of the complete storage group, including its transaction log files. That is the only way you can be sure that your transaction files are matching the status of all stores in the storage group.

A recovery process that means you have to restore a single store (i.e., the EDB file, the STM file, or both) is possible. To do this, you don't have to dismount the other stores in this storage group or the other storage groups. This means that the ongoing recovery process will not affect mailbox users belonging to other stores. When you mount the store after the restore process is done, IS will start the hard recovery process and check the log files for missing transactions that will then be replayed.

Using a Store for Special Needs

Having multiple stores and storage groups also means that you can address the separate needs of your users. Many organizations have groups with special needs, like a management team, a research team, or any other group that places higher demand on the availability of the mail system than the usual mailbox users.

You could use separate stores to address special needs; for example, when:

- Users that accept only very short down times need to be placed in a small store that you take a backup of multiple times per day, backing up to maybe a disk instead of a tape.
- Stores used for transient data, like news group feeds, need to be placed in a separate store where you activate the circular logging feature. Depending on the type of data, you may choose not to take a backup of this store at all.

- Stores used for special applications, like document management systems or help desk applications, are likely candidates for separate stores.
- You use a store for separate companies. Maybe several companies share the same Exchange 2000 server. Then it might be smart to keep each company in its own store, or possibly even its own storage groups.

You still have to think about the transaction log system; remember that all stores in a storage group share the same set of log files and transaction log settings. This means that if you want to activate the circular logging, you must place this store in its own storage group, since this setting is done on the storage group level. For example, you cannot have a storage group with one store using circular logging and another store not using it.

How Many Storage Groups Should I Have?

It is easy to create a storage group and its stores. In fact, it may be too easy, making administrators think that they can create a new one without any real planning. Don't do this. You will only increase the load of the server without achieving anything important. Every mounted store that is created takes about 10MB of memory; if you mount 20 stores, it takes 200MB of memory. And that is simply to mount them. When you start using them, it will place an even greater load on the memory. That said, make sure to have enough memory on your server; the exact amount is impossible to pinpoint, but in a production environment you should have no less than 512MB of memory when multiple stores and storage groups are used. Use the Performance Monitor in Windows 2000 to monitor how much memory is used; if necessary, add more memory to the Exchange server.

The Information Store service (the Store.exe) creates a special process for handling the stores, called the "client instance." Every storage group gets its own client instance, and each of these instances needs virtual memory allocated. This client instance also handles the transaction logs and is the reason why each storage group has its own set of transaction logs. For each new storage group, the load will increase on the virtual memory and the CPU. Microsoft has tested how much load on the virtual memory a normal server can accept and found that four storage groups is an upper practical limit today. This is due partly to the way the Information Store handles these storage groups but mainly to limits in the Windows 2000 Server 32-bit architecture. You can expect to see this number increase as new service packs for Exchange 2000 and Windows 2000 are released. When the next Windows version, "Whistler," is released, it will be based on a 64-bit architecture and therefore be able to handle much more virtual memory than today.

As you may recall, Exchange 2000 has a theoretical limit of 15 active storage groups (and also a 16th storage group used for recovery situations). Each storage group can handle up to six stores, but, at this point in time, you cannot create more than five stores. The reason for the limit of five stores, for the time being, is that if you do a recovery or run the ESEutil.exe utility, the Information Store will need a spare store for its use. By setting the limit to five stores, it will always have the sixth store available for recovery situations.

If you could use all storage groups and stores, you would have 90 stores per server. Even though one of these must function as a public store, 89 are still left for mailbox stores. Whenever it's possible to use all these stores, only a fraction of all companies are usually interested in utilizing all of them. Probably only ISPs or possibly very large corporations would be seriously interested in this. Due to the demand for virtual memory, you should keep to one single storage group as long as you can. If the number of users makes the size of the stores more than what you can accept, maybe 10 to 20GB, or if you have a special need to enable circular logging, you should add an extra storage group. But you should not add storage groups simply because it's possible for you to do it—think hard about your motives before you add a new storage group.

Use Decision Tree 2.1 as a guide to when multiple storage groups should be created. Remember, this is only a recommendation; you must still make the final decision.

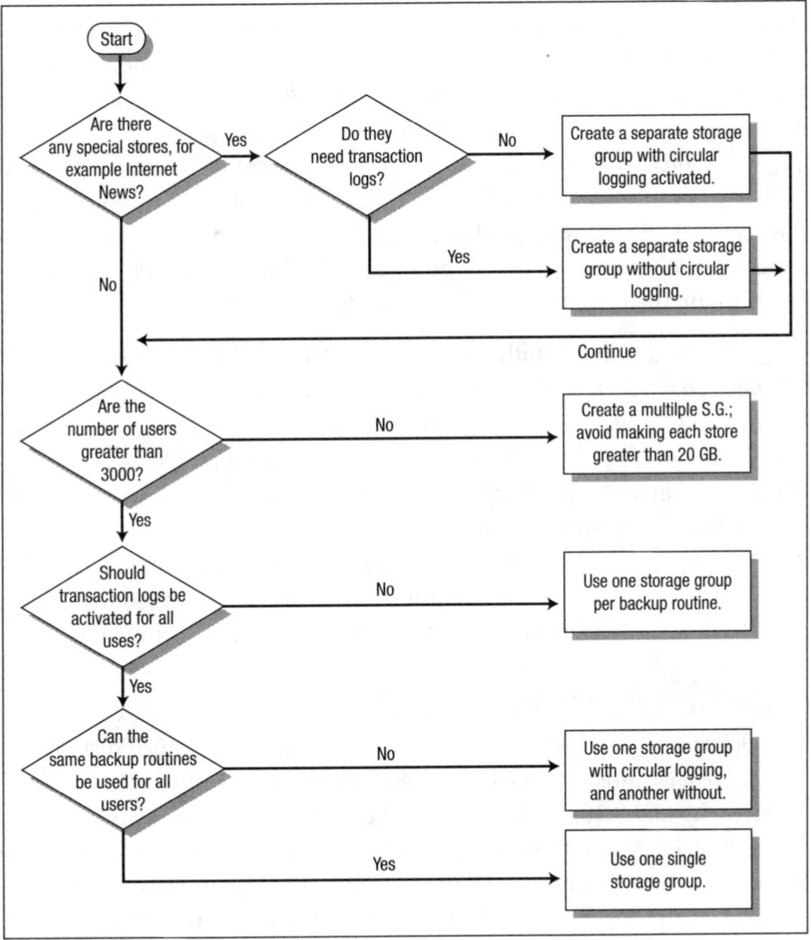

Decision Tree 2.1
When to create multiple storage groups.

Storage Groups and Clusters

Exchange 2000 Enterprise Server is cluster aware. This means that you can install Exchange 2000 on a Windows 2000 cluster environment. With Windows 2000 Advanced Server, you can have up to two nodes in a cluster; with Windows 2000 Datacenter Server, you can have up to four nodes. A cluster is excellent for building solutions with high demand on fault-tolerance and resilience. The cluster solution in Windows NT 4 is based on the active-passive architecture, which means that if you have a cluster with two nodes, only one of them will be active while the other just sits there and waits for the first node to break down. But Windows 2000 has a new active-active architecture, thus making it possible to work with all nodes simultaneously.

This active-active cluster gives you new possibilities for designing your Exchange 2000 environment, but you must not forget the total limit of four storage groups for each server. Let's say that you have a cluster with two nodes. You install Exchange 2000 on both of them, and since they're cluster aware they will know about each other's existence in the cluster. Both of them will look as one, from the client's perspective, and it will only be the cluster itself that knows there are actually two Exchange servers running. So you decide to use two storage groups for the first node and three storage groups for the second node. Everything works nicely until one day when one of the nodes gets some sort of hardware problem. Now you expect that the other node would take over the responsibilities of the faulty node. But if it tried, it would fail since the single node that's left (and is expected to take over all storage groups) would not be able to. Two plus three is five, and this is one more storage group than Exchange 2000 can handle.

In general, you should plan carefully how to use your nodes in the cluster. Make sure that if one node goes down, then the working node will be able to take over all storage groups from the other node. You should also make sure the node that still works has enough memory, CPU, and other system resources available in order to take over the load. Note that this planning can be harder than you first may think. Make sure you understand how the cluster works in both Windows 2000 and Exchange 2000 together. For more information, Microsoft has a good article on its Web site, **www.microsoft.com/exchange/techinfo/deploymigrate.htm** about exactly this subject, titled "Installing Microsoft Exchange 2000 Server on a Windows 2000 Cluster." Read it before you install your first cluster server.

How Much Disk Space Is Needed?

With up to 20 stores at your disposal, you will want to know how much disk space you'll actually need. We have already talked about what your disk layout should look like (refer back to Figures 2.9 and 2.10), but how large should your disks be? This is important to know because you don't want to go back and expand your server after just a few months simply because you underestimated the need for disk space (your boss wouldn't like that either). Several factors affect total disk space; here are the most important:

- The number of users on the server
- The average mailbox size

- The number of stores
- The use of public folders
- Whether or not the soft delete feature has been used
- Whether or not circular logging is being used

Today it is common to accept about 100MB in size for each mailbox user. Certainly some users today have mailboxes over 1GB, but they are still uncommon. However, the need for disk space will increase when email is accepted as a distribution channel for larger file attachments. In just a few years, we will probably send video and voice messages in our mail, which may be more than 100MB each in size. As an Exchange administrator, you must be prepared for that and make sure your mail system can handle all this data.

It has always been very difficult to predict how much mail users will send and receive, but several tools are available that can help you check out how much they use it today. In Exchange, you can set up the server to make a copy of all incoming and outgoing mail with the *Archive All Messages Sent Or Received By Mailboxes On This Store* feature, shown in Figure 2.11, or by using the Mailbox Statistics Tool utility found in the Backoffice Resource Kit. Several vendors sell analysis programs for Exchange usage, like Crystal Report, for example. You don't have to analyze all users' mail; depending on the organization, you should get a good estimate with maybe 25 people randomly selected and measured during a period of one typical month.

When you analyze the mail statistics, you will probably find that some, if not most, people send and receive about 10 to 20 emails per day, with an average size of between 20 to 50K.

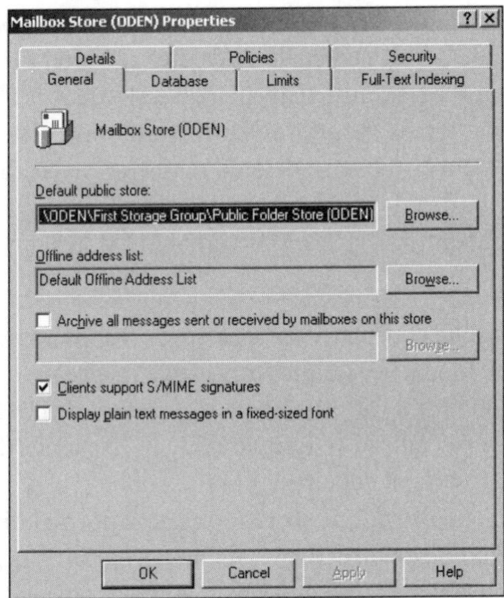

Figure 2.11
Archive all messages sent or received by mailboxes on this store.

If you ask these people, they will probably tell you that they send and receive much more mail than that, including mail with much larger attachments. I remember one MS Mail administrator I posed this question to who responded that the average mail size for his organization of about 2,000 people was over 1MB. This was an extremely large average, so, still curious, I asked him for the mail log from the previous month with all the incoming and outgoing mail; I did a quick calculation and found that the average was 15K, with only 2 percent of all messages larger than 1MB. This administrator didn't believe me, so I repeated the analysis on the preceeding month, and I still came to the same result. I tell you this story because I want you to understand that you should not just ask random users about their mail traffic and then assume that this number is true for the entire organization. You must calculate it for yourself. It is your reputation that will be in trouble if the system is suboptimized.

So once you have all your data, it's time to start calculating. Just to give you a better idea of how all this works, let's assume that your organization has 500 users, and these are the numbers you've found that you must work with:

- Average incoming and outgoing mail: 16 with a size of 30K = 480K/day
- Total disk usage per day = 960K (480 for the store + 480 for transaction logs)
- Total disk usage for 500 users = 480MB/day
- Total disk usage per month = 14.4GB

Notice that I have not calculated with any public folder usage here at all. If we assume that people are storing their mail for up to one month, it would mean that this store must be able to handle up to 14GB, including transaction files. This is, however, not completely true. The transaction logs are normally deleted every night (when the backup runs), so the total monthly size is probably around 8GB. But people don't delete mail after 30 days; they want to keep it forever, right? So even if we assume that the real disk usage is about 8GB per month, we would still need 48GB after six months and 96GB after one year. If we also assume that we use the soft delete feature and store deleted mails for seven days, it would increase the total size to about 1.6GB. When you do calculations like this for yourself, you'll quickly find that you need to think about disk space, the number of stores, and how to back up all this information.

If we then also start to think about public folders, the needed disk space will increase even further. Most organizations today have much smaller public stores than mailbox stores. I would estimate that the ratio is usually around 1:5, with the mailbox stores five times larger than the public stores. However, with the new Web store functionality in Exchange 2000, you can expect that your users will store all sorts of documents in the public stores instead of the file system. Since the ExIFS will make the public store look like a normal disk, it will be easy to read and write from the Web Store directory from any program, such as, for example, MS Word or MS Excel. The advantage that comes with storing information in the public store is higher resilience due to the transaction logs and easier access due to the Outlook Web access. As an administrator, you must take this into account when you calculate the disk space that is needed. It may easily double or even triple whatever sum you have today.

Creating a Storage Group

Use the Exchange System Manager, ESM, to create new storage groups. Remember, this version of Exchange 2000 will only allow you to create up to four storage groups per server. This section will guide you through the steps to installing a second storage group and offer a description of its properties (see Figure 2.12).

To install the new storage group, open the ESM tool, and expand the *Server's* folder. Locate your server; right-click on it and select *New|Storage Group*, then follow these steps:

1. Fill in the *Name* field with the name of the new storage group. Notice that this will also automatically be used as the name of the file directory for the transaction log location and the system path location.
2. Use the Browse button to select another file directory or type in a new path directly. The *Zero Out Deleted Database Pages* option is used if you need to write zero in all deleted pages in all future stores for this storage group. Note that this will decrease the general performance of this storage group and should only be selected if for any reason you want to make sure that pages that are deleted really are overwritten and impossible to read again. This zeroing will be done during the online backup.
3. The *Enable Circular Logging* option should only be selected if you really are sure that all stores in this storage group will use circular logging. If you enable this, you will only get one active log file and four old log files, giving you a total of 25MB.

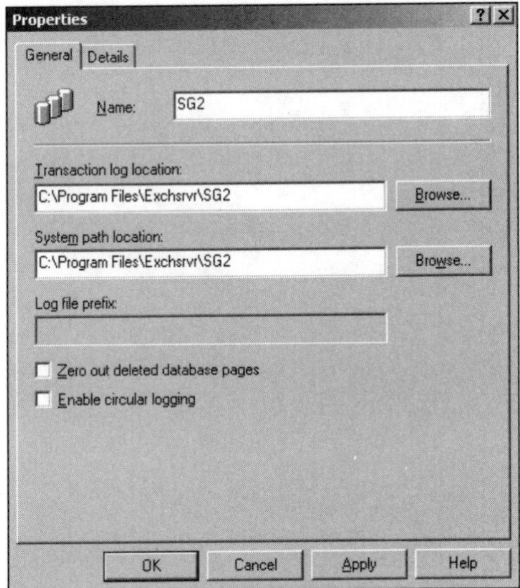

Figure 2.12
Creating the new SG2 storage group.

4. On the *Details* tab, you can write an administrative note about this storage group; you can also see when it was created and when it was last modified. After you click on *OK*, you will find the new storage group under your server. If you don't see it, select the server and press F5 to refresh the ESM tool.

Creating a Store

Now when you have a new storage group, the next logical step is to create a store. Remember that you may have up to five stores within each storage group and that each store is a collection of one EDB file and one STM file. This section will guide you through the steps to create a new store and a description of its properties.

The General Tab

Use the ESM and select the storage group you want to create the new store in; right-click on it and select New. You will have a choice of creating a Public Store or a Mailbox Store. The public store is used for storing public folder data and at least one is needed on every Exchange server. The mailbox store is used for storing mailbox data. For this example, we will create a mailbox store (see Figure 2.13).

Use the *Name* field to give the new mailbox store a name. Although you are free to choose any name, it is common to use names such as PRIV1 or MBX1 because later, names like this make it easier to understand that this is a mailbox store.

The *Default Public Store* field points to the first public store created on this server and is normally accepted. Only if you have more than one public store will you be able to select another store. All mailbox users on this server will use this public store whenever they create a public folder.

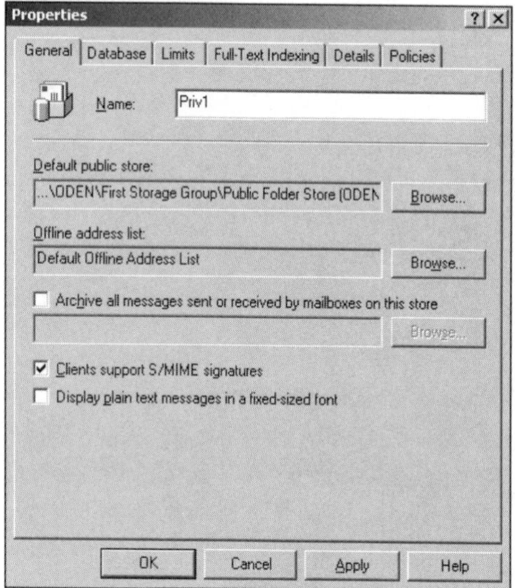

Figure 2.13
Creating a mailbox store—the General tab.

The *Offline Address List* field points to the default downloadable address list, usually used by laptop computers. If you have more than one offline address list, the users will be able to select any of them. Each mailbox store exports address list data to an offline address list, which allows laptop users to browse the complete Exchange organization even when they are offline.

The *Archive All Messages Sent Or Received By Mailboxes On This Store* option creates an archive copy of all messages to or from users on this store. If you select this option, you will then use the *Browse* button to select the receiver of all this archived mail. Please check with your organization's mail policy and make sure it is legal before using this option, since this is a way to get a copy of all mail without the users noticing.

The *Clients Support S/MIME Signatures* option is needed if any of your users are using S/MIME signatures. If this is unselected, the Exchange server will not understand the special attachment that email with a signature has and will make it unusable for the client. Note that your clients can have an S/MIME added without the Exchange server knowing about it. This feature should always be selected. You will learn more about S/MIME in Chapter 14.

The *Display Plain Text Messages In A Fixed-Sized Font* option is used for converting all incoming mail without any formatting to a fixed-size font, i.e., courier. This can be used to avoid displaying ASCII diagrams and pictures.

The Database Tab

Now let's continue with creating our store. Under the *Database* tab in the Properties dialog box (see Figure 2.14), use the *Exchange Database* field to point to the file directory where the EDB file will be stored. Note that the name is inherited from the name of the

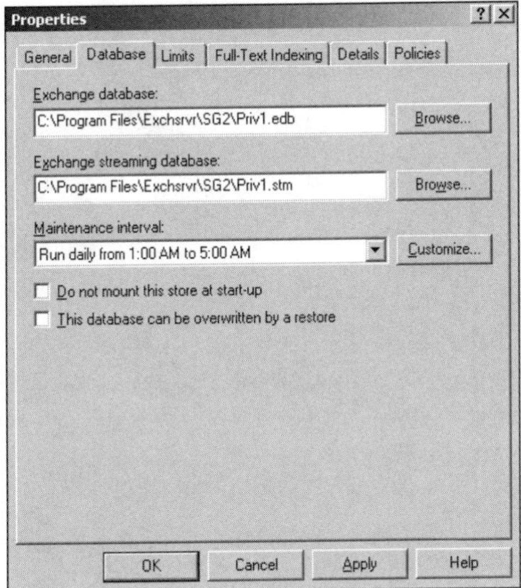

Figure 2.14
Creating a mailbox store—the Database tab.

store itself. Use the *Browse* button to point to another directory or write the new path directory in the field.

The *Exchange Streaming Database* field points to the file directory where the STM file will be stored. This can be a different directory than the EDB file, but usually you keep them together.

The *Maintenance Interval* field is used to specify the time when Exchange will perform online defragmentation and other maintenance operations on this store. If you have several stores, it may be good to use different time schedules for each store; otherwise, Exchange will run this operation on all stores at the same time. Select the *Customize* button to select another schedule. The default schedule is between 1 A.M and 4 A.M.

The *Do Not Mount This Store At Start-up* option can be selected if you don't want this store to be automatically mounted when you start the Information Store service. This could be used when you have a test store or another store that is not a part of the production system; by not starting this store you will decrease the load of the memory.

The *This Database Can Be Overwritten By A Restore* option is a protection to prevent overwriting a store by mistake. Before you can restore a store from backup, this option must be selected. Otherwise, Exchange will not allow you to do an online restore.

The Limits Tab

The *Limits* tab in the Properties dialog box (see Figure 2.15) is mainly used for defining the default values for all users on this mailbox store. If you later change any of these values, all users on this store will be directly affected unless they have been given other explicit values. Note that the default is to have no limits at all; you will probably change

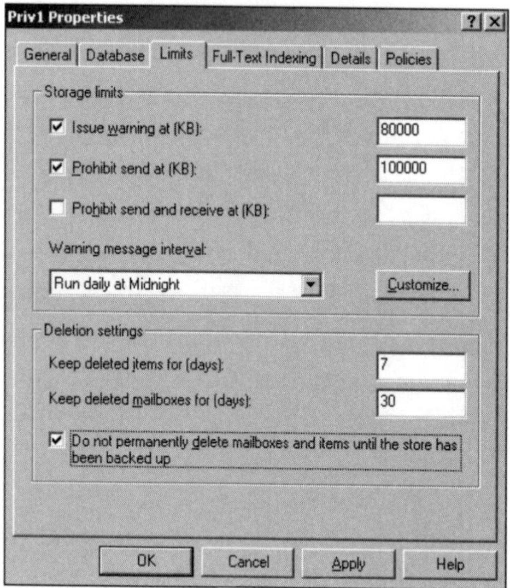

Figure 2.15
Creating a mailbox store—the Limits tab.

some of these values. This tab is very useful and one that you will return to several times. It is one of the best methods for you to control the size of this store.

The *Issue Warning At (KB)* option is used to set a limit on users' mailboxes. If they exceed this value, they will automatically get warning messages from the system at the time defined in the *Warning Message Interval* schedule, saying they have exceeded the mailbox size and by how much. This is default-cleared, which means that there are no defined warning levels. I recommend that you set a warning limit even if you have lots of disk space; users usually don't know how large their mailboxes are, but if you set this, they will be aware of when they pass a certain limit. In Figure 2.15, I have set a warning limit of 80MB.

The *Prohibit Send At (KB)* option is used to set an upper limit on the mailbox. If the users exceed this limit, their send functionality will be temporary disabled, meaning that whenever they try to send a new message or reply to a message, they will get an error message, informing them that they must first delete messages until they get back under this limit before their send functionality can be activated again. This is very effective if you want to keep your users from exceeding a certain mailbox size limit. It is all automatic and as the administrator, you will not need to do anything. In Figure 2.15, I have set a limit of 100MB.

The *Prohibit Send And Receive At (KB)* option will not only prohibit the user from creating new mail if he exceeds this limit, it will also refuse to accept any new incoming mail. New mail will be returned to the sender as with a non-delivery report (NDR). At first, this might sound like it complements the Prohibit Send option very nicely, but in reality it may create more problems than it solves. Let's say that you have your limit set to 110MB. One of your users exceeds this limit and all mail, both internal and external, sent to this user is now generating an NDR. Assume that one person outside the organization has been sending mail to this user for a long time and now suddenly, he gets this NDR message. If this is an ordinary person and not an email expert, he will probably interpret this as just an error message and try to resend the messages, maybe even several times. After a while, he will probably call the intended recipient and tell this person about the problem. Then both of them will now call their respective help desks. If at all possible, I recommend that you try to avoid using this option unless you have a very good reason to.

The *Warning Message Interval* is used to define when the warning message will be sent. You will normally get only one warning per day. The default for this is at midnight.

The *Keep Deleted Items For (Days)* option is not default activated, but in Figure 2.15, I have set this value to 7 days. This option is often referred to as the *soft delete*, and is used to define how many days the store should keep a copy of all deleted message items. This is an excellent feature, saving the administrator the work of restoring a mailbox store when a user has deleted an important message by mistake. The drawback is that it increases the size of the store with the size of all mail during this time period. Usually, though, it's worth this, since a restore is something you want to try to avoid for as long as you can. Buy more disks if necessary, but use this feature unless you have a good reason not to. The normal value for this is usually between 3 and 10 days.

The *Keep Deleted Mailboxes For (Days)* is a new feature for Exchange 2000. It will make the administrator's life even easier, since it will save a deleted mailbox for default 30 days before it is removed from the store completely. This value is usually appropriate as it is, so don't change this unless you have a very good reason.

The *Do Not Permanently Delete Mailboxes And Items Until The Store Has Been Backed Up* option is default on. This means that if you take backups only on the weekends (which, by the way, is not recommended) and you have a Keep Deleted Items value of 5 days, it will still not remove these mail items until the store has been backed up.

This new store object has three more tabs: *Full-Text Indexing*, *Details*, and *Policies*. The *Full-Text Indexing* tab is used for controlling the indexing process of this store. The *Details* tab is used for writing administrative notes, if needed. You can also see when this store was created and find the date of the last modification. The *Policies* tab lists all policies that are enforced on this store. A detailed description of indexing and policies will be given later in the section titled "Full-Text Indexing."

After you have defined all values, click *OK* to create the store. If you are running ESM on any computer other than the Exchange 2000 server itself, you will be warned that ESM cannot check to see that these directories really exist on the server. Just accept that by selecting *OK*. The final question is whether or not you will want to mount it now or not. Usually you'll want to answer yes to this question.

The Installable File System

One of the many new features that come with Windows 2000 Server is the IFS (installable file systems). Previously, you only had a file system for your disks, whether it was physical or logical, and these were fixed. With an installable file system, you can dynamically add a new file system, connecting to something that will look and behave exactly like a disk, even if it is not. This is not a new idea. In fact, Unix has had this for many years; but this is the first time that Microsoft has included this feature in its operating system.

The ExIFS—Exchange Installable File System

Previously, we could select to store our files and documents only in the ordinary file system, in a Web server, or in a public folder. For example, with MS Word, you could save your work in a public folder by using File|Send To|Exchange Folder. If you later wanted to open this document again, it was not possible to browse the public folder structure directly from MS Word—you had to use the Outlook client, locate the document, and double-click it so that MS Word would start with this document, thanks to the DOC file association. It is, as you can see, clearly not the easiest way of accessing your MS Word documents.

The ExIFS changes that completely, making accessing public folders as easy as accessing normal file directories. You can now use any type of application and access all Exchange folders, both public folders and mailbox folders, that you have permission to use. For example, let's say that you use MS Word to save a document to the public folder Projects;

you can later open this public folder with the Outlook client or a Web browser and access the document. It is completely transparent to the user and the application.

The ExIFS will make all data inside Exchange accessible, but all normal permission controls are working. You cannot see anything for which you don't have permission. Regardless of how many stores and storage groups the server has, it will still be presented as one single file system. On the Exchange server itself, you will find the M drive automatically mapped to the ExIFS, with two root folders: "MBX" with the alias name for all mailbox folders, and "Public Folders" with all public folders. Any clients who want to access the Exchange folders need to map a network drive to this M drive. Microsoft also calls this *Web storage*.

Note: *During the Beta phase of Exchange 2000, the development team referred to this ExIFS share as the BackOfficeStorage. You might find references to this share name, but it was removed before the product was released. Share the M drive on the server to give clients access to the Web storage.*

Why Store Information in Exchange Folders?

Why would anyone want to store office documents or similar files in a public store? The reason is two-fold:

- Security
- Access

Since Exchange has the transaction logs that keep a copy of all messages in a store, it is much more resilient than a usual file system. If you save a new document to a server that is running backups every night, you would only have a copy after a backup is taken. In other words, if you created a document at 2 P.M. but at 6 P.M. the disk became corrupted, your document would not have been stored on any backup, and all would be lost. If you instead had saved this document in an Exchange folder, the transaction log would have been able to protect it.

Access to Exchange folders is easier compared with access to ordinary file systems. A document saved in an Exchange folder may be accessed by an Outlook client, the Web client, or by any type of program, such as MS Word. Documents stored in an ordinary file directory can be accessed only by programs, not by Outlook or Web clients (unless you have published the file directory as a Web folder). How important is that? Let's say that you are working outside the office and need to access a document stored on the server. If this document is stored in an Exchange folder, you could use the Web client to get it; if it's stored in the ordinary file system, you would need to use a remote access connection like a modem to access the server. Storing information in Exchange folders makes the information easier to reach from wherever you might be. Of course, you need to plan for security very carefully; you don't want unauthorized people to be able to access this information.

Accessing the Web Storage by Using the Web Client

Besides being able to access the Web storage with the Outlook client and other ordinary programs, you will now also be able to use the Exchange Web client, known as the Outlook Web Access (OWA). This client uses Hypertext Transfer Protocol (HTTP) to communicate with the IIS Web server and gain access to the Web store. Exchange has had the OWA client since version 5 and even though it has been enhanced several times, it still has limitations as to what it can access, like public folders of contact type or calendar type. Today, there's an enhancement to the HTTP 1.1 protocol, called HTTP-DAV, also known as the Web-DAV. DAV stands for *Distributed Authoring and Versioning* and adds commands for searching, copying, deleting, locking, and unlocking resources, such as files and documents on the Web server. It also makes it possible to access an extended number of properties for objects. Web-DAV is an important extension that makes it possible to build Web clients with almost the same look and feel as an ordinary network client like Outlook 2000.

The new OWA server in Exchange 2000 also supports XML, or *eXtended Markup Language*. This protocol is used to describe the data transferred between the server and the Web client and makes it possible to let a user modify and save a document over the Internet with an XML-enabled Web browser, much like a normal network client. All clients are not XML enabled yet, since this is a rather new feature in Web browsers; only version 5 and later MS Internet Explorer understands XML. With both the XML and the Web-DAV features, you can access all information in the Exchange Web store almost as easily as the ordinary Outlook 2000 client can.

Public Folders

Ever since the first release of Exchange, it has been possible to share information by using public folders. A public folder is similar to a mailbox folder, except that it can be visible for all users that have permission to see it. All users are by default granted permission to create new public folders and access other users' public folders; they can add new items, and they can modify and delete their own items. All items in a public folder are stored in a public store, consisting of one EDB file and one STM file, exactly like a mailbox store. Every Exchange server must have at least one public store. All public folders, regardless of what server and store they belong to, will be displayed as one single tree for the clients, as illustrated in Figure 2.16.

The public folder consists of these two parts:

- The name (or hierarchy) of the folder
- The content in the folder

The name is replicated to all servers in the Exchange organization, regardless of how large and distributed it is. The Information Store process is responsible for this replication, not the Active Directory. The content in a public folder is stored by default in one single place: the public store belonging to the server where the public folder was created. This means that the name will be visible (if it's not hidden) to all users in the entire organization.

Figure 2.16
The default public folder tree.

But the content may or may not be accessible, depending on whether the client has access to the public store or not.

The Public Folder Hierarchy

Exchange 2000 allows two possible types of public folders, MAPI folders and General Purpose (GP) folders. When you install an Exchange server, you will, by default, get the *All Public Folder* tree, which is a MAPI folder. It is the same type of public folder tree as in previous versions of Exchange. The MAPI public folder tree is visible to all types of clients who know about public folders, such as Outlook (MAPI) clients, Web clients, IMAP4, and NNTP clients, and applications using ExIFS, like Word and Excel. The GP type of public folder, on the other hand, must be created manually. It is only visible for Web clients, NNTP clients, and applications using ExIFS; it is not visible to MAPI clients.

The names of the MAPI public folders are replicated to all public stores in the organization, making them globally visible. This can be a problem if you don't have strict policies for creating public folders. Any Outlook client can create a public folder, and by default, all users have permission to do that. This could very easily result in public folder chaos. For example, if we assume that you have an Exchange organization distributed over three different countries, and each country has one Exchange server with 300 users each, you would have a total of 900 users. If now every individual user creates one public folder each, the result would be 900 public folders showing up in each and every user's Outlook client! And to make matters worse, depending on how your network is configured, it could be that users are only able to access the content on folders belonging to their own server, giving them an warning message every time they try to access one of the other 600 folders; it's easy to understand how frustrated users could be.

The best thing to do would be to take control of the situation right from the beginning by restricting the permission to create public folders in the top of the folder tree (also known as the *Top-Level folders*) to a small group, making this group your official public folder administrators. This can be done with the ESM tool. Microsoft has an article about this, titled "*Restricting Users from Creating Top Level Folders in Exchange 2000 Server*," in which it describes how to use the *Security* tab for the *Public Folders* folder and deny the group *Everyone* permission to create top-level public folders. But the problem is that this method is not really practical. If you do that, no one will be able to create a top-level folder at all, not even the administrator. This is due to the fact that in Windows 2000, a "deny" permission has priority over all other permissions, and all users belong to the group Everyone. The problem really comes from the fact that the permission to create top-level folders is inherited from the Exchange organization object. So the solution is to remove this permission from the group Everyone. But when you look at the properties for that object, it doesn't have a *Security* tab displayed; however, this tab can be made visible by modifying the registry. Use the following method to make the *Security* tab visible and remove the Create Top Level Public Folder permission from the organization object:

1. Start the Regedit.exe utility.
2. Locate the following key in the Registry: HKEY_CURRENT_USER\Software\Microsoft\Exhange\EXAdmin.
3. On the Edit menu, click Add Value and add this new Registry value:
   Value Name: ShowSecurityPage
   Data Type: REG_DWORD
   Value: 1
   Radix: Decimal
4. Use the ESM and right-click on the Exchange organization object at the top of the tree; select Properties. Now you have the Security page displayed.
5. Locate the Everyone group in the Name pane.
6. Remove the Allow permission for the Create Top Level Public Folder. Don't select Deny since this would create the same result as the first method Microsoft recommends.

The only user that can create a top-level public folder now is the Exchange administrator. I recommend that you create a special security group for the public folder administrators and grant that group permission to add top-level folders.

Note: *The Registry method described above to make the* Security *tab visible for the organization object is local for the computer where you add this new Registry value. If you are using the ESM on more than one computer, you should add this Registry value to all of them.*

If a public folder is mail enabled (by right-clicking on it and selecting *All tasks|Mail Enable*), a new object for this folder will be created in the Active Directory; however, its name will, or will not, be displayed in the global address list, depending on what operation mode this Exchange organization is running in. For example, all MAPI folders will automatically be mail enabled, but hidden, if Exchange runs in mixed mode. Table 2.4 describes the relation-ship between MAPI and GP folders in mixed versus native mode.

Table 2.4 MAPI and GP folders in mixed versus native mode.

PF Type	Mixed Mode	Native Mode
MAPI	Mail enabled by default (cannot be mail disabled). Default hidden from the global address list.	Mail disabled by default, can be enabled. If enabled it will, by default, be visible in the global address list.
GP	Mail disabled by default, can be enabled. If enabled it will, by default, be visible in the global address list.	Mail disabled by default, can be enabled. If enabled it will, by default, be visible in the global address list.

Creating MAPI Public Folders

You can create public folders with clients like Outlook, the Web client, or by using the ExIFS, for example, the File Explorer. But you can also create a folder by using the ESM program. Table 2.5 describes the different methods. Before you can create a folder, you need permission. To create a public folder in the root of the tree, you must have been granted the permission *Create top level public folder* on the *Public Folders* object; this can only be done using the ESM tool. To create a subfolder, you need *Create public folder* permission on the parent folder; this can be granted by using the ESM tool, or by the owner of this parent folder, using the Outlook client.

Note: *If you cannot find an option for creating a new folder, or if it's inactive (gray), you don't have the permission to create a folder there. This is true even inside the ESM tool.*

Creating General-Purpose Public Folders

As you may recall, these types of public folders are not visible to MAPI clients, but you can see and use them with the Web client, ExIFS (the file system), or NNTP clients. However, these GP folders are different from the MAPI folders in how they are made accessible to the clients; default they will not be visible except on the Exchange server where they are created; for example, you can't view a new GP folder with the Web client unless you share it first (more about this in next section).

Table 2.5 Creating public folders.

Program	How to Create the Folder
Outlook (MAPI)	Right-click on the folder where you want to create the new public folder; select New Folder from the menu. Give it a name and define what type of folder it will be (e.g., Contact, Mail items, and so on).
OWA (Web)	If you use Internet Explorer 5.x, use the same method as described for Outlook.
ExIFS	Use the File Explorer, navigate to the folder where you want to create the new public folder, e.g., M:\Humandata.se\Public Folders\ProjectX. Create a folder exactly like an ordinary file folder. Note that you cannot set the type of folder; it will automatically be of mail item type.
ESM	Locate the folder where you want to create the new folder. Right-click on the folder; select New Public Folder. Keep in mind that you cannot set the type of folder; it will automatically be of mail item type.

Before you can use this public folder type, you need to create a new public folder tree and then a corresponding public store; you cannot save a GP public folder tree in the same public store as the MAPI tree. Follow these instructions to create a GP tree:

1. Use the ESM tool and locate the container named *Folders*.
2. Right-click, then select *New|Public Folder Tree*. This will automatically be of *General Purpose* type.
3. Give the new GP tree a name, then click *OK*.

Creating the folder tree was the first part of the process. The next step is to create a public store where all data will be stored:

4. Select the storage group object where you want to create the new public store; right-click, then select *New|Public store*.
5. Give the store a proper name. Click *Browser* and select the GP folder tree created in Step 3 above.

How to Make the GP Folder Visible

If you're using the Outlook client and trying to find the new GP folder tree, you will not find it, since you are using a MAPI client. However, use the File Explorer on the server, and you will find it under the *M:\<organization>*; you can create a share to this folder, and all network clients that map a network drive to this share can then access this GP tree and its subfolders.

If you use the Web client, the GP folder will actually be invisible until you make it visible by sharing it as a Web folder. You can do this by using the *Internet Service Manager* tool or the File Explorer. To make the GP folder visible with the File Explorer, follow these steps:

1. Using the File Explorer, expand the M: drive and select the new GP folder tree.
2. Right-click and select *Sharing* from the menu.
3. Display the *Web Sharing* tab (see Figure 2.17).
4. Make sure you've selected the share feature on the *Default Web Site*; otherwise, select it now.
5. Click *Share This Folder*.
6. Click the *Add* button; enter the name **Public\<folder_tree>**, for example, *Public\GPfolders*.
7. Set the permissions as demonstrated in Figure 2.18.
8. Click *OK* until all pages are closed.

Now you can use the Outlook Web client and open the new GP folder tree by accessing this URL: **http://<server>/Public/<folder_tree>**; refer to Figures 2.17, 2.18, and 2.19 as helpful examples.

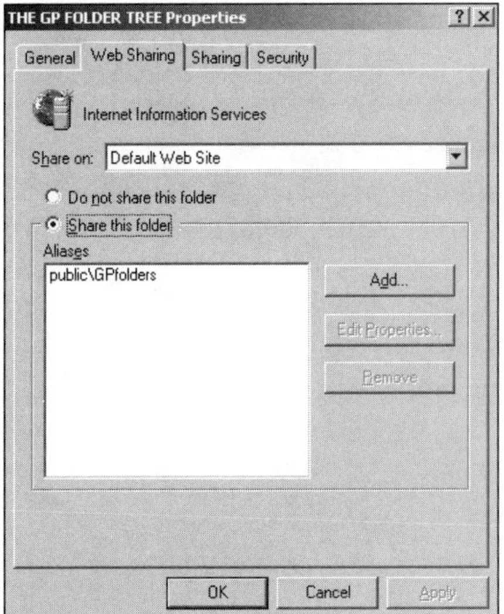

Figure 2.17
The Web Sharing tab.

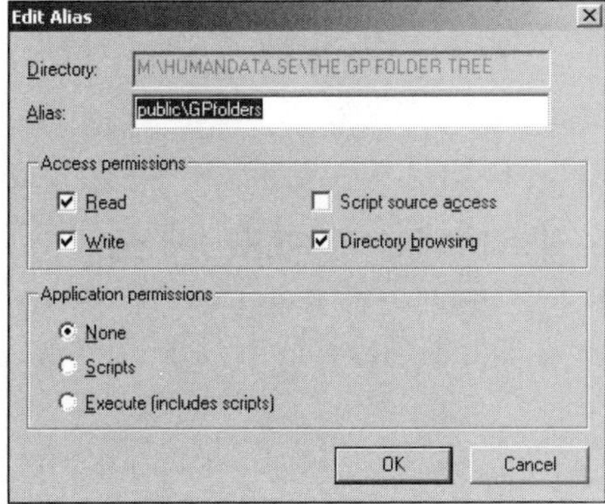

Figure 2.18
Use these settings for your new GP folder tree.

Security Settings in Public Folders

The security settings in previous Exchange versions were simple because you could only set permissions on the folder itself; all items in the folder then automatically inherited these permissions. To set the permission, you used the *Permission* tab for a folder in the Outlook client. This method is still valid today, but the number of permission roles has increased, as you will see in the list below:

- *Owner*—Handles all permissions.
- *Publishing Editor*—Reads, creates, modifies, and deletes all items as well as creates subfolders.

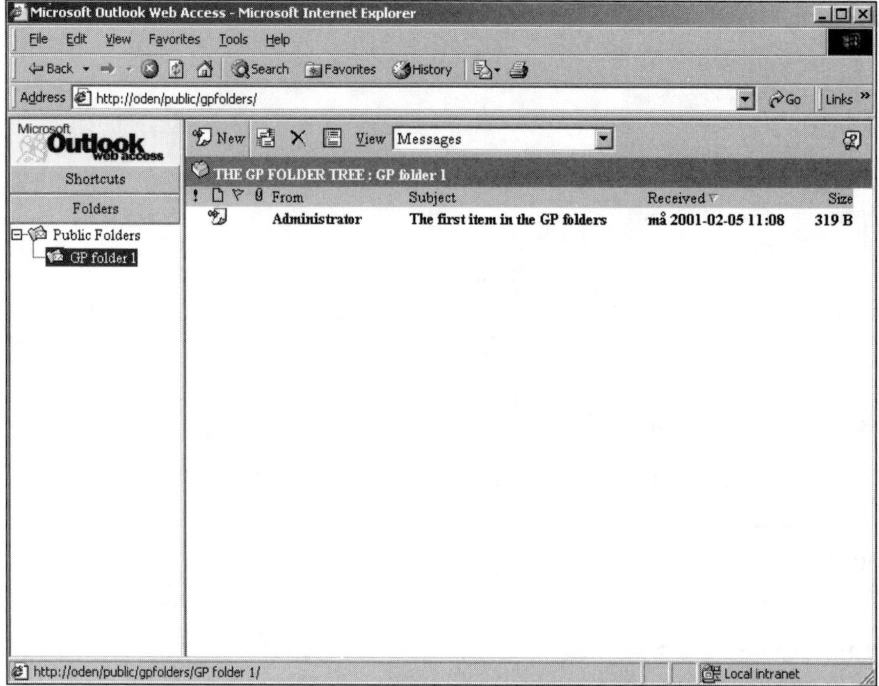

Figure 2.19
How the new GP tree looks with the Outlook Web client.

- *Editor*—Has all the same tasks as the Publishing Editor, except the Editor doesn't have permission to create subfolders.
- *Publishing Author*—Reads, creates, modifies, and deletes own items as well as creates subfolders.
- *Author*—Has all the same tasks as the Publishing Author, except the Author doesn't have permission to create subfolders.
- *Nonediting Author*—Reads, creates, and deletes own items, but doesn't have the power to modify permission.
- *Reviewer*—Read permission only.
- *Contributor*—Create permission only.
- *None*—No permission.

You give these permission roles to users and groups selected from the global address list. On top of that, you can give permissions to two special users:

- Anonymous
- Default

Since Exchange 2000 uses the Active Directory to store information about users and address lists, these two special users have corresponding AD objects:

- *Anonymous* is connected to the AD account *Anonymous Logon.*
- *Default* is connected to the AD group *Everyone.*

Storing users and security settings in the Active Directory allows new possibilities to set permissions not only to folders but to items as well. Now it is possible to set a separate permission on one single item without affecting all other items in that folder. But you cannot do this with the Outlook client; it's still restricted to the old permission roles for a folder with all items within it. You must use the File Explorer and its *Security* permission page to set individual item permissions. But be careful with setting deny permission on the Everyone group, since this will affect all users, including the owner of the folder.

The logic is that items inherit security settings from the folder; this folder has inherited its settings from the parent folder, and the top of the hierarchy is the Exchange organization object. As described before, this object does not have the *Security* tab visible by default, but rather, you must enable it with the Registry before it can be used. The inheritance flow looks like this:

Organization object => Administrative Group => Public Folder tree => Top-level folders

The ESM tool can be used to set permissions on a folder, as with the previous Exchange 5.x Admin program. But ESM also has many more possibilities. With the *Client Permission* button, you can display the same permission window as you find in the Outlook client. The *Directory Rights* button displays the permissions in Active Directory for this folder; use it to set permission to users' accounts to this folder. Finally, the *Administrative Rights* button specifies which users can modify the folder permissions.

It is possible to propagate a new security setting to subfolders in the ESM tool. Right-click on the folder you want to propagate, then select *All Tasks|Propagate Settings*; the picture that follows will let you select what you want to propagate.

***Warning!** Be very careful with this feature. More than one Exchange 5.5 administrator has destroyed individual settings on subfolders by propagating the permissions. Please be aware that the propagated settings will overwrite the previous settings in the subfolders rather than add them.*

Let's say that you have a folder tree with three levels: Folder 1 is the top level, Folder 2 is the middle level, and Folder 3 is the bottom level. In Folder 3, you've set it up so that Anna has the Owner permission. Now you want to add Bill as a new folder administrator to all three of these folders. One way of doing this is to add Bill as an Owner of Folder 1, and then propagate this permission down to Folder 2 and Folder 3; sounds easy, right? Wrong! What will happen is that whatever permission there is in Folder 1 will replace all existing permis-sions on Folder 2 and Folder 3; this means that Anna is no longer an owner of Folder 3, which is probably not what you intended to do.

The following method eliminates the need of propagating permission settings; use this and you will not fall into the propagation trap described above:

1. Make sure that all top-level folders created have an administrative group that is granted owner permissions. All subfolders will inherit this setting.
2. Set whatever user permissions needed to public folders.
3. When a new administrator needs access, make him or her a member of this administrative group.

In Exchange 2000, there's a new possibility to set permissions on individual properties for an item. For example, you could set permission for a user to be able to modify the mail body but not the subject line. This type of property permission is not possible to define with the normal clients or methods described here; you will need to write a special program for this.

Full-Text Indexing

Many Exchange users have been waiting a long time for this feature, and now, at long last, it has been included in Exchange 2000's release. In Exchange 5.5, the only way of creating a full-text index was to install the *Microsoft Site Server* program and use its advanced search engine, or you could buy third-party programs like Fulcrum Find. The new search engine in Exchange 2000 is built upon the index engine in the MS Site Server program; if you are familiar with that, you will also understand how it works now.

The search feature in Exchange 2000 is handled by the MS Search service; it will create a full-text index of both the message text and the content of well-known file attachments (see bullet list below). This advanced search feature is not activated by default; it must be configured before you can use it. Until you do this, your clients will only have the sequential (and therefore slow) search feature that has always been available in all Exchange versions, and this search is not capable of searching any file attachments. However, the advanced search engine can scan file attachments, as long as they are of a certain type:

- MS Word (.doc)
- MS Excel (.xls)
- MS PowerPoint (.ppt)
- HTML (.html, .htm, .asp)
- Text files (.txt)
- Embedded MIME messages (.eml)

It's possible for third-party software vendors to add their search filters to the MS Search engine. So really, you can expect this list to grow larger in the near future.

But even in Exchange 2000, you might sometimes find use for the sequential search, since the full-text index has a serious drawback in that it can only search for complete words.

For example, if you were to search for the word "Admin," it would not be a match for the longer word, "Administrator." Note that wildcard searching does not work; for instance, searching for "Admin*," would still not find "Administrator."

The search engine uses normalized searching, which means that it has the ability to match all possible verb stems; for example, if you were searching for the word "play," it would also be able to find the word "Playing." It's also possible to do combined searching based on properties so that you could, for example, do a search for all messages over 50K with the word "Party."

***Tip:** Only the Advanced Search features in Outlook use the MS Search engine. The basic search will always do a sequential search, even if you have activated full-text indexing, but only on messages, not in attachments.*

Before configuring the full-text index, you should plan for a few things. The fast search is done by indexing the stores (both the EDB and the STM files) and creating an index. This index will be somewhere between 15 and 30 percent in size of the files you are indexing. For example, if you index a 10GB mailbox store, the index could be around 2GB in size, so make sure you have the necessary disk space. Another thing you must be aware of is that it takes CPU and memory resources from your server. Therefore, you probably will not want to run the index process during office hours or when your backup is running.

Configuring Full-Text Indexing on a Store

All indexing is done per store; you do not need to index all stores in a storage group. To enable the index of a store with the ESM tool, you should follow these steps:

1. Use the ESM tool and locate the store that you want to index.
2. Right-click and select *Create Full-Text Index*.
3. Then decide where you want to create the necessary index files in a folder tree; the default is *\exchsrvr\ExchangeServer_<server_name>\Projects*.

Besides creating the index, you must also start the index process. Start by selecting a time for when to run the index process, using the properties for this store and its *Full-Text Indexing* tab (see Figure 2.20). Use the *Update Interval* setting to define when MS Search should run a re-indexing of new and modified items. If your users depend on up-to-date searching functionality, it may be necessary to set this interval to *Always Run*, but remember to configure the server with a fast CPU and extra memory, or else the users on this server will experience noticeable performance drops. Use the *Rebuild Interval* to define when to do a complete re-indexing of all items in the store. This may seem like an unnecessary step, but if the index gets out of sync, the users may not find what they are searching for. This could happen if you restore any information from a backup. It may be a good idea to run this rebuild once a week. You must select the *This Index Is Currently Available For Searching By Clients* option before your clients can take advantage of this full-text indexing. Normally you will always have it selected, but if you do a rebuild of the complete store

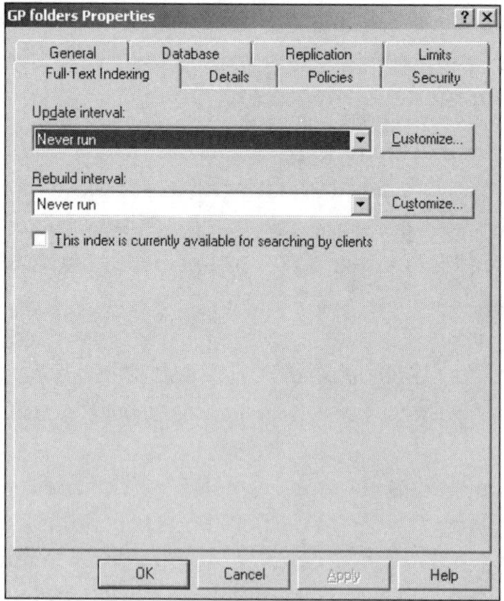

Figure 2.20
Define the time schedule for updating and rebuilding the index from the Full-Text Indexing tab.

index, it could be a good idea to deselect this option during this time, since the system cannot guarantee that the users will find what they're looking for while it does this complete rebuilding of the index files.

You can force start a full indexing by right-clicking on the store and selecting *Start Full Population*. If instead you want to force an update of an already existing index, you would select the *Start Incremental Population*. To remove all indexing for this store, select *Delete Full-Text Index*. Use the ESM tool to see the current status of the index process; under the store object you'll see a *Full-Text Indexing* folder, as in Figure 2.21. In this folder you'll see the following:

- A description of current index status (Idle = done, Crawling = working).
- The number of documents indexed so far.
- The size of the index file in megabytes.
- The last time the index was rebuilt.
- The name of the index—this name will also be used for the gather files.
- The location where the index files are stored.

The Gather Files

The MS Search process can sometimes have problems for several reasons. One problem occurs when it finds file attachments that it cannot scan; for example, when it finds a .doc file that is not actually an MS Word file. Other problems may be that the disk is full or some

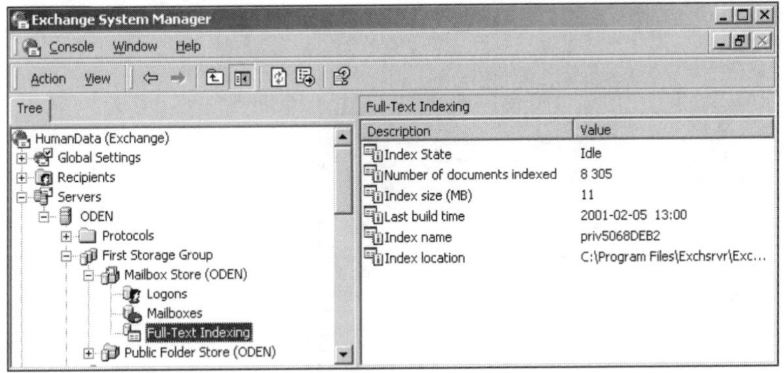

Figure 2.21
The Full-Text Indexing folder.

of the involved services, like the Information Store, have stopped. These problems will be recorded in the Event log application, so you should make sure you check this regularly.

If MS Search has trouble indexing a file or an item, it will make a note of this in a "gather" file. These gather files are created once per night, with the date as the name and .gthr as the file extension; they are stored in the *\exchsrvr\ExchangeServer_<server_name>\GatherLogs* folder. Open these gather files with a text editor to see what items and files it failed to index. A tip is that if these files are under 300 bytes, they will not contain any errors. The first three lines in the file are header information, and each line after that indicates a problematic item, with both an error code and a URL pointing to it. Instead of trying to decode these gather files, use a VB Script utility called *Gthrlog.vbs*; it is stored in the *\\Program Files\Common Files\System\MSSearch\Bin* folder. Use this utility with the syntax: *Gthrlog.vbs <gather-file>*.

***Tip:** Instead of getting a number of dialog boxes from the Gthrlog.vbs script, you could direct all output to a file with this command:* ***Gthrlog.vbs <gather-file> >Output.txt**.*

Using the Full-Text Index in the Client

When the index is built, it can be used directly; there is no need for restarting the Exchange server or the clients. All MAPI clients can take advantage of this full-text indexing. It's also possible to use the search engine with the Web-DAV protocol, but today's Outlook Web client does not yet support this feature.

Remember to use the *Advanced Search* feature in the Outlook client to activate the full-text index. The usual *Find* is still the old sequential, and therefore slow, search method. For example, an advanced search for the words "Disaster Recovery" would take two seconds in a folder with more than 5,300 items (see Figure 2.22), while using the sequential method would take more than five minutes.

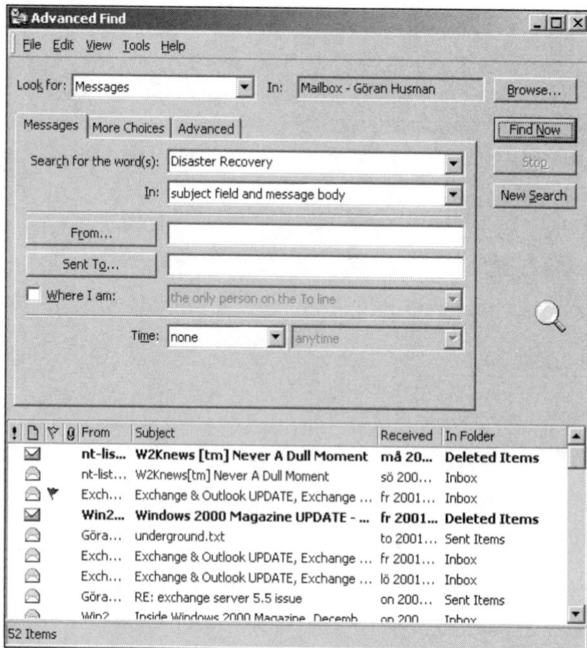

Figure 2.22
Searching for "Disaster Recovery" in a folder with 5,300 items.

Backup and Restore

All information in the Exchange stores is protected by the transaction log file, which also could be described as a continuous online backup that takes a copy of all data transfer and other transactions done on the server. If you get a corrupted database, restore the latest backup of this store; the Information Store process will then check the transaction log files and replace all missing transactions. Unfortunately, even though backup is vital for managing disasters, lots of administrators still take this responsibility very lightly. Not until a disaster occurs do they suddenly start worrying about whether the backups are good and whether they know the procedures well enough to do a restore. Then, however, it could be too late.

It's not just Exchange stores and transaction files that need to be backed up; make sure to take a backup of the index log files, the KMS files, and other special files in the Exchange environment. Since Active Directory has replaced the DIR.EDB and its directory service in the previous Exchange, it is *extremely* important to take backups of the AD database (NTDS), besides the Exchange system. If the AD database were lost, you would not be able to recover any data from the Exchange server.

Since all stores in a storage group share the same set of transaction log files, it's recommended that you take a complete backup of the storage group, even though it's possible to take backups of single stores. Microsoft has a document it regularly updates that describes how to handle different types of disasters; check out **www.Microsoft.com/exchange** for the latest version of the *Microsoft Exchange 2000 Disaster Recovery* document. Since Exchange 2000 is still a rather new product, there isn't yet a lot of real-life experience with disaster, but it will come. Of that, I'm positive.

Different Types of Backups

Backups can be either of two types: offline or online. An offline backup can only be performed if all Exchange services are stopped; otherwise, the files will be locked. However, this is not the way you would take a normal backup of Exchange. An online backup demands that the Information Store is started because the backup program must communicate with the IS in order to access the stores; this is the normal backup type for Exchange.

Before a backup program can perform an online backup procedure, it must understand how to communicate with the IS. If you use a commercial backup program, this is usually an add-on that you must purchase separately. If you don't have this add-on, you must do an offline backup. When you install Exchange 2000 on a server, you will also get an Exchange-aware version of the NTBackup.exe program. This program can be used to take online backups of Exchange, in case your ordinary backup program can't. Since most people use a commercial backup solution I will not describe the NTBackup program further, even though it does an excellent job for Exchange, and is far better than its predecessor in Windows NT. You should check it out—it may be what you are looking for!

Online backups also have several different varieties:

- Normal (full)
- Incremental
- Differential
- Copy

These types differ in what files they back up and what they do with the transaction log files; see Table 2.6.

Table 2.6 Different types of online backups.

Backup	Description
Normal	This is also referred to as *full backup*. It takes a backup of all selected storage groups, i.e., the EDB and STM file, and all current transaction log files. After the log files are copied, they are deleted. This is the most common type of online backup.
Incremental	Copies all transaction log files and then deletes them. No stores are copied. If the incremental backup runs every night, it will only have to back up the last 24 hours, which makes this a fast backup method.
Differential	Copies all transaction log files but does not delete them. If the differential backup runs every night, there will be more and more information to back up, since it won't be deleting the log files.
Copy	This takes a copy of all files and transaction logs without deleting any log files. It's like a snapshot of the files. This is a rather unusual backup method.

One important consequence of these different backup routines is how a restore is performed. For example, if you are running normal backups every night, it will be easier and faster to do a restore, since all information is stored in one tape set. But if instead you are running a full backup on the weekend and then incremental backups every workday, you must first restore the last full backup and then all incremental backups; if only one of these several tapes fails, you will not be able to restore the information. Finally, if you run a full backup on the weekend and then differential backups in between, you will need the latest full backup and the latest differential backup only; this is better than using incremental backups, since the number of tapes needed is smaller, and therefore the risk of a tape failing is less.

If the Exchange server is not using circular logging, the log files will pile up quickly. Exchange will not try to remove any log files; this is the responsibility of the backup program. Make sure that your backup knows how to handle Exchange and its log files; otherwise, the log disk will quickly run out of space.

Note: *It may sound strange, but the most common reason for an Exchange server to halt is because the disk for the log files is full. The reason is often that the backup program couldn't complete successfully, and therefore it could not remove the log files. Make sure to check the status of the backup process every day!*

Single Mailbox Backup

Since a store is shared between hundreds or even thousands of users, it is not an easy task to restore a single message or a mailbox, since you would need to restore the complete store. This, of course, is not acceptable in a production environment; you will need a spare server for this. The general recover procedure goes like this:

1. On this spare server, install Exchange in a test Windows 2000 domain, not the production domain.
2. Restore the database from the backup.
3. Use an Outlook client to copy the lost mail to a personal folder (PST file).
4. Move it to the production server and copy the message to the user.

This is clearly not an easy task, since it may take many hours to complete just for one single message. That is why the *Soft Delete* feature in Exchange is so attractive; when this feature is activated, all deleted mail will be stored in a hidden folder for the number of days that the administrator has configured. Remember that this feature is not activated by default due to the extra disk space needed.

Many commercial backup programs for Exchange have a feature often referred to as *single mailbox backup* or *brick-level backup*. This means that the backup program, after the normal backup procedure of the stores is done, will go back and take a separate backup of each selected user. This makes it possible to restore a single message, or even a single mailbox directly on the production server. The drawbacks are longer backup times and increased tape space. It sounds like an excellent idea, but in practice this can't be done for thousands of users—it would simply take too much time. Use this feature if your backup program has it, but use it selectively. Test it first on maybe 25 users and check to see how much longer it takes and how much more tape is needed; then calculate how many users can be protected by this brick-level backup. Typically it is used to take backups of the management team (and also of your own mailbox, of course).

Restoring Exchange Stores

Luckily, it is unusual for a complete Exchange server to break down, at least if you have followed the recommendations mentioned in this chapter. In most restore situations, you will probably restore only a single store and not a complete Exchange server. This is in fact easy, although it may be time consuming. Follow these steps to restore the store:

1. If the defective store is still mounted, dismount it now. Don't stop the complete server; this is unnecessary and will only slow the process down.
2. Open the properties for the defective store and make sure that you have selected the *This Database Can Be Overwritten By A Restore* option on the *Database* tab.
3. If possible, take a copy of the defective database or move it to another place, just to have the option to go back if needed.
4. Restore the file from tape and make sure it is saved in the correct directory.
5. Mount the store. The Information Store will now begin the recovery phase, which can take a long time depending on how many data and log files there are.
6. When the recovery phase is done, check the properties for the store; make sure everything looks okay. Connect a client to the store and see if it all looks okay.

If you have problems, they will be written to the Event log; check carefully to see what the problems might be. You should start all troubleshooting by inspecting the first error message regarding this problem, since the others could just be a consequence of this. Microsoft's *Knowledge Base* on the Internet is a good resource, as is the *Technet* CD. A good Web site where you can find out more about error messages related to Exchange is **www.Microsoft.com/exchange/en/60/help/default.asp**; be sure to read "Exchange 2000 Server Error and Event Messages."

Some Backup Advice

And lastly, here's some advice about backups. I'll say it again—you can never be too sure about your backups. Remember that it's just a matter of time until it's your system that breaks down. Are you prepared for that?

- Make sure you take backups every night—if possible, take online backups.
- Check the backup status every day—look in the backup program and/or the Event log.

- If you have the time and the tape, take single mailbox backups in addition to the normal backups.
- Take full backups every night, if possible. If not, take a full backup as often as possible and differential backups in between (make sure your disk can handle all log files during this time).
- Test the backup tape regularly, at least once a month, to make sure it is readable.
- Practice going through a recovery situation at least once every 3 months.
- Use high-quality equipment from well-known vendors; it is faster, more reliable, and the chance that you can find spare parts, should you need them, is better.
- Remember that the tapes are expendable supplies; they have limited lifetimes.

Summary

Below is a list of some of the most important topics mentioned in this chapter. Use it as a quick way to refresh your memory.

- The Beta database was based on JET Read—the same as MS Access.
- The first release database, special for Exchange 4, was based on JET Blue.
- *BLOBs*—Binary Large Objects—are the reason Exchange did not use MS SQL.
- The MDBData directory name is a remnant from the Beta period.
- *ACID*—Atomic, Consistent, Isolated, and Durable.
- Dynamic memory allocation takes all memory that is free, but releases it if needed.
- Messages are received in IS memory, written to the transaction log, then written to the store.
- The EDB database is built on B+Tree architecture, with 4K pages.
- A checksum ensures that the data is correct on each page.
- Event ID-1018 is caused by read problems; now IS tries 16 times before it gives up.
- *SIS*—Single-Instance Message Store.
- If there is more than one store, then SIS is only guaranteed on each store.
- MAPI is probably being replaced by Internet protocols soon.
- Each store consists of two files—the EBD file and the STM file.
- The EDB file stores all indexes and data in MAPI format.
- The STM file stores messages in native MIME Internet format.
- The STM file is a complement to and not a replacement of the EDB file.

- Outlook clients primarily use the EDB, but can also get messages from the STM file.
- Internet clients, e.g., Web clients and IMAP4, use the EDB file for indexing but the STM file for storage.
- Transaction log files are like an online digital recorder, taking copies of all transactions.
- Each log file is 5MB in size and is named E00.EDB, E01.EDB, etc.
- All log files should be on a separate disk from the store files.
- Each storage group has its own set of log files.
- You can use ESEutil to dump the header for a store, a log file, and the checkpoint file.
- The checkpoint file helps IS understand what data is written to the store and what is still just stored in the log file.
- Never remove log files or checkpoint files manually—it could make your stores corrupt.
- Circular logging is default off and should only be used in special circumstances rather than for ordinary mailbox stores.
- Reserved log files help IS if the disk space is out—there are two such files for IS to store whatever it has in memory before it shuts itself down.
- You may have up to four storage groups with five stores each, equaling 20 stores total.
- Don't create more storage groups than needed—they need a lot of virtual memory.
- Hosting 3,000 to 4,000 users on the same server and still having acceptable sizes on the stores should not be a problem.
- It is possible to take individual backups and restores on single store files—there is really no need to completely shut down the Exchange server anymore.
- Every mounted store needs 10MB of memory just to start.
- Exchange 2000 is cluster aware—use two or four nodes, all active.
- Try to estimate how much disk space you need before ordering the new server.
- *ExIFS*—Exchange Installable File system, a.k.a. the Web store—makes it possible to use the Exchange information as easily as an ordinary file system, regardless of how many stores you have.
- The Exchange server gets the M disk pointing to the Web store; you can share it with your clients.
- Exchange 2000 has two types of public folders: MAPI and GP.
- MAPI folders are the same "All Public Folder" tree as in previous Exchange versions.
- It's now possible to have more than one public folder tree of type General Purpose (GP).

- Only Web clients and the file system can see GP folders.
- Stop the default top-level folder creation permission that Everyone has before you end up with chaos.
- Use the Registry value to display the *Security* tab for the Organization object.
- Full-text indexing is now possible—you can also index ordinary files like Word and Excel.
- A full-text index can take about 20 percent of the store it has indexed.
- Use the gather files to find out about indexing problems.
- Always use full online backups with Exchange.
- Make sure the backup process has succeeded without any problems.
- If the backup fails, your transaction log files will not be deleted. You can fill the disk quickly.
- Single-mailbox backups or brick-level backups are good but can take a long time.
- Doing a restore is simple, as long as the backup copy is working.
- Practice recovery situations—you may need to call upon your knowledge and experience sooner than you think.

Chapter 3

Routing and Monitoring in Exchange 2000

This chapter is about routing and monitoring messages. It explores how a message moves from one place to another in the shortest possible time using the least amount of bandwidth, equipping you with what you need to know to track down and solve potential problems. Understanding how this works, though, can be complicated. You will encounter three typical routing scenarios:

- *Local message delivery*—Both the sender and the recipient belong to the same Exchange 2000 server.
- *Remote delivery*—The sender and recipient belong to different Exchange 2000 servers.
- *External deliver*—The recipient is on a server outside the Exchange organization.

You will also learn how to monitor the routing links and Exchange servers, getting information you'll need about potential problems so they can be fixed quickly, preferably before any of your users even notice anything is amiss.

Routing is at the heart of any mail system, and Exchange is no different. This has been one of its strengths ever since its first release in 1996. Previous Exchange versions were based on the X.400 protocol, and Exchange continued to follow the rules for X.400 routing. The *MTA*, or *Message Transfer Agent*, service had the sole responsibility for this X.400-based routing. With the MTA service, all messages routed in the old Exchange server were passed to the MTA, which in turn selected the next hop to another Exchange server on the same site or an Internet recipient elsewhere, for example. The MTA used a routing table called *GWART*, or *Gateway Routing Table*, in which all possible routes were listed, along with the cost for each individual route. This information would be saved in each server's directory database (DIR.EDB) and replicated through the complete Exchange organization by the Directory Replication service.

The routing architecture in Exchange 2000 is very different from the old MTA routing. For this newer version, the development team had several goals:

- Having SMTP-based routing instead of X.400
- Making the routing process of SMTP messages twice as quick as in the old Exchange server

- Being able to use the AD instead of the local DIR.EDB
- Being able to use LDAP and DNS instead of RPC

The main reason to change the internal architecture from X.400 to Simple Mail Transfer Protocol, or SMTP, this time around was to adapt to the needs of today; almost none of the modern mail systems are based on X.400. An SMTP-based mail system is much better and handles both internal and external mail traffic more quickly. Because of these changes, much of Exchange 2000 consists of completely new code, optimized for SMTP and MIME, its messaging format. Exchange 2000 has also added some extended ESMTP verbs, like X-LINK2STATE, because it not only uses SMTP for transferring messages, but also for sending link status information that, for instance, signals that a link is not operational.

Previously, the dominating communication protocol was *RPC*, or *Remote Procedure Call*. Although it was a fast and effective protocol for client/server applications, it had several limitations. The most important was its dependency upon high-speed and high-quality network connections. The overhead of establishing an RPC session was high, so previous Exchange releases solved this by keeping the session alive up to five minutes after the last conversation. If the network was slow or unreliable, though, the session would be disconnected, making it necessary to establish a new session again.

Most of today's directory databases, like Active Directory and Novell NDS, have support for LDAP, a protocol used to search and update directories. LDAP is based on the old *DAP* protocol, or *Directory Access Protocol*, first developed for accessing an X.500 database. The DAP protocol was not very effective and would work only on TP4 (Transfer Protocol version 4) rather than on TCP/IP as the transport protocol; (the TP4 protocol is a member of the OSI protocol suite; see note below.) But in 1991, the University of Michigan optimized this protocol, adapting it for TCP/IP and calling it the *LDAP*, or *Lightweight Directory Access Protocol*. It continued to develop, and version 3 was ratified as an IEFT standard in 1997. This version is important because it is the first LDAP version that supports both read and write access to the directory.

Note: *OSI,* Open Systems Interconnection, *is an international standard that defines how different systems should communicate to be able to exchange data. When the OSI standardizing work started in 1977 TCP/IP was still on its experimental level; OSI instead suggested TP4 as a vendor independent network transport protocol, but as we all know now, TCP/IP won that game. OSI is best known for its seven-layer communication protocol, which describes every involved part in a network communication, from the physical layer to the application layer.*

Version 5 of Exchange had a directory database that understood version 1 of LDAP, then used mainly by Internet clients, such as POP3 and IMAP4, to get access to the global address list stored in the directory. Exchange 5.5 was the first release that had full support for version 3 of LDAP. For the first time, you could now use standard LDAP tools to search and update the directory database in Exchange.

The directory database in Exchange 5.5, though, became the foundation for the new Active Directory in Windows 2000, offering full support for LDAP version 3. The Exchange 2000 components use LDAP to communicate with the Active Directory, allowing, for example, a server to more easily find all the possible routes it might need. Because of this, RPC is no longer needed, and Exchange 2000 will not use RPC unless forced to do so, such as when it must communicate with an Exchange 5.5 site connector that is still RPC based.

Before we begin discussing the internal transport architecture, you first need to understand the concept of routing groups in Exchange 2000. Routing within a routing group will always happen directly between the servers, based on SMTP, whereas routing outside a routing group will demand the presence of a special "connector," or communication link. In Chapter 13, you can learn more about these connectors in detail.

Introduction to Routing Groups and Administrative Groups

A routing group, often referred to as an RG, is a group of Exchange 2000 servers that enjoy a permanent and high-speed network connectivity to each other and are also able to communicate by SMTP. Though the concept of routing groups is new for Exchange 2000, it is still very similar to the concept from the old Exchange 5.5 site. One difference is that a routing group deals only with the communication between the servers, whereas the old site also functioned as a boundary for the administrative scope.

The *site* concept has been with Exchange since its first release and has presented challenges for those seeking to design a distributed Exchange organization ever since. Normally, you want to make as few sites as possible, since it is easier to administer fewer rather than too many sites. But this was not always possible, due to the technical conditions needed for a server to belong to a site. For example, let's say you want to install a total of three Exchange 5.5 servers, one in Stockholm and one in London with a 256Kbps-leased line between them, and one in New York with a dial-up connection. Let's say you also decide that you want only one single administrator for all these three servers. Take a look at Figure 3.1.

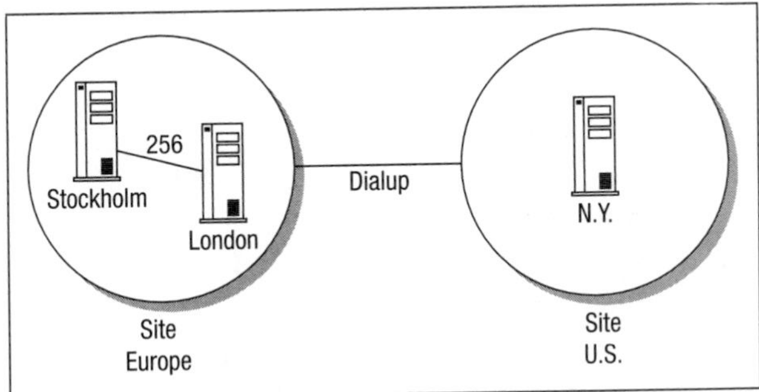

Figure 3.1
Three Exchange 5.5 servers.

But the problem is, this won't work. Because there's only a dial-up connection to New York, it's impossible to build one single Exchange 5.5 site made up of all three servers. In order to make this work, you would need to split your Exchange 5.5 organization into two sites, one European and one U.S., and you would probably end up with one administrator in the U.S. and one in Europe.

Because of such limitations, wouldn't it be great if you could use the ESM tool on any computer and still be able to change the configuration on any Exchange server, regardless of where it is? With Exchange 2000, this is possible. This is how it works: All configurations in Exchange 2000 are stored in a Windows 2000 domain controller and its Active Directory database (all domain controllers have an AD). When you use the ESM tool, you are actually making changes in the AD database. This information is later replicated to all other AD databases in your Windows 2000 forest, regardless of how far away they really are.

This is the reason why you can now create administrative groups and have a collection of Exchange servers that you not only have administrative control over, but also have control over without actually needing to connect them with your ESM. One single administrator can therefore manage all three of your servers, even if one of those servers has only a dial-up connection. Your New York server, as a result, gets the AD replication because the Windows 2000 domain controller in Europe can regularly dial up to a domain controller in New York and replicate the information as SMTP messages. It's all just a matter of time.

Understanding Routing Groups

Let's look at routing groups in more detail. Certain conditions need to be fulfilled before a server can join an existing routing group. These conditions include:

- A permanent network connection (not dial-up) to all other Exchange servers
- Support for TCP/IP and SMTP to the other Exchange servers
- Access to a Windows 2000 domain controller in the same forest
- Contact with the routing group master (usually the first server)

All Exchange servers within one routing group communicate with one another directly. All messages between them are sent through SMTP, which is a fast and resilient protocol. There is no more RPC traffic within this group, as was the case with previous Exchange sites, which is good, since RPC is more demanding as it pertains to the speed and quality of the network connection. One important difference compared to the RPC traffic is that the SMTP messages are not encrypted, like all RPC traffic was. This isn't as bad as one may first think; the SMTP messages between the servers within a routing group are sent in 8-bit binary TNEF format, not in clear text the way usual SMTP traffic is. The *TNEF*, or *Transport Neutral Encapsulation Format*, is Exchange's proprietary binary format used inside the EDB database.

The exact network speed needed to join a routing group is relative to the number of servers in the group. Since the SMTP protocol is very resilient, it can be used with 64Kbps or even less, as long as only a few Exchange servers are in the routing group. But the recommendation is that you have at least 1Mbps for best performance. The SMTP traffic within the routing group cannot be scheduled or limited in size; it is assumed that all servers have the network bandwidth they need.

You may have as many Exchange servers in a routing group as needed. Again, remember that all computers are allowed to talk directly with each other, a process also known as a fully meshed scenario. The number of new possible connections introduced when adding server number N to the routing group will be N minus 1; so, for example, when installing server number 5 in a routing group, the number of possible connections will increase by 5 minus 1, or 4.

Routing Information

Every server in the routing group needs to know how to reach outside destinations, whether they be other routing groups or other mail systems. This information is stored in the Active Directory's configuration naming partition; since all ADs replicate with one another, all Exchange 2000 servers will have access to this routing information. The routing information consists of a list of all Exchange servers' configured connectors, their costs, and the destinations reachable through this connector. A *connector* is a communication link to other routing groups or external mail systems. Whenever a server needs to send a message, it will search the AD for all connectors that can deliver the message to the destination. But before it selects one of them, it must make a selection based on several parameters, like cost and availability. In Figure 3.2, you can see three routing groups with connectors between them; there is also one SMTP connector to the Internet.

Previous versions of Exchange relied on the Gateway Routing Table, or GWART, for routing information. This is not the case in Exchange 2000, except in one special case: If you install an Exchange 2000 server in an Exchange 5.5 site, then the E2K server will take the responsibility of keeping the GWART updated for all Exchange 5.5 servers. This is a process handled in E2K known as the *Routing Information Daemon*, which will keep track of all available connections, both on the E2K side and on the Exchange 5.5 site. Since we may have several Exchange 5.5 sites in our old organization, E2K needs to know about all existing connections in this part of the organization. E2K will collect all connectors from both sides, storing them in Active Directory to be used by all E2K servers; the Routing Information Daemon will create a GWART with the same information and replicate it by the *Active Directory Connector* (*ADC*) to Exchange 5.5. The result will be that all E2K servers know about all connectors on the Exchange 5.5 side and all Exchange 5.5 servers will know about the connectors on the E2K side.

***Note:** The ADC is a Windows 2000 service that synchronizes the Exchange 5.5 directory with the Active Directory. The ADC is installed automatically in Windows 2000 if you join an Exchange 5.5 site with an Exchange 2000 server. This makes it possible to manage the directory in Exchange 5.5 or Exchange 2000, allowing you to add new users or create new connectors while still having this information replicated to both sides.*

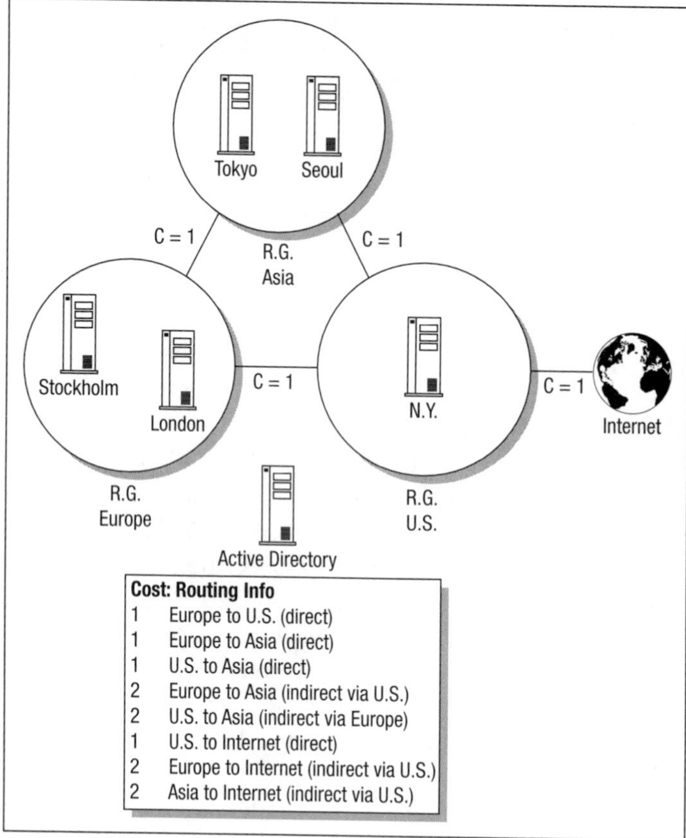

Figure 3.2
Routing groups and connectors are stored in the AD.

This is important since some connectors are available only for Exchange 5.5, like the SNADS and PROFS connectors (see Figure 3.3). Some third-party connectors are still available only for the Exchange 5.5 environment, like fax and voice mail connectors. If your

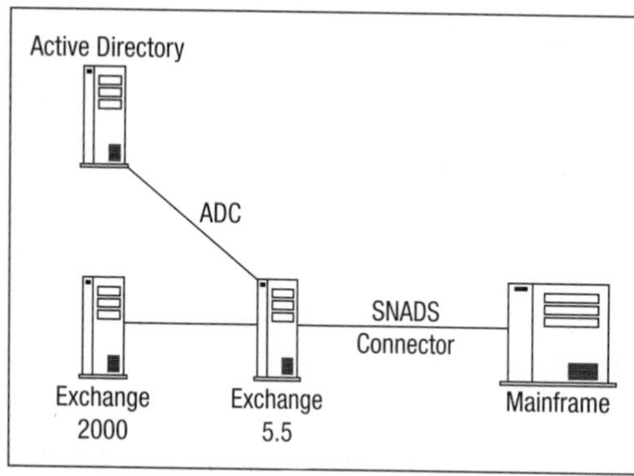

Figure 3.3
Exchange 2000 connected to an Exchange 5.5 with a SNADS connector.

Exchange organization needs one of these, you must keep one Exchange 5.5 server active with this connector. Exchange 2000 will then route all such mail to the Exchange 5.5 server that will, in turn, pass it on to the final destination. You can expect that most, if not all, third-party connectors that exist for Exchange 5.5 will be updated to take advantage of Exchange 2000, so later on you probably won't need any Exchange 5.5 servers anymore.

The Transport Architecture

When you install Windows 2000 Server, you will also get an SMTP protocol stack, called the Internet Mail Service (not to be confused with the IMS in Exchange 5.5), included as part of the operating system. This is a basic SMTP stack, capable of sending and receiving SMTP messages, used by different subcomponents in Windows 2000 Server for replicating system messages, like the Active Directory NT Directory Service (NTDS). This SMTP stack is part of the IIS 5 and executes within the Inetinfo.exe process. If you have ever looked at the Windows NT 4 Option Pack and the IIS 4, you have seen the predecessor of this SMTP service; it is actually the Exchange team that has developed this SMTP stack. Although basic, it still has support for most of the ESMTP verbs, like **8BITMIME**, **CHUNKING**, and **PIPELINING**. These commands make it possible to send messages directly in binary format and faster than normal SMTP traffic.

When you install Exchange 2000, your basic SMTP stack will be upgraded, adding new SMTP verbs with command sets like **X-LINK2STATE**, used for replicating status changes of connectors. You will also get a new advanced queuing engine, an enhanced categorizer agent, and an ExIFS driver that makes it possible for the Information Store service to pick up and drop off SMTP messages directly, instead of through NT File System (NTFS) as before.

The Virtual SMTP Server

The IIS 5 allows multiple virtual SMTP servers to be created, all with their own configurations, like IP addresses, TLS settings, and port numbers. These virtual SMTP servers are used by Exchange when transferring messages in and out of the system. By default Exchange will use the virtual SMTP server that comes with Windows 2000; if you need any special configuration besides the default, you can create one or more new virtual servers. For example, one reason to create an extra virtual SMTP server may be to set up a *Transport Layer Security (TLS)*, an encrypted network connection to a specific server, while the default virtual server will take care of all other SMTP traffic.

All configurations for the virtual SMTP server, along with other Internet protocols that IIS handles, like FTP, IMAP4, and POP3, are stored in the Metabase, not in the Active Directory. This is because the server that is running IIS must not be dependent on the Active Directory to work and also partly because of performance reasons. The Metabase is similar to the Registry, but is smaller, faster, and always loaded in memory, much like the Metabase found in Windows NT 4 and IIS 4. When you use the Internet Service Manager tool (ISM), it will read and write to the Metabase only.

The Metabase lives its own life, and Active Directory knows nothing about its settings; if any modification is done directly in the Metabase, AD will not get this information. When Exchange is installed, you should therefore create and manage these virtual SMTP servers by EMS, instead of ISM. The reason for this is that all Exchange servers in the organization must be able to access the configuration settings for all virtual SMTP servers. A special service called the *Directory Service to Metabase Update Agent* will immediately replicate this information to the Metabase for this particular server.

Warning! *You can use the MetaEdit 2 tool available in the Windows 2000 Server Resource Kit to manage the Metabase. But the replication between AD and Metabase is one-way only (from AD to Metabase), so no modification should be done directly in the Metabase if you want the Active Directory to know about it.*

Several new components are installed with Exchange 2000, besides the enhanced SMTP stack: the Advanced Queuing Engine, the Categorizer, the Router, and the Store drive. These new components are designed for maximum performance and advanced routing features, while still making it possible for you to add your own code to it. Remember that all of these are part of the IIS 5 process, the Inetinfo.exe.

The Advanced Queuing Engine

This is the main component that controls all of the routing and transport process in Exchange 2000; it will call other sub-components when needed. All messages submitted to Exchange are passed to the Advanced Queuing engine, including internal mail, like mail to another user on the same server. It is actually not the message itself that is passed to AQ—rather, it's a file handler, a sort of pointer, to the message that is stored in one of the stores. The AQ will get the complete message if and when it needs it. With the file handler, it can load the complete message directly from the Information Store in case it must route it. Again, if the sender and the recipient are on the same server, there is no need for the AQ to load the complete message. Compare this to how the MTA process in Exchange 5.5 handled message routing; it had a full copy of the message, decided how to route it, and finally delivered it. The AQ is also responsible for maintaining queues for inbound and outbound queues and generating delivery status notifications, like delivery receipts (DR) and non-delivery reports (NDRs).

The Categorizer

This Exchange 2000 component is a part of the AQ and replaces the basic categorizer, the CAT.DLL for Windows 2000, with a more enhanced version, the PHATCAT.DLL. Its job is to analyze, expand, and categorize the messages. The message categorizer receives the message header from the AQ and uses this information to do the following:

1. Get the sender address from the header and look for it in the Active Directory attribute *proxyAddresses*, asking itself, "Is this a sender I recognize?"
2. Get all recipients' addresses from the header and look for all of them in the AD attribute *proxyAddresses*, asking itself, "Do these recipients belong to this server?"

3. If the recipient is a distribution group (previously called a distribution list), then the categorizer will expand the group (if allowed on this server) and repeat Step 2 for all recipients.
4. If any of the recipients cannot be identified, they will be marked as "unknown."
5. Check for limits, like message sizes or delivery restrictions, for each recipient; if a message exceeds the limit, this recipient will get a special mark, and the sender will be notified.
6. Bifurcation, meaning splitting the messages in two or more copies, if needed. For example, a message with both local recipients and external Internet recipients must be separated into two messages due to the difference in the mail format (RTF and MIME, respectively).
7. Categorize each recipient as either Gateway (external) or Local.

When the categorizer is finished, it places the message into a queue, creating a separate queue for each destination domain. You can use the ESM to view the current queues, as in Figure 3.4. In previous Exchange versions, you had the queues in different objects. First, all mail was routed through the MTA, so it had its own queues. Then SMTP mail was transferred to the IMS; it also had its own queues (four of them, two in and two out). But in Exchange 2000, you have all queues in the virtual SMTP server. If you have more than one virtual SMTP server, they all have their own sets of queues.

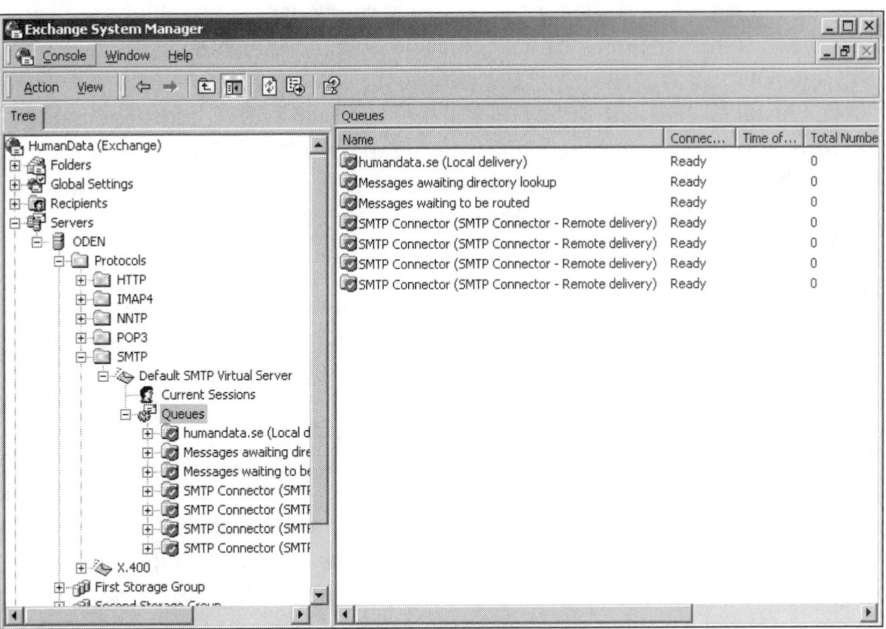

Figure 3.4
The SMTP queues in ESM.

Note: *You can refresh the view by either selecting the Queue folder and pressing F5 or right-clicking and selecting Refresh to make sure you are looking at updated information. For looking at a particular queue, like the local delivery queue, you can right-click on that particular queue and select Enumerate 1000 Messages before each message in the queue will be listed.*

There are actually two more special queues, the *precategorizer queue* and the *postcategorizer queue*. When the AQ passes a message header to the categorizer, it will drop it in the precategorizer queue, whereby the categorizer will pick it up immediately. When the categorizer is done, it will drop the header in the postcategorizer queue. One benefit of this is that we can now create a program that can read and write to the message while it is in either one of these two special queues. This is called an Event Sink and is a new feature of Exchange 2000. If there are no custom event sinks, the message header will go on directly to the next component.

The Router Component

The *Router* component is responsible for finding the best route for the next hop, in case there is more than one route leading to the destination. It will do this by asking Active Directory for a list of all available connectors and their associated cost value. It will also get the link state for each link to see if it is available at that moment.

The Store Driver

This driver makes it possible for the transport components to be able to read and write files directly out of the Information Store and is installed together with Exchange 2000. The basic IMS that Windows 2000 has will use the NTFS file system instead. After Exchange 2000 is installed, you will still be able to see its directory tree under \Inetpub\Mailroot. This directory is no longer used, but a copy of the tree can be found under the \Program files\Exchsrvr\Mailroot directory; it is active and if you drop a correctly formatted SMTP message in the \pickup directory, Exchange will directly try to deliver that message. If it's not formatted correctly, it will be moved to the \Badmail directory instead.

You can use this functionality to send messages from a program or a Web application. Just make sure the messages follow the simple SMTP format and save the messages into the Pickup directory; Exchange will take care of the rest.

The Bigger Picture

Now that you know about all components in the new transport architecture, it's time to see how they relate to one another. In Figure 3.5, you can see all the components mentioned, including the Information Store and a layer called the ExIPC, also known as the Epoxy layer because of the very tight integration it provides. The *ExIPC*, or *Exchange InterProcess Communication*, is a high-speed communication channel that makes IS (Store.exe) and IIS5 (Inetinfo.exe) pass data almost as fast as if they had been one and the same program.

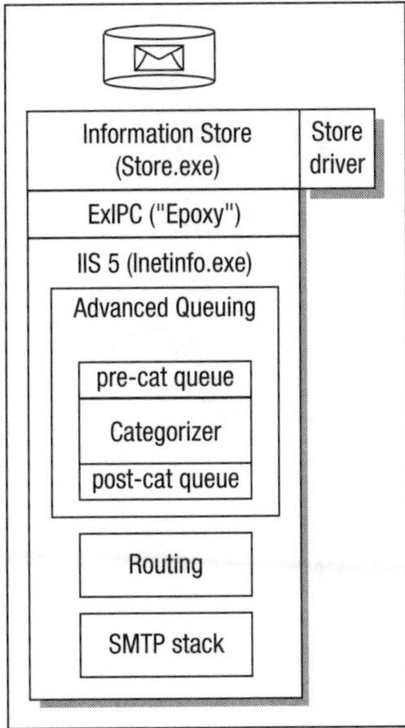

Figure 3.5
The complete transport architecture.

Message Flow in Exchange 2000

Let's look at how Exchange handles different types of message flow in the transport architecture. Remember that the MTA that previously had the sole responsibility for routing and selection is now just a shadow of what it was in its glory days. The only time the MTA is engaged is when it's communicating with the X.400 Connector. Let's look specifically at some scenarios, which describe the normal SMTP-based transport mechanism.

Message Flow for Local Delivery

When a user sends a message to a recipient belonging to the same server, this is how it works (see Figure 3.6):

1. The IS receives the message from the sender.
2. The mail header is passed to the Advanced Queue engine, regardless of whether it's a local or remote recipient.
3. The AQ passes the mail header to the pre-cat queue.
4. The categorizer retrieves the message header and processes it, doing things like expanding distribution groups and checking restrictions like message sizes.
5. The categorizer will see that this is a local recipient and place the message header in the post-cat queue; immediately, it will be moved to the local delivery queue inside the AQ.

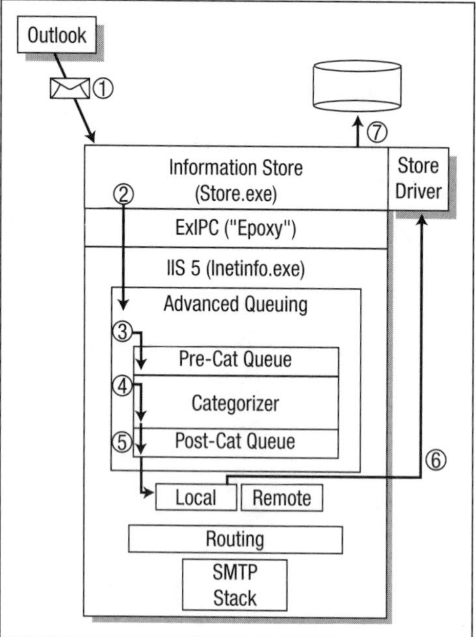

Figure 3.6
Local delivery of mail.

6. The AQ notifies the Store Driver about the recipients in the local delivery queue; it will then pass this information to the Information Store.
7. The IS updates the stores and notifies the recipient.

Remember that the purpose of the pre-cat and post-cat queues is to give custom developed programs a chance to catch the message while in transfer, maybe adding a disclaimer to the message.

Message Flow for Remote Delivery

When a user sends a message to a recipient on another server, Exchange has to route the message through the SMTP stack. The following steps outline this message flow (see Figure 3.7):

1. The IS receives the message from the sender.
2. The mail header is passed to the Advanced Queue engine, regardless of whether it's a local or remote recipient.
3. The AQ passes the mail header to the pre-cat queue.
4. The categorizer retrieves the message header and processes it, doing things like expanding distribution groups and checking restrictions like message size.

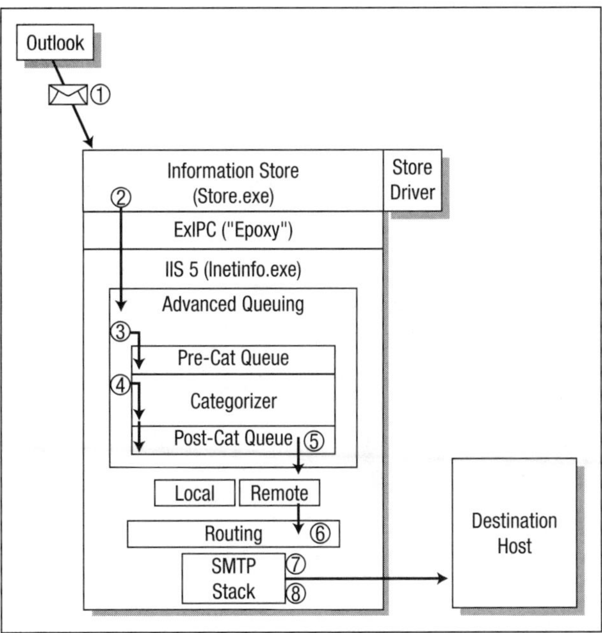

Figure 3.7
Remote delivery of mail.

5. The categorizer sees that this is a remote recipient. Then it checks to see if there are any special settings for this recipient mail domain in the Internet Message Format, determining whether the message is MIME or UUencode formatted, for example (see Figure 3.8). Then it places the message header in the remote queue inside the AQ.
6. The routing engine retrieves the header from the remote queue; it will now look for all possible routes to the destination and select the next hop, based on cost and current link state.
7. The SMTP stack initiates an SMTP session with the remote host, which was selected by the routing engine.
8. When the SMTP session is established, the IS will retrieve the complete message from the store, convert it according to the settings in Step 5, and send the message.

Inbound SMTP Message Flow

This section describes what happens when someone sends an SMTP message into this Exchange server. The following steps outline this message flow (see Figure 3.9):

1. A remote SMTP host establishes a connection to your SMTP stack.
2. The local SMTP stack streams the incoming message directly to the NTFS directory \Program Files\Exchsrvr\Mailroot\Queue, but also to the IS memory and the transaction log. When the complete message is received, Exchange will commit the transaction and write the message to the STM file.

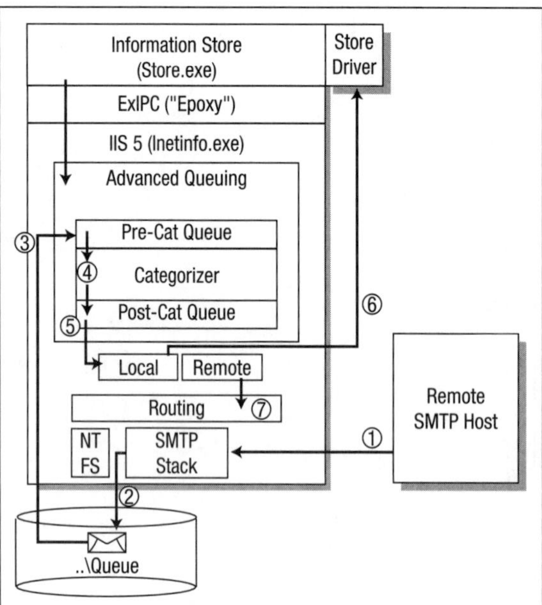

Figure 3.8
The Internet Message Format settings.

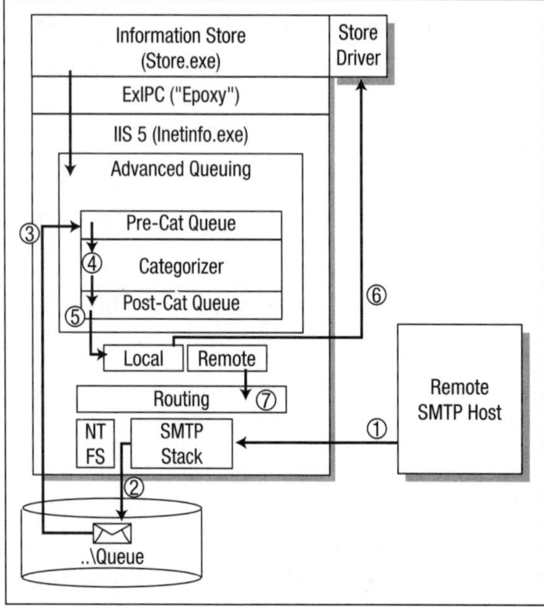

Figure 3.9
Inbound SMTP message flow.

3. The mail header is retrieved from the NTFS directory by the AQ and placed into the pre-cat queue.
4. The categorizer retrieves the message header and processes it, doing things like expanding distribution groups and checking restrictions like message size.
5. The categorizer places the message header in the local delivery queue if this is the final destination. If the mail is to a remote recipient, it will be placed in the destination domain queue.
6. For all recipients in the local delivery queue, the AQ will activate the Store Driver; this will retrieve the recipient names and send them to the Information Store.
7. For all recipients in a remote delivery queue, the routing engine will calculate the best link to the destination, initiate an SMTP session to the remote host, and send the message.

A message received by the MTA, i.e., the X.400 Connector, is treated much like mail submitted from a local user. The Information Store has a hidden mailbox named MTS-IN where the MTA service will store the message. From then on, the IS will handle this as it would any message, regardless of whether it's going to another user on the same server (as in Figure 3.6) or to a remote recipient (as in Figure 3.7).

Note: *The current Exchange 2000 version receives incoming SMTP messages in the NTFS Queue folder, but this may change in future Exchange releases. If the mail was for a local recipient, it would be faster to store the message directly in the ExIFS. But if the message is intended for a remote user, meaning that this server would act like a bridgehead server, it would be faster to store it in the NTFS folder. Future versions of Exchange may have settings in which you determine whether the server is a mailbox server or a bridgehead server, making Exchange use the NTFS or ExIFS system.*

Monitoring the Transport System

The Performance Monitor has about 50 counters directly related to the categorizer and the virtual SMTP server. Each virtual server has its own set of counters. To see these counters, use the Performance Monitor and click Add To Chart on the Edit menu. In the Object box, select SMTP Server to see a list of all the counters in the Counter box. Below are some of these counters, showing what type of information you can get from them; you can use these to keep track of the activity of the categorizer or for advanced troubleshooting:

- Address Lockups/sec
- Address Lockups not found
- Categorizations completed successfully
- Categorizations in progress

- Categorizations failed (DS Connection failure)
- Categorizations completed/sec
- LDAP Binds Failure
- LDAP Connections currently open
- LDAP Pages search completed
- LDAP Pages search failures
- Messages bifurcated
- Messages categorized
- Messages submitted/sec
- Recipients NDR'd (ambiguous address)
- Recipients NDR'd (unresolved)
- Sender unresolved
- Categorizer Queue Length

Some Routing Problems

The routing system in Exchange 2000 is very fast and reliable, but in some rare situations, problems still occur, such as messages being duplicated due to design flaws. This section describes some of these scenarios.

Duplicate Mail

If a user sends a message to two distribution groups (previously called distribution lists), the user may encounter a situation in which some recipients are members of both groups. If these two groups are expanded on different Exchange 2000 servers, due to settings for the distribution group, this might create two messages for the same recipients, depending on the following:

- The Information Store has a built-in detection feature that will be able to discover any duplicates, even if the messages are coming from two different servers. This detection will work only if the second message to the same recipient arrives within one hour of the first.
- If the recipient is an Exchange 5.5 user, this will always cause duplicate messages to be sent, since Exchange 5.5 tracks messages based on Instance ID instead of the Internet Message ID that Exchange 2000 uses. Exchange 5.5 will read it as if the two messages with different Internet Message IDs are in fact two different messages.

You must plan your distribution group expansion servers carefully. The best ways to avoid duplicate messages are to use the same expansion server or not to have any pinpointed expansion servers at all. If the distribution group is expanded on the same server, it will be able to detect duplicate messages and remove all copies except one.

Members in Global Groups Don't Get Any Mail

If you have a multidomain forest, it may happen that none of the members of a global group can have mail sent to the group without generating any NDR or error messages, whether it's a distribution group or a security group. If you try to send a message directly to an individual, though, it will go through just fine. The reason for this is that membership of global domain groups is only visible in the domain each group belongs to; in other domains, the name of the group will be displayed in the Global Address List, but if an Exchange 2000 server in the remote domain tries to expand the group, it will not be able to find any names.

A good solution is to use universal distribution groups rather than global or local domain groups, since the global catalog server in Windows 2000 domain controllers replicates the membership of universal groups to all domains. Another good solution is to make sure the global group can be expanded only on a server in its own domain.

No NDR or Delivery Receipts Are Generated

If you run Exchange 2000 with front-end/back-end design, it may happen that the system will stop sending any NDR or delivery receipts. You may also get several Event log messages, like "Event ID: 6004: The categorizer is unable to categorize messages due to a retry able error" or "Event ID: 6004: Routing table failed to connect to database server." This may happen if the front-end server is running an SMTP connector, but its Information Store process has stopped.

Normally, you wouldn't have the Information Store on a front-end server, since it doesn't have any mailbox users. Microsoft has a white paper called "Exchange 2000 Front-end and Back-end Topoply," which states that the Information Store should be stopped. But the problem here is that the Information Store is needed for routing SMTP messages, as previously described. You can get around this either by creating a storage group and a store to start the Information Store, or by moving the SMTP connector to the back-end server instead.

Link State Information

Inside a routing group, there is no need to keep track of the current status for a certain server; when one server tries to send a message, it will discover if the receiving server is not accessible. The originating server will store messages in a queue, retrying connections until it gets contact and returning an NDR back to the sender if it is still unsuccessful after 48 hours.

Messages that should be transferred to another routing group or to an external mail system are handled differently. You may recall that a connector is a communication link to other routing groups and external systems. The routing system needs to:

- Find out about all possible routes to the destination
- Select the best route if more than one route is possible

The question is, of course, what is the "best" route? This is something that is decided during the design of the Exchange organization. Normally, you want to deliver messages as quickly as possible. But there may be a very fast connection that is so expensive you would only want to utilize it for certain users or perhaps only use it at certain times because of business or political reasons. This section does not deal with design questions; you will find more about that in Chapter 7. In this section, we will look more closely at how Exchange keeps track of the connection status for each connector and see how Exchange replicates changes in this status to all other servers in the organization.

The Link State Table

The Link State Table is new for Exchange 2000. Its purpose is to keep track of the current status of all available links or connectors, both local and in remote routing groups. When a server discovers that a link is down, it will signal this in the Link State Table. This information will immediately be replicated to all other servers with a special protocol called Link State Algorithm (LSA), based on the routing algorithm that Edsger Dijkstra published in 1959. That algorithm has been in use for many years in the router protocol *Open Shortest Path First*, or *OSPF*. The Link State Algorithm will replicate all changes in the link state to all other Exchange servers in the organization almost instantly. This offers several benefits:

- Each Exchange server will be able to select the best available route without first having to send the message to a route only to find that one link is inactive.
- There will be no ping-pong scenarios in which a message is switched between two inactive links. Previous Exchange versions did not keep track of the connection status outside their own sites, and that sometimes resulted in messages being routed back and forth up to 512 times, something also known as the ping-pong problem. This limit of 512 was hard coded into the system and couldn't be changed.
- It prevents looping of messages.

Only two states are possible for a link: Up or Down. The Link State Table will not register any retry state. If a link is marked as Down, its cost value is set to INFINITE, making all routing engines skip to this link.

The Link State Table is only stored in memory, not in any file. If any of the servers restart, it will contact its routing group master (explained in the next section) and ask for a complete table. If the routing group master is restarted, it will ask for updates from any of the remaining servers.

Microsoft is looking into expanding the Active Directory to handle other routing equipment that currently has its own type of Link State Tables, like network routers. If the network equipment can update the Link State Table in Active Directory, the speed and quality of this link state information would be further increased. This is also called *directory-enabled networks*. You can expect that this will be included in a future release of Windows 2000.

The Routing Group Master

In each routing group, there is one *routing group master*, or *RGM*. This server is responsible for keeping the Link State Table with the current status for all connections, showing whether they are Up or Down. All servers within the routing group have a local copy of this table. When a server detects that a link is down, it will send this information to the routing group master. The only type of server that can detect a change in the link state is a bridgehead server or a gateway server. A bridgehead server is an Exchange server with a routing connector installed, like a Routing Group Connector or an X.400 Connector, and a gateway server is an Exchange server with a gateway connector, like an MS Mail connector or a Lotus Notes connector.

It is important that all servers in the routing group have the same version of the Link State Table; therefore, the routing group master will increment a "version number" for each update of the table. Each routing group master has its own version number series. If all servers in the routing group don't have the same table, they will send different updates to the other routing groups, possibly sending contradicting updates about the same link.

If the routing group master goes offline, then all updates of the Link State Table will stop, except for certain special situations. Since all servers still have a copy of the Link State Table, they will continue to use this until the routing group master goes back online again. If this were to take a long time, you should promote another server to operate as the new routing group master. You can do this with the ESM tool, assuming that you are displaying the routing groups (look at the properties for your organization's object). Use the following steps to change your routing group master, and refer to Figure 3.10:

1. Locate the *Member* folder in ESM, looking under Administrative Groups\First Administrative Group\Routing Groups\First Routing Group\Member.
2. Select the server to be the new routing group master.
3. Right-click on this server and select *Set As Master*.

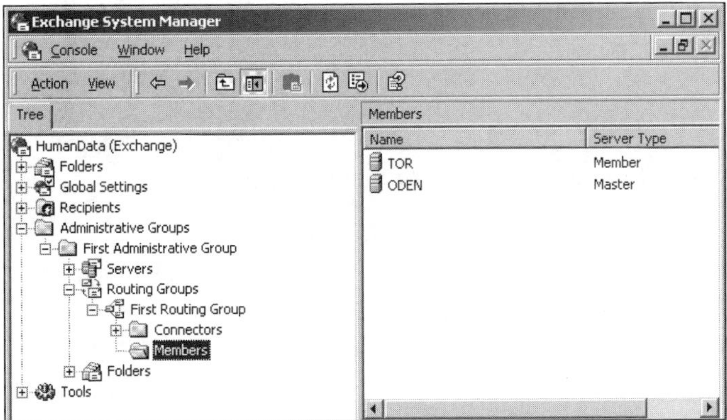

Figure 3.10
Select the routing group master.

As mentioned earlier, there is one special occasion in which a member will update its local copy of the Link State Table even when the routing group master is offline. This is when a bridgehead server (meaning it has a connector installed) may receive a link state update from another routing group; it will then update its local Link State Table. If another server in this routing group then contacts this bridgehead server (while the routing group master is still offline), it discovers that they have different versions and copies the latest table from the bridgehead server.

Replication of Link Status within a Routing Group

When the routing group master needs to replicate a change in a link state, it will connect on TCP port 691 to all members in its routing group and send the data using the Link State Algorithm, a protocol specially developed by Microsoft for this purpose. If a member server in the routing group detects a failed link, it will also use TCP port 691 to send this information to the routing group master, which in turn will replicate this to all other members. This will instantaneously update all servers in this routing group. If you have any filtering routers between the Exchange servers belonging to the same routing group, you should make sure that the TCP port 691 is allowed to pass.

Note: *In the Beta version of Exchange 2000, port 3044 was used instead of port 691. It is no longer used, even though you can still see this port number in previous documentation from Microsoft and other sources.*

Replication of Link Status to Other Routing Groups

When a bridgehead server tries to send a message to another routing group and discovers that it doesn't work, it will continue to try three more times, with a 60-second interval between each attempt before it finally marks this link as Down. This retry period is also known as the *glitch-retry state*. The new link state will then be replicated to all other servers in the routing group, as previously described.

If this routing group has a connector to other routing groups, it will immediately send this link state update to them. It does this by sending a special Microsoft-specific SMTP verb, **X-LINK2STATE**, over port 25. A complete scenario would go something like this (see Figure 3.11):

1. The bridgehead server **N.Y.** with a connector to **R.G. Europe** tries to open an SMTP connection on port 25 to bridgehead server **Stockholm**, but fails.
2. The server waits 60 seconds, and then tries to open the connection again. The server will retry three times and if this still doesn't work, it will mark the link as Down and change its cost to INFINITE. This glitch-retry state will take three minutes. The message, however, is rerouted if possible to another link, directly after the first failed connection.
3. The **N.Y.** server will send the link state update by TCP port 691 to the routing group master **Dallas**.

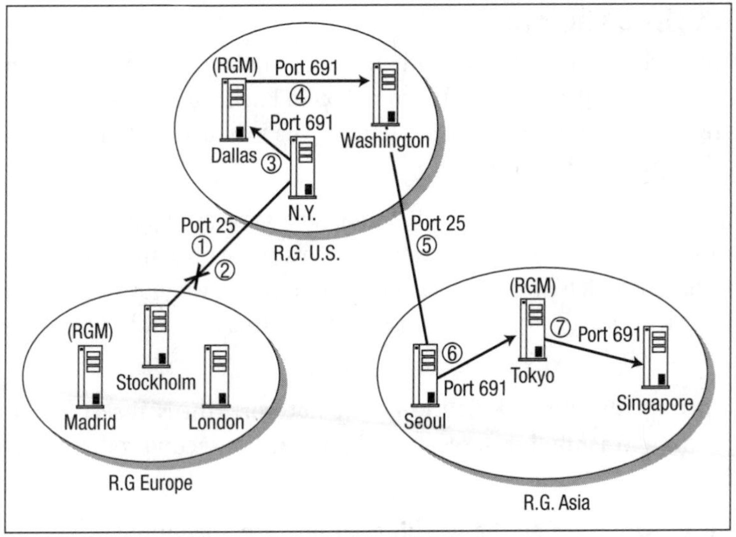

Figure 3.11
Replication of link state updates within and between routing groups.

4. The routing group master will replicate this update to all other servers (**Washington**) in this routing group by TCP port 691.

5. **Washington** is the bridgehead server for routing group **Asia** and will now immediately contact the **Seoul** server on port 25, sending the new link state by using the SMTP verb **X-LINK2STATE**; the link state data is transferred in a special compressed format, a process that normally takes less than one second.

6. The **Seoul** server has an updated link state; it will send this update to its routing group master.

7. The routing group master in **R.G. Asia** will replicate this information to the other servers in this routing group by TCP port 691.

It takes several steps but is actually a very quick procedure; the information sent by port 691 is instantaneous, and the SMTP verb **X-LINK2STATE** sent by port 25 is also very fast, since the data transfer is highly compressed. Any messages to **R.G. Asia** will now wait in the queue on the original server, with no attempt to transfer the message until the link is operational again.

The server that discovered the broken connection will continue to retry to open port 25 according to the settings on the *Delivery* tab for the virtual SMTP server, usually every 10 minutes, until the connector gets active again; then this link state update will be replicated to all servers exactly as described earlier.

Note: *Exchange 2000 does not offer automatic link checking. This means that a link may be down for a long time without any server noticing. It's only when a server tries to open a connection that a link failure will be discovered.*

Multiple Link Breakdowns

The case just described was rather simple with only one single link down. If multiple links are down, however, it could get a little more complex. In Exchange 5.5, this same scenario would probably result in the ping-pong effect, sending the message back and forth between two offline links as many as 512 times.

If you look at Figure 3.12, you'll notice that it's almost the same as Figure 3.10, except with a new route from Asia to Europe. Exchange would try this route now, since the direct route is down. Assume that the link between Asia and Europe is also down, but since no messages have been sent over this link during the last few minutes, this has not been discovered by any server yet. This is what will happen:

1. Since the first route directly to **R.G. Europe** did not work, the **N.Y.** server will reroute the message to the **Washington** server and then over the second route, indirectly passing **R.G. Asia**.
2. The link to **R.G. Asia** is up, so the **Washington** server manages to send the message over to the **Seoul** server.
3. The **Seoul** server sees that the message is destined to **R.G. Europe** and routes it over to the **Singapore** server, since this is the bridgehead server to **R.G. Europe**.
4. The **Singapore** server tries to open port 25 to the **London** server, but for some reason it fails. **Singapore** enters the glitch-retry state and after three retries it notifies all other servers in **Asia** that the link to **Europe** is down and changes its cost to INFINITE.

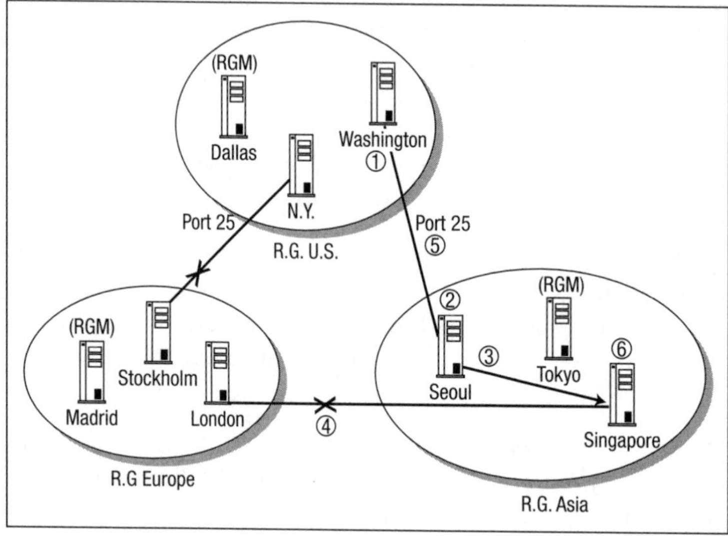

Figure 3.12
Multiple links down.

5. The **Seoul** server contacts the **Washington** server over port 25, sending the **X-LINK2STATE** verb and the compressed data to signal that the **Europe** link is down; **Washington** sends the new link state to **Dallas** (the routing group master), which replicates it to the **N.Y.** server.

6. The mail is still in the **Singapore** server; this server calculates and sees that both routes have a cost of INFINITE, which means that they are down. The server will keep the mail in the queue until one of the routes gets up again; it will not try to reroute the mail.

All subsequent messages to **R.G. Europe** will wait in the originating server's queue, until one of the two possible links becomes operational again. This will eliminate all unnecessary traffic between the servers and on the network.

Link State Updates

A network monitor shows exactly what the communication between the two routing groups looks like when a bridgehead server sends the new link state update to the other side. The unavailable link will be marked as Down using the SMTP verb **X-LINK2STATE**, as shown below:

```
00000030          7B 30 30 30 30 30 30 35 31 7D    {00000051}
00000040 20 44 4D 5F 43 4F 4E 4E 20 37 66 65 31 32 65 66 .DM_CONN.7fe12ef
00000050 65 65 38 66 31 36 35 34 64 62 63 32 37 31 37 35 ee8f1654dbc27175
00000060 38 35 35 64 37 66 37 64 31 20 63 33 38 30 61 62 855d7f7d1.c380ab
00000070 30 66 37 62 37 62 66 66 34 33 38 65 66 62 38 37 0f7b7bff438efb87
00000080 30 37 35 36 38 63 66 38 62 39 20 44 4F 57 4E 20 07568cf8b9.DOWN.
00000090 20
```

Some of the information in this network trace includes:

- The name of the connector: "DM_CONN."
- The hexadecimal number (7FE12EF....), which relates to the GUID of the affected connector, named "DM_CONN."
- The hexadecimal number (C380AB....), which relates to the GUID of the virtual server that detected the change.
- The final word (DOWN), which sets the status of the connector.

As stated earlier, data is transferred between routing groups over SMTP on port 25. The format of the data is roughly similar to that of the intrarouting group communications. However, if you are performing a network trace for link state data, you will notice that the **X-LINK2STATE** command verb denotes the type of data, and the information is sent in compressed binary chunks (FIRST CHUNK, SECOND CHUNK, LAST CHUNK). You can find more information about CHUNK packages in Chapter 4.

Link and Server Monitoring

It's possible to monitor the links between the routing groups and connectors to other mail systems. The ESM tool has a Monitor folder that resembles the previous monitor feature from previous Exchange releases. But in Exchange 2000, this monitoring is more integrated. Under the Tools\Monitoring and Status folder in ESM, you'll see two folders, the Status folder and the Notification folder. Look at the Status folder (Figure 3.13) for an updated view of the current status. All Exchange servers and their connectors are automatically monitored; if all is okay, you will find the status as Available. If it is not available, then right-click on it and select Properties from the menu to see what the problem is.

Depending on the type of object, different status states may be listed for the objects in the Status folder. Two connector link status states you'll find are:

- *Available*—Meaning they function properly.
- *Unavailable*—Meaning that a communication function, such as a routing service, is not working on this connector.

Exchange will perform an automatic link, monitoring all connectors installed on this server and regularly trying to contact the other side of the link to see that it has contact with the receiving server. And as in previous Exchange versions, the System Attendant is the process responsible for performing the monitoring test.

Status states have more possibilities than connector links. They include:

- *Available*—Meaning that a server is online and working normally.
- *Unreachable*—Meaning one of the primary services on the server is down. If the server is in another routing group, it may be the link that is down.

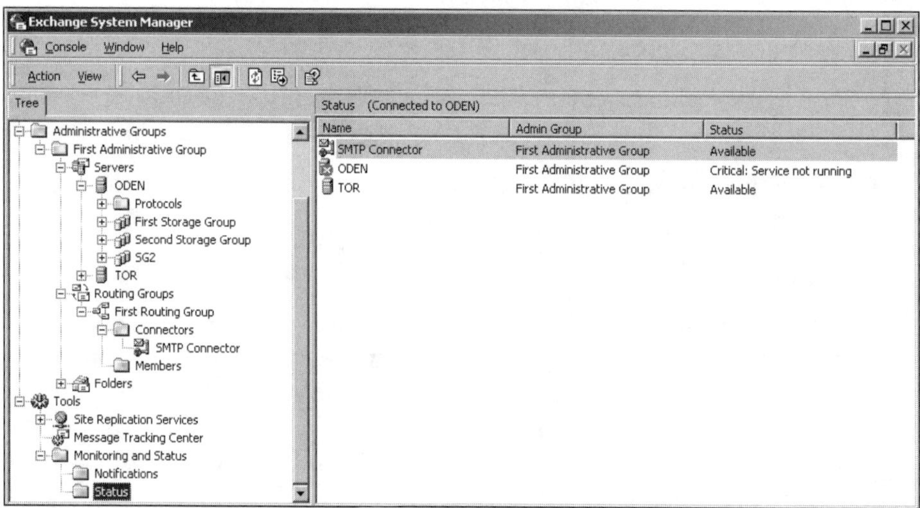

Figure 3.13
Status monitoring of links and servers.

- *In Maintenance Mode*—Meaning that monitoring is temporarily disabled on this server, due to maintenance, backup, repair, or other reasons.
- *Unknown*—Meaning the System Attendant service cannot communicate with the local server.

If you need to do some maintenance service on an Exchange 2000 server, open the properties for the server, select the *Monitoring* tab, and select *Disable All Monitoring Of This Server*. If you don't do this, the monitoring system will start reporting errors and generating notifications.

Warning! *Be aware that if the monitor detects that something happens, you will by default not be notified automatically! You must first create the notification process you want the monitor to use. You can select between two types of notification processes:* E-mail notification *and* Script notification. *Use E-mail notification to send a message when something unexpected happens, or use the Script notification to start a script; for example, to send a Short Message System (SMS) message to your mobile phone.*

You have two levels of notification states: *warning* states and *critical* states. To send a notification by email when you reach a critical state, you would follow these steps:

1. Use ESM and select the *Notification* folder.
2. Right-click and select *New/E-mail Notification* (see Figure 3.14).
3. Fill in the name of the monitoring server that will perform the monitoring process.

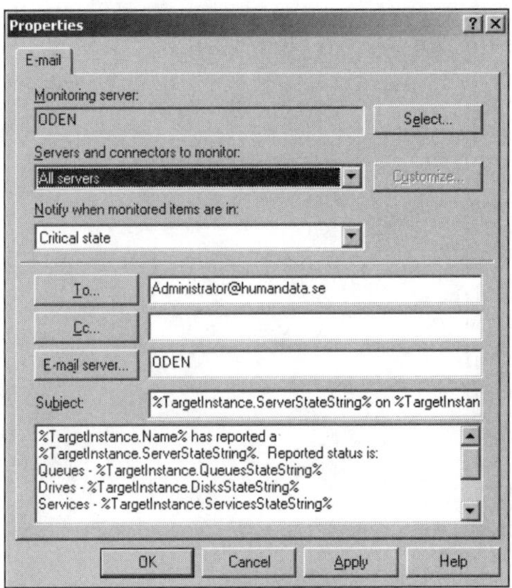

Figure 3.14
Setting up an email notification.

Note: *You may need to do this on an ESM running on an Exchange 2000 server; otherwise, you may get an error message stating* "Object Picker cannot open because no locations from which to choose objects could be found."

4. Select *Servers And Connectors To Monitor*; you may choose between *This Server, All Servers*, and so on; you can also select a custom list of servers.
5. Select what notify state you need with the *Notify When Monitored Items Are In* field; normally, you would select *Critical State* to avoid warning messages.
6. Select who should get these notifications with the *To* and *Cc* fields. You can also select a distribution group instead of individual accounts.
7. The *E-mail Server* field automatically sets to the same server as the *Monitoring Server* field; if you want to send the mail by another server, define it here.
8. Define the *Notify* message. Several variables can be used here; they are all *Windows Management Instrumentation (WMI)* variables. Take a look also at the Windows 2000 Resource Kit.

It is not recommended to run the monitoring and notification process on the same server as the one you are monitoring; if this server goes into critical state, it may not be able to send the notification message. Because of this I recommend you to use the Script notification instead of E-mail notification, in case you only have one Exchange 2000 server. To set up the script notification, you would follow these steps:

1. Use the ESM and select the *Notification* folder.
2. Right-click and select *New/Script Notification*, as in Figure 3.15.

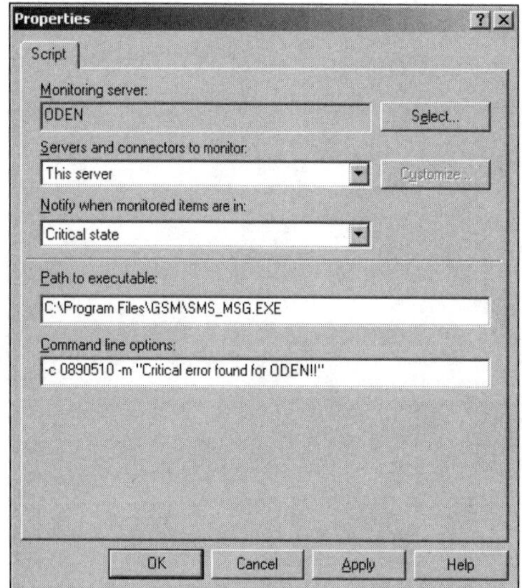

Figure 3.15
Setting up the Script notification.

3. Fill in the name of the monitoring server; this server will be responsible for running the monitoring process and also for running the script.
4. Use *Servers And Connectors To Monitor* to select what to monitor; you may choose between *This Server*, *All Servers*, *All Connectors*, and more.
5. Set the monitor state that should trigger this script with *Notify When Monitored Items Are In*; usually you would accept the default, *Critical State*.
6. Use the *Path To Executable* to define the name of the script (or program), including the full path to its directory.
7. Use the *Command Line Options* to set options for the script (or program). In the example in Figure 3.14, the option is set to call a certain number and send a message to it.

It's important to select the right type of notification, and the most reliable is probably a Script notification, sending all notifications by SMS to a mobile phone; you should not rely on the notification system being able to send E-mail notifications. Use the Decision Tree 3.1 to help you decide what type of notification to select.

Besides the tools that Microsoft offers in ESM, a number of third-party vendors offer very advanced monitoring tools, not only of Exchange 2000 but also of Windows 2000 and other server applications, such as NetIQ (**www.netiq.com**) and MessageWise (**www.messagewise.com**).

Note: *The monitoring tools in Exchange 2000 can only be used to monitor Exchange 2000 servers, not previous Exchange server versions. If you have a mix of both versions running, you need both the monitor tool in ESM and the monitor tool in Exchange 5.x Admin tool if you want to monitor all servers.*

Link States for Gateways

Gateway connectors to other mail systems are treated in a special way. Since one such link may be used to send messages to a number of servers, it is impossible for the link state system to know whether a message is waiting in the queue because the connector link is down or because the particular receiving server is unavailable at the moment.

For example, a message to an external recipient sent over the Internet may not be possible to deliver if the receiving server is temporarily offline for any reason, causing this mail to be stuck in the queue. This is a common situation in the Internet world, and this is the reason Exchange will by default retry 48 hours before the server returns the message to the sender as nondeliverable. Just because one remote server cannot be reached, the complete link should not be marked as Down; other messages can still be delivered with this link.

The result is that all gateways and connectors to external systems are always defined as up, regardless of what state they are in. This means that the Link State Table cannot be used to check such links.

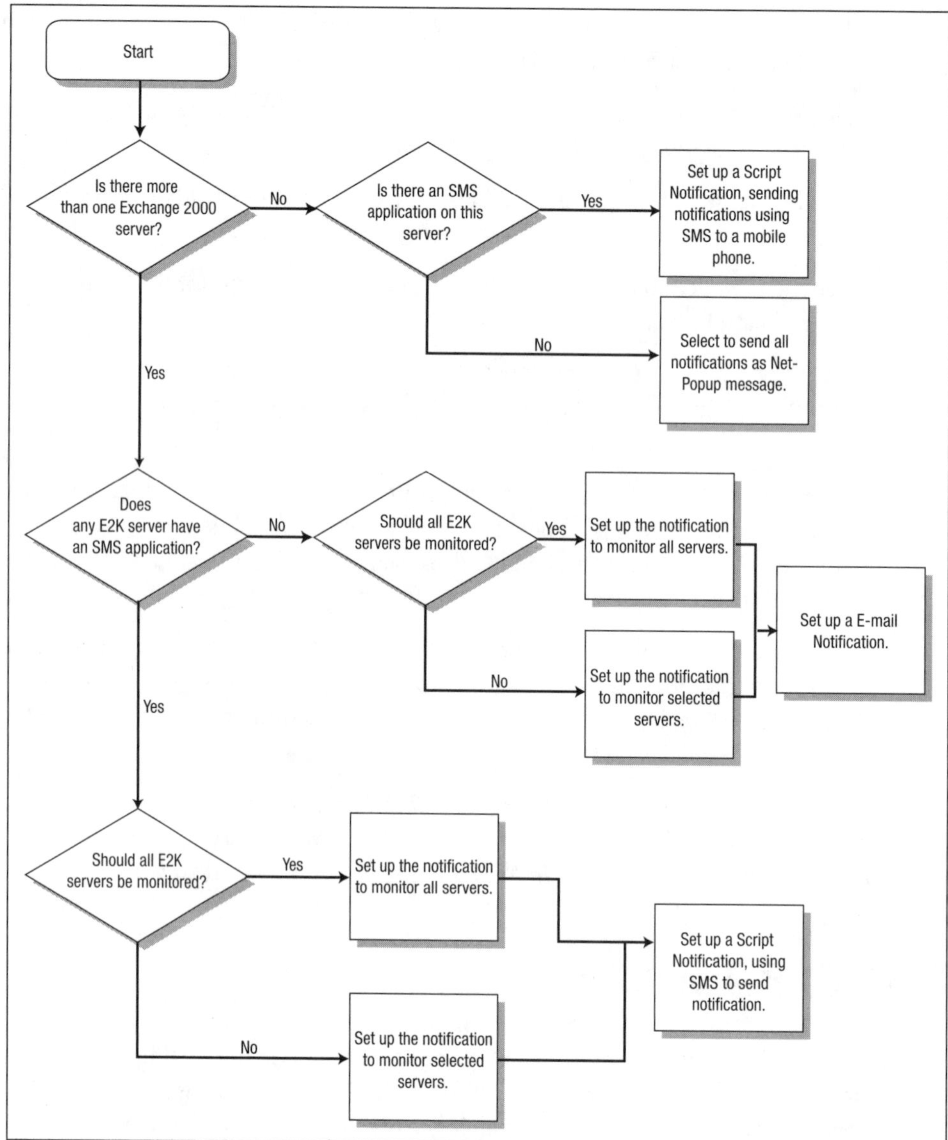

Decision Tree 3.1
Select the right type of notification.

Diagnostic Logging of Links and Services

As in previous Exchange releases, a number of objects can be monitored by the Diagnostic Logging feature. Each Exchange server object has a *Diagnostic Logging* tab as one of its properties, as shown in Figure 3.16. This is an effective method of checking the current status for a server and its connectors, especially when troubleshooting. All logging messages will be written to the Windows 2000 Event log. Note that all errors will automatically be notated in the event log even if you have a logging level set to None.

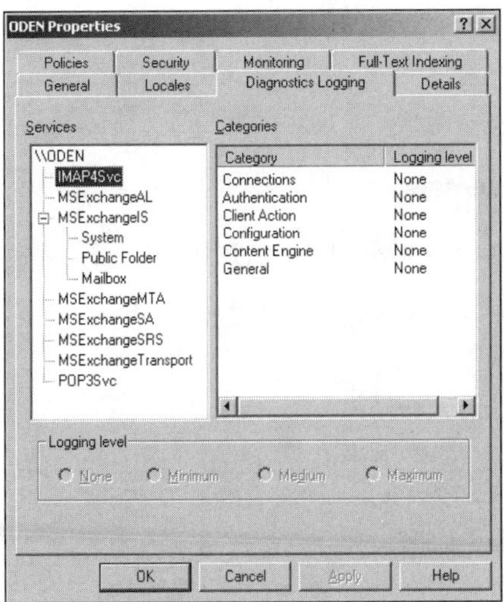

Figure 3.16
Diagnostic logging for a server.

The list of services in Figure 3.16 depends on what connectors you have installed. Table 3.1 lists all available services for diagnostic logging.

Table 3.1 Services available for diagnostic logging.

Monitored Service	Description
IMAP4Svc	Internet Message Access Protocol, version 4 (IMAP4)
LME-GWISE	Lotus Notes GroupWise Connector
LME-NOTES	Lotus Notes Connector
MSExchangeAL	MS Exchange Address List
MSExchangeCCMC	Lotus cc-Mail Connector
MSExchangeDX	MS Exchange Directory Synchronization (for MS Mail)
MSExchangeFB	MS Exchange Schedule Plus Free/Busy Connector (for MS Mail)
MSExchangeGWRtr	MS Exchange Router for Novell GroupWise Connector
MSExchangeIS\System	The Information Store System objects
MSExchangeIS\Private	The Information Store Private mailbox objects
MSExchangeIS\Public	The Information Store Public folder objects
MSExchangeMSMI	MS Mail Connector
MSExchange NSPI Proxy	MAPI Address Book Proxy Service
MSExchangeRFR Interface	MAPI Address Book Referral Service
MSExchangeSRS	Site Replication Service
MSExchangeTransport	SMTP Routing Engine and Transport
POP3Svc	Post Office Protocol, version 3 (POP3)

All the services in Table 3.1 have a number of objects that can be logged. The logging level options include:

- *None*—Only error messages will be logged.
- *Minimum*—Warning messages and error messages will be logged.
- *Medium*—Informational messages, warnings, and errors will be logged.
- *Maximum*—Troubleshooting messages with detailed information, including informational messages, warnings, and errors will be logged.

***Note:** You should not use the Maximum logging level unless needed, since it will quickly fill up the Event log with lots of messages. You usually won't need to have any other setting than None for any of the services mentioned in Table 3.1, except when there is a specific reason you should change the setting, such as when you are encountering problems and intermittent errors.*

Besides the diagnostic logging of server objects, you can also log the SMTP and NNTP virtual servers. This logging will provide detailed information about the commands being sent and received and can be a valuable help in troubleshooting. These virtual servers are not logged by default; you must enable logging by changing the *General property* tab, as illustrated in Figure 3.17. You can select between four types of logging formats with different attributes and file formats, as in Table 3.2. Three of these formats will be stored in a text file that is generated daily with a name that has a prefix as listed in Table 3.2, depending on the type of format, plus the date the file was generated on. The fourth format stores all data directly to a database.

For all three text formats, you can use the *General Properties* tab (see Figure 3.18) to select when the log files will be created. The default is daily, but you could generate them

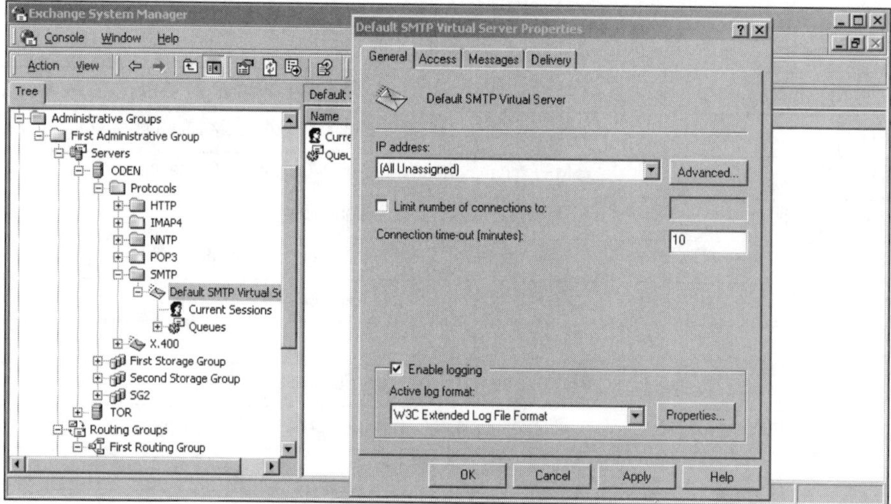

Figure 3.17
The General page for the virtual SMTP server.

Table 3.2 Active log formats.

Log Format	Name Prefix	Description
MS IIS Log File Format	in	Text file; A log file format from IIS 3 with a limited set of attributes.
NCSA Common Log File Format	nc	Text file; The National Center for Supercomputing log file format.
W3C Extended Log File Format	ex	Text file; The World Wide Web Consortium file format—has lots of extended properties (see Figure 3.19). This is the default log format.
ODBC Logging	-	Database; Stores the log info directly in any ODBC-compliant database; needs to be configured before it can be used.

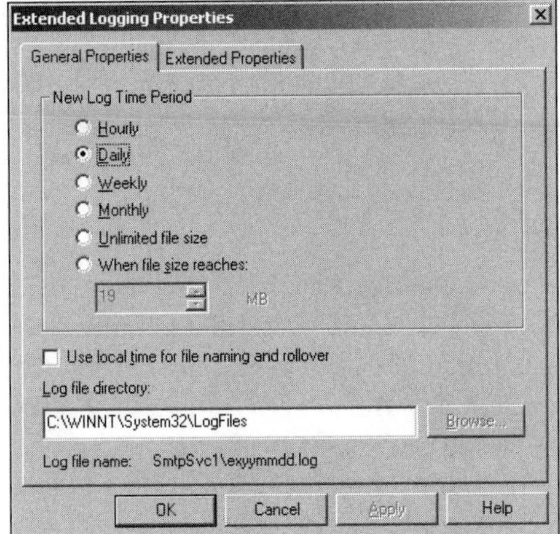

Figure 3.18
The General Properties tab for log formats stored in text files.

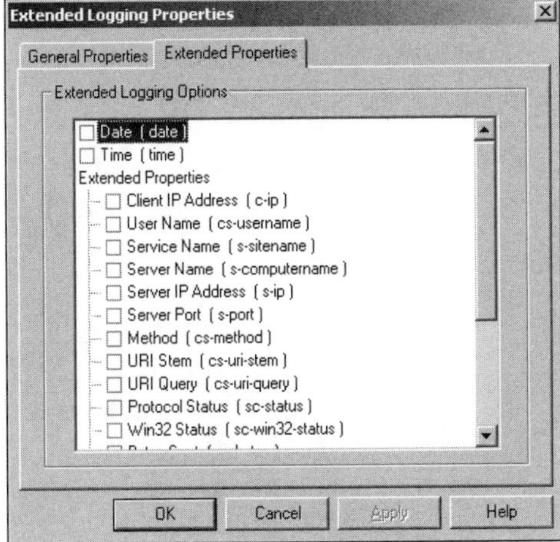

Figure 3.19
The extended properties of the W3C log file format.

as often as once every hour or as seldom as once every month. If you select *Unlimited File Size,* the log system will use the same log file and append all new data to it. If you select *When File Size Reaches,* a new log file will be created when the limit is reached; each log file will be sequentially numbered. On this property tab you can also specify where the log files will be saved.

Note: *Daily generated log files will be created at midnight local time, except for the W3C Extended format; this will be created at midnight Greenwich Mean Time (GMT) by default; you may want to change this to local time by setting the option Use Local Time For File Naming And Rollover.*

As mentioned, the default log format is W3C; it has several extended properties that may be used to get detailed information about the SMTP communication, including all commands being sent. If you don't need this, for example when troubleshooting, you should not set more extended properties than really needed. It will create really large log files that may be hard to handle and interpret.

Configuring Diagnostic ODBC Logging

As listed in Table 3.2, it is possible to store all logging properties directly in an ODBC-compliant database, like MS SQL Server or MS Access. This has the advantage that it is possible to do statistical analysis on any period of choice, like the last week or the last month. *ODBC* stands for *Open DataBase Connectivity* and is a standard for reading and writing to databases; most database vendors have support for ODBC, like Oracle and SuperBase. Before you can log directly to a database, you need to configure the ODBC protocol. Follow these steps:

1. Prepare the database for this logging by creating a table that conforms to the sizes of the fields for your database programs. For example, in Microsoft SQL Server, the sizes of the fields for a table are as follows:
   ClientHost varchar(255),
   username varchar(255),
   LogTime datetime,
   service varchar(255),
   machine varchar(255),
   serverip varchar(50),
   processingtime int,
   bytesrecvd int,
   bytessent int,
   servicestatus int,
   win32status int,
   operation varchar(255),
   target varchar(255),
   parameters varchar(255)
2. Set up a database on your server and create a system *Data Source Name (DSN).*

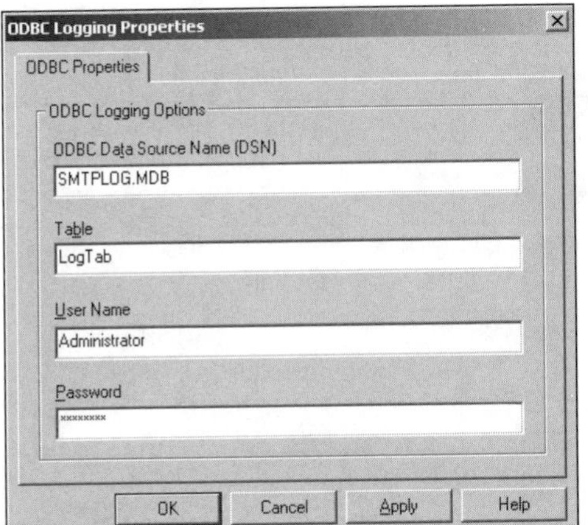

Figure 3.20
ODBC property settings.

Note: *For MS Access, the system DSN is the file name of your database.*

3. To activate the logging to the ODBC database, select the ODBC Logging setting and click the Properties button (see Figure 3.20).
4. Fill in the name of the Data Source Name you added in Step 2.
5. For the Table field, type the name of the table you created in the database.
6. Fill in the User Name and Password fields, if any user security is set on the database.
7. Click *OK* to apply and close this window.

Identifying Potential Bottlenecks in the System

It is impossible to say exactly what values a given Exchange server can accept for CPU utilization, disk usage, and the amount of virtual memory used; it must always be in relation to the hardware configuration, the number of applications running, and the number of users who are using the system. You may need to measure these counters for several days to get a good estimate of their values. However, Microsoft has a few recommendations for some Performance Monitor counters for an Exchange 2000 server. These are listed in Table 3.3; use them as a help when you run into performance problems on your Exchange server.

Table 3.3 Recommended counter thresholds for Exchange servers.

Resource	Object/Counter	Recommended	Comments
Disk	LogicalDisk\%Free space	15 percent	-
Disk	LogicalDisk\% Disk time	90 percent	-

(continued)

Table 3.3 Recommended counter thresholds for Exchange servers *(continued).*

Resource	Object/Counter	Recommended	Comments
Disk	PhysicalDisk\Disk reads/sec	Depends on manufacturer	Check the specifications for this disk. Some SCSI disks can handle 50 to 70 I/O per second.
Disk	PhysicalDisk\Current Disk queue length	Number of spindles plus 2	Check this value over several intervals to get a good estimate.
Memory	Memory\Available bytes	Less than 4MB	Check memory usage and add memory if needed.
Memory	Memory\pages/sec	20	Research paging activity.
Network	Network segment\% Net utilization	Depends on type of network	Ethernet typically has 30 percent as recommended threshold.
Paging File	Paging File\% Usage	More than 70 percent	Find the process that is using a high percentage of processor time; upgrade to a faster CPU or install an extra CPU.
Processor	Processor\Interrupts/sec	Depends on CPU	A sudden increase of this counter without a corresponding increase of system activities indicates hardware problems; check the network adapter or hard disk controller. For current CPUs, use a threshold of 1,500 interrupts/sec.
Server	Server\Bytes total/sec	Depends	If the sum of Bytes total/sec for all servers is about equal to the maximum transfer rates of your network, you may need to segment the network.
Server	Server\Work Item shortage	3	If the value reaches this threshold, consider tuning the InitWorkItems or MaxWorkItems entries in the Registry: HKEY_LOCAL_MACHINE\SYSTEM\CurrentControlSet\Services\lanmanserver\Parameters.
Server	Server Work Queues\Queue Length	4	If the value reaches this threshold, there might be a CPU bottleneck.
Multiple CPUs	System\Processor Queue Length	2	This value changes instantaneously, check it several times.

How to View the Log Files

If the files are stored as text files, you may use any text editor to view them. I recommend that you import them to MS Excel to get a clearer picture of your data and for doing an analysis of the log information by using the following steps:

1. Start MS Excel, select File|Open, and select the log file.
2. You will then get the Text Import Wizard; choose Delimited file type, set Start Import At Row = 4, and click *Next*.
3. Select only delimiters as Space (no Tab or any other delimiter); click *Next*.
4. The next screen offers a possibility to set the column data format. If you need to, change each column to the correct format; for a quick view of your log, you can accept the default General data format. When ready, click *Finish*.
5. Remove the first A1 cell, since it contains a description that you don't need. To do this, select cell A1, right-click and select Delete, then select Shift Cells Left. This is important because the default suggestion Shift Cells Up will destroy your table. After you do this, you are finished.

Tip: *Double-click on the vertical line between column headers to make Excel auto format the size of the left column.*

Since a number of steps are involved in this, I recommend that you create an Excel macro that does this procedure for you, to make it easier next time you want to view a log file.

In the Windows 2000 Server Resource Kit, you can find the free Seagate Crystal Reports for BackOffice under the third-party tools. This is an advanced utility that can create reports from many different types of databases and log files, including Exchange files. It may take a little time to understand this tool, but then it can also offer you lots of information about Exchange.

Monitoring the Exchange Server

A number of critical services for each Exchange server will automatically be monitored: the Information Store, the MTA, the Routing Engine, the System Attendant, the World Wide Web, and the SMTP service. You can add more services to this list, like alerts when the SMTP queue has been constantly growing for a given time or any general Windows 2000 service. They are all added to the server object under the Status folder (as in Figure 3.13); right-click on the server you want to modify and then click Add. See Figure 3.21.

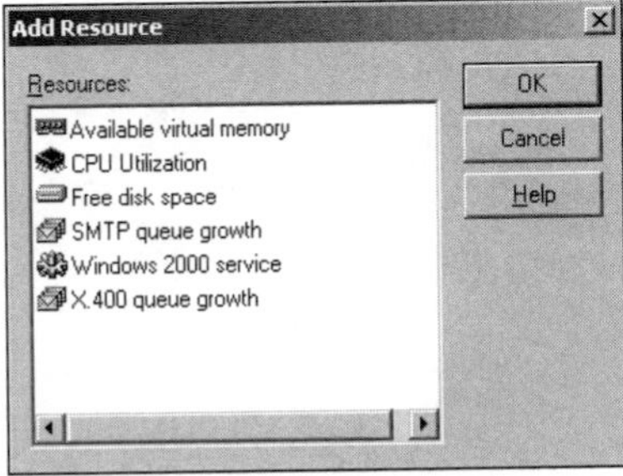

Figure 3.21
Add resources to monitor.

In the following sections you will see all available services that you can add to the monitoring process.

Available Virtual Memory

Use this resource to monitor how much available virtual memory the server has. If it is below a given value (in percentages), the server will enter a warning or critical state; this in turn will generate a notification that you may have configured—see Figure 3.22. The virtual memory is very important for Windows 2000 and Exchange 2000; it is normal to have fluctuations in the amount of available virtual memory, but if the value goes below a certain threshold for the number of times that you have set in the *Duration (Minutes)* field, it will change its state to Warning or Critical.

CPU Utilization Thresholds

Use this resource to monitor the utilization of the CPU. If this value is too high for an extended period of time, it is a sign that this server is overloaded. The solution is to reduce the number of services or to install extra CPUs. This information can be very valuable, since it will indicate when the server is near or at its maximum capacity. The feature of checking the CPU load over a period of time is new; in previous versions you would only have the possibility to trigger when the CPU passed a given threshold of time, making such a trigger in effect almost useless. In Figure 3.23, you see as an example that the duration is set to 5 minutes, the warning state is at 70 percent, and the critical state is at 90 percent. This means that if the CPU is over 90 percent load for more than 5 minutes, a Critical State notification will be generated if a notification has been set for this server.

Free Disk Space

By monitoring this resource, you can receive warnings when the disk is running out of free disk space. The disk that will grow fastest is the disk for the transaction log files; since these log files are created when needed, they can quickly fill the disk if the backup program does not delete the log files as it should, for instance when the backup fails for some reason. Exchange will shut itself down if any of the disks runs out of free disk space. To avoid this, monitor at least the transaction log disk (see Figure 3.24) and set the warning and critical

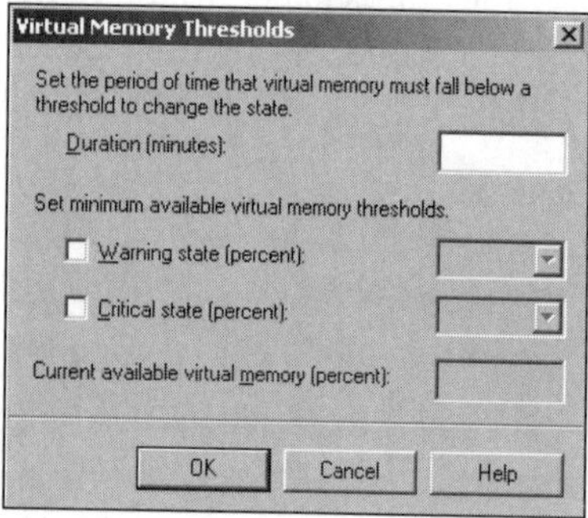

Figure 3.22
The Available Virtual Memory settings.

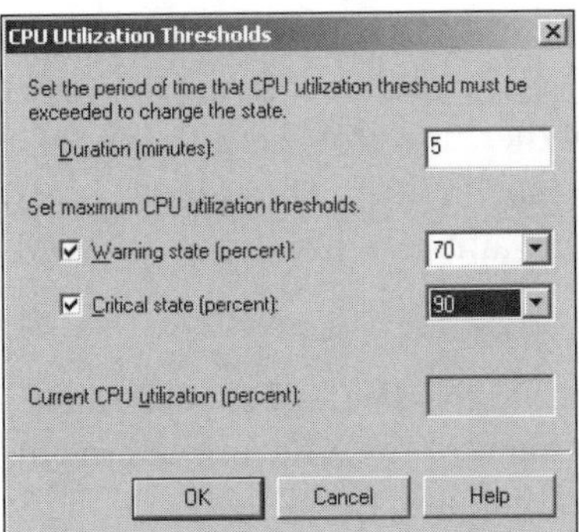

Figure 3.23
Monitoring the CPU utilization.

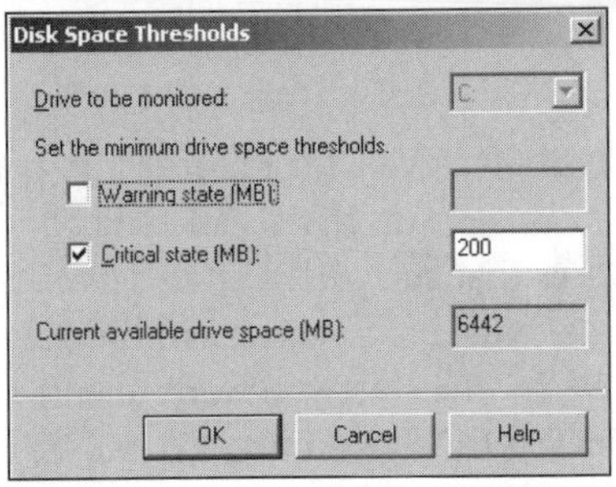

Figure 3.24
The Disk Space Thresholds settings.

state thresholds. If you want to monitor more than one disk, configure as many *Disk Space Thresholds* resources as needed.

SMTP Queue Growth

Use this resource to monitor the SMTP queue growth; if the queue is constantly growing for more than a given number of minutes, this will generate a change to the warning state or the critical state, depending on what you have configured. In the example in Figure 3.25,

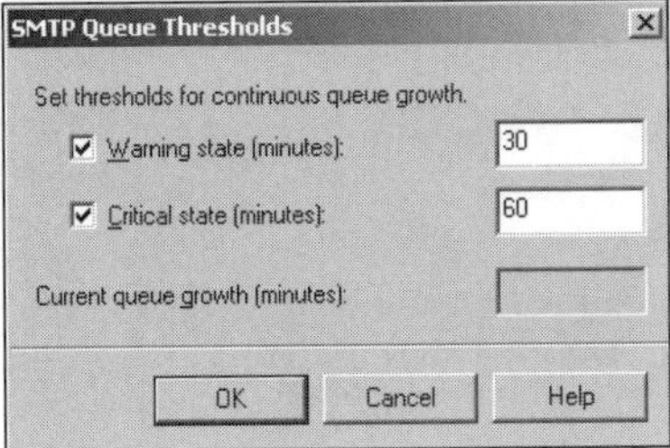

Figure 3.25
The SMTP Queue Threshold settings.

a warning state will be reached if the SMTP queue has been growing for more than 30 minutes; a critical state will be reached if the growth has been occurring for more than 60 minutes. This resource monitoring will tell you if there is a problem with the SMTP connector; it is much more reliable than the old method in the previous Exchange, where you could trigger only on the number of messages waiting in the queue.

X.400 Queue Growth

This resource-monitoring object is exactly the same as the SMTP Queue Threshold, except it checks the X.400 queues. Use this resource to monitor the X400 queue growth; if the queue is growing for more than a given number of minutes, this will generate a change of warning state or critical state, depending on what you have configured. In the example in Figure 3.26, a warning state will be reached if the X.400 queue has been growing for more than 30 minutes; a critical state will be reached if the growth has been occurring for more than 60 minutes.

Windows 2000 Service

This object makes it possible to add any Windows 2000 service for monitoring, not only those directly involved in Exchange 2000 activities. This means that as an extra bonus, you can use Exchange to monitor other critical processes that run on the same server. Select the *Windows 2000 Service*, and then click *Add* to get a list of all services running on this server; add as many as you need (see Figure 3.27). Set the state you want to enter when one of these services stops by using the *When Service Is Not Running Change State To* option. Finally, set a name for this configuration; see Figure 3.28.

Some Advice Regarding Monitoring

All of these monitoring features in Exchange 2000 can be very valuable for keeping track of the Exchange server's status, but don't fall into the trap of adding them just because you can. Nothing in life is free, not even Exchange monitoring. The price equals increased workload both for the Exchange server doing this monitoring and for the servers being monitored. Think before installing and use them with care.

When setting times for checking queues, it is tempting to set short times, like five minutes. But it is normal to have great fluctuations sometime, and you don't want false alarms.

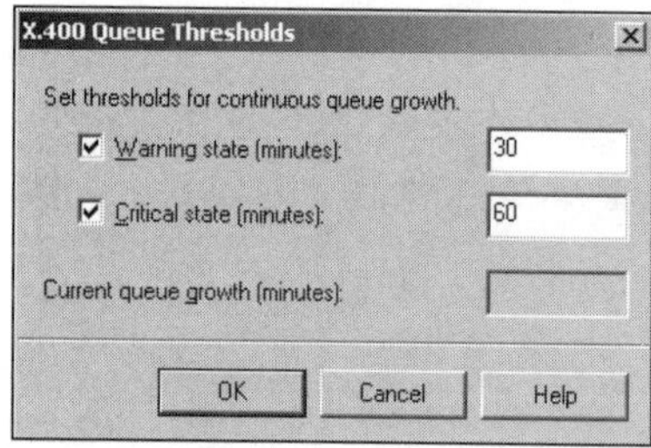

Figure 3.26
The X.400 Queue Threshold settings.

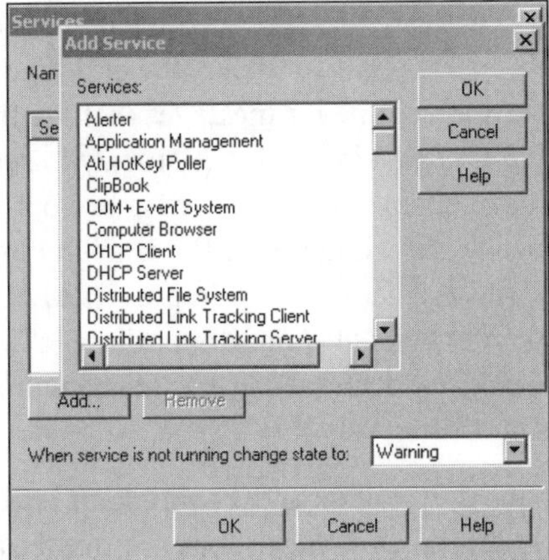

Figure 3.27
Adding new services to monitor.

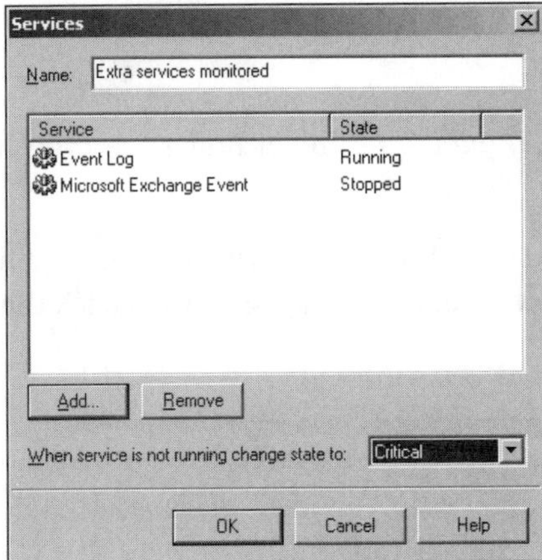

Figure 3.28
An example of monitoring added services.

It is better to select longer times, like 30 minutes or even 60 minutes, to be sure that when these notifications appear, they're really worth checking. If the system generates lots of false alarms, you will stop noticing them.

Message Tracking

The ability to monitor servers and connectors is a great tool, but sometimes you want to know if a message has been delivered and what servers and connectors have been involved in the transportation. This is where the Message Tracking tool in Exchange 2000 comes in handy. For example, with this tracking tool, you can see that a certain user submitted a message to an external SMTP address; this message was first transferred to a server with the SMTP connector and then transferred by ESMTP to the destination server. You can see the time, the subject, the number of bytes, and more.

Before you can use this handy feature, you must activate message tracking on the server. Open the properties for the server, look at the General page, and select the option to enable message tracking. You may also want to see the subject line for messages that are tracked; if so, select the option *Enable Subject Logging And Display*. It is very handy to see the subject line if you want to follow an email virus or spam mail. Below these two options is a setting for how long this particular Exchange server should save the tracking log files; the default is 7 days, which is appropriate for most organizations. In previous Exchange versions, you had to activate message tracking on individual connectors for the MTA object and for Information Store. This is no longer necessary. If the server has message tracking enabled, it will be activated for all connectors on this server.

As soon as the message tracking option is enabled, it will be active; you don't have to restart the server to get it working. If you have several Exchange servers, it may be a good idea to enable message tracking for all servers where you may be interested in tracking a message. The price, as always, is slightly decreased performance. Message tracking requires some resources like CPU and disk space, but it may provide an invaluable tool for solving problems related to mail transfer.

To track a message, follow these steps:

1. Use the ESM and select the *Message Tracking Center* folder under the *Tools* folder; right-click and select *Track Message*.
2. Depending on what you are looking for, choose the *From, Sent To*, or *Servers* fields (or a mix); click the respective *Browse* button and select a name; then click the *Find Now* button. See Figure 3.29.

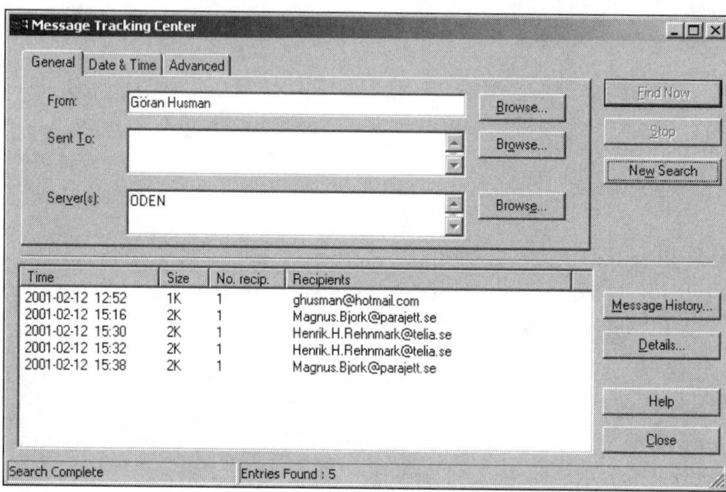

Figure 3.29
Define what mail will be tracked.

3. In a few seconds, you will see a list of all mail from the selected users; select the one you want to track and click *Message History*. This starts tracking this message in all available log files, which can sometimes take a few minutes. If the server has been transferred between different Exchange servers and they all have the tracking log enabled, this tracking monitor will read even those log files. The result will be a message history, like the one in Figure 3.30.

The message story will convey exactly how this message was transferred by the different Exchange services. It ends with the information that the message was sent to the remote SMTP server, mailb.telia.se; select this line and click the Details button to get the exact time of when this happened.

Note: *Warnings about log files not being available can normally be ignored; in Figure 3.30, there is first one warning that the log file from the day before was not found (because tracking was not enabled at that time). Two more appear at the end, warning that the Tracking Center tried to track the message to the destination, but failed since it was a remote SMTP server named MAILB.*

Summary

This is a list of keywords and important features described in this chapter. Use it to refresh your memory.

- Three types of routing scenarios are possible: local delivery, remote delivery, and external delivery.
- Previous Exchange routing was based on X.400, which was controlled by the MTA process.

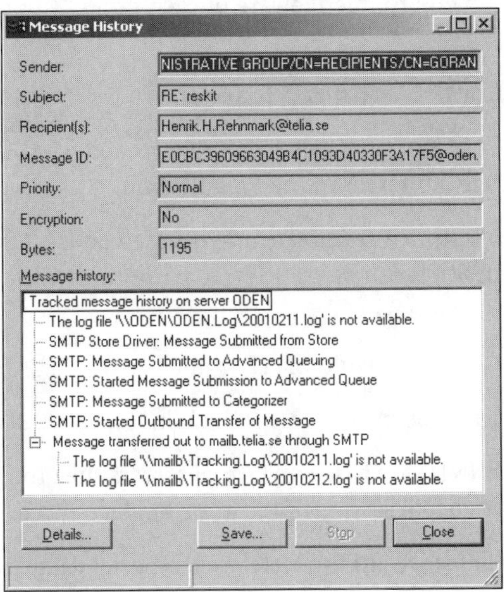

Figure 3.30
The message history.

- The old Gateway Address Routing Table (GWART), is not used in Exchange 2000.
- All Remote Procedure Calls (RPCs) are gone; all communication between servers is now done by SMTP in Exchange 2000.
- There are no more DIR.EDB databases; Exchange 2000 relies completely on the Active Directory in Windows 2000.
- LDAP, or Lightweight Directory Access Protocol, is an enhanced version of the OSI protocol DAP; it is used to search and update directory databases, such as AD and NDS.
- Only LDAP version 3 has support for write operations; it was ratified as an IEFT standard in 1997.
- A *routing group* is a group of Exchange 2000 servers with high and permanent TCP/IP connectivity between them.
- Routing groups are similar to the previous concept of *sites*, except that they're no longer a boundary for Exchange administration.
- Each routing group has a routing group master that keeps the Link State Table updated; it is, by default, the first installed server in the routing group, but can be changed.
- All routing groups and their connectors are stored in Active Directory instead of the old GWART table.
- The Exchange information in AD is replicated to all Exchange servers in the Windows 2000 forest by the global catalog servers.
- An Active Directory connector will replicate AD information to Exchange 5.5 directories by making a mixed Exchange 2000/5.5 environment aware of each others' connectors and routing groups.
- A routing group will be seen as a site by the Exchange 5.5. server.
- Some connectors will not be adopted for Exchange 2000, like PROFS and SNADS; if you need them, you must keep an Exchange 5.5 server in the organization.
- The SMTP transport between servers within a routing group is based on 8-bit MIME format; this means that binary information can be transferred without converting to 7-bit ASCII.
- The previous RPC protocol was encrypted by default; SMTP is not.
- Exchange enhances the SMTP stack that was installed with the Windows 2000 server.
- All Internet protocols, like SMTP and NNTP, are based on virtual servers (like the Option Pack for NT 4). You can install several virtual servers of the same kind if needed.
- All configurations for virtual servers are stored in the Metabase, a special database for IIS similar to the Registry.

- MetaEdit 2 is a tool for manipulating the Metabase in IIS directly. It should be used carefully.
- The Advanced Queuing Engine installs with Exchange 2000; it makes the routing of messages faster, smarter, and more resilient. All messages, including local delivery mail, are passed to the AQ engine.
- The categorizer is a part of the AQ engine; it checks the recipient and the sender, expands distribution groups, and checks for any delivery restrictions like size limits.
- The Router Component finds the best route for the next hop and will check the Link State Table to see what links are up.
- The Store Driver makes the AQ engine able to communicate directly with the Information Store without the need to store information on the NTFS first.
- Local delivery sends messages to a recipient on the same server as the sender.
- Remote delivery sends messages to a recipient on another Exchange server in the same organization.
- External delivery sends messages to recipients outside the Exchange organization.
- Bifurcated mail is split into two or more copies.
- Precategorizer and postcategorizer queues are event sinks directly before and after the categorizer; you may install your own script here to manipulate the message.
- Incoming X.400 messages are first received in a hidden mailbox, called MTS-IN, then treated as normal mail.
- The monitoring of the transport system can be done in many ways; one is to use the Performance Monitor and its more than 50 counters related to the Categorizer and virtual SMTP server.
- No mail to members of distribution groups may result from using global distribution groups instead of universal distribution groups.
- The Link State Table stores current link states and determines if a connector is currently Up or Down.
- The routing group master is responsible for the Link State Table. All members of a routing group get a copy of this table; if a member discovers a link that is down, it reports this to the routing group master by TCP Port 691.
- Replication of link states to other routing groups is done by SMTP port 25 and the verb **X-LINK2STATE**; data is sent in CHUNKS.
- A link is checked only when it's used. It can be down for days without anyone noticing this if it's not used.

- A link that is marked as Down will have the cost value set to INFINITE.
- All links and servers will be automatically monitored by the ESM admin tool, but no notification will be provided.
- Set up notification by email messages or by running an executable, like an SMS program.
- Several third-party tools are available for monitoring Exchange and Windows 2000.
- Gateways or links to external mail systems are always regarded as Up.
- Diagnostic logging can be used to get information about Exchange and its subsystems.
- Four different diagnostics logging formats are possible—W3C is the default.
- You can add more resources to monitor: virtual memory, CPU utilization, disk space, SMTP and X.400 queue growth, and all available Windows 2000 services.
- Use Message Tracking to follow a message through the Exchange organization. Remember that you must activate it first.

Chapter 4

SMTP in Exchange 2000

This chapter will tell you about (SMTP)—its history, how it works in general, and how it relates to MS Exchange 2000 Server. You will also learn about the previous protocols that were replaced by SMTP, like X.400 and Remote Procedure Call (RPC). Since this is the first version of Exchange that is built on the SMTP routing architecture, administrators of previous Exchange systems have several new things to learn. A lot of information about the different Requests for Comments (RFCs) that are used by Exchange 2000 is in this chapter; read it to understand how SMTP works in detail. You will find information about MIME conversion, like Quoted-Printable and Base-64, plus a description of UUencode. The chapter ends by describing how to use Telnet as a tool for testing and troubleshooting SMTP connections. If this is the first time you will be working with an SMTP-based mail system, I recommend you take some time to understand how it works.

The History of SMTP

The first popular program for sending information between computers was File Transfer Protocol—FTP (RFC 165). It was released in 1971 and was based on an even earlier protocol, Data Transfer Protocol (DTP). With FTP, you could send (upload) or receive (download) any file from another computer. People quickly realized that FTP could be used to send files with messages, too, as a rough method of distributing electronic mail. It was a bit tricky, though, so in 1980 the first description of how to distribute email was released—the RFC 772—by S. Sluizer and J. Postel. They called this protocol Mail Transfer Protocol (MTP). It was built partly on the FTP protocol. This MTP was revised several times and in November 1981, J. Postel created the RFC 788, the first SMTP description ever. This was refined in the RFC 821 in August 1982 and it is still considered the SMTP standard. The RFC 822 is also an important standard, released shortly after RFC 821, describing the actual format of a message, like the header and its content. Later, several enhancements and complements to these two RFCs were released—for example, ESMTP and MIME.

As you can see, lots of versions and complements of the SMTP standard are available, but most email vendors claim that their SMTP programs comply with RFC 821 and RFC 822, plus one or more enhancements like ESMTP and MIME. The SMTP standard will continue to develop as the demand increases. Microsoft is committed to the standards relating to SMTP and will continue to add new features in the coming Exchange releases.

One consequence of all these different versions and complements was that only five years ago, it was common to find two SMTP systems that did not always manage to send messages successfully between them. Two problems in particular showed up repeatedly: international characters were not displayed correctly and binary files were frequently corrupted. These kinds of problems gave the SMTP standard a bad reputation, so something had to be done before SMTP was ready for the general public. The solution was MIME—Multipurpose Internet Mail Extensions—a method to convert binary files and national characters so they could safely be transferred to any other MIME-compliant SMTP system. Today all modern SMTP systems are MIME compliant, which has solved these problems.

The SMTP protocol is built to run over TCP/IP; you cannot run SMTP over Novell's IPX/SPX or Microsoft's NetBEUI. This is one of the reasons that Windows 2000 and Exchange 2000 must be TCP/IP-based networks. Today this isn't a problem, but only a few years back, TCP/IP was not generally common on PC-based networks.

A *protocol*, like the SMTP or FTP protocol, is a specification of how the communication between two servers (or programs) should be performed; for example, how to initiate a session, how to transfer data, and how to disconnect. Most of the Internet-based protocols are based on 7-bit ASCII text commands. This makes it very easy to test and troubleshoot these protocols. This chapter describes how you can use an ordinary Telnet session to connect to an SMTP server and manually send the SMTP commands to see exactly what replies you get. Take some time and learn this; it's not just a good troubleshooting tool—you can impress your friends too!

Request for Comments

The Internet world was mainly developed by universities and research institutes. In the academic world, the fundamental idea is that information is free and everyone shares their findings and ideas with each other. ARPANET was the first computer network, started in 1968. It was originally a U.S. military-funded project that later transformed into the Internet as we know it today. During the development of the ARPANET, everyone involved in this project could suggest a new idea; this was sent out to all interested in this matter and was called a "Request for Comments," or RFC.

All RFCs are given a unique number, taken from the same number series; for example RFC 821. An RFC document may be replaced by a newer RFC, but the new RFC will always be given a new number; there will never be several versions of the same RFC. The more popular Internet protocols have several enhancements and expansions, described in their own RFCs; that is the reason why there are so many RFCs describing SMTP, for example. Today, all RFCs are handled by the Internet Engineering Task Force (IETF), which is a subgroup of ISOC, the Internet Society. There are different statuses of an RFC called the *requirement levels* (see Table 4.1), and today you will find some of the most important RFCs also released as Standards (STDs) with a different number series than RFC, such as the

Table 4.1 The different requirement levels of an RFC.

Level	Description
Required	Implementation of this RFC is required to be compliant of a certain standard. For example, IP and Internet Control Message Protocol (ICMP) must be implemented by all Internet systems using the TCP/IP protocol suite.
Recommended	Implementation of this RFC is not required for minimal conformance, but experienced and/or generally accepted technical wisdom suggest its desirability in this domain of applicability of this RFC. Vendors are strongly encouraged to include the functions, features, and protocols of recommended RFCs in their products, and should omit them only if the omission is justified by some special circumstance. For example, the Telnet protocol should be implemented by all systems that would benefit from remote access.
Elective	Implementation of this RFC is optional; that is, this RFC creates no explicit necessity for the subject of this RFC. However, a particular vendor may decide to implement it, or a particular user may decide that it's a necessity in a specific environment. For example, the DECNET MIB could be seen as valuable in an environment where the DECNET protocol is used.
Limited Use	The subject of this RFC is considered to be appropriate for use only in limited or unique situations. For example, the usage of a protocol with the "Experimental" designation should generally be limited to those actively involved with the experiment.
Not Recommended	An RFC that is considered to be inappropriate for general use. This may be because of its limited functionality, specialized nature, or historic status.

SMTP RFC 821 that is also known as STD 10. Finally, you should know one more abbreviation, the For Your Information (FYI) series, which consists of documents with overviews and introductions to different topics. Both the STD and the FYI are regarded as subseries of the RFC.

Different levels of the established standards are described by an RFC, also known as the *maturity levels*. These are, in order, *Proposed*, *Draft*, and finally *Internet Standard*. Most final standard documents are considered to be Draft standard and a vendor should implement such specifications. A few standard RFCs are actually regarded as Internet Standards; these will get an STD number while still retaining their RFC number. Today more than 3,000 different RFCs exist and new ones are created almost every week. Some of the most important RFCs related to SMTP that will be discussed in this chapter are listed here:

- *RFC 821 (STD 10)*—The SMTP protocol describing how to transfer messages between two hosts
- *RFC 822 (STD 11)*—The format of "ARPA Internet Text Messages," meaning the SMTP message structure
- *RFC 1652*—SMTP Service Extension: 8-bit MIME transfer
- *RFC 1869*—SMTP Service Extension: ESMTP
- *RFC 1870*—SMTP Service Extension: Message size declaration

- *RFCs 1891, 1892, and 1894*—SMTP Service Extension: The Delivery Status Notifications (DSN) command; used for delivery receipts and non-delivery reports (NDRs)
- *RFC 1985*—SMTP Service Extension: The Extended Turn (**ETRN**) command; used for de-queuing mail from a secondary mail server
- *RFCs 2045, 2046, 2047, 2048, and 2049*—The MIME format
- *RFC 2197*—SMTP Service Extension: Pipelining
- *RFC 2487*—SMTP Service Extension: transport-level security (TLS) encryption
- *RFC 2505*—Anti-Spam recommendations for SMTP MTAs
- *RFC 2554*—SMTP Service Extension: AUTH for negotiation of authentication method
- *RFC 2645*—On-Demand Mail Relay (ODMR); also known as ATRN
- *RFC 3030*—SMTP Service Extension: BDAT; for transmission of large and binary MIME messages (an alternative to DATA), also known as Chunking

Two excellent sources for looking and searching for RFCs and other types of Internet documents are the RFC Index Search Engine that you can find at **www.rfc-editor.org**, and the Internet Mail Consortium at **www.imc.org**. One of the most active writers of RFCs related to SMTP, the author of RFC 821 and a true Internet pioneer, was Dr. Jonathan B. Postel, who sadly died in October 1998; he had one famous saying: "Be liberal in what you accept, and conservative in what you send," RFC 1122.

Comparing X.400 and SMTP

As mentioned before, previous versions of Exchange were based on the X.400 mail standard. This section compares the differences and similarities between X.400 and the SMTP protocol.

The X.400 protocol was developed by the CCITT (now ITU-TS), a special group under the United Nations. This group was responsible for developing recommendations and standardizations regarding technical specifications for telephone and telegraph systems, and later also standards and recommendations regarding data communication. In 1984, they released the X.400 protocol family, which is a set of standards on how to build a mail system. As we know, Microsoft decided to build the first Exchange release on these standards.

The X.400 world has many similarities to the SMTP world; after all, they both have the same goal of describing how to build a mail system. Each mail organization has a registered Private Management Domain (PRMD); their mail systems are built on one or more Message Transfer Agents (MTAs) that are responsible for the transport, and each client is running a User Agent (UA). Communication to other companies' MTAs is through an Administration Management Domain (ADMD) that is a public X.400 provider; see Figure 4.1.

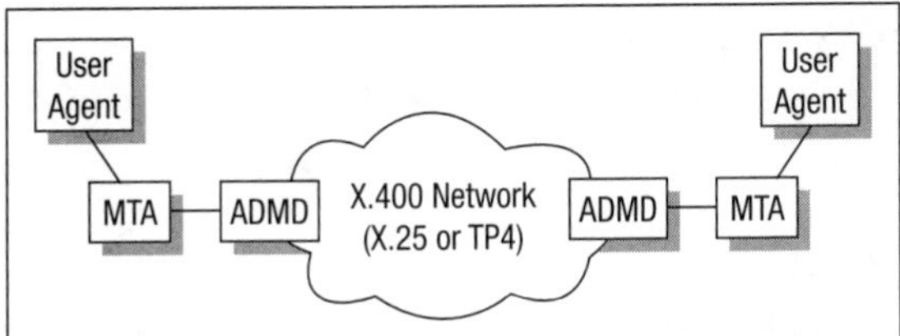

Figure 4.1
An X.400 provider.

If we compare this to an SMTP-based world, it looks almost identical, except for the names: Each mail organization has a registered mail domain, such as "@microsoft.com"; each system is built on one or more SMTP servers; each client is running a mail client, like IMAP4; and communication to other companies' SMTP servers is through an Internet Service Provider (ISP) (see Figure 4.2).

Some more similarities: None of the SMTP or X.400 mail transfers are encrypted, and both of them can transfer file attachments. There are differences in how things are done at the technical level, but the most striking difference is the address standard. An X.400 mail address can have several formats, but the most common are known as the *mnemonic address types*; mnemonic means something that is easy to remember. This is an example of a mnemonic X.400 address:

c=se;a=400NET;p=humandata;o=hq;s=husman;g=goran

Don't you think this address is easy to remember? I guess it depends on what you compare it to. The other X.400 address formats are even stranger, like the hexadecimal network address of the recipient—now that is hard to remember! Regardless of what format you are using, an X.400 address is also known as an Originator/Recipient (O/R) address.

The SMTP address format is well known for most of us: **goran.husman@humandata.se**. Most people consider this type of address much more mnemonic than the X.400 O/R address. However, there is one thing that the X.400 system has that SMTP doesn't: You don't need to use all address attributes, as long as it is a unique address. For example, assume there's only one person with the surname Husman at the HumanData company.

Figure 4.2
An SMTP mail system.

Then you could shorten the O/R address to c=se;a=400NET;p=humandata;o=hq;s=husman. For SMTP addresses, you must use the complete address exactly as it is—no abbreviations are accepted.

LDAP and the X.500 Directory

There is one more thing common to both X.400 and SMTP: Neither of them supports global address lists—all users must keep their own personal address lists. The CCITT group recommended how to design a global directory—the X.500 standard. Such a directory database could be used to store any type of object, including address lists. The CCITT also described a protocol for searching the X.500 database—the Directory Address Protocol (DAP). Most X.400-based mail systems also implemented the X.500 directory database to get a complete mail system with a global address list. The only problem was that DAP was made for the OSI transport protocol TP4/CLNP, a form of TCP/IP, and very few organizations were interested in running TP4 (since it was complicated to install and required much more overhead than TCP/IP). The X.500 directory idea was great, but the DAP was a flop; the solution came when an enhanced version of DAP was adapted for TCP/IP—the LDAP protocol. Now everything was in place for building a global directory that could be used in the TCP/IP world.

From its first release, Exchange had an X.500-based directory database (DIR.EDB), but it was not until release 5 that this database had support for LDAP. This protocol was not used by ordinary Exchange clients, who could read the directory by MAPI calls, but typically by POP3 and IMAP4 clients. Since it was LDAP version 1, it could only be used for searching the Exchange directory, not for writing or updating. The directory in version 5.5 of Exchange finally got support for LDAP version 3; now this protocol could be used for reading and writing the directory database, but still Outlook clients used MAPI calls instead of LDAP.

The Windows 2000 development group used this Exchange 5.5 directory to develop the Active Directory database, which naturally has full support for LDAP version 3. For the first time in the Microsoft world, LDAP is used as the primary protocol. All components in Windows 2000 are talking LDAP with the Active Directory and Exchange 2000 Server is no exception; it uses LDAP to read and write to the AD.

One interesting thing is that the X.500 directory has its own name standard, completely different from both X.400 O/R addresses and SMTP addresses. All objects that are stored in an X.500 directory are identified by a unique X.500 address. Its name standard is called Distinguished Name (DN). Figure 4.3 shows what such a DN address would look like in Active Directory.

Normally, this DN address is not seen by anyone, including the Exchange administrator. The information in Figure 4.3 is read from Active Directory with the ADSI Edit tool; the AD Users and Computers tool will not reveal this information since it's mostly used internally. However, there are situations where you as an administrator must work with the DN names, such as when you export and import accounts. More about this in Chapter 10.

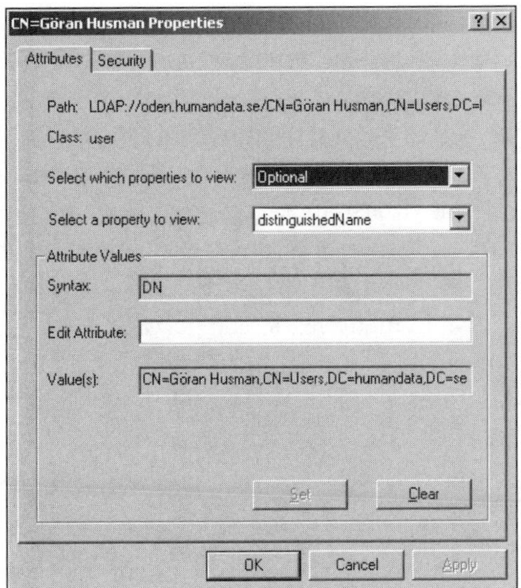

Figure 4.3
The X.500 Distinguished Name.

SMTP Advantages over X.400

The simplicity of the SMTP protocol is a clear advantage over the X.400 protocol when it comes to adding new features. With the X.400 protocol, there is no way to expand the protocol with new commands or feature sets, besides the new version that ITU-TS releases every four years, a long time in the computer world. Compare this to the Internet world; everyone is allowed to suggest a change or added feature to the SMTP protocol, and still new RFC proposals are presented that are related to SMTP.

One of the extensions to SMTP is vendor-specific commands, the X-commands, described in RFC 1869 as local SMTP service extensions. Exchange uses this possibility to add the following three extra commands that can be used in a Microsoft environment:

- *X-EXPS*—For authentication, with support for Kerberos and NTLM.
- *XEXCH50*—For validation and encryption between Exchange 5 and 5.5 servers.
- *X-LINK2STATE*—For signaling that this server understands link states.

An SMTP server that is compliant with RFC 1869 is known as an *ESMTP server*; with these added features, an SMTP server had all the features of X.400 and more. Without ESMTP, it would have been hard to replace the X.400-based mail system in previous Exchange versions because it would mean losing some functionality. All new SMTP extensions have enhanced this protocol even further and there is no question today that SMTP is a much more feature-rich mail system than X.400.

Then we have the question of speed. There have always been discussions about what connector in previous Exchange versions is faster for site communication, the SMTP or X.400

Connector. Since Exchange was an X.400 mail system, the X.400 Connector was a natural choice for many administrators; another advantage of X.400 compared to the SMTP Connector was that the X.400 Connector could transfer 8-bit information without any conversion, whereas the SMTP Connector had to convert 8-bit information to 7-bit MIME or UUencode information before sending and the recipient server needed to do the reverse to get the data back. Of course, this took time. It also increased the information up to 33 percent. But one important thing to remember here is that the overhead involved in establishing an SMTP connection is much less than the overhead for an X.400 connection, so the truth is that they would be about equal in many cases. The new SMTP protocol in Exchange 2000 has support for sending information directly in raw 8-bit binary mode that does not need to be converted during the transport. This will result in SMTP being the absolute fastest protocol for the Exchange 2000 environment.

The SMTP Protocol

The SMTP protocol is a clear text command protocol, typical for most of the Internet-related protocols. This is excellent when you want to troubleshoot any SMTP communication problems since you can type in the commands manually and see exactly what the responses are.

All standard SMTP communications are initiated by one server, the "sender-SMTP" client, which calls the receiving server, the "receiver-SMTP" server, on port 25 (except ODMR, which uses port 366; see RFC 2645). This well-known port number is dedicated for SMTP traffic, but it is possible to use any port number as long as the server and the client agree on what port to use. You can in fact hide a receiver-SMTP server by using a nonstandard port number, but beware—if someone is using a port scanner, this "hidden" server will be discovered! You set the port number by using the properties for virtual SMTP servers; on the General tab, click the Advanced button and edit the TCP port (see Figure 4.4).

As described in Chapter 3, the SMTP protocol stack is controlled by the Internet Information Server (IIS) in Windows 2000. The IIS runs the SMTP stack as a virtual SMTP server by making it possible to have more than one SMTP stack active on the same server. This is very good when you want to run two different SMTP settings on the same server, like one encrypted SMTP session and one unencrypted session. Note that you will gain nothing in performance by creating more than one virtual SMTP server on the same server; it's only for running multiple SMTP configurations.

All settings for the virtual SMTP server are stored in the Metabase that IIS uses; they are not stored in the Active Directory. This is the reason why you must use the ESM tool to make changes to virtual SMTP servers instead of using the ISM tool that is normally used for configuring IIS and its subcomponents.

RFC 821 SMTP

The name of this RFC is "Simple Mail Transfer Protocol." It was written by Jonathan B. Postel in August 1982, and it is the foundation for how two SMTP servers exchange information.

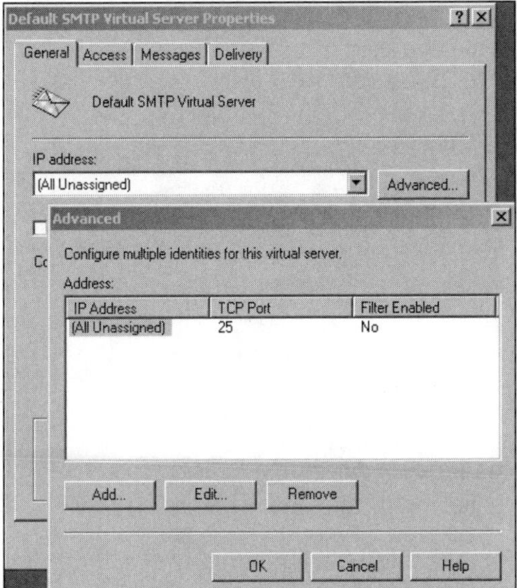

Figure 4.4
Changing the SMTP port number.

An important feature of SMTP is the capability to transfer mail across several networks without any loss of information—for example, to send mail across the Internet.

The SMTP model is simple: When a sender requests mail to be transferred, the sender-SMTP will establish a two-way transmission channel to the receiver-SMTP; this may be the final destination or an intermediate one. The sender-SMTP generates SMTP commands and the receiver-SMTP replies in response to these commands. The first command must always be HELO.

When the transmission channel is established, the sender-SMTP sends a **MAIL** command indicating it will send mail; the receiver-SMTP returns an OK if it will accept the mail. Next, the sender-SMTP sends an **RCPT** command to identify the recipient of the mail. If the receiver-SMTP accepts mail for that recipient, it replies with OK; if not, it returns a **reject** command for this particular recipient (but not the complete mail transaction). The sender-SMTP and receiver-SMTP may negotiate several recipients. When this is done, the data transfer starts with limited numbers of 7-bit ASCII characters per line (1,000 or less). The data transfer ends when a special character sequence is given. The dialog is purposely lock-step, one-at-a-time. See Figure 4.5.

If the final destination SMTP server cannot be reached, the mail may be relayed via one or more SMTP hosts. Each of these relay servers needs to know exactly what the destination is and where the mail is coming from. The argument to the **MAIL FROM** command is a reverse-path, telling whom the mail is from. The RCPT TO argument is a forward-path that specifies whom the mail is for. This forward-path is also known as the *source-route*, whereas the reverse-path is known as the *return-route* that will be used in case there is an

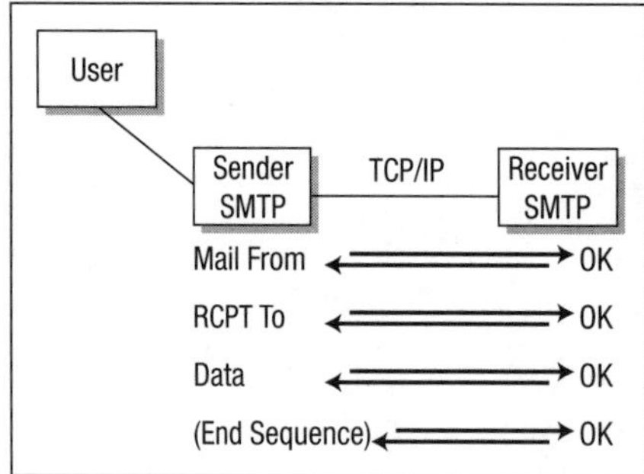

Figure 4.5
The SMTP model.

error message that needs to be returned to the sender. Mail addressed to several recipients is still sent only once if all the recipients belong to the same destination server.

The DATA transfer will contain the complete message, including the mail header items like Date, Subject, To, Cc, and From. Nothing checks to make sure that the To, Cc, or From fields match the **MAIL FROM** or the **RCPT TO SMTP** commands. And nothing checks to make sure that the mail domain from which the mail is sent matches the **MAIL FROM** command or the From item. You can easily fake a sender address without the SMTP protocol noticing.

All mail commands and replies have a rigid syntax. Replies also have a numeric code divided into sections depending on whether they were successful or not:

- *2xx*—Successful replies, like "250: Requested mail action OK"
- *3xx*—Successful replies, like "354: Start mail input"
- *4xx*—Failure replies, like "421: Service not available"
- *5xx*—Error replies, like "500: Syntax error"

Commands and replies are not case sensitive—they can be all lowercase, all uppercase, or a mixture of both. Host names are also not case sensitive. But the original RFC 821 states that sender and recipients may be case sensitive; it depends on the servers! In reality, practically all SMTP implementations are not case sensitive regarding addresses.

All commands are based on the 7-bit U.S. ASCII character set. This is also true for data that is transmitted; a binary 8-bit octet will be right justified and the leftmost bit will be cleared to zero. This means that binary information will be destroyed!

Conclusion about RFC 821

Since the RFC 821 is so important for Exchange 2000 I have summarized the most important conclusions regarding the SMTP protocol:

- There is no checking that the sender address is valid or even that it is giving the domain it was actually sent from.

- All commands and data are 7-bit U.S. ASCII character set. Binary information, like attachments, executable programs, or non-U.S. characters like Ä or ê will not survive the transfer.
- The transfer is simple and robust; it is easy to type these commands manually.

RFC 822 ARPA Internet Text Messages

This document, the RFC 822, was written by David H. Crocker and was released in August 13, 1982; it is a complement to RFC 821 and describes the message that is transferred by RFC 821 protocol. RFC 822 is the protocol that describes the format of the mail itself, what header items it should have, how the mail body should look, and the character set to be used. The name of this RFC, "Standard for the format of ARPA Internet text messages," indicates that this message format was originally for ARPA messages, and the interesting thing is that this format is still the base for all SMTP messages today, although a lot of extensions have been made since 1982.

A message is divided into two parts, according to this RFC: the header and the content. Headers are divided into a number of fields, like Sender and Subject, but the contents are very flexible—there is no fixed format for this part. There must be one empty line between the last header field and the content. One thing that is important to know is that the RFC 822 only accepts text based on 7-bit U.S. ASCII; there is no support for binary messages! This standard has no encryption or compression feature; if this is needed, it must be taken care of before the message is sent by RFC 822. There is no limit on how long a message can be or how long a text line can be, and a message can be without any content at all.

All format description in this standard regards the header (also called the *envelope*) and its fields. Some fields are required and others are optional. There are also "user-defined" fields that may be used if the sender and receiver systems understand how to use them; these types of fields always begin with "X-"; no other field can start with this letter. All header fields are not case sensitive, but the case in the contents must be preserved. Table 4.2 lists some of the many header fields described in RFC 822.

In Listing 4.1, you see the RFC 822 header for mail from **ghusman@hotmail.com** to **goran@humandata.se**. The information tells us a number of things.

Table 4.2 Some of the most common RFC 822 header fields.

Header Field	Description
Return-Path	Trace field: Describes the address and path back to the real sender of this mail.
Received	Trace field: Each server that is transferring this message should add a "Received" field. If there is more than one Received field, the first one in the mail is the latest. It can be used to trace how the mail has been transported.
From	Originator field: The identity of the person who wished this mail to be sent. This could be a person other than the actual sender of this message. This field is mandatory if the Sender field is missing or not equal to the From field.

(continued)

Table 4.2 Some of the most common RFC 822 header fields *(continued)*.

Header Field	Description
Sender	Originator field: The actual sender of this mail. This field is not needed if it is equal to the From field.
Reply-To	Originator field: This field indicates the mail address to which replies should be sent. This field, if declared, has priority over the From field when replying to a message.
To	Receiver field: The primary recipient of this mail.
Cc	Receiver field: The secondary recipient of this mail.
Bcc	Receiver field: "Blind Carbon Copy"; hidden recipients of this mail. These recipients will not be visible to any other recipients, not even other BCC recipients of this mail.
Subject	Other fields: A summary or indication of the nature of this message.
Comments	Other fields: Permits adding text comments onto the message without disturbing the contents of the message's body.
X-	Other fields: User-defined fields. Individual users of network mail are free to define and use additional header fields. Such fields must have names that are not already used in the current specification.

Listing 4.1 Example of RFC 822 headers from Hotmail.

```
01: Received: from hotmail.com ([209.185.241.37]) by oden.humandata.se with
     Microsoft SMTPSVC(5.0.2195.1600); Thu, 15 Feb 2001 13:53:27 +0100
02: Received: from mail pickup service by hotmail.com with Microsoft SMTPSVC; Thu,
     15 Feb 2001 04:53:29 -0800
03: Received: from 194.198.189.150 by lw3fd.law3.hotmail.msn.com with HTTP;
     Thu, 15 Feb 2001 12:53:29 GMT
04: X-Originating-IP: [194.198.189.150]
05: From: "Göran Husman" <ghusman@hotmail.com>
06: To: goran@humandata.se
07: Subject: Test from Hotmail
08: Date: Thu, 15 Feb 2001 13:53:29 +0100
09: Mime-Version: 1.0
10: Content-Type: text/plain; format=flowed
11: Message-ID: <F37xbDBpap6dXmi2psK0000ccc2@hotmail.com>
12: X-OriginalArrivalTime: 15 Feb 2001 12:53:29.0801 (UTC)
     FILETIME=[4B9A2390:01C0974E]
13: Return-Path: ghusman@hotmail.com
```

Look at the three Received fields on lines 1, 2, and 3. Begin with the last Received field, or line 3. It says that the Web client with IP address 194.198.189.150 sent this mail to the server **lw3fd.law3.hotmail.msn.com**. We can tell that it was a Web client because the protocol was HTTP. The time was 12:53:29 GMT.

The second Received field, line 2, says that a mail pickup service on **hotmail.com** received this mail at 04:53:29 (– 8 hours = 12.53.29 GMT); i.e., the mail was instantly received by **www.hotmail.com**.

The Received field on line 1, the last added Received field, tells us that a server on **hotmail.com** with the IP address 209.185.241.37 did send the mail to oden.humandata.se at 13:53:27 (+ 1 hour = 12.53.27 GMT); that is, in fact, two seconds before it was sent! This is because the local time of each mail server is used; the clock for oden.humandata.com seems to be a few seconds behind the Hotmail server.

Line 4 is a user-defined field; it is revealed to us because the name begins with "X-". This means that the receiving mail server can interpret it or skip it; it will not matter. Obviously, this X-Originating-IP tries to tell us what IP number the originating Web client had. Note that this is a user-defined field; other mail servers may not tell you this information.

Line 5 is the From field, telling us who wanted to send this mail. If no Sender field exists elsewhere in the header, this means that it is also the name of the actual sender. Remember, according to RFC 822, you can distinguish between the person who wants to send this mail and the actual sender.

Lines 6, 7, and 8 are self-explanatory—they're the recipient name, the subject, and the time the mail was sent.

Line 9 is an extended field, telling us that the sending server used MIME version 1 to format this mail. If the receiving mail server oden.humandata.se did not understand MIME, we would get an error message when opening this mail. You can find more information about MIME later in this chapter.

Line 10 is a MIME field; it says that this message is a plain text message—there are no attachments.

Line 11 is a message-id, which the Hotmail server has stamped on this message. It could possibly be used to track the message within Hotmail to the originating sender. If you got a message with a virus from a fake sender address, for instance, you could ask the mail administrator on the sending server to track this message internally.

Line 12 is another user-defined field, X-OriginalArrivalTime, that obviously tells us what time the message was received.

Line 13 is the Return-Path field, telling us the complete address and route (if any) to the real originator of this message; this field is added by the sending mail system, not by the sender's client.

All this information is usually not interesting to us, but if we get unsolicited mail (spam) or any other mail that we want to track down, we could do so using this information. Note that many of these headers are defined at the client, making it very easy to fake the sender address, but by using the Return-Path and the Received fields, you can see if it is mail that tries to hide its real origin. The IP address listed in some fields is also rather hard to fake, although it can be done (IP-Spoofing); with this IP address, you can contact the administrator of the originating server and ask him or her to track the malicious sender.

SMTP Service Extensions

The RFC 1869 was released in November 1995 (replacing RFC 1651), and was an important document for the SMTP world. It described enhancements to the RFC 821 SMTP command set, not just a fixed number of commands, but also a way of expanding the command set when needed. Servers that comply with the RFC 1869 are known as *ESMTP-servers*. Since both the sender-SMTP and the receiver-SMTP server need to agree on the extended command set before actually using them, this meant that a new **SMTP** command was needed; it got the name **EHLO** and is an alternative to the old **HELO**. When the sender-SMTP server contacts the receiver-SMTP server, it will send **EHLO** instead of **HELO** to see if the other server understands RFC 1869 service extensions; or in other words, if it is an ESMTP server too. If the reply is "250: OK," then it is an ESMTP server; if the reply is "550: Error," it is not.

The number of **EHLO** commands is growing constantly, so the sender and receiver servers must agree on what commands to use. This is solved like this: When the receiver SMTP server accepts the **EHLO** command, it sends a list of all the **EHLO** commands it supports. It is important to understand that this list may be different between ESMTP servers; newer servers will probably have support for more **EHLO** commands than older servers. Below are more detailed descriptions of the RFCs that are used in Exchange 2000; these extensions are the major reason why SMTP communication between Exchange 2000 servers is so much faster than in previous Exchange releases.

RFC 1652

The RFC 1652 is an **EHLO** command. It describes how to send 8-bit MIME information over SMTP. The command is called **8BITMIME**, and if both SMTP servers agree on using this instead of the ordinary 7-bit ASCII format, the sender server will use an enhanced **MAIL** command; the **8BITMIME** is just a flag, an indication, to send information in 8-bit MIME format. Due to restrictions in the maximum line length (it varies, and can be as low as 1,000 bytes), this **8BITMIME** feature will make it impossible to send any type of 8-bit binary information; by using MIME-formatted content, the lines will never exceed 1,000 bytes—this is why it works.

RFC 1870

The RFC 1870 "Message size declaration" is an **EHLO** command that makes it possible for the sender-SMTP to check if the receiver-SMTP will accept a certain message size, before the actual transfer starts. Without this size control, a sender-SMTP will start sending the message and abort the transmission only after exceeding the limit on the receiver-SMTP. That is a waste of time and network bandwidth.

RFC 1891

The RFC 1891 "Delivery status notification" enhances the simple notification in case of errors in the standard SMTP format. When this RFC is implemented, a client can request a delivery receipt from the receiver-SMTP. Besides this, more elaborate notifications are supported, for both successful and failed transmissions. Exchange 2000 also has support for RFC 1892 and 1894 that complements the RFC 1891. These enhancements replace the previous rather unclear notifications generated by the Internet Mail Service connector in Exchange 5.5. Since MAPI clients have another way of handling notifications, these Internet DSN features are interpreted to give the same type of delivery notifications MAPI has received before, while at the same time give Internet clients the notifications as specified in these mentioned RFCs. All NDRs, non-delivery reports, sent to Outlook 2000 clients are coming from the System Attendant in Exchange 2000, making it possible for the user to resend the message again.

RFC 1952

The RFC 1985 "Extended Turn" (also known as ETRN) is a way of emptying a message queue on another server. In the case that an organization has a dial-up connection instead of a leased line, it cannot have one mail server only, since the line will be connected only occasionally. This is usually solved by pointing the incoming mail to a secondary mail server at the ISP or another organization with a leased line. This secondary mail server will receive all incoming mail when the primary mail server is unreachable. Later, the primary mail server dials into the ISP where the secondary mail servers keep all mail in a queue. By sending the "ETRN <domain>" command (see Listing 4.2) to the secondary server, that will immediately start to empty the queue by forwarding them to the primary mail server, according to the MX record in the DNS; see Figure 4.6 and the steps following Listing 4.2.

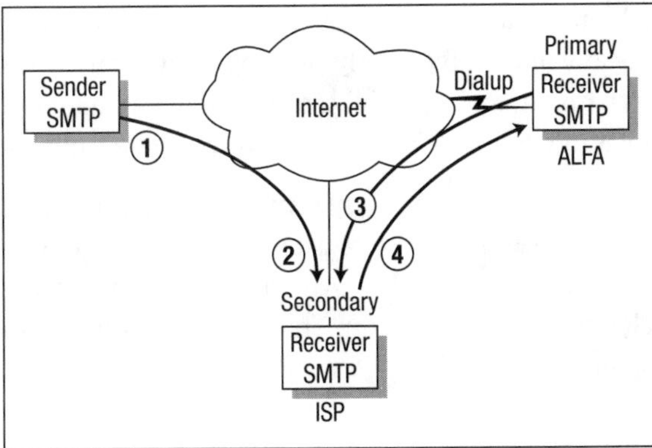

Figure 4.6
An ETRN example.

Listing 4.2 Sending the ETRN command to start de-queuing the mysoft.com domain.

```
S: <wait for connection on TCP port 25>
C: <open connection to server>
S: 220 sigurd.innosoft.com—Server SMTP (PMDF V4.2-6 #1992)
C: EHLO ymir.claremont.edu
S: 250-sigurd.innosoft.com
S: 250-EXPN
S: 250-HELP
S: 250 ETRN
C: ETRN mysoft.com
S: 253 OK, 14 pending messages for node mysoft.com started
C: QUIT
S: 250 Goodbye
```

1. The sender-SMTP server tries to contact the primary receiver-SMTP server. Since this server is not connected to the network at this moment, the sender will check the DNS for a secondary receiver-SMTP; it will find one at the ISP.
2. The sender-SMTP will send the mail to the ISP; since this is not the final destination, the mail will be kept in a queue.
3. Later, the primary receiver-SMTP will connect to the Internet; it will then send an ETRN command to the ISP server.
4. The ISP server is now requested to empty the queue; it will use the same DNS settings as the sender-SMTP, but this time the primary receiver-SMTP will be online and the messages can be delivered.

There are some things you must understand about ETRN; this command is a replacement for the old TURN command, which most administrators consider a security risk since anyone could use the TURN to empty any queue. By simply sending "TURN Microsoft.com" to a server queuing mail for the **Microsoft.com** domain, they would get all mail in return without any checking or authentication. So use ETRN, never TURN, if you can choose.

Another important thing about ETRN is that the primary server (that dials up to the ISP) must have a fixed IP address and this address must be registered in the DNS server. There are a number of installations where the server only has dynamically assigned IP addresses; then it is not possible to use ETRN for this installation. The ATRN is a solution for this; see "RFC 2645," later in this chapter.

RFC 2197

The RFC 2197 "Command pipelining" is an EHLO command that makes it possible to send several SMTP commands to the receiver-SMTP in the same TCP package without waiting for a response to each individual command. For example, it is possible to send "RSET, MAIL FROM, SEND FROM, RCPT TO" in any order in such a pipelined command group. However, the EHLO, DATA, VRFY, EXPN, TURN, QUIT, and NOOP must be the last command (if used at all) in such a group. This makes the communication much faster than ordinary

RFC 821 sessions and is used extensively in Exchange 2000. See Listing 4.3 for an example of a pipelining session where the number of turnarounds is reduced from 9 without pipelining to 4.

Listing 4.3 Example of a pipelining session.

```
S: <wait for open connection>
C: <open connection to server>
S: 220 innosoft.com SMTP service ready
C: EHLO dbc.mtview.ca.us
S: 250-innosoft.com
S: 250 PIPELINING
C: MAIL FROM:<mrose@dbc.mtview.ca.us>
C: RCPT TO:<ned@innosoft.com>
C: RCPT TO:<dan@innosoft.com>
C: RCPT TO:<kvc@innosoft.com>
C: DATA
S: 250 sender <mrose@dbc.mtview.ca.us> OK
S: 250 recipient <ned@innosoft.com> OK
S: 250 recipient <dan@innosoft.com> OK
S: 250 recipient <kvc@innosoft.com> OK
S: 354 enter mail, end with line containing only "."
 ...
C: .
C: QUIT
S: 250 message sent
S: 221 goodbye
```

RFC 2487

The RFC 2487 makes it possible to encrypt the SMTP session with Transport Layer Security (TLS), a standard based on Secure Socket Layer (SSL) 3, which is used to encrypt HTTP traffic. Normal RFC 821 SMTP communication is in clear text, without any encryption at all. However, if two SMTP servers need to transfer sensitive messages over routers and networks they don't control or rely on, the session could be encrypted with TLS for protection.

The TLS will also help to authenticate the servers to each other, avoiding the risk of sending messages to someone you don't trust or accepting messages from rogue SMTP servers. See Listing 4.4 for an example of how a TLS session can be established. Note that before you can configure the SMTP server for TLS encryption, you need an X.509 Server Certificate. You can get one from the MS Certificate Server that comes with Windows 2000 Server. The command name is STARTTLS, but it will not be listed among the supported EHLO commands unless you have installed an X.509 certificate for this SMTP server.

Listing 4.4 Example of a TLS session.

```
S: <waits for connection on TCP port 25>
C: <opens connection>
S: 220 mail.imc.org SMTP service ready
C: EHLO mail.ietf.org
```

```
S: 250-mail.imc.org offers a warm hug of welcome
S: 250 STARTTLS
C: STARTTLS
S: 220 Go ahead
C: <starts TLS negotiation>
C & S: <negotiate a TLS session>
C & S: <check result of negotiation>
C: <continues by sending an SMTP command>
```

Although increasing the security dramatically, a public SMTP server must never require TLS in order to receive mail locally—this would make this server unavailable for practically all public SMTP servers on the Internet today!

RFC 2554

The RFC 2554, or the "SMTP Authentication" command AUTH, adds the possibility to request the sender-SMTP to authenticate itself before sending any information. The AUTH command is listed with all the possible authentication methods it will support; Exchange 2000 supports GSSAPI, NTLM, and LOGIN. The sender-SMTP will then select the authentication method it prefers; after that, the authentication process begins. The recipient-SMTP sends a "challenge" that the sender-SMTP processes with its password and sends back. If correct, the recipient-SMTP accepts the sender as authenticated.

This feature is used when IMAP4 and POP3 clients want to send SMTP messages through the Exchange SMTP stack. By default, Exchange 2000 will not let anonymous clients reroute SMTP messages; they must be authenticated first. This can be changed, although it is not recommended since this would open your SMTP server for relaying of all users on the Internet. This type of "open-relay" SMTP servers are exactly what spam mailers are looking for. Then it will be just a matter of time before they will send mail routed through your server and the recipients will believe that it came from someone in your organization—beware!

RFC 2645

This RFC is also known as On-Demand Mail Relay, or ODMR, and is a solution to the limitations of the ETRN command (RFC 1985) where the mail server needs a fixed IP address. The ODMR works with dynamically assigned IP addresses, which is a common scenario in low-cost Internet connections. In such a scenario, the server may get a new IP address every time it connects to the ISP, so the mail servers outside the organization will never know what IP address the server has.

In order to make this work, the ISP (or the organization that will queue the mail for you) must have an ODMR process that listens on TCP port 366; this process is very similar to the SMTP process, but is activated by port 366 instead of port 25, which SMTP uses. The client (the server who wants to get the mail) contacts the ODMR process with EHLO commands, authenticates with AUTH, and sends an ATRN to request its mail. The roles of client and server now change; the ISP will now use EHLO commands to send the mail back (see Listing 4.5).

Listing 4.5 Example of ATRN communication on port 366 (P=Provider, C=Client).

```
P:  220 EXAMPLE.NET on-demand mail relay server ready
C:  EHLO example.org
P:  250-EXAMPLE.NET
P:  250-AUTH CRAM-MD5 EXTERNAL
P:  250 ATRN
C:  AUTH CRAM-MD5
P:  334 MTg5Ni42OTcxNzA5NTJASVNQLkNPTQo=
C:  Zm9vYmFyLm5ldCBiOTEzYTYwMmM3ZWRhN2E0OTViNGU2ZTczMzRkMzg5MAo=
P:  235 now authenticated as example.org
C:  ATRN example.org,example.com
P:  250 OK now reversing the connection
C:  220 example.org ready to receive email
P:  EHLO EXAMPLE.NET
C:  250-example.org
C:  250 SIZE
P:  MAIL FROM: <Lester.Tester@dot.foo.bar>
C:  250 OK
P:  RCPT TO: <l.eva.msg@example.com>
C:  250 OK, recipient accepted
...
P:  QUIT
C:  221 example.org closing connection
```

RFC 3030

The RFC 3030, "Transmission of large and binary MIME messages," also known as "Chunking" or BDAT, makes it possible to send large binary MIME messages in a very effective way. Normally when you send data with the DATA command, the receiver-SMTP will look for the special character sequence that marks the end of the data transmission, the "CRLF." This has no impact on small or medium-sized messages, but for messages over 1MB, this will slow down the transfer process. Another problem is the 7-bit ASCII format that SMTP enforces on transferred data; this means that binary files must be converted to 7-bit ASCII before being transmitted, transferred, and then reconverted again.

The RFC 1652 was the first suggestion for handling 8-bit information, but the RFC 3030 is much more effective at handling really large files. There is an increasing demand for this, since multimedia information and large office documents like MS Word and MS Power Point files get more and more popular on the Internet. The name of this new EHLO keyword is CHUNKING and the command name is BDAT, used instead of the ordinary DATA command when sending RFC 3030 data. The way Chunking increases the transfer speed is by telling the receiver-SMTP server how much data to expect in the message. The data is then sent in one stream, without the receiver-SMTP trying to interpret the data or looking for the end-sequence. The data is also sent in 8-bit mode; no 7-bit conversion is done. Two Exchange 2000 servers are always sending data by Chunking, making the transfer much faster than previous Exchange versions. Listing 4.6 provides an example where both BDAT (Chunking) and the Pipelining commands are used together to send two chunks of data, the first with 100,000 bytes and the second with 324 bytes. This is exactly how Exchange 2000 servers exchange data.

Listing 4.6 Example of Chunking and Pipelining.

```
R: <wait for connection on TCP port
S: <open connection to server>
R: 220 cnri.reston.va.us SMTP service ready
S: EHLO ymir.claremont.edu
R: 250-cnri.reston.va.us says hello
R: 250-PIPELINING
R: 250-BINARYMIME
R: 250 CHUNKING
S: MAIL FROM:<ned@ymir.Claremont.edu> BODY=BINARYMIME
S: RCPT TO:<gvaudre@cnri.reston.va.us>
S: RCPT TO:<jstewart@cnri.reston.va.us>
R: 250 <ned@ymir.Claremont.edu>... Sender and BINARYMIME ok
R: 250 <gvaudre@cnri.reston.va.us>... Recipient ok
R: 250 <jstewart@cnri.reston.va.us>... Recipient ok
S: BDAT 100000
S: (First 10000 octets of canonical MIME message data)
S: BDAT 324
S: (Remaining 324 octets of canonical MIME message data)
S: BDAT 0 LAST
R: 250 100000 octets received
R: 250 324 octets received
R: 250 Message OK, 100324 octets received
S: QUIT
R: 221 Goodbye
```

Exchange 2000 supports all of the RFCs mentioned above, and more. The easiest way to check if a server is ESMTP compliant, and if so, what EHLO commands are supported, is to connect with the Telnet program on port 25, type in "EHLO", and see what response you get; see Listing 4.7.

Listing 4.7 The ESMTP commands for Exchange 2000.

```
C:\TELNET Oden.Humandata.se 25
220 oden.humandata.se Microsoft ESMTP MAIL Service, Version: 5.0.2195.1600 ready
at  Thu, 15 Feb 2001 19:44:52 +0100
EHLO Loke.humandata.se
250-oden.humandata.se Hello loke.humandata.se
250-TURN
250-ATRN
250-SIZE
250-ETRN
250-PIPELINING
250-DSN
```

```
250-ENHANCEDSTATUSCODES
250-8bitmime
250-BINARYMIME
250-CHUNKING
250-VRFY
250-X-EXPS GSSAPI NTLM LOGIN
250-X-EXPS=LOGIN
250-AUTH GSSAPI NTLM LOGIN
250-AUTH=LOGIN
250-XEXCH50
250-X-LINK2STATE
250 OK
```

The MIME Formatting

All these SMTP extensions are great enhancements to communication between an SMTP client and an SMTP server. But still some things need to be done with the RFC 822, which states that the format of the message should be flat 7-bit ASCII text. True, two RFCs deal with sending 8-bit information, RFC 1652 and 3030, but if you read them carefully you see they assume that the message is MIME formatted. This section will tell you how MIME works in general; later, you will learn about content conversion in detail.

The RFC 2045 is the first in a series of five RFCs where the MIME format is described; it stands for "Multipurpose Internet Mail Extensions" and is a very important format, since without it we could not send binary information seamlessly around the world and to different SMTP implementations. RFC 1431 was the first document that described the MIME format; it was released in June 1992. Since then, there have been several changes and enhancements and currently the RFCs 2045 through 2049 are what to read if you want to know everything about MIME.

The initial RFC 822 assumes only text messages; there is no description of handling nontext messages, like binary files, audio, and images. Even in the case of text, the RFC 822 is inadequate since it can accept only U.S. characters, not international character sets like Swedish, French, or Asian. All lines must be 1,000 characters or less. For gateway connections between SMTP and X.400 mail systems, it was even worse. X.400 states that binary attachments sent to an RFC 822 server must be converted to IA5TEXT or removed. Something obviously had to be done.

The Content-Type Field

The solution was MIME. Due to the addition of several new header fields, such as Content-Type, it is now possible to describe the content and divide the message into any number of parts. Each part is described so the receiving mail system knows how to treat it. For example, an image can be described with the content type "image/tif," which makes it possible for the receiving system, including the mail client, to know that this is an image. This information will be used by the receiving client to decide whether or not to show the user the raw data, or to use a "helper" program like a TIFF-viewer to display the image. There are five top-level media content types; each of these has one or more subtypes:

- *Text*—The subtype "plain" is textual information in plain 7-bit ASCII format, with no formatting commands or directives of any sort. Such information should be displayed "as-is." Other subtypes are HTML and XML. These content types often specify what character set is used, like ISO-8859-1. Example: "Content-type=text/plain; charset= iso-8859-1".
- *Image*—Image data; assumes the recipient has some sort of graphical device to display the image, like a graphical program or a graphical printer. Examples of subtypes are GIF and JPEG.
- *Audio*—Audio data; assumes the recipient has some hardware to play the audio. Examples of subtypes are WAV, MIDI, and BASIC.
- *Video*—Video data; assumes the recipient has a device that can display moving images. Examples of subtypes are MPEG and AVI.
- *Application*—Some other kind of data, typically a binary file that should be displayed with a certain application program. Examples of subtypes are MSWORD and MSPOWERPOINT. A special subtype is OCTET-STREAM, which is used to indicate a body of arbitrary binary data.

All subtypes also have a certain file type extension associated with them; for example, the content type "application/msword" has the file type DOC associated with it. Each mail system can define what content type it supports, including the file type extensions. If you receive a MIME message with the file attachment "MyFile.NEW" with the content type=text/plain, the following will happen:

- Exchange Server 4 and 5 will change the name to MyFile.TXT since the content type is text/plain and its file type is TXT.
- Exchange 5.5 and Exchange 2000 will preserve the name of MyFile.NEW.

The behavior of Exchange 5.5 and 2000 is important, since we otherwise would have problems with some of the new Internet file formats like vCard; such an attachment has the file type .VCF but the content type is text/plain; clearly we don't want this file type to be changed because then our mail program would not understand that this is a vCard file. This behavior can be changed by adding a new Registry key, "RemapExtensions," as described in Microsoft's TechNet article Q182083. I strongly recommend that you don't use this remapping! The MIME content type is applied to MAPI clients only when sending to, or receiving from, Internet clients.

To see what MIME content types Exchange 2000 supports, look at the general properties for the Internet Message Formats object, under the Global Settings; see Figure 4.7. To change the file type associated with a content type, double-click the content type and change the Associated Extension field.

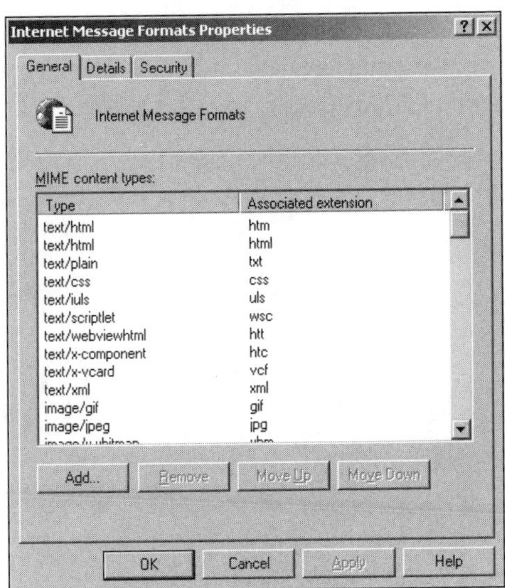

Figure 4.7
The MIME settings for Exchange 2000.

***Note:** In previous versions of Exchange, MIME content types were used only with email clients; in Exchange 2000, MIME content types are used with both email and the Exchange store (for features such as the Web store and Web-DAV).*

The Content-Transfer-Encoding Field

Another new MIME header field is Content-Transfer-Encoding; this is used to describe how the data is encoded. These encoding types exist:

- *7BIT*—All characters are in 7-bit U.S. ASCII format; this is the default value. If there is no Content-Transfer-Encoding field, it is assumed that the mail is in 7-bit format.
- *8BIT*—All data is in raw 8-bit format. No encoding is done—this is just information sent to the receiving mail server. See the RFC 1652 for transferring 8-bit data over SMTP.
- *BINARY*—Same as 8BIT.
- *Quoted Printable*—All non-U.S. characters are translated to index in a translation table, prefixed by a "=" character.
- *BASE64*—All characters, regardless whether they are 7- or 8-bit from the start, are translated using the Base-64 encoding scheme.
- *X-<name>*—User-defined translation methods, like "X-my-own-conversion." This is not recommended since it will hinder the interoperability between systems.

Since the MIME standard makes it possible to divide the content in different parts, it is possible to use individual content transfer encoding for each part; the particular encoding type must then be listed in the header for each part.

Multipart Messages

If a MIME message has several parts, a boundary must be declared in the message header and added to the Content-Type field; this boundary will signal the start and the end of each part. A boundary may look like this:

Content-Type: multipart/mixed; boundary=ThisIsMyBoundary

The boundary must be all 7-bit U.S. ASCII characters and must be unique in this message; the boundary must never exist in any part of the message itself. A simple example of a message with two text parts is shown in Listing 4.8.

Listing 4.8 A MIME message with two text parts.

```
From: <goran@humandata.se>
To: <ghusman@hotmail.com>
Date: Sat, 17 Feb 2001 19:35:48 +1
Subject: Demo MIME multipart message
MIME-Version: 1.0
Content-Type: multipart/mixed; boundary="ThisIsMyBoundary"

This is the preamble; this text will only be visible to clients that don't
understand MIME messages
     ThisIsMyBoundary
This is part one. Since there is no defined content type this part
is assumed to be in plain 7-bit US ASCII text
     ThisIsMyBoundary
Content-type: text/plain; charset=us-ascii
This is part two. As the line above shows, this part
is declared as US-ASCII text

     —ThisIsMyBoundary—
This is the epilogue. It will also be ignored.
```

As Listing 4.8 shows, each part starting after the boundary "ThisIsMyBoundary," is prefixed by two hyphens, "—". At the very end of the message a boundary is listed again, but this time with two hyphens both as a prefix and a postfix, "—ThisIsMyBoundary—". All text before the first boundary and after the last boundary is not displayed for a MIME-compliant email client.

A part can also be an attached binary file or any type of information. Then this part must be declared with a Content-Type header field and a Content-Transfer-Encoding field telling the receiving system how to restore this part back to the original format. The next section will tell you more about conversion methods.

Content Conversion

Since the original RFC 821 does not allow 8-bit binary information, we need to convert all 8-bit information to a corresponding 7-bit format. There has been a demand for sending binary information over SMTP since its beginning, and the most popular method before

MIME was the UUencode—Unix-to-Unix-encode. When MIME was released, UUencode was replaced by the Base-64 and Quoted-Printable methods. These methods are described in the following sections.

UUencode

This method has never been standardized by any RFC; therefore, you can find several different versions of UUencode, some not compatible with others. This is one of the reasons that this method was replaced by the converting methods that MIME offered.

The translation algorithm is known as *four-for-three encoding*. The name comes from the way that this algorithm converts three 8-bit bytes to four 7-bit bytes; this means that all information converted by this method would increase 33 percent. This is how UUencode works. Let's say we have a binary sequence of three bytes looking like this:

```
10001000 10101010 11001100
```

That sequence would never pass an SMTP RFC 821 transfer since all bytes begin with 1; as you may remember, RFC 821 replaces all rightmost 1 bits to 0; by doing so, it destroys our binary sequence. The UUencode method is to break the 24 bytes above into groups of 6 bits:

```
100010 001010 101011 001100
```

Next, we add 100000 (decimal: 32) to these four 6-bit groups and write them as an 8-bit byte with their corresponding decimal value in parentheses, giving us:

```
01000010 (66) 00101010 (42) 01001011 (75) 0101100 (44)
```

Notice that all these new numbers begin with 0, so there is no problem sending this 4-byte sequence by SMTP. The receiving SMTP server will do the reverse, translating it back to the original 3-byte sequence—this is known as *UUdecode*.

Sometimes a user complains that his or her mail contains garbage. This could be a result of a failed UUdecode. If we use these four 8-bit numbers as indexes in the standard 7-bit U.S. ASCII character set, we would get these characters:

```
B*K'
```

If the receiving mail server did not know how to handle the UUencode part, it would just pass it on to the mail client, where it would look something like Listing 4.9.

Listing 4.9 A UUencoded message.

```
From: "Göran Husman" <ghusman@hotmail.com>
To: goran@humandata.se
Subject: Demo of UUencode
Date: Fri, 16 Feb 2001 12:27:30 +0100
```

```
Return-Path: ghusman@hotmail.com

This is the message body,
Below is the Uuencoded file that my mail server
failed to convert for me.

Begin 644 test
#B*K'
'
end
```

The UUencode part is between the "begin" and "end" lines; "644" is a three-digit number specifying the file permission, using a common Unix notation (read/write/execute); "test" is the name of this attachment, and the "#" sign in the first position is the number of converted bytes on this line, 3, plus a constant 32 = 35, corresponding to the ASCII character "#". In fact, most of the lines would probably start with "M" since this indicates a 45-character line (equal to 60 converted characters), the maximum number of characters in a UUencoded line. By tradition, a line containing zero bytes is added to the end and marked with a single apostrophe (').

The UUencode algorithm has done a good job for many years, but some problems can occur with it; some SMTP servers have problems with some of the converted characters when they occur in special places, and not all implementations of UUencode/UUdecode are equal, sometimes making it impossible to restore the original information.

Quoted Printable

MIME was the solution to the shortcomings of UUencode. QP, or Quoted Printable, is one of the converting algorithms in the MIME standard. This is a method wherein the amount of 8-bit information is low, typically used in text parts. To understand how it works, let's first see how a standard RFC 822 message may look; it cannot contain any 8-bit characters or binary attachments (see Listing 4.10).

Listing 4.10 A standard RFC 822 message.

```
From: "Göran Husman" <ghusman@hotmail.com>
To: goran@humandata.se
Subject: A standard RFC 822 mail
Date: Fri, 16 Feb 2001 12:27:30 +0100
Return-Path: ghusman@hotmail.com

This is the message body,
Limited to 7-bit ASCII text
```

The same message using MIME format would look like this; see Listing 4.11.

Listing 4.11 A MIME-formatted message.

```
From: "Göran Husman" <ghusman@hotmail.com>
To: goran@humandata.se
Subject: A standard RFC 822 mail
Date: Fri, 16 Feb 2001 12:27:30 +0100
Mime-Version: 1.0
Content-Type: text/plain; format=flowed
Return-Path: ghusman@hotmail.com

This is the message body,
Limited to 7-bit ASCII text
```

The only difference is two new header fields: Mime-Version and Content-Type. Although there have been updates to the MIME protocol, the version used today is still 1. This field tells the receiving mail server that it's a MIME version 1 formatted message. The Content-Type is set to "text/plain; format=flowed". That tells the receiving server that the content is plain text, i.e., 7-bit ASCII.

If we send some non-U.S. ASCII characters in the MIME message, both in its header and content, it will be more interesting; see Listing 4.12.

Listing 4.12 MIME message with non-U.S. ASCII characters.

```
From: "Noren, Eva (SE - Stockholm)" <eva.noren@deloitte.se>
To: =?iso-8859-1?Q?G=F6ran_Husman_=28E-mail=29?= <goran@humandata.s>
Subject: =?iso-8859-1?Q?Utbildning_Deloitte_-_v=E5rt_tfnsamtal_onsdag?=
Date: Wed, 14 Feb 2001 14:20:56 +0100
MIME-Version: 1.0
Content-Type: text/plain; charset="iso-8859-1"
Content-Transfer-Encoding: quoted-printable
Return-Path: eva.noren@deloitte.se

This is the message body,
With non-US ASCII characters
/G=F6ran
```

We can see "=?iso-8859-1?Q?" written in several header fields; there are also strange character sequences like "=F6" and "=E5," and all space characters seem to be replaced by "_", but there are no non-U.S. ASCII characters anywhere. Why is that? Simply because we are still limited to the 7-bit U.S. ASCII character set that our SMTP transfer allows us to send (unless we are using 8-bit encoding or chunking). By using the MIME format, all non-U.S. characters will be converted; the most common method is "Quoted Printable," or QP. This method will use a special table with 256 characters, similar to an 8-bit ASCII table, and replace all non-U.S. characters with the "=" character plus the corresponding index number (two hexadecimal digits). The table mostly used in Western Europe is "ISO-8859-1," also known as "Latin-1." Complicated? Not really—let's take a look at an example.

Table 4.3 Some of the 256 characters in translation table ISO-8859-1.

Index	Char
28	(
29	)
C4	Ä
C5	Å
D6	Ö
E4	ä
E5	å
F6	ö

The last line in our text body looks like this: "/G=F6ran." Our goal is to convert this to the original text. We have a small section from the ISO-8859-1 character list in Table 4.3; note that the index is in a two-digit hexadecimal form.

We can see from the header fields "Content-Transfer-Encoding=quoted printable" and "Content type=text/plain; Char set=iso-8859-1" that this mail is using QP as the converting method with table ISO-8859-1. An index is prefixed by a "=" sign, so the "=F6" really means the character "ö", according to Table 4.3; thus the original text must be "/Göran."

What about the special character sequence "=?iso-8859-1?Q?" in the header fields To and Subject? It is the same as in the previous example; it is QP-converted characters, using ISO-8859-1. The start of the converted sequence is "=?" and the end is marked with "?=". The "iso-8859-1" tells us what translation table is used; the "?Q?" tells us that the translation method is Quoted-Printable. All non-U.S. characters in this sequence are replaced by an index and all space characters are replaced by "_". Let's try this on the To field; it looks like this:

To: =?iso-8859-1?Q?G=F6ran_Husman_=28E-mail=29?= <goran@humandata.se>

The first part, "=?iso-8859-1?Q?", is just telling us that this line is QP converted with table ISO-8859-1, so we remove this. The "=F6" is "ö", the "_" is a space character, the "=28" is a "(", and the "=29" is a ")" so the complete original text is:

Göran Husman (E-mail) **<goran@humandata.se>**

The subject line is restored by the same method; I suggest that you try this by yourself. The result should be:

Subject: Utbildning Deloitte – vårt tfnsamtal onsdag

The QP method is excellent when there are only a few non-English characters. And as shown in this last example, it can also be used for both header fields and content body. However, the QP method is not good when converting lots of 8-bit binary information, like an attached file or an image. Then another method called Base-64 will be used; see the follow-ing section.

Base-64

The Quoted Printable algorithm is perfect for converting a few 8-bit bytes, but it will replace each 8-bit byte with three 7-bit bytes; this is a 300 percent increase in size. Clearly this can't be used for binary information like an MS Word file or an image. That is where Base-64 enters. It is similar to UUencode in that it converts all bytes, regardless of whether they are 7-bit or 8-bit, with a "four-for-three" algorithm that converts three consecutive 8-bit bytes to four 6-bit groups; each 6-bit group is then converted using a character table. But unlike the UUencode, Base-64 does not use the U.S. ASCII table for conversion; it has a special table with 64 printable 7-bit characters (see Table 4.4). That is the explanation for the name of this algorithm, Base-64.

Table 4.4 The complete Base-64 character table.

Index	Char	Index	Char	Index	Char	Index	Char
0	A	17	R	34	i	51	z
1	B	18	S	35	j	52	0
2	C	19	T	36	k	53	1
3	D	20	U	37	l	54	2
4	E	21	V	38	m	55	3
5	F	22	W	39	n	56	4
6	G	23	X	40	o	57	5
7	H	24	Y	41	p	58	6
8	I	25	Z	42	q	59	7
9	J	26	a	43	r	60	8
10	K	27	b	44	s	61	9
11	L	28	c	45	t	62	+
12	M	29	d	46	u	63	/
13	N	30	e	47	v	-	-
14	O	31	f	48	w	(pad)	-
15	P	32	g	49	x	-	-
16	Q	33	h	50	y	-	-

There is one extra character in this table, the pad that is used when the number of characters is not divisible by three; then the byte sequence to be converted is padded with "=" characters. Let's try the same byte sequence as for UUencode as an example:

```
10001000 10101010 11001100
```

Again, that sequence would never pass an SMTP RFC 821 transfer since all bytes begin with 1, and therefore are not 7-bit transparent. The Base-64 method is to break the 24 bytes above into groups of 6 bits (decimal value in parentheses):

```
100010 (34) 001010 (10) 101011 (43) 001100 (12)
```

Unlike the UUencode, we will now directly use these numbers as indexes in the Base-64 table, thus making this a faster conversion method. The result will be:

```
iKrM
```

Since these are all 7-bit U.S. ASCII characters, they will be transferred by SMTP without any problems. The maximum number of characters per line is 72. As you can see, it's similar to the UUencode algorithm, but by using this special table you can avoid those punctuation characters that are lost or altered by some mail gateways.

SMTP in Exchange 2000

As described in Chapter 3, all communication between Exchange 2000 servers is SMTP based. Information between servers within one routing group is always in binary mode, based on the "Chunking" technique, also known as binary data transfer (BDAT), making the transfer very fast compared to the standard **DATA** command that expects the information to be in 7-bit format. From the information in this chapter, you now understand that the only port number used for data transfer is TCP port 25. It is therefore easier to install systems even when there is a firewall or filtering router between the servers. Compare this to the previous Exchange site traffic, based on RPCs that use several port numbers.

Besides the **BDAT** chunking command, some of the SMTP extensions really do make a difference for Exchange 2000 performance. Pipelining is one very important extension; without this, every SMTP command would need to wait for a response before sending the **next** command. The SMTP history is designed to handle the often slow and sometimes unreliable network connections of 20 years ago. Today, our networks are all much more reliable and faster; the number of dial-up connections decreases every year, and more and more organizations invest in a leased line both for their internal communication to other sites and to the Internet. Another important **SMTP** command is SIZE. Before this command was implemented, a sending SMTP server started to send a large message without any checking; when the limit was reached in the receiving server, it would simply abort the transmission, saying it exceeded the internal size limit. All these SMTP extended commands have made the transport even better than the previous X.400 RCP-based routing.

The way information is transferred between routing groups depends on what type of routing group connector is used. The most recommended are the routing group connectors that send information by the extended SMTP protocol, in binary format (you will learn more about different routing group connectors in Chapter 13). There is in fact an SMTP connector, but this is not used between routing groups, since anything sent through this type of connector will convert the information to 7-bit MIME messages, thereby slowing down the transfer compared to the routing group connector.

Compared to the SMTP functionality in previous Exchange versions, routing group connectors are much richer and faster. Exchange 2000 supports many SMTP extensions that the Internet Mail Service in Exchange 5.5 did not have. Compare the rich SMTP extension set that Exchange 2000 has (Listing 4.13) to Exchange 5.5 and its Internet Mail Service (Listing 4.14).

Listing 4.13 SMTP extensions for Exchange 2000.

```
250-oden.humandata.se Hello [client1.humandata.se]
250-TURN
250-ATRN
250-SIZE
250-ETRN
250-PIPELINING
250-DSN
250-ENHANCEDSTATUSCODES
250-8bitmime
250-BINARYMIME
250-CHUNKING
250-VRFY
250-X-EXPS GSSAPI NTLM LOGIN
250-X-EXPS=LOGIN
250-AUTH GSSAPI NTLM LOGIN
250-AUTH=LOGIN
250-XEXCH50
250-X-LINK2STATE
```

Listing 4.14 SMTP extensions for Exchange 5.5.

```
250-E55.humandata.se Hello [client1.humandata.se]
250-XEXCH50
250-HELP
250-ETRN
250-DSN
250-SIZE 0
250-AUTH LOGIN
250 AUTH=LOGIN
```

Some of the differences are:

- *Binary transfer*—Exchange 5.5 did not send information in binary form; it was always converted to 7-bit MIME format.
- *Pipelining*—Exchange 5.5 has no support for this; all SMTP commands must wait for a response before sending **next** command.
- *Chunking*—Exchange 5.5 has no support for this. All data is sent by the standard command DATA, and all must be in 7-bit MIME format, even between two Exchange 5.5 servers.
- *Authentication*—Exchange 5.5 only supports NTLM and basic clear text validation.
- *Link states*—Exchange 5.5 has no link state; a broken connection in another site will not be advertised to other sites—we have a risk of ping-pong message transfer.
- *ATURN*—Exchange 5.5 does not understand ATURN, which makes it unusable in situations where the server gets a dynamically assigned IP address, very common when using low-cost Internet connections.

Something that is easy to forget if you have been administering Exchange 5.5 is that all SMTP traffic is routed through the Windows 2000 SMTP protocol, which is a part of the Internet Information Server. Before, all SMTP configurations were done through the IMS connector; that has changed in Exchange 2000—there may not even be an SMTP connector installed. For someone from the "old school," it is sometimes confusing to find SMTP-related configuration in several places in Exchange 2000, but it's a consequence of this separation—you will get used to it!

All SMTP stacks in Windows 2000 Server, Advanced Server, and Datacenter are equal. Windows 2000 Professional also has an SMTP stack, but it is limited compared to the server version. Before you install Exchange 2000, the SMTP stack only supports CDO 2, which allows applications to create and submit messages through VBScript. After the installation of Exchange 2000, the SMTP stack will be upgraded to add features like Advanced Queuing and routing, plus several new SMTP extensions. These new features are implemented by adding a new event sink that makes it possible to allow SMTP messages to be sent directly into the Information Store by the ExIFS. The upgrade to Exchange 2000 will also upgrade CDO 2 to CDO 3, known as "CDO for Exchange," which makes it possible for applications to read and write mailbox content.

Because of the enhanced SMTP protocol, in rare situations Exchange 2000 could have problems communicating with older SMTP servers. In such a case, you may need to disable some extended SMTP commands; but since Exchange uses several of them, you can only disable those that are stored in the Metabase, such as the following:

- TURN
- ATRN
- ETRN

- DSN
- ENHANCEDSTATUSCODE
- 8BITMIME
- BINARYMIME
- CHUNKING

Each of these commands has a corresponding value in the Metabase. The total sum of all values represents the various on or off switches for these commands. This sum is stored in the "SmtpInboundCommandSupportOptions" value (in decimal), which can be found in the LM/SMTPSVC/1 folder in the Metabase. If you use the MetaEdit utility for manipulating this sum, you will need to know that the Metabase ID number is 36998. See Table 4.5 for the value of each ESMTP command.

The default value for "SmtpInboundCommandSupportOptions" is 7697601 (0x7574C1H). To disable any of the above commands, subtract its corresponding value from this sum. For example, to disable 8BITMIME, the new sum would be 3503297 (0x3574C1H).

***Tip:** You can use MetaEdit 2 or the Adsutil.vbs to change the Metabase. Metaedit.exe is found in the Windows 2000 Server Resource Kit (must be installed on a server); the Adsutil.vbs is stored on the Windows 2000 Server directory C:\Inetpub\AdminScripts. For more information about these two utilities, read the MS TechNet article Q240225, which is still valid although it was written for the NT 4 Option Pack version of Metabase.*

Using Telnet to Send Messages

Since SMTP is based on text characters, it is very easy to start troubleshooting or checking the SMTP protocol stack. An excellent tool for this is the Telnet application that comes with all Windows versions. Before starting, find out the IP number (or the host name) of the SMTP server and the TCP port that is used on this server. Note that if this server is using more than one virtual SMTP server, they must have different IP numbers or port numbers.

Table 4.5 The value for ESMTP commands in Metabase.

Command	Hex Value	Dec Value
DSN	0x40H	64
ETRN	0x80H	128
TURN/ATRN	0x400H	1024
ENHANCEDSTATUSCODE	0x1000H	4096
CHUNKING	0x100000H	1048576
BINARYMIME	0x200000H	2097152
8BITMIME	0x400000H	4194304

The first thing we will do is check if the SMTP stack is active; this is done by simply using a command prompt or the Run command under the Start button. Then type "Telnet <host name or ip number> <port number>". For example, let's say we want to connect to the host oden.humandata.se on port 25:

```
Telnet oden.humandata.se 25
```

If this SMTP server is active and reachable, the result would be a new window with a response similar to this:

```
220 oden.humandata.se Microsoft ESMTP MAIL Service, Version: 5.0.2195.1600
ready  at  Sun, 18 Feb 2001 22:56:04 +0100
```

This information tells us several things: The SMTP server is active, it's a Microsoft server, and the fully qualified domain name (FQDN) is **oden.humandata.se**. The version number may also indicate what type of Exchange release it is (note that Exchange 2000 has a lower version number than Exchange 5.5). Below is a list of some common SMTP servers on the Internet:

- *Exchange 5.5*—Version number 5.5.x.y
- *Exchange 2000*—Version number 5.0.x.y
- *Sendmail*—Probably a Unix server, many versions, but 8.9.3 is common
- *Sendmail AIX*—Probably an IBM AIX Unix server

Note that it may take a few seconds before you receive a reply from the SMTP server. If you don't get a new window, or if it closes down directly, it is probably because the SMTP server is not available; check again that you have the correct IP number and port number.

Note: *Some ISPs change the IP address to their SMTP servers frequently; in this case try using the FQDN name for the SMTP server instead of its IP address.*

Configure the Telnet Application

The first thing you will want to do is to activate local echo; otherwise, you will not see what you type and since you cannot erase any character by using Backspace or Delete, it is easy to make a typo. Start the Telnet application without any other argument; then type "Help" to get a list of options. Use the **SET LOCAL_ECHO** command to turn on local echo; see Listing 4.14. All new settings will be stored.

Listing 4.14 The settings for Telnet.exe.

```
Microsoft ® Windows 2000 ™ Version 5.00 (Build 2195)
Welcome to Microsoft Telnet Client
Telnet Client Build 5.00.99201.1

Escape Character is 'CTRL+"'
Microsoft Telnet> help
```

```
Commands may be abbreviated. Supported commands are:
close           close current connection
display         display operating parameters
open            connect to a site
quit            exit telnet
set             set options (type 'set ?' for a list)
status          print status information
unset           unset options (type 'unset ?' for a list)
?/help          print help information
Microsoft Telnet> set ?
NTLM            Turn ON NTLM Authentication.
LOCAL_ECHO      Turn ON LOCAL_ECHO.
TERM x          (where x is ANSI, VT100, VT52, or VTNT)
CRLF            Send both CR and LF
Microsoft Telnet> set Local_Echo
Microsoft Telnet>
```

To open a connection to the SMTP server oden.humandata.se on port 25, you type "open oden.humandata.se 25". Notice that Telnet has an escape character (CTRL+") that makes it possible to switch between the Telnet settings and any open connection.

Sending an SMTP Message Using Telnet

Connect Telnet on port 25 to the server you want to send the SMTP message to, then write the SMTP commands as shown in Listing 4.15; remember that during the DATA input, you must follow the RFC 822 message format. First type the header fields, then one empty line, then the message content. Finish the message by typing an empty line, a full period, and another empty line.

Listing 4.15 Sample of Telnet session.

```
220 oden.humandata.se Microsoft ESMTP MAIL Service, Version: 5.0.2195.1600 ready at
Sun, 18 Feb 2001 23:49:38 +0100
ehlo
250-oden.humandata.se Hello [194.198.189.161]
250-TURN
250-ATRN
250-SIZE
250-ETRN
250-PIPELINING
250-DSN
250-ENHANCEDSTATUSCODES
250-8bitmime
250-BINARYMIME
250-CHUNKING
250-VRFY
250-X-EXPS GSSAPI NTLM LOGIN
250-X-EXPS=LOGIN
250-AUTH GSSAPI NTLM LOGIN
```

```
250-AUTH=LOGIN
250-XEXCH50
250-X-LINK2STATE
250 OK
Mail From:<einstein@universe.org>
250 2.1.0 einstein@universe.org....Sender OK
Rcpt to:<goran@humandata.se>
250 2.1.5 goran@humandata.se
Data
354 Start mail input; end with <CRLF>.<CRLF>
From:Dr Albert Einstein <albert.einstein@universe.ru>
To: Mr Husman <goran@humandata.se>
Subject: New findings regarding black holes

Dear Mr Husman,
I must send you a quick note about my new findings!
The holes are in fact blue, not black!

Regards
Dr Einstein

.
250 2.6.0 <ODENAOeIiGXix4A2Dre000000009@oden.humandata.se> Queued mail for delivery
```

Notice that the SMTP command "Mail From" is using a mail address other than the From field used inside the message. As you can see, there is no checking that the sender addresses are real or that they even match each other! When we look at the message received with Outlook 2000, it will look like Figure 4.8.

As you can see, it is the information given inside the RFC 822 message that is displayed. There is no indication that the SMTP command "Mail From" is different from the From

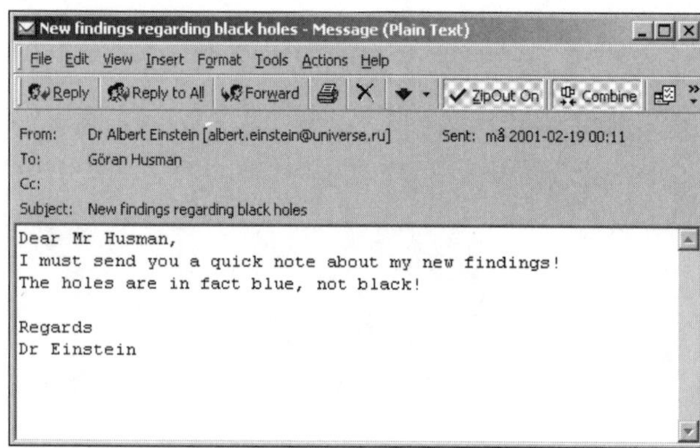

Figure 4.8
How Outlook 2000 will display the message.

field. However, if you look at the message header in Outlook by selecting the menu View|Options for this mail, you will see the Internet headers in Listing 4.16.

Listing 4.16 The Internet headers for this message.

```
Microsoft Mail Internet Headers Version 2.0
Received: from  ([194.198.189.161]) by oden.humandata.se with Microsoft
SMTPSVC(5.0.2195.1600); Mon, 19 Feb 2001 00:09:05 +0100
From:Dr Albert Einstein <albert.Einstein@universe.ru>
To:Mr Husman <goran@humandata.se>
Subject:New findings regarding black holes
Return-Path: einstein@universe.org
Message-ID: <ODENoYAPNXRPmcarcR40000000b@oden.humandata.se>
X-OriginalArrivalTime: 18 Feb 2001 23:10:41.0918 (UTC) FILETIME=[03B401E0:01C09A00]
Date: 19 Feb 2001 00:10:41 +0100
```

Obviously, the SMTP command "Mail From" will be displayed as the "Return-Path" address, but this address will not be used if the recipient will reply to the mail; the Return-Path is used just in case of problems. Outlook will use the reply address found in the From field.

As you can see, there are lots of interesting things you can learn about SMTP by playing with Telnet. I recommend that you practice this; it may be invaluable to have a deeper understanding of the SMTP protocol in case of problems. And you can always impress your friends with this knowledge!

Summary

This is a list of the more important features and keywords described in this chapter. Use it as a reminder and to make sure you have understood the most important concepts:

- *SMTP*—A set of commands for sending information between two SMTP servers or between a POP3/IMAP4 client and an SMTP server.
- *RFCs*—Today many of them are regarded as standards.
- *RFC Levels*—Required, Recommended, Elective, Limited Use, Not recommended.
- *RFC standard maturity levels*—Proposed, Draft, Internet Standard.
- *RFC 821*—The SMTP standard that describes how to transfer mail between two mail servers.
- *RFC 822*—The Internet message standard that describes how the messages that RFC 821 transfers should be formatted.

Note: *There is no checking that the sender address is correct in RFC 821 or in RFC 822. In fact, you can use different sender addresses without any errors or complaints. This is the foundation for spamming.*

- *X.400 and RPC were used in Exchange 5.5*—Encrypted, high overhead to start a session but fast transfer. Need a reliable and high-speed network. Not resilient.
- *Originator/Recipient (O/R)*—The address format in X.400 systems.

Note: *SMTP and TCP/IP are both used in Exchange 2000 and are fast and resilient, with low overhead.*

- *Lightweight Directory Address Protocol (LDAP)*—An enhancement of DAP. Used for searching and updating X.500 databases like Active Directory.
- *DN*—The address format in X.500 directories.

Note: *SMTP is easy to enhance by adding new commands; X.400 is very hard to change.*

- *Extended SMTP (ESMTP)*—An SMTP server that supports RFC 821 and 1869, may also have support for new extended commands.
- *Exchange 2000 uses binary transfer between the servers*—No conversion of 8-bit information is done, making this a very fast transfer.
- *HELO*—The first command for RFC 821 SMTP servers.
- *EHLO*—The first command for RFC 1869 SMTP servers (ESMTP servers).
- *RFC 821*—This was originally built for 7-bit U.S. ASCII characters only. All 8-bit information needed to be converted before it was transferred.
- *RFC 1869*—This extension of RFC 821 made it possible to add new SMTP commands; without it, SMTP would not have been able to manage 8-bit text and binary attachments.
- *Extended Turn (ETRN)*—A way to de-queue mail waiting in a secondary mail server, typically at the ISP. Used when you have a dial-up connection with a fixed IP address.
- *Authenticated Turn (ATRN)*—Similar to ETRN, but can be used when the dial-up connections will give the SMTP server a dynamically assigned IP address.
- *Pipelining*—EHLO command that makes it possible to send several SMTP commands without waiting for a reply for each; makes the SMTP session faster.
- *Transport Layer Security (TLS)*—Built on SSL, used for encrypting the network session between two SMTP servers.
- *Delivery Status Notification (DSN)*—Enhancement to the notification received for successful and failed transfer.
- *Chunking*—Also known as BDAT. Makes it possible to send a large amount of binary data very fast between two SMTP servers.
- *Multipurpose Internet Mail Extensions (MIME)*—An important extension to RFC 822; made it possible to send 8-bit text and binary information in the message.

- *Base-64*—The conversion algorithm used by MIME when converting attached binary files and objects. Uses a special 64-character table for conversions.
- *Quoted Printable (QP)*—The conversion algorithm used by MIME when converting 8-bit characters in the message header and content. Uses a table for conversion, usually the ISO-8859-1 table (Latin-1).
- *Content-Type*—MIME field. Describes what the following message part is, such as text, image, audio, video, or application.
- *Content-Transfer-Encoding*—MIME field. Describes how the following message part is encoded, such as 7BIT, 8BIT, BINARY, QP, and BASE-64.
- *Content conversion*—A method of converting 8-bit information to 7-bit data, like Base-64, QP, and UUencode.
- *UUencode*—Unix-to-Unix-encoding: the old method before Base-64 for content conversion.
- *Uudecode*—Uudecode is the opposite of UUencode; to restore the information back to 8-bit format.

Note: *Exchange 2000 relies on the SMTP protocol stack in Windows 2000 Server; this stack is enhanced when installing Exchange 2000.*

- *Virtual SMTP servers*—The ability to run several SMTP stacks in one Windows 2000 server. Used for different configurations, not for enhanced performance.
- *Telnet.exe*—An excellent utility for testing an SMTP connection.

Chapter 5

Exchange 2000 and Windows 2000

Exchange 2000 is built to run on MS Windows 2000 Server; this chapter will give you all the basic knowledge needed to understand what that dependency means for the Exchange 2000 environment. There is a lot more information about Windows 2000 that goes beyond the scope of this book, not least about the Active Directory; I recommend that you read some of the many excellent Windows 2000 books that Coriolis has released during the last year if you are interested in extending your knowledge in this area—and honestly, you should be!

Previous versions of Exchange were made to run on Windows NT; the relationship between them was rather loose and Exchange really used Windows NT only for running the server processes and mapping NT user accounts to mailbox accounts, thereby controlling access to the mailbox. Exchange has from its beginning been built on the client/server concept, meaning that an active process on the client communicated with one or more active pro-cesses on the server. When the first Exchange version was released in 1996, this was a new concept in the email world; most email applications were built on a concept usually referred to as the Shared File System (SFS), for example MS Mail and cc-Mail.

An SFS email system uses a server only as a central repository for messages and system files, which is often referred to as the post office, while the mail client performs all active functions. When two clients belonging to the same SFS post office send a message to each other, here's what happens (see Figure 5.1):

1. User A creates the message for user B and presses the Send button.
2. User A's mail client stores the message directly in the file system on the SFS server and updates its indexes and system files, but no information is sent to user B.
3. Only when user B uses his mail client to connect to the SFS server will he discover that a message is waiting for him. The message is now retrieved to the mail client.

The important thing to understand here is that user B will not discover any new messages unless his client is looking for one, so most email clients of this SFS type will regularly connect to the mail server and perform this check; this is called "polling" the mail server

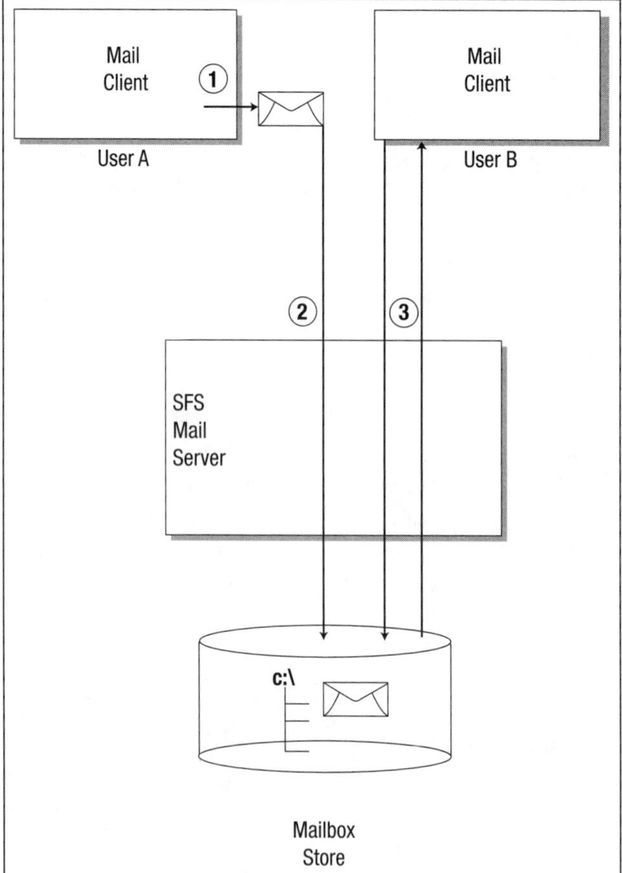

Figure 5.1
Message flow in an SFS mail system.

and is usually performed anywhere from once every minute to once every 10 minutes. The consequence is that all email clients connect to the mail server at the polling interval, thereby increasing the load on the network. It also means that a receiver will not discover any new messages immediately, unless he or she manually forces a polling. Another drawback of the SFS concept is that all mail clients need access to common system files on the mail server, not only to their private mail; the consequence is that a user could easily destroy vital files on the server, either by mistake or deliberately.

With a client/server-based email system, the behavior is very different—a client will register itself with the server when the mail client program starts; when any new message arrives to this user, the server will send a notification to the mail client. The same example as above will now look like this (see Figure 5.2):

1. User A creates the message for user B and presses the Send button.
2. User A's mail client sends the message to a mail process on the server.

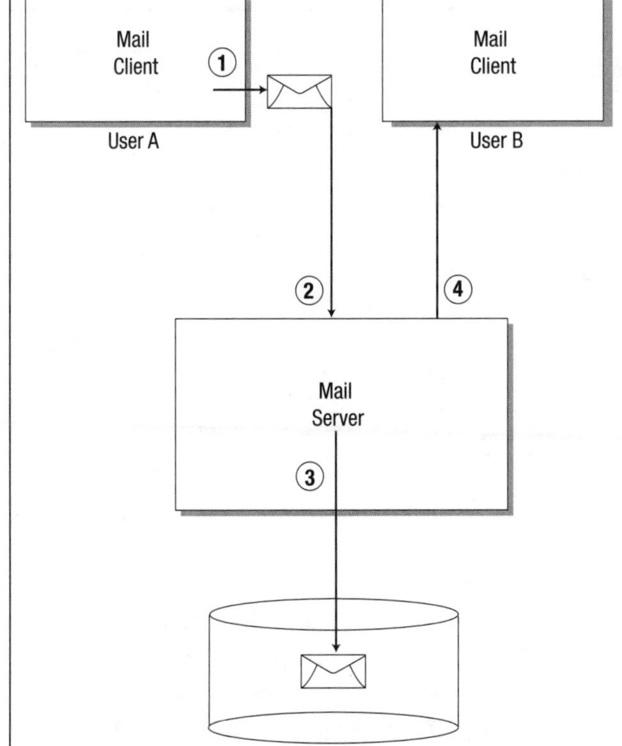

Figure 5.2
A client/server-based mail system.

3. The server process stores the message in its databases; the client will not have any direct access to any of those files.

4. The server checks to see if user B is active; if so, it directly sends notification to the client, informing it about the new message.

This has lots of advantages over the SFS concept. For one thing, there will be no unnecessary network traffic between the mail clients and the server; in fact, unless a new message arrives, there won't be any network traffic at all. Since the mail clients will not have any access to the system files or message databases on the server, there is no risk that these files will be tampered with.

All versions prior to Exchange 2000 had four core processes active on the server, communicating with clients, transferring mail between servers, and managing address lists and configuration settings. These processes, also known as *services*, could be managed by using the Windows NT Control Panel/Services applet; they are described in more detail in Table 5.1.

Table 5.1 The core server processes in previous Exchange versions.

Process	Application	Description
Information Store (IS)	Store.exe	Responsible for all access to the databases PRIV.EDB and PUB.EDB. Receives messages directly from the clients; notifies recipients of new messages.
Directory Service (DS)	DSAmain.exe	Responsible for all access to the DIR.EDB database; stores all address lists, distribution lists, and configuration settings of servers, mailboxes, and other objects.
Message Transfer Agent (MTA)	Emsmta.exe	Responsible for routing all messages, and for sending and receiving messages between servers and Exchange sites.
System Attendant (SA)	Mad.exe	Responsible for several functions, such as updating the routing table, creating proxy email addresses, and link monitoring. All other Exchange processes are dependent on this SA process; if this stops, then all Exchange processes stop.

Besides these four core processes, you could also install extra services—for example, the Internet Mail Service, which provides SMTP connectivity typically used for exchanging messages over the Internet. All these processes were made to run as NT services; if Microsoft wanted, it could also have made them run on Unix or any other operating system, but for obvious reasons they only run on NT. This is the main reason that previous Exchange versions needed the Windows NT Server platform. In Exchange 2000, the bonds to the Windows 2000 Server operating system are even stronger; several vital parts of the messaging structure are now handled directly by subsystems of Windows 2000, including the Active Directory, SMTP connectivity, and client access like HTTP and IMAP4. It would be much harder to convert Exchange 2000 to run on another operating system; in fact, you cannot even make it run on Windows NT 4. This chapter will discuss this dependency on Windows 2000 and its subsystems, and give you the information needed for installing and configuring Exchange 2000 in an optimal way.

Introduction to Active Directory

One major change in Exchange 2000, compared to previous Exchange versions, is the absence of its own directory database, where all address lists and configuration settings are stored. So where is this information stored now? The answer is simple—in the Active Directory, which is managed by Windows 2000.

What is a directory anyway? It is simply a repository for storing different types of objects, like users, groups, and servers, along with information about the objects, called "attributes"; for example, a user object has attributes like first name, last name, and address, and a server object has attributes like the name, shares, and an IP number. Compare this to the ordinary file system. You may have a folder called "My Documents" where you store MS Word documents; each document has a different name, title, author, and so on. The My Documents folder corresponds to the object type, the Word files are objects of this particular type, and the name, title, and author are attributes. The term *schema* is used to define exactly what object types and attributes can be stored in the Active Directory; this schema is extended with many new attributes when you install Exchange 2000—for example, the mailbox name, message limits, and Exchange home server.

Notice that a directory will not store any data besides the object names and their corresponding attributes; all actual data is stored in another database. This type of descriptive information is often called *Meta data*. All database systems have a directory that describes the data stored in the actual database. This is nothing special for Exchange; Windows NT also has several separate directories, like the SAM, the WINS, and the DHCP databases. What Microsoft has done now is to store nearly all these separate directories in one single file, the Active Directory, which makes it easier to administer and manage all Meta information.

Windows NT 4 Domains

In Windows NT, you have the concept of NT domains; each domain has one master, the *Primary Domain Controller (PDC)*, which stores all information about users, groups, and profile configuration for this domain in an encrypted SAM database. SAM is an abbreviation for "Security Account Manager," a less-than-intuitive name. It is limited to 40,000 objects per SAM database, (user and computer accounts are examples of SAM objects); if you have more, you need to create a new domain. One or more servers can have a copy of the SAM database; these are called *Backup Domain Controllers (BDCs)*. The PDC will regularly replicate updates of its SAM database to all BDCs to make sure they have a complete copy of the SAM for the domain. However, it is not possible to make any changes to the SAM database on the BDC—it is used only for the following:

- *Account validations*—For example, when a user logs on to the domain, any BDC or the PDC can validate the username and password.
- *Redundancy and load balancing*—For example, if the PDC gets offline or if there are a lot of logon activities, any BDC will be able to perform validations.
- *Fault tolerance*—If the PDC has a disk crash, any BDC can be promoted to a new PDC.

In Windows 2000 there is also a domain concept, with many features similar to the NT domain. For example, each domain is an administrative boundary; there may be trusts between different domains and domain controllers that validate user logons.

Windows 2000 Active Directory Database

The Active Directory in Windows 2000 is built on the Exchange 5.5 Directory Service and its corresponding Dir.edb database; about 60 percent of the core in AD comes from Exchange 5.5. This heritage is very clear when you look at how AD replicates information between Windows 2000 servers and sites. So although Active Directory is new to Windows 2000, it is based on code that has been used and enhanced for many years; it is a proven concept. The name of the Active Directory database is NTDS.DIT and is stored in the directory C:\WinNT\NTDS on the Windows 2000 server. This database can store more than one million objects, compared to 40,000 for an NT domain. A Windows 2000 server with the NTDS database installed is referred to by several names, all of which have the same meaning:

- The Active Directory server
- The domain controller
- The logon server

The NTDS.DIT database is very similar to the DIR.EDB of previous Exchange versions; it is built on the *Extensible Storage Engine (ESE)*. NTDS.DIT and DIR.EDB have lots of common features, as you can see in Table 5.2. If you look at a domain controller, you will find two NTDS.DIT files, one in \WinNT\System32 and one in \WinNT\NTDS; when you run DCPROMO to promote a server, the first one is used as a template when creating the real NTDS.DIT. After that, the first NTDS.DIT will not be used anymore.

It may look like a step back regarding resilience when Active Directory is using circular logging that cannot be disabled, but the NTDS.DIT and its transaction log files are in fact optimized for circular logging. Because of the redundancy built into Active Directory with multiple domain controllers within a domain, it is still a very resilient system. However, if you have only one single domain controller in a domain (this is not recommended!), you must design your backup routines very carefully—check the backup every day to make sure there are no problems. If you lose this single domain controller and you don't have any backups, your complete domain structure will be lost unless you manage to repair the NTDS.DIT database again. You should always have at least two domain controllers in each Windows 2000 domain!

If needed, you can move the NTDS.DIT and/or its log files by following these steps:

1. Restart the domain controller, press F8 at the Startup menu, and select *Directory Services Restore Mode*.

Table 5.2 Comparing NTDS.DIT with DIR.EDB.

Feature	DIR.EDB	NTDS.DIT
Database engine	ESE-98	ESE-98
Transaction log	Yes, each log is 5MB (or exact 5 242 880 bytes) in size	Yes, each log is 10MB (or exact 10 485 760 bytes) in size
Circular logging	Can be enabled (default) or disabled	Enabled, cannot be disabled
Online defragmentation	Yes, runs every night	Yes, runs every 12 hours as a part of the "Garbage Collection" process
Offline defragmentation	Yes, but the server must be offline	Yes, but the server must be offline
Reserved log files	2 (5MB each)	2 (10MB each)
Checkpoint file	Yes (8KB)	Yes (8KB)
Default file location	\Exchsrvr\DSAData	\WinNT\NTDS

2. Logon as the administrator.
3. Open a command prompt window, and type "*ntdsutil.exe*".
4. At the ntdsutil.exe prompt, type "*Files*".
5. At the *File Maintenance* prompt, do one or both of these:
   - To move a database, type "move db to %s" where "%s" is the new drive and folder.
   - To move a log file, type "move logs to %s" where "%s" is the new drive and folder.
6. To view the log files or databases, type "*Info*". To verify that all is correct after moving the log files or databases, type "*Integrity*".
7. Type "*Quit*" to return to the C:\ prompt.
8. Restart the server in normal mode; make sure to take a backup of the server!

The server roles in Windows NT are inflexible; you must decide when installing a server if it's going to be a PDC or BDC, or a member for a given domain; once this is set, it cannot be changed without reinstalling the server. In Windows 2000 domains, this is very flexible; the utility Dcpromo.exe can be used to promote or demote a Windows 2000 server to a domain controller. It is even possible to move a domain controller from one Windows 2000 domain to another; simply demote the server in the old domain, join the new domain, and promote it to a domain controller again.

Accessing the Active Directory

The Active Directory is based on the X.500 directory recommendation, but not fully X.500 compliant, just like its predecessor, *Directory Service*. The reason for not being fully X.500 compliant is that this would decrease the overall performance of the directory due to the large overhead built in the X.500 recommendation. You can use the LDAP protocol to search and modify the Active Directory; this is used by all Windows 2000 operating systems, like servers and clients, and applications like Exchange 2000 and SQL 2000. Active Directory has support for version 3 of the LDAP protocol that makes it possible to both read and write to the directory; previous LDAP versions only supported reading.

The LDAP protocol is fast and reliable, using TCP port 389 when communicating with Active Directory. But not all clients and applications know how to use LDAP. This is especially true when it comes to email clients like Outlook 97 and Outlook 98. These clients use MAPI and RPC for accessing the Directory Service on Exchange 5.5. When using Exchange 2000, these clients still use the MAPI protocol; however, since Exchange 2000 no longer has any directory, it will proxy the client request by sending an LDAP query to the Active Directory, and then pass the result back to the client. You can find more information about this in Chapter 15.

Active Directory Domain Names

Another difference is that the name for a Windows NT domain is limited to 15 characters, whereas Windows 2000 domains can be a combination of several names, each up to 64 characters long, separated by a period—for example, *microsoft.com* or *ad.telia.se*. The Windows NT limit of 15 characters for domains is because it's a NetBIOS name; this name standard uses 16 characters per name, and the last character is reserved to describe the type of object, such as a domain name, server, or username. The name standard for Windows 2000 domains is the same as DNS names; in fact, you can have exactly the same name for your Windows 2000 domain as the DNS name. The following list summarizes this domain name standard:

- The complete domain name is a combination of one or more name parts, separated by a period.
- Each name field must be less than 64 characters.
- The total length of the domain name must be less than or equal to 64 characters, including period characters.
- The name is not case sensitive.

Note that the total length of the Windows 2000 domain name is actually less than the total limit for DNS names, which is 255 characters. Windows will internally add various prefixes when locating an object, like a domain GUID, site names, and so on, to the domain name, making the longest possible name limited to 64 characters to avoid exceeding the 255-character limit. If you use the Dcpromo.exe utility to create domains, it checks that the domain name is less than or equal to 64 characters; more information about this can be found in the knowledge base article Q245809.

This resemblance with DNS names is no coincidence; AD uses DNS to store information that both domain controllers and AD-aware clients, such as Windows 2000 Professional, need in order to work. The DNS is used for storing names and corresponding IP addresses for servers, as well as for storing information such as who the domain controllers are, and where to find global catalog servers. Basically, the DNS has replaced the WINS service in NT 4.

When you create the first Windows 2000 domain, by an upgrade or a clean install, it will run in *mixed mode* by default; this means that to NT 4 servers, the Windows 2000 domain controllers will behave and look exactly like NT 4 domain controllers—perfect when you want to gradually upgrade an existing Windows NT 4 domain. This has the effect that all Active Directory domain names will also have a NetBIOS name, since only Windows 2000 computers will understand Active Directory domain names. All previous Microsoft operating systems, such as Windows NT 4, Windows 9x, and Windows for Workgroups, recognize only the NetBIOS name. Note that the AD domain name and the NetBIOS name will not be identical, although a part of the AD domain name usually is the same as the NetBIOS name. For example, the AD domain "ad.humandata.se" may have the NetBIOS name

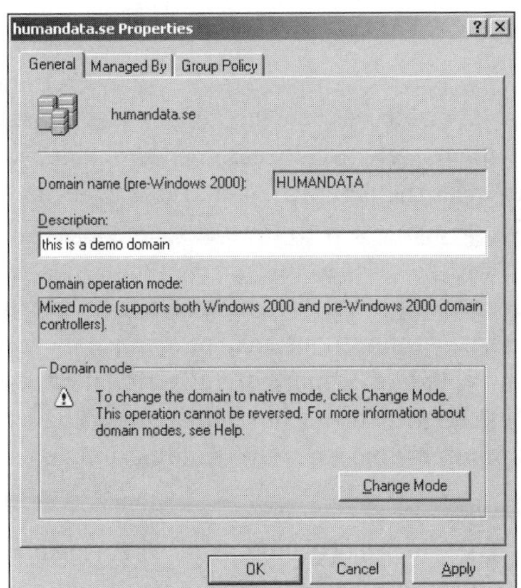

Figure 5.3
The NetBIOS name for an Active Directory domain.

"humandata"; this is also referred to as the *pre-Windows 2000* name. Follow these steps to see the NetBIOS name; see also Figure 5.3:

1. Open the *Active Directory Users And Computers* utility.
2. Right-click on the domain object.
3. The NetBIOS name is listed in the *Domain Name (Pre-Windows 2000)* field.

Notice that you cannot change this NetBIOS name. This is also true for Active Directory domain names; they cannot be changed, so plan carefully before deciding what name to use. As in Figure 5.3, you can change the AD domain from mixed mode to native mode by pressing the *Change Mode* button; this is possible only when no more Windows NT 4 domain controllers are left in this domain. Even after you have changed to native mode, the NetBIOS name will still be valid, thus making it possible to use any pre-Windows 2000 machines as member servers or clients in this domain.

***Note:** If you change from mixed mode to native mode, you will no longer be able to use NT 4 servers as domain controllers in this domain. This operation cannot be reversed!*

Windows 2000 Domains

As previously described, Windows NT domains and Windows 2000 domains share several similarities, but they also have many differences. A Windows 2000 domain is really an Active Directory domain; this type of domain has at least one domain controller, meaning that there is at least one Windows 2000 server that has an Active Directory NTDS.DIT database installed. Unlike Windows NT 4 domains, you can have several writeable domain controllers in one domain; in fact, you should have at least two domain controllers to achieve fault tolerance and load balancing.

The domain is an administrative unit; each domain has its own users and administrators, just like the previous NT domains. NT domains were usually designed based on two goals: to control administrative access and to meet the technical conditions needed for the replication between the PDC and BDC in the domain. With the features that Active Directory offers, you will be able to achieve these goals separately; an AD domain is still the boundary for administrative access, but replication between domain controllers is now performed via Active Directory by RPC or SMTP connections, making it much more tolerant to slow connections. If needed, we can create one or more organizational units (OUs), which are container objects that make it possible to divide our domain into smaller parts. For each OU we can have users and computers, and each OU could have its own set of administrators.

For example, let's assume that we have two Windows NT 4 domains that depend on the needs of two separate administrative groups, the Sales department and the Accounting department. In Windows 2000, we could create one single AD domain, and then create two OUs, one for each department, thereby achieving the goal while still having only one domain (see Figure 5.4).

Trees and Forests

In Windows NT, you can have multiple domains grouped together by creating a trust relationship between them. This makes it possible for a user in one domain to gain access to resources in another domain. In Windows 2000, you can also group domains together in a "tree," and a two-way trust will automatically be created between them—this trust relationship cannot be disabled!

A domain has a name similar to a DNS name—for example, **humandata.se**. If you create a second AD domain, you will have the opportunity to make this a child-domain to the first

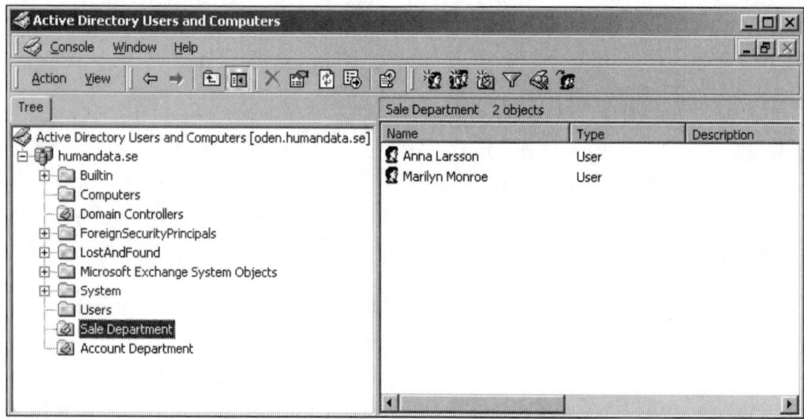

Figure 5.4
One Active Directory domain with two organizational units.

domain, also known as the root domain; the name we give this child-domain will automatically be added to the name of the first domain—for example, **stockholm.humandata.se**. These two domains will now belong to the same AD tree, since they have the same root name, **humandata.se**. You can create as many child-domains to the root as needed, and each child-domain can have its own child-domains, although it's best to keep the number of domains as low as possible for administrative reasons and to avoid unnecessary complexity. All domains belonging to the same AD tree will automatically have a two-way trust relationship between them, thereby making it possible for a user in one domain to gain access to resources in another domain, as long as the user has the correct permissions (see Figure 5.5). If you have more than two domains in the same tree, the trust relationship will be transitive, meaning that if domain A trusts B, and B trusts C, then A and C will automatically trust each other—this is a new feature compared to NT 4 domains.

The beauty of this is that you can design your domain structure based on your business needs. For example, some may use this possibility to create one AD domain for each division, while others will create one single domain and divide it into several OUs. This decision is based on logical and administrative needs; it's not necessarily a technical decision. Regardless of how your domain structure looks, all users will still be able to access all net-work resources, such as servers and printers, if given permission. And administration is easier than ever before—simply connect the administrative tools to any domain controller in the domain and change the settings as needed; this will then be replicated to all domain controllers in this domain.

As we saw, all domains in a tree share the same root domain name, this is called a *continuous name space*. It is possible to create a new tree, with a new root domain name; but still be connected to the first tree; this is known as *discontinuous name space* since we will have different root names for each tree. One reason for creating a separate tree in the forest

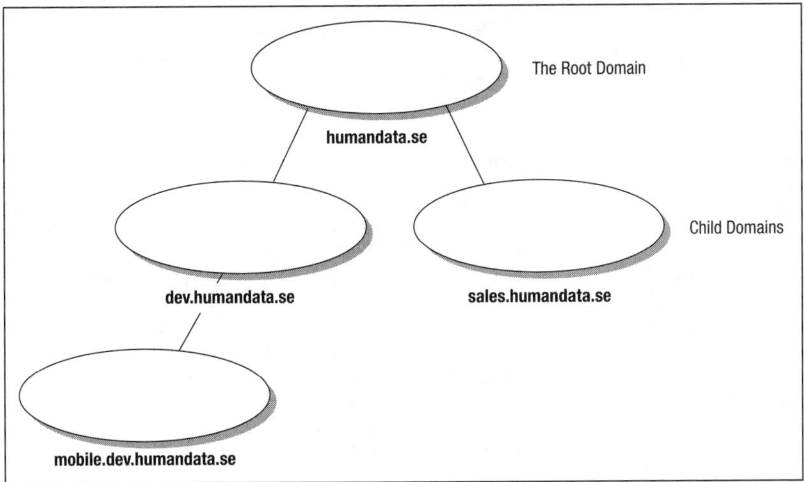

Figure 5.5
Example of AD domain trees.

may be to connect another division or organization that has its own name. Again, you can use the DCPROMO utility to create this new tree; select *Place This New Domain Tree In An Existing Forest*. A *forest* in Windows 2000 is a collection of one or more domain trees, and a *tree* is a collection of one or more domains. You will create the forest when you create your first domain; this domain will also create the first tree. So the smallest forest you can have is one with one single tree, consisting of one single domain; this will be the most common design for small and medium-sized organizations. Table 5.3 summarizes domains, trees, and forests.

Active Directory Domain Partitions

The information in the Active Directory is divided into three parts, or *partitions*. Some of the information will be replicated to all domains in all trees in the forest, whereas some information will be local for the domain. These parts include the following:

- *Domain partition*—Complete information about all objects for a given domain.
- *Configuration partition*—Describes configuration and routing information.
- *Schema partition*—Describes the structure of the AD, what objects can be stored, and what attributes they can have.

All domains belonging to the same forest will have access to the same AD configuration partition and schema partition, but only the domain controllers for a given domain will have complete access to all information in its own domain partition. Let's think about this for a moment. The information in the domain partition will not be seen outside the domain. And this partition stores the names of all users, computers, and other network resources. So how can an Exchange 2000 system see the names for mailbox-enabled users that belong to different domains? The answer is simple—it can't! Not without something that actually replicates at least some of the information in the domain partition between the domains. This something is called the *global catalog*, a service running on a domain controller. It keeps a copy of selected attributes for all objects; you can find more about GC later in this chapter.

Table 5.3 Summary of domains, trees, and forests.

Type	Description
Domain	A group of one or more Windows 2000 domain controllers; each has an Active Directory NTDS.DIT database storing information about network objects, like users and computers, along with their attributes, like names, phone numbers, and departments. A domain must belong to a tree.
Tree	A group of one or more AD domains, sharing the same name space, meaning they all have the same root domain name. All domains in the trees automatically have transitive two-way trust relationships, using Kerberos for authentication.
Forest	A group of one or more AD trees; these trees may have different root names, while still having two-way trust replication between them.

What is the consequence of all domain controllers in the forest sharing the configuration and schema partitions? The answer is: you cannot have any secrets! All applications installed that use Active Directory for storing the configuration will be known all over the forest. One such application is Exchange 2000—this means that there can only be one Exchange 2000 organization per forest. This is new, compared to NT domains and Exchange 5.5; in those versions, it was perfectly okay to install as many Exchange 5.5 organizations as needed, even in the same NT domain. This is something you must be aware of—you can no longer create an Exchange 2000 organization in your Windows 2000 production forest just for testing; you need to create a separate forest for this purpose.

Although the domain controllers are equal, meaning that there is no PDC and BDC anymore, there must be some servers that have particular responsibilities in the forest; these servers were from the beginning referred to as *FSMO servers*; an abbreviation for Flexible Single Master Operation; however, for some reason Microsoft seems to prefer the terms *server roles* and *operations masters* nowadays. The five FSMO roles are:

- Schema master
- Domain naming master
- Relative ID (RID) master
- PDC emulator
- Infrastructure master

The reason Windows 2000 needs these FSMO roles is efficiency and to avoid conflicts, like when changing the schema. Some FSMO roles are global for the whole forest, and others are local for each domain. Note that all FSMO servers are domain controllers. You can at any time move a role from one domain controller to another. Since these roles are needed from the beginning, the first installed Windows 2000 domain controller will by default get all five of these roles.

Schema Master

There must be only one single server in the forest that controls the AD schema partition; this server is called the *schema master* and will by default be the first server installed in the forest. This server has the original schema and this is the only place where the schema can be modified. If you are connected to another domain controller when installing the first Exchange 2000 server, or running the "*Setup /forestprep*," you must wait until the schema update of about 100 new objects and more than 500 new attributes has been completely replicated to all domain controllers in the forest. That is the reason you should update the schema partition directly on the schema master server—to save you time.

Follow these steps to determine the schema FSMO server in the forest:

1. You must register the *Schema DLL* before using the *AD Schema* snap-in. Do this by opening a command window: type "*regsvr32 schmmgmt.dll*"; you should receive a message that the registration was successful.

2. Click *Start*, click *Run*, type "*MMC*", and then click *OK*.
3. On the *Console* menu, click *Add/Remove Snap-in*, click *Add*, double-click *Active Directory Schema*, click *Close*, then click *OK*. Now you have the AD Schema snap-in installed.
4. Right-click on *Active Directory Schema*, then select *Operations Master*, and you will see the name of the schema master; click *Change* if you need to transfer this role to another server; see Figure 5.6.

Note that before you can transfer this role to another server, you must make sure the Operations Master role is attached to that server; do this by using the *Active Directory Domains And Trusts* snap-in; see the next section in this chapter.

***Note:** If you cannot find the Active Directory Schema snap-in, the reason may be that you don't have the Adminpak.msi installed. To install it, locate the file Adminpak.msi on the Windows 2000 CD and double-click to start the installation.*

If the schema master goes down unexpectedly and you are really sure there is no way to get this server online again, you must use the Ntdsutil.exe utility to transfer this schema master role by force; here's how to transfer this role to another domain controller. First make sure you are logged on as an administrator, and then follow these steps:

1. Open a command prompt and type "*ntdsutil*"; this will take you into the ntdsutil command prompt mode.
2. Type "*roles*" and press Return.
3. At the fsmo maintenance, type "*connections*".
4. At the server connections, type "*connect to server*", and then provide the fully qualified domain name to the server to which you want to give the PDC Emulator role.

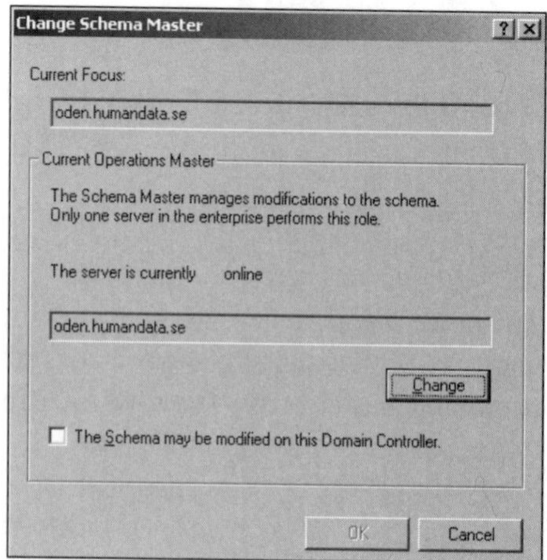

Figure 5.6
Change the schema master.

5. At the server connections, type "*quit*".
6. At the fsmo maintenance, type "*seize schema master*".
7. At the ntdsutil, type "*quit*".

***Warning!** If after you do this, the original schema master gets online after all, you must reformat the disks of that server and reinstall Windows 2000. Otherwise you will have two schema masters and that will corrupt your entire forest!*

Domain Naming Master

This server is responsible for keeping track of domains that are added to or removed from the forest. There is only one domain naming master in the complete forest. This avoids any conflicts by making sure all domain names are unique and fit into the name space in the forest. This information is also used for managing the two-way trust relationships between the domains.

Since there is only one domain naming master in the forest, it is wise to give this role to a server where there is at least one more domain controller on the same subnet; this ensures that any changes will quickly be replicated, and therefore provide you with a backup copy in case the DNM server goes down. It is recommended that you use the same domain controller for both the domain naming master role and the schema master role.

Follow these steps to transfer the domain naming master role:

1. Open the *Active Directory Domains And Trusts* snap-in by clicking *Start|Programs|Administrative Tools*.
2. Right-click *Active Directory Domains And Trusts*, then select *Operations Master*; see Figure 5.7.
3. Change the domain naming master by clicking the *Change* button.

You don't have to pay any special attention to this domain naming master with respect to Exchange 2000.

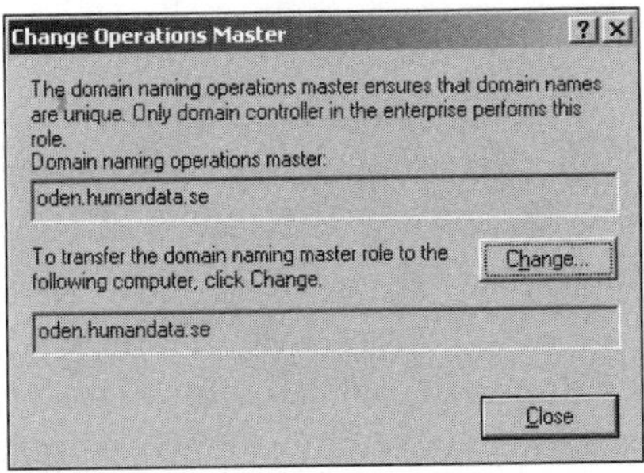

Figure 5.7
Changing the domain naming master.

RID Master

There must be one single RID master for each domain; this server will be responsible for creating an ID that is unique for a given domain. This ID is then combined with a domain-specific security ID, and these two IDs will form the SID given to all objects in this domain. Since all domains have a unique domain security ID, this will ensure that all objects have a SID that is unique throughout the forest.

All domain controllers need to assign a SID for each new object that is created in the domain. They will first contact the RID master, which creates a pool of 512 unique IDs and hands them over to the domain controller. All domain controllers get their own pool of 512 IDs. This means that the RID master will not be contacted unless the pool is almost empty. So if the RID master is unreachable for a short time, this probably won't even be noticed, and there is normally no need to transfer this role to another server, unless it will be disconnected for a longer period. However, if you are creating a lot of new objects—for example, if you import 1,000 users by the LDIFDE tool (described later in this chapter)—then the domain controller needs to contact the RID master.

Follow these steps to transfer the RID master role:

1. Open the *Active Directory Users And Computers* utility by clicking *Start|Programs|Administrative Tools*.
2. Right-click on the domain object and select *Connect To Domain Controller*.
3. Select the domain controller you want to give the RID master role to.
4. Right-click on the domain name object, and select *Operations Masters* from the menu.
5. Look at the RID tab to find out who the current RID master is; change it by clicking the *Change* button. See Figure 5.8.

The Primary Domain Controller (PDC) Emulator

There must be one single server with the PDC Emulator role for each domain. This server will be responsible for creating users, groups, and computers when upgrading an NT 4 domain to an AD domain. This server will emulate a Windows NT primary domain controller; it will support both NTLM and Kerberos protocols, allowing NT 4 backup domain controllers to synchronize with the Windows 2000 domain controllers running in mixed mode.

This PDC Emulator is also responsible for handling password changes, network browser service, and logon requests for pre-Windows 2000 clients (often referred to as *down-level clients*). Yet another important responsibility for the PDC Emulator is synchronizing time in the forest; this is required for the Kerberos authentication protocol. The PDC Emulator is responsible for running the W32Time service within its domain; all domains are synchronized with the PDC Emulator in the root domain. That server should synchronize its time with an external time source.

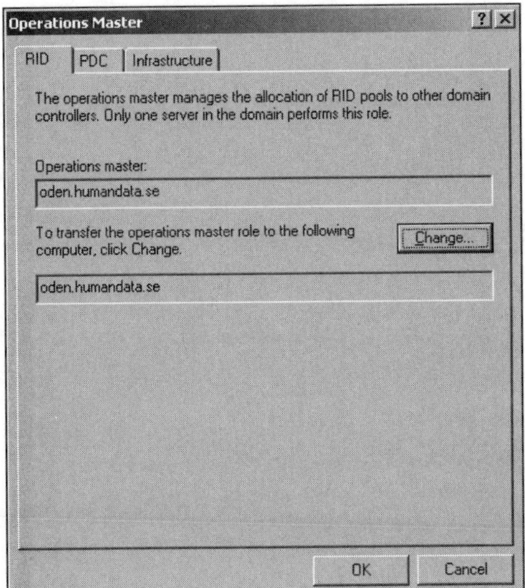

Figure 5.8
Changing the RID master.

If this PDC Emulator gets offline, you will notice several problems; use these steps to give this role to another server if you know you must stop the current PDC Emulator:

1. Open the *Active Directory Users And Computers* utility by clicking *Start|Programs|Administrative Tools*.
2. Right-click on the domain object and select *Connect To Domain Controller*.
3. Select the domain controller you want to give the PDC Emulator role to.
4. Right-click on the domain name object, and select *Operations Masters* from the menu.
5. Look at the PDC tab to find out who the current PDC Emulator is; change it by clicking the Change button. See Figure 5.9.

If the PDC Emulator goes down unexpectedly and you need to transfer this role to another server, you must use the Ntdsutil.exe utility, since the method listed above assumes that the current PDC Emulator is available. Follow these steps to transfer this PDC role by force to another domain controller; make sure you are logged on as an administrator:

1. Open a command prompt and type "ntdsutil"; this will take you into the ntdsutil command prompt mode.
2. Type "roles" and press Return.
3. At the fsmo maintenance, type "connections".
4. At the server connections, type "connect to server", and the fully qualified domain name to the server to which you want to give the PDC Emulator role.

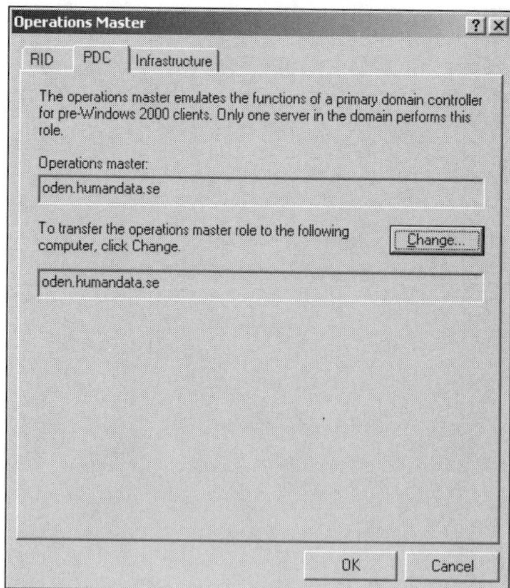

Figure 5.9
Changing the PDC Emulator server.

5. At the server connections, type "quit".
6. At the fsmo maintenance, type "seize PDC".
7. At the ntdsutil, type "quit".

Infrastructure Master

There must be one single infrastructure master in each domain; this server is responsible for keeping track of changes to group memberships in a domain. It will also be responsible for replicating these changes both to its own domain and to other domains. Microsoft recommends that you don't place the infrastructure role on a server with a global catalog, since this could stop updates of group memberships to other domains; you will also get a warning in the Event log file for this domain controller, if this happens.

If this server goes down, it probably won't be noticed—not by users, and not even by administrators. There is no need to give this role to another server, unless the current infrastructure master will be removed. Follow these steps to transfer this role:

1. Open the *Active Directory Users And Computers* utility by clicking *Start|Programs|Administrative Tools*.
2. Right-click on the domain object and select *Connect To Domain Controller*.
3. Select the domain controller to which you want to give the infrastructure master role.
4. Right-click on the domain name object, and select *Operations Masters* from the menu.
5. Look at the *Infrastructure* tab to find out who the current master is; change it by clicking the *Change* button. See Figure 5.10.

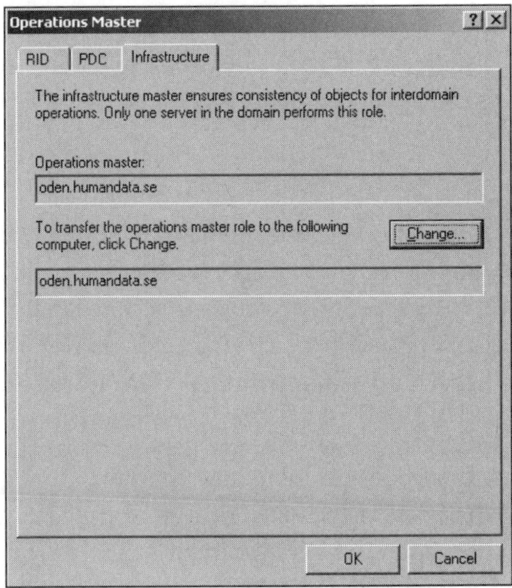

Figure 5.10
Changing the infrastructure master server.

Groups in Windows 2000

Besides users and computers in a domain, there is one more very important object: groups. Instead of assigning individual accounts permissions to perform tasks and access resources, it is a lot easier to create groups and assign them the proper permissions. In Windows NT, you had groups only for security reasons, for example to control who had the permission to access a certain directory. A group could be *local*, meaning it would be visible only on the server on which it was made; *domain local*, meaning it would be visible only in the domain in which it was created; or *global*, meaning the group was visible on all trusted NT domains. The term *scope* is used to describe where a group can be visible and utilized. The NT groups are listed in Table 5.4.

Since none of these groups could be used in the previous Exchange releases, we were forced to use distribution lists to manage access to public folders and mailboxes in an easy way.

Table 5.4 Groups in Windows NT 4 domains.

Group Type	Scope	Typical Usage	Members
Local	On the member server or workstation on which it was made	Used for controlling access to local resources domain	Can contain local and global groups
Domain local	On all servers in the domain in which it was made	Used for controlling access to local resources in this domain	Can contain global groups and user accounts from any trusted domain
Global	On all servers in all trusted domains	Used for creating a group of domain users that would then be given access to resources in other domains	Can contain only users from the same domain

The consequence was that you often had to create two groups with the same members—one NT group controlling access to networks resources, and then a distribution list in Exchange with the same users, for controlling access to Exchange folders and for an easy way to send messages to this group.

For example, let's assume we have a project team that needs to share information on the file system, such as Word files or applications. They also want to have an easy way of sending mail to all members in this group, and to have exclusive access to some public folders. With NT 4 and Exchange 5.5, you solved this by creating a group in NT and a distribution list in Exchange. When the membership of this project team changed, you needed to update both the NT group and the distribution list. This was not practical since it was easy to forget to update one or the other.

In Windows 2000, you have a new group, new rules for membership for existing groups, and a new group type. This makes life much easier for the network administrator in general and the Exchange 2000 administrator in particular. However, Windows 2000 may run in mixed mode or native mode; this will affect how these groups behave and their features. In Table 5.5, you can see how the groups in Windows 2000 work.

If we summarize this, we will find that by running Windows 2000 in native mode, we will have both a new universal group and be able to nest the old global group. This is very good news if you have several domains, but it is not important if you only have one single domain. Besides these changes, Exchange 2000 offers new types of groups: security groups and distribution groups.

Table 5.5 Groups in Windows 2000.

Group Type	Mixed Mode, Can Contain	Native Mode, Can Contain	Can Be a Member Of	Can Be Granted Permission For
Domain Local	User accounts and global groups from any domain	User accounts, global groups, and universal groups from any domain in the forest; and domain local groups from the same domain	Domain local groups in the same domain	The domain in which the domain local group exists
Global	User accounts from the same domain	User accounts and global groups from the same domain	Universal and domain local groups in any domain, and global groups in the same domain	All domains in the forest
Universal	Cannot be used in mixed mode	User accounts, global groups, and other universal groups from any domain in the forest	Domain local and universal groups in any domain	All domains in the forest

Security Groups and Distribution Groups

A *Security Group* is exactly like the standard group type in Windows NT 4; it is used for assigning permissions to network resources, such as applications and folders. But there is one new thing—this group can now be mail-enabled; this means that this group will now show up in the global address list for our Exchange users. If you remember the example with the project team, we now have a very simple way of solving their needs—we simply create one security group for this team and make it mail-enabled; now this group can be used both for controlling access to the file system and to folders in Exchange 2000. This project team group will also be visible in the global address list, making it possible to send mail to all members of this group (assuming they all have mail accounts, of course).

A *Distribution Group* is a completely new concept, compared to the types of groups available in Windows NT. This group is equivalent to *Distribution Lists* in Exchange 5.5. It cannot be used for assigning permission to network resources, like the file system or printers. The whole purpose of distribution groups is to have a way of creating groups of mail accounts, which will be listed in the global address list. In fact, a distribution group cannot be used for assigning permission to public folders; if you try to do so, the group will automatically (and silently) be converted to a security group! Of course, this is logical, if you think about it; only security groups can be assigned access permission to any object, and if you try to use a distribution group for this, it must be converted. An interesting feature, but I wish Exchange 2000 provided some notification of this change.

Note: *If you are used to working with distribution lists in Exchange 5.5, it may be easy to forget that a security group is used for two purposes; to grant permissions and as a mail group. For example, if you have a security group displayed in the global address list, and you add a new member to this mailing group, don't forget that this new member will now also get access to all network resources this security group has been granted access permission.*

For a die-hard Exchange 5.5 administrator, it may come as a surprise that you cannot use the ESM tool to create groups; they are all created by the *Active Directory Users And Computers* tool, even if they are distribution groups meant only for Exchange 2000. To create any type of group in Windows 2000, follow these steps:

1. Start the *Active Directory Users And Computers* tool.
2. Right-click on the *Active Directory Users And Computers* node; connect to the domain where this group will be created.
3. Right-click on the container where this new group will be stored—for example, the *Users* folder—and select *New|Group*.
4. Give the new group a name (the Pre-Windows 2000 group name will be filled in automatically).

5. Select the *Group Scope*: Domain local, Global, or Universal (only available in native mode).
6. Select the *Group Type*: Security (default) or Distribution.
7. If Exchange 2000 is installed, you will then click *Next* (see Figure 5.11); or else click *OK* to close the window.
8. If Exchange 2000 is installed, you will now have the opportunity to mail-enable this group; see Figure 5.12. Note that the alias name will automatically be created, being identical to the group name if possible, but space characters will be removed. You cannot change this name now, but later you can.
9. Click *Finish* to close the window.

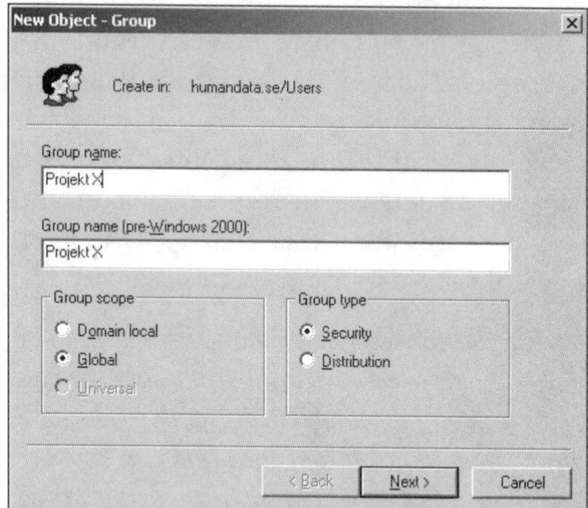

Figure 5.11
Creating a group.

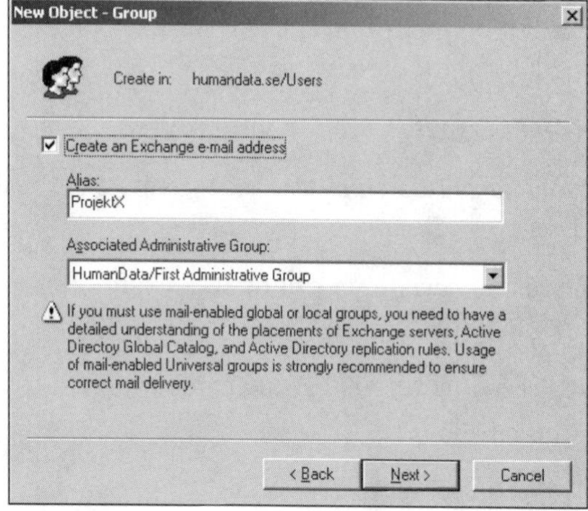

Figure 5.12
Mail-enabling a group.

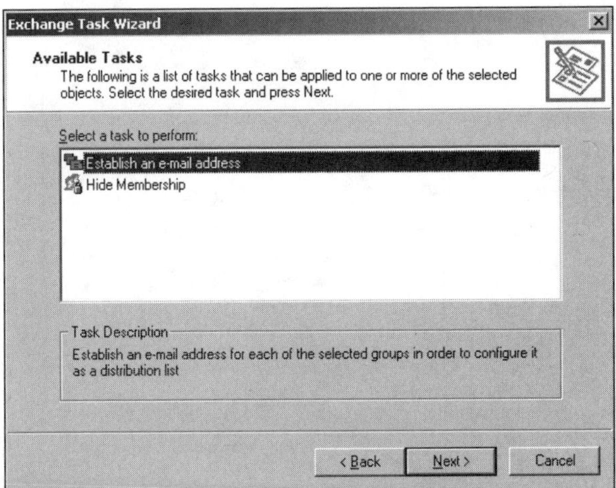

Figure 5.13
Using the Exchange Task Wizard to establish an email address.

Refresh the container where you created the new group; you will see it listed with its name and group type. If you want to mail-enable a group after it is created, just right-click it, then select *Exchange Tasks* to start the *Exchange Task Wizard*. Click on *Next*; select the task *Establish An E-Mail Address* (see Figure 5.13), then click *Next* again. Now you have the same picture as displayed in Figure 5.12 again. Select the administrative group to which you want to assign this group; after a few seconds you will see a summary, click *Finish* to close the window.

A summary: All groups are now created with the *Active Directory Users And Computers* tool; create security groups if you need to assign access permissions to network resources and to use them as groups in Exchange 2000. Create distribution groups if you want to create a group only for mail purposes; see also Decision Tree 5.1.

Visibility of Group Membership

Since all groups are now managed and replicated by Active Directory instead of the replication system in Exchange 5.5, there are some things a mail administrator needs to be aware of. All users and groups are copied from Active Directory to the global catalog; this information will then be replicated to global catalog servers in other domains. However, the membership of local domain and global groups will not be copied to the global catalog! So, for example, if a user in domain A sends a message to a global group created in domain B, then the Exchange server for domain A will not find any members. How is that solved? You have two methods.

- *Method 1*—The Exchange server in domain A will send an LDAP request to a domain controller in B, asking for the members of the global group—this assumes that there is a TCP/IP connection to the domain controller in B.

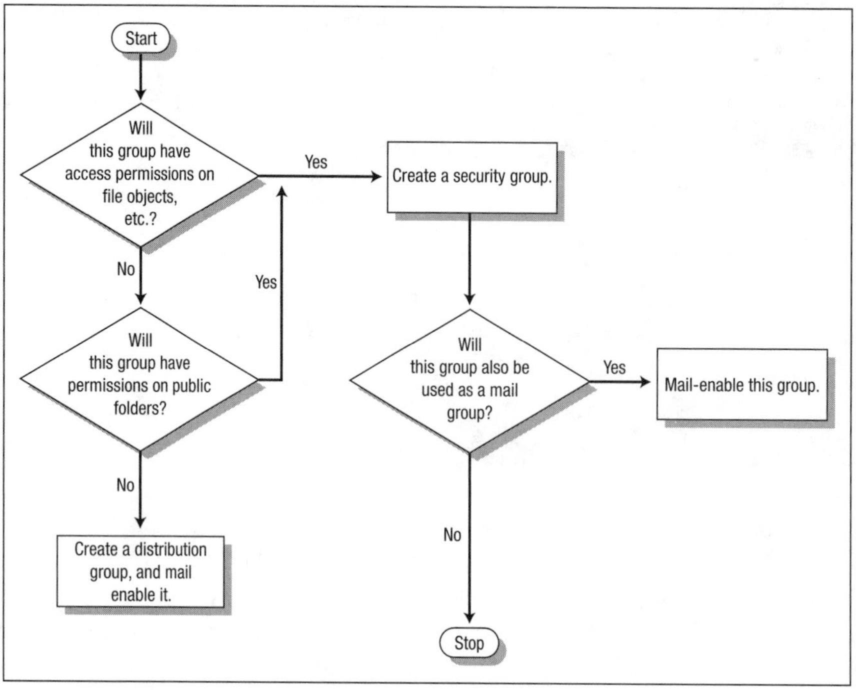

Start

Will this group have access permissions on file objects, etc.?

Yes

Create a security group.

No

Yes

Will this group have permissions on public folders?

Will this group also be used as a mail group?

Yes

Mail-enable this group.

No

Create a distribution group, and mail enable it.

No

Stop

Decision Tree 5.1
Selecting between a security group and a distribution group.

- *Method 2*—Use the properties for the group to define an expansion server; this is a server that takes care of all mail to this group, regardless of where the sender may be. With this method, the mail would be transferred from the Exchange server in A to the given expansion server, which in turn would expand the group and send a mail to each of its members; see Figure 5.14. This assumes there is an Exchange server in the domain where this group is created. Follow these steps to set the expansion server for a group:

1. Start the *Active Directory Users And Computers* tool.
2. Make sure the *Exchange Advanced* tab is displayed: Click on the *View* menu, and select *Advanced Features* if it's not already selected.
3. Open the properties for the group for which you want to set the expansion server.
4. Look at the *Exchange Advanced* tab (see Figure 5.14).
5. Set the *Expansion* server to a given Exchange server. The default is *Any Server In The Organization*, meaning that the sender's server will expand this group.
6. Click *OK* to close the property window.

However, there is a third method; all members of universal groups are copied to the global catalog and therefore are visible for all Exchange servers. This assumes that Windows 2000 is running in native mode, since universal groups are not available in mixed mode.

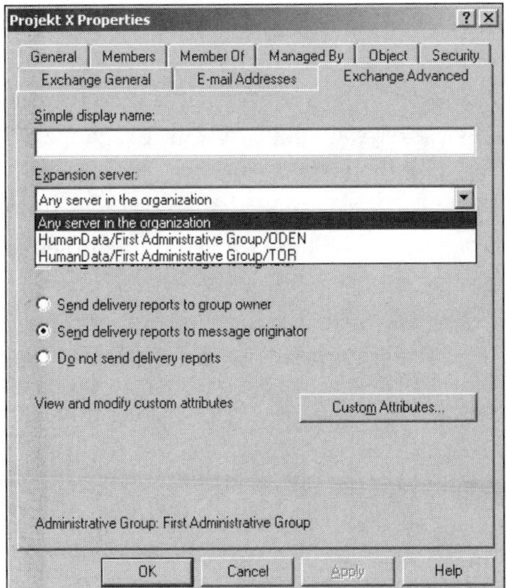

Figure 5.14
Defining an expansion server for a group.

One drawback with universal groups is the replication traffic it will generate every time the group membership is modified. If you have a large Exchange organization with many thousands of users, you must plan for this replication traffic generated by universal groups; it is best to use this type for groups that are fairly static in terms of their membership.

There is a practical limit to how many users you should have in a group, especially if it is used for mail purposes. You should not have more than 5,000 recipients in any one group, due to the overhead of expanding the list. In the Beta version of Exchange, this limit was hard coded, but this is no longer the case. However, if you have, say, 10,000 users, it is most effective to create two groups with 5,000 users each and then create a third group of which the first two groups are members. If the Exchange organization uses several large groups, it would be a good idea to point out an exclusive Exchange server for expanding these groups; that server should not have any other responsibilities since that would decrease their overall performance; for example, avoid using mailbox server or bridgehead server for this role.

The LDIFDE Tool

As previously mentioned, the LDAP protocol is an enhanced version of the older DAP protocol, which was specially designed for accessing X.500 directories. LDAP stands for *Lightweight Directory Access Protocol*, and is faster and easier to use than its predecessor, DAP. The network transport protocol is TCP/IP for LDAP and TP4/CLNP for DAP; this is also an important reason that DAP never made it. TP4 was never a big success in the PC-based network world.

As an Exchange 5.5 administrator, you are used to exporting data from the DIR.EDB database, making updates, and then importing the files again. The file format used in Exchange 5.5 is CSV—a text file with *Comma Separated Values*—a file format easy to import to MS Excel and other spreadsheet applications. Those days are gone now; in Exchange 2000, you will connect to the Active Directory instead, and the format you most probably will work with is a special text file format called LDIF: *LDAP Data Interchange Format*. Instead of separating each value with a comma character, you will get one attribute on each line. Export or import features in the Exchange System Manager or the Active Directory Users And Computers tools no longer exist, as they did in the Exchange 5.5 Admin program; you must use a standalone tool for exporting and importing users and other objects.

You have two tools you can use for exporting and importing data to the Active Directory database; one is the CSVDE tool, which uses the CSV file format, just as in previous Exchange versions. However, this tool cannot be used for creating Contact objects, so my recommendation is that you instead learn the more powerful LDIFDE tool, or the *LDIF Directory Exchange*. This tool is installed in all Windows 2000 servers, in the \Winnt\System32 directory; it can be copied to a Windows 2000 Professional server, if needed. It is a command line tool, with a lot of optional parameters; by typing “LDIFDE”, you will get a list of these commands:

```
C:\>ldifde
LDIF Directory Exchange
General Parameters
------------------
-i                Turn on Import Mode (The default is Export)
-f filename       Input or Output filename
-s servername     The server to bind to (Default to DC of logged in Domain)
-c FromDN ToDN    Replace occurrences of FromDN to ToDN
-v                Turn on Verbose Mode
-j                Log File Location
-t                Port Number (default = 389)
-u                Use Unicode format
-?                Help

Export Specific
---------------
-d RootDN         The root of the LDAP search (Default to Naming Context)
-r Filter         LDAP search filter (Default to "(objectClass=*)")
-p SearchScope    Search Scope (Base/OneLevel/Subtree)
-l list           List of attributes (comma separated) to look for in an LDAP
                  search
-o list           List of attributes (comma separated) to omit from input.
-g                Disable Paged Search.
-m                Enable the SAM logic on export.
-n                Do not export binary values
```

```
Import
------
-k              The import will go on ignoring 'Constraint Violation'
                and 'Object Already Exists' errors
-y              The import will use lazy commit for better performance

Credentials Establishment
-------------------------
Note that if no credentials is specified, LDIFDE will bind as the currently
logged on user, using SSPI.

-a UserDN [Password | *]             Simple authentication
-b UserName Domain [Password | *]    SSPI bind method

Example: Simple import of current domain
    ldifde -i -f INPUT.LDF

Example: Simple export of current domain
    ldifde -f OUTPUT.LDF

Example: Export of specific domain with credentials
    ldifde -m -f OUTPUT.LDF
           -b USERNAME DOMAINNAME *
           -s SERVERNAME
           -d "cn=users,DC=DOMAINNAME,DC=Microsoft,DC=Com"
           -r "(objectClass=user)"
```

As you can see, a lot of parameters are available, both for export and import to the Active Directory. Note that you can define a username and password when connecting—this is important since you want to control who can export the AD information and especially who can modify it. If you don't define any name, LDIFDE will use the account you are logged on as. Since there may be millions of objects with many hundreds of attributes each in the Active Directory, you probably want to select a subset of the information. The parameter –R is used for this; use it for filtering what objects to export. For example, if you want to export all users to a file named Users.ldf, you would type the following:

```
C:\>ldifde -f Users.ldf -r "(objectClass=user)"
Connecting to "oden.humandata.se"
Logging in as current user using SSPI
Exporting directory to file Users.ldf
Searching for entries...
Writing out entries......................
      22 entries exported

      The command has completed successfully
```

The result would be a text file with a subset of the attributes available for all users, 22 in this example; there will be one attribute listed per line, with the attribute name first and then the value. There will be one empty line between each listed user object in this file. If we pick out one single user from the file Users.ldf:, the information will look something similar to this:

```
dn: CN=Göran Husman,CN=Users,DC=humandata,DC=se
changetype: add
homeMDB:
 CN=Mailbox Store (ODEN),CN=First Storage Group,CN=InformationStore, CN=ODEN,
 CN=OServers,CN=First Administrative Group,CN=AdministrativeGroups,
 CN=HumanData,CN=Microsoft Exchange,CN=Services,CN=Configuration,DC=humandata,
 DC=se
memberOf: CN=Info@humandata.se,CN=Users,DC=humandata,DC=se
memberOf: CN=Administrators,CN=Builtin,DC=humandata,DC=se
accountExpires: 0
adminCount: 1
badPasswordTime: 126276546182607088
badPwdCount: 0
codePage: 0
cn:: R802cmFuIEhlc21hbg==
countryCode: 0
displayName:: R802cmFuIEhlc21hbg==
mail: goran@humandata.se
givenName:: R802cmFu
instanceType: 4
lastLogoff: 0
lastLogon: 126279829939637552
legacyExchangeDN:
 /o=HumanData/ou=First Administrative Group/cn=Recipients/cn=goran
lockoutTime: 0
logonCount: 120
logonHours:: ////////////////////////////
distinguishedName::
 Q049R802cmFuIEhlc21hbixDTj1Vc2VycyxEQz1odW1hbmRhdGEsREM9c2U=
objectCategory: CN=Person,CN=Schema,CN=Configuration,DC=humandata,DC=se
objectClass: user
objectGUID:: KHlJLGB9hk2VPiIqouMirA==
objectSid:: AQUAAAAAAAUVAAAAgzOrRg/4YB34n7ROWgQAAA==
primaryGroupID: 513
proxyAddresses: smtp:hostmaster@humandata.se
proxyAddresses: smtp:goran.husman@humandata.se
proxyAddresses: SMTP:goran@humandata.se
proxyAddresses: X400:c=us;a= ;p=HumanData;o=Exchange;s=Husman;g=Goeran;
pwdLastSet: 126259555429412800
```

```
name:: R802cmFuIEh1c21hbg==
sAMAccountName: goranH
sAMAccountType: 805306368
showInAddressBook:
 CN=Default Global Address List,CN=All Global Address Lists,CN=Address Lists
 Container,CN=HumanData,CN=Microsoft Exchange,CN=Services,CN=Configuration,
 DC=humandata,DC=se
showInAddressBook:
 CN=All Users,CN=All Address Lists,CN=Address Lists Container,CN=HumanData,
  CN=Microsoft Exchange,CN=Services,CN=Configuration,DC=humandata,DC=se
sn: Husman
textEncodedORAddress: c=us;a= ;p=HumanData;o=Exchange;s=Husman;g=Goeran;
userAccountControl: 66048
userPrincipalName: goranH@humandata.se
uSNChanged: 14551
uSNCreated: 11388
whenChanged: 20010228155706.0Z
whenCreated: 20010119170205.0Z
homeMTA:
 CN=Microsoft MTA,CN=ODEN,CN=Servers,CN=First Administrative Group,
 CN=Administrative Groups,CN=HumanData,CN=Microsoft Exchange,CN=Services,
 CN=Configuration,DC=humandata,DC=se
msExchHomeServerName:
 /o=HumanData/ou=First Administrative Group/cn=Configuration/cn=Servers/
 cn=ODEN
mailNickname: goran
mDBUseDefaults: TRUE
msExchMailboxGuid:: 0itWvjPy4U+zNED6jNQXyw==
msExchMailboxSecurityDescriptor::
 AQAEgHgAAACUAAAAAAAAAAABQAAAAEAGQAAQAAAAACFAADAAIAAQEAAAAAAAUKAAAAdABhAC4AcwBl
 AAAAAAAAAAAAAAAAAAAAAAAAAAAAAAAAAAAAAAAAAAAAAAAAAAAAAAAAAAAAAAAAAAAAAAAAAAAA
 AAAAAAAAAQUAAAAAAAAAUVAAAAgz0rRg4YB34n7R09AEAAAEFAAAAAAAAFFQAAAIM9K0YP+GAd+J+0d
 PQBAAA=
msExchALObjectVersion: 56
msExchPoliciesIncluded:
 {7FAD2552-59A7-4A81-98E2-317799F3374E},{26491CFC-9E50-4857-861B-0CB8DF22B5D7}
msExchUserAccountControl: 0
```

By default, the LDIFDE tool will list these attributes shown above. However, there are more than 500 Exchange-related attributes for each mailbox-enabled user, and besides these, there are several hundred other standard attributes per user! But let's take a closer look at the default listed attributes. As Exchange administrators, we are usually only interested in a few of them. Table 5.6 offers a short description of these Exchange-related attributes.

Note that attributes that may have a non-U.S. ASCII character will be Base-64 encoded; this is described in more detail in Chapter 4.

Table 5.6 Exchange-related attributes listed as defaults by the LDIFDE tool.

Attribute	Description
dn	Distinguished name (the unique directory name of this object)
changetype	Used mainly when importing a file; can be Add, Delete, Modify
homeMDB	Points to the Exchange server, what administrative group and storage group this user belongs to
memberOf	Lists the groups this user is a member of (may be several lines)
mail	The primary email address
givenName	The first name, will be Base-64 encoded if containing non-U.S. characters
proxyAddresses	Alternative email addresses (may be several lines)
showInAddressBook	Lists the address book where this user will be listed
sn	Surname, i.e., the last name, will be Base-64 encoded if containing non-U.S. characters
homeMTA	Usually the same information as the homeMDB
msExchHomeServerName:	The name of the Exchange server this user belongs to
mailNickname	The email alias name

Sometimes you want to select what users to export, and also to define the attributes you want to list. Again, you use the –R switch for creating a search filter. Let's say you want to list all users with the surname "Husman." But you don't want the default list of 50 attributes; you just want a few of them. Use the –L parameter for defining the attributes to list, like this:

```
ldifde -f Users.ldf -r "(&(objectclass=user)(sn="Husman"))" -l
  "cn,sn,givenname, samaccountname"
```

There are some things you should note here; first, the search filter is a combination of two conditions: (objectclass=user) and (sn=Husman). Note that each condition is defined within a pair of parentheses. Then both of these conditions are in turn also within a pair of parentheses that have an ampersand (&) character in the beginning; this tells LDAP that it is an "Add" operation; we want both of these conditions to be true. It is important that the "&" character comes before the two conditions; LDAP would not give the same search result if you type like this: ((objectclass=user)&(sn="Husman")).

The second thing to note is that the list of attributes wanted, "cn,sn,givenname,sam-accountname," can be in any order; the result would still list them in the order in which they are found in the Active Directory. The result from this LDIFDE search would look like this (and again, some attributes, but not all, containing a non-U.S. ASCII character would be Base-64 encoded, like cn):

```
dn: CN=Göran Husman,CN=Users,DC=humandata,DC=se
changetype: add
cn:: R802cmFuIEh1c21hbg==
```

```
givenName:: R802cmFu
sAMAccountName: goranH
sn: Husman

dn: CN=Marina Husman,CN=Users,DC=humandata,DC=se
changetype: add
cn: Marina Husman
givenName: Marina
sAMAccountName: MarinaH
sn: Husman

dn: CN=Alex Husman,CN=Users,DC=humandata,DC=se
changetype: add
cn: Alex Husman
givenName: Alex
sAMAccountName: alexH
sn: Husman
```


So it's rather easy to pick out the attributes you want listed, now that you know how to use the -L parameter. The trick is to remember all the attribute names, since there are many hundreds of them. Use the Active Directory Schema tool to see them all; this tool was described in the section "Active Directory Domain Partitions," earlier in this chapter.

You can also use the LDIFDE tool to make changes to existing user attributes, just as you could in Exchange 5.5. The method is a bit more complex, due to the format of the LDIFDE file, but it can be done; by the time you read this, somebody has probably made a utility that makes it a lot easier. Until then, use these steps:

1. Export the users you want to modify by using the LDIFDE tool and its search flag -F; define the attributes you are interested in.
2. Use a text editor to make your modifications to the attributes. A tip is to remove users and attributes you don't want to modify; that makes your file smaller and faster to import; it also helps you focus on what you want to change. Note that the attribute dn is used to identify the user during the import process later on—don't remove that attribute!
3. Replace *changetype=add* with *changetype=modify* for all users you want to modify.
4. For each attribute to modify, type a new line with the word *replace:* and the attribute you want to modify; on the next line, type the attribute and its new value (but no quotation marks, unless you really want it; however, 8-bit characters are okay). On the third line, type a single hyphen ("-") to signal that the new definition of this attribute is finished.
5. Make sure there is an empty line between all users you want to modify. The last line in the file must also have a hyphen after the modified attribute.

For example, to modify the company name to MyCompany and the street address to Markörgatan 4 for two users, you would create a file like this:

```
dn: CN=Göran Husman,CN=Users,DC=humandata,DC=se
changetype: modify
replace: company
company: MyCompany
-
replace: StreetAddress
StreetAddress: Markörgatan 4
-

dn: CN=Marina Husman,CN=Users,DC=humandata,DC=se
changetype: modify
replace: company
company: MyCompany
-
replace: StreetAddress
StreetAddress: Markörgatan 4
-
```

If we assume this file is named Users.ldf, you import these changes using this simple line:

```
LDIFDE -i -f Users.ldf
```

***Tip:** Even though some attributes are exported as Base-64 encoded values, you can still type 8-bit characters when you modify them using the method above; the LDAPDE will take care of this conversion, if needed. For example, as you may recall, the givenName will be Base-64 encoded if it contains any non-U.S. ASCII characters; but you can still type any 8-bit character for this attribute in the import file.*

Finally, if you want to delete users using the LDIFDE tool, simply create a list of all users to delete with the **changetype: delete** command and then import it as in the previous example. Note that you must separate each user with an empty line, like this:

```
dn: CN=Christer Wallberg,CN=Users,DC=humandata,DC=se
changetype: delete

dn: CN=Kjell Dyrstad,CN=Users,DC=humandata,DC=se
changetype: delete
```

Replication of Active Directory Information

As we described in the beginning of this chapter, the Active Directory is a directory service built on the Exchange 5.5 directory service and its Dir.edb database. As an Exchange administrator, it is important that you understand the AD replication process, since it contains all mailbox users, groups, and server configurations. Let's compare how these two systems replicate directory updates.

Directory Replication in Exchange 5.5

If you know how Exchange 5.5 manages its Dir.edb database, it will help you understand Active Directory. In Exchange 5.5, all servers had their own directory where users, distribution lists, and server configurations were stored. All servers belonging to the same Exchange 5.5 site shared this information by an automatic replication process running every five minutes; see Figure 5.15. This compares to a small town where everyone knows everything about everyone else; all news, like someone getting married or divorced, will spread to all members of this town within minutes. Exchange 5.5 uses the DS and the RPC protocol to replicate updates, while the townspeople use voice and phone messages instead.

This type of directory design is called *Multimaster*, due to the fact that each Exchange 5.5 server has a complete writeable copy of each server's DIR.EDB database in its site. For example, in the site shown in Figure 5.15, you could:

1. Connect to server "London" with the Exchange 5.5 Admin program.
2. Modify the configuration settings for "Paris"; this will be stored in the DIR.EDB database on "London".
3. Within five minutes, this new setting will be automatically replicated from "London" to "Paris".

This is an elegant feature; connect to any Exchange server and modify any server in that site. However, it is not possible to modify a server in another site. The directory of servers belonging to other sites will be copied as read-only information (see Figure 5.16). But this information is enough to create a global address list with all users from all sites, and all servers can also create an organization-wide routing table, with all possible connections, regardless of where that connector may be installed.

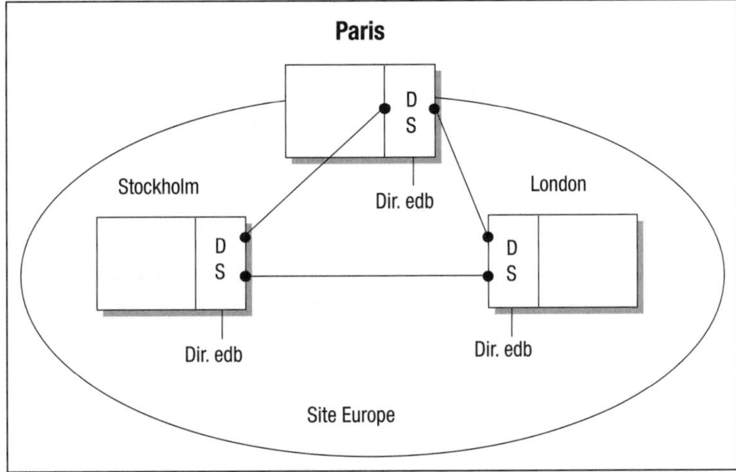

Figure 5.15
Directory replication within an Exchange 5.5 site.

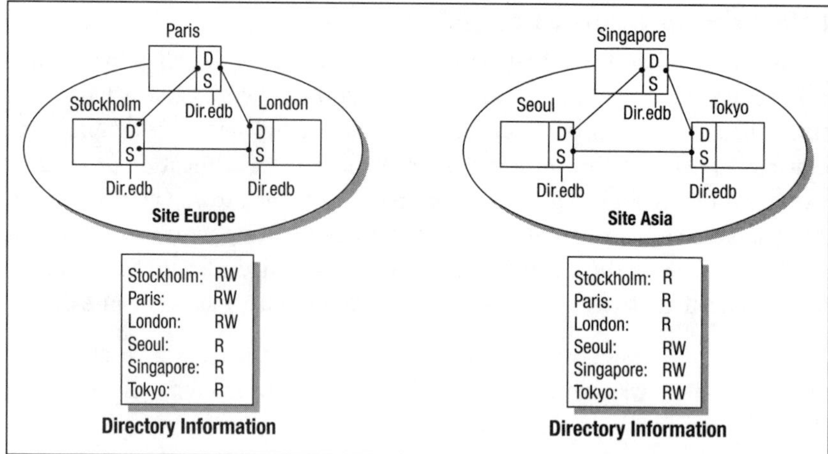

Figure 5.16
Directory replication between several Exchange 5.5 sites.

Note that before the directory information can replicate between the sites, a *directory replication connector* must be installed in one server on each site; this is also called a *bridgehead server*. In Figure 5.16, London and Seoul work in pairs as directory replication bridgehead servers. However, this directory replication connector does not physically move any directory data between these bridgehead servers; all replication data is sent as system messages by a transport connector, like a site connector or an X.400 Connector, which also must exist before the replication can occur.

Directory Replication between Active Directory Servers

Just as Exchange 5.5 uses the site as a boundary for direct directory replication, there is a very similar concept called *sites* in the Active Directory domain, used in the same way. The AD site is usually defined as one or more IP subnets connected by high-speed links. So what is a high-speed link? It depends on how many objects there are in the AD and how many changes need to be replicated between the domain controllers. Large organizations with millions of objects in the AD may need 10Mbps, and a small organization with just two domain controllers may be fine with 128Kbps.

Just as you could create and join Exchange 5.5 sites, you can control the AD domain sites. When you installed the first Windows 2000 domain controller, a site was automatically created; this site is called *Default-First-Site-Name* and the new domain controller will be its first member. Any new domain controller installed on the same IP subnet will automatically be a member of this site.

Intra-Site Replication

Replication within one AD site, also known as intra-site replication, is similar to the replication between Exchange 5.5 servers, but there are also great differences. The similarities are that the domain controllers replicate directly with each other, based on Remote

Procedure Call (RPC), and the server uses Update Sequence Numbers (USNs) to keep track of updates in the directory. These are some of the more important differences:

- All domain controllers will no longer replicate with all others in the same site. The Knowledge Consistency Checker (KCC) process will automatically calculate a routing ring topology between the domain controllers, so there will never be more than three replication hops within this site.
- Replication is triggered every five minutes, except for some important updates like password changes or account lockouts; whenever KCC detects such a change, it will start the replication immediately.
- The replication traffic is uncompressed.
- Only changed attributes are replicated, not complete objects as in Exchange 5.5.

This means that the KCC process is even more important than it was in Exchange 5.5. If one of the domain controllers goes offline, or a new server is installed, it will automatically recalculate a new replication route. The demand for a high-speed network gets a bit clearer when you know that the traffic is uncompressed and all replication is instant. But the fact that AD is only replicating changed attributes instead of the complete object, as in Exchange 5.5, dramatically lowers the size of the replicated data. If you change the display name in Exchange 5.5, this will result in a replication message of around 5K, whereas in Active Directory replication, this will be about 500 bytes.

To force the five-minute replication within the site, as you could in Exchange 5.5, use the Active Directory Sites And Services tool and follow these steps:

1. Open the *Active Directory Sites And Services* tool.
2. Expand the *Sites*, the name of the Site, for example the *Default-First-Site-Name*, and the *Servers* folder.
3. Expand the server you want to update, and select the *NTDS Settings* object under it.
4. In the right pane, right-click on the object *<Automatically Generated>* and select *Replicate Now*.

Inter-Site Replication

If the network connection between two geographical locations is too slow, you need to create a new site. The network speed between sites is expected to be slower than within a site, so the AD replication system is designed to give you several possibilities for controlling this traffic:

- You can define a site link, similar to the DRC in Exchange 5.5.
- You can select between two communication protocols: RPC over IP, or SMTP.
- The replication is scheduled (the default is every three hours).
- All data is compressed with a ratio up to 10:1.

As within a site, you can also force an update of the replication process, if you don't want to wait three hours until the next replication; follow the same steps as described above for updating domain controllers in the same site.

If you need to create a new site, follow these steps:

1. Open the *Active Directory Sites And Services* tool.
2. Right-click on the *Sites* container; select *New Site*.
3. Give the new site a name and select a link object (see Figure 5.17).
4. Click *OK* to close the window. You will get a note that reminds you of all the steps you need to complete before this new site will be operational. See Figure 5.18.

When you install new domain controllers, they will automatically join a site, depending on what IP subnet the server belongs to; the DNS server will keep track of all sites and their subnets. You can also move a server manually between sites by following these steps:

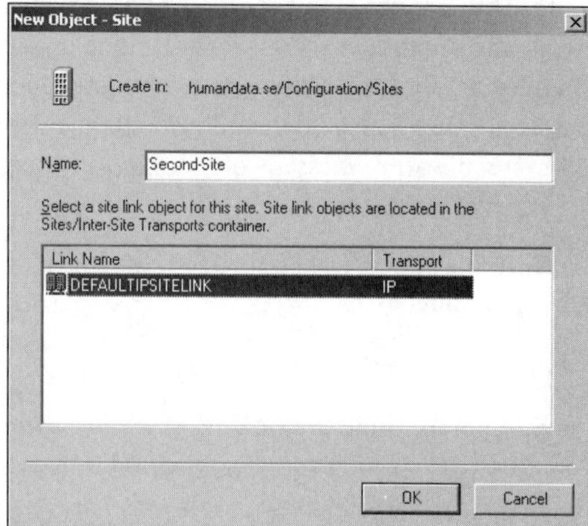

Figure 5.17
Creating a new AD site.

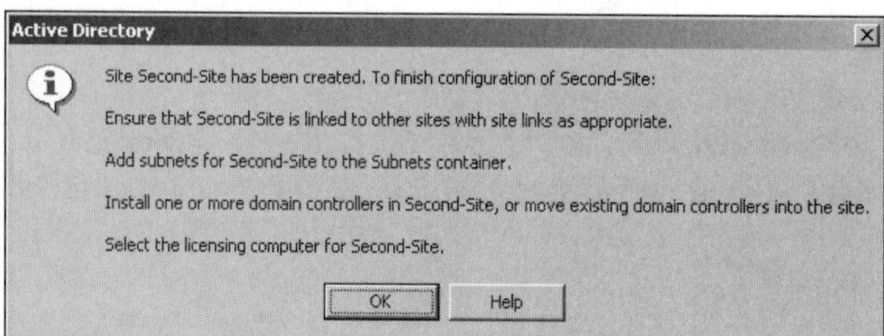

Figure 5.18
A reminder of what needs to be done with the new site.

1. Open the *Active Directory Sites And Services* tool.
2. Expand the *Sites* folder and then the site where the servers are now.
3. Expand the *Servers* folder.
4. Right-click on the server name; select *Move*.
5. Select the new site for this server; see Figure 5.19.

The replication between the sites is by default three hours, as earlier described. This is normally acceptable in most organizations and should only be changed after thorough planning. Since you can force the replication when needed, it is not a good idea to set a short replication interval just to get fast updates between the sites. This will increase the load on the network and the domain controllers, without really gaining so much. If you think about it, how often do you change the attributes of a user or how often will you add or delete users? Large organizations may do updates maybe 20 times per day, and smaller maybe less than 5 times a day. These updates are usually not time critical, so a three-hour replication would be sufficient in most cases; if not, use the manual update method described earlier. If you need to change the replication schedule, follow these steps:

1. Open the *Active Directory Sites And Services* tool.
2. Expand the *Sites* folder and the *Inter-Site Transports* folder.
3. Expand the *IP* folder for RPC links, or the *SMTP* folder for SMTP links.
4. Open the properties for the site link you want to modify—for example, the *DEFAULTIPSITELINK*.
5. On the *General* tab, set the replication interval on the *Replicate Every* field; see Figure 5.20.
6. If needed, you can also use the *Change Schedule* button to set times when the replication process will be active; by default, it will run 24 hours per day.

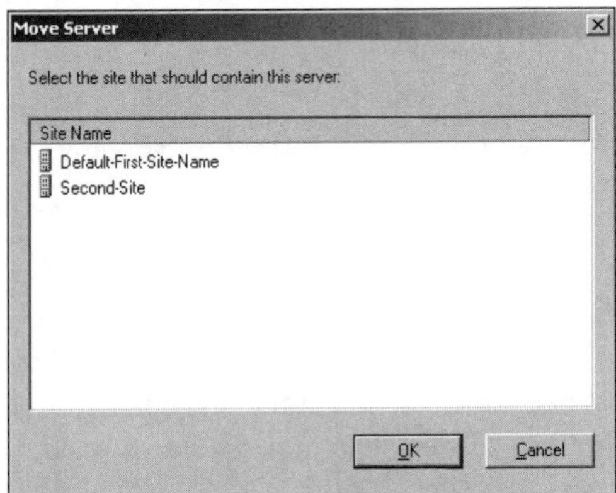

Figure 5.19
Moving a domain controller to a new site.

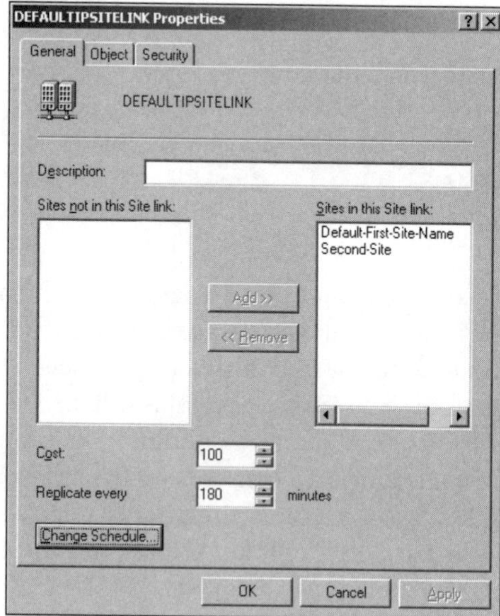

Figure 5.20
Setting the replication interval for a site link.

Global Catalog

Let's summarize what we know about Active Directory and its replication so far:

- A domain is a boundary for the replication of AD data; no domain-specific information, like users and groups, is visible outside the domain.
- The configuration partition and schema partition are, however, replicated to all domains.
- On the physical level, domain controllers are grouped into sites. The KCC process takes care of building a replication topology within the site.
- Most updates in the site are replicated within five minutes; however, some critical information, like password changes and account lockouts, are replicated immediately.
- If the physical network is divided into several IP subnets connected by low network connections, we may need to create new sites for our domain controllers.
- Replications between sites are defined by site links; the default is three-hour replication intervals.

So a natural question now is how can we see users belonging to domains other than ours? The answer is simple: Part of the private domain information is in fact replicated between the domains. This is how it works: At least one server, by default the first domain controller in our forest, has the responsibility to store information about other domains besides itself; this domain controller is called the *global catalog server*, or the *GC*. The information in the GC is used for several purposes, but since this is a book about Exchange, we will focus on mail-related tasks; the GC stores the global address list used by our Outlook clients. Exchange 2000 servers will also use it for checking addresses and expanding mail-enabled groups. However, not all domain-specific information is stored in the GC; that would simply be too much and would restrict how large a Windows 2000 forest could be. Table 5.7 lists some of the more than 100 attributes that are stored in the GC after Exchange 2000 is installed.

As you can see, nearly all of these attributes are replicated to the GC first after you have installed the first Exchange 2000 server. Almost all user attributes that were listed in the global address book in previous Exchange versions are also in Exchange 2000. It is also interesting to see which attributes are not replicated to the GC: Home Postal Address, Assistant, and Employee Number! This means that Outlook clients belonging to domains other than mine will not see my home postal address or my assistant's name. However, users belonging to my domain will see all my information, since the GC has access to the complete domain partition for its local domain.

Table 5.7 Common Exchange 2000-related attributes stored in the GC.

Attribute	LDAP Name	Added by Exchange
First Name	GivenName	Yes
Last Name	Sn	Yes
Display Name	DisplayName	Yes
Alias Name	MailNickname	Yes
City	L	Yes
State	St	Yes
Country	C	Yes
Job Title	Title	Yes
Company	Company	Yes
Department	Department	Yes
Office	PhysicalDeliveryOfficeName	Yes
Telephone	TelephoneNumber	Yes
Home Phone	HomePhone	Yes
Street	Street	Yes
Street Address	StreetAddress	Yes
Manager	Manager	No
SMTP Address	Mail	Yes
Custom Attribute#	ExtensionAttribute#	Yes

Adding New Attributes to the Global Catalog

You can add new attributes that will be replicated to the global catalog, by making this attribute visible to all Exchange users, regardless of what domain they belong to. However, you must select a proper time to do this expansion, since every time a new attribute is configured to be replicated to the GC, this will trigger a complete replication of all objects in the GC database. You must also be aware that each new attribute will result in a larger GC and therefore in increased replication traffic.

The replication process between global catalog servers is much more effective than the directory replication process in Exchange 5.x, where all servers by design are replicating all attributes for a modified user to all servers in its Site, even if just one of the users' attributes has been modified! The network traffic generated by GC replication in Exchange 2000 are considerably less than the corresponding directory replication in Exchange 5.x. This means that if your current network can handle the replication traffic in Exchange 5.x, there will be no problem with the GC replication, when this organization upgrades to Windows 2000 and Exchange 2000. To add new attributes listed in the global catalog, follow these steps:

1. Open the *Active Directory Schema* tool.
2. Expand the *Active Directory Schema* folder and then the *Attributes* folder.
3. Select the attribute you want to add to the GC.
4. Open the properties and select *Replicate This Attribute To The Global Catalog* and then click *OK*; see Figure 5.21.

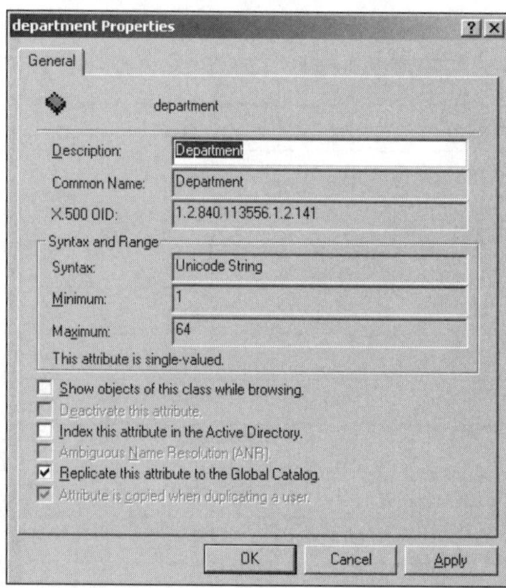

Figure 5.21
Adding new attributes to the GC.

The best time to expand the GC with new attributes is directly after you have installed Exchange 2000, since then there are no mail-enabled users in the organization. If you are using any custom-made application that uses Exchange, check to see if it expects any particular attribute to work; if so, make sure it is added to the GC.

Adding New Global Catalog Servers

If your Exchange organization has only one domain then the global catalog is not interesting for you, since all directory information is available to all users and servers anyway. But if there are several domains, you need to plan for how many GC servers you'll need and which domain controllers should be GCs. As you may remember, there is only one GC by default, even for multidomain forests. So if we have three domains, Europe, U.S., and Asia, and the only GC is in Europe, this would force all clients in U.S. and Asia to connect to the GC in Europe for access to the global address list in their Outlook client. That is not acceptable for performance reasons, and maybe not even possible for technical reasons.

Figure 5.22 depicts an Outlook client connected to an Exchange server in Singapore; when this Outlook client selects the address button, the client will request to see the global address list. However, there is no domain controller in the Asia domain that has the global address list, so the client is directed, by the DNS where the GC servers are listed, to the Stockholm server in domain Europe. Clearly, this is not a good design, but we can improve it by installing more local global catalog servers, at least one per domain.

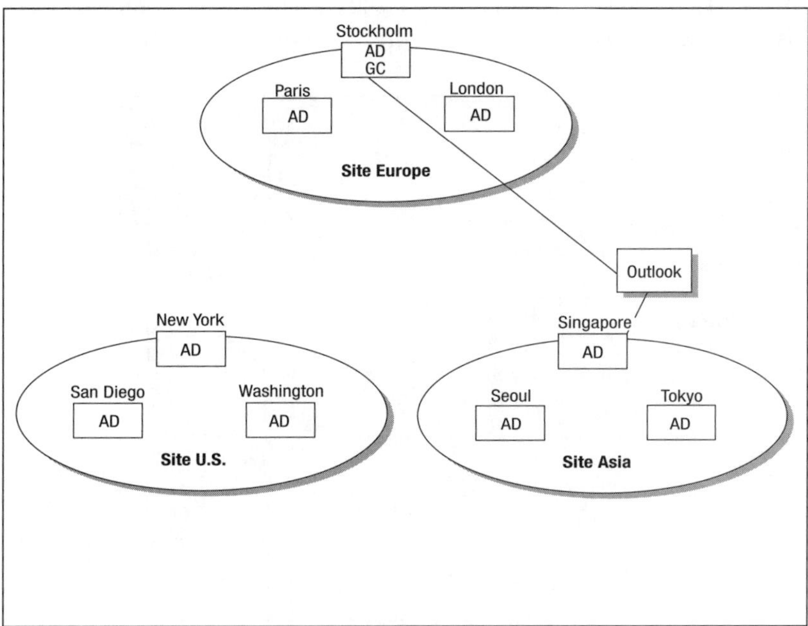

Figure 5.22
Three domains but only one global catalog server.

One more thing—a GC is also used when network clients log on to the Windows 2000 system; if you don't have a local GC, it will take a long time to log on. The general recommendation is to have one GC for each AD site. If you are running Windows 2000 in a mixed environment with Windows NT domain controllers, there must be one GC per domain. It may be tempting to make all domain controllers GCs, but that would increase the replication traffic; as always, it is a balance between trying to get fast access to the data and keeping the replication down to a minimum.

Follow these steps to make a domain controller a global catalog server; see also Figure 5.23:

1. Open the *Active Directory Sites And Services* tool.
2. Expand the *Sites* folder, and then the site where you want a new GC.
3. Expand the *Servers* folder and then the server you want as a GC.
4. Open the properties for the *NTDS Settings*; select the *Global Catalog* checkbox.
5. Click *OK* to close the window.

The actual data in the global catalog is stored in the NTDS.DIT database, i.e. the Active Directory database. When you activate the GC for a domain controller, it gets a new partition in the Active Directory, besides the previous tree partitions: domain, configuration, and schema. The GC will also have a complete copy of all information in the configuration and schema partitions; this means that the GC will have a copy of all objects in the complete forest, but only a subset of attributes for objects in the domain partition. The replication process between GC servers uses the Active Directory replication system.

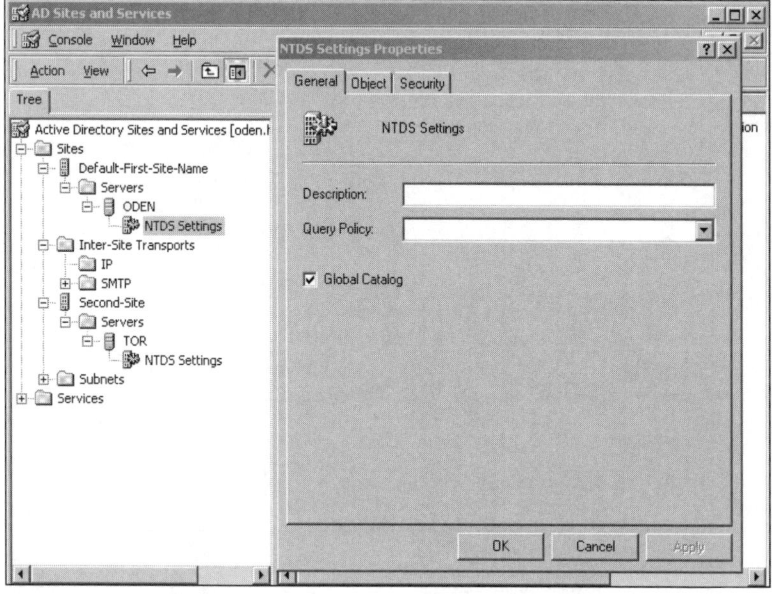

Figure 5.23
Creating a global catalog on a domain controller.

How Exchange 2000 Interacts with Active Directory

All Outlook clients use the global catalog for accessing all address lists, except their own personal contacts or Public Folder contacts. Older versions of Outlook, like Outlook 97 or Outlook 98, have no knowledge about global catalog servers and expect to find the address lists on the Exchange server. When such a client sends a MAPI DS request for the global address list to the Exchange 2000 server, it sends this request to a *DSProxy.dll* process; this, in turn, sends the MAPI request to the nearest global catalog server. The response is received by the DSProxy, who, in turn, sends it back to the Outlook client; see Figure 5.24.

Even though more steps are involved here compared to previous Exchange versions, still very little overhead is required—only six extra network frames; this makes it an acceptable solution for all organizations that still use older Outlook versions, although it is recommended to upgrade to Outlook 2000 when possible.

The Outlook 2000 and later clients know about the global catalog. However, the very first time after you have started an Outlook session, it contacts its Exchange 2000 server when looking for an address list; the Exchange server replies by sending a referral to the nearest global catalog server, and from now on Outlook 2000 uses that GC for all address lookups; see Figure 5.25.

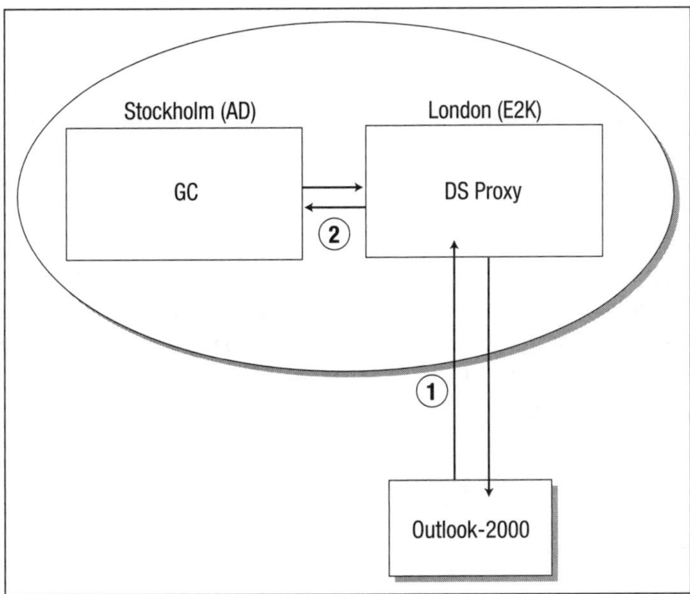

Figure 5.24
How older Outlook clients get access to the global address list.

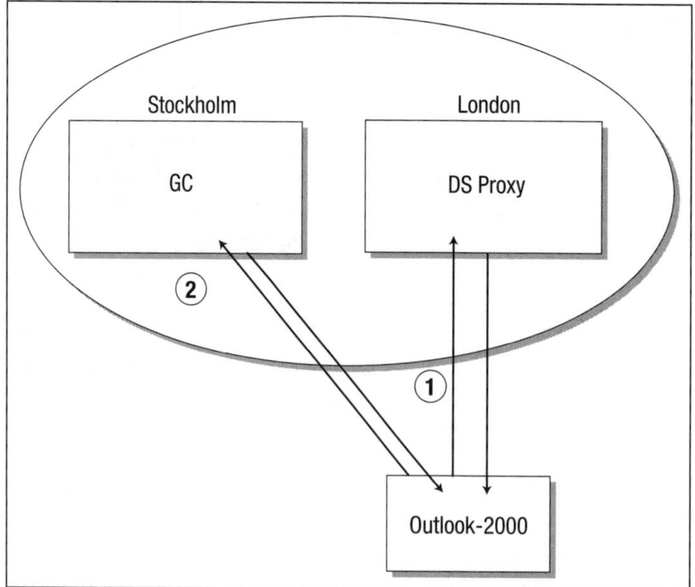

Figure 5.25
How Outlook 2000 clients access the global address list.

Outlook 2000 stores this referral information in its MAPI profile in the Registry:

```
HKEY_CURRENT_USER\Software\Microsoft\Windows NT\CurrentVersion\Windows Messaging
Subsystem\Profiles\<profile name>\dca740…2fe182
Value name: 001e6602
Value type: String
Value data: <The DNS name of the GC server>
```

If this GC server gets offline, you must restart the Outlook 2000 client; it will again ask the Exchange 2000 server for a new referral, meaning another GC server. If needed, you may disable this feature so Outlook 2000 will behave exactly like older Outlook clients; use the Registry parameter for this:

```
HKEY_LOCAL_MACHINE\System\CurrentControlSet\Services\MSExchangeSA\Parameters
Value name: No RFR Service
Value type: DWORD
Value data: 1
```

More about Directory Access

To assist older client protocols in accessing information in the domain controller and the global catalog, and to assist its own message categorizer and store process, Exchange 2000 will proxy such requests. Exchange 2000 servers need to access the domain controller for two primary directory activities: address book lookups and configuration data lookups.

Address Book Lookups

Whenever an Exchange 2000 server needs to look up the address book, for example to expand a mail-enabled group, the server will first try to contact a local domain controller; if this domain controller cannot resolve the query, Exchange sends the request to a global catalog. If there is more than one GC in the same AD site, it will use these on a round-robin basis. The locations of the domain controllers and global catalogs are listed in the DNS server. If you want the Exchange server to go to a preferred domain controller, use the following Registry setting:

```
HKEY_LOCAL_MACHINE\System\CurrentControlSet\Services\MSExchangeDSAccess\
  Profiles\Default\UserGC1
Value name: HostName
Value type: String
Value data: <DNS name to GC server>
```

You must also add this Registry entry to the same folder. Without it this will not work!

```
Value name: IsGC
Value type: DWORD
Value data: 1 (meaning true)
```

Configuration Data Lookups

Whenever an Exchange 2000 server needs to look up configuration data, such as delivery restrictions and routing information, it can connect to any domain controller within its local domain, since the configuration partition is replicated to all domain controllers within the forest. If needed, you could set what domain controller a particular Exchange 2000 server should contact for configuration data; if this server later does not answer any queries, it will resort to the default method of querying the DNS server. Set the preferred domain controller like this:

```
HKEY_LOCAL_MACHINE\System\CurrentControlSet\Services\MSExchangeDSAccess\
  Profiles\Default\UserDC1
Value name: HostName
Value type: String
Value data: <DNS name to DC server>
```

You must also add this Registry entry to the same folder. Without it this will not work!

```
Value name: IsGC
Value type: DWORD
Value data: 0 (meaning false)
```

The Directory Access Cache

In order to improve the performance for address lookups done by the DSAccess.dll on a global catalog, each Exchange 2000 server has a cache for this type of lookup—the *DSAccess Cache*. For each new lookup request, Exchange will first check the cache before sending the request to the global catalog server. This has two positive effects: The network traffic will be lower, since the Exchange server can find the answer in its own cache, and the load on the global catalog will be reduced.

This cache will store any retrieved information for a certain time period, or up to a given size limit. These two values can be set by a Registry entry, and if increased will result in a better effect on the cache. Note, however, that increasing these values will also increase the burden of system resources on the server; so make sure you check this server often after you have made this change. By default, all information will be stored up to 10 minutes in the cache, and a size limit is set to 4MB. Use the Windows 2000 System Monitor to check how effective the cache is by measuring the numbers of cache hits and misses.

Note: *Any MAPI DS address lookups that the Exchange server receives from older Outlook clients will be passed on directly to the global catalog server, without going through the DSAccess and its cache. It's therefore not a good idea to increase these cache settings in an attempt to increase the MAPI address lookups!*

Use this Registry setting to enable or disable the cache:

```
HKEY_LOCAL_MACHINE\System\CurrentControlSet\Services\MSExchangeDSAccess
Value name: CachingEnabled
Value type: DWORD
Value data: 1 (enabled-default) or 2 (disabled)
```

Set the expiry time for cached entries by this value:

```
HKEY_LOCAL_MACHINE\System\CurrentControlSet\Services\MSExchangeDSAccess\
  Instance0
Value name: CacheTTL
Value type: DWORD
Value data: 600 (seconds = 10 minutes default)
```

The size of the cache can be controlled in two ways: by limiting the number of entries in the cache or by limiting the total size of memory the cache will have. Each cached entry takes about 3.6KB of memory; there is a lower limit of 2MB of the cache, due to the memory the cache itself needs to work. If you want to limit the memory demands for the cache, it's better to limit the size of the cache rather than to limit the number of entries. You can set these two entries with these Registry settings:

```
HKEY_LOCAL_MACHINE\System\CurrentControlSet\Services\MSExchangeDSAccess\
  Instance0
Value name: MaxMemory
```

```
Value type: DWORD
Value data: 4096 (KB default)

Value name: MaxEntries
Value type: DWORD
Value data: 0 (number of entries; default=0: no limit)
```


How to Manage Active Directory

As you have seen, there are lots of tools and utilities for managing the Active Directory. In Table 5.8 below, you'll find a short summary of the most common utilities and their uses in an Exchange 2000 environment.

Summary

This is a list of the more important features and keywords discussed in this chapter. Use it as a reminder and to make sure you have understood the most important things:

- Exchange 5.5 runs on Windows NT 4 or Windows 2000, Exchange 2000 runs only in a Windows 2000 domain.

Table 5.8 Tools for managing Active Directory.

Tool	Description
Active Directory Users and Computers	Create users, contacts, and groups. Used for mail-enabling objects (setting email addresses and delivery restrictions). Also used for setting the AD operations masters RID, PDC, and infrastructure. Used almost every day.
Exchange System Manager	Used for setting Exchange 2000 server configurations, creating public folders, storage groups, administrative groups, checking SMTP queues, and more. Used almost every day.
ADSIEdit	Similar to the Exchange 5.5. Admin tool in raw mode; can see and change objects and attributes that are not visible with the AD Users and Computers tool. Used rarely.
Active Directory Sites and Services	Used to create AD sites, to move domain controllers between sites, defining site links, defining global catalog servers, forcing directory replication, and setting directory replication schedule intervals between sites. Can also be used for security setting of Exchange configuration objects. Used mostly for forcing replication, otherwise rarely.
Active Directory Domains and Trust	Used for switching Active Directory to native mode, and to change the AD operations domain naming master. Used very seldom.
Active Directory Schema	Needs to be installed manually. Used for changing the AD schema master, creating new object classes, and to enable and disable attributes for global catalog replication. Used rarely.
RegEdit	Used for different Registry settings related to Active Directory objects and Exchange objects, such as DSProxy settings, preferred global catalog servers for clients, and preferred GC and DC for Exchange servers; setting the DSAccess cache. Used rarely.
LDIFDE	Used for exporting and importing data to the Active Directory. Usage depends on the organization—some use it every day, others never use it.

- Exchange has always been a mail system built upon the client/server model, meaning there are active processes on both the server and the mail client.
- SFS is a mail system like MS Mail and cc-Mail; these are not client/server mail systems.
- Exchange 5.5 has four core system processes: IS, DS, MTA, and SA.
- Exchange 2000 has no DS and therefore doesn't have its own directory.
- A directory is a database where you store information about objects and their attributes. Examples of such objects are Users, Groups, and Servers; examples of attributes are First Name, email addresses, and shares.
- The Active Directory is the Meta directory for Windows 2000. It's built on the DS from Exchange 5.5.
- AD replaces all separate directories and system databases in NT 4, like SAM, WINS, DHCP, and DNS.
- Windows NT 4 domains has one master domain controller, the PDC, and zero or more BDCs; every five minutes the PDC sends out updates to its BDC.
- AD has Multi-master domain controllers; every DC in a domain has a writeable copy of all other domain controllers in its domain.
- The AD database is NTDS.DIT, which is an enhanced version of the DIR.EDB database from Exchange 5.5.
- NTDS.DIT is optimized for circular logging; this cannot be turned off. All transaction log files are 10MB in size.
- To move the NTDS.DIT database or the transaction log files, you need to run the Directory Service Restore Module.
- Use DCPROMO to promote, or demote, a Windows 2000 server to a domain controller.
- LDAP is the protocol most often used for accessing the Active Directory.
- Active Directory names are similar to DNS names, but describe different things; DNS describes IP numbers and host names, whereas AD describes domain objects such as users, groups, and server settings.
- AD names are limited to 64 characters, because there must be room for adding site names and domain GUIDs; the complete name must be less than 255 characters.
- In mixed mode, Windows 2000 domain controllers will allow a mix of Windows 2000 and NT 4 domain controllers.
- In native mode, only Windows 2000 domain controllers are allowed (but the member servers and the clients can still run Windows NT or any other operating system).

- A Windows 2000 domain is an administrative boundary; each domain has its own set of administrators.
- Active Directory is divided into three partitions: the domain, the configuration, and the schema.
- The domain partition stores information about all objects, like users and groups, in a particular domain; this information is not automatically replicated to other domains.
- The configuration partition stores information about Exchange configuration, routes, and AD replication settings. This partition is replicated to all domain controllers in the forest.
- The schema partition stores a description of what objects can be stored, and the attributes available for each object type. This information is replicated to all domain controllers in the forest.
- A domain can have a child domain, which in turn may also have a child domain, and so on. These domains have the first root domain name in common; this is a domain tree. Trusts are automatically configured and are also transitive.
- You can connect several domain trees into one single forest; they will all share the same configuration and schema partition. Transitive trusts will be automatically configured.
- There are some special domain controllers in the forest: the schema master, the domain naming master, the RID master, the PDC master, and the infrastructure master.
- There can be only one schema master per forest; by default, it's the first installed domain controller in the forest.
- There can be only one domain naming master per forest; by default, it's the first installed domain controller in the forest.
- There can be only one RID, PDC, and infrastructure master per domain; by default, it's the first installed domain controller in the domain.
- The universal group is a new group in Windows 2000; its members are visible all over the forest, thanks to the global catalog. This group is not available in mixed mode.
- Global groups can now be nested by other global groups.
- There are two types of groups: security groups and distribution groups. The first is for setting access permission on network resources, the second is purely for mail purposes.
- If you have multiple domains, you need to plan how your groups can be expanded; only universal groups have membership that is visible in all domains. Members in the other groups are only visible in the domain where they are created.
- Define expansion servers to send a local or global group to a particular domain before the group membership is expanded.

- For performance reasons, groups should not include more than 5,000 members; if more are needed, create nestled groups.
- Use LDIFDE to export and import users to the Active Directory.
- Replication of Active Directory information is controlled by AD sites; replication runs each five minutes within a site, and by default every three hours between sites.
- Use the Active Directory Sites And Services tool to force replication.
- RPC is used within a site; between sites, you can select between RPC and SMTP.
- Global catalog is an extra partition on an existing domain controller; this GC stores a subset of all attributes for all domain objects in the forest. It is used by Outlook clients for retrieving the global address list.
- More than 100 attributes are listed in the GC for each domain object.
- You can add new attributes to the GC, but remember, this will increase replication traffic.
- The DSProxy service helps older Outlook clients access the global address list.
- Outlook 2000 will go directly to the GC, using LDAP requests.
- The DSAccess service helps client protocols and internal Exchange services access both the GC and the AD; all information, except MAPI address lookups, is cached.

Chapter 6

Exchange 2000 and DNS

The telephone system makes it possible to connect two phones over a public network; you can make a call anywhere in the world. Every phone is identified by a unique number; when you need to call somebody, but don't have the number, you can look it up in the phone directory. The Internet world is very similar to the phone system in this respect, except that computers use IP addresses instead of phone numbers, and DNS servers instead of phone directories.

You use the Domain Name System (DNS) every time you send an email or surf the Internet, but do you know how it works? The general purpose of a DNS server is to assist TCP/IP applications, like mail servers and Web browsers, that need to find a server that accept email for a particular domain, or a particular Web site. The Internet world is built upon the TCP/IP protocol; in this world, all computers are identified with a 32-bit IP address, such as 194.198.189.160. Since we humans are not good at remembering a lot of numbers, we give all computers an alias name instead, for example, **www.humandata.se**; then we create a DNS database with all these names and IP addresses. Now we can use a Web browser, type the name "www.humandata.se", and our browser will ask the DNS database for the corresponding IP address (194.198.189.160) and connect us to that Web site.

This chapter tells you about the DNS server, how it relates to Windows 2000 and Exchange 2000, and how to install it and troubleshoot DNS problems. It is an important chapter that will help you understand how to manage one of the most fundamental building blocks in the Exchange 2000 world. In previous versions of Exchange, you could often get away with knowing nothing about DNS, but this is not the case anymore. DNS is also absolutely critical for Windows 2000 and its Active Directory; if DNS does not work as expected, then you will experience all kinds of issues, from logon problems to AD replication problems.

A Short History Lesson

The Internet is the successor of the ARPANET, the military research project that ended in 1988. By the way, you should know the difference between *Internet* and *internet*. When spelled with a capital I, we're talking about the successor of ARPANET; when it's not capitalized, we're talking about any network, usually but not necessarily a private IP-based network. Anyhow, the ARPANET used IP addresses for all hosts that could be reached over the network. The term *host* at that time usually meant a server, most often a Unix-based server. Clients did not have any IP numbers in the beginning; they were terminals, connected by a serial interface to a host. In the beginning of the 1980s, more and more terminals were replaced by personal computers, or PCs. Since this was a computer, it could share its resources, like the hard disk or the printer, so it needed its own IP address.

As long as only a few hosts were on the network, all of them could be listed in a file, named "hosts," with the hosts' names and their corresponding IP addresses. This list was managed by the Network Information Center at Stanford Research Institute (SRI-NIC). All computers connected to the ARPANET had a copy of that file so every host could be found. Whenever a change was made to the hosts file, all computers had to download a new copy. As the number of computers with IP addresses increased, it soon became too difficult for SRI-NIC to keep the hosts file updated and to make sure that there were no hostname or IP address conflicts. SRI-NIC soon saw that something needed to be done.

In 1984, Paul Mockapetris of USC's Information Science Institute designed the architecture for the new domain naming system. He released the RFCs 882 and 883, later replaced by the RFCs 1034 and 1035, which described the new DNS. This system made it possible to create a worldwide name hierarchy, where all hosts were guaranteed to have a unique name, no matter how many hosts were added.

The DNS Domain Tree

Mockapetris suggested that the Internet should be divided into parts, called *domains*, which in turn could be divided into child-domains, and so on. This made the domain structure look very similar to a file system tree; see Figure 6.1.

The top of a file system, also referred to as the *root*, has a backslash ("\") as the root symbol; the DNS system uses a single dot, but the correct DNS root name is a null label (" "). What are known as *directories* in the file system are called *domains* in DNS; a *subdirectory* in the file system corresponds to a *subdomain* in DNS.

Every domain has a DNS server that is responsible for all its hostnames and IP numbers; a DNS server can be responsible for more than one domain. The domains for which a given DNS is responsible are called *zones*; that DNS server is then said to have *authority* for that zone. The domains directly under the root are a bit special; they are referred to as *top level domains*, or TLDs. Examples of TLDs include:

- ***.com***—Commercial organizations, like **microsoft.com**, **hp.com**, and **coriolis.com**
- ***.edu***—Educational organizations, like **berkeley.edu**, **kean.edu**, and **stanford.edu**
- ***.gov***—Government organizations, like **nasa.gov** and **whitehouse.gov**
- ***.mil***—Military organizations, like **army.mil** and **navy.mil**

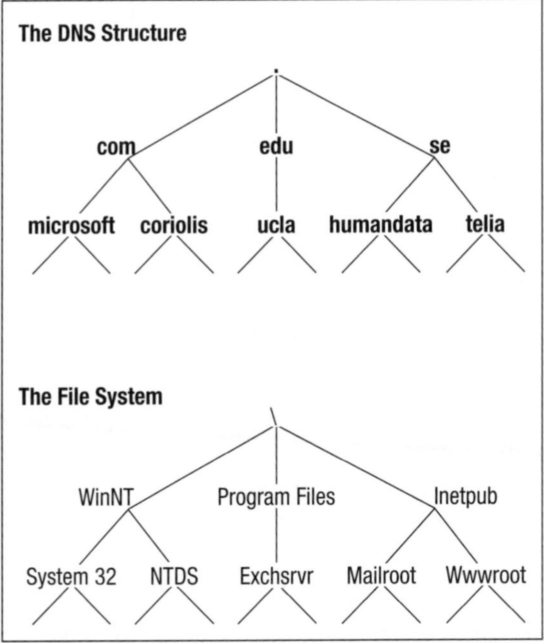

Figure 6.1
The domain structure compared to a file system tree.

- ***.net***—Networking organizations, like **global-ip.net** and **lillnor.net**
- ***.org***—Noncommercial organizations, like **imc.org** and **isoc.org**
- ***.int***—International organizations, like **nato.int**
- ***.se and .fr***—Country-specific TLDs, like **.se** (Sweden), **.uk** (United Kingdom), and **.fr** (France)

All domains, except the root and TLD domains, can have any name, as long as the name is unique within its parent domain. This means that it is okay to have two domains called ***coriolis.com*** and ***coriolis.org,*** since they belong to different TLD domains.

Before you connect your network to the Internet, you must apply for a DNS domain name, for example at your Internet service provider (ISP). Depending on what type of organization you have, or what country you live in, you will get a TLD domain; however, the next level is usually free to name as you wish, as long as it doesn't conflict with any existing domains within this TLD.

The DNS Database

A domain usually consists of computers (hosts) and network services, like SMTP and WWW servers, along with their respective IP addresses. This information is stored in the DNS database responsible for this domain. For example, the **humandata.se** domain has the following hosts and services listed in its DNS database:

```
balder  Host    194.198.189.252
oden    Host    194.198.189.160
tor     Host    194.198.189.163
www     Alias   oden.humandata.se.
```

From this list, we can see three servers—balder, oden, and tor—and their respective IP addresses. We also see that the network service www is listed—since it is listed in the **humandata.se** domain, the complete name is **www.humandata.se**. Note that this entry has a pointer to the **oden.humandata.se** host, instead of an IP address; that must be a Web server. The process that queries a DNS server for an IP address is called a *resolver*, and it is often built into the client application.

So how does it work when somebody, for example in England, wants to look at this Web server? Here's what happens:

1. First, the user types "www.humandata.se" in his or her Web browser.
2. The browser now needs to find which server to connect to on the Internet, so it sends a request to its own resolver, asking it to resolve the IP address to **www.humandata.se**.
3. The resolver has the IP address to a preferred DNS server, and sends the request to it.
4. The DNS receives the request, and starts by looking at the TLD domain. All DNS servers have a list of *root DNS servers*, which know what DNS server is responsible for a given TLD (.se in this case). Our local DNS queries one of the root servers and gets the IP address to the DNS server responsible for the .se domain.
5. The local DNS contacts the DNS server responsible for the .se domain, asking it what DNS server is responsible for **humandata.se**, and gets the IP address to that server.
6. The local DNS contacts Human Data's DNS, asking it about **www.humandata.se**; the reply is a pointer to **oden.humandata.se**.
7. The local DNS now needs to find the IP address to **oden.humandata.se**, so it sends a request for that IP address; Human Data's DNS will reply with 194.198.189.160.
8. Finally, this IP address is returned back to the resolver on the client, which opens a TCP connection (on port 80 since it's a Web site) to the IP address 194.198.189.160.

This is a lot of steps that obviously take time to complete; to increase the performance of name resolution, the DNS server will cache the retrieved information. The next time any client asks this DNS server for the IP address to **www.humandata.se**, it will find it in its cache; our local DNS now also knows the IP address of the DNS server responsible for **humandata.se**, which will make all queries for hosts in that domain very quickly.

Standard DNS Naming Rules

Below are some of the most important naming rules that apply to DNS domains. Be sure to follow these, or you may end up changing these characters sooner rather than later. Note that Active Directory also follows these rules, except the length; an AD domain name must not exceed 64 characters, as described in Chapter 5.

- The only allowed characters are 0 through 9, A through Z, and hyphen; the name is not case sensitive.
- A domain name must be less than 64 characters, not including the dot.
- The complete name, or the *fully qualified domain name (FQDN)*, must not exceed 255 characters.
- There must not be more than 127 levels in the domain tree.

In a Microsoft Windows NT/2000 network, all computers have a NetBIOS name; its name standard is very different from DNS, which could result in a computer having different DNS hostnames and NetBIOS names. The name standard for NetBIOS includes the following guidelines:

- Must be less than or equal to 15 characters.
- More characters are accepted than in DNS; for example, the space character is okay.
- There is no hierarchy, like in DNS domains; it's a flat name space.
- All names must be unique within one NT/2000 domain.

Make your existing NetBIOS names follow the DNS naming rules so that these names can be identical, if possible; this will avoid future name confusion and mistakes. This is especially true for the Windows 2000 environment, since all domain controllers are completely dependent on the DNS.

Warning! *Do not change the NetBIOS name for an existing Exchange server! Some applications, like Exchange, will stop working if you change the NT server's NetBIOS name. Make sure no application on the NT server is dependent on the NetBIOS name before you change it!*

A Real-Life Experience

I helped one customer migrate from Windows NT 4 and Exchange 5.5 to Windows 2000 and Exchange 2000; the Exchange 5.5 server NetBIOS name was "Server Alfa," and the hostname was "serveralfa." The Windows 2000 domain controller had no problem communicating with this server using its hostname, but when I installed an Active Directory connector, it did not accept the space character in the NetBIOS name. Now I had a delicate problem: I could not change the NetBIOS name, since that would stop the Exchange 5.5 server from working, and I could not install the AD connector needed to get Exchange 5.5 and Active Directory to replicate with each other.

The quick solution was to install a new Exchange 5.5 server in a Windows 2000 server (without any space in its name!), and join the existing 5.5 site. Now the directory replication was possible—first between the two Exchange 5.5 servers, then between AD and the new Exchange 5.5 server. Another solution could have been to run the Exchange 5.5 Move Server Wizard utility and change the name of the Exchange server, and then change the NetBIOS name of the NT server itself.

The DNS Architecture

You may remember that all domain zones have one authoritative DNS server. This server is a master, also known as the *primary* DNS name server; all changes must be made on this primary name server. If this server becomes unavailable, then all information about this zone will be unreachable. To avoid this, you install one or more *secondary* DNS servers, which poll the primary name server at regular intervals to see if any updates have been made to the name database. If any have been made, the secondary DNS servers will request a copy of the complete database; this is known as a *zone transfer*. The secondary name servers can answer any questions about this zone, since they have a read-only copy of the name database.

A DNS that is a secondary name server for one zone can simultaneously be the primary name server for another zone; in fact, a DNS server can be both a primary and secondary name server for more than one zone at a time. It may sound confusing, but this system is actually very practical; for example, in Figure 6.2, you see two DNS servers, A and B. DNS

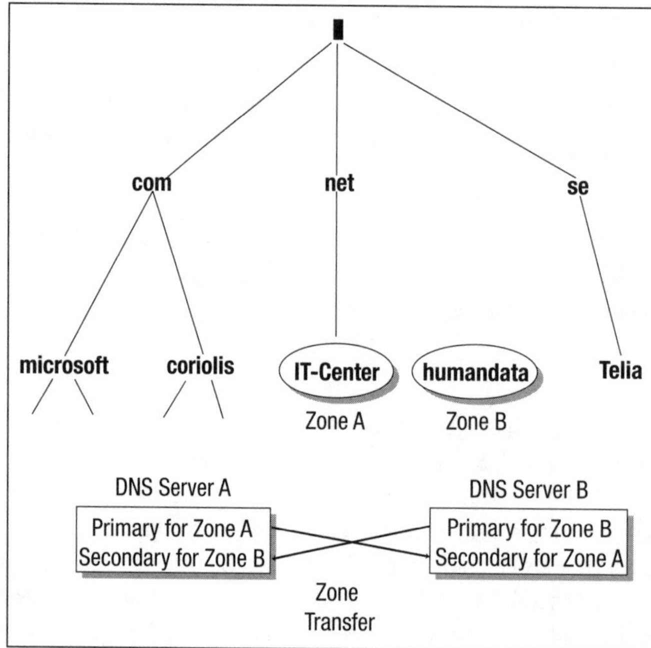

Figure 6.2
Primary and secondary name servers.

A is the primary name server for zone A, **it-center.net**, and at the same time this server is the secondary name server for zone B, **humandata.se**. The DNS server B is primary for zone B and secondary for zone A.

Besides the primary and secondary name servers, there may also be cache-only name servers. A *cache server* does not do any zone transfer; the only thing it does is cache all names and IP numbers it has been asked to find out. After the cache-only name server has been active for some time, it will have the most requested information in its cache, by improving the performance of name resolution without requiring any zone transfer, which means less network traffic.

Internal and External DNS Servers

It is customary for most organizations to have one external DNS, accessible from the Internet, and one internal DNS, accessible only from the inside. The idea behind this is to avoid exposing all internal hosts to the Internet, thereby increasing the security of your network. The firewall is also usually configured to stop access to the internal DNS from the Internet, while at the same time accepting outgoing DNS requests from the internal DNS; see Figure 6.3.

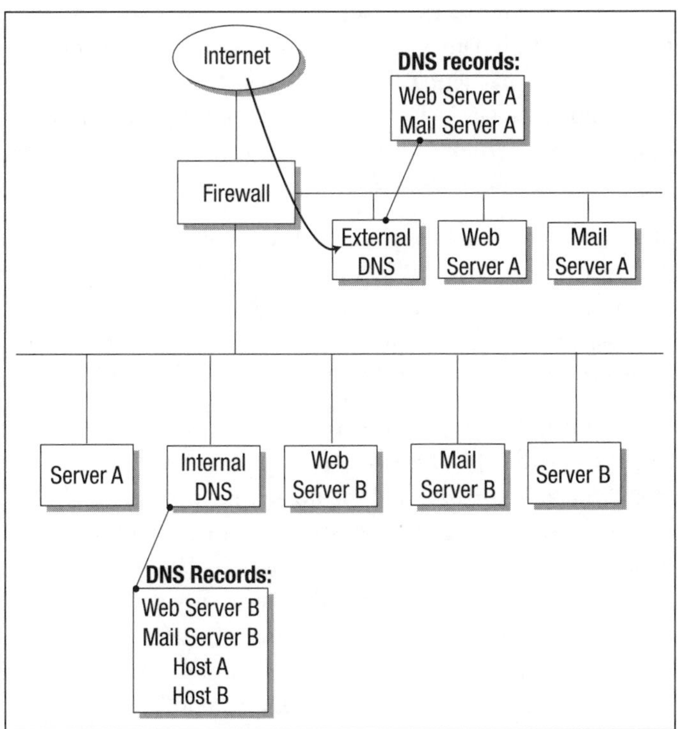

Figure 6.3
Internal and external DNS servers.

DNS Resolvers

In the beginning of this chapter, we saw an example of a Web client that needed the IP address for a certain Web site; this process was performed by a *resolver*. This may be a separate program that is built into the client's TCP/IP stack or it may be code that is part of the application itself, or the Web browser in this case. A resolver handles the following tasks:

- Querying a name server
- Interpreting responses from this query (could be a successful response or an error message)
- Returning the information to the application that requested it

The resolver will simply be contacted by an application, create a query, send it to the name server, and then return the result to the application. The resolver runs in the client computer, and the name server does all of the work of finding an answer for the query.

Reverse Name Resolution

Sometimes we need to find the name for a given IP address; this is called *reverse name resolution* or *address-to-name mapping*. This is a trickier task than one first may think, since the DNS domain tree is built on names, not IP addresses. One way of doing this is to search all domains, looking for this particular IP address; clearly not a practical solution. To perform this reverse resolution effectively, another branch in the domain tree is designed, the ***in-addr.arpa***, that is actually a branch in the Internet domain name space; this is also referred to as the *Reverse lookup zone*.

The nodes in the **in-addr.arpa** domain are named after the numbers in the dotted-octet representation of IP addresses; for example, 194.198.189.0, a class-C IP address. The **in-addr-.arpa** domain has up to 256 subdomains, one for each possible value of the first octet in the IP address; each of these subdomains in turn also has 256 subdomains for the next octet, and so on for the two remaining octets in the IP address.

A domain name, like **oden.humandata.se**, must be read backward to see where in the domain this host belongs, since the DNS tree is like an upside-down tree. The TLD domain is ***se***; the subdomain is ***humandata***, and the hostname in this domain is ***oden***. The **in-addr.arpa** domain is constructed in the same way; the most significant octet is in the top (directly under the in-addr.arpa), then the next-most significant octet, and so on. However, unlike the domain names that are notated with the least-significant part in the beginning (oden) and the most significant part in the end (se), the IP address has the most significant octet in the beginning (194) and the least significant octet last (160); this is the reason we must reverse the IP numbers for the in-addr.arpa domain.

For example, the **oden.humandata.se** host has the IP address 194.198.189.160; its position in the **in-addr.arpa** domain will be 160.189.198.194.in-addr.arpa, as is depicted in Figure 6.4.

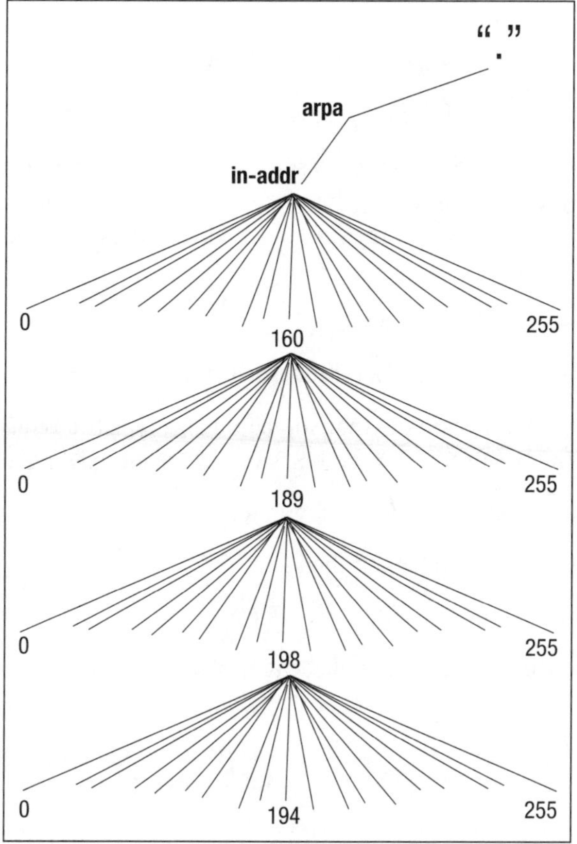

Figure 6.4
The **in-addr.arpa** domain.

The reason for building the in-addr.arpa tree like this is that it makes it possible to delegate authority for the in-addr.arpa domain, much like the delegation of name domains; to do it the other way around would mean that the first subdomain in **in-addr.arpa** would be 160 in the example above; this is actually the octet pointing to a host, not the network number, and there are lots of hosts on the Internet that end on octet 160, so that would make it impossible to delegate this subdomain.

When you, as a DNS administrator, add new hosts to the primary name server, you will also have a choice of adding the IP number of this new host to the in-addr.arpa domain; you should do this, since some problems may arise later if you don't, especially with domain controllers in the Active Directory domain. If you miss adding the IP address, you can do it afterwards, by following these steps (based on the DNS server on Windows 2000):

1. Start the *DNS* management tool for Windows 2000.

2a. Expand the *Reverse Lookup Zones* and check to see that there is a subfolder for your IP network address. If not, you must create it before you continue. Follow Steps 2b-2f; otherwise continue with Step 3.

2b. Right-click on the *Reverse Lookup Zones*.

2c. Select *New Zone*. This starts the *New Zone Wizard*; click *Next*.

2d. Select the type of zone (AD-integrated, Primary, or Secondary); click *Next*.

2e. Type in the network part of the IP address, exactly as it is (no reverse order; the wizard will make this change for you—look at the bottom when you type in the address). Remember that the Class A network uses one single octet, class B uses two, and class C uses three octets. Click *Next*.

2f. Click *Finish* to complete the New Zone Wizard.

3. Right-click on the corresponding reverse lookup zone; select *New Pointer*.
4. Click *Browse* to list all available hosts; note that you could also type the remaining octets for this host, but using the Browse button helps you avoid any spelling errors.
5. Click on your DNS server and then click *OK*; see Figure 6.5.
6. Click on the *Forward Lookup Zones* folder and then click *OK*.
7. Click on the domain the host belongs to and then click *OK*.
8. Browse the list of hosts for this domain and select the host you want to add to the reverse lookup zone; then click *OK*. See Figure 6.6.
9. Now you are back at step 4 again, but this time with the IP address and the fully qualified domain name; see Figure 6.7. Fill in the empty octets in the IP address and then click *OK* to add the host to the reverse lookup zone.

This was the long way to create reverse lookup pointers to hosts. There is actually a much simpler method, if you are sure the reverse lookup zone exists for this network address; follow these steps:

1. Start the DNS snap-in for Windows 2000.

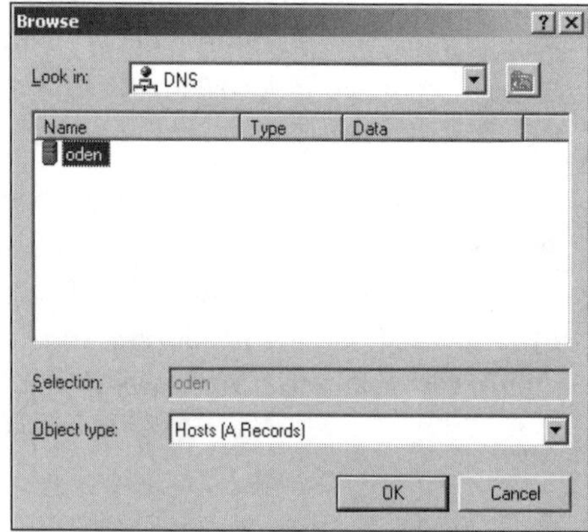

Figure 6.5
Select the primary DNS for the domain.

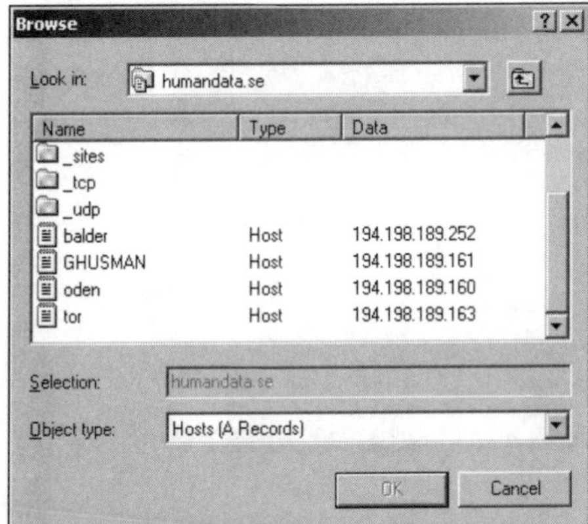

Figure 6.6
Browse the list of available hosts in this domain.

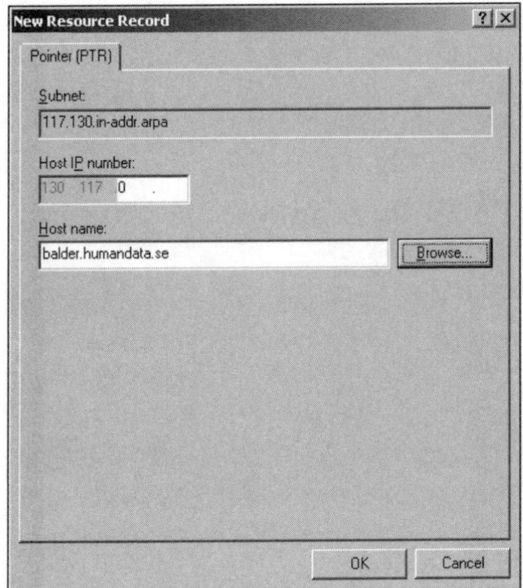

Figure 6.7
Fill in the remaining part of the IP address to this host.

2. Expand the *Forward Lookup Zones* and the domain the host belongs to.
3. Locate the host in the right pane; see Figure 6.8.
4. Open the properties for this host, and click on the *Update Associated Pointer (PTR) Record* checkbox, then click *OK*; see Figure 6.9. You're done!

The SOA Record

Every primary name server has a special record for the zone in its database: the *Start Of Authority*, or SOA. This is a very important record that describes a lot of information about

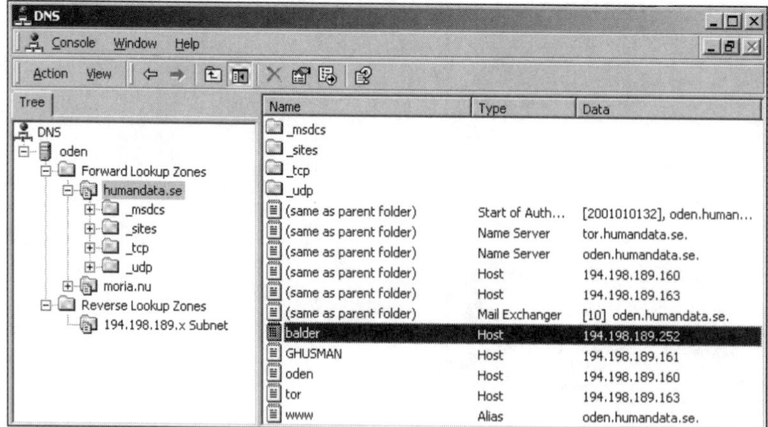

Figure 6.8
Locate the host for whom you want to add a PTR record.

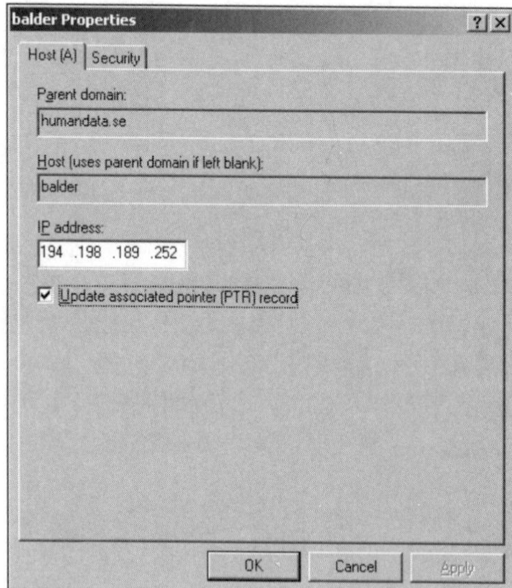

Figure 6.9
Check the PTR record.

this zone, for example the name servers, along with the polling settings and the SMTP address to the responsible person. Let's take a closer look at the SOA record; we can use the **NSLOOKUP** utility to list this information as described below:

```
C:\>nslookup
Default Server:  ns.global-ip.net
Address:  194.52.1.10

> set type=soa
```

```
06: > humandata.se
07: Server:  ns.global-ip.net
08: Address:  194.52.1.10
09:
10: Non-authoritative answer:
11: humandata.se
12:         primary name server = marilyn.humandata.se
13:         responsible mail addr = hostmaster.humandata.se
14:         serial  = 2001030603
15:         refresh = 3600 (1 hour)
16:         retry   = 600 (10 mins)
17:         expire  = 86400 (1 day)
18:         default TTL = 3600 (1 hour)
19:
20: humandata.se    nameserver = oak.itcenter.net
21: humandata.se    nameserver = marilyn.humandata.se
22: oak.itcenter.net        internet address = 195.54.129.10
23: marilyn.humandata.se    internet address = 194.198.189.11
```

NSLOOKUP is clearly a useful tool for exploring DNS servers. Let's look at each line.

- *Lines 01-03*—We start **NSLOOKUP**; it connects to the client's default DNS server, which in this case happens to be **ns.global-ip.net**.
- *Line 05*—We type "set type=SOA", which tells **NSLOOKUP** to give us only the SOA record; however, we can retrieve much more information from a DNS, as we will see later in this chapter.
- *Lines 06-08*—We type "humandata.se", since this is the domain we are interested in. The result will be retrieved from the **ns.global-ip.net**, since this is the DNS we are connected to; if we want, we can switch to another DNS server.
- *Line 10*—Starts the listing of the SOA record for **humandata.se**; the phrase *Non-authoritative answer* is a warning to us, saying that the current DNS is not primary, or authoritative, for this zone; it could be incorrect.
- *Line 11*—The name of the queried domain.
- *Line 12*—The primary name server for this domain is **marilyn.humandata.se**.
- *Line 13*—The SMTP address to the responsible person for this domain. Since the @ character has a special meaning in the DNS database (it's an alias for the domain name), we write the address with a period instead; however, the real address should be interpreted as **hostmaster@humandata.se**. This address is not used by the DNS server itself; this is for anyone having questions for a given domain.
- *Line 14*—How does a secondary DNS server know if there are any changes to pick up? This is solved by incrementing a *serial* number for each update. All secondary servers keep track of the latest serial number they have received; at the next polling, they check

to see if this number has increased. If it has, they request a zone transfer of the complete zone database. This is similar to the way directory replication works in Active Directory, with USN numbers incremented for each update. However, for name servers, this serial number is manually updated by the administrator; it can be set to anything but it is customary to set this serial number equal to the date for this update, and a change number for this date. In the example above, the serial number is 2001030603; this means that the last time this primary DNS was updated was the year 2001, month 03, day 06, and this was the third update on that particular day.

- *Line 15*—The Refresh field defines how often the secondary DNS server will poll the primary server for updates; in this case, 3,600 seconds.
- *Line 16*—The Retry field says how long the secondary server should wait before it retries a new polling, if the first one did not succeed; in this case, 10 minutes.
- *Line 17*—All information that secondary servers poll from this particular primary server should be saved for 24 hours (86,400 seconds); after that, the information has expired and must be removed. A new zone transfer will then take place.
- *Line 18*—The TTL, or Time To Live, field tells how long any name server should cache this information; after this time, the information must be discarded and new information must be retrieved from the primary name server. Be careful how you set this value; for example, if this value is 7 days, it means that it will take up to one week before new information will be retrieved by the secondary and cache-only name servers. If you set it to 1 minute, the name servers will discard all values from the cache too quickly.
- *Lines 20 and 21*—The names of all name servers, both primary and secondary. The first is our primary name server, so the next must be a secondary name server.
- *Lines 22 and 23*—The IP address to the name servers listed on lines 20 and 21.

MX Records

Besides using DNS for finding hostnames and IP addresses, you can also use it for finding Internet resources, like mail servers. This is a special type of record in the DNS database—the MX record. MX stands for *Mail eXchanger* and points any incoming SMTP mail to a certain host. Since this is a book about Exchange 2000, we use this MX record to point external mail servers to the Exchange server that accepts mail for a given DNS domain. For example, to find out what server accepts mail to users on the **@humandata.se** domain, we again will use the **NSLOOKUP** utility (by now you may have guessed that "ns" stands for "name server," right?). Since we are only interested this time in MX records, we tell **NSLOOKUP** to make a query only for this type of record by the **set type=MX** command; on the next line we type in the domain we are interested in, **humandata.se**:

```
C:\>nslookup
Default Server:  ns.global-ip.net
Address:  194.52.1.10
```

```
> set type=MX
> humandata.se
Server:  ns.global-ip.net
Address:  194.52.1.10

humandata.se    MX preference = 10, mail exchanger = oden.humandata.se
oden.humandata.se       internet address = 194.198.189.160
```


The line listed above, starting with "humandata.se MX . . ." is what we are interested in. This line tells us that all mail to the **@humandata.se** domain should be sent to the host **oden.humandata.se**; on the next line, we get the IP address to this host. Look again at this line—there is a part in the middle that is very interesting: "preference = 10". This preference value is really only useful when we have more than one mail server accepting incoming mail to a domain. In our example, we actually have one more Exchange 2000 server that we could use for receiving mail to the **humandata.se** domain; let's add an MX record pointing to this server to our primary name server, using the following steps:

1. Open the *DNS* management tool.
2. Expand the *Forward Lookup Zones*.
3. Right-click on the **humandata.se** domain where we want to add this new MX record.
4. Select *New Mail Exchanger*.
5. We can now type the fully qualified domain name to the new mail host, or we could use the *Browse* button, as described in the steps for adding reverse PTR records. This time we simply add the name manually, **tor.humandata.se**; see Figure 6.10. Note: leave the *Host Or Domain* field empty.

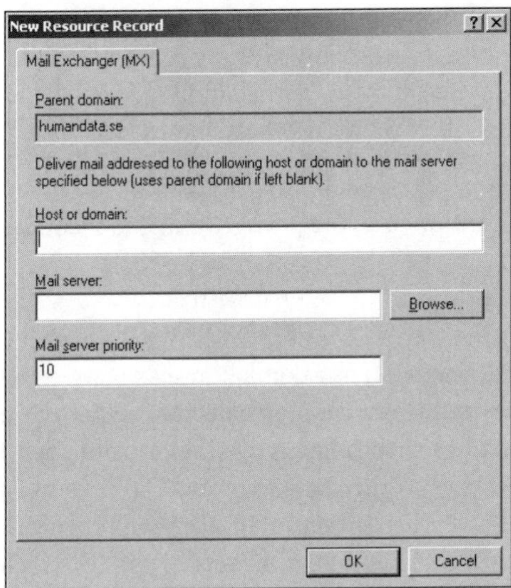

Figure 6.10
Defining a new MX record.

6. In the *Mail Server Priority* field, type in the preference value, for example 20.
7. Click *OK* to close the window.

Now let's use the **NSLOOKUP** utility again, and query for MX records for the **humandata.se** domain, to see if there is any difference:

```
C:\>nslookup
Default Server:  ns.global-ip.net
Address:  194.52.1.10

> set type=MX
> humandata.se
Server:  ns.global-ip.net
Address:  194.52.1.10

humandata.se    MX preference = 10, mail exchanger = oden.humandata.se
humandata.se    MX preference = 20, mail exchanger = tor.humandata.se
oden.humandata.se        internet address = 194.198.189.160
tor.humandata.se         internet address = 194.198.189.163
```

Indeed, we now have two MX records for the **humandata.se** domain; one pointing to **oden.humandata.se** and the other to **tor.humandata.se**. So when a remote mail server wants to send a message to anyone at **humandata.se**, it will find two possible choices. The preference value will tell the sending server to use **oden.humandata.se** first, since it has the lowest preference value; if **oden** does not answer, the sending server will connect to **tor.humandata.se** instead.

Preference Values

The preference value is a way to define multiple mail servers, but only for receiving messages—it will not affect outgoing messages from any of these servers in any way! If there is more than one MX record for the same domain, any sending server will always try the server with the lowest preference value first; if two MX records have the same preference value, the sending server randomly selects one of them. To summarize this:

- Use different preference values if you want to have one primary and one secondary mail server.
- Use the same preference value if you want load balancing.

There is no limit to how many MX records can be in one domain; use as many as needed. The preference value can be anything between 0 and 65535. The actual values themselves are not important; they are only compared to each other. A preference value of 1 for one MX record and 65535 for the other will result in the same as a preference value of 10 for one MX record and 11 for the other. However, it is common to use preference values in steps of 10, 20, 30, and so on, since then you can add a new MX record with the preference value of 15, if this would be necessary.

Dial-up Connections and DNS

Any mail organization should have at least one primary and one secondary receiving mail server. In some situations, this is a necessity, for example when your network uses dial-up connections by modem or ISDN. You may remember the extended SMTP command ETRN from Chapter 4, which is used for de-queuing a secondary mail server at the ISP, or another organization with a permanent Internet connection. Since the DNS works like an announcement of what receiving email servers there are for a given domain, we must make sure that the external DNS, the one that is visible to the Internet, has two MX records: one primary mail server pointing to our server on the internal network, and one secondary pointing to the mail server at the ISP.

At first, this may seem strange—why not make the ISP mail server the primary, since it's always connected? The answer is that when our mail server later connects to the Internet, it will send the **ETRN humandata.se**, or whatever the domain is called, to the ISP mail server; that server will in turn check the external DNS to see who the primary mail server is. So the MX record with the lowest value must point to our mail server, else it will not receive any mail.

This is also the reason why our internal mail server must have a known IP address; otherwise, we could not enter an MX record for this server on the external DNS. In Chapter 4, we also discussed another new extended SMTP command—the ATRN. By using this command, we don't need any predefined IP address for our server; it will simply regularly connect to the ISP mail server, authenticate itself, and activate a message transfer. The ISP mail server would then reverse the roles of sender and receiver, and make a standard SMTP connection back to our mail server. This is often the case for the new low-cost dial-up ADSL connections and similar techniques.

The BIND Implementation

The first DNS implementation was called JEEVES, developed by Paul Mockapetris, the man behind the DNS. However, another implementation of DNS that quickly became more popular was Berkeley Internet Name Domain (BIND), originally developed by Kevin Dunlap for Berkeley's 4.3 BSD Unix operating system. BIND is still the most common DNS on the Unix platform today. There have been many versions of BIND since its first release, and the most common is probably version 4.9, since it was stable and did its job well.

However, that release does have some security problems—for example, there are several unchecked buffers in this version of BIND that may let attackers execute any type of code or command on the operating system it runs on. It also has a data leak that lets intruders access the system's memory, allowing them to inspect system variables and programs loaded into the memory.

Computer Emergency Response Team (CERT), **www.cert.org**, is an organization that specializes in documenting computer-related security problems; they have documented 12 different vulnerabilities for BIND version 4.9 since 1997. Even version 8 has reported buffer overflow problems, but still many administrators have failed to upgrade their BIND implementation to version 9 or later, which doesn't have these problems. There are also implementations of versions 4 and 8 of BIND for Windows NT, and both of them have the same problems as the Unix version.

This is serious, since the servers running BIND are exposed to the Internet; somebody could access information they shouldn't, or change information in the DNS database, or simply bring this server down, thereby making your organization unreachable for external access. If you have a server running BIND, check its version and upgrade if necessary, or at least apply the patches that are available for most BIND versions!

DNS and Windows 2000

Since Exchange 2000 is an SMTP-based email system, it is completely dependent on a DNS server. In fact, even Windows 2000 itself, without any Exchange, needs a DNS to work; it is used, for example, for Active Directory replication based on SMTP messages, and to list domain controllers and global catalog servers. When the first Windows 2000 domain controller is installed in a new forest, it will check for an existing DNS server; if it doesn't find any, the installation wizard program will suggest that you install one before completing the installation of the domain controller.

A Replacement of WINS

In Windows NT 4, a client needs a domain controller (PDC or BDC) to log on to the domain, but there is no particular domain controller set for the client. One way of finding a domain controller is to broadcast a NetBIOS call; any domain controller listening to this broadcast would then reply back to the client. This technique does not work over routers, since they most often don't forward broadcasts. If the network is TCP/IP based, the client can instead ask a given WINS server (whose IP address is set in the client's TCP/IP settings); the WINS server keeps a list of all available domain controllers and their IP addresses, and will return them to the client. This will work over routers since it is a direct call.

The nice thing about WINS servers is that they accept dynamic updates; this is an absolute necessity when clients get dynamically assigned IP addresses from a DHCP server, instead of fixed addresses. When the DHCP server has assigned an IP address to any computer, it will automatically update the WINS server with this new information. The WINS server will also register the names and addresses of domain controllers. Most NT 4 domains running DHCP would also run WINS for these reasons, since they complement each other.

Dynamic DNS

The problem with WINS is that it's made for NetBIOS names, not for DNS domain names and hostnames. Windows 2000 still supports NetBIOS, but only to be backward compatible; this means that NetBIOS names are still valid, and you can still run a WINS server to assist all pre-Windows 2000 computers. However, even with clients like Windows 2000 Professional, the network must be able to handle dynamically assigned IP addresses received from a DHCP server. If we don't want to use WINS, what should we use? The answer is an enhanced version of DNS, the Dynamic DNS, also known as the DDNS. This version will dynamically add new entries—for example, a Windows 2000 Professional client that is assigned an IP address from a DHCP server.

The DNS that comes with Windows 2000 Server has a lot of new features, and one is particularly important—the Dynamic DNS. This enhancement of the DNS is described in RFC 2136, and was released in 1997; other DNS implementations exist that also support RFC 2136—for example, BIND 8.1 and later versions. But how is the new information entered into this DDNS? It depends on what type of operating system it is; Windows 2000, both professional and servers, will send information about itself to the DDNS, regardless whether it's a static or dynamically assigned IP address. The DDNS will store this information in the DNS database. Pre-Windows 2000 computers don't know about DDNS; they need help. The new DHCP server in Windows 2000 is enhanced so it will automatically add all IP numbers it has assigned to the DDNS server, for all NT and Windows 9X computers.

There is still one more thing that we need to take care of before the WINS server becomes superfluous: Where will the system store the names of the domain controllers? Again, the solution is our new DDNS; it will accept dynamically assigned IP addresses, but it can also register the Internet services that Active Directory offers, like the names and IP addresses of domain controllers and global catalog servers. This type of information is called *Server Resource Records (SRV RRs)*.

Since DDNS supports both dynamic updates of hosts and IP addresses, and resource records to locate domain controllers, does that mean we can remove our WINS server now? The answer depends on what clients you have. If you still have pre-Windows 2000 clients or servers, they simply don't understand how to use the information in the DDNS resource records; the only thing they understand is WINS, NetBIOS broadcasts, and LMHOSTS files. Our only intelligent choice is WINS in this case, since the other two a) will not work over routers, or b) are too labor-intensive to manage. This means that most organizations will continue to use WINS for a long time.

Server Resource Records, SRV RRs

In 1996, RFC 2052 was released, describing how DNS could handle server resource records. Microsoft's DDNS in Windows 2000 supports this RFC, and so do others—for example, BIND 8.2 and later versions. These server resource records provide a general mechanism for locating and advertising Internet services, not only for client logon services. Since these are new records, in comparison with the standard DNS, they must be easy to recognize; they all start with an underscore, like ***_ldap*** and ***_gc***. These resource records are added dynamically by the NetLogon service on the Windows 2000 domain controllers; restart the NetLogon service if you need to update these resource records. In Table 6.1, you can see all resource records that NetLogon may add in the Windows 2000 DNS.

Table 6.1 Server Resource Records in DNS.

Service	Description
_ldap._tcp.*<DnsDomainName>*	Allows a client to find an LDAP server in the domain named by ***<DnsDomainName>***. For example, **_ldap._tcp.humandata.se**. The LDAP server is not necessarily a DC. Registered by all domain controllers.
_ldap._tcp.*<SiteName>*._sites.*<DnsDomainName>*	Allows a client to find an LDAP server in the domain ***<DnsDomainName>*** and the site ***<SiteName>***. For example, **_ldap._tcp.second-site.human-data.se**. Registered by all domain controllers.
_ldap._tcp.dc._msdcs.*<DnsDomainName>*	Allows a client to find a DC of the domain named by ***<DnsDomainName>***.
_ldap._tcp.*<SiteName>*._sites.dc._msdcs.*<DnsDomainName>*	Allows a client to find a DC of the domain ***<DnsDomainName>*** and the site **<SiteName>**. Registered by all domain controllers.
_ldap._tcp.pdc._msdcs.*<DnsDomainName>*	Allows a client to find the primary DC (PDC) of the domain ***<DnsDomainName>***. Only the PDC of the domain registers this name.
_ldap._tcp.gc._msdcs.*<DnsForestName>*	Allows a client to find a global catalog (GC) server. For example, **_ldap._tcp.gc._msdcs.humandata.se**. Registered by all GCs of the forest ***<DnsForestName>***.
_ldap._tcp.*<SiteName>*._sites.gc._msdcs.*<DnsForestName>*	Allows a client to find a global catalog (GC) server that is in the site ***<SiteName>***. For example, **_ldap._tcp.second-site.gc._msdcs.human-data.se**. Registered by all GCs of the forest ***<DnsForestName>***.
_gc._tcp.*<DnsForestName>*	Allows a client to find a global catalog (GC) server for this forest. For example, **_gc._tcp.humandata.se.** Registered by all LDAP servers serving a GC of the forest ***<DnsForestName>***. The LDAP server is not necessarily a DC.
_gc._tcp.*<SiteName>*._sites.*<DnsForestName>*	Allows a client to find a global catalog (GC) server for this domain that is in the site ***<SiteName>***. For example, **_gc._tcp.second-sites.human-data.se**. Registered by all LDAP servers serving a GC of the forest ***<DnsForestName>***. The LDAP server is not necessarily a DC.
_ldap._tcp.*<DomainGuid>*.domains._msdcs.*<DnsForestName>*	Allows a client to find a DC in a domain with a GUID of ***<DomainGuid>***. This operation will only be done if the ***<DnsDomainName>*** of the domain has changed and the ***<DnsForestName>*** is known. This is an unusual operation. Registered by all domain controllers.
_kerberos._tcp.*<DnsDomainName>*	Allows a client to locate a Kerberos Key Distribution Center (KDC) for the domain. All DCs providing the Kerberos service will register this name.
_kerberos._udp.*<DnsDomainName>*	The same as **_kerberos._tcp.<DnsDomainName>** except that the UDP is used.
<DnsDomainName>	Allows a client to locate a Kerberos KDC for the domain ***<DnsDomainName>*** that is in the site ***<SiteName>***. All DCs providing the Kerberos service will register this name.
_kerberos._tcp.dc._msdcs.*<DnsDomainName>*	Allows a client to find a DC running a Kerberos KDC for the domain ***<DnsDomainName>***. All DCs providing the Kerberos service will register this name.

(continued)

Table 6.1 Service Resource Records in DNS *(continued)*.

Service	Description
_kerberos._tcp.*<SiteName>*._sites.dc._msdcs.*<DnsDomainName>*	Allows a client to find a DC running a Kerberos KDC for the domain ***<DnsDomainName>*** and is in the site ***<SiteName>***. All DCs providing the Kerberos service will register this name.
_kpasswd._tcp.*<DnsDomainName>*	Allows a client to locate a Kerberos Password Change server for the domain. All DCs providing the Kerberos service will register this name.
_kpasswd._udp.*<DnsDomainName>*	Same as _kpasswd._tcp.***<DnsDomainName>*** except that the UDP protocol is used.

The Logon Process in Windows 2000

When a Windows 2000 client wants to log on to the domain, it will send a query to its DDNS server, asking for a domain controller; the DDNS server will locate all domain controllers in its database and return this information back to the client. The client uses this information and connects directly to a domain controller.

Let's see how these resource records work by looking at exactly how the logon process works for Windows 2000 clients; we assume that we have two domain controllers in our Windows 2000 domain, **oden.humandata.se** and **tor.humandata.se**. The client will contact the domain controller by LDAP, using the TCP protocol, so let's look at a DNS server in this domain and see what information it has in the _TCP folder for **humandata.se**:

```
Name          Type              Data
_gc           Service Location  [0][100][3268] oden.humandata.se.
_kerberos     Service Location  [0][100][88] tor.humandata.se.
_kerberos     Service Location  [0][100][88] oden.humandata.se.
_kpasswd      Service Location  [0][100][464] tor.humandata.se.
_kpasswd      Service Location  [0][100][464] oden.humandata.se.
_ldap         Service Location  [0][100][389] tor.humandata.se.
_ldap         Service Location  [0][100][389] oden.humandata.se.
```

This folder has a complete list of all TCP-based services; note that the same servers will also be listed under other folders in this DNS, depending on the service offered; for example, all domain controllers will also be listed under the subfolder _msdcs/_dc/_tcp. The Data column above contains the following information:

- [0] is the priority, similar to a preference value; lower value means higher priority.
- [100] is the weight; if there are two records with the same priority, but different weight, the one with the highest weight will be used. If they are equal, they will both be used, in a round-robin fashion.
- The third [xx] lists the TCP port number to be used for this protocol. For example, the GC must be contacted on TCP port 3268, and LDAP with port 389.
- The last part of the Data column is the fully qualified domain name to the host offering this service.

The following will now happen when the client wants to log on:

1. The Windows 2000 clients sends a query for **_ldap._tcp.dc._msdcs.humandata.se** to the DNS server; this folder will list all available domain controllers for this domain.
2. The DNS server looks in its database for any _LDAP resource records in the _TCP folder for the **humandata.se** domain; it finds two such records, and returns them back.
3. The client picks one of them (see below), for example **oden.humandata.se**, uses the LDAP protocol on port 389 (as listed in the resource record), and connects to the domain controller.

Since both of these domain controllers have the same priority and weight, the client can select either of them. If the selected domain controller does not answer in a timely fashion, the client will try the second domain controller. When the client gets in contact with a domain controller, this server will check the client's IP address to see if it is the closest domain controller, based on the IP subnet the server belongs to; if it isn't, the server will refer the client to the closest domain controller. This information is then cached by the client. Remember that these steps are valid only for a Windows 2000 client; older clients don't know how to use resource records.

Tip: *If you should ever need to disable the dynamic registrations of the DNS server in Windows 2000, you can do so with some Registry settings. The MS TechNet article Q246804 describes how to disable dynamic updates for different components.*

DNS and Exchange 2000

Without DNS there would be no SMTP traffic; all receiving email servers are listed in the DNS as MX records. The DNS works like an advertisement, telling the Internet what mail domains we accept and what email servers to use. All the new features in the Windows 2000 DDNS are really not important for the SMTP traffic; you could do perfectly well with any standard type of DNS. However, some parts of Exchange 2000 definitely use the new features of the DDNS, for example when Exchange needs to communicate with the Active Directory to see the address lists and Exchange configuration settings; then it needs to query the resource records in the DNS to locate the domain controllers and the global catalog servers.

If the DNS server becomes unreachable, this will prohibit the Exchange server from contacting the Active Directory; this is something that must be avoided. When creating a new DNS zone in Windows 2000, you can configure it as a *Standard primary zone* or *Standard secondary zone* DNS server, which use text files for storing all information; or as an *Active Directory integrated zone*, using the NTDS.DIT database for storing its information. The last method, to make the zone AD integrated, will replicate all DNS information to all domain controllers, thereby making all of them DNS servers. This will make the zone more resilient, and will probably also increase the performance of Exchange, since it uses DNS so extensively. If you install the standard zone type, you must make sure there are secondary DNS servers placed on each subnet, unless the network speed between your subnets is very high.

Note that this setting of zone type is individual for each DNS zone. You can have two zones in one DNS server; one of them can be AD integrated, the other can use standard DNS files. If you want to change the type of DNS installation afterward, it's easy to do; follow these steps:

1. Open the Windows 2000 DNS tool.
2. Expand the *Forward Lookup Zones*.
3. Right-click the zone you want to change, and select *Properties*.
4. At the *General* tab, you can see what type it is now; see Figure 6.11.
5. To change the type, click the *Change* button and set the new zone type; see Figure 6.12.
6. Click *OK* two times to complete the changes.

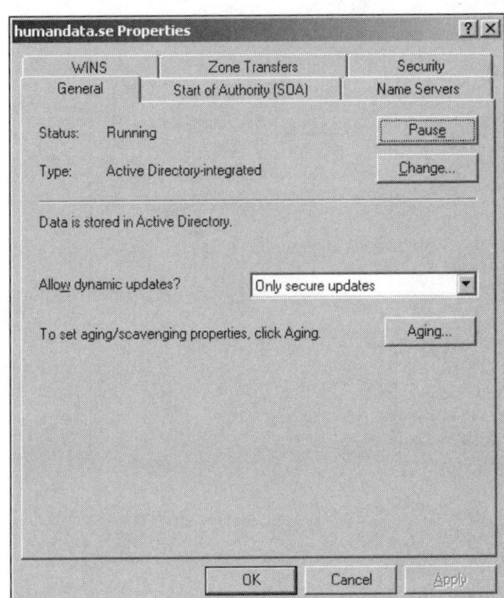

Figure 6.11
The General tab for a DNS domain.

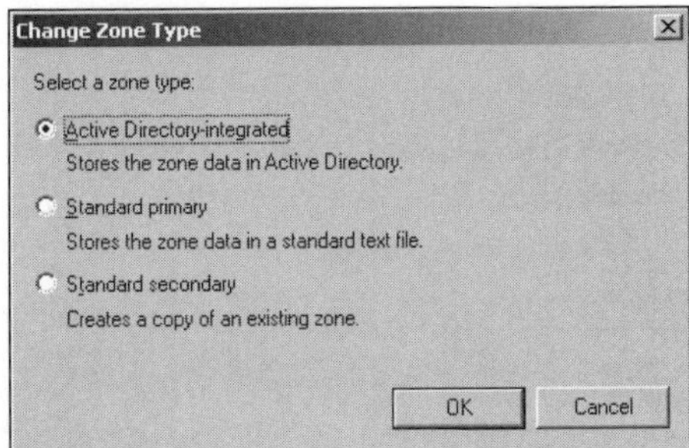

Figure 6.12
Setting a new zone type.

Make sure your Exchange servers, and all other clients and servers that are dependent on the DNS in Windows 2000, are actually using the right DNS. I have seen some installations of Windows 2000 and its DNS server, configured with all the right zones and settings, that still had problems; some clients could not log on, some admin tools like Exchange System Manager and Active Directory Users and Computers did not work at all. The problems were all due to errors in the DNS settings for these clients and servers; they were still configured to use the old DNS server.

Use the following Decision Tree 6.1 to help you select the right type of zone type for a DNS server; just remember that the same DNS can be primary for one zone and secondary for another zone simultaneously.

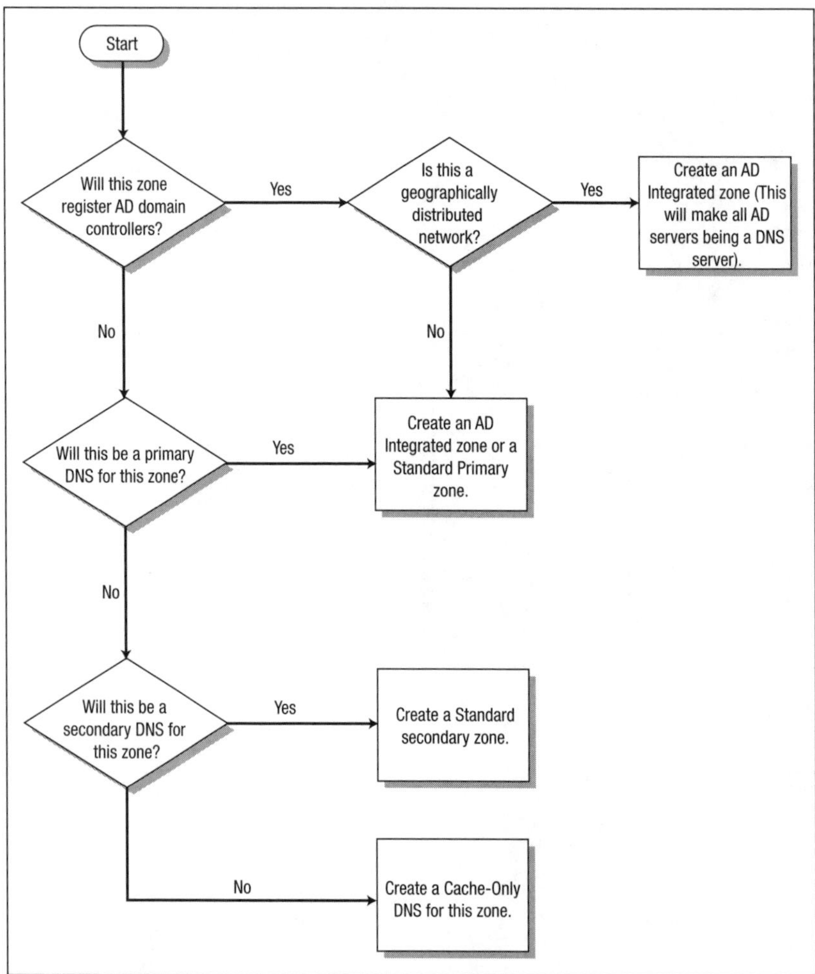

Decision Tree 6.1
Selecting the DNS zone type.

More New Features in Windows 2000 DNS

Besides the dynamic updates, resource records, and AD integration described earlier, this DNS version offers several other new features; below is a list of the more important ones. All these features together make this DNS server a very good implementation of DNS, especially for Windows 2000 domains; you should have a really good reason for not using this DNS, at least for your Windows 2000 domain.

Secure Dynamic Update

Since the information in the DNS is so critical, we must be able to control the update process. Any DNS zone that is integrated with Active Directory can be configured to use a *secure dynamic update*; this makes it possible to define what Windows 2000 groups or users have permission to update resource records in that zone. This secure dynamic update is based on the *GSS Algorithm for TSIG*, an Internet draft standard. The default method is to first try a non-secure dynamic update; if this fails then negotiate a secure dynamic update.

Controlling Update Access to Zones and Names

By default, any authenticated user can dynamically create an A or PTR resource record in a new zone. If you define an owner for a hostname, then only users and groups with write permission are enabled to modify this record. The computer that created this record will be its owner. This could sometimes be a problem, for example when there are two DHCP servers that write dynamic updates to the DNS server on behalf of pre-Windows 2000 clients. If the first DHCP server goes down, the second DHCP server will not be able to update these records if necessary. This can be solved by adding both of these DHCP servers to a special Windows 2000 group called *DnsUpdateProxy*. Any member of this group will not take ownership of names written to the DNS, and therefore they are not locked for updates.

By default, the DNS Admins group has full control of all zones and records in a Windows 2000 domain; this group is configurable through the Active Directory Users and Computers tool in the Users folder.

Aging and Scavenging

The dynamic updates of the DNS server automatically create a lot of records as computers and domain controllers are added to this zone. But these records are not always automatically deleted when the computers are removed from the network. These orphan records take up space and could also give a querying client the wrong answer.

Windows 2000 solves this problem with the ability to *scavenge* these orphan records; this means that DNS can search its database for resource records that have aged and delete them. This process is controlled by the administrator, who controls which servers and zones can be scavenged, and which records must be scavenged if they become orphans.

The DNS uses an algorithm that ensures that no records are deleted by mistake, provided you have configured all the parameters correctly. Note that this scavenge process is disabled by default. Microsoft recommends that you do not enable scavenging before you understand exactly how to configure all the settings, otherwise you may delete resource records by mistake. You can enable scavenging per DNS server, per zone, or per resource record. You define these settings on the General property tab for the zone.

Unicode Character Support

The RFC for DNS states that a subset of the 7-bit U.S. ASCII character set are the only characters accepted. Since NetBIOS names allow more characters, it could mean that some computers' NetBIOS names are not accepted by the DNS server. RFC 2181 describes an extension of the character set allowed by DNS; it specifies that a DNS label can be any binary string, possibly not even interpreted as ASCII. Microsoft has proposed that DNS names should be able to handle the UTF-8 character encoding, defined in RFC 2044; this would make it possible to use most of the characters in any language. The DNS server in Windows 2000 has support for this UTF-8 character encoding, if and when this should be accepted by the Internet world.

How to Install DNS

When installing the first domain controller in the first Windows 2000 domain in the forest, the setup wizard will look for a DNS server that offers support for dynamic updates and resource records. If it cannot find one, it will suggest creating one before continuing the domain controller setup. The most used tool for creating a domain controller is DCPROMO; this tool can also create the DNS on this server, if needed. This will be an automatic process that will update all settings necessary in this domain controller.

Preparing TCP/IP Protocol and Installing DNS

If you want to install the DNS manually instead, you can do so. However, before you begin, you must prepare the TCP/IP settings and the DNS domain name for this server; follow these steps:

1. Click *Start|Settings|Network And Dial-up Connections*. You will find at least one *Local Area Connection*.
2. Right-click the *Local Area Connection* object you want to use; select Properties.
3. Locate the *Internet Protocol* (TCP/IP) and open its properties.
4. Click the *Advanced* button, and open the *IP Settings* tab.
5. Look at the *IP settings* for this server; make sure the *IP Number*, *Subnet Mask*, and *Default Gateway* settings are correct.
6. Open the *DNS* tab; Click *Add* for adding the IP address to the preferred DNS server. Since this server will be a DNS, you add its own IP address here. If you have another DNS, you can add its IP number too, in case its own DNS service is down; just make sure its own IP address is at the top.

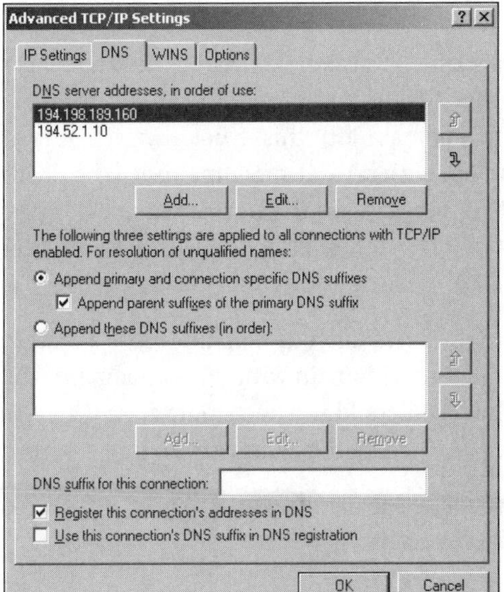

Figure 6.13
The DNS tab.

7. Still on the DNS tab, make sure the *Append Primary And Connection Specific DNS Suffix* and *Append Parent Suffixes Of The Primary DNS Suffix* options are selected; see Figure 6.13.

8. Click *OK* to close the window; close the *Network And Dial-up Connection* window.

That concludes the TCP/IP settings of this server. Now we must also check the DNS hostname and domain name used for this server; follow these steps:

1. Right-click on the *My Computer* icon on the desktop, then select *Properties*.

2. Open the *Network Identification* tab; here you see the current name for this host and domain.

3. Click *Properties* to make any changes necessary, then click *OK* to close this window. You must reboot before these new settings will take effect.

Now everything is ready for you to install the DNS server on this computer. The easiest way of doing this is probably to use the *Configure Your Server* Web tool that comes with all Windows 2000 servers. Here's how:

1. Click *Start|Administrative Tools|Configure Your Server*.

2. Click *Networking* in the left column, then click *DNS*.

3. Click *Set Up DNS* and follow the instructions.

Creating DNS Zones

Now that you have the DNS installed, it's time to create the DNS zones that this server will be responsible for. You may recall that a zone is a subset of the DNS domain tree; often you see that the zone is identical to a domain. But this is not always true; a zone can contain several domains, and a large domain with several subdomains can be divided into several zones. For example, in Figure 6.14 you can see the **humandata.se** domain with two subdomains; this domain is divided into two zones, although it could have been one large zone.

The question if you should have one or more zones for your domain tree is a matter of how complex the domain is; for example, if you have a domain with one subdomain, and there are a limited number of servers and clients, you could use one single zone. One common reason for using several zones is the need to delegate the administration to several groups.

The dynamic DNS version in Windows 2000 is special, in that it can be integrated with Active Directory. This has lots of benefits, for example:

- Host records and their PTR records are added dynamically; you don't need to manually update the DNS server unless there are some special needs.
- If the zone will be AD integrated, then all domain controllers in this domain will be a name server for this zone; they will all be multi-masters, and this means you don't have to create any primary or secondary name servers.
- If one AD-integrated name server goes down, then any other domain controller will still be able to answer all DNS queries and accept any new records for this zone.

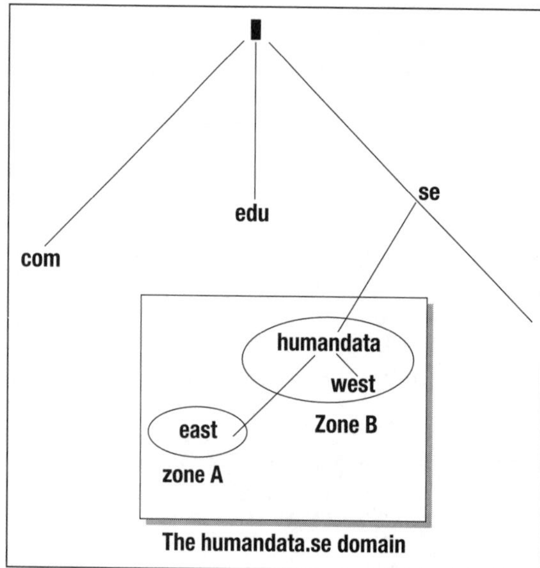

Figure 6.14
A domain tree divided into two zones.

- You don't have to make separate backups of the DNS database; when you back up the AD, you will also back up the DNS information.

Let's go ahead and create our first zone for our new DNS. Follow these steps, assuming you are running these steps on the new name server:

1. Open the DNS tool (*Start|Programs|Administrative Tools|DNS*).
2. Right-click the *DNS* object in the left pane; select *Connect To Computer* and then select *This Computer*; click *OK*.
3. You will now see a new folder with the server name; right-click on the server and select *New Zone*. This will start the New Zone Wizard.
4. Click *Next* to continue the wizard.
5. Define the zone type for the new zone. You can select between AD-integrated, Standard Primary, and Standard Secondary, but since this name server should be authoritative for the new zone, we must select between AD-integrated or Standard Primary. The Standard Primary zone type is default; however, by selecting AD-integrated, this zone will take advantage of all benefits mentioned earlier. Make your choice and then click *Next*.
6. Define what type of zone to create—forward or reverse lookup zone. Normally you create a forward lookup zone first and then a reverse zone; click *Next*.
7. Type the DNS name for the new zone, for example **myzone.com**, and then click *Next*.

8a. If this was an AD-integrated zone, continue with Step 9 below.

8b. If it was a Standard Primary zone, you must now create the zone file; see Figure 6.15. I recommend that you accept the default file name. Note that you can also import an

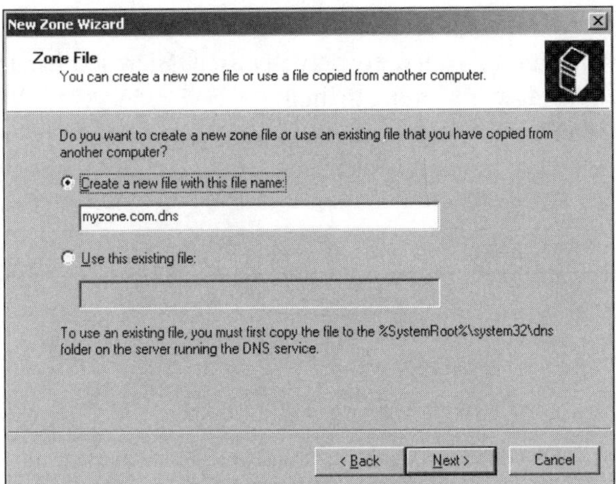

Figure 6.15
Creating the Standard zone file.

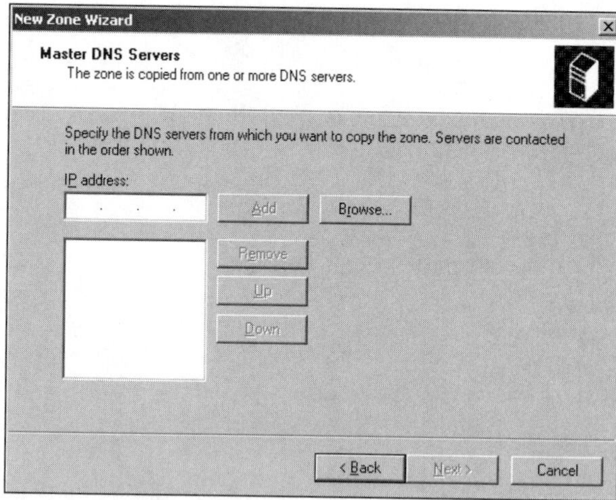

Figure 6.16
Selecting the Master DNS Servers for a secondary name server.

existing zone file by first copying it to the *\%SystemRoot%\System32\dns* folder. When ready, click *Next*.

8c. If it was a Standard Secondary zone, you will now see the Master DNS Servers window, see Figure 6.16. Type in the IP address to the Primary name server, or browse the existing DNS servers to locate it. Then click *Next*.

9. Click *Finish* to complete the New Zone Wizard and create the zone. The new zone will now be visible under the Forward Lookup Zone folder.

Adding Records to the New Zone

If the name server is authoritative for this new zone, i.e., you have created a standard primary or AD-integrated zone, the next logical step is to start adding records. A number of different records are available, but only a few are actually used. Microsoft has tried to simplify the process of adding records by renaming them in the DNS manager for Windows 2000. Table 6.2 lists all these records, with both names and a short description of each.

Table 6.2 DNS records.

Microsoft Name	Standard Name	Description
AFS database	AFSDB	Andrew File System Database server record. (RFC 1183)
Alias	CNAME	Indicates an alias DNS name for a name already specified in other resource records. (RFC 1035)
ATM	ATMA	Maps a DNS domain name to an ATM address.
Host	A	Maps a DNS domain name to a standard 32-bit IP address. (RFC 1035)
Host Information	HINFO	Used for describing CPU type and OS version. (RFC 1035)

(continued)

Table 6.2 DNS records *(continued)*.

Microsoft Name	Standard Name	Description
IPv6 Host	AAAA	A host record for IPv6 hosts; maps a DNS name to a 128-bit IPv6 address. (RFC 1886)
ISDN	ISDN	Maps a DNS domain name to an ISDN phone number. (RFC 1183)
Mail Exchanger	MX	Pointer to an email server for a given DNS domain. (RFC 1035)
Mail Group	MG	Adds domain mailboxes, specified by an MB record in the current zone, as members of a domain mailing group. (1035)
Mailbox	MB	Maps a specified domain mailbox name to a mail server.
Mailbox Information	MINFO	Specifies a domain mailbox name to contact, in case of error messages relating to the mailing list or mailbox specified in this record. (RFC 1035)
Pointer	PTR	Reverse lookup record. Lists the name for a given IP address. (RFC 1035)
Renamed Mailbox	MR	Specifies a domain mailbox name, which is the proper rename of an existing specified mailbox. (RFC 1035)
Responsible Person	RP	Specifies the domain mailbox name for a responsible person and maps this name to a domain name for which text resource records exist. (RFC 1183)
Route Through	RT	Provides an intermediate-route-through binding for internal hosts that do not have their own direct WAN address. (RFC 1183)
Service Location	SRV	Allows administrators to use several servers for a single DNS domain, to easily move a TCP/IP service from one host to another host with administration, and to designate some service provider hosts as primary servers for a service and other hosts as backups. DNS clients that use SRV-type queries ask for a specific TCP/IP service and protocol mapped to a specified DNS domain and receive the names of any available servers. (RFC 2052)
Text	TXT	Holds a string of characters that serves as descriptive text to be associated with a specific DNS domain name. (RFC 1035)
Well Known Services	WKS	Describes the well-known TCP/IP services supported by a particular protocol on a particular IP address. (RFC 1035)
X.25	X25	Maps a DNS domain name to a Public Switched Data Network (PSDN) address, such as X.121 addresses, which are typically used to identify each point of service located on a public X.25 network. (RFC 1183)

Host Records (A)

The most commonly used record is *Host*, also known as *A records*, used for recording hostnames and their IP addresses. Note that this step may not be necessary in a Windows 2000 domain, since all Windows 2000 computers will dynamically add their A records. Any IP address assigned by a Windows 2000-based DHCP server will also be added to the zone; this is also true for pre-Windows 2000 computers. If you need to assign a host record manually, follow these steps. See also Figure 6.17:

1. Right-click on the zone name, then select *New Host*.
2. Add the name of the host you want to register.

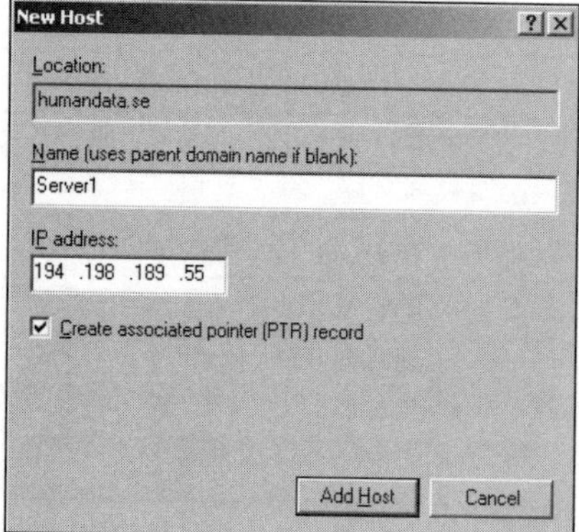

Figure 6.17
Creating a host record.

3. Fill in the IP address for the host.
4. Probably you want to create a reverse lookup record too; select the *Create Associated Pointer (PTR) Record*. Note that you cannot create PTR records until you have a corresponding reverse lookup zone for this IP subnet address.
5. Click *Add Host*, then click *OK* when informed that the new host is created; then click *Done* if there are no more hosts to create at this time.

Note that there is no control if this IP address is correct, or if it is unique; in fact, you can have several hosts with the same IP address or even the same hostname with different IP addresses. This can be used when you want to make a host known by several names; however, if you later want to change this IP address, you must update all corresponding host records. There is actually a special record for this situation, the *alias* record, where you refer to a hostname instead of an IP address.

Alias Records (CNAME)

For example, let's say you have a server named **oden** in the **humandata.se** domain; you have installed a Web service and an FTP service on this server, and you need to create DNS records, to make them known to the world. The bad solution would look like this:

```
humandata.se:
     oden      Host     194.198.189.160
     www       Host     194.198.189.160
     ftp       Host     194.198.189.160
```

It would be much easier to use the alias record; then the DNS table would look like this:

```
humandata.se:
     oden       Host    194.198.189.160
     www       Alias    oden.humandata.se
     ftp       Alias    oden.humandata.se
```

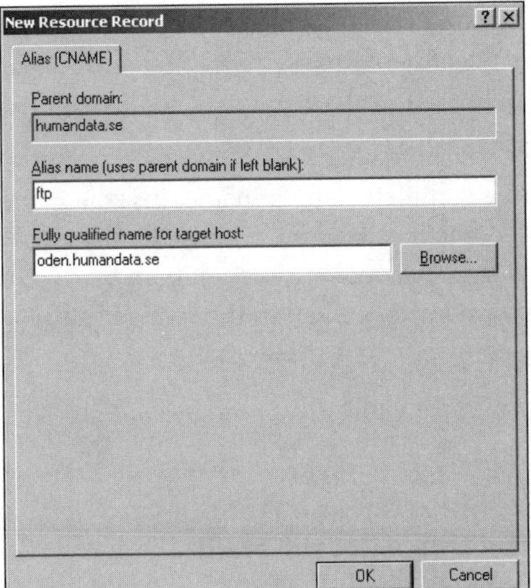

Figure 6.18
Adding the alias record.

If the IP address for oden changes, then only the host record needs to be updated; all alias records will still point to the right server. To create an alias record, right-click the zone where you want to add the new record, and select *New Alias*; see Figure 6.18.

Different Record Names in Microsoft's DNS

There is one thing that the observant reader has probably detected; the DNS management tool in Windows 2000 does not present the records as they will appear in a standard DNS file, for example in BIND. As described before, this is an attempt by Microsoft to make it easier to work with these DNS records; see Table 6.2 for a list of both the standard names and Microsoft's names. The standard way of presenting the same host records and alias records as above would look like this:

```
humandata.se:
     oden     IN A           194.198.189.160
     www      IN CNAME       oden.humandata.se
     ftp      IN CNAME       oden.humandata.se
```

If you don't use an AD-integrated DNS zone, the database will be written as a text file at *\%systemroot%\System32\DNS*; the names of the files were set when you created the standard zone. In these files, the standard names of records are used, not Microsoft's names.

Delegating Domain Names

If your organization has a large DNS domain with several subdomains, you may want to delegate the administration of some or all of these subdomains by creating different zones, as depicted in Figure 6.14. It is important that these zones have a continuous name space, or in other words, that the subdomains contained in the zone belong to the same root domain. You cannot create a zone consisting of subdomains from different root domains; in that case, you must create different zones.

To create a subdomain, right-click on the root domain and select *New Domain*; then add the name of the subdomain. Don't add the complete domain name, just the name of the subdomain. For example, to create a subdomain called *moria* under **humandata.se**, you would right-click on **humandata.se**, and then select *New Domain*; then type "moria" as the new domain name. The result would be an empty folder in the **humandata.se** domain. To delegate the authority of this new subdomain, follow these steps:

1. Right-click on the **humandata.se** root domain and select *New Delegation*. This starts the New Delegation Wizard.
2. In the *Delegated Domain Name* page, type in "moria" in the *Delegated Domain* field. Note that the *Fully Qualified Domain Name* below will be filled in automatically; it should now say **moria.humandata.se**; see Figure 6.19. Then click *Next*.
3. In the *Name Server* page, click *Add* and fill in the IP address of the DNS server that should be authoritative for this zone, and then click *Add*. Or use the *Browse* button and locate the new name server; see Figure 6.20. Then click *OK*.
4. Now you have returned to the *Name Server* page; now you can add more name servers, or click *Next* to continue.
5. Click *Finish* to complete the new delegation.

If you now look in the new subdomain moria, you will see a *Name Server* record, pointing to the server defined in Step 3 above. The next step now is to add hosts to this subdomain; this can be done dynamically, by making the clients have **moria.humandata.nu** as their DNS domain setting, or it could be done manually, as described before.

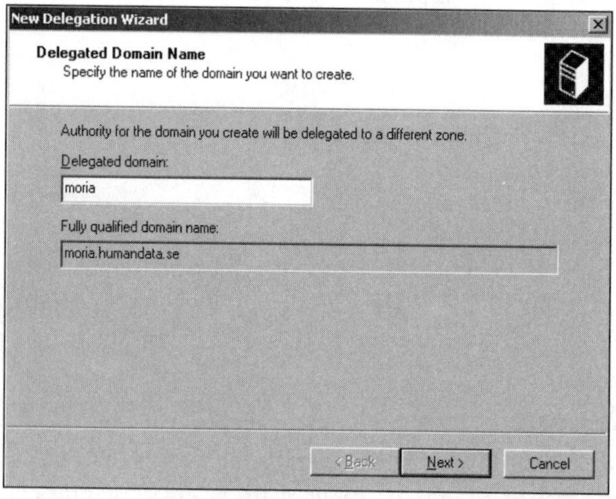

Figure 6.19
The Delegated Domain Name page.

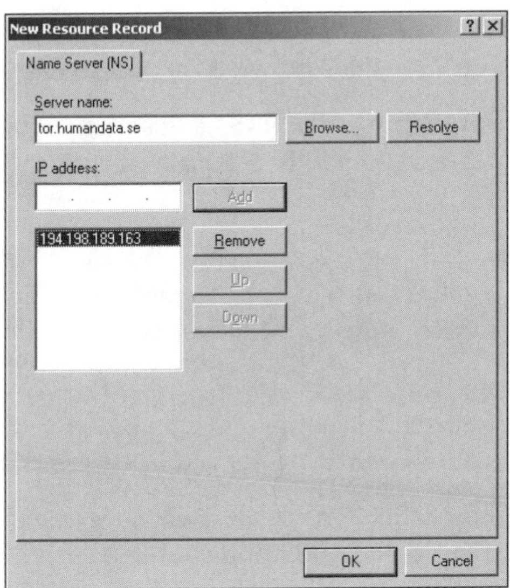

Figure 6.20
Defining the IP address of the new name server.

Note: *If the name server you referred to in Step 3 above does not have any PTR records, this step will fail! It is important that all DNS servers have both a host and PTR record; otherwise this server will not work properly.*

Moving an Existing DNS to Windows 2000

After inspecting your current DNS server implementation, you may find that it does not meet the requirements of the Windows 2000 domain. In this situation, you have two options:

- Create a separate DNS in Windows 2000 for all servers and clients that will participate in the new Windows 2000 domain. Continue to use the current DNS for all other computers.
- Migrate the current DNS to Windows 2000 DNS.

The first solution is often preferred when an organization has a complex DNS structure that they don't want to touch; the drawback will be that you now have two different DNS structures to administrate—this solution is error prone.

The second solution will give you a unified DNS structure, where you can benefit from all the new and advanced features in the Windows 2000 DNS server. The drawback will be that you need to perform a migration. It is important that this period is short and carefully planned; you don't want any servers unavailable just because the DNS information is not available.

Migrating to Windows 2000 DNS

Follow these steps to migrate from a Unix DNS to the Windows 2000 DNS server:

1. Start by preparing a Windows 2000 server; then install DNS on this server. If you later want this migrated zone to be AD integrated, it must be a domain controller; if not, it can be a stand alone server.
2. Copy all forward and reverse lookup zone files to the directory *\%systemroot%\system32\dns*. Unix has a special file called *named.boot* or *named.conf* in the */etc* directory that tells you where these files are stored; zone files usually begin with *db.* in Unix.
3. If the Unix domain name is different from the AD domain, you must rename the copied zone files; open each of them and update all domain names to the new name.
4. Use the DNS management tool in Windows 2000 and create a new zone for each zone that was copied from the Unix DNS; right-click the *Forward Lookup Zone* and select *New Zone*—this will start the New Zone Wizard.
5. Create a *Standard Primary* zone type; on the next page, type the name of the zone.
6. On the *Zone File* page, select *Use This Existing File* and type the name of the zone file that you copied before.
7. Complete the New Zone Wizard to create the zone.

After the zone is created, it is important that you check to make sure that it will allow dynamic updates; open the properties for the new zone, and look at the *General* page. Make sure that *Allow Dynamic Updates* is enabled. You must also create the reverse lookup zone; this is done exactly as listed above, except that you select *Reverse Lookup Zone* in Step 4. If you plan to stick with this standard primary zone type instead of Active Directory integrated, you must now create at least one more secondary name server.

Last, but not least; unless the Windows 2000 server name and IP address are identical to the Unix DNS, you must update this DNS information at InterNIC, or at your ISP. All computers that have the old IP address in their DNS settings must also be updated, unless they are using DHCP, in which case you must update the DNS setting for this IP scope. It is also wise to take this opportunity to migrate from any Unix-based DHCP to the Windows 2000 DHCP, since this version will dynamically add all IP addresses assigned to non-Windows 2000 clients.

Troubleshooting DNS

As we have seen several times in this chapter, one good tool for troubleshooting DNS servers is **NSLOOKUP**. This utility comes with all Windows 2000 versions, including Professional. There are also plenty of free implementations of this tool for other operating systems on the Internet. Besides this tool, a number of others are available. Table 6.3 lists some free DNS tools. All of these utilities can be found at the Web sites **www.dns.net/dnsrd/tools.html** or **www.dns.net/dnsrd/mark/wintools.html**.

Table 6.3 DNS troubleshooting tools.

Tool	Description
nslookup	The most commonly used tool; available for all operating systems. Used to query DNS servers. Note that the NSLOOKUP in Windows NT 4 does not have all the features of its counterpart in Windows 2000.
dig	Used for querying DNS servers. Similar to NSLOOKUP, but more general and will present the results in a format easier for parsing by scripts and other tools. No Windows version is available as far as I know.
host	An enhanced version of NSLOOKUP and dig. No Windows version is available as far as I know.
Cyberkit	A Windows NT/2000/ME utility with networking tools, such as Ping, TraceRoute, Finger, NslookUp, Time synchronizer, Quote of the day, NetScanner, and DBScanner.
Netinfo	Has several utilities like Ping, TraceRoute, and Local Host Info; this tool also has the ability to scan a range of IP addresses for the presence of hosts, and a service scanner that will detect DNS, HTTP, and so on.
PingPlotter	An enhanced trace route program for Windows 9x/NT/2000; does everything a standard trace router does, but with a graphical presentation, including statistics, alerts, and long-term monitoring.

Besides these free utilities, I want to mention one more tool—DNS Expert. This tool helps you analyze your DNS server, whether Unix, Linux, or Windows 2000. It has a built-in check for more than 70 different DNS problems, ranging from "more than one A record with the same IP address" to "same mail server listed with a different preference value."

Using the NSLOOKUP Tool

Since the **NSLOOKUP** utility comes with all Windows 2000 computers, I want to describe how to use it in some common troubleshooting situations. Please note that this is not a complete description of how to use **NSLOOKUP**; plenty of Internet sites and books go into much more detail than I will here.

NSLOOKUP works with only one name server at a time; the default is the DNS that your client's TCP/IP stack uses as its primary DNS server. It can be run either interactively or in non-interactive mode. If you only want to retrieve one piece of data, use the non-interactive mode; for more advanced work, use an interactive session.

To start **NSLOOKUP** in interactive mode, just type "nslookup". For help, type "?" or "help". To quit, type "exit". As you can see, the first information given is the name of the connected name server, or **oden.humandata.se** in this example:

```
C:\>nslookup
Default Server:  oden.humandata.se
Address:  194.198.189.160

> help
Commands:   (identifiers are shown in uppercase, [] means optional)
NAME            - print info about the host/domain NAME using default server
NAME1 NAME2     - as above, but use NAME2 as server
help or ?       - print info on common commands
```

```
set OPTION       - set an option
    all                 - print options, current server and host
    [no]debug           - print debugging information
    [no]d2              - print exhaustive debugging information
    [no]defname         - append domain name to each query
    [no]recurse         - ask for recursive answer to query
    [no]search          - use domain search list
    [no]vc              - always use a virtual circuit
    domain=NAME         - set default domain name to NAME
    srchlist=N1[/N2/.../N6] - set domain to N1 and search list to N1,N2, etc.
    root=NAME           - set root server to NAME
    retry=X             - set number of retries to X
    timeout=X           - set initial time-out interval to X seconds
    type=X              - set query type (ex. A,ANY,CNAME,MX,NS,PTR,SOA,SRV)
    querytype=X         - same as type
    class=X             - set query class (ex. IN (Internet), ANY)
    [no]msxfr           - use MS fast zone transfer
    ixfrver=X           - current version to use in IXFR transfer request
server NAME      - set default server to NAME, using current default server
lserver NAME     - set default server to NAME, using initial server
finger [USER]    - finger the optional NAME at the current default host
root             - set current default server to the root
ls [opt] DOMAIN [> FILE] - list addresses in DOMAIN (optional: output to FILE)
    -a           -  list canonical names and aliases
    -d           -  list all records
    -t TYPE      -  list records of the given type (e.g. A,CNAME,MX,NS,PTR etc.)
view FILE            - sort an 'ls' output file and view it with pg
exit             - exit the program

> exit
C:\>
```

To run **NSLOOKUP** in noninteractive mode for querying for the IP address of a given host, for example **balder.humandata.se**, simply type "nslookup" and the host; you will get the result and then return to the command prompt:

```
C:\>nslookup balder.humandata.se
Server:  oden.humandata.se
Address:  194.198.189.160

Name:    balder.humandata.se
Address:  194.198.189.252
C:\>
```

Below is a list of common tasks for **NSLOOKUP**; the first looks up different data types, such as the address for a name or the name for an IP address; this is the default data type. Use *Set Type* or *Set Query* to select another data type. See examples below:

```
C:\>nslookup
Default Server:  oden.humandata.se
Address:  194.198.189.160

> balder.humandata.se
Server:  oden.humandata.se
Address:  194.198.189.160

Name:    balder.humandata.se
Address:  194.198.189.252

> 194.198.189.161
Server:  oden.humandata.se
Address:  194.198.189.160

Name:    ghusman.humandata.se
Address:  194.198.189.161
```

Above are examples of querying default data types. Below is an example of querying for a particular type, in this case the MX records; then we will ask for any type of records:

```
> set type=mx
> humandata.se
Server:  oden.humandata.se
Address:  194.198.189.160

humandata.se    MX preference = 20, mail exchanger = tor.humandata.se
humandata.se    MX preference = 10, mail exchanger = oden.humandata.se
tor.humandata.se        internet address = 194.198.189.163
oden.humandata.se       internet address = 194.198.189.160

> set type=any
> humandata.se
Server:  oden.humandata.se
Address:  194.198.189.160

humandata.se    internet address = 194.198.189.163
humandata.se    internet address = 194.198.189.160
humandata.se    nameserver = oden.humandata.se
humandata.se    nameserver = tor.humandata.se
humandata.se
```

```
        primary name server = oden.humandata.se
        responsible mail addr = admin
        serial  = 2001010162
        refresh = 900 (15 mins)
        retry   = 600 (10 mins)
        expire  = 86400 (1 day)
        default TTL = 3600 (1 hour)
humandata.se    MX preference = 20, mail exchanger = tor.humandata.se
humandata.se    MX preference = 10, mail exchanger = oden.humandata.se
oden.humandata.se       internet address = 194.198.189.160
tor.humandata.se        internet address = 194.198.189.163
tor.humandata.se        internet address = 194.198.189.163
oden.humandata.se       internet address = 194.198.189.160
```

Sometimes you can see that the result is from a non-authoritative name server. You can switch to another name server any time in interactive mode; just type the command "server" and the new server or its IP address. Sometimes the new server is not fully operational, or you have switched to a host that doesn't have any name server installed; then you can't return back again if you don't use a little trick. Look at this example:

```
C:\>nslookup
Default Server:  oden.humandata.se
Address:  194.198.189.160
```

The default name server is obviously **oden.humandata.se**, as listed above. Now let's switch to the server **loke.humandata.se**, which doesn't have a DNS, and then try to query for the IP address of **balder.humandata.se**:

```
> server loke.humandata.se
Default Server:  loke.humandata.se
Address:  194.198.189.169

> balder.humandata.se
Server:  loke.humandata.se
Address:  194.198.189.169

*** loke.humandata.se can't find balder.humandata.se: No response from server
```

Of course this does not work; we get the error message *No response from server*. This is a common scenario when you are debugging newly installed DNS servers and are switching back and forth. Now let's try to return to our first name server:

```
> server oden.humandata.se
*** Can't find address for server oden.humandata.se: No response from server
```

Again we get the same error message. But there is a special command, *lserver*, used for querying our local name server that we can use instead:

```
> lserver oden.humandata.se
Default Server:  oden.humandata.se
Address:  194.198.189.160
```

You can use the command *ls* to make **NSLOOKUP** perform a complete zone transfer. This feature is especially good when you're troubleshooting name servers—for example, if a server has a spelling error that prohibits you from querying about this server, or to get a complete list of all hosts that are in a remote domain:

```
> ls humandata.se
[oden.humandata.se]
 humandata.se.                A      194.198.189.163
 humandata.se.                A      194.198.189.160
 humandata.se.                NS     server = oden.humandata.se
 humandata.se.                NS     server = tor.humandata.se
 gc._msdcs                    A      194.198.189.160
 balder                       A      194.198.189.169
 demo1                        A      194.198.189.150
 demo2                        A      194.198.189.161
 moria                        NS     server = tor.humandata.se
 oden                         A      194.198.189.160
 slow                         A      194.198.189.253
 tor                          A      194.198.189.163
```

If the output is more than you can see in one screen, you can redirect this to a file instead: **ls humandata > /tmp/zone.txt**. It is important to use the front slash (/) instead of the backslash (\). Later you can view this file from within **NSLOOKUP** by typing "view /tmp/zone.txt". Again, it's important to use front slashes. The *ls* command can also be used to list certain records, for example MX records, by using the *–t* parameter:

```
> ls -t mx humandata.se
[oden.humandata.se]
 humandata.se.                MX     20   tor.humandata.se
 humandata.se.                MX     10   oden.humandata.se
```

Finally, some tips about using **NSLOOKUP** in troubleshooting situations:

- Make sure you are using the right name server; it is easy to simply continue with the default name server instead of switching to the one you are troubleshooting.
- If you are looking for a particular data type, for example A records, that does not exist on the name server, you will get an error message saying "No such records available"; in this case, try *set type=any* and make a new query to see what records exist.

- If **NSLOOKUP** says that the default name server has the IP address 0.0.0.0 when you start it, then it could not find any name server; check the DNS settings for this client.
- If **NSLOOKUP** exits with the error message "Can't find server names for address" when you start it, the problem might be that the name server does not have any PTR record; add it and try again.

Summary

Below is a list of some of the most important topics and keywords mentioned in this chapter. Use it as a quick way of refreshing your memory.

- DNS stands for Domain Name System; it was designed by Paul Mockapetris and released as RFCs 882 and 883 in 1984.
- These RFCs were later replaced by RFCs 1034 and 1035.
- ARPANET was the predecessor of the Internet, running from late 1960 to 1988.
- The standard version of DNS is a database with names and IP addresses; these are manually updated.
- A DNS server is also referred to as a *name server*.
- All clients use a process called the resolver to query the name server.
- In the DNS world, all Internet computers are divided into smaller parts, or domains.
- Every domain has a DNS server that is responsible for its names and IP addresses.
- A DNS zone consists of one or more domains, belonging to the same name space; each zone has one authoritative name server.
- The root domain in the DNS tree is marked with a period.
- All domains under the root domain are known as Top Level Domains (TLDs); examples are **.com**, **.edu**, and country codes such as **.se**, **.uk**, and **.fr**.
- There is only one authoritative name server per zone—the primary name server.
- Secondary name servers have a read-only copy of the DNS database; they are used for load balancing and fault tolerance.
- The SOA record in the zone database describes the name servers, responsible persons, and polling settings.
- Reverse name resolution means to find the name for a given IP address; this can only be done if the name is listed in the reverse lookup zone.
- **in-addr.arpa** is the reverse name domain; it consists of IP octets (bytes) in four levels. The most significant octet is listed directly under the in-addr.arpa domain.

- MX records are used for listing email servers that accept incoming SMTP messages.
- Preference values are used by sending email servers to prioritize between different MX records; if the preference values are equal, there will be a random selection.
- Host records, also known as A records, are used for listing hosts in the DNS database.
- BIND is the most common Unix implementation of DNS. There is also a BIND version for MS Windows.
- Windows 2000 domain controllers use DNS extensively—if they don't work, you will have all sorts of problems.
- The Windows 2000 DNS has support for Dynamic DNS (DDNS; RFC 2136) and Server Resource Records (SRV RR; RFC 2052).
- All Windows 2000 computers dynamically add their IP addresses to the DDNS.
- Any IP address that is assigned to a non-Windows 2000 computer from a Windows 2000 DHCP will also be dynamically added to the DDNS.
- SRV RRs are used to define general Internet services, like domain controllers and global catalog servers.
- If there is more than one server with the same resource, the client will compare their priority and weight to select one of them.
- Exchange 2000 uses DNS for SMTP address resolution and for querying the Active Directory for address lists and configuration settings.
- The DNS in Windows 2000 has support for secure dynamic updates, control of updates, aging, and scavenging, and Unicode UTF 8.
- Windows 2000 uses simpler but nonstandard names of records; for example, Alias instead of CNAME.
- You can delegate a subdomain to another name server.
- The standard utility for troubleshooting a DNS is **NSLOOKUP**, available in all versions of Windows 2000 and most other operating systems.

Chapter 7

Designing Your Exchange 2000 Organization

It's easy to install Exchange 2000 Server, but to make it an effective and optimized Ex change 2000 system you need to plan your installation carefully. This chapter is about designing and planning an Exchange 2000 organization; the goal is to meet both users' needs and administrative needs, without creating more technical demands than necessary. This may seem like an easy task at first, but when you start looking at all the details you need to take care of, and then try to find the technical specifications for the current environment, you will quickly realize that it will take time.

Most Exchange installations fall under one of two categories: the first type is carefully designed and planned out, and the other type is completed by administrators who simply skip this step and start the installation directly, hoping for the best and solving each problem as it arises. Since I am a senior Exchange consultant, I love both of these groups; the first since the administrators are serious and understand they need an experienced Exchange designer; the second because they soon discover that their Exchange system is a mess and they now need an experienced Exchange consultant to clean it up. Since you are reading this chapter, you hopefully belong to the first group.

I have done a number of Exchange designs since its first release in 1996, for different types of organizations. When designing, I recommend you start by defining the objectives for your Exchange system; then continue by checking the current status of network connections, servers, and the locations of your users. Your objectives should meet these types of needs:

- Organizational needs, also referred to as users' needs
- Administrative needs

It's easier to create a design plan when you know what's important for the organization, and what the objectives are. After all, you've invested in an Exchange system based on needs that this software will be able to satisfy. In my opinion, the sheer number of clients is not the most critical factor; a system for 250 users can in fact be harder to design than a system for 25,000 users. More important is how distributed the organization is, and the available bandwidth between the different sites. If the organization has the luxury of a

10Mbps high-speed network connection, then it will only be a matter of calculating the number of servers needed and making sure it's a secure email system with multiple connections for fault tolerance. However, this is seldom the case; it's more often a number of network sites with just a handful of users, connected by overloaded 64Kbps lines and a number of ISDN connections. Designing a good Exchange organization on top of such a network is more an art form than it is just following some simple guidelines. I remember an old Chinese saying: "You will not be a good doctor until you have placed a hundred patients in the graveyard!" Drastic, but probably true; the same is valid for designing Exchange organizations—the more experience you have, the better probability for a successful design.

During the five years Exchange has existed, I have returned many times to designs I made a few years back; I can honestly confess that some of my first efforts would be designed differently today, but most are still valid. However, due to the rapid technical development in computer hardware, and especially the cheaper and faster Internet connections available today, I have changed my presumptions for building an Exchange organization. All the new features in Windows 2000 domains, with Active Directory, along with the enhancements in Exchange 2000, give the designer much more freedom of choice, compared with just a few years back. Another thing that strikes me when I have returned to some of my previous Exchange designs is that the basic ideas I had when designing these organizations, such as keep it simple with as few Exchange sites as possible, have been forgotten when the organizations themselves continued to expand the system. Now some of them have developed into something I always tried to avoid: complex systems with a large number of Exchange sites, some of them consisting of just five to 10 users each. The bad thing is that it will most likely happen again, unless the people taking over the responsibility for the Exchange system have the knowledge to make the right choices in the future.

Define User Needs

The number one objective in design should always be to meet the users' needs, and if possible to exceed them. Sounds easy, right? Just ask them what they want and build the Exchange organization based on that. Wrong! This is one of the most difficult questions to answer. If you ask 10 users, you will probably get 10 different answers. One good piece of advice is to start with the current mail system, and try to find out how it's used. If you are going to design an Exchange 2000 organization, and they currently use Exchange 5.5, this will be an easier task compared to the case where the current mail system is MS Mail, cc-Mail, or HP Open Mail, since these types of mail systems do not have many of the features that the new Exchange 2000 environment offers. It's hard for a user to know whether they need a feature they have never tried. However, from my own experience I can say that users prioritize, in order, these features:

- Email functionality
- Calendar
- Public folders

Analyzing User Behavior

Try to identify different users' groups—for example, different departments, managers versus non-managers, headquarters versus remote office sites, and so on. Take a survey of these groups; for example, ask them what the three best features are in the current mail system. Ask them also about three features they are missing today. If you pick at least five people from each group, you will get a good estimate of what the users like most and what they are missing. Use this information to prioritize what to focus on when designing the mail system and its features. Below are some common questions that your analysis should be able to answer:

- *Who are the users sending messages to*?—In most cases, the 80/20 rule is valid, i.e., a user sends about 80 percent of the messages within his or her own group, and 20 percent outside it. This is also true within the department, the division, and the company itself. Investigate the log files of the current email system to analyze this.
- *How many messages are sent every day*?—Microsoft has suggested three categories of users: light, medium, and heavy. For the new Exchange 2000 environment, a new category has been introduced: *MAPI Message Benchmark 2*, or MMB2; see below for more information about these categories.
- *How are attachments used*?—Are all users sending attachments, or just some users? What types of attachments are used most? What is the average attachment size? What are their future needs for attachments?
- *How will calendars be used*?—Will free/busy information be used within its own group or all over the company? How about detailed information about bookings? Which users need access to other users' calendars? Is there a need for a group calendar, beyond the scope of Outlook? If there is, you must look for add-on products. Will the calendar be used for booking resources? If yes, should everyone be able to book the resource directly or will there be a single person responsible for all bookings?
- *What is the need for email security*?—Will the Key Management System fulfill the needs? Are S/MIME or PGP needed for external message transfer? Does the Outlook Web Access client need SSL protection? Does the traffic between SMTP servers need TLS protection?

Analyzing Public Folder Usage

Public folders may be a new concept to users, depending on the mail system they used before Exchange 2000; this means that it can be very hard to estimate and analyze the public folder usage, but you still must answer some questions. If public folders are new to them, let a test group of users use them to see how they can address the needs of their organization; make sure to train them in how to use public folders—for example, how to store different types of contents, like messages, contacts, and calendar bookings; also show them how permissions can be used to control the information, how the content can be available to all users in the organization, and what electronic forms can do. Some important questions regarding public folder usage are:

- How will public folders be used? Just for ad-hoc occasions, sharing information when needed, or is there a need for a clear public folder tree structure, for example with a branch for each division?
- Should everyone have permission to create top-level folders?
- Should the content be available outside the routing groups?
- How much information will be stored in the public folders?
- How long will the information be stored in the folders? Should information be automatically removed after a given time? For example, should all messages older than 30 days be cleaned out?
- Will some folders use electronic forms to present their information? If yes, for what type of clients—just MAPI or OWA clients, or both? If both, an HTTP form must be designed. Note that Outlook 97 does not have any support for HTTP clients.
- Is there a need for creating general-purpose public folders, for example to be used for storing MS Office documents or special applications like Help Desk systems? If yes, what users will need access to this information? They must belong to the same Exchange server or have a replicated copy of this GP store.
- Will there be a need for Usenet news groups, stored in a public folder? If yes, how often should there be a news feed replication? For how long will information be stored? Can circular logging be used for this store?

Analyzing Cyclical Usage Patterns

Try to find out if there are any cyclical patterns in the usage of Outlook or the network; this is important since your planning of bandwidth usage must take into account regular peaks. Try to find out patterns like:

- Are all users starting Outlook at about the same time; for example, does everyone start working at 9 o'clock?
- Are there any regular usage peaks? There is often one peak in the morning, one right after lunch, and one more at the end of the day.
- Are there any special applications running at regular times, like file transfers or backup procedures?

It is also important to know what type of formatting your users prefer; three different types are available: Plain Text, Rich Text Format (RTF), and HTML. They differ in both features and size. If your users don't mind sending messages without any formatting, they should use Plain Text, since this will work with any type of client. The Rich Text Format adds just a little overhead, but only works for Microsoft clients and Lotus Notes clients. HTML

Table 7.1 The different types of message formats.

Format	Features	Works With	Size
Plain Text	No formatting features	All types of message clients	100%
RTF	Lots of formatting features	Only Exchange, Outlook, and Notes clients	110%
HTML	Lots of formatting features	Practically all modern clients	120-140%

adds the most overhead, but works for most modern mail clients. But this is only half the truth—actually sending the message generates a much larger network traffic size, compared to the size of the message itself, depending on the type of client. Table 7.1 offers a summary of the different format types, looking only at the message itself; later in this chapter you will find information about how different client protocols affect the transferred message size.

Another important factor when analyzing user behavior is to find out where the message will be stored. In Exchange, messages can be stored in two places: the Exchange server store, or in a personal store.

Storing Messages in the Exchange Store

This is the preferred storage for all types of messages, for many reasons. First, all information in Exchange stores will enjoy the transaction log system and the daily backups; information stored here will be much safer than if stored in a personal storage file. If all user information is stored in the Exchange store, you can also take advantage of the *single instance store* feature, where a message to any number of users belonging to the same Exchange store is stored only once. By using this central storage, your users can share their private information, like calendar, inbox, or contact folders. This type of storage is also necessary if users want to get access to their messages by Web clients or move between different clients; see Figure 7.1.

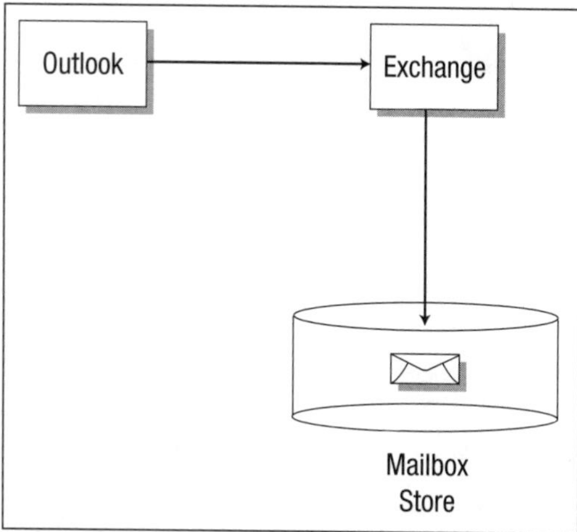

Figure 7.1
Central storage of mailbox data.

Storing Information in the Personal Store (PST File)

This type of storage requires that each client create a personal store, or PST file, on their local hard drive or possibly in their home directory on a server. If a PST file is the primary storage for the Outlook client, this will have several drawbacks:

- The information is not protected by the transaction log system.
- If the PST file is stored on the local computer, it will be harder to take a backup.
- No more single instance storage; a mail to 10 persons will exist as 10 copies.
- Users cannot share their private folders, like calendars or inboxes.

The PST file is most often used in situations where users have notebooks or are connected by slow network links; in the last example, all new messages are transferred in the background to the PST file, without the user noticing. Later, when the user opens the message, it will open instantly. But if the messages were centrally stored in the Exchange store, large messages could take a long time to open, due to the slow link. Although the PST file does offer some advantages, this type of storage is normally something to avoid due to the many serious disadvantages; see Figure 7.2.

Offline Storage Files (OSTs)

So what do you do if you want to use a central Exchange store, but still need access to information offline, like for notebook computers? There is a third solution; you can have a copy of all your mailbox information replicated from the Exchange server to a local OST file. Later, when using the notebook in offline mode, you will see all messages in this OST file; you can reply or create new messages, read calendar bookings and create new ones, and so on. The next time you get a connection to the Exchange store, every modification will automatically be replicated back to the Exchange server; see Figure 7.3.

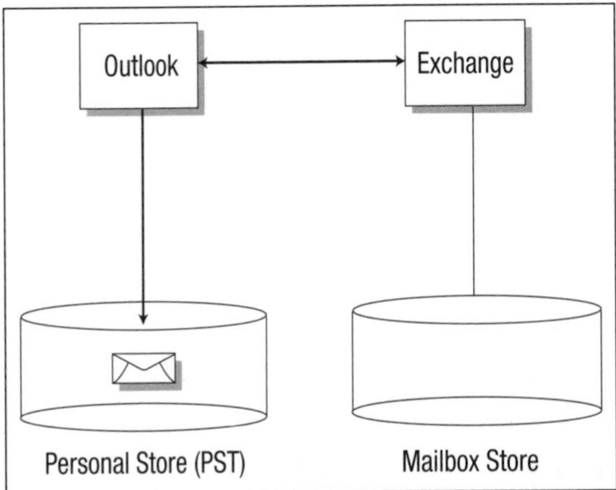

Figure 7.2
Using PST files for primary storage.

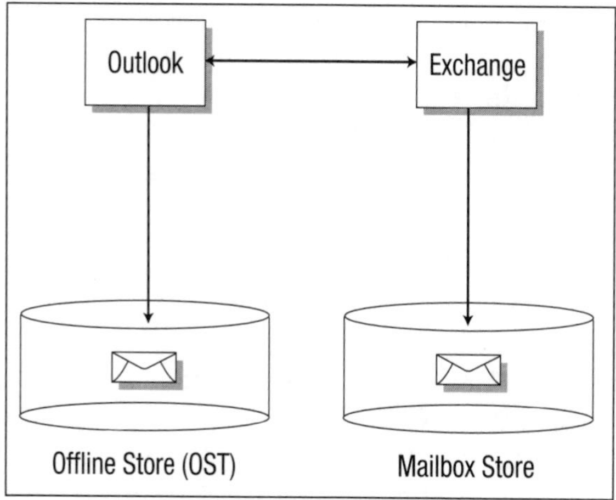

Figure 7.3
Using OST files for synchronizing mailbox data.

This means that all the advantages of the central Exchange store are available, and at the same time offline storage is possible. This replication process is also known as *synchronization*, and works in both ways. The synchronization from the client to the server is always automatic and is performed as soon as the client gets in contact with the server. However, the synchronization from the server to the client may be configured in many ways; the default is manual activation by the F9 key, or menu: *Tools|Synchronize*. Outlook can also be configured to synchronize at regular intervals automatically, like every 60 minutes. This OST synchronization technique can also be used for small branch offices with slow network links, like ISDN; configure Outlook for central storage, run Outlook in offline mode, and use synchronization to update the local copy of the Exchange mailbox information.

Different Client Access Methods

Exchange has always been a MAPI-centric email system, but has also supported Internet clients like POP3, IMAP4, and Web clients. When designing the Exchange organization, you must also try to find out what type of messaging clients will be used, and how many of each type will be included; they will all have different requirements regarding the network bandwidth and the TCP ports used. The message format is also something that will affect network bandwidth; for example, 300 Outlook clients using RTF will generate the same amount of network traffic as 100 Outlook clients using HTML formatting. Another important factor is the number of remote access users that use ordinary modems or ISDN to get connected to the Exchange system.

Outlook Clients (MAPI)

Outlook 2002 is the recommended standard client for Exchange 2000; it's the most advanced client type, in terms of available features. It is also the most demanding client, in terms of network speed, since it uses MAPI on top of the RPC protocol; anything below 64Kbps makes this client almost unbearably slow. The time to start up this client depends on the size of the mailbox and the number of calendar bookings; I have done tests showing that a mailbox with about 2,000 messages in the inbox and about one daily calendar booking will result in a data transfer of about 60KB between the server and the client, which adds up to 60KB = 60,000 bytes × 8 = 480,000 bits. Add some overhead for start and stop bits and you have about 640,000 bits. With a 64Kbps connection, it will take about 10 seconds just to start this client.

This calculation assumes that the Outlook 2002 preview feature is not activated; otherwise, this data transfer could take much longer, depending on the message displayed in the preview window. The data transferred is message headers, like To, Subject, and Date fields; every message header itself is about 100 bytes in size. Attachments in messages are not downloaded until opened; this is true only for Outlook 2000 and 2002. For each name resolution there will be around 1K for manual name checking and 3.5K for automatic name checking; this difference is due to the fact that manual checking uses a built-in name cache in Outlook 2002, but the automatic check will always generate an LDAP query to the global catalog server. Another interesting thing is that checking detailed information for a user using the *To* field generates 70 percent more network traffic than checking the same detailed information using the Address Book. In general, Outlook 2002 querying the global catalog generates about the same network traffic as Outlook 97 querying the Exchange 2000 server.

Warning! *Outlook can format messages using one of three formats: RTF, HTML, and Plain Text; note that the same message will result in very different network traffic usage. The Plain Text format and RTF generate approximately the same amount (RTF is in fact smaller!); however, the HTML version of the same message will be between three and five times higher! Make sure your users stay with RTF unless it's necessary to send HTML-formatted messages.*

All MAPI clients, such as Outlook 2002 and its predecessor, use the Remote Procedure Call (RPC) protocol. RPC uses several TCP and UDP ports when communicating with the server; if there is a firewall or filtering router between the client and Exchange, they must allow traffic on these ports, otherwise Outlook will not work. Exactly what ports depends on the type of client—Outlook 2002 uses both RPC and LDAP ports, Outlook 98 uses only RPC unless the client has installed the *Outlook 98 Archive Patch*; if so, then both RPC and LDAP ports will be used. All other MAPI clients, including the old Exchange client, will use only the RPC ports. When the client starts, the following will happen:

1. Outlook uses the MAPI profile stored in the Registry to find the name and the IP address of the Exchange server (and the global catalog server if LDAP is used).

2. The client contacts the Exchange server on TCP port 135, asking for the port numbers to the Information Store and Directory Service; these two port numbers are returned to the client. The server also registers what port number the client is using.

3. The client then connects to the Directory Service first and then to the Information Store, using the given port numbers.

4. When this RPC session is established, it is used for a user account validation and a mailbox connection. Next, the client requests all message headers in the Inbox folder and checks the calendar and task for any reminder that should be notified to this mailbox user.

To summarize, the port numbers are 135 plus two more for the IS and DS; by default, they are randomly set to any available port number above 1023 when starting the Exchange server. These port numbers will be valid until the next time the server is restarted. This is not acceptable when there is a firewall between the client and the server. Follow the Microsoft TechNet article Q155831 to set the DS and IS port to a fixed number, then configure the firewall to open these two port numbers.

Post Office Protocol POP3

The simplest client available for Exchange 2000 is the Internet protocol POP3, or Post Office Protocol, version 3. This POP protocol is designed to move data from the server before making the messages available to the user. This means that the server is used as a temporary storage for the messages; the messages will be deleted on the server, unless a special flag for storing a "copy" is set on the client. The only information that can be retrieved with a POP3 client is the Inbox folder; no access is possible to any other folder, including the calendar, the contacts, or public folders. In fact, the POP3 client does not even have support for a central address list, like the global address list (GAL) in Exchange 2000. However, by using the LDAP support found in most POP3 clients, it is still possible to search the GAL. Microsoft offers POP3 support in its Outlook Express client, but it is also possible to use a standard Outlook 2000 client using POP3 in Internet Mode Only; the only folder available will still be the Inbox. The POP3 client needs to poll the server to find any new messages; you can configure this polling to be performed at regular intervals.

The network traffic generated by the POP3 client is minimal; there is no traffic when the client launches, unless it's configured to download new messages at logon. The only traffic is generated when the user selects the Send/Receive action. When downloading messages from the POP3 server, i.e., Exchange 2000, the overhead is low. POP3 can only use Plain Text or HTML format; be aware that HTML messages will be at least twice the size of messages in Plain Text format!

The port used for POP3 is TCP 110 for normal unencrypted traffic or port 995 for POP3 with SSL encryption; no other ports are used. Note that all communication over port 110 is in clear text, including the domain account name and password, used for authenticating the user. It is not recommended that you run POP3 over port 110 on a public network like the Internet, since it is easy to use a network monitor to read the account name and its password (see also Chapter 14 for a discussion about network monitors.)

Internet Message Access Protocol, IMAP4

IMAP4 is an enhancement of the POP3 protocol, designed to take advantage of the multiple folders available on modern mail servers like Exchange. Besides that, IMAP4 can also read messages without downloading every one of them to the local disk first. This makes this client protocol much better suited for the Exchange environment and also for remote access situations. However, the IMAP4 protocol is limited to folders of mail type, like the Inbox or any private mail folder and public mail folders, but no other folder types, like calendar or contact folders. Also, the IMAP4 protocol has the same limitation as POP3 regarding access to server-based address lists. It can only access its own personal address book, unless the LDAP protocol is installed; then it can access the global catalog and its global address list, exactly like the POP3 client. Outlook Express has some extra features not found in other IMAP4 clients: The server can notify the client of new messages, and the server uses three mailbox folders for the IMAP4—Inbox, Sent Items, and Draft. The description below is based on the Outlook Express client.

The network traffic generated by the IMAP4 protocol is slightly higher than for the POP3 protocol; when the client is launched, it generates 2K of traffic because it connects to the Exchange server. When selecting the Inbox folder, it downloads the message headers; obviously the number of messages will affect the size of the network traffic generated. When sending messages, a copy of the message will also be sent to the Sent Item folder on the Exchange server; this means that all messages are sent twice! If you disable this option, you will decrease the network load in this operation by 50 percent. The reason for this is that the first message is sent to an SMTP server, which could be a machine other than the Exchange server; still, you would normally prefer to have a copy of all sent items on the server in case you are using more than one client.

When a message with an attachment opens, both are first downloaded to the client; next time you read the same message or open the attachment, the client will use the locally stored copy. The server will send all new message headers automatically to the IMAP4 client; there is no need for generating a refresh. As the POP3 protocol, IMAP4 can only use Plain Text or HTML format; again, HTML messages will be twice the size of messages in Plain Text format!

The port used for IMAP4 is TCP 143 for normal unencrypted traffic or port 993 for IMAP4 with SSL encryption; no other ports are used. As with the POP3 protocol, all communication over port 143 is sent in clear text, including the domain account name and password. It is not recommended that you run IMAP4 over port 143 on a public network like the Internet, since it is easy to use a network monitor to read the account name and its password.

Outlook Web Access Client, OWA

This is the Web client, used to get access to almost all Exchange information by using a standard Web browser. There is a great performance difference between standard Web browsers, like Netscape and Opera, and XLM, Web-DAV, and DHTML-enabled browsers, like Internet Explorer 5. This new version of OWA can access all types of folders, both in the private mailbox and in public folders. However, since it is a Web browser, it does not have an online session with the Exchange server; any new messages will not show up until you refresh the inbox in the OWA client.

This client generates more network traffic than the others, due to the fact that all information from the server must be converted to Web pages; for example, each message header generates about 600 bytes, compared to 100 for Outlook 200x. Still, much of the traffic is reduced by the XML content; without it, the network load would be even bigger.

The way attached files are treated by the OWA client differs, depending on what you are doing:

- When you *create* a message and want to add a file to it, this file will immediately be uploaded to the Exchange server when it is attached, before the message is sent.
- When *reading* a message with an attachment, this file will stay on the server until the attachment is opened.
- If you *forward* a message with an attachment, the way the attachment is treated will depend on the message format. An attachment in an RTF-formatted message will be downloaded to the client before being forwarded; an attachment in an HTML message will stay on the server.

Tip: *Use the Check For New Messages button instead of the Refresh button, since this will result in less network traffic.*

Several protocols are used for the OWA client—in fact, more than in previous Exchange releases, due to the new support for LDAP and Kerberos. As previous OWA clients, all HTTP network traffic is by default not encrypted; this is also true for the logon sequence. This means that you must configure the OWA server to use SSL encryption or use IPsec between the client and the server. SSL is easiest and most common. Port 443 must be open for an OWA client to work over an SSL connection; for standard HTTP traffic, port 80 is used. The scenario becomes more complicated when front-end and back-end configurations are used; see more about this in Chapter 15.

Lightweight Directory Access Protocol, LDAP

This protocol is mentioned here because all types of Exchange clients use it to query the global address list (GAL) on the global catalog server. The port used for LDAP is 389 for accessing the Active Directory, and port 3268 for accessing the global catalog. Since the Active Directory only stores information about local objects in its domain, any query on port 389 is limited to local users. So it's best to use the LDAP port 3268 since the global catalog is the only one that has access to the GAL in a multi-domain environment.

The traffic generated by LDAP queries using Check Names and Find Addresses in the POP3 and IMAP4 client are exactly the same; they generate the same query. The Outlook Web Access client uses LDAP queries for resolving names, but does not store the results in any cache; all queries will therefore generate the same amount of network traffic.

Tip: *When using the OWA client, you should check the names before typing in the text in the message body, since the time for name resolution is related to the size of the message. Or, you can avoid name checking before sending the message, if you know that the recipient address is unique.*

Remote Access Clients

Many users have dial-up connections for temporary access, most often road warriors with notebook computers. Your analysis must take this type of access into account when you're designing the Exchange organization. Check to see how many such users exist today; try to estimate how many there will be within a year or two. You should answer a number of questions before you can create an optimized Exchange design:

- How many users will use a dial-up connection occasionally? How many will use it as the primary connection?
- What type of connection is it? Asynchronous modem, ISDN, or ADSL?
- If a RAS connection will be used, how many RAS servers are needed? Where should they be located?
- What kind of client will they use—MAPI, POP3, IMAP4, or OWA?
- What message format will be used, Plain Text, RTF, or HTML?
- Will they use personal store (PST) or offline store (OST) files?

What is the best solution? There is no single solution for remote access usage; it all depends on the available hardware, the connection type, and what type of information the user needs access to. However, here are some guidelines:

- Users with a Pentium-based notebook running Windows 9x/2000, which connects only occasionally to the office by a 56Kbps modem, could use the OWA client or the Outlook 2000 client configured with an OST file.
- Users that most often use dial-up connections, who are not interested in anything else besides mail folders, like the Inbox and some public folders, could use IMAP4. If they need access to the calendar, they should use Outlook 2000 with an OST file.
- Roving users, who need access to the Exchange information from different computers, should use the OWA client.

As a general rule, you should avoid using POP3 clients—use IMAP4 instead. Also avoid using PST files, since this will remove all mailbox data from the server; use the OST file instead. To avoid excessive network traffic, teach your users to use RTF or Plain Text format instead of HTML.

Selecting the Right Client

As you can see from above, there are a number of different clients that can access all or parts of the information in the Exchange 2000 server. To help you decide what client to use, I have made the Decision Tree 7.1. Remember that today the richest client is the MAPI/RPC based Outlook 2002, released in June 2001; the next generation of clients may well be based on HTTP instead, using XML and Web-DAV for messages, and LDAP for address queries.

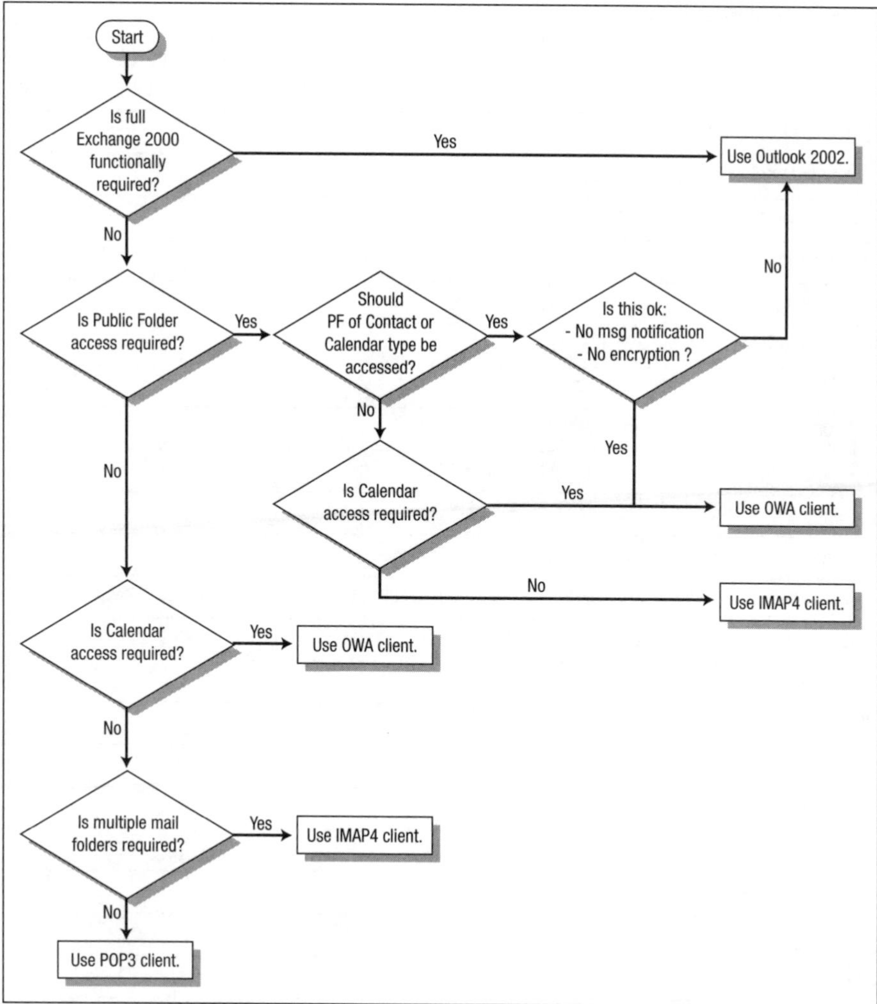

Decision Tree 7.1
Selecting the right client.

Investigating the Users' Need

You can use the worksheet below as a guide when investigating and analyzing the users' need. Let the users fill in how they rate each feature, assuming the users understand Exchange concepts like web clients and public folders and so on. It makes no sense to use more than a three graded scale, since the idea behind this worksheet is to understand what features in a mail system your users think are important or not important. Remember that this is just a sample; you may have to adjust it to your own organization.

Investigating the users' need worksheet.

Statement	Do You Agree with This Statement? No	Partly	Yes
1: I need access to the mail system all day long.			
2: The mail system must never be down more than one hour.			
3: More than 25 percent of the messages I send contain an attachment.			
4: I need to see immediately when new mail arrives.			
5: I send messages over the Internet.			
6: I need to send formatted messages to external users.			
7: I send messages to other mail systems in our organization.			
8: I need web access to our mail system when I'm traveling.			
9: I need POP3/IMAP4 access to our mail system when I'm not at the office.			
10: I use a laptop computer, and I need to read mail also when offline.			
11: I need to share some mailbox folders with others in the organization.			
12: I need to access other users' private folders, such as their inboxes and calendars.			
13: I need to access public folders of all types, like mail items, calendars and contacts.			
14: I need to be able to create public folders.			
15: I need to access the content of public folders also when offline.			
16: I need the calendar in Exchange for my personal use.			
17: I need the calendar to view other people's free/busy time.			
18: I need the calendar to view and book resources, such as conference rooms.			
19: I need to view the calendar for several users simultaneously.			
20: I want to use customized forms, such as reports for traveling expenses, time reports.			
21: I need to share contact information with others.			
22: I often use distribution groups when sending messages.			
23: It's important for me to send encrypted messages.			
24: I must be able to electronically sign outgoing messages.			
25: I need Instant Messaging in my work.			
26: I need Chat features in my work.			
27: I need a computerized conferencing system in my work.			

The reason I have chosen these statements in the worksheet are explained below; the number refers to the statement above:

1. How many of the users are actually using the mail system every day? People only using it a few times a week will not place a great load on our systems; you can group a large number of these users on one single server, if necessary.

2. How many users really need the mail system constantly? It could be help desk people, or sales people and so on. This will give you a hint of what will happen when the mail system unexpectedly goes down. It will also be an indicator of how many stores and storage groups you may need, including the backup routines you must use for this category of users. Assume we find 50 people who can't work without the mail system; one design suggestion could be to place these 50 users on the same storage group, which is backed up more often than the other stores.

3. Indicates how important attachments are; if the number is low, say less than 25 percent, the average message size should be around 20-40KB. You must also compare this value with the statistical analysis you have done on mail logs from the legacy mail system.
4. A user who needs to see directly when new mail arrives must use an MAPI client like Outlook 2002; the other types of mail clients will have a delay before the new mail shows up. This statement will also indicate if the user needs a permanent online connection, or if a dial-up connection can be acceptable.
5. These users are dependent of the Internet connection; they expect this line to be constantly available. If this is a large group, you should design your Internet connection to have more than one in-and outgoing link.
6. Try to analyze if they need to use HTML or RTF formatting; note that HTML will work for most types of Internet clients, but will increase the message size several hundred percent, compared to RTF formatted messages; this will increase the network load. Make sure your network can handle this traffic.
7. These users are dependent of connectors to other mail systems in this organization; it may be MS Mail, Lotus Notes, or GroupWise, for example, during a migration period. If the number is large, make sure to have at least two links to these other mail systems.
8. The Outlook Web Access client is a good choice for these users; here you will see how many of users are actually interested in this type of client.
9. This will tell you how many users will run POP3 or IMAP4 clients; for example, from their home computer.
10. This will list the number of laptop computers; you should configure these laptops to use an OST file instead of the PST file, whenever possible.
11. To share a private mailbox folder, these users must not use a PST as their primary storage file; all messages must be stored on the Exchange server.
12. Almost the same as statement 11. The users that will share their mailbox folders need to be configured to use Exchange as the primary storage place.
13. To access all types of public folders, the user must use a MAPI client or the OWA client; in other words, here you will find out how many users absolutely need the MAPI or OWA client.

14. These users must have been granted the permission to create top-level folders. Note that default all users have this permission; in Chapter 2 you have a description of why you should remove this permission, and how to do it.

15. These users must have an OST file configured that synchronizes public folders. They are probably laptop users, or use a dial-up connection. Note that only MAPI clients support the possibility to synchronize all types of public folders; an IMAP4 client can only synchronize public folders of message type.

16. They need access to the calendar; they need the MAPI client or the OWA client.

17. These users expect other users to update their calendar; if this is a small number, you may expect that the calendar feature will only be used for personal use. Also, to be able to view other people's free/busy calendar status, they must not use the PST file as the primary store.

18. This shows how many users expect to find resources created in the calendar system; unless there are only a few users requesting this, you must plan for adding resources to the calendar.

19. These users expect to be able to easily view a number of calendars simultaneously; typically these are team leaders, managers, and receptionists. Although Outlook 2002 has better group calendar functionality than its predecessors, you should look at the many third-party group calendar applications available, like the *Exchange Central* (**www.ms-add-on.com**) and *LOOK* (**www.symprex.com**).

20. This indicates if you need to create custom Outlook forms; do you have the resources needed to create these forms? If not, start looking for consulting companies that develop such forms.

21. To share personal contacts, a user can do one of two things: a) share his personal contact folder with the other users, or b) create a public folder of contact type; this folder should only be available to this group of users. I recommend solution b), since this will work even on a distributed organization.

22. This indicates how important distribution groups are. You must decide if you need to create distribution groups or security groups; if the group will also be granted access to public folders, it must be a security group.

23. These users need S/MIME or PGP (see Chapter 14). If there are just a few users, you may select to configure their particular clients only; if there are more users interested in this, you should plan for configuring the KMS system in Exchange. Note that the OWA client can't handle encryption or signing; avoid this client type for these users.

24. Really the same question as 23; this is an indication of the interest of S/MIME or PGP configurations on the Outlook clients.

25. This indicates the interest in Instant Messaging; if it's required, you must plan for its design and how to install IM servers and deploy IM clients (see Chapter 17 for more information).

26. This indicates if you need to install the MS Exchange Chat server; if it's required, you must plan for its design and how to install Chat servers and deploy Chat clients (see Chapter 16 for more information).

27. This indicates if you need to install the MS Conferencing Server; remember that this is an add-on that requires you to run Exchange 2000 Enterprise edition (see Chapter 18 for more information).

The Different User Categories

Since it is impossible to look at the exact behavior of each individual mailbox user, users are usually divided into different categories. Exchange has in the past used three MAPI Messaging Benchmark (MMB) user categories called *light*, *medium*, and *heavy*. These three types differ regarding the number of messages sent and received; they are described in Table 7.2.

The MMB categories have been criticized for not giving realistic results when used in simulations with tools such as Microsoft's LoadSim. To overcome this, Compaq (together with Microsoft) has suggested a new and much more demanding user category called *MAPI Messaging Benchmark version 2*, or MMB2, that gives much more realistic simulations. This new category is actually built on the MMB medium category, but enhanced to take into account all the new features of the Outlook 2000 client and the features of Exchange 2000. As a comparison, the medium category calculates with an average message size of 15KB and MMB2 with 75KB; the number of sent messages increased from 15 to 44 per day, and the average number of messages received per day increased from 66 to 162. A Compaq ProLiant 6400R with four Pentium III Xeon 550 MHz, capable of simulating 26,000 MMB medium users, is able to handle 4,000 MMB2 users with about the same read response time. The new LoadSim tool for Exchange 2000 uses the MMB2 category for its simulations, and it's important to understand how different this simulation model is, compared to the old LoadSim.

Planning for User Training

No matter how many nice features Outlook and Exchange may have, if users don't know how to use them, or use them improperly, then clearly the users need training. This may also be one of the conclusions you reach from the user survey; for example, if a lot of people complain that it's hard to find a given address, then they probably don't know how to use the address list and its search features. Training is something you must plan for, with

Table 7.2 The different user categories.

Category	Sent Per Day	Received Per Day
Light	7	20
Medium	15	66
Heavy	40	120

respect to both money and time. Training must also be provided at the right time—if possible, the day before users get access to the new system. Training given a week before, or longer, is usually just a waste of time, since most people will forget what they have learned. If it is given after the users have already been migrated to the new system, then they will experience unnecessary frustration and irritation, and the support team will have to address more questions.

Most organizations can't allow all their users to be away for a full day of training, but in my experience a two-hour presentation, along with short documentation, where an instructor demonstrates and explains the most common tasks, will be satisfactory, under the presumption that this presentation is given directly before they get migrated. The documentation should be about 10 pages long, with a clear and easy description of how to perform tasks such as the following:

- *Messages*—How to read, send, forward, and delete them; how to use message flags, views, and sorting; how to add new columns like Size; how to use Read/Delivery Receipts and Tracking; how to recover deleted items.
- *Attachments*—Opening and saving; how to include them in messages.
- *Address list*—Searching; difference between To, Cc, and Bcc; difference between GAL and Contacts.
- *Contacts*—How to add, modify, and delete personal contacts; how to use categories and the different views; how to create personal distribution lists.
- *Searching*—How to search for items; difference between standard search (nonindexed) and advanced search (indexed).
- *Calendar*—How to add, modify, move, and delete bookings; recurring bookings; inviting attendees; difference between detailed and free/busy information; booking of resources.
- *Tasks*—How to add, modify, and delete tasks; differences between tasks and calendar bookings; delegating tasks.
- *Notes*—How to add, modify, and delete notes; color-coding; different views.

How to Group the Students

One of the difficulties that you may experience if you are planning an Exchange or Outlook training is to group the students with approximately the same level of previous knowledge. Since Exchange and Outlook have existed for a number of years, it's likely that some people in your organization already have experience of these applications. It's easiest for both the students and the teacher if all students in the class are on the same level; then a class with mostly new beginners can go a bit slowly, while a class with more experienced users can focus more on difficult tasks, and tips and tricks. Use the worksheet below to investigate the level of knowledge of your users; let them fill in this form and later group your users based on the results. In my experience, it's better to have two small classes with equal students than one large class with large differences. This sample spreadsheet will also help you to focus on the right features, regarding the MS Outlook client; for example, if this worksheet shows that all users know how to add read receipt you don't have to mention this feature.

A similar worksheet for Exchange administrator courses is not really needed at this time, since Exchange 2000 is such a new and different application, compared to previous Exchange releases; you can probably assume that all administrators want to start from the beginning in their Exchange 2000 training.

Define the Administrative Needs

By now you should have a clear picture of the objectives and needs of your users. Now it's time to learn how the system should be administrated. This is also a very important task; if this isn't investigated and planned for, you may end up using more administrators than necessary, and this will be expensive! Many companies I have talked with look only at the initial cost for buying the hardware and the Exchange server and its user licenses; often this is used as the most important point when comparing different mail systems. Compare this to buying a car—if you were to choose between two different cars, one a little more expensive but a lot more reliable and one cheaper car that needed constant service, I am sure you would select the first. Interestingly enough, when the same people choosing the first car are deciding what mail system to buy, they look only at the initial cost, not at the service costs. So if mail system A costs $5,000 and requires three administrators, and mail system B costs $10,000 but requires only two administrators, it would be much cheaper to

Investigating the students' experience of MS Outlook worksheet.

Statement	Do you agree with this statement? No	Partly	Yes
1: MS Outlook is a new experience for me.			
2: I know how to request Read and Delivery Receipt.			
3: I know how to add, save, and open file attachments.			
4: I know how to sort inbox by Sender and Subject.			
5: I know how to use Views, such as "Last Seven Days."			
6: I can format my message with bold text, larger fonts, etc.			
7: I can search messages using the Find button.			
8: I have used the Inbox Assistant.			
9: I know how to use the Out-of-Office Assistant.			
10: I know how to add new sub-folders for my messages.			
11: I can make the messages from my boss be displayed in red, using the Organizer feature.			
12: I know how to resend messages.			

(continued)

Investigating the students' experience of MS Outlook worksheet *(continued).*

Statement	Do you agree with this statement? No	Partly	Yes
13: I know what the To, CC, and BCC fields are used for.			
14: I know the difference between Contacts and the Global Address List.			
15: I know how to create, modify, and delete Contact items.			
16: I know how to send copies of my Contact items to other users.			
17: I know how to create personal distribution lists.			
18: I know how to add, modify, and delete normal meetings in the calendar.			
19: I know how to create recurring meetings.			
20: I know how to invite others to meetings.			
21: I know how to move or copy meetings.			
22: I can create, modify, and delete tasks.			
23: I can delegate a task to another user.			
24: I can open and access information in public folders.			
25: I can create, modify, and delete public folders.			
26: I can change the permission for a public folder.			
27: I know how to use the "Favorites" folder.			
28: I can add and remove delegates for my mailbox folders.			
29: I can open other users folders.			
30: I can add and remove PST files.			

buy system B, since the extra $5,000 would be saved in only one or two months by requiring two administrators instead of three. And of course you want to run the mail system for years, not just for a few months.

Exchange has always been easier to administrate than most other mail systems, at least if it was built on a good design. Exchange 2000 is even easier than previous versions, and the new feature of administrative groups makes it possible to design the management of the Exchange system without caring about the network connections and the domain structure. A small organization will most probably consist of only one Windows 2000 domain, and usually there will be one single group of Exchange administrators. It is important to understand that even if the Exchange organization is small, it is still important that there be at least two Exchange administrators—maybe not working full time with this administration, but to be able to handle situations like sickness, vacations, and attrition.

Maybe the last situation is the worst; I have seen a number of small and medium-sized organizations where there in effect has been only one single administrator; this person has been running the show for several years; he or she knows the configuration by heart and also knows how to fix the most common problems and situations. Usually there is one more person engaged in this type of scenario who assists the administrator, for example, running the backup system and performing trivial administration tasks like creating and modifying users. The primary administrator is a very critical person here; if he or she quits, the organization will not only lose one of its employees. This person will also take the configuration of the mail system with them, since there is no updated documentation of the system and its configuration! The poor assistant will now be asked to take over the responsibility, but doesn't have the skills or access to all the information needed to perform all tasks; it's often just a matter of time before chaos ensues.

The Exchange Administrator

For Exchange 2000 organizations, we talk about two different administrators—the mailbox administrator and the Exchange configuration administrator. Let's talk about the Exchange configuration administrator first.

This type of administrator typically has all the permissions needed to change any configuration related to the Exchange system, like site link connectors, server configurations, and the routing group configuration. The new feature of administrative groups in Exchange 2000 makes it possible to divide the Exchange 2000 organization into groups of servers that are managed by one or more Exchange administrators. It is important to understand that these administrative groups can consist of any Exchange server, regardless of where they are located and the network connection type. This is possible because all Exchange configurations are stored in the Active Directory and its configuration partition; this partition is then replicated to all other Active Directory servers in the Windows 2000 forest, regardless of how many domains there may be. This is very similar to how the Exchange 5.5 directory replication works within an Exchange 5.5 site; connect the Exchange admin program to any server and update the configuration. When the directory replication within the site is done, all servers know about this new update. The important difference is that in Exchange 2000, this replication will work all over the Exchange organization.

How Many Administrative Groups?

One important question you must answer in the design is how many administrative groups this Exchange 2000 organization will require. The most common answer will probably be one; if there is no need to divide the administration of Exchange servers between different groups, you should avoid it! There is absolutely no point in using this feature just because it is available. However, in some situations you will definitely need several administrative groups. For example:

- The Exchange organization consists of one company with one or more subsidiaries, each wanting to manage their own Exchange servers.
- The Exchange organization hosts several independent companies.
- A company has several large divisions or departments that demand to be in control of their own Exchange servers.

You can create as many administrative groups as you like, but again, avoid creating more than needed; if necessary, a new group can always be created, or deleted, later. Some Exchange 2000 documentation says that a server must be installed into its final administrative group from the beginning, and continues to say that servers cannot be moved later. This is in fact wrong, although you must use the ADSI Edit tool to move servers between the administrative groups; see Chapter 11 for more information about administrative groups and how to use ADSI Edit to move servers.

Different Administrative Roles

For each administrative group, you use the Exchange Delegation Wizard to create and remove administrators. Three types of administrative roles are available:

- *Exchange View Only Administrator*—Which can only view configuration settings, not modify them.
- *Exchange Administrator*—Has all permissions to this administrative group. However, this role cannot add new administrators or remove existing ones.
- *Exchange Full Administrator*—Has all accesses that the Exchange Administrator has, plus the permission to add new and remove existing administrators.

All administrative groups also inherit permission from the organization top folder; this means that any administrator created by the Exchange Delegation Wizard on the organizations top folder will have the same permissions on each administrative group. You should therefore be very careful who gets any permissions on the organization level; use the wizard to create super Exchange administrators, with full permissions on all administrative groups, or to create global View Only administrators, giving them the permission to view configuration settings in all administrative groups.

***Tip:** Avoid assigning administrative permissions to individual user accounts; always use a special security group for this purpose. If you do this, it will be easy to remove administrative permissions for a person leaving the company, and add a new administrator.*

The Mailbox Administrator

A mailbox administrator is the person responsible for mailbox-enabling users, distribution lists, and contacts. In small and medium-sized organizations, this will be the same person as the Exchange administrator; however, it doesn't have to be. This administrator will use the Active Directory Users and Computers tool for all Exchange-related work. He or she does not need permission to the Exchange system, but often has at least View Only Administrator permissions. The number of mailbox administrators will depend on the organization, but you should have at least two mailbox administrators for exactly the same reason that there should be at least two Exchange administrators.

It is common to have a support team, or a help desk, to assist users; they are usually mailbox administrators, helping users reset passwords, change email addresses, and update attributes like names, addresses, and phone numbers. This team usually needs to be able to check the message queues, if a user complains that messages have not been delivered.

To meet this need, give this team View Only Administrative permission on one or more administrative groups in the Exchange organization.

A large organization will probably have more than one OU folder for its users. These OUs will inherit the permission settings from their parent folders; the result is that the same persons who are granted administrative permissions to the parent folder will also have administrative permissions on these OU folders. To add a new administrator for a particular OU folder, follow these steps:

1. Start the *Active Directory Users And Computers* tool.
2. Select the OU folder with the users. Right-click and select *Delegate Control*; this will start the *Delegation Of Control Wizard*.
3. Click *Next* to continue to the *Users Or Groups* page.
4. Click *Add* and select the security group (preferred) or the user name that will be the new mailbox administrator; then click *OK* to close this window. You will be returned to the *Users Or Groups* page again.
5. Click *i* to continue to the *Active Directory Object Type* page.
6. If the new administrator should have full control of all users, groups, and contact objects in this folder, accept the default *Delegate Control Of*. If not, select *Only The Following Objects In The Folder* and then use the list below to set exactly what objects this administrator will be able to control in this folder; see Figure 7.4. When ready, click *Next*.
7. This is the *Permission* page; use it to set the permissions this administrator will have on the objects. Depending on what checkbox you select on *Show These Permissions*, you will see a number of permissions listed; see Figure 7.5. A mailbox administrator should have full access, but you can also create a *View Only Administrator* by selecting the *Read* permission only.
8. Click *Next* and then *Finish* to complete this wizard.

Define a Name Standard

I have seen a number of test installations of Exchange systems that used a temporary organization name and server names that almost imperceptibly have turned into a production environment. Eventually the administrators realize that the names must be changed, and unfortunately, at that point it may be hard or even impossible to change them. There are some important names in the current version of Windows 2000 and Exchange 2000 that cannot be changed once they are in use:

- Windows 2000 domain names
- The Exchange 2000 organization name
- NetBIOS names for Exchange servers and domain controllers

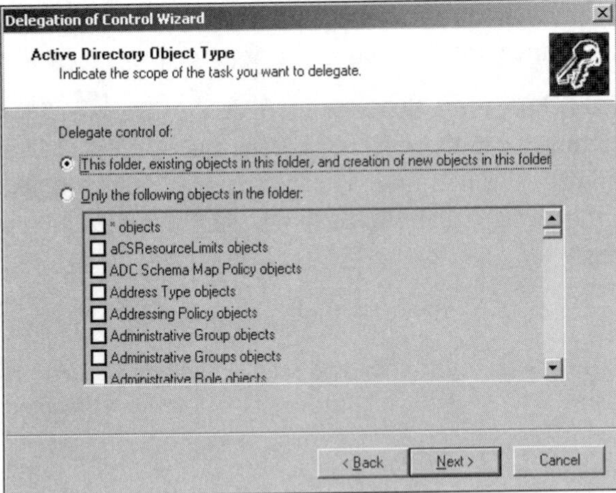

Figure 7.4
The Active Directory Object Type page.

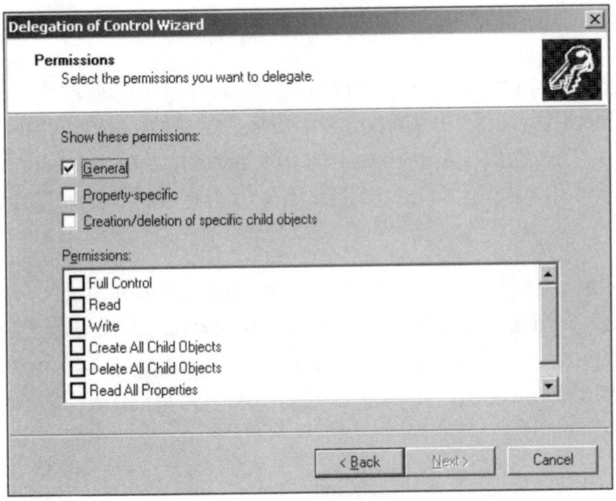

Delegation of Control Wizard
Permissions
Select the permissions you want to delegate.
Show these permissions:
General
Property-specific
Creation/deletion of specific child objects
Permissions:
Full Control
Read
Write
Create All Child Objects
Delete All Child Objects
Read All Properties
< Back
Next >
Cancel

Figure 7.5
The Permissions page.

The Windows 2000 Domain Name

Many large organizations have a special design team for the Windows 2000 forest and its domain, and another design team for Exchange; and most medium-sized and small organizations use the same design team for both Windows 2000 and Exchange 2000. The Windows 2000 domain name does not affect the Exchange organization; you can still set any organization name or any other Exchange-related names you like. However, if the name of the Windows 2000 domain will be changed later, Exchange will be affected. The only way known today to change a domain name is through a complete reinstallation of all domain controllers; this will also remove any existing Exchange servers! So my recommendation is to make sure the domain names will stick before installing your Exchange environment!

The Exchange 2000 Organization Name

Exactly as in previous Exchange versions, the Exchange 2000 organization name is limited to 64 characters. You are allowed to use most characters for this name, even 8-bit non-U.S. ASCII characters, but I recommend you avoid this. Sometime later these characters might give you problems—for example, when you're connecting to other systems or using third-party software add-ons for Exchange. For Exchange 5.5, there exists a utility called Move Server that can change the existing organization name (and the site and server name). There is no such tool for Exchange 2000 yet; hopefully it is in the works. So whatever name you select for the organization, you will have to live with it, unless you are willing and able to do a complete reinstallation of all Exchange servers in this organization. When I say a reinstallation, I mean that you first have to remove the Exchange server software completely, and then do a clean installation again; there is no way you can make a reinstall of Exchange and keep the existing data and configuration!

What is a good Exchange organization name? They are usually identical or similar to the company name, and that is often acceptable as long as we avoid using non-U.S. ASCII characters, as we explained above. However, since this name cannot be changed, it must be a name that is highly unlikely to change. Is this true for company names? The answer is no! The business world is full of mergers and acquisitions. Also, other types of organizations change names now and then. Are there any other names that can be used instead? Hard to say, and it's really up to the organization, but one suggestion is to use a completely fictitious name, like "Email," "Exchange," or "The Messaging System." Such names will be valid even if the name of the company changes. The only drawback is that the Exchange organization name is used as the default SMTP domain name (and the X.400 Private Management Domain name), but this can easily be changed, using the Recipient Policies in the ESM tool, as opposed to the organization name.

NetBIOS Server Names

All Windows 2000 servers still have a NetBIOS name, along with its hostname. This name must not be changed after the installation of Exchange 2000, or a domain controller; this would prevent Exchange from starting. This means that you must select a name for the Windows 2000 server before installing Exchange. If you must change the name afterward, you must first remove the Exchange server software completely, then make a clean installation again. All user data and configuration settings will be lost unless you first move all users to another Exchange server and then remove the server.

Selecting a Name Standard for Users

Two types of names are particularly important for the user: the display name, used in the global address list, and the SMTP email address. If your organization is small, with just a few users, this may not be so important, but for large organizations, this is crucial. Even if this type of name standard can be modified anytime, it is still much easier to plan this before the installation than it would be to modify all existing users.

The Display Name

The layout of this name type is important, mainly because it will be displayed in the global address list stored in the global catalog; this list will be sorted by the display name. The default name standard is:

First name, Last name, for example: "Jessica Choi"

This has the effect that the global address list is sorted after the first name. However, organizations with more than 100 names usually prefer a global address list sorted after the last name, like this:

Last name, First name, for example: "Choi, Jessica"

Many organizations also want to sort by what department, office, or division a user belongs to. This could be achieved by using a name standard that looks like this:

Last name, First name (department), for example: "Choi, Jessica (Editing)"

The name standard must also take care of the situation where several people have the same name, possibly also working in the same department. A common technique is to use the initial for this. Some organizations will use an initial only if there is more than one person with the same name, while other, often larger organizations, will use initials for all users, regardless whether the names are unique or not. The idea behind this is that even if a name is unique today, it may well be ambiguous tomorrow; here is an example:

Last name, First name Initial, for example: "Choi, Jessica A"

It is much easier to change the default display name generation before you start adding users. Since all users are now stored in the Active Directory, and the global address list is built on these names, this means that the new display name generation must be set even before you start adding users to Windows 2000! That was not necessary in previous Exchange releases, since it had its own directory. To change the default display name generation to "Last, First," follow these steps:

1. Start the *ADSI Edit* tool.
2. Expand the *Configuration Container/DisplaySpecifiers*.
3. Locate the subfolder *CN=409*.
4. In the right pane, locate the *CN=user-Display* and double-click to open its properties; see Figure 7.6.
5. Change the *Select A Property To View* to *createDialog*.
6. Type in these LDAP attribute names, exactly like this: "%<sn>, %<givenName>" and press *Set*; then click *OK* to save.

The attribute **<sn>** stands for surname or the family name, and **<givenName>** stands for the first name. You will find more information about these LDAP names in Chapter 5,

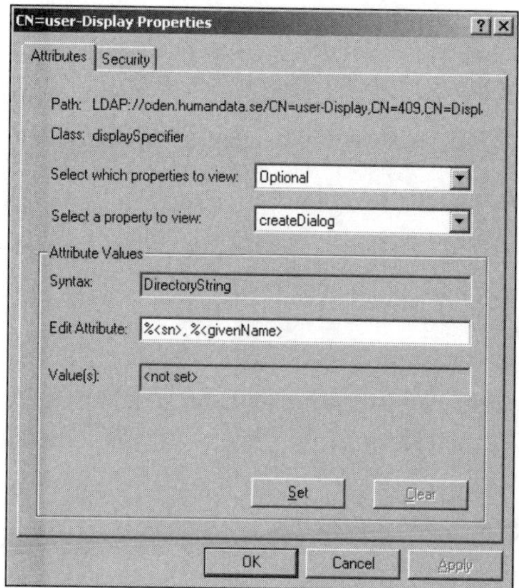

Figure 7.6
Defining a new display name generation rule.

Table 5.5. If you need to change the display name for existing users, you can use the LDIFDE tool, as described in Chapter 5.

Please observe that every user has a full name in the Active Directory and a display name listed in the global address list; it is perfectly okay to have one full name and a different display name, although this should be avoided since it will create confusion and generate mistakes; if possible, use the same name for both. The method described above will set the name generation standard for both names.

SMTP Email Addresses

We have similar problems for the SMTP names as for the display names; we must make sure the names are unique. If fact, an SMTP name must be unique in the whole Internet world! The default SMTP name generation is built on the alias name plus the SMTP domain name, and the alias name is equal to the user logon name, given when you create this account.

For example: A new user account in the Windows 2000 domain **abc.se** with the first name=Jessica and last name=Choi, and a user logon name=Jessica, will default result in an alias **name=Jessica** and **SMTP address=Jessica@abc.se**.

For many organizations, it's common to have a name standard that looks like this:

First.Last@domain.tld, for example: "Jessica.Choi@abc.se"

To change the default SMTP name generation to this standard, use the Exchange System Management tool, and follow these steps:

1. Open the ESM tool.
2. Expand the *Recipients/Recipient Policies*.
3. Open the properties for the *Default Policy*, and switch to the *E-Mail Addresses* tab.
4. Select the *SMTP* address type and click *Edit*.
5. In the *Address* field, add the following *before* the @ sign: "%g.%s". For example, if the SMTP domain is **@abc.se**, the new value should be **%g.%s@abc.se**.
6. Click *OK* twice to close the default policy.
7. Last, you will be asked if you want to update all corresponding email addresses; answer *Yes* to update all existing users' SMTP addresses, or *No* if you want this new setting to be valid only from now on; see Figure 7.7.

As in previous versions, you are using special placeholders (or variables) for some attributes that can be used to create the SMTP name generation rule:

- ***%g***—Given name, or the first name; will be picked from the First Name field.
- ***%s***—Surname, or the last name; will be picked from the Last Name field.
- ***%i***—Initial; will be picked from the Initial Name field.

When you create a new user with the Active Directory Users and Computers tool, it will directly check to see if the logon name or the full name is unique; if not, you will get a warning about this. There is no check that the alias name is unique, but you should avoid having multiple instances of the same alias name. If you by accident try to create an SMTP email address that already exists, you will get a warning about this; see Figure 7.8.

A large organization can use the same technique for creating unique SMTP addresses as for creating unique display names; use the initial name. Since the Active Directory does not allow you to create multiple users with the same full name, this ensures that all names are unique, regarding both display names and email addresses. To create an email generation rule that creates SMTP names like **first.initial.last@<domain.tld>** (for example, "Jessica.A.Choi@abc.se"), type this in the Address field:

%g.%i.%s@<domain.tld>

You can also pick a given number of characters from the first, initial, and last name. For example, if you want to make a generation rule that creates email addresses with the com-

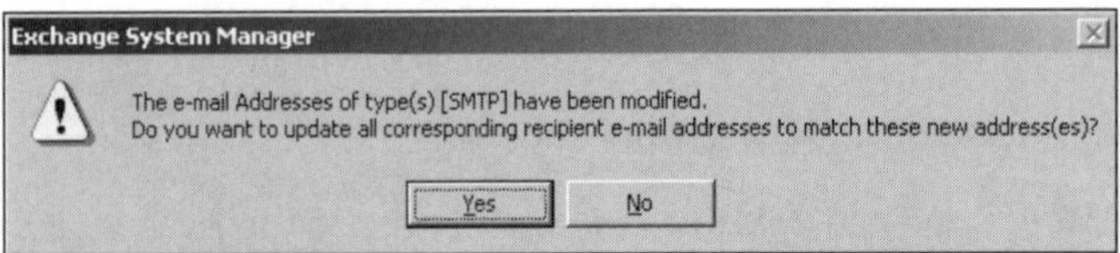

Figure 7.7
Updating the SMTP email address.

plete first name and only the first character of the last name (for example, "JessicaC"), use this rule:

%g%1s@<domain.tld>

It is also possible to substitute one character for another. This is often used to replace uppercase characters with the corresponding lowercase character. In the Unix world, it has always been customary to use only lowercase characters for the SMTP address; however, the SMTP protocol is not case-sensitive regarding email addresses. Any of these addresses will be treated alike:

- **jessica.choi@abc.se**
- **Jessica.Choi@abc.se**
- **JESSICA.choi@ABC.se**

Since the generation rules for SMTP addresses will create an address built on the exact string of characters in the first and last name fields for the user, the generated SMTP address will be constructed of names with an initial capital, like **Jessica.Choi@abc.se**. This can be modified by using a replacement rule, %r; the format for this rule looks like this:

%rAa

This will replace the uppercase "A" with the lowercase "a"; such replacement rules must be written at the beginning of the line, preceding the %g and %s placeholders. By using this replacement rule, we could replace all uppercase characters for an SMTP address format like **first.last@<domain.tld>** (since it's such a long line, I will only type the first and the last replacement rules; you understand the rest):

%rAa%rBb%%rCc%rDd%rEe%Ff ....%rXx%rYy%rZz%g.%s@abc.se

Name Standards for Public Folders

The important thing to remember about public folder names is that top-level folders (the folders in the root of the public folder tree) will by default be visible for all users in the whole organization. Depending on network connections and user permissions, a client may or may not have access to the content. For example, if you have a dial-up connection between the routing groups in Spain and South Africa, any top-level folder created in Spain will be visible in South Africa, but the content will not be accessible since there is no direct

Figure 7.8
The system detects if the email address already exists.

connection between the routing groups. So the users get an error message when they try to look at the content. This is very irritating and should be avoided. The most obvious solution to this is to use the Permissions tab under Property for this folder, and disable the Folder Visible option for the Default group if this public folder is not open to public access; see Figure 7.9.

However, in some situations it's impossible or impractical to hide a public folder; using clear and descriptive names of these public folders helps users understand why they cannot see the content, and also quickly navigate to the folders intended for them. Below is an example of public folder trees for a medium-sized company. Create a security group of the different kinds of users; use the Permissions tab for each top-level folder and make sure only the correct security group has access to the folder. That will also protect the subfolders from being displayed to users not belonging to this group:

```
All Public Folders
     Management
          Discussion
          Ongoing projects
          Finished projects
          Economy
     Sales
          District A
                    Customers
                    Sales activities
                    Economy
          District B
                    Customers
                    Sales activities
                    Economy
     Account
          Time reports
          Travel reports
          Invoices
     Production
          Current Goals
          Documentation
          Result
```

The example above uses departments as a base for constructing the public folder tree. An international company would instead use countries at the top level, like this:

```
All Public Folders
     Public information
          Discussion
          Company Policies
```

```
          Activities
U.S.
          Sales
          Economy
          Reports
England
          Sales
          Economy
          Reports
Denmark
          Sales
          Economy
          Reports
```


In this example, all folders except the Public Information folder would be accessible only to members of the respective country; for example, only employees of Denmark would have access to the top-level folder Denmark.

Other Important Name Standards

Besides the names mentioned above, other name standards should be defined in the design document. The purpose of these standards is to define how these names should be constructed; this will make things easier to understand and will help you avoid confusion and mistakes. A good rule is to let the name describe what type of object it is, and what it is used for. Table 7.3 presents a list of objects that should have a standardized name.

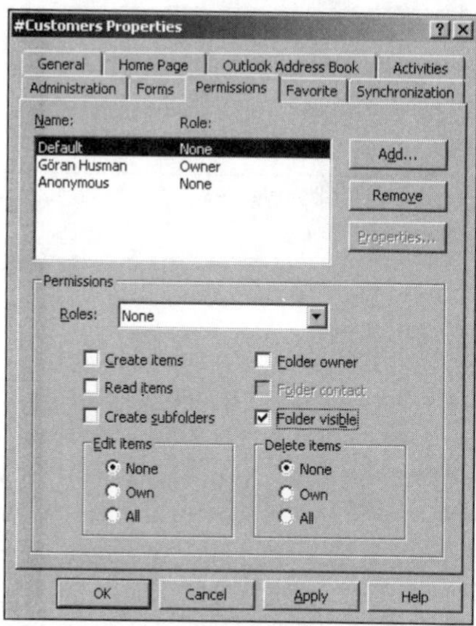

Figure 7.9
Clear the Folder Visible checkbox to hide the public folder.

Table 7.3 Name standards for Exchange objects.

Object	Examples
Administrative groups	AG 1, AG 2 or AG Sweden, AG Finland.
Routing groups	RG 1, RG 2 or RG Stockholm, RG London.
Storage groups	SG 1, SG 2 or Storage Group 1, Storage Group 2. (Yes, you can rename the First Storage Group.)
Stores	MBX 1, MBX 2, PUB 1, or MBX Sales and PUB Helpdesk; make sure that you can see directly on the name what sort of store it is. MBX is commonly used as an abbreviation for mailbox stores, and PUB for public folder stores. It may also be a good idea to give the name a description of how it is used.
Virtual SMTP servers	VS-SMTP-1 ODEN, VS-SMTP-2 ODEN; use the name of the server (Oden in this example).
Virtual IMAP4 servers	VS-IMAP4-1 ODEN, VS-IMAP4-2 ODEN.
Virtual POP3 servers	VS-POP3-1 ODEN, VS-POP3-2 ODEN.
Virtual NNTP servers	VS-NNTP-1 ODEN, VS-NNTP-2 ODEN.
Distribution groups	#Grp Team A, #Grp Team B; the # in the beginning causes all groups to be listed together on top of the GAL.
SMTP connectors	SMTP Connector 1, SMTP Connector 2, or use the bridgehead servers name instead; SMTP Connector Oden, SMTP Connector Tor, and so on. (Yes, you can rename the Default SMTP Virtual Server.)
X.400 connectors	X400 Connector from PARIS to LONDON; use the names of the two bridgehead servers.
Routing group connectors	RGC from RG1 to RG2, use the names of the routing groups connected by this RG.
Address lists	IT Department, Stockholm office, or any other descriptive name.
Offline address lists	"OAL: Sales Dept," "OAL: San Diego"; make sure the users will understand what this list contains just by looking at the name.
Recipient policies	Recipient Policy: Scandinavia; don't abbreviate, it will not save any space and it will only be harder to understand what this object is.
Public folder trees	PF-Tree: Helpdesk, PF-Tree: DocMan; you should also give the corresponding public store a similar name, like PUB Helpdesk and PUB DocMan.

Define the Current Environment

By now you should have a clear picture of what users expect from your mail system. You have also defined the administrative groups and name standards to be used; in short, now you know the objectives for this Exchange 2000 organization. Next, it's time to look at the current environment, to see what has to be done in order to meet the objectives, or decide whether some objectives cannot be met. This part is at least as labor intensive as the previous parts, but if you are lucky you'll have good and updated documentation that you can rely on—but you must make sure you really can trust it. I have met several network administrators who were absolutely sure they knew all about some or all parts of the environment, but once I started checking, their information wasn't accurate. Maybe it was correct at one time, but the modifications that had been made since weren't documented. Sometimes the person who knew all the details of the network left the company. This investigation can also be a fun and challenging part, since it resembles a detective story; personally, I follow the old adage, "Don't trust anything you hear, and only half of what you see."

The Current Network Topology

Start by looking at the current physical network; it's very important that you're familiar with all IP subnets, as well as all WAN connections and their bandwidth, both the max value and the current load. Since the Active Directory servers will be of extreme importance for the Exchange 2000 servers, you must know where these are. If possible, make sure there are at least two domain controllers on each IP subnet where there is an Exchange 2000 server; at least one of them should also be configured as a global catalog server. If there are several subnets, you must investigate the WAN connections carefully—how fast are they? What is the average network load? Do traffic peaks occur at regular intervals? How much of the current traffic is generated by the current mail system? How much network load can this WAN connection manage, without disturbing the other network traffic? Must the bandwidth be increased to manage the new traffic load?

Investigate the WAN connection very carefully; sometimes it looks like there are redundant connections between locations, but when you look at the physical network more closely, you find that they all pass through a common router, possibly at the ISP. This is something you must take into account when designing routing group connectors; if you think that you have created redundant connections and in reality you have not, unexpected behavior will be the result if the network goes down.

When calculating how much network traffic the new Exchange system will generate, you cannot simply estimate the number of kilobytes per second, since that would assume that the network load is evenly distributed over time, and in reality there will be a number of peaks. The best tool for testing and analyzing the response time for message clients is the LoadSim tool, available for all versions of Exchange. It has now been updated for Exchange 2000 and should always be used before you install real users. The last thing you want is complaints from users that the mail system is too slow. You have already analyzed user behavior; you know how many there are in every location, you also know what clients they use and how much mail they send. Now it's time to use the LoadSim tool to run a simulation of these users.

The LoadSim Tool

This utility can be downloaded from **www.microsoft.com/exchange**; search for LoadSim and you will find it. Before using this tool, make sure to read the included documentation, since it's an advanced simulator with lots of configuration settings. The basic idea is to use this tool to simulate your real users. You configure settings like the number of users to simulate, the amount of mail sent and received each day, how large the messages are, how often the calendar is used, how often public folders are used, and so on. You can define your own values (see Figure 7.10) or you can use one of three predefined groups—MMB2, medium, or heavy—as described earlier in this chapter.

When this configuration is complete, the simulation begins. Usually it runs for eight hours, sometimes even longer. The first step is to create the environment on the Exchange server; LoadSim will create all users and groups, and populate the mailboxes and public folders. Next, LoadSim will use an Outlook 2000 client to create a number of MAPI sessions to the server, one for each user; after that, these clients start to behave as real users, i.e., they send and receive messages, look at calendars, and update public folders. The LoadSim program registers all activities, and the time for every task is measured.

After the simulation period is over, an analysis program called LSLog creates statistics from the simulation logs; it presents the response times in milliseconds for activities like opening a message, sending a message, and checking the calendar. This will give you a true picture of how long common activities will take. For example, the list below presents results from an LSLog analysis; we can see that the average time for sending messages is 840 milliseconds, 95 percent of all send operations take less than 1.237 seconds, and 95 percent of all reading operations take less than 435 milliseconds:

```
Category         Weight  Hits  50th Pctile  95th Pctile  Mean   Std. Dev.
SEND             1       11    765          1237         840    230
READ             10      246   219          435          235    92
REPLY            1       27    313          578          376    199
REPLY ALL        1       14    531          750          517    104
FORWARD          1       17    735          1250         797    178
MOVE             1       44    375          609          389    24
DELETE           2       78    312          546          324    113
S+ CHANGE        0       16    451          1824         555    361
DELIVER          0       119   170          611          642    2089
RESOLVE NAME     0       28    187          375          234    115
SUBMIT           0       69    390          672          394    142
LOAD ATTACH      0       10    78           266          95     59
NDR              0       9     0            0            0      0
EMPTY FOLDER     0       10    859          1266         862    254
CREATE PROFILE   0       10    2281         4281         2103   1074
OPEN MSG STORE   0       20    1438         5234         1552   1334
LOG ON           0       10    14625        16375        12700  3551
Weighted Average 0       17    738          325          584    257
112<-"score"
```

The LoadSim program will probably be your most valuable tool when estimating the performance of the Exchange 2000 system, from a user's point of view. By using a network monitor during this simulation, you will also get information about how much network traffic it generates, and thereby also get an idea of whether you need to increase the available bandwidth.

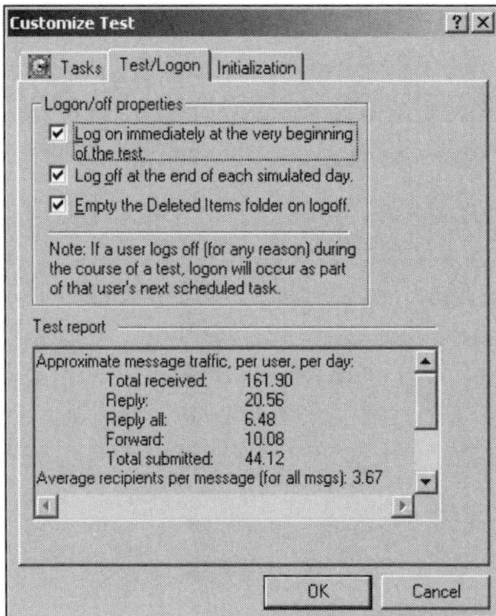

Figure 7.10
Customizing user behavior in LoadSim.

The Current Computer Configuration

It's important to know what types of computers the users have, and also how the current servers are configured. Here we assume that the Windows 2000 design is done; and since you are designing an Exchange system, you need to know the following:

- Will the users' current computers be able to handle the new messaging clients? You must look at CPU speed, memory, and available hard disk space. Will their current operating system allow them to run the messaging client? Specify what the new messaging client requires; investigate if there are any computers that need to be upgraded or replaced. Several products on the market can help you with this; Microsoft's SMS is just one of them. Make sure you plan for this upgrade; it can take a substantial amount of time.

- Will the upcoming Exchange servers be able to handle the new load? If you plan to use existing servers for running Exchange 2000, you must make sure they have the CPU speed, memory configuration, and disk layout needed. Before you can decide this, you must know how many users and how much disk space you will need on each server. Get prepared by investigating the configuration of the current servers; some may need to be upgraded or replaced. Again, this can take a substantial amount of time.

- Will the current backup system handle Exchange 2000? Since this is a new program, not even previous Exchange backup systems understand how to back up Exchange 2000. Also look at the backup hardware; is it fast enough and is the storage capacity enough to back up all Exchange 2000 data?

- Will the current anti-virus program be enough? The new Exchange 2000 server needs updated anti-virus programs; again, not even Exchange 5.5 anti-virus programs will be able to run on Exchange 2000. You most likely need to upgrade.

- Are there any other server-based applications that may be affected by the Exchange 2000 system? Are there mainframe-based mail systems that must be connected to Exchange 2000? Are there any special applications running today that utilize the current mail system; if so, do they need to be modified in order to run with Exchange 2000?
- Do you need to change the firewall configuration? For example, will the current open ports and IP addresses be sufficient? What about if you need to install an Exchange 2000 front-end server on the DeMilitarized Zone (DMZ) segment?
- Will the current Internet connection be enough? If the message traffic will increase, you may have to get a faster Internet connection. If the Internet connection will be business critical, you may need an extra network connection for fault-tolerance and load balancing.

The Current Organization

Now we know the current network and we know what computers and software are on it; next we need to know where all the users are located and whether any changes are planned for the next two years—for example, new offices or acquisitions of other companies. Interview the management and the HR department to determine the following:

- Where are all the users located? Get a list of all available offices in the organization.
- How many users are there in each location?
- Do all users have their own computers or do they share equipment?
- How does the information flow? Is it mainly within the group, or from branch offices to headquarters, or how?
- Are there any external users? For example, do any customers or suppliers need access to the Exchange information?

When you have all this information, make a map to get a clear overview of the organization. Add the Windows 2000 domain topology, with its domain controllers, DNS servers, and global catalog servers, along with the physical network topology, and you will be ready to define the numbers of Exchange servers and routing groups needed.

Servers, Routing Groups, and External Connections

With the map of user locations and network topology, together with the list of objectives for the Exchange system, it's time to define the Exchange topology, i.e., the number of Exchange servers, routing groups, and connections to external mail systems like the Internet. Remember that it's easier to manage fewer servers and routing groups than many. Your goal should always be to keep the numbers of these to a minimum, even at the expense of increasing WAN connections. In previous versions of Exchange, it was hard to move users between Exchange sites; this is not the case anymore. With Exchange 2000, you can move your users freely between any Exchange servers all over the organization. The move feature is even capable of keeping the single instance storage principle; if a message for the moved user already exists in the new server, it will not be copied. Instead, a new pointer to this message will automatically be created. That gives you a new freedom when designing server and routing groups; if needed, users can be moved between servers anytime.

The Number of Exchange Servers

The total number of users per server depends on both the hardware capacity and the type of user activities. Compaq has a free Exchange 2000 sizing tool that can be used for this; you can download it at **www.Compaq.com/activeAnswers**. A state-of-the-art server can handle several thousand users without any performance problems. Since a server with lots of users, let's say 5,000, is also a single point of failure, you must make every precaution to protect this server from any hardware failures. With the Windows 2000 cluster feature and RAID5 disk sets, you can build very resilient Exchange servers. The size of the database was previously a problem; if it grew too large, it was hard to maintain, and especially to restore. With the storage groups and their multiple stores, you can have up to 20 stores per server; share the users between them to lower the average size of the stores. For example, let's say we plan to have a server supporting 5,000 users with 100MB each; this is a total size of 500GB. Divide these between 20 stores and they will be about 20GB each, a large but still manageable size.

Other important factors that often determine how many servers are needed are the network connectivity and its speed to the user locations. A quick-and-dirty solution is to install an Exchange server at every user location, regardless of how many users there are. True, this will make the local users happy, since they have fast access to the server; however, if the design is based on this policy, you will get a messy system with lots of servers and routing groups that will be hard to administrate. The replication of public folder data will increase, and it will be more expensive since it will require more Exchange server licenses and more servers. Add to that the increased complexity of the Windows 2000 domain design that will follow, since the Exchange servers need constant contact with a domain controller and all messaging clients need access to a global catalog. Don't succumb to this temptation; it will result in more problems than you solved in the first place. If the network connection to a user location is low, consider these possibilities instead:

- Increase the network speed. It will probably need to be upgraded anyhow for other reasons within a year or two.
- Use Outlook 2002 in offline mode; configure it to synchronize each 15 minutes. This will give your users access to locally stored messages.
- Use lighter clients, such as IMAP4 or Outlook Web Access. The first is fast but cannot access some mailbox information like calendars or tasks; the other gives you access to all Exchange information, but is sometimes regarded as clumsy by users, since they must refresh manually.

The Number of Routing Groups

A *routing group* is a collection of one or more Exchange 2000 servers. It is similar to the Exchange 5.5 site concept, in that all servers communicate directly with each other. All servers in a routing group must be able to transfer SMTP messages between them at any time, and the network speed should be at least 64Kbps, although the SMTP protocol is resilient enough to handle much lower network speeds.

There is no traffic between these servers besides user messages, replication messages, and link state messages; compare this to the Exchange 5.5 site, where all servers besides the message traffic also replicate directory information every 5 minutes, 24 hours per day! The network traffic is in fact much lower in a routing group. The consequence of this is that a routing group can span a larger and more distributed group of servers than a site ever could.

Use your map and look at the network topology. Look at the numbers of Exchange servers planned for the organization and where they will be located. Look at the results from the LoadSim simulation; do you need to change the number of servers or their location? Maybe you need to run some more simulations? If so, don't hesitate, do it now. It is always easier to change your design now rather than later after all the servers are installed and the users are active.

Routing Group Connectors

It is time to decide what type of connectors to use between the routing groups. A routing group connector is a transport link between two routing groups; without it, there will be no message traffic between them. Unlike previous Exchange versions where you usually selected between the Site Connector and the X.400 Connector, the choice is now easier; it will almost always be the Routing Group Connector, or RGC. However, let's have a quick look at the three choices available:

- *Routing Group Connector*—Uses SMTP; can be scheduled to run at intervals; can be instructed to send large messages at night, has all configuration settings you need. Can also be used for communication with a Site Connector in an Exchange 5.5 site; in this case, the RGC will automatically switch over to RPC instead of SMTP. This connector is the fastest and easiest of them all—however, it is limited to communication between routing groups belonging to the same Exchange 2000 organization.
- *X.400 Connector*—Needs a transport stack to work; there are three different types: TCP/IP, X.25, or RAS. This type of connector is mainly used for connections to Exchange 5.5 sites with an X.400 Connector, or to other X.400-based mail systems. There are really no advantages to this connector and it should not be used unless you have a good reason.
- *SMTP Connector*—Uses TCP/IP; usually used for connection to the Internet or other SMTP-based mail systems, but can also be used as a routing group connector. This connector will be slower than the RGC, since it uses standard SMTP communication with MIME conversion of binary information. Again, there is no reason to select this connector over the RGC.

A good design must be able to handle network problems by rerouting messages over alternative connections. Depending on what type of routing group connector you select, you may need to configure more than one of the same type between the same routing groups. However, the most common choice, the RGC, will let any local server in its routing group use this connector, much like the Site Connector in previous Exchange versions; see Figure 7.11.

7

If the RGC is configured like Figure 7.11, this will take care of the situation where one of the sending servers goes down; all other local servers will still be able to use this connector. Depending on how you have configured the RGC, it will also be able to handle a situation in which one of the servers in the remote routing group goes down. Use the Remote Bridgehead tab for the RGC, and list the remote servers that can accept mail from this connector. If you want to make this connector fault tolerant, make sure to add all remote servers to this list; see Figure 7.12.

But you will still be in trouble if the network link goes down. This can be solved if your network topology allows alternative routes; time to look at your map again. Remember, this information is often hard to get; you may have to contact the ISP or the telecom company responsible for the leased WAN lines to get the information you want. There is absolutely no point in creating multiple routing group connectors in order to get redundant links if they will be dependent on the same network link; it will only create a false sense of security. For example, in Figure 7.13 you see three routing groups connected by a routing group connector to each (the thick lines); the idea is to create redundant connections. However, since all physical network connections (the thin lines) pass the router in the middle, there is no real redundancy; if any network links go down, both routing group connectors will fail.

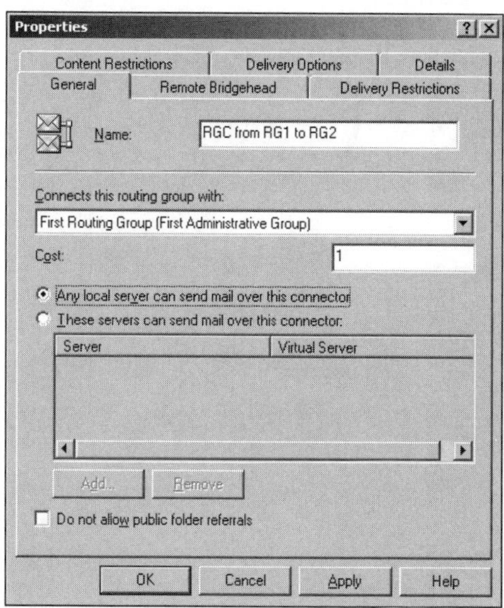

Figure 7.11
Defining local remote bridgehead servers for the RGC.

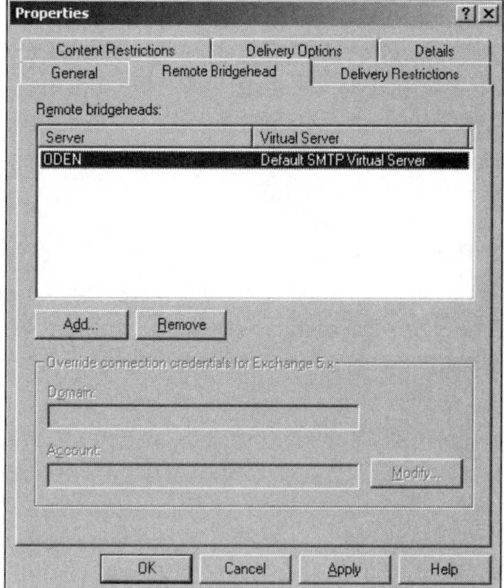

Figure 7.12
Defining remote bridgehead servers for the RGC.

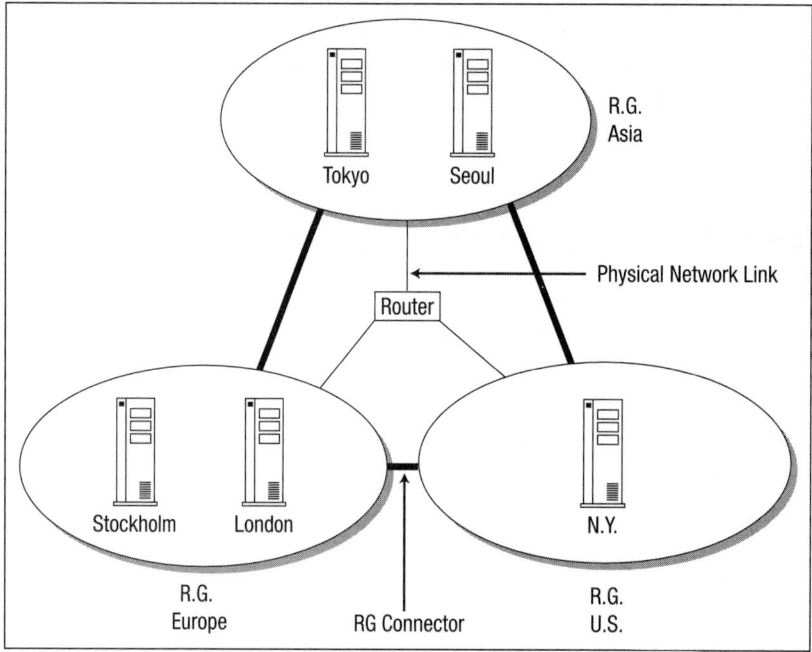

Figure 7.13
False redundant connections.

Internet Connections

Besides the connectors between routing groups, you must also plan for Internet connections. Since Exchange 2000 is SMTP based, it will be able to communicate directly by SMTP without any configuration. However, if you want to control which servers are responsible for outgoing SMTP messages to the Internet, you must install the *SMTP Connector*. This connector has lots of settings for outgoing SMTP, such as what users can send messages over this connector, when they can connect to the Internet, ETRN settings, address space, and connector scope (see Chapter 13 for more details about this and all other routing group connectors).

If the Internet traffic is intensive or business critical, you should make sure that more than one server is listed as *local bridgehead*, meaning they are responsible for all outgoing SMTP messages. To make a fault-tolerant design, you need at least two different Internet connections to two different ISPs, if possible. Again, make sure that both of these lines are not dependent on some common link on their way out. Note that Exchange 2000 will automatically monitor any connector, but there will be no notification if any problems occur; read more about link monitoring in Chapter 3.

Other Messaging Connectors

If another mail system exists (for example, MS Mail or Lotus Notes), you may need to set up a connector to it. This is common when you migrate from one mail system to Exchange 2000; if you can't migrate all users at once, Exchange 2000 has to coexist with the old mail system for a period of time; Chapter 8 has more information about migration. Your design plan must also take into account any migration phases and how these two mail systems can exchange messages and address lists between each other.

Exchange 2000 Server Enterprise includes a number of connectors to other mail systems:

- *SMTP Connector*—Used for connection to SMTP-based mail systems.
- *X.400 Connector*—Used for connection to other X.400-based mail systems.
- *MS Mail Connector & Dirsync Requestor*—Used for message transfer and address replication (known as *Directory Synchronization*) between MS Mail and Exchange.
- *CC-Mail Connector*—Used for message transfer and address replication between cc-Mail and Exchange.
- *Lotus Notes Connector*—Used for message transfer and address replication between Lotus Notes and Exchange.
- *Novell GroupWise*—Used for message transfer and address replication between GroupWise and Exchange.

Note that two connectors are no longer available in Exchange 2000—the *SNADS Connector* and the *PROFS Connector*; both of them are mainframe computer mail systems. If you need a connection to one of these mail systems, you need to keep at least one Exchange 5.5 server, since this can work as a gateway between the mainframe mail system and Exchange 2000.

Define Your Backup Strategy

Your design should also describe the backup strategy for the Exchange system. It is of utmost importance that you have a reliable backup system, and that the administrator knows how to use it. The backup is your last defense line; if this doesn't work, you will be in trouble, big trouble! A friend once asked me, "Do you know what they call an Exchange administrator who does not take backups?" "No," I replied. "Unemployed!" he answered.

The backup strategy is basically the same as for previous Exchange versions; use transaction log files and take a full backup every night. Exchange allows online backups, which means that the system will be backed up while running as normal, although a bit slower. But what is it that you need to take a backup of? The answer is, a lot of things. In fact, it's a bit more complicated now, compared to previous Exchange versions, since our directory with the address lists and Exchange configuration settings are stored in the Active Directory, and not in the Exchange server. However, the most important data is stored in our mailbox stores and public stores; let's recapitulate the store architecture:

- An Exchange server may have up to four different storage groups.
- Every storage group has its own set of transaction log files, shared by all stores in this storage group.
- Each storage group can have up to five stores.
- Each store can be up to 16TB in size.
- Each store consists of one EDB database and one STM streaming file.
- The total amount of data that can be stored in one Exchange server is $4 \times 5 \times 16\text{TB} = 320\text{TB}$.

That could easily be a lot of data to back up. But you will most likely never see an Exchange server with even half that amount. The idea behind all these stores is not to be able to save hundreds of terabytes, it is to be able to distribute users between different stores and storage groups, using different configuration settings for transaction logging and indexing of data. In Exchange 2000, you may take a backup of individual stores or complete storage groups; you can also restore them individually, without the need to stop the complete Exchange server or even other stores in the same storage group. This is very elegant, and makes it possible to manage single stores without affecting the complete server; for example, users belonging to other stores will not even notice that you are restoring one of the stores.

What Should I Back Up?

Besides the Active Directory and all Exchange stores that must be backed up, there are also configuration settings in the Registry, and more; below is a list of Exchange-related information that should be backed up:

- Stores in the storage groups
- Transaction log files
- The Registry on the Exchange server
- Message-tracking log files
- The Active Directory database and its configuration settings

Let's start with the last bullet, the Active Directory. This information is stored in the server's System State folder. You can use the backup program that comes with Windows 2000 for this, but you must run it locally on the domain controller; you cannot run a backup of the System State from another computer. See Figure 7.14. This will create a backup of:

- The Active Directory database
- All boot files
- COM+ class registration

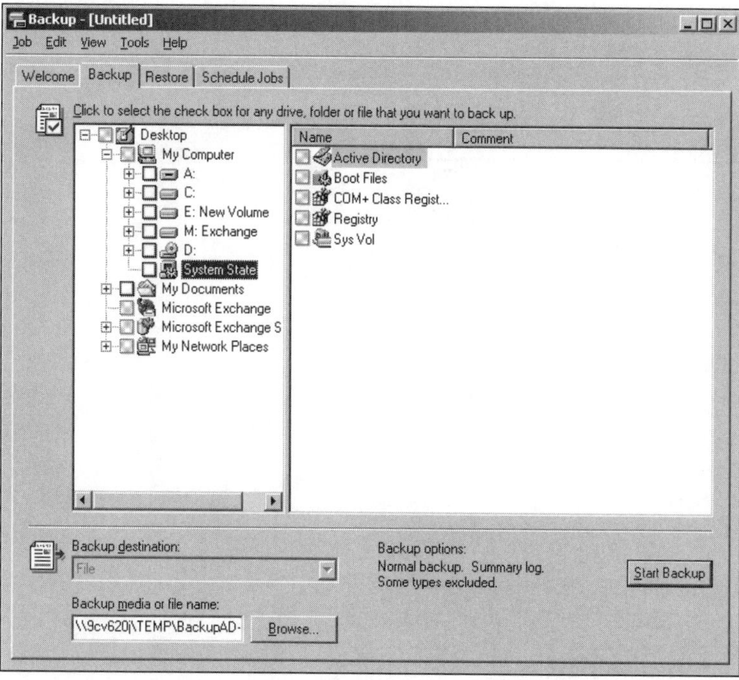

Figure 7.14
Taking a backup of the System State folder.

- The Registry
- The SYS Volume
- The Certificate Services database (if installed)

The size of this information is related to the number of objects in the Active Directory, but even a small Windows 2000 domain will generate a backup file of 400MB or more.

***Tip:** Since you cannot take backups of the System State folder over the network, you can do this instead: Run the Backup program locally, taking a backup of the System State, save this backup file locally, then use your ordinary backup program and take a backup of this file over the network.*

Exchange 2000 requires that the backup program understand the new features of stores and storage groups. You can upgrade your favorite backup application to a version compatible with Exchange 2000, or use the backup program that comes with Windows 2000 for this. To take a backup of all Exchange stores, make sure you select the Microsoft Exchange Server folder checkbox; see Figure 7.15. You can also drill down to a certain storage group or even a certain store.

Different Types of Backups

There are several types of backup processes that can be performed with the Windows 2000 backup program; they differ in what they will back up, what files they will remove from

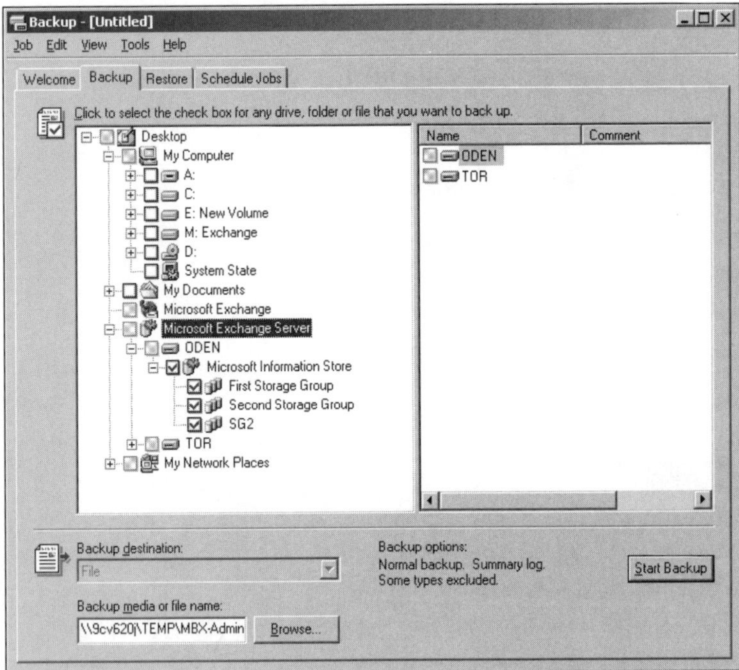

Figure 7.15
Backing up all Exchange 2000 stores.

the server, and how fast they run. See Table 7.4 for more details. You may wonder how the backup program knows if a file has changed, and therefore should be backed up. The answer is the Archive flag, which has been an attribute of all files since the dawn of MS-DOS. If this flag is set, it means that this file has changed since the last backup. When the backup program has made a backup of this file, it clears the Archive flag. Use Windows Explorer and make the Archive flag visible by selecting View|Choose Columns.

If possible, you should always select to run the normal backup procedure, since any restore operation later will be easiest to perform. The problem with normal backup procedures is of course that it could be a lot of data. Depending on how fast the backup hardware is and the amount of data, you may or may not have the time to perform this backup each night. Let's say your backup system manages to back up 10GB per hour and the total amount of Exchange data is 50GB; it will take approximately five hours for this backup, and the backup hardware must be able to store 50GB for this to work.

If there is no time for a normal backup every night, select to run *incremental* or *differential* backups instead. The incremental option is faster, since the data volume will be smaller, but will be harder to use in case of a restore scenario, since you must then restore first the latest normal backup and then all incremental backups after that. Let's say you take a full backup every Sunday and the rest of the week you run incremental backups. On Wednesday you need to restore a store; you must now start by restoring the normal backup from Sunday, and then the incremental backups from Monday and Tuesday.

Differential backups will take a backup of all changed files since the last normal backup so every day the size of the data volume will increase. If you take normal backups every Sunday, and differential backups every weekday, a restore scenario will be easier than for incremental backups, since there are always only two backup sets that need to be restored: the normal backup plus the latest differential backup. Below is a summary of the three types of backups available for Exchange servers:

Table 7.4 The different types of backups.

Type	Archive Flag	Files that are Backed Up	Effect on Exchange Files
Normal	Cleared after backup	Will take a backup of all selected files, without checking the Archive flag first	Selected Exchange stores are backed up, and transaction log files are removed
Copy	Will not be changed	Will take a backup of all selected files, without checking the Archive flag first	Selected Exchange stores are backed up, but no transaction log files are removed
Daily	Will not be changed	Will take a backup of all files that have changed this day; the modification date is used to identify these files, not the Archive flag	Does the same thing as a Copy backup
Incremental	Cleared after backup	Will take a backup of all files with the Archive flag set	Only transaction log files will be backed up, and then removed
Differential	Will not be changed	Will take a backup of all files with the Archive flag set	Only transaction log files will be backed up, but not removed

- *Only normal backups*—Easiest in case of a restore scenario, but take the longest time to perform. This is the recommended backup procedure.
- *Normal backups on weekends plus incremental backups on weekdays*—Incremental backups are fast, since they include only the changes made during the last 24 hours, but they take the longest time to restore.
- *Normal backups on weekends plus differential backups on weekdays*—Faster than normal backups every day, but not as fast as incremental backups; in case of a restore scenario, only two backup sets will be needed—the normal backup and the latest differential backup.

In the design plan, decide what backup procedure to use. Remember that you can take a backup of single stores or whole storage groups. You should always try to back up a complete storage group, since all stores within share the same transaction log files. Make an estimate of how much data to back up every night; make sure the backup system can handle this amount of data. Estimate how much data will be on the server if the number of users increases or the average mailbox size grows over the current max limit. You must never allow a server to collect more data than it is possible to back up!

Tip: *If you have a store with business-critical information, you can take a differential backup at regular intervals, for example every hour. Since this will only back up any changes, the amount of data will be small, compared to the complete store. If you also save this backup set to a disk instead of tape, it will be even faster.*

Single-Mailbox Backup

Many commercial backup systems allow backup of single mailboxes, as a complement to backing up the complete store. This feature is sometimes called *brick-level backup*. It usually works like this: After the normal backup is done, the backup system will connect to the Exchange server as a mailbox user, copying all content for this user to the backup set. This feature makes it very easy to restore a single mailbox or even a single piece of mail, depending on the features offered by the backup program. But don't expect that you can both do a full backup of all stores and then a backup of every single mailbox, unless it's a very small organization. Single-mailbox backups take a long time to perform. Do you remember that Exchange has the single item store feature, where messages are stored only once, even if there are a number of recipients of this message? A normal backup procedure will copy this message only once, since it is stored only once; however, the single mailbox backup will copy this message once for every recipient. Use these as guidelines:

- Run a test to see how much time it takes to perform a single-mailbox backup; use this information to calculate how many mailboxes can be backed up like this.
- Select only important mailboxes for this type of backup, like management and key persons (and yourself?).
- Monitor this backup type regularly; make sure it's not growing due to larger mailboxes. Check to see how long it takes and make sure the data fits onto the backup tape.

Backup of Metabase

The Internet Information Server 5 is now a critical part of the Exchange server; the IIS is responsible for all Internet protocols, like POP3, IMAP4, NNTP, HTTP, and SMTP. The Active Directory is not used for storing the configuration settings; instead, IIS has its own Metabase where all settings are stored. But every change of these Internet protocols made with the ESM will first be stored in the Active Directory and then copied to the Metabase. However, the Active Directory will not have a complete copy of the Metabase information. To make a backup of the Metabase, follow these steps:

1. Start the *Internet Service Manager* (*ISM*).
2. Right-click on your server and select *Backup|Restore Configuration*.
3. Click *Create Backup*.
4. Type a name for this backup, and then click *OK*.
5. Make sure this file is included in the normal backup procedure.

Disaster Recovery

This is every Exchange administrator's nightmare: having to restore a corrupt store or even worse, a complete server. However, if the backup routines are working, this is not as bad as you might first think. The keys to success are two:

- The backup tape is readable and contains what you expect.
- The administrator knows how to restore the tape.

So how hard can it be? In reality: Very hard! There are many administrators that never check the log of the backup program, and therefore never discover any errors or warnings. I have been at installations where the backup program had not been working for five months without anyone noticing, until the system crashed. The other problem is that many administrators have never performed a restore procedure, and when the first time comes, they make disastrous mistakes. But all this can be easily avoided by following some simple rules, which should be described in the design plan:

1. Check the backup log for warnings or errors every day!
2. Test the backup tape at least every month, by performing a restore on a separate server—but not the production server!
3. Use several tapes; don't overwrite them too often. An absolute minimum is one separate tape for each workday; if possible, use more. Tape is cheap, but data is not.
4. Store the backup tapes in a location separate from the server; anything can happen, like fire, flooding, and theft.
5. Don't use backup tapes longer than the manufacturer recommends; remember that tape is an error-prone media that easily gets destroyed.

The restore process itself is very simple if everything else is okay; select what to restore and start. The backup program will automatically dismount the store in question, perform the restore, and then mount it again. Other stores on the same server will not notice this procedure, except for a slight drop in the performance.

***Tip:** When restoring a store, you should first make sure that the checkbox This Database Can Be Overwritten By A Restore is selected; you will find it at the properties for the store, on the Database tab. If you don't select this checkbox, it may take up to 15 minutes to mount this store after it has been restored; see Figure 7.16.*

The design document should describe routines for recovering from different disaster scenarios. It should also describe how the administrators should practice these routines, for example how often, under what conditions, and what servers to use. Some companies have a really tough drill for their administrators; without warning, someone will come to the administrator, tell him that it's an emergency, and ask him to restore a single store or perhaps a complete server. A timer will then be started to see how much time the administrator needs to perform this restore. When the time comes for a real restore scenario, this administrator will perform this operation fast and without any mistakes.

Any restore of a single mailbox or a message must be performed on a separate server, since we don't want to restore a complete store on the production server. In the design plan, there must be a reserved server to be used for situations like this; this must not be a production server, since the restore operation may require a complete reinstallation of the operation system. This server may have less CPU and memory than the production servers, but it must be able to handle all the stores in the largest available production

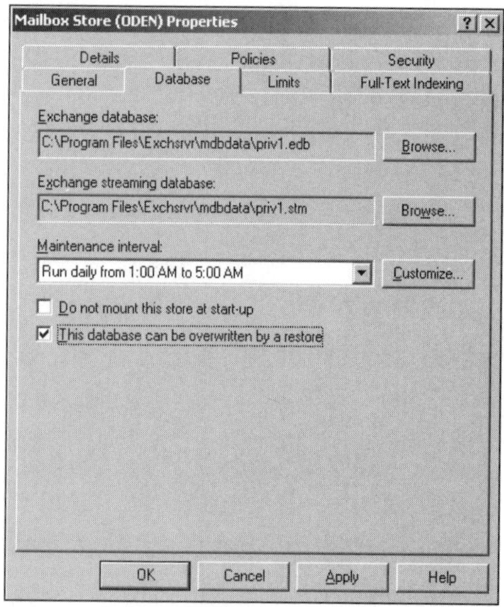

Figure 7.16
The This Database Can Be Overwritten By A Restore checkbox.

server. It is sometimes hard to explain to a CFO why this standby server is needed, but it is absolutely necessary if you need to be able to do certain restore procedures without disturbing the production environment.

Daily Routines For the Administrator

In order to avoid or at least decrease the risk of disasters and problems, you should take care of the Exchange system as if it was a patient and you were the doctor. Make sure to follow routines every day, looking for strange error messages and unexpected behavior and you will likely find and solve problems before they grow into disasters. Use the following worksheet as a checklist, every day. In case you find something, you must make a note on what you have found, which components are affected, and the time and date. If you manage to fix the problem, describe how you did it. If you do this, you will after a while have excellent documentation of your system and its behavior, and you will also have a description on how to fix the usual problems.

Summary

This is a list of the more important features and keywords mentioned in this chapter. Use it as a reminder and to make sure you have understood the most important things:

A basic daily checklist for the administrator worksheet.

What to Check	Status/Value	Comments
The Event Log, Application section		Look for error and warnings related to E2K
The Event Log, System section		Look for errors and warning related to E2K
The Event Log, Security section		Look for indications that someone is hacking
Check all SMTP Queues in ESM		No mail should be older than 48 hours
Check all X.400 Queues in ESM		Only if there is X.400 traffic
Check the Monitoring and Status folder in ESM		Are there any problems reported?
Check the Link Status Table		Are any links down? If so, why?
Check all Exchange services		Has anyone of them stopped? When? Why?
Check the CPU load		Notate its average value (skip peaks)
Check the Memory Usage		Notate its average value (skip peaks)
Check *Exchsrvr\mailroot\vsi 1\Queue*		Should be empty
Check *Exchsrvr\mailroot\vsi 1\Pickup*		Should be empty
Check *Exchsrvr\mailroot\vsi 1\BadMail*		May contain items, open any *.BAD or *.EML
Check the available free disk space		Both for the Trans.log and the database
Check the Backup program		Are there any errors or warnings?
Check the Administrators/Postmaster mailbox		Are there any errors or warnings?
Send a message to an Internet recipient		Use an echo mailbox, such as **echo@swip.net**

- A good design plan is the key to a successful Exchange organization.
- The number one objective for the design is to make a mail system that meets or exceeds users' expectations.
- Start your design by analyzing the users' needs.
- The most popular features in Exchange are, in order: email, calendar, and public folders.
- Select representative groups of users and ask them about good and bad things about the current mail system; ask them what features they would like the new mail system to have.
- Analyze the current mail traffic—how much, to whom, what features are used; is S/MIME or PGP used or asked for?
- Analyze the interest in public folders; let users test it and show them what they can do with it.
- Is there any need for general purpose folders? For example, document management applications?
- Is Usenet news of interest?
- Are there any cyclic patterns in behavior; for example, does every Outlook user start the client at 9 o'clock in the morning?
- What messaging format will the users prefer: Plain Text, RTF, or HTML?
- How will the messages be stored—in the Exchange store, PST file, or OST file?
- What client type is preferred—POP3, IMAP4, OWA, or MAPI?
- Are there any remote access clients? How will they connect? What client will they use?
- Previous Exchange versions defined three user profiles: light, medium, and heavy.
- Exchange 2000 has a new profile called MMB2: MAPI Messaging Benchmark version 2, which is much more demanding than any previous user profiles.
- A design plan must describe how to educate the users and support team.
- Administrative needs are easier to fulfill in Exchange 2000, regardless of the network topology.
- There are two types of administrators: Mailbox administrators and Exchange administrators.
- Mailbox administrators use the Active Directory Users and Computers tool.
- Exchange administrators use the Exchange System Manager, ESM.
- Create one administrative group for each set of administrators that want to manage their own Exchange servers.

- There are three Administrative roles: View Only, Exchange Administrator, and Exchange Full Administrator.
- A clear and good name standard is of paramount importance.
- Some names cannot be changed: Windows 2000 domain names, Exchange 2000 organization names, and NetBIOS server names.
- The default display name is First, Last; consider changing this to Last, First, using the ADSI Edit tool.

- The default SMTP email address is **alias@domain.tld**; consider changing this to **first.last@domain.tld** using the ESM.
- Define name standards for distribution groups, public folders, administrative groups, routing groups, storage groups, stores, virtual servers, connectors, address lists, and so on.
- Make a map of the current network topology, with all network links, speed, routers, firewalls, and IP subnets.
- Use the LoadSim tool to simulate a number of users with a given behavior.
- Investigate the current server and client computer configuration; do any computers need to be replaced or upgraded?
- Add the organizational layout to your network topology map, showing where the users are located and how many there are.
- Use a few but large Exchange servers before many small servers.
- Do you need higher speed on some or all of the WAN connections?
- Use as few routing groups as possible; this makes the system less complex, and will increase the transport performance.
- There are three different routing group connectors: RGC, X.400 Connector, and SMTP Connector.
- The Routing Group Connector, RGC, will be used in most cases.
- Use the SMTP Connector for controlling outgoing external SMTP messages.
- Create multiple connectors if you are sure there are true redundant WAN connections.
- Will there be any other mail system that Exchange 2000 will connect to? For instance, MS Mail, Lotus Notes, or GroupWise.
- Make sure you take a backup of everything that is related to Exchange: stores, AD, Registry, Metabase, and tracking logs.
- Back up the System State folder on the domain controller to get all-important data, like AD, Registry, and boot files.

- There are five types of backups; only three of them are normally used for Exchange: Normal, Incremental, and Differential.
- Normal backup is recommended every night; if this is not possible, select Normal plus Differential.
- Single-mailbox backups, or brick-level backups, are nice to have, but take a long time and require a lot of extra space on the backup tape.
- Disaster recovery is easy if the backup tapes are working and the administrator knows how to do the restore.
- Describe the backup and restore procedures in the design document.
- Make sure the backup logs are read every day; look for warnings and error messages. Remember, this is your last line of defense!

Chapter 8

Migrating to Exchange 2000

Most companies and organizations today already have mail systems that have been in use for many years. Their reasons for upgrading to MS Exchange 2000 are usually because their old system doesn't offer the features they need today, and also because it is hard to administrate; another common reason is that their current product is dead, or at least dying. By now you should agree that Exchange 2000 has many advanced features that make it possible to share information in an easy and intuitive way, while at the same time it is easy to administrate, regardless of how small or large the organization is. In my opinion, no other mail system offers the same number of features for messaging and collaboration, combined with highly resilient data stores and Internet connectivity.

I often tell my customers that they should look at more factors than features and price when they're selecting a new mail system. A new system should stay in the company for years, it must give the organization what it needs today and tomorrow, and it must allow the organization to grow and expand, or else a lot of money and time are wasted. In many companies, the messaging system is a business-critical application, if not the most important. So you should select the new messaging system very carefully—you don't want to have to change again after a year. Questions you should ask before selecting such a system are:

- Does it have the features our organization needs?
- How many administrators are needed to run this system?
- Will this vendor still be on the market in five years?
- Will this messaging system continue to develop?
- Do lots of third-party vendors make add-on products for this messaging system?
- Do lots of independent consultant companies support this system?
- Are training and courses offered on both user levels and administrative levels?

All of these questions are more important than the initial cost! It is not easy to select the perfect messaging system for an organization; a number of products are on the market today. The questions mentioned above are important signs to look for when comparing messaging systems; some of the messaging systems that have been around for years are now slowly moving away from the market—products like MS Mail and CC-Mail, and also big players like ICL TeamWare and HP Open Mail, who recently announced that they have stopped developing the Open Mail product.

Since I am a trainer, I have good insight regarding courses offered by training institutes and requested by customers. If you use this as a critical factor for selecting a mail system, several other big players are showing clear signs of trouble, such as Novell GroupWise. On the other hand, the number of courses available for MS Exchange has increased since the start, and the interest for these courses is high. Also look at the number of books available for these mail systems, the number of third-party products, and the number of consulting companies offering services; if you look at all these factors together, MS Exchange wins hands down, in my humble opinion!

Expect Chaos

So you have decided to migrate to Exchange 2000. Congratulations, you've made an excellent choice! However, if your organization is large, and you will not be able to migrate all users at once, Exchange 2000 will have to coexist with the old mail system for a while. This will be a time of chaos, not because of problems with mail communication, but because of the ongoing process of moving users and groups from one mail system to another. Every day, users will disappear from the old system and show up in Exchange. If the address lists are not constantly updated on both sides, your users will constantly receive *Non-Delivery Reports (NDRs)* when sending messages.

Perhaps the hardest, and simultaneously the most neglected problem during migration is mail groups or distribution lists, as they are called in previous Exchange versions. If you don't migrate all users in a mail group at once, the group will no longer be valid, since some of its members don't exist anymore on this mail system. And people tend to be members of more than one group at the time, so if you can't migrate all groups and their members at once, you cannot use these groups during the migration phase.

During the migration period, messages must be able to pass freely between the two mail systems. This is no problem if they have a common mail protocol, like SMTP. Exchange 2000 is rich on connectors, or gateways as they really are, to other mail systems. This is a smart move from Microsoft; there should be no excuse for not implementing Exchange 2000 in the organization. Exchange 2000 Server Enterprise edition has connectors to the following mail systems:

- *SMTP Connector*—Used for connecting to SMTP-based mail systems; no address replication available.

- *X.400 Connector*—Used for connection to other X.400-based mail systems; no address replication available.
- *MS Mail Connector and Dirsync Requestor/Dirsync Server*—Used for message transfer and address replication (known as *Directory Synchronization*) between MS Mail and Exchange.
- *CC-Mail Connector*—Used for message transfer and address replication between cc-Mail and Exchange.
- *Lotus Notes Connector*—Used for message transfer and address replication between Lotus Notes and Exchange.
- *Novell GroupWise*—Used for message transfer and address replication between GroupWise and Exchange.

Previous versions of Exchange also supported two mainframe computer mail systems: the SNADS Connector and the PROFS Connector. These are not supported in Exchange 2000. You must keep at least one Exchange 5.5 server as a gateway if you need a connector to either of these two systems.

If SMTP or X.400 is the only mail protocol that can be used for message traffic between Exchange 2000 and the old system, you must also solve the problem of how to replicate address lists between these two systems; remember that none of the SMTP Connector or the X.400 Connector has an address replication feature similar to the cc-Mail Connector or Lotus Notes Connector. In this case, I would recommend searching the Internet for any third-party solutions to this problem, checking mailing lists or newsgroups, or asking the vendor of your old mail system if they know of any solutions. If you still cannot find any solutions to the address replication problem, you must develop your own replication procedure. This will probably take a long time and will also be expensive. In such a case, look at the migration process again; is there any way to speed this migration up? Do you really need to have address replication during this time? If you come to the conclusion that address replication is necessary, you can use the LDIFDE tool for Exchange 2000 to export and import users. Hopefully, the old mail system also has some sort of export and import function; then it will "only" be a matter of adjusting the address file format to each mail system. Look at Chapter 5 for more information about exporting and importing users with the LDIFDE tool.

If you have one single connector between the two mail systems, it must be carefully monitored. If that connector or any of its bridgehead servers go down, this will stop all message traffic and address replication between them. It may be a good idea to have at least two connectors, both for fault-tolerance and load balancing. A large organization with thousands of users may generate a lot of traffic over this connector; you can reduce this traffic by following this advice:

- Users who send lots of mail between them, like teams, groups, and departments should be migrated at the same time.

- Reduce the maximum message size over this link.
- Instruct the users to avoid sending large messages if it's not absolutely necessary.

You must have a clear picture of how to perform the migration before you begin; otherwise you will be lost, and more chaos than necessary will result. If you have not performed any migrations before, it is wise to hire an experienced consultant to assist in this delicate matter.

Define the Migration Plan

No migration should ever start without a detailed plan on what to do, and how to do it. Migrations involve lots of steps, and you must be very careful when designing this plan. Your migration plan must include answers to the following:

- How should the migration process be performed?
- How should Exchange and the old mail system communicate?
- How should address replication be performed?
- How many users can be migrated per day?
- Which users should be migrated and when?
- What data should be migrated to Exchange?
- What will we do if the migration does not work?
- What do we do when the migration is complete?
- How should users, administrators, and the help desk be trained?

Let's look at these questions in more detail.

How Should the Migration Process Be Performed?

Together with the Exchange 2000 server program comes the *Migration Wizard*, a tool for migrating users from different mail systems to Exchange 2000. This tool is constantly updated; you should check Microsoft's Web page to make sure you have the latest version. The current version supports migration from the following mail systems:

- MS Mail for PC Networks
- Lotus cc-Mail
- Lotus Notes
- Novell GroupWise 4.x
- Novell GroupWise 5.x
- Collabra Share

- Internet Directory (LDAP)
- IMAP4

The Migration Wizard is an excellent tool for migrating users; it will connect to any of the mail systems listed above, read all messages for a given user, create this user in Exchange 2000, and copy (not move!) all messages to the new Exchange system. For most of these mail systems, the Migration Wizard will also copy any calendars and personal address lists. It is important to understand that all data is copied from the old system—it will not be removed, and the mail accounts on the old system will still be active. You must disable the account manually, if this is necessary; otherwise these accounts can still receive messages that make the sender believe that the message has reached its recipient, while in reality it has gone to an inactive mailbox.

Migrating by the Client

If you have a mail system that Migration Wizard doesn't know how to migrate, like First Class or QuickMail, you should first look for any available third-party migration tools. If you can't find any, you may still be able to migrate users if they can use an Outlook client, by following these steps:

1. Replace the existing client with MS Outlook (any version).
2. Configure Outlook to use personal stores (PST) files; make sure all messages are stored in the PST file.
3. Reconfigure the Outlook client to connect to Exchange 2000.
4. Change the primary delivery point to *Mailbox* - ***<User Name>***; see Figure 8.1.
5. The PST file should now automatically be copied to the Exchange server and you should be finished; if not, you must import the PST file manually.

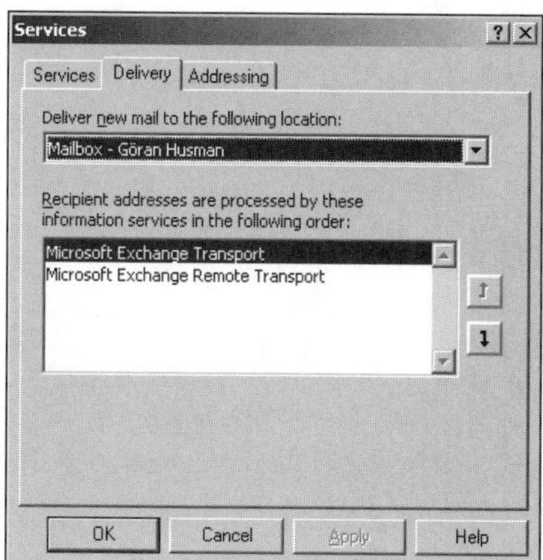

Figure 8.1
Setting the primary delivery point of messages.

If the PST file was not automatically copied in Step 5 above, then you must import it manually by selecting the Outlook menu:

1. Select *File|Import And Export.*
2. Select *Import From Another File.*
3. Select *Personal Folder File.*
4. Browse to find your PST file, select it, and click *OK* to continue.
5. Select the options you want. The default is *Replace Duplicates With Items Imported*; click *Next* to continue.
6. Make sure you have selected *Import Items To The Same Folder In . . . Mailbox* ***<User Name>****;* see Figure 8.2; then click *Finish* to start the import process.

How Should Exchange and the Old Mail System Communicate?

This is usually the easiest question to answer, due to the multitude of connectors Exchange 2000 offers, but for some mail systems, like First Class, it can be a problem. If so, ask the vendor of the old mail system for help, or search the Internet for all available third-party connectors. If nothing else is found, SMTP gateways are usually available for any mail system.

How Should Address Replication Be Performed?

This topic was mentioned before, but let's repeat it anyway. If you are lucky, you can use one of the connectors available in Exchange 2000 that has address replication built in. If not, you must 1.) look for available third-party add-ons, or 2.) develop your own address replication process.

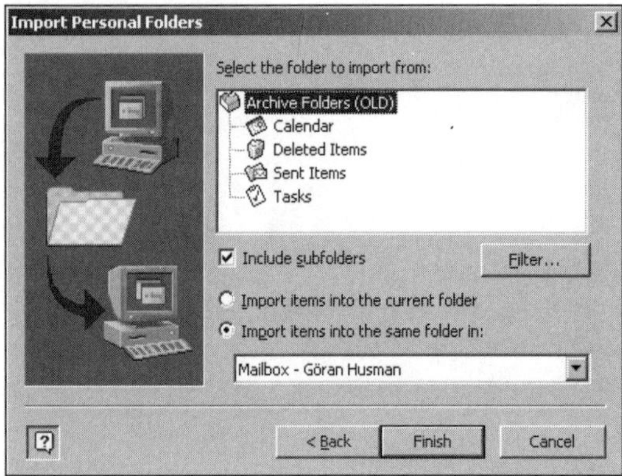

Figure 8.2
Configure where to store imported items.

How Many Users Can Be Migrated Per Day?

This question is hard to answer without knowing anything about the old mail system, the migration tools being used, and the amount of data to be migrated. Let's take an example from the real world: if you use the Exchange Migration Wizard and migrate from MS Mail, you will be able to migrate about 50 to 100 users per day. Running the Migration Wizard on several computers simultaneously will increase this number, but this is a rather CPU-intensive operation for the Exchange server, so you may reach the maximum number of migrations that the server can manage simultaneously.

Which Users Should Be Migrated and When?

In Chapter 7, we discussed design topics and how important it is to understand how information flows in the organization. This information is also very valuable when selecting which users to migrate together; always try to migrate a group of users that send lots of messages to each other—for example, a complete office or smaller departments. During the migration process, these users will not be allowed to use either the old mail system or Exchange 2000; they must wait until their mailbox is completely migrated. This makes it hard to perform the migration process during office hours for some organizations; if this is the case, then migration must be performed during nights or weekends.

Before migrating a user, he or she must have the Outlook client installed; as soon as the migration is done, the user must be able to start working with the new system. The user must also be trained in the new system a day or two before the migration is done. As you can see, several time factors are critical if you want to perform an optimized migration. Here are the steps I usually follow:

1. Start by installing the Outlook client (or whatever type of client this user should have). This can be done weeks before the actual migration process.
2. Decide on a date when this user will be migrated; plan this several weeks ahead, and inform the user what will happen and when.
3. Make sure this user has training in Outlook, preferably the day before the migration.
4. On the given date, migrate this user to Exchange 2000.
5. Create a user profile in Outlook so the client is ready to be used; you can do this by manually adding the profile, or by using tools like NewProf.exe in the logon script.

What Data Should Be Migrated to Exchange?

Depending on the type of mail system, you may select to migrate all data or just some of it. Users may have saved a lot of messages during the years and this will be a good opportunity to clean some of it out, before the migration. This may also be true for personal address lists, calendar bookings, and other types of information stored in the old mail system. If the users have lots of information, several hundred megabytes each for instance, the migration will take a long time. If the users for any reason can't clean out the old mailboxes and reduce their sizes, another solution is to move all old mail to a PST, rather than migrating this data to the Exchange server. Follow these steps to move the old messages to a PST file:

1. Install the new Outlook client, connect to the old mail system, and move all data to a locally stored PST file.
2. When migrating the user, do not copy any data from the old system; just create a mailbox-enabled user account in the new system.
3. Create an Outlook profile to Exchange 2000; then add the old PST file to this profile.
4. Add an Outlook shortcut to the old PST file to make it easily accessible for the user.

This user will now have access to both the new mailbox in Exchange 2000 and all old messages and addresses. You should also instruct the user how to access the old information, and how to move or copy it to the new system, if necessary.

What Will We Do If the Migration Does Not Work?

This is an extremely important question that must be answered before the migration process starts. For example, let's say that a few weeks after we have started to migrate, we discover that the servers will not be able to store all users, or the clients may not be able to run Outlook; the migration team must now abort the migration process. If the problem can't be solved in a satisfactory way, we may have to return to the old mail system again. If this isn't possible, we will have a big problem. This must never happen. By planning the migration, you can avoid this. The basic idea is that for everything that is migrated, you must be able to reverse the operation without losing any data. Here are some recommendations for how to plan for a recover.

1. Always make a backup of the old mail server before migrating its first user. If you are migrating by upgrading an existing mail server to Exchange 2000, you must take a complete backup of the whole server.
2. For each user migrated, make sure their data is copied, not moved, from the old server.
3. If the user has locally stored information, for example POP3 mailbox data and personal addresses, then take a backup of this information before installing Outlook.
4. Make a plan for how to restore the complete old mail system, with step-by-step instructions on what to do and how to do it.

I can't stress this point enough: Do not ever start a migration without a plan for how to restore the old mail system. In most organizations, the message system is business critical, and users will not accept losing any data whatsoever, so please take this task seriously!

What to Do When the Migration Is Done

The first thing to do when the migration process is done for the day is to back up the new system; after all this work, you don't want to lose it due to a disk crash. Check this backup and make sure it is okay; remember that too often backup tapes are unusable, due to technical problems or because the backup doesn't contain all the data that you expect.

You should also disable the mail account on the old system to avoid anyone continuing to send mail to that account, but be careful not to remove any data! On some systems, you cannot disable accounts. In those situations, you must try to find another way of stopping data from entering the old system; for example, if you have migrated a complete MS Mail post office, you can disconnect this server from the network, or rename its folder. Sometimes you can't do this, so mail will continue to enter the old mail account, usually from external users. This is a tricky situation, since you have moved the user to Exchange 2000 and all messages going to the old mailbox must somehow be forwarded to the new one. Depending on the type of mail system, you can solve this problem several different ways:

- If possible, create a server rule that will forward all mail to the new mail server.
- If this does not work, maybe a client rule can forward this mail.
- Some mail systems have add-on products that make it possible to create forward rules, even if the server or normal client can't do it—for example, MS Mail.
- The mail server that receives all incoming Internet mail—for example, Sendmail, may rerout SMTP messages to the new address.

In the worst case scenario, you can configure the user's Outlook client to connect to both the old mail system and Exchange 2000 at the same time; this is not so good, since this will give the users two active mail systems, and everyone who still uses the old mail account will not understand that they should start using the new one instead. This should be avoided, or you will have to support two different mail systems instead of one.

How Should Users, Administrators, and the Help Desk Be Trained?

If your organization is not properly trained for the new environment, users will not understand how to use Outlook properly; this will lower their productivity and create irritation. After working so hard with the migration process, we want our users to be excited by the new Exchange 2000 environment, not irritated. Training is the way to produce happy and productive users. Most often, full-scale user training is not necessary; a short presentation, maybe two to three hours, is usually satisfactory, during which an experienced teacher presents the most important features of the new system. Since this may be the first time many of these users come in contact with Outlook and Exchange, it is important that the teacher gives an interesting and fun, although serious, presentation; we want the users to be keen on starting with this new system, and interested in its new features and possibilities.

However, users aren't the only ones who must be trained. Regardless of how much training they receive, many new situations will arise where they need help and support. Larger organizations usually have a help desk or a support team; these groups will need much more training than the users, making them ready and able to support the organization. They must receive this training shortly before the first users are migrated. I would suggest at least a two-day training, with hands-on exercises combined with a deeper explanation on how the Exchange system works, and how to solve usual support tasks like:

- Creating or deleting mailbox-enabled users
- Modifying user attributes, like department, phone number, family name
- Modifying users' email addresses
- Resetting passwords
- Sharing private mailbox folders with other users
- Modifying permissions on public folders
- Creating rules and out-of-office messages

Besides users and help desks, the upcoming Exchange and Mailbox administrators need proper training as well. The Exchange administrator needs at least a one-week training; I recommend Microsoft's official course number 1572: "Implementing and Managing Microsoft Exchange 2000," or course 2355: "Upgrading from MS Exchange Server 5.5 to MS Exchange 2000," or any other course with corresponding content. Even if a mailbox administrator doesn't need the full 1572 course, it still gives them a good understanding of Exchange that helps them avoid mistakes caused by lack of knowledge of Exchange.

Migrating Distribution Groups

As previously stated, migrating distribution lists, mailing lists, or mail groups, whatever they are called in the old system, can be very hard or sometimes almost impossible. One problem is that as soon as the migration starts, users will be moved from the old mail system to the new Exchange 2000; all groups that this user was a member of will now be incomplete. The other problem is that in both the old system and the new, users expect to find these groups. When creating the migration plan, these problems can be solved in one of three ways:

- Make sure these groups are complete, even if you must add and remove members of all groups manually; this may be very labor-intensive in larger organizations.
- Tell your users that they can't trust the membership of distributions lists during the migration period; this is clearly an unsatisfactory solution for most organizations.
- Disable all distribution lists during the migration period.

Let's look more closely into these different options.

Make Sure the Distribution Groups Are Updated

For larger organizations using lots of distribution groups, this is most often the only solution. In this case, the migration team must be prepared for the extra work involved in keeping these groups updated. A deeper look into the problem will explain the challenge we have before us; I will describe two methods.

Method #1—Migrating Distribution Groups

With this method, we assume that we have full address replication between these two mail systems; all users in Exchange 2000 will be listed as remote email addresses in the old system, and all users in the old system will be registered as mail-enabled Contact objects in the Active Directory. Here's how the first method works:

1. The old mail system has a distribution group named X-Team, with the following members: Johan, Beatrice, Marielle, Thomas, and Anna. This group is replicated to Exchange 2000 as a mail-enabled Contact. The result is that users on both sides can send messages to the X-Team.
2. Next, Johan will be migrated to the new system, so the old account will be disabled; this means that the X-Team is not complete anymore. However, since Johan's new account in Exchange 2000 will show up in the old system as a remote mail address, we can solve this problem by adding Johan's new remote address to the X-Team group. The result is that users on both sides can send messages to the X-Team. The consequence is that an Exchange 2000 user who sends a message to this group will generate two messages: one is delivered to the Contact address, pointing to the old system, and since one of its members was removed, the old mail system will send a copy of this message back to Exchange 2000 again.
3. Finally, all members of the X-Team will be migrated. The next logical step would be to remove this group from the old system and create it as a distribution group in the Exchange 2000 environment. Then this distribution group will be replicated back as a remote address, making this group accessible for users in the old mail system.

One thing to consider here is the amount of manual work involved in keeping these groups updated. As described in Step 2, for each migrated user you must wait until their new Exchange 2000 address shows up in the old mail system and then manually add them to all groups they used to be members of. Assuming that we migrate 50 users every day, and we have 200 groups, we will have lots of groups that need manual updates every day. If these are not updated, users will think they have sent messages to recipients, whereas in reality they may have missed some.

Method #2—Migrating Distribution Groups

Another important conclusion is the increase in mail traffic that groups will generate; as described in Step 2, for each message sent to a group with a removed mail recipient, a copy of this message will be sent back again. This may or may not be a problem, depending on the connection between the mail systems. Let's say that the old system is MS Mail and you are using one MS Mail connector for message traffic; if this connection gets overloaded, the result will be queues and long delivery times. Clearly you want to avoid this double message traffic generated by groups during the migration process. One way of solving this is to create two groups, one on each side that will not be replicated between the systems. Using the same example as above, we would now get this result:

1. The old mail system has a distribution group named X-Team, with the following members: Johan, Beatrice, Marielle, Thomas, and Anna. This group will not be replicated to Exchange 2000; instead, a distribution group with the same name is created in the Exchange 2000 environment. This distribution group consists of the members Johan, Beatrice, Marielle, Thomas, and Anna; all of them are mail-enabled Contacts created by the address replication process between these two systems. The result is that users on both sides can send messages to the X-Team. A message sent to this group from the old mail system will not generate any traffic to Exchange 2000; a message sent from an Exchange 2000 user will generate one transferred message to the old mail system.
2. Next, Johan will be migrated to the new system, so the old account will be disabled; this means that the X-Team is not complete anymore. Again, Johan's new account in Exchange 2000 will show up in the old system as a remote mail address, and we add Johan's new remote address to the X-Team group. Next we update the X-Team distribution list in Exchange 2000, replacing the previous Custom object for Johan with the new mailbox-enabled User object. The result is that any messages sent to either of these two groups will generate one single message transferred over the connector, since both instances of this X-Team group contain members from the other side.
3. Finally, all members of the X-Team group are migrated to Exchange 2000; then we can remove this group from the old mail system. Instead, we start replicating the X-Team group from Exchange 2000 to the old mail system, thereby making this group available to its users.

By this method we have solved the problem of doubled message transfer for groups, but at the price of more manual work, since we now must update two groups (one on each side) instead of one. However, if we can use the Exchange Migration Wizard, it will automatically detect if a migrated user is listed as a Contact, and replace this object with the newly created mailbox-enabled User object, wherever it is used. This means that the Migration Wizard will update the X-Team distribution group automatically, and no extra work is required except the update of the group in the old system. This method is preferred when using the Migration Wizard, but even if you are not, you could create an LDAP script searching for all migrated users and replace their contact objects wherever found.

Migrating from Exchange 5.5

The migration from Exchange 5.5 to Exchange 2000 is probably the easiest upgrade to perform. This should come as no surprise, of course, since Microsoft realizes that this type of update is very common. There are several methods of upgrading to Exchange 2000, and you should take the time to understand the differences between them:

- In-place upgrade
- Move-mailbox upgrade
- Swing upgrade
- Exmerge upgrade

You can choose a migration method rather freely, but it's common to use one method before another in given situations. Use the Decision Tree 8.1 as a guide to when a given method should be used. In the following sections you will read more about each migration method and how to perform it.

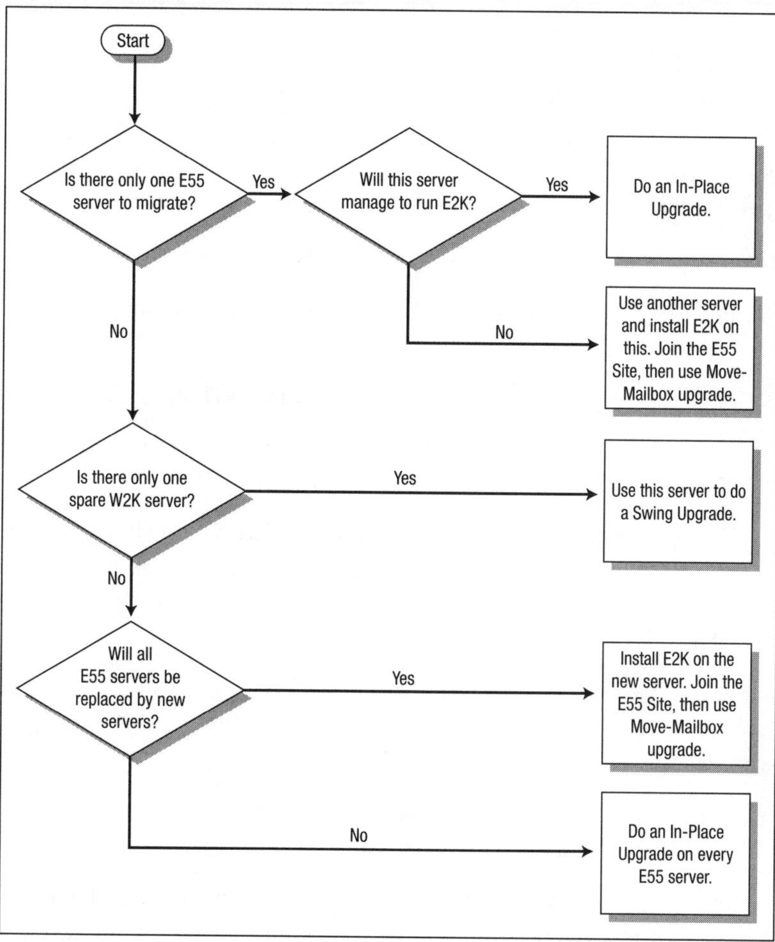

Decision Tree 8.1
Selecting a migration method.

One thing that is common to all methods is that you must make sure the Exchange 5.5 server is okay before any migration starts. You should run the *DS/IS Consistency Adjuster* on both the mailboxes and the public folders; this feature is activated on the *Advanced* tab, in the properties for the Exchange 5.5 server, using the Exchange 5.5 admin tool. Although the migration from Exchange 5.5 may be the easiest, it's more complicated than, for example, an upgrade from Exchange 5 to 5.5, since Exchange 2000 doesn't have its own directory anymore. All users that are migrated from Exchange 5.5 must get a user account created in the Active Directory, which is part of a Windows 2000 domain. If your Windows 2000 forest has multiple domains you must plan the migration carefully to make sure these users will be created in the correct domain. Let's continue by looking more closely at these four methods available for migrating from Exchange 5.5.

Note: *Before any migration is started, you must make a backup of the old system; Make sure you have a backup of all files and directories necessary to roll back a failed migration!*

In-Place Upgrade

This method upgrades an existing Exchange 5.5 server to Exchange 2000; all data is converted to the new store, and all users are converted to mailbox-enabled User objects. It is a fast and convenient method, but must be planned ahead of time since several conditions must be met before this method can be used successfully, for example:

- Only Exchange 5.5 with Service Pack 3 or later can be upgraded.
- This server must be running Windows 2000, and be a member of an Active Directory domain.
- This server must have an IIS 5, including the SMTP and NNTP protocols installed.
- A dynamic DNS server must be installed for this Active Directory domain, but not necessarily on this server.
- An Active Directory connector must be installed in the forest, and all mailbox accounts in Exchange 5.5 must be synchronized by a *Recipient connection agreement*. (You must also change the port number used by Exchange 5.5 for LDAP to something else than 389, for example 388.)
- No connector can be installed on this Exchange 5.5 server that is not supported by Exchange 2000, such as SNADS or PROFS. If one is installed, the setup program will abort the upgrade.
- You must use a Windows 2000 account that is a member of the Domain Administrators, Schema Administrators, and Enterprise Administrators groups.

If all of these conditions are met, you upgrade by running Setup on the Exchange 2000 CD; it will automatically detect the old Exchange 5.5 server and suggest an in-place upgrade. After the *last* server is converted, you should remove the AD Connector, since it's not useful anymore. This may be trickier than one first may think. Follow these steps:

1. Use the *AD Connector* snap-in and remove all *User Connection Agreement* (but you will not be able to remove the *ConfigCA* object, because it's still active).
2. Use the *Exchange 5.5 admin* program that comes with the Exchange 2000 setup program; connect it to the now converted Exchange 5.5 server (yes, it's strange, but you must learn to like this).
3. Look into the *Directory Replication Connector* folder; you will see a connector to the Exchange 2000 Site Replication Service (SRS); remove all connectors in this folder, then close the Exchange 5.5 admin tool.
4. Use the *ESM* tool; expand the *Tools* folder, right-click on the *Site Replication Service* object, and select *Delete*.
5. Use the *AD Connector* snap-in again; now you can remove the *ConfigCA* object; then you can uninstall the AD Connector by using the *Add/Remove Programs* applet in the *Control Panel*.

If you don't perform the steps mentioned above you may not be able to convert the Exchange 2000 organization to operate in native mode; you can read more about this in Microsoft's TechNet article Q260781.

How to Roll Back a Failed Upgrade

You must also make sure that the server has the hardware configuration needed to run Exchange 2000. Since you will replace the complete Exchange 5.5 installation on this server, you must make sure you have a backup of the server itself, in case you must restore the previous environment. Remember, any migration must be reversible in case something unexpected happens. To roll back a failed upgrade, you must follow a number of steps, described in detail in TechNet article Q264309; here is a summary of these steps:

1. Remove all references to Exchange 2000 in the Registry.
2. Rename all ..*Exchsrvr* folders.
3. Uninstall the IIS 5 server, restart the server, and install the IIS 5 again.
4. Remove the renamed ..*Exchsrvr* folders.
5. Run *Setup /R* from the Exchange 5.5 CD; create a new site with the same organization and site name.
6. Restore Exchange 5.5 from the latest backup.
7. Start Exchange 5.5; make sure it replicates within its own site.
8. Use the *AD Connector* to force a replication.
9. Use the *Exchange 5.5 admin* program to rename the alias name, admin display name, and email address for the *Site Replication Service* to *Directory Service*, and change the email address *SRS* to *DSA*.

10. Use the Exchange 5.5 admin program to change the *Serial-Number* attribute to *"Version 5.5 (Build 2650.24 Service Pack 3)"* or whatever it was before.
11. Create an LDAP object in the Exchange 5.5 server.
12. Restart the *Directory Service* on the Exchange 5.5 server.
13. Use the *ADSIEdit* tool to change the *Serial-Number* attribute on the Exchange 5.5 server to the same as in Step 10.
14. Force intrasite replication and AD Connector replication.

Again, for complete details, read the Q264309 article. As you can see, this is a lot of steps just to restore the previous Exchange 5.5 server, but all this is due to the dependencies of Windows 2000 and the Active Directory. Clearly, you should be very careful when performing this upgrade, even though it's the easiest one as long as nothing goes wrong.

Move-Mailbox Upgrade

The *move-mailbox upgrade* involves adding a new Exchange 2000 server to an existing 5.5 site, and then moving mailbox accounts to Exchange 2000. This method is a bit more complicated than the in-place upgrade, but it has some advantages, including:

- Not all users have to be migrated at the same time.
- The only downtime is during the migration of a mailbox; other mailboxes will continue to work.
- Any users on Exchange 4 or 5 servers in the same site can also be migrated.
- In case the migration does not work, you still have the Exchange 5.5 environment up and running; by restoring the Exchange 5.5 databases, you will be back to the previous state.

The prerequisites for this method are few: There must be at least one Exchange 5.5 server with SP3 or later in this site; otherwise, you can't install Exchange 2000 as a member. All 5.5 users must also have a Windows 2000 account; use the Active Directory Connector to replicate the accounts from Exchange 5.5. There are some drawbacks with the move-mailbox upgrade compared to the in-place upgrade method:

- Key Management Server (KMS) can't be migrated
- Older version connectors can't be migrated

How to Use the Move-Mailbox Upgrade Method

This method requires you to have a new machine for the Exchange 2000 server. As always, you must take a backup of the existing Exchange 5.5 server in case you need to restore the old environment. Follow these steps to migrate with the move-mailbox upgrade method:

1. Install Exchange 2000 Server on the new machine; make sure to join the existing Exchange 5.5 site.

2. Start the *Active Directory Users and Computers* tool.
3. Right-click the user to move, and then select *Exchange Tasks*. You can select more than one user to move. Make sure these users are logged off before moving them; otherwise, you may have permission problems during the move operation.
4. In the *Move Mailbox* window, select the Exchange 2000 server and its storage groups and mailbox store where you want to move the new user.
5. Let all Outlook users log on to Exchange at least once; their profiles will automatically be updated to point to the new Exchange 2000 server.

You may be tempted to use the *Move Mailbox* feature in the Exchange 5.5 admin program instead of the *Active Directory Users and Computers* tool, but this must be avoided since the 5.5 Admin tool does not know about storage groups and multiple mailbox stores.

Warning! *Disable all anti-virus programs during the migration. This is especially important for any programs using the anti-virus API provided in Exchange 5.5 Service Pack 3, since it will be triggered by some of the operations performed by the Move Mailbox feature and therefore will terminate these operations.*

Besides moving users, you probably also want to move public folders to Exchange 2000; log on with an account with administrative rights in both the Exchange 5.5 site and Exchange 2000 server, then follow these steps:

1. Use the *AD Connector* to create a *Public Folder Connection Agreement* between the Exchange 5.5 server and the Active Directory. This is necessary to inform the Active Directory about the permission settings on the public folders.
2. Use the *Exchange 5.5 admin* tool to replicate the public folders to the Exchange 2000 server; on the properties for each public folder, use the *Replication* tab.
3. Wait until the public folder is successfully replicated. The amount of time this takes depends on the replication schedule, how fast the connection is, and how much data is in this folder.
4. Change the *Home server* to the Exchange 2000 server for these public folders; use the *Advanced* tab on each public folder's properties.
5. Remove the replicated instance of this folder on the Exchange 5.5 server, using the Exchange 5.5 admin tool.

In previous Exchange versions, you needed to be very careful not to create an orphan object, i.e., a public folder that doesn't have a home server. However, in Exchange 2000 this concept has been changed; a public folder does not have a home server and it is not possible to create a public folder orphan anymore. For example, if you later remove the Exchange 5.5 server, you will still be able to administer the replicated public folders in Exchange 2000.

Swing Upgrade

This method makes it possible to upgrade a number of Exchange 5.5 servers without requiring that there be a new machine for each new Exchange 2000 server, except one new machine that is required to start this "swing" upgrade. This method is basically the same as the move-mailbox method, and works like this:

1. A new server is installed; all users are migrated from an old Exchange server.
2. This old server is then reinstalled as a new Exchange 2000 server.
3. All users from another old Exchange server are moved to this new server.
4. Then this old server is reinstalled as a new Exchange 2000 server, and so on.

The advantages of this method are the same as for the standard move-mailbox method plus three more:

- Only one extra machine is needed to upgrade any number of Exchange servers, presuming that all servers have the hardware configuration necessary to run Exchange 2000 Server.
- Short downtime for the users. Only the user that is currently being moved will be offline; as soon as they are moved, the user can begin to use the new Exchange 2000 environment.
- It is possible to migrate Exchange 4 and 5 without having to upgrade them to 5.5 first.

The disadvantages are the same as for the move-mailbox method, i.e., KMS and older version connectors cannot be moved.

Exmerge Upgrade

The Exchange tool *Mailbox Merge*, or *Exmerge.exe*, is used for copying data between two Exchange servers. This tool has been around for several years and is now updated for the Exchange 2000 environment; you will find it in the *\Support Tools* folder on the Exchange CD.

This tool extracts a copy of a user's mailbox folder, and stores it temporarily in a number of PST files; then the data is copied from the PST file into a mailbox in the new Exchange server. You can run Exmerge in one of two modes: *One-Step* and *Two-Step*.

- *One-Step mode*—The program copies all selected mailboxes from server A to the PST files, and then looks for a matching mailbox account on server B; if one is found, the data is merged into this mailbox account. A matching mailbox account is one that has an identical *Distinguished Name* for the mailbox, and the same recipient container path.
- *Two-Step mode*—The program copies all selected mailboxes to PST files and then stops (Step 1). Move these PST files to the new server, and use Exmerge to merge them into the new mailboxes.

The advantage of Exmerge is the ability to migrate mailboxes from any Exchange version, and the ability to migrate servers with no or slow network connectivity to the new Exchange 2000 server. Another advantage is that there are no changes on the old server; if the migration process does not work, simply activate the old servers again and you are back where you started. Unfortunately Exmerge also has some disadvantages:

- It will not migrate Inbox rules, forms, or Schedule+ data. However, it will migrate user folders, messages, Outlook calendars, and contacts.
- Copied messages lose the single instance storage; this may result in a significant increase of the new mailbox store.

Before you run this tool, make sure you are logged on as an account with permission to open all Exchange mailboxes—for example, the Site Service account. You must also have the Exchange 5.5 admin tool and an Exchange client installed on this computer. This method can also be used to migrate an Exchange server with a corrupt Priv.edb or Pub.edb database, which prevents the Information Store service, IS, from starting; assuming we have a production server called PROD and a test server called TEST, we can follow these steps:

1. Move all files from the *Exchsrvr\Mdbdata* folder on the PROD server. This will force Exchange to create new files, and will make the IS service start.
2. Restore the old information from PROD to server TEST.
3. Stop the IS service on both the PROD server and the TEST server.
4. Rename the *..\Mdbdata* folder to *..\Mdbdata.OLD* on server TEST.
5. Create a new *Exchsrvr\Mdbdata* folder on server TEST.
6. Rename the *..\Mdbdata* folder to *..\Mdbdata.NEW* on server PROD.
7. Create a new *Exchsrvr\Mdbdata* folder on server PROD.
8. Copy the files PRIV.EDB and PUB.EDB from *\\PROD\Exchsrvr\Mdbdata.NEW* to *\\TEST\Exchsrvr\Mdbdata*.
9. Copy the files PRIV.EDB and PUB.EDB from *\\TEST\Exchsrvr\Mdbdata.OLD* to *\\PROD\Exchsrvr\Mdbdata*. The result is that you have swapped the databases between these two servers.
10. Run *Isinteg –patch* on server PROD and server TEST.
11. Make sure both servers PROD and TEST start Exchange without any problems.
12. Run *Exmerge* and merge all mailboxes from server TEST into server PROD.

In versions prior to Exmerge 2000, there was a problem regarding the naming of mailbox folders that would be created in English instead of the selected regional settings of the clients. This is a problem because the previous Exmerge program used parts of the English-language version of the Exchange admin program. Since Exmerge was often the first "client" to access the new mailbox, all folders got English names. The latest version of Exmerge has improved support for different language mailboxes; by specifying a default locale (a national setting), Exmerge will use this locale when logging on to the new mailbox, hence creating the corresponding folder names. If you have this problem, use the older Exchange Client to rename these mailbox folders (Outlook will not allow you to change these names).

***Note:** Exmerge 2000 will only work on a Windows 2000 Server or Professional, not on Windows NT 4. However, it will support mailbox merging between Exchange 5.5 servers and Exchange 2000.*

The Active Directory Connector (ADC)

This connector is needed to replicate mailbox accounts, public folders, and Exchange server configuration settings between the DIR.EDB database in Exchange 5.5 and the Active Directory in Windows 2000. For most of the migration methods mentioned above, except the Exmerge method, this AD Connector is a prerequisite before the migration can be started. When Windows 2000 was released, it had an AD Connector that made it possible to replicate user accounts between AD and Exchange 5.5. However, this version did not know about Exchange configurations. When Exchange 2000 was released eight months later, it had an enhanced AD Connector included on the CD that allowed a replication of Exchange 5.5 configuration data to the Active Directory; this makes it possible to run Exchange 2000 in mixed mode. You should always use the enhanced version; if you have the older AD Connector, simply upgrade it with the Exchange 2000 version.

The AD Connector can replicate information either one-way or two-way; one-way replication is typically used for replicating Exchange 5.5 information to Active Directory, in order to prepare for a migration to Exchange 2000. Two-way replication is typically used when you have a mix of Exchange 5.5 and Exchange 2000 servers coexisting, and you want a new object created on either side to be replicated to the other side. Table 8.1 describes how different objects will be replicated with the AD Connector. Remember that in Exchange 5.5 you have two separate objects, one for the 5.5 mailbox accounts and one for the NT user accounts, whereas in Windows 2000 and Exchange 2000 you have only one mailbox-enabled user object.

Table 8.1 Replicating objects with the AD Connector.

Exchange 5.5	Active Directory
Mailbox	If the NT account that owns this mailbox maps to an existing Windows 2000 user account, that user object will be mail-enabled with directory information from Exchange 5.5.
Custom Recipient	Mail-enabled Contact object.
Distribution List	Mail-enabled Universal Distribution Group (if Windows 2000 is in native mode).

If the AD Connector is used for replicating Exchange 5.5 accounts that belong to an untrusted Windows NT 4 domain, you must decide how these unknown user accounts should be registered in the Active Directory domain. By default they will be mapped to disabled Windows 2000 user accounts, but this can be changed to create new Windows 2000 users, or to create Windows 2000 contacts. Use the *Advanced* tab for the connector agreement to configure this setting; see Figure 8.3.

The AD Connector is implemented as a Windows 2000 service that can be stopped or started like any other service. Any errors or warnings will be registered in the Event log. If the organization is large, i.e., there is a large number of objects, the replication process may be resource intensive; in that case, it may be wise to install the AD Connector on a member server instead of a domain controller.

Connection Agreements (CAs)

You define how the AD Connector will operate by a *connection agreement*, or *CA*. Such an agreement defines what directory objects to replicate, between what servers, and how they will replicate. One AD Connector can contain multiple connection agreements; for example, one for each Exchange 5.5 Site. There are two different connection agreements:

- *Recipient CA*—For replicating mailbox accounts, custom recipients, and distribution lists.
- *Public Folder CA*—For replicating public folder names.

The recipient CA may be configured to replicate directory information one-way only, or two-way. The question about configuring one-way or two-way recipient replication can

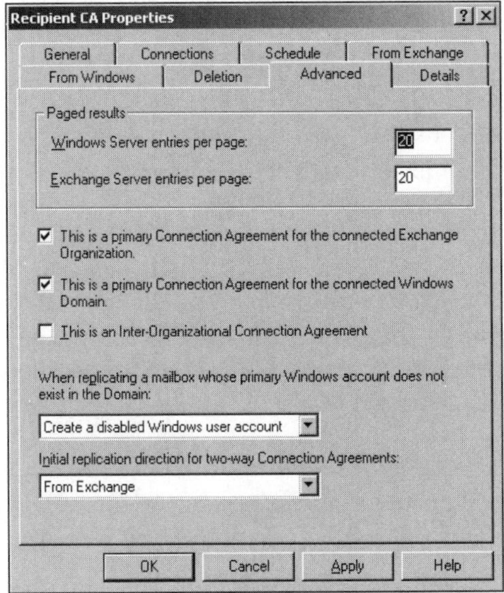

Figure 8.3
The Advanced tab for a connector agreement.

only be answered when you know how information should flow. There are three possible combinations for the recipient CA replication:

- *One-way, from Exchange 5.5 to AD*—This will make all changes in the 5.5 directory visible in the AD, but any changes in AD will not be replicated to 5.5. That means AD is the only complete directory. This type of replication is common when an Exchange 5.5 site will be migrated to Exchange 2000, and you need to populate the AD with all 5.5 mailbox accounts.
- *One-way, from AD to Exchange 5.5*—All updates of mail accounts, contacts, and distribution groups will be replicated to Exchange 5.5, but no updates of 5.5 will be visible in the AD. This could be used when you want Exchange 2000 and 5.5 to coexist for a shorter time, and all mailbox updates will be done in the AD only.
- *Two-way, between AD and Exchange 5.5*—All mail-related directory updates in either side will be replicated to the other. This is typically used in situations when Exchange 2000 and 5.5 coexist for a longer period, and there will be updates on both sides.

The public folder CA is hard-coded to be a two-way replication; in fact, most of the settings for this CA are hard-coded and cannot be changed. If you don't install the public folder CA, the names of mail-enabled public folders will not be replicated between the AD and Exchange 5.5; for example:

- Mail-enabled and visible public folders will show up in the 5.5 global address list (GAL), but not in the Exchange 2000 GAL, or vise-versa; this will make these GALs look different.
- Applications may not be able to send messages to public folders that belong to the other side; for example, an Exchange 5.5 application will not be able to find the email address of a mail-enabled public folder in Exchange 2000.
- An upgrade of Exchange 5.5 will be harder, since not all objects are known to the AD.
- Microsoft has issued a warning that not configuring a public folder CA could result in Exchange 2000 public folders being rehomed to Exchange 5.5; this can happen if an Exchange 5.5 administrator runs the DS/IS consistency adjuster.

In short, you should always configure a public folder CA, together with the recipient CA. If there is more than one Exchange 5.5 site, create one public folder CA for each of them; if there is more than one AD domain in the forest, all public folder CAs don't need to connect to the same AD domain, since the intrinsic Active Directory replication will make sure the whole forest will get this information.

Note: *Public folder CAs will not affect the view of the public folder tree in the MS Outlook client; nor will they prevent public folder replication or affect public folder permissions. They are only used to control which mail-enabled public folders will be visible in the global address list.*

Configuring AD Connectors and Connection Agreements

Below are step-by-step instructions for configuring the Active Directory Connector and a Recipient Connection Agreement. This configuration is common in a migration scenario, and in most cases you will set up a one-way replication from the Exchange 5.5 to the AD; however, in case you want this CA to be two-way, you have one extra step (Step 11) added to these instructions:

1. Log on as a Windows 2000 domain administrator.
2. Open the *Active Directory Connector Manager*, ADCM (*Programs|Administrative Tools*).
3. Right-click on the *Active Directory Connector* folder in the left pane; select *New|Recipient Connection Agreement*.
4. In the *Name* field, type a clear and intuitive name, like "CA to ServerA"; see Figure 8.4.
5. Configure this CA as either *One-Way* or *Two-Way*, depending on how you want this CA to operate.
6. Open the *Connections* tab (see Figure 8.5); click on the *Modify* button in the *Windows Server Information* window. Select the admin account and password you want to use for this ADC; then click *OK*.
7. In the *Exchange Server Information* field, type the NetBIOS name of the Exchange 5.5 server. Click *Modify* and add the Site Service account with password; then click *OK*.

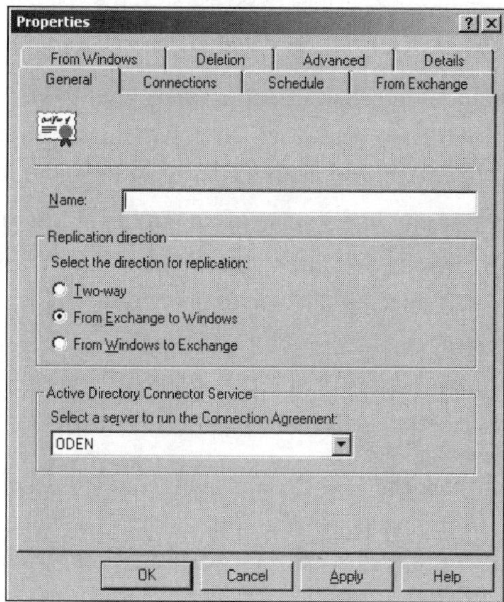

Figure 8.4
The General tab for CA.

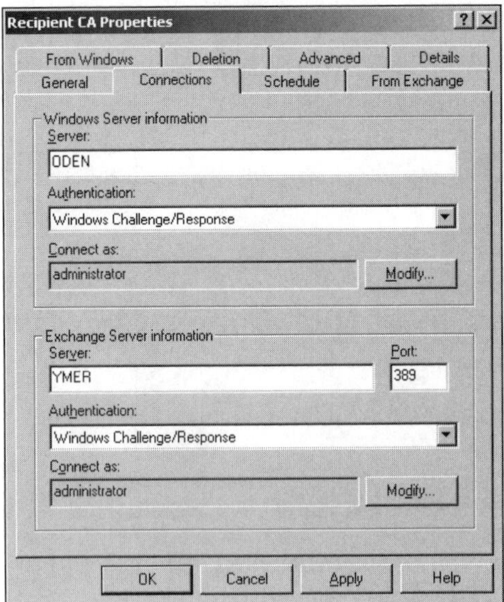

Figure 8.5
The Connections tab for CA.

8. Open the *Schedule* tab and set the schedule to *Always*; this will activate the replication every 15 minutes. Alternatively, you can set the replication schedule to run at specific times if needed.

9. Open the *Advanced* tab, and set the *Paged Results* values to 99 for both the *Windows Server Entries Per Page* and *Exchange Server Entries Per Page*; refer back to Figure 8.3.

10. Open the *From Exchange* tab; click *Add* and select the containers to import to AD. Click *Modify* and select the OU container where these new accounts should be created. You can also select what type of objects to replicate from Exchange 5.5; see Figure 8.6.

11. If this CA is two-way, you then open the *From Windows* tab. Click *Add* and select what OU containers to replicate to Exchange 5.5; click Modify to set where this new account should be created. You can also select what type of objects to replicate; see Figure 8.7.

12. Open the *Deletion* tab; configure how this CA should handle replicated delete instructions; see Figure 8.8.

13. Click *OK* to save changes. Then right-click the new CA and select *Replicate Now* to force the first replication. Check that user objects will show up in the selected containers. You should also check to see that there are no error or warning messages in the Event log.

In the *Advanced* tab (see Figure 8.3 again), you can configure this CA to be a primary CA or not; in this case, it would be a secondary CA. You configure this for the Windows 2000

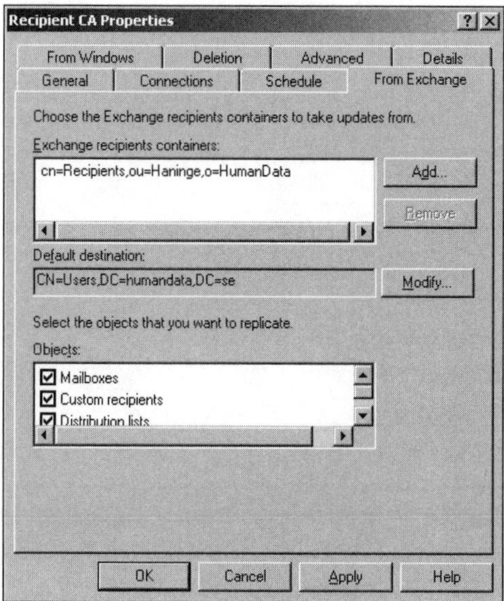

Figure 8.6
The From Exchange tab for CA.

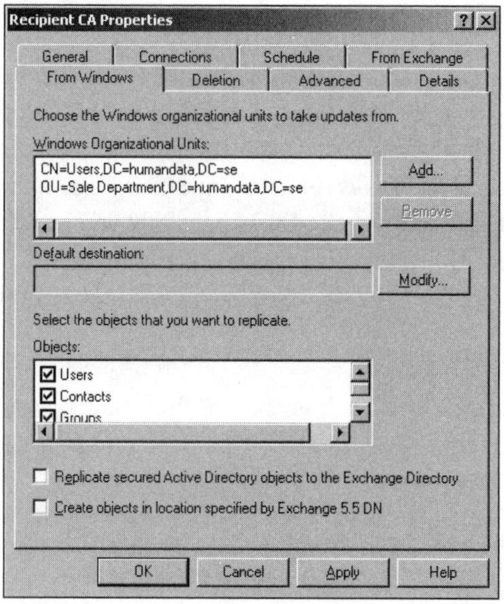

Figure 8.7
The From Windows tab for CA.

domain, and for the Exchange 5.5 organization, respectively. The differences between primary and secondary CAs include:

- The *primary CA* is able to create new objects in the *Default Destination* folder, defined in the *From Windows* or the *From Exchange* tab.

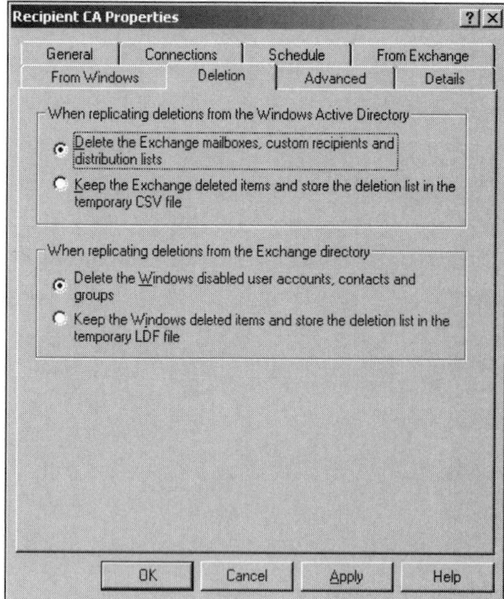

Figure 8.8
The Deletion tab for CA.

- The *secondary CA* will only be able to update existing objects in this destination folder.

You should only have one primary CA per destination folder. By default, the first configured CA will be primary and the following will be the secondary CA; this prevents duplication of replicated objects. The *Advanced* tab also gives you the ability to configure this CA to another Exchange 5.5 organization by selecting *This Is An Inter-Organizational Connection Agreement*; note that this feature is only available in the Exchange 2000 version of the AD Connector, not the Windows 2000 version. However, this requires careful planning, in order not to disturb the deployment of Exchange 2000; follow these step-by-step instructions:

1. Select one of the Exchange organizations as being primary.
2. Migrate this organization to Exchange 2000, as described in this chapter, using standard AD Connectors and connection agreements without selecting *This Is An Inter-Organizational Connection Agreement*.
3. When the primary Exchange organization has successfully replicated with the Active Directory, it's time to continue with the other Exchange 5.5 organizations.
4. Configure a new CA from this AD domain to the other Exchange organization, making sure you have selected *This Is An Inter-Organizational Connection Agreement*.

Replicating Mailboxes with the Same NT Account

In Exchange 5.5, it is common to create multiple mailboxes that have the same primary NT account—for example, resource mailboxes. This is possible since NT accounts and Exchange 5.5 mailbox accounts are different objects. However, in Active Directory, a user account can be mail-enabled, thus it is impossible to create multiple Exchange 2000 mailboxes for the same AD account. What happens when the AD Connector replicates multiple 5.5 mailboxes to the Active Directory? When the first of these mailboxes is replicated, all is okay, since a unique NT account will be identified. However, when the following mailboxes are replicated, they will be created as *Disabled Users*, new *Enabled Users*, or *Contacts*, depending on the settings in the *Advanced* tab in the recipient CA. To avoid this, you should change the primary NT account for these mailboxes, making them unique, before the replication. If this was not done, you may find a number of new or disabled users in the Active Directory; follow these steps to clean up these user accounts:

1. Stop the *AD Connector* service.
2. Use the *ADSI edit* (or the LDP tool) to delete the values from the *msExchADCGlobalNames* attribute on the affected mailbox account.
3. Start the Exchange 5.5 Admin program in raw mode: *Admin /R*; remove all values for *ADC-Global-Names* for each of the mailboxes that corresponds to the user account.
4. For each mailbox that you do not want matched to the user account, set *Custom Attribute 10* equal to *NTDSNoMatch* on the mailbox; this will force the AD Connector to create a disabled user account. Set *Custom Attribute 10* equal to *NTDS Contact* if you instead want to create a Windows 2000 Contact object for this mailbox.
5. Wait for the replication to be successfully completed within the AD domain and Exchange 5.5 organization, respectively.
6. Restart the AD Connector; when the replication is done between AD and Exchange 5.5, check the mailbox accounts in question.

Warning! *Using the ADSI Edit or LDP tools incorrectly may cause serious problems in the Active Directory, which can be fixed only by doing a complete reinstallation of Exchange 2000 or Windows 2000! Also, running the Exchange 5.5 Admin program in raw mode incorrectly may cause serious problems in the Exchange 5.5 system. Use these tools very carefully!*

Microsoft has a special tool called *NTDSNoMatch*, also known as the *NTDSAtrb*. You can use this tool for searching for all mailboxes in Exchange 5.5 that have duplicate primary NT accounts; for each such mailbox found, NTDSNoMatch will create an entry in a CSV file with the *Custom Attribute 10* set to *NTDSNoMatch*. Then use the Exchange 5.5 Admin program to import this CSV file before configuring the recipient CA.

Site Replication Service (SRS)

The AD Connector will make sure the mail accounts are visible in both Exchange 2000 and Exchange 5.5; however, it will not transfer messages between these mail systems. If these two systems must coexist during a migration period, you must be able to send messages between them. We discussed before how the Routing Group Connector could be used to connect an Exchange 2000 routing group with a site connector in an Exchange 5.5 site.

But how can we transfer messages if our Exchange 2000 server is a member of a 5.5 site? By using the MTA service, just like we always have in previous Exchange versions. This brings up a new question: How does the Exchange 2000 server replicate configuration settings with all the Exchange 5.5 servers in this site, so they all know about each other? The answer is: through the *Site Replication Service*.

The Site Replication Service, or SRS, is responsible for replicating the configuration naming partition of Active Directory for an Exchange 2000 server that has joined an Exchange 5.5 site. The SRS is a Windows 2000 service that emulates the Exchange 5.5 Directory Service; the configuration data is stored in a special database named SRS.EDB, which is identical to the DIR.EDB database in Exchange 5.5, with the same set of transaction log files. These files are stored in the *..\Exchsrvr\srsdata* folder. The SRS will be installed automatically in these situations:

- When the first Exchange 2000 server joins an Exchange 5.5 site
- When the first Exchange 5.5 server is upgraded to Exchange 2000
- Whenever any Exchange 5.5 Directory Replication bridgehead server is upgraded to Exchange 2000

With this SRS, an Exchange 2000 server will behave exactly like another Exchange 5.5 server; for example, all directory replications are RPC based and run every five minutes. For example, let's say we have a site with two Exchange 5.5 servers, Server-A and Server-B; next, we install an Exchange 2000 server that joins this site. These three servers will now replicate directory information between them, every five minutes, exactly like any other 5.5 site; see Figure 8.9.

If any more Exchange 2000 servers will be joining this site, their SRS will not be activated, since there will be enough with one single SRS; however, if you need to activate one more SRS, you can do so. You will find more information in the TechNet article Q266147. To avoid name resolution errors, use the *Name Service Provider Interface*, or NSPI, disabled on this SRS; this service prohibits Outlook clients from querying the SRS for the global address list.

The configuration information that SRS connects must be replicated to the Active Directory in order to make it known for all other Exchange 2000 servers in this organization. This is done by a special type of AD Connector Connection Agreement, the *ConfigCA*, which is automatically installed by the SRS. Just to make it clear to you, this CA is between the SRS and AD, contrary to the other types of CA that are between the AD and Exchange 5.5. The ConfigCA is a read-only agreement that will show up in the AD Connector Management (ADCM) tool; all such configuration CAs can quickly be identified by their names; they will all be named "ConfigCA_<server_name>". Since it's a read-only CA, you cannot modify any settings; if you look at its properties, you will see that it is a two-way connection, and this cannot be changed.

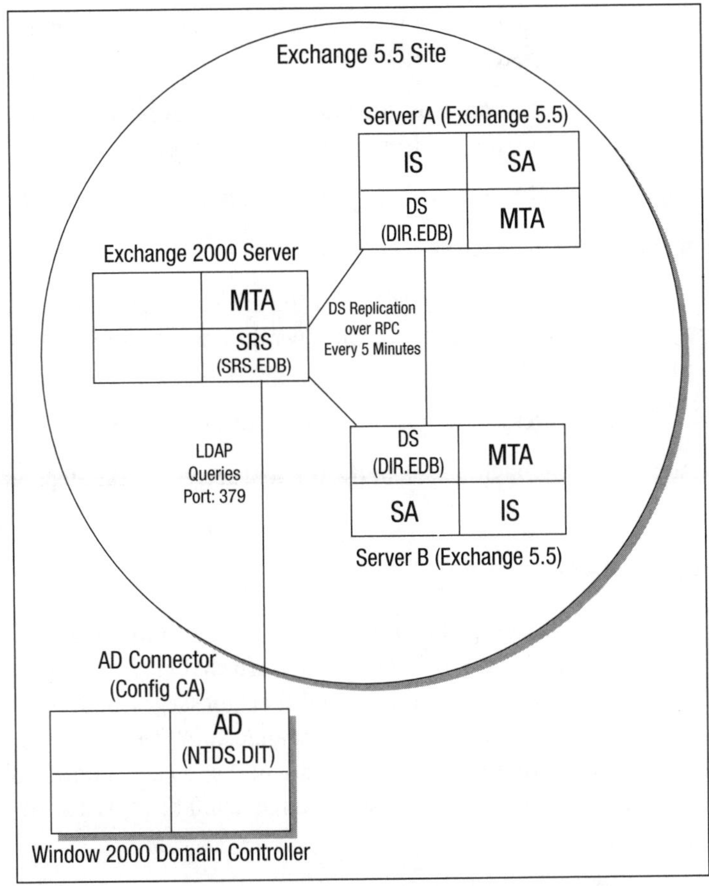

Figure 8.9
Replication within a 5.5 site with an Exchange 2000 server.

In Figure 8.9, you can see how the SRS will replicate its configuration settings to the Active Directory by using the LDAP protocol over port 379; the normal LDAP port 389 is locked for queries to the Active Directory. Everything is set up automatically—you don't have to configure anything regarding the SRS and its ConfigCA replication. If you should remove the ConfigCA from the AD Connector, you must recreate it, or the replication will stop. Since the ConfigCA is automatically installed when SRS is installed, you need to install a new SRS to create the new ConfigCA. Since you are not allowed to remove the existing SRS, if it's the last one in this site, you must have one more Exchange 2000 server. Create a new SRS on this server, then you can remove the first SRS.

If you lose the whole SRS and not just the ConfigCA—for example, due to a hard disk failure, and you don't have a backup, you must also recreate this SRS. Again, you must have at least two Exchange 2000 servers joined to this Exchange 5.5 site; if you don't, install one now, then follow these step-by-step instructions:

1. Start the *ESM* tool; this must be done on the Exchange 2000 server itself, since the SRS configuration cannot be performed from a remote computer.
2. Open the *Tools* folder, then select the *Site Replication Service* folder.
3. Open the *View* menu and make sure the *Site Replication Service View* is selected.
4. Right-click the *Site Replication Service* folder, and then select *New|Site Replication Service*. This may take several minutes, since this operation will be similar to adding a new 5.5 server to a site.
5. After the new SRS has been created, remove what is left of the first SRS.
6. *Optional*: If you want to move the SRS back to the original server, repeat Steps 4 and 5 again.

Migrating from MS Mail

The migration from MS Mail to Exchange 2000 is almost identical to the migration process in previous Exchange versions. The Migration Wizard that comes with Exchange 2000 is the best tool for migrating all users and their messages, address lists, and Schedule Plus data from the MS Mail system to Exchange 2000. However, you will have the same problem as migrating from any other system; if you can't migrate all users in one single operation, you must configure Exchange 2000 to coexist with MS Mail during the migration period.

Before you migrate the MS Mail users, you must plan the migration process, as described earlier—for example, which users should be migrated together, name standards, and which client they will use. In this case, when migrating from MS Mail, you should strive to migrate complete MS Mail post offices; if this is possible, you can then move or rename the *Maildata* folder after a successful migration. The Maildata folder is where the post office keeps its files; renaming or moving it in effect makes this post office unreachable for all clients and other post offices. If you need to activate this post office ever again, just restore the old name.

All users in MS Mail have an MMF file, similar to a PST file, where all messages and personal address lists are stored. Make sure these MMF files reside in the *Maildata\MMF* directory on the mail server; otherwise, the Migration Wizard will not find them, and therefore no message data can be migrated. The directory where this MMF file is stored is configured on the MS Mail client; make sure your users set the MMF file to be stored on the server, i.e., the MMF directory.

Follow these instructions to migrate from MS Mail to Exchange 2000, using the Migration Wizard:

1. Start the *Migration Wizard*, in the *Programs|Microsoft Exchange*.
2. Continue to the *Migration* window; select *Migrate From MS Mail For PC Networks*, then click *Next*.
3. Continue to the *Migration Procedure* window; select *One Step Migration* if you want to migrate the users directly into the AD, or *Two Step Migration* if you need to adjust things like user names and account names. In this example, we select One Step Migration. Click *Next*.
4. In the *Migration Destination* window, you can select to migrate the users directly to an Exchange 2000 server, or to PST files; see Figure 8.10. We will continue to discuss this later, but for now select to migrate directly to the Exchange server.
5. In the *Access Information* window, define the path to the MS Mail post office (in our case M:\), and the administrator account Admin and its password (usually "password"); see Figure 8.11.
6. In the *Migration Information* window, you select what to migrate. The default setting is *All User Information*; see Figure 8.12.
7. In the *Account Migration* window, select which users to migrate. Select all or just some; use the standard Windows technique with the *Control* button to select discontinuous sections, or *Shift* to select a list of sequential users; see Figure 8.13. Then click *Next*.
8. In the *Container For New Windows Accounts* window, select in what OU container these new users should be created; see Figure 8.14. You can use the *Options* button to select how the passwords should be created; if this MS Mail post office has used

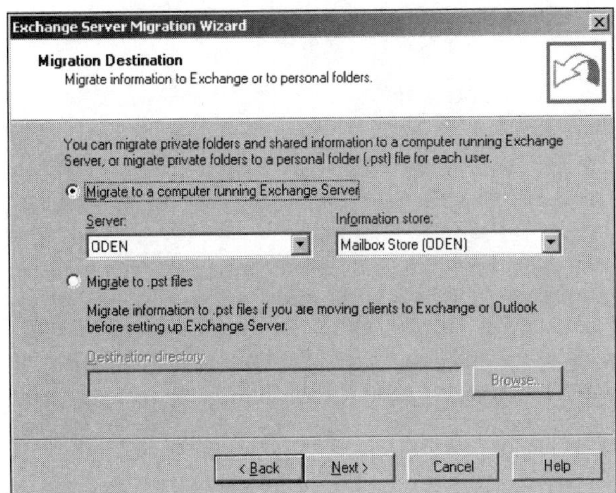

Figure 8.10
Setting the migration destination.

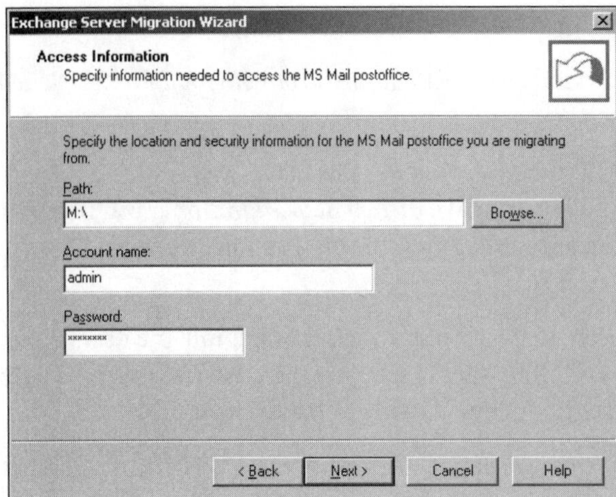

Figure 8.11
Defining access information to the MS Mail post office.

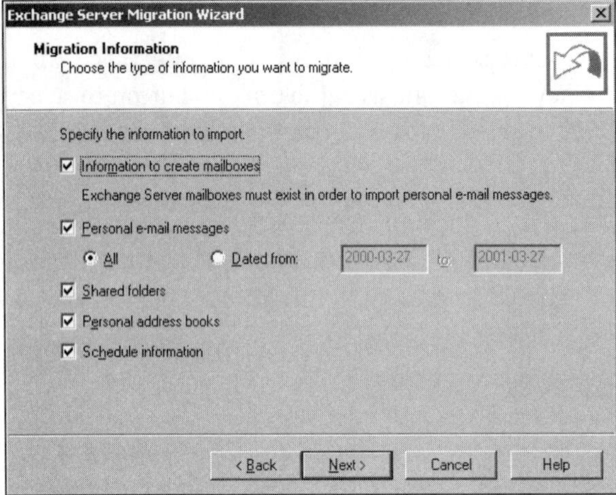

Figure 8.12
The Migration Information window.

Templates for extended user properties, you can select to import this file now. See Figure 8.15.

9. In the *Windows Account Creation And Association* window, you decide whether these migrated users should have new Windows 2000 user accounts, or have the Migration Wizard find any existing account that matches; make sure the users get the right user account here, it will save you time later. See Figure 8.16.

10. In the *Access Permission* window, select the access permission for the migrated public folders; default is *No Access*. MS Mail doesn't offer many access types, besides full access or restricted; if you are not sure exactly what the imported public folders will

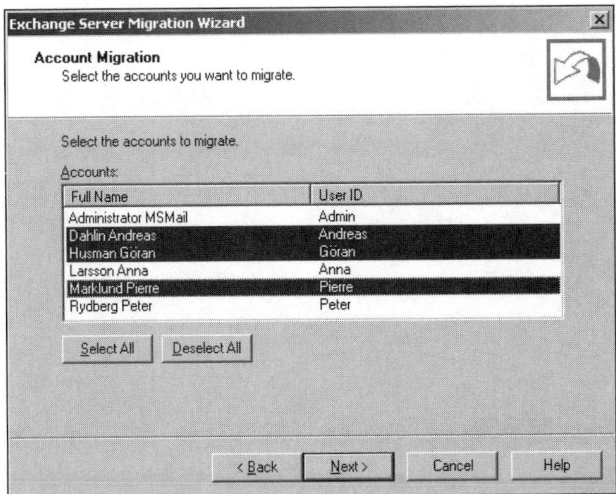

Figure 8.13
Select which users to migrate.

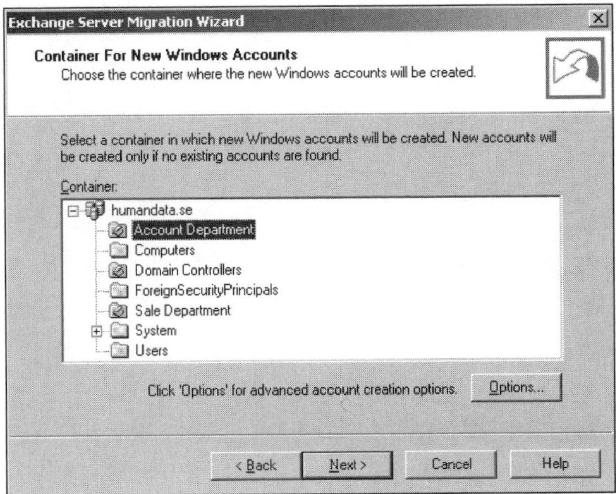

Figure 8.14
Define the container for new Windows accounts.

contain, it's safest to go with the default *No Access*, and if necessary you can change this later. See Figure 8.17.

11. In the *Account Owner* window, select the owner of the migrated public folders; you should usually use the Exchange Administrator account; see Figure 8.18.

12. Next, the migration process will start; you will see the name of the user currently migrating and how many total users to migrate. This process can take a considerable amount of time, depending on the number of users to migrate and the size of their mailboxes. When the migration process is done, you will see a summary of everything

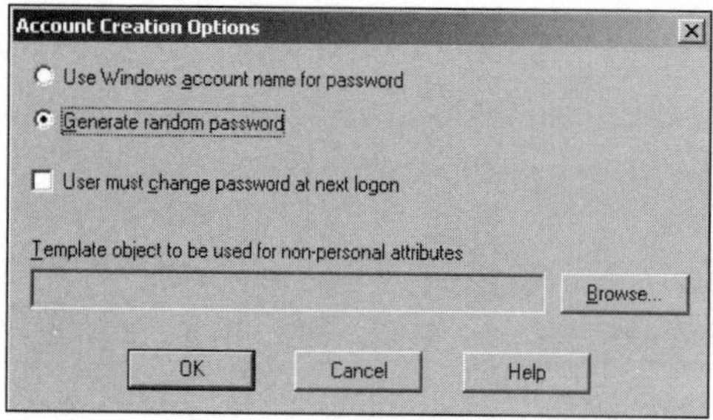

Figure 8.15
The options for new user accounts.

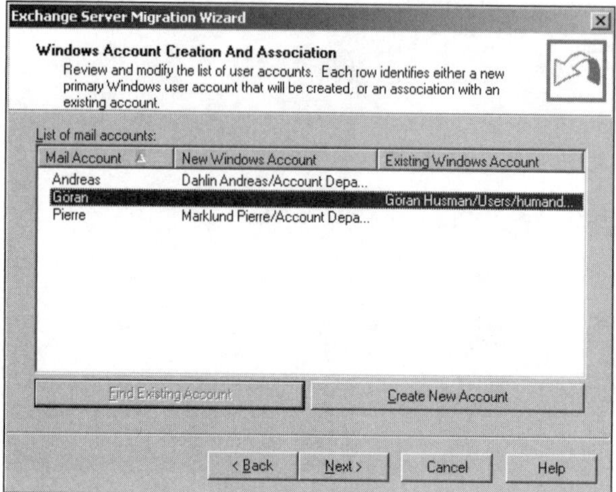

Figure 8.16
Mail accounts and their Windows 2000 accounts.

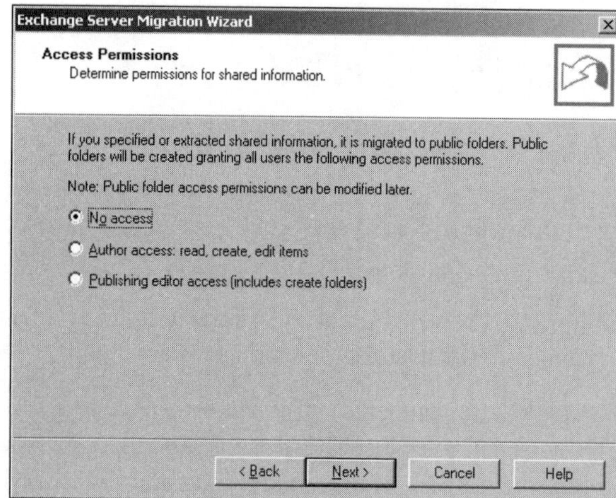

Figure 8.17
Setting access permission for migrated public folders.

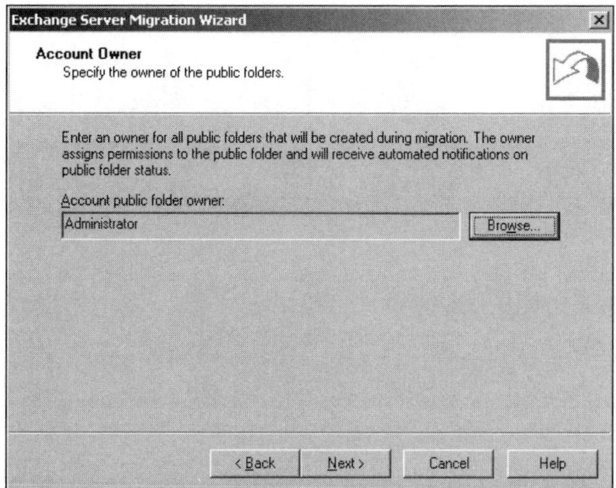

Figure 8.18
Setting the owner of the public folders.

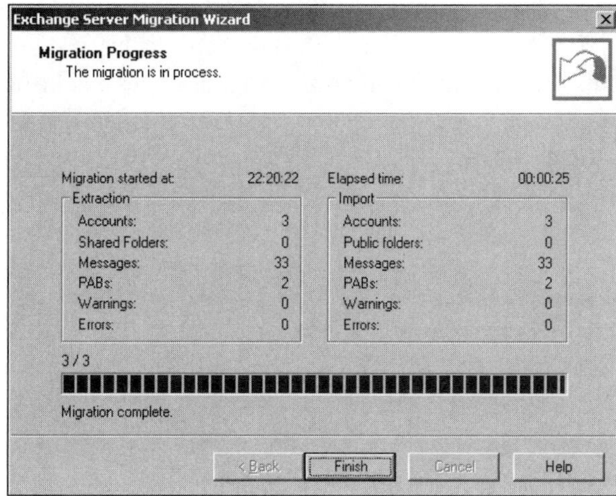

Figure 8.19
The result of the migration process.

migrated, including the number of warnings and errors; see Figure 8.19. Click *Finish* to exit the Migration Wizard.

If you encountered any warnings or errors, they will be listed in the Windows 2000 Event log. If all went well, the next step is to check the new accounts and make sure they have the correct properties set. Use the Active Directory Users and Computers tool for this; see Figure 8.20. Use Outlook with some of the migrated users and check that it works with Exchange 2000; for example, send messages, look at the global address list, and browse the public folders.

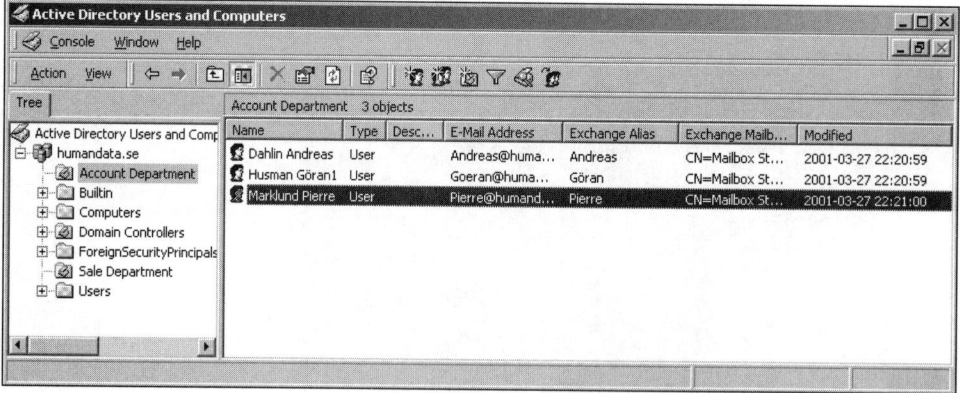

Figure 8.20
Check the newly migrated users.

An Introduction to MS Mail

In order to make Exchange 2000 coexist with MS Mail during a longer migration process, you need to understand the basics about this mail system. This type of mail system is usually referred to as a *Shared File Mail System*, since the post office is just a public file share that all mail clients connect to for sending and retrieving messages and browsing the global address list. The default root folder name for the post office is MailData, and it's usually shared with the same name. It consists of these 19 directories; the most important has a short description:

```
\Maildata
      \ATT          :attachments
      \CAL          :Schedule Plus calendar files
      \FOLDER       :Shared folders
      \GLB          :MS Mail system files
      \GRP          :Groups
      \HLP
      \INF
      \INI
      \KEY          :Index of read messages with pointers to MBG files
      \LOG
      \MAI          :Mail body
      \MBG          :Mail Header with pointers to MAI files
      \MEM
      \MMF          :Clients MMF files
      \NME          :Global Address List & post office lists
      \P1
      \TPL
      \USR
      \XTN
```

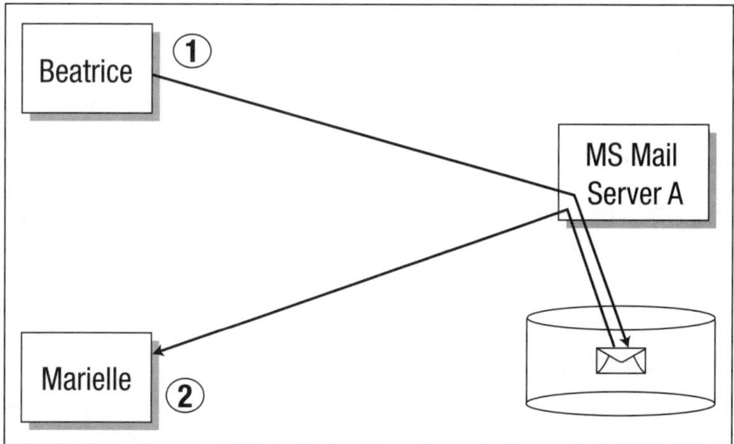

Figure 8.21
Messages between two users belonging to the same MS Mail post office.

To understand how MS Mail works, let's take a look at an example: If the user Beatrice is sending mail to Johan (another user belonging to the same MS Mail post office), the following will happen; see also Figure 8.21:

1. Beatrice writes the message to Johan, and clicks the Send button (#1).
2. The mail client now checks to see if this recipient exists; if so, the message will be stored in a mail folder on the server (usually named MailData).
3. This message waits on the server until Johan's mail client checks for new messages; this is done at regular intervals, usually every 10 minutes. Now the client detects a new message (#2).
4. Johan's client now moves this message to the client's MMF file (similar to a PST file), which is usually stored in the MMF folder on the server, but could also be stored on the local client machine.

There are some things you should be aware of here: First, no mail process is running on the server; clients perform all activities in this case. Second, since there is no server process, every client needs to check for new messages regularly; this is also known as *polling*. Third, messages are moved from the mail server to the user's MMF file; every user has his or her own MMF file.

Next example: Now Beatrice wants to send a message to Marielle, a user who belongs to another MS Mail post office. Since there are no server processes in MS Mail, we need help moving the messages between the post offices. There is one such program, usually called the *MTA*, not to be confused with the MTA in Exchange. The real name for this program is External.exe and it works similarly to a client, in the sense that it connects to a post office and looks for new messages. However, the External program is connected to multiple post offices, and regularly connects to each and every one of them (by default every five minutes) in a round-robin fashion, looking for any messages that should be transferred to another of its connected post offices. This will now happen; see also Figure 8.22:

1. Beatrice sends a message to Marielle, a user on another MS Mail post office (#1).
2. Beatrice's client stores the message in a special queue file.
3. After some time, the External program connects to Beatrice's post office and checks the queue file; it will now find one message. Next, this message is transferred to the other MS Mail post office (#2).
4. When Marielle's client later polls her MS Mail post office, it discovers the new message and moves it to the MMF file (#3).

Sending Messages between MS Mail and Exchange

When we need Exchange to coexist with MS Mail, we can use the MS Mail Connector as a transport mechanism between them. It will create a shadow MS Mail post office on the

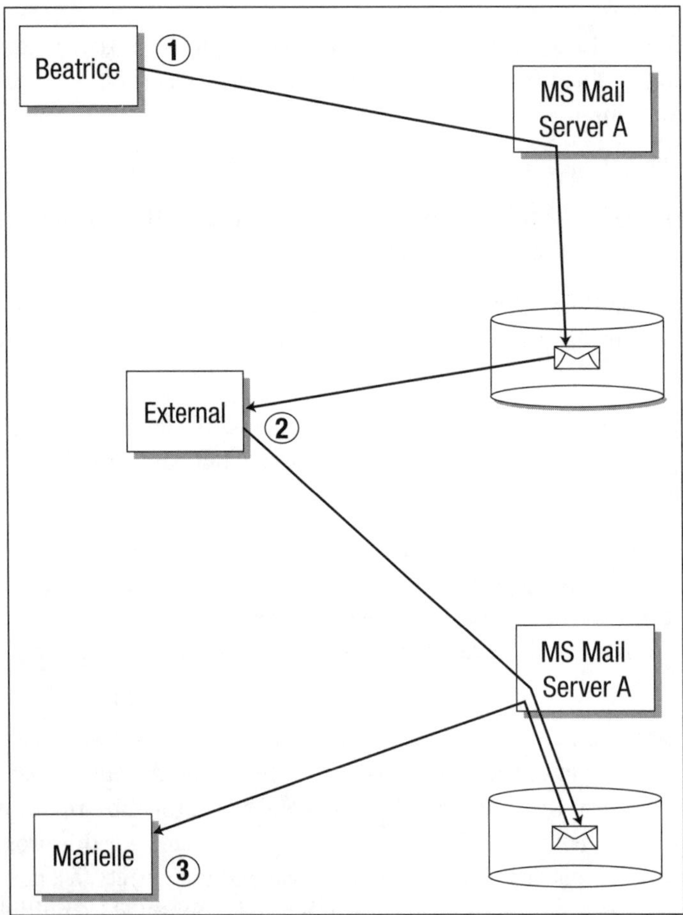

Figure 8.22
Messages sent between different MS Mail post offices.

Exchange server that is almost identical to a standard MS Mail directory structure, except it doesn't have the folders and files necessary for an MS Mail client to connect to it; however, it has all the folders needed for transferring messages with the External.exe or a similar program. See Figure 8.23.

The idea behind this shadow post office is to make Exchange look like MS Mail, thereby making Exchange able to communicate with any MS Mail post offices. The shadow post office will be used as a temporary storage area for mail passing between Exchange and MS Mail. But instead of transferring messages between the post offices using the External.exe program as normal, the MS Mail Connector has a special *MSM MTA* process that transfers messages between any post offices, including the shadow post office. However, it's not enough just to transfer the messages to the Exchange server; we must also convert incoming messages to Exchange format, and outgoing messages to MS Mail format. The MSM Interchange process, also a part of the MS Mail Connector, performs this task. To summarize, the MSM Connector contains these three parts:

- The shadow post office, almost identical to an ordinary MS Mail post office.
- The MSM MTA, which replaces the External.exe program that is normally used in MS Mail.
- The MSM Interchange, a gateway process that converts messages between Exchange and MS Mail format.

Let's look at an example to illustrate how this works: MS Mail user Beatrice sends a message to Exchange user Alex. We have the MS Mail Connector configured between these mail systems (see also Figure 8.24), and this is what will happen:

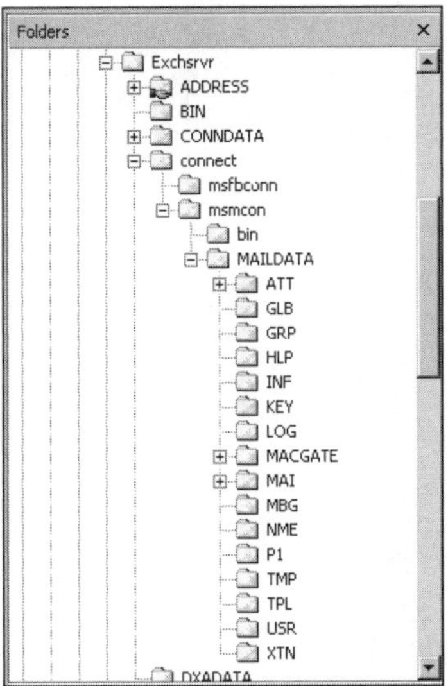

Figure 8.23
The shadow post office on the Exchange server.

1. Beatrice (on MS Mail) creates the message for Alex (on Exchange), and sends it to the MS Mail post office.
2. Since the recipient Alex is on an external MS Mail system (remember that Exchange looks like an MS Mail post office), the message will be placed in a queue file.
3. The MSM MTA process checks the queue file on the MS Mail post office every five minutes for any new messages, and now it finds one. The destination is the shadow post office on the Exchange server, so the MSM MTA transfers the message to that post office.
4. The MSM MTA notifies the MSM Interchange process to immediately take this new message and convert it to Exchange format, and then transfers the messages like any other Exchange message. Since this message is to a local user, the Information Store notifies Alex's client.

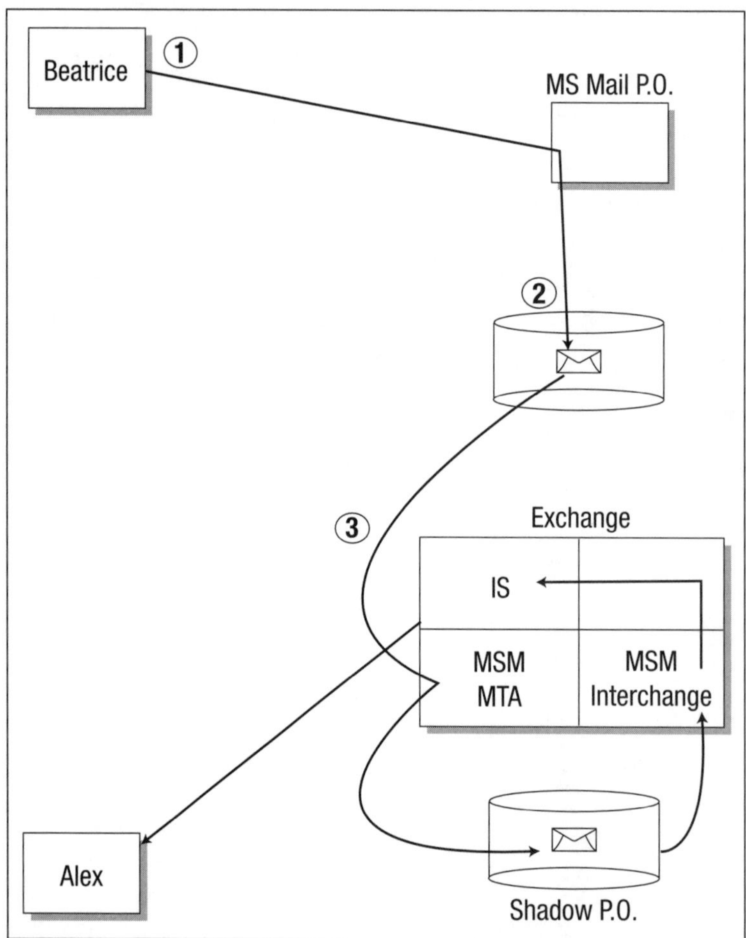

Figure 8.24
Sending messages from MS Mail to Exchange.

Since the MSM MTA replaces the External.exe program, we won't need External.exe anymore. If we compare Figure 8.24 with Figure 8.22, we can see that they are very similar, except that there is a gateway process converting the message and address format, before the message enters the normal Exchange transport system.

Configuring the MS Mail Connector

Use the Exchange 2000 Setup program to install the MS Mail Connector. This will make the MS Mail Connector show up automatically in the Connectors folder, under the First Routing Group (see Figure 8.25), together with the Connector or MS SchedulePlus FreeBusy (more information about that later). Follow these step-by-step instructions to configure the MS Mail Connector:

1. Start the ESM and open the properties for the *MS Mail Connector*.
2. The *Interchange* tab: See Figure 8.26. Define the administrator's mailbox; this user will receive any error messages or warnings. You can use a distribution group if you need to. Define the primary language for clients; this will make sure the proper character sets will be used when converting messages over this connector. This setting also determines the language used for sending status messages to MS Mail. The Maximize MS Mail 3.x Compatibility option controls how embedded objects in messages should be handled; if this checkbox is cleared, MS Mail clients will not be able to view or save embedded objects, since it only supports older version of OLE. If this checkbox is set, all embedded objects will be sent in two formats, one standard and one older format,

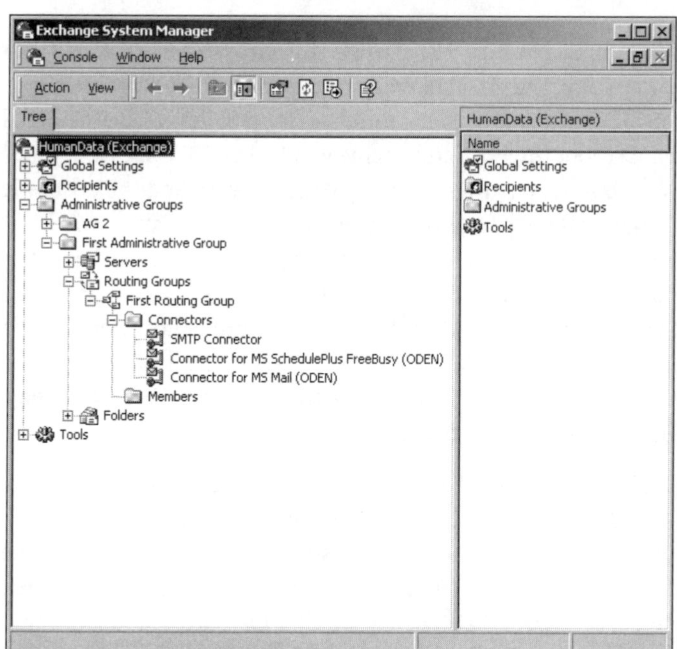

Figure 8.25
The MS Mail Connector in ESM.

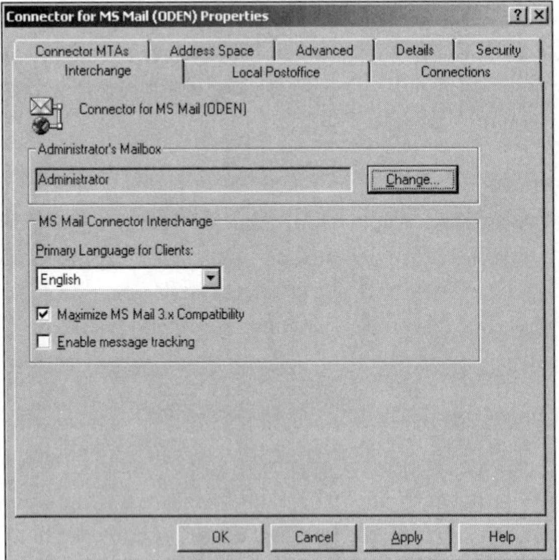

Figure 8.26
The Interchange tab.

suitable for MS Mail. By setting the Enable Message Tracking checkbox, it will be possible to use the Tracking Monitor for tracking MS Mail messages passing this connector.

3. The *Local Postoffice* tab: See Figure 8.27. Define the name of this shadow post office and its network name, using the MS Mail name standard (max 10 characters, no spaces, no non-English ASCII characters). By default, the network name will be equal to the Exchange organization; the Postoffice name will be the 10 first characters of the first administrative group. The names chosen for the network and the post office will not affect how MS Mail and Exchange coexist; you can have any name you like here, but do remember them! The sign-on password and sign-on ID are used when an external MS Mail post office connects by modem to transfer messages; if all connections to MS Mail are over LAN or WAN links, this password is not used. The *Sign-on ID* is the serial number of the MS Mail post office. It's actually a simple copy protection; if the External.exe or MSM MTA programs detect that two post offices have the same serial number, they will refuse to start.

4. The *Connections* tab: See Figure 8.28. The first time this tab is configured, you will only see the name of the shadow post office. This means that the MS Mail Connector is not aware of any MS Mail post office so far. To show the connector what other MS Mail post offices are available, click the *Create* button; this will open the *Create Connection* window (see Figure 8.29). Click the *Change* button and add the path to the MS Mail post office directory (usually named Maildata); you can use a network mapped drive, or a Universal Naming Conversion (UNC) path, like *\\ServerA\Maildata*. If the MS Mail post office is stored in a Novell network, you must add a username and password with the administrative rights to the MS Mail folder tree; if the MS Mail post

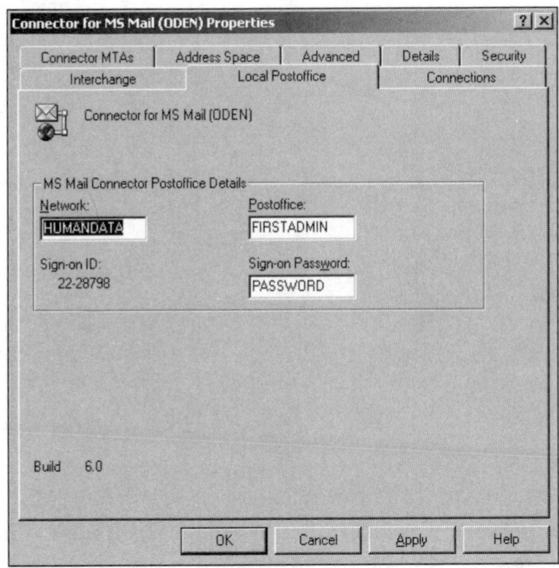

Figure 8.27
The Local Postoffice tab.

office is stored in a trusted NT or AD domain, you normally don't have to fill in any name or password here, since the connector will use your currently logged on admin account. Click *OK* to close this window.

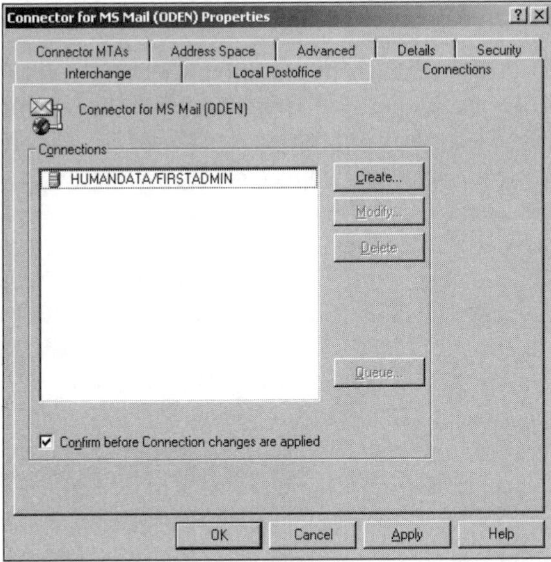

Figure 8.28
The Connections tab.

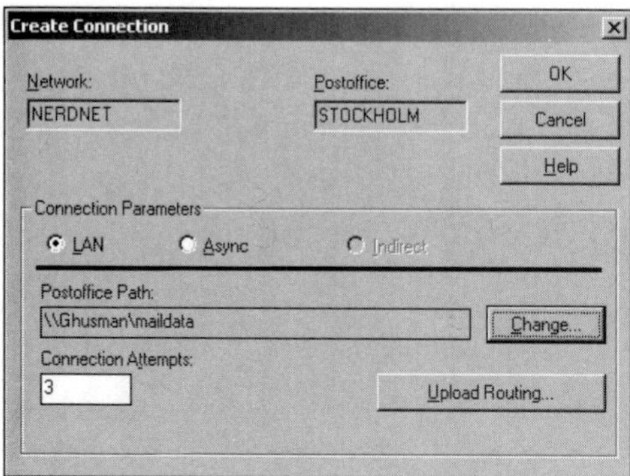

Figure 8.29
The Create Connection window.

You will now return to the *Create Connection* window; it will list the post office name and its network name, found on the given path. If this post office has contact with other *downstream post offices*, i.e., post offices that can be reached indirectly through this post office, and you want Exchange to know about them, click the Upload Routing button to import their names. Click *OK* to close this window.

You will now return to the *Connections* tab; in the *Connections* pane all known post offices are now listed, with the shadow post office on top (see Figure 8.30). If you need to create a direct connection to another MS Mail post office, click *Create* again. You can also modify or delete any connection. To see any messages awaiting delivery to an MS Mail post office, click its connection name and then click the *Queue* button.

5. The *Connector MTAs* tab: This tab is used to create one or more MSM MTA services, and define what MS Mail post offices each of them will service. The first time you open the tab, these two panes are empty. Start by creating an MSM MTA service. Click the *New* button; this will take you to the *New MS Mail Connector MTA Service* window (see Figure 8.31). Add the service name for this MSM MTA. Note: This name will later be listed in the Windows 2000 Service Manager. If you want to create log files for sending and receiving files on the MS Mail post offices, set their respective checkboxes. Set the period interval for checking any updates of users and MS Mail networks; usually every 60 minutes will do fine. Set the polling interval time with the *Check For Mail Every* field; default is five minutes. It may be tempting to set this value lower, but this will increase the network load, since it will force the MSM MTA to connect to the MS Mail post office more often. If you connect over a LAN, then select this choice under *Connection Parameters*; if you connect using an asynchronous modem, select *Async And LAN*. This will display more options—for example, what COM port to use, what modem script, and how to communicate.

   To configure advanced options, click the *Options* button; see Figure 8.32. Set the maximum message size allowed (default is unlimited size) that will be transferred by this

MSM MTA. If the network load is high, setting a lower max size may decrease it; however, you must make sure the size will not prohibit important messages from being transferred between Exchange and MS Mail. The *Free Disk Space* option is used to set the lowest available amount of free disk space (default is 100KB); if it's lower than this limit, the post office will be disabled. The *NetBIOS Notification* checkbox is used to instantly notify MS Mail clients about new messages, relieving them from polling the post office; this requires that both the server and the client use NetBIOS. You may also disable the distribution of messages within the MS Mail post office by setting the *Disable Mailer* checkbox. However, then there must be another External.exe program that takes care of this; I recommend that you don't set any of these options.

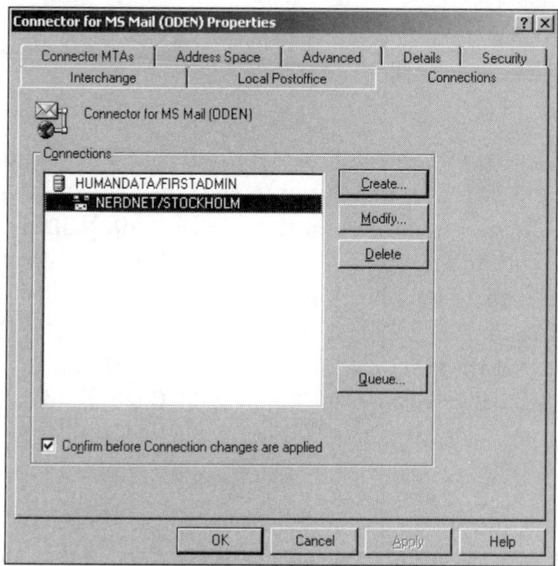

Figure 8.30
The Connections pane, with all known post offices listed.

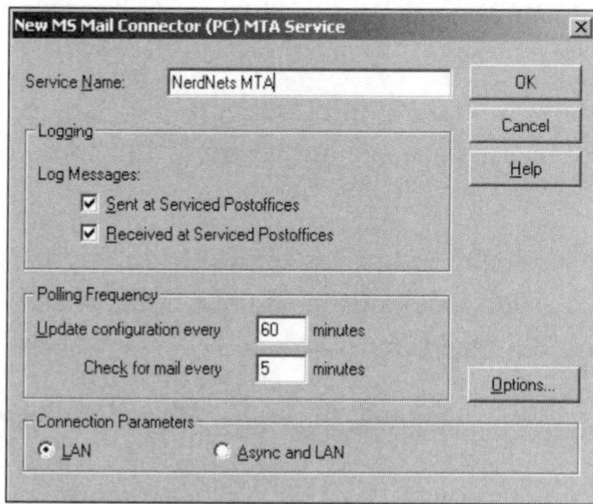

Figure 8.31
The MTA Service window.

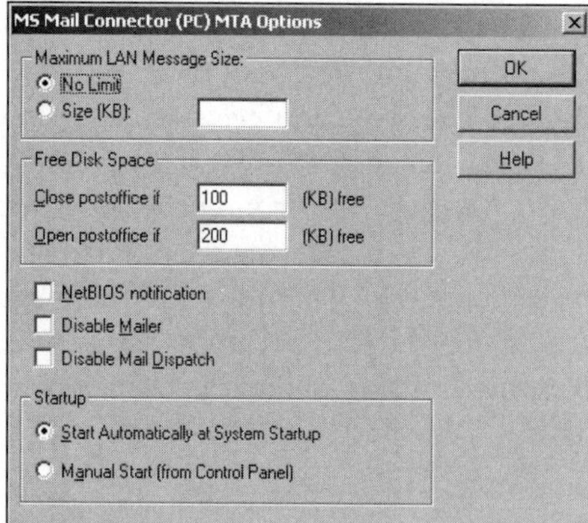

Figure 8.32
The MTA Options window.

Click *OK* until you are back at the *Connector MTAs* tab. To reconfigure an existing MSM MTA, click *Configure*; to see its current log status, click the *Log Status* button. By now we have one MSM MTA service; next we must define what MS Mail post offices it will service. Click the *List* button; this will display the available post offices. If you don't see your post office here, go back to the *Connections* tab and add it first. Select the post office this MSM MTA should service and click *Add*. One single MSM MTA can service up to 50 post offices, but the practical limit is about 10 to 15, since higher numbers mean longer message delivery times; see Figure 8.33. Click *OK* to close this window and return to the *Connector MTAs* tab; it should now look similar to Figure 8.34.

6. The *Address Space* tab: It should contain an address space of type MS (for MS Mail) to all post offices. If needed, you can limit the scope, or the visibility, of this address space to this routing group only; the default scope is *Entire Organization*. Normally you don't need to change anything here.
7. The *Advanced* tab: You can set a global message size limit for all MSM MTA connections in this tab; the default is *No Limit*.
8. The *Details* tab: Lists the creation date and last modification date. You can also type in an administrative note here, which will be visible only from within this MS Mail Connector.
9. The *Security* tab: Define what Windows 2000 account has administrative rights; inherit permissions from the administrative group it belongs to. Usually not changed. Click *OK* to finish the configuration of this MS Mail Connector and close the window.

Your next task is to check the MSM MTA service created in Step 5; open the Windows 2000 *Services* MMC snap-in and locate this new service. Make sure it's started; you must also start the *MS Mail Connector Interchange* service. If either of these two services is not started, no messages will be transferred over this connector!

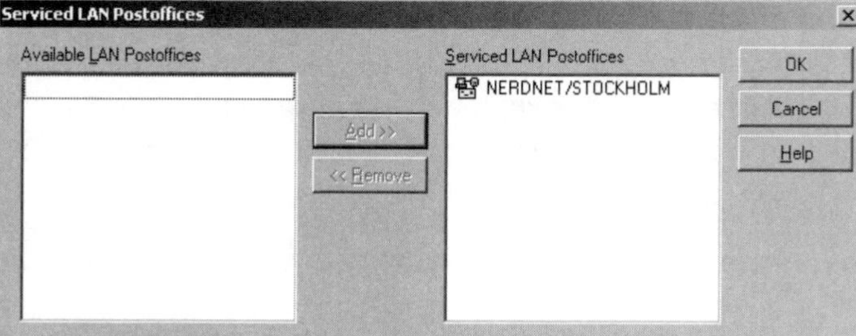

Figure 8.33
Serviced post offices.

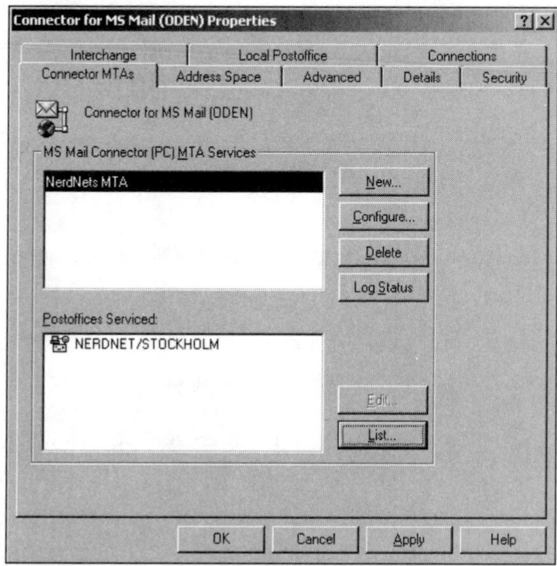

Figure 8.34
The completed Connector MTAs tab.

Tip: *Whenever this MSM MTA service is restarted, it will immediately connect to all MS Mail post offices served, and check if there is any mail in queue. This can be used to force the MS Mail Connector to check the MS Mail post offices, instead of waiting five minutes, or whatever the polling time is set to.*

Configuring the MS Mail Post Office

The previous set of steps made Exchange 2000 aware of MS Mail, but you also need to configure MS Mail so it will know about the shadow post office on Exchange. This must be done with the MS Mail admin tool *Admin.exe,* usually found in the Mailexe directory on the MS Mail server. Follow these step-by-step instructions to add the Exchange shadow post office FIRSTADMIN with the network name HUMANDATA as an external post office to the MS Mail post office STOCKHOLM and the network name NERDNET:

***Note:** In MS Mail it's common practice to map the M: drive to the Maildata directory on the post office; most system utilities default expect the M: drive to be mapped to this directory. You can use other drive letters, but then you must always specify what drive you are using. This is the reason it's easiest to use M: and in the following examples I have assumed that M: is mapped to Maildata.*

1. Open a command prompt and change the directory to *Mailexe* (where the *Admin.exe* tool is).
2. We assume that the M: drive is mapped to the Maildata directory; start the MS Mail admin program by typing "Admin". Log in as mailbox Admin (the password is usually *password*), then enter the admin program; see Figure 8.35. Note that you cannot use the mouse here; use the arrows or the highlighted characters to navigate. Press Return to select, and Esc to go back.
3. Press E (External-Admin) and C (create); see Figure 8.36. Type in the network name and the post office name of the shadow post office; set route type to Direct, and the Direct Connection Via to MS-DOS, which means a LAN connection. Press Return to create this external post office.
4. Now you are done; press Esc two times to step back to previous windows; when asked if you want to quit this program, select *Yes*.

Now both sides know about each other, and we have a transport service (the MSM MTA) that will move messages between them; it's time to test this connector. First, configure an MS Mail address for your users by changing the recipient policy in EMS: Open the properties for the *Default Policy*, look at the *E-mail Addresses* tab, set the *MS* checkbox, and click *OK*. You will be asked if you want to create an MS Mail address for all users; if this is okay, click *Yes*. If not, you must manually add an MS Mail address for all users that need one. Use an Outlook client connected to Exchange and send a message to the administrator's mailbox by using the address *[MS:Nerdnet/Stockholm/Admin]*. The square brackets must be included since they tell Outlook not to check this address (we know it doesn't exist in

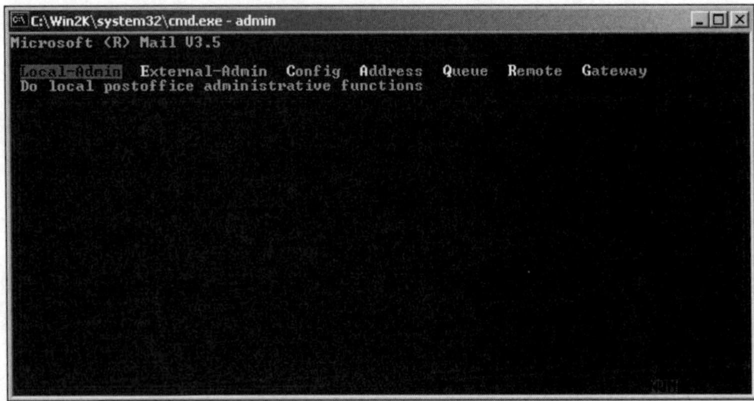

Figure 8.35
The MS Mail admin program.

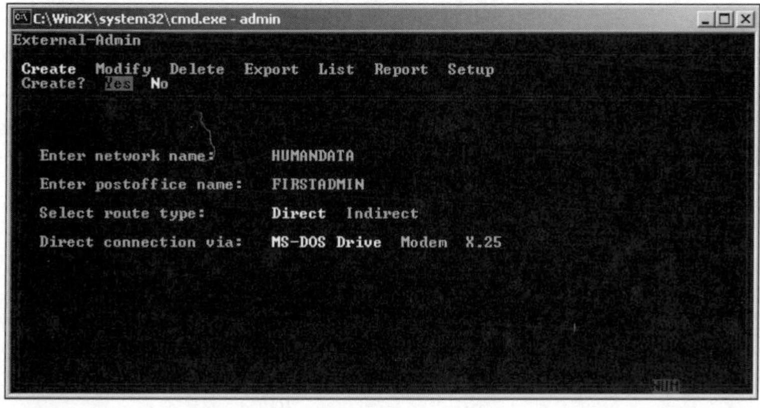

Figure 8.36
Creating the shadow post office as an external post office.

Exchange since we don't have any address replication to MS Mail yet); the address format is MS: for the MS Mail address type, and "network/postoffice/mailbox"; see Figure 8.37.

This message will now be passed over to the MS Mail Connector; if we are fast, we can see it in the message queue. Start the ESM, and expand the administrative group and the routing group where this connector is created. Look at the properties for the *Connector For MS Mail* and look at the *Connections* tab; select the MS Mail post office name and click the *Queue* button (see Figure 8.38). Within five minutes, or whatever your MSM MTA polling time is, the message will be delivered; you can also force a connection by restarting the MSM MTA service. Click on the *Refresh* button to see the current status.

Address Replication between MS Mail and Exchange 2000

When messages can be transferred back and forth between these mail systems successfully, it's time for the next step: address replication. Again, Exchange is adapting to the method used on the MS Mail side, so you need to have a basic understanding of this method tool.

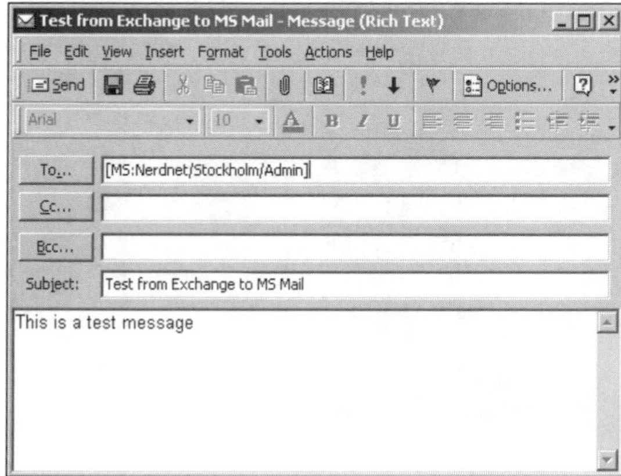

Figure 8.37
Sending a test message to the MS Mail administrator.

The first address replication method in MS Mail was a manually initiated export. This method does not work with Exchange. The second method was a more advanced method that made it possible to automatically replicate address lists once per day; this was called *Directory Synchronization*, or Dirsync for short. This is the method that Exchange can use. Dirsync works like this: One of the MS Mail post offices is promoted to a Dirsync server; this means that this post office is responsible for keeping and updating the global address list. All other post offices send their address updates to the Dirsync server, and receive the global address list in return; these post offices are referred to as *Dirsync requestors*. There can only be one single Dirsync server in the MS Mail world, but the number of requestors is unlimited. Let's look at the steps in the Dirsync process.

We assume the post office *Master* is our Dirsync server; we also have two more post offices, configured as Dirsync requestors, called *Req1* and *Reg2*. Normally this Dirsync process is active during the night, so in our example, we start at 10 P.M.; this time is often referred to as *Time 1* (*T1*), and the other two times are called T2 and T3. This is what will happen (see Figure 8.39):

- *T1*—At 10 P.M. each requestor, i.e., Req1 and Req2, creates a system message with all local address updates since the last Dirsync run; these messages are sent to Master, the Dirsync server.
- *T2*—At 11 P.M. the Master merges all address updates, including its own, to a file called the *Master Change List (MCL)*; this list is then sent back to all the requestors.
- *T3*—At 12 A.M. each requestor imports the received MCL file and rebuilds its own global address list (GAL).

You're probably wondering where these time settings came from. The answer is that the administrator sets them at will. As mentioned, it's best to run the Dirsync process during

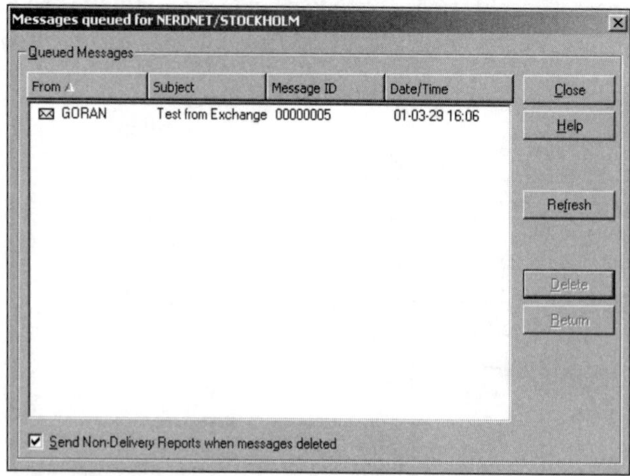

Figure 8.38
The MS Mail message queue.

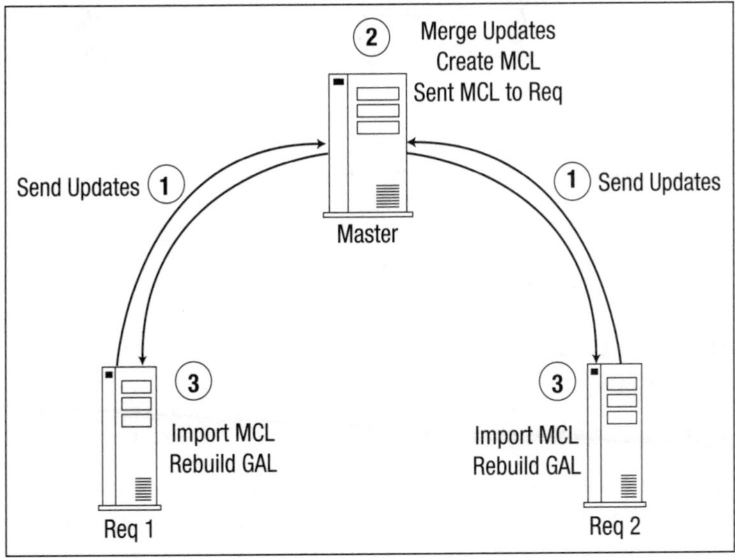

Figure 8.39
The Dirsync process.

off-hours; you don't want to rebuild the GAL while people are working with their MS Mail clients. First you select a time to start T1, for example 10 P.M.; then select a later time to run T2; in most cases one hour is enough for letting all requestors create the update file and send it to the Dirsync server, but in larger MS Mail organizations, you may need more time. Then, finally, you select a time for T3, when all requestors should have received the MCL file, again usually one hour after the previous step, or 12 A.M. in our example. These time settings are defined in the Dirsync configuration, as you will see shortly.

Since the MS Mail post office is nothing but a number of directories and files, what process will create the update files for the requestors? Who will create the MCL file on the Dirsync server? And what will import this MCL file and rebuild the GAL on the requester? Lots of questions, but the answer is simple: the Dispatch.exe program. This program is actually not doing any of the above; instead, it's responsible for starting other programs at the right time and in the right order, programs like Reqmain.exe, Srvmain.exe, Import.exe, and Rebuild.exe. All these programs are doing their part in this rather complex Dirsync process.

Configuring Exchange 2000 as a Dirsync Requestor

Exchange 2000 can be a Dirsync server or a requestor. If the MS Mail system already has one Dirsync server, then configure Exchange to be a requestor. If they don't have a Dirsync method implemented yet, I recommend that you make Exchange the Dirsync server. Many administrators love to hate the Dirsync method, since it is hard to understand and easily gets out of sync unless you care for it like a baby; however, then it works very well. And since you need the Dirsync method for replicating addresses between Exchange and MS Mail, you need to understand how to configure it properly on both systems.

***Note:** You must perform the steps below directly on the Exchange server; they cannot be performed on a remote ESM tool, due to the updates they must make on the server and its directories.*

If the MS Mail system is running the Dirsync process, you must configure the Exchange servers as requestors by following these step-by-step instructions:

1. Make sure you know the name of the Dirsync server, whether a password is required for the requestor, and the times for T1 and T3 (T2 is not relevant now, since Exchange in this case is a requestor).
2. Start the EMS tool, expand *First Administrative Group/First Routing Group*; right-click the *Connectors* folder, select *New|Dirsync Requestor*.
3. In the *New Requestor* window, select the *Dirsync server*, and click *OK*.
4. On the *General* tab, type a name for this requestor. This is usually enough; see Figure 8.40. Use the *Address Type* field to import address types other than MS Mail from the Dirsync server. You can select the language used for Dirsync log messages with the *Requestor Language* field; you can also select which Exchange server will be the requestor (default is the current server).
5. On the *Import Container* tab, click *Modify* and define in which OU container imported MS Mail addresses will be stored. You will be informed that the machine account must have access to that folder; this is normally acceptable. Define what the Dirsync process will do when the imported MS Mail users don't exist in the Windows 2000 domain; default is to create a Contact. See Figure 8.41.

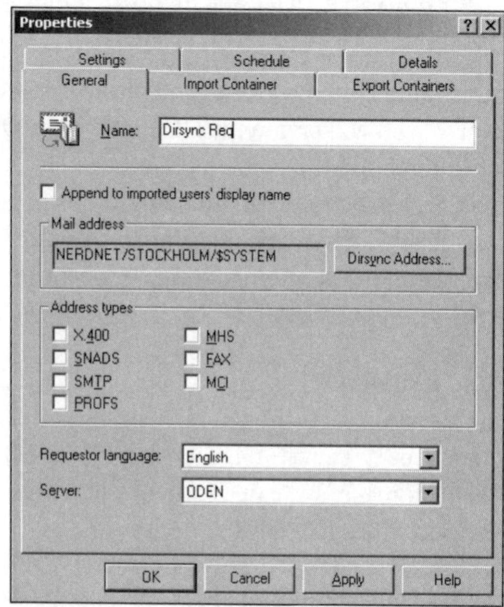

Figure 8.40
The General tab for Exchange Dirsync requestors.

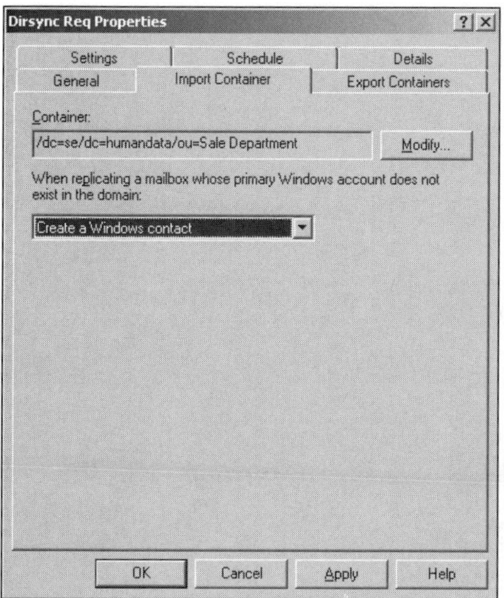

Figure 8.41
The Import Container tab for Exchange Dirsync requestors.

6. On the *Export Containers* tab, click *Add* and select the OU containers you want to export to MS Mail; again, you will be asked if it's okay to grant permission to the machine account. Select the OU containers you want to export to MS Mail; again, you will be asked if it's okay to grant permission to the machine account. Select *Yes*. Be careful to add all OU containers you want to export. You can also export Contacts and Groups to MS Mail; check each box that is appropriate. See Figure 8.42.

7. On the *Settings* tab, set the password that the Dirsync server requires. By default no password is set. Configure if you want to both send and receive updates, and how to use template information (i.e., extended properties for mailboxes), if any; usually there is no template information. You can also force a complete import and export on the next Dirsync cycle by setting the respective checkboxes. See Figure 8.43.

8. On the *Schedule* tab, set the T1 and T3 times for this requestor. Normally the Dirsync process runs once every night during the week; make sure the Dirsync servers are running every day—sometimes administrators skip weekends. See Figure 8.44.

9. If you want to add any notes, use the *Details* tab; you can also view the creation date and the last modification date. Click *OK* to complete the configuration of this requestor.

The Dirsync requestor is now configured; you will find the new object under the *Connectors* folder. Next, you must notify the MS Mail Dirsync server that it has a new requestor. Use the MS Mail admin program again, following these steps:

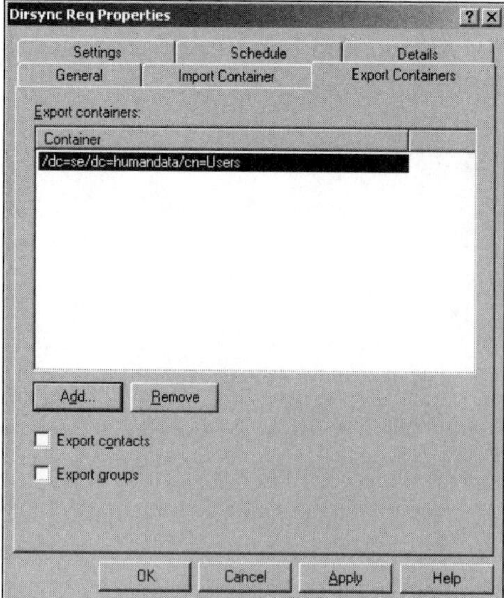

Figure 8.42
The Export Containers tab for Exchange Dirsync requestors.

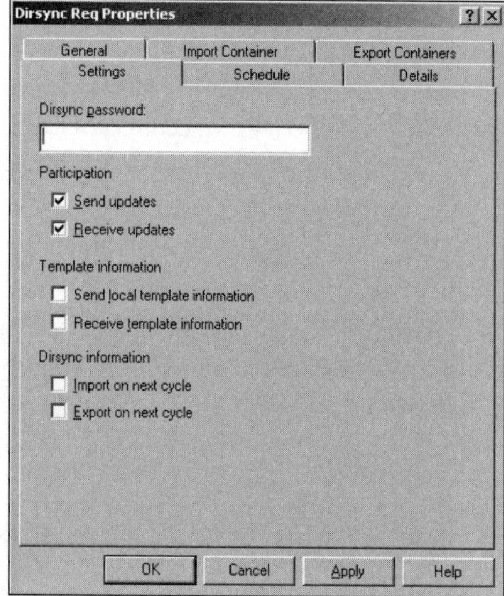

Figure 8.43
The Settings tab for Exchange Dirsync requestors.

1. Start the *MS Mail Admin* program, and log on as the Admin mailbox, as previously described.
2. Press the characters C (Config), D (Dir-Sync), S (Server), R (Requestors), and C (Create).

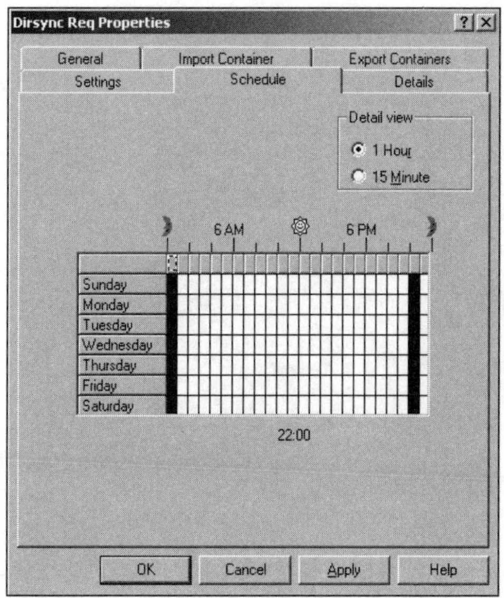

Figure 8.44
The Schedule tab for Exchange Dirsync requestors.

3. Select the network of the shadow post office, then the post office (if there is only one post office, the Admin program will automatically select this). Next you have the option to set a password for the requestor. However, you should avoid doing so; it doesn't provide any protection, and it only makes it harder to get the Dirsync process to work! See Figure 8.45. Next click *Yes* to register the post office.
4. Press Esc several times until you have exited the Admin program.

The registration of the shadow post office as a requestor is now completed. Now you must start the Microsoft Exchange Directory Synchronization service on the Exchange server, and change it to start automatically. If you don't want to wait until the scheduled Dirsync process starts, you can force it to start now. However, it's not recommended to do this in a production environment! Follow these step-by-step instructions to force Dirsync on the requestor:

1. To force the Dirsync process on the Exchange requestor, first pause the *Microsoft Exchange Directory Synchronization* service. You will receive a warning (see Figure 8.46), but this is normal; just click *OK* to close it. The requestor has now created a message with all updates; since this is the first time we've run the Dirsync process, it will contain all addresses from the selected OU container.
2. To speed up the transfer of this message to the Dirsync server, restart the MSM MTA service; otherwise you have to wait until it occurs automatically.
3. Open the text file *M:\Log\Recv.log* on the Dirsync server; if it has received two messages from the shadow post office and a user called *$System*, then it has received the updates

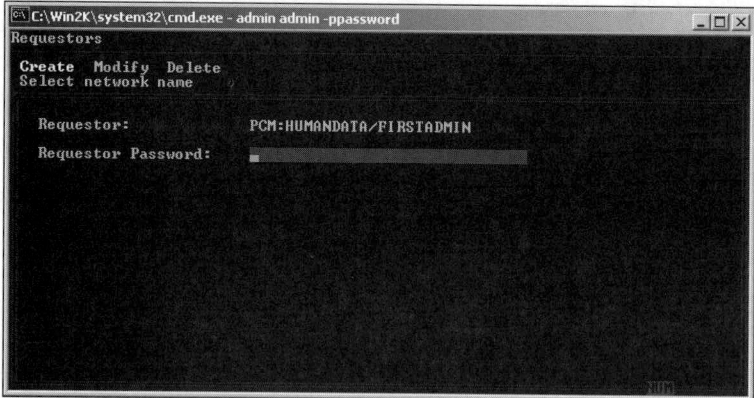

Figure 8.45
Register a requestor post office.

from the requestor; if not, wait some more, or run Steps 1 and 2 again (make sure the Microsoft Exchange Directory Synchronization service is running!).

By now, the update messages have arrived at the Dirsync server; this means that the T1 process mentioned earlier has been successfully performed. Next we need to force the T2 process; this is done on the Dirsync server alone, like this:

4. Open a command prompt and change the directory to Mailexe (or wherever the MS Mail Dirsync programs are located).
5. Make sure that M: is mapped to the *MailData* directory (or else you must specify what network drive is used for this directory). Type:

   Srvmain –R
   Srvmain –T

   This completes the T2 process and a *Master Change List* file should now be sent back to *all* requestors (not only the one we forced T1 for!).
6. To speed up the transfer of the MCL message, restart the MSM MTA.
7. Open the text file *M:\Log\Sent.log* and look for messages sent from user *$System* to the requestors. It should happen within one minute after Step 6; otherwise, try Step 6 again.

Figure 8.46
The warning message received when you pause the Dirsync process.

When the T2 process is successfully completed, it's time to force the T3 process. This is done on the requestor. Since this requestor is an Exchange server, it is intelligent enough to run the T3 process automatically, as soon as the MCL is received from the Dirsync server. That completes all three steps of the manual Dirsync process. Now you should be able to see the updated address list on the requestor.

Configuring Exchange 2000 as a Dirsync Server

If the MS Mail system doesn't have a Dirsync process running, you must now set one up. Since there is no existing Dirsync server, you should configure Exchange 2000 to act as one. Then all MS Mail post offices must be configured as requestors. Follow these step-by-step instructions to make Exchange a Dirsync server (again, do this directly on the Exchange server):

1. Make sure you know the times for T1, T2, and T3.
2. Start the *EMS* tool, expand *First Administrative Group/First Routing Group*; right-click the *Connectors* folder, and select *New|Dirsync Server*.
3. On the *General* tab, type in a descriptive name for this object. Click *Modify* and select the mail account that will receive error messages, usually the administrator. When troubleshooting, you may want to see the replication messages sent; if so, select *Copy Administrator On Outgoing Messages* and *Forward Incoming Dirsync Messages To Administrator*; however, normally they should not be selected. See Figure 8.47.
4. On the *Schedule* tab, set the T2 time (remember, this is the Dirsync server so we aren't using T1 or T3 here); see Figure 8.48.

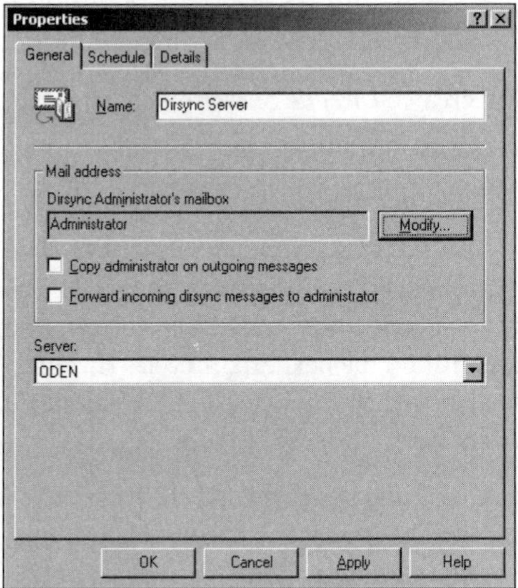

Figure 8.47
The General tab for the Dirsync server.

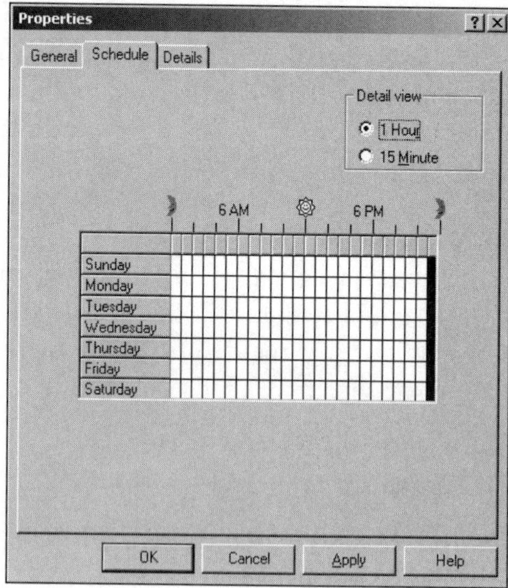

Figure 8.48
The Schedule tab for the Dirsync server.

5. If you want to add notes to this object, use the *Details* tab. When ready, click *OK* to complete this configuration of the Dirsync server.

A Dirsync server must also know the names of the requestors; in Exchange 2000, this is called *Remote Dirsync Requestors*. You must add one such object for each requestor; for example, if you have five MS Mail post offices and Exchange is the Dirsync server, you must configure one Dirsync server and five remote Dirsync requestors. Follow these step-by-step instructions:

1. Using the *ESM*, right-click the newly created *Dirsync Server* object, and select *New|Remote Dirsync Requestor*.
2. You will see a list of all known MS Mail post offices; select the first of them that will be a requestor; next click *OK*.
3. On the *General* tab, type in a descriptive name; this is normally all you do. However, if you want to force this requestor to use a password, type it here. You can also force Dirsync to export the complete address list on the next export cycle. The *Mail Address* field should not be modified—it displays the user ($System) on the requestor to whom the Dirsync server will send the *Master Change List*. See Figure 8.49.
4. On the *Import Container* tab, click *Modify* and select the OU container where the MS Mail addresses from this requestor will be stored. You can also define how these addresses should be registered, if they don't have any Windows 2000 accounts in this domain. The default is to create Contact objects. See Figure 8.50.

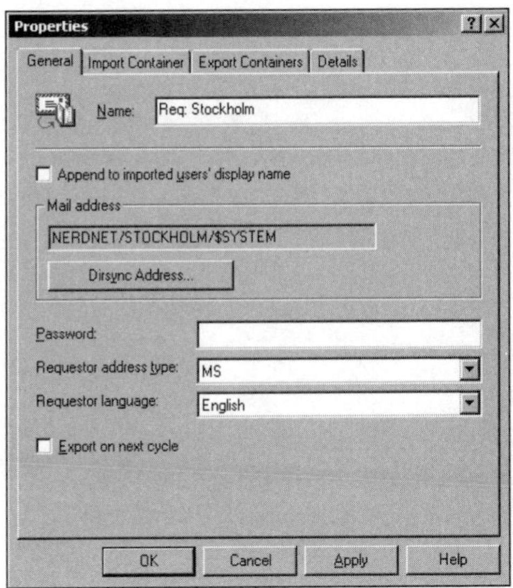

Figure 8.49
The General page for remote Dirsync requestors.

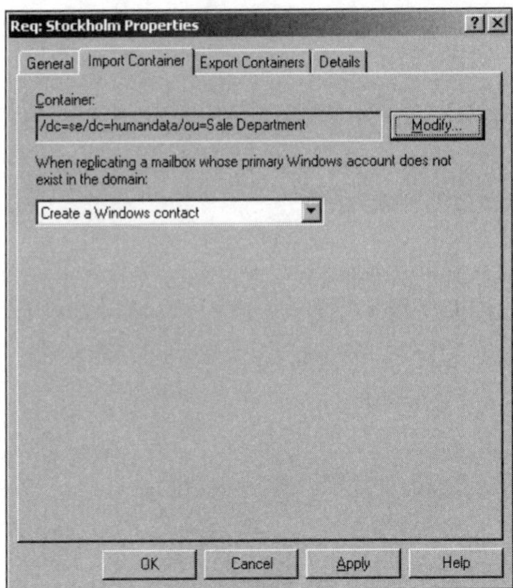

Figure 8.50
The Import Container tab for remote Dirsync requestors.

5. On the *Export Containers* tab, click *Add* and select the OU containers that should be exported to this requestor. You can also select to export Contacts and Groups; see Figure 8.51. Click *OK* to complete this remote Dirsync requestor.

Repeat all the steps above for all requestors. When this is done, you must configure each MS Mail post office to be a requestor, using the MS Mail Admin program. Follow these steps:

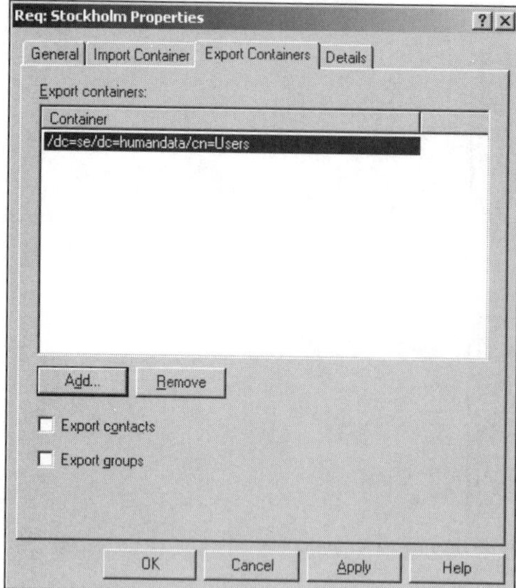

Figure 8.51
The Export Containers tab for remote Dirsync requestors.

1. Start the *MS Mail Admin* program, and log on as the Admin mailbox, as previously described.
2. Press the characters C (Config), D (Dir-Sync), R (Requestors), and R (Registration).
3. Press N (Name) and select the network name of the shadow post office (i.e., the Exchange server); then select the name of the shadow post office. Finally, type the password, if any is set on the Dirsync server. When ready, press Esc to return.
4. Press S (Schedule) for each day that the Dirsync process will run and define the T1 time (Send Request) and the T3 time (Process Updates); see Figure 8.52. When finished, press Esc to return.

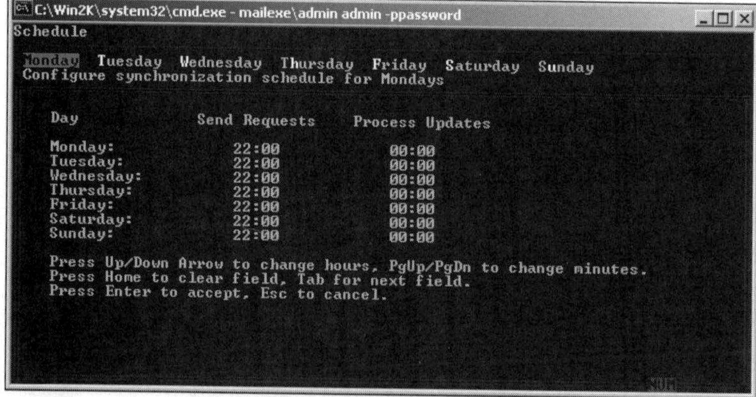

Figure 8.52
Defining the T1 and T3 times for MS Mail requestors.

5. Normally, this is all that is needed; you may also force a full import or export on the next Dirsync cycle, if needed. Press Esc two times to return to the Config window.
6. Press G (Global-List) and then Yes to enable the global address list on this requestor.
7. Press Esc until the Admin program exits.

All of these steps must be repeated for all MS Mail requestors. And that completes the configuration of the Dirsync process, where the Exchange server is the Dirsync server. However, there is still work to do. Since this scenario was based on an MS Mail system without a previous Dirsync process, the next thing we need to do is to start the MS Mail program that will perform all steps in the Dirsync process, the Dispatch.exe program.

You may remember that the MSM MTA replaced the External.exe program for MS Mail. However, there is no Exchange process that will replace the Dispatch.exe program; this is still needed for all MS Mail post offices! But it's rather simple to run; it is very similar to the External.exe. Follow the instructions in the MS Mail Admin manual to create a Dispatch.ini file, which defines what post offices it should be responsible for.

Now just wait for the Dispatch program to do its work. If you need to force the Dirsync process, it can be done manually; follow these step-by-step instructions to force the T1 process on all MS Mail requestors:

1. To force the T1 process on an MS Mail requestor, you need access to the Dirsync program's *Reqmain.exe* file (usually stored in the Mailexe directory). Open a command prompt and type:

   Reqmain –T

   This will create a message with all address updates. It now waits to be delivered to the Dirsync server.
2. To speed up the transfer of this message to the Dirsync server, restart the MSM MTA service.
3. Open the text file *M:\Log\Sent*.log on the requestor; if it has sent two messages from a user called $System to the Dirsync server, then this message has been successfully delivered; if not, wait some more, or run Steps 1 and 2 again (make sure the Microsoft Exchange Directory Synchronization service is running!).

By now, the update messages have arrived at the Dirsync Server; this means that the T1 process mentioned before has been successfully performed. Next we need to force the T2 process; this is done on the Dirsync server alone.

4. Pause the *Microsoft Exchange Directory Synchronization* service. You will receive a warning as previously described (refer back to Figure 8.46), but this is normal; just click *OK* to close it. The requestor has now created a message with the Master Change List for all requestors.

5. To speed up the transfer of the MCL message, restart the MSM MTA.
6. Open the text file *M:\Log\Recv.log* and look for messages sent from user System to the requestors. It should happen within one minute after Step 5; otherwise, try Step 5 again.

This completes the T2 process. By now you also see all updates received from the requestor post offices in the OU container. Next, we force the T3 process; it's done on all requestors:

1. Open a command prompt and change the directory to Mailexe (or wherever the MS Mail Dirsync programs are located).
2. Make sure that M: is mapped to the MailData directory. Type:

   Reqmain –R
   import Admin –P*password* –Q –Y
   Rebuild –F

That completes all three steps of the manual Dirsync process. Now you should be able to see the updated address list on all requestors.

Migrating from Other Mail Systems

Migrations for mail systems other than previous Exchange versions and MS Mail are often very straightforward. Use the Migration Wizard if possible—it will take care of most tasks and make sure they are performed in the right order. In the section "Define a Migration Plan" earlier in this chapter was a description of what other mail systems the Migration Wizard could handle, and how a client-based migration could be used as an alternative in many cases. Remember that a migration requires that you have a good understanding not only of Exchange 2000, but also of the current mail system. Make sure that you have the knowledge available when planning and performing the migration, otherwise you could easily create chaos instead of happiness for the organization.

Migrations that can't be performed in one "big-bang" process mean coexistence. As earlier described, coexistence requires some form of connection between the mail systems, for transferring messages in between; it also requires some sort of address replication between them. Exchange 2000 has the ability to coexist with the following vendor-specific mail systems, besides Exchange and MS Mail:

- cc-Mail
- Lotus Notes
- GroupWise

All of them also offer address replication; this means that it is reasonably easy to configure for coexistence. Exchange 2000 will again emulate these post offices, and use their protocols and techniques for message transfer and address replication; this makes the other mail system believe that Exchange is just another post office of the same kind. That is very practical since we don't have to make any changes in the existing mail system, except configure it to communicate with one more post office. However, there are lots of versions of these three mail systems; you must carefully test to ensure that the tools and connectors that come with Exchange 2000 are really working with this particular mail version. Never start a migration of the production environment without first testing all tools and utilities in a lab environment!

What should you do if you need to coexist with another mail system during the migration period? I would look for an SMTP connection; if you find one, then you have at least solved the problem of how to transfer messages between Exchange and this system. But you still need to solve the problem of address replication. Exchange 2000 has its LDAP export and import format, as previously described. But what about the other mail system? Look for the following:

- Are there any export and import features? If so, what format? How hard is it to convert to the LDAP format? Search the Internet for any third-party tools; ask the vendor, including Microsoft, if they know about any tools that can help you with this. Ask other organizations that have migrated; maybe they have developed their own utilities that you can buy from them.
- What directory protocols are supported by the other mail systems? For example, LDAP, NDS, MAPI-DS, or XDS? Is there anything you could use for importing and exporting addresses? Again, search the Internet for possible solutions.

If you can't find a tool for migration and coexistence, then it must be a rather unusual mail system. As an emergency solution, investigate whether your organization can accept simply dropping the old system and starting fresh with Exchange 2000; or in the worst case consider running them simultaneously. The last option should be avoided, since it is very inconvenient to have two separate mail systems, and it's just a matter of time before you'll have to drop your old system anyway. If you have an aching tooth, it's better to pull it out quickly than to pull little by little for days on end.

Prepare Administrators and Help Desk

As described in the section on migration planning, there is one important task that must not be forgotten—training the administrators and the support and help desk teams. Even if you are an experienced Exchange 5.5 administrator, you will be completely lost in Exchange 2000 without proper training; you already know this, which is why you are reading this book, right? How about the other administrators in your organization? Do they get trained properly, or are you going to be the single person responsible for configuring Exchange 2000 and solving every problem? If so, I hope you don't get sick or decide to change jobs, because you will be a very important person for your organization, with almost divine status.

Regardless of which mail system you migrate from, there is much to learn, simply because Exchange 2000 is very rich in features and possibilities; use them wisely and your users will love you. Use them incorrectly and you may become highly unpopular. I recommend that all Exchange 2000 administrators take at least one of the following Microsoft courses:

- 2355 *Upgrading from MS Exchange Server5.5 to MS Exchange 2000*—This two-day course is a good choice for the experienced Exchange 5.5 administrator who needs a quick introduction to Exchange 2000.
- *1572 Implementing and Managing Microsoft Exchange 2000*—This is the five-day entry-level course; you don't need any experience with any other mail systems, although experience will make it easier to understand the features described.
- *1573 Designing Microsoft Exchange 2000 for the Enterprise*—This is level two; you need the 1572 course for this course. This three-day course describes how to design and plan an Exchange 200 organization. It's a more theoretical course compared to the previous two; the number of hands-on labs are much less.

If you are an experienced Exchange 5.5 administrator, you may be interested in 2355 that explains the differences between Exchange 5.5 and Exchange 2000. But if you want to know more about Exchange 2000 I recommend taking 1572 since it contains more information than 2355. The 1573 course is for administrators who need to know how to design Exchange 2000 organizations; normal administrators usually don't need this course.

Any mailbox administrator, meaning personnel that is responsible for managing mailbox-enabled users only, doing no configuration of the Exchange server, and support personnel may also take the 2355 or 1572 course if possible, even if it contains more information than they really need. It is very helpful to have a good understanding of how Exchange 2000 works, even for this type of administrator.

Summary

This is a list of the more important features and keywords mentioned in this chapter. Use it as a reminder and to make sure you have understood the most important things:

- The initial price of the mail system is not as important as the question of how expensive it is to run, also known as the Total-Cost-of-Ownership, or TCO.
- Migration means chaos—be prepared.
- The connectors that come with Exchange 2000 include SMTP, X.400, MS Mail, cc-Mail, Lotus Notes, and GroupWise.
- PROFS and SNADS connectors have been removed from Exchange 2000.
- You must define a migration plan before you start the migration; this is extremely important! Your plan should answer questions like:
  - How should the migration process be performed?
  - How should Exchange and the old mail system communicate?
  - How should address replication be performed?
  - How many users can be migrated per day?

- Which users should be migrated and when?
- What data should be migrated to Exchange?
- What will we do if the migration does not work?
- What will we do when the migration is done?
- How should users, administrators, and help desk personnel be trained?

- The Migration Wizard is a great tool for migrating from the following mail systems: MS Mail, cc-Mail, Lotus Notes, GroupWise 4.x and 5.x, Collabra Share, LDAP systems, and IMAP4 systems.
- You can migrate by using the Outlook 2000 client and its PST files too.
- Create a short description of the new system for the users.
- Train the administrators and support personnel how to use the Exchange 2000 system.
- Train the help desk to solve all common problems.
- Train users the day before they get the new client.
- Migrating mail groups, distribution groups, or distribution lists is harder than you might first expect!
- Upgrading from Exchange 5.5 can be done using several methods:
  - *In-place upgrade*—Upgrade an existing Exchange 5.5 installation to Exchange 2000.
  - *Move-mailbox upgrade*—Install a new Exchange 2000 server and join an existing Exchange 5.5 site; then move users to the new system.
  - *Swing upgrade*—Similar to move-mailbox upgrade, but needs only one extra server to upgrade any number of Exchange 5.5. servers.
  - *Exmerge upgrade*—Similar to move-mailbox upgrade, but does not make any changes on the old system; therefore, it's easy to restore the old environment, if necessary.
- Replicated mailbox users from 5.5 that do not have a known Primary NT account in the AD domain will by default be created as disabled user accounts.
- Migration from MS mail is done with the Migration Wizard.
- Active Directory Connector, ADC—Replicates user and group information between Exchange 5.5 and AD; however, no configuration settings are replicated.
- Connection Agreements, CA—A configuration setting for the ADC; it defines what object to replicate, when, and between which servers.
- Recipient CA—Special CA for replicating recipient objects; may be one-way or two-way replication.

- Public Folder CA—Special CA for replicating mail-enabled public folder addresses; always two-way replication.
- Site Replication Service, SRS—Responsible for replicating server configuration settings between Exchange 5.5 and AD.
- The first Exchange 2000 server in a 5.5 site will automatically have the SRS installed.
- If the SRS stops working, it may result in problems transferring messages between Exchange 5.5 and Exchange 2000.
- MS Mail clients use one MMF file each, for storing messages and personal addresses.
- The MS Mail post office is just a number of directories and files, and is usually shared to the MS Mail clients as Maildata.
- MS Mail uses a program called External.exe to transfer messages between post offices.
- The MS Mail Connector contains a replacement for the External program, called the MS Mail MTA, also referred to as the MSM MTA; this will show up as a Windows 2000 service.
- The shadow post office is an MS Mail look-alike directory on the Exchange 2000 server; this is used for temporary storage of messages going between Exchange and MS Mail.
- The MS Mail Interchange service is a gateway process, converting messages and addresses between MS Mail format and Exchange format; this will show up as a Windows 2000 service.
- Address replication is called Directory Synchronization, or Dirsync, in MS Mail.
- Exchange 2000 uses Dirsync to replicate addresses to and from MS Mail.
- The Windows 2000 service Microsoft Exchange Directory Synchronization is responsible for the Dirsync process in Exchange 2000.
- Exchange 2000 can be configured as a Dirsync server or a Dirsync requestor.
- Besides configuring Exchange for MS Mail traffic, you need to configure the MS Mail post office; use its Admin.exe program for this.
- Migration from systems other than those that Exchange directly supports may be a challenge; make sure to find any available utilities before writing your own.
- Training your administrators and support personnel is a key factor for a successful migration.

Chapter 9

Creating and Managing Users

The most important objects in our Exchange system are our users, of course. They're the reason why we implemented a mail system in the first place. This chapter discusses the different types of users, how to create and manage them, and how to configure these objects for different needs and uses. In previous Exchange releases, a mailbox was a separate object from the NT user account, whereas in Exchange 2000 with Active Directory, a user is an AD security principal that is mailbox enabled; that difference is important and results in new ways to manage and configure them. You might be a user management expert in Exchange 5.5, but you will still encounter a lot of new features and routines in Exchange 2000 that you'll need to learn about and understand.

Besides managing our Exchange users, we must also be able to register external email accounts and create groups of users for email purposes. The management of these features and objects is new compared to previous Exchange releases, and it is important that you understand how to work with them properly. There are new types of email groups that behave completely differently from the distribution list groups in Exchange 5.5. These new types of groups offer new solutions to problems and needs that previously were hard to solve. We will also cover shared resource mailboxes, like public info and support mailboxes—how to create and manage them, and how to get the most out of them. Finally, we will look at how recipient policies can be used to manage and control users all over the Exchange 2000 organization; this gives the administrator unprecedented control of all users, regardless how large and distributed the organization is.

The Different Recipient Types

First, we don't have any separate mailbox accounts in Exchange 2000 anymore; all our users are created in the Active Directory. Second, there are several new or modified types of recipients. Let's take a quick look at all the different types of objects that can be mail recipients in Exchange 2000; see Table 9.1.

As you can see, there are several new objects compared to Exchange 5.5; in the following section we will discuss these objects in more detail.

Table 9.1 Different mail recipients in Exchange 2000.

Object	Description
Mailbox-enabled user	A user (or *AD security principal*, as they are called in Windows 2000) that has a mailbox in Exchange 2000. This is the same as a mailbox account in previous Exchange versions.
Mail-enabled user	A user security principal that has an external email address but not an Exchange 2000 mailbox.
Mail-enabled contact	A reference to an external email address. This type of recipient cannot log on to the Windows 2000 domain; i.e., it's not a security principal object.
Distribution group	A group with an email address. It can contain users, contacts, mail-enabled public folders, or other groups.
Mail-enabled security group	Same as a distribution group, except this group can also be used to set access permissions on Active Directory objects, like files, directories, and public folders.
Mail-enabled public folder	A public folder in Exchange 2000 that is mail-enabled.

Mailbox-Enabled Users

A user account in Windows 2000 is called an *AD security principal*; this is an account that logs on to the AD domain to access resources like files and applications. Windows NT 4 offered only *user* accounts; all of them were enabled to log on to the Windows NT 4 domain. However, since a Windows 2000 domain is based on Active Directory, and this type of directory allows more than just logon-enabled user accounts, Microsoft decided to rename the standard user account *security principal*. So, in short, an AD security principal is a user that can log on to the Windows 2000 domain, just like an NT 4 user account.

When a security principal user is mailbox-enabled, an entry in Exchange 2000 is created. Information about the Exchange server's name, storage group, and the name of the mailbox store the user belongs to are registered in the Active Directory. A lot of other Exchange-related information is also created, like the email address, mailbox limits, and delivery restrictions. Using the *ADSI Edit* tool, you can look at these properties by following these steps:

1. Start the ADSI Edit tool (a Windows 2000 support tool).
2. Expand the Domain NC, then the OU folder that contains the user you want to look at.
3. Find the username in the left pane; right-click and select Properties.
4. Use the Select A Property To View option to select HomeMDB; in the Value field you will see the name of the store, the storage group, the administrative group, and more. Place the cursor in this field and use the arrow keys to view the rest of this value text, as shown in Figure 9.1.
5. Click Cancel to close this window without accidentally changing any values.

The HomeMDB value must not be changed manually; update it by using the Move Mailbox features in Exchange Tasks. A user that becomes mailbox-enabled will also be displayed in the global address list, stored in the global catalog.

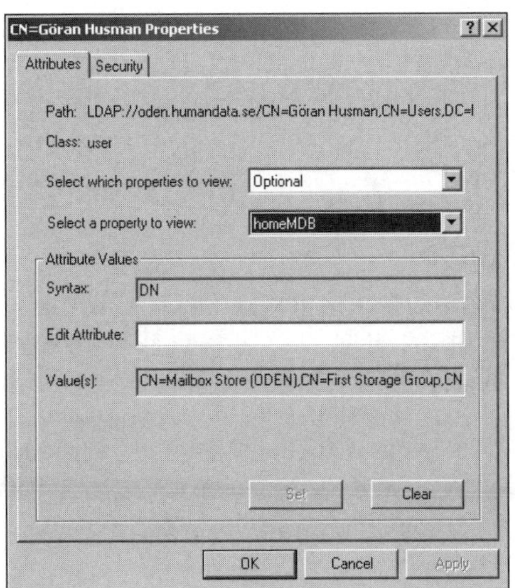

Figure 9.1
The HomeMDB value field for a mailbox-enabled user.

Tip: *If you need to delete the mailbox from a user, and the original Exchange server can-not be contacted, you can't use the Exchange Tasks Wizard in the AD Users and Computers tool that normally is used for this type of operation. However, by clearing the HomeMDB value, Active Directory will believe that this user is not mailbox-enabled; it can now be mailbox-enabled again. This type of scenario might occur if the Exchange server crashes and we don't have a backup (bad, bad!); we install a new Exchange server, but we are not able to mailbox-enable the users again, or use the move-mailbox feature, since there is no contact with the original Exchange server!*

Mail-Enabled Users

This is also a user object of the security principal type; i.e., this user account can log on to the AD domain. However, this user is only mail-enabled, not mailbox-enabled. This means that this user has an external email address; here "external" means an account that doesn't belong to the Exchange 2000 organization in this Windows 2000 forest. This type of user object is typically used for hired consultants or external users that need to be able to receive mail and access some of the resources in the domain, but don't need an Exchange mailbox. Mail-enabled users don't have any value set for the HomeMDB property. This user will be listed in the global address list.

Mail-Enabled Contacts

This is not a security principal object and this account cannot log on to the AD domain; this means that this object doesn't have a SAMAccountName, objectSID, userAccountControl, or userPrincipalName property. However, if this object is mail-enabled, it will have an email address—for example, an SMTP address. If it's not mail-enabled, this contact object will only be visible in the Active Directory, not in the global address list. By mail-enabling this user, you can create an email address that will be displayed in the GAL. All contact users must belong to an administrative group in Exchange; this will affect how this user will be replicated to a coexisting Exchange 5.5 environment. You may recall that an administrative group is equal to an Exchange 5.5 site, regarding directory replication.

Mail-Enabled Distribution Groups

This object is used to create a group of user objects, contacts, public folders, and other groups. If this group is mail-enabled, it will be displayed in the global address list; if it doesn't appear there, it's not mail-enabled. The distribution group is not security-enabled, and no permissions can be assigned to this type of group. A distribution group that is not mail-enabled is of little practical use; normally it's mail-enabled—it corresponds to the distribution lists in previous Exchange, except that it can't be used for assigning permissions to public folders or other mail folders. If you try to do so, this group will automatically (and silently) be converted to a security group.

The distribution group can contain any type of AD objects, even users and contacts that are not mail-enabled; you won't receive any warnings about this. If a message is sent to this group, it will successfully deliver the messages to the members who have an email address, and return non-delivery reports for those objects that don't have an email address, as shown in Figure 9.2. That means you must make sure to include only mail-enabled objects in a distribution group that should be used for email purposes!

Note: *An interesting thing to notice is that although a distribution group can contain both mail-enabled and non–mail-enabled Contact objects, only mail-enabled contacts will be visible when an Exchange client, like Outlook, looks at its members.*

Mail-Enabled Security Groups

This type of group is very similar to the distribution group, with one important exception: Security groups can be assigned permissions to network resources, like files, directories,

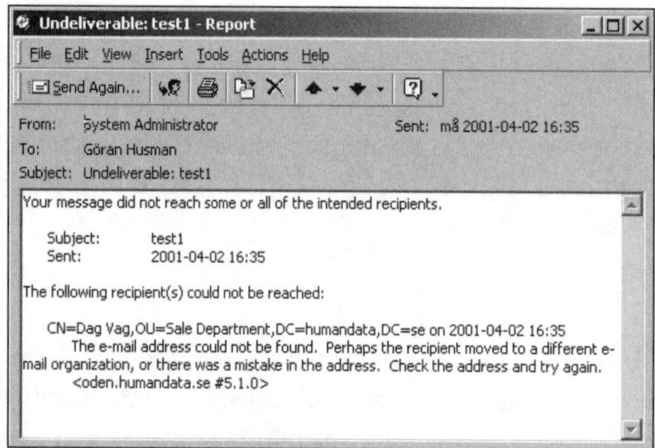

Figure 9.2
Non-delivery reports are received by distribution group members that are not mail-enabled.

and public folders. A security group can be mail-enabled; this will make it display in the global address list. This is a new feature compared to Exchange 5.5 and Windows NT 4; now you can create a security group for assigning permissions. You can also use it as a mail-enabled group, whereas previously you needed to create one group in NT 4 and one distribution list in Exchange 5.5 to get the same functionality. If you have two groups, but for different purposes, it's easy to forget one of them when updating the membership. However, in Windows 2000 it may also be easy to forget that one group has two functions. For example, let's say you have a group called Managers, mainly used for email purposes. A new manager is employed and her name should be included in the Managers security group so she will get all messages sent to this group. Assume that this security group also has access to some sensitive files; the new manager will now also be able to access these files. Sometimes this is exactly what you want, sometimes it's not; just make sure you remember how mail-enabled security groups work.

Mail-Enabled Public Folders

Public folders are created only in the Exchange server; they will not be displayed in the Active Directory and its OU containers. However, if you mail-enable a public folder, an instance of this object will be stored in the Active Directory and the global catalog; thus the name will be visible in the global address list in Exchange.

When talking about public folders, we must know whether the Exchange organization is running in native or mixed mode; we must also distinguish the ordinary MAPI folder from general purpose (GP) folders, since they have different characteristics. Table 9.2 summarizes the different combinations.

A GP folder that is mail-enabled will by default be visible in the global address list; you don't need to unhide it. A MAPI folder is hidden by default; follow these instructions to change this setting for both MAPI and GP folders:

1. Start the ESM.
2. Expand the administrative group this public folder belongs to; next expand the Folders folder. Locate the public folder you want to change.
3. Open the properties for the public folder and look at the Exchange Advanced tab. Change the setting of Hide From Exchange address lists as needed.
4. Click *OK* to save and close.

Table 9.2 Public folders in native and mixed Exchange 2000 mode.

Mode	MAPI Public Folders	GP Public Folders
Mixed mode	Mail-enabled by default, can't be disabled.	Mail-disabled by default, can be enabled.
Native mode	Mail-disabled by default, can be enabled.	Mail-disabled by default, can be enabled.

New Features Compared to Exchange 5.5

The many new recipient features in Exchange 2000 are mainly due to the Active Directory taking over the responsibility of all types of recipient objects from the DIR.EDB in the previous Exchange release. In the last section, we saw all objects that can be displayed in the global address list: Users, Contacts, Groups, and Public Folders. As before, a mail-enabled object can still receive messages, even if its email address is hidden from the global address list. Below is a list of some of the new features related to recipient features in Exchange 2000:

- Multiple public folder trees
- Multiple global address lists
- Smarter address lists
- Multiple email addresses created automatically
- Multiple languages preinstalled for Details templates and Address templates
- System policies
- Recipient Update Service
- Extended mailbox properties
- New ways of creating folders
- New ways of accessing folders

This section describes the new features and methods related to recipients in Exchange 2000; let's take a closer look at these new features.

Multiple Public Folder Trees

The previous Exchange releases had only one public folder tree. This was sometimes inconvenient—for example, when a mail-enabled application like a document-handling system needed public folders to store its information. Such folders could easily grow in size and make the PUB.EDB database hard to manage; or maybe there was a need to hide its existence to everyone except its users. With the General Purpose public folder tree in Exchange 2000, this is much easier. You can create as many GP folders as needed; they will still have unlimited size (or 16TB, that is) and be protected by transaction log files, just like the ordinary MAPI-based All Public Folder tree. However, GP folders are not visible for all kinds of clients, most notably the standard Outlook client, due to hard-coded limitations in the MAPI protocol. The following types of clients can access a GP folder tree:

- Outlook Web Access (OWA) clients
- NNTP clients
- Standard applications like MS Word and Excel by the file system

However, none of these clients can view a GP folder by default; in fact, the folders are accessible only on the Exchange server itself and its ExIFS, or the Exchange Installable File System. See Chapter 2 for more information about how to create and access GP folders. Each GP folder tree must have its own public store; it cannot be shared with the standard MAPI folder tree.

Remember that GP folders by default are not mail-enabled; you can change that by using the ESM, right-clicking on the GP folder, and selecting All Tasks/Mail Enable. This makes it possible to send messages to the GP folder by email, even from MAPI clients that can't view its contents or external sources, like the Internet. But perhaps the most interesting access method for GP folders is through the file system. Thanks to the ExIFS, any folder in Exchange, including the mailbox folders, MAPI public folders, or GP folders can be shared like any other file system resource. If necessary, you can map several drives to different parts of the ExIFS tree.

For example, in Figure 9.3 you see a network client that has mapped its M: drive to a specific GP folder, named THE GP FOLDER TREE, with one subfolder called GP folder 1. At the same time, the N: drive is mapped to the root of the ExIFS; within that, you see the Exchange organization **Humandata.se** and its branches MBX (mailbox folders), Public Folders (standard MAPI type), and the GP Folder Tree (the same GP folder that M: is mapped to).

Since these folders are now accessible as directories, they can be used from within any application for storing and retrieving any type of file document. For example, in Figure 9.4 you see the ordinary Save As feature in MS Word listing the contents of the N: drive. Don't confuse this with the much restricted Send To |Exchange Folder that has always been a feature in Exchange; with the ExIFS, you can work with the shared Exchange folders like any file directory—you can save, rename, move, or delete any of its files, as long as you have the proper access permissions.

If we use the File Explorer and display the contents of the GP Folder 1 where the Word document was saved, it looks like Figure 9.5; you can see the MS Word document Proposal.doc along with three ordinary mail messages. Any of these files, including the messages, can be opened by double-clicking, as well as modified or deleted, just like normal files. If we consider the superior security Exchange is offering with its transaction log protected messages stores, compared to the ordinary file system, and the easy access of its content through Web clients like OWA and ExIFS, we quickly understand how attractive it is to be able to store all of our information in the Exchange stores; you'd better be prepared for this when designing the Exchange organization!

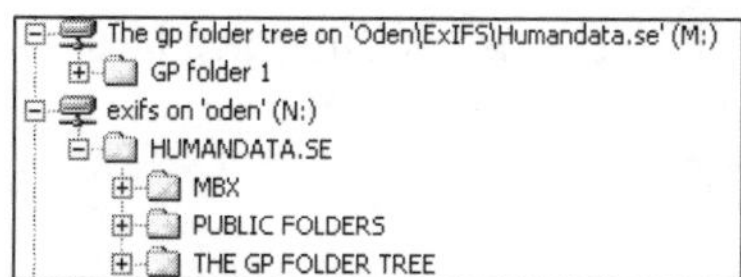

Figure 9.3
Multiple network drives mapped to the ExIFS.

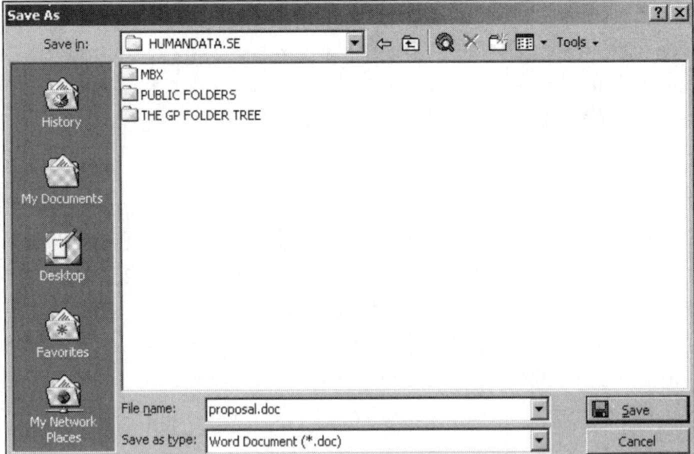

Figure 9.4
Saving Word documents directly to a GP folder.

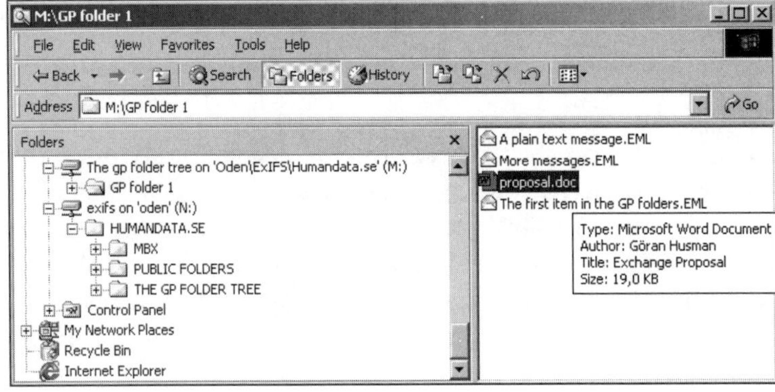

Figure 9.5
The documents in a public folder displayed with the File Explorer.

Multiple Global Address Lists

Previous Exchange versions had only one single global address list, or GAL. That made it hard to host several organizations in the same Exchange 5.5 system. Only by using a rather bizarre configuration of the search permissions for the organization object, combined with address book views, was it possible to hide addresses for particular NT groups of users; for more information about that, read the TechNet article Q182902. This is completely modified in Exchange 2000; you can now easily create as many GALs as needed. However, if you have multiple global address lists, only one will be shown in the user's Outlook address book; the selection is based on:

- The GAL to which the user has access
- The GAL of which the user is a member
- The GAL that is the largest

For example, if there are two lists, A with 200 names and B with 300 names, and a user has access to both, and is a member of both, then this user would see the list B, since it's the largest list. However, if the user has access to both, but is only a member of A, then that list will be used in the Outlook client. And if the user has access only to list A, this list will be used, regardless of membership or size; see also Decision Tree 9.1.

Let's assume that we have two companies hosted in our Exchange 2000 organization: Human Data and Moria. We want to create one global address list each, showing only members of the same company. If we look closer at the access permissions of the default global address list configuration in Exchange 2000, here's what we find:

- All users belong to the security group, Authenticated Users.
- Authenticated Users has access permission to the Default Global Address List.
- All mail-enabled users are members of the Default Global Address List.

Using the selection order above, all users will have access to the Default Global Address List; if we create a new global address list, all our users will still only see the default GAL, not the new GAL. Since one of the selection rules is "The GAL of which the user is a member," we could try solving this problem by changing the membership of the default GAL; however, it's not possible to change the membership of the default GAL, so this can't

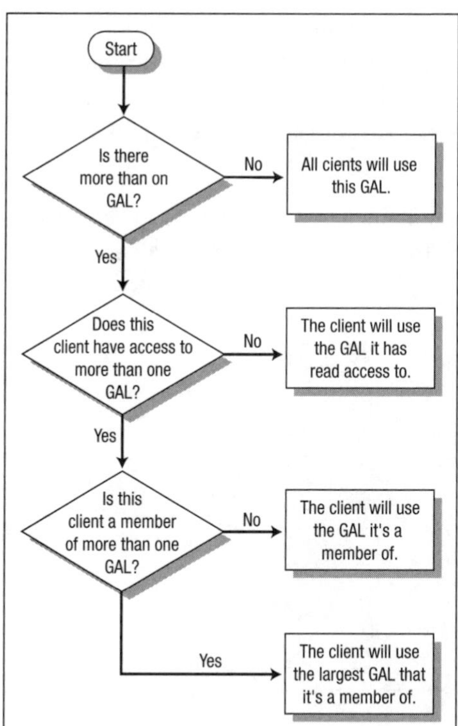

Decision Tree 9.1
Selecting what GAL will be visible for an Outlook client.

help us. Another solution would be to change the access permission; this will work as expected. Follow these step-by-step instructions to create two global address lists, one for each company:

1. Start the ESM tool, expand the Recipients, right-click All Global Address Lists, and select New|Global Address List.
2. Give this list an intuitive name, for example "GAL Human Data."
3. Click Filter Rules, and look at the Advanced tab; click the Field button and select which names this GAL should contain—for example, Company Is (Exactly) = Human Data. Then click Add, as shown in Figure 9.6.
4. Click *OK* and then Finish to complete the creation of this new global address list.
5. Create one more global address list called Moria, where the filter rule is Company Is (Exactly) = Moria.

Now we have our new global address lists, one for each company. Open the properties for each user and make sure they have either Human Data or Moria as their company name. Notice that the rule we created expects the company name to be spelled exactly, including capital letters. The next thing we need to create is a security group for each company: Human Data Group and Moria Group. Here's how:

6. Start the AD Users and Computers tool, and create two security groups, one for each company. Add members to these groups, employees of Moria in the Moria Group, etc. It doesn't matter in which OU you create them, but these companies probably have their own OU containers; if so, it may be logical to store the group together with its members.
7. Use the ESM and open the properties for the Human Data global address lists; click the Preview button on the General tab to ensure that it displays all employees of this company and nobody else.

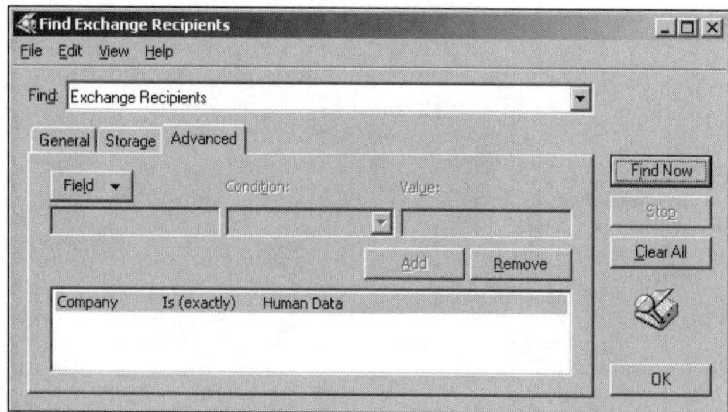

Figure 9.6
Creating a filter rule.

8. Look at the Security tab; click Add and select the Human Data Group. Click Add to make it appear in the bottom pane, then click *OK* to return.
9. Select the Human Data Group, and change its allowed permission to Open Address List only. Next, click *OK* to close this window.
10. Make the corresponding change for the other GAL, giving Moria Group permission to add the Open Address list to this global address list.
11. Open the properties for the Default Global Address List; look at the Security tab.
12. Select the Authenticated Users group, and Deny the Open Address List permission. Click *OK* to save and close this window.

From now on, only users belonging to the Human Data Group will be able to see the users and contacts from the company Human Data. The last step, number 12, is necessary to disable the default global address list. Another solution would be to delete it completely.

As you can see, there are two items to define when using multiple global address lists: who will have access to this list, and what this list should contain. To control the contents of the GAL, you create LDAP rules, as described in Step 3 above. Instead of creating the rule for the GAL by selecting search conditions, you can write the LDAP search rule directly, using the Custom Search and its Advanced tab, as shown in Figure 9.7, where we search all users with the attribute Company equal to Moria.

Smarter Address Lists

Previously, Exchange had the Address Book View, or ABV, that was used to create lists of users belonging to a certain category—for example, departments or countries. In Exchange 2000, we have the following lists, besides the global address list:

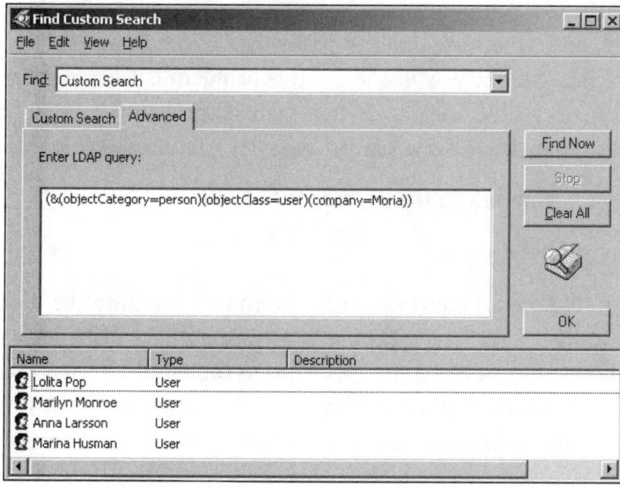

Figure 9.7
Writing custom LDAP search rules.

- The default address lists
- Custom address lists
- Offline address lists

These lists can be hidden from a user if necessary—for example, a user may only see the address lists belonging to a given department or company. This is controlled by the access permissions, as described for the global address lists in the previous section. Beware that the security group Authenticated Users, which all users belong to, will by default be without any given access, neither Allow nor Deny; the effect will be that all users can see the list's contents. If you change the access permission to Deny, this will prohibit all users from listing its contents, since Deny permission has priority over Allow. One way of solving this dilemma is to remove the Authenticated Users group from the address list in question; but before doing this, you must clear the checkbox Allow Inheritable Permissions From Parent To Propagate To This Object (make sure to copy the permission, when asked); otherwise, this group cannot be removed.

The Default Address Lists

These lists are created when Exchange 2000 is installed; you can use them as they are, or modify them if necessary:

- *All Contacts*—Lists all mail-enabled contacts in the organization.
- *All Groups*—Lists all mail-enabled groups in the organization.
- *All Users*—Lists all mail-enabled and mailbox-enabled users in the organization.
- *Public Folders*—Lists all mail-enabled public folders that are not hidden.

Custom Address Lists

These are lists that you create as a complement to the default address lists. You may have any number of address lists, but remember that too many lists make it hard for the users to find the list they are looking for. One way of solving this problem is to hide address lists from general view, making them visible only for certain security groups. The Allow permissions that a group must have in order to access an address list from Outlook include:

- *Open Address List*—Makes the names in the address list visible.
- *List Content*—Makes any sublists visible.

Similar to top-level public folders, an address list at the top level cannot be hidden, although its contents and sublists can. This means that you must first create a top-level address list, that only certain groups have Allow permission to; below this list you can create any number of address lists that will be displayed only for users with List Content permission—in other words, users belonging to other groups will see an empty top-level list, and nothing more.

Follow this step-by-step instruction to create a top-level address list named Demo AL, which has two sublists named Customers and Private Addresses. These lists must be visible only to members of the security group Moria Group:

1. Start the ESM tool, and navigate to the Recipients/All Address Lists folder.
2. Right-click on the All Address Lists, and select New/Address List.
3. Give this top-level address list the name "Demo AL."
4. Click on the Filter Rules button and create a search rule of your choice (this is the same technique as when creating search rules for global address lists, as described earlier). Next, click *OK* to complete the creation of this address list.
5. Open the properties for the new Demo AL, and switch to the Security tab. Since this will be a list that only Moria Group will have access to, we must remove the group Authenticated Users, for reasons previously mentioned. But first, clear the Allow Inheritable Permissions From Parent To Propagate To This Object checkbox; make sure to select to copy inherited permission when asked. After that, select the Authenticated Users group and click Remove.
6. Click Add, browse the list, and select the Moria Group; click Add again, and then OK. You have now returned to the Security tab, and the new group is by default given all permissions. This is not necessary; you can clear all permissions except the Open Address List and List Content if you want. Then click *OK* to close this window.

Now we have our new top-level address list, with permissions that allow only the Moria Group to view its content, although all users will see the name of the address list. Next, we will create the two sublists; they will automatically be hidden for all users except Moria Group members:

7. Right-click the Demo-AL object; select New|Address List. Name this list Customers. Click on the Filter Rules and create your search rules; click *OK* when you're finished to complete the creation of this address list.
8. Right-click the Demo-AL object again; select New|Address List again and name this new list Private Addresses, and create a filter search rule.

Test these three new address lists by logging on as a user that's not a member of the Moria Group; you should only see an empty address list, as shown in Figure 9.8.

Then log in as a user that is a member of the Moria Group; this user will not only see the names in the Demo AL, but also its sublists Customers and Private Addresses, as shown in Figure 9.9.

Offline Address Lists

Mobile users and others with temporary access to the Exchange server need access to the address list, also when in offline mode. The Offline Address Lists, or OALs, are used for this purpose; by default there is one offline address list that is a copy of the complete Default Global Address List. A user can download this list to his or her computer when

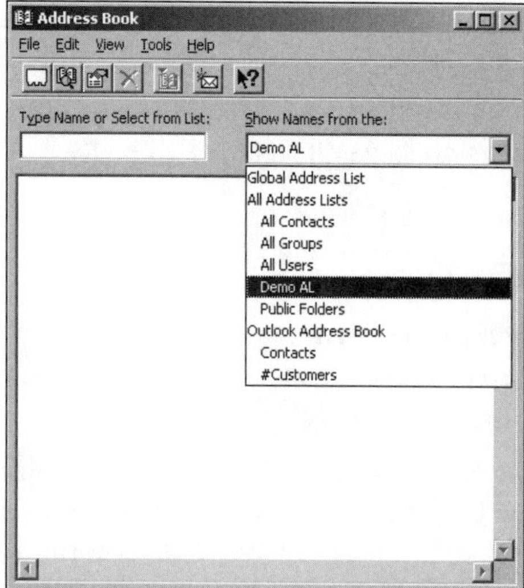

Figure 9.8
How the new address list looks for users without access.

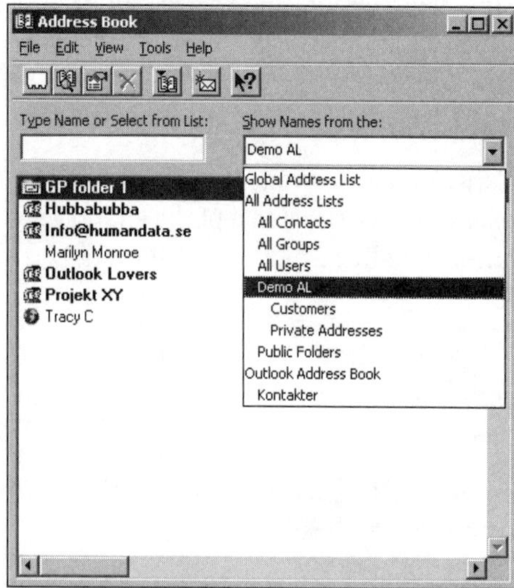

Figure 9.9
How the new address list looks for users with access.

online, and later when using Outlook offline, this list will be used instead of the ordinary GAL. The downloaded OAL file will have the extension .OAB, as in Offline Address Book. Each OAL can consist of a number of address lists—for example, both the default global address list and a list for each department. When an Outlook user selects to download an OAL containing several address lists, the user can choose any of these lists, as shown in Figure 9.10.

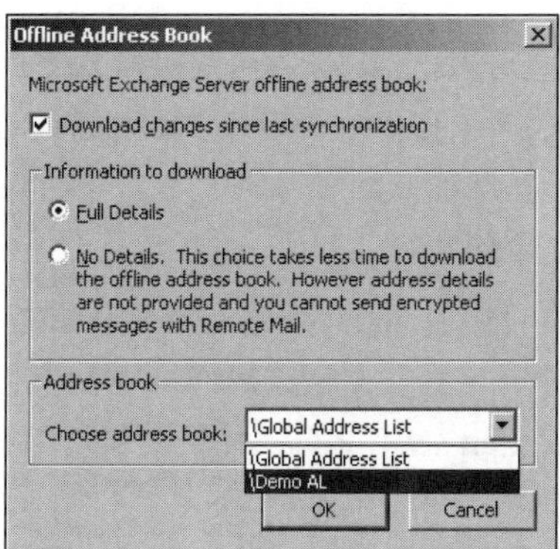

Figure 9.10
Downloading OAL with multiple address lists.

If the organization is large, it may be necessary to create several subsets of the global address list—for example, one OAL for each department or country. Access to these OALs is controlled by permissions, in the same way as the previously mentioned lists; this means that you can create OALs that are accessible only by certain groups of users. Follow these step-by-step instructions to create extra OALs:

1. Start the ESM, navigate to the Recipients|Offline Address Lists. By default there is one OAL named Default Offline Address List in the right pane.
2. Right-click the Offline Address Lists; select New|Offline Address List.
3. Give this list an intuitive name; remember that the users will see these lists.
4. Click Browse and select the Offline Address List Server, i.e., the Exchange server responsible for updating the OAL. When ready, click *Next*.
5. In the next window, you select which address lists to include in this OAL; if you have more than one GAL, they will all be listed by default. Remove the ones you don't need for this particular OAL. You can also add new address lists to this OAL by clicking the Add button, and selecting between all available address lists. Click *Next* to continue.
6. You might receive a warning that this OAL will be created during the store maintenance period of the Exchange server selected in Step 4; therefore, this OAL will not be available to clients until that time. Click *Next* to continue.
7. The next window summarizes what this OAL will contain; if this is okay, click Finish to complete this OAL. Otherwise, click Back and adjust this OAL definition.

The newly created OAL has several properties that can be used to control when this OAL should be rebuilt and what address lists it will include. Open the properties for the new OAL and you will find:

- *The General tab*—You can change the server that is responsible for rebuilding this OAL by clicking the Browse button. In the Address List pane, you can see which address lists it currently contains; use the Add or Remove buttons to modify this list. In the Update Interval field, you can see when this OAL is rebuilt; default is once every day at 5 A.M. If this Exchange 2000 server is a member of an Exchange 5.5 site that also has Exchange 4 or 5 servers, you must also set the checkbox for Exchange 4 and 5; if not, avoid setting this checkbox since it will decrease the OAL performance.

- *The Details tab*—Lists the creation date and the last modification date; you can also add administrative notes.
- *The Security tab*—Select which groups of users can see this OAL; the default is Authenticated Users, i.e., all logged-on users.

Multiple Email Addresses Created Automatically

In previous Exchange versions, only one SMTP address could be created automatically when a new user was created. Many organizations have two or more SMTP addresses, and the way to solve this was to use one of the following methods:

- Manually add the second address.
- Export all users to a Comma Separated Value (CSV) file, add the second address, and import the file again.

Exchange 2000 offers a new feature called Recipient Policies that decides what email addresses to create; by default, it creates one SMTP address and one X.400 address. This recipient policy can be modified to add extra email addresses. Follow this step-by-step instruction to configure the default recipient policy to add a second SMTP address:

1. Start the ESM tool and navigate to the Recipients/Recipient Policies.
2. Right-click on the Default Policy object in the right pane; select Properties.
3. Open the E-Mail Addresses tab; you will find the two default email addresses that the system creates currently.
4. Click the New button, select what type of email address to create—for example, SMTP Address—and click *OK*. Add the new SMTP address, including the @ sign. Also note the This Exchange Organization Is Responsible For All Mail Delivery To This Address checkbox; you must set this checkbox if this Exchange organization indeed should accept messages for this SMTP address. Next, click *OK* to continue.
5. You have returned to the E-Mail Addresses tab again; the new SMTP address is displayed, but its checkbox is not. If you leave it like this, you must manually add all new addresses; if you set this checkbox, all new users will have this SMTP address besides the default SMTP address. Click *OK* to close this window; you will then see a question asking if you want this new setting to apply only to new users, or if it should also apply to existing users.

Tip: *If your Exchange organization will host more than one company, then Exchange must be configured to accept multiple SMTP domains; for example, both* ***humandata.se*** *and* ***taurnet.se****. To make this work, you must first create a new recipient policy for the new company (use the filter rules to make sure it only contains members of that company); next, add the new SMTP domain as described above and (important) make sure to set the checkbox described in Step 5! If you don't do this, Exchange will see this as rerouting and will refuse to accept messages for this new domain, unless you accept rerouting (which you shouldn't do)!*

In Chapter 7, you will find more information on how to control the name standard—for example, how to automatically create SMTP addresses like **first.last@domain.tld**, instead of **alias@domain.tld** by default, by typing "%g.%s@domain.tld" as the SMTP address in Step 4 above.

In previous Exchange releases, you defined inbound SMTP domains using the Routing tab for the Internet Mail Service. As described in Step 4 above, this is now defined in the recipient policy and the This Exchange Organization Is Responsible For All Mail Delivery To This Address checkbox.

Multiple Languages Preinstalled for Details Templates and Address Templates

In Exchange 5.5, you had to manually add support for languages other than the Exchange server software, for example English; this was important to get the correct national settings of date and time formats, alphabetic sort order of the GAL, etc. To do this, you imported a nationalized Template.csv file with the Exchange admin program. Exchange 2000 comes with 30 preinstalled language templates, which makes this import superfluous. As in previous Exchange versions, there are two types of templates:

- *Details Templates*—These are used when an Outlook client requests the properties of a mailbox, contact, group, or public folder, or when the Outlook user wants to search the GAL for a name. Outlook will tell the Exchange server about its regional settings, so the server knows what templates to use.
- *Address Templates*—These are used when the Outlook client wants to add an email address (that doesn't exist in the GAL or the Contact folder) to a message. There are templates for SMTP, X.400, MS Mail, and cc-Mail address types.

It is possible that you might want to modify or extend the Outlook client's search template; the default template makes it possible to search for attributes like first and last name, department and companies, but not, for example, phone number or email address.

The way to change a template is exactly the same as in previous Exchange releases; follow these step-by-step instructions to add the phone number to the search template:

1. Start the ESM, and navigate to *Recipients* ***/Details Templates <language>***.
2. Open the properties for the Search Dialog object and go to the Templates tab.
3. Click the Test button to see its current design. Click *OK* to close the test window.

4. Locate the line Cit&y (look in the right-most column, almost at the end of the list); click once on this line.
5. First, we add the label Phone (with n underlined) to the search dialog: click Add; select a Label and give it the following values: X=183, Y=90, Width=70, Height=8, Text=Pho&ne. Click *OK* when ready, as shown in Figure 9.11.
6. Second, we add the phone number attribute; it's called the Telephone-number. Click Add, select Edit, and fill in the following values: X=254, Y=90, Width=100, Height=12, Field=Telephone-Number, Length=64. Use the Move Up and Move Down buttons, if needed, to list the Edit field after the Label field, as shown in Figure 9.12.
7. Test the new search template by clicking the Test button; it should now look similar to Figure 9.13. If all is correct, click *OK* twice to close the search dialog box; otherwise, make the necessary modifications.

Use the Outlook client and test the new search dialog in the address book; it should find all numbers listed on the user's General tab and Telephone Number attribute. Note that you can search for incomplete numbers—for example, searching for "08-556" will find all numbers beginning with 08-556.

System Policies

Creating global configurations like mailbox limits or delivery options was not possible in previous Exchange versions; the best you could do was default settings for all users

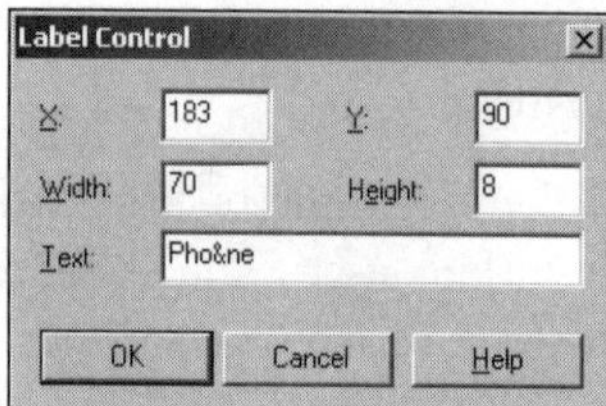

Figure 9.11
The new search label.

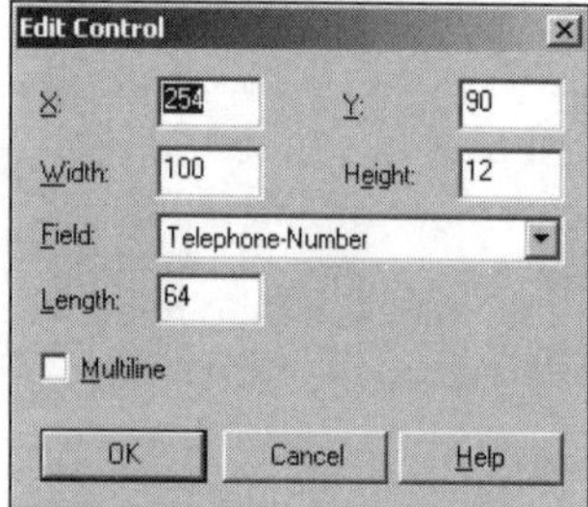

Figure 9.12
The new Edit field.

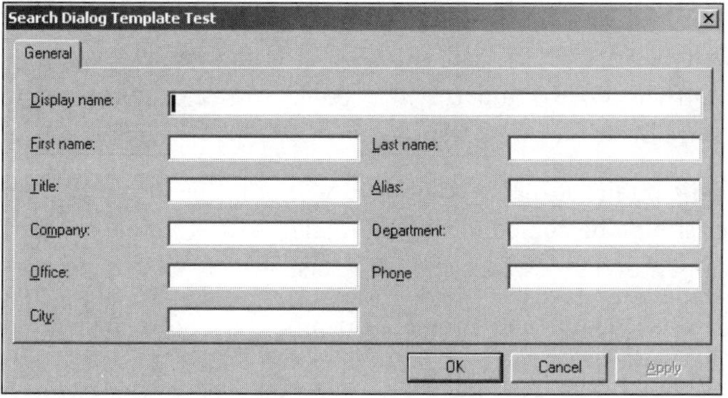

Figure 9.13
The modified search dialog.

belonging to the same Exchange site. But Exchange 2000 comes with the new feature of System Policies that you can use to create preconfigurations of many attributes of:

- Mailbox stores
- Servers
- Public stores

This makes it very easy to apply configuration settings on any store or Exchange server in the organization. This policy may be modified at any time, and these new settings will automatically apply to all its stores or servers. You can add or remove stores and servers to an existing policy at any time. Before any of these policies can be created, you must first decide which administrative group should be responsible for setting these preconfigured values. Next you must create a system policies folder in that administrative group. Finally, you are ready to create one or all of the policies listed above. Follow these instructions to create the system policy folder:

1. Start the ESM, and navigate to Administrative Groups and the administrative group that you have decided to be responsible for these policies. Note that although only one administrative group is responsible, these policies can be applied to all Exchange servers in the organization, regardless of what AG they belong to!
2. Right-click the AG of your choice, and select New|System Policy Container. This will result in the creation of new folder System Policies in this AG.
3. Right-click the System Policies folder; select New, and choose between these types of policies: Server Policy, Public Store Policy, and Mailbox Store Policy.

For each type of policy, you can select one or more property pages. Make sure not to select more pages than you really want to configure; if you select a page without configuring it, then this page will be locked on the server where this policy is applied! The following section describes each policy in more detail.

Mailbox Store Policies

When creating this mailbox store policy, you must first give it a name; try to make it intuitive, for example "MBOX Store Standard." This policy can be used to preconfigure settings for a mailbox store by its four property pages:

- *General*—Configure the public store the mailboxes will use, the offline address list, whether all messages should be copied to a given mailbox, whether clients support S/MIME, and whether plain-text messages should be displayed in a fixed-size font.
- *Database*—Configure the schedule and interval for running the store maintenance.
- *Limits*—Configure storage limits for mailboxes (warnings, prohibit send, prohibit send and receive), when to send warning messages, deleting settings (how long to keep deleted items, and how long to keep deleted mailboxes), and whether the delete operation should wait until the backup process is done.
- *Full-Text Indexing*—Configure when to run updates of the index, and when to rebuild the index.

To apply this policy, right-click the new policy and select Add Mailbox Store. Then select all mailbox stores you want to apply this policy to, as shown in Figure 9.14.

Note: *If you first apply a policy, just as a test, and then remove the policy, all its preconfigured values will still be set; there is no way to undo a policy setting, except to manually restore these settings to their original values.*

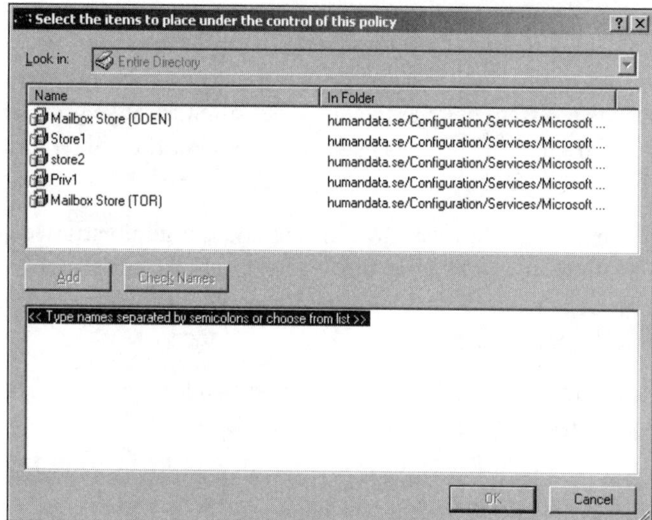

Figure 9.14
Add mailbox stores to the new policy.

Server Policies

Again, when creating this policy, you must start by giving it a name—for example, SRV Bridgehead. There is only one property page for this server policy—the General page. Use it to preconfigure the following: enabling subject logging and display, enabling message tracking, and determining how long log files should be kept, as shown in Figure 9.15.

As for the mailbox store policy, apply this server policy by right-clicking on it and selecting Add Server. Then select any server in the Exchange organization.

Public Store Policies

Start by giving this policy a name—for example, PUB Store Standard. This policy has five property pages:

- *General*—Configure whether these clients support S/MIME, and whether plain-text messages should be displayed in a fixed-size font.
- *Database*—Configure when to run the maintenance of the public store.
- *Replication*—Configure the default replication time for public folders, how many minutes the setting Always should be, and the size limit for replication messages.
- *Limits*—Configure these storage limits: Warning, Prohibit Send, and Prohibit Send and Receive; when the warning messages should be sent out; how long to store deleted items; whether the permanent delete operation should wait until the backup is done; and the default age limits for all folders in this public store. See Figure 9.16.
- *Full-Text Indexing*—Configure how often to run the update of the index, and when to run a rebuild of the index.

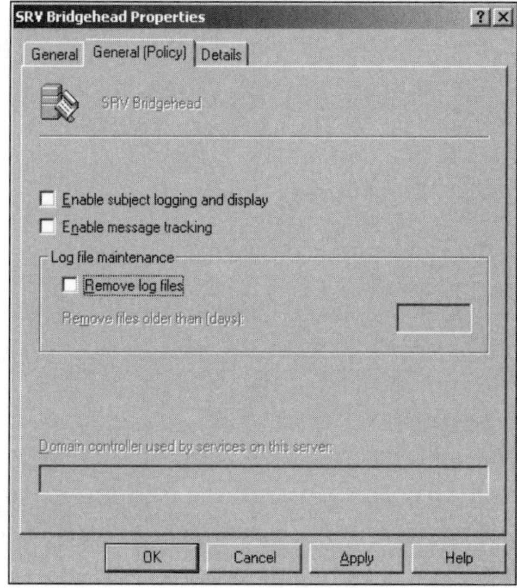

Figure 9.15
The General (Policy) property page.

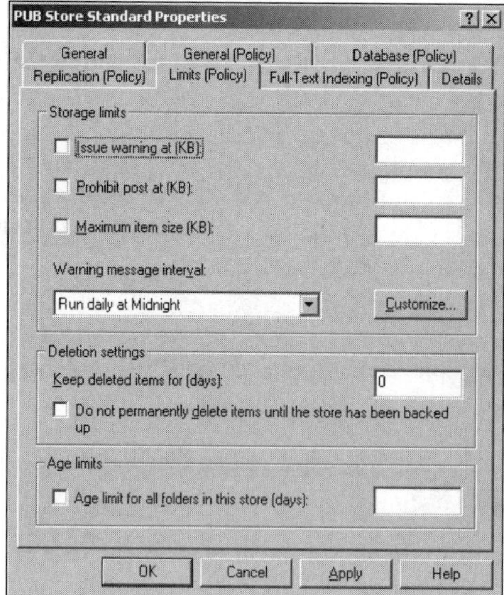

Figure 9.16
The Limits (Policy) property page for the public store policy.

To apply this policy, right-click it and select Add Public Store; select any public store in the Exchange organization.

Recipient Update Service

The Recipient Update Service, or RUS, is new for Exchange 2000. This service is responsible for updating email addresses and address lists. This RUS is a part of the System Attendant service and runs at regular intervals. It replaces the View Consistency Checker in Exchange 5.5 that was used for updating the Address Book Views. Responsibilities of the RUS include:

- Populating and updating address lists, global address lists, and custom address lists.
- Populating and updating AD with the email address of mail-enabled and mailbox-enabled objects, like users, contacts, public folders, and groups.
- Setting the homeMDB, homeMTA, and msExchHomeServerName attributes.
- Setting the LegacyExchangeDN, msExchMailboxGuid, and displayName attributes.
- Setting the ACL on the Exchange objects for permissions set by the Exchange Delegation Wizard.

The RUS service looks for the showInAddressBook attribute for those objects that control whether a name should be displayed in a list or not. By default the RUS service runs once every minute, but this can be modified if needed. You can also force the RUS service manually. Here's how:

1. Start the ESM, and navigate to the Recipients/Recipients Update Service.
2. In the right pane, you can see two RUS services; right-click on the RUS service with the domain name. Select Update Now, as shown in Figure 9.17.

There will be one RUS service for the enterprise configuration, and one more for each AD domain with Exchange 2000 servers. The enterprise RUS updates the email addresses of objects in the configuration partition of AD, such as SA, MTA, and IS system objects. Usually you are more interested in updating users' email addresses, address lists, etc; use the RUS domain for this purpose. Instead of updating, you can rebuild all object attributes that RUS is responsible for; however, this operation may take a long time to complete for a large organization. Use this option only when you are sure that the normal update operation will not be sufficient!

The RUS service (both the enterprise and the domain versions) may be configured to run on different intervals. Open the properties for the RUS object and change the Update Interval if needed; see Figure 9.18.

Note: *Be careful with setting the Update Interval to Never Run. This will prohibit the RUS service from operating, and this means that no updates of address lists or email addresses will occur.*

Extended Mailbox Properties

A mailbox in previous Exchange versions had about 100 attributes, such as first name, last name, email address, and phone number. A mailbox-enabled user object in Active Directory has more than 500 attributes; luckily enough, you don't need to see or manage most of them. By using the ADSI Edit tool, you can see all these objects. Here's how:

1. Start the ADSI Edit tool.
2. Expand the Domain **NC|DC=<domain>** and the OU container where the user is—for example, the Users container.

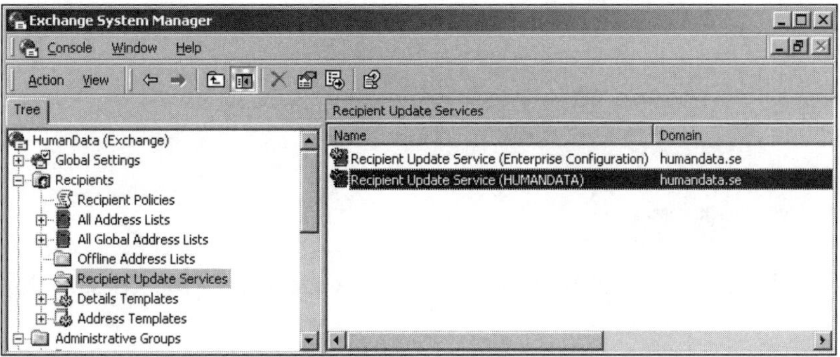

Figure 9.17
The Recipient Update Service objects.

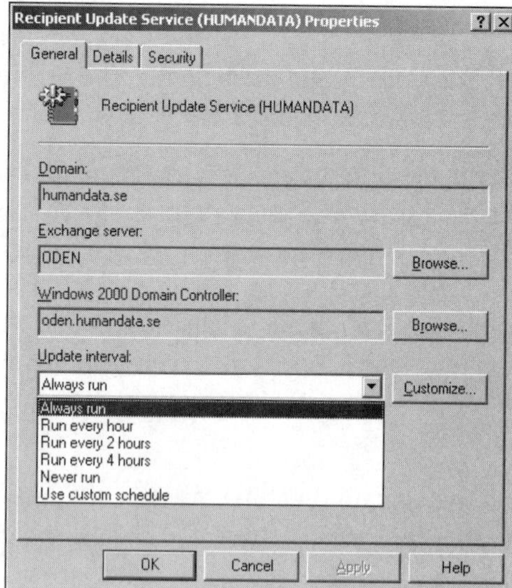

Figure 9.18
Properties for the RUS object.

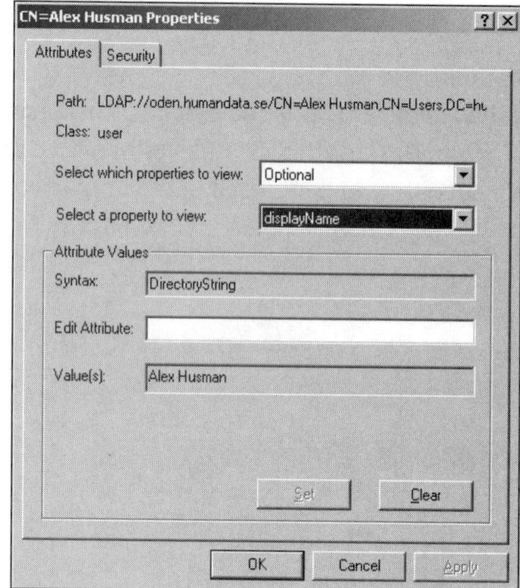

Figure 9.19
The attributes for a mailbox user.

3. Locate the user you want to inspect, right-click and select Properties, as shown in Figure 9.19.

4. Select which properties to view: Optional (default), Mandatory, or Both.

5. Select a property to view; be careful with changing any property, unless you are very certain of what you do! When you are done, click *OK* or Cancel to close this window.

If necessary, you can modify an attribute directly in ADSI Edit; when you have listed the attribute, as described in Step 5, type the new value in the Edit Attribute field and then click Set. However, you must be very careful with this type of modification! There is no spelling check or other control mechanism that will look at the value you add; using the ADSI Edit tool corresponds to running the Exchange 5.5 Admin.exe program in raw mode.

Some of the new mailbox attributes that you may configure as an administrator include:

- *Web page*—For example, a home page for a user.
- *IP phone*—The IP phone number to a user.
- *Exchange features*—For example, Instant Messaging.
- *Custom attributes*—There are now 15 such attributes instead of 10, as in previous versions.
- *Mailbox rights*—Are now changed to take advantage of the Windows 2000 security system; many more can be controlled now, compared to previous Exchange versions.
- *Mailbox store*—The name of the database where this user has his or her mailbox.
- *Delivery options*—Set the maximum number of recipients for outgoing messages.
- *Email addresses*—Can be automatically updated based on recipient policies.

As in previous Exchange releases, only a small subset of all attributes will be visible for the Outlook client. You can change what attributes they see, as shown in Figure 9.20, by changing the details template for the user object; see a previous section in this chapter to learn how to change a template.

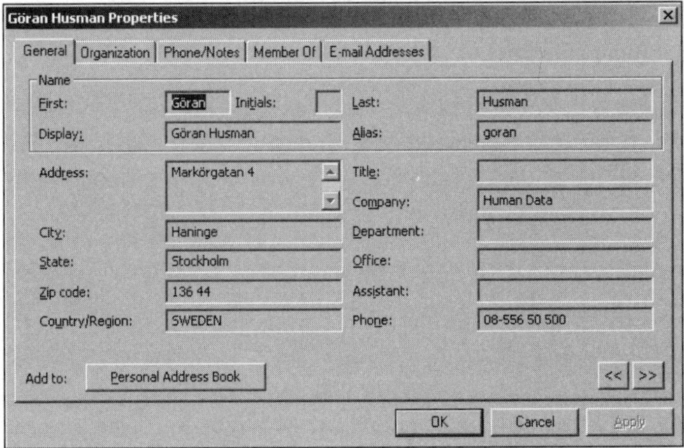

Figure 9.20
The default user template, as seen from Outlook.

New Ways of Creating Folders

In previous Exchange releases, the only way to create a public folder was with the Outlook client; for example, it was not possible to use the Exchange 5.5 Admin program, not even for deleting public folders. In Exchange 2000, there are several new ways to create and delete public folders:

- By MAPI (for example, the Outlook client)
- By the ESM tool
- By the Outlook Web Access client
- By IMAP4 (for example, Outlook Express)
- By the ExIFS (for example, the File Explorer)

The following sections provide descriptions of how to work with public folders using all of these methods.

Creating Public Folders with MAPI Clients

This is the same method as in all previous Exchange releases. For example, to create a public folder in Outlook 2000, navigate to the public folder tree (remember, MAPI clients like Outlook can only view the standard MAPI public folder tree), and select where the new folder will be created. Right-click on the parent folder—for example, All Public Folders—and select New Folder. Give the folder a name, select what the folder will contain, and select where to create the new folder.

Next, configure the permissions to this folder; by default, all users will have the right to create, modify, and delete items. This means that the permissions to this new folder are very open; make sure your users are aware of this, and that they understand how to modify them. Follow this step-by-step instruction to modify public folder permissions:

1. Use the Outlook client, and navigate to the public folder in question.
2. Right-click on the folder, and select Properties.
3. Go to the Permissions tab. These are the default settings. Default (i.e., the group Everyone) can read all items, and create, modify, and delete their own items. The owner (the user that created this folder) has all access. Anonymous is a Contributor, meaning that anyone can send a message to this folder.
4. Start by modifying the Default permission; select a role or set the checkbox manually if there is no matching role. To restrict the default permission, select the None role and uncheck the Folder Visible checkbox to make this folder invisible for people who cannot see its contents.
5. Add any new security group or user by clicking the Add button. It's always best to use groups before individual accounts, since this will make it easier to add or remove

users' permissions to this folder later on. Remember, if you give a distribution group permission to a public folder, this group will automatically (and silently) be converted to a security group.

6. Make sure the Anonymous group has the correct permissions; if not, change them. Click *OK* when finished.

Creating Public Folders with the ESM Tool

This feature is new for Exchange 2000; it makes it possible to use the admin tool ESM to create and delete public folders, both for MAPI and General Purpose (GP) types of folder trees. However, with the ESM tool it's only possible to create folders of Mail Items type; you cannot create folders of contact, calendar, or task types, for example. However, you can move and copy any type of folder, including contacts and calendar, without modifying their type; the ESM tool can also delete any type of folder. Follow these instructions to create a mail-item public folder:

1. Start the ESM tool; navigate to the Administrative Groups/Folders and the public folder tree where the new folder should be created.
2. Right-click on the parent folder for this new folder; select New|Public Folder.
3. Give the new folder a name, and fill in a description, if needed. Notice that by default the folders keep track of the individual read-status for users; if this is not okay, un-check the Maintain Per-User Read And Unread Information For This Folder checkbox.
4. Go to the Replication tab; by default this folder will only be stored on the public store in which this user is configured to save public folders. You can create a replica (a copy) of this folder to be stored in another server, for performance or for fault-tolerance reasons. To make an extra replica, click the Add button and select one or more servers.

   If you selected to replicate this folder, continue by selecting the replication schedule, using the Public Folder Replication Interval settings. Later, when the replication has started, you can open this folder again and see when the last replication occurred by checking the Last Replication Message Received field. Finally, you can change the priority of the replication messages; for example, you can set the priority to Urgent and have a routing group connector that transfers only urgent messages.
5. Go to the Limits tab; define the storage size limits for this folder—Issue Warning and Prohibit Post. You can also define the maximum item size that can be stored in this folder. Notice that no default limit is set!

   Use the deletion settings to configure if and how long to keep deleted items. You can also set the age limit for items in this folder; default is both of these settings configured to use the default public store settings. Click *OK* to complete the creation of this folder.

Creating Public Folders with the OWA Client

This is the first version of the Outlook Web Access client that can create both private folders and public folders, at least with XML and Web-DAV compliant Web browsers. This client can create exactly the same folder types as the ordinary Outlook 2000 client—for example, mail items, calendar, and contacts. Follow these instructions to create a public folder with the OWA client:

1. Start the OWA client; click Folders in the right pane and expand the public folder tree (if you receive an error, see the tip further down).
2. Right-click on a public folder; select New Folder.
3. Give the folder a name, select the type of folder, and choose where to create it. Click *OK* to create the folder.

Notice that there is no way to modify folder properties with the OWA client—for example, the permissions or replication settings. However, you can use the OWA client to move, rename, copy, and delete any folder for which you have the proper access permissions.

Tip: *If you receive an error message stating that the security settings of the browser prohibit the OWA client from displaying the public folders, you have found a bug. The problem is the NavBar.js file on the OWA server; there is a fix for this, released in Service Pack 1 for Exchange 2000 Server.*

Creating Public Folders with IMAP4 Clients

Using IMAP4 clients like Outlook Express, you can also create and delete public folders, in much the same way as the ordinary Outlook client. However, the IMAP4 client can only create folders of the type Mail Items. Follow these step-by-step instructions to create a public folder with an IMAP4 client like Outlook Express:

1. Start the Outlook Express client; select any of the public folders.
2. Right-click a folder, and select New Folder.
3. Give the folder a name, and select where this folder should be stored. It will automatically be synchronized to the IMAP4 client.

Again, there is no access to the properties of a public folder, like permission or replication settings. The only thing this IMAP4 client can do is to rename or delete it.

Creating Public Folders with ExIFS

ExIFS is a new feature for Exchange 2000, compared to previous Exchange releases. It makes it possible to work with all the Exchange stores as if they were just another file system. By default an M: drive will be mapped to the Exchange stores, but only on the Exchange server itself. To make this M: drive accessible to other clients, you must share it, just like any other disk or file system. The client must then map a network drive to this M: share, as described earlier in this chapter. Refer back to Figure 9.3.

For example, let's say we have a client that mapped N: to the ExIFS share on the Exchange server. This client can now use the File Explorer, command prompt, or any application to exploit the Exchange folders. Follow these step-by-step instructions to create a folder with the File Explorer, using the ExIFS:

1. Start File Explorer; navigate to the N: drive (mapped to the ExIFS share).
2. Select the folder where the new folder will be created.
3. Right-click in an empty area in the right pane (not on the folder!); select New|Folder.
4. By default this folder will be named New Folder; change it to its real name. (It may accidentally change its folder icon; press F5 to refresh the pane.)

The new folder looks and behaves like any other file directory—you can move, rename, copy, and delete the folder, as long as you have the proper access permissions. Using the ExIFS share, you can also change the access permissions for this folder; right-click on the folder, select Properties, and go to the Security tab, as shown in Figure 9.21.

Some behavior regarding how the permissions of an Exchange folder are presented by the File Explorer is unexpected: The user that created this folder has full control, but is shown as only having List Folder Content permission on the Security tab. However, if we click the Advanced button, we will find that the creator has full control of the directory and almost full control of its files. If we look at the permissions for this folder in the ESM tool or in Outlook, we will see that the creator has the Owner role, as expected. If you modify the permissions for this user to Full Control permission with the File Explorer, you will in fact decrease the permission for the creator to the role of Publishing Editor, and the Default is changed to the role of Reviewer, as shown in Figure 9.22. All of this is true for any Exchange folder, regardless of how it was created!

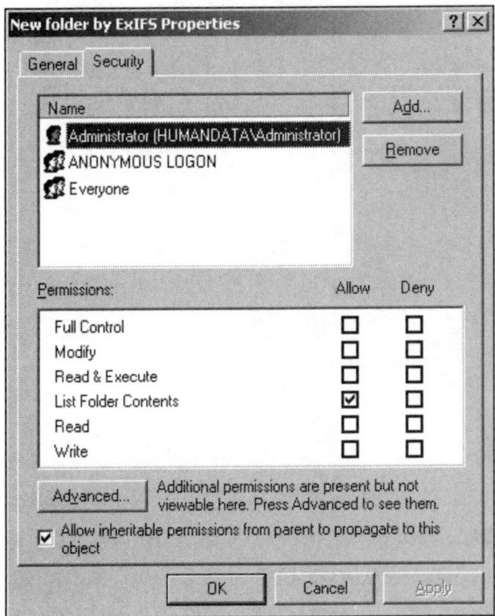

Figure 9.21
The Security tab for an Exchange folder viewed with the File Explorer.

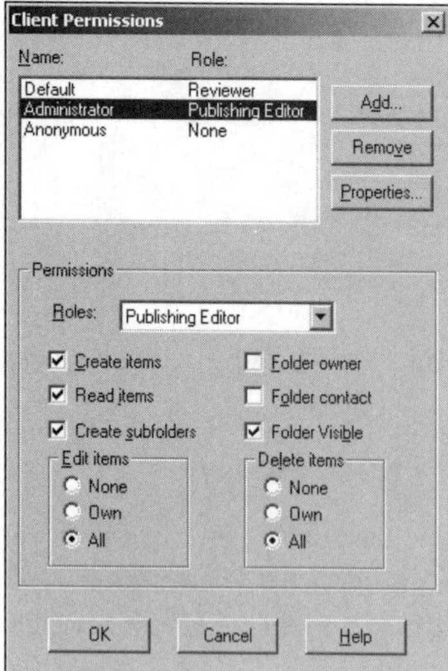

Figure 9.22
Viewing the modified permissions with the ESM tool.

One interesting thing that can be done only via the ExIFS interface is to set individual permissions on items; for example, if we have a folder with four messages, where Default has Write permissions on all messages, we can use the File Explorer and remove the Write permission for one of these messages by following these steps:

1. Start the File Explorer and navigate to the folder where these four messages are stored.
2. Right-click on the message item you want to change, select Properties, and go to the Security tab.
3. Notice that the security group Everyone (corresponding to the Default group in Outlook) has inherited permissions; clear the checkbox Allow Inheritable Permissions From Parent To Propagate To This Object, select to Copy the permissions, and remove both the Read and Read & Execute permissions, as shown in Figure 9.23. Then click *OK* to close this window.

The reason we have to remove the inherited permission for the group Everyone instead of just denying it is that all users belong to the group Everyone, and Deny permissions have priority over Allow permissions; it would affect all users, making this message invisible for all users.

New Ways of Accessing Folders

As described in earlier sections of this chapter, Exchange 2000 offers new ways of accessing the contents of public folders. For example, in Exchange 5.5 you could not view public folders of any type other than Mail Items (although it was possible to see some of the contents in a Contact folder). In Table 9.3, you will find a list of what the different clients can see and do with public folders in Exchange 2000.

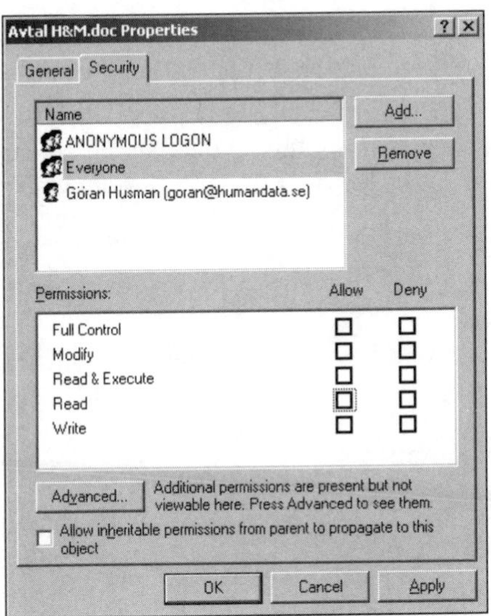

Figure 9.23
Changing the read permission to Deny for a message item.

As you can see in Table 9.3, the client that can view the most information is the Outlook Web Access client. The MAPI protocol is in fact limited by its design and will not be able to view general-purpose folders; this is also the reason why Microsoft tries so hard to develop the Web client, and to get away from MAPI as the client protocol. However, it will probably be several years before we see an Exchange release that doesn't have any support for MAPI, due to the large installed base of Outlook clients.

Create and Manage Users

This section describes how to create and manage mail-enabled and mailbox-enabled users in Exchange 2000. The step-by-step instructions in the following sections describe the most common tasks an administrator will perform. As you may recall from previous sections,

Table 9.3 Public folder access with different clients.

Client Type	Can View	Cannot View
Outlook	All MAPI public folders of all types	GP public folders
OWA	All MAPI and GP folders of all types but limited access to journals and task folders	-
IMAP4	All MAPI public folders of Mail Item type	GP public folders and any folder that is not of Mail Item type
POP3	-	No access to any type of public folders
ExIFS	All MAPI and GP folders, but with limited access to folders other than Mail Items	-
NNTP	Public folders of Mail Item type, shared as news folders	-

users in Exchange 2000 are created in the Active Directory and then mail- or mailbox-enabled. The primary tool for this type of work is the Active Directory Users and Computers snap-in for MMC. In special situations, it may be necessary to use the ADSI Edit tool to modify attributes not displayed in AD Users and Computers. When you need to update a lot of users, you may need the LDIFDE export and import tool; for more information on exporting and importing, see Chapter 5.

Creating a New User

Let's start by creating the user Thomas in our Windows 2000 AD domain; follow these instructions:

1. Start the Active Directory Users and Computers tool.
2. Locate the OU container where this user will be created—for example, the Support container.
3. Right-click on the Support container, select New|User.
4. Fill in the first and last names; notice that the Full Name is created automatically, but can be changed if necessary. Give the user a unique User Logon Name; notice that the User Logon Name (Pre-Windows 2000) field will be identical to the user logon name. Then click *Next*.
5. Add a password for this user; make sure to communicate this password to this user in a secure way. It is recommended that you request that the user change the password the first time he or she logs on. Then click *Next*.
6. Since Exchange 2000 is installed in this domain, you will be asked if this new user should have a mailbox created; usually you accept this. Fill in the Alias name for this mailbox; select the Exchange Server and an Administrative Group for this user. Finally, select the Mailbox Store where the mailbox will be created. Then click *Next*.
7. Finally, you see a summary of the selections you have chosen for this new user. If the information is okay, click Finish to complete this operation; otherwise click Back and make any modifications now.

Mailbox-Enabling an Existing User

That completes the creation of the new mailbox-enabled user. Let us now assume that we have an existing user named Henrik who doesn't have a mailbox. We need to mailbox-enable this user; follow these step-by-step instructions:

1. Start the Active Directory Users and Computers tool.
2. Locate the OU container where this user is stored.
3. Right-click on the user Henrik and select Exchange Tasks. You will have three options: to create a mailbox, to establish an email address, or to enable Instant Messaging. Select Create Mailbox, and then click *Next*.

4. Fill in the mailbox Alias, the name of the Exchange Server and Administrative Group, and the Mailbox Store that this user will belong to. Then click *Next*.
5. You will now see the Task In Progress, showing the creation process; when this is done, you see a Task Summary where the result will be given. If the creation was successfully completed, then click *Finish*. Otherwise click Back and correct the problem.

Mail-Enabling an Existing User

Now let's assume we have a consultant that we have hired for two months; he needs access to the Windows 2000 domain and its server and printer, but we don't want to give him an Exchange mailbox. A manager asks you to fix an email address to this consultant so people in the organization can send mail to him; since he has an email address at his company's mail system, we will only mail-enable his user account. Follow these step-by-step instructions:

1. Start the Active Directory Users and Computers tool.
2. Locate the OU container where this user is stored.
3. Right-click on the consultant's user account, and select Exchange Tasks. Select Establish E-mail Addresses and click *Next*.
4. Check that the suggested Alias name is okay; click on the Modify button, select what type of email address this is (usually SMTP Address), and fill in his email address. Select what administrative group this external address will belong to. When ready, click *Next*.
5. You will now see the Task In Progress, showing the creation process; when this is done, a Task Summary appears in which the result is shown. If the creation was successfully completed, click *Finish*. Otherwise click Back and correct the problem.

Managing a Mailbox Account

Our manager now asks us to check the configuration settings for *Thomas*, our Mailbox user *Thomas*; she want us to set his mailbox size limits to 100MB, with a warning at 95MB. We should also make sure he is not able to send messages over 2MB, with a maximum limit of 50 recipients. Since this is a single user, we must configure this mailbox directly; if our manager had wanted these settings for many users, we would have used mailbox store policies. Since we are modifying this mailbox, let's look at all available properties. Follow this step-by-step instruction to look at all settings for an Exchange mailbox-enabled user; only tabs that are Exchange related will be depicted:

1. Start the Active Directory Users and Computers tool. Click on the View menu and make sure the Advanced Features are selected; otherwise, we will not see all Exchange-related tabs.
2. Locate the user, then open the properties for this account.
3. *General* tab: Make sure all relevant fields are correctly filled in.

4. Address tab: Make sure all relevant fields are correctly filled in.
5. Account tab: Check the logon name, the logon hours, and what machine this user is allowed to log on to. Make sure the account options are okay, and that the settings for Account Expires are correct.
6. Profile tab: Check the profile path, the logon script, and home folder, if any.
7. Telephones tab: Make sure these phone numbers are correct; some of them will be displayed in the global address list.
8. Organization tab: Fill in the title, department, company name, and the manager's name.
9. Exchange Features tab: View the status of the Instant Messaging feature. It can be enabled if necessary, as shown in Figure 9.24.
10. Exchange Advanced tab: The Simple Display Name may be used if the mailbox name has non-ANSI characters, like Kanji. You may select to hide this mailbox from the GAL, but make sure that the user has created an Outlook profile first! All X.400 messages can be forced to normal priority, even if they were sent as high-priority messages by using this special checkbox, as shown in Figure 9.25.

    Click the Custom Attribute button to view and edit any of the 15 custom attributes available.

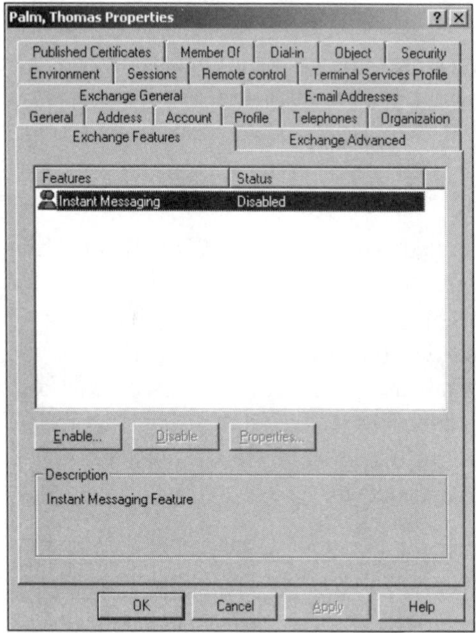

Figure 9.24
The Exchange Features tab.

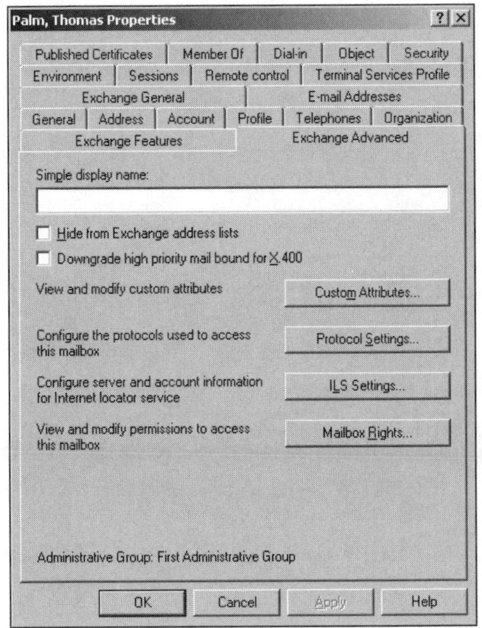

Figure 9.25
The Exchange Advanced tab.

Click the Protocol Settings button to enable or disable any of the client protocols HTTP, IMAP4, or POP3; by default they are enabled. You can also set the message encoding for these client protocols, like MIME, UUencode, and default character set. By default the settings of the corresponding protocol (under the server object) are used. The use of Rich Text Format can be enabled or disabled here.

Click the ILS Settings button to define what Internet Locator Service server this mailbox account will use, along with the ILS Account name used in that server. This is for Internet applications like Chat services and NetMeeting.

Click the Mailbox Rights button to define what users have access to this mailbox. By default only SELF is listed, as the mailbox owner.

In the bottom of this tab, you will find the name of the administrative group this user mailbox belongs to.

11. Exchange General tab: At the top of this tab the name of the Exchange Server/Storage Group/Mailbox Store is listed. Next comes the Alias name for this mailbox, as shown in Figure 9.26.

    Click the Delivery Restrictions button to set the maximum incoming and outgoing message size. Our manager wanted this user to have a limit of 2MB; use the Outgoing

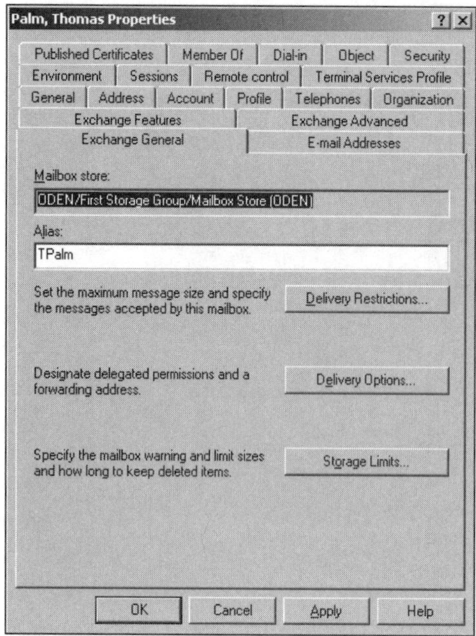

Figure 9.26
The Exchange General tab.

Message Size setting for that. We can restrict who can send messages to this mailbox account with the Message Restrictions option; this could be used for a CEO of a large company to restrict who can send messages to him or her.

Click the Delivery Options to set Send On Behalf Of permission to other users; for example, an assistant to a manager may need to send messages on behalf of the manager. The recipient will clearly see who sent this message, but the From field will list the manager's name. The Forwarding Address is used when you want messages sent to this user to be forwarded to another recipient—for example, if a user has left the company and wants all messages still coming to this old address forwarded to the new address. Our manager wanted this user to be limited to a maximum of 50 recipients. This is the place to set this limit; use the Maximum Recipients field for this.

Click the Storage Limits to set mailbox size limits; our manager told us to restrict this user's maximum mailbox size to 100MB with a warning at 95MB. Use the Issue Warning and the Prohibit Send At fields for this. Avoid setting the Prohibit Send And Receive At field, since this could create more support problems than it solves. For example, assume that this user receives mail regularly from another user, and we have this limit set to 110MB; when this user exceeds this limit, all mail to him will return with a Non-Delivery Report, stating that the message could not be delivered. The sender is surprised, since he has sent many messages to this user before, so he assumes there is a technical problem and therefore calls the support; you get the idea.

Generally, you should avoid setting individual limits for mailboxes; try to set default values on the mailbox store or try using mailbox policies. You can also set the time for how long deleted messages should be stored before being physically removed from the system; if you have the extra disk space, I recommend three to seven days for this setting.

12. E-Mail Addresses tab: Use this to manually add extra email addresses of any type this Exchange system supports—for example SMTP, X.400, and MS Mail. If you have more than one address of the same type, only one of them will by default be the primary address; for example, if you have two SMTP addresses, one of them will be the primary SMTP address. This address will be used as the default reply address on outgoing SMTP messages. At the bottom of this tab you can see a checkbox where you can control if this mailbox should be automatically updated by the recipient policy or not; this checkbox is set by default, as shown in Figure 9.27.
13. Environment tab: Used to configure Terminal Services startup environment.
14. Sessions tab: Used to configure Terminal Services timeout and reconnection settings.
15. Remote Control tab: Used to configure Terminal Services remote control settings.
16. Terminal Service Profile tab: Used to configure the Terminal Services user profile.
17. Published Certificates tab: Used to list the X.509 certificates issued to this user. These certificates are a sort of electronic passport, used to prove the identity of this user when sending electronically signed messages with S/MIME or PGP, as shown in Figure 9.28.

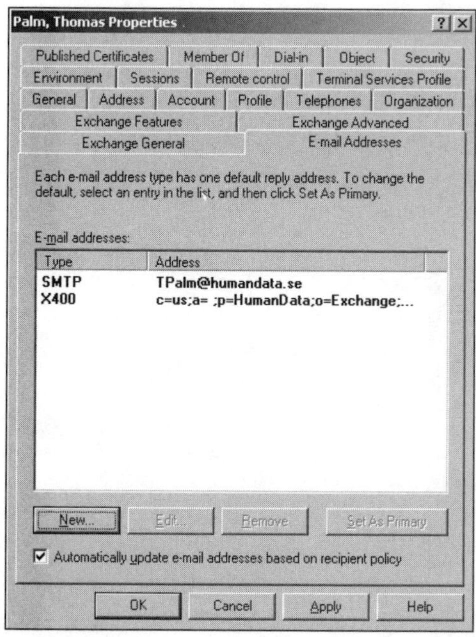

Figure 9.27
The E-mail Addresses tab.

18. Member Of tab: Lists the groups this user is a member of, both security and distribution groups. Click the Add button to add this user to a new group, or click the Remove button to remove this user from a group. Toward the bottom of this tab the Primary Group is listed, together with a button to change it; changing it is not necessary unless you have Macintosh clients or POSIX-compliant applications, as shown in Figure 9.29.

19. Dial-in tab: Used to set the remote access permissions for dial-in or VPN access.

20. Object tab: Lists information about the current and original Update Sequence Number (USN) for this user object, the X.500 version of Fully Qualified Domain Name for this user, and the dates when it was created and modified, as shown in Figure 9.30.

21. Security tab: Lists the users and groups that have any permission settings on this user object. This can be used to control who can modify this user, and who can just read its properties. By default the Account Operators, Administrators, Domain Admins, Enterprise Admins, and the SYSTEM will have administrative rights to all user objects.

Create and Manage Contacts

As for users, the standard administrative tool is the Active Directory Users and Computers snap-in; in special situations it may be necessary to use the tool ADSI Edit to modify attributes not displayed in AD Users and Computers. The LDIFDE tool may be used for

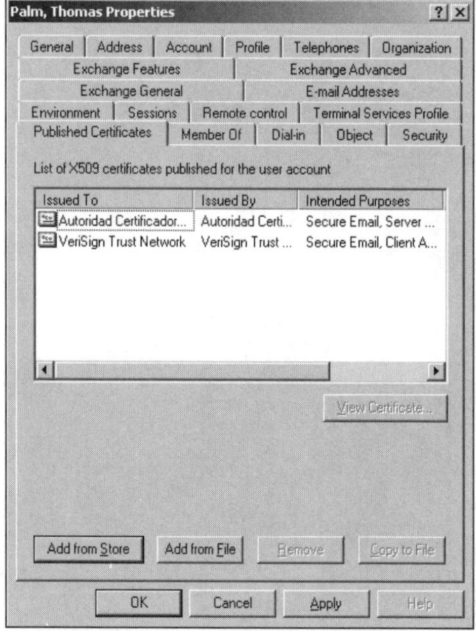

Figure 9.28
The Published Certificates tab.

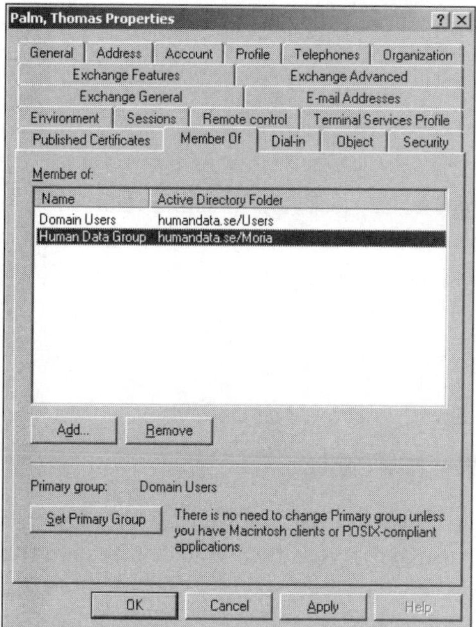

Figure 9.29
The Member Of tab.

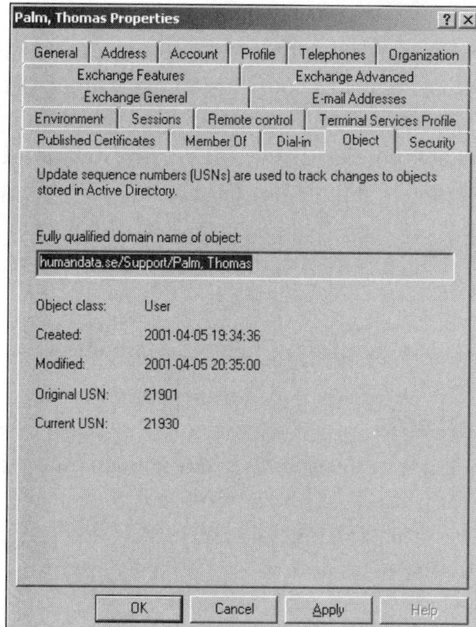

Figure 9.30
The Object tab.

bulk updating Contacts, as for the users. Note that the tool CSVDE cannot be used for creating Contact objects; you must use LDIFDE for this. You can find more information on these tools in Chapter 5.

Creating a New Contact

Let's continue our tour through typical day-to-day tasks for an administrator by creating a Contact. Your manager once again comes to you and asks you to add the name of an important customer to the global address list in Exchange. Do this by following these instructions:

1. Start the Active Directory Users and Computers tool.
2. Select the OU container where this new Contact will be created.
3. Right-click on the container and select New|Contact.
4. Fill in the name of this new Contact. Note that the Full Name is the name of the object in Active Directory, and the Display Name is the name displayed in the global address list. Click *Next* to continue.
5. The next question is whether you want to create an Exchange email address; the default is Yes, and we accept that. Look at the Alias, and adjust it if necessary; avoid spaces and special characters for the Alias field, since it's used as a default value when creating other fields later.

   Click the Modify button; select what email address type the Contact should have. The most common is SMTP, but could also, for example, be an MS Mail or Lotus Notes address. Next, fill in the complete email address to this Contact, then look at the Advanced tab; use it to configure any nondefault settings regarding message format. For example, if the Contacts mail client cannot handle HTML, you could change the format of the message body to Plain Text only, instead of both Plain Text and HTML, as is the default. Click *OK* to close this window, and then click *Next* to continue.
6. The last window is a summary of this operation; click Finish to complete it.

Managing a Mail-Enabled Contact

A Contact is not a security principal, meaning it cannot log on to our domain. And it doesn't have a mailbox in our Exchange 2000 organization—its only purpose is to be listed in the global address list, thus making it easy for our Exchange users to send messages to this Contact. Still, this type of object has a number of attributes. Let's take a closer look at all the available tabs and attributes:

1. Start the Active Directory Users and Computers tool. Click on the View menu, and make sure the Advanced Features are selected; otherwise, we will not see all the Exchange-related tabs.

2. Locate the Contact and open its properties; go to the *General* tab first.
3. *General* tab: This is the same tab as for a user object, described earlier; make sure its attributes are correct. The Other button for the Telephone Number field and the Web Page makes it possible to add more phone numbers and Web pages, or any text you like; however, none of this other information will be displayed for the Outlook client.
4. *Address* tab: (Identical to the User object) Used for address information to this contact. Information will be displayed to the Outlook client.
5. *Telephone* tab: (Identical to the User object) Used to note phone and fax numbers, including notes about this contact. This information is displayed to the Outlook client. 9
6. *Organization* tab: (Identical to the User object) Used to note the title, department, company name, and the manager. The Direct Reports field automatically lists all names that have noted this contact as their manager; this information is displayed to the Outlook client.
7. *Member Of* tab: (Identical to the User object) Lists all groups this contact is a member of. Use the Add button to make this contact a member of a new group. You can actually make a contact a member of a security group, but this will not be meaningful unless this group is mail-enabled. This information is displayed to the Outlook client.
8. *Object* tab: (Identical to the User object) Displays the current and original USN number, object class (Contact), and the date and time this object was created and last modified. This information is not displayed to the Outlook client.
9. *Security* tab: (Identical to the User object) Lists the security principal objects that have administrative permissions on this contact object. Not displayed to the Outlook client.
10. *Exchange General* tab: Lists the Alias name and the email address for this Contact. Also defines the incoming message size limits. The default is the most restricted value on the virtual SMTP server and its *Messages* tab, and the global setting Message Delivery, and its *Default* tab. Both of these values are set to No Limit by default, as shown in Figure 9.31.

    Use this tab to restrict who can send messages to this contact; select between From Everyone (the default), or Only From a given user. You may also say that only the listed users are prohibited from sending a message to this contact by using the From Everyone Except setting.
11. *E-mail Addresses* tab: (Identical to the User object) It may seem strange at first, but the Contact object can in fact have several email addresses, besides its true destination address. This could be used to make this contact reachable from other mail systems that don't send SMTP messages directly, or that don't want to add this contact manually to their mail system, as shown in Figure 9.32.

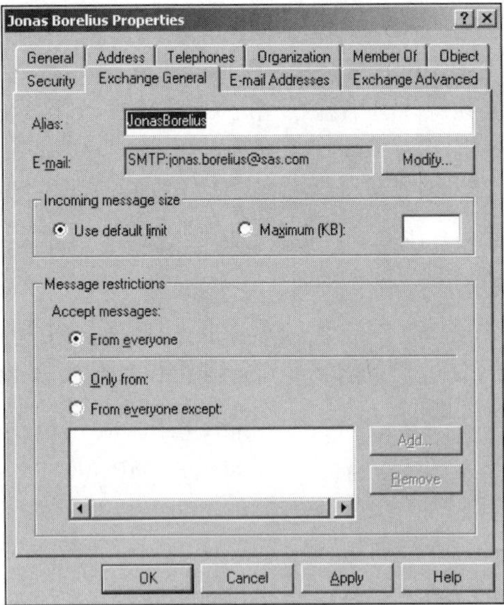

Figure 9.31
The Exchange General tab for a Contact.

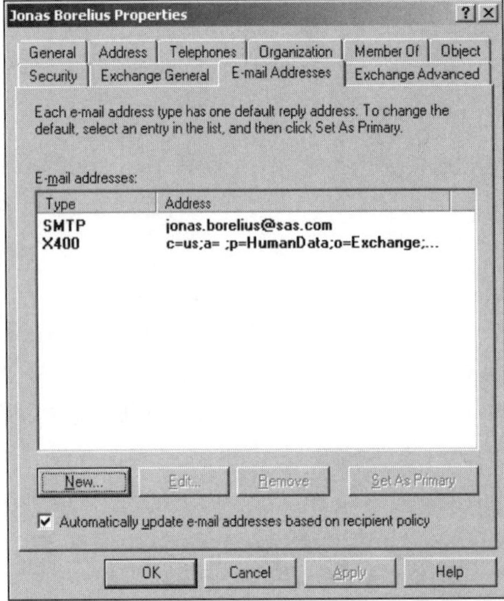

Figure 9.32
The E-mail Addresses tab for a Contact.

For example, assume that we have an MS Mail system coexisting with the Exchange 2000 system; all users on the MS Mail side must also be able to send messages to this contact, but they will only use SMTP addresses to reach names in the global address list (where this contact resides); if we add an MS Mail address to this contact object, it can be replicated by the Dirsync process to the MS Mail side, thus making its name show up in the MS Mail global address list. When an MS Mail user sends a message to this contact, it will first be transferred to the Exchange server, and then to the final destination.

By default, this Contact object will be automatically updated by recipient policies; this can be deselected by clearing the Automatically Update E-mail Addresses Based On Recipient Policy checkbox.

12. *Exchange Advanced* tab: Use the Simple Display Name field to add a name for contacts created with non-ANSI characters, like Kanji. You can hide this contact from the address lists in Exchange by setting the Hide checkbox, as shown in Figure 9.33.

    The Use MAPI Rich Text Format checkbox is unchecked by default. If you are sure that this contact is using a rich text format compliant client, like Outlook 2000 or Outlook Express, set this checkbox. If you are mistaken, this user will receive an attachment with every message, called Winmail.dat or application/ms-tnef, which contains the format description of this message. If you are not sure what client this Contact is using, let this checkbox remain unchecked. Note: This setting will override any per-domain Internet Mail Format setting you may have configured!

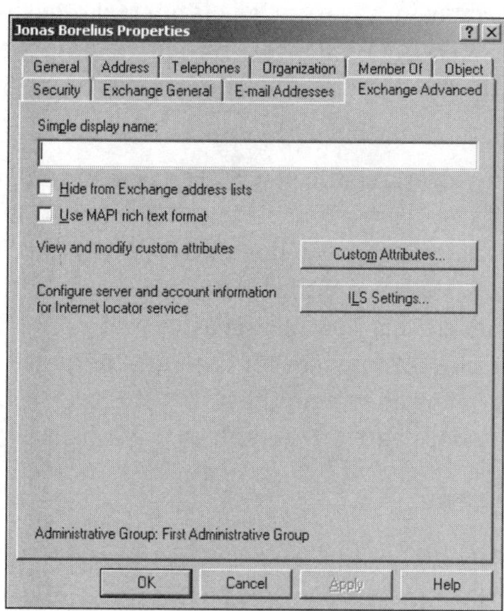

Figure 9.33
The Exchange Advanced tab for a Contact.

Use the Custom Attributes button to add extra information about this Contact—15 different custom attributes are available. They will be displayed to the Outlook client.

Use the ILS Settings button to define what ILS server and what ILS account this Contact uses; these settings are used for Internet applications like NetMeeting and Chat systems.

Create and Manage Groups

When talking about Exchange, we are most interested in mail-enabled groups. As you may recall, there are two types of groups: security groups and distribution groups. The security group can be given access permissions to objects in the AD domain, like files or directories, but also to public folders. The distribution group is only used for mail purposes. Since Exchange 2000 is integrated with Windows 2000 and its Active Directory, we can create a security group both for the purpose of setting access permissions and to be used as a mail group. Remember that if a distribution group is used for setting access permissions on public folders, it will automatically be converted to a security group.

Besides these two types, groups can also have different scopes:

- *Global Groups*—Can be used in any domain in the forest. Can be converted to universal groups, if Windows 2000 is in native mode and it doesn't contain any other global groups. Its members are *not* replicated to the global catalog!
- *Domain Local Groups*—Can only be used in the domain where they are created. Its members are *not* replicated to the global catalog!
- *Universal Groups*—Can be used in any domain, and its members *are* replicated to the global catalog. However, if the AD domain is in mixed mode, only distribution groups may be a universal group; when the domain is converted to native mode security groups can also be a universal group.

For more information about groups and scopes, see Chapter 5. When creating a group you must decide what type of group and scope is required. If the forest consists of one single AD domain, it doesn't matter what type of group you use, since both types, including their members, will be visible everywhere. However, if the forest consists of multiple domains, it is very important that you understand how mail-enabled groups work, in relation to Exchange 2000. The most flexible group scope for Exchange purposes is the Universal, since its members are visible in any domain in the forest. However, you must take into account the impact Universal groups have on replication traffic before implementing this group in a large organization.

Creating a Mail-Enabled Group

Your dear manager comes to you again; this time she wants you to create a group of mail-enabled users that will work on a new project called *Zero-Gravitation*. She also gives you a list of the members that should be included in this new group. Follow these instructions to create a mail-enabled distribution group:

1. Start the Active Directory Users and Computers tool.
2. Select the OU container where this new distribution group will be created.
3. Right-click on the container and select New|Group.
4. Give the group a name, for example *Zero-Gravitation*; make sure both the AD name and the pre-Windows 2000 name are identical. Make this a distribution group with Universal scope, then click *Next*.
5. Create the Exchange email address; the Alias field will by default be used as the first part of the email address. Make sure this new group belongs to the right administrative group, then click *Next*.
6. The last page is a summary of your selections; click Finish to create this group, or Back to change any errors.

Now we have a new universal distribution group; however, it doesn't have any members yet. You can add members several different ways:

- Open each user's properties, and add to this group by using the *Member Of* tab. This method is used to add only one or two members, not many.
- In the AD Users And Computers, right-click on User Name, and select Add Members To A Group. This method can be used while several names are selected; it's a fast way to add many names simultaneously.
- Open the group's properties, and add the members by using the *Members* tab. This will be demonstrated in the next section.

Managing a Group

Like Users and Contacts, several property pages are used to configure this group and its behavior. Below is a description of each page:

1. Start the Active Directory Users and Computers tool and click on the View menu. Make sure the Advanced Features are selected; otherwise, you will not see all the Exchange-related tabs.
2. Locate the Group, and open its properties; go to the General tab first.
3. *General* tab: You can change the pre-Windows 2000 group name, if necessary. You can also add a description, although it will not be displayed to the Outlook client. The automatically generated email address is listed here; change it if needed. You can also see what type of group it is, and the scope. Note that we cannot change the group type because it's a universal distribution group created in an AD domain of mixed

mode, and this mode doesn't allow security groups in universal mode! Use the Notes pane to write comments; observe that these notes will be displayed to the Outlook client.

4. *Members* tab: Click Add or Remove to modify the members of this list. Most types of AD objects can be a member of any group in Windows 2000; however, since this will be a group for mailing purposes, it should contain only mailbox- or mail-enabled users, contact, groups, or public folders. If you send a message to a group with objects that are not mail-enabled, these objects will result in non-delivery reports returned to the sender.
5. *Member Of* tab: Lists all groups that this group is a member of.
6. *Managed By* tab, as shown in Figure 9.34. Lists the manager of this group, if any. Also displays the address, phone, and fax number for this manager. Parts of this information will be displayed to the Outlook client, like the name, phone number, and office. In previous Exchange releases the mailbox account defined as *Manager* could use the Outlook client to modify the membership of a distribution list. Unlike previous Exchange releases, the m*anager* of a distribution group will not have the permission to modify its membership from the Outlook client! This is now controlled by the *Security* tab; see below.
7. *Object* tab: (Identical to the User object) Displays the current and original USN number, the object class, and the date and time this object was created and last modified.
8. *Security* tab: (Identical to the User object) Lists the security principal object that has access permissions on this group. Any user or group that has the access permissions Read, Write, and Add/Remove Self As Member has the rights needed to modify this

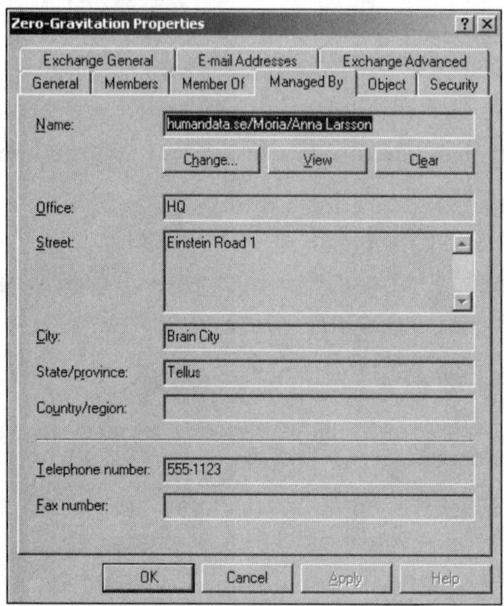

Figure 9.34
The Managed By tab for a group.

list from an Outlook client; as shown in Figure 9.35, where the user Anna Larsson has been given these permissions.

9. *Exchange General* tab: Defines the Alias and Display Name; You can set a maximum message size (default is No Limit), and you can restrict who can send messages to this group. This last feature can be very handy sometimes; for example, if you have a group where only the members of this group should be allowed to send messages to this group, change this setting to Only From and add the name of this group. Large groups are also important to restrict; if you have a group with 50,000 users, you probably don't want everyone to be able to send messages to this group, as shown in Figure 9.36.

   Microsoft has a recommendation regarding the size of groups: Due to performance reasons, you should avoid creating groups with more than 5,000 members. Instead, create several smaller groups, each with fewer than 5,000 members, and then create one group that consists of all the smaller groups.

10. *E-mail Address* tab: (Identical to the User object) Lists the email addresses for this group; you can add new addresses, and edit or remove existing email addresses, to this list. If there is more than one address of the same type, one of them must be the primary address, used as the default reply address for outgoing messages.

11. *Exchange Advanced* tab: You can set a simple display name if the original name is created with non-ANSI characters, like Kanji. The Expansion Server field is used to define what Exchange 2000 server should expand this group. The default is Any Server In The Organization, which means that the home server for a mailbox user will by

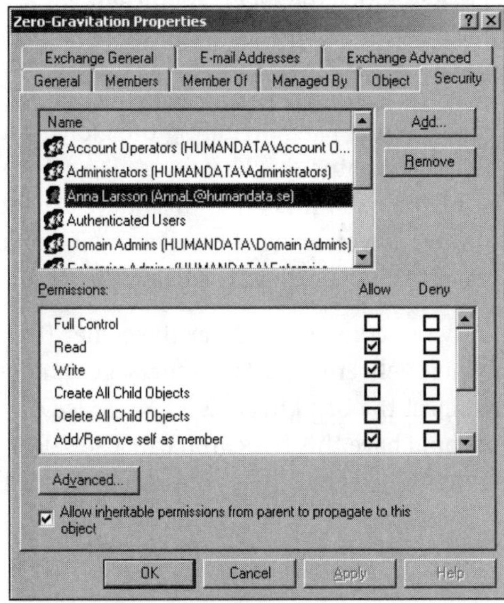

Figure 9.35
The Security tab for a group.

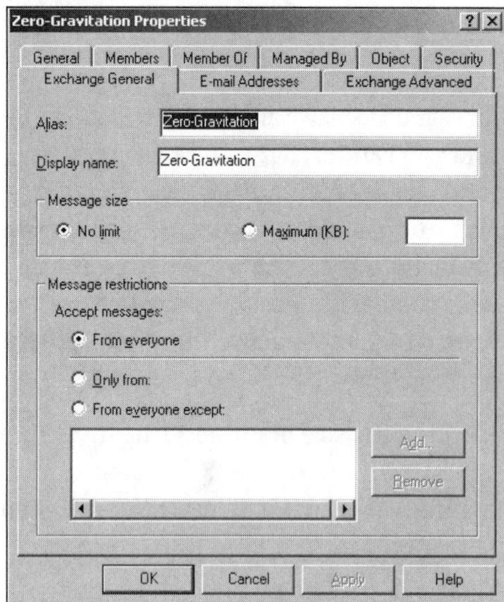

Figure 9.36
The Exchange General tab for a group.

default expand this group, and this is usually satisfactory. However, if the Exchange organization has several large groups that are heavily used, it may be smarter to send all messages to these groups to one particular Exchange server that doesn't have any users or other demanding responsibilities. Or, if the forest has multiple domains and your group has the scope Global or Domain Local, its membership will not be available to AD domains outside where it was created, since the membership will not be replicated to the global catalog. In both these situations, the solution would be to define a given expansion server, as shown in Figure 9.37.

You can hide this group from Exchange address lists, including the global address list. The Send Out-Of-Office Messages To Originator checkbox is used to control how to handle out-of-office messages that members of this group may have activated; if someone sends a message to this group, do you want to receive any individual member's out-of-office message? If yes, set this checkbox. The default is off.

The Send Delivery Reports To Group Owner controls whether the owner (the Manager) of this group should receive any non-delivery reports if a message can not be delivered to this group. Default is on. Select the Send Reports To Message Originator instead if the sender of this message should have this NDR. You can also select not to send any NDRs in case of delivery problems; however, this is not recommended.

The Custom Attributes button lets you modify any of the 15 available custom attributes for this group.

At the bottom of this page is the name of the administrative group that this group belongs to.

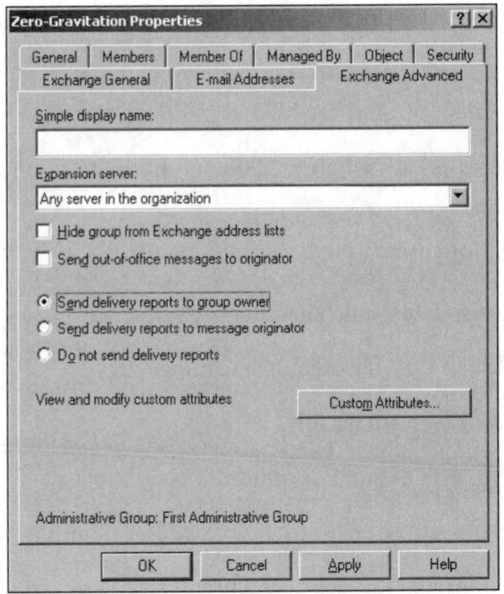

Figure 9.37
The Exchange Advanced tab for a group.

Summary

This is a list of the more important features and keywords mentioned in this chapter. Use it as a reminder and to make sure you have understood the most important things:

- There are six types of mail recipients in Exchange 2000:
  - *Mailbox-enabled user*—A security principal with an Exchange mailbox.
  - *Mail-enabled users*—A security principal with an external email address (no mailbox).
  - *Mail-enabled contact*—Only an external email address that will be listed in the GAL.
  - *Mail-enabled distribution group*—Contains (normally) other mail-enabled objects; corresponds to distribution lists in Exchange 5.5.
  - *Mail-enabled security group*—A security principal; usually contains other mail-enabled objects.
- *Mail-enabled Public Folder*: Is default hidden from the GAL. Both MAPI and GP folders may be mail- *Mail-enabled Public Folder* enabled.
- The HomeMDB attribute is set for mailbox-enabled users; remove this and Exchange thinks that this user doesn't have a mail server.
- Don't forget that mail-enabled security groups are used both for setting access permissions and for mail purposes.
- Distribution groups will be automatically and silently converted to security groups if they are used to control access to public folders.

- MAPI public folders in mixed mode are default mail-enabled; in native mode, they are by default not mail-enabled.
- General-purpose public folders are always not mail-enabled, regardless of mode.
- There are many new and enhanced features in Exchange 2000 compared to previous versions. These features include:
  - Multiple public folder trees—MAPI and GP types.
  - Multiple global address lists—perfect for hosting several companies.
  - Smarter address lists that can be hidden for all except a specific group.
  - Multiple email addresses will be created automatically.
  - Multiple languages preinstalled for Details templates and Address templates.
  - System policies to control global settings of servers, mailbox stores, and public stores.
  - The Recipient Update Service, which forces updates of the email addresses and other settings.
  - Extended mailbox properties.
  - New ways of creating mailbox and public folders: by MAPI, ESM, OWA, IMAP4, and ExIFS.
  - New ways of accessing mailbox and public folders: by MAPI, ESM, OWA, IMAP4, ExIFS, and NNTP.
- Default address lists are: All Contacts, all groups, all users, and public folders.
- Access permission needed to view an address list is: Open Address List and List Content.
- Use the AD Users and Computers tool to create and manage users, contacts, and public folders.
- Use the ADSI Edit tool for updating attributes not listed with AD Users and Computers; this tool is similar to running Exchange 5.5 Admin in raw mode.
- Use LDIFDE for bulk updates to users, contacts, and groups.
- Avoid sending MAPI Rich Text Formats to external users, unless you are sure they have a mail client that understands this format. Otherwise they will receive the file attachment Winmail.dat with every message, but they will not see the contents of the message itself.
- Use Universal Groups if there are multiple domains in the Windows 2000 forest.
- Membership of Global Groups and Domain Local groups are not replicated to the global catalog; this must be solved in a multidomain forest.

- Using an Expansion-server for a group will solve the problem above; this is also a solution when the organization has many large groups that are used heavily.
- Restrict who can send messages to large or sensitive groups; for example, set a restriction that allows only group members to send messages to this group.
- Avoid creating groups with more than 5,000 members; if you need larger groups, create several smaller groups and then make one group that consists of these smaller groups.

Chapter 10

Installing Exchange 2000

It's finally time to install your Exchange environment. So far, we have covered the pre-requisites, regarding important concepts, features, and planning. When I first began writing this book, I first thought of placing this chapter very early on; however, since the Exchange 2000 system together with the Active Directory domains are a bit unforgiving, for example regarding AD schema expansion, I came to the conclusion that it was probably better to give you the basic facts that you would need before you began your installation.

In previous Exchange releases, it was easy to set up a test environment, play with it, and then replace it with a production installation. This was possible, due to the fact that Exchange then had its own directory, the DIR.EDB database, controlled by the Directory Service, or DS. No irreversible modifications of the NT user account database were made during the installation of the Exchange server. As you are aware, this is not the case anymore. The Exchange 2000 server and Active Directory server are like the left and right halves of the brain; you need both of them to be fully functional, and things you do to one half will affect the other. When installing the first Exchange 2000 server, you need to make irreversible modifications to the Active Directory database; so if you want to have a test environment for Exchange 2000, you must also set up a test AD domain, or several, to mimic the production environment. Under no circumstances should you start playing with the Windows 2000 production environment, unless you are an experienced Exchange 2000 administrator.

So what important concepts have we covered so far? Let's make a list:

- The Storage Architecture, with multiple storage groups and stores
- The Routing Architecture, with multiple routing groups and the routing engine
- The SMTP protocol, how it works and how to troubleshoot it
- The Active Directory, its relationship to Exchange 2000, and features like global catalog
- The DNS server, how it works, and how to troubleshoot it
- How to plan the Exchange 2000 organization

- How to migrate from other mail systems
- How to create and manage users and other types of recipients

In the following sections we will discuss these features and concepts, and how they affect the planning and installation of the new Exchange 2000 system.

Before You Install

The old saying "Think before you act" is especially true when it comes to Exchange 2000 installations. This will probably be one of the most business-critical systems in your organization, so we don't want it to be unreliable or suboptimized; we want to install the best messaging system this organization has ever seen, right? Because of the many features and possibilities of Exchange 2000 together with Active Directory, we must start off by planning this messaging system.

Planning the Installation

Chapter 7 covers Exchange planning in detail, but let's summarize the information you should know by now, before the actual installation starts:

- *The objectives with this Exchange installation*—The users' needs today (for example, messaging, calendar, and public folders); how the system will be used one year from now; what type of messaging clients will be used; migration plans; Internet connections; estimated traffic volumes.
- *A clear picture of the current environment*—The number of users, their locations, and current client computer hardware; the LAN and WAN connections, types of network protocols used today; bandwidth usage; current server configurations; current mail system; Internet connections and ISP; applications that use the current mail system.
- *The future name standard*—How to name user accounts, display names, email addresses, public folders, groups, servers, exchange organizations, routing groups, administrative groups, storage groups, and stores, just to mention a few names.
- *The future server layout*—The number of servers needed; where they will be installed; their configuration; the number of stores and storage groups; the number of users, groups, and public folder trees; permission to create top-level public folders; what other applications will run on these servers; if there are any special roles besides being an Exchange server (like a domain controller, responsible for Internet connections, gateway to old systems, or an Outlook Web access server).
- *Backup routines*—How the servers will be backed up, how often, what media, how long to store backup sets, where to store backup sets; how to perform a restore; whether there are any special restore servers?
- *Migration plans*—If a migration is needed, how it will be performed, when to start the migration, when it will be finished, what users should be migrated and when, how to set up the coexistence between Exchange 2000 and the current mail system.

- *The integration with Active Directory*—Who is the schema master? Where will the domain controllers and global catalog servers reside? How many AD domains? How long will it take to replicate AD information to all domain controllers in the forest? Do you have a Dynamic DNS server installed?
- *The administrative needs*—How many administrative groups? What Exchange servers should belong to what AG? Will there be different types of administrative access, like full and view-only administrators?

It's possible to change most of these configurations and settings even after the installations, but some will be very time consuming or even impossible to modify without a new installation. The things that must be correct from the start include:

- The Exchange 2000 organization name
- The names of the Exchange server
- The names of the Windows 2000 domain controllers

Most other things can be reconfigured after the installation; however, the more users have started to work with the new system, the harder it will be to modify things like:

- *User name standard*—Full name, display names, email addresses
- *Group name standard*—Full names, display names, email addresses
- *Public folder name standard*—Display names, email addresses
- *Public folder structure*—The tree layout and permission to create top-level folders
- *Network bandwidth*—Slow or overloaded connections to remote office sites and Internet connections

If at least those things are taken care of, you will be in a much better position if something needs to be reconfigured or restructured. However, as always it's much cheaper to do the installation correctly in the first place. Any modifications that need to be done on a production environment, even if it's not complete yet, will probably result in irritating breaks and delays in the message system.

Prepare for the Exchange Installation

Before the first Exchange server in the organization is installed, there are some steps that must be taken: The Windows 2000 forest must be prepared, the access permissions must be set, and the server itself needs to be configured in a proper way before the Exchange server software can be installed.

Prepare the Windows 2000 Forest

The schema partition of the Active Directory describes what objects can be stored, and their properties. When installing Exchange 2000, a large number of new attributes need to be added for the existing objects; also, the configuration partition needs to be modified.

A totally new Exchange installation will result in 1,959 modifications to the Active Directory. This will also force a rebuild of the global catalog server, resulting in a network-intensive replication phase; this is the reason why you should avoid performing this update of the Active Directory during working hours and, if possible, before the complete Windows 2000 system is up and running.

The AD schema partition is extended by a set of commands contained in 10 LDIF Files (LDF), located in the \Setup\I386\Exchange directory on the Exchange 2000 server CD; these files are named SCHEMA0.LDF, and SCHEMA1.LDF through SCHEMA9.LDF. The Setup.exe program uses the LDIFDE tool (stored in the C:\Winnt\system32 directory) to read these files; an example of the update commands for adding the ms-Exch-Home-Server-Name attribute looks like this:

```
dn: CN=ms-Exch-Home-Server-Name,<SchemaContainerDN>
changetype: add
adminDescription: ms-Exch-Home-Server-Name
adminDisplayName: ms-Exch-Home-Server-Name
attributeID: 1.2.840.113556.1.4.7000.102.47
attributeSyntax: 2.5.5.12
isMemberOfPartialAttributeSet: TRUE
isSingleValued: TRUE
lDAPDisplayName: msExchHomeServerName
name: ms-Exch-Home-Server-Name
oMSyntax: 64
objectCategory: CN=Attribute-Schema,<SchemaContainerDN>
objectClass: attributeSchema
schemaIdGuid:: DvOEopOwOhGqBgDAT47t2A==
searchFlags: 0
```

Actually, just installing the Active Directory Connector, necessary when running an Exchange 5.5 server in a Windows 2000 domain, will result in 435 updates to the AD schema partition; if you install an Exchange 2000 organization later, it will perform the remaining 1,524 schema updates.

You may recall that there is one single AD schema master in a Windows 2000 forest; if possible, you should perform the schema update directly on this server, although it's possible to make this update on any Windows 2000 domain controller. However, then you must wait until this information is first replicated to the schema master before continuing with the installation of Exchange 2000. Only an administrator who is a member of the Schema Admins security group is allowed to perform any updates of the AD schema, as shown in Figure 10.1.

Besides this access permission, the administrator also needs to be a member of the Enterprise Admins group; also, administrative rights are needed on the local server on which the schema preparation is performed. There are two ways to perform this update:

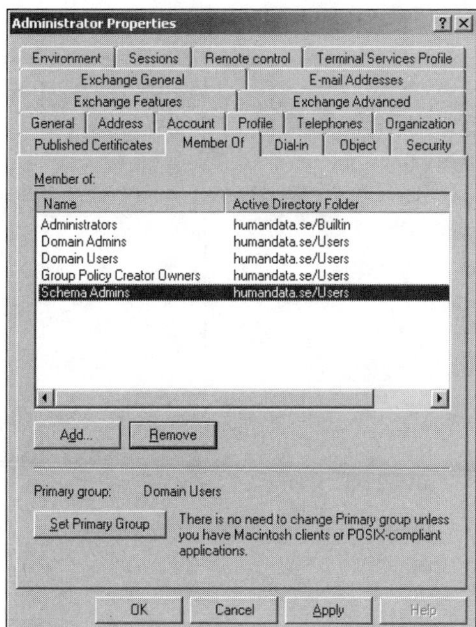

Figure 10.1
Membership in the Schema Admins security group is necessary to upgrade the schema.

- Run the schema update only.
- Run a standard setup of Exchange 2000.

The first method is performed by running two commands—**ForestPrep** and **DomainPrep**. The second is a standard setup procedure. The next sections describe these methods more closely.

Running the ForestPrep Command

The first method is preferred, since you can perform this update at any time, without the need to install a complete Exchange server. In a large Windows 2000 organization, you may even have special administrators responsible for schema updates; only they have the permissions necessary to perform this type of update, not the Exchange administrator. Then this method is the only solution that works. When performing a schema update, you will also create the Exchange 2000 organization; make sure you have the correct organization name before running this update, since it's not possible to change it later on!

Note: *When you put the Exchange 2000 Server CD in the CD-ROM, it automatically starts a menu where you can select to set up Exchange, Instant Messaging, or the Active Directory Connector, as shown in Figure 10.2. This menu cannot be used to run the* ***ForestPrep*** *or* ***DomainPrep*** *commands; instead, follow the instructions below!*

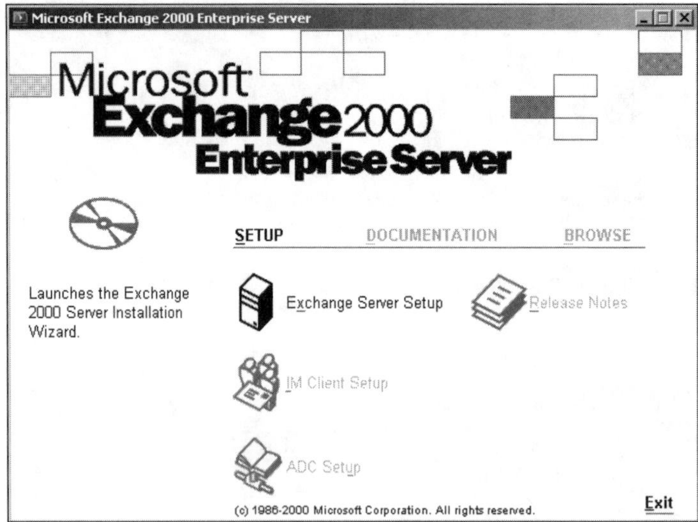

Figure 10.2
The Exchange 2000 installation menu.

Use the **ForestPrep** command to perform an update of the schema and create a new Exchange organization by following these instructions:

1. Log on locally to the AD schema master server (usually the first installed server in the forest) as an administrator with the proper access permissions. If you can't use the schema master directly, use any domain controller; however, you must wait for the replication of all AD updates to be completed before continuing with the **DomainPrep** (see below).
2. Use the Exchange server Setup.exe program, located on the CD. On the server, open the Start|Run command; in the Open field, type *"Drive:\Setup\I386\Setup.exe /forestprep"*, where *Drive* is the CD-ROM drive, and click *OK*, as shown in Figure 10.3.
3. This will start the Exchange 2000 Installation Wizard; click *Next* to continue.
4. Next is the *End-User License Agreement*, or the *EULA*. Read it and if you accept it (do you really have a choice?), select *I Agree* and click *Next*, as shown in Figure 10.4.

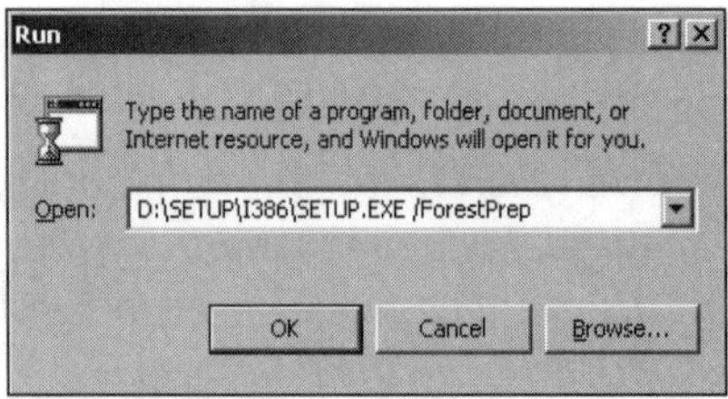

Figure 10.3
Running the **ForestPrep** command.

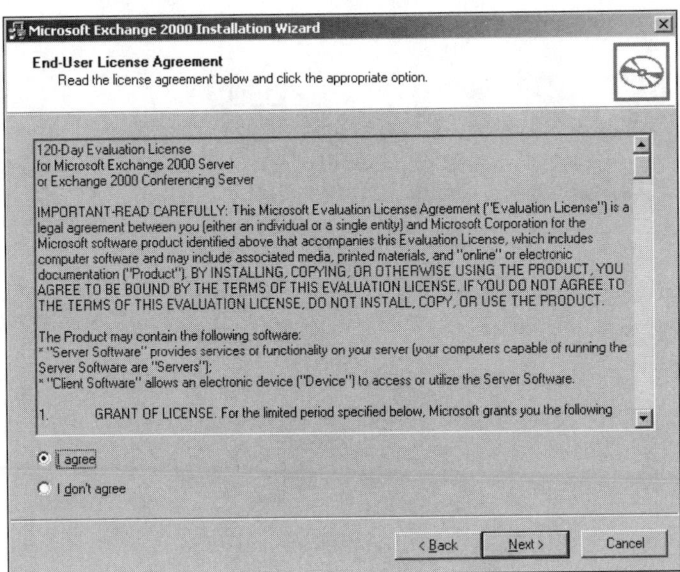

Figure 10.4
The EULA page.

5. The next page is the *Product Identification* page; type the server CD key (not case sensitive; usually located on the back of the CD case), and click *Next*, as shown in Figure 10.5.

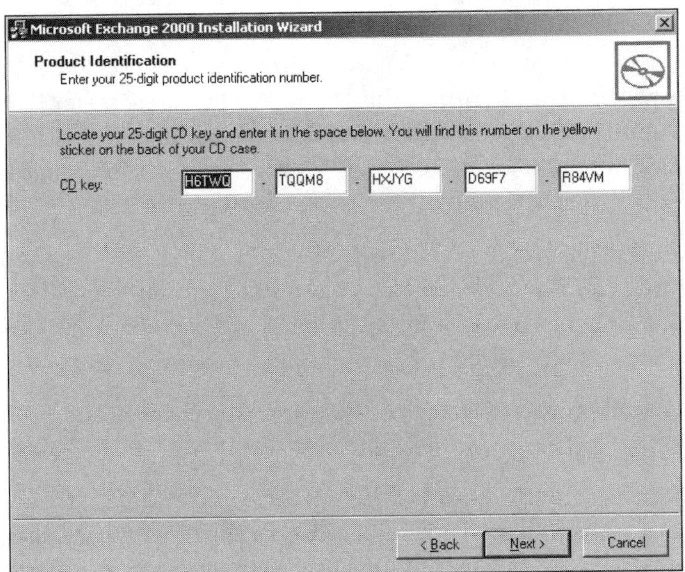

Figure 10.5
The Product Identification page.

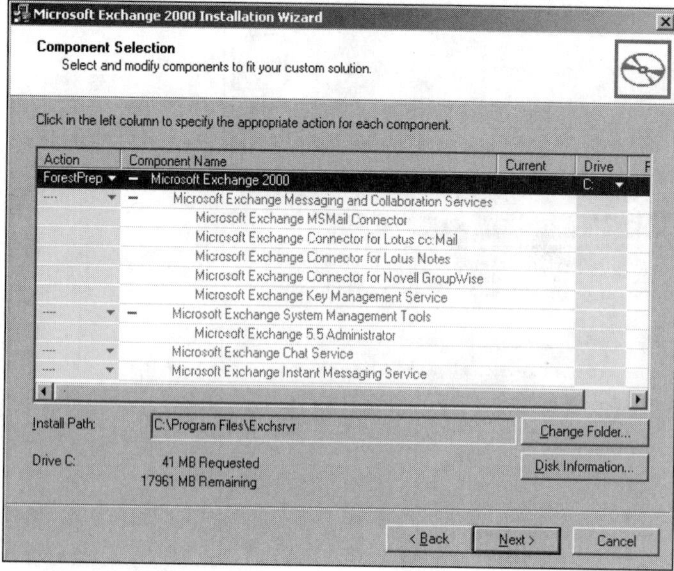

Figure 10.6
The Component Selection page.

6. Next is the *Component Selection* page; make sure the *Action* is set to *ForestPrep*, as shown in Figure 10.6. If you encounter any problems—for example, if you cannot reach the domain controller, you can't even manually set the action to **ForestPrep**; if so, make sure you are running this command directly on the schema master server.

   On this page you also define on what disk and directory Exchange will be installed. The default is *C:\Program Files\Exchsrvr*; this will also be the directory for the *First Storage Group* (named *C:\Program Files\Exchsrvr\MDBdata*), and the first *Priv1* and *Pub1* stores. You might want to change this disk—if so, do it now before you continue to the next page. Click *Next* when ready.

7. Next is the *Installation Type* page; select *Create A New Exchange 2000 Organization*, as shown in Figure 10.7. This means that the setup program could not find any previous Exchange 2000 installations in this Windows 2000 domain. On this page you can also select to join an existing Exchange 5.5 site.

8. Type the new organization name; remember this cannot be changed later! See Figure 10.8.

9. On the *Exchange 2000 Administrator Account* page, type in the name of the Windows 2000 user (or security group) that will be responsible for the new Exchange organization; in other words, this user will be the initial Exchange administrator, as shown in Figure 10.9. By default, this will be the currently logged on account. It might be a good idea to change this value to a security group instead. For example, create a group called Exchange Admins before you start the **ForestPrep** command; make sure your current account is a member of this group. Click *Next* when ready.

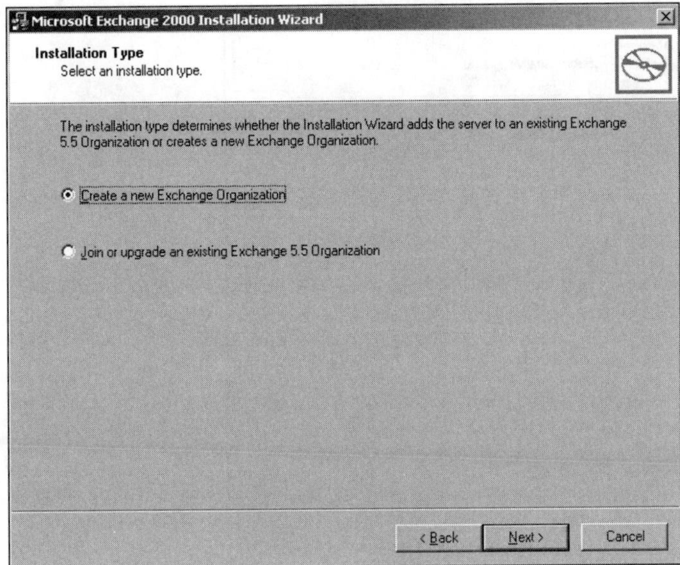

Figure 10.7
The Installation Type page.

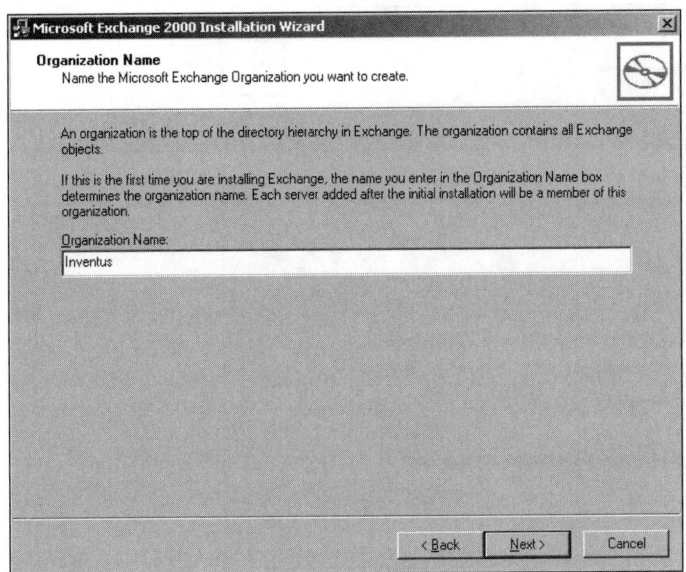

Figure 10.8
The Organization Name page.

10. Wait for the **ForestPrep** to complete; it may take 30 minutes or more. You will see a progress bar indicating the status of the upgrade process; as shown in Figure 10.10. When the update is done, click *Finish* to complete the operation.

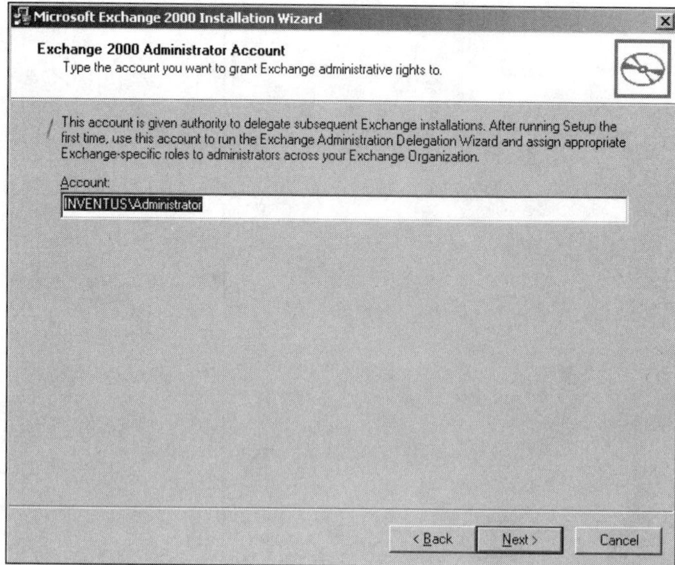

Figure 10.9
The Administrator Account page.

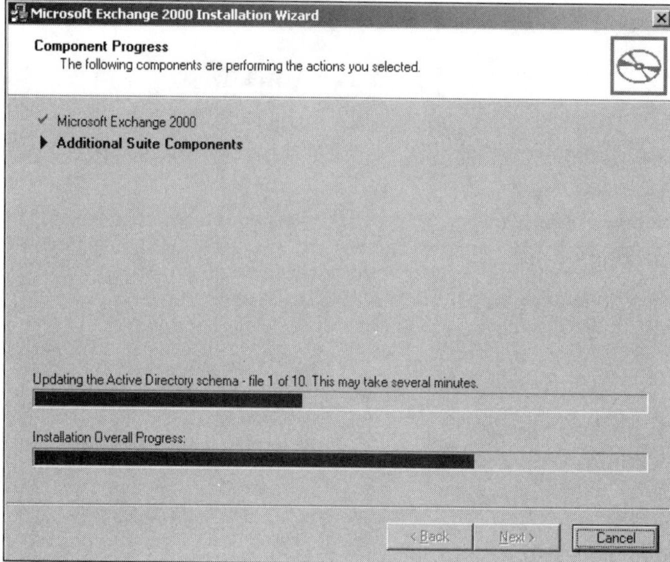

Figure 10.10
The Component Progress page.

Running the DomainPrep Command

The next step after running the **ForestPrep** command is to prepare the domain for Exchange 2000; for example, create special groups needed to run Exchange 2000, and assign them permissions on various OU containers in the AD domain. This command must be executed on all Windows 2000 domains where one or more Exchange 2000 servers reside; it must also be executed on the root domain, even if no Exchange servers are installed in that domain! The **DomainPrep** command performs the following tasks:

- Creates the Exchange Domain Servers domain global group, and adds all servers running Exchange 2000 in this domain as members.
- Creates the Exchange Enterprise Servers domain local group, which will contain all Exchange 2000 servers in the complete organization; this group will only be created when you run **DomainPrep** the first time.
- Gives these two groups the access permissions needed on all relevant OU containers in this Windows 2000 domain.
- Creates a special user account called EUSER_EXSTOREEVENTS that will be used to execute Exchange Event service scripts. This account will actually have fewer permissions than the Guest account; for example, it will not be allowed to access any files or Exchange folders.

To run this command, you need to be a member of the security group Domain Admins plus have administrative rights on the server this command is executed on. This command will be completed quickly; you don't have to wait 30 minutes like you would for the **ForestPrep** command. Follow these step-by-step instructions to run **DomainPrep** on a Windows 2000 domain:

1. Log on locally on any domain controller in this domain; make sure you have the access permissions needed.
2. On the *Start* menu, select *Run* and type *"Drive:\Setup\I386\Setup.exe /DomainPrep"*, where *Drive* is the CD-ROM drive, and click *OK*.
3. Click *Next* on the *Welcome* page.
4. On the *End-User License Agreement* page, select *I Agree* (if you do) and click *Next*. (This question will not be asked if this is the same domain as where you ran **ForestPrep** earlier.)
5. On the *Production Identification* page, add the product CD key. (This question will not be asked if this is the same domain as where you ran **ForestPrep** earlier.)
6. On the *Component Selection* page, make sure the *Action* is set to *DomainPrep*; if not, you might have problems reaching the domain controller, as shown in Figure 10.11. Click *Next*.
7. On the *Recipient Update Server* page, type the name of the server that will be responsible for running the *Recipient Update Service* for this domain; see more about this RUS service in Chapter 9. Note that this Exchange server doesn't need to exist, but its computer account must; when later installing Exchange 2000 in this domain, you must use this computer account! Click *Next*.
8. On the *Completion* page, click *Finish* to complete this **DomainPrep** command.

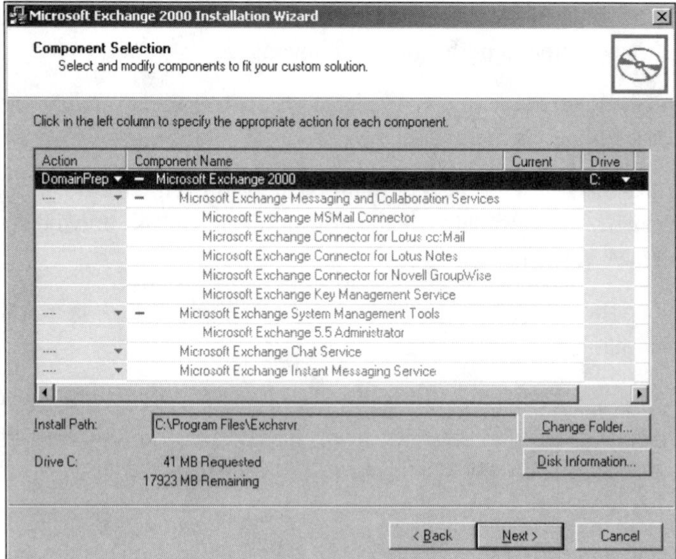

Figure 10.11
The Component Selection page for **DomainPrep**.

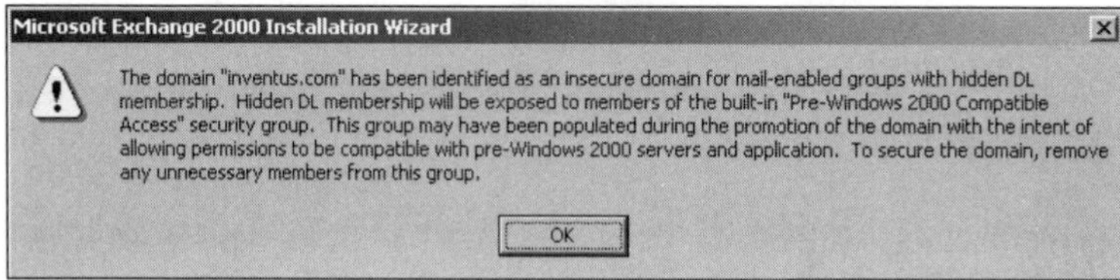

Figure 10.12
The warning about an insecure domain.

If the Windows 2000 domain is running in mixed mode, you will get a warning stating that this is an *Insecure Domain For Mail-Enabled Groups With Hidden DL Membership*, as shown in Figure 10.12. This warning is due to the fact that there is a special group named *pre-Windows 2000 Compatible Access* that will be able to look at membership of hidden distribution lists; by default the group *Everyone* is a member of that group. You might want to modify that membership.

Remember to run this **DomainPrep** command on every domain where there is an Exchange server installed, plus the root domain in the forest, even if there is no Exchange server in that root domain. Even if you have already run the **ForestPrep** command, you still need to run **DomainPrep**.

Standard Exchange 2000 Installation

If we don't run the **ForestPrep** and **DomainPrep** commands first, the same steps will be taken automatically when you install the first Exchange 2000 server in the forest. However, the drawbacks compared to running these commands separately include:

- The administrator needs to be a member of the following groups to run this first Exchange setup: Schema Admins, Enterprise Admins, and Domain Admins. The administrator also needs full access to the local computer. Probably there will only be a few administrators that are members of the Schema Admins group.
- If this Exchange server is not the same as the schema master, you must wait until the replication of all AD updates to the schema master has been completed, as well as the rebuild of the global catalog; this might take a long time.
- The setup process of this first Exchange server will take a long time to complete, since it will update the schema, create the new security groups, and install the Exchange server files. Updates of the schema are not recommended during working hours, so this process should be done in the evening or the weekend.
- If you want to assign this Exchange server to a certain administrative group, you must use the ForestPrep/DomainPrep method, since that makes it possible to rename the default First Administrative Group and create new administrative groups; during the installation of the Exchange server later on, you will be asked what administrative group this server should be assigned to.

To summarize, run the **ForestPrep** and **DomainPrep** commands, unless it's a small installation with just a few Exchange servers in one single AD domain, and you don't mind waiting for the setup program to be completed.

Installing Exchange 2000 Server

In this section, we assume that the Windows 2000 domain has already been prepared with the **ForestPrep** and **DomainPrep** commands. We will concentrate on the installation of the Exchange server itself: the hardware and software requirements, and the steps to perform the installation.

The Hardware Requirements

The server on which you install the Exchange 2000 Server software needs the following *minimum* hardware configuration:

- A server with a Pentium 133MHz or higher CPU
- A CD-ROM drive
- A VGA monitor
- At least 128MB RAM
- At least 500MB of free hard disk space on the drive where Exchange 2000 will be installed
- At least 200MB of free hard disk space on the system drive

The above configuration is needed to install the Exchange 2000 software, but it will not be sufficient for any production environment. The most critical factors here are RAM memory and disk space, though the speed of the CPU and the number of CPUs are of course also important for the overall performance of this Exchange server.

Let's look at an example; assume you have 100 users that will be allowed to have up to 150MB of mailbox space each (equals 15GB); we also assume that we will have about 4GB of public folder data, and an Internet connection. The RAM memory should under no circumstances be less than 256MB, even for smaller organizations; the more memory, the better performance. In this situation, I would suggest 384MB or more. The hard disk layout should have one system drive, one drive for transaction logs, and one RAID5 set for the Exchange stores. You should go for fast SCSI drives, since Exchange is a typical database application, which constantly writes and stores information onto the disks. If we can afford it, we should have mirrored drives for both the system drive and the transaction log drive. The recommendation for this example looks like this:

- A server with 800MHz Pentium III CPU, plus a CD-ROM drive and 17-inch VGA monitor
- 384MB of RAM memory
- One SCSI 9GB system drive (mirrored, if we can afford it)
- One SCSI 9GB drive for the Exchange transaction logs (mirrored, if possible)
- One SCSI RAID5 drive set, with at least 20GB of free disk space (30GB, if possible)

Besides this configuration, I would also add the following:

- A 100Mbps network card
- An uninterrupted power supply (UPS) that can hold the server for at least 30 minutes
- Backup hardware, with at least 40GB of storage capacity, capable of backing up at least 10GB per hour

The Software Requirements

The operating system that needs to be installed on this server is one of the following Windows 2000 versions:

- *Windows 2000 Server*—For a server with up to four CPUs
- *Windows 2000 Advanced Server*—For a server with up to eight CPUs and two-node cluster support
- *Windows 2000 Datacenter Server*—For a server with up to 32 CPUs and four-node cluster support

Notice that the Windows 2000 Datacenter Server is not for sale as a standalone product; you must buy a server with this software installed on it—for example a Compaq ProLiant 8500. Besides the operating system, there are some special configurations that need to be set before the installation of Exchange 2000 software:

- This server must have joined a Windows 2000 domain; however, it doesn't need to be a domain controller. A member server is okay, and often preferred.
- This server must be able to contact a dynamic DNS server.
- Internet Information Server (IIS) 5 or higher must be installed.
- The TCP/IP protocol must be installed.
- The SMTP protocol must be installed.
- The NNTP protocol must be installed.
- You must apply the Service Pack 1 (or higher) for Windows 2000.

There are a few recommendations too; these will make the Exchange system more secure and run faster:

- NTFS should be used as the file system
- The Page file should be twice the size of the physical RAM memory

The Installation Process

You have the server ready, with the suitable hardware and software configuration. It's time to perform the actual installation process. Follow these instructions to install the first Exchange 2000 server:

1. Log on to the server as an administrator with the proper access permissions.
2. On the Start menu, select Run and type "*Drive*:\Setup\I386\Setup", where *Drive* is the CD-ROM drive, and click *OK*.
3. This will start the MS Exchange 2000 Installation Wizard; on the Welcome page, click *Next* to continue.
4. On the End-User License Agreement page, select I Agree (if you do!) and click *Next* to continue.
5. On the Product Identification page, fill in the 25-digit CD Key (usually written on a yellow sticker on the back of the CD case).
6. On the Component Selection page, click on the Action column and set it to Install for all components you want to install. The default is Typical and corresponds to installing the MS Exchange Messaging And Collaboration Services and the Exchange System Management tools, as shown in Figure 10.13.

   On this you can also change the installation path; the default is C:\Program Files\Exchsrvr. A typical installation needs about 257MB of disk space. Click *Next* to continue.
7. On the Licensing Agreement page, select I Agree if you have read the license agreement for Exchange 2000, as shown in Figure 10.14. Then click *Next*.

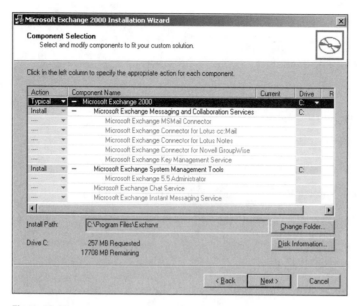

Figure 10.13
The Component Selection when installing an Exchange server.

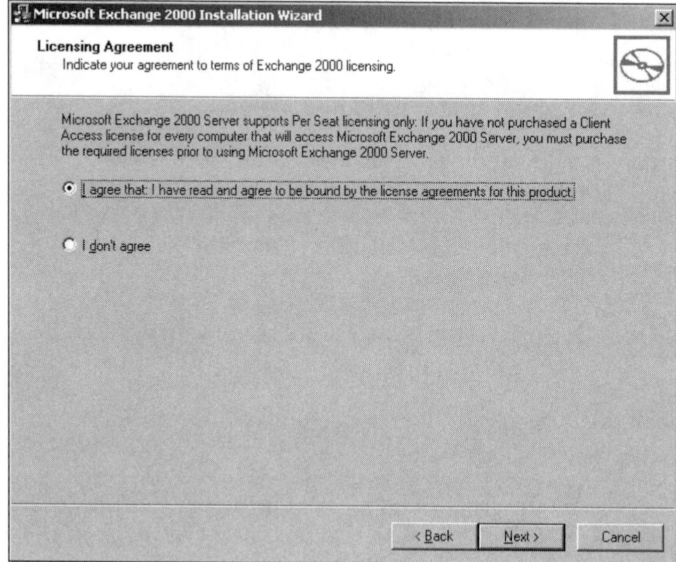

Figure 10.14
The Licensing Agreement page for Exchange 2000.

8. On the Component Summary page, check to see that the installation selections are correct, as shown in Figure 10.15. If they're not correct, click the Back button and correct the error; if they are correct, click *Next* to start the installation. This process will take about 15 to 30 minutes, depending on how fast the computer is.

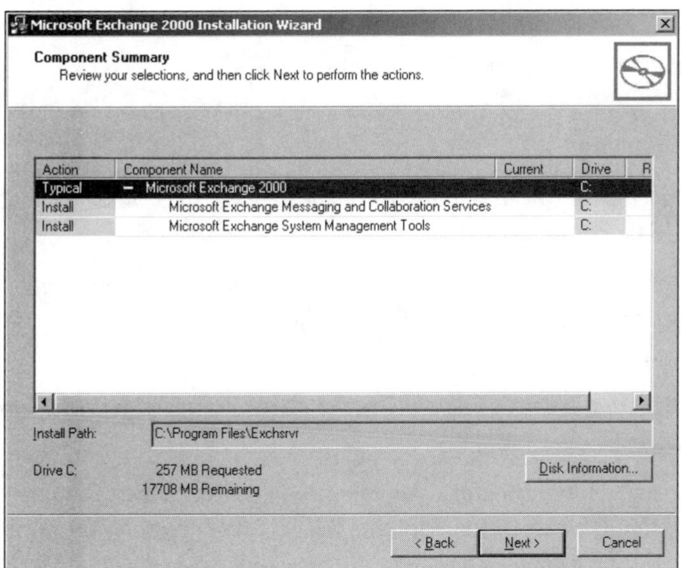

Figure 10.15
The Component Summary page.

9. When the installation is done, click Finish to complete the installation.

After the installation is completed successfully you should also install the latest service pack for Exchange 2000. Since this is the first version of this new Exchange server it's unavoidable that it will have some flaws and bugs. In Service Pack 1, for example, you will find updates of the Outlook Web Access server, fixing the bug in OWA that prohibits some web clients from viewing public folders.

The Available Exchange 2000 Components

On the Component Selection page mentioned in Step 6, you will find a list of different components that can be installed. You should not install more than necessary; for example, installing the cc-Mail Connector if you don't intend to connect Exchange to such a mail system will result in all users getting a cc-Mail email address automatically. If you later would like to add or remove any components, run the installation process again, as described above; when you reach Step 6, select to Install or Remove any components. The following is a list of all available Exchange components, if you have the Exchange 2000 Enterprise Server edition:

- *MS Exchange Messaging and Collaboration Services*—This is the core Exchange 2000 module, needed to run the Exchange server and communicate with other Exchange 2000 servers in this organization.
- *MS Exchange MS Mail Connector*—This is the gateway to MS Mail, including its address replication process Dirsync.

- *MS Exchange Connector for Lotus cc-Mail*—The gateway to cc-Mail, including its address replication process.
- *MS Exchange Connector for Lotus Notes*—The gateway to Lotus Notes, including its address replication process.
- *MS Exchange Connector for Novell GroupWise*—The gateway to GroupWise, including its address replication process.
- *MS Exchange Key Management Service*—This is the Exchange service for email encryption and electronic signing, using X.509 certificates; it can be used for standard S/MIME communication.
- *MS Exchange System Management Tools*—The standard administrative tool for Exchange 2000 servers.
- *MS Exchange Server 5.5 Administrator*—An enhanced version of the Exchange 5.5 Administrative tool that is aware of the Windows 2000 Active Directory. You should use this tool to administrate Exchange 5.5 servers from a Windows 2000 computer, instead of installing the original Exchange 5.5 admin program on this computer.
- *MS Exchange Chat Service*—The Internet Relay Chat Server service.
- *MS Exchange Instant Messaging Service*—The Instant Messaging Server service.

The number of available components for the Exchange 2000 Server edition is smaller, compared to the Enterprise Server edition; this version also has other restrictions, including:

- The store is limited to 16GB in size.
- The number of mailbox stores is limited to one; however, you can create up to four general-purpose public stores, besides the default MAPI public folder.
- The server is limited to one storage group only.
- This version doesn't have support for Windows 2000 active/active cluster.
- Front-end and back-end configurations are not allowed.
- Chat is not allowed.

Installing Exchange 2000 in Unattended Mode

It is possible to install Exchange 2000 in unattended mode, by creating a predefined initialization file. You can create this file by running the setup program with the command-line switch **createunattend**; you will be asked all the installation questions, and your answers will be stored in the initialization file. Later, this file is used to run an unattended setup on another server. This initialization file may also be encrypted to protect its content, if needed. Run the command **Setup /?** to see all available command-line switches:

- **Setup /disasterrecovery**—Allows you to recover missing files, Registry keys, and deleted folders. You will need a valid backup of the data to be recovered. If you don't have such a backup, this operation will only be successful if the Exchange stores are consistent.
- **Setup /forestprep**—Prepares the AD schema for Exchange 2000.
- **Setup /domainprep**—Prepares the AD domain for Exchange 2000.
- **Setup /createunattend <*file name*>.ini**—Creates an initialization file for unattended setup of an Exchange 2000 server.
- **Setup /unattendfile <*file name*>.ini**—Runs setup of Exchange 2000 server in unattended mode, using the initialization file.
- **Setup /password <*password*>**—Logs the current user on.
- **Setup /encryptmode**—Runs with the **/createunattend** switch to create an initialization file that uses encryption, (but the file will still be readable with a text editor).
- **Setup /showui**—Will make the unattended setup show the user interface during the installation process. Must be used together with the **/unattendfile** switch.
- **Setup /noeventlog**—Turns off event logging.
- **Setup /noerrorlog**—Turns off error logging.
- **Setup /all**—Enables all components for installations, upgrades, or reinstallation.

Running an unattended setup can be an excellent choice in situations where an administrator without Exchange experience needs help to install a server. For example, if you have a geographically distributed Exchange organization, without experienced Exchange administrators on each local site, you can create one initialization file for each site and distribute them to the local administrator.

Before you can run the setup in unattended mode, the Windows 2000 domain must be prepared for Exchange. There are no command-line switches for **/ForestPrep** or **/DomainPrep** in the unattended setup mode. A number of operations are actually not possible to perform using an unattended setup, including the following:

- **ForestPrep**
- **DomainPrep**
- Upgrading Exchange 5.5 servers
- Uninstalling Exchange 2000
- Disaster recovery, using the forklift method
- Installing cluster nodes
- Maintenance mode, for adding or removing components
- Installing the first Exchange 2000 server in an Exchange 5.5 organization

- Installing the Exchange 2000 Chat component
- Installing the Exchange 2000 Instant Messaging component

As you can see, the real purpose of an unattended setup is to perform completely new standard Exchange 2000 server installations; in those situations this is an excellent installation method.

Creating an Initialization File

Generating an initialization file is almost identical to running a standard setup. However, don't generate this file on a server where Exchange 2000 or any subcomponent, like the ESM tool, is installed; even if you add the **/createunattend** switch, the setup program will still think you want to modify the existing components on this server. Follow these instructions to create an initialization file for unattended setup of Exchange 2000:

1. On the Start menu, select Run and type "*Drive*:\Setup\I386\Setup /createunattend c:\tmp\e2ksetup.ini" where *Drive* is the CD-ROM drive; this will create an initialization file named e2ksetup.ini in the C:\tmp directory. Note: This file must not already exist; if it does, you get an error and the setup program will abort.
2. On the Welcome page, click *Next* to continue.
3. On the End-User License Agreement page, select I Agree (if you do) and click *Next* to continue.
4. On the Product Identification page, type in the 25-digit CD Key, and click *Next* to continue.
5. On the Component Selection page, click on the Action column and set it to Install for all components you want to install. The default is Typical and corresponds to installing the MS Exchange Messaging And Collaboration Services and the Exchange System Management tools.

   On this page you can also change the installation path; the default is C:\Program Files\Exchsrvr. A typical installation needs about 257MB of disk space. When ready, click *Next* to continue.
6. On the Licensing Agreement page, select I Agree if you have read the license agreement for Exchange 2000. Then click *Next*.
7. On the Component Summary page, check to see that the installation selections are correct. If they're not correct, click the Back button and correct the error. If they are correct, click *Next* to start the generation of the initialization file; this will go very quickly.
8. When the installation is done, your screen will look like Figure 10.16. Note that it says Setup Created The Following Unattended File **<File Path>**, instead of creating an Exchange server installation! When ready, click *Finish*.

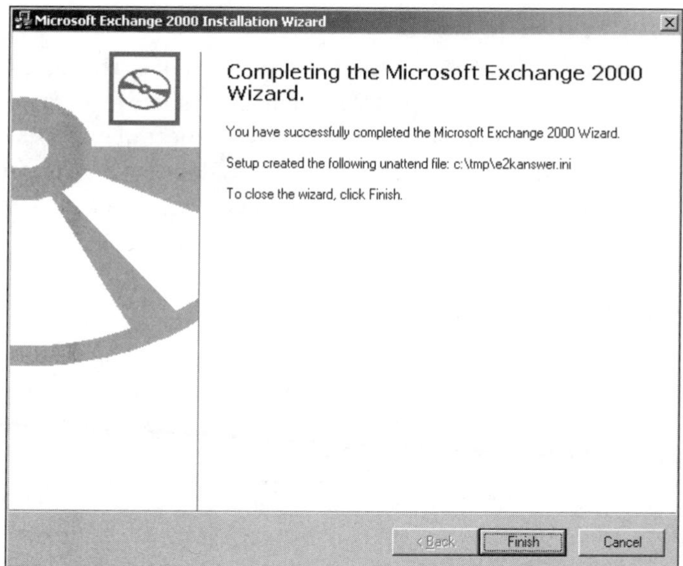

Figure 10.16
Generating the initialization file.

Performing an Unattended Setup of Exchange 2000

To perform an unattended setup of Exchange 2000, use the previously created initialization file, along with the Exchange CD used to create it; the CD key is stored in that initialization file. Follow these instructions to perform this unattended installation:

1. On the Start menu, select Run and type "Drive:\Setup\I386\Setup /unattendfile c:\tmp\e2ksetup.ini", where *Drive* is the CD-ROM drive; this will start the installation of Exchange 2000 Server, using the initialization file named e2ksetup.ini in the C:\tmp directory.

   If this is the first Exchange server in the organization, you will have to confirm that you want to create this new Exchange organization.

   The installation process will not show any dialog pages—you will only see the Component Progress page, showing the current status during the installation. This will take the same amount of time as a usual setup, or about 15 to 30 minutes, depending on what components you install and the speed of the server.

2. When the installation is done, the setup process will quietly exit.

After the installation is finished, use the ESM tool to make sure everything looks good. Notice that the administrator account used to create this server will automatically be mailbox enabled, if it wasn't before.

A Guide to Install Exchange 2000

You have now seen the different methods that can be used to install Exchange 2000, including the possibilities to run Forestprep and Domainprep separately. You can also see that it's possible to perform an unattended installation; which is perfect when inexperienced administrators should perform the installation; for example, in domains that are far away from you. The question is when should these different options be used? Look at Decision Tree 10.1 for a guide of when certain installation should be performed.

Removing an Exchange 2000 Server

If you need to remove the first Exchange 2000 server, for example to change the Exchange organization name, you simply uninstall Exchange 2000; when you run setup again you will be asked about the new Exchange organization name. However, if you want to clean out

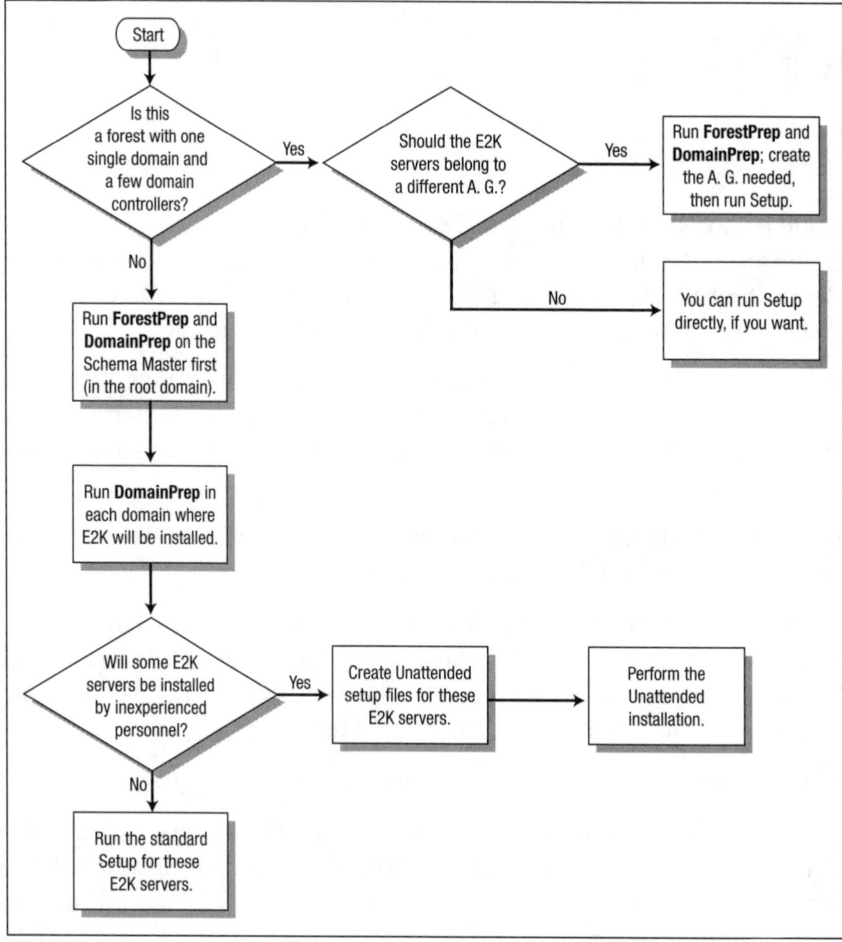

Decision Tree 10.1
When to use a particular installation option.

all entries in the Active Directory about Exchange 2000, it's not enough to just uninstall; you must also manually clear the parts of Active Directory that contain information about Exchange. But you can never restore the Active Directory completely; all extensions to the schema that **/ForestPrep** made cannot be undone, unless you reinstall all the Windows 2000 domain controllers from scratch again! Follow these instructions to clean out Exchange 2000 from a Windows 2000 forest.

Warning! *The operation described here will destroy the Exchange 2000 organization completely! Do not complete these steps unless you are absolutely sure you really want to remove Exchange 2000!*

1. Start by removing all mailboxes in the Exchange organization; it's not possible to remove an Exchange server if there are any mailbox-enabled users left. Use the *Active Directory Users and Computers* tool, and select all users that are mailbox-enabled. Then right-click and select *Exchange Tasks*, then *Delete Mailbox*.

   If any mail-enabled contacts or groups don't matter, or if there are any public folders with data, you will still be able to remove the Exchange server.

2. Remove all Exchange 2000 servers by running the Exchange Setup program on the *Component Selection* page. Click on the *Action* column for the first component, Microsoft Exchange 2000, and set it to *Remove*. Click *Next* until the remove process starts. This takes almost as long as installing an Exchange server.

   When the Exchange 2000 software is removed, you need to reboot the server.

3. Use the *File Explorer* and remove all directories that are related to Exchange 2000; they are usually in the *\Program Files\Exchsrvr* directory. Note that the Exchange server might be using several disks; make sure all directories are removed.

4. Start the *ADSI Edit* tool, and navigate to the *Configuration\Services\Microsoft Exchange*. First make sure there are no *Active Directory Connectors* of type *Config_CA*. Look in the Active Directory Connections folder—if there are any connectors that start with *Config_CA*, right-click on them and select *Delete* and then click *OK*. (If the *Config_CA* object can't be removed, you may have a *Directory Replication Connector* still configured in Exchange 5.5 that is connected to the SRS in Exchange 2000; if so, start by removing the DRC with the E2K version of the Exchange 5.5 admin tool, and then remove the *Config_CA*.)

5. Locate the folder with the Exchange 2000 organization name; right-click it and select *Delete*, and then OK, as shown in Figure 10.17.

6. Step back in the folder tree to the Microsoft Exchange object again; right-click it and select *Properties*. Select to view the *Heuristics* property; click *Clear*, and set the value to 0 (zero). Then click *Set* and then *OK*. See Figure 10.18.

7. Shut down the server on which Exchange 2000 was installed.

8. Reboot the domain controller that you were using to delete the AD containers.

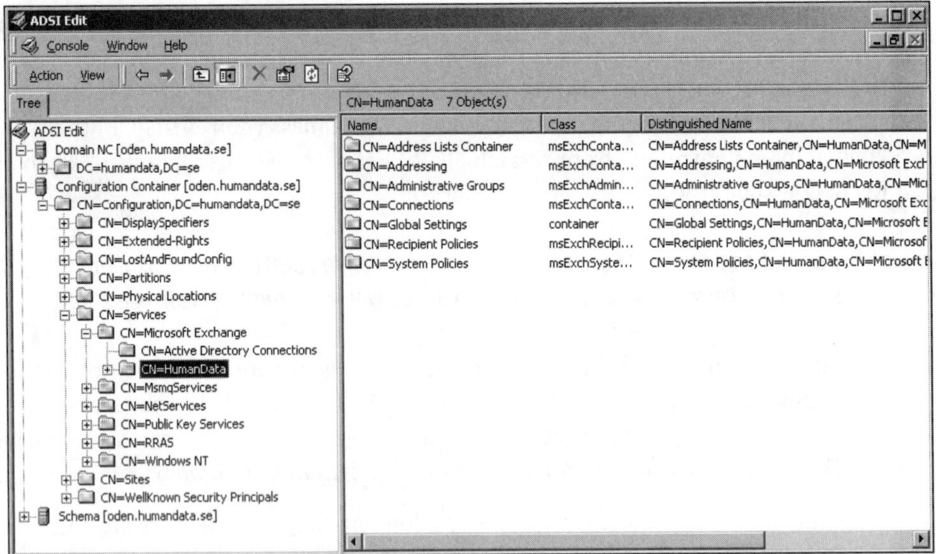

Figure 10.17
Deleting the Exchange organization from Active Directory.

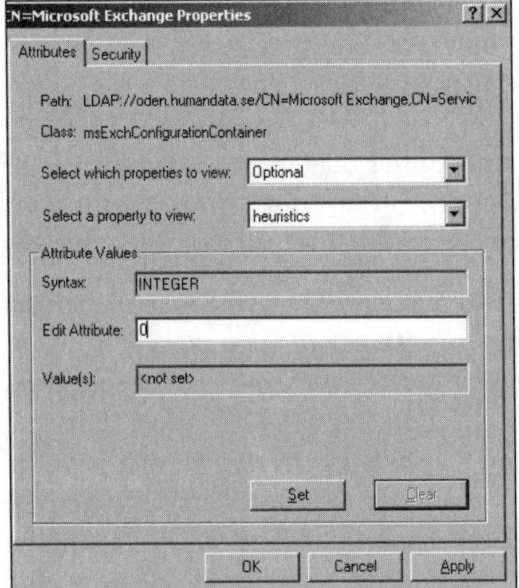

Figure 10.18
Clearing the Heuristics attribute of the Exchange container.

9. Start the servers that previously had Exchange 2000 on them.
10. Remove the Exchange System Manager tool from all computers.

Now the Exchange 2000 organization will be completely removed from this Windows 2000 forest. If you want to install a new Exchange organization, you must first start with **ForestPrep** and then **DomainPrep**, as described earlier in this chapter.

Removing an Exchange 2000 Server Installation Manually

In some rare cases, you can't remove the Exchange 2000 server software using its setup program, as described above in Step 2. In this case, you must manually remove the files and a number of Registry settings in order to remove the Exchange server from a computer. Follow these instructions to remove the server:

1. Delete the following Registry keys:

```
HKEY_LOCAL_MACHINE\SOFTWARE\Microsoft\ESE98
HKEY_LOCAL_MACHINE\SOFTWARE\Microsoft\Exchange
HKEY_LOCAL_MACHINE\SYSTEM\CurrentControlSet\Services\DAVEX
HKEY_LOCAL_MACHINE\SYSTEM\CurrentControlSet\Services\ESE98
HKEY_LOCAL_MACHINE\SYSTEM\CurrentControlSet\Services\EXIFS
HKEY_LOCAL_MACHINE\SYSTEM\CurrentControlSet\Services\ExIPC
HKEY_LOCAL_MACHINE\SYSTEM\CurrentControlSet\Services\EXOLEDB
HKEY_LOCAL_MACHINE\SYSTEM\CurrentControlSet\Services\IMAP4Svc
HKEY_LOCAL_MACHINE\SYSTEM\CurrentControlSet\Services\MSExchangeAL
HKEY_LOCAL_MACHINE\SYSTEM\CurrentControlSet\Services\MSExchangeDSAccess
HKEY_LOCAL_MACHINE\SYSTEM\CurrentControlSet\Services\MSExchangeES
HKEY_LOCAL_MACHINE\SYSTEM\CurrentControlSet\Services\MSExchangeIS
HKEY_LOCAL_MACHINE\SYSTEM\CurrentControlSet\Services\MSExchangeMTA
HKEY_LOCAL_MACHINE\SYSTEM\CurrentControlSet\Services\MSExchangeSRS
HKEY_LOCAL_MACHINE\SYSTEM\CurrentControlSet\Services\MSExchangeSA
HKEY_LOCAL_MACHINE\SYSTEM\CurrentControlSet\Services\MSExchangeTransport
HKEY_LOCAL_MACHINE\SYSTEM\CurrentControlSet\Services\MSExchangeWEB
HKEY_LOCAL_MACHINE\SYSTEM\CurrentControlSet\Services\POP3Svc
HKEY_LOCAL_MACHINE\SYSTEM\CurrentControlSet\Services\RESvc
```


2. Remove and reinstall the Internet Information Server component, including the SMTP and NNTP protocols; after this, you have to reboot the server.

3. Delete the *\Exchsrvr* directory structure; make sure to check all hard disks on this server for other Exchange-related directories that you don't want anymore.

4. Use the *ADSI Edit* tool to manually clear the user attribute *HomeMDB* for all mailbox-enabled users on this server; otherwise they will still be configured to look for their mailboxes on the now removed Exchange server, and you cannot use the *Exchange Tasks|Remove Mailbox* command because that presumes access to the Exchange server. (See also the section about mailbox-enabled users in Chapter 9.)

5. If this was the last Exchange server in the organization, you should now continue with Step 4 in the previous step-by-step list. If not, continue with the next step to remove this Exchange server object from the Exchange organization.

6. Log on to any one of the remaining Exchange 2000 servers, start the EMS tool, and locate the manually deleted Exchange server object in one of the administrative groups and its Server folder.

7. Right-click on the server object—make sure it's the deleted server! Select *All Tasks| Remove Server*. You will get a warning; click *Yes* to remove the server from this Exchange organization.

Wait for this modification to be replicated to the complete Exchange organization. The server is now completely removed. If you want to reinstall the Exchange server again, it will be like doing it for the first time.

Installing Any Subsequent Exchange 2000 Servers

Any subsequent installations of Exchange 2000 server will be easier, since you don't have to prepare the Window 2000 forest. However, if this is the first Exchange server in this Active Directory domain, you should run the **DomainPrep** command, unless it has been done before. You must plan for what administrative group this server will belong to; during the installation of subsequent servers, you will be able to select administrative groups, in case there are more than one, as shown in Figure 10.19. Otherwise, the server will automatically belong to the First Administrative Group. Besides that, you can follow the instructions for installing the first Exchange server, since these installation procedures are almost identical.

After the Installation

When you have successfully installed the Exchange 2000 server, several new directories, file shares, and services will have been added to this Windows 2000 server. A number of new administrative tools and groups will also have been added. Let's take a closer look at these new objects.

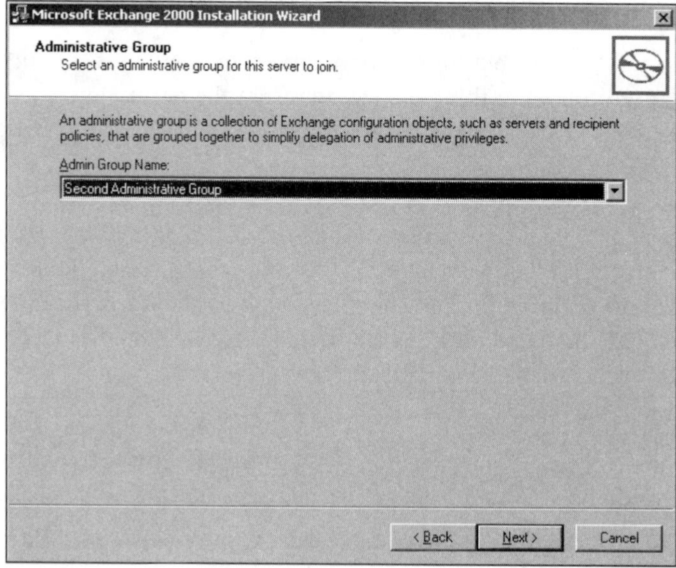

Figure 10.19
Selecting an administrative group for the new server.

The New File Directories

The setup program will create a number of directories on the Exchange 2000 server; by default they will all be stored in the C:\Program Files\Exchsrvr directory. Table 10.1 describes these directories and their contents.

Depending on what connectors you have installed, you will find other directories, too; for example, when installing the MS Mail Connector, you will also find directories like DXAData, where all Dirsync files will be stored. Any new storage groups that you create will get a file directory with the same name.

New File Shares

The number of file shares that the setup program creates is smaller than for older Exchange releases; in fact, there will now only be two shared folders:

- *Address*—Points to the Address folder. This will give access to the Exchange address object over the network.
- ***<server-name>**.log*—Points to the directory with the same name. This will give access to the tracking log files on this server over the network.

By default, the Administrators group has full control regarding access permissions, and the Everyone group has read access to these two file shares. Do not modify these permissions or Exchange may not operate properly.

Table 10.1 The new file directories.

Directory	Contents
Address	Email address generators for cc:Mail, Lotus Notes, GroupWise, MS Mail, SMTP, and X.400
Bin	Exchange 2000 binary files and administrative tools
Conndata	Routing files
Connect	Support directories and files to installed Exchange connectors—for example, the MS Mail Connector (like the shadow post office and Free/Busy connector)
ExchangeServer_***<name>***	Configuration files and indexing files
Exchweb	Root file for Outlook Web Access files
Mailroot	The message queue files for virtual SMTP servers, including the BadMail folder
MDBData	The database folder for the First Storage Group and its log files
MTAData	Configuration files and log files for the X.400 MTA service
RES	DLL files for event viewer and performance monitor
SCHEMA	Schema files for the OLEEDB process
Srsdata	Files for the Site Replication Service process
<server>.log	Stores the Tracking Log files

New Groups

Two new security groups are created during the setup; they are used by the Exchange server when performing updates of recipient addresses and populating the global address list, using the Recipient Update Service; for more information about RUS, see Chapter 9. The two groups are:

- *Exchange Domain Servers (EDS)*—A Global security group containing all Exchange servers in this domain. This group is populated by the Setup process. It is needed for the *Recipient Update Service*. (This group was previously known as *Domain EXServers* in the beta version of Exchange 2000).
- *Exchange Enterprise Servers (EES)*—A Domain Local security group, containing all EDS groups from all other domains running Exchange 2000. This group is first populated with the local EDS group by the DomainPrep; EDS groups from other domains are then added by the *Recipient Update Service*. (This group was previously known as *All Exchange Server* in the beta version.)

Both of these new groups are given access permissions on different containers in each domain where an Exchange 2000 server is installed. You should not add users or modify the membership of these groups; they are only for internal use.

New Exchange 2000 Services

The total number of Exchange services that can be installed on an Exchange 2000 Enterprise Server is impressive; they will all be installed as Windows 2000 services, and can be stopped or restarted through the Windows 2000 service manager; see Table 10.2 for a list of all available services. Note that not all of them will be started automatically, even if they are installed—for example, the MS Exchange Directory Synchronization service and the MS Mail Connector Interchange. If the services are needed, make sure they will start automatically.

Table 10.2 The Exchange 2000 services.

Service	Description
MS Exchange Chat	The IRC chat server service.
MS Exchange Connectivity Controller	Adds support services for the other Exchange connectors.
MS Exchange Connector for cc-Mail	Adds gateway and address replication functionality with cc-Mail.
MS Exchange Connector for Lotus Notes	Adds gateway and address replication functionality with Lotus Notes.
MS Exchange Connector for GroupWise	Adds gateway and address replication functionality with GroupWise.
MS Exchange Directory Synchronization	Adds address replication functionality with MS Mail.
MS Exchange Event	Monitors folders, starts Exchange 5.5 compatible scripts at given events.
MS Exchange IMAP4	Adds IMAP4 functionality to Exchange 2000.
MS Exchange Information Store	Manages Exchange 2000 information storage, i.e., the storage groups and all stores.

(continued)

Table 10.2 The Exchange 2000 services *(continued)*.

Service	Description
MS Exchange Message Transfer Agent (MTA) Stacks	Manages X.400 functionality in Exchange 2000. Will only be used when communicating with Exchange 5.5 sites or when using the X.400 Connector.
MS Exchange POP3	Adds POP3 functionality to Exchange 2000.
MS Exchange Router for Novell GroupWise	Adds support to Exchange 2000 for scheduling collaboration with GroupWise.
MS Exchange Routing Engine	Manages Exchange 2000 message routing.
MS Exchange Site Replication Service	Simulates an Exchange 5.5 Directory Service; makes it possible for Exchange 2000 to coexist with an Exchange 5.5 server.
MS Exchange System Attendant	Manages system-related services for Exchange 2000; the base service that all other services depend on, directly or indirectly.
Microsoft Search	Manages full-text indexes on message content, attachments, and properties.
MS Mail Connector Interchange	Is a MS Mail gateway, responsible for converting messages and addresses between MS Mail format and Exchange 2000 format.
MS Schedule Plus Free-Busy Connector	Allows sharing of Schedule Plus Free-Busy information between MS Mail and Exchange 2000 servers.

New Administrative Tools

During the installation of an Exchange 2000 server, a number of administrative tools and utilities are added to the server. Here is a list of these tools, and a short description of what they are used for:

- *Exchange System Manager (ESM)*—The main configuration tool for Exchange 2000. Replaces the Exchange Admin.exe tool in previous releases.
- *Active Directory Users and Computers (ADUC)*—The main administrative tool for managing users, groups, and contacts. Replaces both the previous Exchange 5.5 Admin.exe tool for creating mailboxes, and the User Manager for Domains tool in Windows NT 4.
- *Active Directory Cleanup Wizard*—Searches the Active Directory for multiple accounts for the same user; this can happen during a migration to Exchange 2000 from NT 4 and Exchange 5.5.
- *Migration Wizard*—The premium tool for migrating to Exchange 2000 from mail systems other than Exchange 5.5—for example, MS Mail, Lotus Notes, and GroupWise.

These tools should also be installed on all computers that are used to administrate the Exchange organization and its users; use the Exchange 2000 setup program to install them on any type of Windows 2000 operating system, including Windows 2000 Professional. However, you cannot install these tools on a computer with Windows NT 4, Windows ME, or older Windows versions. To install only the administrative tools on a computer, follow these instructions:

1. On the *Start* menu, select *Run* and type "*Drive:\Setup\I386\Setup*", where *Drive* is the CD-ROM drive.
2. On the *Welcome* page, click *Next* to continue.
3. On the *End-User License Agreement* page, select *I Agree* (if you do) and click *Next* to continue.
4. On the *Product Identification* page, type in the 25-digit CD Key, and click *Next* to continue.
5. On the *Component Selection* page, click on the *Action* column for the MS Exchange 2000 component and set it to *Custom*; next, set the *Action* column to *Install* for the *Exchange System Management* tools only! You will need about 88MB of free disk space for these tools. When ready, click *Next* to continue.
6. On the *Component Summary* page, check to see that the installation selections are correct. If not, click on the *Back* button and correct the error; if they are correct, click *Next* to start the installation of the management tools. This process will take about five minutes to complete.
7. When the installation is done, click *Finish*.

Checking the Installation

When the installation of the new Exchange server is finished, you should check it; follow this instructions:

1. Restart the new Exchange server.
2. When the server is running again, check the *Event Log* monitor for any warnings or errors; if there are any, investigate them and solve the problems.
3. Verify that the Exchange services listed in Table 10.3 have been installed (assuming you have done a typical installation).

Table 10.3 The default Exchange services.

Service	Status	Startup Type
MS Exchange Event	Not started	Manual
MS Exchange IMAP4	Started	Automatic
MS Exchange Information Store	Started	Automatic
MS Exchange MTA Stacks	Started	Automatic
MS Exchange POP3	Started	Automatic
MS Exchange Routing Engine	Started	Automatic
MS Exchange Site Replication Service	Not started	Disabled
MS Exchange System Attendant	Started	Automatic

4. Verify that the Exchange file directories are created and stored on the correct drives.
5. Start the ESM tool; locate the new server and make sure it's installed in the right administrative group and routing group.
6. Apply the latest service pack for Exchange 2000 server, along with any important hot fixes Microsoft recommends that you install.

Troubleshooting the Installation Process

Usually, the installation of Exchange 2000 server is very smooth and simple. But since there are a number of dependencies for the installation process, something could go wrong. In this section, we list the most common problems and how to solve them.

Common (and Not So Common) Installation Issues

Below are some common, and in the end, not so common installation issues:

- *Not logged on to the domain*—Log off from the local server's administrator account, and log on to the administrator for this domain.
- *Improper Windows 2000 Permissions*—The account used during the installation must be a member of the Windows 2000 security groups Domain Admins, Enterprise Admins, and Schema Admins.
- *The MDBData directory is not empty*—Exchange will not allow a new installation until the old data is manually removed; this is a security precaution. If you are sure you don't need it anymore, remove the complete Exchsrvr directory and restart the Setup program.
- *Unable to contact Access Directory*—The server must have contact with a domain controller that will register the new configuration settings in the Active Directory. Find out why this server doesn't have contact with the domain controller, fix the problem, and start the setup process again.
- *Incorrect Exchange 5.5 Service Account password*—If the Exchange 2000 server will join an Exchange 5.5 Site, you must have the Site Service account and password used in this Site.
- *Unable to access the Windows 2000 AD*—This is a common error message, stating that the setup program cannot contact the Active Directory. The most common cause is a communication problem, but it could also happen if you try to install several Exchange 2000 servers at the same time; if so, complete one installation before starting the next.
- *The Directory Service is busy*—This is a problem that could occur if the Exchange server is installed in a child domain and is affected by the way that *Named Pipes* work. Simply rerun the setup program again and add any components that weren't installed the first time; then this installation will be complete.
- *Administrator can't run ForestPrep*—If the administrator has been denied access to a global address list, then he or she can't rerun the **Setup /ForestPrep** command; neither can he or she administrate those address lists.

- *Administrator can't run DomainPrep*—If the administrator doesn't have the access permissions to view the Configuration container in the Active Directory, he or she cannot run the **Setup /DomainPrep** command.
- *Setup failed while installing subcomponent Site Replication Service*—This can happen if there is a problem with the connection to the Active Directory. It might also be due to missing entries for this domain in the DNS. Resolve the problem and click Retry to continue the installation of Exchange.

Optimizing the Exchange Server

After a successful installation of Exchange server, you might want to optimize it for maximum performance and stability. There are no single steps to take that will fit all organizational needs, but there are some rules of thumb that you can use. The first thing an Exchange 5.5 administrator will notice is that the Exchange 5.5 Optimizer program is missing; that was an important tool in the previous Exchange environment. The new Exchange 2000 has lots of auto-tuning settings that to some extent eliminate the need for an optimizer program. Besides, optimizing Exchange 2000 is not just an Exchange question anymore since all our users today are stored in the Active Directory database; this means that we must optimize the Active Directory too.

Optimizing the Active Directory

This section is about optimizing Active Directory, with respect to Exchange 2000. The AD is a repository not only for all users, groups, and contacts, but also for mail-enabled public folders and Exchange server configurations. Our AD forest can contain one or more domains, structured into one or more AD trees. The structure that is easiest to manage and that replicates AD information fastest is the single-domain structure. Even companies and organizations today that have a multitude of Windows NT 4 domains can benefit from consolidating all of them to one single AD domain. The structure will affect the Exchange 2000 environment greatly, since the Active Directory has taken over the role that DIR.EDB and DS played in previous Exchange releases. So try to keep the number of AD domains down to a minimum—if possible just one.

One common reason why companies created several Windows NT 4 domains was the need for administrative control. The NT 4 domain is essentially a flat structure; if you are an administrator of an NT 4 domain, you can administrate all of its objects. In contrast to that, Windows 2000 has a hierarchical structure within its AD domain; you can create a tree structure of organizational units (OUs), and for each OU you can create an administrator. If there is a tree structure of OUs, an administrator can be delegated administrative control of the complete tree structure, if necessary. Try to migrate the NT 4 domains to OUs, thereby making it possible to keep down the number of AD domains in the forest.

Remember that one Windows 2000 forest can contain only one single Exchange 2000 organization, and one Exchange organization cannot span more than one Windows 2000 forest. This means that companies with two or more Windows 2000 forests need to have two or more Exchange 2000 organizations! And no tools are available from Microsoft as of today that will help you replicate address lists, public folder data, and mailbox information like Calendar Free/Busy information between two Exchange 2000 organizations. However, the Microsoft Metadirectory Server (MMS) can be used to replicate directory content using LDAP, and that may be a solution for companies with several Exchange 2000 organizations; contact Microsoft for more information about this product.

Some of the Windows 2000 domain controllers (i.e., a server with Active Directory installed) have special roles, besides being a domain controller. You will find more information about this in Chapter 5, but here is a quick overview:

- *Global Catalog*—Stores a copy of all objects in the forest, with a limited set of attributes. Stores the global address list for Exchange 2000.
- *Schema Master*—The server that controls all updates and modifications of the AD schema for the complete forest. There is only one schema master per forest. To update the schema, you must be a member of the security group Schema Admins.
- *Domain Naming Master*—Controls the addition or removal of AD domains in the forest. There is only one such server per forest.
- *Relative Identifier Master*—Responsible for allocating sequence of RIDs to each domain controller in its domain. There is one RID Master per domain.
- *PDC Emulator*—This server is used to emulate an NT 4 PDC so that pre-Windows 2000 servers and clients can log on to the AD domain. There is one such PDC Emulator per domain.
- *Infrastructure Master*—This server is responsible for updating the group-to-user reference whenever group membership changes. There is one such server per domain.

Global Catalog Servers

Of all these roles, the global catalog (GC) role probably has the most impact on our Exchange environment. By default, only one single GC is installed in the forest—the first installed domain controller. In a distributed environment, with several WAN connections, you should definitely make sure there is at least one GC per IP subnet. All Windows 2000 domain controllers can be configured to be a GC, besides its usual responsibilities; however, this will increase the burden of this server, since it now will have a copy of all objects in the forest, and participate in the GC replication process; so make sure the server will be able to handle this increased load. Here is a list of considerations when placing GC servers:

- The GC stores the address books; Exchange 2000 servers and Outlook 2000 clients access the GC to resolve address queries. If the access to the GC is slow, this will affect both Exchange servers and clients.
- If the GC cannot be contacted, a computer will not be able to log on; only the cached local logon credentials will be available. Make sure you have a GC at remote sites.

- Membership of universal groups is stored in the GC; when the Exchange server needs to expand such a group, it will contact a GC.
- Domain controllers only perform authentication and expansion of domain local groups, not universal groups.
- Too many GCs generate unnecessary replication traffic.
- In a single-domain forest, the GC will have the same information as any other domain controller.
- The rule of thumb is to have at least one GC per Windows 2000 site.

Schema Update Considerations

When the **ForestPrep** command is executed, it expands the AD schema with lots of new attributes for many object types, like users, groups, and contacts. It will also affect what attributes will be listed in the GC. You can add new attributes to be exposed by the GC by using the Active Directory Schema snap-in; however, you must be aware that every time the exposed attributes are modified, a complete replication is forced between all GCs in the forest. In a large organization, this could take a long time to complete and the network traffic will be intensive during this time, possibly affecting other network applications.

The reason for this complete replication is the way the Active Directory keeps track of modifications of its objects. Each domain controller has an Update Sequence Number (USN) that increases for each modification (a 64-bit counter). When a new attribute is tagged for being replicated to the GC, this resets the USN number to 0. As a result, all objects in the Active Directory, not just the modified attribute, must be replicated to each global catalog again. The lesson here is to make any modifications to the GC attributes very early in the deployment of Exchange 2000, or at least to make any such modification during off-hours.

Optimizing Exchange 2000 Server

Depending on what the Exchange organization looks like, what clients are used, and what features have been implemented, there are different types of optimizations. The following section looks at some common situations and offers some tips on how to optimize them.

Front-End and Back-End Servers

In case the organization uses the Outlook Web Access (OWA) client, you can increase the overall performance by installing one or more front-end Exchange servers, which handle client access, and back-end servers, which store all data. A front-end server is an Exchange 2000 Enterprise server that doesn't host any local mailboxes; instead, it forwards any requests coming in from the OWA clients to the back-end server. The performance hit may be substantial if SSL encryption is used (and it should be!); by installing one or more front-end servers, you will get much better overall performance. Even for small organizations, a front-end/back-end solution can be beneficial since the front-end can be installed on the DeMilitarized Zone (DMZ) segment on the firewall, and the back-end server on the internal network; this will increase network security.

***Note:** Only Exchange 2000 Enterprise Servers can be used when installing front-end / back-end solutions; the Exchange 2000 Server version cannot be used for this. You must therefore purchase two Enterprise server licenses, one for the front-end and one for the back-end server; which makes it an expensive (but good) solution.*

Full-Text Indexing

If your clients need to search their mailboxes or any public folders for messages or attachments for certain keywords, you should implement full-text indexing. This feature comes with Exchange 2000, but is not installed by default. The ordinary search feature in Outlook will not be able to search any attachments—it can only search the message's header and body. The attachments that can be indexed by the full-text index features include:

- Embedded MIME messages (.eml)
- HTML files (.html, .htm, .asp)
- MS Excel (.xls)
- MS PowerPoint (.ppt)
- MS Word (.doc)
- Text files (.txt)

You can expand this list by adding new search filters for other types of attachments; ask your vendor if they have any such filter for Exchange. The full-text index is accessed in Outlook by selecting the *Advanced Search*; it can also be accessed from an IMAP4 client. However, there is one little quirk here—the full-text index engine that comes with Exchange 2000 can only search for complete words. For example, if you search for the word *Admin*, it will not return messages with the word *Administrator*; there is no possibility to use wild-cards, such as "Admin*", when searching, unfortunately.

The indexing process is very CPU intensive. You configure when to run an update of the index by the ESM; each store can be indexed individually. You should select the schema for updating the index with great care; running it all the time will decrease the server performance as would running it every hour. I recommend that you run an update every night, unless you have a server with lots of extra resources. Microsoft recommends that the server running full-text indexing should have at least 512MB of memory; however, in my experience 256MB will do fine for a smaller organization, as long as the index is updated during off-hours. Note that the index file will be about 20 to 30 percent of the size of the store; for example, if you have a store that is 20GB, the index file may be between 4GB and 6GB in size. Make sure enough free disk space is available for the index file. Read more about full-text indexing in Chapter 2.

Hard Disk Layout

Exchange 2000 is a database application. This means that constant writing and reading operations will be made to the hard disk. Even small improvements of these operations might result in large gains in overall performance of the Exchange server. The things we must consider include:

- *The Stores*—.EDB and .STM files
- *The transaction log files*—.LOG and CHK files
- *The operating system page file*—Pagefile.sys

The worst disk layout would be to place all of these files on the same hard disk! Not only would this slow down performance, but it would also in effect prohibit the transaction system from working as designed, since you would place both the stores and the transaction logs together; one disk crash would destroy both of them!

Instead, you should have a disk layout that takes into account both the constant disk access and the security aspects. Then you would get a solution like this:

- A mirrored disk for the operating system and its page file
- A mirrored disk for the transaction log files
- A RAID5 disk set for each storage group

This would increase the initial cost of the server, but it would also increase its performance and security! It is absolutely worth the extra money to build a good and reliable disk layout; if you don't believe me, ask anyone who's had a disk crash where they stored both the stores and the transaction log files on the same disk!

Not only should you go for multiple disks, but they must also be fast. I recommend that you look for Ultra SCSI drives or faster. They will give the Exchange server much better performance compared to IDE drives. The multiple disks should also have separate disk controllers, making it possible to read and write independently to these disks; since Exchange 2000 is a multithreaded application, it will take advantage of this ability, if available. However, you should avoid activating write-ahead caches on those disk controllers, even if you have a battery-backup. Even they will fail from time to time, and when this happens your Exchange stores will crash!

The DSAccess Cache

Another important factor that influences overall Exchange performance is the DSAccess cache. This is a cache that every Exchange server has to improve its performance regarding queries to the global catalog server. Every time an Outlook client earlier than Outlook 2000 accesses the global address list, it will send a request to the Exchange server. However, since the Exchange 2000 server doesn't have its own directory anymore, this query is forwarded by the server to the GC; the result is later passed back to the client. If we have 1,000 clients on one single server, this could affect performance dramatically. To overcome this, each Exchange 2000 server caches the results from the global catalog server; the next time a client asks for the same address list, Exchange already has it in the cache.

Table 10.4 Some of the Performance Monitor counters for the DSAccess cache.

Counter	Description
Cache Expires/sec	Number of objects expired from the cache per second
Cache Hits/sec	Number of hits, i.e., objects found in cache, per second
Cache Inserts/sec	Number of new objects inserted into the cache per second
Cache Misses/sec	Number of misses, i.e., objects not found in cache, per second
Cache Misses Total	Number of misses since system initialization
Total Memory Size	Total shared memory size of the cache (in bytes)

The name of the cache is DSAccess Cache; it is default 4MB in size, and will store information up to five minutes. After that, the data is removed. A number of special counters in the Performance Monitor are available for this cache, which can be used for monitoring how effective it is. See Table 10.4; see also KB article Q246271.

When analyzing these counters, you may find that you want to modify the size of the cache or the amount of time the objects are stored there. When doing this, you must take into account a number of things; for example, if the time objects are stored in the cache is too long, it may prohibit the server from retrieving new updates quickly. If the size of the cache is too large, it will increase the system load. Change the values of the cache, then use the Performance Monitor again to see the result, and make new adjustments if necessary; repeat this until you have found an optimized cache.

Use the Regedt32.exe tool to optimize the parameters for the cache for your organization. There are three such parameters: CacheTTL, MaxEntries, and MaxMemory.

Note: *Microsoft recommends that you configure the cache size using the MaxMemory Registry key. This will give you a higher degree of control over the memory usage of the server, compared to using the MaxEntries.*

The CacheTTL controls how long a cached object will be stored in the DSAccess cache. It is defined in the Registry hierarchy:

```
HKEY_LOCAL_MACHINE\System\CurrentControlSet\Service\MSExchagneDSAccess\
  Instance0
CacheTTL = 0x600 (REG_DWORD) : sets the TTL to 600 seconds, or 10 minutes.
```

Note that you might have to create both the Instance0 and the CacheTTL entries manually.

The MaxEntries parameter sets a limit on how many objects can be stored in the cache. The default is 0, meaning an unlimited number of entries. The MaxEntries is stored in the hierarchy:

```
HKEY_LOCAL_MACHINE\System\CurrentControlSet\Service\MSExchagneDSAccess\
  Instance0
MaxEntries = 0 (REG_DWORD) : sets number of entries to unlimited
```

Finally, the last parameter that controls the cache is MaxMemory; it will set a limit on how large the cache is allowed to grow. This parameter is stored in the hierarchy:

```
HKEY_LOCAL_MACHINE\System\CurrentControlSet\Service\MSExchagneDSAccess\
  Instance0
MaxMemory = 4096 (REG_DWORD) : sets the max cache size to 4096KB, or 4MB.
```

Tuning the SMTP Transport

Incoming SMTP messages to an Exchange server are temporarily stored in the *C:\Program Files\Exchsrvr\Mailroot* directory. For an organization with many mail-intensive users, a large number of messages will temporarily be stored on this directory. Practical tests on an organization with more than 30,000 users showed that moving this mailroot directory to another disk greatly improved the SMTP transport performance. Follow these instructions to move the mailroot directory to another disk:

1. Shut down all Exchange server services.
2. Take a backup of the *\Program files\Exchsrvr\mailroot* directory.
3. Move the *VS1* directory, including all subdirectories, to the new location.
4. Start the *ADSI Edit* tool.
5. Navigate to Configuration container\CN=Configuration, CN=Services, CN=Microsoft Exchange, CN=<organization name>, CN=Administrative Groups, CN=<admin group>, CN=Servers, CN=Protocols, CN=SMTP, CN=1.
6. Right-click the *CN=1* object, and then select *Properties*.
7. Select *Both* from the *Select Which Properties To View* list.
8. Modify the path of the following attributes, making them point to the new location:
   - msExchSmtpBadMailDirectory
   - msExchSmtpPickupDirectory
   - msExchSmtpQueueDirectory
9. Wait for AD to replicate these new settings to the other domain controllers in the forest.
10. Start the *MS Exchange System Attendant* service; this will replicate the new settings in the AD to the Metabase that IIS and its virtual SMTP servers are reading.
11. Open the *Event log*; you should get three 1005 events, indicating that the replication to the Metabase was successful.
12. Restart the Exchange 2000 computer.

Summary

This is a list of the more important features and keywords mentioned in this chapter. Use it as a reminder and to make sure you have understood the most important things:

- Since Exchange 2000 doesn't have its own directory anymore, we must configure both the Exchange server and the Active Directory.
- Before installing Exchange 2000, there are a number of things we must take care of and plan for. "Think before you act!"
- Plan the installation carefully; make sure you understand the objectives of this messaging system. Document how the current system looks; will it be able to manage the new system?

- Do you have a name standard? Create one before you install your first Exchange server. It will be a lot of work to change the name standard after half the organization is up and running on the new system.
- How many servers will there be? Where will they be located? How many users will be on each server?
- How many administrative groups and routing groups will there be?
- Some settings must be decided before you install the first Exchange server, since they cannot be changed: the organization name, the name of the Exchange server, and the names of the Windows 2000 domain controllers.
- Prepare the Windows 2000 forest by running the **ForestPrep** command; this will expand the number of attributes of users, groups, and other objects.
- You need to be a member of the Schema Admins group to run **ForestPrep**.
- Prepare each local Windows 2000 domain that will have Exchange 2000 servers by running the **DomainPrep** command.
- You need to be a member of Domain Admins and Enterprise Admins groups to run **DomainPrep**.
- **DomainPrep** creates two new security groups: Exchange Domain Servers and Exchange Enterprise Servers; these are special groups for Exchange servers—you should not add an administrator account to these groups.
- A special user account called EUSER_EXSTOREEVENTS will be created, which is used when executing Exchange Event service scripts; this type of user has fewer permissions than the Guest account.
- Small Exchange organizations, with only one Windows 2000 domain, don't need to run **ForestPrep** and **DomainPrep**; the Exchange setup program will do it automatically. But make sure you are logged on as an administrator that is a member of the Schema Admins group.

- The minimum hardware configuration for installing Exchange 2000 is Pentium 133MHz with 128MB of RAM and 500+200MB of free disk space.
- The more practical minimum configuration is Pentium III 850MHz, with 256MB of RAM and 10+10+20GB of disk space.
- Never ever forget the backup solution to the Exchange server!
- *Windows 2000 Server*—For a server with up to four CPUs.
- *Windows 2000 Advanced Server*—For a server with up to eight CPUs and two-node cluster support.
- *Windows 2000 Datacenter Server*—For a server with up to 32 CPUs and four-node cluster support.
- The Windows 2000 server must have IIS, SMTP, NNTP, and TCP/IP installed. There must also be a domain controller with a Dynamic DNS server reachable.
- Use NTFS to be able to secure your directories and files.
- The Page file should be twice the size of the physical memory.
- There are two versions of Exchange: Exchange 2000 Server, and Exchange 2000 Enterprise Server.
- The Enterprise version has 10 different components that can be installed, including Exchange core features, MS Mail connectors, cc:Mail Connector, Lotus Notes, GroupWise, Key Management service, ESM Management tools, Exchange 5.5 Admin tools, Exchange 2000 Chat service, and Instant Messaging.
- Exchange can be installed in unattended mode, using the **/createunattend** switch to create the initialization file, and **/unattend** to run an unattended setup.
- Unattended setup is very handy when the person installing Exchange lacks Exchange experience.
- A number of things can't be done with an unattended setup, like **ForestPrep**, **DomainPrep**, upgrading, uninstalling, adding, or removing components.
- To remove Exchange 2000 completely from the Windows 2000 forest, you must manually modify objects in the Active Directory.
- Removing a crashed Exchange 2000 server is even more tricky; it involves removing keys in the Registry and modifying attributes for mailbox-enabled user objects.
- Installing subsequent Exchange servers is easy; just decide what administrative group it will belong to (if there is more than one).
- After the installation, you will see a number of new directories, file shares, groups, services, and administrative tools, including the following:

    - *Exchange System Manager (ESM)*—The main configuration tool for Exchange 2000. Replaces the Exchange Admin.exe tool of previous releases.
    - *Active Directory Users and Computers (ADUC)*—The main administrative tool for managing users, groups, and contacts. Replaces both the previous Exchange 5.5 Admin.exe tool regarding creating mailboxes, and the User Manager for Domains tool in Windows NT 4.
    - *Active Directory Cleanup Wizard*—Search the Active Directory for multiple accounts for the same user; this can happen during a migration to Exchange 2000 from NT 4 and Exchange 5.5.
    - *Migration Wizard*—The premium tool for migrating to Exchange 2000 from mail systems other than Exchange 5.5—for example, MS Mail, Lotus Notes, and GroupWise.
- Restart the Exchange server after the installation, and check the Event log for errors and warnings.
- Optimizing Exchange also means optimizing the Active Directory.
- The global catalog server is very important for the Exchange server and its clients.
- If you need to update the global catalog with new attributes, do it very early in the deployment process.
- Use front-end/back-end servers to increase performance of OWA clients, and to improve security.
- Activate full-text indexing for your clients, but remember to run the update process off-hours.
- Spend as much money as you can on the disk layout; you'll be repaid later with a fast Exchange server that is more resilient.
- Modify the DSAccess Cache to improve the pre-Outlook 2000 clients' querying of the global address list.
- Large organizations can benefit from moving the mailroot directory to another disk.

Chapter 11

Administrative Groups and Permissions

When selecting a mail system, it's easy to focus on the initial price for the product and forget about how it will be administrated. No approach could be worse, in my opinion. We usually pay only once for the product, but the administration of the product is an ongoing process, and those expenses quickly exceed the initial price. Therefore we should look for messaging products that are easy to administrate and require a minimum of people working as administrators. Previous Exchange releases were among the best in this respect, and the new Exchange 2000 is even better. One of the reasons is the new concept of *Administrative Groups*, or AGs, that gives us the means to build and design the messaging system from two independent points of view: the technical view, where we create routing groups with Exchange servers, and the administrative view, where we create administrative groups that define who can manage objects like servers and policies.

Another new feature in Exchange 2000 is that it utilizes the permission system in Windows 2000. In previous releases, Exchange managed its own access permissions for administration of mailbox accounts and server configuration settings, storing them in its own DIR.EDB database. In Exchange 2000, however, access permissions are stored in the Active Directory database. The ESM administrative tools are used to set administrative access permissions for parts of the Exchange system, such as server configurations, address lists, and public folders, and all administration of user accounts is done with the Active Directory Users and Computers tool. The number of access permission types has increased, compared to previous Exchange versions, making it possible to define the access permissions in detail, if necessary.

One aspect of administration is how to handle large and/or distributed organizations; how can we make sure that all remote sites have the same configuration settings without too much manual administration labor? Previously this was difficult; in Exchange 5.5 we had the *site* concept, that in many ways corresponds to an administrative group—we could create some configuration settings that were shared between all servers within one site, but each site had to be managed separately. With the new concept of *policies* in Exchange 2000, we have the means to define configuration settings of servers and users for the complete organization, regardless of how distributed or big it may be.

We start this chapter by looking at how administration was done in previous Exchange releases. Next we continue with a general description of the administrative groups in Exchange 2000; after that we investigate how permissions work in Windows 2000 and Exchange 2000, and then we look at how to create and manage administrative groups, including policies.

Comparing with Exchange 5.x Sites

All three of the previous Exchange versions were built on the same administrative concept, the *site*. A site is a group of one or more Exchange servers, expected to have a high bandwidth and a permanent network connection between them, capable of transferring Remote Procedure Call (RPC) network packages. The site is also an administrative boundary, meaning that each site has its own set of administrators; of course it can be the same person, and even the same administrative account, as long as the sites are within the same Windows NT 4 domain or a Windows NT trust exists between the domains. In Exchange 5.5 and previous versions, it was not possible to create a super-administrator who had access to all sites; if you were given administrative access to the organization object, you would be allowed to modify the display name of the organization, but nothing more.

Three different administrative roles are available for an Exchange 5.x administrator within a given site:

- *View Only Admin*—Can start the Admin.exe tool and view the settings of the site, but can make no modifications.
- *Admin*—Full administrative access, but no permission to add or delete new administrators.
- *Permissions Admin*—Full administrative access; can also add or delete new administrators.

These three roles can be assigned to three different levels within the Exchange organization tree, resulting in different types of administrative access:

- *The Organization object*—Makes it possible to change the display name of the organization, but only for users belonging to this site.
- *The Site object*—Makes it possible to manage mailbox users, custom recipients, public folders, and address book views; will also give View-Only access to the configuration settings for the servers and the connector objects in this site.
- *The Configuration object*—Gives full administrative access to all configuration settings for this site.

Usually, these three roles and three levels of administrative access are used for creating the following types of administrators for a given site:

- *The View-Only Administrator*—Has View-Only access to the Site object only; this type of administrator can start the admin program and view its configuration and queues. Usually granted to first-line support or power users.
- *The Mailbox Administrator*—Has Admin permission on the Site object only; this type of administrator can start the admin program and create, modify, and delete mailbox users and custom recipients.
- *The Full Exchange Administrator*—Has Permission Admin permissions on the Site, Configuration, and Organization objects; this type of administrator can do everything in this site.

For smaller organizations, this was just fine—there was seldom a need for a finer degree of administrative control. However, for larger or more distributed organizations this was sometimes not enough; for example, an Exchange 5.5 site with two Exchange servers might have two groups of administrators that want to administrate one server each. This is not possible, since the two servers belong to the same site. The only way of solving this is to split the site into two separate sites, with one server each; this would result in delayed replication of directory information and an unnecessarily complex Exchange environment.

Another example of the problems with the administrative concept in Exchange 5.5 is when you want to define global settings, or configuration settings that should be set on more than one server. Some configuration settings are possible to define for all servers within a site—for example the SMTP address—but others will be valid only for a particular server. For example, let's say you want to set a maximum mailbox size limit of 50MB globally, and the Exchange organization consists of several sites. In this case, you must configure each server in each site individually to set this limit; if you want to modify that value later, you need to change each server again.

Most of these problems are due to the way configuration settings are stored in Exchange 5.5 and previous versions. Everything is kept in the server's DIR.EDB database; every server has its own DIR.EDB, and its Directory Service will replicate all changes to all other servers within this site. However, between sites only a subset of the information is replicated. But even for the information that actually is replicated, Exchange servers in other sites are not designed to import those settings.

In Exchange 2000, however, it works like this: All configuration settings are stored in the Active Directory; instead of sites we now have AD Domains (that may be divided into several Windows 2000 sites). All domain controllers within a given domain replicate everything in their Active Directory database between them; a subset of this information, including the Exchange configuration settings, will be replicated to the global catalog. Since the content of the GC is replicated to all other GCs in the forest, this information is truly global. All Exchange servers read the GC, and if any updates are made to their configuration setting, they will get this information. This is exemplified in Exchange 2000 by the new concept of *system policies*, configuration settings that can be applied to just a single server or to all servers in the organization, regardless of how many domains there may be.

Easier Administration in Exchange 2000

The new concept of *Administrative Groups*, or AGs, in Exchange 2000 makes it easier to administrate even a distributed Exchange organization with lots of Exchange servers. It makes it possible to group objects together, regardless of their physical location. We can assign very detailed access permissions to the administrators for this administrative group, and even to any of its subfolders. An administrative group can contain these standard objects (see also Figure 11.1):

- *Folders*—Both MAPI public folders and GP (general purpose) folders.
- *Servers*—Exchange servers and their protocol containers and storage groups.
- *System Policies*—Defining configuration settings for server, public, and mailbox stores.
- *Routing Groups*—Groups of well-connected Exchange servers that can transfer messages directly between them.

Besides these standard objects, an administrative group can also contain Chat Server networks and Conferencing Server objects, if they are installed in this Exchange organization.

Note: *It may be easy to confuse security and distribution groups in Windows 2000 with administrative groups; however, they have nothing in common, except that they are both collections of objects. An administrative group is purely a logical concept that is used only for grouping Exchange 2000 objects for administrative purposes; it will not affect message transfer or any physical configuration.*

Exchange 2000 Mixed Mode vs. Native Mode

A new Exchange 2000 organization will by default be configured to run in mixed mode, as you may recall from previous chapters. The reason for this is that Exchange 2000 must be able to join an Exchange 5.5 organization; this also has the consequence that not all

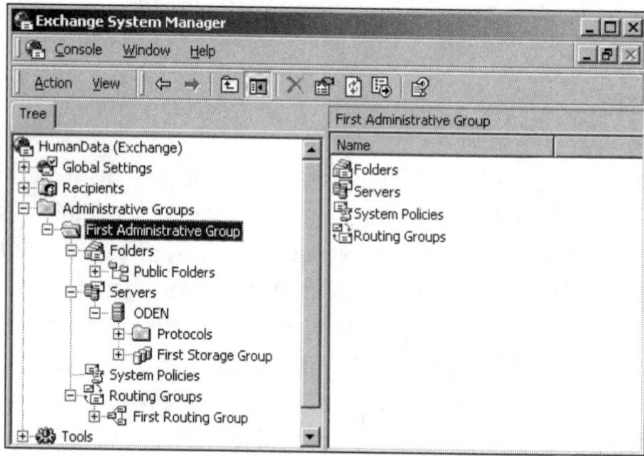

Figure 11.1
Objects within the administrative group.

features in Exchange 2000 are enabled, making these two versions compatible. When only Exchange 2000 servers are left, and you have no plans to add any Exchange 5.5 servers later on, you should convert the organization to run in native mode. To perform this conversion, open the properties for the Exchange 2000 organization object, look at the General page, and click on the button to switch to native mode operation.

Warning! *The conversion to native mode is a one-way street; you can never return to mixed mode again! Remember that native mode does not allow a mix of Exchange 2000 and Exchange 5.5 servers in the same organization.*

Once you have a clean Exchange 2000 organization, you should not hesitate to switch over to native mode; the benefits are several, including:

- You can move mailboxes between servers that belong to any routing group in the organization (in mixed mode, they can only be moved to other servers in the same routing group).
- One single administrative group can contain all routing groups within the organization; this will make it possible to create administrators that can manage all routing groups.
- You can create administrative groups and routing groups freely; for example, an Exchange 2000 server can belong to a routing group in one administrative group, but at the same time this server can belong to a *Server* folder that is managed by another administrative group.

Later in this chapter we will discuss different administrative models for Exchange 2000; it is important to understand that an organization must operate in native mode before you can select between these types of models.

Note: *There is no correlation between Windows 2000 native or mixed mode operation and Exchange 2000 native or mixed operation; you can have any type of combination—for example, a Windows 2000 forest in mixed mode, running Exchange 2000 in native mode.*

The First Administrative Group

When the first Exchange 2000 server is installed in the organization, or the **ForestPrep** command is executed, a default administrative group will be created called the First Administrative Group, as depicted in Figure 11.1. All subsequently installed Exchange servers will automatically belong to this AG, unless a new administrative group is created; if so, you will see an extra dialog page during the installation, asking what AG this new server will belong to. If you want to split the servers into several administrative groups, it is of paramount importance that you create all administrative groups before installing these servers. Microsoft doesn't support servers moved between AGs, even though it technically can be done, as described later in this chapter; you must install the server directly into the final administrative group!

The default setup of the ESM tool does not display administrative groups or routing groups. To make them visible, follow these steps:

1. Start the *ESM* tool.
2. Right-click on the *Organization* object and select *Properties*.
3. On the *General* page, set the checkbox for *Administrative Groups And The Routing Groups*; note that you cannot display routing groups if the Exchange 2000 organization is running in mixed mode, (see Figure 11.2). Click *OK* when ready.
4. Restart the ESM tool; now you will see the *Administrative Groups* folder, and within it, you'll find the *First Administrative Group*.

In the old Exchange 5.5 site concept, there is no difference between the administrative boundary and the routing topology; if an Exchange 2000 server wants to join an Exchange 5.5 organization, its administrative groups must behave exactly like a 5.5 site. That is the reason an Exchange 2000 organization running in mixed mode will create one routing group within each administrative group. Since you cannot create more than one routing group per AG, there is no point in displaying them.

If you are running Exchange 2000 in mixed mode and one of its servers has joined an Exchange 5.5 organization, each 5.5 site will be displayed as an administrative group, but with a special icon. It will be white, compared to the ordinary AG icons that are yellow. If you look at its Server folder, you will also see that all Exchange 5.5 servers have white server icons, whereas Exchange 2000 servers have gray server icons. Both these white icons clearly indicate that this organization is running in mixed mode instead of native mode.

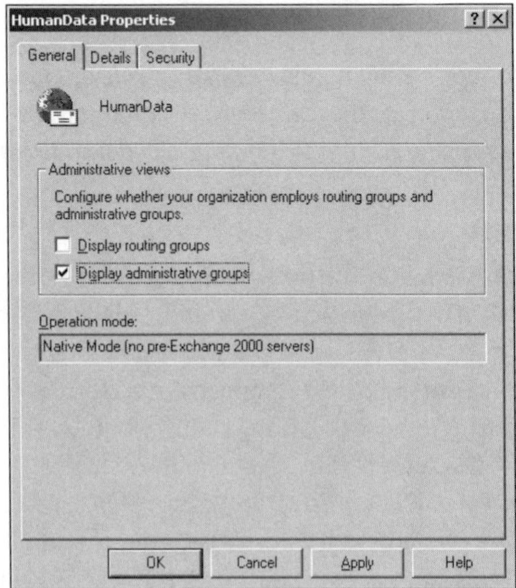

Figure 11.2
Displaying administrative groups.

Setting Access Permission to the Administrative Group

The First Administrative Group will inherit the access permissions set on the organization object. This means that the account used to install the first Exchange server will have full access to this first administrative group. Use the Delegation Wizard to add new administrators; however, you cannot remove any inherited administrator accounts, except by removing them from the parent container, i.e., the organization object. Follow these steps to add a new administrator to the First Administrative Group:

1. Open the ESM tool, and navigate to the *First Administrative Group*.
2. Right-click on this object, and select *Delegate Control*.
3. On the *Welcome* page, click *Next*.
4. On the *Users Or Groups* page, click *Add*.
5. On the *Delegate Control* page, use the *Browse* button to select the new administrator (or preferably a group of Exchange administrators); then select the administrative role this user (or group) will have. See more about roles in the section about permissions later in this chapter. Click *OK* when ready.
6. Go back to the *Users Or Groups* page and click *Next* to continue.
7. Click *Finish* to complete this operation.

If you need to remove this administrator, or change its role, use the Delegation Wizard again.

Creating Subsequent Administrative Groups

You can create any number of administrative groups, but you should always have a good reason to do so; there is no point in creating extra AGs just because it is possible. Small-to medium-sized organizations will probably do fine with one single administrative group; however, if the organization is large or geographically distributed, it may be necessary to create extra administrative groups. If that is the case, I recommend that you create all the administrative groups needed immediately after the First Administrative Group is created (which was created by using the **ForestPrep** command or when the first Exchange server was installed); when installing subsequent Exchange servers, you can select to install them into the correct AG directly. To create a new administrative group, follow these instructions:

1. Start the *ESM* tool.
2. Navigate to the *Administrative Groups* folder.
3. Right-click on this folder, and select *New|Administrative Group*.
4. In the *General* page, type the name of the new AG; remember to follow the naming standard for AGs. Click *OK* when ready, and this will create the AG.

Moving a Server between Administrative Groups

The new administrative group will not contain any objects initially; you can create a routing group container, a system policy container, and a public folder container by right-clicking on the new AG and selecting *New*. However, you cannot create a server container! This container will be created automatically when the first Exchange server is installed into this AG; this container will also be created if a server is moved into this AG. Officially, Microsoft says that it's not possible to move servers between administrative groups; however, this is not completely true—you can move them by using the *ADSI Edit* tool. But this is dangerous! If you move a server to another administrative group, the following problems could arise:

- The *Information Store* could have problems managing the store databases, since they have a distinguished name (DN) that refers to the administrative group.
- There could be a problem with permission settings.
- Outlook may have a problem trying to publish *free/busy* information to the store.
- In mixed mode operation, where Exchange 2000 servers have joined an Exchange 5.5 site, strange things could happen if you move the server to another AG.
- "Things will break, it's just a matter of time!" according to one Exchange specialist I talked to at Microsoft.

The bottom line is that Microsoft absolutely does not support moving servers between administrative groups! And as far as I know, no plans are in the works to change that in the next release of Exchange. However, during practical tests I have done in small organizations running in native mode, I have not seen any problems so far.

Warning! *If you want to test this, do it at your own risk; use a test environment, preferably a mirror of the production environment, and check if you encounter any of the problems mentioned above. Remember, this is a nonsupported operation!*

To manually move an Exchange server into the new AG, follow these instructions:

1. Start the *ADSI Edit* tool.
2. Navigate to *Configuration Container/Configuration/Services/Microsoft Exchange/<organization name>/Administrative Groups*. In this container, you will find each created administrative group.
3. Expand the first AG containing the server that will be moved; look into its *Servers* folder.
4. Right-click the server to be moved, and select *Move*; this will give you the same folder tree as in Step 2. Navigate to the new administrative group this server will be moved to and select its *Server* container. See Figure 11.3. Click *OK* to move the server.

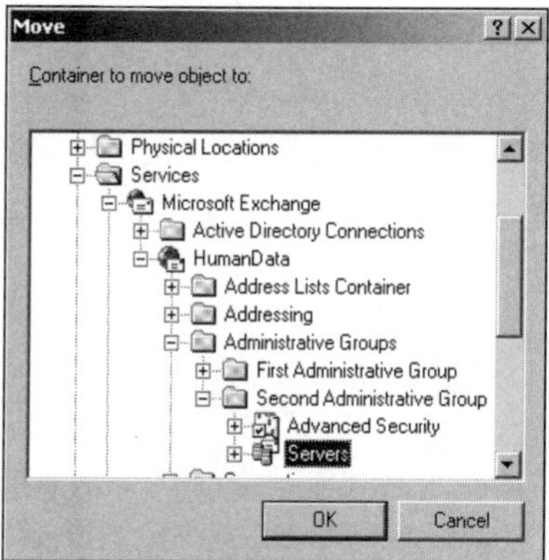

Figure 11.3
Selecting the new administrative group into which to move the server.

5. Exit the *ADSI Edit* tool.
6. Open the ESM tool again, and select the *Administrative Groups* folder. Click Refresh, and open the new administrative group; you will find the server folder containing the moved server.

Common Administrative Models

The simplest model is an Exchange organization with one single administrative group, but in some situations it may be necessary to create more than one AG. In general, three different administrative models are possible for Exchange 2000 organizations:

- *Centralized administration*—One group of administrators managing the complete Exchange organization.
- *Delegated administration*—Different groups of administrators managing different locations or parts of the Exchange organization.
- *Mixed administration*—A mix of the two models above.

The choice of model depends on how the IT department wants to manage and control the Exchange system; the model selected will determine how many administrative groups there will be.

Centralized Administration

This is by far the most common model, due to the many benefits it offers. Even large organizations may prefer to use this model to achieve central administration of the Exchange organization. In this model, you typically have only the First Administrative Group, since you don't need any more administrative groups. However, if you have a mix of Exchange 5.5 servers and Exchange 2000 servers, each 5.5 site will be created as an administrative group containing one single routing group. In this case, you will need to give your Exchange administrator group global access permission using the Delegation

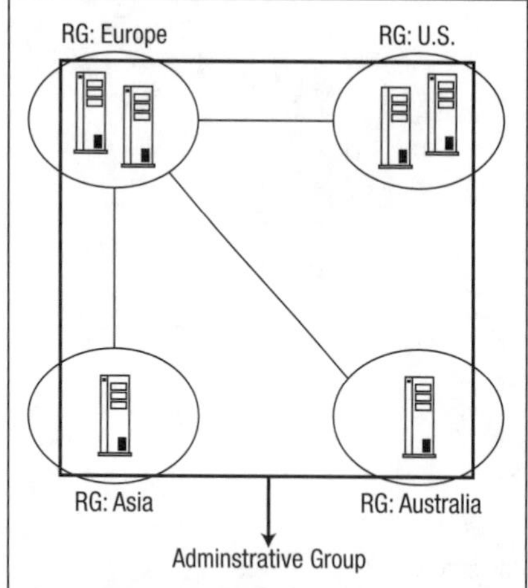

Figure 11.4
Example of a central administrative model.

Wizard on the organization object in ESM. Make sure this group of Exchange administrators includes only reliable people, since they will have unlimited power within this Exchange organization! See Figure 11.4 for an example of a company with a centralized administrative model; this organization has four routing groups, one for each geographical site, but only one administrative group, which manages all servers.

Delegated Administration

This model is common for organizations that are geographically distributed, or typically a company with several subsidiary companies that each want to have their local IT staff manage their own set of Exchange servers. In this case, create one administrative group for each subsidiary and one for the headquarters; then create a security group of administrators for each, giving them full access permissions within their respective AGs. For example, in Figure 11.5 you see an organization with one headquarters and three subsidiary companies, A, B, and C; each of them has their own administrative group, AG-A, AG-B, etc., giving them full control of their local Exchange servers.

The drawback of this model is that it offers no central control; in this situation, it's important to define rules and guidelines that each local group of administrators should follow. This type of administration model is equivalent to what you have in Exchange 5.5 organizations with multiple sites. Use this model only if each subsidiary company has local administrators with the required technical knowledge of Exchange 2000; otherwise, this model could result in a chaotic or suboptimized Exchange system, as several large Exchange 5.5 multisite organizations have experienced.

A Mixed Administrative Model

This model is a mixture of the two previous models; first there is a central group of administrators, with full access permissions to all administrative groups in the Exchange

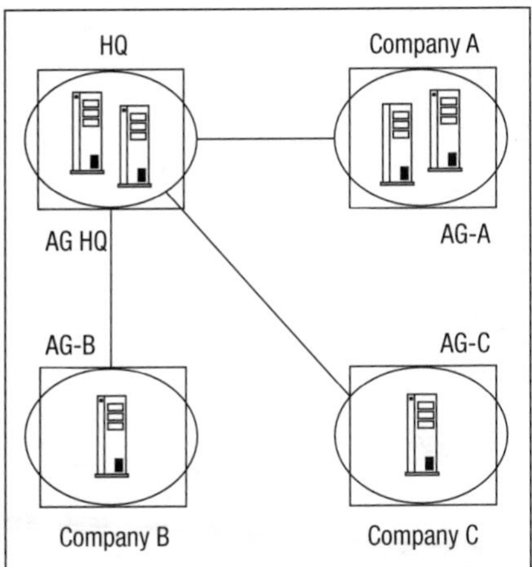

Figure 11.5
Example of a distributed administrative model.

organization. Then there is one administrative group with its local group of administrators for each subsidiary company. This will make it possible for the local administrators to manage their own Exchange servers, but when necessary the central administrators can make adjustments to the local Exchange settings. This model is probably more popular with the central administrative group than the local IT groups, since it ensures that the central group has the power to make adjustments, if needed. However, the local administrators may think of this model as some sort of "Big-brother is watching you" scenario, so make sure the organization accepts the consequences before implementing this mixed model.

In Figure 11.6, you can see an example where the headquarters (HQ) has their own AG, but is also given administrative power of all other AGs, while at the same time each local subsidiary company has their own AG, managed by their local administrators.

To configure the permissions as shown in Figure 11.6, you would start by giving the administrators at the headquarters full access permissions to the organization, using the Delegation Wizard on the Exchange organization object. This will give them full access to all existing and future administrative groups. Next, use the Delegation Wizard on each administrative group object, giving each local admin group the permission role Exchange Administrator. This will give them full access to all objects in this AG, but doesn't allow them to add or remove administrators to this AG.

Another type of mixed administration is when each subsidiary company has administrative permissions to their local AG, but another group, usually the IT staff at the headquarters, has the permissions to create system policies for all servers, regardless of what AG they belong to.

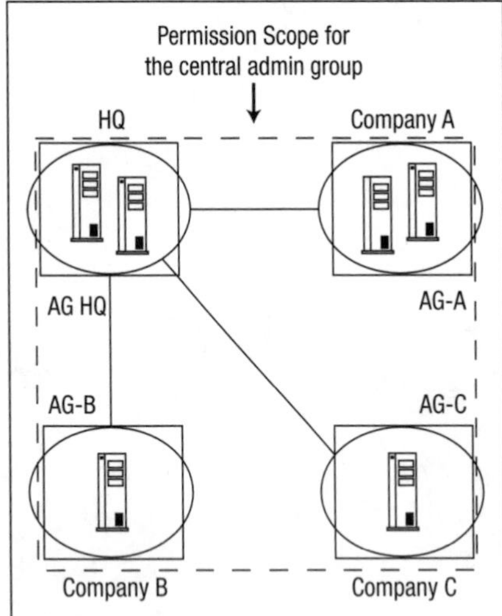

Figure 11.6
Example of a mixed administrative model.

Other Administrative Design Considerations

Besides selecting the proper administrative model, there are more things to consider regarding administration of Exchange 2000. For example, if you have migrated from Exchange 5.5, you must make sure the new configuration and permission settings allow the persons that previously had any form of administrative role to continue their tasks. However, you should also take this opportunity to look over the current administrative roles, to see if the system could be made simpler and require fewer administrators. Remember, if you can reduce the total number of administrators by one or more, you have saved the company a lot of money.

The following topics must be considered when deciding the new administrative model for Exchange 2000:

- Mailbox administration
- Recipient policies
- Address lists
- Server configurations
- Routing issues
- Public folders
- Collaboration issues

Mailbox Administration

The primary tool used for creating, modifying, and deleting mailbox-enabled users is the Active Directory Users and Computers tool; this was previously done with the Exchange 5.5

Admin tool. Who will administer these users' accounts now? It's not necessarily the same group of people as before. With Windows 2000, it's easier to manage large and complex organizations, and mailbox administration is now managed by configuring the users' extra property pages for Exchange. Maybe the same people that managed Windows NT 4 accounts before can now manage all user and group administration, including Exchange properties? Or maybe we should train the Human Resources department to do this type of work, since they are responsible for all employees? In some organizations, this is music to the Exchange administrator's ear, whereas in others this will not be acceptable. How much training is needed before we can allow people with no previous Exchange experience to administrate user accounts? Don't underestimate the political problems this question could create, it may be a "hot potato" for larger companies.

A related topic is the administration of mail-enabled contacts and groups; who will administrate these? Remember that in Windows 2000, you can have mail-enabled security groups that can be used both for assigning access permissions and as message groups. It is always best if a single group of administrators can be responsible for the management of all users, groups, and contacts, since this requires fewer administrators, creates faster response times, and lowers the risk of errors; but again, in a large organization this may be hard to implement due to political problems.

Recipient Policies

A recipient policy is used to define rules for generating email addresses of users. It is also used to control what SMTP domains this organization accepts. An email address rule can be applied to the complete Exchange organization, not just a single Exchange 5.5 site, as before. Your administrative model must cover who will be able to manage recipient policies; this should probably be an administrator in a central position, since typically all users share the same SMTP domain name, like **@microsoft.com**. This type of policy is covered in more detail later in this chapter.

Address Lists

In Exchange 5.5, there is one *Global Address List (GAL)* that displays every visible user, group, and public folder in the organization. There are also one or more recipient folders in each site, which are visible to the Outlook users. Finally, there is a possibility to create lists of users based on properties such as *Department* and *Company*; this feature is called *Address Book Views (ABV)* and is also visible to the Outlook users. Any *Mailbox Administrator* for a site could modify these recipient folders and ABVs.

Exchange 2000 offers a number of new address lists, based on LDAP search filters, so this task is now more complex than in previous Exchange versions. You need administrative rights in the Exchange organization to be able to create, modify, and delete these lists. These lists are very important to users, since they are displayed to the Outlook client; they also provide a measure of security, since they can be used to filter what addresses a user can see. Only an experienced Exchange administrator should be given the responsibility for managing these lists due to their importance and the complexity that the LDAP search filter adds to them.

Server Configuration

This is one of the most fundamental configuration issues in Exchange 2000; the administrator that manages a server must be able to configure server properties, such as monitoring and tracking logging. This administrator also controls all virtual servers for the Internet protocols: HTTP, IMAP4, NNTP, POP3, SMTP, and X.400. Besides being able to configure and mange these virtual servers, this administrator can view and manipulate the servers' message queues. And more, this administrator manages the storage groups on this server and their stores, configuring, for example, transaction log files and circular logging. These are indeed important tasks.

With the new permission model that Windows 2000 offers us, we could create different administrators for each single store database! That opens up a number of new administrative possibilities that were impossible in previous Exchange versions; for example, you may have one group that administrates an AG, but only one of these administrators is allowed to manage the mailbox store and control operations like mounting, indexing, and defining the location of the database files. Only experienced Exchange administrators should be allowed to manage server configurations.

Routing Issues

Another truly fundamental issue is the configuration and management of routing groups and connectors, including connections to other mail systems like the Internet and any older mail system Exchange coexists with. It will not be enough to understand the routing features in Exchange 2000; these administrators must also have knowledge about the underlying physical network, like the WAN connections, routers, switches, and firewalls. Again, only experienced Exchange administrators are expected to manage routing issues. Since message routing is at the heart of a mail system, probably only a few administrators should be allowed to manage routing issues.

Public Folders

Managing public folders is also an important task; it involves managing public folder stores and permissions to create top-level folders. It might be easy to forget the administration of public folders, but don't! Make sure the public folder administrator fully understands how public folders work, the difference between MAPI folders and GP folders, and the importance of controlling who is allowed to create top-level folders. You may recall that by default, everyone is allowed to create top-level folders; if we have an organization with 300 users, and each of them creates a public folder just to test it, all users will then see 300 new public folders displayed in the Outlook client, regardless of what Exchange server they belong to.

Another common mistake that a public folder administrator must avoid is erroneous replication of access permissions down a public folder tree. For example, assume that after the Exchange system is installed, users create a number of public folders in the carefully structured top-level folder structure. These subfolders probably have different access permissions, defined by the users when they created these folders. Now, let's assume that you need to assist some users with their public folders; to do this you need to grant yourself access permissions. Using the ESM tool, you open up the top-level folder for this tree, add your own account to the permission tab, and select to propagate the new settings to all subfolders. The result will be that the permissions for all subfolders will be replaced by whatever permission setting there was for the top-level folder! This could be very hard to repair since most users don't document or remember what permissions they define for their folders.

It may not be necessary to use a senior Exchange administrator for this task, but make sure whomever you do choose is well trained in this subject; otherwise he or she could easily create chaos!

Collaboration Issues

Besides administering the core messaging issues mentioned above, there may also be some special applications that utilize the Exchange server for storing and sharing information, like a Help Desk application, or a Customer Relationship Management (CRM) system. Who will administer these systems? Responsibility for this task may require extra training, besides Exchange expertise. You may also have installed Instant Messaging, the Chat Server, or the Conferencing Server into the Exchange system; these products must also be administrated. Again, it may require extra training, besides basic Exchange knowledge. Make sure the administrator of these systems gets the proper training before taking on the responsibility to manage and configure them.

Defining Permissions

Since Exchange 2000 runs on the Windows 2000 platform, it will utilize its rich set of access permissions to enforce security on Exchange 2000 objects. When installing Exchange 2000, the Windows 2000 permission model will be extended by a number of new messaging-specific permissions, like *Create Top-Level Folders*. With the granular permissions now available, it is possible to customize the access permission for almost all needs. However, with all these new possibilities, it might also be easy to make mistakes; this section describes how to use the Windows 2000 permission system to control access to Exchange objects in an optimal way.

Some of the possibilities that the new security model offers are:

- You can set access permission on any Exchange object, not just public folders.
- You can set access permission on single items in a folder.
- You can set access permission to individual properties for an item.
- You can set access permissions to security groups, distribution groups, or user accounts.
- You can deny permissions; this always takes precedence over granted permissions.

Another feature in the Windows 2000 permission system is inheritance; when an object is created, it will inherit the permissions from its parent object. For example, if you create a system policy container in an administrative group, it will contain exactly the same permissions as the administrative group, due to inheritance. This will simplify administration in the following ways, not least for Exchange administrators:

- It simplifies permission settings when creating new objects, since all child objects inherit permissions from their parents.
- Inheritance ensures that all permission settings for all child objects are consistent.
- To modify permissions for a group of object, for example an administrative group, change the parent object and all child objects will automatically inherit the new permission setting.

You can set some of these permission settings with the ESM tool, others with the File Explorer, and some with the ADSI Edit tool. Let's start by looking at how public folder permissions are managed in Exchange 2000.

Public Folder Permissions

Previous Exchange versions used two special "groups" to control general access to public folders: *Default* and *Anonymous*; they are still used in Exchange 2000 when setting permissions for public folders of MAPI type, in order to be backward compatible with MAPI clients like Outlook. However, in the new Windows 2000 security model, they correspond to the security groups *Everyone* and *Anonymous Logon*, respectively. For example, when you set the *Default* access permissions for a MAPI folder, you can then view the corresponding Windows 2000 permission settings for the group *Everyone*. To compare the MAPI permissions and the corresponding Windows 2000 permissions, follow these instructions:

1. Start the *ESM* tool; select any MAPI public folder under the *Folders* container.
2. Right-click on this MAPI folder and select *Properties*.
3. Click the *Permissions* tab.
4. Click the *Client Permissions* button.
5. Note the current permission role for *Default*. In this example it's *Reviewer*; see Figure 11.7.
6. Click *Cancel* to close this window; you are back to the *Permissions* page again.
7. Press the *Control* key on the keyboard, and click the *Client Permissions* button again. This time you will see the corresponding Windows 2000 permissions; see Figure 11.8.

Public Folder Permission Roles

Exchange 5.5 has its own set of permissions, optimized for the control of administrative access and public folder access. The administrative access was described in the beginning of this chapter, so let's look at how public folder access works in Exchange 5.5. Both Outlook clients and the Exchange 5.5 Admin program can be used to set access permission roles to public folders; see Figure 11.9.

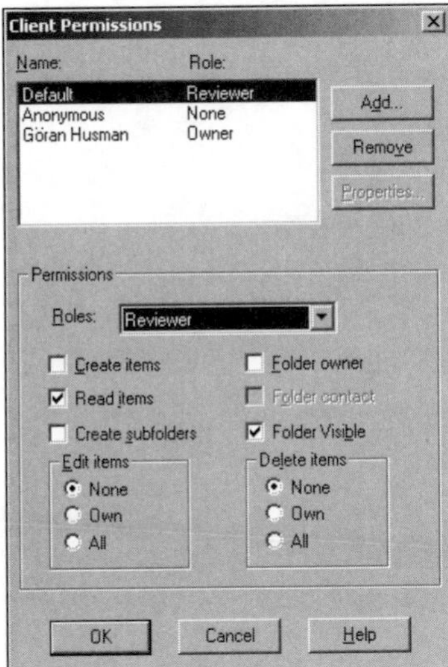

Figure 11.7
The standard MAPI permissions.

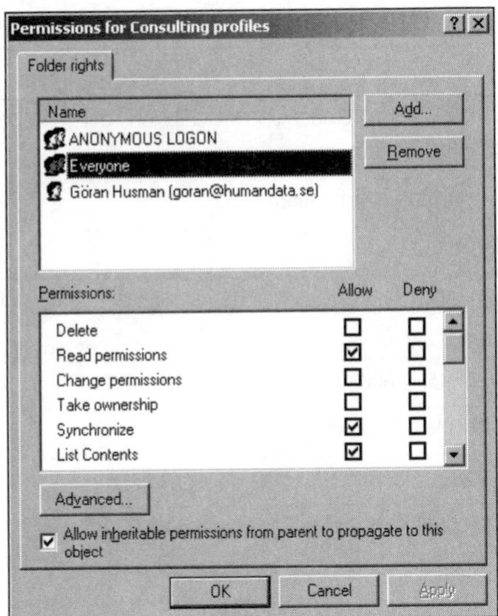

Figure 11.8
The corresponding permissions in Windows 2000.

These permission roles are still valid for public folders of MAPI type in Exchange 2000; they are the only means by which an Outlook client can control access to a public folder. An administrator can also use the ESM tool to modify these permissions, just like it was possible to use the Admin.exe program in Exchange 5.5. The permission roles available in Exchange 2000 have been extended with one new role, the *Contributor*; they are all described in Table 11.1.

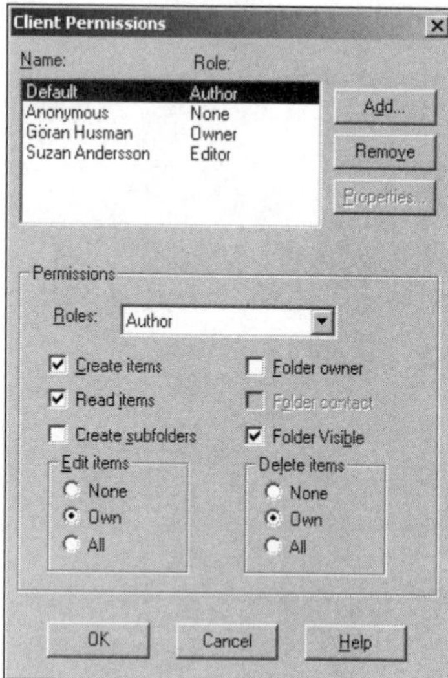

Figure 11.9
The permission roles for public folders.

Table 11.1 Permission roles for public folders.

Role	Permission
Owner	Has full access to this public folder and its objects. Can create, read, modify, and delete all items and files; can create subfolders; can also modify the permissions on this folder.
Publishing Editor	Can do everything an owner can, except modify the permissions.
Editor	Can create, read, modify, and delete all items and folders.
Publishing Author	Can create and read all items and files; can modify and delete own items and files; can create subfolders.
Author	Can create and read all items and files; can modify and delete own items and files.
Nonediting Author	Can create and read all items and files; can delete own items and files.
Reviewer	Can read items and files.
Contributor	Can create items and files; cannot view the contents of this folder. This is new for Exchange 2000.
None	No access to this folder or its contents.

More Public Folder Permissions in ESM

Besides using these predefined permission roles, an administrator can set more granular access permissions using the *Security* property page for a public folder. You can apply three different types of permissions to a public folder with the ESM tool; you can find them in the properties for the public folder, on the Permissions page:

- *Client Permissions*—Controls the access to the folder and its contents as described above.

- *Directory Rights*—Controls the access to this folder in the Active Directory. This could be used to prohibit an administrator from viewing the properties for this folder. Figure 11.10 shows the error message you'll receive in ESM if you try to open the properties for a folder you don't have directory rights to view; however, this folder will still be visible for Outlook clients, if the Client Permissions allows it.
- *Administrative Rights*—Controls the administrative access to this folder; can be used to prohibit an administrator from modifying the size limits, for example.

These different permissions make it possible to control the access to each public folder in great detail, which was never possible in the previous Exchange releases. You could, for example:

- *Prohibit an administrator from viewing a public folder's properties, although he or she has full access to the administrative group*. To do this, use the Directory Rights button on the Permissions page for this folder; select the name of this administrator and deny Read Properties access; see Figure 11.11.

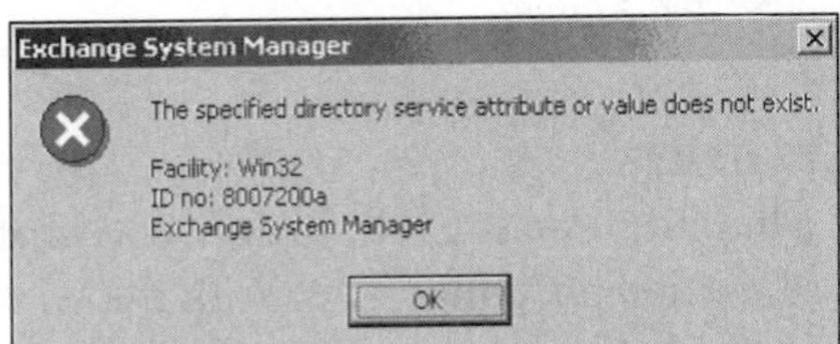

Figure 11.10
You'll receive this error message if you don't have the directory rights to a folder you're trying to access.

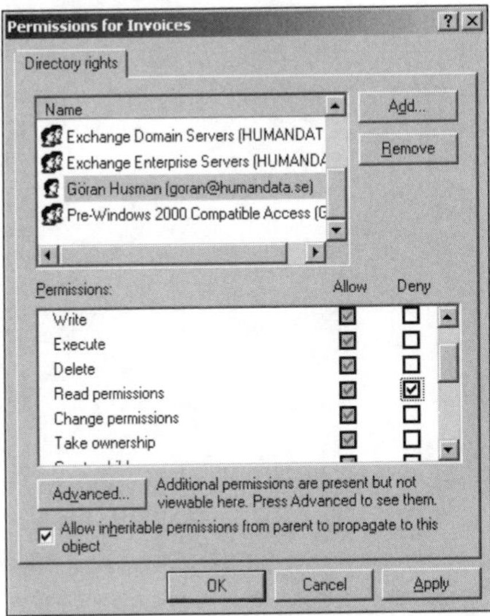

Figure 11.11
Denying access to read properties for a public folder.

- *Prohibit an administrator from taking ownership of a public folder*. To do this, use the Directory Rights button, select the name of this administrator, and deny Take Ownership permission.
- *Prohibit an administrator from modifying the deleted item retention setting for a folder, while still allowing administration of other properties of this public folder*. To do this, use the Administrative Rights button, select the name of the administrator, and deny the Modify Public Folder Deleted Item Retention permission; see Figure 11.12.
- *Prohibit all clients without explicit permission from adding new items in this public folder*. To do this, use the Client Permission button, without the Control key, and set Default permission to Reviewer. This will grant read-only permission to all users that don't have any specific permission setting on this folder; see Figure 11.13.

Warning! *If you once used the Windows 2000 security system to set the client permissions (by pressing the Control button when you click on the Client Permission), you cannot use the normal MAPI permission roles for this folder anymore, not even if you restore the permissions to their original state! If this happens, you must continue to use the Windows 2000 permissions for this folder in the future.*

Setting Access Permissions on Individual Items

The permissions mentioned so far affect the administration of public folders, and what users can do with their contents, like viewing, reading, and updating items. With the Windows 2000 permission system, you can also define exactly what access permissions users have on a single item inside a folder, regardless whether it's a mailbox folder or a public folder. However, this permission can't be set with the ESM tool—you must use the File Explorer for this.

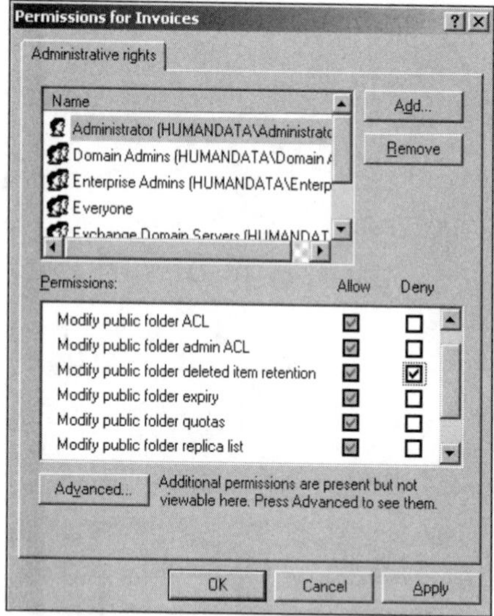

Figure 11.12
Denying access to modifying particular properties for a public folder.

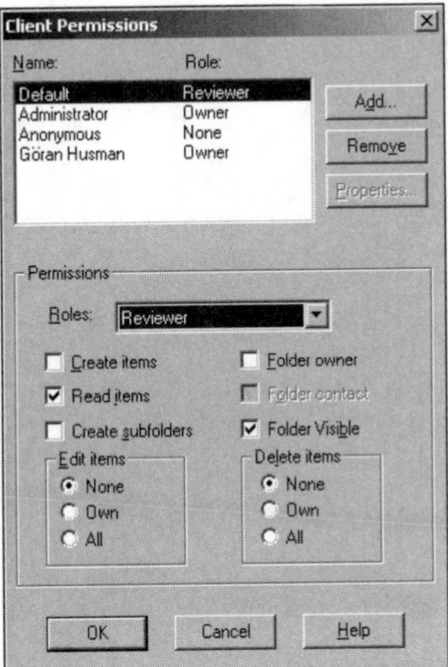

Figure 11.13
Set the default permission to the role Reviewer.

For example, assume you have a public folder named *#Customers* with the permission role *Editor* for the group *Team-X*; this grants all members of this group read and write permission for all items, not only their own. Now, one of the items in this folder is more sensitive than the others, and only the user Suzan Andersson should be allowed to update this item. In this example, we assume that the client computer has a network drive M: mapped to the shared Exchange Web store. Follow these steps to set up this permission:

1. Use the client access permissions, and make sure that *Team-X* has been granted the permission role *Editor* on the *#Customers* public folder.
2. Open the *File Explorer* and, assuming the Exchange organization is **Humandata.se**, navigate to *M:\Humandata.se\Public Folders\#Customers*; see Figure 11.14.
3. Note that all items are listed as .EML files in the right pane; locate the item you want to modify, right-click on it, and select *Properties*.
4. Open the *Security* page, locate the *Team-X* group, and set permission *Deny* to this item. See Figure 11.15. When ready, click *OK* to close this window.

With the Windows 2000 permission model, it's even possible to control the read and write access permissions to a specific property for an object; for example, all users have the permission to read the office phone number for contact items, but only the HR department has permission to modify it. However, this cannot be done with any standard tool—it must be done programmatically.

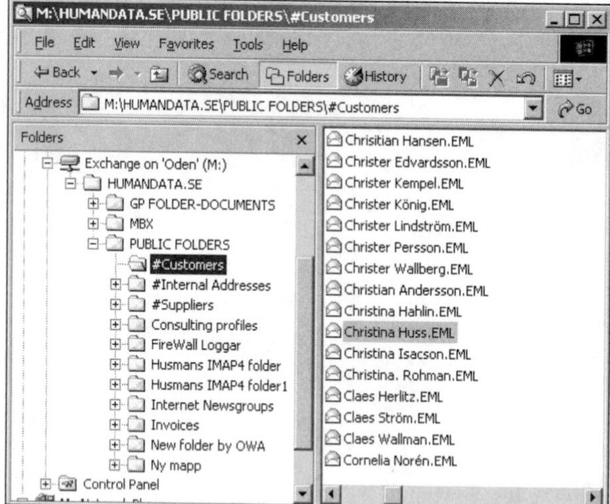

Figure 11.14
Exploring the public folder #Customers.

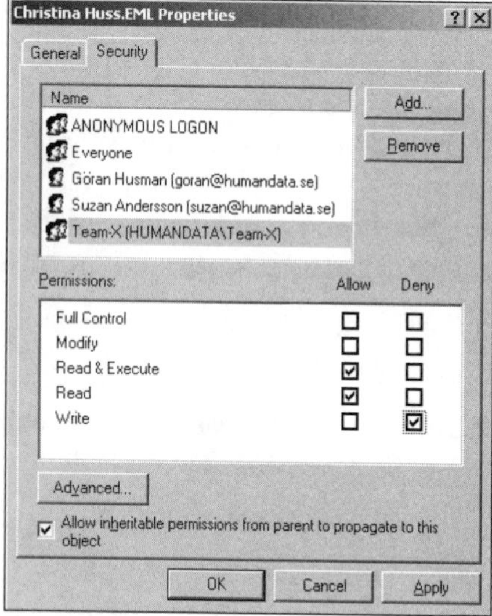

Figure 11.15
Deny access to a single item in a folder.

Setting Access Permissions to the Exchange Administrator

Besides these access permissions to folders and their contents, Windows 2000 permissions are also used to control the administrative control of Exchange configuration settings, and administration of users and groups. Previously we discussed how to use the *Delegation Wizard* in the ESM tool to delegate administrative permissions to Exchange objects—for example, the organization object or an administrative group object. The administrative roles that can be defined with the Delegation Wizard are:

- View-only administrator
- Administrator
- Full administrator

View-Only Administrator

This type of administrator role has the permission to view, but not modify, the object in question; for example, having view-only permission on the Exchange organization object will make it possible to view all settings in this Exchange organization. Or, having view-only permission on a particular administrative group will make it possible to view this administrative group and its subcontainers, but no other AG. However, you will automatically also get view-only permission on the other root folders in the Exchange organization, like the Global Settings, Recipients, and Tools.

Administrator

This administrator will have all access permissions to the object in question, except the permission to add or remove new administrators. For example, a user or group granted the Administrator role on the organization object will have full access to all objects in this Exchange organization, thanks to the inheritance of the Windows 2000 permission model.

Full Administrator

This is the highest access permission role available; a user or group that is granted this role on a particular object can do anything on this object or its subcontainers. This role also permits adding and removing new administrators on this object and below. If you have this role on the organization object, you are Godlike within this Exchange organization.

The Delegation Wizard

This wizard provides a simple method of defining permissions, and should always be used whenever possible. However, most objects don't have the Delegation Wizard; for those objects that don't, you must use their Security property page to set the permissions. The only two objects that have the Delegation Wizard are:

- *The organization object*—This permission will affect the complete organization.
- *Each administrative group*—This permission will affect this particular administrative group and all subcontainers.

When deciding what role a user or group should have, you must take into account a number of things, for example: what objects should they be allowed to administrate? On what objects are view-only permissions enough? Does this user have the necessary skills and understanding to take on the responsibility of administering these objects? Use the Decision Tree 11.1 to find the right administrative role for a user or group.

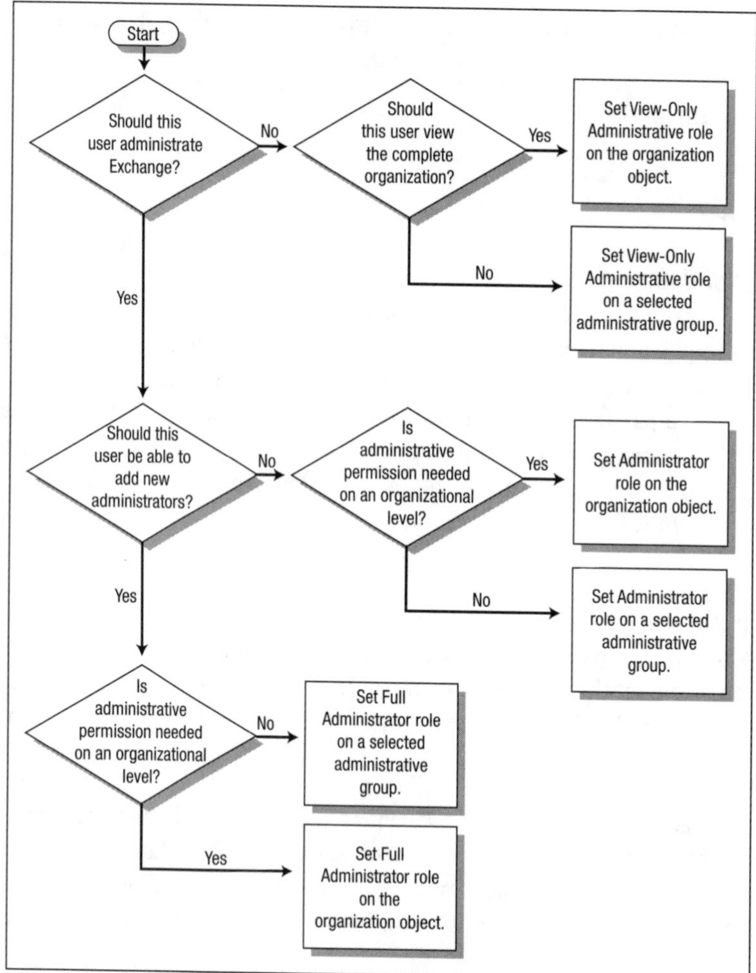

Decision Tree 11.1
Selecting the administrative role.

Setting Access Permissions for the Mailbox Administrator

The mailbox administrator uses the *Active Directory Users and Computers* tool for adding, modifying, and deleting mail-enabled users, groups, and contacts. This type of administrator does not need any form of administrative permission on the Exchange organization, not even view-only administrator permissions. Similar to the Exchange organization, you can get administrative permissions for the whole Windows 2000 forest, or for just one single container folder. Larger organizations will probably have separate groups of mailbox administrators, responsible for one or more user containers each. The Active Directory Users and Computers tool has a similar type of Delegation Wizard as the ESM tool, called the *Delegation of Control Wizard*; however, the number of permissions and options is much larger in this version. For example, to grant a user administrative permission on the Users container, follow these instructions:

1. Open the *Active Directory Users and Computers* tool; navigate to the *Users* container.
2. Right-click on this object, and select *Delegation Control*; this will start the *Delegation of Control Wizard*. Click *Next* to continue.
3. On the *Users Or Groups* page, click *Add* to add the new mailbox administrator; click *Next* to continue.
4. On the *Active Directory Object Type* (see Figure 11.16), select the scope for this permission. Default is the current folder and its contents and any subfolders. You could also select a particular type of object, as described later in this chapter. In this example, we select the default; click *Next* to continue.
5. On the *Permissions* page (see Figure 11.17), select the permissions you want to delegate. Since there is a large number of permissions, this page will by default display only general permissions; if the administrator should be granted full access to the objects selected in Step 4, then select *Full Control*, which will check all types of permissions available. In this example, we select *Full Control*; click *Next* to continue.
6. On the *Completion* page, check to see that the granted permissions are correct; click *Finish* to complete this operation, or *Back* to make any adjustments.

This user can now use the Active Directory Users and Computers tool and administrate all objects within the Users folder and any subfolders. To view the permissions granted, open the properties for the folder, and use the *Security* page to get a summary. For a detailed description, click the *Advanced* button, select the user again, and then click the *Edit* button; see Figure 11.18. If the *Security* page is not visible, open the *View* menu and make sure

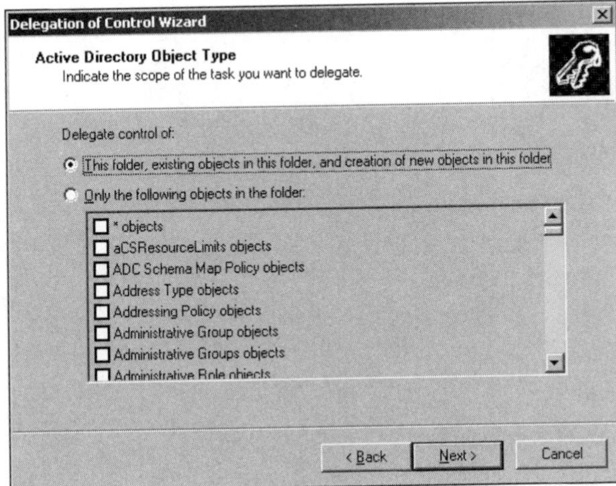

Figure 11.16
The Active Directory Object Type page.

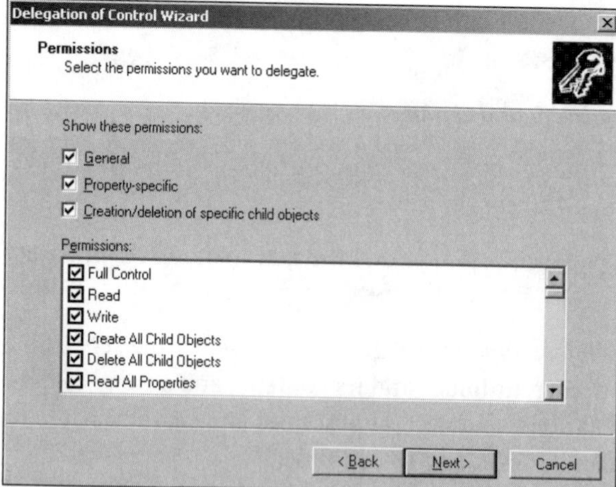

Figure 11.17
The Permissions page.

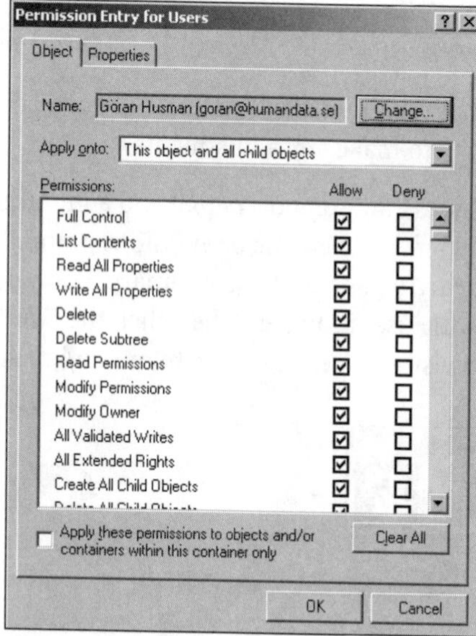

Figure 11.18
View the granted permissions in Windows 2000.

Advanced Features is selected. To remove a granted permission, use the *Delegation Control Wizard* again, and select to remove the user; or use the *Security* page to remove the user.

Delegation Wizard Options for Created OUs

There is an interesting difference between the standard folder *Users* and the new folder you create; all OU folders that you create in the Windows 2000 forest will have access to the *Delegation Control Wizard*, but the *Users* folder will not. An OU folder is typically created to contain users, groups, and contacts; most often, these objects will also be mail-enabled. For example, you may want to create one OU per department or subsidiary company; each of these OUs can then be managed by different administrator groups. Using the Delegation Control Wizard on the OU object folder gives you the ability to select any of the following predefined common tasks (see also Figure 11.19):

- Create, delete, and manage user accounts
- Reset passwords on user accounts
- Read all users' information
- Create, delete, and manage groups
- Modify the membership of a group
- Manage group policy links

If you don't want to delegate any of these predefined permissions to the administrators, you can instead select to create a custom task where you have more than 160 different types of permissions.

Delegation Wizard Options for Other Folders

The Delegation Control Wizard can also be used to assign permissions to the root domain folder in the Windows 2000 forest; however, there are only two predefined common tasks (see Figure 11.20):

- Joining a computer to the domain
- Managing group policy links

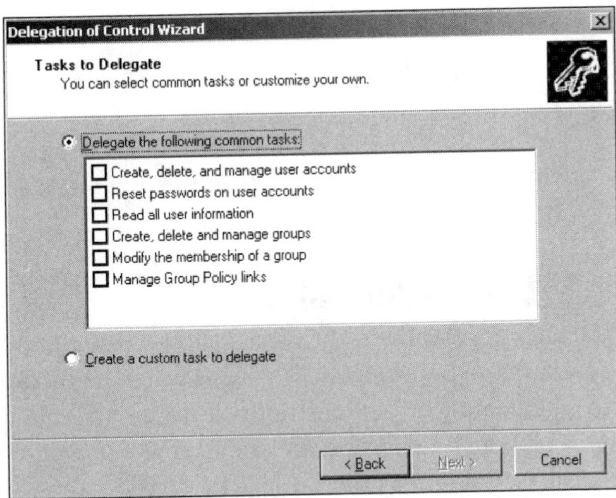

Figure 11.19
Common tasks for the created OU folder.

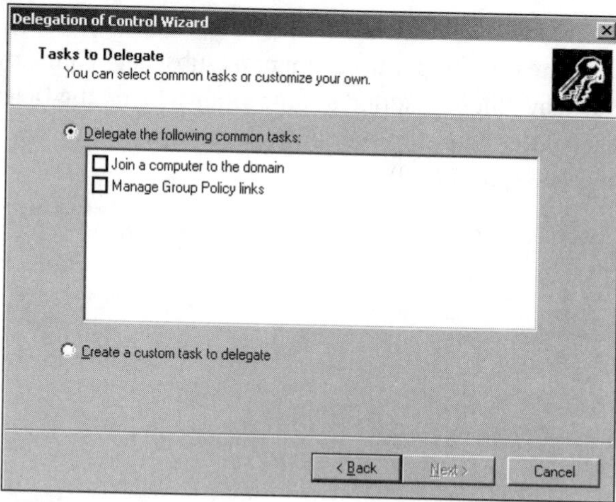

Figure 11.20
Common administrative tasks for the root domain.

The *Domain Controller* folder can also use the Delegation Control Wizard; it will actually have the same predefined common tasks as a created OU. However, some folders don't have any predefined common tasks at all:

- *Computers*—Contains all computers that have joined this Windows 2000 domain, but are not domain controllers.
- *ForeignSecurityPrincipals*—Special group accounts from NT 4 domains, like Everyone and Interactive.
- *System*—A number of subfolders for the Windows 2000 domain, for example policies, DNS, and file replication services.

The remaining folders can't be configured with the Delegation Control Wizard; instead you must use the *Security* page in their properties to set permissions. The folders mentioned in this section are seldom interesting for an Exchange or mailbox administrator; if you want more information about what you can do with them, I recommend any of Coriolis's excellent Active Directory books.

Common Tasks for the Mailbox Administrator

With all these options given by the wizard and the security page, it may be hard to grant the permissions necessary for a mailbox administrator. The easiest is an administrator with full permissions, of course, but creating an administrator with a limited number of permissions can be harder. In this section, we look at some of the more common types of mailbox administrators, besides the full administrator; see also the Decision Tree 11.2 for a quick overview of what permissions to grant:

- *Full administrator for a specific OU folder*—This type of administrator can create, modify, and delete all types of both mailbox-enabled and non–mail-enabled objects, like users, contacts, and groups. Use the Delegation Control Wizard and select to create a

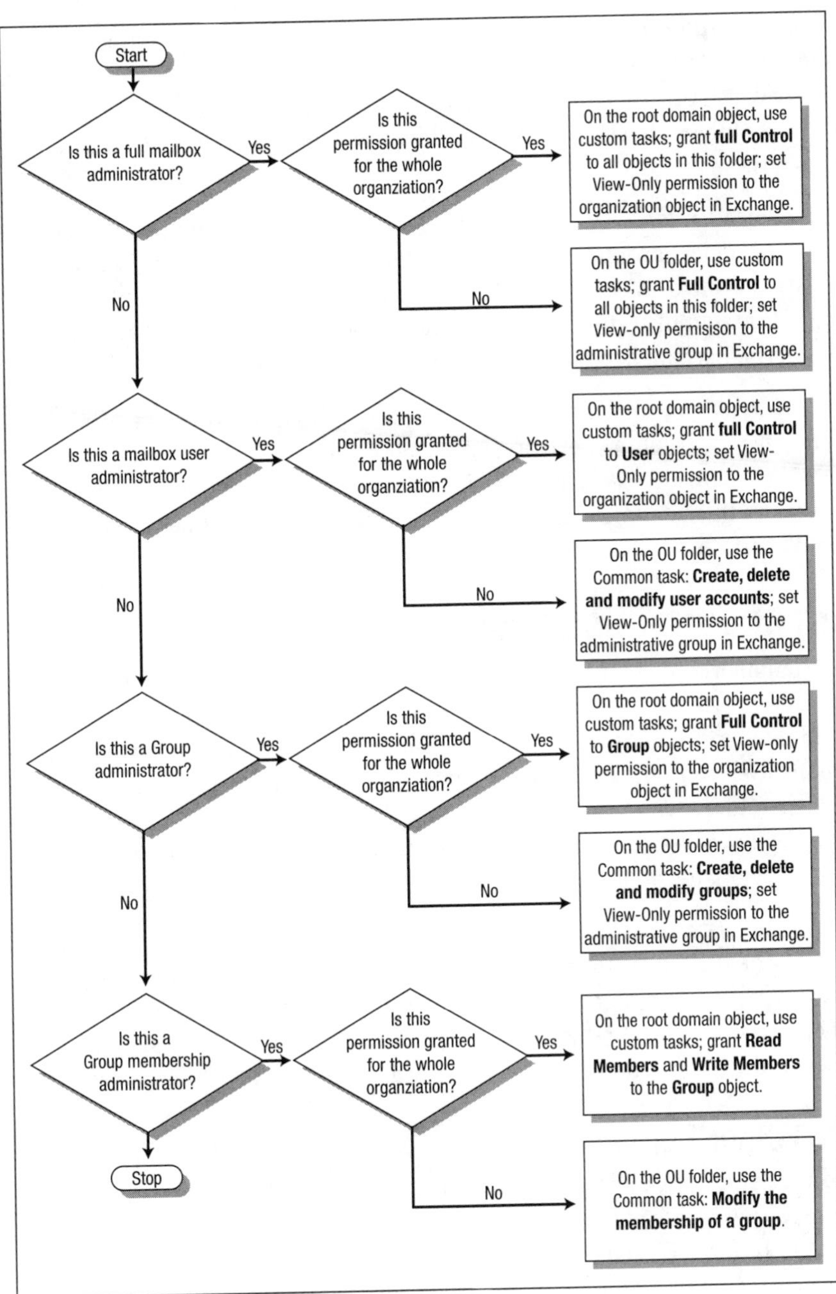

Decision Tree 11.2
Defining different types of mailbox administrators.

custom task for all objects in this folder, granting Full Control permissions to this administrator. This administrator must also have View-Only permission on the administrative group in the Exchange organization these users belong to; if not, Exchange-specific properties cannot be modified, for example email addresses.

- *User administrator for a specific OU folder*—This type of administrator can create, modify, and delete user objects only. Use the Delegation Control Wizard and select the predefined task Create, Delete, And Manage User Accounts; this administrator must also have View-Only permission on the administrative group in the Exchange organization to which these users belong.
- *Group administrator for a specific OU folder*—This type of administrator can create, modify, and delete group objects only, including modifying the membership. Use the Delegation Control Wizard and select the predefined task Create, Delete, And Manage Groups; this administrator must also have View-Only permission on the administrative group in the Exchange organization to which these groups belong.
- *Group membership administrator for a specific OU folder*—This type of administrator can modify membership of existing groups, but cannot create or delete groups. Use the Delegation Control Wizard and select the predefined task Modify The Membership Of A Group; this administrator doesn't need View-Only permission in the Exchange organization.

Managing an Administrative Group

Due to the importance of this topic, I will mention this once again: You must create all administrative groups before you start installing Exchange servers in the organization. Microsoft does *not* support using the ADSI Edit tool to move servers between administrative groups. You simply must know how many administrative groups your organization will need in the future, before you start installing Exchange servers! If you aren't sure how many you will need, stick with one; you will still be able to control the administration of this Exchange organization in much higher degree than in previous Exchange versions.

When the administrative groups are created, there are no particular properties to configure besides the previously mentioned folders that can be created: one or more routing group containers, one system policy container, and one public folder container. In the next chapter, we'll look into the details of recipient containers, and system policies will be described in the next section, so let's look now at the public folder containers.

Public Folder Containers

There can be only one public folder container per administrative group; its purpose is to store public folder trees of both MAPI and General Purpose types. You may have only one MAPI folder tree per Exchange organization, but unlimited numbers of GP folders. To create a new public folder tree, follow these instructions:

1. Start the *ESM* tool, and navigate to the administrative group where this folder tree should be created.
2. Right-click on the administrative group object, and select *New|Pubic Folder Container*.
3. Right-click on the newly created folder container, and select *New|Public Folder Tree*; see Figure 11.21. Note that this folder will always be of type *General Purpose*, since

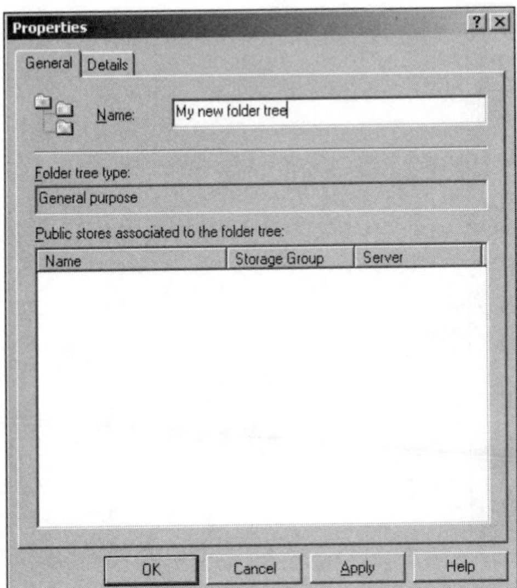

Figure 11.21
Creating a new public folder tree.

the default MAPI folder is automatically created when you install the first Exchange server. The pane *Public Stores Associated To The Folder Tree* is always empty at first, but when you return to this property page later on, it will list the public store database used for this folder tree. Click *OK* to create this folder tree now.

Before this folder can be used, it must first be associated with a public store; this will be created in one of the storage groups for the server. Follow these instructions:

1. Using the *ESM* tool, navigate to the server object (regardless of what administrative group it belongs to).
2. Expand the storage group, or create a new storage group where this new public store will be created.
3. Right-click on the storage group, and select *New|Public Store*.
4. On the *General* page, give this store a name, and click *Browse* to select the previously created public folder tree; see Figure 11.22.
5. For more information on how to configure this new public store, see Chapter 2 and its section of public folders; when ready click *OK* to complete this operation. You will be asked if you want to mount this new store; answer *Yes*.

The new public folder trees are now ready to be used. Note that the tree itself can be created in one administrative group, while at the same time be associated with a public store on an Exchange server that belongs to another administrative group. This is one example of how free the administrative group concept is from the physical layout of the Exchange system. The only administrators that can manage this new folder tree are the ones who have been granted administrative permission to the administrative group this tree belongs to.

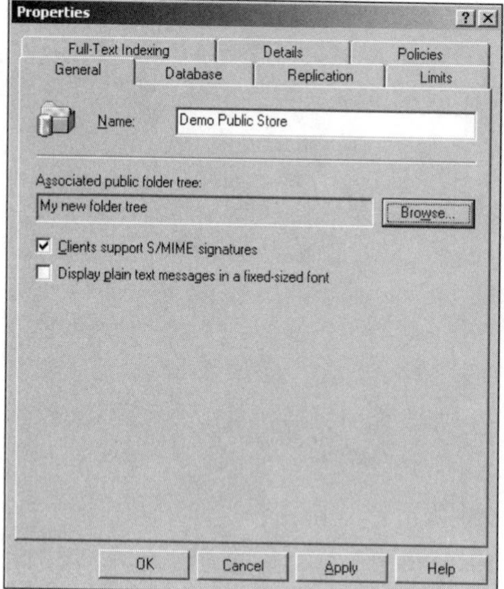

Figure 11.22
Create a public store and associate it with the new folder tree.

The same principle works for both system policies and routing groups; any policy or server created in one of those folders will be under the control of its administrative group, regardless of which servers they affect. Administrative groups are only used to logically group objects together for administrative purpose, regardless of what the physical layout looks like. This gives the Exchange designer lots of possibilities when working with the administrative model.

Removing Administrative Groups

In rare cases you may need to remove an existing AG; for example, if a company has sold a subsidiary that had its own AG. Before you can remove an administrative group, you must first remove all subfolders in it; there must not be any objects contained in this AG, or ESM will not remove this group; Figure 11.23 shows the error message you'll receive if the AG is not empty.

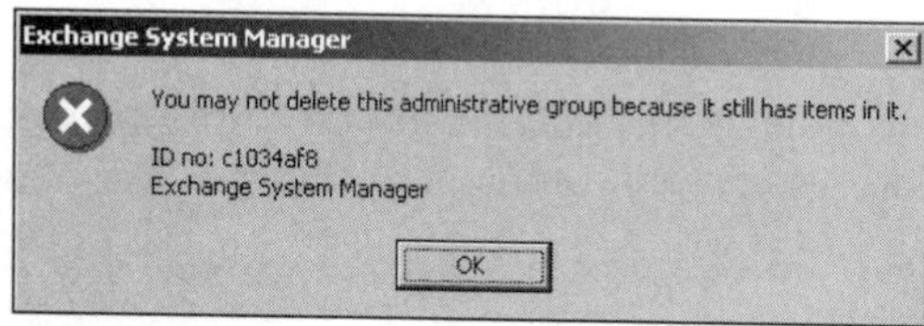

Figure 11.23
Error message you'll receive if you try to remove a non-empty AG.

The same is valid for most folders; if they contain any objects, they can't be deleted. For example, if we try to delete the newly created Folder container while it still contains our new public folder tree, we also get an error message. To delete an administrative group, follow this instructions:

***Warning!** These steps will permanently remove the administrative group and all its objects. Make sure you have a working backup of the complete Exchange server before continuing with these steps; you cannot undo these delete operations!*

1. Using the *ESM* tool, right-click on public store and select *Delete* on each store that is associated with a public folder tree that belongs to this administrative group. You don't have to dismount them first, but the database files must be manually removed from the disk; make sure you know their names before deleting them (look at the properties for the public store, on the *Database* page).
2. Right-click on the public folder tree and select *Delete*; repeat this for all public folder trees.
3. When all public folder trees are deleted continue by right clicking on the *Folders* folder; select *Delete* to remove this object.
4. Right-click the *System Policies* folder, and select *Delete*. Note that this folder can be deleted even if it contains policies!
5. Expand the *Routing Groups* folder, and make sure all defined routing groups are empty; if not, make sure to move them to another routing group first by dragging the server objects from the subfolder *Member* to another routing group's *Member* folder. When this is done, right-click on the routing groups and delete them.
6. When the *Routing Groups* folder is empty, right-click it and select *Delete*.
7. If there is a *Server* folder, make sure it contains no server objects; if so, uninstall them (or move them to another administrative group, but remember this is not recommended by Microsoft). When the *Server* folder is empty, delete it.
8. Now this administrative group should be empty; right-click and delete it.

Working with System Policies

The new concept of system policies will greatly ease the administrative burden for many organizations; a *policy* is a predefined configuration setting. This feature makes it possible to enforce configuration settings on any Exchange server, regardless of where in the Exchange organization it is located or what administrative group it belongs to. A system policy is always created as a subfolder under an administrative group, but the server does not need to belong to the same administrative group. The configurations that can be set with system policies include:

- Server policies

- Public store policies
- Mailbox store policies

A system policy setting that is enforced on a server cannot be modified by the server's property pages; instead you must change the policy or remove this server from the scope of this policy. If the policy is removed from a server, all its settings will still be valid; the configuration will *not* be restored to any default values. This is important to understand; you shouldn't test a policy on a production server just to see how it works. The only way to restore the previous property settings for this server is by manually restoring these settings again, once the policy has been removed.

You can create several system policies of the same type; however, you can't apply several conflicting policies on the same object. For example, you cannot have two mailbox store policies that are applied to the same mailbox store. However, there is one exception—if these two policies don't conflict with each other, there will be no problem. For example, if one policy defines the mailbox size limit and the other the databases, then it will be okay to have two policies applied to the same server.

This section describes how to create these different policies and how to use them. Remember that even if you have only one administrative group for all servers in the organization, it is possible to create a new AG later where system policies are created and enforced to any server, regardless of what AG they belong to.

Server Policies

The server policy controls one single property page: the *General* page, on a server. To create this policy, follow these steps:

1. Right-click the *System Policies* folder, and select *New|Server Policy*; see Figure 11.24.
2. Check the *General* box and click *Next* to continue.
3. Give this new policy a descriptive name; make sure to follow the name standard, if one has been defined in your organization.
4. Open the *General (Policy)* page—this is where the policy is defined. As you can see, only three properties can be preconfigured on this page: subject logging, message

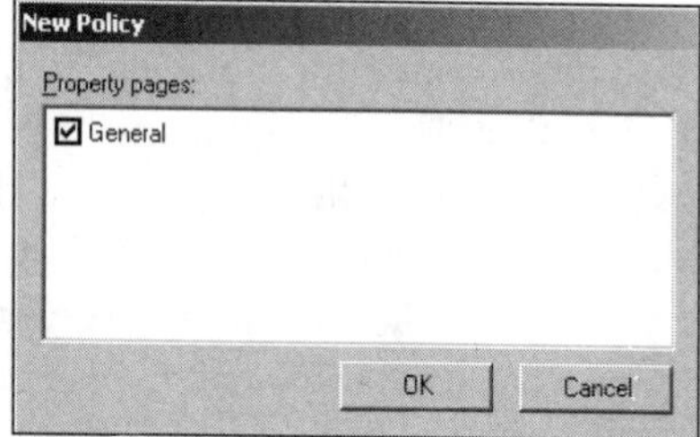

Figure 11.24
The New Server Policy.

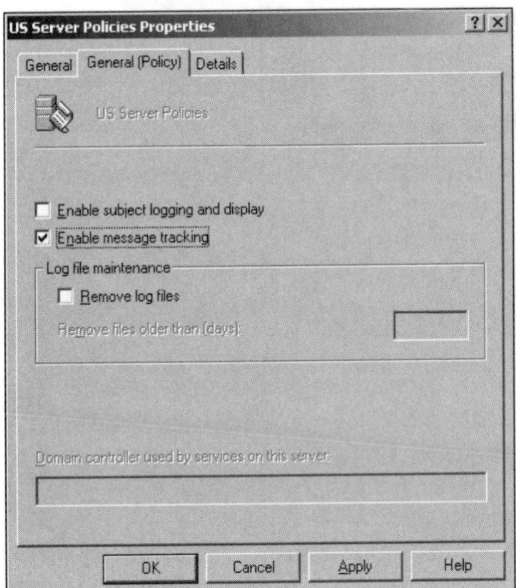

Figure 11.25
The General (Policy) page.

tracking, and the length of time that log files will be stored. See Figure 11.25. Whatever settings you select on this page, they will be enforced on the server this policy is applied to. For example, if you set *Enable Message Tracking*, but leave the other two options cleared, this will enforce the setting of message tracking but also ensure that the other two options will always be cleared! Leaving an option unchecked means that this setting is cleared; it doesn't mean that this property can be configured freely on the server. Click *OK* when you're ready to complete this operation.

It is important that you understand that any property you leave unchecked on a policy means that this policy will be cleared, regardless of the setting it had before this policy was applied to the server. You can't just configure one or two properties on a page; you must configure all the available properties that the policy has.

Applying the Policy on a Server

When the policy is created, it should be applied to one or more servers. Follow these steps:

1. Right-click on the new system policy object, and select *Add Server*.
2. From the list of available servers (see Figure 11.26), add the servers that this policy will be applied to. Note that if a server already has a system policy applied, its name will not be displayed in this list; a server can have only one system policy applied.
3. When all servers this policy should be applied to are added, click *OK* to save and close this window.

The policy is now applied; we can verify this by opening the properties for the server and looking at the General page (see Figure 11.27). Note that the three properties listed on

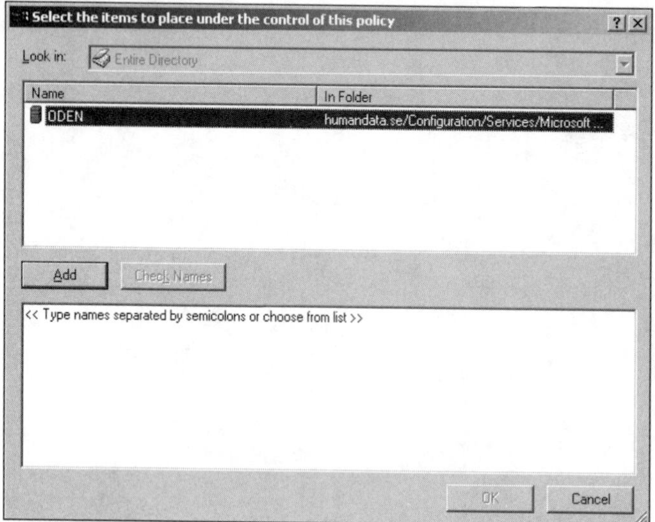

Figure 11.26
Selecting the server this server policy will be applied to.

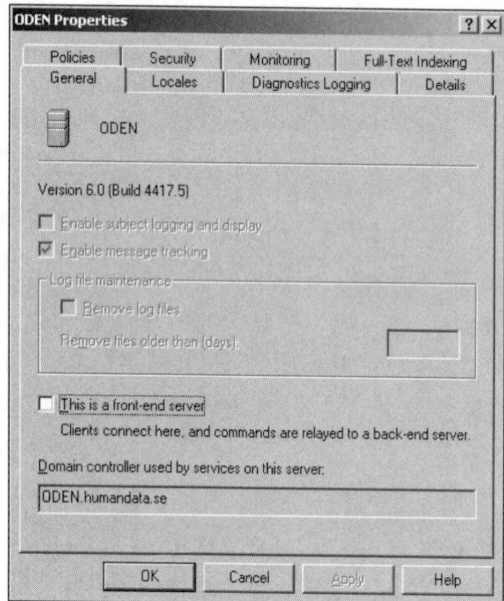

Figure 11.27
The General page on a server with a policy.

the policy are grayed-out, indicating that they can't be modified. Also note that there is one more property on this page that cannot be controlled by a policy, the front-end setting.

Next, switch to the *Policies* page for this server; there you will see exactly what policies are applied to this server. This is just for informational purposes—you can't remove the policy from there; it can only be done from the policy itself. See Figure 11.28.

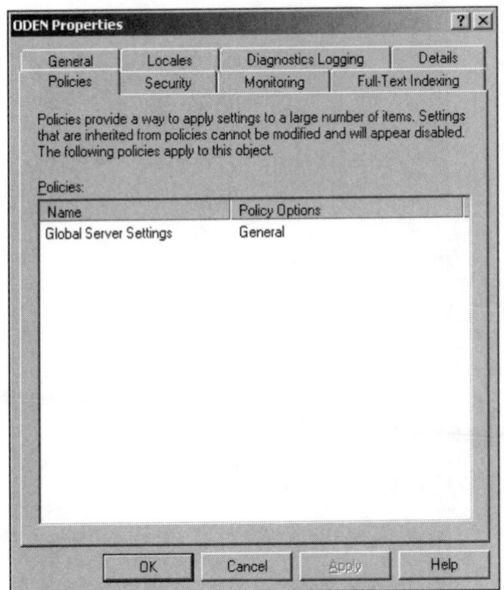

Figure 11.28
The Policies page, listing the policies applied to this server.

Removing a System Policy

To remove a system policy from a server, follow these steps:

1. Select the policy object; all servers it is applied to are listed in the right pane.
2. Select the server it should be removed from.
3. Right-click on the server and select *Remove From Policy*; accept *Yes* when prompted if you want to continue with this operation. The server will now be removed from this list.

But let's check the server again, and its *General* page, now that the policy is removed; see Figure 11.29. As you can see, the latest settings enforced by the policy are still active; however, it is now possible to modify any of these settings again. And looking at the *Policies* page, we can see that this is now empty; no policies are applied to this server anymore.

Public Store Policies

Public store policies work exactly like server policies, in that the policy controls a number of property pages, and all definitions, regardless of whether you set or clear an option, will be enforced on the object this policy is applied to. Public store policies are of course applied to public store databases. This type of policy controls the following property pages:

- General
- Database
- Replication

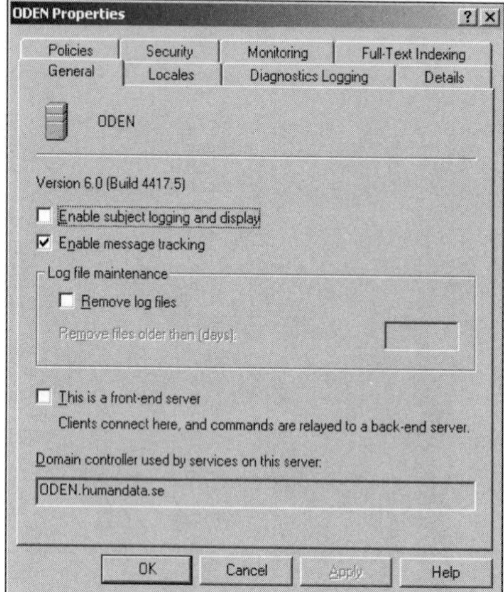

Figure 11.29
The General page after the policy has been removed.

- Limits
- Full-text indexing

A public store policy is created like any other type of policy; right-click on the *System Policies* folder, and select *New|Public Store Policy*. The first thing you will see is a list of all available property pages that this policy can control; see Figure 11.30.

Don't select a property page that you won't use; this would have the effect of enforcing cleared property settings for this particular page! Only select pages you want to configure.

The General (Policy) Page

This policy page controls the settings of clients supporting S/MIME signatures and whether plain-text messages should be displayed with a fixed-sized font; see Figure 11.31. Note that you cannot modify the associated public folder tree, since this would prohibit this policy from being applied on more than one single public store.

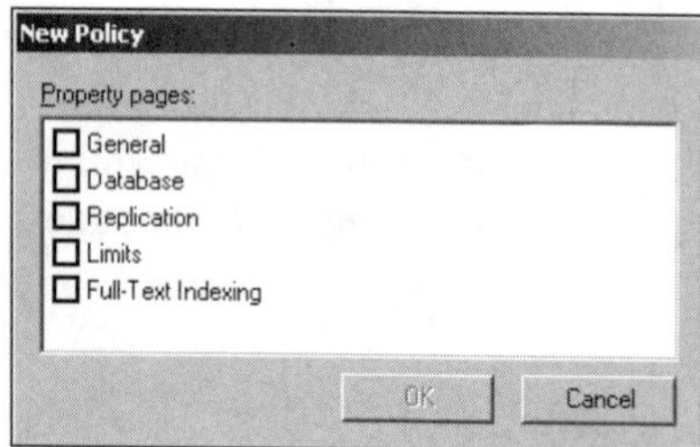

Figure 11.30
The Property pages for a public store policy.

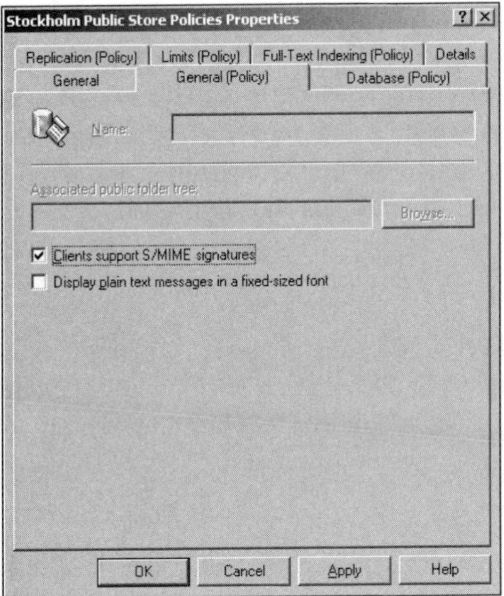

Figure 11.31
The General (Policy) page.

The Database (Policy) Page

This policy page controls when the online database maintenance process should run. Default is once every night, between 11:00 P.M and 3:00 A.M. Click *Customize* to modify this interval setting; see Figure 11.32.

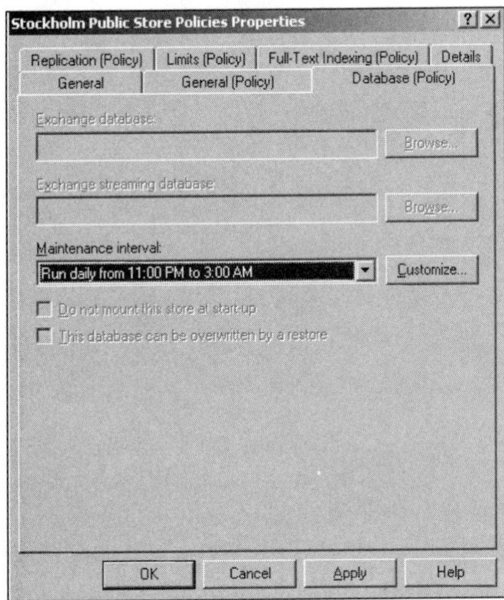

Figure 11.32
The Database (Policy) page.

The Replication (Policy) Page

This policy page controls the default settings of the public folder replication schedule; use the Customize button to select another default schedule—you can select between *Always Run* to once every week. Use this page to configure exactly what "*Always*" means (default is every 15 minutes), and the size limit of replication messages (default is 300KB). Click *Restore Defaults* to set these values to 15 minutes and 300KB, respectively. See Figure 11.33.

The Limits (Policy) Page

This policy page is probably the most-used page for the public store policy; it controls the public folders' default values for storage limits, deletion settings, and age limits; see Figure 11.34. By default all public folders are configured to follow the settings on this page; however, a single public store can always exceed these settings.

The Full-Text Indexing (Policy) Page

This policy page controls when the full-text index should be updated and when it should be rebuilt; see Figure 11.35. Click the *Customize* button to configure any special settings, using a week-long schedule; or click on the arrow and select any of the preconfigured settings.

Applying the Public Store Policy

When this public store policy has been configured (make sure you only check pages that you want to configure!), click *OK* to save and close. Right-click on this new policy, select *Add Public Store*, and select what public store this policy will be applied to; see Figure 11.36.

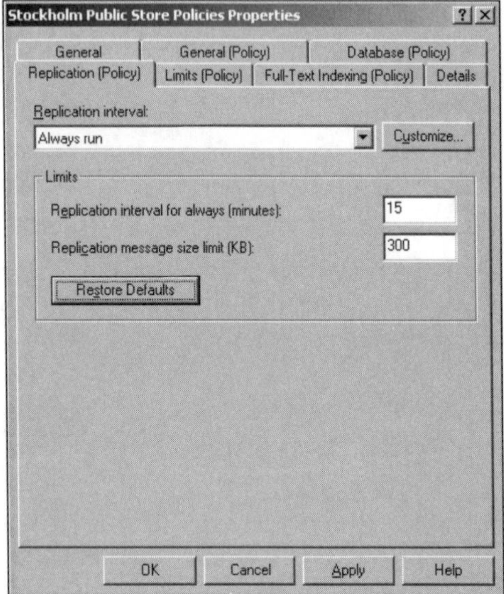

Figure 11.33
The Replication (Policy) page.

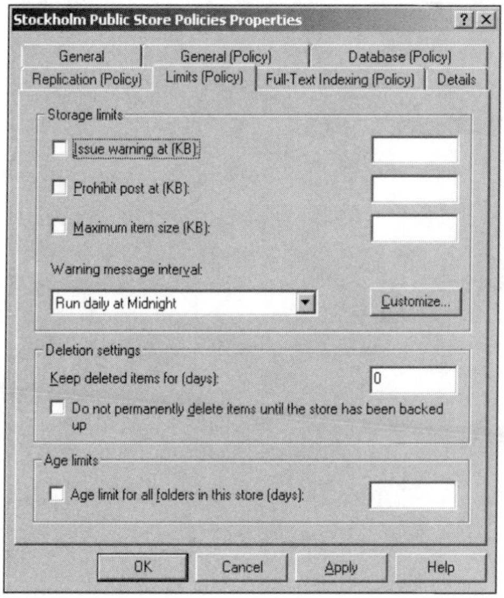

Figure 11.34
The Limits (Policy) page.

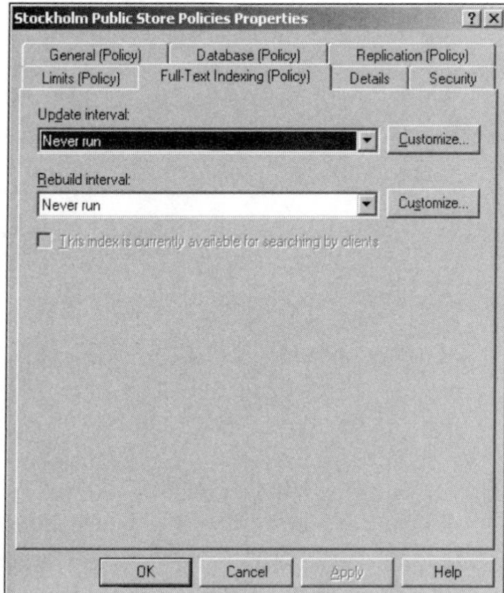

Figure 11.35
The Full-Text Indexing (Policy) page.

Removing a Public Store Policy

This is done exactly like other types of policies. Select the policy; from the list of public stores in the right pane, right-click on the public store that should be removed from this policy and select *Remove From Policy*. Again, remember that any property settings this

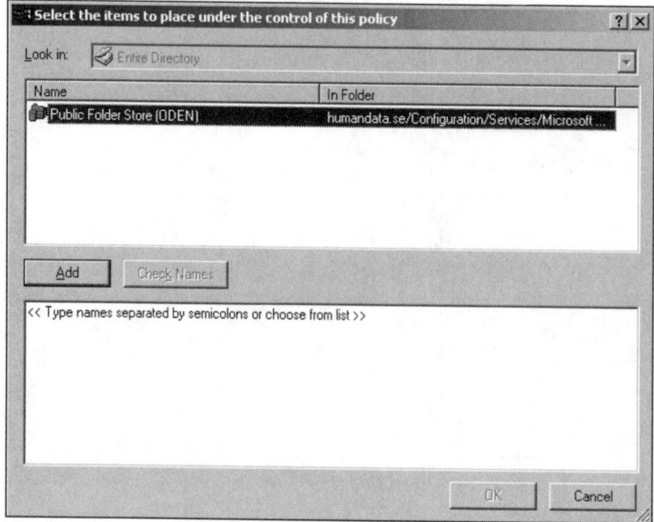

Figure 11.36
Applying a public store policy.

policy has enforced on this public store will still remain; you have to manually check the settings to make sure it is configured properly, or apply a new policy with the right settings.

Mailbox Store Policies

This is an important and powerful policy since it controls the settings of the mailbox stores, thereby enforcing settings for our mailbox users. As the public store policy, this type of policy can control several property pages:

- General
- Database
- Limits
- Full-text indexing

Once again, don't select property pages that you don't intend to configure; it would only clear any settings on the mailbox stores this policy will be applied to. Create this policy by right-clicking on the *System Policies* folder, and selecting *New|Mailbox Store Policy*; select what property page to configure, and give this policy a clear and intuitive name. Make sure to follow any established name standards in your organization. The property pages that can be configured with this policy are described in the following sections.

The General (Policy) Page

Use this policy page to control the default public store that all users belonging to this mailbox store will use when creating public folders. This page also controls the default offline address list for Outlook clients that want to download the address list.

By checking the *Archive All Messages* checkbox, you can make a copy of all messages passing this server; click the *Browse* button to select what user or public folder will have these copies. Make sure you have the necessary free disk space available for this recipient, since it will most likely be a large volume of data.

Select whether the messaging clients, like Outlook, support S/MIME signatures. If so, set this checkbox. You can also configure the mailbox store to display all plain-text messages in a fixed-size font; see Figure 11.37.

The Database (Policy) Page

This policy page controls when to run the regular mailbox store maintenance process; default is every night, from 11:00 P.M. to 3:00 A.M. No other property can be set by this policy page; see Figure 11.38.

The Limits (Policy) Page

As for the public store policy, this *Limits (Policy)* page is popular for enforcing different types of limits on an Exchange organization; see Figure 11.39. Use it to define the default values for storage limits and deletion settings. By default, all users will be configured to follow these settings, unless they are configured individually. Even if your organization doesn't have any size limits, it's always a good idea to set a warning limit, just to inform the users that they have a large mailbox size. I also recommend that you select to keep deleted items for at least three days, to avoid restore operations due to someone deleting a message by mistake.

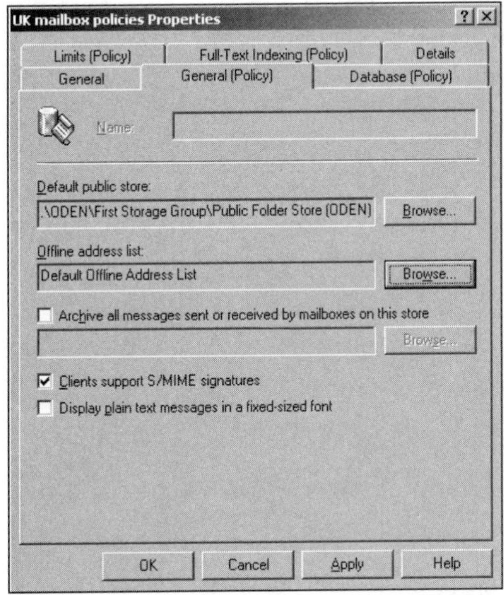

Figure 11.37
The General (Policy) page.

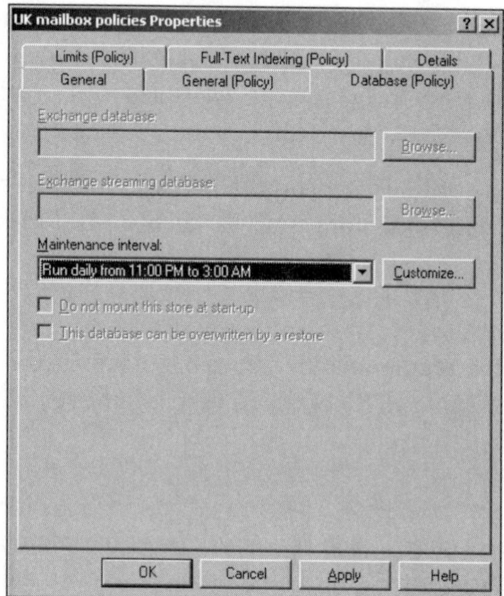

Figure 11.38
The Database (Policy) page.

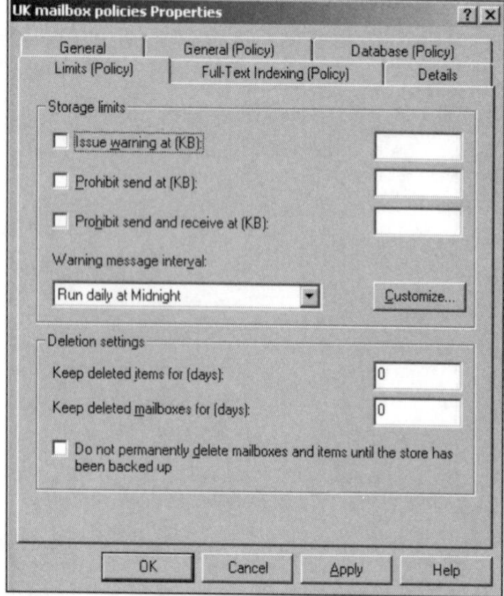

Figure 11.39
The Limits (Policy) page.

The Full-Text Indexing (Policy) Page

This policy page is identical to the public store policy; it controls when the full-text index for this mailbox store should be updated and when it should be rebuilt; see Figure 11.40. Click the *Customize* button to configure any special settings, using a weeklong schedule; or click the arrow and select any of the preconfigured settings.

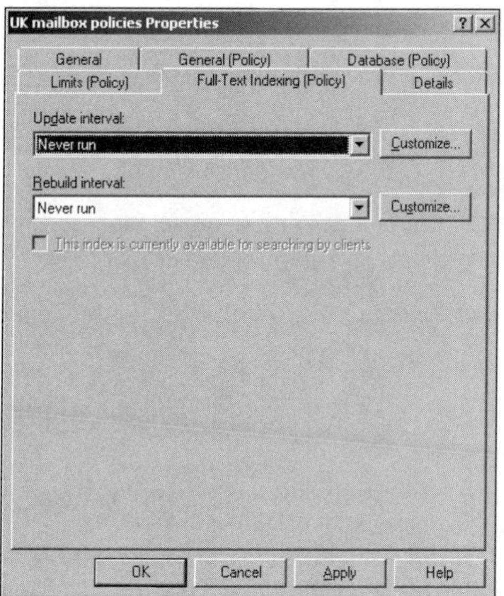

Figure 11.40
The Full-Text Indexing (Policy) page.

Applying and Removing a Mailbox Store Policy

When this mailbox store policy has been configured, click *OK* to save and close. Right-click on this new policy, select *Add Mailbox Store*, and select what mailbox store this policy will be applied to; this is exactly the same procedure as for public store policies.

Removing a mailbox from a policy is also done the same way as a public store policy; select the policy, right-click on the mailbox store in the right pane that should be removed from this policy, and select *Remove From Policy*. Again, remember that any property settings this policy has enforced on this mailbox store will still remain; make sure these settings are what you expect.

Summary

This is a list of the more important features and keywords mentioned in this chapter. Use it as a reminder and to make sure you have understood the most important things:

- Select the mail system that is cheapest to maintain, not necessarily to buy.
- Exchange 5.5 sites are equal to an administrative group with one routing group.
- Previous Exchange versions had three types of administrator roles: View-Only, Admin, and Full Admin.
- The typical administrators in Exchange 5.5 are Mailbox Admins and Configuration Admins.
- Exchange 5.5 uses the Exchange Admin.exe program for all types of mail administration.

- All configuration settings in Exchange 5.5 are stored in the DIR.EDB database.
- Exchange 2000 stores its configuration in the Active Directory database.
- Exchange 2000 has lots of new features that make administration easier to perform and administrative models easier to define.
- An Administrative Group (AG) is used to group a number of objects for administrative purposes; it has nothing to do with the physical layout of servers or routing groups.
- An AG can contain these types of subfolders: Public folders, Servers, System policies, and Routing Groups.
- An Administrative Group has nothing to do with the Windows 2000 objects Security Groups and Distribution Groups.
- An Exchange 2000 organization can run in either native mode or mixed mode.
- Mixed mode is default; it creates the AG with its single routing group, and behaves exactly like an Exchange 5.5 site. This makes it possible for Exchange 2000 and Exchange 5.5 to coexist.
- Native mode makes it possible to use AG much more freely; you can create one AG that controls all routing groups in the organization.
- In mixed mode, users can be moved only within the AG; in native mode, users can move to any server.
- The First Administrative Group is created when you run the **ForestPrep** command or when you install the first Exchange 2000 server in the organization.
- You can have any number of AGs, but don't create more than you need; it will only increase the complexity of your system.
- AGs will not be displayed by the ESM default; use the properties for the organization object to make them visible.
- All new AGs, including the First Administrative Group, will inherit the permission settings from the organization object.
- Use the Delegation Wizard in ESM to configure access permissions.
- Make sure you have all the AGs created before installing Exchange servers; a server must belong to an AG, and it can't be moved to another AG later on.
- You have the ability to move servers between AGs with the ADSIEdit tool, but beware—Microsoft warns that several things might go wrong if you move a server!
- There are three types of administrative models: Central, Delegated, and a mix of these two.

- Decide what administrative model to use before creating the AGs and starting to install the Exchange servers.
- There are several topics that must be considered when you're selecting an administrative model—for example, mailbox administration, recipient policies, address lists, routing issues, and public folders.
- All mailbox, group, and contact administration is done with the Active Directory Users and Computers tool.
- Will the same people that create users also manage their Exchange configuration settings? Do they have the necessary skills?
- Exchange 2000 utilizes the security model in Windows 2000; this results in much more advanced and rich permission settings, for both mailbox users and public folder settings.
- Using the EMS, you can configure three types of public folder permissions: client permissions, directory rights, and administrative rights.
- Press the Control button when opening the client permission on a public folder to see the corresponding Windows 2000 permissions; but don't change any permissions, this will force you to use these Windows 2000 settings forever, for this particular public folder.
- Permissions are inherited—this makes them easier to set. By modifying the parent object permissions, all subfolders will inherit the new permissions.
- Deny has priority over Allow Permissions.
- The Windows 2000 group Everyone corresponds to the Exchange group Default.
- You can set access permissions on individual items in a folder, using the File Explorer.
- Programmatically, it is possible to set per-property specific permissions.
- The Delegation Control Wizard is used in the Active Directory Users and Computers to set administrative access permissions.
- The standard Users folder does not have the Delegation Control Wizard; however, any new OU you create will have this wizard.
- There are predefined administrative roles for several (but not all) folders.
- You can create very specific administrative roles—for example, an administrator that can modify membership of groups, but can't create or delete groups.
- You can remove an AG only if all its subfolders are removed first.
- A system policy is a general configuration setting that can be applied to one object, like a server, or all objects of this type in the organization.
- There are three types of system policies: Server policies, Public store policies, and Mailbox store policies.

- First you create the policy, then you select what object this policy will be applied to.
- Removing a policy will not restore the configuration settings!
- Don't include a property page in your policy.

Chapter 12

Routing Groups and Link States

The ideal Exchange organization, from a routing perspective, consists of one single server. In such an organization, there is no mail-related traffic besides clients sending and receiving messages, and the connection to other messaging systems (typically the Internet). However, for many reasons, this design may not be practical and sometimes not even possible for large or distributed organizations. When the Exchange organization is divided into several Exchange servers, these servers are compiled into *routing groups*. Routing groups are groups of one or more Exchange servers that can transfer SMTP-based messages directly between each other, without having to pass these messages over another link or server. If more than one routing group is needed, a connection must be configured between them manually; such a connection is often referred to as a *routing group connector*.

The routing group concept originally developed from the *site* concept, which was used in previous Exchange releases. I assume that many readers have experience with Exchange 5.5 and earlier releases, so this chapter will begin by comparing routing groups and sites. Later on, we will discuss how to design routing groups, and how to install and manage them. This chapter will also discuss how Link State Routing works in relation to routing groups.

The goal of this chapter is to help you understand exactly what a routing group is, how it works, and how to use it in your organization. You will see that some of the information here repeats material covered in other chapters, but this time it is adapted to provide a complete description of how routing groups work in Exchange 2000.

Comparing with Exchange 5.x Sites

The site concept has been the fundamental building block of Exchange organizations ever since its first release. An Exchange 5.x *Organization* is a collection of one or more sites that share the same organization name; each site is a collection of one or more Exchange servers. All servers that belong to a site must share the same *Site Service Account*, have a relatively high-speed network connectivity, and be able to use Remote Procedure Call (RPC) for communication. As we saw in Chapter 11, the Exchange 5.x site is a boundary for administration, but is also a boundary for direct message transfer; all servers in a site can transfer messages directly to any other server in this site, using RPC. No messages can leave the site unless a connector is installed, not even to other sites in the same Exchange 5.x organization.

Message Traffic Within a Site

Besides message traffic, an Exchange 5.x site also transfers directory replication messages; these are system messages with updates of directory information, like new or modified mailbox users, and new server configuration settings. This information is stored in the DIR.EDB database and managed by the DSAMAIN.EXE service, also known as the *directory service*. Every Exchange 5.x server has its own DIR.EDB database and directory service, and this service is configured to contact other directory services every five minutes, 24 hours per day, which makes 288 messages per day. The directory replication topology is fully meshed, meaning that all servers send replication messages to all other servers in this site. For example, a site with two servers will send 288 × 2 = 576 replication messages per day, and a site with three servers will send 288 × 2 × 3 = 1,728 messages per day, due to the fully meshed topology, even if there are no directory updates whatsoever. If there are updates, the message traffic will be even greater, since there will be more data to transfer. It is easy to see that large sites generate a lot of traffic, and this is the reason they demand high-speed networks, whereas a small site with just two servers may do just fine with a 64Kbps connection.

Besides the replication messages in the site, you must also take into account all the messages transferred between users, also known as Inter Personal Messages (IPM). The traffic volume for IPMs depends on the number of users in the site, and the average message size. When designing Exchange 5.x organizations, we have to take all message traffic into consideration; if we have the required bandwidth, all servers can be kept in one site. If not, we have to create several sites. The result is that the typical Exchange 5.x site has a 10Mbps network connection, meaning all servers in the site are connected to the same LAN, since not many organizations can afford high-speed WAN connections between their different locations.

Another factor that influences whether the organization will have one or more sites is the *Site Service Account*. This is a standard NT 4 user account that is used extensively in Exchange 5.x; and all Exchange servers in a site must use the same account. This account is used, for example, when an Exchange server establishes an RPC connection to another server in the same site; it will then authenticate using this account. Another example is the Exchange services on a server; all these services run in the security context of this service account. If you have one Exchange site with two Exchange servers that belong to different NT 4 domains without any NT trust between them, you must create one site each, even if the network connection is fast.

Message Traffic between Sites

When an Exchange organization has more than one site, a connector must be configured to transfer messages between them. Exchange 5.x offers four different types of connectors, which differ in terms of transport protocol, the number of configuration options, and speed. The different connectors include:

- *Site Connector*—RPC based; the fastest connector of all; but with only a few configuration settings.
- *X.400 Connector*—Can be used with TCP/IP, X.25, or TP4 transport protocols; 30 percent slower than the Site Connector, but with lots of configuration settings.
- *Internet Mail Service*—TCP/IP based; slower than the other connectors due to the gateway nature of this connector (Exchange 5.x is X.400 based).
- *Dynamic RAS Connector*—Used for dial-up connections with asynchronous modems or ISDN; similar to the X.400 Connector regarding its configuration settings.

Using one of these connectors, messages can be transferred between sites; for all types except the *Site Connector*, one single Exchange server in each site is responsible for the connector and its message transfer. This server is called a *bridgehead server*, since they work in pairs, similar to bridges with two bridgeheads. If one of these servers, or their intermediate connection, breaks down, the message transfer between these two sites gets interrupted. The Site Connector works differently; if this connector is installed on one server in the site, all servers in this site can see this new configuration and will be able to run this connector independently of the other servers. The result is that the connections between the sites are much more resilient with a Site Connector compared to the bridgehead connector like the X.400 Connector. However, organizations often want to control the message traffic, which makes the X.400 Connector the first choice, before the Site Connector. A combination of the best features of these two would be nice, wouldn't you agree?

It is possible to create more than one connector between two sites—for example, one X.400 Connector and one Site Connector, or two X.400 Connectors. This is a common technique that creates redundant and more fail-tolerant connections. Each connector has a *Cost* value associated with it; this is a value between 1 and 100 that is used to control which connector to use primarily. A connector with a lower cost is always preferred (as long as it works) over a connector with a higher cost value. If there are two connectors with the same cost, the server will load-balance the message traffic over them.

These four types of connectors are used for one single task—transferring messages. However, they will not take on the responsibility of replicating directory updates between sites. It is important that directory replications also exist between sites, not just inside them; remember that the directory stores information about mailbox users, address lists, and server configuration settings. Directory replication is needed to create an organization-wide global address list, and to make each server aware of the configuration of all other servers, regardless of what site they belong to; for example, if you configure one server in Site A to have an Internet connection, you want this information to be known by the servers belonging to all other sites.

The *Directory Replication Connector* is used for replicating directory information between sites. However, it doesn't transfer the replication messages itself; they will be transferred with whatever type of transport connector exists between the sites—for example, an X.400 Connector. The Directory Replication Connector uses the bridgehead technique; one server in each site is configured to replicate the directory information, and if this server breaks down, the directory replication between these sites will also be interrupted.

The Gateway Address Routing Table (GWART)

All Exchange 5.x servers have a routing table, known as the *GWART*, that describes all known routes to other sites and mail systems, including the total cost for all connectors involved in each route. In this way a server in Site A will know about all Internet Mail Connectors that exist in this Exchange organization, regardless of where they may be; the server will then use this information to select the route with the lowest total cost whenever a message should be sent to the Internet.

However, the GWART design does have a flaw—it doesn't keep track of the connection status. The GWART table itself is rather static; it will be rebuilt once every night, unless the server discovers a new connection. To be honest, this is enough since this table stores only static information anyway. But this flaw makes it possible to create looping messages; for example (see Figure 12.1), assume there are two routes from a server in Site A to the destination Site D, one passing over Site B and the other over Site C. If the server in Site D goes down, both of these routes are disabled, but the sending server cannot see this since it is not directly connected to Site D. A message sent to this destination will first try one route (over Site C, since its total cost is lowest), but since it won't work, the message will be returned to the origination server in Site A, which immediately tries the second route over Site B. However, since that route is also disabled, the message will be returned once more; the server will now try the first route again, since it has no way of knowing that the remote link is still down. This message will be transferred 512 times between these two routes, until a hard-coded limit stops it.

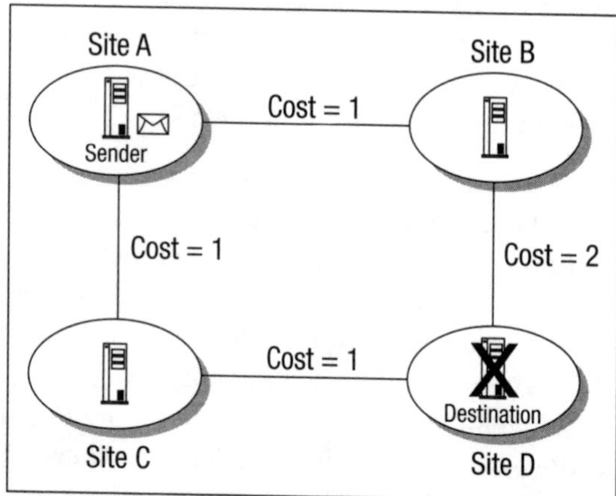

Figure 12.1
Looping messages due to flaws in the GWART design.

Comparing the MTA in Exchange 5.x with the MTA in Exchange 2000

The service that had the sole responsibility for routing in previous Exchange versions was the *Message Transfer Agent*, or the MTA. This service used the GWART table to find all possible routes to the destination, and then selected the best route, using a number of selection criteria, tested in this order:

1. Eliminate inbound connectors.
2. Compare the retry counter against the *Max Open Retries* settings.
3. Eliminate any connector with delivery restrictions that prohibit transfer of this message.
4. Check the activation schedule; select the connector with the earliest activation.
5. Compare the retry counter for the connectors; select the one with the lowest value.
6. Eliminate any connectors that are currently in a retry state.
7. Compare the connector cost; select the one with the lowest cost.
8. Select local connectors over remote connectors.
9. If there is more than one connector passing all previous steps, randomly select one of them; this will result in load balancing.

The MTA in Exchange 5.x was also responsible for expanding distribution lists, corresponding to distribution groups and security groups in Exchange 2000. The MTA process is still there in Exchange 2000, but its role is now much less important. It will not perform any routing functions, and it will not expand any groups. Its major function is to assist the X.400 Connector in its work, in case this connector should be used. However, it will still perform fan-out procedures for X.400 and EDK-based connectors, and for messages that are destined for native Exchange 5.x MTAs over RPC connections. For example, if two Exchange 5.5 sites are connected to this Exchange 2000 routing group, and a message is destined for users on both sites, the MTA in Exchange 2000 will split, or fan out, the message in two, one for each X.400 Connector. There is one more thing that the Exchange 2000 MTA still does—it converts between X.400 P2/P22 messages format and the internal MDBEF format.

All routing decisions are now made by the new routing engine, which will use the LST to find all routes to the destination; if there are multiple routes, the routing engine will make its selection based on the following criteria, tested in this order:

1. Identify all possible routes to the destination.
2. Any connector that is flagged as *Down* will be discarded.
3. Remove any route that has a restriction that prohibits this message from being delivered.

4. Select the route with the closest address space; i.e., a connector that has an address space that matches the destination is preferred over a connector with a general address space.
5. Select the route with the lowest total cost value.

Note: *Exchange 2000 does not consider connector activation schedules during the selection process, as Exchange 5.x did!*

The expansion of distribution lists is now performed by the Message Categorizer in Exchange 2000, a subcomponent of the Advanced Queuing Engine.

Summarizing the Weak Points in Exchange 5.x

If we summarize all this information about routing in previous Exchange versions, we can see that several weak points could create problems sometimes:

- The site is a boundary both for routing and administration.
- All servers in the site replicate directory status every five minutes to all other servers in this site.
- The RPC traffic between the servers in the site is not resilient.
- All servers in the site must use the same Site Service account.
- The fastest site connector doesn't have any settings for controlling the traffic.
- The GWART table is static; it doesn't keep track of the current status of connections.
- It's impossible to move servers between sites, unless you use special tools like Move Server, released in Service Pack 2 for Exchange 5.5.

In Chapter 11, we saw how administrative groups have simplified administration; in the next section, we will see how Exchange 2000 solves all the remaining problems related to message routing.

Easier Routing Design

Exchange 2000 does not have sites anymore; they have been divided into two new concepts, the *Administrative Group* and the *Routing Group*. This split means that we no longer have to reach two design goals at the same time, one regarding the routing topology and the other regarding the administrative model. The administrative group and its consequences are described in Chapter 11, so in this section we will look into the details of routing groups.

A routing group, or RG, is a collection of Exchange servers that:

- Share a reasonably fast permanent network connection
- Can use SMTP to transfer messages
- Can send messages directly to any member server in this RG

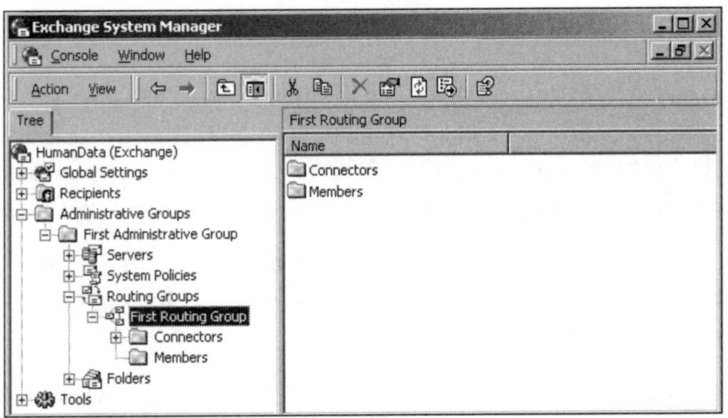

Figure 12.2
The first routing group.

This is very similar to the conditions for an Exchange 5.x site; however, a lot of restraints have been removed, as we will see shortly. In Exchange 2000, a routing group is always under the control of an administrative group, as depicted in Figure 12.2. This routing group is automatically created when the first administrative group is created, but as described in Chapter 11, neither of these two groups will be displayed in the ESM tool, unless you specifically configure ESM to show them, by using the General property page for the Exchange organization object. This routing group is by default named First Routing Group, and has two subcontainers: Connectors and Members.

Routing in Exchange 2000 Compared to Exchange 5.x

Let's look at how routing groups make the routing system in Exchange 2000 easier to manage and more resilient, compared to previous Exchange versions.

No More Directory Replication

Exchange 2000 does not have a directory database anymore; all configuration settings and user lists are now stored in the Active Directory database. This means that Exchange 2000 does not replicate directory information; this removes a large burden from the Exchange server, at the same time reducing network traffic. For example, assume we have three Exchange 5.x servers that all replicate directory information between them every five minutes; when these servers are upgraded to Exchange 2000, they will stop this directory replication. Now all of them will probably contact the same Active Directory server instead. The only network traffic left is message transfers and directory lookups in the Active Directory.

At the same time Active Directory takes care of the directory replication, it also makes each Exchange 2000 server extremely dependent on the contact with the AD. Previously, we could install our Exchange 5.x server without too much concern for the NT 4 domain controllers, whereas Exchange 2000 stops working if it loses contact with a domain controller. The design of the Active Directory structure is very important and the Exchange 2000 system must be designed in cooperation with the AD design.

No More RPC Traffic

Exchange 2000 uses SMTP for transferring all types of messages between the servers inside the routing group; no more RPC traffic exists, as with previous Exchange sites. This has a lot of benefits, but also one drawback; let's take a look. All RPC traffic inside a site is encrypted; when we start sending messages with SMTP, it will not be encrypted anymore. However, we could protect this message transfer using either of these two methods:

- *IPSEC encrypted network transfer*—This is the preferred method, because it is the fastest; this will also encrypt all network traffic over this link, not just messages. It will also be transparent to the Exchange servers.
- *Transport Layer Security (TLS)—A derivative of the SSL encryption method*—Each server must be configured to run TLS before this encryption can be used.

The problem with RPC is that it requires a reliable network connection with relatively high bandwidth. If too many network packages are dropped, due to an unreliable network connection or too low bandwidth, the RPC connection will fail and a new connection must be established. The SMTP protocol is much more resilient than RPC; it handles both unreliable network connections and lower speeds better. And this will make it possible to create routing groups that span a larger group of Exchange servers than was possible with sites.

No More Site Service Account

The Site Service account no longer exists in Exchange 2000. All its services run in the security context of the *Local System account*; see Figure 12.3 for an example. This will increase the security in our system, since the old Site Service account had full access to

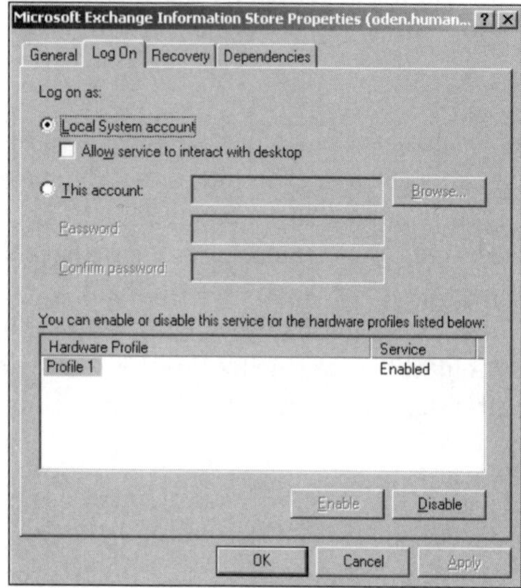

Figure 12.3
Exchange 2000 services use the Local System account.

the site; someone that logged on as this account could take control of any mailbox and read its content. And to make it worse, most organizations never changed its password since it was a bit tricky. This account was often also a member of the *Domain Admin* group, making it a primary target for anyone who wanted to get administrative access to this NT 4 domain and its Exchange site!

The Site Service account was also a delimiting factor when building sites, since all members in the site must use the same account; if some of the servers were members of other NT 4 domains, trust needed to be configured. If that wasn't possible or acceptable, a new site needed to be created for each NT 4 domain that had Exchange servers. No corresponding dependencies exist in Exchange 2000; as long as the server has a reasonably fast TCP/IP connection to the other servers, it can be a member of their routing groups. Again, we see one obstacle removed, opening up possibilities for us to create routing groups that span large areas.

Smarter Site Connectors

In Chapter 13, we will look more into connectors between routing groups, so let's just take a brief look here. The site connector (spoken in general terms and not to be confused with the particular *Site Connector*) is used to create a message transfer link between sites. When you create multiple routing groups, a similar connector must be configured in order to transfer messages between these groups. However, the number of connectors in Exchange 2000 is one less than in previous Exchange versions, since the *Dynamic RAS Connector* is gone. In Exchange 2000 there is mainly one connector that is used, unless there is a special need for the other; this primary connector is called the *Routing Group Connector* and has the best features from both the *Site Connector* and the *X.400 Connector* in Exchange 5.x. The available routing group connectors in Exchange 2000 are:

- *The Routing Group Connector*—Uses SMTP, but can also use RPC if it is connected to an Exchange 5.x Site Connector. It has lots of control features, like a schedule for when to send large messages, and message priority.
- *The SMTP Connector*—Uses SMTP for transferring messages in standard MIME format. Mostly used for connection to the Internet, but could be used to connect two routing groups.
- *The X.400 Connector*—Can use TCP/IP or X.25 as transport protocols. Mostly used to connect to X.400 Connectors in Exchange 5.x sites, but could also be used to connect routing groups.

No More GWARTs

Yes, it's true—Exchange 2000 does not have any GWARTs, or *Gateway Address Routing Tables*. Instead, it has the much more advanced *Link State Table (LST)*, that keeps track of all things that the old GWART did, and more; such as keeping track of the current connection status of each connector, regardless of where this connector is installed in this organization. This prevents looping of messages and reduces unnecessary network traffic;

never again will messages be transferred over a connector only to find that the link further down is broken. Later in this chapter we will delve more deeply into the link state table, but first let's make a comparison with Exchange 5.x.

Do you remember how the old GWART system could be fooled into sending messages like ping-pong balls between two alternative routes? This cannot happen with the link state system, since it will keep track of the current status. If we take the same example as for the GWART earlier (see Figure 12.1), the LST will work like this:

1. An Exchange 2000 server will first send the message over *Site C* (since it's still the cheapest).
2. When *Site C* fails to deliver this message it will try the link over *Site B*, just like in Exchange 5.x.
3. However, when *Site B* also discovers that it can't send the message to *Site D*, it will queue this message, instead of trying with *Site C* again, since all available routes have been tried and all have failed. As soon as one of them is operational again, the message will be sent over that route.

Easier to Move Exchange Servers

An Exchange 5.x server could not be moved to another site or organization until Microsoft released a special utility called *Move Server* in Service Pack 2 for Exchange 5.5. The problem was that the name of the site and the organization was written into the distinguished name, or the DN, for every object in the server's DIR.EDB database. To move a server from one site to another, the Move Server utility works like this: Search the directory database for all DNs where the old site name is listed; when found, change it to the new site name. Depending on how large the organization is, the number of changes will be at least several thousand, up to millions. And only Exchange 5.5 SP2 or later can use the Move Server utility.

Exchange 2000 can easily be moved between routing groups, as long as they belong to the same organization. Today there is no feature or utility that can move a server to another Exchange 2000 organization, although I am certain such a utility will be released in the future. As long as the organization is operating in mixed mode, a server can only be moved to routing groups belonging to the same administrative group. However, when the organization is switched to native mode, a server can be moved to any routing group, regardless of what administrative group it belongs to.

Although it is easy and painless to move servers between routing groups, it should not be done without careful planning. If the organization is operating in mixed mode, all the Exchange 5.5 servers will recognize only the members of the first routing group in each administrative group. However, even in mixed mode, is it possible to create new routing groups; this could be useful in a situation where the organization is still running in mixed mode, but only Exchange 2000 servers are installed. Since it's so easy to move servers, you should check the routing topology regularly to see if a server needs to be moved. For example, if the average delivery time for messages between servers within a routing group exceeds one minute, or the delivery time between routing groups is more than 15 minutes, it may be time to redesign the routing topology.

New Routing Design Possibilities

If we summarize all the new features of the routing system in Exchange 2000, we find that it is now much easier to use and more flexible than ever before. This is of course good news when designing the routing topology in the first place, but it also opens up new possibilities for redesigning and adjusting our topology as the system and our user base develop. But as long as our Exchange organization is operating in mixed mode, many of these new features are restricted; we should therefore switch to native mode operation as soon as possible.

If the Exchange 2000 system will join an existing Exchange 5.5 organization, or you have plans to add Exchange 5.5 servers later, the organization must continue to operate in mixed mode. As you may recall, during mixed mode each administrative group is associated with one routing group, in order to simulate an Exchange 5.5 site; when joining an Exchange 5.5 organization, all sites will be displayed as an AG with one RG. In this situation, you should not move servers between routing groups, since that would prohibit the cooperation between Exchange 5.5 and Exchange 2000. In Figure 12.4, you can see an example of a mixed mode organization, with one standard Exchange 5.5 site, one mixed 5.5 site and Exchange 2000 AG/RG, and one AG /RG that contains only Exchange 2000 servers. The *Routing Group Connector* is used to transfer messages between these sites and routing groups.

When there are no more Exchange 5.5 servers in this organization, and no plans to add new ones, it's time to switch Exchange 2000 over to native mode operation. But remember that this is a one-way conversion—it can't be undone unless you reinstall the entire Exchange 2000 organization. Note that there is no correlation between the Windows 2000 operation

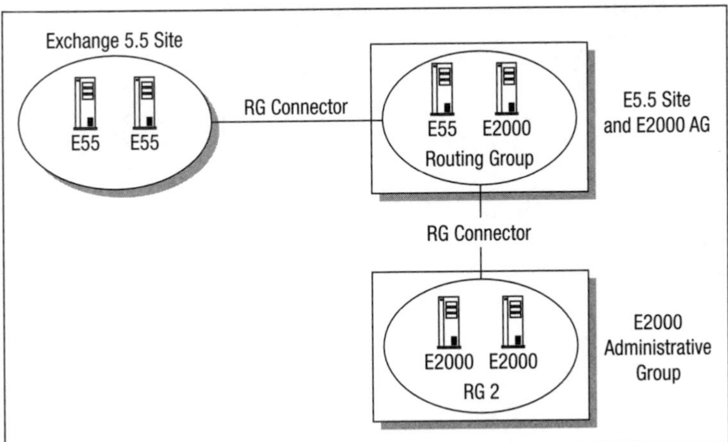

Figure 12.4
Example of a mixed mode organization with both sites and administrative groups.

mode and Exchange 2000; for example, it is perfectly okay to run Exchange 2000 in native mode while Windows 2000 is running in mixed mode.

In native mode operation, Exchange 2000 offers all the new routing possibilities; servers can now be moved between any routing groups and users can be moved between any servers, regardless of what administrative group they belong to. In native mode, you are not restrained to create a routing group within a particular administrative group; if necessary, a routing group could contain servers belonging to any administrative group. See Figure 12.5—in this picture you can see RG 1 and RG 3 within each administrative group, while RG 2 is shared between two administrative groups.

However, the routing group *folder* must always be created within an administrative group. It is the *member servers* of a routing group, not the actual folder itself, which can be shared between multiple administrative groups.

For example, look at Figure 12.6; in this picture you can see an Exchange 2000 organization operating in native mode with two administrative groups, *First Administrative Group*

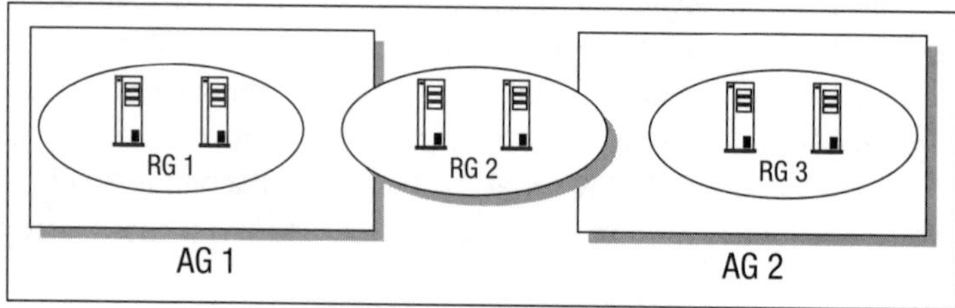

Figure 12.5
Routing groups are independent of administrative groups in native mode.

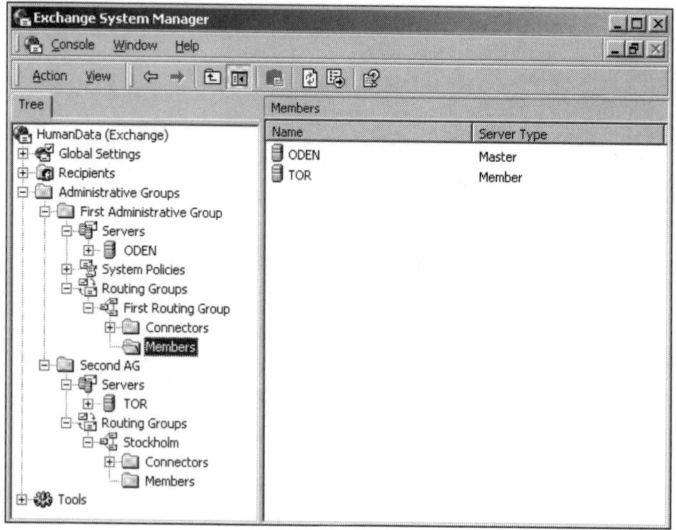

Figure 12.6
A routing group that is shared between two administrative groups.

with the server *Oden*, and *Second AG* with the server *Tor*. These AGs also have one routing group each, the *First Routing Group*, and *Stockholm*, respectively. In this figure, you can see that even though *Oden* and *Tor* belong to different administrative groups, they are still members of the same *First Routing Group*. This is an example of a routing group that is shared between two administrative groups.

The consequence of sharing a routing group is that the administration of each server is under the control of the administrative group, whereas the routing group controls the physical routing of messages; in other words, they work independently of each other.

Creating and Managing Routing Groups

The first routing group is created when the first server is installed, or when the **ForestPrep** command is executed, whichever comes first. The name of this default routing group is First Routing Group, and it contains two subfolders:

- *Connectors*—Contains all routing group connectors for this routing group.
- *Members*—Contains all Exchange servers that belong to this routing group.

All subsequently installed Exchange servers will automatically be members of this routing group, unless you create more routing groups; in this case, you will be asked a question during the installation of the new Exchange server asking what routing group it should join. As you may recall from the previous section, servers cannot be moved to routing groups in other administrative groups while the organization is operating in mixed mode; make sure the new server is installed in the right routing group!

Creating a New Routing Group

All routing groups belong to the Routing Groups folder, and that folder is always a subfolder to the administrative group; see for example Figure 12.6 again. Note how the First Routing Group is a subfolder of Routing Groups, which in turn is a subfolder of the First Administrative Group. This means that if we want to create a new routing group, we must first create the Routing Groups folder, unless one already exists. Follow these instructions to create such a routing group in an existing Routing Group folder:

1. Start the ESM tool, and navigate to the administrative group where this routing group should be created.
2. Right-click on the Routing Groups folder, and select New|Routing Group.
3. Give this routing group an intuitive name; make sure to follow the organization's name standard, if there is one.
4. Click *OK* to create the new routing group.

There are two interesting questions regarding the creation of routing groups: what is an intuitive name, and when should a routing group be created?

Intuitive Routing Group Names

If there will be only one single routing group in our organization, the question about using intuitive routing group names is irrelevant, since the routing group already has a name anyway, and no server will ever be moved. By the way, it is simple to rename a routing group; just right-click it, and select *Rename*. When the organization has three or more routing groups, it is important that all administrators understand the purpose of each routing group. Avoid naming them *First Routing Group, Second Routing Group*, etc.; these names are clearly not intuitive and don't say anything about what they are used for. Since the membership of routing groups is primarily based on network speed, they are often geographically oriented—for example a subsidiary company, a city, or a country. If the name also contains anything that makes you associate it with routing groups, the object's purpose will be even more intuitive; below are some examples of intuitive routing group names:

- Routing Group Human Data
- Routing Group Gävle
- Routing Group Italy
- RG: London
- London (RG)

You can use 8-bit characters in the routing group name, such as *Gävle*; usually I recommend that you stick with 7-bit U.S. ASCII characters only, but so far I have not seen any problems with these 8-bit characters.

When Should a New Routing Group Be Created?

If the network speed allows it, all servers should belong to the same routing group. There is absolutely no point in creating a new routing group just because it is possible; doing so will only make the system more complex and slow down the average message delivery time. These are indications when you should create a new routing group; see also Decision Tree 12.1:

- The available bandwidth is less than or near 64Kbps; note that a 512Kbsp WAN-connection that is heavily utilized may have less than 64Kbps of free bandwidth!
- The quality of the network is not ideal; for example, if it's an unreliable network, or if there is no permanent network connectivity.
- There is a need to schedule the transmission of messages, especially large messages.
- There is a need to control the connections to certain servers.

Contrary to previous Exchange versions, the routing topology can be changed whenever needed. For example, if the initial design for this Exchange organization resulted in one routing group, and 12 months later your company expands with a new office in another country, that's probably a good time to create a new routing group. Maybe some of the

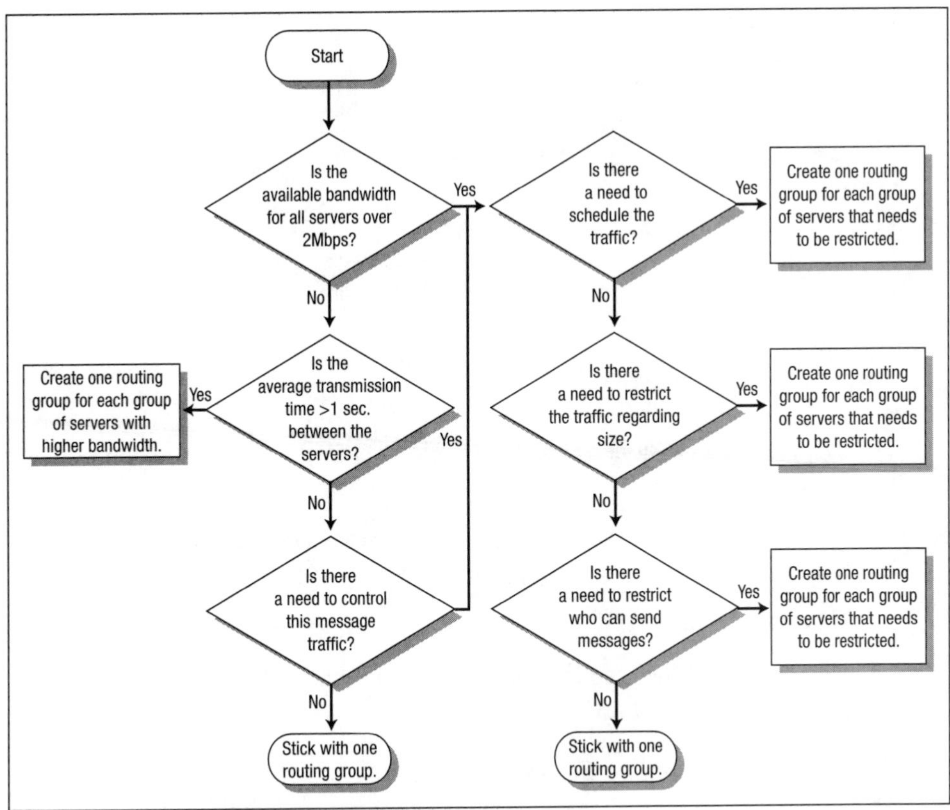

Decision Tree 12.1
When to create new routing groups.

12

employees from the headquarters will move to this new office; if so, use the ESM and move their mailboxes to a server in that routing group.

The Routing Group Master

In every routing group there must be one server acting as the routing group master. By default, the first member of the routing group will be the master; however, the administrator can at any time give this role to another member. The routing group master is responsible for maintaining the LST, or the link state table, an in-memory table that keeps track of the current connectivity status of all servers within the routing group, as well as all connections, i.e., if they are *Up* or *Down*. Every time a message is to be transferred, the server's internal routing engine will consult the LST table to select a route. Whenever a bridgehead server in this routing group discovers any status changes in a local connection, or receives such information from other routing groups, the information is transferred over to the routing group master, which updates its LST. Every time the master updates its LST, it will also replicate this information to all members of this routing group, who in turn will update their local copy of the LST.

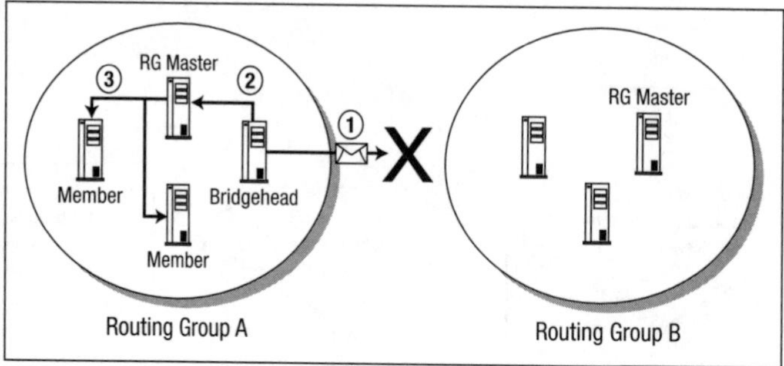

Figure 12.7
How the routing group master operates.

For example, here's what happens when a bridgehead server detects a connection problem; see also Figure 12.7:

1. The bridgehead server in Routing Group A discovers a connectivity problem to Routing Group B.
2. This information is replicated to the local routing group master, which updates its LST.
3. The master will then replicate the update information to all members of the routing group, who will update their local LST.

Assigning a New Routing Group Master

The information in the LST table is only stored in memory; if this server is restarted, the LST table will be rebuilt from the information stored in the other member servers. If the routing group master goes offline, no updates of connector status will be sent to the members of this routing group; however, all information they have received so far will be available to them. If you know that the current routing group master will be offline for a longer time, or permanently removed, you must assign this role to another server in this routing group, by following these steps:

1. Open the ESM tool, and navigate to the routing group to be changed.
2. Select its Member folder. You will see all members in the right pane; see Figure 12.8. You can also see who the current routing group master is—in Figure 12.8, it's the server Oden.
3. Right-click the new master; select Set As Master.

There are actually two special cases where member servers will continue to learn about link state updates, even if the routing group master is down. The first case is when the bridgehead server receives any link state updates from another routing group; it will always update its own LST, even if it fails to contact the routing group master. The second case is when two member servers transfer a message between them; if they don't have the same LST version, the newest LST will be replicated to the other server, even if the routing group master is down.

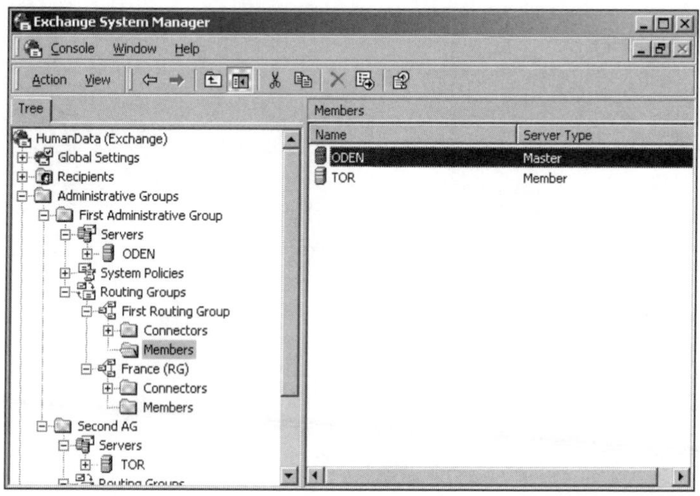

Figure 12.8
Selecting a new routing group master.

Managing the Routing Group

Not much can be done with an existing routing group, except adding or removing members, assigning a new routing group master, or creating routing group connectors. This last task is significant enough to deserve its own chapter; see Chapter 13 for more information about routing group connectors.

Moving a Server to a New Routing Group

As you may remember, a server can be moved to another routing group whenever necessary, although this should not be done just for fun. To move a server, follow these steps:

1. Open the ESM tool, navigate to the routing group, and expand the Member folder that the server will be moved to; you will later drag the server to this folder, so it's important that the Member folder is visible.
2. Navigate to the routing group and Member folder the server currently belongs to.
3. Use the mouse and drag the server icon to the new Member folder (the one you made visible in Step 1). Done!

A server that is acting as a bridgehead server, i.e., one that has any type of routing group con-nector, can't be moved; see Figure 12.9. You must start by modifying the connector to use another server, or remove this connector, before the server can be moved.

Removing a Routing Group

If you need to delete an existing routing group, its subfolder must be emptied first, in a specific order. Follow these instructions to remove a routing group:

1. Open the ESM tool, and navigate to the routing group to be deleted.

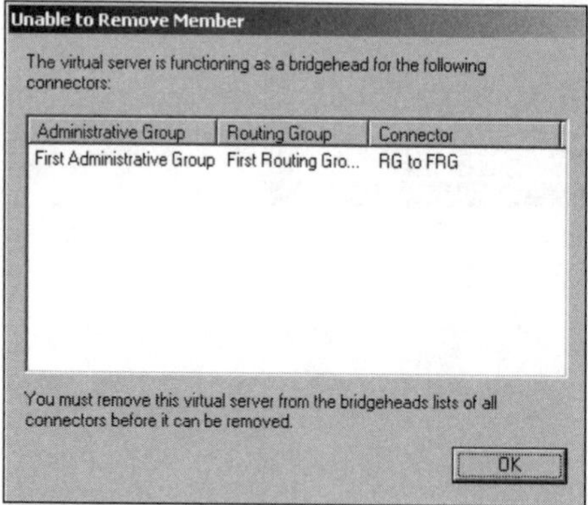

Figure 12.9
The error message you'll receive if you try to remove a bridgehead server.

2. Open the Connectors folder; note what other routing groups this routing group has a connection to.
3. Delete all routing group connectors.
4. Go to each of the other routing groups that has a connector configured to this routing group; delete that connector.
5. Go back to the first routing group and its Member folder; move its servers to a new routing group. Note that you cannot delete a server from the Member folder, you can only move them. If you missed deleting any connectors in Step 4 above, and then try to move the bridgehead server for this connector, you will receive an error message; see Figure 12.9. This message will tell you which connector must be deleted before this server can be moved; it will also tell you which routing group this connector belongs to.
6. Right-click the routing group to be removed and select Delete; if any server is still remaining in the Member folder, you will get an error message stating that all servers must be removed first.

The Link State System

Large or geographically distributed messaging systems are in a constant state of flux; servers, routers, and WAN connections may go offline at any time due to technical problems or maintenance. The more complex the message system is, the more often something will happen that affects the connectivity between the different parts. The link state system is covered in detail in Chapter 3; here we will repeat some of the most important concepts, along with some new information related to routing groups.

The GWART table that is used in 5.5 and previous Exchange releases was not designed to cope with these constant changes; GWART only stores a list of configured connectors and their destinations, along with their Cost value, used by the administrator to control what connector to prioritize. The MTA process is responsible for message routing in Exchange

5.x and uses the GWART at any time a message will be routed; the MTA will detect if the selected route is not working, and select another one, if available. Otherwise the message will be stuck in a queue. However, the MTA cannot detect connectivity problems in removed sites, since no status information is stored in the GWART, and would happily try to send a message over a route that is down somewhere on the way to the destination.

The LST

In Exchange 2000 the LST has replaced the GWART. The LST can be viewed as an enhanced version of the GWART and contains the following information:

- The name of the connector
- The cost for the connector
- The routing group and administrative group this connector is connected to
- The address space of this connector, i.e., the destination that can be reached
- The type of address space, for example, RG or X.400
- The current status of the connection (up or down)
- The restriction—Maximum Message Size and Accept Message From

There is actually even more information than this in the LST, like the name of the organization and version numbers. Unfortunately, the LST table can't be displayed with the ESM tool, as the GWART could be displayed in the Exchange 5.5 Admin program; however, with the *WinRoute* utility, you can view the complete LST information.

The WinRoute Utility

This utility is necessary to view the LST table and the current status of all connections. WinRoute can be found on the Exchange 2000 Resource Kit CD, in the *\exreskit\tools\admin\winroute* folder. You don't have to install the complete resource kit to use this tool—simply copy this utility to your hard disk and it's ready to use. If you install the resource kit, what you get is a number of help files, not the utilities themselves. The help text for WinRoute is short—it simply tells you how to install the utility and lists the contents of the three different panes.

When you start the WinRoute utility, you must first open a connection to an Exchange 2000 server; select *File|New Query*, then enter the server name. If the server belongs to another domain, click the *Bind Options* button and fill in the information needed; click *OK* to open the connection to the Exchange server. You will see something like Figure 12.10; adjust the panes by dragging their borders until you see all three panes.

The three panes consist of the following information:

- *The top pane*—Displays the current status of the LST of this server. This information is presented in a tree structure, with descriptive headlines that make it easier to understand what this data is. The tree branches can be collapsed and expanded, as needed.

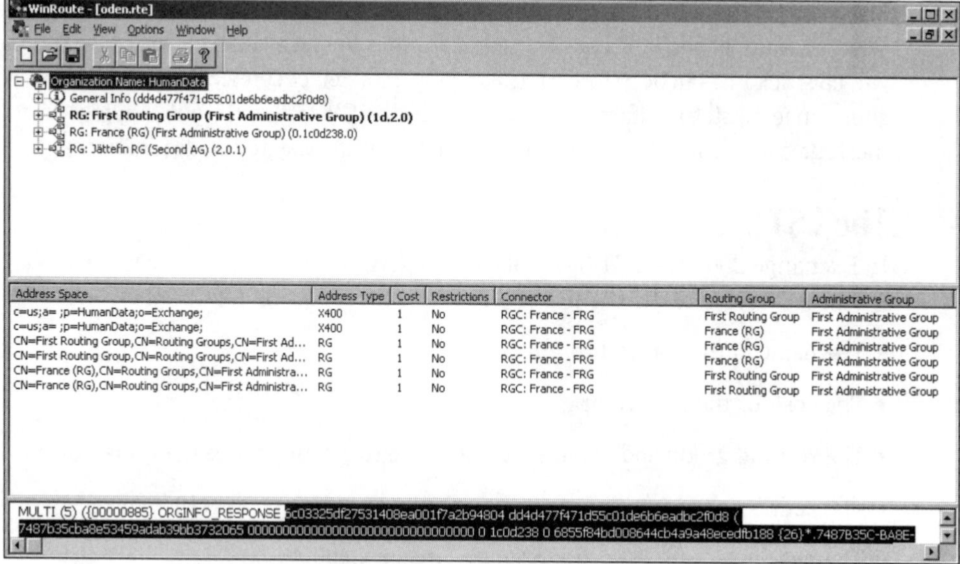

Figure 12.10
The WinRoute utility.

- *The middle pane*—Displays the routing information in a layout similar to the old GWART table; it shows the address space, address type, cost, restrictions, connector name, and the routing and administrative groups.
- *The bottom pane*—Displays the LST data in raw format; all information in the top and middle panes comes from this pane.

Usually the top and middle panes are the most interesting, since they're easiest to understand. To see if a connection is *Up* or *Down*, click the routing group it belongs to, and expand the *Connectors* folder; any routing group connector with a *red cross* (see Figure 12.11 and *RGC: France - FRG*) is *Down*; if it has a *green check mark*, it is *Up*.

To see if a server is Up or Down, expand the routing group folder this server belongs to, then expand the RG Members folder. Servers that are Down are flagged with a red cross; servers that are Up are flagged with a green check mark; see Figure 12.12.

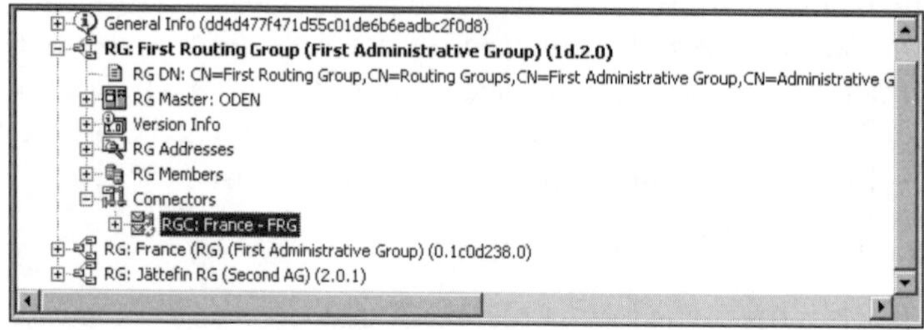

Figure 12.11
A connection flagged as Down in WinRoute.

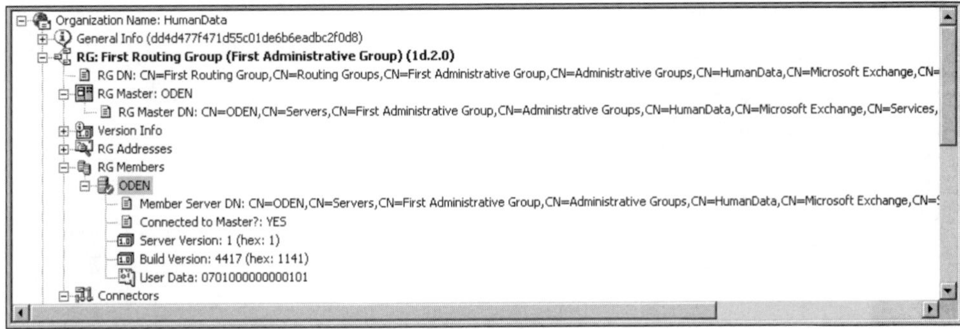

Figure 12.12
A server flagged as Up in WinRoute.

The information displayed in WinRoute is by default not updated; use the F5 key to see the latest information. You can configure WinRoute to update itself at regular intervals; use the Options menu, select Auto-Refresh, and select the update interval (see Figure 12.13). In the same menu, you will also find the option Get Statistics that will display a summary of the number of routing groups, servers, etc.; see Figure 12.14. As you can see, lots of interesting information is available with the WinRoute program; any administrator responsible for routing should use this tool.

Updating the LST

In Exchange 5.5, one server in each site was responsible for updating the GWART table; this was the *Routing Calculation Server*. Once per day, or whenever a new server or connector

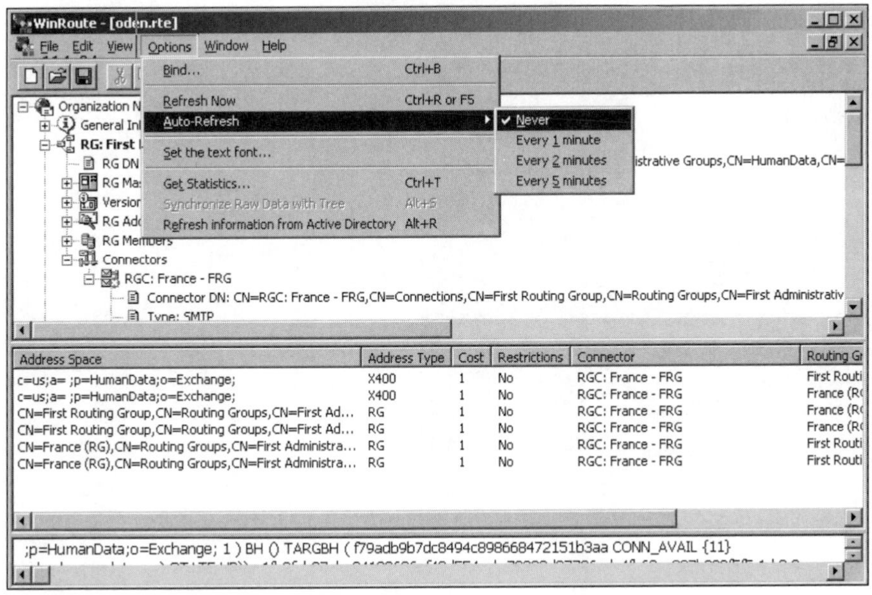

Figure 12.13
The Auto-Refresh option in WinRoute.

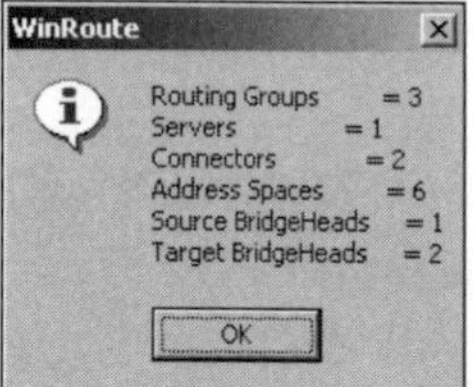

Figure 12.14
The Get Statistics option in WinRoute.

was installed, the GWART was rebuilt. The administrator could also force a rebuild of the GWART, using the Exchange 5.5 Admin.exe program. As we have seen, in Exchange 2000, we have the *Routing Group Master* in each routing group that is responsible for keeping the LST updated; this master is responsible for updating all member servers in this routing group whenever there is a status changed detected.

The process in Exchange 2000 that is responsible for the link state system is the *MS Exchange Routing Engine Service*, or the *RESvc*. The link state system uses TCP port 691 to communicate with the RESvc service. By default this service is configured to run in the *Inetinfo.exe* process; you should not tamper with this service, or the link state system will stop working. The RESvc service is actually independent of the other Exchange services, and will start as soon as the InetInfo.exe process starts (see Figure 12.15); however, it's dependent of the *IIS Admin* service.

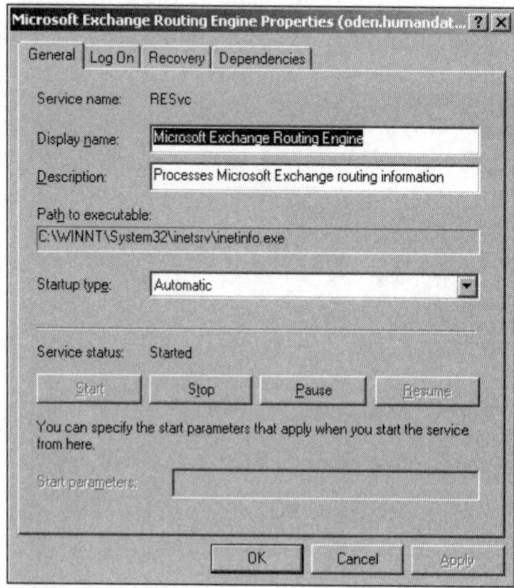

Figure 12.15
The Routing Engine Service.

Updating Link State Information in the Local Routing Group

Any server that detects a change in connectivity will send a TCP package on port 691 to the routing group master. The routing group master will immediately update its LST and then send the new information on TCP port 691 to all members in this routing group. This is an extremely fast way to pass information about LST updates; we could in fact say that it's instantaneous. It's important to understand that the link state system is designed to detect connectivity problems in links to other routing groups, as well as when a member server goes offline. Because of that, all servers have an LST that is updated in real-time to help them select the best available route to the destination, whether it's a local delivery or a remote delivery.

The link state update uses a Microsoft-developed protocol called *Link State Algorithm (LSA)* when transferring messages over TCP port 691. Microsoft has proposed to the Internet Engineering Task Force (IETF) that this will be a standard RFC protocol for all link state updates between SMTP servers. However, if IETF instead recommends another protocol for this purpose, LSA is designed to be able to replace the current protocol with whatever IETF suggests.

There are two important exceptions to this detection of link states; the first is when an *SMTP Connector* is configured to use DNS. Such a connector will always be regarded as up, even if a message can't be delivered to the destination. The reason for this is that Exchange doesn't know if the failed delivery of a message is due to the remote mail system being down or if the link is down. We surely don't want our *SMTP Connector* to stop sending messages to the Internet simply because one of the receiving SMTP servers is down at the moment.

The second exception is when a *Routing Group Connector* is configured to use *Any* as the source bridgehead server; in this case, any server in the routing group will be able to use this connector independently of the other servers; if one server fails to deliver over the *Routing Group Connector*, we don't want to prevent the other servers from using this connector.

Updating Link State Information between Routing Groups

The goal of the LST system is to keep the complete Exchange organization aware of any connectivity problems; a problem detected in one routing group must therefore be replicated to all other routing groups. The question is: How should the link status information be transferred between the routing groups? The answer is: It depends on what type of routing group connector is used. We basically have three types of connectors—the Routing Group Connector, the SMTP Connector, and the X.400 Connector.

The first two use the SMTP protocol for message transfers; both will also send link state updates using ESMTP commands. The third connector uses an X.400 dummy message for transferring the link state update to the other routing group. Note that only between routing groups with Exchange 2000 will link state updates be valid; Exchange 5.5 does not understand these messages since it doesn't have an LST. Neither can these update messages be transferred to other Exchange 2000 organizations; this is a design restriction that has been built into the link state replication system; whenever a link state message is transferred, the name of the organization and a *digest* are also sent, to make sure the two routing groups belong to the same organization. The digest consists of a mathematical hash sum, based on the organization name and its version number; this digest will always have the same number of characters, regardless of how long the organization name is. If the receiv-ing routing group doesn't have the same organization name or digest, the transferred link state update will be discarded.

The two SMTP-based connectors, the Routing Group Connector and the SMTP Connector, send the link state update like this:

1. The sending bridgehead server in the site that has detected the connectivity problem connects to the receiving bridgehead server on TCP port 25.
2. The sender sends an **EHLO** command to check that ESMTP is supported; if not, the link state update is aborted.
3. The sender sends an **X-LINK2STATE** command to inform the receiving server that a link state update, using a Microsoft specific command, will be transferred.
4. The receiving server must acknowledge this command, or the transfer will be aborted.
5. The actual link state update, consisting of the state (up/down), configuration data, and organization name plus digest, is transferred in a compressed format; usually this takes less than one second.

When the link state update is transferred, any other normal SMTP messages that are waiting to be transferred to this remote routing group will also be sent; the link states are always sent first. The size of the link state update is 32 bytes per object; for example, if you have an organization with 30 servers, 10 routing groups, and 15 connectors, the total size will be $32 \times (30+10+15) = 1{,}760$ bytes.

The X.400 Connector cannot use SMTP commands; instead, an X.400 dummy message is created, containing the link state update, including the configuration data, organization name, and digest. The receiving X.400 connector will treat this message in a special way to make sure the receiving server immediately updates its LST.

When Is Link State Down Detected?

So now we know that within the routing group, the LSA protocol over TCP port 691 is used to send updates, and between routing groups the **ESMTP** command is used; but one question remains: When is a change in the link state detected? The answer is: When it's used the first time after the change. For example, assume that a link to another routing group goes down at 10:30 A.M.; at 11:15 A.M. a server tries to use this link, but fails. This is when the changed link state is detected. Exchange 2000 does not test each server or connector constantly to see what the current link state is; that would generate too much network traffic. Instead, a link that is down will go undetected until a server tries to transfer a message over this link.

When the link has failed, the sending server will try three more times (the "glitch-retry" state), with 60 seconds between each retry; if it still fails the third time, this server will flag this connector as down. However, it will wait five more minutes before sending a link state update message over port 691 to the routing group master. This means that a few minutes elapse before the information about the failed link is replicated, first inside the routing group, and then to other routing groups. The reason behind this five-minute delay is to prevent replication of a link down status for a connector that is temporarily down; for example, maybe the remote bridgehead server is restarted.

It is possible to change this five-minute delay using the *StateChangeDelay* Registry setting; but remember that a delay shorter than five minutes will probably generate a lot more "false" link down states; for example when an Exchange server is restarted. The *StateChangeDelay* registry value must be created the first time you want to use it, and is configured like this:

```
Hkey_LocalMachinge\System\CurrentControlSet\Services\RESvc\Parameters
Type = REG_DWORD
Name = StateChangeDelay
Value = <seconds to wait>, default is 300 seconds, or 5 minutes.
```

You can also prohibit any link state to be generated from a given Exchange 2000 server. Use this Registry parameter for this; note you must create it first:

```
Hkey_LocalMachinge\System\CurrentControlSet\Services\RESvc\Parameters
Type = REG_DWORD
Name = SuppressStateChanges
Value = [0=no suppress/1=suppress]
```

When Is Link State Up Detected?

The server that detected the failed link will continue to retry a connection according to the retry schedule settings on the Delivery page for this particular connector (see Figure 12.16 for an example), until the connection goes up again. This will result in a new series of link state updates replicated around the Exchange organization, informing all servers that the link is now operational again.

The RID Master

Exchange 2000 has introduced a new concept called the *RID Master*, or the *Routing Information Daemon Master*. This is an Exchange server that is responsible for updating the GWART table in an Exchange 5.5 site and publishes it to the other servers. By default, the first Exchange 5.5 server in a site will be its RID Master. If an Exchange 2000 server joins an existing Exchange 5.5 organization, it could take over this responsibility. The

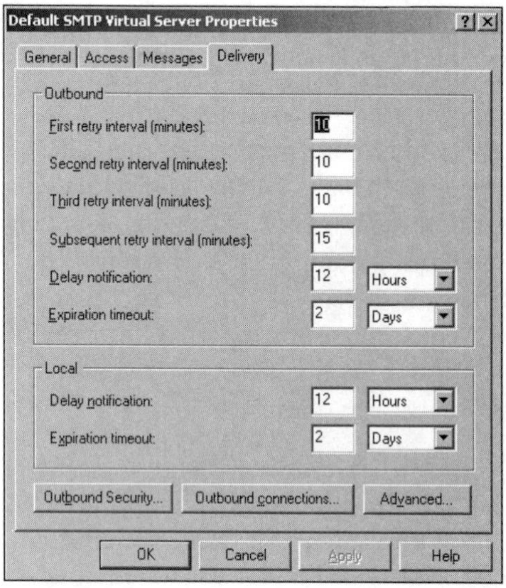

Figure 12.16
The retry schedule is controlled by the connector's Delivery page.

benefit of using an Exchange 2000 server as the RID Master is that it will be able to update the GWART table whenever a link state change is detected, thereby improving the quality of routing information in the Exchange 5.5 site. The RID Master will also make sure the GWART table in the Exchange 5.5 site is replicated to the LST table in the Exchange 2000 routing group.

However, Exchange 2000 does not recognize the Exchange 5.x concept of sub sites. These sub sites were used in Exchange 5.x to limit the scope of the address space for a connector to a group of servers within the site; by default the address space visible for all servers was in the site. If sub sites are used in a site, you must avoid having an Exchange 2000 server as a RID Master, since this server will ignore any restriction of the scope, and will basically flatten the sub sites. To change the RID Master for an Exchange 5.5 site, follow these steps:

1. Open the Exchange 5.5 Admin.exe program; connect it to the site in question.
2. Expand the *Configuration* container, then double-click on the *Site Addressing* object.
3. Select the *General* page.
4. Select the RID Master by setting the *Routing Calculation Server*. If any subsites are defined in the site, make sure to select an Exchange 5.5 server. If there are no subsites, you should select an Exchange 2000 server instead.
5. Click *Apply* to activate the change.
6. Select the *Routing* page.
7. Click *Recalculate Routing*.

Summary

This is a list of the more important features and keywords mentioned in this chapter. Use it as a reminder and to make sure you have understood the most important things:

- A routing group is a collection of servers that enjoys a permanent and relatively high bandwidth, capable of transferring SMTP messages directly between all servers.
- Routing groups are a holdover from the Exchange 5.x site, but have no relationship to any administrative functions.
- Create each routing group only from a routing perspective; do not look at the administrative boundaries.
- Exchange 5.x sites are both routing and administrative units.
- The directory replication alone in a site generates a lot of messages, 24 hours a day.
- A site with three servers generates 1,728 messages per day.
- The site uses RPC to communicate between its member servers, regarding both directory replication and message transfer.
- IPM, Inter Personal Message, refers to normal mail between users.
- Messages between sites need to be transferred using one of the four available site connectors.
- The Site Connector in Exchange 5.x is the fastest connector, and uses RPC.
- The X.400 Connector is slower, but has lots of options; it uses TCP, X.25, and TP4.
- The Internet Mail Service (formerly Internet Mail Connector) is an SMTP-based connector.
- The Dynamic RAS Connector is used for dial-up connections.
- The Directory Replication Connector is used to control the replication of directory messages between sites. It will only create the replication messages; these will still be transferred with one of the four site connectors.
- The GWART, or the Gateway Address Routing Table, is the routing table in Exchange 5.x.
- The GWART contains all connectors and their address spaces, including the total costs to reach the final destination.
- The Address Space describes what destinations this link leads to.
- The Cost value is used by the administrator to control what connector to prioritize.
- The GWART is almost static; it's rebuilt once every 24 hours, unless a new server or connector is installed.

- GWART does not recognize any link status; it's up to each server to detect any connection problems.
- The MTA, or Message Transfer Agent, is responsible in Exchange 5.5 for routing and selection; it uses the GWART to find all possible routes to a given destination. One of these routes will then be selected by the MTA.
- The MTA in Exchange 2000 is no longer responsible for routing or selection; it's mainly used whenever an X.400 Connector is installed.
- The LSR, or the Link State Routing system, uses the routing engine in the Advanced Queuing Engine to route and select messages in Exchange 2000.
- Exchange 2000 doesn't consider the schedule during the selection process.
- The Message Categorizer in Exchange 2000 now handles expansion of groups, which was previously performed by the MTA in 5.5.
- The Exchange 5.5 site concept has a number of weak points; for example, it's a boundary both for administration and routing. It has the directory replication where all servers will send replication messages each five minutes to all other servers, and all servers must share the same Site Service account.
- Exchange 2000 offers much more freedom for designing the routing topology.
- There is no directory replication in Exchange 2000.
- There is no RPC traffic.
- There is no Site Service account.
- There are smarter site connectors.
- The GWART is replaced by the Link State Table (LST).
- When the Exchange organization is operating in native mode, servers can move to any routing group.
- Mixed mode organization has a restriction; servers can only be moved within an administrative group.
- Convert to native mode as soon as you are 100 percent sure that all Exchange 5.5 servers are (and will stay) gone.
- The First Routing Group is created when the Exchange 2000 organization is created.
- It always has two subfolders: Connectors and Members.
- A routing group is always under the control of an administrative group, but its members can belong to any AGs, when operating in native mode.
- Select intuitive and good names for the routing groups; "First Routing Group" says nothing about what it contains.

- Try to stick with one single routing group for as long as possible; this eliminates the need for any routing group connectors, and will result in the fastest average times for message transfers.
- Create new routing groups when the bandwidth is too low or the network connectivity between the servers is intermittent, when a dial-up connection is used, or to control the message traffic over a link.
- The RGM, or the Routing Group Master, is the server in each routing group that is responsible for updating the LST and replicating all changes in the link state to the members of this routing group.
- Avoid being without an active RGM for long periods; it's easy to assign this role to another server in the routing group.
- Move a server between routing groups by dragging it between the Member folders.
- Removing a routing group can be done only when all subfolders are empty.
- The link state system has a lot more information than its predecessor the GWART.
- Use the WinRoute utility, found in the resource kit, or the Exchange server CD to inspect the current status of a server's LST.
- Link state updates within a routing group use the LSA protocol over TCP port 691.
- The RESvc, or the Exchange Routing Engine Service, is responsible for the link state process in each Exchange server; this is an IIS 5 process.
- Exceptions to the link state update: SMTP Connectors using DNS will always be considered up; likewise, Routing Group Connectors that have configured all servers as source bridgeheads.
- Link state updates between routing groups are sent by X-Link2state ESMTP messages or by X.400 dummy messages, depending on the type of connector.
- Link state messages are small, only 32 bytes per object.
- A link that is down is detected when a server tries to transfer a message.
- First the server will retry sending the message three times within 60-second intervals, then the connector's Delivery page will control how often the server will retry the connection.
- When a server has detected that the link is down, it waits five minutes, then it notifies the RGM.
- The RID Master is used to make the GWART aware of Exchange 2000 links, and to make Exchange 2000 aware of routes in the GWART.

Chapter 13

Routing Group Connectors

This chapter continues and concludes the discussion of message routing that started in Chapter 12. If your Exchange 2000 organization consists of one single routing group, with no connection to the outside world, then you don't need this information. However, if you want to understand how routing is performed between routing groups, or to the Internet or other messaging systems, this chapter is for you.

As soon as we have more than one routing group in our organization, we must connect them using a routing group connector. This is a configured transport mechanism, the main purpose of which is to transfer messages from one routing group to another. But routing group connectors also have another purpose; they are used to refer Outlook clients looking for public folders to other routing groups, in case they can't find a local copy. In Exchange 2000 we have three types of connectors:

- The Routing Group Connector
- The SMTP Connector
- The X.400 Connector

The reason for having three connectors instead of just one is that they differ in transport mechanism and configuration possibilities; they also differ in speed, the Routing Group Connector being the fastest. It's easy to get confused when talking about these connectors; they are often referred to as "routing group connectors," and at the same time we have a particular connector called the *Routing Group Connector*. To make sure you understand the difference, I will use capital letters for the specific *Routing Group Connector*, and small letters only when I talk about the general term.

In Chapter 8, we discussed migration and how connectors were used to configure an Exchange 2000 organization to coexist with legacy mail systems, for example MS Mail or Lotus Notes. In this chapter, we will summarize the use of these connectors to other mail systems and discuss when to use them.

Have you, as an administrator, ever been asked by a user whether a certain piece of mail has been delivered, or have you ever tried to find what route a specific message has taken? If so, then you will love the *Message Tracking Center*. At the end of this chapter, we will look at how the message tracking system works in Exchange 2000; the good news is that it has been extended, compared to previous Exchange releases. For example, you can now see the subjects of messages that you are tracking.

Connectors in Exchange 5.x

The sites in Exchange 5.5 and previous versions also needed to be connected in order to exchange messages; these communication links were referred to as *site connectors*. There is one major difference between the connectors in Exchange 2000 and Exchange 5.x: The routing group connectors in Exchange 2000 also control what servers a client will use when accessing a public folder; this is not the case with site connectors in Exchange 5.x. Exchange 2000 has three types of connectors, compared to four in Exchange 5.x:

- *The Site Connector*—RPC over TCP/IP, IPX/SPX, and NetBEUI
- *The X.400 Connector*—TCP/IP, TP4, or X.25
- *The Internet Mail Service Connector*—SMTP over TCP/IP
- *The Dynamic RAS Connector*—Asynchronous modem or ISDN

The Dynamic RAS Connector and the X.400 Connector were basically the same connector; the difference was the connectivity method. The RAS connector was used for dial-up connections, whereas the other was used for LAN/WAN connections. In Exchange 2000, the Dynamic RAS Connector has been removed completely.

The two most commonly used site connectors in Exchange 5.x were the Site Connector and the X.400 Connector. The Site Connector was the fastest, but had practically no configuration settings for controlling the message traffic; the X.400 Connector had lots of configuration settings, but was up to 30 percent slower. The IMS Connector was mainly used for Internet connections and was very seldom used as a connector between two sites. Let's take a closer look at the first two in the following sections.

The Site Connector

This connector is the fastest of them all, but at the same time, the most demanding. Since it uses the RPC protocol to transfer messages, it's very sensitive to low bandwidth and bad network connections; if such conditions occur, the RPC network session will fail, and a new session has to be established, resulting in a retransmission of the message. This would show up as an error message in the Exchange server's Event log. The consequence of this sensitivity was that administrators most often used this connector to connect 5.5 sites over high-speed LAN connections or fast WAN connections, but never over slow WAN links.

Another disadvantage of the Site Connector is its lack of configuration settings; for example, it's not possible to set a maximum size limit for messages, or to schedule the connections. If this were necessary, you would instead select to install the slower X.400 Connector. However, the Site Connector has one interesting feature that the X.400 Connector lacks—even if this connector is installed on one server, all servers in this site can use it, independently of the others. For example, if we had two sites called Sweden and Finland, with three servers each, and these sites were connected with a default-configured Site Connector, then any server in either of these sites could send a message directly to any server in the other site. That gives us both fault tolerance and load balancing. However, it's possible to configure it so that only a certain local server should be responsible for transferring messages over this connector; it's also possible to select what servers shall receive messages—these are called the *target servers*. Using these configuration settings, we can create an environment where one local server is solely responsible for transferring messages to a single target server in the remote site; or in other words, to make the Site Connector work with the bridgehead technique.

Target Server Cost

Not many Exchange 5.x administrators understand how the concept of target servers and their special cost value works, so let's take a closer look at this mystery. By default, all servers in the remote site are designated as target servers, meaning any one of them could be selected to receive a message from this site. However, using a feature called *target server costs*, you could balance the traffic between the target servers—for example, making one of them the primary target server and the rest backup target servers. The target server cost interval was from 0 to 100, interpreted this way:

- *0*—This server will always be used, making it the primary target server.
- *100*—This server will never be used, unless all other servers have failed, making it a backup target server.
- *1–99*—Load balance the message transfer between these servers, using the servers with low target server cost more often (but not solely) than servers with higher cost.

The last interval, 1 to 99, is interesting. It is used to distribute the load between the target servers, making some of them more utilized than others, but all of them were used. Compare this to ordinary connector costs; the one with the lowest cost is always used first; if it fails, then the next lowest connector is used.

For example, let's say that there is one site called Sweden, with two servers: Stockholm and Uppsala, and another site called Norway with three servers: Oslo, Trondheim, and Narvik (see Figure 13.1). A Site Connector is configured between these sites. Both servers in the Swedish site share the same configuration settings of target servers, as seen in Figure 13.1: Oslo, with a target server cost of 0; Trondheim, with a cost of 10; and Narvik, with a cost of 20. A message from server Stockholm is to be delivered to the server Narvik; here's what will happen:

1. The MTA process in the Stockholm server looks in the GWART table to see if there is any routing to the destination site; it finds the Site Connector described earlier.
2. Next, the MTA consults the configuration settings for the Site Connector; it finds the three targets servers and their respective target server costs.

3. Since Oslo has the target server cost 0, it will always be used as long as it works. In this example, let's assume that Oslo is offline; this leaves us with two remaining servers, Trondheim and Narvik.

4. The MTA will now calculate which of these servers to select to receive this message, using a weighted average formula:

   First, subtract the target server cost for each server from 100, giving us: 100–10=90 and 100–20=80; these are called the *preference values*. Next, add these values to get the *divisor*: 90+80=170. Third, divide each preference value with the divisor to figure out the delivery probability of each target server. Trondheim gets 90/170=0.53 and Narvik gets 80/170=0.47.

   In other words, the probability that our MTA selects Trondheim is 53 percent, and Narvik (the final destination) is 47 percent!

5. If the message was delivered to Trondheim, we assume that this server will immediately route this message to its final destination, which is Narvik.

As you can see from these steps, the final destination server is not necessarily selected as the target server. In other words, there is no guarantee that the server receiving messages over Site Connectors is the final destination server—it's completely dependent on the configured target server costs. However, it will never be more than two hops before the message reaches the final destination.

The X.400 Connector

This connector is popular because of its many configuration settings; you can configure a connection schedule, maximum message size limits, and more. This connector doesn't understand target servers or target server costs; it works only with the bridgehead technique, meaning that two designated servers, one in each site, transfer messages between them using the X.400 Connector. If one of them fails, the complete connection stops.

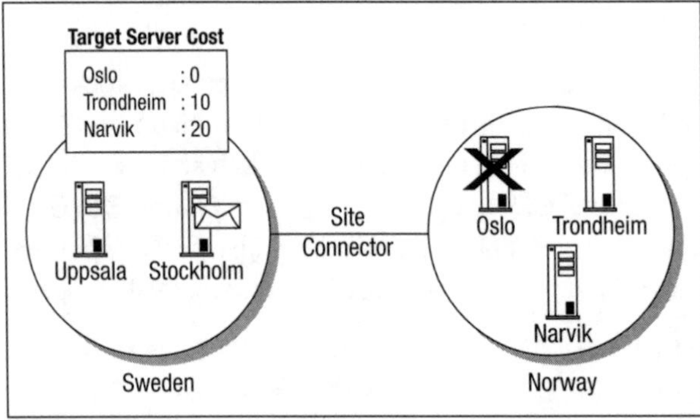

Figure 13.1
Selecting a target server in Exchange 5.5.

Many Exchange 5.x administrators think that this connector is hard to configure, mainly because of its many options, but also because of the many X.400-related settings, like the X.400-based address space, and OSI parameters, like TSAP and NSAP. However, if this connector is used between two Exchange sites, you don't have to mess with any OSI parameters at all, and the initial address space will be created automatically if you configure the connector to connect to a given site. This X.400 Connector can also be used to connect to external X.400-based mail systems; then you may need to configure both OSI parameters and the address space manually, and this can be tricky.

The Routing Group Connector

The Routing Group Connector, RGC, has replaced the Site Connector, and is designed to be the primary connector between routing groups. It offers a number of enhancements, compared to the Site Connector, regarding the transport protocol used and the number of configuration settings. This connector is the fastest of all three; it's also the easiest to install and configure. Unless there is a special reason, you should always use the RGC for connecting routing groups. Routing group connectors always work in pairs—i.e., you must configure an RGC in both routing groups, connected to the other, before they can start transferring messages.

Note: *The Routing Group Connector can be used only between routing groups that belong to the same Exchange 2000 organization; if you need to connect two routing groups in different organizations, use the SMTP Connector or the X.400 Connector.*

The RGC can also be used to connect a routing group to an Exchange 5.5 site configured to use a Site Connector. In that situation, the RGC will use the RPC protocol, and send messages over a 40-bit encrypted link, like the standard RPC connections in Exchange 5.5. The RGC will in this case use the MTA process in Exchange 2000, which actually will establish an RPC session with the MTA process on the Exchange 5.5 server. All this makes the routing group connector behave exactly like a Site Connector, thus making it very easy to communicate with 5.5 sites.

How to Set Up the Routing Group Connector

You don't have to install this connector separately; it will be available in all Exchange 2000 servers. Follow these instructions to set up an RGC:

1. Start the *ESM* tool and navigate to the routing group and the *Connectors* folder where this new RGC will be created.
2. Right-click the *Connectors* folder, and select *New|Routing Group Connector*. Note that you must have at least one Exchange server as a member of this routing group before you can configure a new RGC; otherwise you will receive an error message stating "You must have at least one SMTP VSI in this routing group to create a routing group connector."

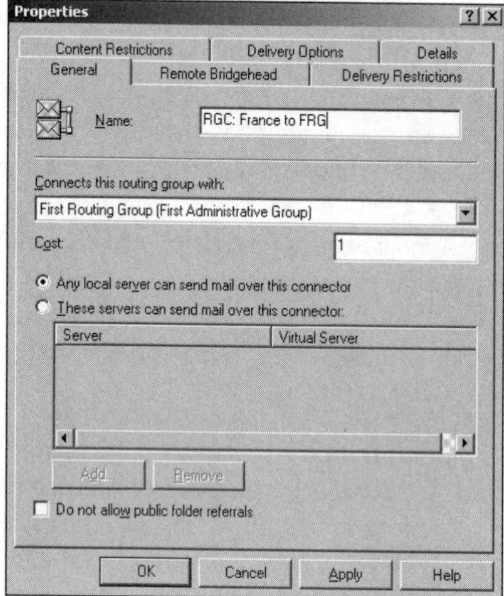

Figure 13.2
The General tab for a Routing Group Connector.

3. On the *General* tab (see Figure 13.2), give this RGC an intuitive name. Be sure to follow the name standard in your organization, if one is defined; this name will show up in many places—for example, in Event log messages and in the tracking log—and a good name for the connector will make troubleshooting situations easier.

   Select what routing group this RGC will connect to, using the pull-down menu; it will list all available routing groups in this organization, regardless of what administrative group they belong to.

   Set a cost value for this connector; remember that the routing engine uses this value to prioritize one connector before another; i.e., make sure to set a low value for a primary connector (the default cost is 1).

   Set the local bridgehead servers to be used; default is *Any Server Can Send Mail Over This Connector*, making this connector work similarly to the Site Connector. If you want to utilize specific local bridgehead servers for this connection, select *These Servers Can Send Mail Over This Connector*, and click *Add* to add these servers. If there is more than one server, the message traffic will be load balanced automatically between these servers.

   Define whether this connector will do public folder referrals or not; this feature is described in more detail in the design section, later on in this chapter.

4. On the *Remote Bridgehead* tab (see Figure 13.3), you must manually add all remote bridgehead servers; you cannot leave this tab empty. Click *Add* and select all servers in the remote routing group that will receive messages from this RGC. If more than one server is selected, automatic load balancing is activated. Note that the RGC

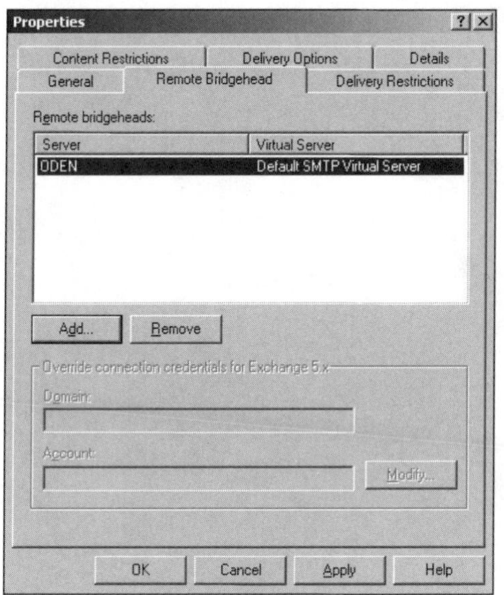

Figure 13.3
The Remote Bridgehead tab.

doesn't use target server costs, like the Site Connector does; the message traffic will be distributed between all servers equally.

The pane called *Override Connection Credentials For Exchange 5.x* is used when this RGC will be connected to an Exchange 5.x site; in this case, you must add the NT Domain name, the Site Service Account, and its password, by clicking the *Modify* button. If you don't specify an account, Exchange 2000 will use the Windows 2000 account that has administrative rights on the administrative group this routing group belongs to. You must also configure the *Override* tab for the Site Connector in the 5.5 site to use the account that has administrative rights for this routing group, unless the Site Service account in 5.5 has been granted administrative permissions for this routing group. When the RGC is connected to a site, it will then use the RPC protocol, instead of SMTP, as described previously in this section.

Warning! *The Windows 2000 account that the Site Connector will declare on its Override tab must not have a blank password; this would prevent the Exchange 5.5 MTA process from connecting to the Exchange 2000 MTA over the RGC! You will get an error message in the Event log that reads: "An RPC communications error occurred. Unable to bind over RPC." Make sure no administrative accounts have blank passwords, which is a really bad idea anyway.*

5. On the *Delivery Restrictions* tab (see Figure 13.4), messages from all users are accepted by the RGC. In some situations, you may want to restrict what messages this connector will deliver. Use the *Accept Messages From* pane to declare all users that specifically will be accepted; use the *Reject Messages From* pane to declare all users that

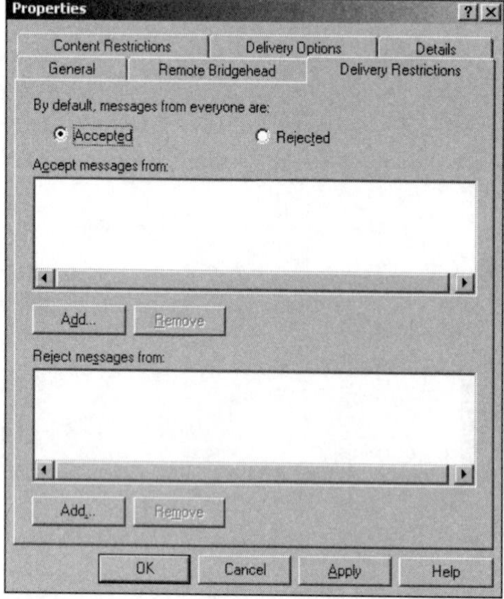

Figure 13.4
The Delivery Restrictions tab.

specifically will be rejected. Any declaration in one of these panes will override the default configuration.

6. The *Content Restrictions* tab (see Figure 13.5) gives you control over what messages will be accepted by this RGC. The default is to accept all types of messages, regardless of priority, type, or size.

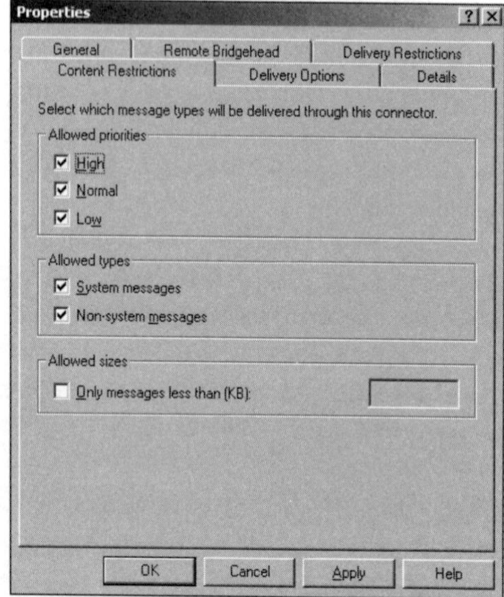

Figure 13.5
The Content Restrictions tab.

Use the *Allowed Priorities* pane to set any combination of *High, Normal,* or *Low* priority messages that are accepted by this connector; for example, clear the *Low* checkbox to prohibit messages with low priority from being transferred with this connector.

Use the *Allowed Types* pane to set any combination of *System Messages* or *Non-System Messages* that will be accepted by this connector. System messages are all messages coming from Exchange services, like replication messages, delivery reports, Monitoring Tools messages, or Windows 2000 messages, whereas Non-System Messages are standard Inter Personal Messages (IPMs), meaning messages between users, groups, and contacts.

Use the *Allowed Sizes* pane to set the maximum size for outgoing messages that this connector will accept for delivery; note that this will not prohibit large incoming messages!

7. The *Delivery Options* tab (see Figure 13.6) gives you control over two things: first, when this connector will connect to the other routing group, and second, when large messages will be sent.

   Use the *Connection Time* schedule to define when this connector will send messages. The default is *Always Run*, meaning that all messages will be sent without any delay. In some situations, you may need to schedule the connections; if so, use the pull-down menu and select *Always Run, Run Daily At 11:00 P.M., Run Daily At Midnight, or Run Daily At 1:00 A.M.* If none of these alternatives is appropriate, click the *Customize* button and select the exact time for each day in the week when this

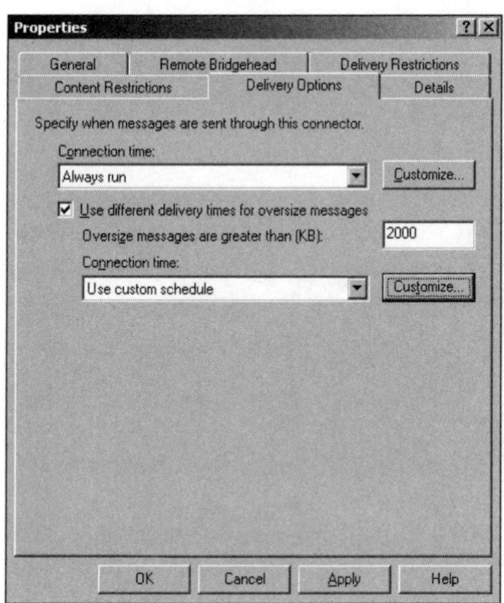

Figure 13.6
The Delivery Options tab.

connector should run; this will be displayed as *Use Custom Schedule* in this pull-down menu.

Check *Use Different Delivery Times For Oversize Messages* if you want to control when large messages will be delivered. By default, this option is not activated, meaning that all messages will be delivered according to the *Connection Time* on the top of this tab, regardless of how large they are. If you check this option, you must also define what an oversized message is; default is 2000KB. Use the special *Connection Time* parameter to set when to send oversized messages; the predefined schedules are *Run Every 2 Hours*, *Run Every 4 Hours*, *Never Run*, or *Use Custom Schedule*; the last alternative is defined by using the *Customize* button, and specifying exactly what times on what day of the week to send these oversized messages.

Note: *When the checkbox for oversized messages is set, the default schedule will be Use Custom Schedule; be sure to set this schedule by using the Customize button, since the schedule is by default empty, meaning oversized messages will never be sent!*

8. The *Details* tab (see Figure 13.7) allows you to see when this connector was created, and when it was last modified. You can also write an administrative note here, for example, describing the purpose of this connector and the name of the person responsible for managing this RGC.

9. When all tabs are configured, click *OK* to complete the setup of this RGC. You will next be asked whether a corresponding RGC should be created in the remote routing group; select *Yes* if this is what you want, and you have the administrative permissions required on that routing group, or *No* if you want to create that RGC manually.

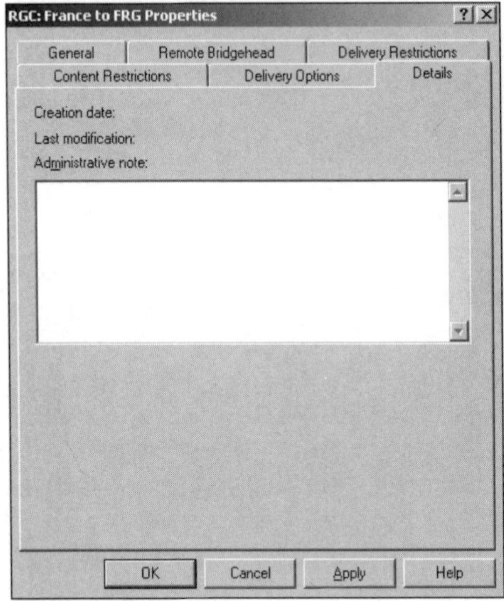

Figure 13.7
The Details tab.

One thing to remember is that the automatically generated RGC will have exactly the same configuration settings, including the name of this RGC. For example, if the first RGC is named "RGC From France to Germany," the other RGC will also have the same name; since you have used a direction in the name (From, To), you probably want the second connector to have the name "RGC From Germany to France"; if so, remember to rename that second connector.

Managing the Routing Group Connector

When the routing group connector is configured, you usually don't have to do much to keep it running. Just make sure the configuration settings are correct and the defined bridgehead servers are running, and this connector will be fine. However, sometimes you may need to modify its settings—for example, the name of the RGC, or the connection schedule. If so, open the properties for this RGC (it will be stored under the *Connections* folder for this routing group), and make any adjustment needed. These settings may need some time before the Active Directory has replicated these new values to all Exchange servers in the organization, depending on how complex the AD design is. All settings may be modified; you can even reconfigure this RGC to connect to another routing group, if necessary. If so, you must also make sure a corresponding RGC exists in the new routing group.

When looking at the properties for an existing RGC, you will find a new property tab called *Security* (see Figure 13.8); this is the standard Windows 2000 security tab that all objects have. It shows the permission settings inherited from the administrative group object and the organization object. If necessary, it can be modified, but usually you don't change these settings.

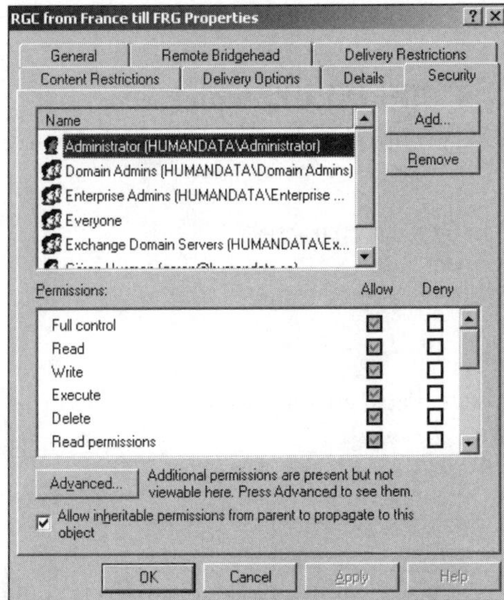

Figure 13.8
The Security tab.

To view the queues of the RGC, expand the *Protocols* folder of the server running this connector. Then expand the *SMTP* folder and the virtual SMTP server; right-click on the *Queues* folder and select *Refresh*. You will then see the RGC and any messages waiting in this queue.

When to Use the Routing Group Connector

As stated, the RGC is the first choice when connecting two routing groups belonging to the same Exchange 2000 organization. The reasons for this are:

- It's the fastest connector.
- It's very resilient and can handle both low bandwidth (in extreme cases down to 16Kbps) and unreliable network connections, thanks to the SMTP protocol.
- It's easy to set up.
- It has lots of configuration options.
- It can be used to connect to Exchange 5.5 sites, using the Site Connector.

It really doesn't have any drawbacks, as long as the SMTP protocol can be used (unless it's connecting to an Exchange 5.5 site; then RPC will automatically be used). Use the Routing Group Connector in these situations:

- To connect two routing groups belonging to the same organization, if you have at least 16Kbps of free bandwidth.
- When the fastest possible connector between routing groups is needed.
- To connect an Exchange 2000 routing group to an Exchange 5.5 site that has a Site Connector installed.

What You Must Know Before Setting Up the RGC

When you have decided to set up the routing group connector, you must be able to answer a few questions before you start:

- What will the name of this RGC be (up to 64 8-bit characters)?
- What local bridgehead servers should be used?
- What remote bridgehead servers should be used?
- What cost value should this connector have (between 1 and 100)?
- Are any special configuration settings needed?

The SMTP Connector

The SMTP Connector also uses the SMTP protocol, just like the Routing Group Connector; so what is the difference between those two connectors? The answer is control—the SMTP Connector has more configuration options than the RGC, but it's also slower and a bit more complicated to configure. The normal use for an SMTP Connector is external SMTP traffic, typically to the Internet. However, it can also be used to connect two routing groups, and they don't have to belong to the same Exchange organization. Another thing that differs is that the RGC never uses MX record in the DNS server to find the remote bridgehead servers, whereas the SMTP Connector needs them; instead, the RGC will look up the destination bridgehead server in the Active Directory.

The SMTP Connector must follow all usual RFC standards for the SMTP protocol, since it can be used both for connecting routing groups, and for transferring messages to any external SMTP server. It must therefore convert 8-bit binary information to 7-bit MIME format before transferring messages, regardless of what type of server is on the other end. The RGC will utilize the fact that both the sending and receiving servers are Exchange 2000 servers belonging to the same organization, and send 8-bit information directly in binary format, without converting it to 7-bit MIME format first. This is the reason the RGC is faster than the SMTP Connector.

A *smart host* is an SMTP server that receives messages from other SMTP servers and takes the responsibility of routing these messages to their final destination, using DNS lookups. This is an old concept in the SMTP world, and is often used today when outgoing SMTP messages should be brought together to a central point before they are delivered—for example, to scan for viruses, or to have disclaimers added to outgoing messages. The SMTP Connector can be configured to send all messages to a smart host, and it can also be a smart host for other SMTP servers.

How to Set Up the SMTP Connector

Follow these step-by-step instructions to set up the SMTP Connector between two routing groups:

1. Start the *ESM* tool and navigate to the routing group and its Connectors folder where this new SMTP Connector will be created.

2. Right-click the Connectors folder, and select *New|SMTP Connector*. Note that you must have at least one Exchange server as a member of this routing group before you can configure a new SMTP Connector; otherwise you will receive an error message stating "You must have at least one SMTP VSI in this routing group to create an SMTP connector."

3. From the *General* tab (see Figure 13.9), give this SMTP Connector an intuitive name; make sure to follow any defined name standards.

   Select to use DNS if this connector should be able to send messages to the destination servers, using MX records. If this connector instead will send all messages to a smart host, select the option *Forward All Mail Through This Connector To The Following Smart Hosts*; if you want to enter multiple smart hosts, seperate them with a semicolon or comma character. Type the Fully Qualified Domain Name (FQDN) for the smart host—for example, **server1.humandata.se**. You can also define the IP address to the smart host, instead of its name; make sure to enclose the IP address in brackets, like

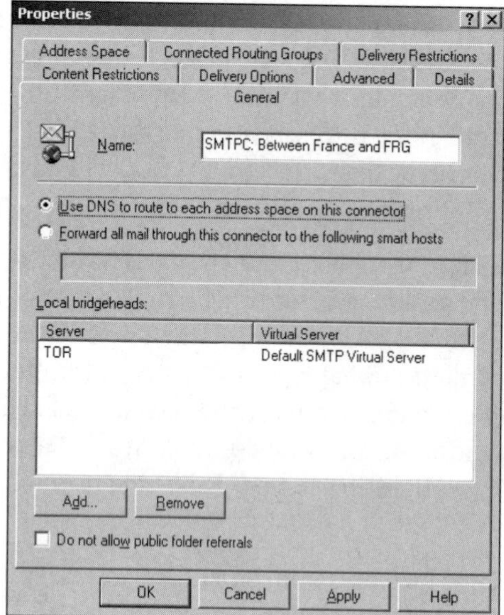

Figure 13.9
The General tab for an SMTP Connector.

this: [192.168.15.10]. The brackets tell Exchange to interpret this as an IP address, instead of looking this up in the DNS.

If this SMTP Connector will be used for connecting two routing groups, you must configure one Exchange server in the other routing group as a smart host; otherwise you can't create this object. In this case, don't forget to use the *Connected Routing Groups* tab to define what routing group to connect to; see more information about that later on in this section.

Note that any smart host defined in an SMTP Connector will override any smart host settings that may exist in the virtual SMTP server on this Exchange server. Microsoft recommends that you use the smart host settings on the *SMTP Connector* instead of the virtual SMTP server, since the connector can handle message delivery on a per-domain basis.

Use the *Local Bridgeheads* pane to declare the local bridgehead server. You must have at least one; if there is more than one, Exchange will automatically load balance the message traffic between these servers. This will also create fault tolerance, since they will run independently of each other.

At the end of this tab, you'll see a *Do Not Allow Public Folder Referrals* checkbox; set this checkbox if you don't want to refer Outlook clients to that remote routing group, looking for a public folder they can't find in their local routing group.

4. Go to the *Content Restrictions* tab. This tab is identical to the same tab in the RGC (refer to Figure 13.5); use it to control what messages will be accepted by this SMTP Connector. The default is all types of messages, regardless of priority, type, or size.

   Use the *Allowed Priorities* pane to set any combination of *High*, *Normal*, or *Low* priority messages that are accepted by this connector; for example, clear the *High* checkbox to prohibit messages with high priority from being transferred with this connector.

   Use the *Allowed Types* pane to set any combination of *System Messages* or *Non-System Messages* that will be accepted by this connector. System messages are all messages coming from Exchange services, like replication messages, delivery reports and Monitoring Tools messages, or Windows 2000 messages, whereas Non-System Messages are messages between users, groups, and contacts.

   Use the *Allowed Sizes* pane to set the maximum size for outgoing messages that this connector will accept for delivery. Note that this setting will not affect incoming messages!

5. The Delivery Options tab is also identical to the same tab in the RGC (refer to Figure 13.6); it gives you control over when this connector will connect to the other routing group, and when large messages will be sent.

   Use the *Connection Time* schedule to define when this connector will send messages. The default is *Always Run*, meaning that all messages will be sent without any delay. In some situations, you may need to schedule the connections; if so, use the pull-down menu and select *Always Run, Run Daily At 11:00 P.M., Run Daily At Midnight*, or *Run Daily At 1:00 A.M.* If none of these alternatives is appropriate, click the *Customize* button and select the exact time for each day of the week when this connector will run; this will be displayed as Use *Custom Schedule* in this pull-down menu.

   Check the *Use Different Delivery Times For Oversize Messages* checkbox if you want to control when large messages will be delivered. By default this option is not activated, meaning that all messages will be delivered according to the *Connection Time* at the top of this tab, regardless of how large they are. If you check this option, you must also define what an oversized message is; the default is 2000KB. Use the special *Connection Time* parameter to set when to send oversized messages; the predefined schedules are *Run Every 2 Hours, Run Every 4 Hours, Never Run,* or *Use Custom Schedule*; the last alternative is defined by using the *Customize* button, and specifying exactly what times on what day of the week to send these oversized messages. As for the RGC, make sure to set the schedule manually since the default schedule is to never run!

   Use the *Queue Mail From Remote Triggered Delivery* Option to make this SMTP Connector accept mail for other SMTP domains; these other domains will later use the **TURN** (or **ATRN**) command to dequeue these messages. Both of these commands

13

(contrary to the more common **ETRN**) require the remote computer to authenticate itself before this Exchange server will send all queued messages back. Click *Add* and select the Windows 2000 account this remote server must use for authentication.

6. The *Advanced* tab (see Figure 13.10) is used to control if ESMTP is allowed or not; it is also used to control how to dequeue messages temporarily stored in another SMTP server.

   Use the *Send HELO Instead Of EHLO* checkbox if you want this SMTP Connector to avoid using **ESMTP** commands; this should be set only in the rare occasion that the receiving SMTP server doesn't understand **ESMTP** commands. Even then, it's normally not needed, since the SMTP protocol itself usually detects whether the receiving server can't handle **ESMTP** commands; see Chapter 4 for more information about ESMTP.

   The *Outbound Security* button displays a new dialog box (see Figure 13.11) where you can configure how this SMTP Connector will authenticate itself when connecting to other SMTP servers. It is normal to use *Anonymous Access*, unless this connector will connect to a well-known server at the other end; in this case, that server may require this SMTP Connector to logon, using *Basic Authentication* (sending account name and password unencrypted) or *Integrated Windows Authentication* (using NTLM or Kerberos to protect the account name and password during the authentication process; this works only with Windows NT or Windows 2000 servers). You can also configure this SMTP Connector to use Transport Layer Security (TLS), an encryption method almost identical to Secure Socket Layer (SSL) that is used frequently in HTTP communications. The TLS system will encrypt the complete SMTP session between

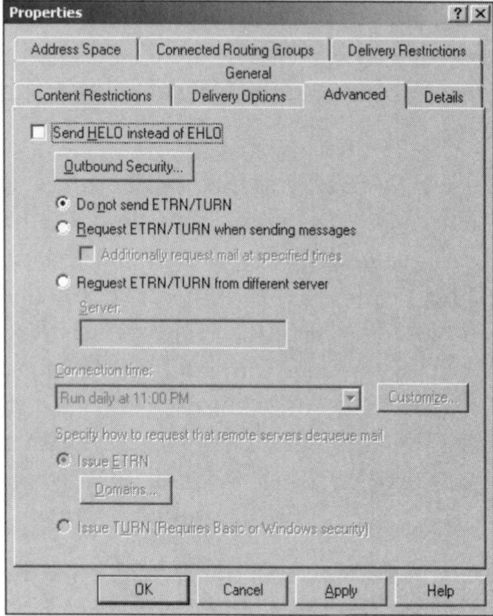

Figure 13.10
The Advanced tab for the SMTP Connector.

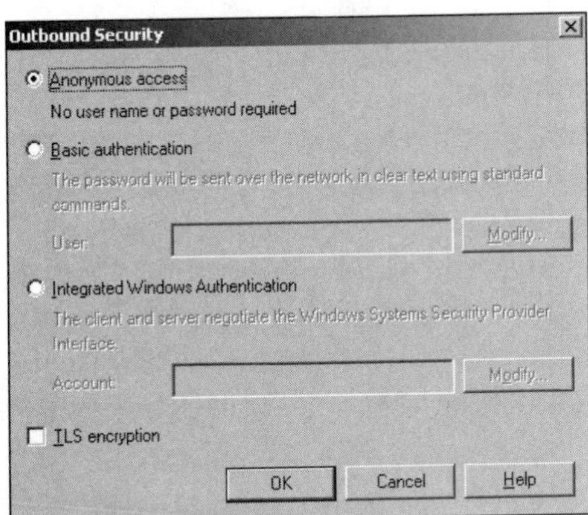

Figure 13.11
Configuring outbound security for the SMTP Connector.

the two servers, prohibiting network analyzers and similar systems from viewing the information transferred. Before the TLS encryption will work, an X.509 certificate must be installed; for more about configuring TLS encryption, see Chapter 14 and the Windows 2000 Server documentation.

Note: *Whatever you select on this tab will override any security settings for the virtual SMTP server.*

The rest of this tab is used whenever you want this SMTP Connector to pick up messages temporarily stored at another SMTP server, typically an Internet Service Provider (ISP). The default setting for this option is *Do Not Send ETRN/TURN*, which disables this dequeuing feature. To enable this, select *Request ETRN/TURN When Sending Messages* or *Request ETRN/TURN From Different Server*. The first option will force this SMTP Connector to send an **ETRN** or **TURN** command (depending on what command is selected at the bottom of this tab; the default is **ETRN**) whenever it connects to the remote server. The second option will force this SMTP Connector to send the **ETRN** (or **TURN**) command to another server. For both of these options, you can configure a connection schedule by using the *Connection Time* pull-down menu and the *Customize* button; however, for the first option, you must check *Additionally Request Mail At Specific Times* before the *Connection Time* can be defined. For more information on how to use this dequeuing feature, see the design section later in this chapter.

7. The *Details* tab is identical to the same tab in the RGC; refer to Figure 13.7. Use it to see when this SMTP Connector was created, when it was last modified, and to add administrative notes.
8. The *Address Space* tab (see Figure 13.12) is one of the two tabs used for defining what destinations can be reached with this SMTP Connector, also known as the *address space*. In Figure 13.12, you can see an example of the address space *SMTP: **, meaning this connector can deliver mail to all SMTP destinations, a typical configuration for an SMTP Connector that is connected to the Internet. By default, this tab will not

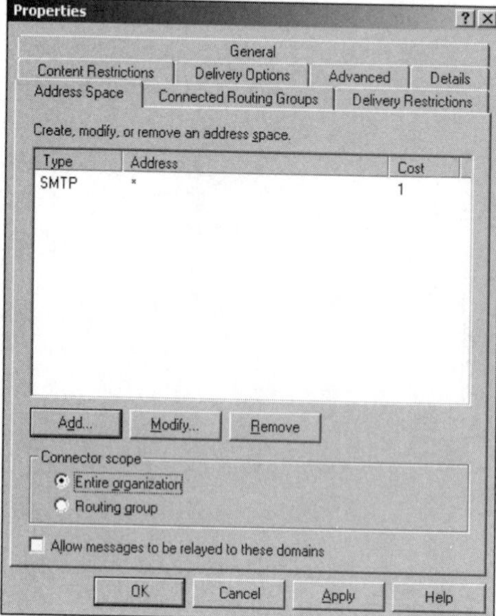

Figure 13.12
The Address Space tab.

have an address space configured. However, you can restrict this connector to accept messages only for a specific domain, for example, to microsoft.com, by using an address space of **SMTP:microsoft.com**, or **SMTP:*.microsoft.com**. The difference between these two address spaces is that the first will only accept messages to SMTP addresses like name@microsoft.com, whereas the second will accept messages like name@subdomain.microsoft.com. Use the *Add* button to add new address spaces; you can also modify or delete existing address spaces.

If this SMTP Connector will be used to connect two routing groups in the same organization, you would leave this tab blank; instead, you define the address space from the *Connected Routing Groups* tab.

Use the *Connector Scope* to define how far this SMTP Connector and its address space will be visible in the Exchange organization. The default setting is the *Entire Organization*, making all Exchange servers aware of this connector, regardless of what routing group they belong to; if an Exchange server is aware of a connector, it can also route messages through it. Sometimes it can be necessary to restrict the knowledge about this SMTP Connector, then set the connector scope to this routing group; this will only make Exchange servers in this routing group aware of this connector. Exchange 5.5 actually had a third scope option, *This Location*, where a large site could be divided into sub-sites. Exchange 2000 doesn't support the concept of sub-site, and therefore not that scope either.

The last option is the *Allow Messages To Be Relayed To These Domains* tab. Its purpose is to make this SMTP Connector relay incoming messages to the address space defined earlier. For example, if you use this SMTP Connector for Internet traffic, you will have the address space *SMTP:**; if you set this checkbox, all SMTP servers (including sending POP3 and IMAP4 clients) on the Internet can reroute messages through this connector. This is a very dangerous configuration, since all messages will look like they originated from your Exchange organization—exactly what producers of junk (a.k.a. spam) email and unsolicited commercial email are looking for. Maybe you think (or hope?) they won't find your relaying server? Sorry, these types of people have special scanner programs that look for open relay servers over the whole Internet; it will only be a matter of days before they find your server, and then you will have to answer all the angry messages coming from people receiving this junk mail from your server! In other words, don't allow relay of messages, unless you have a very good reason to do so, and you know exactly what you are doing.

9. The *Connected Routing Groups* tab (see Figure 13.13) is the other tab that is used to define address spaces, or destinations, for this SMTP Connector. This tab should be used instead of the *Address Space* tab when this connector connects two routing groups belonging to the same organization. Figure 13.13 shows an example of what happens when one routing group is added, the *First Routing Group*; this SMTP Connector will connect this routing group (France) with the *First Routing Group*. In this situation, you would normally leave the *Address Space* tab empty, since this tab is all that is needed for routing messages between these two routing groups.

   To add a routing group, click the *Add* button, then select what routing group this SMTP Connector will connect to, using the pull-down menu on the *General* tab (see Figure 13.14). This menu lists all known routing groups in the organization, including

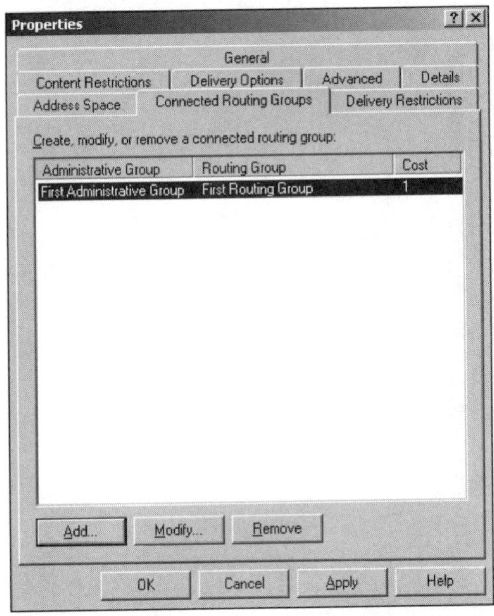

Figure 13.13
The Connected Routing Groups tab.

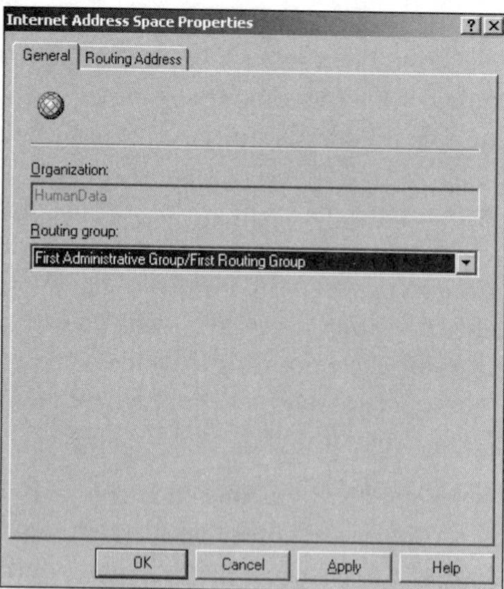

Figure 13.14
The General tab, used when adding new routing groups.

an option to connect to a server in an Exchange 5.5 site, which has an *Internet Mail Service Connector* installed. Note that you cannot change the organization name; the reason for this is that all routing groups must belong to the same organization. On the *Routing Address* tab, you can set the SMTP domain name used in the other routing group, including a cost value (see Figure 13.15). This tab will probably not be interesting if all users have the same SMTP domain (for example, **humandata.se**); but

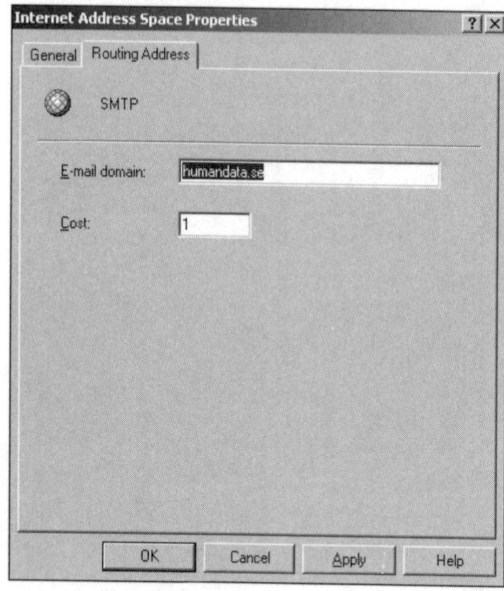

Figure 13.15
The Routing Address tab, used when adding new routing groups.

if different SMTP domains are used for your routing groups, you must configure this *E-mail Domain* accordingly. When you're finished, click *OK* to return to the *Connected Routing Groups* tab.

10. The *Delivery Restrictions* tab is identical to the same tab in the RGC (refer to Fig-ure 13.4). By default, messages from all users are accepted by the SMTP Connector. However, you can also restrict which users can send messages by this connector. Use the *Accept Messages From* pane to declare all users that specifically will be accepted; use the *Reject Messages From* pane to declare all users that specifically will be rejected. Any declaration in one of these panes will override the default configuration, whatever it may be.
11. When all configuration settings are complete, click *OK* to complete this operation. Note that the SMTP Connector will not give you an opportunity to create a corresponding SMTP Connector in the other routing group, like the RGC did; it must be set up manually.

Managing the SMTP Connector

If you need to modify any settings of an existing SMTP Connector, open its properties and modify whatever is needed. Everything, including its name, can be modified. You don't need to restart the SMTP services to activate the new settings—just wait for the replication of AD to complete.

To view the queues of the SMTP Connector, expand the *Protocols* folder of the server running this connector, expand the SMTP folder and the virtual SMTP server, right-click the *Queues* folder, and select *Refresh* to see any messages waiting in the queue.

When to Use the SMTP Connector

This connector will probably be used mainly for SMTP traffic to the Internet, although it can also be used as a routing group connector. Actually, to send messages to the Internet, you don't even need the SMTP Connector, since Exchange itself is based on SMTP; all servers can send any SMTP message, using their virtual SMTP servers. So why do we need the SMTP Connector? The answer is this: to get control over the outgoing SMTP traffic. For example, let's say you have an Exchange organization with two routing groups and five Exchange 2000 servers. You probably don't want all these servers to send messages to the Internet; it's more likely that you want one or two servers connecting to the Internet. Another important reason is that you can configure the SMTP traffic in much greater detail, compared to the virtual SMTP server.

Use an SMTP Connector in these situations:

- To centralize outgoing SMTP messages to a particular server.
- When you need to use **ETRN** or **TURN** commands to pick up messages on a remote SMTP server (the ISP scenario).

- When TLS encrypted SMTP sessions are required.
- When outgoing messages must pass a smart host.
- When more control over the SMTP traffic is needed than the RGC can offer.
- To connect two routing groups belonging to the same organization, and you have at least 16Kbps of free bandwidth.
- To connect an Exchange 2000 routing group to an Exchange 5.5 site that has an Internet Mail Service Connector installed.

What You Must Know Before Setting Up the SMTP Connector

When you have decided to set up the SMTP connector, you must be able to answer a few questions before you start:

- What will the name of this SMTP Connector be (up to 64 8-bit characters)?
- Will this server use a DNS to look up receiving servers, or should all messages be passed on to a smart host?
- What local bridgehead servers should be used?
- Should messages be picked up by **ETRN** or **TURN** commands?
- Will this connector be used for Internet traffic? If so, what address space should be defined?
- Will this connector be used as a routing group connector?
- What cost value should this connector have (between 1 and 100)?
- Are any special configuration settings needed?

The X.400 Connector

The last type of routing group connector is the X.400 Connector; it is almost identical to the X.400 Connector in Exchange 5.x. It's unlikely that you'd find this connector in a pure Exchange 2000 environment, since the Routing Group Connector will almost always be a better choice for connecting routing groups. Still, in some situations, the X.400 Connector will be the best choice—for example, if we want to connect a routing group with an Exchange 5.5 site that uses an X.400 Connector, or if we need to communicate with an external X.400-based mail system like All-In-One from Compaq (formerly Digital Corporation).

There is a special situation where the X.400 Connector will be a better choice than the Routing Group Connector or the SMTP Connector; if the available bandwidth between two routing groups is less than 16Kbps, and the average message size is large, then the X.400 Connector offers the best performance. What makes the X.400 Connector slower than SMTP connections is the higher overhead the X.400 protocol requires; the actual transfer of messages is very fast. However, studies comparing the X.400 Connector with the SMTP

Connector sending normal-sized messages over fast network connections show that an SMTP Connector in some situations can be up to 300 percent faster than the X.400 Connector.

This connector is full of configuration options, just like its predecessor in Exchange 5.x; this will probably again lead to administrators avoiding this connector, if possible. However, you don't have to configure all its settings; for example, all the OSI parameters that most Exchange administrators find hard to understand are not even used when the X.400 Connector is used between two routing groups. But if these OSI parameters are used in your environment, make sure to set these values exactly, otherwise the X.400 traffic will fail.

The X.400 Connector in Exchange 2000 is designed to use the bridgehead technique, just like its predecessor in Exchange 5.x, meaning that two servers, one in each routing group (or site), are exchanging messages over an X.400 connection. If either of these two servers goes down, this connection will fail. For that reason, it's common to configure two X.400 Connectors between the same pair of routing groups, or to design multiple routes between the routing groups, to achieve fault tolerance.

Step 1: Create a Transport Stack

Before an X.400 Connector can be set up, a transport stack must first be created. The X.400 Connector is protocol independent, meaning that it can create X.400 messages, but it will not transfer them; instead, a transport stack handles this. In previous Exchange releases, you had three transport stacks to choose from: TCP/IP, X.25, and TP4. Then you had the Dynamic RAS Connector, which was an X.400 Connector for dial-up connections. In Exchange 2000, only two transport stacks are available: TCP/IP and X.25.

Only one transport stack per server is needed; it can serve any number of X.400 Connectors. If you need a dial-up link to the remote server, use the Routing Remote Access Server (RRAS) feature of Windows 2000, which will do a dial-up connection on demand.

To create a TCP/IP-based transport stack, follow these steps:

1. Start the *ESM* tool, and navigate to the Exchange server that will be the local bridgehead server for the X.400 Connector later on. Expand its *Protocols* folder.

2. Right-click on the X.400 folder and select *New|TCP/IP X.400 Service Transport Stack*.

3. Go to the *General* tab (see Figure 13.16). This new TCP/IP stack will get a default name of type *TCP (server)*; if you don't have any special reason to change it, stick to this name.

   The OSI address information can normally be left as is, unless this transport stack will be used to connect to an X.400 system that demands special OSI settings. If you need to define any of these OSI parameters, make sure to set the right type first, *Hexadecimal* or *Text*, otherwise they will not be valid. Ask the administrator of the other system what parameters to use. If possible, just leave them blank; it is still possible to set up X.400 connections to external X.400 systems, as long as all involved servers have agreed to use blank values.

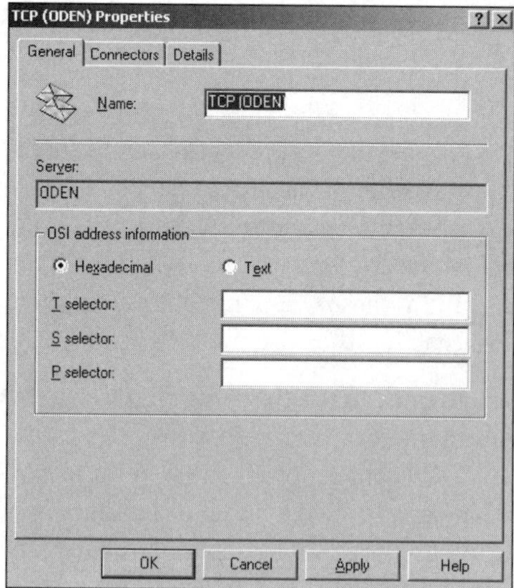

Figure 13.16
The General tab for the transport stack.

4. The *Connectors* tab is initially empty; later it will display all X.400 Connectors that use this transport stack. You will not modify this tab directly.
5. The *Details* tab shows when this object was created, and last modified. You may also add administrative notes here.
6. Click *OK* to complete the creation of this transport stack.

The newly created transport stack will be listed in the X.400 folder, under the *Protocols* folder for the server. As you can see, creating a transport stack is extremely easy; nothing needs to be configured, not even its name. Now you are ready to set up the X.400 Connector.

Step 2: Create an X.400 Connector

This step cannot be completed unless you have created the transport stack first; you must also make sure the transport stack is created on the Exchange server that this X.400 Connector will use as a local bridgehead server. When this is done, then follow these steps to create an X.400 Connector, in this example using a TCP/IP transport stack:

1. Start the *ESM* tool and navigate to the *Member* folder in the routing group where this new X.400 Connector will be created.
2. Right-click the *Member* folder, and select *New|TCP X.400 Connector*. It's important that you select the correct version of X.400 Connector; it must match the type of the transport stack previously created.
3. Go to the *General* tab (see Figure 13.17). Start by giving this connector an intuitive name that will clearly tell all administrators its purpose; as always, follow any name standard, if one is defined.

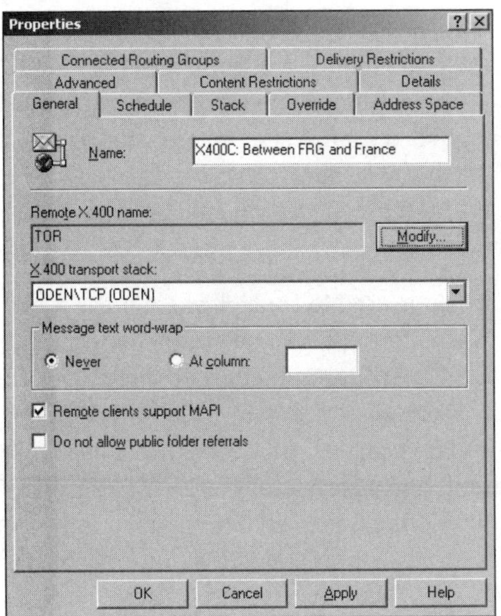

Figure 13.17
The General tab for the X.400 Connector.

Click the *Modify* button to define the remote X.400 bridgehead server this connector will communicate with (see Figure 13.18). If it's an Exchange 2000 or 5.x server, use its NetBIOS name; if it's an external X.400 mail server, ask the administrator of that system. The password you are asked for in Figure 13.18 is the remote X.400 system's MTA password; this is not a user account, but a special password for the X.400 connector that is used to verify that our X.400 Connector has the permission to send and receive messages with the remote X.400 server. However, it's normal to use blank passwords here, since it doesn't really create any higher security; it's just makes it harder to get the X.400 traffic to work.

The *X.400 Transport Stack* option is used to define what transport stack this X.400 connector will use. Make sure it's the correct stack, on the right server; otherwise this X.400 Connector will simply not work.

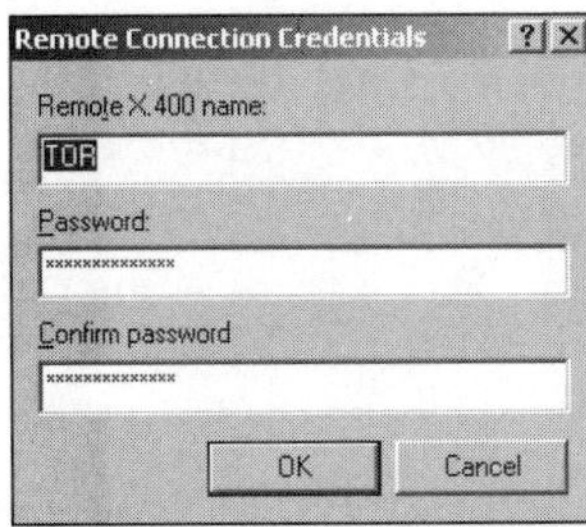

Figure 13.18
Defining the remote X.400 server along with its password.

The *Message Text Word-Wrap* pane is used to force word wrapping at a given column. This can be necessary if the receiving X.400 mail server cannot handle lines longer than a given number of characters. Today, this is seldom a problem, especially when the remote X.400 server is an Exchange server (any version); but when connecting to older X.400 systems that follow the 1984 X.400 standard, it may be necessary to use this setting. Typically, the older X.400 system will demand a line wrap at column 75 or 78; by default there is no word wrapping.

The *Remote Clients Support MAPI* option is used to control whether the X.400 messages should accept messages with MAPI's formatting system called *Rich Text Format (RTF)*—it includes, for example, bold, underline, and different character sizes. The formatting instructions are sent in a separate attachment called *WinMail.dat*. If the receiving clients don't understand this MAPI format, they will still see the WinMail.dat attachment, but when they try to open it, it will appear to be empty. This usually makes the users very frustrated. If this X.400 Connector is used for connecting to another Exchange server, we can safely assume that MAPI is supported; if it's not Exchange at the other end, you must check to see what client that system is using.

The X.400 Connector has, like the two other routing group connectors, a checkbox to disable public folder referrals; by default this feature is not set, meaning that referral is activated. See the design section later in this chapter to read more about this referral feature.

4. Use the *Schedule* tab (see Figure 13.19) to configure the connection schedule, or in other words, when this X.400 Connector will connect to the remote X.400 bridgehead server. Default is *Always*, meaning all messages will be delivered without any delay.

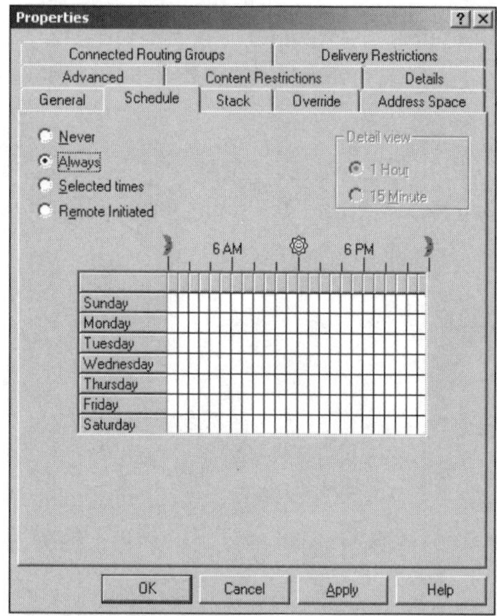

Figure 13.19
The Schedule tab for the X.400 Connector.

To set a specific schedule, set *Selected Times*, and use the time grid below. You can set this time grid to display 15-minute or one-hour resolution. Note that if you define one hour, the X.400 Connector will connect four times for each such one-hour period, one for each 15-minute period.

You can also set this schedule to *Never*, in effect disabling this X.400 Connector. This may be useful when you want to temporarily disable a connector without removing it completely.

The last choice, *Remote Initiated*, will prohibit this X.400 Connector from making contact with the remote bridgehead server; all messages passing over this connector will wait in queue until the remote server connects to this local server; then all messages are dequeued. This feature could be handy if you have an Exchange design with one central hub routing group, and several spoke routing groups with X.400 Connectors configured for remote initiated. All connections are now controlled by the X.400 Connectors in the hub.

5. The *Stack* tab (see Figure 13.20) is used to define the address to the remote X.400 server. You can type the server's IP address or its host name in FQDN format—for example, *oden.humandata.se*. By using the IP address instead of the host name, you will gain some performance, since the Exchange server doesn't have to look up the host name in the DNS server.

   If this X.400 Connector is using an X.25 connection instead of TCP/IP, this tab will display X.25 address parameters instead of IP numbers or host names.

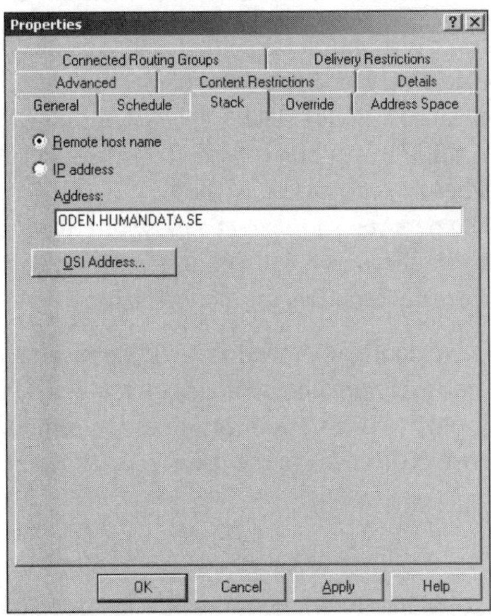

Figure 13.20
The Stack tab for the X.400 Connector.

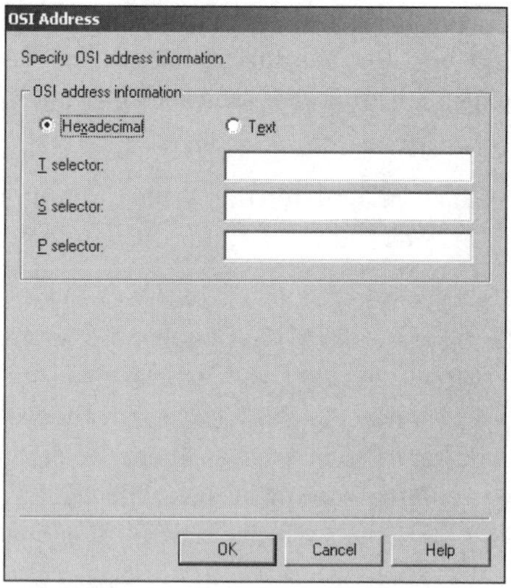

Figure 13.21
The OSI address parameters.

If the remote X.400 system requires that you define any OSI parameters, click the OSI Address button, and type in whatever you are required to enter (see Figure 13.21). Just make sure to select the correct data type, either *Hexadecimal* or *Text*, before you start defining any OSI parameters. The T selector, S selector, and P selector are also known as *TSAP*, *SSAP*, and *PSAP* in the OSI world. Note that this is the preferred way of configuring OSI parameters, instead of using the OSI tab in the transport stack.

6. Use the *Override* tab (see Figure 13.22) to give your local X.400 server a name other than the NetBIOS name. This may be necessary when the local name is longer than the remote X.400 system can handle; the typical limit for older X.400 systems is eight characters maximum, all 7-bit U.S. ASCII. If this option is used, then this name must be defined in the remote X.400 bridgehead server, instead of the local NetBIOS name. Click *Modify* to change the name. From here you can also set a password that the remote X.400 server needs to know before the local X.400 Connector will accept any connections; see also Figure 13.23. Normally you leave this option blank.

   The *Connection Retry Values* are used to configure how this X.400 Connector will do when retrying to send a message. The *Maximum Open Retries* (default: 144) defines how many times this connector will retry to open a connection to the remote server before sending an Non-Delivery Report (NDR) back to the user.

   The *Maximum Transfer Retries* (default: 2) defines how many times the connector will try to send a message over an open connection before generating an NDR.

   The *Transfer Interval* (default: 120 sec.) defines how long a message should wait before retrying to send a message over an open connection.

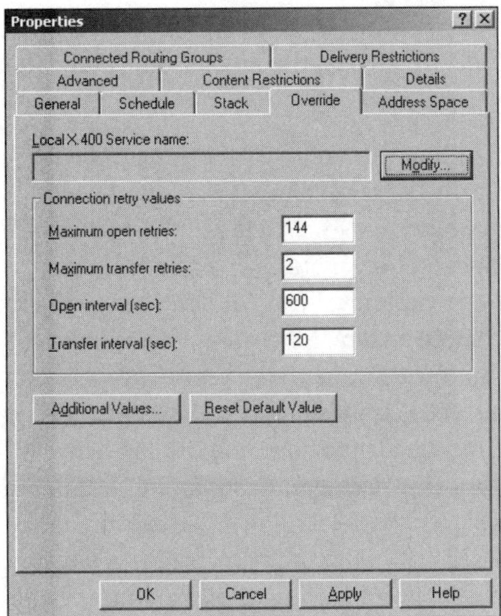

Figure 13.22
The Override tab.

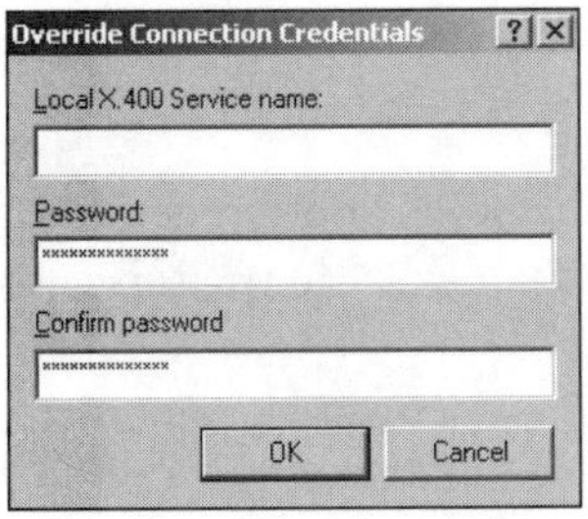

Figure 13.23
The Override Connection Credentials dialog box.

The *Open Interval* (default: 600 sec.) defines how long the connector will wait before trying to reopen a connection that previously ended in error.

All these retry values will control how long a message will wait in queue before retrying a connection; however, if there is an alternative route to the destination, the routing engine will always immediately reroute the messages over that route instead of waiting for this connector to get connected.

Note that if this connector is the only route to the destination, and it fails one time, it will wait 10 minutes (the default *Open Interval setting*) before retrying to connect. This means that if you have an easily solved network problem—for example, the network cable is loose—and you quickly fix this problem, all messages will still have to wait up to 10 minutes before a reconnection will be attempted. Since life is too short to wait for long reconnection timeouts like this, force a reconnection by restarting the *MS Exchange Message Transfer Agent* service; the X.400 Connector will then immediately retry all connections.

If you like to configure values like this, there are more where those came from; click the *Additional Values* option and you will have nine other *Reliable Transfer Service* (*RTS*) values—see Figure 13.24. They determine message reliability parameters, like the *Checkpoint* to include in data and the amount of unacknowledged data that can be sent. You can also configure association values that determine the number and duration of connections to the remote system; for example, an established X.400 session will by default be open for 5 minutes (300 seconds) before it gets disconnected. This will save the connector from constantly establishing new X.400 sessions whenever there's a message to send. Transfer timeouts define how long the connector will wait before sending an NDR for different priority messages; this is an interesting feature. It basically says that an urgent message will have less time to be delivered than a non-urgent message. The time is also related to the size of the message—a large message will have more time than a small message. If you mess up these parameters, click *Reset Default Values* to restore the standard settings.

7. The *Address Space* tab is identical to the same tab in the SMTP Connector; refer to Figure 13.12. This is one of the two tabs used to define what destinations can be reached with this X.400 Connector. The other tab is the *Connected Routing Groups* tab that is described in Step 8.

   Use the *Address Space* tab when the X.400 Connector is used for external connection, outside the Exchange organization—for example, if you want to use this connector

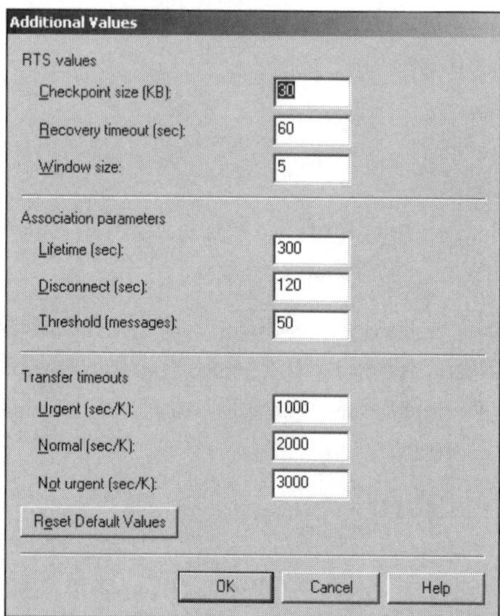

Figure 13.24
The Additional Values on the Override dialog box.

for transferring messages to another Exchange organization. When defining X.400 address space, you will normally use the X.400 name standard, also known as the *Originator/Recipient* (*O/R*). Click the *Add* button and select to create an X.400 address space; you will then see the O/R tab (see Figure 13.25). In the example shown in this figure, you will see that some, but not all, values are defined; the O/R address standard works like this in Exchange 2000 (including all previous versions):

- *Organization (o)*—Add the name of the remote routing group or 5.5 site.
- *Private management domain name (p)*—Also known as the PRMD; add the name of the remote Exchange organization.
- *Administrative management domain name (a)*—Also known as the ADMD; add one space character here! This field is not allowed to be empty, but since we don't want to use it, it's common practice to use a space character instead.
- *Country/Region (c)*—Add the country code here, or select from the pull-down menu.

The tricky part here is to understand that the O/R field *Organization* is used to define the remote routing group, and the *Private Management Domain Name* is used to define the Exchange organization.

If this X.400 Connector will be used to connect two routing groups in the same organization, you would leave this tab blank; instead, you define the address space from the *Connected Routing Groups* tab.

8. Use the *Connector Scope* to define how far this X.400 Connector and its address space will be visible in the Exchange organization. The default is the *Entire Organization*,

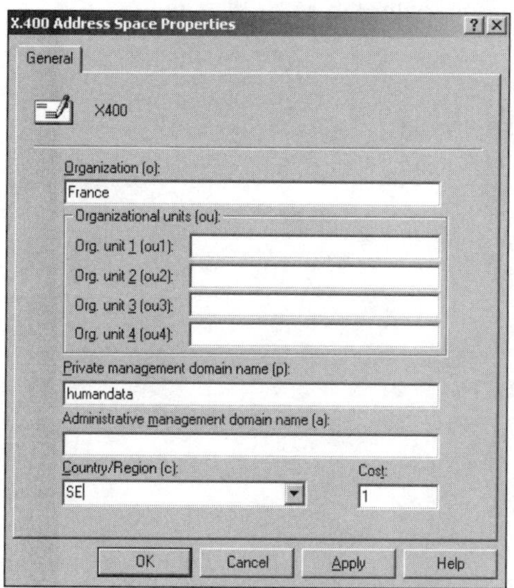

Figure 13.25
The O/R Address Space dialog box.

making all Exchange servers aware of this connector, regardless of what routing group they belong to. Remember, if an Exchange server is aware of a connector, it can also route messages through it. Sometimes it can become necessary to restrict the knowledge about this SMTP Connector. If this is the case, then set the connector scope to *This Routing Group*; this will only make Exchange servers in this routing group aware of this connector.

9. The *Connected Routing Groups* tab is identical to the same tab in the *SMTP Connector* (refer to Figure 13.13). This is the other tab that is used to define address spaces, or destinations, for this X.400 Connector. This tab should be used instead of the *Address Space* tab when this connector is connecting two routing groups belonging to the same organization. In Figure 13.13, you see an example where one routing group is added, the *First Routing Group*; or, in other words, this X.400 Connector will connect this routing group (France) with the *First Routing Group*. In this situation, you would normally leave the *Address Space* tab empty, since this tab is all that is needed for routing messages between these two routing groups.

   To add a routing group, click the *Add* button, then select what routing group this X.400 Connector will connect to using the pull-down menu on the *General* tab (refer to Figure 13.14). This menu lists all known routing groups in the organization, including an option to connect to a server in an Exchange 5.5 site that has a corresponding X.400 Connector installed. Note that you cannot change the organization name; the reason for this is that all routing groups must belong to the same organization. On the *Routing Address* tab, you can set the X.400 O/R address space for the other routing group, including its cost value (see Figure 13.26); make sure you don't forget to add a space character for the *Administrative Management Domain* field. When done, click *OK* to return to the *Connected Routing Groups* tab.

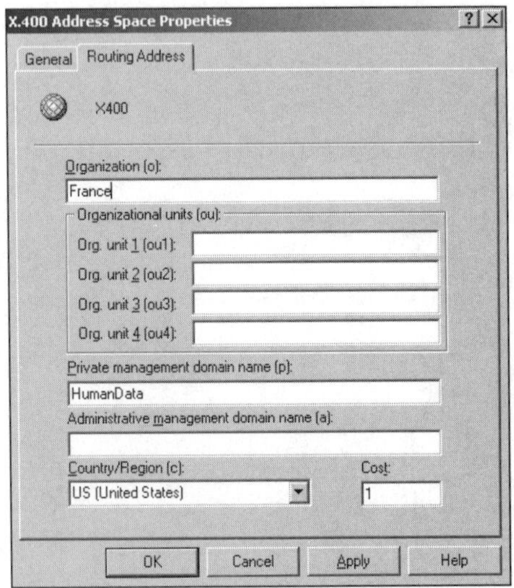

Figure 13.26
The X.400 Routing Address tab.

10. The *Delivery Restrictions* tab is identical to the same tab in the *SMTP Connector* and the *Routing Group Connector*; refer to Figure 13.4. By default, messages from all users are accepted by the *X.400 Connector*. However, you can also restrict which users can send messages by this connector. Use the *Accept Messages From* pane to declare all users that specifically will be accepted; use the *Reject Messages From* pane to declare all users that specifically will be rejected. Any declaration in one of these panes will override the default configuration, whatever it may be.

11. The *Content Restriction* tab is identical to the same tab in the RGC and the *SMTP Connector* (refer to Figure 13.5); use it to control what messages will be accepted by this X.400 Connector. The default is all types of messages, regardless of priority, type, or size.

    Use the *Allowed Priorities* pane to set any combination of *High*, *Normal*, or *Low* priority messages that are accepted by this connector; for example, clear the High checkbox to prohibit messages with high priority from being transferred with this connector.

    Use the *Allowed Types* pane to set any combination of *System Messages* or *Non-System Messages* that will be accepted by this connector. System messages are all messages coming from Exchange services, like replication messages, delivery reports and Monitoring Tools messages, or Windows 2000 messages, whereas Non-System Messages are messages between users, groups, and contacts.

    Use the *Allowed Sizes* pane to set the maximum size for outgoing messages that this connector will accept for delivery. Note that this setting will not affect incoming messages!

12. Use the *Advanced* tab (see Figure 13.27) to configure the format of the message, what X.400 standard to be used, and any global domain identifier.

    The *Allow BP-15* checkbox is used for controlling whether this connector will send messages in *Body Part 15* format, causing attachments to be displayed in the message exactly the way the sender formatted them. If this switch is cleared, all binary attachments will be renamed to names like *Bdypart01.p14* instead of the original names. Older X.400 systems usually cannot handle BP-15, but all Exchange versions can.

    The *Allow Exchange Contents* checkbox is used to control whether messages including attachments should be converted to standard *X.400 P2/P22* messages or transferred in the internal Exchange format MDBEF. If this X.400 Connector is used between Exchange servers, this checkbox should always be set; otherwise it should be cleared.

    The *Two-Way Alternate* checkbox is used to control whether the message transfer can be two-way or not; older X.400 standards only supported one-way, meaning that only the server that opened the X.400 session was allowed to send messages, even if other messages were waiting to be transferred the other way. If this connector is used between Exchange servers or to another X.400 system that is compliant to the 1988 X.400 standard, this checkbox should be set.

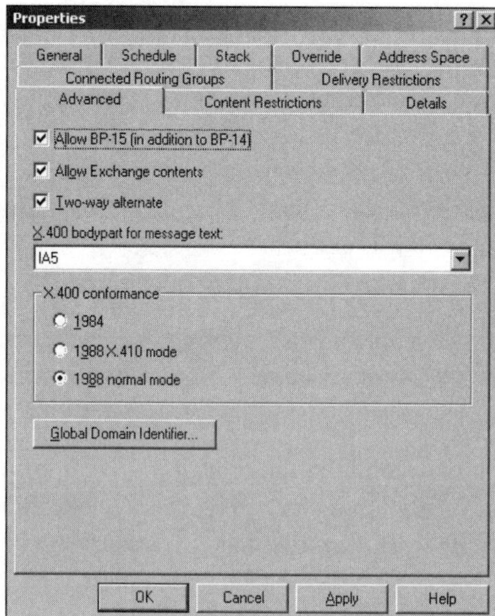

Figure 13.27
The Advanced tab for the X.400 Connector.

The *X.400 Bodypart For Message Text* pull-down menu is used to define the character set for the message body. This will be important if you use this X.400 Connector for connecting to older X.400 systems; ask the administrators of that system what character set to use. Between Exchange servers (all versions), this parameter should always be set to *IA5*, even if you find your local country table in the pull-down menu; for example, Sweden has the *IA5 (Sweden)*, but will still use the *IA5* here.

The X.*400 Conformance* pane is used to define what X.400 standard this connector should use; default is *1988 normal* mode. Use the *1988 X.410* mode when connecting to an *HP Open Mail* system, or the 1984 standard when connecting to older X.400 systems.

The *Global Domain Identifier* button will display a new window; see Figure 13.28. These parameters are used when this Exchange server will receive X.400 messages for its local use and for another in-house X.400 system. For example, assume you have a company that migrates from *Digital's All-in-one* system to Exchange 2000; for a while, both of these systems will coexist. All incoming external X.400 messages can be received by Exchange 2000; the X.400 Connector can be configured to reroute those messages destined for the legacy X.400 system, if it has some parameters that can make Exchange differ between its own X.400 messages. It must be one of these O/R parameters: PRMD, ADMD, or Country. Consult with the administrator for the legacy X.400 system to configure this tab correctly.

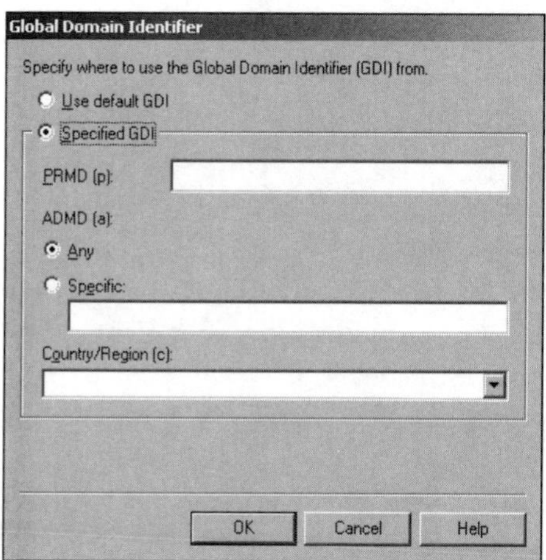

Figure 13.28
The Global Domain Identifier dialog box.

13. The *Details* tab is the same tab as for the other two routing group connectors. Use it to see when this connector was created and when it was last modified. You can also add administrative notes on this tab.
14. When all tabs are correctly configured, click *OK* to complete the creation of this connector. Don't forget to create the corresponding connector on the remote X.400 bridgehead server.

Managing the Routing Group Connector

Whenever needed, you can modify any settings of an existing X.400 Connector; simply open the properties for the connector (stored in the *Connectors* folder, under the routing group). If you want to force Exchange to read the new settings immediately, be sure to restart the *MS Exchange Message Transfer Agent* service; otherwise just wait until Exchange discovers the new settings automatically.

To view the queues of the *X.400 Connector*, expand the *Protocols* folder of the server running this connector. Then expand the X.400 folder, right-click the *Queues* folder, and select *Refresh* to see any messages waiting in the queue. You should see the name of your X.400 Connector as a separate queue (see Figure 13.29).

When to Use the X.400 Connector

The most common use for this connector will be as a connection to Exchange 5.5 sites that have X.400 Connectors, and also as a connector to external X.400-based systems. As demonstrated in the configuration settings earlier, this connector can also be used as a routing group connector; although it's safe to believe that this will apply only in very special situations, for example at extremely low available bandwidth, such as 9.6Kbps. True, the X.400 protocol is very resilient and handles unreliable network conditions very well, in some situations even better than the SMTP protocol.

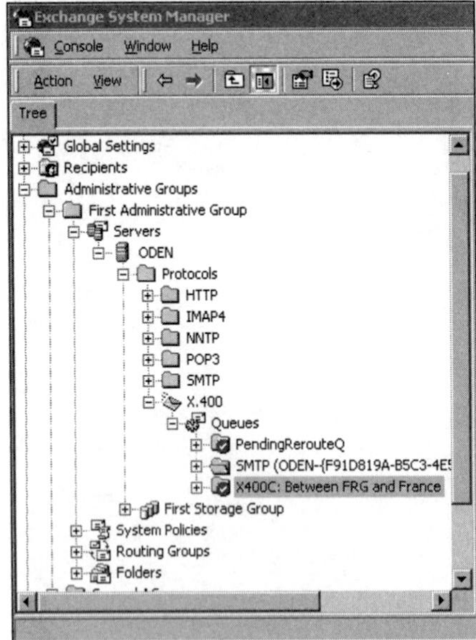

Figure 13.29
Viewing the queues of the X.400 Connector.

When it comes to the number of configuration options, this connector wins over the others. The fact that you can control session parameters and retry settings in detail makes it possible to adjust this connector to most network conditions. Remember that you don't have to set all configurations to use it; most settings can be left as is, and you will still have a highly functional *X.400 Connector*. Just remember that when using this connector between routing groups in the same Exchange organization, make sure to use the *Connected Routing Groups* tab instead of the *Address Space* tab.

Use an X.400 Connector in these situations:

- When more control over the message traffic is needed than any other connector can offer.
- To connect two routing groups belonging to the same organization, and you have less than 16Kbps of free bandwidth.
- To connect an Exchange 2000 routing group to an Exchange 5.5 site that has an X.400 Connector installed.
- To connect an Exchange 2000 organization to an external X.400 system.

What You Must Know Before Setting Up the X.400 Connector

When you have decided to set up the X.400 connector, you must be able to answer a few questions before you start:

- What will the name of this connector be (up to 64 8-bit characters, but stick to 7-bit ASCII characters if possible)?

- What type of transport stack will be used?
- What local bridgehead servers should be used?
- Will this connector be used for external X.400 traffic? If so, what address space should be defined?
- Will this connector be used as a routing group connector?
- What connection schedule should be configured?
- What cost value should this connector have (between 1 and 100)?
- Are any special configuration settings needed? For example, if the remote server is an older X.400 system, you must change several parameters on the Advanced tab.

Design Goals for Routing Group Connectors

In Chapter 7, we discussed design topics in general; here we will look specifically at how to design connections between routing groups and also connections to external systems. The golden rule is still to keep the number of routing groups down to a minimum. If you can make do with one, please do so! This will make the Exchange organization much simpler, lessen message traffic, and result in the best performance for your system. Of course, this may not be possible for large or distributed companies; in those cases, we must divide the Exchange organization into several routing groups.

In the following sections, we will look at how these three routing group connectors work in different scenarios. We will use an Exchange organization with four routing groups, as an example (see Figure 13.30); they have 128Kbps WAN connections between three of them, and one is a dial-up ISDN connection. This organization also has a connection to the Internet. Our goal is to create a resilient and fault-tolerant routing structure, while keeping the structure simple and easy to manage.

Let's start by examining what the most common connector can do for our organization.

Routing with the Routing Group Connector

This is the most commonly used connector in Exchange 2000—it's fast and easy to set up, it uses the SMTP protocol for message transfer, and it's restricted to use between routing groups belonging to the same organization. This connector has a special feature that none of the others has; any server in the routing group can use this connection, unless you have configured it to use a particular server (there may be more than one). As you can see from Figure 13.30, our routing groups contains between one and four servers each.

What will happen if we try to stick with the RGC for this organization, configuring this connector to allow all local servers to send messages (using the *General* tab) to all remote servers in the other routing groups (using the *Remote Bridgehead* tab)? See Figure 13.31. The result will be that only the routing groups Sweden, the U.S., and Norway are connected; the RGC cannot be used for dial-up connections, making Iceland unconnected to the other routing groups. This is clearly not an acceptable situation.

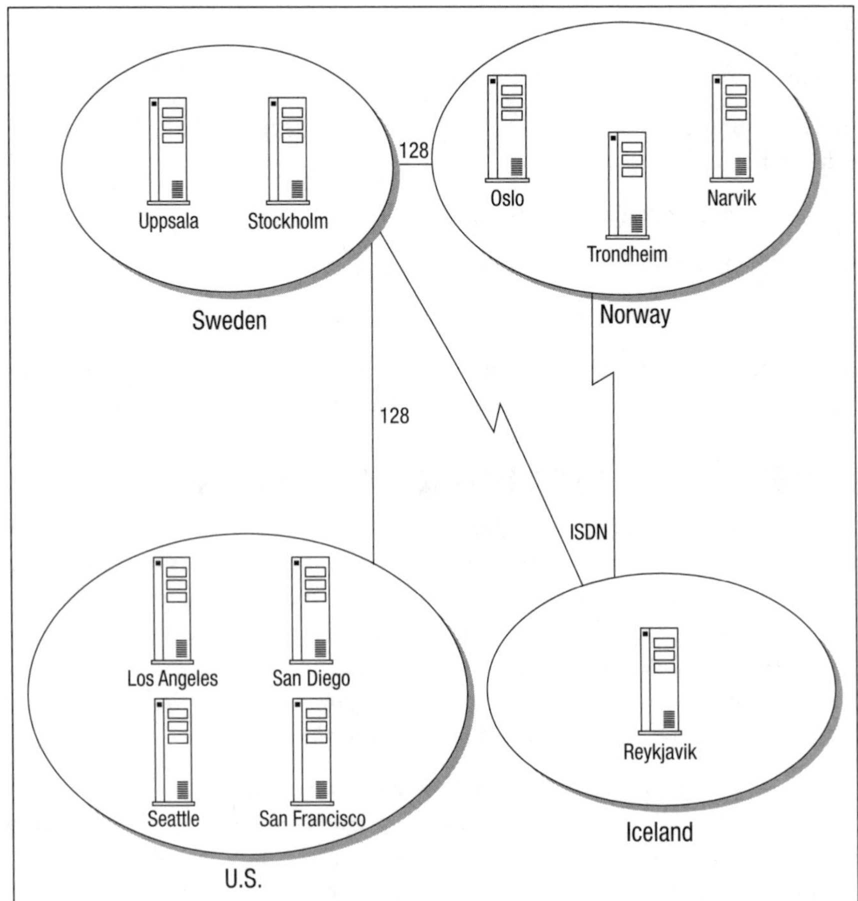

Figure 13.30
Our example organization.

However, since our RGC is configured to let all local servers in one routing group communicate with all servers in the remote routing group, we have at least accomplished some fault tolerance and load balancing between the U.S. and Sweden, and between Sweden and Norway. If one of these servers goes down, it will not affect any of the other servers. But if the WAN connection goes down—for example, between Sweden and Norway—it will make Norway unreachable for all the other routing groups. This problem arises due to the fact that we only have one WAN connection between these three routing groups; it could be solved by creating a new WAN connection between the U.S. and Norway, but for now, let's assume we don't have the money for this.

Pros and Cons of the RGC

The following are some of the pros and cons of using the RGC:

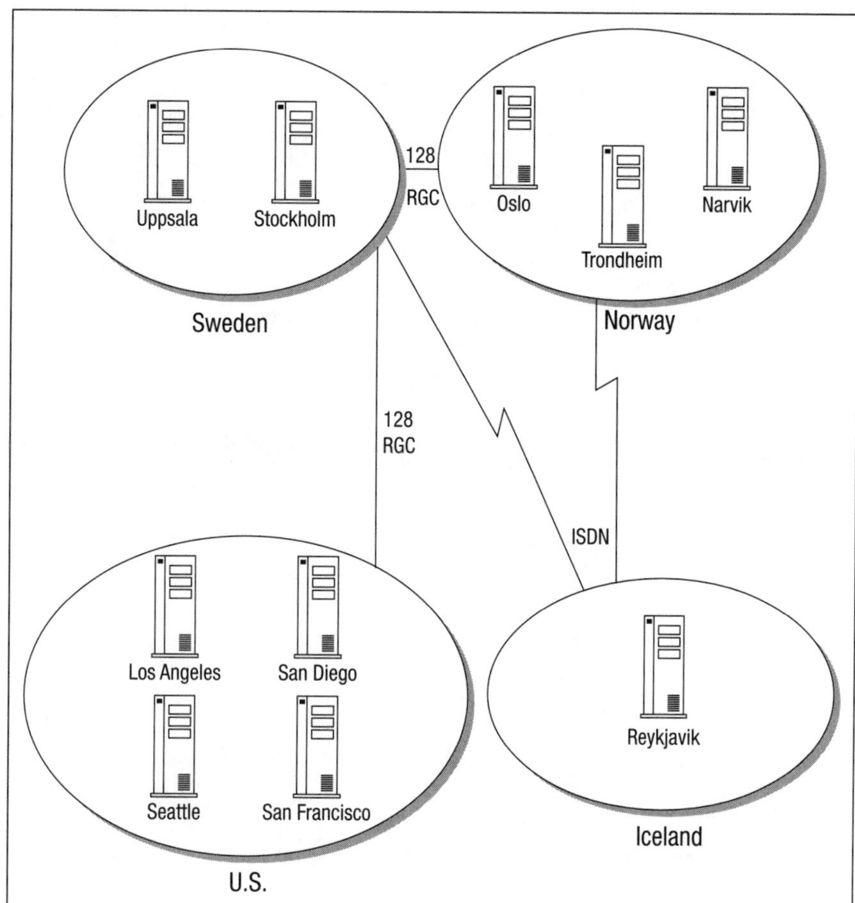

Figure 13.31
Using only RGC in our organization.

- *Pro*—Between each routing group we have fault tolerance and load balancing.
- *Pro*—This is the fastest connection available in Exchange 2000.
- *Con*—The Iceland routing group is isolated, since the RGC can't handle dial-up connections.
- *Con*—No backup routes exist between the U.S. and Norway.

Routing with the SMTP Connector

This connector also uses the SMTP protocol for message transfer; it's slower than the RGC, due to the fact that it has to convert binary information to standard 7-bit MIME format, but it can handle dial-up connections, by using the Windows 2000 Routing and Remote Access Service (RRAS).

If we replace all RGC connectors in our example with SMTP Connectors, we will in fact be able to connect all four routing groups in our organization, an important improvement

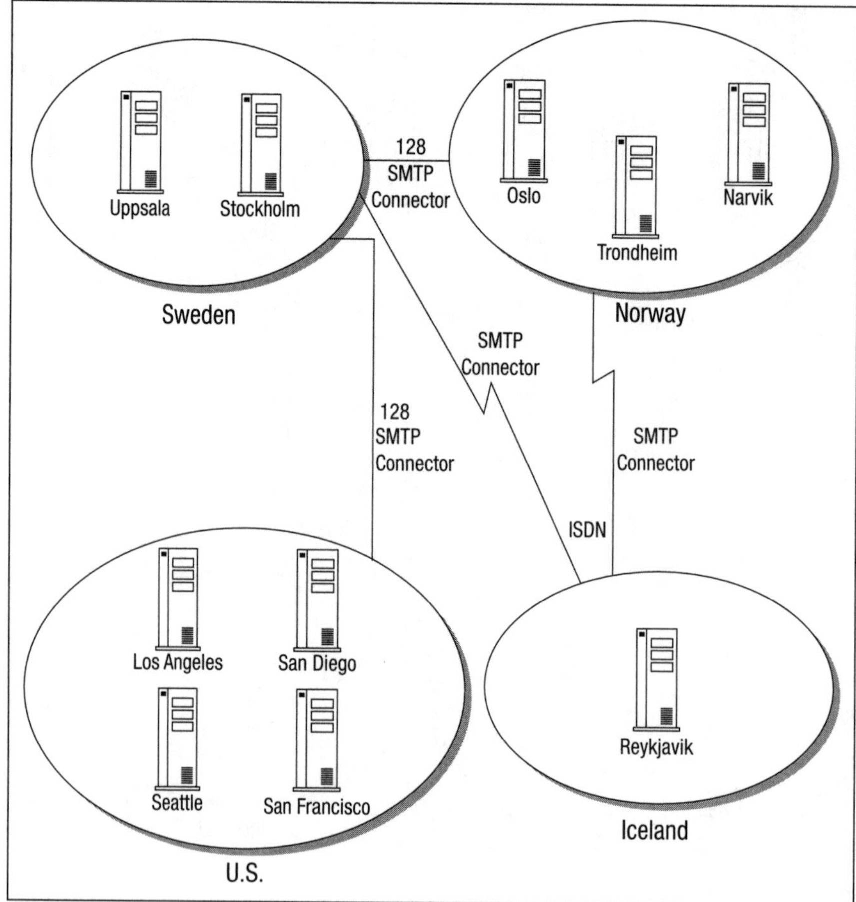

Figure 13.32
Using only SMTP Connectors in our organization.

compared to the previous design; see Figure 13.32. With this new design, the Swedish routing group will have a connection to three other routing groups, whereas Norway and Iceland have two connections and the U.S. has only one; now we must decide if we want multiple SMTP Connectors in Sweden, Norway, and Iceland, or only one. If we configure each connector to use the DNS for looking up the remote bridgehead servers, we can manage with one single SMTP Connector per routing group; however, if we configure the connector to send all messages to a smart host (the *General* tab), we must configure one SMTP Connector for each destination.

However, we have lost speed, since the SMTP Connector is slower than the RGC connector; we have also lost some of the fault tolerance, since we now work with the bridgehead technique. For example, if one of the bridgehead servers for the connector between Sweden and the U.S. goes down, all connectivity to and from the U.S. are lost. But if one of the bridgehead servers for the connector between Sweden and Norway goes down, messages can take the alternate route over Iceland.

Pros and Cons of the SMTP Connector

The following are some of the pros and cons of using the SMTP Connector:

- *Pro*—All routing groups have a working connection.
- *Pro*—Backup routes exist between Iceland, Sweden, and Norway.
- *Con*—No backup route exists to the U.S.
- *Con*—Message transfer over the WAN links is slower compared to the RGC.
- *Con*—No load balancing exists between the routing groups.
- *Con*—This configuration is a bit more complex than with RGC.

Routing with the X.400 Connector

Let's try to solve this example with X.400 Connectors only. That would be very similar to the SMTP Connector case, since the X.400 Connector is also working with bridgehead servers, and it can also use a dial-up connection, using the RRAS service in Windows 2000.

With only X.400 Connectors, we could create connections to all routing groups, including the ISDN links to Iceland (see Figure 13.33). This connector is faster than the SMTP Connector, but it will work only with specified bridgehead servers; there is no way to create more local bridgehead servers than the SMTP Connector allows, so this will make this solution a bit less fault tolerant.

Since the X.400 Connector must connect to a specific server, we have to create one such connector for each connected routing group. This means that the U.S. will have one X.400 Connector, Iceland and Norway two, and Sweden three connectors. Since this type of connector has lots of configuration options regarding communication parameters, it could be used to optimize the message traffic over the ISDN link, if necessary, making it more resilient and effective.

Pros and Cons of the X.400 Connector

The following are some of the pros and cons of using the X.400 Connector:

- *Pro*—All routing groups have a working connection.
- *Pro*—Backup routes exist between Iceland, Sweden, and Norway.
- *Pro*—It's possible to optimize the message traffic over the ISDN links.
- *Con*—There is no backup route to the U.S.
- *Con*—Message transfer over the WAN links is slower as compared to the RGC.
- *Con*—No load balancing exists between the routing groups.
- *Con*—There is no fault tolerance built into this connector.
- *Con*—This configuration is a bit more complex than with RGC.

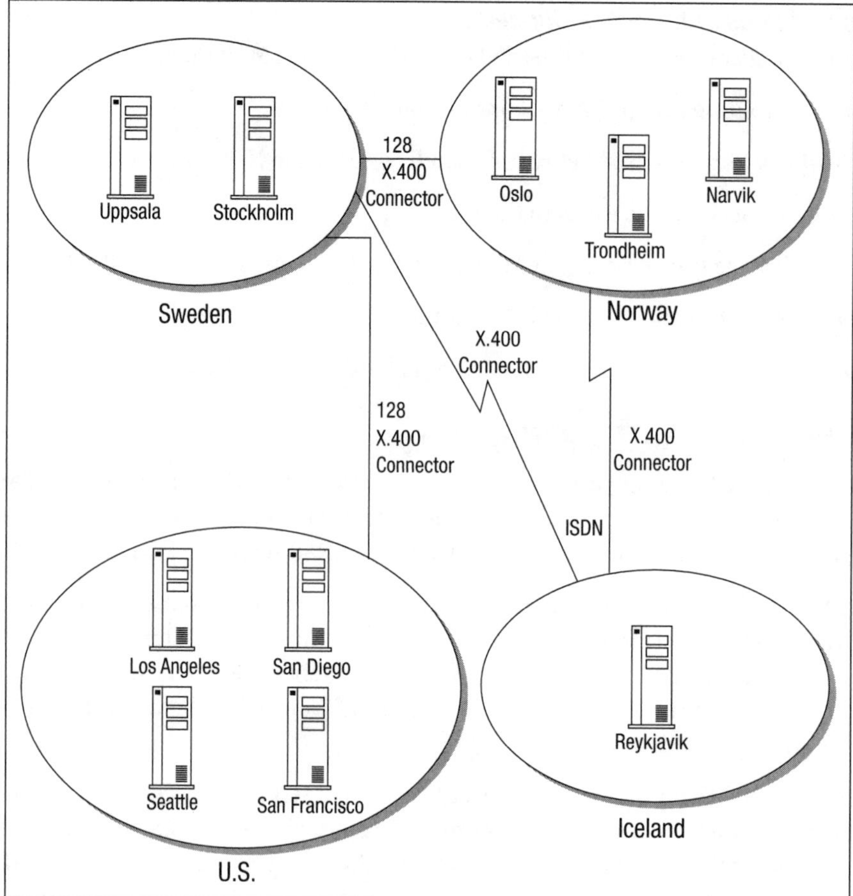

Figure 13.33
Using only X.400 Connectors in our organization.

The Conclusion

Since none of these three routing group connectors could solve all the problems or needs for this example organization, we should look for a fourth design solution that uses a combination of the different connectors. We must divide this design problem into two parts: the first concerning the WAN connections, the other concerning the ISDN connection.

The WAN Connection

If this connection were a bit faster than 128Kbps, say 512Kbps or higher, there would be no question that the *Routing Group Connector* would be the best choice. However, we have to analyze this a bit more first. Look at the routing groups Sweden and the U.S.—they have two and four servers, respectively. If we assume there is a lot of traffic between these routing groups, this network link could easily get saturated. For example, if we have an RGC between these two routing groups, configured so that all servers can send messages to all remote servers, and in both directions, then 128Kbps will be too little. We could still use an RGC if we configure it to communicate between one bridgehead server in each routing group. The consequence would be that the average delivery time will increase; you would have to monitor this traffic to see when it gets too slow. The solution to this problem is of course to increase the network speed—at least double it, or make it 512Kbps, if possible.

Another solution would be to use the slower X.400 Connector, since it uses the bridgehead server technique only, and has several configuration options regarding network traffic. If we look at these different solutions, I would choose the RGC with a bridgehead configuration, i.e., using one particular server in each routing group.

The ISDN Connection

This link is special—both because it's a relatively slow dial-up connection that needs about one second for establishing a network session, and because you pay for each connected minute. We must take these features into consideration when selecting what routing group connector to use.

The network speed for an ISDN link is 64Kbps per channel; usually you can use two channels simultaneously, giving you 128Kbps total. But the time to establish a network session over an ISDN link should also be considered; it's usually around one and two seconds. Since you pay for this link for each connected minute, the ISDN modem is usually configured to disconnect after a few minutes of inactivity. If we assume that we have one message every five minutes, we will end up with an ISDN link that goes up and down constantly; this will be both expensive (the ISDN links usually aren't cheap), and much slower than a corresponding 128Kbps WAN connection.

The RGC is out, since it requires a permanent connection; this leaves us with the SMTP Connector and the X.400 Connector. Either of these two would do the job, assuming we use a pure bridgehead configuration. Both of them can configure a connection schedule, for example, making one ISDN connection every hour. The X.400 Connector has one advantage over the SMTP Connector; it can be optimized regarding the network session, like its settings for checkpoint size and how long a session should be kept open. Personally, I would select the X.400 Connector, but the SMTP Connector would probably do fine too; Figure 13.34 depicts the new design.

If You Have the Money

We still have one unsolved problem—there are no backup routes to the U.S. routing group. This can only be solved in one way: set up an extra link, for example between U.S.A. and Norway. If possible, this should be a WAN connection of at least 256Kbps, but even an ISDN link would give us a backup route, thereby making the complete organization much more fault tolerant. For example, such an extra route to the U.S. can be used by Sweden, if its primary connector to Norway should go down; it will also reduce the number of hops from U.S.A. to Iceland to two; see Figure 13.35.

A common mistake when designing organizations like this is when the administrator configures a backup route without checking the physical wide area network. For example, assume that there are no WAN connections between the U.S. and Norway. You can still

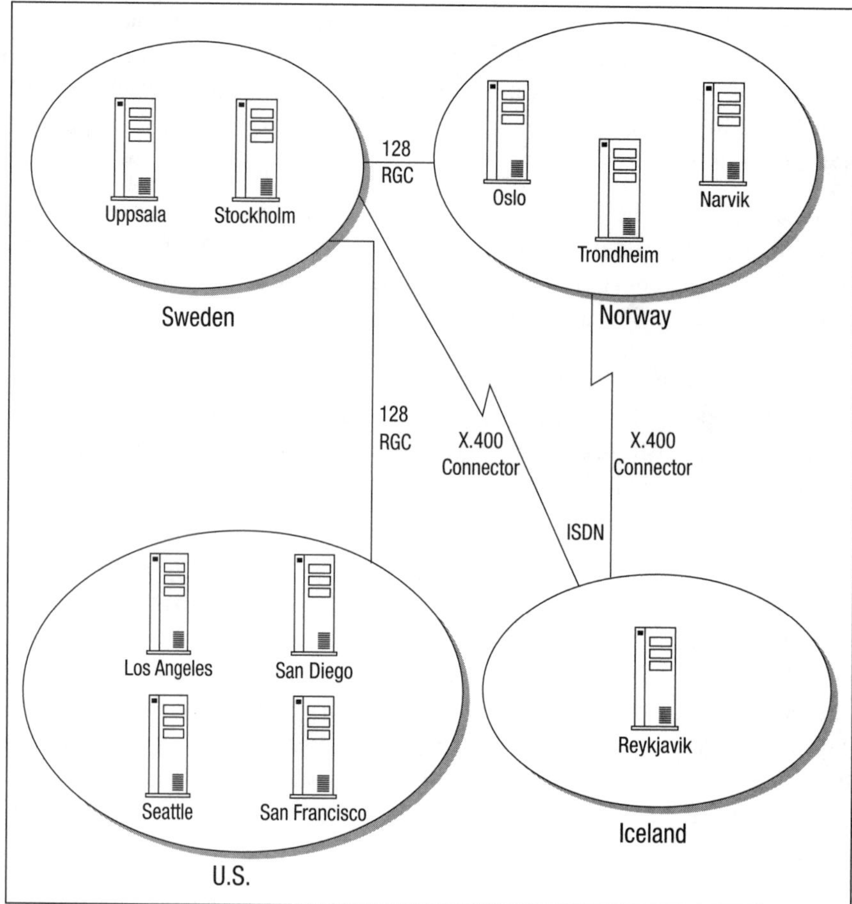

Figure 13.34
The suggested design for this example organization.

create a connector between those two routing groups—however, this will give you a false sense of security, because the U.S. routing group will have two connectors actually using the same physical network connection. If this physical link goes down, both of these connectors go down. It is easier to make this mistake than you might think at first, since in reality it's often very hard to get a complete and updated network map; make sure to ask the telecom company or whichever company who owns the physical network for such a map.

What Connector Should I Select?

This question is impossible to answer without detailed information about the underlying physical network structure, the number of routing groups and servers in this organization, and how much traffic there will be between these servers. As you have seen, there are a lot of options and possibilities for all three connectors, but here are some guidelines to help you make your selections (see also Decision Tree 13.1):

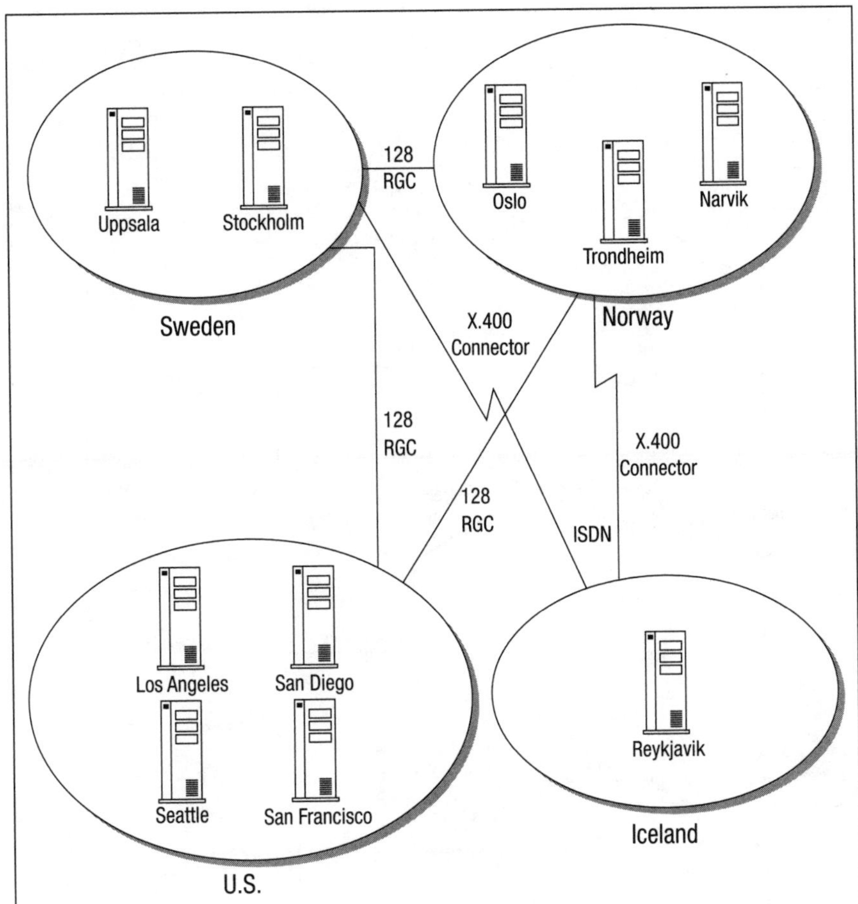

Figure 13.35
The final design suggestion.

- *For dial-up connections*—You should select the SMTP Connector or the X.400 Connector, depending on the need to have multiple local bridgehead servers for load balancing and fault tolerance.
- *For WAN connections faster than 256Kbps*—You should select the Routing Group Connector, unless you have a special need to schedule the connections.
- *For WAN connections slower than 16Kbps*—You should select the X.400 Connector.
- *For WAN connections between 16Kbps and 256Kbps*—You can choose any of the three connectors. Make your selection based on the need for control, scheduled connections, and whether multiple local bridgehead servers are needed; if you don't have any special configuration needs, select the RGC. You can always create another connector later, if this was the wrong choice.

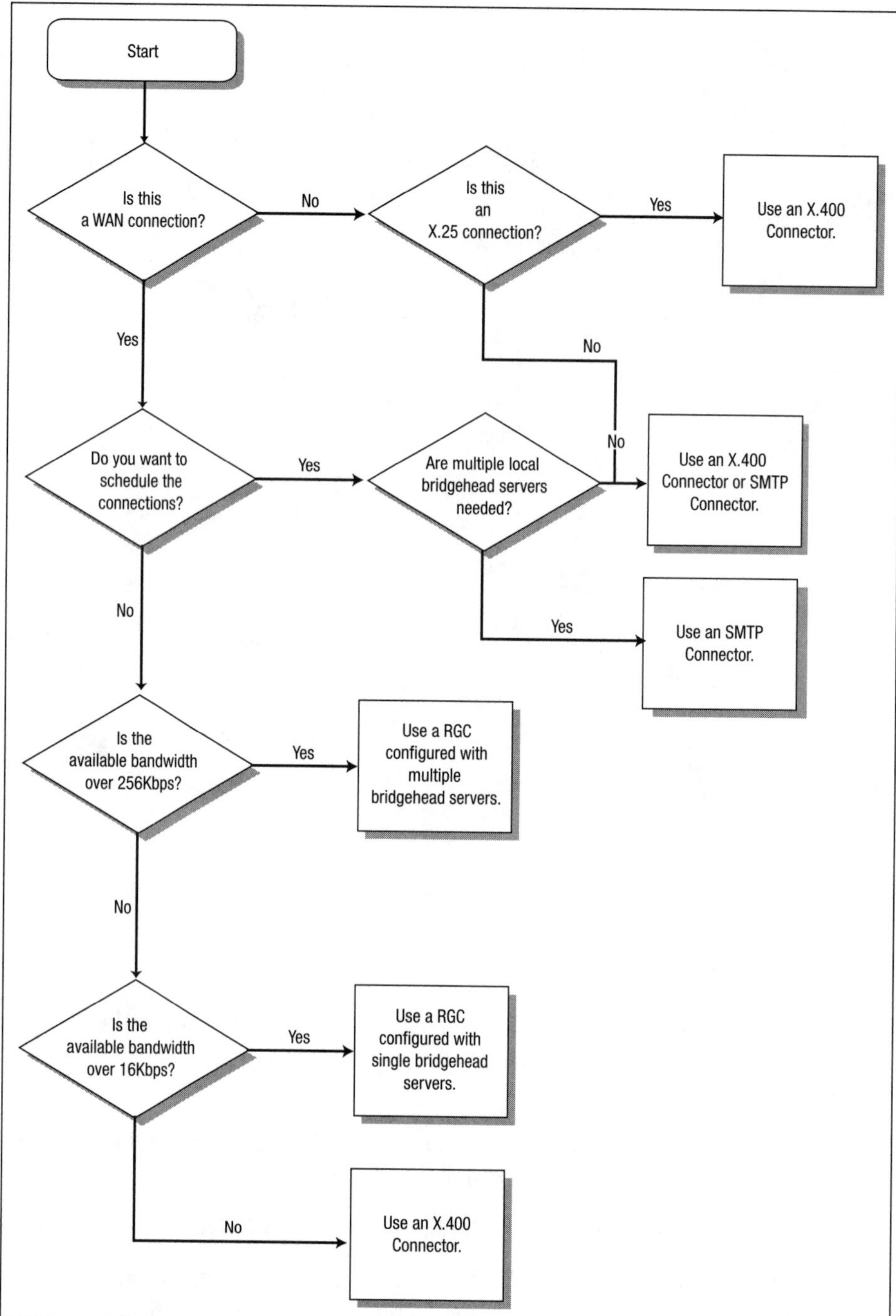

Decision Tree 13.1
Selecting a routing group connector.

Public Folder Referrals

A routing group connector also controls how clients can access public folders not available in their local routing group. Regarding public folder access, a routing group behaves very similar to the Exchange 5.x site, meaning that a client will always have access to all public folders in their home RG, regardless of what Exchange server it is stored on.

However, when the client can't find a local copy of this public folder, it will start looking in other routing groups. In previous Exchange versions, you could define an *Affinity* that directed Outlook users to other sites; each affinity also had a cost value associated with it that prioritized what sites the clients should contact first. Exchange 2000 doesn't have affinity values; instead, each routing group connector can be a referral to other routing groups. By default, all routing groups have this referring activated, meaning that a client can connect to the remote routing group this connector points to. It's important to understand that the connector itself will not transfer any messages for the client; it only works as a reference. The client will then connect to the remote server, using RPC and MAPI.

Example 1: One Single Copy of the Public Folder

The referral is also transitive, meaning that if you have one connector between the U.S. and Sweden, and one between Sweden and Norway (using the previous examples), then any client in U.S.A. will be referred to Norway, if this is the only place this particular public folder exists; see Figure 13.36. In this example, an Outlook client connected to the server *San Francisco* is looking for a particular public folder, and the following will happen:

1. The client tries to open the public folder *Sales*.
2. The Exchange server sends an LDAP query to the Active Directory, asking for all copies of this particular public folder; it finds out that there aren't any local copies of the *Sales* folder in this routing group. However, there is a copy on the remote server Trondheim, in the routing group Norway. Since both the RGC and the X.400 Connector have allowed *Public Folder Referral*, the Exchange server will now pass the name of this server back to the client.
3. The client will now open an RPC/MAPI session to the server Trondheim and access the public folder *Sales*.

If one of these routing group connectors had disabled their public folder referral, the client would not be able to contact the remote server.

Example 2: Two Copies of the Public Folder

The first example assumed that there was only one single copy of the public folder. If we instead assume that there are two copies of this public folder, one in Sweden and one in Norway, the following would happen (see Figure 13.37):

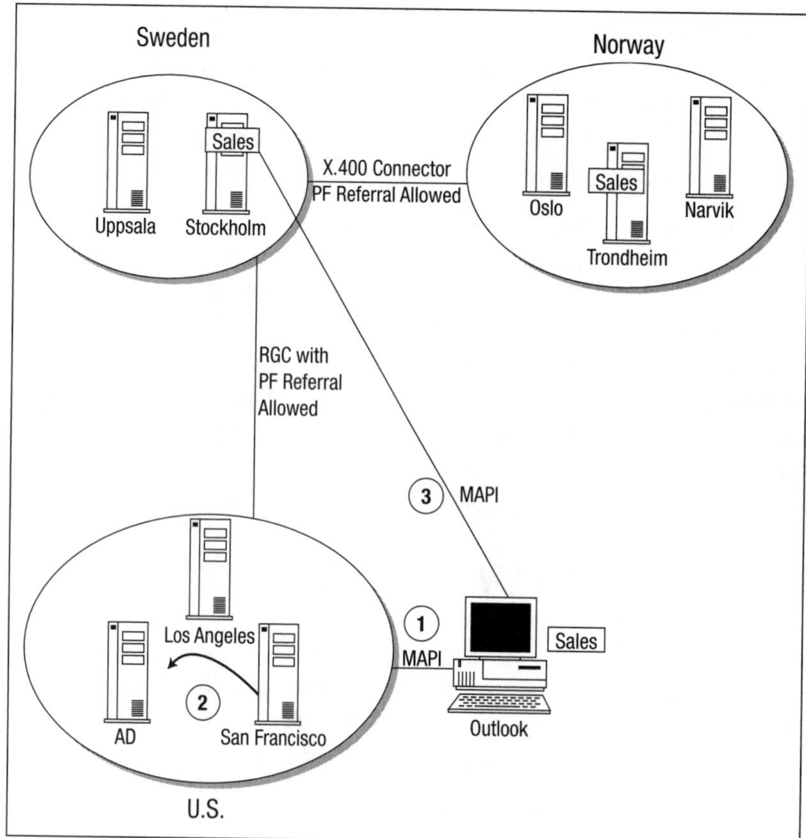

Figure 13.36
Transitive public folder referrals to a remote server.

1. The client tries to open the public folder *Sales*.
2. The Exchange server sends an LDAP query to the Active Directory, asking for all copies of this particular public folder; but again, there aren't any local copies of this folder in the U.S. routing group. However, there are two remote copies, one on the server Trondheim in the routing group Norway, and one on the server Stockholm in the routing group Sweden. Since both the RGC and the X.400 Connector have allowed *Public Folder Referral*, the Exchange server will now compare the total connector cost to each routing group; since the connector cost to Sweden is lowest (it must be, since it's only one hop away), the server will refer the client to the server Stockholm.
3. The client will now open an RPC/MAPI session to the server Stockholm and access the public folder *Sales*. If the client for any reason can't get in contact with this server, it will ask San Francisco for another referral, and get the server Trondheim in return.

As you can see, the cost value for each connector is also used to prioritize what public folder server the clients are referred to; this is something you must not forget when setting cost values for connectors.

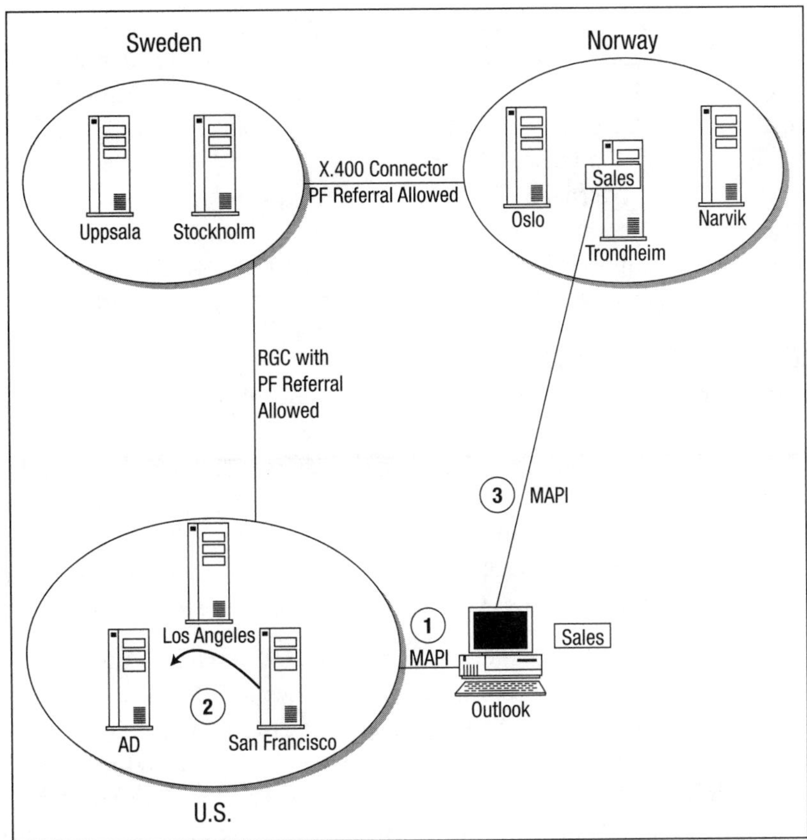

Figure 13.37
Public folder referrals when two copies of the folder exist.

Note: *In previous Exchange releases, all referrals (then called Affinity) were default disabled; you had to manually create them if you wanted to refer local clients to other sites. In Exchange 2000, all referrals are default enabled and transitive, enabling clients to look for public folders on any Exchange server in the organization, as long as the network connections allow this.*

Designing a Route Outside the Exchange 2000 Organization

So far, we have only discussed how to create and configure connectors between routing groups belonging to the same organization. We must also look at how to create connections outside this organization; the primary example is a connection to the Internet. Since Exchange 2000 is built to run on Windows 2000, which has the SMTP functionality built-in, you don't have to do anything special to enable Exchange 2000 to send SMTP messages to the Internet or any other SMTP destination; the virtual SMTP servers in IIS 5 take care of that. We have looked at this virtual server in Chapter 3 and how to configure it, so in this section, we will discuss how to create a good connection to the Internet with the SMTP Connector.

As described earlier in this chapter, the SMTP Connector can be used both between routing groups and for external SMTP traffic. The real benefit you get from using this connector, instead of simply using the virtual SMTP server, is control! Before installing the SMTP Connector, all Exchange servers with the proper network connections will be able to send any SMTP messages to the Internet. However, when this SMTP Connector is installed, it takes control over this external SMTP traffic; any settings configured in this connector have priority over any conflicting settings in the virtual SMTP server. For example, assume the virtual server is configured not to use a smart host for outgoing messages, but the SMTP Connector is; then all outgoing SMTP messages will go to that smart host.

Internet Connections for Centralized Organizations

When the Exchange organization is centralized, meaning all servers belong to the same routing group, you need to think about fault tolerance when designing the Internet connection. You basically have two options for doing this: one SMTP Connector with multiple local bridgehead servers or multiple SMTP Connectors. In previous Exchange releases, one Internet Mail Service Connector could only be used by one server, and each server could have a maximum of one single IMS connector; to achieve fault tolerance, you needed to set up at least two Exchange 5.x servers with one IMS connector each.

The SMTP Connector for Exchange 2000 is much smarter; if you install this on one server in the routing group, you can still configure it to have two or more local bridgehead servers. All of these servers are independent of each other, or in other words, if one of the local bridgehead servers goes down, the other servers will still be able to use the SMTP Connector. This is due to the fact that the configuration of an SMTP Connector is stored in the Active Directory, which makes this information available to all Exchange servers in this routing group.

So my recommendation to this type of organization is to create one SMTP Connector, but configure it with at least two local bridgehead servers; see Figure 13.38. This will give the organization both fault tolerance and load balancing.

Internet Connections for Distributed Organizations

For organizations with multiple routing groups, it may be beneficial to use a local SMTP Connector in each routing group. The most common reason to create multiple routing groups is the lack of high-speed connections between the Exchange servers. For example, say you have one office in Thailand and one in Germany; the network line between them is too slow to create one single routing group. If you want to control all traffic going in and out to the Internet, you must create one SMTP Connector, let's say in Germany, which both routing groups will share. But this also means that all incoming and outgoing Internet messages to the office in Thailand must pass this slow link, making it even slower, since this link will now transfer both messages between the routing groups and Internet messages. Depending on the network speed for this link, and the company policy regarding Internet traffic, it may or may not be acceptable.

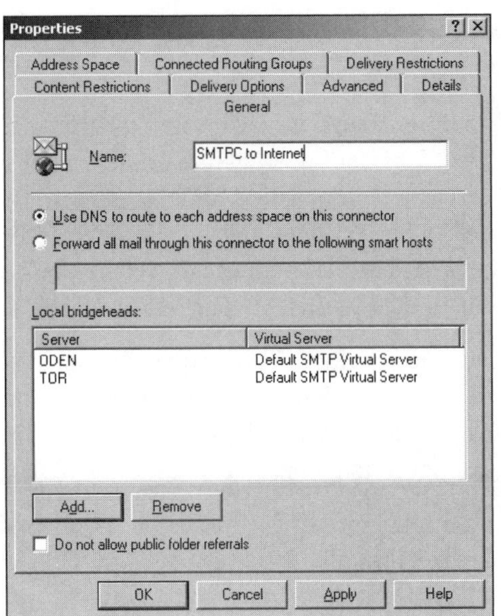

Figure 13.38
Configuring multiple local bridgehead servers for the SMTP Connector.

If we instead configure one SMTP Connector in each routing group, they will work independently of each other. Remember, an SMTP Connector controls outbound messages only. The benefit of this design is:

- *Fault tolerance*—Each routing group will have an independent Internet connection.
- *Load balancing*—Each routing group takes care of its own Internet traffic.
- *Faster delivery*—Most messages will probably be to individuals in the local region, i.e., the Thailand office will most likely communicate with other individuals in Thailand. To first pass this message over to Germany, then over the Internet back to Thailand, takes extra time, and is less resilient, since it involves a more complex route.
- *Less network traffic*—There will be less traffic on the link between the routing groups.

The only serious drawback will be that you lose control over the organization's complete Internet traffic; maybe all outgoing messages should pass a virus-scanner first, or all outgoing messages should have a disclaimer attached, or you want to have one log file for all Internet traffic; the reasons may be several for not letting each routing group have their own SMTP Connector to the Internet. This is really a question of company policy.

Multiple Inbound SMTP Servers

Remember that these multiple bridgehead servers will affect only outgoing SMTP messages, not incoming. The configuration of the external DNS is what controls how many incoming SMTP servers there will be, and who they will be. Make sure to configure the external DNS (not the internal!) to have at least two MX records for your mail domain (assuming you also have at least two Exchange 2000 servers).

One thing that may confuse Exchange 5.x administrators is how incoming SMTP mes-sages are handled. As stated above, an SMTP Connector is for outgoing messages; so what should we configure to make an Exchange 2000 server accept incoming SMTP messages? The answer is this: Nothing! It doesn't even need an SMTP Connector installed. Remember that Exchange 2000 is an SMTP-based system now; the medieval times of X.400 now belong in the dark history of Exchange, only to be told to our children on long winter nights.

Chapter 6 discussed DNS in great detail, but we conclude this discussion by looking at an example of how a DNS could be configured to have two Exchange servers for inbound SMTP messages; in this example, our domain is humandata.se and the two servers are Oden and Tor. Let's look at what the external DNS configuration looks like (see Figure 13.39).

In this figure, you can see two Mail Exchanger (MX) records for the DNS zone humandata.se, pointing to Oden and Tor; notice that Oden has the value 10, whereas Tor has 20. From Chapter 6, you may remember these are called *preference values* and are used to prioritize what server an external SMTP system should contact first; lower preference values have higher priority than higher (spanning between 0 to 65535). Since Oden has the lowest preference value, it will be the primary server for incoming SMTP messages. However, if Oden fails to answer a connection request in a timely fashion (don't you just love that phrase?), the external server will try to contact Tor instead. If both MX records have the same preference value, the remote SMTP server would randomly select one of them, thereby load balancing the incoming SMTP traffic.

A common problem when configuring a connection to the Internet is that outgoing messages are fine, but the server will not receive any incoming messages. This means that the

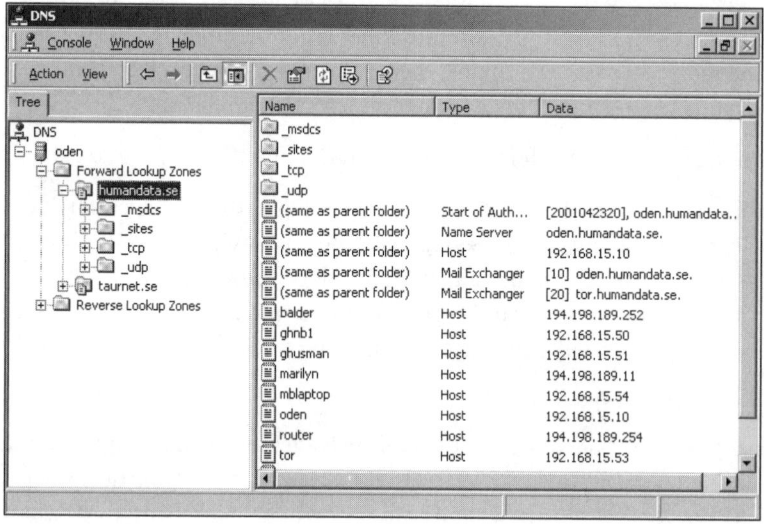

Figure 13.39
A DNS configuration with two MX records.

SMTP Connector is okay, but the DNS is not. Remember that it's the external DNS that counts here, not the internal. The external DNS works like a billboard, telling all external systems on the Internet what services we have and what type of connection we accept. The easiest way of testing this is to use the NSLookup.exe program; it was described in detail in Chapter 6, so here we'll just give you a quick reminder on how to look up MX records on a DNS server:

```
C:\>nslookup
Default Server:  oden.humandata.se
Address:  192.168.15.10

> set type=mx
> humandata.se
Server:  oden.humandata.se
Address:  192.168.15.10

humandata.se     MX preference = 20, mail exchanger = tor.humandata.se
humandata.se     MX preference = 10, mail exchanger = oden.humandata.se
tor.humandata.se          internet address = 192.168.15.53
oden.humandata.se         internet address = 192.168.15.10
> exit
```


In this code, you can see how NSLookup is asked to list all MX records for the domain **humandata.se**; it replies by listing the two servers Oden and Tor, including their preference values and IP numbers.

RRAS Dial-Up Connections

For dial-up connections to the Internet, you must now configure the *Routing and Remote Access Service (RRAS)* in Windows 2000; Exchange 2000 does not have its own dial-up service, as did previous versions. The RRAS feature is a large topic, so here you will find only a short description on how to set up a dial-up connection with an analog modem or ISDN to the ISP for an Internet connection.

The RRAS will basically make the server behave like a network router between two links; one link goes to the internal network, through the *Network Interface Card (NIC)*, and the other link goes to the ISP and the Internet, through the modem. See Figure 13.40, where Stockholm is the RRAS server.

Before you can follow these instructions, you must have an agreement with an ISP. Then continue by installing the Windows 2000 optional component RRAS on the Windows 2000 server that will be used for dial-up connections:

1. Install the ISDN (or analog) modem on the server; make sure it has contact to the phone line system.
2. Log on as the administrator on the server; click *Start|Programs|Administrative Tools*, then select *Routing And Remote Access*. This will start the RRAS manager.

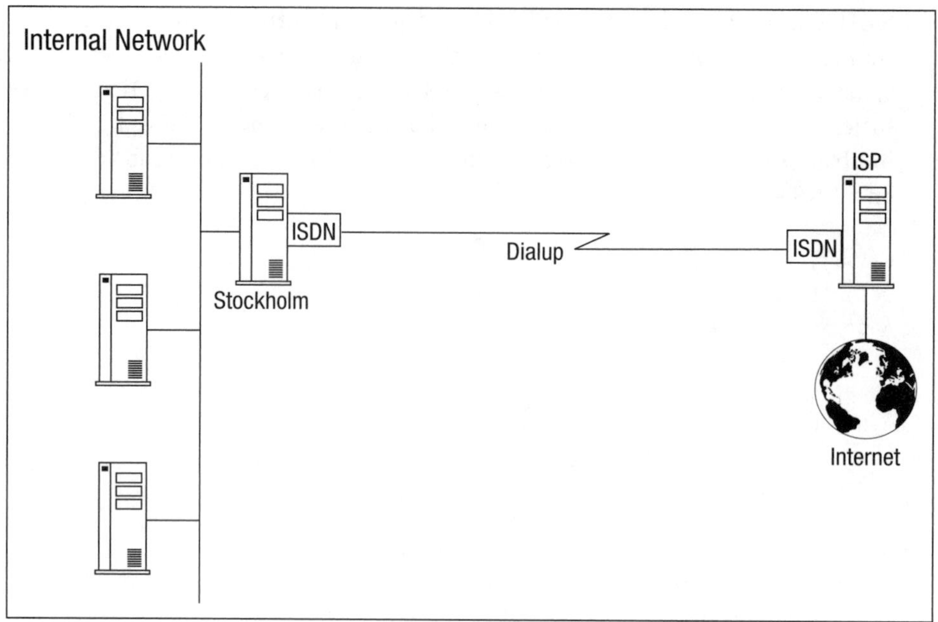

Figure 13.40
The RRAS server.

3. Right-click on the server and select *Configure Routing And Remote Access Service*; this will start the *RRAS Setup Wizard*. Click *Next* to continue.
4. Select *Set Up Router With The Network Address Translation (NAT) Routing Protocol*; this will make the RRAS translate all internal IP addresses to an external (and official) IP address, thereby increasing the security of the network. Then click *Next*.
5. From the *Internet Connection* tab, select *Create A New Demand-Dial Internet Connection*, and click *Next*. This will start the *Demand Dial Interface Wizard*.
6. Give the new *Demand Dial Interface* object a descriptive name, then click *Next*.
7. Next, you will see a list of devices; select your modem (analog or ISDN), and click *Next*.
8. Enter the phone number to the ISP, and click *Next*.
9. Accept the defaults for desired protocols and security (=*Route IP Packets On This Interface*) and click *Next*.
10. Type in the logon name and password you have received from the ISP; if the remote system isn't a Windows system, leave the domain field empty and click *Next*.
11. Click *Finish* to complete the *Demand Dial Interface Wizard*.

That concludes the creation of the RRAS dial-up interface. Next, we have to configure the TCP/IP parameters for the modem object; this can be done from the RRAS manager, or by opening the properties for My Network Places. Here we assume that the ISP has given us a static IP address for our dial-up connection; we must now configure our modem to use this IP address:

12. Open the properties for the dial-up network object; select the *Network* property tab.
13. Open the TCP/IP properties, select *Use The Following IP Address*, and type the *static* IP address you have received from the ISP.

Now the dial-up network interface is ready to go. If the SMTP Connector sends all messages to a smart host on the ISP, all you need to do now is type the static IP address to that smart host (don't forget the square brackets [] around the IP address); otherwise make sure that the server running the SMTP Connector has configured its TCP/IP settings to use a DNS that can search the Internet—for example, it could be a DNS at the ISP.

However, the RRAS will solve only half the problem, namely outgoing SMTP messages. Incoming SMTP messages will most likely have to be queued at the ISP, since your system is connected only occasionally. And to dequeue these mails, you must configure the *SMTP Connector* to use **ETRN** or **TURN**, depending on what the ISP can offer you. If you get a static IP number from the ISP, you will probably also use **ETRN** for dequeuing messages. Follow these instructions to configure the SMTP Connector for dequeuing the domain **Humandata.se** using **ETRN** every third hour:

1. Open the *ESM*, navigate to the *SMTP Connector*, and open its properties.
2. On the *Advanced* tab (see Figure 13.41), select *Request ETRN/TURN When Sending Messages*.

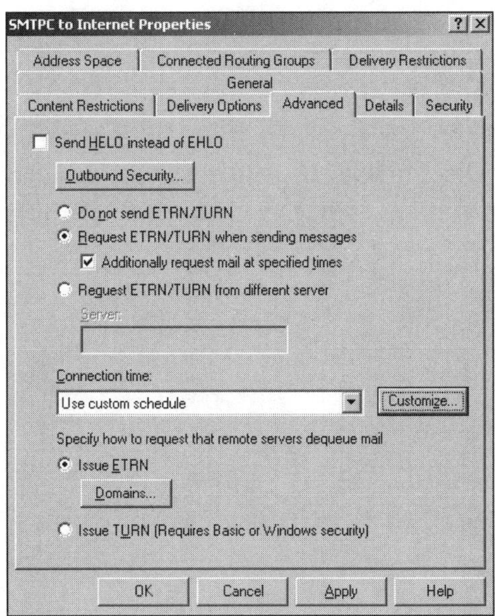

Figure 13.41
Configuring the SMTP server for **ETRN**.

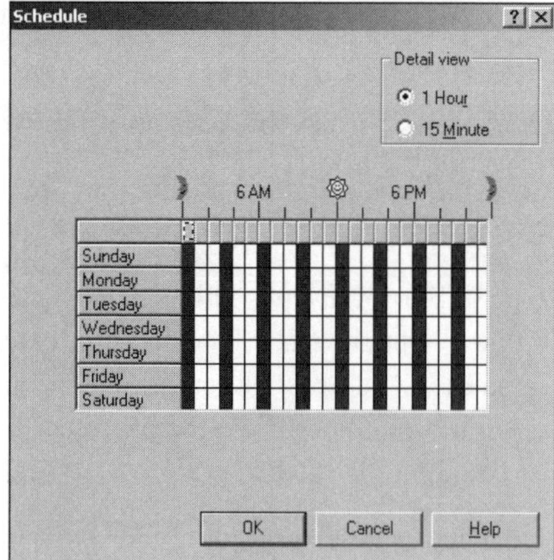

Figure 13.42
Selecting the time schedule for requesting mail.

3. Check *Additionally Request Mail At Specific Times*, and click the *Customize* button further down; select the time schedule for connecting to the ISP and sending the **ETRN** command. See Figure 13.42.
4. Click the *Domain* button, and then add the domain you want to dequeue (you can add more than one domain); see Figure 13.43. Then click *OK* to store these new settings.

Now your *SMTP Connector* should be able to send messages to the Internet and receive them; this concludes the dial-up description.

The Message Tracking Center

A chapter about message routing would not be complete without a description of the *Message Tracking Center (MTC)*, an excellent tool for tracking messages through the Exchange 2000 system. With this tool, you can see when a message has been submitted

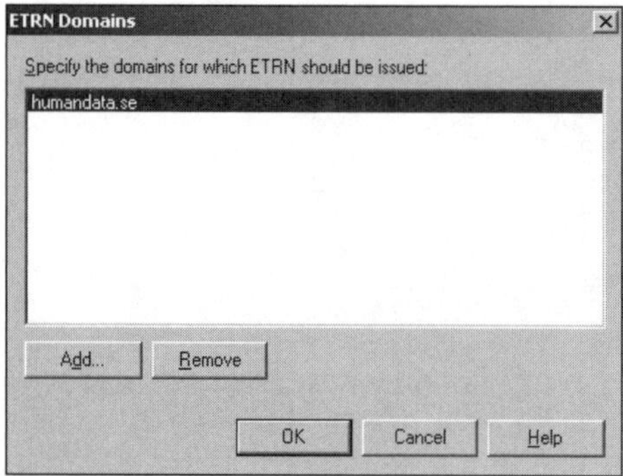

Figure 13.43
Selecting the mail domain to dequeue with **ETRN**.

(i.e., sent), what route and connectors it has passed, and when it was delivered to the destination. You can see the name of the sender and the recipient, along with the subject of the message. The MTC is an enhanced version of the *Message Tracking* system in previous Exchange releases; this new version is slightly easier to work with and it displays more information—for example, the message subject.

Enabling Message Tracking

In Exchange 5.x, you had to activate tracking on each respective object in the site that could route messages—for example, the *Message Transfer* object, the *Information Store* object, and the *Internet Mail Service* connector. In Exchange 2000, it's much easier; you can configure each individual server to enable or disable tracking logs (see Figure 13.44); by default, tracking is disabled, just like in Exchange 5.x.

When the tracking is enabled for a server, all its routing activities will be logged; this information will be stored up to 7 days by default (see Figure 13.44 again—*Remove Files Older Than*). If only the message tracking is enabled, your log files will be smaller, but you will not be able to view the subjects of the messages, something that can be extremely valuable when you are looking for a particular message. I suggest that you enable both tracking logs and subject logging, if you have the available disk space. Beware that Exchange servers connected to the Internet will also register all in and outgoing Internet messages; for a larger organization, this could be a lot of messages, so make sure you have enough space. If the number of messages routed is large, the tracking log will decrease the overall performance of the server; you may have to monitor those servers more carefully in the beginning when tracking is enabled, to make sure they will not have any problems.

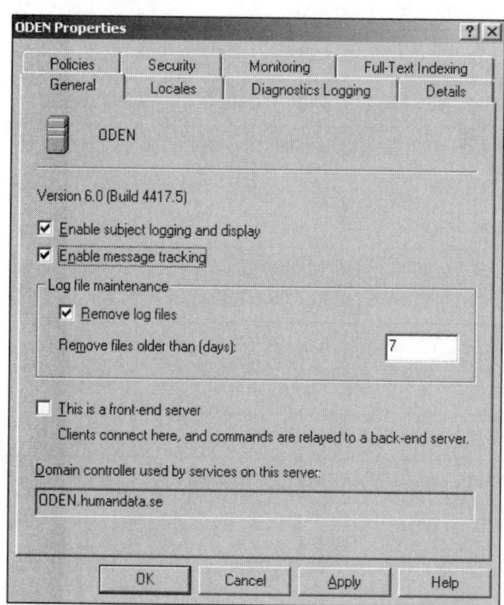

Figure 13.44
Enabling tracking logs and subject logging for a server.

Each tracking log file will be stored in the *\\Program Files\Exchsrvr\<server_name>.log* directory. When the Exchange 2000 server was installed, it automatically created a network share to this directory, called *<servername>*.log; you can map a network drive to this share by typing "Net Use L: \\Oden\Oden.log", assuming you want to map the L: drive to the Exchange server Oden. There will be one log file for each day, named *<yyyymmdd>*.log, for example 200010510; the size of these log files depend on the number of messages routed.

Interpreting the Raw Tracking Log Format

The tracking log files are now in a standard tab-separated ASCII format, which makes it much more handy than the rather esoteric format used in previous Exchange releases. You can in fact use these raw log files for statistical analysis by importing them into MS Excel or any similar program. Table 13.1 describes the format of this log file if subject logging is enabled.

Table 13.1 The raw log file format.

Field Number	Name	Description
1	Date	The date for this record, adopted to the regional setting
2	Time	The time for this record, adopted to the regional setting
3	Client-ip	The IP number for the sending client
4	Client-hostname	The hostname for the sending client
5	Partner-Name	The partner or messaging service; for example, the IS that received this message
6	Server-hostname	The name of the sending server
7	Server-IP	The IP address of the sending server
8	Recipient Address	The recipients of this message, in SMTP or X.400 format
9	Event-ID	The event ID that describes what processing has occurred
10	MSGID	The unique message ID; will be created by the sender; will not change on its way to the recipient
11	Priority	0=normal, 1=high, 5=low, according to what I have seen, but Microsoft's documentation says –1=low, 0=normal, and 1=high
12	Recipient-Report-Status	0=delivered, 1=not delivered; valid only for NDR and DR
13	Total-bytes	The total number of bytes in this message
14	Number-Recipients	Number of recipients for this message
15	Originator-Time	Date and time when this message was submitted by the sending system
16	Encryption	0=not encrypted, 1=signed only, 2=encrypted message
17	Service-version	The version of the service making the log entry
18	Linked-MSGID	The message ID from another service, if any

(continued)

Table 13.1 The raw log file format *(continued)*.

Field Number	Name	Description
19	Message-Subject	The message subject, truncated to 256 characters—note: In Excel, non-U.S. characters may be wrongly converted
20	Sender-Address	The sender address, in SMTP, X.400, or Distinguished Name (DN) format

Tracking Messages

When the tracking log is enabled, it will soon be activated—you don't have to restart any services (however, in some rare cases it can take a longer time; if you want to speed it up, restart the Exchange services). Use the ESM tool to activate the MTC, or create a separate MTC snap-in, for help desks or similar groups.

Let's look at an example. Assume that one of our users, Jessica Rabbit, calls the support and says she is missing some important messages that a colleague has sent her. We must check to see if those messages have been transferred and if so, when. Here's what we would do:

1. Open the ESM tool and expand the *Tools* folder (usually at the bottom of the ESM).
2. Right-click on the *Message Tracking Center* object, and select *Track Message*. This will display the start window for the MTC; see Figure 13.45.
3. Since we are looking for messages sent to Jessica Rabbit, we click the *Browse* button to the right of the *Sent To* field, and select this user (as displayed in Figure 13.45).
4. Before we can start our search, we must also define what server to start searching from; it should be the server the messages originated from. If you select to start from Jessica's home server, you will only see messages coming from other users on this server!

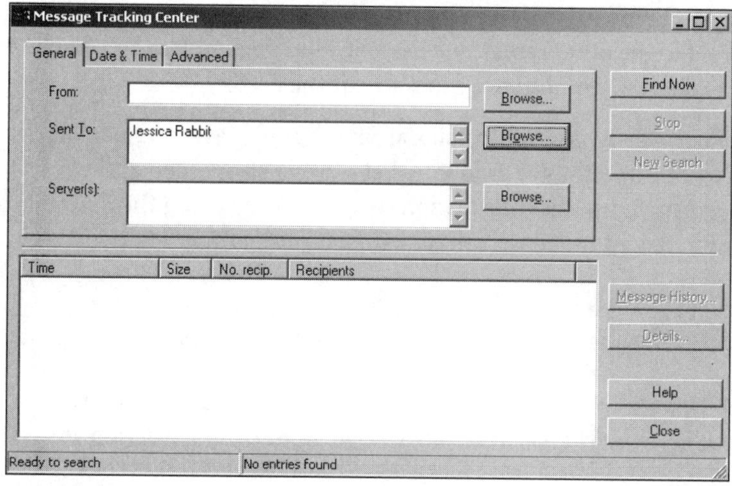

Figure 13.45
The start tab for the Message Tracking Center.

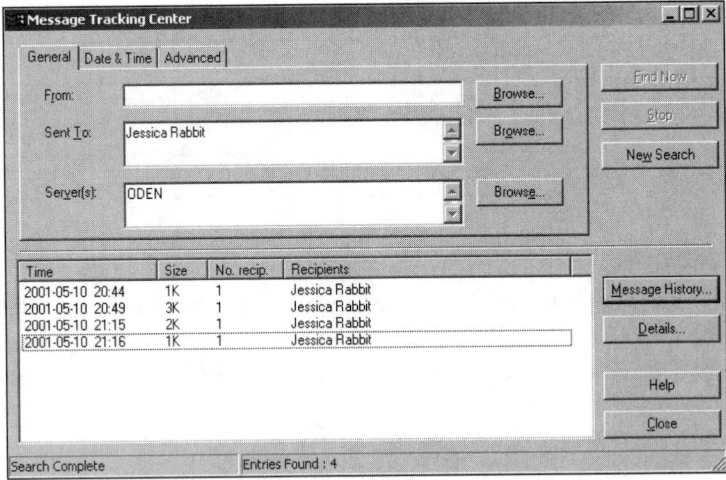

Figure 13.46
The search result.

We know that the messages were sent from the server Oden, so we select that server.

5. Next, we click on *Find Now* to start scanning the tracking logs. The result will look something similar to Figure 13.46; a number of messages are destined for Jessica.

6. The messages we are looking for contained the words *Important Message*, according to Jessica. By looking only at the search result, we don't know which messages these may be. Each message has a link to its routing history, so simply click on the message and you will find more details, like the subject line (this is the same as clicking the *Message History* button). After checking some messages, we finally find one we are looking for; see Figure 13.47.

7. From this information, we can see exactly when the message was submitted, how it was transferred to the other server, and when it was stored in Jessica's mailbox store. When you are done, click *Close* two times to exit the MTC.

The message history may look a bit complex at first, but it's easy to understand it when you start to look into the details of each line. Let's take a closer look at the result from Figure 13.47. You can dump this information to a text file by using the *Save* button (see Figure 13.47 again); the information looks like this:

```
01: 2001-05-10  21:16 Tracked message history on server ODEN
02: 2001-05-10  23:28 The log file '\\ODEN\ODEN.Log\20010509.log' is not
                      available.
03: 2001-05-10  21:16 SMTP Store Driver: Message Submitted from Store
04: 2001-05-10  21:16 SMTP: Message Submitted to Advanced Queuing
05: 2001-05-10  21:16 SMTP: Started Message Submission to Advanced Queue
```

```
06: 2001-05-10  21:16 SMTP: Message Submitted to Categorizer
07: 2001-05-10  21:16 SMTP: Started Outbound Transfer of Message
08: 2001-05-10  21:16 Message transferred out to tor.humandata.se through SMTP
09: 2001-05-10  23:28 The log file '\\tor.humandata.se\tor.Log\20010509.log'
                      is not available.
10: 2001-05-10  21:17 SMTP Store Driver: Message Delivered Locally to Store
```

Referring to the line number at the beginning of each line, we can interpret this information like this (plus finding a bug for the log system):

01: At 21:16, the first tracking info for this message is found on the server Oden.

02: At 23:28, the MTC tried to find yesterday's log file, but didn't find any. This is no problem, since the message was submitted today. However, the time is very suspect; it's actually two hours before the correct time. Both of these servers have the correct time and the same time zone, but the reason for this time difference is that all log files are generated by the IIS 5, which always use Greenwich Mean Time (GMT), regardless of what time zone the server has.

03: At 21:16, the message was submitted, i.e., sent from the client, and received by the SMTP Store driver. (The rest of these activities take place immediately so we don't put out the time for each line below.)

04: The message is passed on to the Advanced Queuing (A.Q.) engine.

05: Immediately it was received by the A.Q.

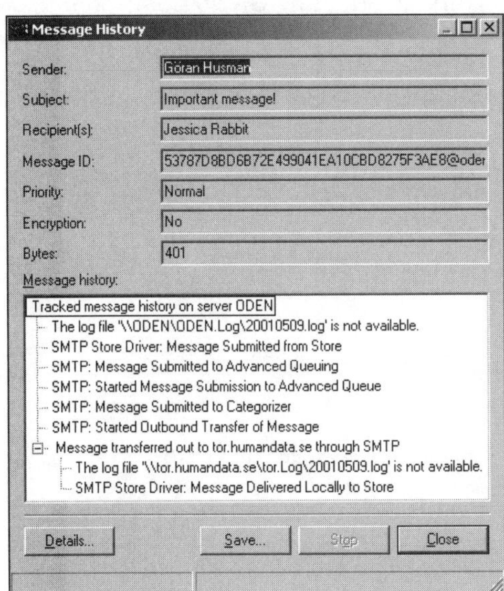

Figure 13.47
The message our user is missing.

06: Then the message is passed on to the Categorizer (a subcomponent of the A.Q.), which checks for message restrictions, size limits, if there are any groups to expand, and so on.

07: The routing engine in the A.Q. has discovered that the message must be transferred to another server (Tor), and starts to send the message by SMTP.

08: The message has now been transferred to the server Tor.

09: The tracking system must now try to look for a tracking log in that server. It starts by looking at yesterday's log file, but it doesn't exist; this is no problem. Notice that the same time difference shows up again as in Step 2 above, and for the same reason!

10: The message has finally reached the destination server, and the message is delivered to her mailbox store. This completes the tracking.

As you can see, we can tell when messages were submitted to the store, and when they were delivered to the destination store, but we can't see if the user has read the message. In this example, our user Jessica probably failed to notice when this message arrived, since we now have proof that it actually was delivered to her mailbox store. So the case is closed!

Summary

This is a list of the more important features and keywords mentioned in this chapter. Use it as a reminder and to make sure you have understood the most important things:

- Routing groups need a connector to transfer messages between them.
- Exchange 2000 has three such connectors: the Routing Group Connector, the SMTP Connector, and the X.400 Connector.
- They differ in speed, configuration options, and method of transporting messages.
- Exchange 5.x had a Dynamic RAS Connector—that is gone now, but using RRAS, we can still connect using dial-up links.
- Target Server Cost was a special feature for the Site Connector in Exchange 5.x that made it possible to distribute the transfer load in a sophisticated way (but most people didn't understand how to use it).
- Exchange 5.x used the Gateway Routing Table (GWART). This doesn't exist in Exchange 2000.
- A target server is a server that may be selected to receive a message.
- Most Exchange 5.x administrators thought the X.400 Connector was complex.
- The Routing Group Connector is the fastest and easiest connector in Exchange 2000; it replaces the Site Connector in previous Exchange versions.
- The RGC uses SMTP, compared to the Site Connector that uses RPC; however, the RGC will automatically use RPC if it connects to an Exchange 5.x site with a Site Connector.

- The RGC can be used only between routing groups that belong to the same Exchange organization.
- The RGC has the most commonly used configuration options, like maximum message size, and time schedules for connections.
- The RGC can use multiple local bridgehead servers; it can also be configured to use multiple remote bridgehead servers—this makes it similar to the Site Connector.
- Oversized messages can be scheduled for transfer during off-hours, in the RGC.
- The RGC is perfect even when you have slow network connections, but 16Kbps is a lower limit.
- The SMTP Connector is mostly used for connecting to the Internet, although it can be used between routing groups too.
- The SMTP Connector will use DNS (or a smart host) when sending messages; the RGC will instead query the AD.
- The SMTP Connector sends messages in standard ESTMP 7-bit MIME format.
- A smart host is perfect if all outgoing messages should be tunneled through a specific server—for example, for virus checks or for adding disclaimers.
- The SMTP Connector has priority over any conflicting settings in the virtual SMTP server.
- The SMTP Connector is the only connector that can dequeue messages with **ETRN** and **TURN** commands.
- The Connector Scope will control how far the connector's address space will be visible; the default is the whole organization.
- Use the Address Space tab when connecting to external systems.
- Use the Connected Routing Groups when connecting two routing groups.
- The X.400 Connector from Exchange 5.x is still alive in Exchange 2000; it has some small enhancements, but is still mostly identical to its predecessor.
- A transport stack (TCP/IP or X.25) must be configured before an X.400 Connector can be installed.
- Use the X.400 Connector in situations where you want almost complete control over the transfer session, or when the available bandwidth is lower than 16Kbps.
- Try to create backup routes between all routing groups in the Exchange organization; a dial-up connection is better than no backup route.
- In most organizations, the RGC will be the only type of connector used; but for dial-up, or very slow network situations, an X.400 Connector may be perfect.

- Don't create backup routes passing over the same physical network links as the primary routes; they will only give you a false sense of security.
- All routing group connectors are also used to refer clients looking for remotely stored public folders; this referral is default enabled.
- In Exchange 5.x, a referral was called an *Affinity*.
- The SMTP Connector can be configured to use multiple local bridgehead servers, making it fault tolerant and load balanced, perfect for Internet connections.
- For inbound SMTP connections, use DNS with multiple MX records to achieve fault tolerance and load balancing.
- For dial-up connections, configure the RRAS service in Window 2000 Server; it will work as a router to the Internet and the ISP, making it possible to also use the SMTP Connector in dial-up situations.
- The Message Tracking Center (MTC) is now better and easier to use than the tracking system in previous Exchange versions.
- All tracking log files are now in ASCII files; you can import them into Excel and use them for statistical analysis of the traffic.

Chapter 14

Email Security

When the message system becomes an important application in your organization, you must make sure the system is safe regarding day-to-day operations and the information in the system. In previous chapters, we have discussed how to design and manage a reliable Exchange 2000 organization; in this chapter, we will focus on the different forms of email security available to Exchange 2000 and its clients: S/MIME, PGP, and the KMS system—Exchange's own email security system. You will learn what these security systems are, and how you can use them in the Exchange 2000 environment. But first, let's discuss why email security is important and how an unauthorized person can gain access to your messages.

In my experience, most users believe their email messages are safe as long as they send messages between clients belonging to the same Exchange 2000 organization; the same users have a feeling that the Internet is a bit more insecure, but not too much. After all, why would so many people send all sorts of information over the Internet? A former colleague of mine was in contact with a law firm in New York; they often sent messages to their clients, asking them to transfer money into given bank accounts, often in amounts over $100,000. A large company used to send important business documents, like sensitive financial analyses of the company, to his accountant. And I know several friends that use free mail systems, like Hotmail or Yahoo, because they want to send messages anonymously at times.

The law firm stopped sending these types of messages when they realized that anyone could intercept their messages, change the account number, and pass the message on. The large company was informed that it was possible for someone outside the company, such as a journalist or a competing company, to scan for these messages and discover sensitive financial information. And my friends now know that they aren't so anonymous using Hotmail and Yahoo!, because the IP number of their client (or their firewall) is listed in the mail header, available to the recipient.

All of these examples are real, and I guess that you too have some interesting stories. The real point I'm trying to make here is that people trust their mail systems. Completely! And not just their own mail systems, but also public mail systems. That is interesting, and can only mean one of two things: either these people are ignorant about the true level of security regarding email messages, or they don't care. But again, it's only human to react this way. For example, ask people if they feel safe when talking on the phone, and most people will say yes. But the truth is that a lot of people can listen to the phone conversation; it doesn't have to be the secret police. Many employees of the telecom company have the knowledge and the technical equipment needed to listen to other peoples' phone conversations. In short, people like to think they can trust any system, regardless of what type of system it is, when that is simply not the case.

Why Is Security Important?

It may seem like a silly question—of course security is important, no one will argue with that, right? So, let me rephrase the question: Why do we need to secure our mail systems? This question may be more legitimate, since many users believe that their messages must be completely uninteresting to anyone except themselves. The answer may differ depending on the organization, but the common reasons are these:

- To prevent *unauthorized access* to the information in the message system. Only legiti-mate users should be able to view the information, regardless of whether it's sensitive.
- To prevent *tampering*. When the message arrives, the recipient must be sure that no one has modified its content in any way.
- To prevent *forgery* by using another person's mail account to send out messages.
- To prevent *spoofing*—impersonating another user by using his or her email address when sending messages.
- To prevent *virus* attacks distributed by email.
- To prevent *Trojan horses*, malicious programs disguised as a game or something similar, that are passed along with the message. When the program is opened, it installs a security-breaking program that, for example, registers all your passwords and sends them to another user.

Besides these threats, there are others, like *Denial-of-Service (DoS)* attacks, where some part of the mail system is overloaded, making it crash or halt; and mail-relaying, where your server is used to disguise the true origin of unsolicited messages and such. But let's continue by looking at different types of unauthorized access.

How to Access Other Peoples' Messages

We all want to trust our computer systems completely, especially in the sense that we want to be sure that there is no way to gain unauthorized access to information. The truth is you can't trust any system completely, in this sense; this is also true for messaging systems, regardless of the vendor. For example, there must always be at least one person who has complete access to the messaging system, the mail administrator. She can take ownership of any mailbox, including her manager's or the CEO's. But it doesn't have to be an administrator who can gain unauthorized access to the message system; if you leave your desk for three minutes, do you always lock your computer? Even in this short amount of time, someone could sneak into your office and view your mail, and even send a message in your name! This person could also add himself as your delegate, giving himself permission to access all your personal folders, like the inbox and contacts; he doesn't have to be an administrator to do this.

Social Engineering

The best trick may still be based on social engineering; call the user, pretend to be a person working with the computer system, such as an administrator or a consultant, and ask the user for their password. In the majority of cases, you will get it. Or even better, call the Help Desk and pretend to be a user who has forgotten his password; ask them to reset the password and then you have what you need. The only things required are a phone and some nerves. A very interesting book about hacking and social engineering is the *Underground*, by Suelette Dryfus; it's a true story about a group of hackers and crackers from all over the world who band together to exploit security holes and social engineering to get access to thousands of highly sensitive computer systems. One part in this book is especially interesting when discussing social engineering; it describes exactly how one of these teenagers calls a manager in a company, pretending to be working at the computer department, and makes the manager give his password over the phone. Read this story—you will laugh and cry at the same time. It's free to download from the Internet at **www.underground-book.com**.

How to Listen to the Message Traffic Using the Network

The transport of messages is also a weak security point. For example, let's assume that we have a curious person called Jan working in our company; this Jan has more technical skills than morals, and he wants to know all about your message conversations. We assume that Jan isn't an administrator, and that he doesn't dare sneak into your computer and add himself as a delegate for your mailbox. Still, he has several other options; for example, Jan can use a network-monitoring program to listen to all your message traffic. Several network tools are available that are specialized for collecting email messages and browser traffic to and from a particular user. Since Jan is working from the inside of the organization, he can select to listen to the traffic between your computer and the server; he also could listen to your incoming and outgoing Internet traffic, or he could do both.

The type of network traffic between the client and the server depends on the type of message client; if it's an Outlook 2000 client, it will be an RPC/MAPI session that is hard, but not impossible, to interpret. If it's an OWA client, it will be much easier, since all messages will be formatted using HTTP, and sent in clear text. If it's a POP3 or IMAP4 client, it will also be in clear text. All network analyzer programs will let you view the HTTP, POP3, and IMAP4 traffic, since these protocols send all information in clear text (or Base-64 encoded, which is almost as easy to interpret), including user accounts and passwords! The problem with Outlook clients is that they send messages in 8-bit format; not many parsers are available for this, at least not freely available.

All messages sent over the Internet use SMTP format; such messages are almost always in clear text and are very easy to capture, as long as you have a network connection to the links transferring these messages. Since Jan is an employee, he has access to the internal network; it's an easy task for him to record whatever SMTP conversation he likes. But now you get a bit suspicious; someone seems to be reading your mail. You decide to use a Hotmail account for sending more sensitive messages. However, it's equally easy for Jan to scan your HTTP traffic; every time you read or send a message, Jan will be able to see this, too. We simply can't stop people like Jan from scanning messages, since he has access to the internal network; the only thing that would hinder Jan would be to encrypt our messages.

Is It So Bad If Someone Can Read My Mail?

The answer is yes! Definitely! Even if you think that your messages aren't sensitive, the information in your mailbox could be used to collect information about your company that a competing company could take advantage of—for example, to get access to names and home phone numbers of employees, or to simply send out messages in your name to create confusion and conflicts. A message doesn't always have to be top-secret material to be interesting to other people; different groups have different interests.

The threats discussed so far have assumed access to the internal network, so they must be done by employees, contracted workers, or hired consultants. The following is a summary of these threats:

- An administrator gains unauthorized access to the message system.
- An employee gets access to an unattended client.
- An employee scans the network traffic.

The natural question is: How can we stop this? The answer is: We can't! There will always be weak spots in our systems that someone can take advantage of; we need to trust our administrators and employees to a certain degree, or else we can't run a messaging system, or in fact any computer system. But we can make it harder to misuse the system by following some simple guidelines, described in the following sections.

Selecting an Exchange Administrator

Make sure that the people working as administrators are highly trustworthy since they have almost divine status in your Exchange 2000 organization. Before being granted total access to the message system, they should be scrutinized: Do they have any problems regarding drugs, criminal records, financial debt, or similar issues that could make them an interesting target for other people who want information from this company? This person should also be continuously scrutinized during the employment period; just because he or she was suitable once doesn't mean that this is still the case two years later. Make sure that the administrators sign a legal contract regulating what they are allowed to do, and how they should treat information they get access to.

If your company has outsourced its messaging system, those questions mentioned above could be extremely hard to answer. What people are working in that outsourcing company? Do you know their names? Are you informed when they hire new employees? Do you know which people in that company have administrative access to your Exchange organization? Who has access to the Exchange servers? Even if it may be a good idea financially to outsource all or parts of the mail administration, it's a bad idea from a security perspective; you have no direct control over these people, and it doesn't improve the situation that these types of companies often have a high rate of new employees.

If I wanted full access to a company's message system, I would try to get employment as an administrator; one day would be enough. Or, I could take an assignment as an Exchange consultant, fixing some problem that required me to have the administrator password. If I just get some time alone with the Exchange server, I could add myself as an administrator, take ownership over some interesting mailboxes, or install a script that sends a copy of all messages to me over the Internet. Not long ago, this actually happened to a company with military connections in Sweden; a consultant installed a script on an SMTP smart host that made a copy of all Internet messages to and from this company. Fortunately they discovered this very quickly, but it's amazing how easy it is to get a hold of an organization's email, if you just have the right opportunity. (No, it wasn't me!)

Prevent Unauthorized Access to Message Clients

This is really a question about educating the users; this is the only way people can understand how important it is to protect their message client from unauthorized access. I suggest that all users have some form of training about this topic, or even better, when giving them a general Outlook course, give them a practical demonstration of how easy it is to get unauthorized access. For example (assuming you have a suitable training facility), when all the users leave the classroom, maybe for a coffee break, let one user secretly go back and send some messages on other users' clients, trying to make them look realistic. When people return to the classroom, start talking about security and the importance of locking their computers before leaving them unattended; then tell them that some fake messages have been sent, and ask them to identify which ones are fake. (If they are smart, they will look at the time stamp!) Silly demonstrations like this will make security easy to remember, even for users who normally take it lightly.

Make sure all users know how to lock their computers—for example, by using a screen saver with a lock feature, or the usual Ctrl+Alt+Del key sequence and then selecting Lock Computer. This last method is preferred, since it locks the computer immediately, whereas the screen saver method may take 10 minutes or more to activate, depending on the configuration.

Unauthorized Scanning of the Network

It's almost impossible to detect whether an employee is using a network monitor for scanning the internal network; this will not show up in any log or warning messages—it's simply a transparent network operation. The only thing that is needed is a computer connected to the internal network and a network scanner. That makes this method very nasty, and the fact that these network scanners can easily be found on the Internet make it even worse. I think that the only way to protect the organization from this is to implement strict company policies that explicitly forbid all kinds of unauthorized network scanning.

On the technical side, there are a few things you can do. Dividing your network into different IP subnets will delimit what the scanner can see. But the best solution may be to use network switches instead of ordinary hubs, since this will prohibit the user from seeing any other network traffic besides his or her own. In this case, the user must gain access to the network cable to the Exchange server; only then can he or she scan all messages. Make sure to keep all servers in a locked server room; this will make unauthorized network scanning much harder.

Threats from the Outside

So far we have discussed the threats from insiders, or people who have access to our internal network. What about the outside? Could anyone gain access to our messages or give us any problem using our message systems? I'm sorry to say this, but yes; not only can it be done, but it is done every day! External threats for message systems are usually these:

- Message theft or tampering
- Spoofing
- Denial-of-Service attacks
- Relay of messages
- Virus attacks
- Trojan horses

The following sections describe each threat and what you can do to avoid them. But remember, you can never be 100 percent sure; protection is an ongoing process that must be scrutinized and updated constantly.

External Message Theft or Tampering

When reading newspapers and watching TV, it's easy to get the impression that any teenager with a home computer can get a hold of whatever information they want. Fortunately, this is not true! However, if this teenager knows how to exploit security holes in a particular system, he or she might get access to whatever information is passed over the system. What these people really want is access to the network links that transfer the messages to and from the Internet. For example, employees working at an ISP have this access. They also have access to any Smart Host or secondary mail servers, making it easy to install a script that makes a copy of certain messages, like all mail to the CEO of a particular company.

Do you remember Jan from the previous example? Let's assume that he gets fired, and now he wants revenge. The best thing Jan can do now (from his twisted perspective) is to get employed by the ISP that his former employer uses for Internet connections; once he is inside the ISP, he can install his network scanner program again, configured to listen only for messages going to and from his former company. But Jan doesn't just want to view messages—he wants revenge! An effective way of creating chaos and confusion is to modify inbound messages; this can be done several ways: he can use any secondary mail server for this company hosted at the ISP, or redirect all incoming SMTP messages to a new server by changing the external Domain Naming Service (DNS) and its Mail Exchanger (MX) record.

The first method, using secondary mail servers, is easiest for Jan and hardest for the company to detect. This method is normally used only when the company has a dial-up connection, for example an ISDN link; if the company has a leased line, then the ISP will probably not host any secondary mail servers. If so, Jan could instead use the second method—modifying the external DNS to point incoming SMTP messages to a new SMTP server that receives mail destined for this company, and then forwarding them to the final destination server. This method allows Jan to capture some messages, and modify their content before they are passed on to the company. But this method also exposes Jan to a greater risk of detection, since incoming SMTP messages will reveal to an observant user that a new server is part of the transport link.

These methods of tampering could also be used for outgoing messages. For example, Jan could change bank account numbers, prices in offers, and so on, which could easily make the company lose money and customers; by modifying the text of outgoing messages to contain offending statements, Jan also could make this company lose credibility and damage its reputation.

Message Spoofing

This type of attack is very easy to accomplish; any Internet client, like POP3 and IMAP4, can be used for this purpose. This is how it's done: A user configures his Internet client to use another person's email address as the reply address (see Figure 14.1).

All users receiving messages from this client will believe that this message came from this sender, or in my example, George Bush **<president@whitehouse.gov>**; see Figure 14.2.

Only by looking at the message header can you see that this message doesn't come from the alleged originator. To view the header, you have to open the message. Select View|Options; in the Internet Header pane, and you will see the header:

```
Microsoft Mail Internet Headers Version 2.0
Received: from ghnbl ([192.168.15.50]) by oden.humandata.se with Microsoft
SMTPSVC(5.0.2195.1600);
      Tue, 15 May 2001 14:24:18 +0200
Message-ID: <008e01c0dd39$f6c390e0$320fa8c0@humandata.se>
From: "George Bush" <President@whitehouse.gov>
To: =?iso-8859-1?Q?G=F6ran_Husman?= <goran@humandata.se>
```

```
Subject: World Peace at last
Date: Tue, 15 May 2001 14:24:18 +0200
MIME-Version: 1.0
Content-Type: multipart/alternative;
     boundary="----=_NextPart_000_008B_01C0DD4A.B9D3AE70"
X-Priority: 3
X-MSMail-Priority: Normal
X-Mailer: Microsoft Outlook Express 5.50.4133.2400
X-MimeOLE: Produced By Microsoft MimeOLE V5.50.4133.2400
Return-Path: President@whitehouse.gov
X-OriginalArrivalTime: 15 May 2001 12:24:18.0995 (UTC)
     FILETIME=[F6CE1830:01C0DD39]
```

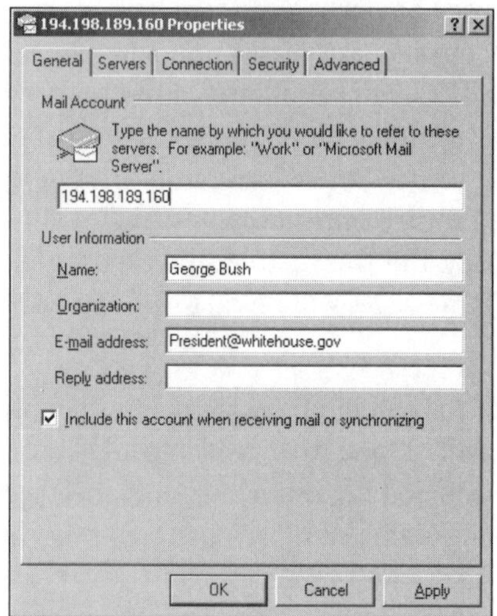

Figure 14.1
Faking the originator address.

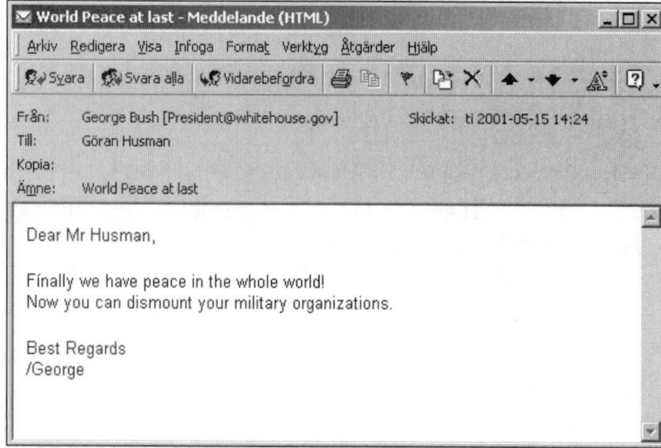

Figure 14.2
A fake message.

If you look at the second line, it appears that George Bush has been connecting directly from the computer *ghnb1* to **Oden.humandata.se**. This looks strange; there should be a server belonging to **whitehouse.gov** listed here. This is most likely a fake address. What will happen if the recipient answers this mail? Well, since the reply address is **president@whitehouse.gov**, the mail will actually go to that address, and the true owner of this email address, Mr. Bush, will probably start wondering what this mail is all about.

As you have seen, spoofing is extremely simple to perform; anyone with an Internet client can do it. The whole point is to make the recipient of this mail believe it came from another user; the person doing the spoofing is not interested in getting replies, and he will not get any, either. The reasons to send spoofed messages include:

- To misinform or confuse someone—for example, a competing company, or a journalist
- To discredit someone
- To joke with someone (this is the most common reason, I believe)

Denial-of-Service Attacks

This is a cheap trick; the simple idea is to overload a system until it breaks down. You don't need knowledge of message systems to use a DoS attack; free programs are available on the Internet that will do it for you. The question is whether a DoS is a teenage prank or if it's a terrorist attack. In a world with 100 million Internet users, many people think this cheap trick is funny; if they don't like someone (for example, often the local telecom company), or they just want to impress their friends, a DoS attack is often performed. However, this form of attack could also be an effective weapon when you want to discredit a company or disable their normal operations. For example, assume someone is mad at their bank; by sending thousands of messages every minute to the bank's mail system, he will effectively disable their mail system, at least for a while. Or, in warfare situations, one side could perform DoS attacks on the other side's mail system, to make sure they can't receive Internet messages.

A DoS attack on a mail server is normally combined with message-relay (see the next section). If you are an attacker, you don't want to leave a trail that leads back to you; you must make all these messages look like they're originating from another source. Otherwise, it will be an easy task for the victims to see where these mails came from.

It's hard to defend yourself from a DoS attack. Some firewalls and SMTP servers are able to detect whether they are under a DoS attack. They count the number of messages coming from the same source; if it's over a given number per time unit, they shut down their service. This is far better than accepting these messages into the production environment, since that will in the end halt the Exchange server, and this in turn will stop all internal message traffic, too. You should never let an Exchange server that hosts users to accept inbound messages directly from the Internet; it's an all too easy target for DoS attacks.

Relay of Messages

Message-relay is a feature on SMTP servers that must be active to assist POP3 and IMAP4 clients sending messages to the Internet; without relay, they can only send messages to the internal Exchange system. The relay technique has been around since the early days of SMTP; it was used when a sending party was unable to reach a destination directly, and had to pass the message through one or more other SMTP servers on its way. A few years back, senders of messages who wanted to disguise their true origin discovered that they could send their messages through an SMTP server belonging to another company, making these messages appear to originate from that company. For example, see Figure 14.3; here you see how the original sender of these messages uses the SMTP server in Company A as a relay server. For the recipient of these messages, it will look as if they originate from Company A, instead of the true origin.

Nowadays, most SMTP servers have disabled message-relay, because of this risk of being used for relaying large volumes of unsolicited commercial messages. However, previous versions of Exchange had their Internet Mail Service connector open by default for message-relay; but in Exchange 2000, message-relay is by default disabled, unless the sender authenticates first, using a valid Windows 2000 account. This is configured by the properties for the virtual SMTP server and its *Access* page; click the *Relay* button (see Figure 14.4) to control the message-relay feature. Note the *Allow All Computers Which Successfully Authenticate To Relay* checkbox at the bottom. All POP3 and IMAP4 clients must then be configured to log on before sending SMTP messages over the Exchange 2000 server; make sure to set the *My Server Requires Authentication* checkbox; see Figure 14.5 in the account's *Servers* property page.

The difference between the unrestricted message-relay illustrated in Figure 14.3 and our authenticating POP3 and IMAP4 clients is that our clients will authenticate before sending any SMTP messages; see Figure 14.6. This will still make these messages appear to come

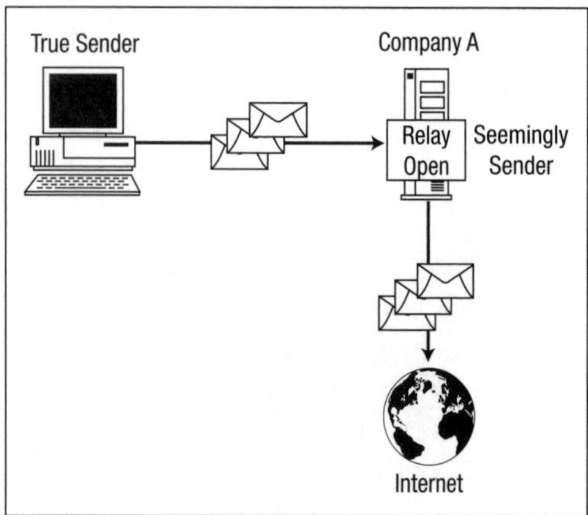

Figure 14.3
A relay making messages seem to come from Company A.

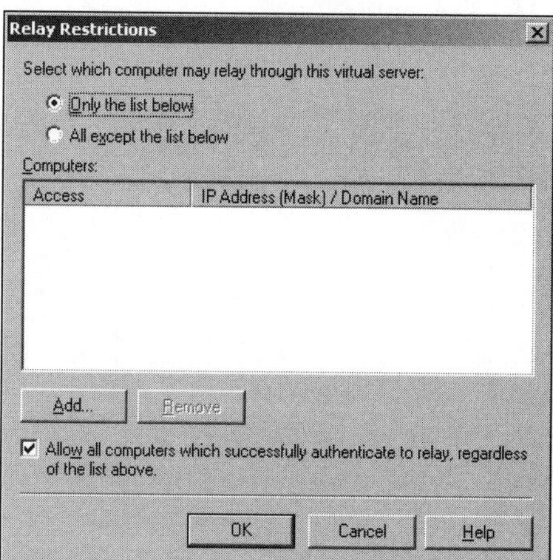

Figure 14.4
Configuring Exchange 2000 to prohibit relay unless the client authenticates.

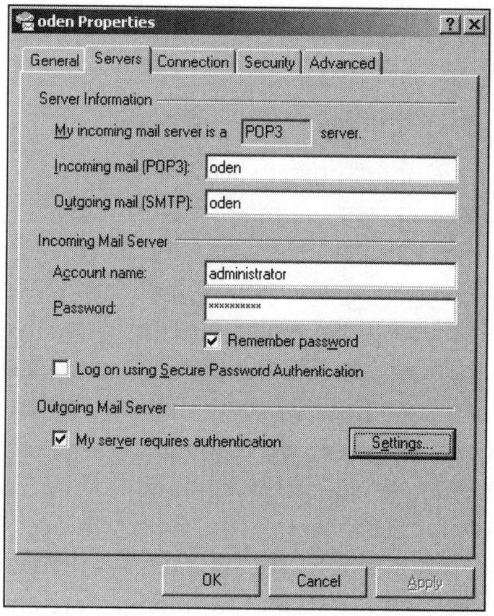

Figure 14.5
Configuring Internet clients to log on before sending SMTP messages.

from Company A, but this time it's actually true; these clients belong to our organization since they have a valid Windows 2000 account.

An interesting question is how do they find SMTP servers that are open to message-relay? Again, by using utilities available on the Internet. This time it's port scanning programs that will connect to a large number of SMTP servers and check their message-relay settings. You simply can't hide, even if you are a small organization that nobody knows about; if your server is connected to the Internet and open for message-relay, it will only be a matter of weeks before someone finds your server. So the recommendation is simply to keep the

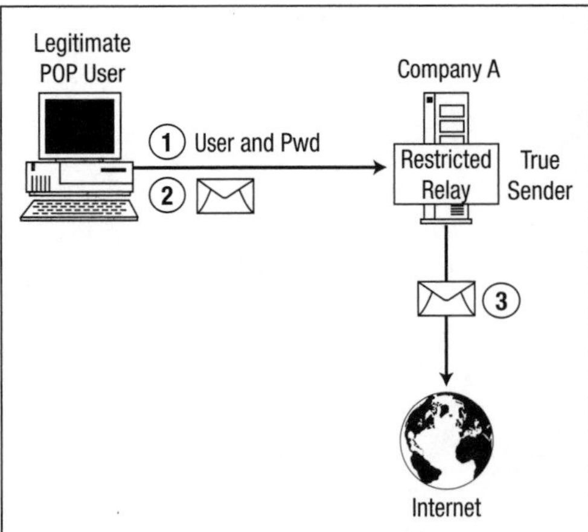

Figure 14.6
Authenticated POP3 and IMAP4 clients are allowed to relay messages.

message-relay settings in Exchange 2000 as they are—never ever change this to an open relay unless you are very sure of what you are doing!

Virus Attacks

Emails that have virus-infected attachments are unfortunately becoming more and more common, and they can create a lot of damage and force companies to stop their mail systems for a day or more. Their effectiveness is based on the fact that this type of virus attack can replicate so quickly over the whole Internet. The usual virus looks something like this: A message is sent to the first attacked user, carrying a virus disguised as something interesting, for example a particular game or a nude picture of some celebrity; when the user opens the attachment, the virus executes. Exactly what damage the virus will do differs; many are actually harmless, but some will destroy certain files or wipe out a complete disk. But the way this virus spreads is interesting; it will make a copy of itself and send the copy to each registered contact this user has in his or her Outlook client. That means that this virus uses social engineering to replicate itself—all new virus messages will appear to come from a known person; this makes recipients more apt to relax their security and open the attachment without too much concern.

All files use the last three characters to indicate what type of files they are; for example, Word files use .doc, program files use .exe, and Visual Basic scripts use .vbs. A virus must be able to execute when the user opens it; that delimits the number of file types a virus can use to a handful. In Outlook, it's common to use Visual Basic scripts to build viruses. So why doesn't the receiver understand that it's not an normal attachment, but instead a dangerous Visual Basic script? Because the true file type can be hidden behind a more innocent type, like .txt or .bmp. For example, the ILOVEYOU virus that hit the Internet in April 2000 was an email attachment named LOVE-LETTER-FOR-YOU.TXT.VBS; but since the standard configuration in Windows is to hide some file types, such as the .vbs, the recipient only saw an attachment that seemed to be named LOVE-LETTER-FOR-YOU.TXT.

Microsoft has released several security patches for Outlook 97 and Outlook 98 that can be downloaded from **www.Microsoft.com/download** and installed on these types of clients; this will warn the user before opening certain types of file attachments, or even prohibit the user from opening them from within Outlook. You must instead save these files to disk and then execute them from outside Outlook. Microsoft has also released special security updates for Outlook 98 and Outlook 2000 that will prohibit viruses using similar techniques to ILOVEYOU from executing. Both Outlook 2000 SR1 and Outlook 2002 are pre-configured to disable features that are necessary for these types of email-borne viruses; for example, .vbs files will not execute, nor will it be possible for any type of script or program to be executed inside Outlook and use the addresses in the Contact folder for sending out messages.

This means that it's now much harder to distribute computer viruses using the Outlook client than ever before. However, this optimistic attitude presumes that people have upgraded their Outlook clients, and the truth is that a horrifying number of organizations are still using Outlook versions without any security patch whatsoever. This is obvious, since outbreaks still occur of new viruses that are built on the same principle as the ILOVEYOU virus. Use Decision Tree 14.1 as a guide for what to do with the current Outlook versions to increase their security.

Trojan Horses

A Trojan horse is a program that looks innocent, but that actually hides malicious code that will do things that are hidden from the user. The term "Trojan Horse" refers to the ancient trick described in Homer's *Iliad*, in which the Greeks give a giant wooden horse as a peace offering to their enemies, the Trojans. However, inside the horse Greek soldiers are hiding; the Trojans drag the horse inside the city walls, and during the night, the soldiers get out of the horse and open the city gates, allowing the Greek army to enter and capture Troy.

An example of a Trojan horse is the Resume worm that steals passwords from the computer under attack and sends them to an external email address; this particular Trojan message can be recognized by its subject, Resume, with the attached file, RESUME.TXT.VBS, which is the real worm.

Note: *A computer worm is a special type of virus that can replicate itself and use computer memory, but can't attach itself to other programs the way a virus can. The difference is subtle to most people, but it's important to know that both viruses and worms are threats to your systems and that both can be distributed by email. All anti-virus programs will also identify worms; there are no special anti-worm programs.*

Some Things Were Better in Exchange 5.x

Exchange 2000 has numerous enhancements and new features compared to the previous Exchange versions, but regarding security, some things were actually better in the old Exchange versions. I am referring specifically to the Remote Procedure Call (RPC)-based communication used within Exchange 5.x sites, and between sites using the Site Connector.

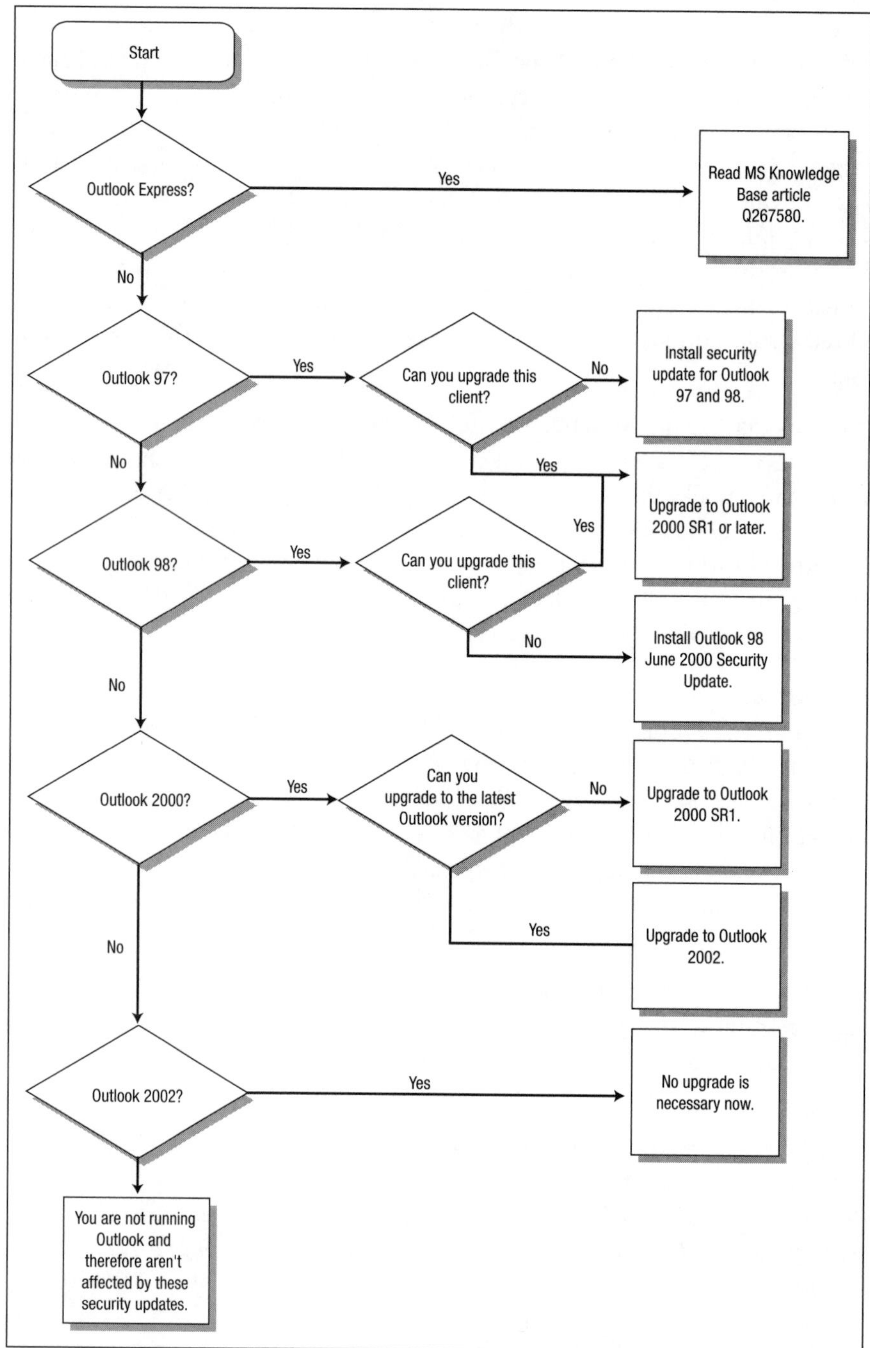

Decision Tree 14.1
Security upgrades for Outlook clients.

Since all traffic in Exchange 2000 by default uses SMTP as the transfer protocol instead of RPC, we have actually decreased our security regarding the network traffic.

One of the nice features with RPC when used between Exchange servers and sites is its built-in encryption. This is also known as *Encrypted RPC*. It uses a 40-bit RSA algorithm called RC4 to encrypt the data transferred on the network. It's important to understand that encrypted RPC protects only the *transfer* of messages. When the message has arrived at the destination, it is no longer encrypted; at that point, it becomes the responsibility of the receiving computer to protect the messages.

RPC Traffic Between the Client and the Server

All MAPI clients from Microsoft, for example, Outlook 2000, use RPC when communicating with the Exchange server. In previous versions of Exchange, it was possible to enable encryption of this RPC traffic as well as the server-to-server encryption. Since Exchange 2000 also allows MAPI clients, like any Outlook version, it too can accept encrypted RPC traffic to and from the clients. Follow these instructions to enable encrypted RPC between any Outlook client version and any Exchange version, including Exchange 2000:

1. Start the Outlook client.
2. Open the *Tools|Services* menu.
3. On the *Services* page, open the properties for the Microsoft Exchange Server.
4. Switch to the *Advanced* page (see Figure 14.7). Use the *Encrypt Information* pane and set the *When Using The Network* checkbox to enable encrypted RPC between the client and the server.

   You can also enable encryption when using a dial-up network connection to the Exchange server by setting the *When Using Dial-Up Networking* checkbox.

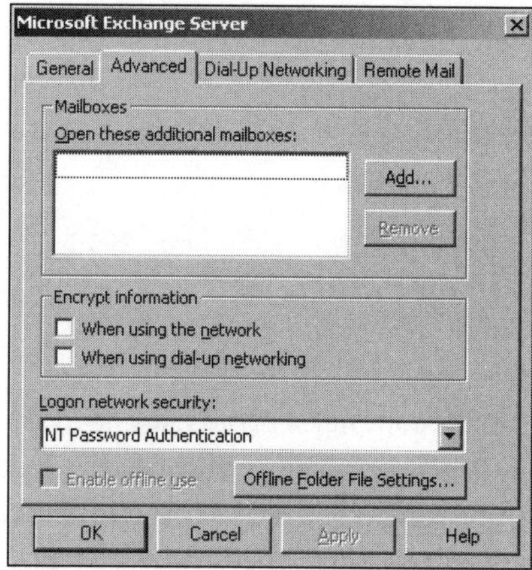

Figure 14.7
The Advanced page for Outlook's Exchange service.

By default, there will be no encrypted RPC traffic between clients and Exchange servers, and the reason is simply performance. If all clients use encrypted RPC, the server performance decreases; I have not seen any figures from Microsoft regarding how much resources encryption takes, but compared to other encryption forms, like SSL, I would guess that it takes at least 50 percent more resources.

RPC Traffic Between Exchange 5.x and Exchange 2000

The network traffic between two Exchange 2000 servers will never use encrypted RPC. However, in some special situations, Exchange 2000 can use encrypted RPC between servers:

- If an Exchange 2000 server joins an existing Exchange 5.x organization, it will communicate directly with the Exchange 5.x servers in its site, using encrypted RPC. If it didn't have this capability, an Exchange 2000 server could not join a 5.5 site.
- Also, when the Routing Group Connector is used to connect with an Exchange 5.x site that uses the Site Connector, it will also use encrypted RPC, for the same reason mentioned above.

How to Encrypt Network Traffic in Exchange 2000

Since SMTP traffic has replaced RPC traffic in Exchange 2000, encryption is no longer a feature. But the situation is not so bad as you might first think. First, messages sent between Exchange 2000 servers belonging to the same routing group are passed as 8-bit MIME messages, not in clear text. You will not be able to use a network monitor to scan such traffic and understand anything from it; however, if you have a *Message DataBase Encoded Format (MDBEF)* parser, you can decode the Exchange traffic. As described earlier, the MDBEF is the internal Exchange database format, used for both standard user messages and system messages. When sending messages between routing groups using the Routing Group Connector, you will have exactly the same type of network traffic.

Second, it's possible to encrypt the message traffic, if necessary; the cost will be a decrease in performance, as it always is when extra code is involved in the transfer process. The two standard methods of encrypting message traffic in Exchange 2000 are:

- *Transport Socket Layer (TLS)*—An encryption method that's almost identical to the SSL encryption method used for Web traffic.
- *Internet Protocol Security (IPSec)*—This type of encryption takes place beneath the SMTP protocol layer. In other words, this is not configured on the Exchange server.

IPSec and Exchange 2000

The recommended method is IPSec, since it's faster, completely transparent to the Exchange servers, and can encrypt all TCP/IP-based network traffic between these servers, not just Exchange messages. IPSec is a feature that is configured in the Windows 2000 security system by using security policies. It's a framework of open standards developed by the Internet Engineering Task Force (IETF), for ensuring secure communications over IP networks, using cryptographic security services.

If you were to use IPSec between two Exchange 2000 servers called Stockholm and London, the following would happen (see also Figure 14.8):

1. Stockholm sends a message to London.
2. The IPSec driver on Stockholm checks its stored *IP Filter Lists* to see if this IP package should be encrypted; the answer is yes.
3. The driver then notifies the *Internet Key Exchange (IKE)* process to start negotiations with the London server.
4. The IKE process on London receives a message requesting a security negotiation.
5. Stockholm and London establish a Phase I *security association (SA)* and share a master key.
6. Two Phase II SAs are negotiated: one inbound SA and one outbound SA. The SA includes the encryption keys used to secure the communication, including the *Security Parameters Index*.
7. The IPSec driver on Stockholm uses the outbound SA to sign and encrypt the IP packets.
8. The driver passes the signed and encrypted IP packets to the IP layer, which routes the packets to the London server.
9. London's network card receives the signed and encrypted IP packets; it passes them directly to the IPSec driver.
10. The IPSec driver on London now uses the inbound SA to check that the signature is valid and then decrypts the IP packets.
11. The driver then passes the decrypted packets up to the standard TCP/IP driver, which in turn passes them to the receiving Exchange 2000 virtual SMTP server.

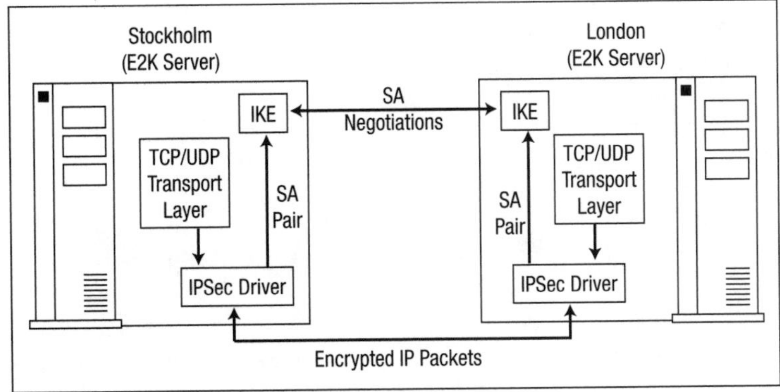

Figure 14.8
Two Exchange 2000 servers using IPSec for encrypted network traffic.

***Tip:** An excellent guide for troubleshooting network connections using IPSec is the* MS Windows 2000 Server Manual*, and its Security page, in the section titled "Troubleshooting IP Security." This document can be found on the MS Technet CD or in the Windows 2000 Server documentation.*

Introduction to Encryption and Signing

As we have seen in the previous sections in this chapter, dedicated hackers have plenty of opportunities to listen to message traffic, modify its content, hide the true origin of a message, and get unauthorized access to the mail system as an administrator. We have also seen that part of the problem is the SMTP-based network traffic, which, by default, is not encrypted; however, this can be solved by using TLS or IPSec. But these two methods do not solve all problems! For example, they can't stop someone from capturing SMTP messages going in and out to the Internet, since we usually can't use TLS or IPSec on external SMTP servers.

However, other methods will solve these security problems; they all use client-based encryption. This means that all messages will be encrypted before leaving the client, and they will not be decrypted until the recipient opens the message using his or her client; see Figure 14.9.

This method protects the message transfer the whole way, not only between the servers or between the client and the server. Sounds great, doesn't it? So what's the catch? The answer is that both the sender and the receiver must exchange something called a *public encryption key* first; you can't just send an encrypted message to anyone on the Internet. Then both clients must be configured to use encryption; for example, an Outlook 2000 client uses the *Tools|Options* menu and the *Security* page to set up secure email.

There is an extra bonus: Not only can you encrypt messages with this client-based method, you also can electronically sign outgoing messages, thereby proving to the recipient that you are the originator of the message. Even someone sneaking into your room when you were out for a few minutes wouldn't be able to send a secure message, pretending to be you.

The beauty of this method is that a standard exists; this means that you can use this method today to send encrypted and electronically signed messages to anyone, as long as

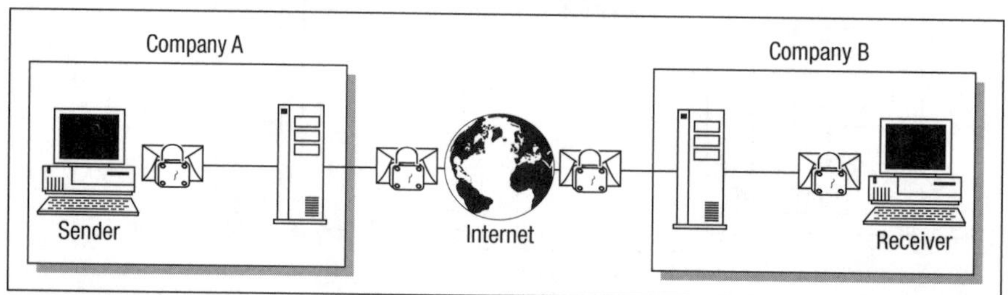

Figure 14.9
The client-based encryption principle.

the recipient also understands and uses this standard. However, to make this a bit more complicated, we have two more methods similar to the standard; one that is used for exchanging encrypted and signed messages with external recipients, and one that is used only within the Exchange organization. Before we describe each method, I must explain how the basic technique works. Please note that this is a very large (and disputed) topic, so I will only be able to provide the overall picture. If you want to know more about electronic encryption and signing, a number of books are available, for example *E-mail Security: How to Keep Your Electronic Messages Private*, by Bruce Schneier (John Wiley & Sons, 1995).

How Encryption and Signing Works

The history behind encryption is almost as old as mankind; the need to hide information from enemies, curious eyes, and sometimes even your partner has always existed. Really interesting encryption methods have been invented that could hide information from one party, but reveal it to another. For example, 2,500 years ago a Greek named Histiaios wanted to instruct Aristagoras of Miletos to start a revolt against the Persian king; to pass information to Aristagoras, he shaved the head of one of his slaves, wrote the secret message on his head, and waited for the hair to grow out. Then this slave could travel safely, since he seemingly didn't carry anything with him. When the slave arrived, he shaved his head and showed the secret message.

A more modern example is the Enigma, used by the Germans during World War II; this was a code machine that looked similar to a large typewriter. The Germans used the Enigma to type in a message; this was then encrypted using a secret key (a sequence of numbers and characters). Then it was safe to transfer this encrypted message, even over public lines like radio broadcasts. The only person who could decode this message was someone with another Enigma machine and the same secret key used in the first place. To increase the security, the Germans changed the secret key every day, making it extremely hard to decode any messages, even if you managed to obtain one Enigma machine. You can read much more about this story, and others; a great number of books have been written on this subject. One good introduction is *The Code Book: The Science of Secrecy from Ancient Egypt to Quantum Cryptography*, by Simon Singh (Anchor Books, 2000).

Both of these examples have one particular thing in common: The sender and receiver must share a common secret. Aristagoras needed to know where the secret message was hidden, and both the sender and receiver of the Enigma code had to use the same secret key when decoding the message. That's exactly the problem with all types of encryption—a shared secret! The slave was instructed to tell this secret to Aristagoras, but the Germans had to find another way to distribute all their secret encryption keys; they did it by creating a codebook with all the secret codes for one month. This codebook was then distributed to all German fighting units, like the submarines, the battle fleets, and the armies. It's easy to understand the interest the Allies had in this codebook, and their struggle to capture it.

The History of Asymmetric Encryption

The true weakness in all encryption algorithms is the sharing of the secret key; it doesn't matter how complex the encryption is if some unauthorized party discovers the secret key. This method is often referred to as a *symmetric* encryption, and its biggest problem is how to distribute the secret key securely. But a break-through in encryption came at the end of 1969, when the English military asked James Ellis, one of England's best cryptologists, to look at this key distribution problem. He discovered that there was a way to send encrypted messages without having to exchange keys first. But since this was a military project, none of this was ever published.

In the United States, other people were thinking about exactly the same problem—how to avoid key distribution. Two researchers, Whitfield Diffie and Martin Hellman, came to a similar solution to the problem in 1975, completely unaware of the results of James Ellis. This was the birth of *asymmetric* encryption, a method whereby information can be encrypted and distributed in a secure way to the recipient, without first exchanging a secret encryption key. This is rather interesting; it has only been about 25 years since mankind took one of its greatest leaps in the ancient science of cryptography. The method of asymmetric encryption has actually been known for a long time, but it only works under certain conditions; the problem was to find a way to make it work when using mathematical algorithms.

A Manual Asymmetric Encryption Method

Imagine that we have two people, Alice and Bob, who need to exchange secret messages between them. They don't have a computer system; they will instead use the standard (snail) mail system. The problem is that the unpleasant man Jan, from our previous examples, is now working at the mail company. He is as curious as ever; he secretly opens all messages that pass between Alice and Bob, so they must protect their messages. This is how they will do it:

1. Alice puts her secret message in a box, and locks it with a padlock. The box is then transferred to Bob. Jan cannot open this box, since he doesn't have the key to the padlock.

2. Bob adds a new padlock to Alice box; now there are two padlocks. Bob returns the box to Alice. Once again, Jan can't open the box.

3. Alice receives the box with two padlocks; she removes her own padlock and sends the box back to Bob.

4. Bob is the only person with the key to the remaining padlock, which makes him the only person who can access its content.

This method allowed the transfer of a message without Alice or Bob having copies of one another's keys. The method is simple, and has been known for a long time. But if we apply this technique to mathematical encryption algorithms, we will have a problem: Alice encrypts the message with her secret key, and sends the result to Bob. He encrypts the already encrypted message with his secret key, and passes it back to Alice. Here's where the problem arises: Alice can't remove her encryption, since Bob's encryption locks her out. This prohibits us from using this method in the computer world.

An Asymmetric Encryption Method That Works for Computers

What Diffie and Hellmand discovered was a new method that also worked with mathematical algorithms. The solution was to create an encryption key consisting of two parts: one private and one public. The private part should be guarded carefully—only you should know about your private key. However, the public part could be freely distributed to everyone. Mathematically, you could check to see if a private key matched a public key; the probability of finding another private key matching your public key is extremely low, to the point of not existing. From a given public key, it's impossible to find out the matching private key.

Let's look at an example where Alice and Bob use the asymmetric method to send an encrypted message. Note that this is just the basic principle; later in this section, you will see exactly how it works:

1. Alice wants to send an encrypted message to Bob, using this new asymmetric method. Before she can start, she needs to obtain Bob's public key; she sends an email to Bob, asking him to return his public key.
2. Bob returns his public key. But Jan somehow manages to get a copy of this email; he now also knows Bob's public key. Is this a problem? No—in fact, Bob wants the world to know about his public key; you will soon understand why.
3. Alice now has Bob's public key. She encrypts the message using Bob's public key with an asymmetric encryption method. The result is now transferred as a standard email to Bob. Once again, Jan gets a copy of this message too.
4. Bob (and Jan) have received the encrypted message. But (now comes the trick) only Bob will be able to decrypt the message, since he is the only one that has access to the private key that matches the public key Alice used. Jan doesn't have it, and therefore can't decrypt it.

All this is based on the mathematical area called modulus functions, and the level of security is dependent on how long the key is. Instead of trying to find the correct secret key, an attacker could try a brute force attack, trying every available combination. For example, a key consisting of four binary digits has 2^4, or 16 combinations; a key with five binary digits has 2^5, or 32 combinations, and so on. A common key length is 128 bits, which gives us 2^{128}, or 10^{38} combinations, a number consisting of 39 figures. If you had a really fast computer and tried every combination, it would still take too long to find the correct key. We can assume that the speed of our computers continues to increase every year; Table 14.1 estimates the time it would take to crack the key using a brute-force attack for different key lengths, with respect to the development in computer technology, using state-of-the-art decryption hardware.

Table 14.1 Brute-force attack using specially designed decryption hardware.

Year	40 Bits	56 Bits	64 Bits	80 Bits	112 Bits	128 Bits
1995	.2 sec	3.6 hrs	38 days	7,000 yrs	10^{13} yrs	10^{18} yrs
2000	.02 sec	21 min	4 days	700 yrs	10^{12} yrs	10^{17} yrs
2005	2 ms	2 min	9 hrs	70 yrs	10^{11} yrs	10^{16} yrs
2010	.2 ms	13 sec	1 hr	7 yrs	10^{10} yrs	10^{15} yrs
2015	.02 ms	1 sec	5.5 min	251 days	10^{9} yrs	10^{14} yrs
2020	2 mcs	.1 sec	31 sec	25 days	10^{8} yrs	10^{13} yrs
2025	.2 mcs	.01 sec	3 sec	2.5 days	10^{7} yrs	10^{12} yrs
2030	.02 mcs	1 ms	.3 sec	6 hrs	10^{6} yrs	10^{11} yrs

The figures mentioned in Table 14.1 may scare you since they are surprisingly short, at least for any key length less than 128 bits. If we instead perform a brute-force attack using commercially available computer systems we will get completely different figures. For example, if we buy the fastest computer we can get for about $1 million U.S., the time to crack the same encryptions would look like this; see Table 14.2.

Again, these times are estimates when using the fastest commercially available computers; using standard personal computer equipment will take at least 10 times longer. This means that a 40-bit encryption key will only take about half an hour to crack today, using standard computers! It's not long, so if possible, you should upgrade to 128-bit key lengths which will make it impossible even for special security organizations like the National Security Agency (NSA) in the United States and similar organizations around the world that have access to specialized decryption equipment. The asymmetric encryption algorithms that are common in the PC world today are developed in the United States, which places them under the control of U.S. export regulations. Until recently, the U.S. government only allowed 40-bit keys outside the United States. This means that the NSA and similar organizations could decrypt messages using 40-bit encryption keys almost in realtime.

Table 14.2 Brute-force attacks using a million-dollar commercial computer system.

Year	40 Bits	56 Bits	64 Bits	80 Bits	112 Bits	128 Bits
1995	33 min	3 yrs	1,000 yrs	10^{7} yrs	10^{17} yrs	10^{22} yrs
2000	3.3 min	225 days	100 yrs	10^{6} yrs	10^{16} yrs	10^{21} yrs
2005	20 sec	15 days	10 yrs	700,000 yrs	10^{15} yrs	10^{20} yrs
2010	2 sec	1.5 days	1 yr	70,000 yrs	10^{14} yrs	10^{19} yrs
2015	.2 sec	3.6 hrs	38 days	7,000 yrs	10^{13} yrs	10^{18} yrs
2020	.02 sec	21 min	4 days	700 yrs	10^{12} yrs	10^{17} yrs
2025	2 ms	2 min	9 hrs	70 yrs	10^{11} yrs	10^{16} yrs
2030	.2 ms	13.sek	1 hr	7 yrs	10^{10} yrs	10^{15} yrs

This export regulation has now eased, and many European countries are now allowed to use 128-bit keys, but many organizations still use 40-bit encryption. By upgrading the security to use 128-bit keys, we find that it would take the NSA between 10^{16} to 10^{17} years (see Table 14.1) to crack such a message using brute-force, and that is longer than the universe has existed.

The Encryption Algorithms

A brute-force attack is not possible if you don't know what encryption algorithm has been used. Still, most algorithms are published. Why? Because before an organization selects to use a particular algorithm, they must know it's secure. If a company claims they have found the unbreakable algorithm, there is no need to keep it a secret; when they do insist on keeping it a secret, there must be something fishy about it. For example, if a national security organization releases an encryption algorithm to the public, but refuses to reveal its working details, many would suspect that this security organization has a back door implemented in this algorithm, making them able to decrypt messages without the need to use brute-force methods.

When talking about encryption algorithms, we must differentiate between symmetric and asymmetric algorithms: A symmetric algorithm works only if both parties use the same encryption key; an asymmetric algorithm uses one public key to encrypt a message, and another key (the corresponding private key) to decrypt it.

Symmetric Encryption Algorithms

This type of encryption is the old type; both parties must use the same key. We have a number of publicly available encryption algorithms that we can use when encrypting email messages:

- *Data Encryption Standard (DES)*—This is an international standard encryption method, developed by IBM, and released to the world as a nonexclusive, royalty-free license; the National Bureau of Standards (NBS) proposed it as a standard. Outside military organizations, this is the most widely used encryption algorithm, although it was met with suspicion when it was first released, due to the fact that the NSA was involved in the evaluation of this algorithm, and that IBM refused to explain certain parts of the algorithm (like the S-boxes). The key length used for DES encryption was set to 56 bits (although the original algorithm used 128 bits), making it an easy target for specially designed brute-force encryption hardware (like the NSA has); however, using an extremely fast standard computer, it will take at least three months to break it.

- *Triple-DES, a variant of DES*—The message will be encrypted three times, one after the other; every encryption will also use a different 56-bit key to make this encryption algorithm very secure. However, it's half as fast as DES.

- *International Data Encryption Algorithm (IDEA)*—Invented in 1991 by James Massey and Xuejia Lai of ETH Zurich, in Switzerland. This algorithm is faster than DES, and has a longer encryption key than the Triple-DES three keys combined. In February 2001,

RFC 3058 was released, which described how to use IDEA in S/MIME for encryption of SMTP messages.

- *RC2, RC4, and RC5: Rivest Cipher (or Ron's Code)*—A very fast encryption algorithm; it has support for key lengths between 40 and 256 bits—for example, RC4-40 (40 bits). Ron Rivest, a cryptographer at MIT, developed these algorithms. He was also one of the founders of the security company RSA Data Security Inc. (together with Adi Shamir and Leonard Adleman). From the beginning, these algorithms were trade secrets, but today you can find the source code for an RC4-emulating encryption algorithm on the Internet. The RC4 algorithm is used in many applications, such as Netscape and Internet Explorer, and email applications such as Exchange.
- *Blowfish*—This algorithm was designed by Bruce Schneier, a cryptologist of the highest quality (and also the founder of Counterpane Security). It has support for key lengths up to 448 bits, and is used in several applications, such as PGPfone and Nautilus.

Besides these symmetrical algorithms, there are several others, like Red Pike, CAST, and more. What you should consider before selecting a particular algorithm is that this algorithm is well known and has been in use for at least a few years. Many new algorithms are invented all the time, but after a while, someone discovers weaknesses and then the particular algorithm dies.

Asymmetric Encryption Algorithms

The asymmetric public-key encryption technique that Diffie and Hellman developed required new types of encryption algorithms; it was not possible to use DES or any other symmetric algorithm. Some of the most commonly used asymmetric algorithms are:

- *Rivest, Shamir, and Adleman (RSA)*—RSA Data Security Inc. is the company that developed the first working version of the asymmetrical public-key encryption. Key lengths used with this algorithm start with 512 bits; however, it's recommended to use 2,048-bit keys, whenever possible.
- *Diffie-Hellman Key Agreement Method*—Developed by Diffie and Hellman, the two researchers who developed the theory behind asymmetric encryption. This algorithm is also described in RCF 2136.
- *Digital Signature Algorithm (DSA)*—This is also the underlying algorithm for Digital Signature Standard (DSS), which is endorsed by the U.S. government. These are widely used and accepted as good algorithms.

Besides these asymmetric encryption algorithms, we have a special class of algorithms used for calculating a checksum on a message:

- *Secure Hash Algorithm (SHA)* also known as *Secure Hash Standard (SHS)*—This is a cryptographic hash algorithm published by the U.S. government. It produces a 160-bit hash value from an arbitrary length string.
- *Message Digest Algorithm 5 (MD5)*—This is a hash algorithm developed by RSA Data. It produces a 128-bit hash value from an arbitrary length string.

How Encryption Is Used in Reality

So now we have two types of algorithms, symmetric and asymmetric. And we also have the hash algorithms. A relevant question now is why do we need all these types? The answer is that they all solve different problems. In the previous examples, I raised the asymmetric algorithms to the sky, since they gave us the possibility to encrypt information without the need to distribute secret keys first. But the truth is that we still need the symmetric algorithms. Below is a summary of the different features of these three types of algorithms:

- *Symmetric algorithms*—Are very fast; they encrypt large messages (including their attachments) in just a few seconds. The result (also known as *ciphertext*) is just slightly larger than the original plain-text message. The drawback is that both the sender and the recipient must have access to the same encryption key.
- *Asymmetric algorithms*—Are much slower, and the resulting ciphertext is much larger than the original plain text. But its advantage over symmetric algorithms is that it doesn't require a shared secret.
- *Hash algorithm*—Has a special use; it's excellent when you want to make sure that no one has tampered or changed anything in a message. This type of algorithm calculates a sort of checksum on the message; this hash value will always have the same number of bits, regardless of how small or large the message is. For example, using the MD5 hash, the result is always a 128-bit value.

So in reality, we are using all three of these types of algorithms, dependent on what we are doing. To help us understand how they really work, we'll look at an example:

1. Alice wants to send an encrypted email message to Bob, using her MS Outlook client (which is configured for secure email).
2. Alice retrieves Bob's public encryption key by downloading it from the Internet.
3. Her Outlook client now generates a random symmetric encryption key; let's call this SEK.
4. This symmetric encryption key is used to encrypt the message to Bob, using a symmetric algorithm such as DES. (So far we are using the same methods as Enigma.)
5. Next, Alice's Outlook encrypts the SEK, using Bob's public key and an asymmetric algorithm, such as RSA. At this stage, Alice has two encrypted parts—the message and the SEK that was used to encrypt this message.
6. Outlook creates an email containing the ciphertext and the encrypted SEK; this email is now sent over the Internet to Bob.

This message might be captured by Jan or anyone else, including security organizations. The information is protected by the encryption algorithms; however, this protection is only as good as the algorithms, and they are dependent on the key length used!

7. Bob now receives this message from Alice. His Outlook client is also configured for secure email. As long as Bob doesn't try to open this message, nothing more happens.
8. Bob opens the message; this is a signal to Outlook to decrypt the SEK. This can only be done if a.) he has access to his *private* key, and b.) Outlook knows which asymmetric algorithm has been used. In this example, we assume that Bob has his private key stored in a local file, protected by a password. The algorithm Alice used will be listed in the clear text part of the message. So Bob has everything he needs; he is first requested to type in the password to unlock his private key, and then Outlook will decrypt the SEK.
9. Since Bob's Outlook now has access to the SEK, it will use this key to decrypt the actual message from Alice. Finally Bob can read the message.

As you can see from this example, the asymmetric algorithm is only used to encrypt the symmetric encryption key (SEK). The reason for not using the same algorithm to encrypt the actual message is the drawbacks that asymmetric encryption algorithms have when used on large messages; however, since the SEK is so small, typically 128 bits, using this type of encryption won't pose any problems. This means that symmetric encryption is still used to encrypt the actual message and its file attachments, so in reality, we are using both symmetric and asymmetric encryption. This is an elegant solution to the problem of sending encrypted information without the need to first distribute secret keys, don't you think?

Electronic Signing of Messages

It's not only encryption that is sometimes necessary when we send messages; an equally important question is how to prove that the sender is actually the one he or she claims to be. Do you remember the spoofing example earlier in this chapter where we sent a message claiming to be from George Bush? It illustrated the weakness in email communication; we can never be sure who the sender of a message really is. However, once again, asymmetric algorithms come to our aid. They work similarly to encryption, but we use the public and private keys the other way around, like this:

1. Alice wants to send a message to Bob, and she wants to prove her authenticity.
2. She (or her Outlook client, really) calculates a *hash* value for her message to Bob, using a hash algorithm, such as MD5. This hash value is very similar to a checksum, typically 128 bits long.
3. Next, her Outlook now encrypts this hash value using an asymmetric encryption algorithm, such as RSA, and her *private* key.
4. Outlook creates a new message consisting of the actual message, information about what algorithms have been used, and the encrypted hash. This is called a *signed message*; it's then sent to Bob.
5. Bob receives Alice message; his client notices that this is a signed message and starts the process of evaluating the signature.

6. His client first calculates a hash code on the actual message, using the same hash algorithm that Alice used.
7. Next, Alice's *public* key is retrieved; in this example, we assume that Bob has received it before.
8. Using Alice's public key and the same asymmetric algorithm that she used, his client is now able to decrypt Alice's hash value.
9. Bob's client compares the two hash values; if they are equal, then it must have been Alice who sent this message. No other person has access to her private key. He can also be sure that no one has modified the message after it left Alice's client.

As you can see, once again we are using two types of algorithms: first the hash algorithm, and then the same type of asymmetric encryption algorithm we used before. Of course, there are a number of presumptions before this electronic signing of messages can really be trusted. For example:

- *Only Alice should have access to her private key*—Typically, this key is stored in a password-protected file on Alice's computer; she will unlock it by typing her password *every time* she signs a message. If someone gets a hold of this password, then we can't trust this signature.
- *A hash value must be one-way*—In other words, it must be impossible to use a hash for calculating the original message. MD5 and SHA/SHS are examples of one-way hash algorithms.
- *The probability that two messages generate the same hash must be almost zero*—This is important; if this isn't true, then a fake sender could capture the message during its transport, modify the message still using the same hash, and then send the message to Bob. He would then not be able detect that the message had been changed. This is the responsibility of the hash algorithm; the two mentioned, MD5 and SHA/SHS, are generally accepted as good hash algorithms.
- *Bob must be able to trust Alice's public key*—Otherwise, a fake sender could give Bob a fake public key that seems to belong to Alice. Then this fake sender could send any number of signed messages to Bob, and they all would look authentic.

Maybe the biggest problem is how to create public-private key pairs that we can trust. This is described in the next section.

Certificates

If we think about the last bullet above, what is stopping us from creating our own private and public keys? Well, nothing really. The email world simply can't trust just any key pairs; they must be proved somehow. This is actually the same problem as in the real world; for example, how do you prove that your drivers license is authentic? A number of steps have been taken to make the license trustworthy—it has your picture on it and it has your signature. A police officer can compare the picture and your signature to see if they match.

The actual drivers license is made in a special way that is very hard to tamper with or to replicate. And the police officer can also see what authority has given you the license. For example, if I use my Swedish drivers license in the United States and a police officer stops me, he must judge if he can trust the Swedish authority (they usually do!). But let's say that instead I show a driver's license authorized by some authority in a corrupt banana republic, will he still believe it's authentic? You get the idea.

In the computer world, we also have a sort of drivers license where our public key is listed, together with our name, email address, and more (see the bulleted list below). This is called a *certificate*. There have been a number of different types of certificates over the years, but the standard that is most commonly used today is the *X.509 Certificate*, developed by the OSI standard commitment (the same group that gave us X.400 and X.500, if you remember); see Figure 14.10.

An X.509 certificate usually contains the following information:

- The name of the person
- The person's email address
- The DNS name to the directory this email address belongs to
- The dates between which the certificate is valid
- The public key for this person
- The authority that guarantees that this certificate is authentic

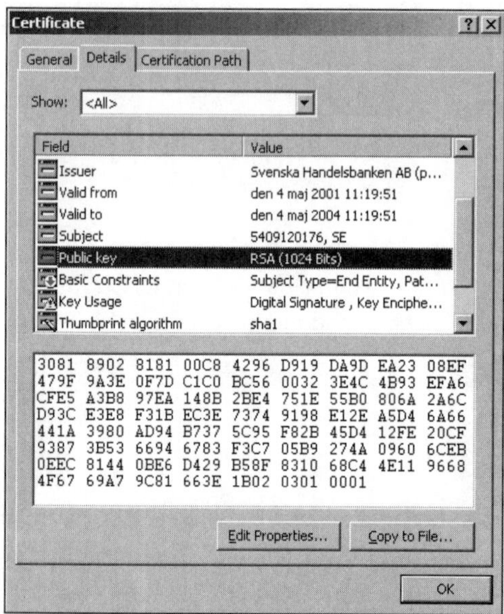

Figure 14.10
Example of an X.509 certificate.

- A serial number that is unique to each X.509 authority
- The electronic signature of certification authority
- The location of the revocation list, which would indicate whether the certificate has been revoked

So the X.509 certificate says something like this: "The person *Frida Holmberg* has the email address **Frida@hotmail.com**; her public key is: ***<09234 034...>***. This certificate is valid until the *1 of June 2002*. If you need to check if this certificate has been revoked, follow this URL link. We, VeriSign, guarantee that this information is correct."

Are you still with me? I know I've given you a lot of theoretical information so far, but we are almost done now. The final question is: Who are these certification authorities? The answer is not completely satisfying—it could be you! Anyone could install the MS Certificate Server program that comes with Windows 2000 and start generating genuine X.509 certificates. That brings us back to the police officer who had to decide whether to trust my drivers license. Now it's up to you to judge whether an X.509 certificate is trustworthy. But in reality, it's not as hard as it might seem.

For example, let's say that your company wants to create X.509 certificates for all its employees; these certificates will be used for signing emails sent within the company. The company installs the MS Certificate Server (MSCS) and configures themselves as the Root Certificate Authority (Root CA). This means that they alone have divine power to create whatever X.509 certificate they need; but on all these certificates, the name of this CA will be listed. If Alice wants to send a signed message to Bob, and they both work for this company, she will do what we described before; the only difference is that her X.509 certificates will be sent along with the signed message. Since this certificate also contains her public key, Bob doesn't have to retrieve that public key elsewhere as long as he trusts the CA that created Alice certificate; Bob knows this CA, so he trusts it and accepts Alice certificate and public key; everyone is happy.

Another example: Wanda sends a signed message to me; we don't work for the same company, and I have never met her before. Can I trust her X.509 certificate? Here my Outlook tries to help. When you install the Outlook client, it will have a number of preinstalled CAs that it trusts, such as:

- Baltimore Ez by DST
- C&W HKT SecureNet
- Certisign
- Deutsche Telecom
- Entrust
- VeriSign
- Microsoft

If Wanda's certificate is generated by one of these CAs, my Outlook client will automatically trust her certificate. But if it's not, I will get a warning, similar to the one you see in Figure 14.11.

However, this is just a warning. If you judge that the CA is trustworthy, you can still open the message by clicking the *View Message* button. If you want to know more about this CA, click the *Details* button and you will see something similar to Figure 14.12, where it clearly states that "This certificate cannot be verified up to a trusted certification authority." This means that this CA (or **www.tenfour.net**) is not known and that no other CA can certify that this CA is trustworthy.

Remember that trust here is very relative; it's dependent on the CA that has been added to your Outlook client. If you judge that you can trust a CA that is unknown to Outlook, this is perfectly okay. To add a new CA, click the *Edit Trust* button shown in Figure 14.11 and you can make Outlook explicitly trust all certificates generated by this CA in the future; see Figure 14.13.

Figure 14.11
A warning that this CA is unknown to Outlook.

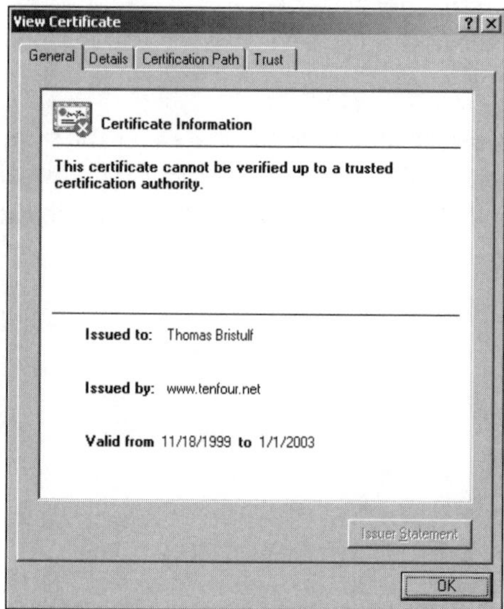

Figure 14.12
Details about the untrusted CA.

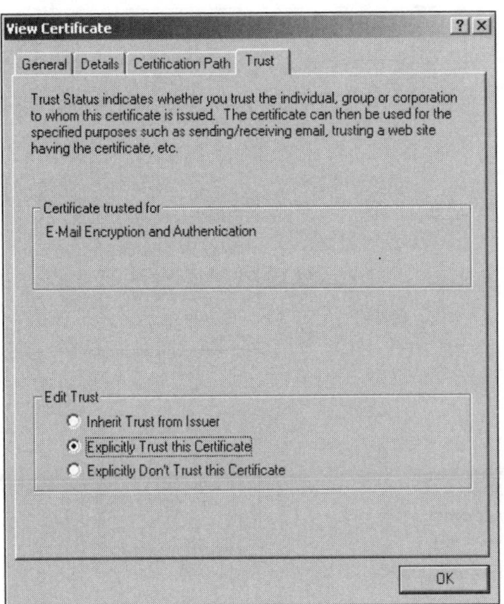

Figure 14.13
Add this CA to your list of explicitly trusted CAs in Outlook.

14

Next time you open the same message, or any other message signed with certificates from this CA, you will not receive any warnings. Of course, it's much easier if all Outlook clients on the Internet recognize the CA—then they don't have to manually add them. This is the reason why many organizations select to purchase X.509 client certificates, instead of creating them with their own certificate server; it's simply more convenient. While we are still on this subject, yes, it's possible to get your own CA to be certified by a more well-known CA, such as VeriSign; this is expensive, but now all your "homemade" certificates will indirectly be signed by VeriSign. This will make all clients accept these certificates without questioning the CA. Contact your favorite CA to get more information about the procedures and prices.

Sending Encrypted and Signed Email Messages

We conclude this section about general email security by describing how a message can be both encrypted and signed, using X.509 certificates. Note that it's perfectly okay to send a message that is only encrypted, or only signed, or both. Remember that if you send a message that is only signed, it will not be encrypted. Jan (our unpleasant villain) could still read these messages, although he could not modify them in any way without invalidating the signature. So if we want to be really sure, we should both encrypt the message and sign it, thus making the intended recipient the only person who can read our message and be sure where it came from. This is how a message is treated when both encrypted and signed; in this example, we assume that Alice obtained Bob's X.509 certificate earlier (maybe by mail from him, or maybe from a key distribution server on the Internet); see also Decision Tree 14.2:

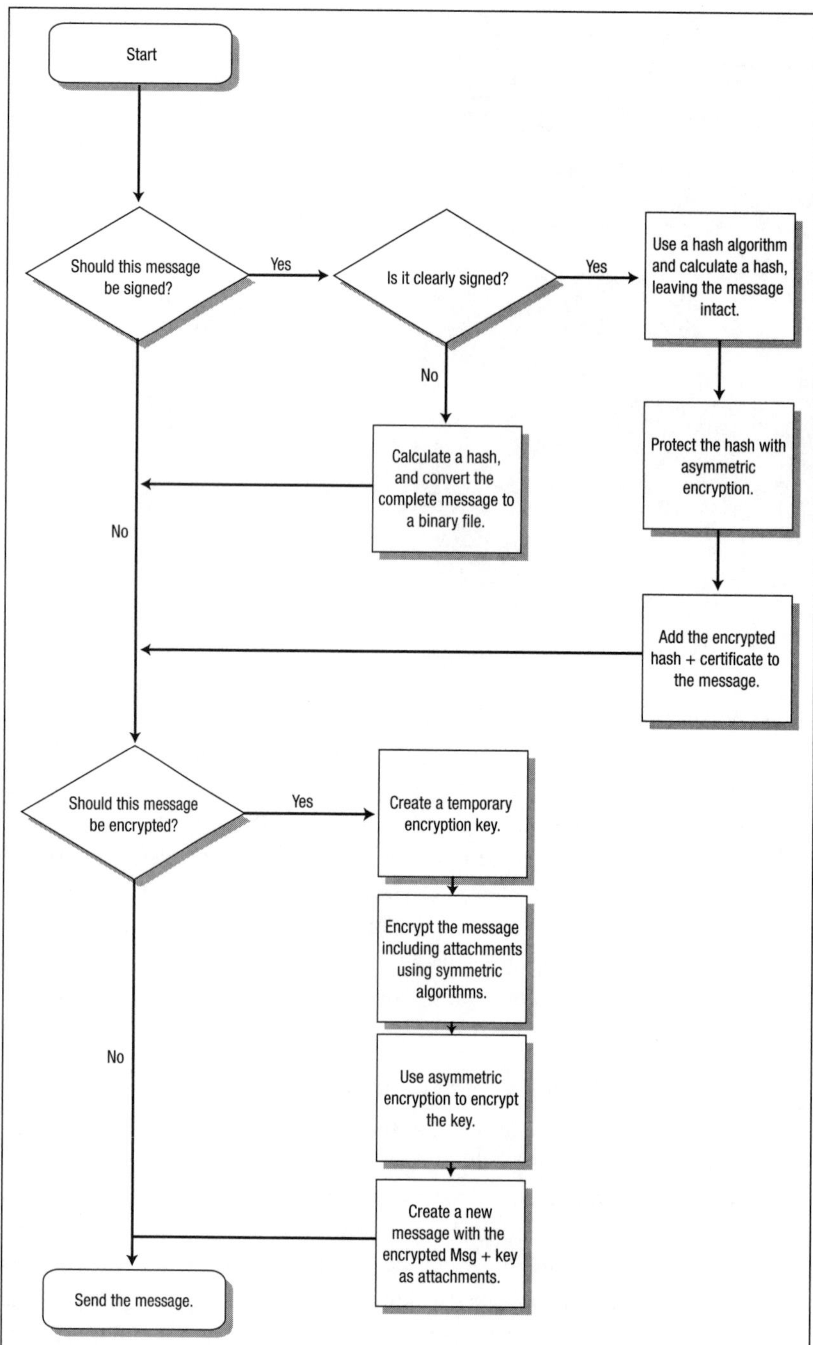

Decision Tree 14.2
How a message is signed and encrypted.

1. Alice wants to send an encrypted and signed message to Bob. Her Outlook must first calculate a hash for her message, using a hash algorithm (such as MD5).

2. She then signs this hash, by encrypting it with an asymmetric algorithm (such as RSA), using her private key (she has to type in a password to unlock this key).

3. Then her Outlook creates a new message, consisting of the original message, the signed hash, and Alice's X.509 certificate (containing her public key).

   We now have a signed message; the next step is to encrypt the message.

4. Next, Alice's client generates a random encryption symmetric key (the SEK). Using a symmetric algorithm (such as DES) and the SEK, Alice encrypts the signed message.

5. Alice now encrypts the SEK, using an asymmetric algorithm (such as RSA) and Bob's public key (found in his certificate).

6. A new message is created and is sent over to Bob that consists of the encrypted message (the ciphertext) plus the encrypted SEK.

That was Alice's part. Now it's time for Bob to restore the message and recalculate the hash to see if the sender is really who she claims to be:

7. Bob receives the message; his Outlook extracts the encrypted SEK, and by using his private key (again, it's password-protected) and the same RSA algorithm, he is able to decrypt the SEK.

8. Using the SEK and the DES algorithm, Bob can now decrypt the ciphertext; now he has the signed message, including its encrypted hash and Alice's certificate.

9. Bob separates the actual message from the hash; he then calculates his own hash for this message, using the same MD5 algorithm that Alice did.

10. Using Alice's public key (found in her certificate) and the RSA algorithm, Bob is able to decrypt Alice's hash value.

11. Bob compares his own calculated hash with Alice's hash value; if they are equal, the message must be genuine. If not, Bob cannot trust this message.

As you can see from this process, this involves a lot of steps. Lucky for us, we don't have to perform this procedure manually; our Outlook client does it for us. In the following sections, we will look into two of the most popular types of client-based security standards that are used today, S/MIME and PGP.

Secure Mime (S/MIME)

Secure MIME (S/MIME) is a security extension to the basic *Multipurpose Internet Mail Extensions (MIME)* standard. It's not a separate program that you run for secure email; instead, it's an add-on to standard email clients, such as Outlook 2002, that makes these clients able to send and receive encrypted and signed messages. You may recall from Chapter 4 that MIME has defined a number of content types, such as Text, Word, and Excel, which help the receiving mail system understand how to treat these types of contents. What S/MIME does is to add new content types that are used when sending secure email messages:

- Application/pkcs7-mime
- Multipart/signed
- Application/pkcs7-signature

When sending an encrypted or signed message, these parts are added as attachments to the message; if the content is Application/pkcs7-mime, the attached file type is .p7m, and content type Application/pkcs7-signature is attached as .p7s files. These special file types signal to the receiving mail system that this is a S/MIME message and should be treated accordingly.

S/MIME-Compliant Clients

As you may remember from Chapter 4, the keyword *Application* means that the receiving system (both the server and the receiving client) must use an application to process this type of content, before it can be presented to the recipient. This means that not all email clients understand how to use S/MIME; they simply don't have the application necessary to process these types of S/MIME contents. Listed here are some of the clients that are able to handle S/MIME content:

- Outlook 98
- Outlook 2000 and 2002
- Outlook Express 5.*x*
- Netscape Messenger 4

In the Exchange 2000 environment, just like previous Exchange versions, it's possible to use the Key Management Server (KMS) for enrolling users for email security; this will be described in detail later in this chapter. As you will see, the KMS system makes it very easy to handle certificates, enrollments, and recovery of certificates. But it's also important to know that you don't need the KMS system to make the Outlook client able to use S/MIME for encryption and signing; you don't even have to use the MS Certificate Server for generating certificates. It's perfectly okay to configure each Outlook client to use S/MIME with certificates acquired from third parties such as VeriSign or Entrust. In fact, if just a few clients in your organization need the ability to encrypt and sign email messages, it's probably easier to configure these Outlook clients separately, instead of installing the KMS server. However, from the information received in this chapter, you should really be concerned about the lack of security on the Internet; I strongly suggest that you look at the possibility of enrolling all your users for S/MIME security using KMS. Even if they don't need it today, they will probably need it tomorrow!

Outlook 2000 SR1 Tips

As with most other protocols, even S/MIME has different versions. The latest version is 3, which is described in RFC 2633. Outlook 2000 with Service Release 1 (SR1) and Outlook 2002 support S/MIME V3. However, Outlook 2000 SR1 will not display its new features, unless you request it by adding a new entry called *EnableSRFeatures* in the Registry. Before this entry can be added, you must first create a new key called *Security*:

```
Hkey_Local_machine\Software\Microsoft\Office\9.0\Outlook
Add Key: Security
```

Then add the new entry in this Security key (see also Figure 14.14):

```
Hkey_Local_machine\Software\Microsoft\Office\9.0\Outlook\Security
type: DWORD
name: EnableSRFeatures
value: 1 = display; 0 = hidden
```


This new Security key can be used to control several security settings—for example, to hide warnings about invalid signatures, to accept certificates only from a given CA, and to force all outgoing messages to be encrypted (AlwaysEncrypt = 1) and/or signed (AlwaysSign = 1). You can find more information about this in the *MS Office 2000 Resource Kit* and *MS Outlook 2000 Service Release 1 White Paper* on the MS TechNet CD or on the Web at **www.Microsoft.com/office/ork/xp** for Outlook 2002 and **www.Microsoft.com/office/ork/2000** for Outlook 2000.

Clear and Opaque Signing

From the previous section about encryption and signing, you learned that the sender of a piece of mail could sign the message by calculating a hash value on the message, which

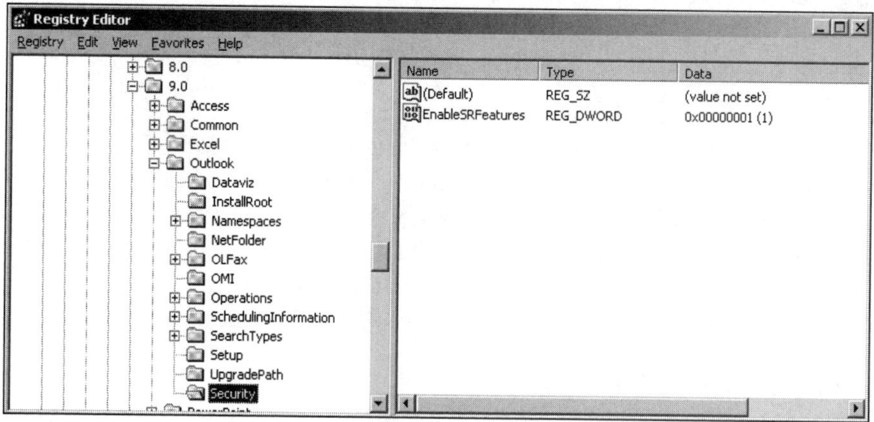

Figure 14.14
Enabling the new SR1 security features in Outlook 2000 SR1.

then was encrypted by an asymmetric algorithm using the sender's private key. However, two types of signing exist, *Clear* signing and *Opaque* signing; the differences between these two types are described here:

- *Clear signing*—The message and any attachments will still be in their native format after signing the message; the encrypted hash value is added as an extra attachment. A clear signed message can be read by the recipient, even if their client doesn't understand S/MIME.
- *Opaque signing*—The message, including any attachments, will be combined with the encrypted hash value to a binary file. If the recipient doesn't have an S/MIME-compliant client, he or she will only see this message as an SMIME.P7M file.

In Outlook 98 and later, it is possible to set the type of signing on a per-message basis; if you will send a signed message outside the organization, and you don't know what type of client your recipient uses, select *Send Clear Text Signed Message* when signing the message. By default, Outlook uses opaque signing. The OWA client cannot display opaque signed messages—they will appear blank; however, clear signed messages are visible, although there is no support in OWA-2000 to check if the signature is valid. The same is also true for encrypted messages; OWA will display them as blank messages, since it cannot decrypt messages.

S/MIME and Certificates

The S/MIME standard is just one of several methods, such as PGP and PEM, for securing email traffic, both for encryption and signing. One thing that differentiates S/MIME from the other methods is how this standard expects the certificates to be treated. In S/MIME, all certificates are generated by a CA, as described earlier; we may have a hierarchy of CAs, where one *root CA* certifies the *sub-CA*. The only entity that can create or revoke a certificate is the CA. This means that the administrator that controls the CA application has great power; but some people don't like the idea that one CA should be able to control these certificates—they want more personal control over whose certificates to trust. These people often choose PGP or PEM instead of S/MIME.

However, companies and larger organizations that have contact with lots of people, such as customers and suppliers, accept the certificate idea behind S/MIME. Many (but not all!) of them would even like to have a government-controlled CA, instead of a commercial CA; they argue that we don't have any idea what happens with our certificates inside these commercial CAs and question whether we should trust their employees unconditionally. But others use exactly the same arguments as the reasons why we should not let the government control a CA. I guess that whatever the outcome, many people will not like it.

Recovering Certificates

Every user needs a personal certificate for securing email conversations. But one certificate is enough for both encryption and signing. However, when using the *KMS* for assigning certificates to our Exchange clients, all users will in fact get two certificates, one for encryption and one for signing. The reason for this is the need to open encrypted messages in special situations. For example, assume that your organization has used S/MIME security for a while, but you are not running Exchange. So all users have one certificate only; one user tells you that he has lost his secret password for his private key. The problems he will encounter include:

- Old encrypted messages can't be opened anymore
- New encrypted messages can't be opened
- He can't send any signed messages

However, he can still open all signed messages that he receives. Now assume your CA allows a certificate to be recovered. Fine—you recover this particular user's certificate, he selects a new password for it, and everyone is happy, right? Not really! The whole idea behind the signing process is that one and only one person in the world should be able to sign this user's outgoing messages (also known as *nonrepudiation of message origin*); otherwise, the recipients can't be absolutely sure who the sender is, don't you agree? But if an administrator can recover the certificate, he could also do this in order to get a copy of this user's certificate, thereby being able to send signed messages in his name. Clearly, this is not acceptable.

This dilemma is often solved by not allowing recovery of certificates. But this means that every time a user forgets a password (and we all know how often this happens, right?), we have to create a new certificate; that means this user cannot open previous encrypted messages, plus he must now distribute his new certificate with the new public key to everyone who wants to send encrypted messages to him.

Microsoft's solution is more elegant: give the user two certificates, one for encryption and one for signing. By making sure that only the certificate for encryption can be recovered, we solve the dilemma of non-repudiation versus recovery; if the certificate for signing is lost, we will simply generate a new one. The consequence of this strategy is:

- By recovering the certificate for encryption, the user will still be able to view his previously received encrypted messages, including any new encrypted messages.
- We will not compromise the concept of non-repudiation since the certificate for signing cannot be recovered.
- If the user loses his signing certificate, we can create a new one (not recover it). This will not affect his ability to read or send encrypted messages, since that operation requires a separate certificate that has not been replaced.

If we have an administrator who really wants to send a signed message in another person's name, he could create a new certificate for signing for this user; but in order to do that, he must revoke the old certificate first. This will soon be detected by the true owner of this certificate since it's now marked as invalid; this owner can also show that he is using another certificate, in case this should be needed in a court case.

Storing the Certificates

If someone can access your private encryption and signing keys, the security is gone. This makes it extremely important to protect these keys. In previous Exchange versions, these keys were stored in a password-protected .EPF file (a heritage from the Entrust code that KMS was built upon in previous Exchange versions). This made it hard to support growing users, unless the user could access this file on all computers.

In Exchange 2000, the client's private keys are stored in different places, depending on the type of client:

- *Outlook 97 and the Exchange client*—Stored in an encrypted .EPF file, as in previous Exchange versions.
- *Outlook 98*—Stored in the client's Protected Store, an encrypted database stored on the local computer.
- *Outlook 2000 and 2002*—Stored in an encrypted part of the Registry. This makes it possible to support growing users, by configuring roaming profiles.

The public keys are always stored in the Active Directory, regardless of client type. A copy of the user's private encryption keys (in order to be able to recover these keys) are stored on the Exchange server's Protected Store, a highly secured database, based on Microsoft's CryptoAPI architecture for Windows 2000.

PGP

Besides the S/MIME standard, another system called *Pretty Good Privacy (PGP)* is commonly used for email security. PGP is not a standard; it's a security product that can be attached to email clients like Outlook. PGP was first released in June 1991 by its developer Philip Zimmermann, who wanted to create an email security system that was free of charge for everyone. The first version of PGP used the RSA algorithms without permissions from RSA Data Security Inc., but later versions have licensed the algorithm. Although Zimmermann created the first release, a lot of people have taken part in the subsequent releases. To avoid export restrictions, PGP 2 was developed outside the United States, which made it possible for non-U.S. organizations to use longer encryption keys than 40 bits. Because it was one of the first free email security products with really strong encryption, it became very popular in the computer world, especially with nonprofit organizations, smaller companies, and private persons. Today, even large companies use PGP, although many have switched to S/MIME because it's a standard.

Microsoft doesn't provide any direct support for PGP in any of its products, but the developers of PGP has adapted it to many email clients, including Microsoft's. Today you can use PGP as a plug-in with clients such as:

- Outlook 97/98/2000
- Outlook Express 4.*x*/5.*x*

- Qualcomm Eudora 4.*x*
- Claris Emailer 2.*x*

Today, the *Massachusetts Institute of Technology (MIT)* has the patent for PGP; for more information about where to find PGP, you can go to their Web site at **web.mit.edu/network/pgp.html** and follow the many links listed there.

Security Features of PGP

The PGP product offers security features similar to what you can get with an S/MIME-configured Outlook client:

- Confidentiality
- Data origin authentication
- Message integrity
- Non-repudiation

With the PGP product, all of these features are automatically activated when sending messages; however, you can select what features to activate for outgoing messages. For example, you can send a PGP-protected message without providing confidentiality.

Confidentiality

This protects the contents of the message from unauthorized disclosure by encrypting the complete message including any attachments. This prohibits any third party from reading this information during its storage on the sender's local mailbox, when it's transported to the recipient's mailbox, and until the recipient opens the message.

Data Origin Authentication

This feature permits the authorized recipient of this message to check whether the sender is authentic. This is equal to signing in S/MIME; however, in PGP, it's only the authorized recipient that has this control, whereas in S/MIME, anyone can check the signature.

Message Integrity

This feature gives the authorized recipient of this message an assurance that the contents of this message have not been modified in any way during its transport. Again, only the authorized receiver will be able to get this information, not any eavesdropper who manages to intercept the message. This is comparable to the hash feature used when signing messages with S/MIME.

Non-repudiation

This is a feature that allows one person to forward a message to another person, who can then verify the identity of the original sender. For example, Jessica can send a message to Wanda, and Wanda can forward this message to Frida. The non-repudiation feature in PGP will allow Frida to verify that Jessica sent the original message to Wanda.

Key Handling in PGP

PGP doesn't use certificates the way S/MIME does; in fact, PGP doesn't use certificates at all. You may recall that the certificate in S/MIME was used to authenticate the public encryption and signing keys, and that all certificates were generated by a Certificate Authority. This is maybe the greatest difference between S/MIME and PGP. The basic idea in PGP is that people trust their friends; if you don't know someone, you don't trust him—a basic social concept. This is how PGP handles keys:

1. Jessica and Wanda are friends. They create their own key pair, one public and one private key, used for both signing and encryption.
2. Jessica signs Wanda's public key; and Wanda signs Jessica's.
3. Now a third person, Frida, wants to send email with PGP, so she creates her own public and private keys.
4. Frida is a friend of Jessica's, so she asks Jessica to sign her public key.
5. Frida sends a PGP-protected message to Wanda, a person she has not met.
6. Wanda receives the message from Frida, and since Frida's public key is signed by Jessica, whom Wanda trusts, she accepts Frida's message.

What happens if you receive a PGP-protected message from someone that you don't know, and no mutual friend has signed the key? You can still accept the message, even if you don't know this person. Again, this is like real life—you may meet someone at a conference that you don't know anything about, but you both decide to trust each other for secure email. PGP has support for more advanced sharing of keys, through rings of trusts, making it possible to trust people you have never met before, but this goes beyond the scope of this book; you can read more about PGP in *The Official PGP User's Guide*, by Phil Zimmermann (MIT Press, 1995).

Key handling in PGP is both its strength and its weakness, depending on whom you talk to. The problem is public key distribution to many people; for example, how can you make it possible for anyone outside your circle of friends to send PGP-protected messages to you, if they don't have your public key? One way is through *Public PGP Key Servers*; these are servers available on the Internet on which you can add your own public key, or search for others. One such server can be found on **pgpkeys.mit.edu:11371**.

Key Management Server

The KMS is an add-on to Exchange 2000; it's not a standalone product. Exchange has always had a KMS system, but not until Exchange 5.5 SP3 was it possible to use KMS with standard X.509 Version 3 S/MIME certificates; before that, KMS generated its own certificates, thereby making it impossible to send encrypted messages outside the Exchange organization. When using KMS in Exchange 2000, clients can communicate with any other party using S/MIME.

Note: *Both the sender and receiver of secure email must use the same type of security system; for example, it's not possible for a PGP client to exchange secure email with an S/MIME client!*

The KMS system works only for MAPI clients like Outlook 98 and 2002; you cannot use the KMS system for OWA or Internet clients such as POP3 and IMAP4. The KMS system also has its own administrators and passwords, due to the sensitivity of this type of system. When you install KMS the first time, the administrator account used during the installation will also be the first KMS administrator. You can then add and remove administrators as needed, although you should carefully limit the number of KMS administrators.

The KMS system has its own service: KMServer.exe, which you can find on the Processes tab using the Task Manager. You should not end this process by using the Task Manager; instead, use the Services applet in the Control Panel to start and stop the *Microsoft Exchange Key Management Services*. All KMS files are stored in their own directory: *Exchsrvr\KMSData*; the data is stored in an encrypted ESE database called *KMSMDB.EDB*. This version of KMS is protected by transaction logs, contrary to previous Exchange versions; each log file is 1MB, and there is also a checkpoint file and two reserved log files (1MB each), similar to a storage group protected by transaction logs.

KMS Features

KMS is an excellent add-on when you want to deploy email security to more than just a few Exchange users in the organization. It will give you the following benefits:

- Easy enrollment of users
- A secure way to distribute private and public keys
- The ability to use standard X.509 S/MIME certificates from any source
- The ability to integrate with the MS Certificate Server, available in Windows 2000 Server
- Easy recovery of encryption keys
- Easy revocation of keys
- Two key pairs, one for signing and one for encryption

The following sections provide more details about each feature; later in this chapter, you will find a set of step-by-step instructions that describe how to install and activate KMS and MS Certificate Server, plus how to enroll the clients.

Easy Enrollment of Users

With the KMS, you can use its management tool (which is integrated in ESM) to enroll Exchange 2000 users. You will receive a list of all users, to which you simply add the ones that should be able to use S/MIME, and select Enroll. However, no encryption or signing key pairs are generated until the Outlook client activates the secure email feature.

Secure Distribution of Private and Public Keys

When an Exchange user wants to configure his or her Outlook client for KMS-integrated S/MIME security, here's what happens (see Figure 14.15):

1. When an Outlook client activates her secure email features, a request is sent by email to the user's home Exchange server.
2. The home server passes on this request to the *Key Management Server*.
3. KMS checks to see if the administrator has enrolled this user; if not, an error message is returned to the user. If the user is enrolled, KMS then sends a request for two certificates for this user to the MS Certificate Server (MSCS).
4. The MSCS generates these signing and encryption certificates, and returns them to the KMS server.
5. The KMS server stores a copy of these certificates, plus the private encryption key (for recovery reasons) in its *Encrypted Store* on the Exchange server's directory: *\\Program Files\Exchsrvr\KMSData*. Copies of the public keys are also sent to the Active Directory, to make them globally available within this Exchange organization.
6. The KMS server creates an encrypted message using a temporary 12-character-long encryption key. This message contains the two certificates and the two key pairs; these are sent back to the user's home server.
7. The home server passes this encrypted message back to the client.
8. The client can decrypt this message only if she has the temporary 12-character encryption key. This key will be given to her by the KMS administrator that enrolled her.

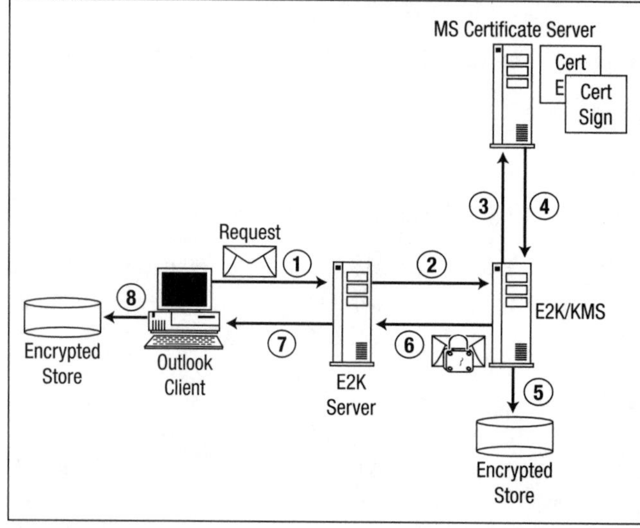

Figure 14.15
Activating secure email on Outlook.

When she opens this message, the certificates and key pairs are stored in the client (the exact location depends on the Outlook version, see the previous S/MIME section). The client is now ready for secure S/MIME communication.

Ability to Use Standard X.509 Certificates

With the KMS server in Exchange 2000, you can use any X.509 version 3 certificates; they don't have to be from the MS Certificate Server; see the next section.

Ability to Integrate with the MS Certificate Server

Instead of generating its own proprietary certificates as in previous KMS versions, KMS can now use standard X.509 version 3 certificates. You can select to purchase these certificates from a third party, such as VeriSign, or you can set up the MSCS and generate as many certificates as you will need. The KMS will automatically find the MSCS by searching the Active Directory. This last choice, to integrate with MSCS, is simple and easy, and you don't have to spend money on certificates. As you may recall from earlier sections in this chapter, a certificate made by your own CA will not be automatically accepted by external email clients outside your organization; they will receive a warning about an untrusted CA (but they can still use the S/MIME features). If you want to avoid these warnings, you could ask a third-party CA (such as VeriSign, Entrust, etc.) to authorize your CA; this will give your own certificates the same status as the third-party CA.

Easy Recovery of Encryption Keys

If a user loses his private encryption key, or forgets the password that unlocks it, the KMS administrator can generate a copy of this encryption key for the user. This is possible since the KMS has a copy of all users' private encryption keys (but not private signing keys) in its Encrypted Store.

If the user loses his private signing key, a new signing key pair, including certificate, must be generated. The reason for this is to make signing a non-repudiation operation; there must be only one single private signing key, and only the true owner of this key must be able to access it.

Easy Revocation of Keys

All certificates and keys have a limited life span, usually between one and two years. Sometimes you must revoke a certificate before this time period ends, for example, when a user leaves the company. The KMS management module (located in the ESM tool) makes this revocation operation very easy; simply point out the certificate to revoke, and click the Revoke button.

Two Key Pairs, One for Signing and One for Encryption

As mentioned several times, the KMS system will generate two keys pairs instead of one, as is customary. The reason for this is to make it possible to recover the private encryption key without compromising the non-repudiation concept. The private signing key cannot be recovered.

Installing MS Certificate Server

If you want to install the Key Management Server, it's highly probable that you want to use the MSCS that comes with Windows 2000 Server. KMS uses MSCS to generate certificates for each Exchange user. It's important that you select the right server for this MSCS; after the installation, you can't rename this server or move it to another domain.

Requirements for Installing the MSCS

You will need a Windows 2000 Server CD (not necessarily the same one that you used to install Windows 2000) for this; after the installation, there is no need to restart the server (thank you, Microsoft!). You can install MSCS on the same computer as the KMS server, or on a separate Windows 2000 server. If you have upgraded an NT 4 server with MSCS 1 to Windows 2000, you can also upgrade MSCS 1 to the new version that comes with Windows 2000 server.

Step-by-Step Instructions for Installing MSCS

Follow these steps to install MSCS and configure it for later use with KMS:

1. Start the *Control Panel* and select the applet *Add/Remove Programs*, then select *Add/ Remove Windows Components*; this will start the *Windows Components Wizard.*
2. Check the *Certificate Services* component (see Figure 14.16) and click *Next*; you will then receive a warning (see Figure 14.17) that this server can't move to another domain or be renamed.
3. The next page is the *Certification Authority Type* (see Figure 14.18). This page is used to select the type of CA you are going to create. If this MSCS will be used for Exchange 2000 KMS only, you should select the *Enterprise Root CA*. This will store all entries later in the Active Directory. If this CA will be used for Exchange 5.x KMS, you must

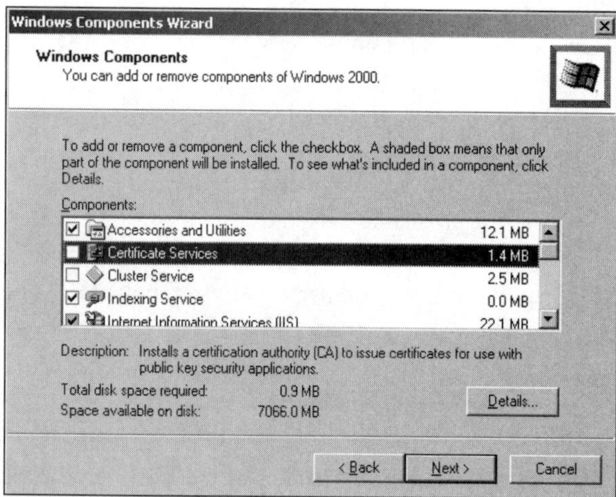

Figure 14.16
Selecting to install the Certificate Services component.

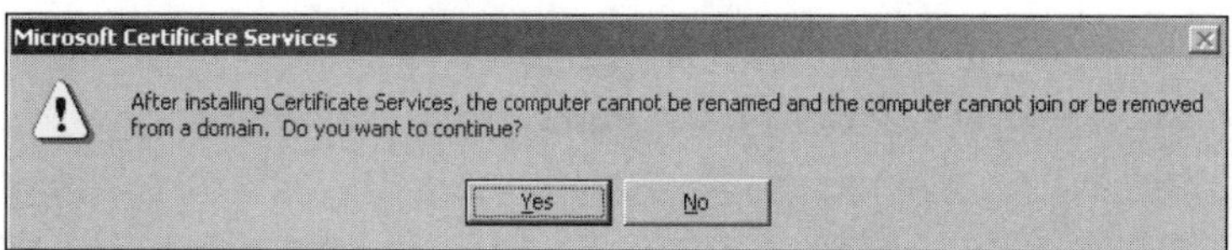

Figure 14.17
The warning you receive before installing MSCS.

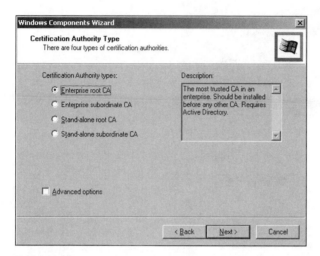

Windows Components Wizard
Certification Authority Type
There are four types of certification authorities.
Certification Authority types:
Enterprise root CA
Enterprise subordinate CA
Stand-alone root CA
Stand-alone subordinate CA
Description:
The most trusted CA in an enterprise. Should be installed before any other CA. Requires Active Directory.
Advanced options
< Back
Next >
Cancel

Figure 14.18
The Certification Authority Type page.

instead select *Stand-Alone Root CA*, which will store the information in files instead of in the AD.

If this CA will be subordinate to another CA (similar to a NT 4 Backup Domain Controller), you should instead select the *Subordinate CA* that corresponds to the type of existing root CA you had before.

If you want to be able to select the type of available encryption and signing algorithms, or import root certificates, you must check *Advanced Options*; this will give you a few extra pages during the installation. For the purpose of installing a common *Enterprise Root CA* used for KMS, you can skip this advanced option for now; but just to let you see one of its extra pages, check out Figure 14.19.

4. If you don't select the advanced options, the next page will be the *CA Identifying Information* page (see Figure 14.20). In this page, you fill in the information about this CA and the company responsible for it. This information will later be visible in the certificates, so type in something that will be valid for at least two years, or however long you will use this CA. As you can see at the bottom of this page, you can set how long the self-generated CA certificate you are creating will be valid; the default is two years. Click *Next* when ready.

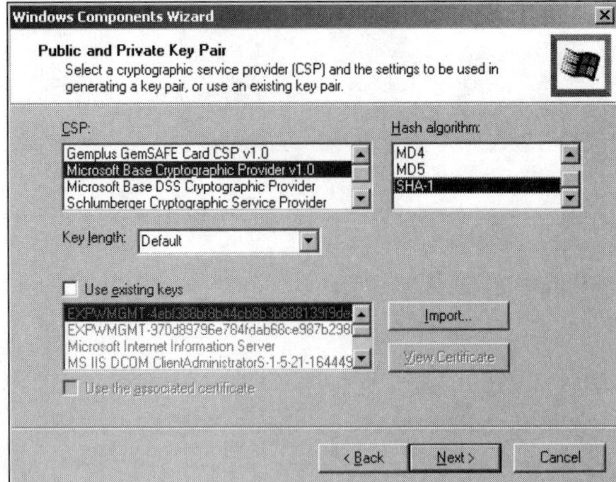

Figure 14.19
Examples of advanced options.

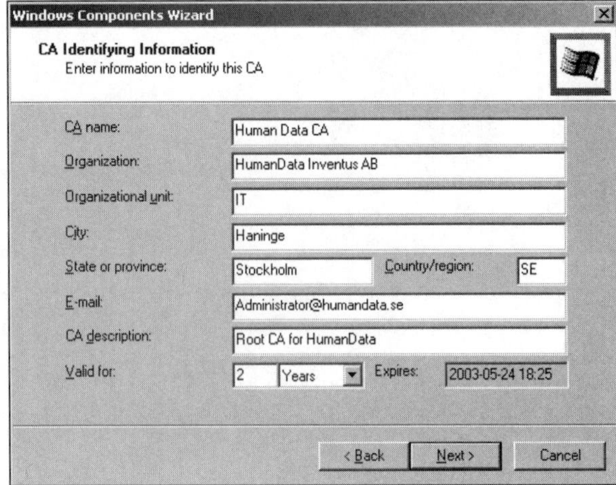

Figure 14.20
The CA Identifying Information dialog box.

5. The *Data Storage Location* page (see Figure 14.21) is where your certificates and log files for the MSCS will be generated.

   You should select the checkbox St*ore Configuration Information In A Shared Folder*, and then click *Browse* to select this folder. It's common to call this folder *CAConfig*. When ready, click *Next*; you will receive a warning that IIS will stop during this installation. Click *OK* to continue (see Figure 14.22).

6. Next, you will see a progress bar, showing you the current status of the installation of MSCS. Wait a few minutes until it's done. After that, you will see the completion page for this installation wizard; click *Finish*.

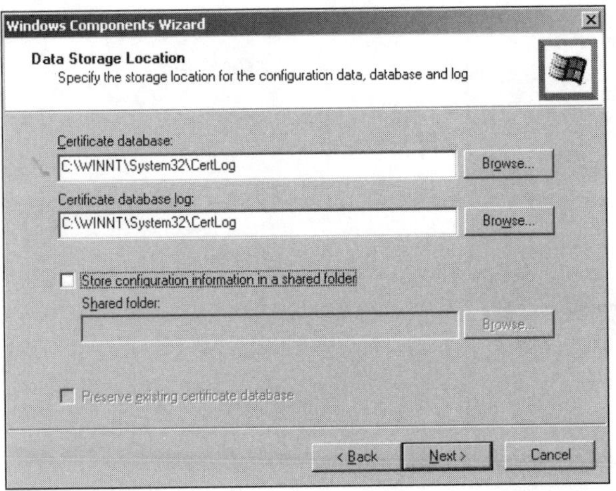

Figure 14.21
The Data Storage Location dialog box.

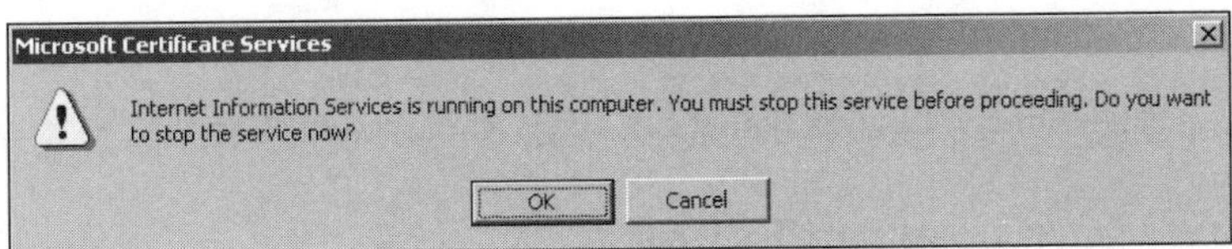

Figure 14.22
The warning that IIS will be stopped.

Step-by-Step Instructions for Configuring MSCS for Exchange 2000

That concludes the installation of MSCS; however, this server is not yet ready for the KMS server. If you try to install KMS now, you would receive the error message shown in Figure 14.23.

1. Start the management tool for MSCS by selecting *Start|Programs|Administrative Tools|Certification Authority*.
2. Right-click the *Policy Settings* folder and select *New|Certificate To Issue*.
3. In the *Select Certificate Template* pane (see Figure 14.24), press the Ctrl key first and then select the following three templates:
   - *Enrollment Agent (Computer)*—Don't select the Enrollment Agent.

Figure 14.23
The error message you receive if you install KMS without first configuring MSCS.

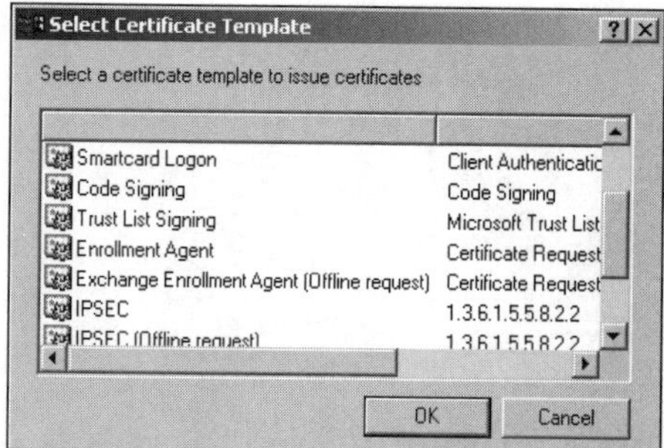

Figure 14.24
Selecting Exchange certificate templates.

- *Exchange User.*
- *Exchange Signature Only.*

  Next click *OK* to copy these into the Policy Settings folder.

4. Your *Certification Authority* manager now shows the installed templates.

Now the MSCS is ready for Exchange 2000 and its Key Management Server!

Installing Key Management Server

Now it's finally time to install the KMS. This is very easy and the only thing you need is an Exchange 2000 Server CD (Enterprise or standard version), and you must be logged on to the domain as an Exchange administrator. Then follow these steps to install the KMS on an Exchange 2000 server:

Note: *The Key Management Server is not cluster aware! You cannot install KMS on a cluster node. This is because the start-up password is needed for the KMS service, which makes it hard to do a cluster state transition without storing the password on a file, and also because the KMS files aren't stored on a cluster-shared device!*

1. Start the *Control Panel*, and select the applet *Add/Remove Programs*, then select *Microsoft Exchange 2000*, and click *Change/Remove*. This will start the Exchange 2000 Installation Wizard.
2. Continue in this wizard until you come to the *Component Selection* page. Select *Action|Change* on the Microsoft Exchange 2000 object, then *Microsoft Exchange Messaging And Collaboration Services*, and select *Action|Install* on the Microsoft Exchange Key Management Service object.
3. From the *Administrative Group* page, select the administrative group the KMS server will belong to; this will control who can administrate this object later. Note that there can be only one KMS per administrative group.
4. From the *Key Management Service Information* page, select how you want to enter the startup password for the KMS service. The safest method is to type it in manually

each time this service is started, but you can also select to store this code in a file on the hard disk or a diskette that this server later will use automatically to retrieve the password when starting. If you select manual password entry, *you must now write down the password* (it can't be copied and pasted!). A tip is to write this password in a text file—that will make it easier for you to copy and paste it later when starting this service. If you selected to create a shared folder for the MSCS before, it will automatically contain a copy of this password in a file called *KMServer.pwd*; make sure to protect this file—move it if necessary!

Note that this KMS service is used only when certificates are created, recovered, or revoked, or when an administrator needs to use the KMS management module in ESM. This means that if the server is restarted, without KMS services automatically restarting, it will not be a problem; clients don't need the KMS service to perform their encryption or signing operations.

5. From the *Component Summary* page, you will see that you are going to install the KMS service; click *Next* to start copying the files.
6. When the installation is done, click *Finish* to complete the installation.

And that concludes the installation of the KMS! Now everything is set for enrolling users and configuring the Outlook clients. The next thing we must do is start the new Microsoft Exchange Key Management Service, using the *Control Panel|Services* applet, as usual. If you just try to start it like any other normal service, you will get an error message.

The reason for this error message is that you haven't entered the special KMS service startup password that you received when installing the KMS system earlier (refer to Figure 14.29). The proper way to start this service—assuming you selected to enter the password manually—is to open the properties for this service and type in the password in the *Start Parameters* field; see Figure 14.25. When this password is entered, click *Start* on the same property page. This is how to start the KMS service manually.

But before we do that, let's take a look at the new KMS object we have in the ESM tool.

Configuring the KMS Object

Microsoft has included the KMS feature to make it possible for you to install and manage email security for your users in a highly secure fashion. This will affect how the management of KMS works; at first it may seem a bit quirky, but remember that this is a highly sensitive security operation, and nothing should be taken lightly. You may remember my advice for selecting a trustworthy Exchange administrator? Well, the administrator that will have control over the KMS system must definitely be trustworthy, or else the whole point with this security system fails! By default, there will only be one person who has access to the KMS system, the administrator who installed KMS. He or she will now also be the KMS administrator for this Exchange 2000 organization. To make it even more secure, KMS has its own password for accessing the different property pages of the KMS objects in the ESM tool. By default, this password will be, yes, you guessed it, "password." And the first thing you should do is to *change this KMS password* to something that only

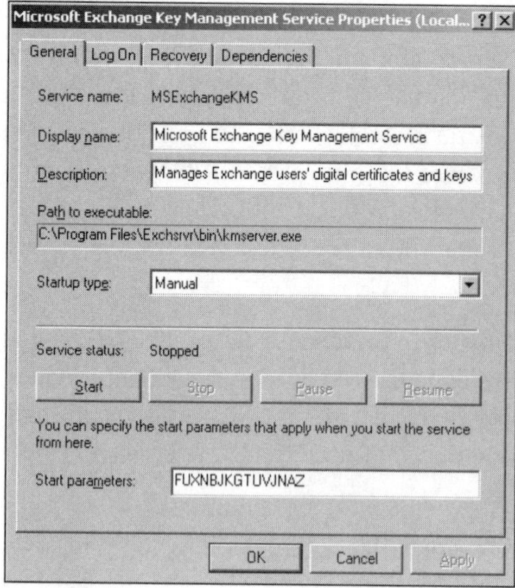

Figure 14.25
The properties for the KMS service object are used to enter its password.

you and other KMS administrators know about! Please don't forget to do this. If I ever come out to your system one day and find that you are still using this default password, I will give you a calling down!

Okay, enough said about that. Let's move on and look at the property pages for the KMS object.

Start the ESM tool and expand the *Administrative Groups* and the AG that KMS belongs to. You will find a new object, *Advanced Security*, that contains two objects: *Encryption Configuration* and *Key Manager*; see Figure 14.26. We will start by looking at the *Encryption Configuration* object; despite its name, it doesn't contain anything that you usually modify.

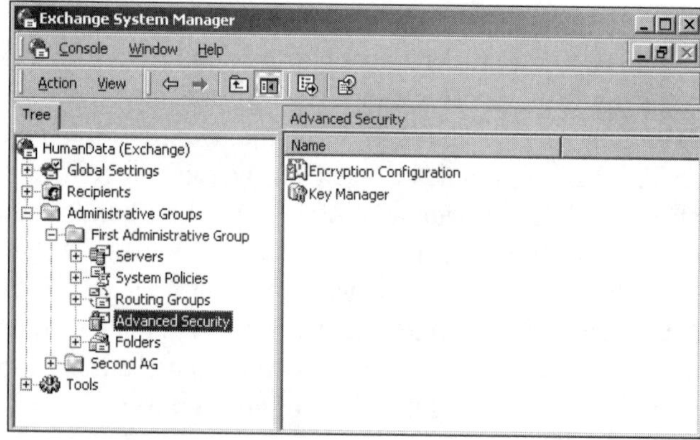

Figure 14.26
The new Advanced Security folder.

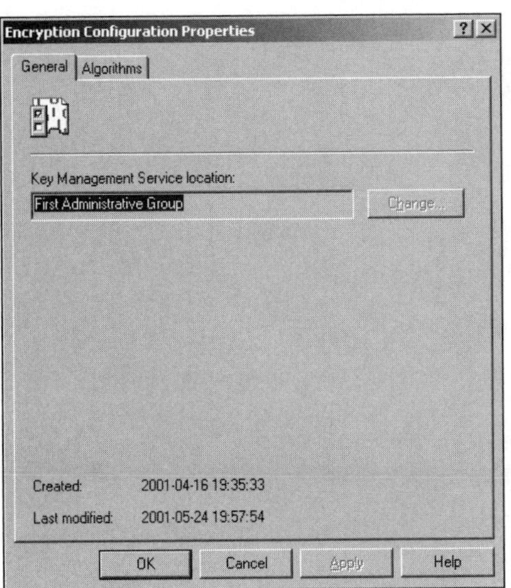

Figure 14.27
The General page for the Encryption Configuration object.

1. Open the properties for the *Encryption Configuration* object first. On the *General* page (see Figure 14.27), you will find the *Key Management Service* location that lists what administrative group this KMS object belongs to. If you have multiple AGs, you can click *Select* to change to another AG.

   At the bottom of the page, you can see when this object was created and when it was last modified.

2. On the *Algorithms* page (see Figure 14.28), you can select what type of encryption algorithm should be used. Note that there are two listings, one for Exchange 4/5 and one for Exchange 5.5 SP1 and Exchange 2000.

   You can see that for Exchange 2000, the default algorithm for systems belonging to North America is 3DES (Trippel-DES), whereas the rest of the world has to be satisfied with RC2-40, which uses only 40-bit long encryption keys.

   At the bottom of the page, you can set the *Security Message Format*; unless you are running KMS with an old Exchange 5.x system, you should stick with S/MIME here. When ready, click *OK* to close this object.

The other object, *Key Manager*, is much more interesting. Here you can add and remove KMS administrators, enroll new users, revoke certificates, and recover keys. Since this object is so sensitive, you must enter the special KMS password for each property page you want to look at. Note that this is not the same password as is used when starting the KMS service, and it's not the administrator's Windows 2000 account password; this is a special password, used only for this object. As I told you before, the default is set to "password," but should immediately be modified to something else (but remember it, since it can't be recovered). The window prompting you for this password looks like

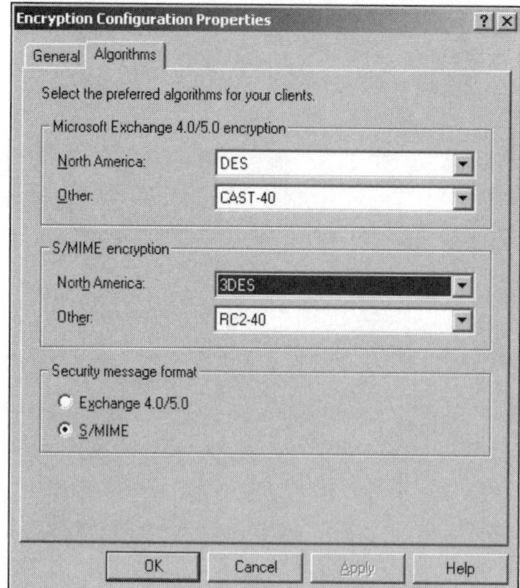

Figure 14.28
The Algorithms tab for the Encryption Configuration object.

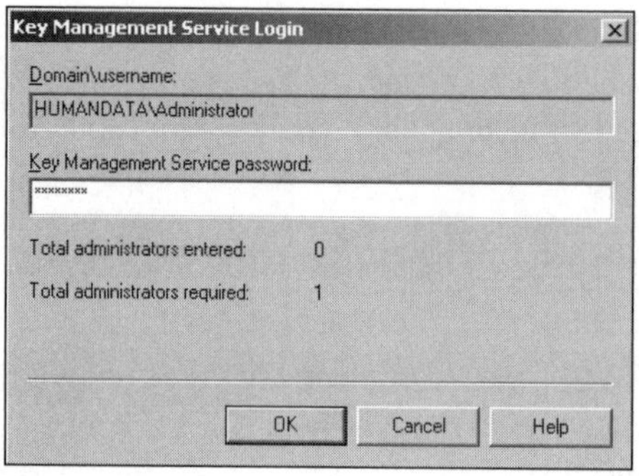

Figure 14.29
The dialog box for entering the KMS password.

Figure 14.29; note that it will tell you the total number of KMS administrators, and also how many administrators that are needed for this particular operation (you can set up some operations to require two administrators; more about this later).

If you right-click the *Key Manager* and select *New*, you have a number of interesting options to select from:

- *Start & Stop KMS Service*—Remember that you must enter the KMS Service password before starting the KMS service.
- *Enroll Users*—This means you should configure them to be security enabled. However, this will not be enough for enabling high security; their clients must also be configured for this. When this option is selected, you must first enter the KMS password; then

you will go to a new window where you can select to enroll individual users or complete servers or stores; see Figure 14.30.

- *Revoke Certificates*—This is used to disable a user certificate, for example, when an employee leaves the company. Again, you must first enter the KMS password; then you get a new window that looks like Figure 14.31. Select the users to revoke in the left pane; click *Add* to move them to the right pane, and then click Revoke.
- *Recover Keys*—This dialog window is very similar to the *Enroll Users* window. Again, after you enter the KMS password, you get a window that's almost identical to the window in Figure 14.30.
- *Export and Import Users*—After entering the KMS password, you can export all enrolled users to a file that can then be imported into another Exchange 2000 organization's KMS system; see Figure 14.32. Before this export operation can be performed, you must have a copy of the CA certificate of the destination KMS; see Figure 14.33. The reason for this is that the export function must adapt the users to the certificate used on the destination KMS, otherwise they can't be imported to that server.

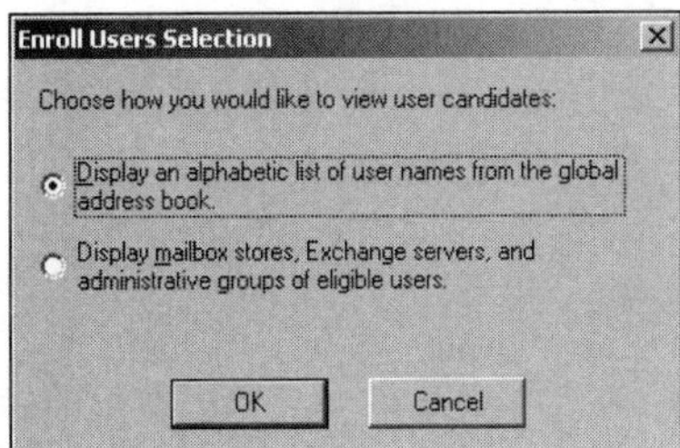

Figure 14.30
Enrolling users.

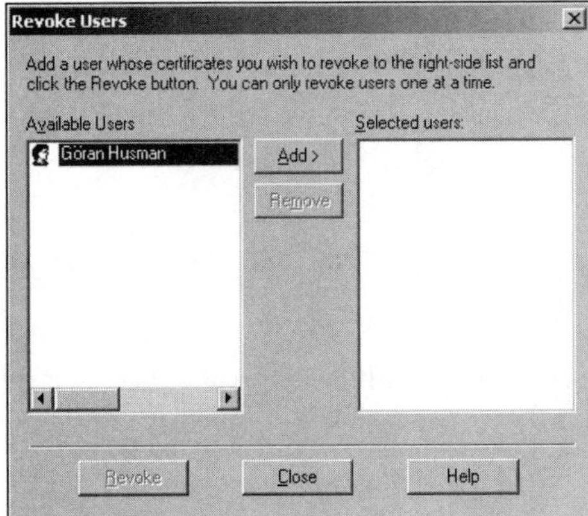

Figure 14.31
Revoking users.

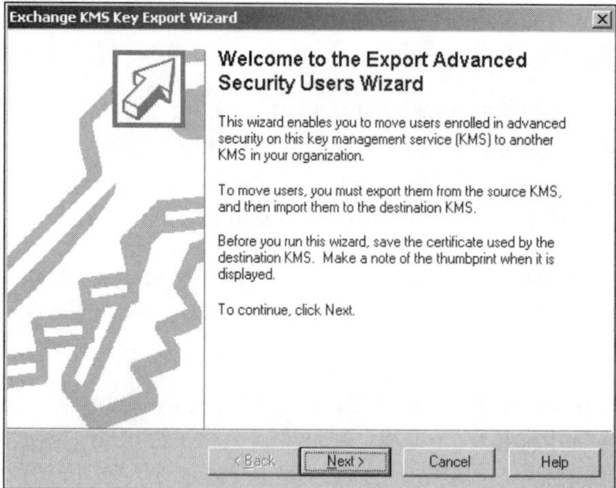

Figure 14.32
Exporting users enrolled in high security.

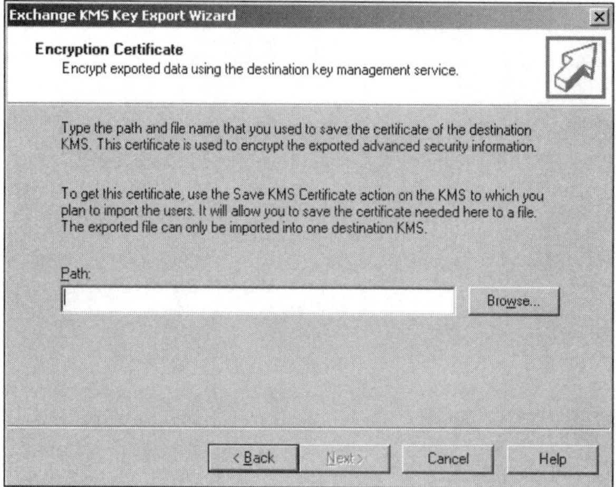

Figure 14.33
Enter the password of the destination KMS.

- *Save KMS Certificate*—This is what has to be done on the destination KMS before we can export our enrolled users from our KMS; see Figure 14.34.

These operations are the most common operations you will perform as a KMS administrator. But the properties for the Key Manager object are also very interesting, at least for an Exchange nerd:

1. On the *General* page (see Figure 14.35), you will see what CA this KMS knows about, and when its certificate expires. By clicking *View Details*, you can see all the details for this certificate. At the bottom of the page, you can see when this object was created and last modified.

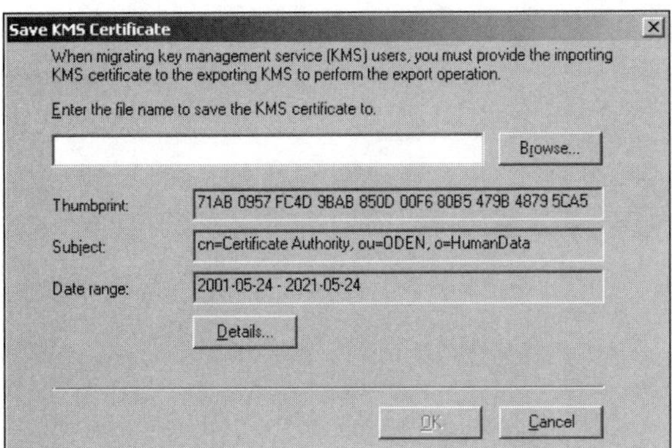

Figure 14.34
Saving the KMS certificate.

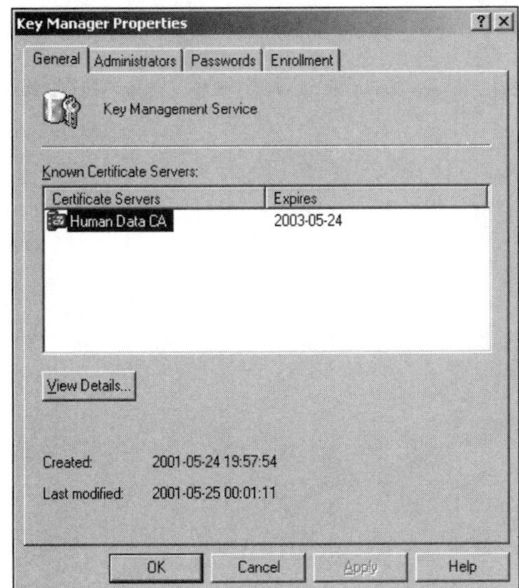

Figure 14.35
The General page for the Key Manager.

2. On the *Administrators* page (see Figure 14.36), you can see all the KMS administrators. You can add or remove administrators, and you can also change the KMS password used for each administrator. This is where you change the password I so nicely begged you to change before. Note that each KMS administrator has its own KMS password; these passwords have nothing to do with the ordinary Windows 2000 account passwords!

3. On the *Passwords* page (see Figure 14.37), you will see how many administrators are needed to perform certain security operations, such as recovering a key. This is also known as *Missile SILO style* multiple password policy.

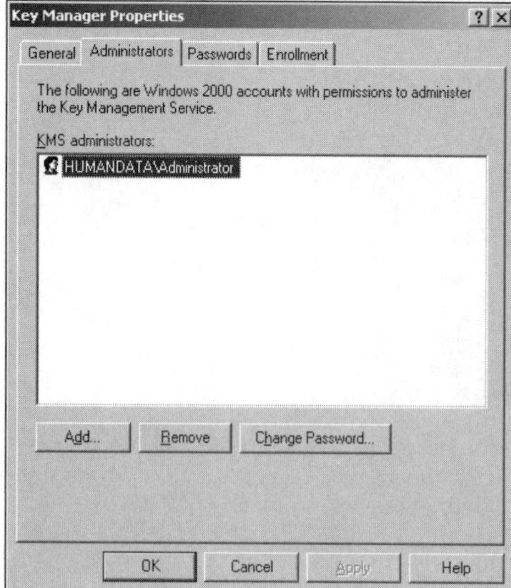

Figure 14.36
The Administrators page for the Key Manager.

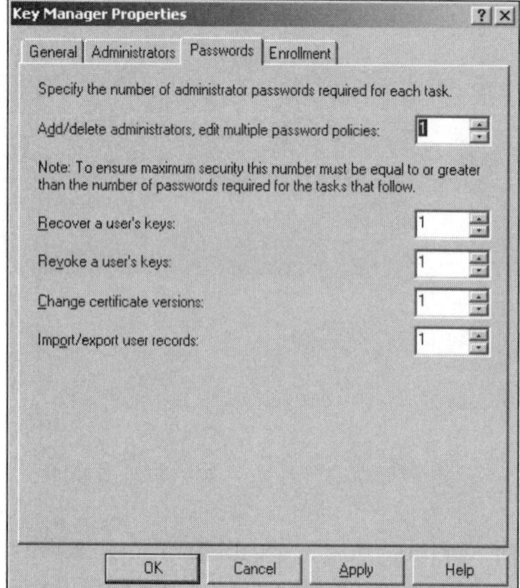

Figure 14.37
The Passwords page for the Key Manager.

4. On the *Enrollment* page (see Figure 14.38), you can configure how to deliver the one-time temporary password for activating KMS features on the Outlook client. By default, this password is not sent by email; instead, the KMS administrator must deliver it by

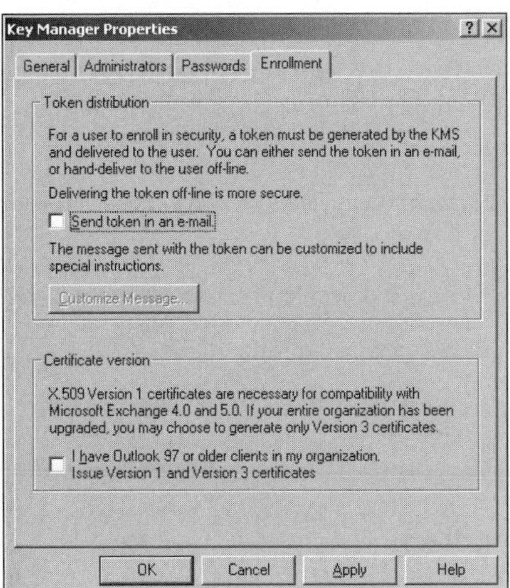

Figure 14.38
The Enrollment page for the Key Manager.

hand or tell the user the password. If this default setting is used, all enrolled users' passwords will be listed in the text file *Enroll.log*, which is stored on the Exchange server's directory *\Exchsrvr\KMSData*; make sure this directory is protected from all but KMS administrators! If you instead set the *Send Token In An E-mail* checkbox, this password will be sent in a clear text message, which is much less secure.

A tip here is to set this checkbox and modify the message (click *Customize Message*) that all enrolled users will get; by removing the %TOKEN% from this message, no password will be listed in the mail, but you can still send the users a confirmation or any other information you want to give them.

In the *Certificate Version* pane, you can set a checkbox if you want KMS to generate X.509 version 1 certificates to any Outlook 97 client you may have in the organization, but still generate X.509 version 3 certificates to other Outlook versions. Remember that version 1 certificates can't use them for secure email outside this organization!

Activating High Security for Users

So now we have our MS Certificate Server up and running, and we have the KMS service activated; now it's time to see how this secure email feature works in practice. The first thing that must be done is to enroll the user; remember that the KMS administrator is the only user account that can enroll users (also known as *enable advanced security* in Exchange 5.5). When this is done, the user's client must be configured to use high security. We start off by enrolling our users.

Step 1: Enroll Users for High Security

Follow these step-by-step instructions to enroll users for high security; remember that you must be logged on as a KMS administrator, and that you must know the special KMS password used for this KMS administrator:

1. Start the *ESM* tool and navigate to the *Advanced Security* object in the administrative group.
2. In the right pane, right-click the *Key Manager* object, and select *All Tasks|Enroll Users*.
3. Enter the password for your KMS administrator account and click *OK*.
4. Now you will see the *Enroll Users Selection* dialog box (refer back to Figure 14.37). It shows two options:
   - *Display an alphabetic list of user names from the global address book*—This option is used for selecting individual users that will be enrolled. You can select any number of users, using the global address list; see Figure 14.39. The names that have the read sign on their icons are either already enrolled, or can't be enrolled, such as distribution groups.

Tip: *If this option can't be displayed, try performing this operation directly on the Exchange 2000 server.*

   - *Display mailbox stores, Exchange servers, and administrative groups of eligible users*—This option makes it possible to bulk-enroll users, for example, all users belonging to a certain administrative group or a certain server.

And that's it! Wasn't too hard, was it? Now comes the next part, configuring the users' Outlook clients.

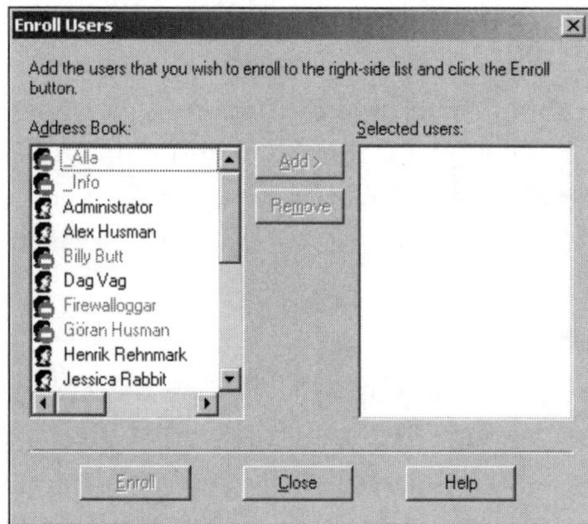

Figure 14.39
Enrolling individual users.

Step 2: Configuring the Outlook Client

This process must be performed for every security-enabled user using their Outlook client. Preferably, the user can perform these steps without the administrator, especially the step where the user enters the special password that protects his or her private keys; no one, not even the administrator, should know about this password! This is extremely important, or the whole point of nonrepudiation will be lost.

Follow these instructions to enable a user (in this example Anna) and her Outlook 2000 client:

1. Anna starts her Outlook client as normal.
2. Select the *Tools|Options* menu, and switch to the *Security* tab (see Figure 14.40).
3. Click the *Get A Digital ID* button; this will give you a choice to select where your X.509 certificate will come from (see Figure 14.41). Select *Set Up Security For Me On The Exchange Server* (*Note:* This is not the default). Click *OK* when ready.
4. Next, Anna must enter her token, or the temporary password, given to her by the KMS administrator (see Figure 14.42). Click *OK* when ready.
5. Next, Anna must select a personal password for her digital ID that will protect her private keys in the future; make sure this password is at least six characters long and that it is hard to guess (see Figure 14.43). *This password should not be the same as the user logon password!* There are two reasons for this: a) It will not be updated if the user changes her logon password, and b) For higher security, this digital ID password

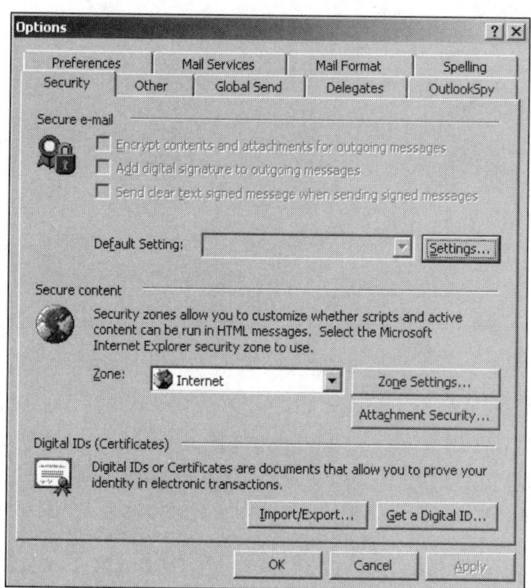

Figure 14.40
The Security tab for Outlook 2000.

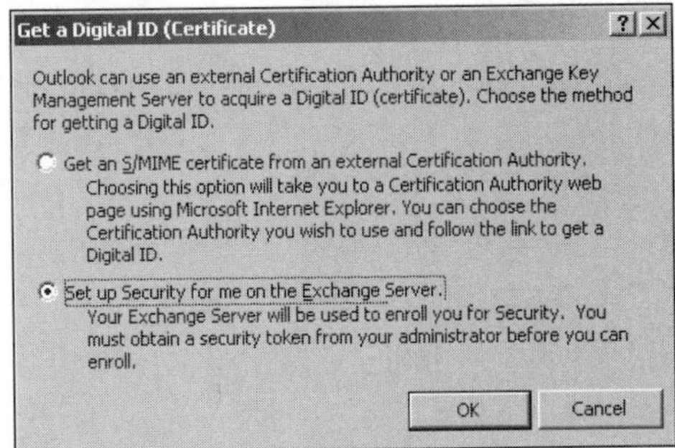

Figure 14.41
Selecting where to get the X.509 certificate.

Figure 14.42
Entering the personal token.

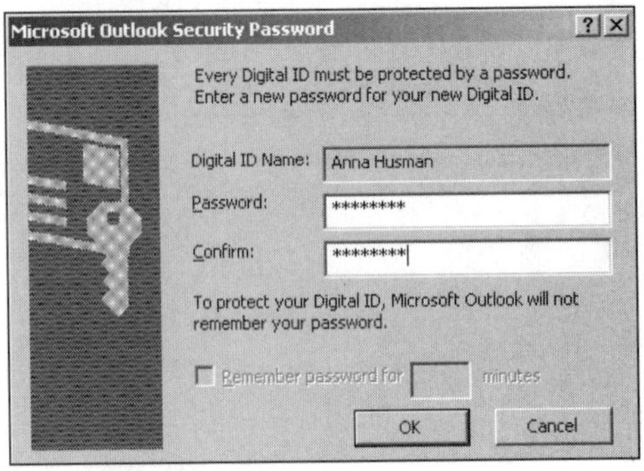

Figure 14.43
Selecting a password for her digital ID.

should be different. Enter the password twice, and click *OK*. This will generate a message sent to the KMS service that will check to see if Anna is enrolled and if the token was correct; if so, she will get an encrypted message back (see Figure 14.44). Click *OK* to close this information window, and OK again to close the Options dialog box.

6. After a few minutes, Anna will receive an encrypted message from the Security Authority (see Figure 14.45); notice that this message does not display in the Preview Pane. When this message is opened, Anna must enter her digital ID password (from Step 5) and click *OK*.

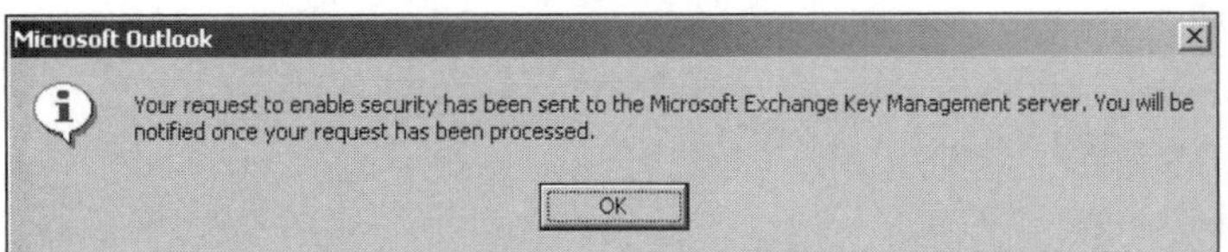

Figure 14.44
This request has now been sent to the KMS.

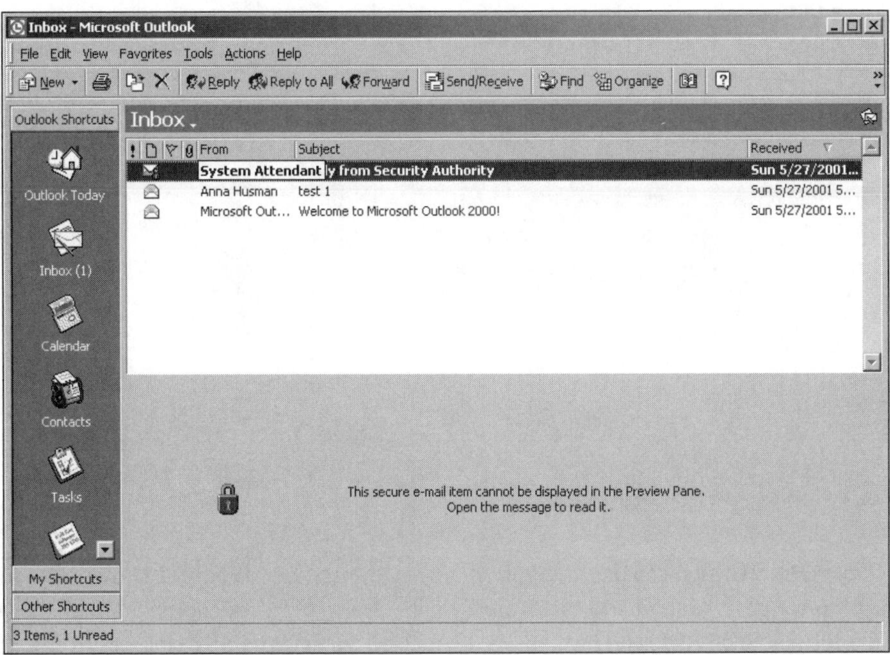

Figure 14.45
A new message from the System Attendant.

7. When prompted to add the certificate to the root store (see Figure 14.46), click Yes. Again, Anna must enter her digital ID password; Anna can finally read the message, stating (hopefully) that her account is successfully security enabled. When ready, close this message; see Figure 14.47.

Now the user and her Outlook client are configured for high email security. It's time to see how to send and receive encrypted and signed messages.

Sending and Receiving Encrypted and Signed Messages

Sending encrypted and signed messages is easy; it's like requesting any option, such as a delivery receipt. You can select to use encryption or signing (or both) for all outgoing messages, or for individual messages. This is up to the user to decide; some users should always encrypt and sign their messages, while others use it just when needed. Remember that OWA clients can't view encrypted or opaque signed messages.

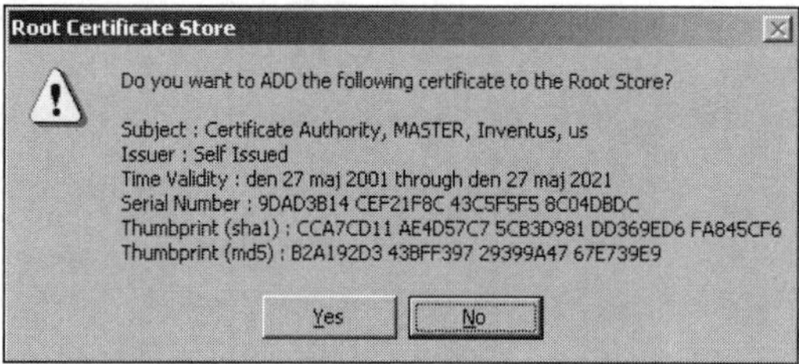

Figure 14.46
Adding the new CA certificate to the root store.

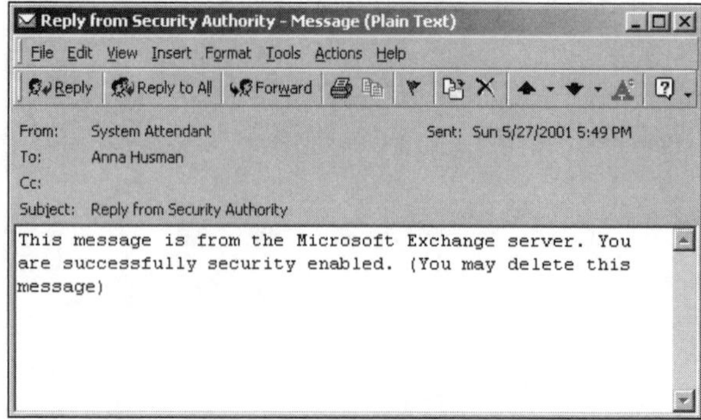

Figure 14.47
The actual message from the Security Authority.

To configure Outlook to use encryption and/or signing for all outgoing messages, open the *Tools|Options* menu and the *Security* page. Note that these options are only available for Outlook 2000 SR1, and that you have enabled to view the SR1 features in the Registry, as described earlier in this chapter. Here you can select to:

- *Encrypt contents and attachments*—This will encrypt all outgoing messages.
- *Add digital signature*—This will sign all outgoing messages.
- *Send clear text signatures*—This will avoid Opaque signatures, and make it possible to view these signed messages even if the client doesn't understand S/MIME signed messages; this will also let OWA clients view these messages. Unless you have a good reason, you should keep this setting as is.
- *Request secure receipt*—This will return a receipt that the recipient trusted your certificate; if you don't receive this receipt, you know that the recipient did not trust your certificate! This will affect all outgoing secure messages.

Instead of encrypting or signing all outgoing messages, you can activate these options for individual messages. In this case, don't set the encryption or signing. Instead, follow these steps to send a signed and encrypted message:

1. Use the Outlook client, and start writing a new email message.

2. Before sending the message, click the *Options* button.

3. From the *Options* dialog window, select to encrypt and/or sign this message. Click *Close* when ready.

4. Click *Send* to send the message. You will now be requested to enter the digital ID password. This is how you prove that you are actually the true sender of this message; no one other than you knows this password. Even if someone manages to find your computer unlocked and unguarded, they still will not be able to send any messages in your name.

When you receive a secure message, you'll notice that it looks a bit different from other messages; if it's encrypted, its content will not display in the preview pane (but signed will). These types of messages will also have special icons:

- Encrypted messages have a blue padlock symbol.
- Signed messages have a red symbol.
- Encrypted and signed messages will have the same symbol as encrypted messages.

Note: *Even encrypted messages display their subject line during transport between servers and over the Internet, so the lesson is this: Don't write anything sensitive on the subject line; it will not be protected by the encryption process!*

All secure messages also indicate that they carry an attachment. This is the secure part (i.e., the encrypted message and/or the signature) of the message; this means that you can't tell if this message also has a normal attachment.

To complete this long walk-through of secure email in Exchange 2000, follow these steps to open a secure message:

1. Double-click to open the secured message. You will be prompted for your digital ID password; then the message will open (see Figure 14.48). The reason for this is that you must prove you are the legitimate recipient of this message. Every time an encrypted message is opened, this password must be entered. This will ensure that no one besides the legitimate recipient, not even the administrator, can read these encrypted messages.

2. Notice the two icons in the circle in Figure 14.48; the blue padlock indicates that this message is encrypted, and the red ribbon shows that it's signed. Click the blue symbol; this will tell you that this is an encrypted message, and what algorithm and key length has been used. If you want to look at the certificate, click the *Encryption Certificate* button. Click *OK* to close.

3. Click the red icon to view its signature status; it will show whether this message is authentic, and whether the certificates are okay. Click *OK* to close.

All encrypted messages are protected during all phases of the processing of this email—from the moment it was sent (including the copy in the sender's *Sent Items* folder), during

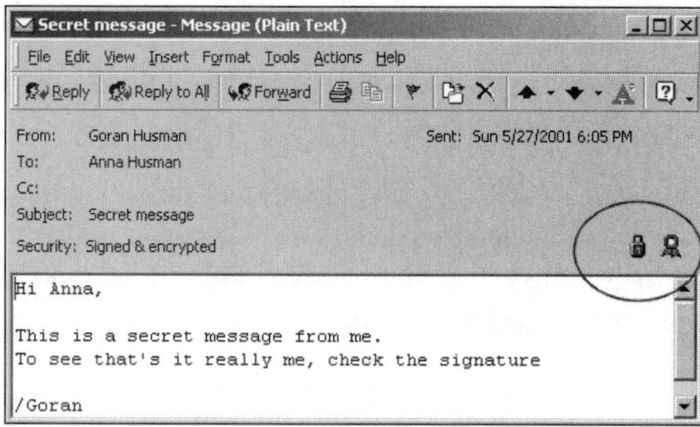

Figure 14.48
An opened secure message.

the transport over any links, including the Internet, between Exchange servers, and when stored in the messages stores. There is simply no way to access the contents of this message without the user's digital ID password. Make sure this password is well protected!

Drawbacks to Security

Doesn't security have any drawbacks? Sure, it has some, but compared to what you gain, it's worth it. The drawbacks of high email security are these:

- *Slower*—Since the sender and recipient clients must encrypt and decrypt, or sign and verify signatures, the process of sending secure mail takes extra time and is more demanding for the CPU and memory of these clients. However, this extra burden is usually not noticeable, unless it's a large message over 500KB; then it will show up as a delay when opening messages.
- *You can't do virus scans on encrypted messages*—This is maybe the most important drawback. An encrypted message can't be scanned by virus programs, not on its way out, and not when entering the recipient's mail system. Not until the user decrypts the message is it possible to scan for viruses; this means that the clients must have virus scanning activated on their Outlook clients. A similar problem is to scan for content (is the user sending sensitive information to a competitor?) or checking that the message is following company policies.
- *Clumsier*—A small drawback is that security makes sending and receiving messages a bit clumsier for users; they have to enter their password whenever they want to open an encrypted message, or whenever they send an encrypted or signed message.

Summary

This is a list of the more important features and keywords mentioned in this chapter. Use it as a reminder and to make sure you have understood the most important things:

- The Internet is completely insecure! All standard messages are sent in clear text, which is possible for others to view if they have access to the network used for transporting these messages.
- Security is very important—to avoid unauthorized access to information, to avoid forgery, and to avoid spoofing.
- There are also problems with email-distributed viruses, Trojan horses, and Denial-of-Service attacks.
- Social engineering is the easiest way to obtain other peoples' passwords.
- A network monitor can view the messages sent over the network.
- MAPI clients send messages over RPC; it's harder to interpret, but it can be done.
- Threats to email include an administrator gaining unauthorized access, an employee sneaking into your computer, and an employee scanning the network with a network monitor.
- Make sure to select trustworthy administrators; make them sign a contract about what they are allowed to do.
- Be aware of temporary personnel with access to the network and servers, such as contractors and consultants.
- If you have outsourced your mail servers, do you know who runs them now?
- Teach users to lock their computers when they leave them.
- It's hard to prevent scanning of the network; but with a switch configuration, it may be possible.
- Make sure to place servers in a locked room, open only to authorized personnel.
- Threats from the outside include message theft, spoofing, DoS, relay of messages, viruses, and Trojan horses.
- Note that all POP3 and IMAP4 users can simply change their reply address to impersonate someone else; you don't have to be an expert hacker to do this!
- Make sure you have at least two incoming SMTP servers to decrease the risk of being damaged by DoS attacks.
- Make sure that your SMTP servers do not allow relay of messages, unless the clients are authenticated first.
- Virus attacks are something we must live with (like in real life); make sure you have the best available virus protection on the server.
- If you haven't upgraded to Outlook 2000 Service Release 1 or later yet, do it! It will protect you from the many .vbs viruses, like ILOVEYOU.

- RPC in Exchange 5.x was always encrypted, except between the client and the server, but this could, and can, be activated.
- Server traffic in Exchange 2000 can be protected by Transport Layer Security (TLS) or Internet Protocol Security (IPSec).
- TLS is very similar to the SSL encryption used for Web traffic.
- IPSec is a standard describing how to encrypt network traffic. This method is preferable to TLS since it's faster and you don't have to configure the E2K server.
- Symmetric encryption assumes both parties have the same key; this is the method that has always been used in the past.
- Asymmetric encryption uses one key for encrypting and another key for decrypting; this method is less than 30 years old.
- Whitfield Diffie and Martin Hellman discovered how to use a public and private key to encrypt messages; this was the birth of the asymmetric encryption method.
- James Ellis, who was in the English military, found a similar method 10 years before Diffie and Hellman, but it was kept a secret.
- The strength of encryption algorithms depends on the length of the key; 40-bit keys were okay five years ago, but today you need 128 bits to be secure.
- Remember that our national security organizations, such as NSA, *are* scanning the Internet for messages with suspicious content; it's their job.
- Symmetric algorithms include DES, 3DES, IDEA, RC2, RC4, RC5, and Blowfish; these are only a few (but the most popular) of all available algorithms.
- Asymmetric algorithms include RSA, Diffie-Hellman, KAM, and DSA; these are very popular.
- Hash algorithms include SHA (SHS) and MD5; this type of algorithm is used to calculate a hash, or a checksum, on a message. This will be recalculated by the receiver and then compared; if they are alike, the message is intact.
- Ciphertext is the encrypted message.
- In reality, all three types of algorithms are used—symmetric is used for encrypting messages, asymmetric is used for protecting the symmetric key, and hash is used for calculating a checksum on the message.
- The reason asymmetric encryption is not used for everything is that it's slow and its resulting ciphertext is much larger than the original message.
- To encrypt messages, the sender uses the recipient's public key.
- To sign messages, the sender uses its private key.

- Certificates are used to prove that public keys are authentic.
- X.509 is the standard used for S/MIME certificates.
- X.509 certificates are generated by a Certificate Authority (CA).
- Windows 2000 contains an MS Certificate Server that can be used to create your own CA.
- MS Outlook recognizes a number of commercial CAs, but not the CA that you set up yourself. However, you can import your CA certificate into Outlook to make it recognize it.
- Outlook doesn't have to explicitly trust a CA. A message from an unknown CA will generate a warning to the user; he or she can still decide to view the message.
- S/MIME, or Secure MIME, is an extension of the MIME protocol to handle encryption and signing. Such messages have attachments like P7M and P7S.
- Outlook 97 doesn't understand today's S/MIME standard (yet another reason to upgrade!).
- Outlook 98, 2000, 2002, and Outlook Express are Microsoft clients that understand S/MIME.
- Service Release 1 for Outlook 2000 contains several important enhancements regarding S/MIME; you should upgrade.
- *Clear Signing*—The actual message is still in clear text, making it readable even for receiving clients that don't understand S/MIME (including the OWA client).
- *Opaque signing*—The message is converted to a binary file (but not encrypted!); only S/MIME clients can see its content.
- *Nonrepudiation*—The term used to describe a signed message that is coming from a given sender, without any doubt. No one in the world should be able to send a message signed with another person's private key.
- Outlook 98 stores its private keys in an encrypted file; Outlook 2000 stores it in an encrypted part of the Registry. Set up roaming users, and the Registry settings will follow the user.
- *PGP*—Stands for Pretty Good Privacy; it was developed in 1991 by Philip Zimmermann, using RSA encryption algorithms. It's used as an add-on to mail clients. It can also be used with Outlook 9x/2000. It offers strong protection due to its long keys.
- The key distribution in PGP is based on a social concept: I trust my friends! All PGP clients generate their own keys; no CA is involved.
- *KMS*—Stands for Key Management Server, the built-in security feature in Exchange 2000. It's an enhancement of the KM Server of previous Exchange versions, and it has lots of features that make it easy to enroll and manage S/MIME security in an organization.
- The Microsoft Exchange Key Management Service is actually the KMServer.exe process.

- KMS uses two key pairs, one for signing and one for encryption; the reason is that the administrator must be able to recover encryption keys but not signing keys (because of the demand of nonrepudiation).
- Install the MS Certificate Server (MSCS) before installing KMS.
- MSCS must have these policies installed: Enrollment Agent (Computer), Exchange User, and Exchange signature.
- The KMS service password is listed during KMS installation; make sure to write it down. (If you have shared a directory for MSCS, it will be copied to a file named KMServer.pwd in this directory.)
- There is a special password for KMS administrators used to configure the Key Manager object; this is by default "password"—make sure to change it!
- You can configure Key Manager to require more than one administrator for a given operation, such as recovering a user.
- You can export user certificates to another Exchange organization, using the Key Manager object; you will need the new KMS certificate for this.
- When users have been enrolled, they must configure their Outlook client before they can use S/MIME security.
- The password for the user's digital ID must be well protected! No one besides the user should know this password, or nonrepudiation will be invalidated.
- Secure messages are secure at all times, from the time they are created, until the recipient opens them; every time one is opened, the recipient must enter his or her password.
- Secure messages have special icons, and always carry an attachment, making it impossible to see if there is also another, normal, attachment included.
- Drawbacks of secure messaging include the following: slower performance, clumsier to use, and impossible to virus scan or content scan!

Chapter 15

Exchange 2000 Clients

This chapter will tell you about all the clients that can be used with Exchange 2000, including the first MS Exchange clients and Schedule Plus. We have mentioned many of these clients in this book, but this time we will go into detail about the clients themselves, how to install them, and how to configure them. The goal with this chapter is to tell you everything that's worth knowing about these clients; some of this information has already been mentioned, but here we'll consolidate all the information about these clients so you don't have to go hunting around for bits of information in the other chapters.

The clients in Exchange 4 were limited to the MS Exchange client, used for messaging and Schedule Plus, the calendar client. Since then, several new clients have been added, and Exchange 2000 now has support for all these different types of clients and protocols:

- *MAPI Clients*—MS Exchange client, Schedule Plus, Outlook 9x, and Outlook 200x
- *POP3 Clients*—Any POP3-compliant client, such as MS Outlook Express, Pegasus, and Gmail
- *IMAP4 Clients*—Any IMAP4-compliant client, such as MS Outlook Express, Netscape Messenger, and Pegasus
- *NNTP Clients*—Any NNTP-compliant client, such as MS Outlook Express, Pegasus, and GRN
- *HTTP Clients*—Any HTTP-compliant Web browser that supports frames and Java scripts, such as MS Internet Explorer, Netscape, and Opera

A natural question is what the difference is between these clients and when to use a particular client. There is no single answer to this question; it depends on many different parameters, such as:

- The operating system for the client; for example, Windows 2000 Professional, Macintosh, or Linux
- The type of connection; for example, LAN, WAN, or dial-up

- The type of usage; for example, stationary computers, notebooks, or temporary access using a Web client
- The type of information needed; for example, only email, email and public folders, or email, public folders, and calendar
- The need for offline storage

However, only one type of client gives you access to all of Exchange 2000's features—it's the MS Outlook 2000 and later versions. The other types are subsets of the Outlook client, which limit what the user can see and do, but also have fewer requirements on the client computer. Let's start this chapter by looking into the oldest client type still available for Exchange, the MS Exchange client.

The MS Exchange Client and Schedule Plus

When Exchange 4 was released in 1996, it came with one messaging client and one calendar client. The name for this messaging client was *MS Exchange client*. It was based on the new MAPI 1 release that replaced the Simple MAPI version that was used in MS Mail; this new MAPI 1 was built to be used in the client/server model that Exchange 4 used. Since Exchange 2000 also supports MAPI 1, this old client can actually still be used.

The MS Exchange Client

When this client was released in 1996 many people were confused because in MS Windows 95, there was also a program called *MS Exchange client* that used exactly the same icon as the type of client that came with the Exchange server. However, this Windows 95 version of this client didn't have support for communicating with an Exchange server, and it lacked the advanced MAPI 1 protocol that had replaced the Simple MAPI used for MS Mail post offices. Microsoft renamed the Windows 95 client version to *Windows Messaging Client* to avoid confusion with the real Exchange client.

This Exchange client had the basic messaging features, like an inbox, public folders, and access to the Global Address List (GAL) on the Exchange server. However, it didn't understand the calendar, to-do list, journals, or contact folders. Some of this was solved by using another client, the Schedule Plus, which was actually a heritage from the MS Mail environment. Schedule Plus made it possible for the user to view the calendar and the to-do list, and also to view other users' calendars (if granted the proper permissions).

The Exchange client officially died when Outlook 97 was released in January 1997, together with the MS Office 97 package. After that release, it wasn't possible to get the Exchange client from Microsoft anymore. However, when installing both Outlook 97 and Outlook 98, the user also got the Exchange client installed, but there was no indication of its existence. Its name was Exchng32.exe and it was stored in the *\Program\Windows Messaging* directory; but no Schedule Plus came with these Outlook versions. I don't really know the reason behind Microsoft's decision to add the Exchange client with Outlook 9x, but at least it was good for one thing that Outlook couldn't do: It could rename the users mailbox folders, such as Inbox and Calendar.

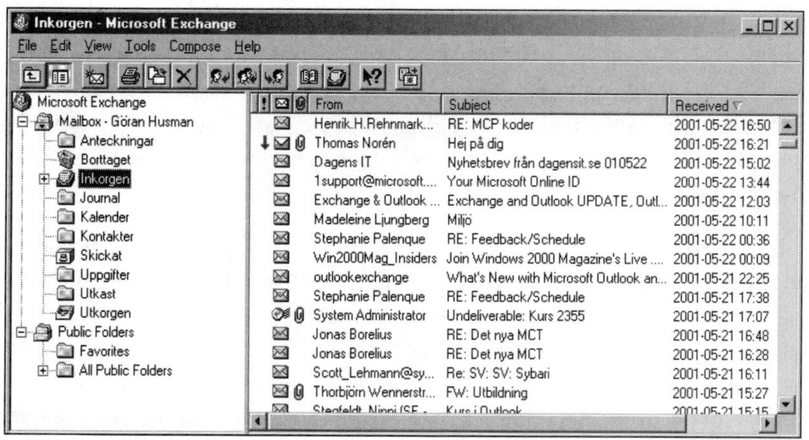

Figure 15.1
The Exchange client.

For example, assume that the names of our mailbox folders are in a language other than what we want (a common problem in non–English-speaking countries); for instance, *Inbox* was named *Inkorgen* in Swedish (see Figure 15.1). These folder names have never been possible to change using an Outlook client, not even today. But with the Exchange client, it was no problem—just right-click on the folder and select *Rename*.

The Exchange client can even be used today, with Exchange 2000. And you can still use it for renaming folders. But this client is no longer included in Outlook 2000 or 2002, so you will need to install an Outlook 9x.

Note: *The problem with erroneously labeled folders is due to the way Exchange gives them names. The first time a mailbox is accessed by a client (usually Outlook), Exchange looks at the regional settings for this client; if it's Swedish, then the folder names will be in Swedish, etc. The language of the client software does not affect these labels, only the regional settings.*

The Schedule Plus Client

As mentioned, the Schedule Plus 7 calendar client was an adaptation of the Schedule Plus 1 client used in the MS Mail environment. Schedule Plus 7 could access the user's mailbox in the Exchange PRIV.EDB database, for reading and updating calendar information. This information was stored in a hidden folder in each user's mailbox on the Exchange server, in a special Schedule Plus calendar format; by default, a *.CAL file was also created locally on the client computer, which regularly synchronized with the server folder.

When Outlook 97 was released, it integrated the messaging features with both the calendar and to-do features. It also had a new calendar format, and so as not to destroy any Schedule Plus calendar information, the Outlook calendar was stored in a separate folder (but still in the user's mailbox). When a user upgraded from Schedule Plus to Outlook 97, the calendar info was imported to the new Outlook calendar folder, and all was well. However, if the organization had a mix of Schedule Plus and Outlook calendar users, you got in trouble; they could not see each other's detailed information, because Outlook clients only looked in the Outlook calendar folder and vise versa. The typical user never noticed this problem, since they were usually only allowed to view other users' Free/Busy Schedule information; this is stored in a special public folder, regardless of what type of calendar client is used.

Another little problem with the Schedule Plus 7 calendar client was that it had its own contact folder; a user could use this as an alternative to the Personal Address Book (PAB) that was used in the Exchange Client. However, since Outlook 97 had integrated the calendar, it didn't need any extra databases for personal addresses; all these conflicts forced companies to migrate quickly to the Outlook client and abandon the Schedule Plus client, to many users' sorrow since Schedule Plus was regarded as a much better calendar client than the one provided by Outlook.

Migration Problems with Schedule Plus 1

If you must migrate an MS Mail organization to Exchange and Outlook, you usually use the MS Exchange Migration Wizard, described in Chapter 8. However, if the MS Mail users have used the Schedule Plus 1 calendar, the wizard will fail to migrate these calendars to Exchange and Outlook calendar format! This problem has several solutions:

- Use the Outlook client and import the original .CAL file. However, in some situations this can be a problem; check the TechNet article Q165873.
- Install Schedule Plus 7 on this computer, convert the Schedule Plus 1 *.CAL file to 7 *.SCD file format, save this information in a file, and then import it into Outlook.
- Use Outlook 200x to import Schedule Plus 1, 7, and *.SC2 files.

The reason for this problem is that the migration wizard doesn't understand the Schedule Plus 1 format that is used in the MS Mail environment.

The MS Outlook Client

This is the primary message client for Exchange server, and has been since 1997. This is also a MAPI client, like its predecessor, but has lots of new features. In this chapter, we will only look at MS Outlook as an Exchange client, although it's possible to use Outlook as an Internet client using, for example, POP3 or IMAP4. Four major Outlook versions have been released:

- Outlook 97 (released January 1997)
- Outlook 98 (released April 1998)
- Outlook 2000 (released May 1999)
- Outlook 2002 (released May 2001)

Even though there are many differences between these versions, not least regarding security and performance, they still offer the same set of basic features, including:

- Email
- Calendar
- Contacts
- To-do lists
- Journals
- Notes
- Public folders
- Synchronization between the client and the Exchange server
- Dial-up features
- Global Address List

Outlook started as a development project in 1992, and a lot of people have been involved in the many different versions. Just for fun, you can see a bit more about these people, and their pictures, by visiting their Web site at **www.creditsite.com/outlook**.

In the following sections, we will look a bit more into each Outlook version to learn about their features, differences, and quirks. Another excellent Web site regarding Outlook is Sue Mosher's **www.slipstick.com**; you will find almost all the add-ons mentioned in this Outlook section in Sue's Web site; it also contains very good tips and tricks—a true gold mine for the Outlook nerd!

MS Outlook 97

In January 1997, the MS Office development team released Office 97—with it came the new Outlook 97 client that would replace the old Exchange Client and Schedule Plus calendar. This client was released a few months before Exchange 5 was released in April 1997, and the consequence of this was that this first version of Outlook 97, also known as version 8, lacked some features that Exchange 5 offered. During its lifetime, several versions came out, from 8.01 to 8.04.

When Exchange 5.5 was released in December 1997, it also had a new Outlook 97; version 8.03. Exchange 5.5 had a new feature called *Soft Delete* that made it possible for users to recover deleted messages. That feature required version 8.03 of Outlook, so most Outlook 97 versions still in use today are usually 8.03 or higher. The final version of Outlook 97 was 8.04; this was mainly a fix to make the client Y2K compliant.

Problems with Outlook 97

Although a number of updates have been made to this client, it was still the first Outlook version and it lacked some functionality that later Exchange server versions offered. The main problems with using Outlook 97 in an Exchange 2000 environment are:

- *Security*—Outlook 97 cannot handle S/MIME and X.509 V.3 certificates, making it a bad choice for organizations that want to implement advanced email security.
- *Virus attacks*—Outlook 97 is vulnerable to script-based virus attacks.
- *Contact*—Outlook 97 uses both the PAB and the Contacts folder; the only reason for keeping the PAB file is that Contacts in Outlook 97 can't create personal distribution lists, whereas this is possible in the PAB file.
- *Format*—Outlook 97 doesn't support HTML-formatted messages.
- *Forms*—Outlook 97 has its own format for electronic forms; this client cannot view forms created with later Outlook versions or HTML forms.
- *Missing features*—Outlook 97 doesn't support all features in Exchange 2000—for example, voting buttons, follow-up flags, and some remote-access features.

The conclusion is that Outlook 97 is not recommended for use in an Exchange 2000 environment.

Note: *Although Outlook 97 was released with MS Office 97, there are no dependencies between them; for example, it is perfectly okay to run a later version of Outlook together with MS Office 97.*

System Requirements for Outlook 97

These are the minimum requirements necessary to install Outlook 97; however, you should at least double or triple many of these values to get a high-performance Outlook client:

- *Hardware*—486/33MHz or higher
- *Memory*—Win 95: 8MB, Win NT 3.51 with SP5: 16MB
- *Operating system*—Windows 95 or later; or Windows NT 3.51 with SP5, Windows NT or Windows 2000

Outlook 97 Easter Egg

An *Easter egg* in the software industry is a hidden bit of software that usually lists the names of the developers of the application. Outlook 97 has an Easter egg that you can see by following these steps exactly:

1. Create a new contact named *Ren Hoek*.
2. Select this new contact, then select *Help|About*.
3. Press Ctrl+Alt+Shift and click the OK button on this *Help* dialog box.

You should see a list of all developers, testers, and so on scroll before your eyes.

MS Outlook 98

In March 1998, the new Outlook 98 was released as a free download, and later maintained as a free upgrade for registered Outlook 97 users. This time it was a stand-alone version, not included in an MS Office package. Outlook 98 has also been upgraded a number of times, solving serious problems regarding security and Y2K; if your organization is running Outlook 98 today, you should apply some, if not all, of the fixes listed in Table 15.1.

Problems with Outlook 98

If you apply these patches, Outlook 98 will be safer and much more suitable for Exchange 2000 than Outlook 97. But this client still has a number of problems that should encourage your organization to upgrade to a newer Outlook client; for example:

- *Resource booking*—Outlook 98 lost a feature that Outlook 97 had—to automatically accept calendar bookings for resources, such as conference rooms. In Outlook 98, you must either have a client logged on as this resource, or install a script, such as the AutoAccept Utilities (**www.exchangecode.com**).
- *Contacts*—Outlook 98 uses both the PAB and the Contacts folder; the only reason for keeping the PAB file is that Contacts in Outlook 98 can't create personal distribution lists, whereas this is possible in the PAB file.
- *Features*—Outlook 98 doesn't support all the features available in Exchange 2000; for example, it can't use LDAP to access the global catalog server in Windows 2000.

Enhancements in Outlook 98 Compared to Outlook 97

The Outlook 98 release is a much better client for the Exchange 2000 environment; it has several enhancements compared to Outlook 97, such as:

- *Formats*—Outlook 98 allows HTML-formatted messages, besides plain text and Rich Text Format (RTF).

Table 15.1 Important Outlook 98 updates.

Release Date	Name	Description
August 1998	Outlook 98 security update	Fixes a problem where long file names in attachments make Outlook 98 crash; these long file names could also be followed by arbitrary code, which then could be executed after the crash had occurred.
June 1999	Outlook 98 email attachment security update	Increases the security regarding attachments of certain file types, such as executables, that are opened. This patch warns the user about opening such an attachment, and the users must save the file to disk before opening it.
June 1999	Outlook 98 archive patch	This update fixes an archive fidelity issue in Outlook 98 that involves potential data loss during an archive process.
June 2000	Outlook 98 SR-1 email security update	Adds protection against email viruses such as Melissa by prohibiting access of executable file types.

- *Outlook Today*—Outlook 98 has introduced the Outlook Today page, an HTML page that summarizes information in one page, such as the number of new messages, upcoming appointments, and current tasks. You can customize this page, although it's a bit tricky.
- *Outlook Bar*—Outlook 98 has a shortcut bar with the most common message folders listed; this makes it much easier for users, compared to viewing the complete folder tree, as in Outlook 97 (although many advanced users still prefer the old way, which can still be made visible if they like).
- *Features*—Outlook 98 allows the user to customize the toolbar; there is a new Folder Size button, and you can select to spell check with different languages, just to mention a few new features.
- *Performance*—Outlook 98 is faster than its predecessor Outlook 97.

When Outlook 98 is installed, you will also get Internet Explorer 4 together with Outlook Express 4; the reason for this is that the HTML engine in Outlook is shared with the Internet Explorer, and Outlook Express is added as a Usenet News client. You cannot install Outlook 98 without these added programs; however, after the installation is done, they can be removed without problems.

System Requirements for Outlook 98

These are the minimum requirements necessary to install Outlook 98; however, you should at least double or triple many of these values to get a high-performance Outlook 98 client:

- *Hardware*—486/66MHz or higher
- *Memory*—Win 95: 8MB, Win NT 4 with SP 3: 16MB
- *Operating system*—Windows 95, Windows 98, Windows 2000, Windows ME, or Windows NT 4 with SP3

Outlook 98 Easter Egg

The Easter egg for Outlook 98 is identical to the Easter egg for Outlook 97:

1. Create a new contact named Ren Hoek.
2. Select this new contact, then select Help|About.
3. Press Ctrl+Alt+Shift and click the OK button on this Help dialog box.

Once again, you should see a list of all developers, testers, and so on scroll before your eyes.

MS Outlook 2000

In June 1999, the new Outlook 2000 was released as a free upgrade for all users with a registered Client Access License (CAL) for Exchange servers (any version). Outlook 2000 was first released as a member application to the MS Office 2000 package. However, running this client without the Office 2000 products poses no problems; in fact, you can run Outlook 2000 with Office 97 if necessary. Exactly like its predecessors, Outlook 2000 has some

Table 15.2 Important Outlook 2000 updates.

Release Date	Name	Description
June 2000	Outlook 2000 SR-1 email security update	Use this patch to protect against viruses spread via email attachments. This patch will prevent users from accessing several file types; it prompts the user when an external program attempts to access their Contacts folder, or send email on their behalf.
July 2000	Outlook 2000 CDO security update	This patch updates the Collaboration Data Objects (CDO) library, thereby increasing protection against mail viruses, such as ILOVEYOU and Melissa. This update requires the Outlook 2000 SR-1 email security update.
December 2000	Office 2000 update SP-2	This is a multipurpose fix; it includes the two updates mentioned above, plus a large number of other updates and fixes.

updates, mostly regarding security patches. Some of the most important patches are listed in Table 15.2.

This Outlook version is an excellent client for Exchange 2000 environments, especially if you apply the Office 2000 update SP-2. This update is necessary because Outlook 2000 was released more than a year before Exchange 2000 was released (in October 2000).

Exactly like Outlook 98, this version also includes Internet Explorer (version 5) and Outlook Express (version 5); the reason again is the same—to get the HTML functionality in Outlook 2000 and to have a Usenet News client.

Enhancements in Outlook 2000 Compared to Outlook 98

Outlook 2000 has a number of enhancements, compared to Outlook 98. Many users were a bit disappointed with Outlook 98, but they love Outlook 2000; despite all its new features, it's actually even easier to use this client than both its predecessors. Besides the performance increase and bug fixes, these are some of the features that have been added to this version:

- *Office integration*—Now all Office applications, such as Word and Excel, can send messages without loading WordMail as the email editor; the Office applications will display the To, Cc, and Subject fields for you to fill in and convert the document to HTML or RTF format.
- *Expansion of DL*—Add a Distribution List as an attendee and Outlook will automatically expand; you can then remove any names if necessary.
- *Resource Booking*—At last this feature that disappeared in Outlook 98 is back; a resource can automatically accept booking requests without requiring an active client.
- *Calendar Color*—It's now possible to change the background color for the daily planner view, just like the good old Schedule Plus.

- *Personal DL*—Now you can create Personal Distribution Lists in the Contacts folder; this means that the Personal Address Book is no longer necessary. Consequently, the Outlook 2000 setup program will ask you if it's okay to migrate all users in your PAB file to the Contacts folder if you upgrade from Outlook 9x.
- *Mail Merge*—This feature has existed since Outlook 98, but this version is enhanced to make it even easier to use names in the Contacts folder to generate mail merge documents in Word, or to create individual email messages.
- *Remote Mail*—Now you can define a group of mail folders that you want to synchronize, instead of just having the option of synchronize one or all folders.
- *Rules Wizard*—The new feature Run Now! is an excellent button to use when you have created a new rule and want to apply it on the current folder and its messages.

System Requirements for Outlook 2000

These are the minimum requirements necessary to install Outlook 2000. As usual, these values are way too low for a production environment—you should at least double or triple many of these values to get a high-performance Outlook 2000 client:

- *Hardware*—Pentium 75MHz or higher
- *Memory*—Win 95/98/ME: 24MB, for NT 4 with SP3: 40MB, Win2K: 64MB
- *Operating system*—Windows 95 or later, Windows NT 4 with SP3

Outlook 2000 Easter Egg

The Easter egg for Outlook 2000 is a bit different than for Outlook 98; follow these steps exactly to see the Easter egg for Outlook 2000. Note: It may not work with SR-1 installed!

1. Search for the name "Ren Hoek" (without the quotes) in the Find A Contact box on the toolbar and press Enter; Outlook will say it can't find this contact.
2. Select Tools|Macro|Macros.
3. Enter **OL2KRocks** in the Macro Name field.
4. Click the Create button.
5. The About Microsoft Outlook dialog box appears.
6. Press Ctrl+Alt+Shift and click the OK button on this Help dialog box.

This will start a game; try to catch the names of the developers as they fly across in the mailbox.

MS Outlook 2002

On May 31, 2001, Outlook 2002 was released, and exactly like all previous Outlook versions it's a free upgrade for all users with a registered CAL for Exchange 2000 servers; however, if you only have CALs for Exchange 5.5 and earlier releases you will need to purchase an Outlook 2002 or Office XP license. Outlook 2002 was first released as a member application to the MS Office XP, but there is no problem with running this client without the Office XP products. In fact, you can run Outlook 2000 with any Office version if necessary. However, to get the most out of Outlook 2002, such as the nice new WordMail, you must run it together with the Office XP. As of this writing, Outlook 2002 is a new release and Microsoft has so far only released one update to Outlook 2002, described in more detail in TechNet article Q300550; below is a short description of the fixes in this update:

- Fixing a bug when using Outlook 2002 for opening an Instant Messaging message
- Fixing a bug where the users were prompted for passwords that are already saved
- Fixing a bug in the rules wizard
- Fixing a bug related to Japanese character set
- Fixing a bug that makes the client send an RPC request to the Exchange server every minute!

Only the last bullet is enough reason for implementing this Outlook 2002 update immediately, since without it you will have an extra 20 percent load on your Exchange 2000 server!

Enhancements in Outlook 2002 Compared to Outlook 2000

The Outlook 2002 client has several enhancements, compared to Outlook 2000. Many of those who liked Outlook 2000 will love Outlook 2002, although some have mixed feelings regarding its behavior. Besides the usual performance increase and bug fixes, here are some of the features that have been added to Outlook 2002:

- *Addresses*—Now you have auto completion of addresses in the To, Cc, and Bcc fields, making it work more like Outlook Express.
- *Web*—Outlook 2002 has support for Web DAV-compliant HTTP-based email.
- *No Modes*—You no longer have to choose between several modes when installing the client; in previous versions, you had to select between Corporate Workgroup and Internet Mail Only; Outlook 2002 works with all protocols.
- *Reminder*—There is now one single reminder pop-up window, instead of multiple pop-up windows; this is great when you have been away from your computer for a few days and you don't want your screen filled with pop-up reminders.
- *Synchronization*—Now you can see the progress of synchronization, and cancel it, without any problems. This will be appreciated by those who work a lot with remote mail clients.
- *Group Calendar*—Although not too fancy, it's still a group-scheduling feature that makes it possible to view the calendar of a group that the user has created, not the administrator.

- *Wordmail*—Now Word XP is the default email editor; this will make it easier since Word XP offers a lot of new and time-saving features. And it's much faster than the old Wordmail you saw in previous Outlook versions.
- *Calendar Colors*—This new feature makes it possible to define different colors for different meetings and appointments in the new Outlook 2002 Calendar; however, it's not completely intuitive to do this—prepare to spend some time understanding how this feature works.
- *Preview Pane*—Now voting buttons and meeting requests appear directly in the preview pane; you don't need to open these messages anymore.
- *Security*—Outlook 2002 has similar email security features as Outlook 2000 upgraded with Service Release 1; this means that this version of the client will let the user have more control over what file types are blocked. By changing the Registry, the user can receive them, but they still have to be stored on the disk before opening.
- *Search*—The Find feature is improved, and you can cancel a search.
- *Script*—Now it's possible to run VBA scripts as a part of a Rules Wizard rule.

System Requirements for Outlook 2002

These are the minimum requirements necessary to install Outlook 2000; as usual, these values are way too low for a production environment—you should at least double or triple many of these values to get a high-performance Outlook 2000 client:

- *Hardware*—Pentium 133MHz or higher
- *Memory*—Win 98: 24MB, Win ME or NT: 32MB, Win2K: 64MB
- *Operating system*—Windows 98, Windows 98 SE, Windows 2000, Windows ME, or Windows NT 4 with SP6

Outlook 2002 Easter Egg

Since this client has just been released as of this writing, I haven't found any Easter eggs for it yet. But I'm sure they're hiding there, somewhere. A good Web site for Easter eggs is **www.eeggs.com**.

What Is RPC Really?

All of these Outlook versions are based on the MAPI protocol, running on top of an RPC session between the client and the Exchange server. The previous Exchange servers used Remote Procedure Calls (RPCs) extensively to communicate between computers and processes. The RPC is a general method to establish a synchronous session between two processes, either running in the same computer or in different computers. This makes RPC a good choice for building client/server applications like mail systems and database applications.

An RPC session is similar to a voice conversation in an ordinary phone call: When you call a friend, you need the phone system to take care of converting your voice to digital packages, find the destination phone, transport the packages to the other side, and convert them back to an analog voice again; without the phone system, your friend will not hear your voice.

RPCs are also a way of "talking" to another process; however, they need a transport system, such as TCP/IP, IPX/SPX, or NetBEUI. If the client computer is running multiple network protocols, RPC will have a list in the Registry that says what protocol to use first; if the other computer doesn't use that transport protocol, the initialization of the RPC session will fail after a few minutes of time-out, then the next available transport protocol will be used, and so on.

When you call your friend on the phone, each of you addresses the other—"Hi! It's Jessica." When the RPC protocol establishes a session (calls its server friend), it too presents itself—"Hi! It's the XX Account." In the computer world, the server process that is contacted must be able to authenticate the caller; this is done by checking the account database: Active Directory in Windows 2000, and SAM in NT 4. If the caller cannot be validated, the session will not be established. The caller must also be able to identify (or validate) the contacted process before the session is established.

As you understand, this takes some time, so when the session is established, Exchange will keep it up and running for five minutes, even if there is no data to send. This is exactly what you do when you talk on the phone; just because neither of you says anything for a few seconds, you don't hang up and then call back, right? The RPC protocol is fast when the session is established, but it does not like glitches on the network; if there are any intermittent network problems, the RPC session will fail, which generates a warning in the Event log, and then a new connection will be established. This is one reason that Exchange 2000 has abandoned RPC and instead uses the much more resilient SMTP protocol. Previ-ous Exchange versions used RPC in these situations:

- Between servers in the same Exchange site
- Between MAPI clients and the Exchange server
- Between the Exchange administrator program and the Exchange server
- Between Exchange sites when using the Site Connector

In the Exchange 2000 environment, RPC is almost gone. The ESM admin tool uses LDAP, and the Exchange 2000 servers communicate by SMTP within a routing group and usually also between routing groups (depending on the type of routing group connector), but RPC is still used in some situations:

- Between MAPI clients and the Exchange 2000 server
- Between an Exchange 2000 routing group and an Exchange 5.5 site

The RPCPING Utility

As an Exchange administrator, you must understand that your Outlook clients will still use RPC to send and receive their MAPI messages to the Exchange 2000 server. If a client cannot reach the Exchange server, it may be because of RPC problems. An excellent tool for troubleshooting RPC sessions is the RPCPING utility, found in the Exchange 2000 CD directory \\Support\RPCPING\WINNT. Use this tool like this:

1. Start the *RPINGS.EXE* on the Exchange server—this will initiate a server process in a command window, listening for RPC traffic on all network protocols available, including Named Pipes.
2. Start the *RPINGC.EXE* on the client—this is a Windows program that is used to test the RPC traffic using different network protocols.
3. Using the *RPINGC.EXE* tool, type the name of the server that is running *RPINGS.EXE* in the Exchange Server field. Select the network protocol you are using, typically TCP/IP, in the *Protocol Sequence* field and make sure the *Endpoint* field is set to Rping.
4. Click the *Start* button to send one RPC Ping; view the result. It should look something similar to Figure 15.2 if the RPC traffic was successful, and like Figure 15.3 if unsuccessful.

You can also use this RPINGC.EXE program without the RPINGS.EXE server process to test whether you can reach the *RPC Endpoint Mapper* service on an Exchange server. Simply start the RPINGC.EXE, type in the name for the Exchange server, change the

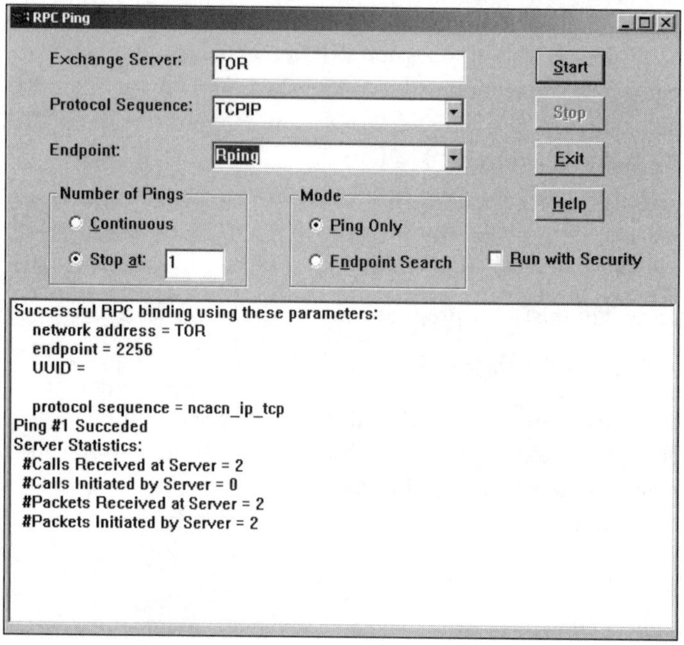

Figure 15.2
Successful RPC Ping responses.

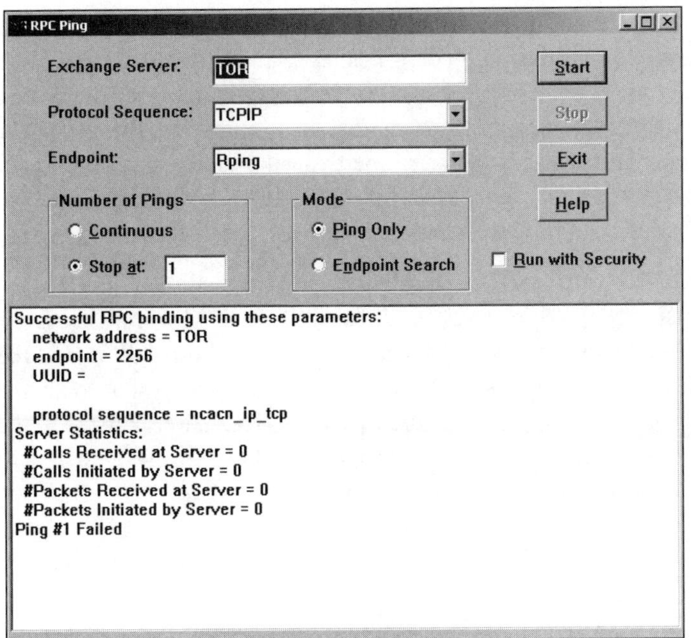

Figure 15.3
Unsuccessful RPC Ping responses.

Endpoint setting to *Store*, and change the mode to *Endpoint Search*; then click *Start* to test whether you can get an RPC contact with the *Information Store* process on the Exchange 2000 server. More information about the RPCPING utility can be found on the CD in the file RPCPING.RTF.

RPC Binding Order

Sometimes a client can look as if it hangs when starting Outlook, then after a long time it finally starts and then behaves normally. If a client always takes one minute or longer to start up, it usually depends on one of two things:

- The client can't reach the proper DNS server (because the client is configured to use the wrong IP number for the DNS, or the wrong DNS server, or there may exist a local *hosts* file on this client that has an entry for the Exchange server pointing to the wrong IP address).
- The client has multiple transport protocols installed, but the Exchange server and/or AD controller has only TCP/IP installed.

If the client doesn't start up at all, you should always start by checking whether you can ping the Exchange server and the DNS server from this client; if so, use the RPC Ping utility to test the RPC traffic. Make sure the client and the server are using the same transport protocol!

However, here we assume that the clients actually get in contact with the server, but only after a delay of one or two minutes (often described as 30 minutes by the user). Looking at the first possibility mentioned above, the client will simply not find the Exchange server using its DNS settings; however, after nearly two minutes the DNS search will time out and a broadcast or Wins search will occur, and this will find the server. An incorrectly configured *hosts* file is especially nasty since all DNS settings will look perfectly okay; however, this problem is due to the fact that *hosts* files are used before any DNS settings.

The other reason is also a bit tricky. This problem is normally not seen often today, but in organizations still using NetBEUI or IPX/SPX, it can still occur. The problem here is that the client has more than one transport protocol—for example, both TCP/IP and IPX/SPX. When Outlook starts up, it initiates an RPC session, which must have a transport protocol; if more than one is installed, which should RPC use? The answer is listed in the RPC Binding Order, a definition in the Registry of the client that determines in what order an RPC session should use a particular transport protocol:

```
HKEY_LOCAL_MACHINE\SOFTWARE\Microsoft\Exchange\Exchange Provider
Value name: Rpc_Binding_Order
Value data: ncalrpc,ncacn_ip_tcp,ncacn_spx,ncacn_np,netbios,ncacn_vns_spp
```

From the Value Data field, you can see what transport protocols RPC can use, and in what order the client will try them (a protocol will only be tried if it's installed). The "ncac" means Network Computing Architecture Connection, and the protocols and their binding order are:

1. *ncalrpc*—Local RPC, for communication between processes within one computer
2. *ncacn_ip_tcp*—TCP/IP
3. *ncacn_spx*—SPX (from the protocol stack IPX/SPX)
4. *ncacn_np*—Named Pipes
5. *netbios*—NetBIOS
6. *ncacn_vns_spp*—Banyan Vines IP

This is the default binding order for a 32-bit client like Windows 98 or Windows 2000; for Windows 3.x and DOS clients (do they still exist?), the binding order is different. So what can go wrong? Assume that one client is configured to use this binding order:

```
Rpc_Binding_Order= ncacn_spx,ncacn_ip_tcp
```

This means that the client will first try with the IPX/SPX protocol, and if the RPC session can't be established, the client will try the next protocol, or TCP/IP in this case; this should work because Exchange 2000 is a TCP/IP-based mail system.

If you think that the binding order is wrong for a client, simply modify the order in this line. You don't have to use all protocols, if you are sure they aren't used; for example, if you know that there is no Banyan Vines IP in the network, you can remove the ncacn_vns_spp.

The MS Outlook Express Client

This is Microsoft's Internet client; it can be used to talk with any messaging server on the Internet, using one of its communication protocols. It's also possible to use Outlook Express with the Exchange 2000 server; however, this client will offer much less functionality compared to MAPI clients like Outlook 2002. The Internet protocols that Outlook Express can handle include:

- *POP3*—Post Office Protocol, version 3
- *IMAP4*—Internet Mail Access Protocol, version 4
- *SMTP*—Simple Mail Transfer Protocol
- *NNTP*—Net News Transfer Protocol
- *LDAP*—Lightweight Directory Access Protocol

Notice that MAPI is missing here; this is the reason why Outlook Express doesn't have the same functionality as a full Outlook client. Outlook Express simply isn't made for Exchange. So why are we talking about this client in this Exchange 2000 book? Because Exchange 2000 Server has support for all the Internet protocols mentioned above, and in some situations, this client can be an excellent replacement for the full Outlook client.

The POP3 Protocol

One of the oldest mail protocols available is the Post Office Protocol (POP). Several versions of this protocol have been released, and the version used today is 3, also known as POP3. This message protocol was first described in RFC 918, released in October 1984, and it has gone through a number of upgrades; the latest RFC about POP3 is RFC1939, released in May 1996.

Originally, the purpose of the POP protocol was to support clients to download messages from a mail server, instead of reading these messages directly on that server. If we go all the way back to the beginning of the 1980s, it was common for organizations to run their mail systems on a time-sharing multiuser computer system, like DEC PDP-11, where the clients used terminals for reading their messages. When people got personal computers instead of terminals, they also wanted to download their messages to their local disks, instead of being connected to the server all the time; this was particularly true for those lucky users who had a PC at home, using a modem for connecting to the server. The Post Office Protocol described how a user's message could be moved from the server to the user's PC, thereby reducing the time needed for being connected over the modem; see Figure 15.4.

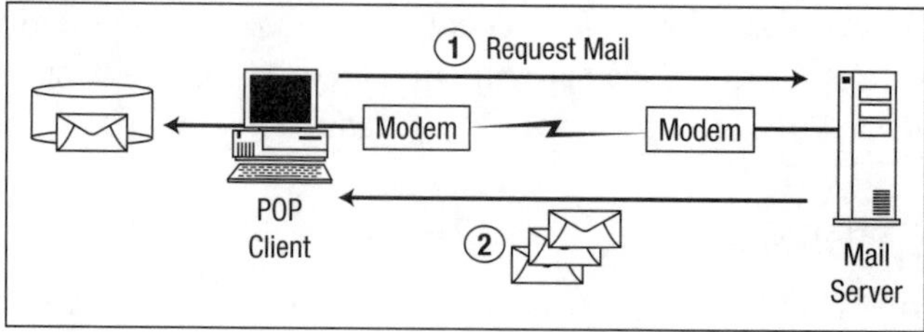

Figure 15.4
Using a POP client to download messages from the mail server.

Notice that the POP protocol is designed to *move* the messages, not copy them; that made the mail server just a temporary storage for emails, since all the messages were stored on the user's PC. All POP commands are sent over TCP port 110, using clear text commands.

The POP protocol is not used when sending messages from the user's PC to the mail server; such a protocol already existed—the SMTP protocol. So every POP client also runs SMTP for sending messages, using TCP port 25 as usual. That is the reason why you must configure two servers in POP3 clients like Outlook Express (see Figure 15.5). These two servers can be different (that's why you can define two servers); for example, in Figure 15.5 you can see that **Oden.humandata.se** is used as the POP3 server, whereas **Tor.humandata.se** is used when sending messages with SMTP.

POP3 Features

This is simple; the Post Office Protocol supports downloading the primary inbox folder. And that's it. The reason for this is that POP was designed when mail systems allowed only one

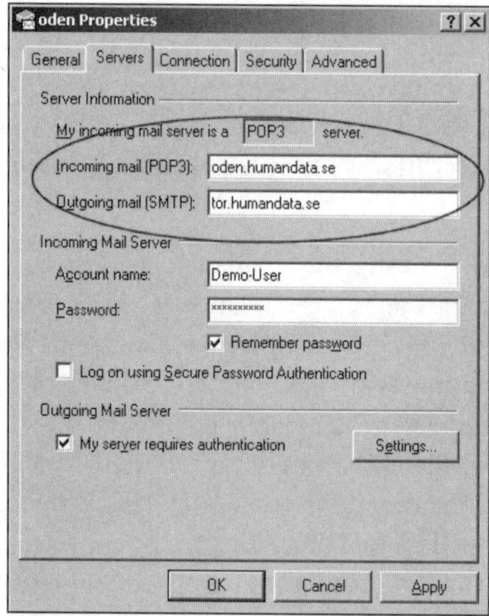

Figure 15.5
Configuring a POP3 server and an SMTP server for a POP3 client.

inbox per user. Today, with mail systems like Exchange 2000, users have a number of folders, but POP can still see only the inbox folder. It is actually easier to describe what POP3 cannot do:

- It's not possible to download any other folder besides the primary inbox that the user may have on the mail server.
- It's not possible to read anything besides emails, such as calendars or contacts.
- It's not possible to use POP for accessing global address lists.

So why are people still using POP3 clients, like Outlook Express or Eudora? Because they are very thin clients; if you are satisfied with reading only your new messages, then it does the job. Besides, POP3 clients are usually free, and POP3 clients exist for every imaginable computer system, from Atari home computers to IBM mainframes.

The IMAP4 Protocol

The Internet Mail Access protocol was described in RFC1730, released in December 1994. It was an upgraded version of the POP3 protocol, which solved many of the requests for a more advanced Internet mail client. Since the IMAP protocol was thought of as an upgrade of POP3, it got 4 as its first version number (same logic as when Exchange 4 replaced MS Mail 3.5). About 15 extensions and enhancements of the IMAP4 protocol exist, described in RFCs; one of the latest is RFC2971, released in October 2000, so this protocol is still developing.

IMAP4 clients work similarly to POP3 clients; you connect to the mail server and request to download messages to the local client computer (see Figure 15.4 again). However, with the IMAP4 protocol, you can download headers only; then you double-click a message to completely download it, including any attachments. That makes IMAP4 much better than POP3 when a modem connection is used. For example, if you just want to check for any new important mail, using your laptop computer and a mobile phone, you don't want to download everything as the POP3 would do; with IMAP4, you can see the header information like sender, subject, and size, before you select what messages to download.

IMAP4 Features

There were two problems with POP3 that IMAP4 solved:

- It made it possible to view multiple folders, not just the inbox.
- It made it possible to download copies from the server, instead of moving the messages.

But still the IMAP4 could not retrieve information from a global address list. The IMAP was designed to use TCP port 143 (instead of port 110 for POP); and it's only used for downloading messages from the server, just like POP. To send messages, SMTP is used, so when configuring an IMAP4 client, two servers must be set; see Figure 15.6.

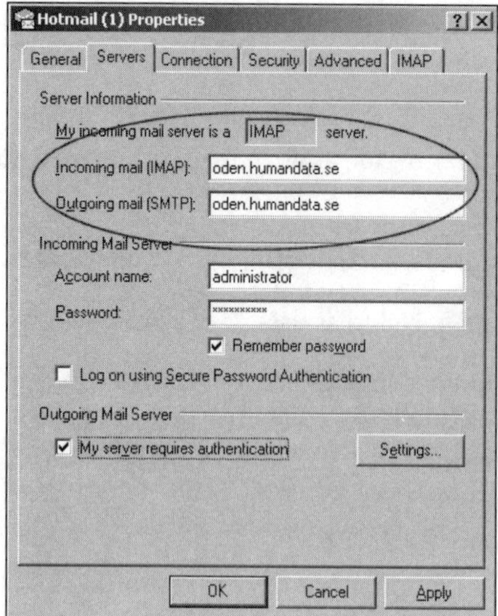

Figure 15.6
Configuring an IMAP4 and SMTP server for an IMAP client.

How to Install an IMAP4 Client

The first time Outlook Express is started, it must be configured. Follow these steps to install MS Outlook Express 5.5 as an IMAP4 client:

1. Start the MS Outlook Express client by selecting *Start|Programs|Outlook Express*.
2. If this is the first time Outlook Express is started, you will now see the *Internet Connection Wizard*. Select how you want to set up this connection (in this example, we will use a LAN connection), and click *Next*.
3. Select how to connect to the Internet (here we will use LAN), then click *Next*.
4. Select how to detect any proxy settings; if you are sure there is no proxy, don't fill in any of these options. If you are unsure, select *Automatic Discovery Of Proxy Server*. Click *Next* to continue.
5. Next, you will be given the option of creating a mail account; if you answer *No* here, Outlook Express will be installed, but it will not connect to a mail server. If so, you must later configure a mail account before this client can communicate with a mail server.

   If you answer *Yes* (which is the default), you will now see a number of dialog boxes to help you set up this new mail account. In this example, we chose this option. When ready, click *Next*.
6. The first dialog is about the user's display name. This name will later be used in outgoing messages as the sender's address, so be sure to select the proper name here. When ready, click *Next*.

7. Then enter the reply email address; make sure to enter the correct address here, since if this is wrong, no one will be able to reply to your messages. Note that there is no check that this email address (or the display name in Step 6) is genuine and correctly spelled.

8. On the *Email Server Names* page, select what type of mail protocol to be used and the FQDN names to these servers; or, you can also enter the IP address to the server instead.

   Outlook Express 5.5 has support for POP3, IMAP4, and HTTP mail servers. The first two are self -explanatory, but the HTTP protocol is new for version 5.5 of Outlook Express. This protocol makes it possible to connect this client to a Web-based mail system, such as Hotmail. Make sure to select the right protocol here; when ready, click *Next*.

   Notice that incoming mail may be POP3, IMAP4, or HTTP, but outgoing mail servers are always SMTP; make sure to type the correct names for these servers, and that they are listed in the DNS server.

9. On the *Internet Mail Logon* page, enter the account logon name and password. If you set the *Remember Password* checkbox, this client will remember this password in the future; if it's cleared, you must enter the password every time you connect to the mail server with this mail account. For highest security, you should clear this setting, but if you trust that no one can sneak in to use your computer, or if you don't care, keep this setting.

   The *Secure Password Authentication (SPA)* is a method of sending the password with a challenge/response method, such as *Windows NTLM Challenge/Response*; if this option is not selected, the password will be sent in clear text. Before this option can be used, you must make sure that the IMAP4 (or POP3) mail server understands SPA validations; however, all versions of Exchange support SPA.

   Note that when SPA is selected, another account that you may select will be used! For example, assume that your client is logged on to the network as Anna, and you want to use Outlook Express for reading the mail account Administrator; if you set the checkbox for SPA, Outlook Express will use the logged on account, regardless of what account and password you have listed on this Internet Mail Logon page!

10. The next page completes the installation of Outlook Express.

Rerouting of Outgoing Messages from IMAP4 and POP3 Clients

Outlook Express is now ready to use; if you also created an IMAP4 account, you can now connect to the IMAP4 server. However, if this is an Exchange 2000 server, you must complete one more step before you can actually send messages from this client—you must configure the Outlook Express client to use logon authentication when sending messages. Here's how:

1. Start Outlook Express, select the *Tools|Accounts* menu, and switch to the *Mail* tab.
2. Select the new mail account and click *Properties*; open the *Servers* tab (see Figure 15.7).

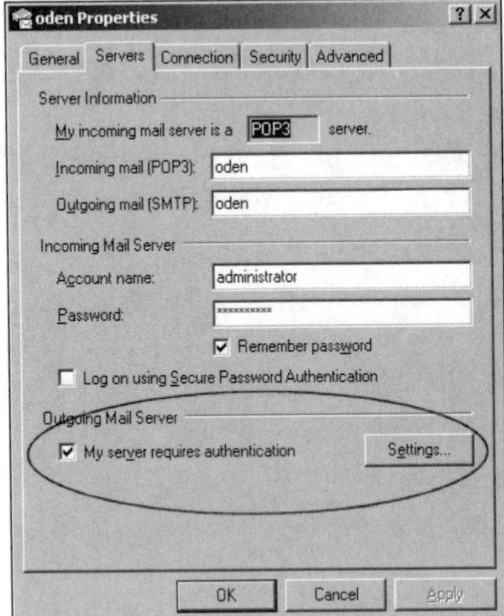

Figure 15.7
The Servers tab.

3. Set the *My Server Requires Authentication* checkbox. Normally you use the same account for retrieving messages as sending; if this is correct, then you are finished now. If not, you must enter the other account and password; click the Settings button and change to Log On Using (see Figure 15.8).
4. Click *OK* to close all dialog windows.

The reason why POP3 and IMAP4 clients must set this authentication for sending messages is that Exchange 2000 by default doesn't allow anonymous rerouting of messages. "What is rerouting?" you may ask. This is when someone uses an Internet client and connects to your SMTP server, requesting that this SMTP server reroute messages from this client to external addresses, which will make these messages look like they originate from your server.

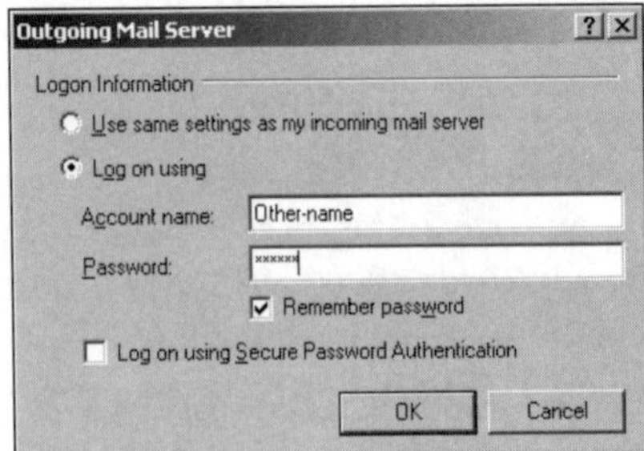

Figure 15.8
Enter the account name and password for sending messages.

Let's look at an example; if I use an IMAP4 client and connect to Human Data's SMTP server to send a message to someone outside this organization, such as Microsoft.com, this is rerouting. The recipient at Microsoft will see that this mail is sent from Human Data's mail server, whereas in fact it could have been sent from an IMAP4 client anywhere in the world. This rerouting feature is often used for sending unsolicited commercial messages, also known as *spam* mail. If the recipient at Microsoft gets mad at this mail, he or she may send a request to the postmaster at Human Data, asking them to stop sending spam; however, since the true sender is not a member of this organization, there is not much the postmaster can do, except of course to disable the relay feature.

To see this setting in Exchange 2000, follow these steps:

1. Use the *ESM* tool and navigate to the Exchange server object; then select *Protocols|SMTP|Default SMTP Virtual Server*.
2. Open the properties for this virtual SMTP server, and select the *Access* tab.
3. Click the *Relay* button (see Figure 15.9). This figure shows the default settings; it says that the only computers that can relay messages through this SMTP server are the ones listed—and this list is empty! But below you can also see a checkbox set for *Allow All Computers Which Successfully Authenticate To Relay, Regardless Of The List Above*. This is the setting that will make IMAP4 and POP3 users that authenticate before sending messages able to reroute, but will stop all others. If you don't have an account in this Windows 2000 forest, you will not be able to reroute any messages. This will prevent the spammers from using this server. Do not clear this checkbox unless you know exactly what you are doing!

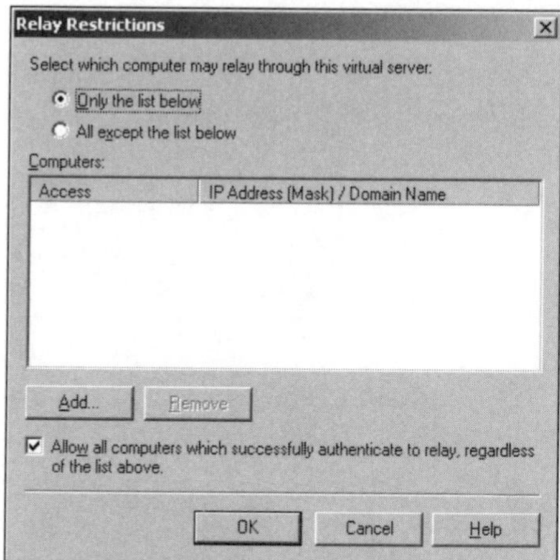

Figure 15.9
The Relay Restrictions for the virtual SMTP server.

Leaving Copies of Messages on the Server

You may recall that POP3 is designed to physically move messages from the server to the local POP3 message file (stored in the file Inbox.dbx deep down in your profile; it's easiest to search for it). This means that if you just want to test and play with the POP3 account to see how it works, using your own mailbox account, you will soon discover that all your mail is moved to Outlook Express; when you use the Outlook 2002 (or whatever client you use), it will show empty folders. Now, that is not something you want, right? So before playing with POP3, you should configure it to leave a copy of messages on the Exchange server, to avoid this irritating little mistake. Follow these steps to activate this setting:

1. Start *Outlook Express*, select the *Tools|Accounts* menu, and switch to the *Mail* tab.
2. Select the mail account to modify and click *Properties*.
3. Open the *Advanced* tab (see Figure 15.10), and set the *Leave A Copy Of Messages On Server* checkbox. You can also configure Outlook Express to automatically clean the server mailbox after a given number of days, or when deleted from the *Deleted Items* folder. Click *OK* to save and close this dialog window.

But what if the damage is already done? All your messages are already moved to Outlook Express, so what can be done now? Well, of course you can forward all messages back to your mailbox, but this is not a good solution since all the messages will list your name as the sender, and the delivery date and time are also modified. There is actually a much better solution available in Outlook Express 5.5; you can export messages back to the Exchange server by following these steps:

1. In *Outlook Express*, select *File|Export|Messages* menu.

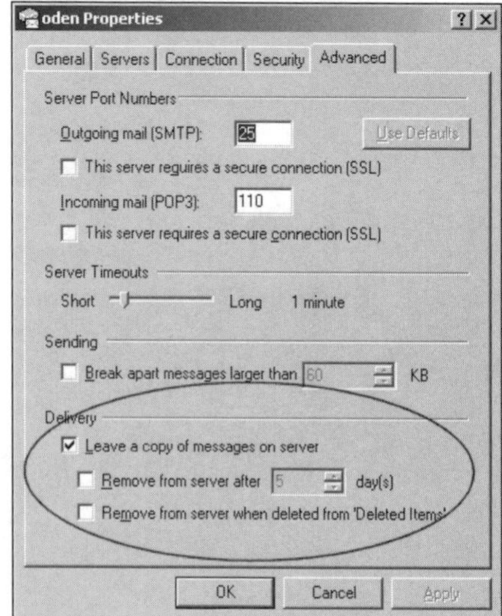

Figure 15.10
The Advanced tab for POP3 properties.

2. That will display a dialog box saying that this will export these messages to Outlook (PST file) or the Exchange server; click *OK* to continue.
3. Next, you will need to select the Outlook profile to be used (only if you have configured Outlook to prompt for profiles); select the profile you want to export these messages to. Click *OK* when ready.
4. The *Export Messages* page will be displayed. Default is to export all folders. However, if you just want to restore your messages back to the *Inbox* (remember, POP3 only knows about the Inbox; it can't move any other messages), change to *Selected Folders* and select the *Inbox* folder. Click *OK* when ready.
5. This will start the export. Wait until the process is completed, and your messages are back in the Inbox again.

A note for users who have non-U.S. folder names; the export will always go to a folder in Exchange with the same name as the Inbox folder in Outlook Express; if this folder doesn't exist, it will be created. So if you have an Inbox folder in Outlook Express that is labeled Inbox, but the corresponding folder in your Exchange mailbox is labeled Inkorg, then you will have a new Inbox folder where all messages are stored; you will have to move these messages manually to the correct folder.

The OWA 2000 Client

The Outlook Web Access (OWA) client makes it possible to view your mailbox from any Web browser in the world, while still being protected from both unauthorized access and network monitors scanning for passwords and messages. However, this is true only if the system is configured correctly. The default settings will give you an OWA client that sends the account name and password in clear text, and all messages in clear text. In this section, I will show you how to configure OWA properly.

First, let's look at the background of the OWA client. Its first release was with Exchange Server 5, in April 1997; that version was limited in what folders it could access and its performance was low. With Exchange 5.5 in December 1997 came a much better OWA client; it has since then been upgraded with each Exchange service pack, making it faster and able to access more folder types. But still this client was a long way from being comparable to the MAPI Outlook client.

The OWA 5.x Architecture

All versions of OWA in Exchange 5 and 5.5 were built on basically the same type of architecture. The client accessed an IIS 4 Web server, which impersonated the user and established a MAPI/RPC session with the Exchange server; see Figure 15.11.

This is what happens in this architecture when a user opens his or her mailbox:

1. The user's Web browsers request to open the mailbox; the user must first authenticate by entering the account name and password.

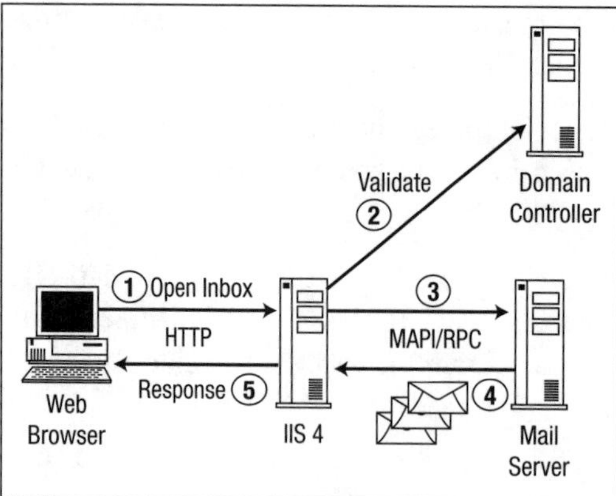

Figure 15.11
The OWA architecture in Exchange 5.x.

2. The IIS Web server must first validate this user account with a domain controller.
3. If the validation is okay, this Web server then establishes an RPC session with the Exchange server, and sends MAPI commands (just like any Outlook client does) requesting the first 25 message headers.
4. The Exchange server passes this information back to the Web server, using standard MAPI calls over this RPC session.
5. The Web server converts the information received from the Exchange server to HTML-formatted files, and sends them back to the Web client.

Since the Web server has to convert the client's HTTP requests to MAPI calls, and messages to HTML files, the number of simultaneous clients this Web server can handle are much less than the number of MAPI clients an Exchange server can handle. Depending on the hardware configuration, up to 800 simultaneous OWA users may be served.

To make the IIS Web server understand how to talk MAPI over RPC, and how to convert messages to HTML format, it must be extended with new Dynamic Link Libraries (DLL) files; these are installed using the Exchange Server setup program. The Exchange server itself doesn't have to be configured in any way (however, you can configure it to refuse Web access if necessary).

The largest weakness with the OWA client is its lack of security; all information, including the account password, is sent in clear text (or really Base-64 encoded, but that's no encryption; it's just a solution to accept 8-bit characters in the password). At the same time, OWA's greatest strength is that it will allow access to the mailbox from almost anywhere in the world, as long as the IIS Web server is connected to the Internet.

The OWA Architecture in Exchange 2000

When Exchange 2000 was released in October 2000, many people expected an improved OWA client; Microsoft didn't disappoint. The new OWA 2000 was much faster, and it could access nearly all folders. A part of the reason for this increased performance was that Exchange left the responsibilities for all Internet protocols, like HTTP and LDAP, to the IIS 5 Web server that comes with all Windows 2000 servers, including the server where the Exchange 2000 is installed. Another reason was that Exchange 2000 has the new STM stores, described in Chapter 2; these stores can store MIME-formatted messages without the need to convert them to Exchange database format.

Yet another reason was that the IIS server no longer had to convert messages to HTML or use RPC sessions for these OWA clients. The default configuration in Exchange 2000 is to let the OWA client access the Exchange server almost directly, by first accessing the IIS layer that uses a very fast communication layer called *ExIPC* to talk with the Exchange server. Besides that, the new OWA client also supports Web-DAV and XML protocols, including Dynamic HTML, which all make this client faster and give it more features. When an OWA client accesses Exchange 2000 with the new architecture, this is basically what happens; see Figure 15.12:

1. The user's Web browsers request to open the mailbox; the IIS Web server replies by asking the user to authenticate by entering the account name and password.
2. The IIS Web server then validates this user account with an Active Domain controller.
3. If the validation is okay, this Web server retrieves the contents of the Inbox folder directly from the Exchange stores, requesting the first 25 message headers, and sends them back to the Web browser.

This OWA version has many more features than its predecessors, and it's a great client to use for temporary access or when you just occasionally need to access the mailbox.

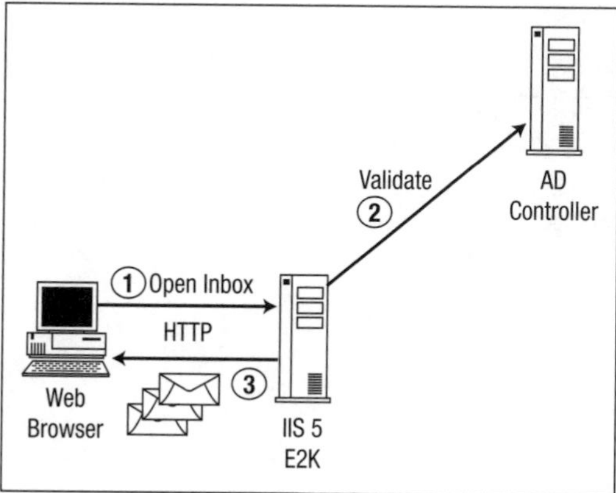

Figure 15.12
The OWA architecture in Exchange 2000.

However, some features require that you have a Web browser that supports Web-DAV, XML, and Dynamic HTML. New features in this version include:

- *Public Folders*—Now it's possible to view public folders of Contact and Calendar type.
- *Address List*—Is easier to use than before (see Figure 15.13).
- *Preview Pane*—You can preview messages without opening them first, just like in the standard Outlook client.
- *Right-click*—If you right-click the folder tree, you can move, copy, rename, delete, or create new folders.
- *Windows*—When opening a message now, it will open in a window that looks very similar to the standard Outlook message window.
- *Drag-and-Drop*—Now it's possible to drag files to other folders in the OWA client (but you can't drag files outside the OWA client).
- *Calendar*—Improved; for example, it's now possible to view other peoples' free/busy schedule.

But some features were still missing, compared to the MAPI Outlook client, such as:

- *Tasks*—You can view, but not create or modify tasks (also known as to-do lists).
- *Rules*—OWA doesn't allow you to create rules; however, you can run the Out-of-Office assistant (see Figure 15.14).

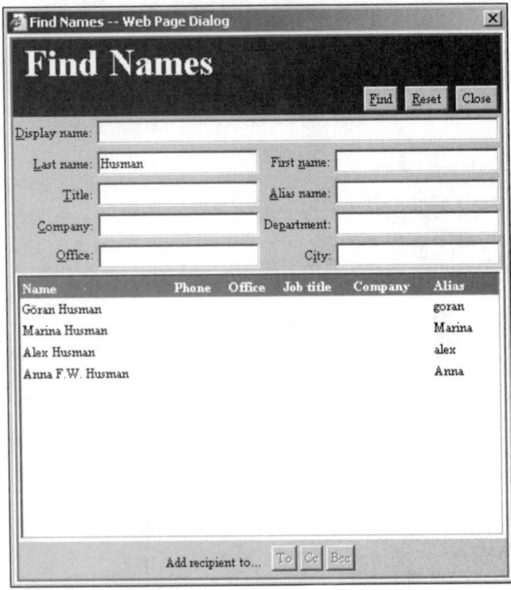

Figure 15.13
The Address feature in OWA 2000.

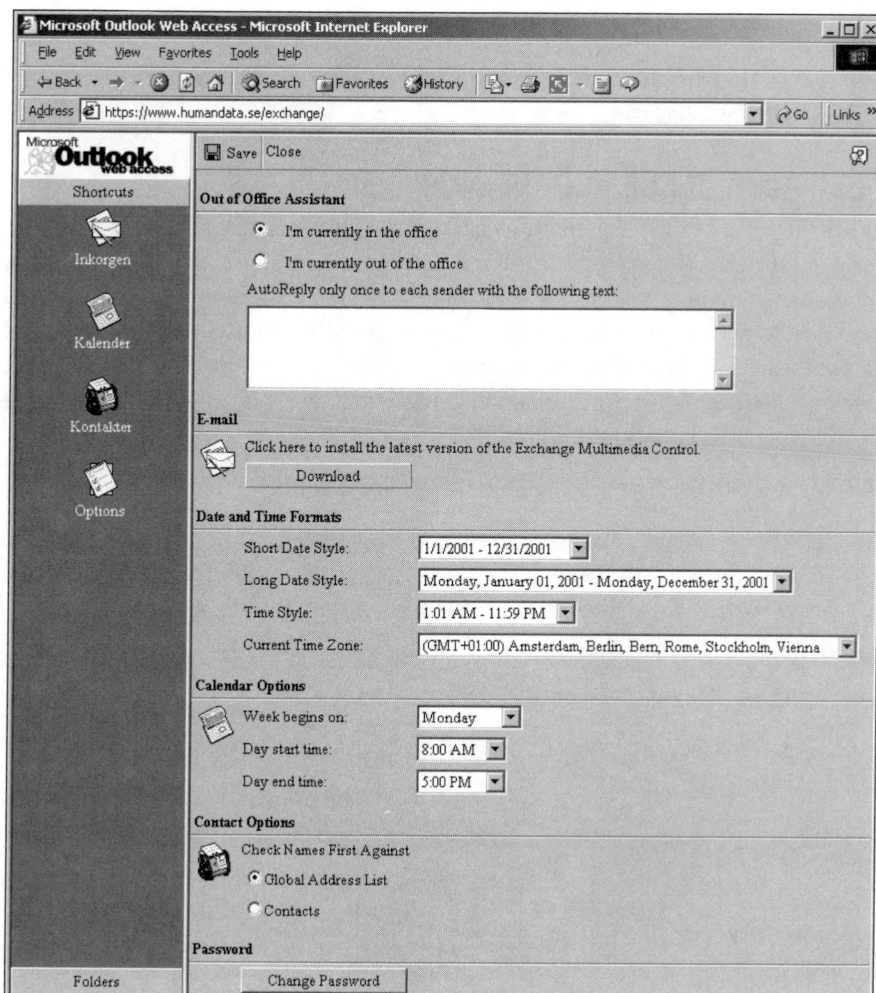

Figure 15.14
The Options page in OWA 2000.

15

- *Views*—It's not possible to modify the preconfigured views or create new views.
- *Search*—Although Exchange 2000 has the new advanced search engine, no search feature exists in the OWA client.
- *Polling*—The user must manually update the OWA client; new messages will not show up automatically.
- *Address lists*—As in previous OWA versions, there is no way to browse the global address list; but it's easier to search addresses in this OWA version.
- *Settings*—The number of configuration settings is very low, compared to the standard Outlook client.

- *Security*—There is no support for S/MIME.
- *Options*—There is no support for voting buttons, sending messages a given number of times, follow-up flags, etc.

Installation of SSL in OWA 2000

It's easy to activate the OWA client in Exchange 2000; no installation is actually necessary if you accept the default configuration described above. However, if you want to protect the OWA client and its traffic, you must configure SSL encryption. Another thing that you may want to do is to separate the IIS 5 server from the Exchange 2000 server. But let's start with the SSL configuration; this is easier than you first may think, especially if you have installed the MS Certificate Server, as described in Chapter 14. Follow these steps to protect your OWA clients with SSL:

1. Start the *Internet Service Manager (ISM)*, located in *Start|Run|Administrative Tools*.
2. Open the properties for the *Default Web Site* and switch to the *Directory Security* tab; see Figure 15.15. We will start by installing an X.509 Web certificate that later can be used in any of the virtual directories of this Web server.
3. Click the *Server Certificate* button on this page; this will start the *Web Server Certificate Wizard*. Then click *Next* to continue.
4. On the *Server Certificate* page (see Figure 15.16), select *Create A New Certificate*; then click *Next*.

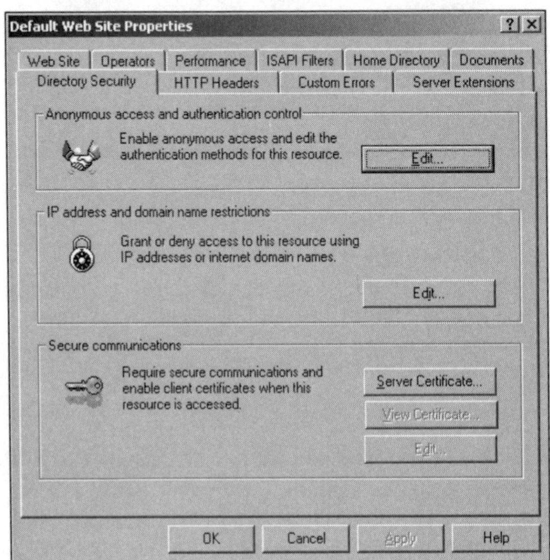

Figure 15.15
The Directory Security tab for the default Web site.

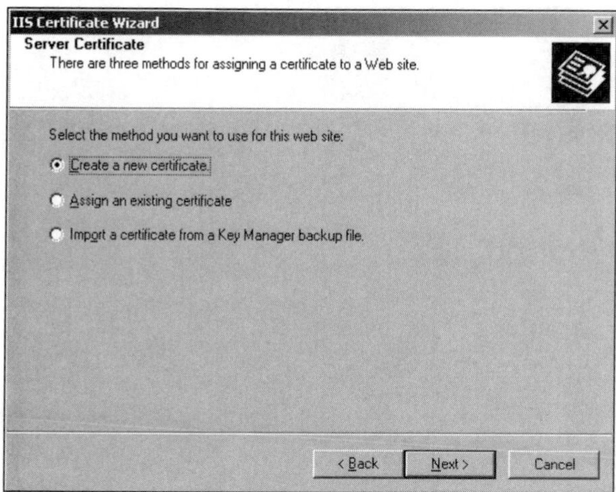

Figure 15.16
The Server Certificate page.

The *Assign An Existing Certificate* option is used when you have acquired a certificate from a CA. The *Import A Certificate* option is used in emergency situations to restore a certificate. Use the *Keyring.exe* program in Exchange 5.5 to create a backup file; this file can then be used to import the certificate with the option mentioned on this page.

5. On the *Delayed Or Immediate Request* page (see Figure 15.17), select how to request the new certificate. If you have an *MS Certificate Server* in the domain, you should use the *Send The Request Immediately To An Online Certification Authority* option.

   You can also use the *Prepare The Request Now, But Send It Later* option. This will create the request that should be sent to the CA; you can store this request in a text file, if necessary. Click *Next* to continue.

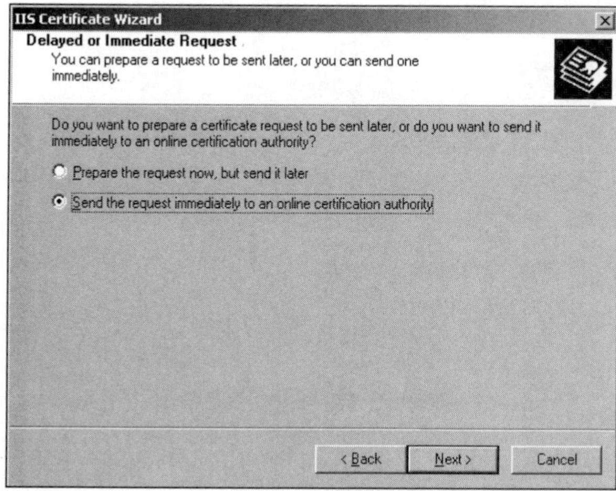

Figure 15.17
The Delayed Or Immediate Request page.

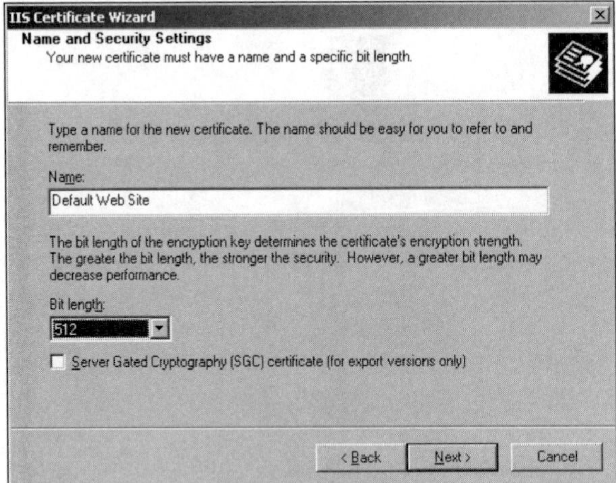

Figure 15.18
The Name And Security Settings page.

6. On the *Name And Security Settings* page (see Figure 15.18), enter a descriptive name for this certificate, and select the encryption key length. Default is 512 bits, but longer keys give higher protection at the cost of decreased performance.

   The *Server Gated Cryptography* is an extension of SSL that provides strong 128-bit encryption for Internet banks and other approved users. The difference between SSL and SGC is that SSL can be used for all purposes, but SGC can only be used for approved applications (such as online banks). We don't use the SGC for our OWA certificate, so leave this option cleared.

7. On the *Organization Information* page (see Figure 15.19), enter the name of your organization and the organizational unit.

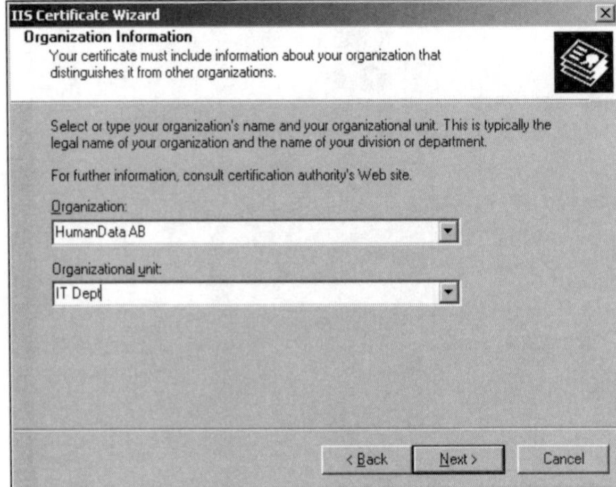

Figure 15.19
The Organization Information page.

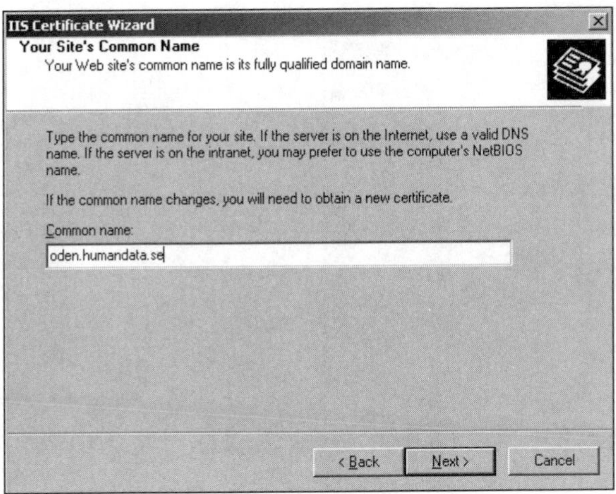

Figure 15.20
The Common Name page.

8. On the *Your Site's Common Name* page (see Figure 15.20), enter the fully qualified domain name (FQDN) for your Web server; however, if this Web server is only used on your intranet, you can enter the server's NetBIOS name instead.
9. On the *Geographical Information* page (see Figure 15.21), enter the country, state, and city for your location.
10. The *Certification Authority* page (see Figure 15.22), since we selected to send our request to an online CA, lists all available certification authorities; you should see the MS Certificate Server here.

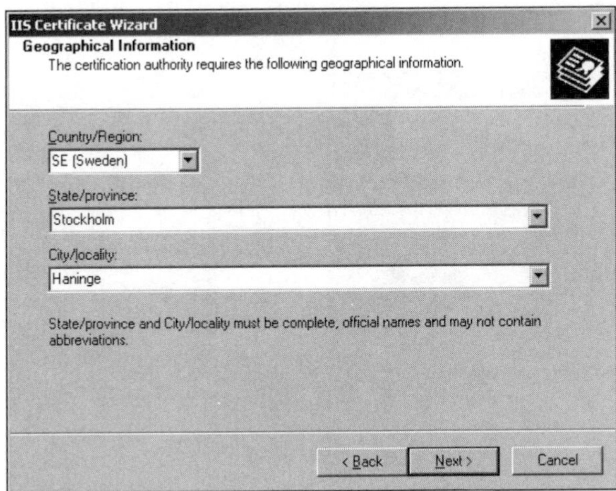

Figure 15.21
The Geographical Information page.

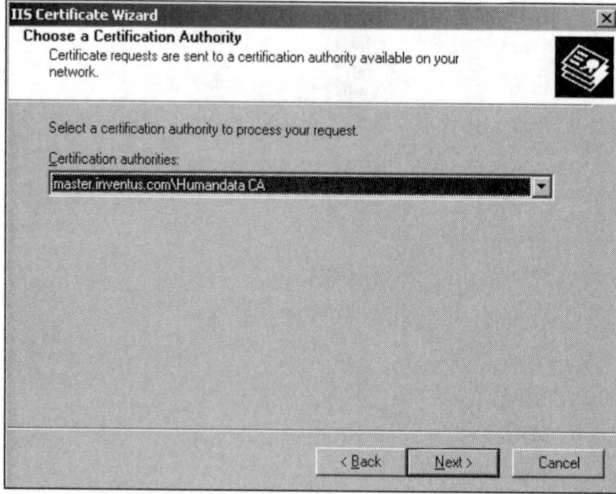

Figure 15.22
The CA page.

11. Finally, on the *Certificate Request Submission* page (see Figure 15.23), you will see a summary of your certificate request; if all is okay, click *Next* to send the request, otherwise click *Back* to correct any errors.

Configure the Exchange Virtual Directory for SSL

That completes the request; now this request is sent to the online CA (our MS Certificate Server), and when the X.509 certificate is returned, it will automatically be installed. However, we have not yet used this certificate for our OWA. This is done by modifying the properties for the virtual Web directory labeled Exchange; see Figure 15.24. Don't worry about the red stop sign for this directory; this is the result of the Inetinfo.exe process (IIS 5) starting up before Exchange 2000 has started its stores and ExIFS services.

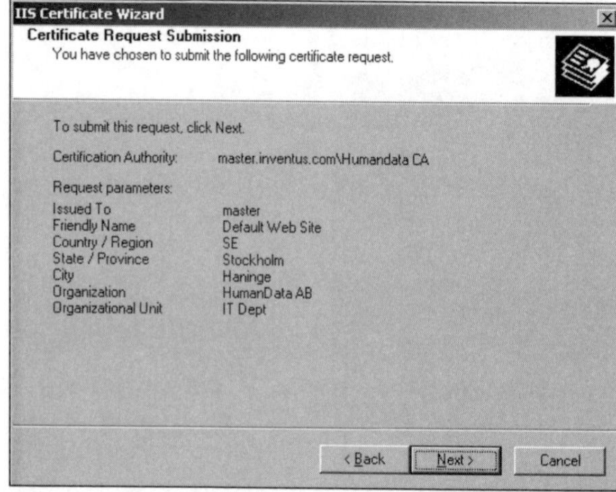

Figure 15.23
The Certificate Request Submission page.

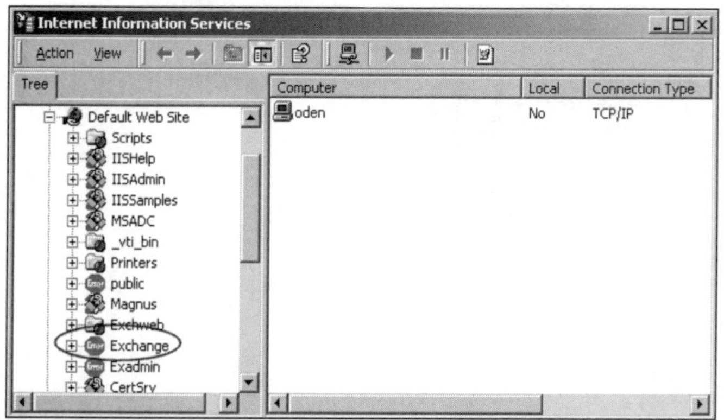

Figure 15.24
The virtual directory used for OWA access.

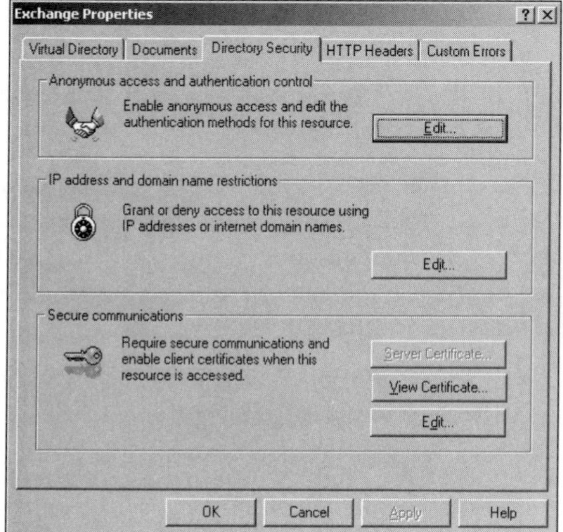

Figure 15.25
The Directory Security page for Exchange virtual directory.

Open its properties and switch to the *Directory Security* page (see Figure 15.25). Click the *Edit* button and set the *Require Secure Channel (SSL)* checkbox; see Figure 15.26. Now you have an SSL-protected OWA client! That wasn't so hard, was it?

Using the OWA Client with SSL Encryption

To start the OWA 2000 client, you need a Web browser that is at least HTTP 3.2 compliant and understands Java Script; if it also understands Web-DAV, XLM, and Dynamic HTML, it will be even better, since it will be faster and give OWA some extra features, such as the ability to right-click on folders and drag items between folders. But the basic features will still exist without these extra protocols; for example, it's okay to run OWA on MS Internet Explorer 4 or Netscape 3, but for maximum performance and to take full advantage of all available features in OWA 2000, you should select MS Internet Explorer 5.x or later.

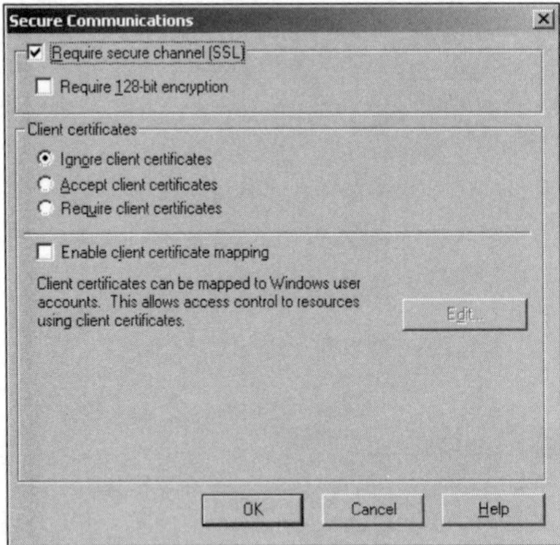

Figure 15.26
Requiring SSL encryption for OWA access.

To start the OWA client without SSL, browse to **http://www.humandata.se/Exchange** (assuming our Web server is named **www.humandata.se**).

This will lead you to the default Web site and its virtual directory Exchange (refer back to Figure 15.24). Since we have entered **http** at the beginning of this URL, we are requesting to start the OWA client using non-encrypted communication. However, since we now have configured our OWA to be protected by SSL, we will get a warning stating that this is a protected page that must be viewed over a secure channel; see Figure 15.27.

From this error message, we also get a tip to use *https* instead of *http* when accessing this page, so let's try this instead: **https://www.humandata.se/Exchange**.

Now that was better! First we must authenticate ourselves, using the standard Windows 2000 account, password, and domain; then we will have access to our Exchange mailbox (see Figure 15.28).

***Tip:** If this Web site belongs to the same domain as our user, you don't have to enter this domain—you can leave this field empty. If the Web server belongs to another domain, you can make it easier for your users by changing the default domain setting. Open the Directory Security property page for the virtual directory Exchange (as depicted in Figure 15.35); click the Edit button in the Anonymous access and authentication control pane; finally, click the Edit button in the Authenticated Access pane, and enter the default domain.*

Look carefully at Figure 15.28—notice the yellow padlock at the bottom of this window. This is an indication that this page is encrypted using SSL. The only thing users need to remember is to type HTTPS instead of HTTP when starting the OWA client. No configuration is required on the Web client, which means that you can use any publicly available Web browser, like in an Internet café, and still enjoy an encrypted connection. An SSL-secured connection protects everything that is sent between the Web client and the Web

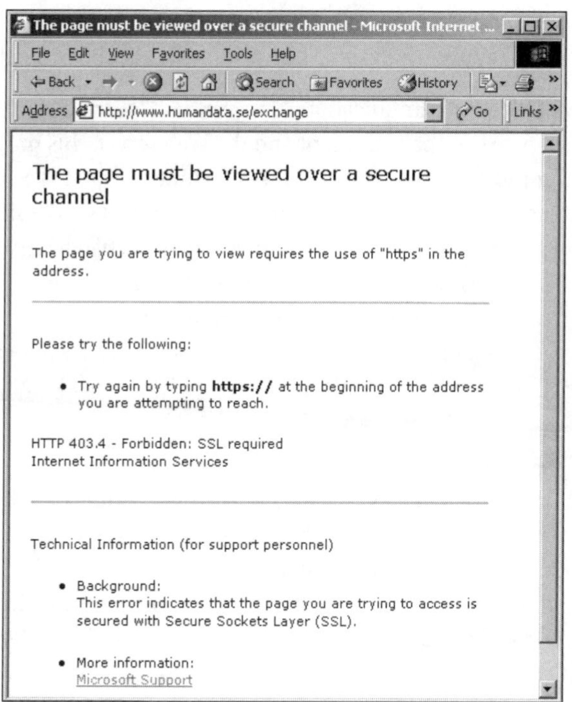

Figure 15.27
The error message you'll receive when trying to open an SSL-protected page.

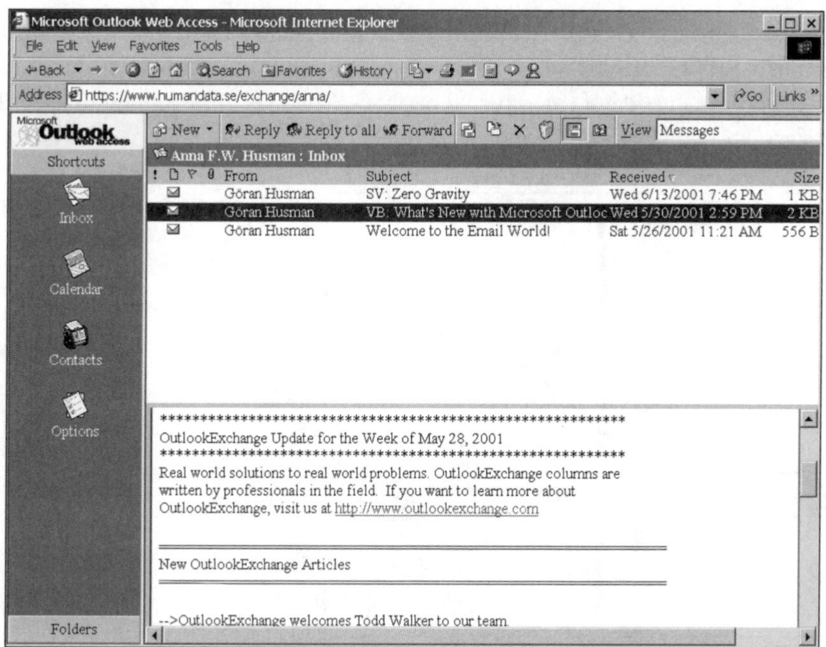

Figure 15.28
Accessing OWA using SSL encryption.

server—from the logon dialog box to the transfer of messages and attachments. Even if you use a Basic Clear Text logon procedure, this communication will also be protected.

Normal HTTP traffic uses TCP port 80 for communication; however, HTTPS traffic uses TCP port 443 instead. If a firewall exists between the Web client and the Web server, this must have port 443 enabled or else this SSL communication will not work. No other ports will be used when an OWA server is used that also has the Exchange 2000 system installed on the same physical server. However, many organizations don't want to expose their Exchange server on the Internet; they want to use an OWA server on the firewall's DMZ segment, communicating with Exchange 2000 on the internal network. This is how it was done in Exchange 5.x; refer back to Figure 15.21. So how do we configure Exchange 2000 to use one external OWA server and one internal Exchange server? The answer is: by using a front-end/back-end design.

Front-End/Back-End Scenarios

A *front-end/back-end (FE/BE)* scenario is used when you want to separate the Exchange server with the mailbox stores from the OWA server that handles the Web clients. This was rather simple in previous Exchange versions; you just used an IIS and installed the necessary DLL files. Exchange 2000 is more complicated; in this version you must install an Exchange 2000 Enterprise server configured as a *front-end* server to make it an OWA server. This FE server will then communicate with the normal Exchange servers, also known as the *back-end* servers; see Figure 15.29.

When a Web client accesses the Exchange 2000 server using OWA, this is what happens (assuming the Web server is **www.humandata.se**); see also Figure 15.29:

1. The Web client connects to **www.humandata.se/exchange** using HTTP over port 80 if it's normal HTTP, or port 443 if it's HTTPS. This URL points to the front-end server, located on the outside of the internal network. The user is prompted to enter his or her account name, password, and domain.

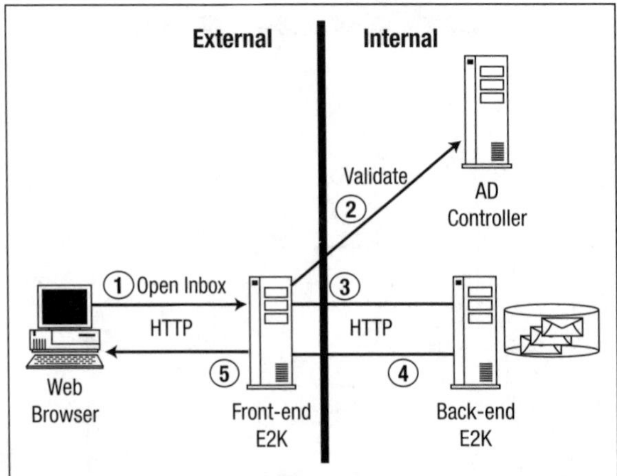

Figure 15.29
A front-end/back-end scenario.

2. The FE server queries an Active Directory server to determine the back-end server this user belongs to.
3. When the FE knows which BE to contact, it forwards the user's HTTP request to the BE server, using port 80. Note that the traffic between FE and BE servers will always be over port 80, even if the client uses SSL over port 443 to communicate with the FE server.
4. The BE server is processed in a normal way, and the response is sent back to the FE server.
5. The FE server forwards the response to the client, using port 80 if normal traffic or port 443 if it's SSL encrypted.

The BE server handles the requests from the FE server exactly as if it were a standard Web client; all HTTP packages are simply forwarded to and from the FE server without any modification. As noted in Step 3 above, all traffic between the FE and BE servers is standard HTTP communication, using port 80; this means that SSL is never used between FE and BE servers, regardless of what communication is used between the client and the FE server.

Performance Issues

The front-end server caches the responses, thereby radically decreasing the number of queries to Active Directory servers and BE servers for both mailbox and public folder access; this increases the overall performance.

When a BE server is unreachable, the FE server marks this server as *unavailable* for a period of 10 minutes; however, the FE immediately sends the request to another BE server that is available. During this 10-minute period, no further connection retries are attempted to this BE; this means that if the BE server comes back online quickly, it may take nearly 10 minutes before the FE server will use it.

When using FE/BE scenarios, the FE server must be configured for *basic* authentication; neither *Windows Integrated Security* (with NTLM and Kerberos authentication), nor *Digest Authentication* is supported by Exchange 2000 front-end servers. To protect the user's password from being captured by network scanners, the FE server must be configured to use SSL. This decreases the performance of this server and lowers the number of simultaneously supported OWA users up to 40 percent, depending on the behavior of these users. Special hardware is available to be used for SSL-encrypted communication; this hardware takes care of all encryption and decryption processing, thereby offloading this burden from the Web server's CPU—for example AEP 1000 SSL Accelerator (**www.aep.ie**) and Compaq AXL300 (**www.Compaq.com/protucts/servers/security/AXL300**).

Configuring a Front-End and Back-End Server

To set up a front-end server, you only need to make a very simple modification to a back-end server; open the properties for an Exchange 2000 server, using the ESM tool, and set the *This Is A Front-End Server* checkbox (see Figure 15.30). Restart the computer and that's it!

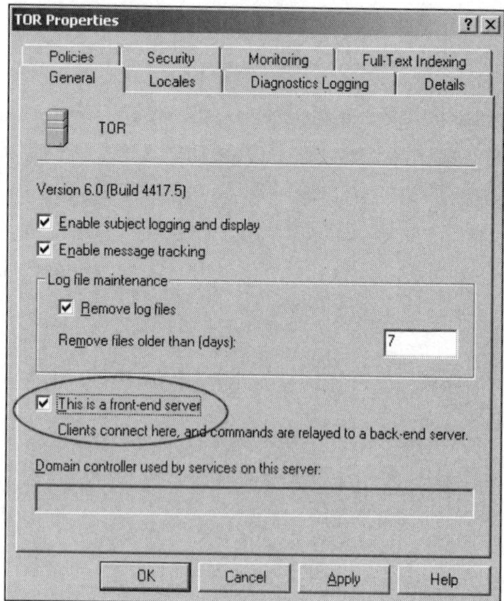

Figure 15.30
Configuring a front-end server.

The back-end server must be configured to support the front-end server. You must create one new virtual HTTP server that maps to each front-end server's namespace (such as **humandata.se** and **highrad.org**) by following these steps:

1. Start the *ESM* tool. Navigate to the HTTP folder (in the *Protocols* folder under the server object).
2. Right-click the HTTP folder and select *New|HTTP Virtual Server*.
3. On the *General* page (see Figure 15.31), Microsoft recommends using names similar to Exchange FE VS TOR (assuming the FE server is named TOR), to make these special virtual servers easy to identify.
4. Still on the *General* page, click the *Advanced* button (not the *Access* tab!), and then the *Add* button (see Figure 15.32). Enter a *Host Name*, but don't modify any other parameters; then click *OK*.
5. Click *OK* to close the *Advanced* dialog box, and *OK* again to close and create the new virtual HTTP server.
6. Expand the HTTP folder, right-click on the new virtual HTTP server, and select *New|Virtual Directory*.
7. On the *General* page (see Figure 15.33), enter the name **exchange**, make sure the *Mailbox For* option is selected, and note that the gray marked namespace listed is the one this FE server supports (if not, click *Modify* and select another one). Then click *OK* to complete the creation of this virtual directory.

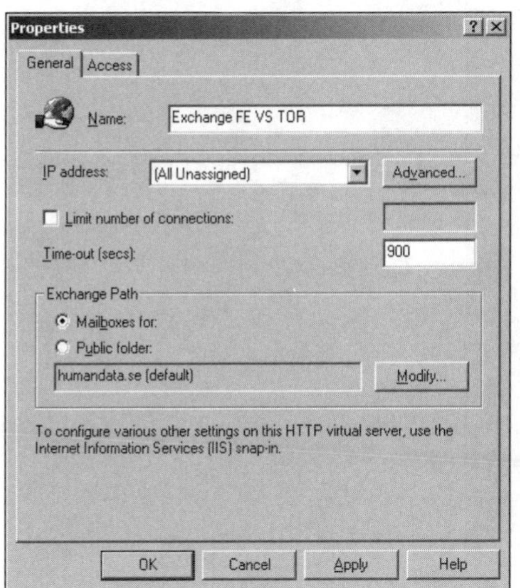

Figure 15.31
The General page for the new HTTP server.

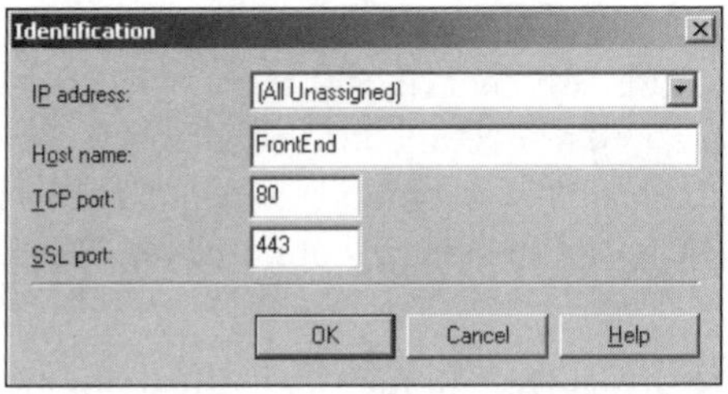

Identification
IP address: (All Unassigned)
Host name: FrontEnd
TCP port: 80
SSL port: 443
OK Cancel Help

Figure 15.32
Adding an identity for the front-end server.

8. Repeat Steps 6 and 7 again, this time creating a virtual directory named "public"; change the *Exchange Path* option to *Public Folders*; click *OK* when done.

If you support more than one namespace, for example both **humandata.se** and **highrad.org**, you must create one virtual HTTP server each, both with an Exchange and Public virtual directory.

What you also might find interesting is how many FE servers you may need. Microsoft generally recommends having one FE server for every four BE servers. Of course, this is dependent on the hardware configuration of both the FE and BE servers, as well as the users' behavior—how many messages they send and how large these messages are on average. Microsoft has a server sizing tool that can be used to calculate the number of users; you can find this tool on Microsoft's Web site at **www.Microsoft.com/Exchange/Techinfo/exchangecalculator.htm**. However, this tool will not take the increased load of SSL encryption into consideration when calculating the number of users.

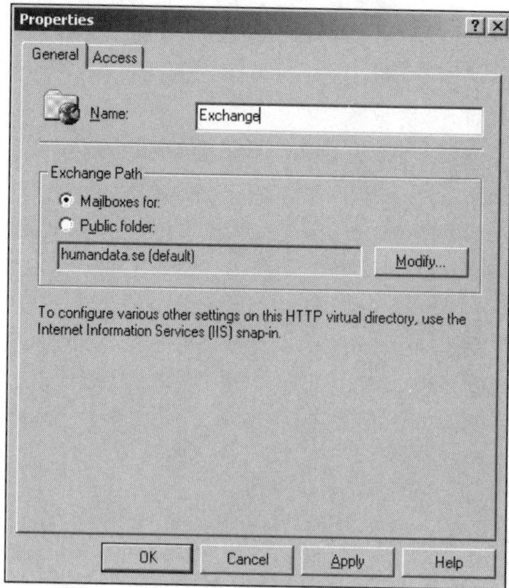

Figure 15.33
Creating the virtual directory Exchange uses for mailbox access.

Firewalls and Front-End/Back-End Scenarios

The usual configuration when setting up an FE/BE scenario is that there is a firewall between the front-end and the back-end server, to protect the internal network. This firewall must be configured to have certain ports open for communication, at least from the front-end server to the back-end servers. The port numbers that are used for OWA traffic are listed in Table 15.3.

Use Decision Tree 15.1 to select what ports to open, assuming that we have an FE server on the DMZ segment and the BE servers on the internal network; see Figure 15.34.

Table 15.3 Network ports used in OWA connections.

Port	Description
80/TCP	Used for standard HTTP 1.x communication between the client and FE, and also between the FE and BE.
443/TCP	Used only between the Web client and the FE in case SSL (i.e., HTTPS) is configured.
389/TCP	Used for LDAP requests from FE to the Active Directory server.
3268/TCP	Used for LDAP requests from the FE to the global catalog server.
88/TCP & UDP	Used for Kerberos authentication between the FE and the AD.
53/TCP & UDP	Used for DNS queries from the FE to the DNS server (the AD is usually the DNS server in the Windows 2000 environment).
135/TCP	Used as the RPC Endpoint Mapper between the FE and the AD server (to perform AD service discovery and client authentication).
>1023/TCP	Used for RPC communication between the FE and the AD.
445/TCP	Used for NetLogon between FE and AD servers.

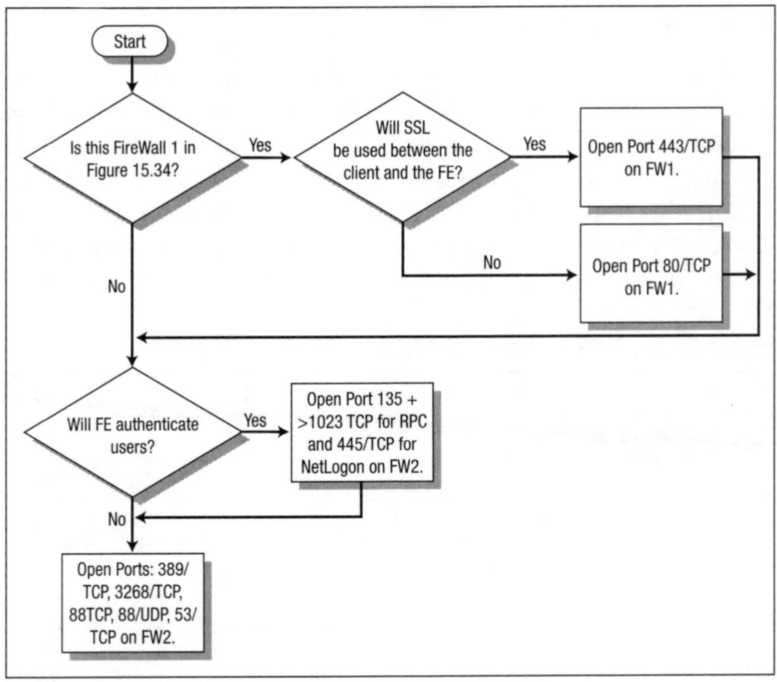

Decision Tree 15.1
Select what ports to open on the firewall.

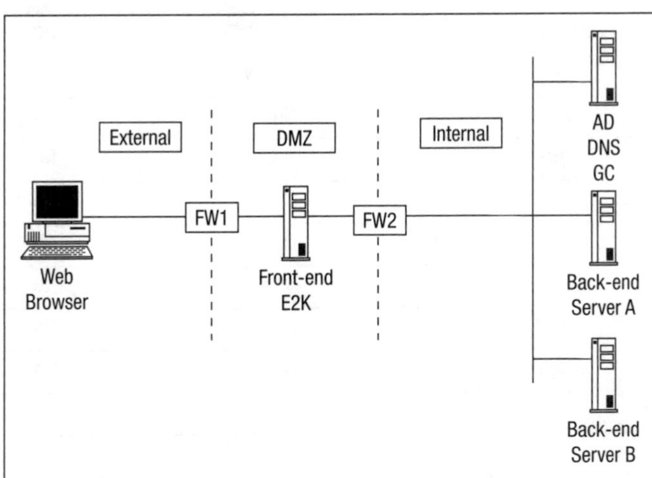

Figure 15.34
A typical FE/BE design protected by a firewall using a DMZ segment.

15

What Clients Should I Use?

So what client should you use? It depends on what features you need, what operating system and computer you have, and whether it's a permanent or dial-up connection. My general recommendation is to use the full Outlook 2002 if possible, and the Outlook Web Access client for temporary use. Try to stay away from POP3 and IMAP clients, since they are very limited in what features they offer. Use Table 15.4 to compare the differences between Outlook 200X and OWA 2000; just for comparison, I have also added the OWA in Exchange 5.5 to help you see how much better the new OWA in Exchange 2000 is.

Table 15.4 Comparison between Outlook 200X and OWA.

Feature	Outlook 200X	OWA 2000	OWA 5.5
Email	Yes	Yes	Yes
Calendar (private)	Yes	Yes	Yes
Calendar (Public folder)	Yes	Yes	No
Contact (private)	Yes	Yes	Yes
Contact (Public folder)	Yes	Yes	No
Tasks	Yes	No	No
Access to embedded objects	Yes	Yes	No
Rich Text Format	Yes	Yes	Yes
HTML format	Yes	Yes	No
Drag-and-Drop editing	Yes	Yes (with IE5)	No
Short-cut menus	Yes	Yes (with IE5)	No
Offline use	Yes	No	No
Journal	Yes	No	No
Printing templates	Yes	No	No
Timed delivery	Yes	No	No
Expiration of messages	Yes	No	No
Spelling checker	Yes	No	No
Reminders	Yes	No	No
Outlook rules	Yes	No	No
Preview pane	Yes	Yes	No
Collapse and expand folder tree	Yes	Yes	No

Summary

This is a list of the more important features and keywords mentioned in this chapter. Use it as a reminder and to make sure you have understood the most important things:

- Exchange 2000 has support for the following Internet message protocols:
  - *MAPI*—Messaging Application Programming Interface, such as Outlook 2002
  - *POP3*—Post Office Protocol, version 3, such as Outlook Express
  - *IMAP4*—Internet Mail Access Protocol, version 4, such as Outlook Express
  - *NNTP*—Net News Transfer Protocol, such as Outlook Express
  - *HTTP*—Hypertext Transfer Protocol, such as Internet Explorer
- You select the "right" client depending on the type of operating system, connection, type of usage, what features are needed, and the need for offline storage.
- The Exchange client was the first available message client for Exchange 4; this client was based on MAPI, and could also access public folders and the global address list.
- Schedule Plus 7 was a companion to Exchange Client, a MAPI client used for calendar, tasks, and contacts.
- Schedule Plus 1 was the predecessor, used in MS Mail systems.
- MS Outlook 97 was released in January 1997, and has been upgraded a number of times; the last version was 8.04. The first version came together with Office 97.
- MS Outlook 98 was released in April 1998, and has been upgraded several times.
- MS Outlook 2000 was released in May 1999. Several upgrades to this client are available; SR2 was the last major upgrade. This Outlook version came with Office 2000.
- MS Outlook 2002 was released in May 2001, together with Office XP (also known as Office 2002, or release 10).
- One of the best resources on the Internet for Outlook is **www.slipstick.com**.
- Outlook 97 has several drawbacks, especially with regards to antivirus features. You should upgrade this client.
- It is free to upgrade Outlook to a later version as long as you are a registered Exchange user, i.e., you have a Client Access License for Exchange.
- Easter eggs are hidden code that usually list the names of the developers and testers of a product; most Microsoft products have such Easter eggs.

- For each new release of Outlook, the hardware and software requirements have increased, from 486/33MHz with 8MB for Outlook 97 to Pentium 133 with 64MB in Outlook 2002.
- Outlook 98 is much better than Outlook 97, but still has several problems, such as not supporting automatic resource booking and the Contacts folder not supporting personal distribution lists.
- Outlook 2000 upgraded with SR2 is a very good and secure client. You should use this client before using Outlook 98.
- Outlook 2002 has a number of new features compared to Outlook 2000; if you need one or more of them, you have a reason to upgrade now!
- RPC, Remote Procedure Call, involves synchronous sessions between two programs in the same computer, or between two different computers. RPC is very similar in its logic to a standard voice phone session.
- RPC Binding Order defines what network transport protocol should be used first; if it's wrong, the client will take several minutes to start up.
- Use the RPC Ping tool to test RPC connectivity between computers, such as the client and the Exchange server.
- MS Outlook Express is not really built for communicating with Exchange servers; however, since it can talk to POP3, IMAP4, and NNTP, it can be used as a client, but with severely limited features. Use this only when no other client works.
- IMAP4 is an upgrade of POP3; use IMAP4 before POP3—It will allow you to view multiple folders, like public folders.
- POP3 is designed to move, not copy, messages from the server to the local disk on the client computer; however, it can be configured to store a copy on the server.
- You can export messages from the POP3 inbox directly to an Exchange mailbox.
- Both the IMAP4 and POP3 clients use SMTP for sending messages.
- The SMTP server that these clients use must be configured for rerouting, otherwise these clients cannot send messages outside this Exchange organization.
- An SMTP server should never be configured to allow all clients to reroute messages; only authenticated users should be able to do that! Otherwise, your SMTP server will soon be used for sending spam messages.
- The Outlook Web Access (OWA) client is perfect for occasionally accessing the Exchange mailbox, but it's not good enough for replacing the standard Outlook client permanently (yet!).

- The OWA 2000 client has been greatly enhanced compared to the OWA 5.5 client. It's also faster and easier to use.
- All HTTP applications use port 80 for sending information in clear text; to protect the OWA client session, SSL encryption must be configured.
- The Secure Socket Layer (SSL) is configured on the server only; no configuration is necessary on the Web client.
- SSL is CPU intensive—it decreases the overall performance of the server; however, SSL Accelerator hardware is available if this is a problem.
- Use *https* instead of *http* when accessing an SSL-protected Web site. You will also see a yellow padlock in the browser's status row that indicates an SSL session.
- Use the front-end/back-end scenario when you want to put the OWA server outside the internal network, typically on the DMZ segment.
- The front-end computer is an Exchange 2000 Enterprise installation that has been stripped to only proxy HTTP requests between the Web client and a back-end server.
- The back-end server must be configured to use the front-end server.
- The FE server will use a number of TCP ports (and some UDP ports) when communicating with the AD server—the DNS, the GC, and the BE servers.

Chapter 16

Exchange 2000 Chat Service

An email system such as Exchange 2000 is perfect for asynchronous communication; the sender and recipients don't have to be online simultaneously. Sometimes it's necessary to have a realtime discussion between groups of people, however, and email systems are not designed to meet this need. The usual solution is to arrange a meeting during which all members of a group can get together and talk directly to one other. But if the members of this group are located in different geographical areas, it can be impractical or even impossible for all members to join a meeting. The problem increases with the number of members in the group; this is an issue well known to all medium or large organizations. Two ways of solving this problem of distributed members are:

- Voice phone conferences
- ISDN videoconferences

However, these solutions introduce new problems. With phone conferences, it's impossible to share documents and illustrations unless they have been distributed to all the attendees before the phone meeting; it's not possible to share new or updated printed information. The quality of the voice system may be low, making it hard to hear and easy to misunderstand each other.

Videoconferencing is a much better alternative, but the problem is often the cost; video conference systems are generally expensive, and all members must have their own video systems. You must also have an ISDN connection, since an ordinary phone system can't handle the large volume of information. As a result, videoconference systems are installed in specially prepared locations; they can't be moved around to arbitrary places. Videoconferences are also used between two parties only; it's hard to arrange a videoconference between three or more locations simultaneously.

The History of Conferencing Systems

Sharing information among a large group of people is even more problematic if you don't know exactly who the members will be. This has always been a big problem for people who share the same interests, and this is one reason open conferences take place about every subject you can think of. But for a computer nerd (like me), this problem was solved around 1980 with a program that allowed a standard personal computer (connected to a modem) to act as a message central, to which the users would dial in and read other peoples' postings and post their own. This was called a *bulletin board system*, or BBS. The first BBS is usually credited to Ward Christianson, who developed his system around 1977.

Bulletin Board Systems

Since all users were connected to the same BBS server, any new posting was immediately visible to all active users. Anyone with a personal computer and a modem could set up their own BBS, and many did; the numbers of BBSes that have existed over the years is very large, although many of them only existed for a month or even less.

The problem with BBSes was the limited number of simultaneous users; you needed one modem and one phone line for each active user. Around 1990, several large BBS-like conferencing systems started that were open for public access; these systems were often managed by telecom companies and other commercial organizations that wanted to make a business out of this idea.

Usenet

The Unix world has had a conferencing system for a very long time, even before the BBS became popular. This system was often referred to as the *Usenet*, an abbreviation for the User Network, and also known as the *News* system. It started in 1979 as an application for replicating messages between the University of North Carolina and Duke University. Usenet was designed to be a global conferencing system, not a centralized system like the BBS. A Usenet community is a group of servers (usually Unix based) running the News conferencing system; the information is stored in different newsgroups for different content, such as comp.ms.exchange for MS Exchange discussions. The News servers then replicate all new postings to the other members in this community. That means that a posting you make in a newsgroup on your News system will be replicated around the world to all other News systems in this Usenet community, making your posting globally visible.

Still, none of the BBS or the News systems were able to offer an environment in which a group consisting of any number of users could share information in realtime; a new type of application was needed that allowed any number of users, anonymously or authenticated, to share information freely. The base for this application was the Internet; when all users were connected to the same communication network (i.e., the Internet), you could set up a server anywhere in the world and let the users share their information there. This new type of groupware for realtime sharing was called *chat systems*.

The History of Chat Systems

It's hard to find any particular chat system that was the true ancestor to all others, but the Bitnet Relay Chat was an inspiration for the first really popular chat system, Internet Relay Chat (IRC). This system was developed by Jarkko Oikarinen from Finland in August 1988, on a server called tolsun.oulu.fi. After a slow start (mainly because Finland at that time didn't have an Internet connection to other countries), it spread quickly around the Internet world. The IRC system really became famous in 1991 when Baghdad was bombed; people in Baghdad reported live using IRC about what happened, and other IRC users could comment and talk to these people.

Internet Relay Chat

The IRC today is a connection of more than 20 networks where people meet on *channels* (also known as *chat rooms* and *virtual places*) to discuss a certain topic. These channels have names that start with # or &; the # channels are globally available, whereas & channels are restricted to users on your own IRC server. You can talk in groups or switch over to a private one-to-one conversation. There is no limitation on the number of simultaneous users in a group, or the number of channels that can be formed on the IRC.

As a user, you run a client program that connects to the IRC server; all IRC servers are members of an IRC network. All IRC servers are interconnected and are able to pass messages between users over the IRC network; see Figure 16.1. The largest IRC network is the Eris Free Net (EFNet), with more than 150,000 users; two other popular IRC networks are the Undernet (100,000+ users) and Dalnet (80,000+ users).

A number of IRC clients are available; the most popular are mIRC, Virc, and Pirch. You can download an IRC client from many Web sites, such as **www.tucows.com** and **download.cnet.com**. IRC network traffic uses TCP port 6667 (but some, for example Dalnet, use port 7000). The IRC world is basically a virtual meeting place where users anonymously log on, using fake names if they want, and sometimes even fake genders. On the IRC, you are known to others by a nickname of your choice; note that several users can have and use the same nickname, which of course can create confusion.

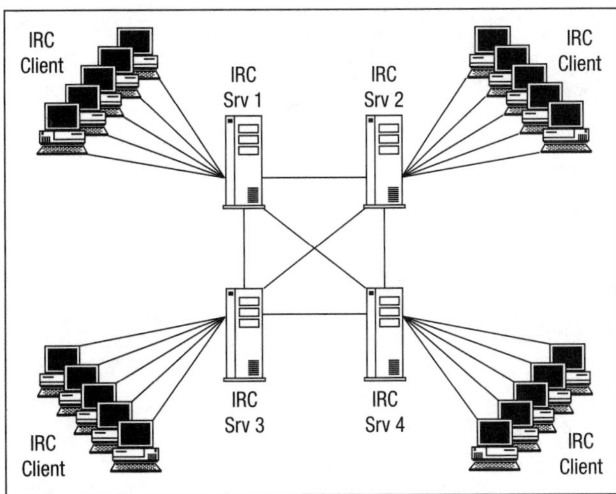

Figure 16.1
The fully meshed structure used in IRC.

Each IRC channel has one or more administrators, called ChanOp or just Op, who can ban an IRC user who doesn't behave according to the often unspoken rules of that particular channel. A banned user will not be able to use this IRC channel until the ChanOp removes this ban. An IRC Operator (IRCop) administers the whole IRC server and can ban you from the IRC server completely.

Acronyms Used When Chatting

To make conversation faster and reduce the number of characters to type, a large number of acronyms and special character sequences are often used. You don't have to use them, but they will help you understand what others are saying (and it will also make you look like an experienced IRC user :-); see Table 16.1 for some of the most common acronyms. For more acronyms and smileys, look at **www.solscape.com**.

Table 16.1 Common smileys and acronyms used in chat conversations.

Acronym	Interpretation
:-)	smiley face (tilt your head to the left to see it properly)
:)	small smiley face
:-))	very happy smiley
:-(	sad face
;-)	wink
lol	laughing out loud
rofl	rolling on the floor laughing
roflmao	rolling on the floor laughing my ass off
r u	are you
brb	be right back
bbl	be back later
afk	away from keyboard
ltns	long time no see
cu	See you
cul	See you later
ic	I see
imho	In my humble opinion
irl	In real life
<G>	grin
<S>	smile
<EG>	evil grin
<BEG>	big evil grin

Microsoft Exchange Chat Server

Microsoft's first release of Chat Server came with Exchange 5.5. It has been enhanced in Exchange 2000 to support up to 20,000 users per Chat server, compared to 5,000 users in Exchange 5.5. This Chat server is based on the IRC protocol, which is described in RFC1459 (and is extended in RFC 2810, 2811, 2812, and 2813). Besides some extensions to this protocol that Microsoft calls IRCX, this Chat server is fully IRC compliant; it could join other IRC networks and it will accept any standard IRC client, like mIRC. The communication in Exchange Chat Server uses TCP port 6667 (like the standard IRC servers), although it's possible to use other port numbers too.

I haven't actually seen an Exchange Chat server in a production environment yet, but I think the reason for this is that Exchange administrators don't know how to set up and run the Chat server, since this is a completely new ball game compared to Exchange. This chapter will help you do this, and maybe you will find it to be an invaluable complement to your organization's messaging features; if you don't try it, you will never know for sure. It's easy to install and it will not affect the overall performance unless you have thousands of Chat users, so give it a shot.

Exchange 2000 Chat Server Architecture

When Chat Server is installed on an Exchange 2000 server, it will create a new service called MSExchangeChat, and the executable file is called Chatsrv.exe; see Figure 16.2. This chat service controls the chat communities and their channels. Any standard IRC client can contact the chat service over TCP port 6667 to join any of these channels.

This chat service is not dependent on any other service, not even any Exchange 2000 services. You may therefore stop and start Exchange without affecting the Chat server.

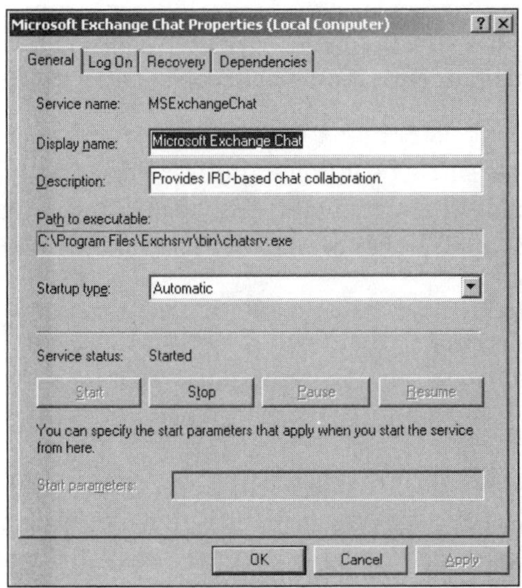

Figure 16.2
The new MS Exchange Chat service.

Note: *Previous Exchange 5.5 Chat servers supported Microsoft's proprietary chat protocol called Microsoft Internet Chat (MIC). This protocol is no longer supported in Exchange 2000 Chat Server.*

The IRC protocol described in RFC 1459 has undergone several upgrades since its release, but unfortunately not all IRC networks (such as Underworld, EFNet, and Dalnet) have chosen to follow the same IRC upgrade path; the result is that they can't link with each other. Microsoft has suggested an RFC draft that enhances RFC 1459 to create a standard with a rich set of features and commands. This is known as the Extended IRC, IRCX, which adds new functionality to the standard IRC protocol; however, these features will only be used when both sender and receiver understand IRCX, otherwise the standard IRC protocol will be used. Examples of clients that understand IRCX are Microsoft Chat 2.1 and Chat 2.5. These are some of the new commands found in Microsoft's IRCX:

- *Access*—Grants or denies access to an object
- *Auth*—Authenticates clients
- *Create*—Creates a new channel or joins an existing channel
- *Data*—Sends instructions, banners, or other data to clients
- *Ircx*—Enables IRCX mode on the server
- *Isircx*—Queries the server if it supports IRCX
- *Listx*—Lists channel properties and searches for strings of characters
- *Prop*—Adds, changes, or deletes channel properties
- *Whisper*—Sends a message to one or more members in this channel

Besides these new commands, several new enhancements have been added to the IRC protocol to handle Unicode text, Simple Authentication and Security Layer (SASL), and increased security.

Every administrative group can host one single Chat Communities folder. This folder by default contains one folder labeled Default-Chat-Community, also known as a virtual chat community, and each of these can host any number of *channels* (also known as *chat rooms*); see Figure 16.3.

These virtual chat communities are governed by their own administrative controls; using the ESM tool, you can assign individual administrators and sysops for each chat community.

Channels in Exchange 2000 Chat Server

As described previously, a channel (or a chat room) is a virtual meeting place where members can communicate. If you join an existing channel, you can see what all the other members of this channel are writing. There are two types of channels:

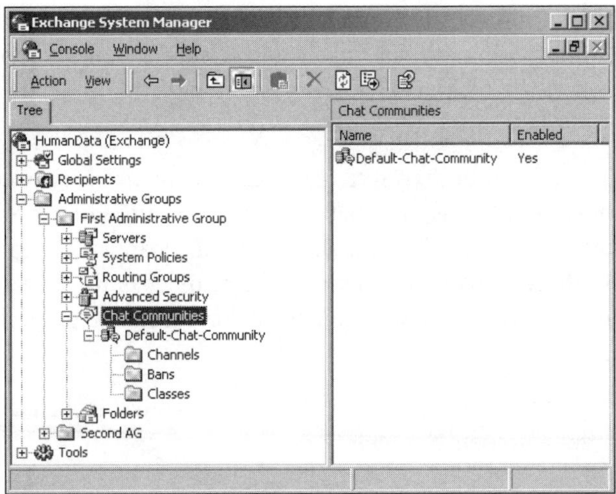

Figure 16.3
The default chat folder structure in ESM.

- *Registered channels*—These are created by the administrator, so they can't be removed by a user. Two types exist: one that starts automatically when a user joins this channel, and another that starts when the chat service starts.
- *Dynamic channels*—These are created by the users by the command Join (IRC) or Create (IRCX). The user that created the channel will be its *channel operator* (chanop); this role is referred to as *host* on the security tab in the channel properties. A channel may have more than one chanop.

The channel operators aren't the only persons with power in a channel; the *sysop*, or system operator, monitors and controls a dynamic channel (and registered channel if granted permissions). He or she can use a chat client to ban users or even close the channel by using the Kill command. Any user can be granted the role sysop by the channel operator. A sysop is recognized by its name; it usually begins with one of the following strings:

- sysop
- orwell
- ChanServ
- CodeServ
- HelpServ
- MemoServ
- NickServ

For example, a name might be sysopGoran or CodeServeGoran. Only a system operator can have these nicknames; ordinary users will not be able to take such a name. For example, though it's perfectly okay to take the nickname Goransysop, it will still be visible to all that this user is no sysop.

A channel can be secure, cloneable, or both. A *secure* channel is one to which access is restricted; the chatop can invite users, or require that the user must authenticate, or enter a secret password before accessing this secure channel. A *cloneable* channel is a registered channel that will split itself into two channels whenever the number of users reaches a limit, determined by the administrator. The new channel will have identical properties to the original channel.

Enough said about channels; it's time to install the product so we can test its behavior and configure the chat communities and their channels.

Installation of Exchange 2000 Chat Service

Installing Chat Server for Exchange 2000 is easy; it takes about five minutes and requires only 2MB of disk space. Before installing Chat Server, you should plan the installation and decide how to use this chat service; use the Sample Worksheet 16.1 as a guide for your planning.

Sample Worksheet 16.1 Planning the Chat Server installation.

Activity	Description	Example
Number of chat communities	Controls the channels	One chat community is enough for small- to medium-sized organizations, but two eliminates the single point of failure.
Name standard	Establish a name standard for communities and channels; a channel must begin with # or & for IRC channels, or %# or %& for IRCX channels	**#Mailnerds**, **%&Support**
Select server	Select an Exchange 2000 server for the chat service	**Oden.humandata.se**
Install server	Select when to select the Chat server	August 15, 2001.
Upgrade server?	If this server has a Chat server from Exchange 5.5, it can be upgraded; follow the TechNet article Q262210	No upgrade necessary.
Configure chat community	Create and configure virtual chat communities, set access permissions and default topics, language, and other properties	**#Sales** require a password, **#Support** is open to all and no whispering is allowed.

(continued)

Sample Worksheet 16.1 Planning the Chat Server installation *(continued).*

Activity	Description	Example
Create registered channels	Use ESM to create all registered channels and configure them	Create these registered IRCX channels: **%#Support**, **%#Sales**, **%#Free-forum**
Grant administrative access	Create administrators and sysops for this organization	Administrators: Anna, Frida; sysops: Thomas and Johan
Client software	Select the chat client to be used	The mIRC client

Setting Up the Chat Server

Installing the Exchange 2000 Chat Server is easy, as long as you do it the right way. You must complete at least two steps before the clients can actually connect to the Chat server:

- Install the Chat Server
- Create a new IRCX protocol instance

When this is done, the clients can connect. However, you probably also want to create and configure one or more registered channels (these are permanent channels, if you remember from the previous sections).

16

Installing the Chat Server Software

Just add the Chat Server software to an existing Exchange 2000 server by following these steps:

1. Start the installation wizard for Exchange 2000; click *Next* until you come to the Component Selection page (see Figure 16.4).

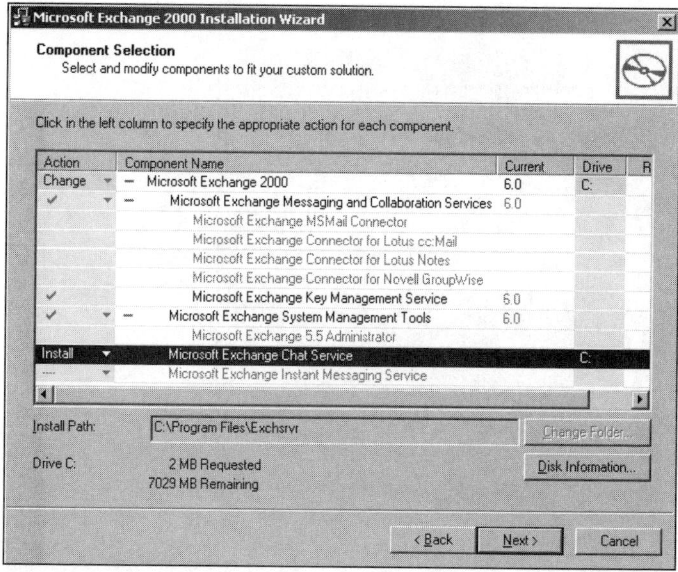

Figure 16.4
The Component Selection page when installing Chat Server.

2. Set the Action to Change for Microsoft Exchange 2000, then set the Action to Install for the Microsoft Exchange Chat Service. Notice that the default file directory to store the chat files will be /Exchsrvr/bin; there will not be a separate chat directory. If necessary, change this directory. All files together will be less than 2MB in size. When ready, click *Next*.
3. On the Administrative Group page (see Figure 16.5), select what AG this Chat server will belong to. Note that this Chat server can't be moved to another AG later. Click *Next* when ready.
4. On the Component Summary page (see Figure 16.6), make sure all settings are correct; if not, click Back and make any necessary corrections, otherwise click *Next* to start the installation.
5. Then a Component Progress will be displayed, showing the current status. After a few minutes, the Completion page for this installation wizard will display; click Finish to complete the installation of Chat Server.

Note: *I have experienced a few mishaps during installation of Chat Server (see Figure 16.7); in this situation, I have solved this problem by manually restarting the World Wide Web Publishing Service and the Network News Transport Protocol service. When I run the setup program again, it has always succeeded.*

6. Optional step: Restart the complete Exchange 2000 server! The setup program doesn't force you to complete this step, but in a few occasions I have experienced problems connecting clients to the Chat server that were solved by a complete restart.

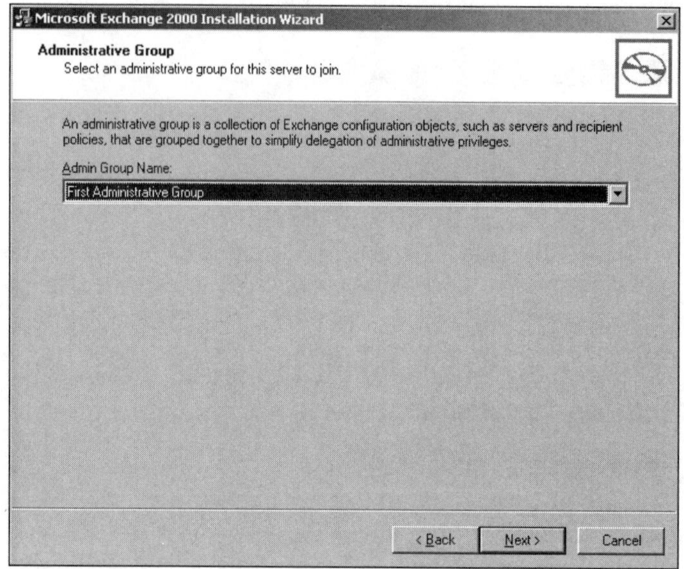

Figure 16.5
Selecting what Administrative Group this Chat server will belong to.

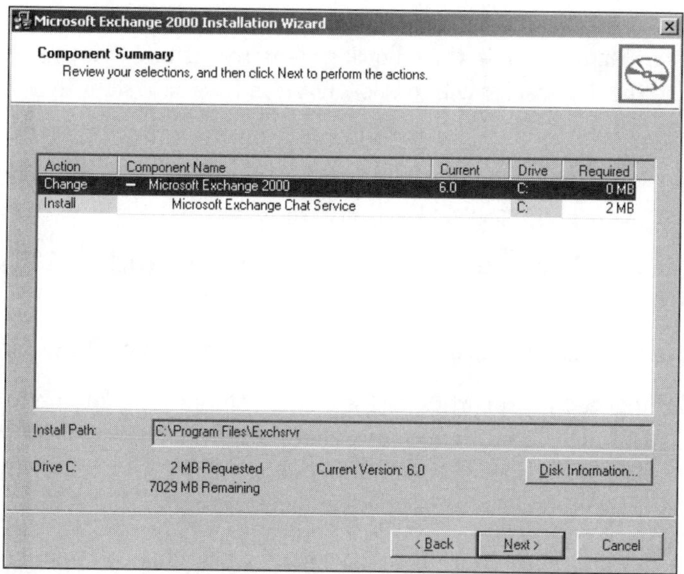

Figure 16.6
The Component Summary page for the Chat installation.

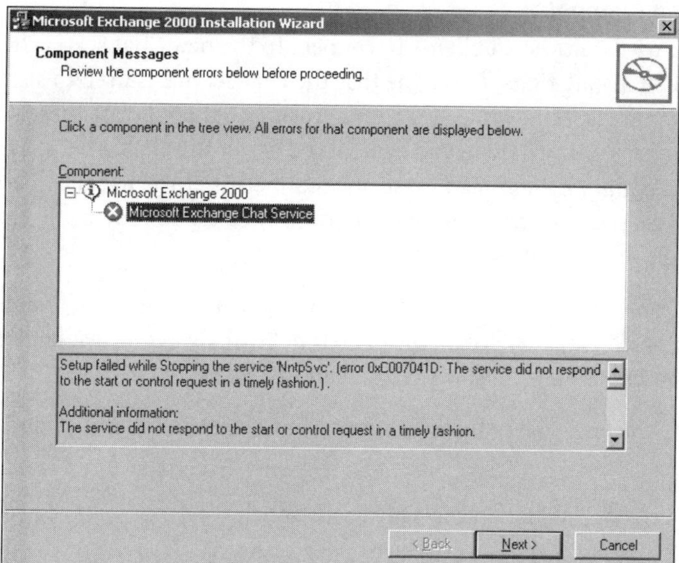

Figure 16.7
Problems when installing the Chat server.

Configuring an IRCX Protocol Instance

The next step is to connect the Chat server to an IRCX protocol, thereby making this Chat server available to the clients. Before this can be done, you must know what port number this Chat server will use (port 6667 is standard); we also must know the name of the chat community. All default created Chat servers will have the Default-Chat-Community, as illustrated previously in Figure 16.3. In the following steps, we assume that this name has not been changed, and that this server will use port 6667; follow these steps to configure the IRCX protocol:

1. Start the ESM tool and navigate to the Administrative Group and its server object, to which the Chat server belongs; expand the Protocols folder.
2. You should now see an IRCX folder; if not, refresh ESM. Right-click the IRCX folder and select Properties.
3. On the General page, click Add and select the chat community; click *OK* to continue.
4. Next you must configure the properties for the chat community; make sure to set the Enable Server To Host This Chat Community checkbox. Unless you have more than one chat community, or any special reason to do so, you don't have to modify any other parameters here; click *OK* to close this window.
5. Now you're back to the General page; it will now list the new chat community. Since there are no more chat communities, click *OK* to complete the configuration of this IRCX protocol.

Adding a Registered Channel

This step isn't necessary to allow chat clients to connect to the new Chat server; however, in most Exchange 2000 installations, I imagine that the chat service is used to share real-time information regarding specific topics. If so, you probably want to create these channels before the clients connect; this will help you control the use of the chat service. The other types of channels are *dynamic channels*; these are channels that the users can create whenever they like. You can configure the chat community to prohibit dynamic channels, if necessary; by default they are allowed.

In the following example, we assume that we want to create one registered channel (or permanent channel), #Mailsupport. This type of channel will always be available to the user, unless denied access. Follow these steps to create such a channel:

1. Start the ESM tool and navigate to the Default-Chat-Community and its subfolder Channels.
2. Right-click the Channels folder and select New|Channel.
3. On the General page (see Figure 16.8), add the following name for this channel: **#Mailsupport**. A channel must always begin with one or two special characters; the default IRC standard requires that channel names begins with # (or &, but it's more unusual), and the IRCX standard requires that these names begin with %# (or %&); you must also avoid characters like space, backslash, and comma. A tip is to avoid ending the name with a number, since this will make the name look confusing when cloning this channel!

   Add a Topic description; this will be displayed for clients who join this channel.

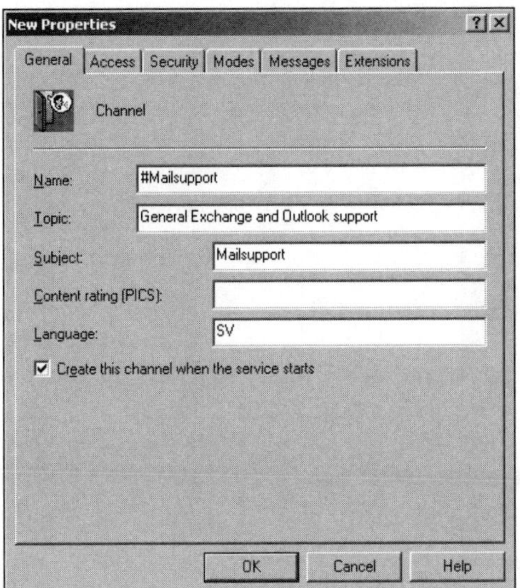

Figure 16.8
The General page for a registered channel.

Add a Subject; this will be a description of the subject of the conversation on this chat channel. This is not shown to the client.

Use the Content Rating (PICS) to classify this channel, if necessary, This is the same type of content information classification that is used for Web servers. Normally you leave this empty unless you have a special reason to set a value here. For more information about PICS, see **www.w3.org**.

Use the Language field to define what primary language is used on this channel. You can leave this empty, but if you use it, follow the ISO 639 code table (find it at **msdn.Microsoft.com/workshop/management/iso639.htm**); for example: **sv**=Swedish, **en**=English, **fr**=French.

If you want this channel to be created when the chat service is started, set the checkbox Create This Channel When The Service Starts; otherwise it will be started when the first user accesses it.

4. The Access page (see Figure 16.9) is used to control the access and the visibility of this channel. Depending on what type of client is used, IRC or IRCX compliant, you must configure this property page accordingly. The most important thing to remember is that authentication isn't allowed in non-IRCX clients.

   Use the Visibility To Users pull-down list to select whether this channel will be publicly visible or not. There are four different options for the visibility:

   - *Public*—Default; the channel description and its content are visible to all users.
   - *Private*—The name and the number of users will be visible, but not its content.

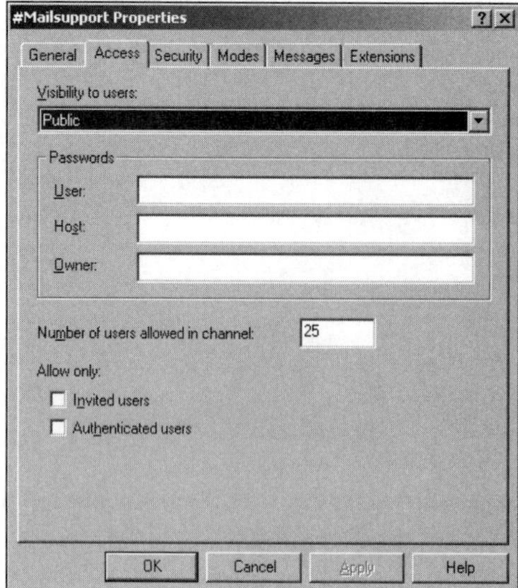

Figure 16.9
The Access page for registered channels.

- *Hidden*—This channel is hidden from the List command, but if you know its name, you can still query this channel for its name and description.
- *Secret*—This channel cannot be located by a channel search or any other query.

In the Passwords pane, you can set an access password for User, Host (sysop, that is), or Owner. Space and tab characters are not allowed. The default is no password. These passwords work with both IRC and IRCX clients.

Set the maximum number of users in this channel; default is 25. To make it unlimited, set this number to zero. If the number of users reaches this limit, the channel will be cloned, if this is allowed (default is no cloning).

Use the Allow Only options to restrict the access to Invited Users and/or Authenticated Users only. If you set any password to be required, Authenticated Users will be automatically checked. However, this requires that any chat client must authenticate before accessing this channel; most non-Microsoft Chat IRCX clients, such as mIRC, can't authenticate against the Exchange 2000 Chat server, because they lack the IRCX command Auth. If this type of client is used in your chat community, you should avoid setting Authenticated Users and instead set an access password for the user, host, or owner.

5. Use the Security page (see Figure 16.10) to control which users can be granted User, Host (i.e., sysop), or Owner status. Default is that the group Everyone can be a user, and no denying permissions are enforced.

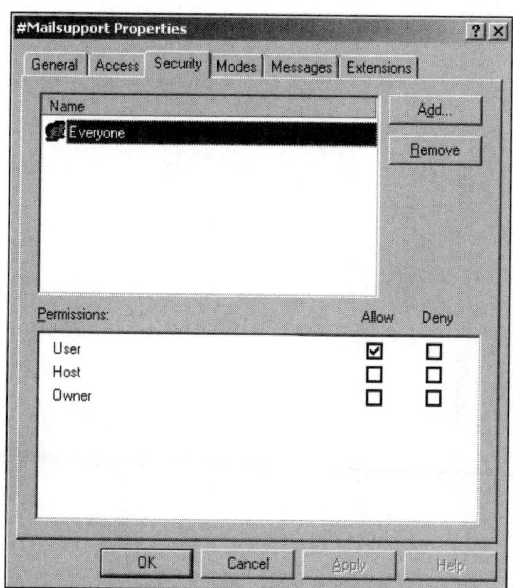

Figure 16.10
The Security tab for registered channels.

Note that before you can use this page for controlling user status, they must be authenticated; to be authenticated, they must have an IRCX-compliant chat client. In other words, if your organization uses IRC clients (such as mIRC), you should not use this tab.

6. The Mode page (see Figure 16.11) configures the channel's messaging and speaking restrictions and some other channel settings. There are three different groups of settings:

   a. In the Message pane, there are three options to control channel messages:

      - The option Accept Only From Channel Members controls whether anyone other than the members can send messages to this channel; the default is yes.
      - Set the option Do Not Format Client Messages if you want to prevent the chat client from displaying the From Alias prefix in channel conversations. This will increase the performance when clients use graphical extensions, since the load of the server will be decreased.
      - Set the option Notify Host When Users Cannot Join; this will send a notification to the channel host (sysop) if a user can't join.

   b. In the Speaking Restrictions pane, you have four options to control who can send messages to this channel:

      - Set the Authenticated Users Only option if you want to prohibit all nonauthenticated users from sending messages to this channel. Note that this requires IRCX-compliant chat clients!

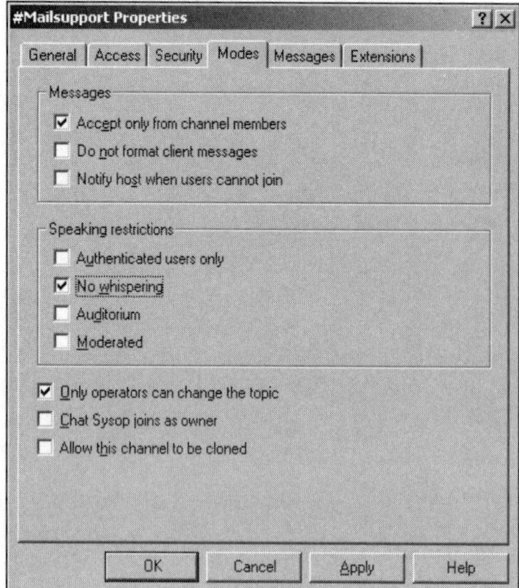

Figure 16.11
The Modes page for restricted channels.

- Set the No Whispering option to prohibit a channel member from sending a private message to one or more other members, for example using the IRC command **Privmsg**, or the IRCX command **Whisper**.
- Set the Auditorium option to allow any user to view messages in this channel, but restrict these users from sending messages to channel hosts only. The only people allowed to send messages are the channel hosts. This option is often implemented when the channel is used as a large public chat forum, for example a department meeting. By giving the speakers host status, they can talk to the complete channel, and users can send messages with comments and questions to these speakers.
- Set the Moderated option to restrict users to view-only access; only channel hosts are allowed to send messages to the channel. A user can be granted speak-permissions by using the IRC command /mode ***<channel>*** **+v** ***<nickname>*** by a channel host. This option is similar to the Auditorium, but this is often used for smaller public chat events.

c. The other settings on this property page include:

- *Only Operators Can Change The Topic*—This option is used to control who can modify the topic description for this channel. By default this option is set, making sysops and owners the only ones who can change the topic.
- *Chat Sysop Joins As Owner*—This option controls the power of the channel host (i.e., the sysop). If this checkbox is set, all sysops for this channel will have full control; they can ban users, close down the channel, and add new sysops. If you set this checkbox, make sure to be careful regarding who will be granted sysop permissions.

- *Allow This Channel To Be Cloned*—This option is used to control whether this channel will automatically be split into two if the number of users reaches the maximum limit. For example, assume our #Mailsupport channel is limited to 25 users. When user number 26 joins this channel, an automatic split will take place; the first 25 users will be members of the #Mailsupport01 channel, and the 26th user (and the following users) will be members of the #Mailsupport02 channel. The maximum number of clones is 99; each clone retains the properties of the original channel.

7. The Messages page (see Figure 16.12) defines the messages received when joining and leaving this channel. Note that a chat client can be configured to skip these messages!
8. The Extensions page (see Figure 16.13) lists any extension added to this channel; you can also configure existing extensions. By default there is no extension to a channel; however, with Exchange 2000 there are two: the Profanity Filter and the Channel Description. To add an extension, see the upcoming section, "Adding a Channel Extension."
9. When ready, click *OK* to create this channel. Then restart the IRCX protocol and activate these settings by right-clicking the IRCX folder, then selecting Stop, and then Start; see Figure 16.14. Note that this will make all chat clients lose their connection to this Chat server; avoid doing this when people are using any channels on this Chat server!

This concludes the basic configuration for enabling an Exchange 2000 Chat server and making it ready to be used.

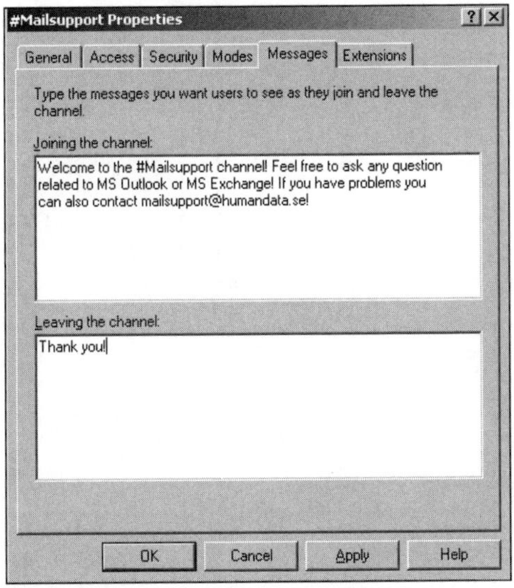

Figure 16.12
The Messages page for restricted channels.

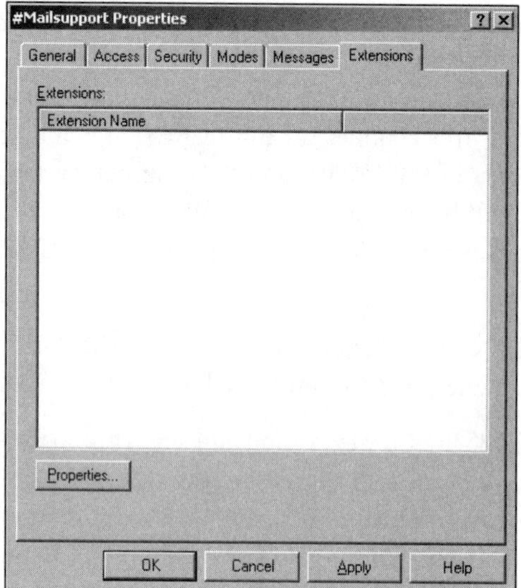

Figure 16.13
The Extensions page for restricted channels.

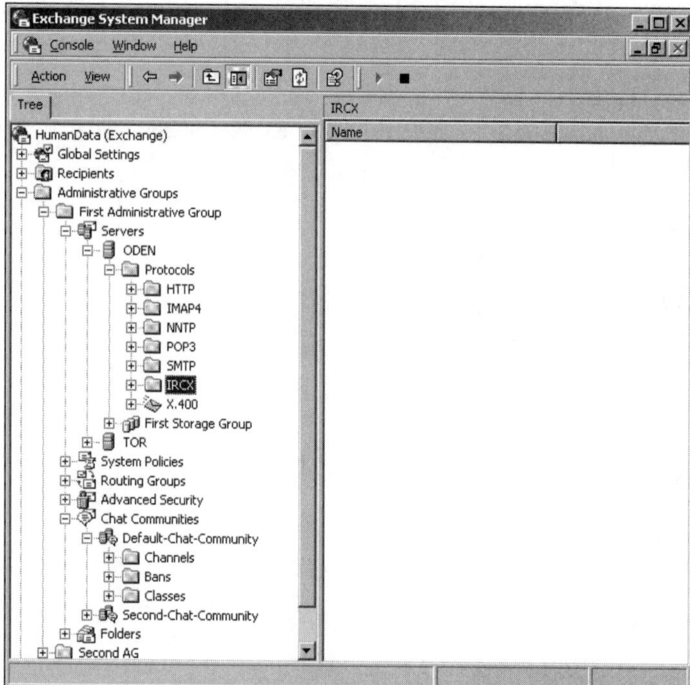

Figure 16.14
Restarting the Chat server.

Adding a Channel Extension

It is possible to add extensions to the channels; these are DLL files that add functionality to the channel. Exchange 2000 offers two such extensions:

- *The Profanity Filter*—Makes it possible to detect and filter words that your organization considers offensive, abusive, or inappropriate for a given channel.
- *The Channel Transcription*—Makes it possible to record chat sessions and save them to the hard disk.

Installing a Channel Extension

These extensions are always added to the Chat Community object, never to the channels directly; when this is done, the channels must be configured to use these extensions, if necessary. Follow these steps to add the two channels extensions that come with Exchange 2000:

***Note:** This must be done directly on the Chat server; you can't do this from a workstation that has the EMS tool installed. The reason is that these DLL files are installed and visible only on the Chat server itself.*

1. Open the ESM tool, navigate to the IRCX protocol folder, and open its properties.
2. Select the chat community to which to add these extensions (typically it's the Default-Chat-Community); then click on *Properties*.
3. In the Property page for the chat community, click the Extensions button.
4. In the Extensions page, click *Add*.
5. You will get a list of all available chat extensions; select one and click *OK*.
6. This will take you back to the Extensions page again; repeat Steps 4 and 5 for every extension you want to add to this chat community. When ready, click *OK* twice to close this IRCX object.
7. Restart the IRCX protocol to activate these extensions.

The chat community now has these extensions installed, but they need to be configured before they can be used. Exactly what you can or should do depends on the type of extension; following are the configurations of the Profanity Filter described.

The Profanity Filter Extension

The Profanity Filter can be used on all channels in this chat community, or on individual ones. It will detect whether any forbidden words are used in the regular chat conversation, in private messages, invitations, quit messages, part messages, whispers, nicknames, and channel names. To use the Profanity Filter, you must first create a list of forbidden words that this filter will scan for; you can also create a list of exceptions, or words that actually will be allowed even if they exist on the list of forbidden words.

Before a channel can use this filter extension, it must be configured regarding what words to look for and what to do when they are detected. Follow these steps for this configuration:

Note: *Make sure to do this on the Chat server; you will not see any channel extensions using a workstation with the ESM tool installed. Note that you must restart the IRCX protocol to be able to configure this filter extension!*

1. Use the ESM tool and open the Property page for the IRCX protocol again (the same one we just used to install these extensions); open its properties.
2. On the Property page for the chat community, click the Extensions button.
3. On the Extensions page, you will see a list of all installed extensions (if not, restart the IRCX protocol); select PFilter and click the Properties button.
4. On the General page (see Figure 16.15), you can select what filter to apply to different types of conversations, such as private messages and channel names. By default, only one filter is labeled Default; this filter is empty. You must add your own words before this filter will do anything useful. Click Edit Filters to configure the filter.
5. On the Edit Filters page (see Figure 16.16), you can define filters, add new filters, create filter exceptions, and more.

   To add words to the Default filter, make sure it's selected in the Selected Filter field, then click the Add button; add the new forbidden word without space characters. Select whether it should be treated as a wildcard expression or not, and define what message the user should get if they use this word; then click *OK*. Repeat this step for all words you want to add to this list of forbidden words. You will return to the Edit Filters page again.

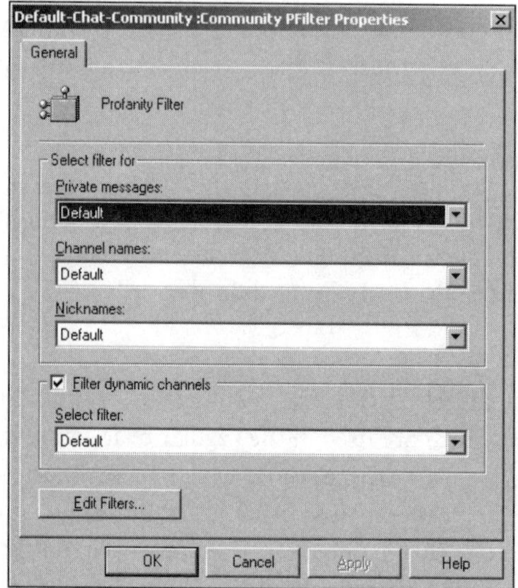

Figure 16.15
The General page for the Profanity Filter.

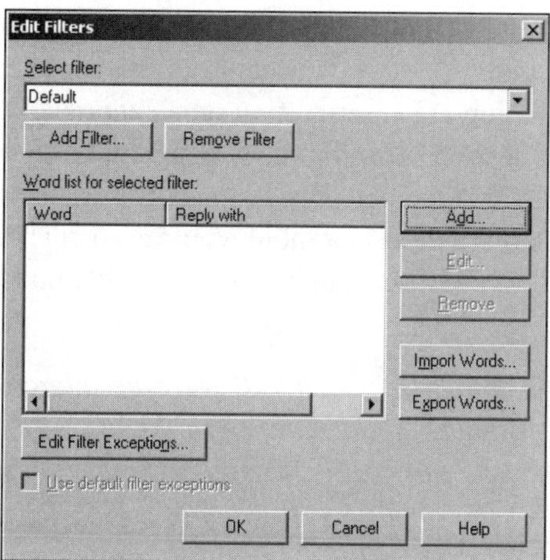

Figure 16.16
The Edit Filters property page.

If you want to add an exception, click the Edit Filters Exceptions button and add the words that will be accepted even if they occur on the forbidden list, then click *OK* to close this dialog box. For example, assume that you have defined a filter that prohibits all words that *Notes* is a part of, but you would accept the word *Notes-Killer*; you would add the word *Notes-Killer* to the Filters Exceptions field.

It's possible to both import and export text files with forbidden words and filter exceptions; use the Import Words/Export Words buttons for this; however, there is no example list of words to import on the Exchange server CD-ROM, you must create this list manually, or achieve it from an external source.

6. Click the *OK* button a number of times to close all the dialog boxes.

Now we have defined our filter list; next we will apply this filter to one of our channels. Remember that the default configuration for a channel is to not activate any extensions. Follow these steps to activate the filter extension to our #Mailsupport channel:

1. Use the ESM tool; navigate to the channel #Mailsupport, then open its properties.
2. Switch to the Extensions page and you will see all available extensions; PFilter is the Profanity Filter and TScript is the Transcription extension. Select the PFilter and click the Properties button.
3. This General page is used to control whether this extension will be active on this channel, and if so, what this filter will be applied to.

   Default is Do Not Filter Messages. Change to Filter Messages to activate the filter for this channel. Select the filter to be used, and how to apply it; All Messages really does mean all messages, including private and whispering messages. Select Only Messages Sent To Entire Channel if you only want to apply this filter on open chat conversations. Click *OK* to close this window.

The Channel Transcription Extension

The second extension that comes with Exchange 2000 is the Channel Transcription. This extension makes it possible to record the complete conversation on a channel. A good example of when to use this is when a chat session is used to inform all employees about some important topic; by recording this session, you can give a copy of this information to the people who missed the session. If you are more paranoid, you can easily think of more interesting scenarios where this feature might be handy (you remember our villain Jan from Chapter 14, don't you?).

Note: *The Transcription feature is a bit CPU and disk intensive; if you have a large chat community with lots of active chat users, activating this feature could decrease the overall performance so much that the users will notice. The default setting is to make a transcript of all dynamic channels. Change this if you aren't sure that you really need this default setting.*

Just like the Profanity Filter, we must configure the Channel Transcription on the IPCX object before it can be applied to a channel; follow these steps to do so:

1. Use the ESM tool and open the properties for the IRCX protocol.
2. On the Property page for the chat community, click the Extensions button.
3. On the Extensions page, you will see a list of all installed extensions (if not, restart the IRCX protocol); select TScript, and click the Properties button.
4. On the General page, select where these transcript files will be stored. The root path is in the Exchsrvr\ChatData\Transcript; below this folder, a new folder will be created with the same name as the chat community, and below this you will find one folder for each channel. The files will have names based on dates with the following name standard: *yyyymmdd_hhmm*.log—for example, 20010604_1600.log. These log files must be manually removed when no longer needed.

   The default setting is to take a transcript of all dynamic channels, but not registered channels. Unless you really need this default setting, I recommend that you clear this set-ting to preserve CPU and disk resources on the Exchange server.

   Click *OK* several times to close all the dialog boxes for the IRCX protocol. Then restart the IRCX protocol to activate the new settings.
5. The IRC protocol is now prepared; it's time to configure the channels. Open the properties for the channel you want to run, and switch to the Extensions page.
6. On the General page, set this checkbox if you want to transcribe this channel.
7. Click *OK* several times to close all dialog boxes.

The log files created by the transcript feature will give you a detailed description of the conversations and commands given. Use a standard text editor to view this log file; it will look similar to this:

```
#Summerparty
2001-06-04 16:00 [START  ]
2001-06-04 16:00 [TOPIC  ]
2001-06-04 16:00 [ENTERS ]Husse
2001-06-04 16:00 [MEMBER ]Husse is ~goran@192.168.15.50 Real Name: Göran Husman
2001-06-04 16:00 [ENTERS ]FridaH
2001-06-04 16:00 [MEMBER ]FridaH is ~Frida@192.168.15.51 Real Name: Frida H.
2001-06-04 16:01 [MESSAGE]Husse Hi! IT IS SUMMER - AND IT'S PARTY TIME!!!
2001-06-04 16:01 [MESSAGE]FridaH Yeah! With lots of Sun and bath... and
dancing!
2001-06-04 16:02 [MESSAGE]Husse Maybe you want something cold to drink? ;-)
2001-06-04 16:03 [MESSAGE]FridaH Some ice tea would be nice, thanks!
2001-06-04 16:03 [MESSAGE]Husse OK, 10-4. What system are you on? Lotus Notes?
2001-06-04 16:05 [MESSAGE]FridaH Reality check, please! It's Exchange 2000 of
course. Where have you been the last year?
2001-06-04 16:07 [MESSAGE]Husse Sure! I just wondered. Sorry, got to go, CUL!
2001-06-04 16:07 [MESSAGE]FridaH CU!
2001-06-04 16:07 [LEAVES ]FridaH
2001-06-04 16:09 [LEAVES ]Husse
2001-06-04 16:09 [STOP   ]
```


Some Tips Regarding Transcription of Channels

Even if the transcript of channels is disabled by default, you can temporarily activate this feature if you are an administrator and you have logged on to the Chat server. Use any of these commands to control the transcription of a channel:

- *Extmsg Tscript Start|Stop Dynamic*—To start or stop transcripts of all dynamic channels.
- *Extmsg Tscript Start|Stop Persistent*—To start or stop transcripts of all registered channels.
- *Extmsg Tscript Start|Stop Name=*<channel>—To start or stop transcripts of a given registered channel.
- *Extmsg Tscript Set Directory=*<path>—To designate a location for the transcripts.
- *Extmsg Status Channel=*<channel>—To see if a particular channel is transcribed or not.

Using the Chat Client

Now the time has finally come to install the chat client. A number of clients are available for the IRC protocol, such as mIRC, Virc, and Pirch; these are often shareware, meaning you can download these clients and test them for a limited time, then you are supposed to pay a (usually) low fee to register this client. If you use these shareware clients, please do pay these developers this registration fee; it will help them continue to develop new versions. You can find these chat clients on many places on the Internet, for example at **www.tucows.com**.

Since Microsoft developed the Extended IRC (IRCX), it's only natural that it was the first to offer IRCX-compliant clients; the latest version is MS Chat 2.5. However, now a few other clients are IRCX compliant, such as the shareware TurboIRC 2000 (**www.turboirc.com**). Many experienced chat users running standard IRC clients, such as mIRC, get irritated at users that have the MS Chat 2.1 clients since this version generates a lot of "garbage" characters in the beginning of each text line. The reason for this is that MS Chat, also known as the "Comic Chat" client, has a graphical feature that makes it possible to send drawings of people in different modes. The idea behind this is probably to make it more intuitive to the casual chat user. However, in a corporate environment, I don't believe that this type of client is the one your users will prefer; for example, I have a hard time imagine that the president of a company wants to present something important using the character Xeno :-). So in this section I describe how to install and use the most popular general IRC client as of today, the mIRC.

It's common for IRC servers on the Internet to have a name similar to **irc.domain.com**. If you want the Exchange 2000 Chat server to follow this name standard, then add a new Alias record to the DNS server that your clients are using. Follow these steps to create this new alias:

1. Open the DNS manager in Windows 2000.
2. Expand the DNS server and the Forward Lookup Zones, and then your DNS domain name where this Chat server belongs.
3. Right-click your domain name, and select New Alias.
4. Fill in the dialog box: Enter **irc** as the alias name, then enter the complete server name in the Fully Qualified Name For Target Host field or click the Browse button to locate the server hosting this chat service. When ready, click *OK*.
5. You are done! Close the DNS tool.

The mIRC Client

This client is probably the most popular IRC-compliant Windows chat client available today. It was developed by Khaled Mardam-Bey and has been adopted by most popular operating systems, such as all versions of MS Windows, Macintosh, and Unix. You can tell it has its root in Unix by all the command switches, but you can also use menus or buttons to perform any activity. It's also highly adaptable; many users love this client because of its rich script functionality.

Installation and Configuration of the mIRC Client

You can download a shareware version of this client from many Web sites, but **www.mirc.co.uk** may be preferred one since this Web site also has a lot of information about IRC in general and mIRC in particular. The download file is roughly 1MB in size and usually has a name similar to *mirc59t.exe*. Double-click this file to start the installation; this will display five dialog windows with easy-to-understand questions.

Before you can use this client with the Exchange 2000 Chat server, you need to configure some settings; follow these steps:

1. Start the mIRC32 client; this will display an About mIRC window. You can click the Introduction to read the help file, or click How To Register to get information about how to register this client. Click the upper-right X-button to close this window.
2. Since this is the first time you're starting mIRC, it will automatically start the mIRC Options dialog box. This dialog is used to configure which IRC server to connect to.
3. Click the Add button, then fill in the following values:
    - *Description*—Exchange 2000 Chat Server
    - *IRC Server*—irc.humandata.se (Replace this with your real domain name.)
    - *Port*—6667 (Unless you have configured the IRCX protocol to use another port.)
    - *Group*—(Leave this field blank.)
    - *Password*—(Leave this field blank.)
4. When ready, click the Add button to close this dialog box.
5. While you're still in the mIRC Options dialog box, fill in the Full Name, E-Mail Address, Nickname, and Alternative fields. In the real IRC world outside your Exchange organization, it's common to type in fake names and addresses here; however, this will only be your internal Chat server so I recommend that you enter correct names and addresses.
6. This is all you need to configure mIRC with Exchange 2000 Chat; click the Connect To IRC Server option to start the chat session.
7. You will now be connected to the Chat server (if not, see the section "Troubleshooting the Chat Server," later in this chapter). You will first see the client displaying the connection status, number of channels, users, and the Message Of The Day (MOTD). You will also see a separate window displaying a number of channels; these are not Exchange 2000 chat channels! If you select one of these, the Exchange Chat server will create a dynamic channel (if this is allowed) with this name. If you instead want to join a registered channel, simply type in its name and click Join; this will open a new window in the mIRC client in which you can start chatting with the members of this channel. To exit from a channel, simply close its window.

16

Some mIRC Tips

That wasn't so bad, was it? The trick is to understand how to make mIRC connect to the Exchange Chat server and how to join a channel. The next time you start the client, it will remember the Exchange Chat setting; just click Connect to establish a chat session with the Exchange Chat server again. To make it easier for the user, you can configure the mIRC to connect to the Exchange Chat server automatically; follow these steps:

1. Start the mIRC client (you don't have to connect). You will be listed with the mIRC Options.
2. Click the Options; set the option Connect On Startup and clear the other three options. When ready, click *OK*.

Test this by restarting the mIRC client; you should now be connected directly to the Exchange Chat server. Another related tip is to clear out all suggested channels and add the ones used by your organization. Here's how:

1. Open the mIRC Channels Folder. This will open automatically when you start the mIRC client, otherwise click on the third left icon on the toolbar.
2. Mark all preconfigured channels and click Delete.
3. Click Add and enter the following information:
   - *Channel*—Enter the channel name.
   - *Password*—Enter the password for this channel, if any, or to get sysop permissions.
   - *Description*—Enter a short description.
   - *Network*—Leave it as All.

   Set the option Auto-Join Channel On Connect if you want this client to automatically join this channel when connecting to Exchange Chat; it's okay to have more than one auto-join channel.

   Set the option Auto-Minimize On Join if you want to minimize the window for this channel.

   When ready, click *OK* to save this channel definition.
4. When you have configured all channels needed, set or clear the checkbox for Pop Up Folder On Connect as you want it to be.

These customized channel settings are stored in the file \mIRC\mirc.ini, together with a large number of other personal settings for this client. You can copy the channel information and paste it into another client's mirc.ini file instead of adding them manually. Look at the end of the mirc.ini file for the [*chanfolder*] section—all lines that start with "n" are named channels; for example:

```
[chanfolder]
n0=#Mailnerds,"Werd mail nerd conversation"
n1=#Mailsupport,"General mail support"
n2=#PartyTime,"Dynamic channel for party discussions"
n3=#Project_X,"Team discussions",Team
```

Warning! *Any passwords for the channels are written in clear text in the mirc.ini file; for example, Team above is the password needed to enter the #Project_X channel!*

By now you may have started wondering what all these PING? PONG! lines in the status window are. This is a test that the connection is alive; you can hide these lines if you want by using the same option dialog box as before. Select the File|Option menu, expand the IRC option, select Options, and check the Hide Ping? Pong! event.

As you may understand from this short introduction, the mIRC is a client full of features but is still rather easy to use. But let me just show you one more feature available in mIRC—the Direct Client-to-Client (DCC) chat; this is a feature that makes it possible to connect two mIRC clients directly, without any chat server. This will bypass any profanity filtering or transcription of the chat service. The DCC also has a feature for sending files between two users; you don't have to have a chat connection for this to work. Simply use the DCC menu on the mIRC client and select to chat or send files; use the other person's nickname as the recipient address for both DCC chat and DCC file transfer.

Warning! *Be careful when accepting files from unknown senders; they may contain viruses or Trojan horses disguised as ordinary files!*

The MS Chat Client

Let's compare the mIRC client with Microsoft's chat client. This client is fully IRCX compliant, and has both a standard text-based user interface and a graphical user interface known as the Comic Chat. It's actually hard to find this client, but look in the Exchange 5.5 Service Pack 3 (but not in SP4!) CD-ROM, under the directory \Eng\Chat\Setup\I386; start the setup.exe program to install MS Chat 2.1.

The new version, MS Chat 2.5, is installed as a part of the Windows 98 SE, ME, or NT4 operating systems. You will find it under the Windows Setup/Communications option; click on Details to find the MS Chat 2.5 as a subcomponent. However, if you are running Windows 2000, you will not find the MS Chat 2.5 version; you have to download it from a Web site, such as **filedudes.ozbytes.net.au/win95/irc/mschat.html**. (I have not managed to find it on Microsoft's own download center any longer.)

Installing MS Chat 2.x

This client runs on Windows 9x, ME, NT, and 2000; it requires about 4.5MB of disk space. Follow these steps to install this client:

1. a) To set up MS Chat 2.1: Put in the Exchange 5.5 SP3 CD-ROM; start the \Eng\Chat\Setup\I386\MSChat21.exe program.

   b) To set up MS Chat 2.5: Download the file MSCHAT.EXE from the Web; double-click it to start the installation. If you already have MS Chat 2.1 installed, it will retain all configuration settings.

2. On the Welcome page, click *Next* to continue.
3. On the Registration page, enter your name and company name; click *Next* to continue.
4. On the Choose Destination directory, select the directory where this chat client will be installed; the default is C:\InetPub\Chat. Click *Next* to continue.
5. On the Select Component page, select Microsoft Chat 2.1 Client; clear all other components (they aren't needed). Click *Next* to continue.
6. On the Folder Selection page, select what program folder this item should be added to. Default is Microsoft Exchange Chat Service. However, if you only install the MS Chat client, this folder selection will be ignored! Your MS Chat client will always be listed directly under the Start|Programs folder. Click *Next* to continue.
7. Next, confirm the setup information; if it is okay, click *Next* to start the installation, otherwise click Back and correct the error. After this, the files are copied to the com-puter, followed by a Setup Complete page; click Finish to complete the installation of the MS Chat 2.1 client.

Using the MS Chat 2.X Client

The next step is to test this new client. Versions 2.1 and 2.5 of this client are almost identical in their look and feel; follow these steps to start and configure the MS Chat client:

1. Start the new client by selecting Start|Programs|Microsoft Chat. This will automatically start the Chat Connection dialog box, used for configuring the Chat server, personal information, preferred character, and background.
2. On the Connect page, enter the URL to the Chat server—for example, **irc.humandata.se**. You can also configure the client to automatically join a channel, or to list all avail-able channels. If you aren't sure which channel to start using, select to list the channels.
3. On the Personal Info page, enter the name, nickname, email address, personal Web page (if any), and a brief description of yourself. Note that in real chat scenarios, it's common to fake these names and addresses; however, since this is an Exchange 2000 Chat server used only within your own organization, you should enter your correct information here.
4. On the Character page, select the character that you like; you can choose among three female, four male, and five fantasy characters.
5. On the Background page, select the background you prefer for your characters. When ready, click *OK* to close this dialog box.

Now the MS Chat client is ready to use. When you close the Chat Connect dialog box, you automatically connect to the Chat server. You will see a Message of the Day (MOTD). It will list the number of Chat servers in this chat network (usually one), the numbers of users, and the number of active channels.

This MOTD will always show up when you connect to the Chat server; clear the Show This Whenever Connecting option if you don't want this. If you configured the chat client to list available channels (in Step 2 above), you will now see this list; to join any of these channels, select it and click Go To or double-click the channel.

Instead of joining an existing channel, you can create a new (dynamic) channel; click Create Room and enter the channel name and a short topic (if any). You can also configure the access to this channel, by using these options:

- *Moderated*—Only the room host (i.e., sysop) and users granted speak permission by the sysop will be allowed to send messages to this channel; all other users can only view the messages.
- *Set Topic anyone*—Allows any user to change the topic description for this channel.
- *Invite only*—This channel is closed for all users except the ones the sysop invites.
- *Hidden*—This channel is not publicly listed. Only members of this channel will see this name listed.
- *Private*—This option controls whether the information about the users inside this channel will be available to users outside this channel.

Mixing MS Chat and Standard IRC Clients

The MS Chat client starts in Comic Chat mode, making the chat conversation look like a comic strip. Although this mode is fun to use for a short while, it is not suitable for more serious chat sessions, like project meetings or department discussions.

If there is a mix of MS Chat 2.1 and standard IRC chat clients (such as mIRC), some annoying character strings result from this mix; for example, messages that the MS Chat 2.1 client sends in Comic Chat mode will look a bit strange on mIRC clients. Look at Figure 16.17; this is the MS Chat 2.1 client sending a message to AnnaH, who is using a mIRC client. When AnnaH receives this message, it will look like Figure 16.18. All replies from the mIRC client will, however, look normal on the MS Chat 2.1 client. This problem is fixed in MS Chat 2.5, making it possible to use this version with standard IRC clients.

Note the extra character string (#G4:0E710M1) in Figure 16.18 that initiates messages from the MS Chat 2.1 client; these characters describe the sender's selected comic character and mode setting, such as happy or angry. Users of standard IRC clients usually get very irritated about these extra characters; you should instruct users of the MS Chat 2.1 client to avoid the Comic Chat mode when using channels with mixed clients, or upgrade to MS Chat 2.5 doesn't generate these characters.

Another problem with mixing these client types is that IRC clients don't understand channel names using IRCX names—for example %#MyIRCXChannel—since the initial % character in IRCX names isn't allowed in IRC channels. The result is that IRC clients cannot join IRCX channels.

Figure 16.17
The sender uses MS Chat 2.x in Comic Chat mode.

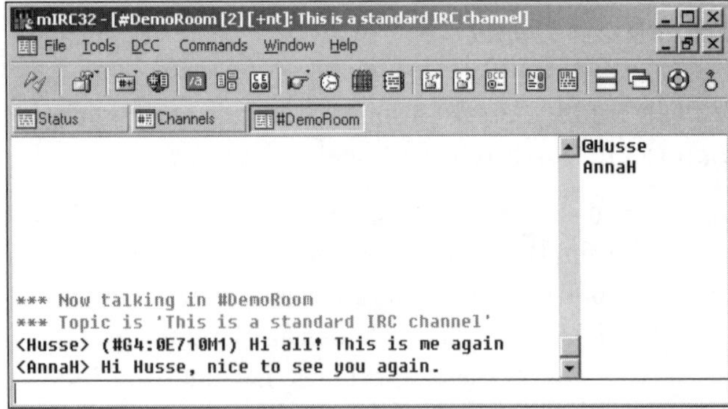

Figure 16.18
The receiver uses mIRC in standard mode.

Tips Regarding the MS Chat Client

Here are some tips regarding the MS Chat 2.x client. Note that this client refers to channels as "rooms":

- *Plain text*—You can switch to standard IRC text mode by selecting the View|Plain Text menu. This will also remove the extra character strings displayed for standard IRC clients, as described in the previous section. However, in version 2.1, you must do this before joining a channel; otherwise, all new messages will still only be visible in the Comic Chat mode. In version 2.5, you can switch back and forth between these two modes.

- *Multiple rooms*—You can join multiple rooms simultaneously; use the Room|Enter Room menu to join a new room.
- *Room Settings*—To modify the access settings for a room, use the Room|Room Properties menu. Note that you must be a sysop to do this.
- *Change user status*—If you are the sysop for a room, you can change the status for a member user between Host (i.e., sysop), Speaker (normal user), and Spectator (view-only). In the upper-right pane of the MS Chat client, right-click the user and select Status. You can also ban or kick out a user with this menu.
- *Whispering*—Send secret messages by right-clicking the user's character (or select the Member menu) and selecting Whisper Box. No one besides you two can see these messages.
- *Send Files*—Send a file to a member by right-clicking the user's character (or selecting the Member menu) and selecting Send File. This will work with mIRC and other DCC-compliant clients. Note that many standard IRC clients have restrictions on what files they can accept; for example, they usually don't accept *.exe, *.vbs, or other executable files (this can be modified in the mIRC client by using the File|Options|DCC|Folders menu; use the DCC Ignore pane to modify which files are ignored.
- *Create new characters*—You can download a special designer program to create new characters by using the Help|Microsoft On The Web|Free Stuff menu. This doesn't seem to work in MS Chat 2.1 or 2.5 anymore—maybe it can be found on the Internet?
- *Selecting room properties*—There are a number of room properties, such as Moderated, Invite only, etc. Use Decision Tree 16.1 to help you set up the right room properties.
- *Macros*—Version 2.5 of the MS Chat client has support for macros; these can be defined to run when you enter a new room, or to avoid IRC attacks like flooders (someone sending a large number of messages), or to be notified when a particular nickname joins the room. Use the View|Macros menu to create and manage macros.

Administration of Exchange 2000 Chat Service

In this chapter, we have already covered a large number of the administrative tasks you have for the Exchange Chat server, such as:

- Creating a chat community
- Creating and configuring a registered channel (i.e., a permanent channel)
- Creating and configuring an IRCX protocol
- Installing and configuring channel extensions, such as PFilter and TScript

In this section, we will cover the rest of Chat server administration.

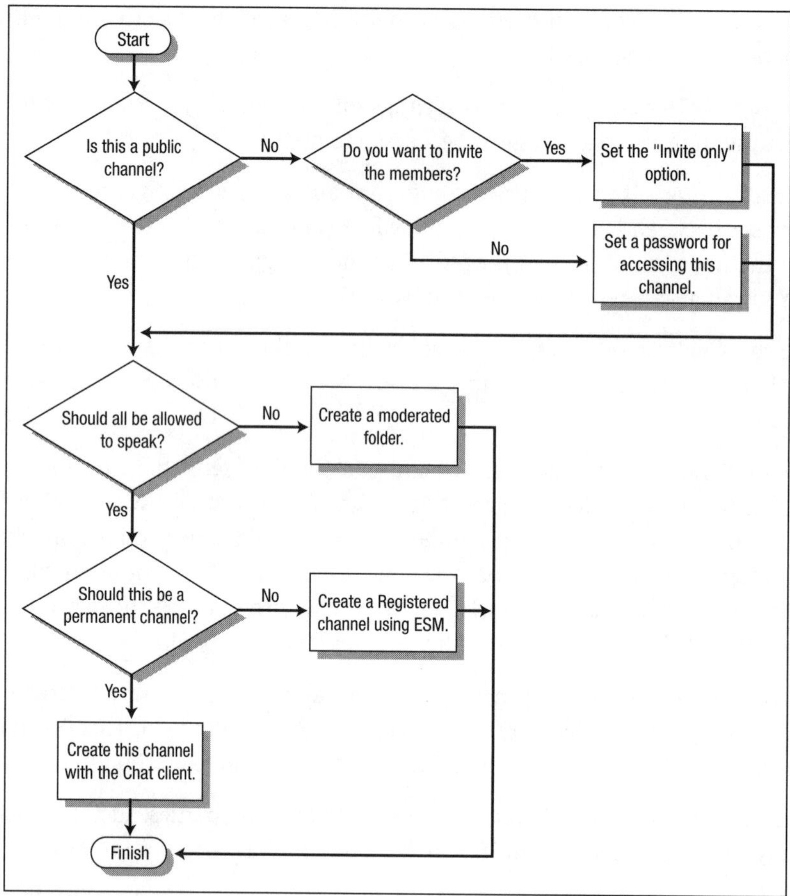

Decision Tree 16.1
Selecting the room properties.

Configuring the Chat Community

This is very similar to the configuration of channels we covered earlier in this chapter. What you set in this object will be regarded as default values for the new channel. These types of objects are known as *virtual chat communities*, since they are subfolders to the root folder Chat Communities. The first virtual chat community is created automatically when you install the Chat server; its name is Default-Chat-Community. This name will be visible to all users connecting to this Chat server; you may want to change this to a more descriptive name. You can also delimit the number of simultaneous users and enable or disable this Chat server. Follow these steps to configure a virtual chat community:

1. Start the ESM tool; navigate to the Default-Chat-Community object and open its properties.

2. On the General page (see Figure 16.19), enter a descriptive name for this virtual chat community. The Title field will be displayed every time a chat client connects to this Chat server.

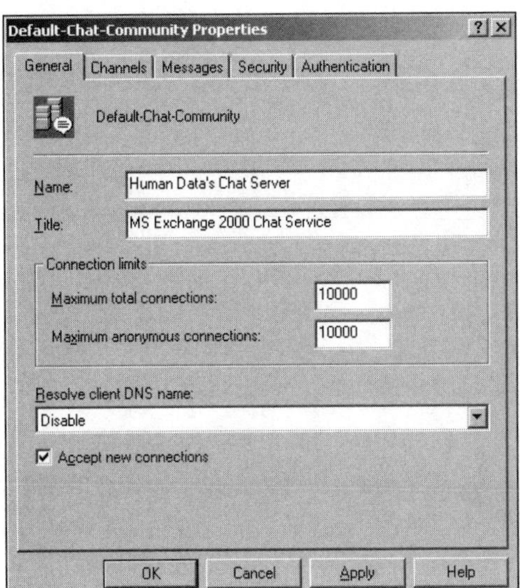

Figure 16.19
The General page for the virtual chat community.

The Connection Limits pane is used to set the maximum total connections and maximum number of anonymous connections, when counting all channels together.

The Resolve Client DNS Name option is default disabled, because it decreases the performance of the Chat server and could deny clients access to the channels. However, if you set this value to Attempt, the Chat server will try to resolve the client's IP address; still, if the resolution fails, the client will get access to the channels anyway. By setting this value to Require, you will deny access for clients that can't be resolved; this is the most secure alternative, since you now are pretty sure which clients can connect to this Chat server. Note that this resolve setting affects all channels on this Chat server.

Use the Accept New Connections option to control whether this Chat server will accept new client connections or not. If this setting is cleared, no more connections are accepted, but all current clients will still be able to use their connection.

3. On the Channels page (see Figure 16.20), set the default maximum number of users for registered channels. Default is 25; you may want to increase this number if you have a lot of chat users. You can select any value up to 99,999; zero means no limit. Each registered channel can change this default value if necessary.

   In the Language field, set the default language for all channels, using ISO 639; for example, **en**=English and **sv**=Swedish. Each registered channel can change this value if necessary.

   The Allow An Owner Or Host For Channel option controls whether the user that creates a channel will also be its host and owner.

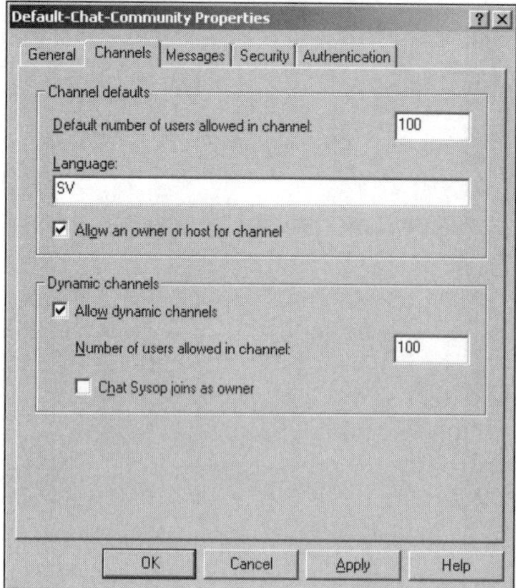

Figure 16.20
The Channels page for the virtual chat community.

The Dynamic Channels pane is used to control basic features of the dynamic channels that users create with their clients. You can deny the ability to create such channels with the Allow Dynamic Channels option. You can also define the default maximum number of users for dynamic channels. And finally, you can set an option that grants a sysop (i.e., host) of a dynamic channel owner's permissions.

4. On the Messages page (see Figure 16.21), define the MOTD users will see when they connect to this chat community.

   You can also define a message given to users that run the IRC command **Admin**; the maximum message size is 119 characters.

5. On the Security page, you can control which users can be granted user, host (i.e., sysop), or owner status. By default, the group Everyone can be a user, and no denying permissions are enforced.

6. On the Authentication page (see Figure 16.22), you can control how authentication is performed; this will affect all channels, both registered and dynamic. Default is to accept Anonymous connections (which is standard in IRC networks). If this option is cleared, then all users must authenticate before accessing any channels.

   It is possible to authenticate using Basic Authentication (an insecure clear text validation) and the Windows Security Package (using the Windows 2000 Security Support Provider Interface, or SSPI). If you use an SSPI package to authenticate users, then you should clear the Basic Authentication option! To install an SSPI package, follow the guidelines in the ESM Help and the Set Up User Authentication section.

   When ready, click *OK* to close this dialog box.

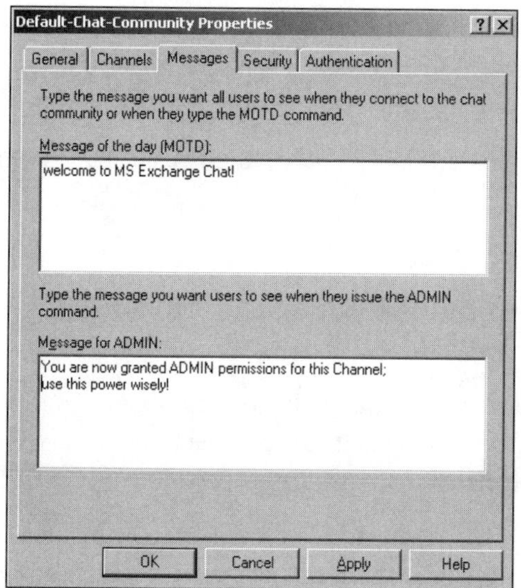

Figure 16.21
The Messages page for the virtual chat community.

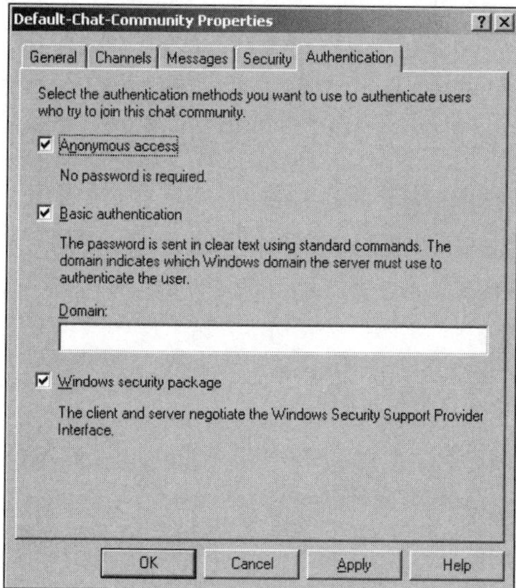

Figure 16.22
The Authentication page for virtual chat communities.

Configuring Bans

To ban a user is to stop him or her from joining a particular channel. In normal IRC networks, this is usually done if a user is abusive or behaves inappropriately. In the Exchange Chat server environment, you have much more control, and this situation will seldom occur, hopefully. Any sysop for a channel can activate the ban feature; you can also configure permanent bans using the ESM tool. For example, assume that you have extra personnel working in your company, and you don't want them to access any chat channels; you would use the ESM tool to ban these people. Follow these steps to create a permanent ban:

1. Start the ESM tool and navigate to the Bans folder (under the virtual chat community folder).
2. Right-click the Bans folder and select New|Ban.
3. There is only one property page here, the General page (see Figure 16.23). You can identify the user to ban several ways, such as:
   - *Nickname*—Use this field to enter the nickname to be banned. Default is the wildcard *, meaning all nicknames. Note that this is not very secure; it's easy for the user to simply choose another nickname.
   - *User name*—Use this field to enter the "real name" of the user to be banned. This is also insecure because the user has often not been authenticated, i.e., he or she is logged on as anonymous users.
   - *Domain name or IP address*—This identifies the user by his or her client's domain name or IP address.
4. Use the *Time Active* field to define when this ban is active; default is 24 hours. This option could be a way of controlling when a group of users is banned; for example, you could choose to ban all consultants from the chat community during office hours.

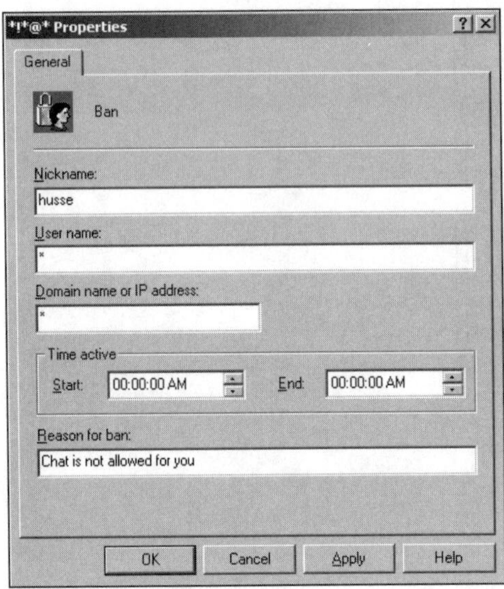

Figure 16.23
Banning a user with the ESM tool.

5. Enter a reason for banning these users; however, this message will not be displayed for the users. You don't have to enter any reason; this entry is optional. A banned user will only discover that he or she can't connect to the server.

Don't test this ban feature without actually entering any values; the default is to ban all users at all times! When you have defined a new ban, you must restart the IRCX protocol; beware, this will disconnect all current users, so make sure to select a proper time for this restart. To remove a ban, right-click it and select Delete.

User Classes in the Chat Community

A *user class* is a group of users identified by a property, such as a common domain name (**@humandata.se**), IP address (192.168.15.0), or if the user is authenticated or anonymous. These user classes can then be used to protect your server from flooding and other types of attacks. You can also use these user classes to control the users' ability to log on to the server, create or join dynamic channels, or become a sysop or channel owner.

Follow these steps to create a user class:

1. Start the ESM tool and navigate to the Classes folder (under the virtual chat community folder).
2. Right-click this folder and select New|Class.
3. On the General page, enter a descriptive name for this class, making it easy to understand which users belong to this class; note that space characters aren't allowed in this name. Next, select how to identify these users—by Identity Mask or IP Address:

   a) By using the Identity Mask: Identify the user based on his or her nickname, user name, or Domain or IP address. For example, if you set these values:

   - **Nickname=Husse, User name=*, Domain or IP address=***—This will create a user class with all users with the nickname **Husse**.
   - **Nickname=*, User name=Goran Husman, Domain or IP address=***—This will create a user class with all users named **Goran Husman**.
   - **Nickname=*, User name=*, Domain or IP address=humandata.se**—This will create a user class with all users belonging to the **humandata.se** domain.

   b) By using the IP Address: Identify the user based on his or her IP address and subnet mask. If you are looking for a particular host, click DNS Lookup to browse to the DNS server. For example, if you set IP Address=192.168.15.0, subnet=255.255.255.0, this will create a user class with all users belonging to the class-C IP net 192.168.15.0.

4. On the Access page: This page is used to impose restrictions on this user class.

The Logon Method pane: Use one of these three options to restrict how members of a user class can log on to a chat community:

- *Authenticated or anonymous*—Any of these two options will be okay for accessing the chat community.
- *Authenticated only*—The users in this class must authenticate to access the chat community.
- *Anonymous only*—The users in this class must log on as anonymous to access the chat community.

The *Restrictions* pane: Use these options to restrict this user group from the following activities:

- *Log on*—Users belonging to this class cannot log on to this chat community.
- *Own or host channels*—Users in this class cannot own or host a channel.
- *Create dynamic channels*—Users in this class cannot create dynamic channels.
- *Join dynamic channels*—Users in this class cannot join dynamic channels.

Use the Time Active option to define when these restrictions are valid; default is 24 hours.

Use the Hide Class Member's IP Addresses And DNS Names option to hide the IP address and domain name from other users in this channel.

Note: *None of these restrictions will be applied to a sysop or owner of the channel, except for the log on restriction!*

5. Use the Settings page to establish general security settings for members of this user class.

   The most advanced option on this page is the Attack Protection Level. You can set one of four different protection levels: None, Low, Medium, and High. The idea behind this security feature is to prohibit users from attacking the channels of this chat community by looking for certain types of events; when they happen, the system will create a delay for this user for a given number of seconds. The events that will be detected are:

   - *Data message*—Someone is trying to send a data message to the channel.
   - *Invitation*—Someone tries to send an invitation to other users.
   - *Wrong channel password*—Someone uses the wrong password for a channel.
   - *Standard message*—Someone sends a standard message; this also includes messages sent by the commands **Privmsg**, **Notice**, or **Whisper**.
   - *Message from host to channel*—A host (sysop) sends a message to the channel.

Table 16.2 The delay in seconds for different attack protection levels.

Event	None	Low	Medium	High
Data msg	0 sec	1 sec	2 sec	3 sec
Invitation	0 sec	2 sec	4 sec	5 sec
Join	0 sec	2 sec	3 sec	4 sec
Wrong password	0 sec	2 sec	4 sec	5 sec
Standard msg	0 sec	1 sec	2 sec	3 sec
Msg from host to channel	0 sec	1 sec	1 sec	2 sec

If the selected Attack Protection Level is something other than None, the user will experience a delay for a number of seconds when a certain event happens; see also Table 16.2.

In the Limits pane, you can set restrictions for this user class and their use of this chat community:

- *Maximum IP connections*—Set a maximum limit of simultaneous client connections; default is 0, which equals an unlimited number of connections.
- *Maximum channels user can join*—Default is 10.
- *Output saturation limit (KB)*—Set the maximum amount of data that the Chat server will buffer for a client before dropping the connection. Default is 64KB.

In the Delays pane, you can set these types of time interval delays for this user class:

- *Ping delay*—By default, these users must wait 90 seconds between every ping.
- *Message processing delay*—By default, these users must wait zero seconds between sending messages.
- *Nickname change*—By default, these users must wait zero seconds between changing nicknames.

When ready, click *OK* to save this User Class object.

Troubleshooting the Chat Server

The Chat server is easy to install and configure, but problems can still crop up from time to time. If you experience trouble connecting to the server, restart the complete Exchange server, not just the MS Exchange 2000 Chat service. If you still have problems connecting, you can use a Telnet session to connect to the Chat service and see if it's alive.

Do your test like this: Click Start|Run and enter **Telnet *<chat server or ip number>* port**. You should then be able to type in the command **USER . . .** (including the three periods and space characters in between), and then **NICK**. In the following example, I am using the nonexistent name DUMMY for the user and DUMMYNIC as the nickname; this will tell us if a) this Chat server works, and b) if it's open for anonymous access. Note that HD-Chat is the name of this chat community:

```
TELNET irc.humandata.se 6667
USER DUMMY . . .
NICK DUMMYNIC
:HD-Chat 001 DUMMYNIC :Welcome to the Microsoft Exchange Chat Service, DUMMYNIC
:HD-Chat 002 DUMMYNIC :Your host is Default-Chat-Community, running version
6.0.4417.0
:HD-Chat 003 DUMMYNIC :This server was created Aug  2 2000 at 02:20:57 GMT
:HD-Chat 004 DUMMYNIC HD-Chat 6.0.4417.0 aioxz abcdefhiklmnopqrstuvwxz
:HD-Chat 251 DUMMYNIC :There are 1 users and 0 invisible on 1 servers
:HD-Chat 254 DUMMYNIC 2 :channels formed
:HD-Chat 255 DUMMYNIC :I have 1 clients and 0 servers
:HD-Chat 265 DUMMYNIC :Current local users: 1 Max: 1
:HD-Chat 266 DUMMYNIC :Current global users: 1 Max: 1
:HD-Chat 375 DUMMYNIC :- HD-Chat Message of the Day -
:HD-Chat 372 DUMMYNIC :- welcome to MS Exchange Chat!
:HD-Chat 376 DUMMYNIC :End of /MOTD command
```

Obviously, this Chat server works and anonymous access is allowed. If you get another response other than the one listed here, you should interpret it like this:

- *No response*—The Chat server is unreachable. Try to ping the server, using its IP address and then its FQDN name. If this works, restart the complete Exchange server and try again.
- *Class denied access*—You are a member of a user class that has restricted access to this Chat server.
- *No IRC client permitted*—This Chat server only accepts MIC clients.
- *No more connections*—Either this Chat server only accepts authenticated users or the maximum number of connections has been reached.

Summary

This is a list of the more important features and keywords mentioned in this chapter. Use it as a reminder and to make sure you have understood the most important things:

- Mail systems are not designed for realtime communication.
- Phone systems allow realtime communication, but lack the capability to display pictures.
- ISDN videoconference systems make it possible to present both voice and picture information, but they're expensive systems that demand ISDN connections and special hardware. Only two parties can share information with this type of system.

- Bulletin Board Systems (BBSes) were the embryo to realtime chatting; the first one started in 1977.
- Usenet was the Unix world's equivalent to the BBS system, but it lacked a true realtime communication feature.
- Bitnet Relay Chat was one of the first really popular chat systems, designed for realtime communication between large groups of users.
- Internet Chat Relay (IRC) was designed in 1988 by Jarkko Oikarinen of Finland; this is the true chat standard of today.
- The IRC protocol is described in RFC1459 (and extended in RFC 2810, 2811, 2812, and 2813).
- An IRC network is a group of IRC servers that share their information and appear to the user as one large system.
- The user joins a channel, also known as a chat room, to converse with other members of this channel. No information is stored unless someone has activated a log (which can be done on the server or the individual chat client).
- The largest IRC networks today are Undernet, EFNet, and Dalnet.
- The most popular chat clients are mIRC, Virc, and Pirch.
- The chat culture has its own language; learn the basic acronyms and special character sequences, such as :-) before joining the Chat servers on the Internet.
- Microsoft's Chat server was first released with the Exchange 5.5 Server.
- Microsoft has applied an RFC draft for extending the IRC protocol, IRCX, to overcome the differences that make it impossible to share information between IRC networks today; for example, users on Undernet cannot talk with users on Dalnet.
- The Exchange 2000 Chat service is named Chatsrv.exe; it is not dependent on any Exchange 2000 service.
- Use port 6667 when connecting to an MS Chat server (this can be changed).
- The old Microsoft Internet Chat (MIC) protocol is no longer supported in this version of the Chat server.
- A registered channel is a permanent channel that is always available; these are created using the ESM tool.
- A dynamic channel is a temporary channel, created by the chat client.
- A powerful user in a channel is the sysop; this role is also referred to as the channel operator, or the host. This user can kick users out of the channel and ban them (prohibit them from entering again).

- The installation of Exchange 2000 Chat server is easy and requires very few resources, unless you have a very large organization. This version can handle up to 20,000 users.
- The Chat server installation will create a Default-Chat-Community; these objects can contain any number of channels, both registered and dynamic.
- After the Chat server is installed, you must create an IRCX Protocol object, which must be connected to the newly created chat community.
- Lots of security settings and restrictions can be applied to a channel; for example, it can be moderated, invitation-only, or protected by passwords.
- A channel extension provides added functionality; Exchange 2000 Chat server has two: the Profanity Filter (which filters forbidden words) and the Transcript Extension (which logs chat sessions to a file).
- One of the most popular IRC clients today is the mIRC, developed by Khaled Mardam-Bey. This client is not IRCX compliant.
- Microsoft Chat Client exists in two versions today: 2.1 and 2.5. Avoid using the 2.1 version if you have a mixed client environment with standard IRC clients. It's hard to find a version of this client for download, unless you have Windows 98 SE, ME, or NT4; if you have Windows 2000, try this Web site: **filedudes.ozbytes.net.au/win95/irc/mschat.html**.
- The MS Chat 2.x client can be used in both plain-text mode (i.e., standard IRC mode) and Comic Chat mode, which makes the chatting conversation look like a comic strip.
- The chat community can be configured to set default values for all its channels. It can also be configured to control the connections to this community.
- It's possible to configure permanent bans using the ESM tool; this could be used to disable the chat service for a group of people, such as hired consultants, during office hours.
- User classes provide a method of grouping users and placing restrictions on the group. For example, you can group all users coming from a given IP subnet and prohibit them from creating dynamic channels during a given time period.
- Troubleshooting Chat Server installation is best performed with the Telnet application. Connect to the Chat server on port 6667 and try the USER and NICK commands; if this works, your server is alive!

Chapter 17

Exchange 2000 Instant Messaging

Have you ever needed to check to see if a person is online and available for a quick question? And if he's not, have you wondered where he is? Then Instant Messaging (IM) is something you will appreciate. IM is a new type of messaging application that focuses on the presence status of other users, often referred to as *contacts* or *buddies*. One of Microsoft's Exchange development gurus, Thomas Rizzo, once described Instant Messaging as "the virtual water cooler," in the sense that this system is used for getting in contact with your buddies for quick conversations. IM has its roots in the chat system, but is still very different. The basic features offered by IM are:

- *Presence* information of other users
- *Status* information of other users
- *Realtime private conversations* between two or more users
- *File transfer* between two users

Instant Messaging might sound very similar to a chat system, but in fact it's not. There are many differences, but the most fundamental are:

- Chat servers allow a group of any size to exchange information
- Chat servers don't provide *presence* information for their clients
- Chat servers don't provide *status* information for their clients

With IM, you can see if another user is sitting at his or her computer and able to talk with you at this moment. For example, assume you get a phone call from a customer asking you a question about Java programming that you can't answer; however, you know that Johan is a guru on this topic and you want to ask him for advice. You would use your IM client to see if Johan is working at his computer right now, and if so you'd send him a quick question. Johan will immediately see that you want to talk with him using Instant Messag-ing, and he'll decide to accept the message and help you with this question. Within a few minutes, you have the answer and can pass it on to the customer.

So what's the difference compared to a chat session? In a chat session, you would have to join a channel and hope that Johan also joined this channel; that's not so practical. How about email? Then you wouldn't know if Johan was sitting at his computer or not. This is also impractical. But you could call him on the phone, right? Yes, this could be one solution, assuming your telephone switchboard allows you to put calls on hold and start a new call. But assume that Johan needs to send you a file to answer the customer's question—then the phone alternative would fail. The only way of solving this need of combining realtime conversation with status and presence information, as well as file transfer capability, is Instant Messaging.

History of Instant Messaging

There have been several predecessors to Instant Messaging systems, but the first really popular program was the ICQ (pronounced *I Seek You*) developed by the Israeli software company Mirablis in November 1996. The ICQ client was a free instant messaging utility that anyone could use for realtime conversations with other ICQ clients. The architecture of the ICQ system is illustrated in Figure 17.1.

As you can see from this figure, all ICQ clients connect to an ICQ server; this server keeps track of all ICQ clients that are online, including the IP address of each of them. Whenever you want to call another ICQ user, just select his or her name from the list of online users. Since this list can be very large, you can select a few of these names and add them to your personal contact list, thus making it easier to find them.

Shortly after the ICQ had become popular, America Online (AOL) released its IM client called AOL Instant Messaging (AIM). This quickly became even more popular than ICQ since this free AIM client made it possible to have realtime conversations with any one of the more than 20 million AOL users, as well as users not belonging to AOL. A third very

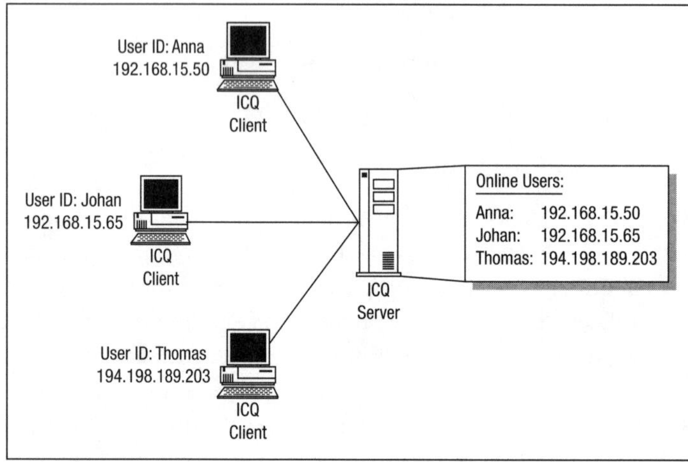

Figure 17.1
The ICQ architecture.

popular IM client is the Yahoo! Messenger, which combines IM features with the other Yahoo! services and content.

Microsoft couldn't stay out of this new Internet technology for long; around 1998, they released an IM client called MSN Messenger Service (MMS) for users connected to the Microsoft Network (MSN). This IM client is also built into MSN Explorer, making it available when using this Web client.

The IM Protocol

The ICQ and MMS, as well as other IM systems, use proprietary protocols, which makes it impossible to establish IM connections between these systems. You simply must have the "right" client when using a particular IM system. In February 2000, the first specification regarding IM was released as RFC 2779: Instant Messaging and Presence Protocol (IMPP). At least one Internet draft has since been released that extends the features described in RFC 2889: A Common Profile for Instant Messaging (CPIM). Hopefully, IM developers will agree on using this protocol, thus making it possible to use any IM client, regardless of the IM system.

Microsoft has chosen to implement its own Rendezvous Protocol (RVP) for the IM service included in Exchange 2000. This protocol is an extended subset of the WebDAV protocol, which is an extension of the HTTP 1.1 protocol. The RVP uses TCP port 80 for all standard HTTP connections, which makes it easy to configure firewalls for this IM communication.

None of these IM protocols are truly secure; most in fact send information in clear text. That makes IM sessions vulnerable to the kind of eavesdropping that was discussed in Chapter 14. You should inform your IM users that even if they have a private conversation, others could still use a network monitor and look at the conversation!

Presence and Status Information

One of the differences between IM and other messaging applications is the presence information available for each active IM client. When you first start the IM client, it will register with the IM server; usually you authenticate yourself first by logging on. This client will then check your online status and report any changes to the IM server. For example, if the screen saver on your computer gets activated, it will be detected by the IM client, which then reports this new status to the IM server. All IM users that subscribe on your IM information will be notified about this new status.

The following presence settings are available for an IM client; some will be automatically triggered by events such as the screen saver starting, while other presence settings are set by the users themselves:

- Online
- Appear offline
- Busy

- Be right back
- Away
- On the phone
- Out to lunch

It's not just users who can benefit from these presence settings; you could also use this information in applications that need realtime responses. For example, you could develop an Exchange application that accepts purchase orders by email from external users; when such an order is received, it must be taken care of immediately. Assume your application is IM aware; then this application could check the current status of everyone in the sales department and hand the purchase order to the first salesperson online.

Instant Messaging Architecture

Similar to other IM systems, all IM clients are connected to an IM server that keeps track of the user's current status. The IM server included in Exchange 2000 has the following components:

- The *IM client*
- The *IM home server*
- The *IM routing server*

These components work together to make it possible to design an *IM domain* for all types and sizes of organizations, from small companies with just a handful of users to large international companies with many thousands of users.

The IM Client

The IM client is light and doesn't require much disk or many CPU resources on the client com-puter. Exchange 2000 has its own IM client that works only in the Exchange environment, but version 3.5 of the MSN Messenger Service client can be used both for IM sessions with MSN and with Exchange 2000.

The IM clients use Microsoft's proprietary RVP protocol, which uses port 80 for communication with the IM server and other IM clients. The presence information sent between the client and the server is very small and will not affect network traffic unless you have many thousands of IM users. However, port 80 is only used to establish the IM session with the server; after that, the server selects a random TCP port over 1023 for this traffic; any firewall must therefore allow all ports over 1023 for incoming traffic. If a proxy server is used between the client and the server, this will prohibit the external IM client from receiving messages from the internal network, since a direct connection is required between these two computers. This could be solved by establishing a virtual private network, or by using a remote access connection directly into the network.

All IM clients are registered with one IM server; this is known as the user's *IM home server*. In small IM domains, all IM clients connect directly to the home server; however, in large or distributed IM domains, the clients initially connect to an *IM routing server*, which either proxies the client's request or refers the client to its home server.

The IM Home Server

An IM home server is the server that clients connect to in order to become authenticated (if authentication is required). This server maintains a database containing all the registered names for this server, their IP addresses, and current presence status. It also contains any subscriptions that IM users have set up on other users' presence status. The name for this node database is msimnode.edb, and it's stored in the Exchange 2000 server's \Exchsrvr\Imdata directory, together with its transaction log files.

The home server is also involved in the transfer of IM messages. For example, when IM user Alex sends a message to another IM user, this message will be sent to the IM home server from Alex's client; then the IM server passes this message directly to the recipient if both users belong to the same IM home server. There is no direct transfer between the IM clients.

One home server can host up to 15,000 IM clients simultaneously, and there is no limit on the number of home servers in one IM system. This makes it possible to create very large IM systems, if necessary. It is also possible to send IM messages to other organizations that also use the Exchange 2000 IM server. If an IM client requests the presence status of a remote user, i.e., a user that belongs to another home server, this client will be referred to the routing server.

The IM home server runs on the MS Internet Information Server 5 as an Internet Server Application Programming Interface (ISAPI) extension, so if you stop the Inetinfo.exe process, you will also stop the IM server. The IM server consists of three major modules, besides the node database; see also Figure 17.2.

- *The Firewall Topology Module (FTM),* which retains information about each IM server, regardless of whether it is inside or outside the firewall. This module also has information about how to pass RVP messages through the firewall; this is something the administrator must configure.
- *The Locator module,* which sends status notifications to the right home server when messages are passed through IM router servers; the Locator module gets this information from the Active Directory.
- *The Server Application Layer,* which is the central module; all information between the other modules, including the node database, is passed through this module.

To administrate the IM server, use the Exchange System Manager (ESM) tool and configure a Virtual IM Server object that is located under the Exchange server's Protocol folder. Since the IM server is an ISAPI extension to the IIS 5, you will also find an object called InstMsg

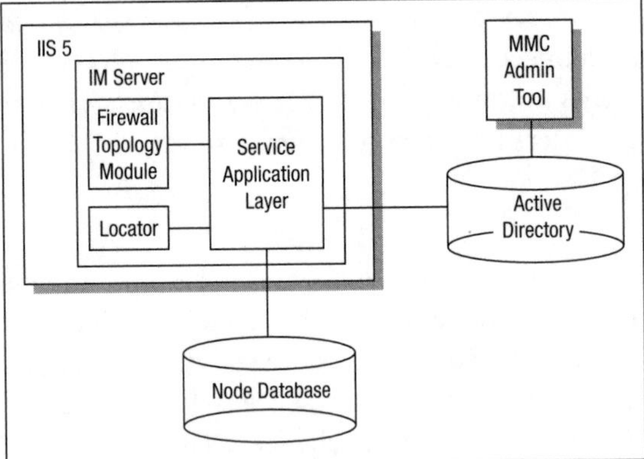

Figure 17.2
The IM server architecture.

under the Default Web Site in the ISM administrative tool; however, you should only use the ISM tool for configuration settings when specifically instructed to do so, for example, by a TechNet article. The ESM tool will use the Active Directory for managing the virtual IM server; this information is then passed over to the IM modules by the Server Application Layer.

The IM Router Server

The IM router server is used when you have more than one home server, or to accept calls from external IM clients, such as users in other organizations. For example, if user Alex wants to check the status of user Beatrice, and they belong to different home servers, the IM routing server will be passed the request from Alex's home server, which queries the AD for Beatrice's home server, and passes Alex's request to that server; see Figure 17.3.

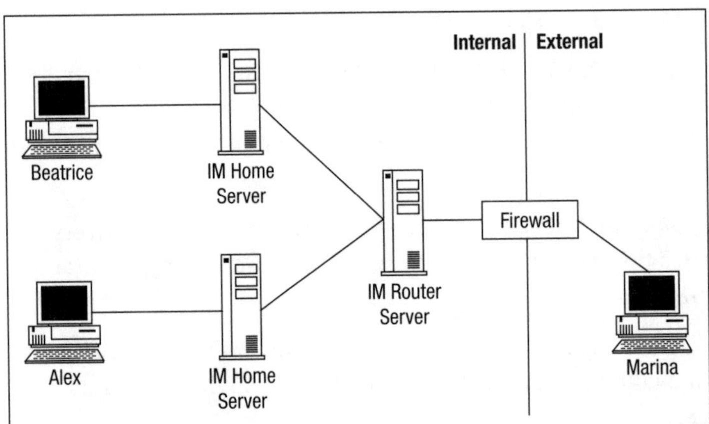

Figure 17.3
Using IM routing servers when you have multiple home servers and accept external IM connections.

A message or status request coming from the outside of this organization is also handled in the same way; for example, if the external user Marina wants to know the presence status for Alex, her request will be received by the IM routing server, which then will look up Alex's home server in the AD and pass the request to that server; this is also illustrated in Figure 17.3.

The only real difference between a router server and a home server is that the router server doesn't have any IM users. The primary use of a routing server is to find out what home server the IM users belong to in this IM domain and to route messages between IM servers. One IM routing server can handle up to 50,000 IM clients; Microsoft recommends that you have one such routing server for every two or three home servers.

Configuring DNS for IM

To follow the common practice for Instant Messaging, you should configure the Domain Naming Service (DNS) for this new IM domain before installing any IM servers. This is a straightforward three-step process:

1. Enter an A record for each IM server into the DNS database; if this will be a single IM server domain, it's common practice to name this service **im.<domain>.<tld>** for example, **im.humandata.se**. If you don't complete this step, the users must enter the fully qualified domain name (FQDN) to the IM server instead—for example, **oden.humandata.se**. However, experienced IM users expect the IM domain to be similar to **im.humandata.se**.
2. If there are one or more IM routing servers in this domain, it's common for these IM routing servers to have an IM server name such as im.**<domain>.<tld>** (and the ordinary home servers get other names).
3. Create an _rvp SRV resource record for the RVP protocol to enable it to work over TCP port 80; map this record to the IM routing server if this exists, or else to the IM home server. When an IM client tries to log on to the IM server, it will query the DNS for an _rvp SRV record; if this record exists, the client will connect to that server and refer to this server as its home server.

The _rvp SRV Record

The third step may seem a bit strange, but it will make the logon process for all IM clients more natural and easier to understand. To add this _rvp SRV record, follow these steps:

1. Open the DNS administrative tool and expand your DNS lookup zone—for example, **humandata.se.**
2. Right-click the domain and select Other New Records.
3. Select the record type Service Location (SRV), and click Create Record.

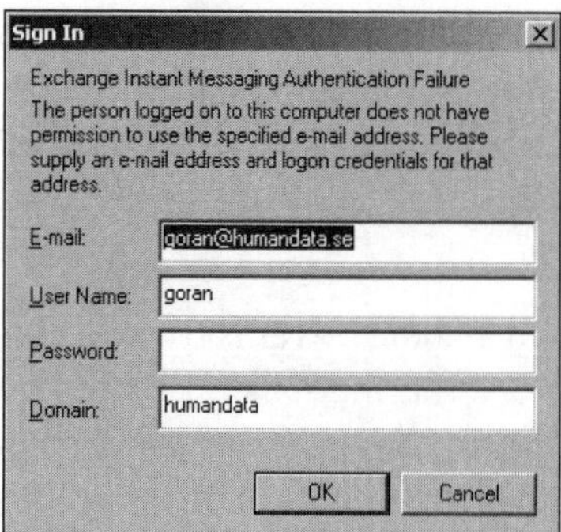

Figure 17.4
The logon dialog box for IM clients.

4. On the SRV page (see Figure 17.4), make sure the domain is correct (if not, cancel and select the right domain); then set the following values:
   - In the Service field, manually enter the text **_rvp**.
   - In the Priority field, enter **0**.
   - In the Weight field, enter **0**.
   - In the Port Number field, enter **80**.
   - In the Host Offering This Service field, type the FQDN name for the IM server.

   Click *OK* when ready.
5. Check in the TCP folder; you will find the new _rvp record there.

The challenge we face is that there are two domain names now: one for the email, and one for the IM; the user's email address follows the name standard **<user>@<DNS-domain>**, whereas the IM domain address follows the name standard **<user>@<IM Domain>**. We all know what an email address looks like, but how does it differ from an IM domain? This is where the _rvp SRV record comes in; if you *don't* configure this resource record in Step 3, then the IM domain will look like this: **<user>@<server>.<domain>**—for example, **goran@oden.humandata.se**. But if we *do* create the _rvp SRV record, we can allow our users to have IM domain names that are identical to their email names—for example, **goran@humandata.se**.

Let's look at how the connection process works in more detail, including how the _rvp SRV resource record will be used:

1. When the user starts the IM client, he or she must log on to the IM domain; see Figure 17.4. The E-mail field is what confuses the user; they think it's the SMTP email address, while in fact it's the IM address.

2. Next, the IM client looks at the domain part of the entered "E-mail" address; for example, if the user entered **goran@humandata.se**, the IM client assumes the IM domain to be **humandata.se**.
3. Next, the IM client contacts the DNS and queries about the _rvp SRV record for the domain **humandata.se**.
4. If the DNS server finds this _rvp SRV, it will reply with the name of the IM server and the port number (usually TCP port 80).
5. The IM client will then contact the given IM server over this port, using HTTP to send a subscribe request. The client also sends the IP address and TCP port number that it wants the server to use for sending messages back.
6. The IIS service on the server will call its InstMsg ISAPI application and query the AD account for this particular user's IM account. Then an authentication process takes place. The user first tries to authenticate using NTLM; if this doesn't work, it will try Digest authentication.
7. If the authentication was successful, the IM server will now query the AD to find out the home server for this IM user; if you only have one single IM server in your system, then this connection process is finished now.
8. However, if this IM server is a routing server, there will be an extra step: The routing server will pass the URL to the user's home server back to the client; in the future, the client will use this server instead.
9. The IM client issues a Proppatch request to inform the server that this client is now online.

Using Multiple IM Domains Connected to the Same Home Server

A special case regarding DNS configuration is when one IM home server will be used for multiple IM domains. For example, assume that you have two companies sharing the same computer environment: **humandata.se** and **taurnet.com**; then your DNS server will have two zones. To set up the DNS and IM domain environment, you would follow these steps:

1. Set up one IM home server that both companies will use.
2. Set up one IM router server, and add one A record to the DNS to this server; use a name such as **im.humandata.se** (this doesn't matter for the taurnet.com users; they don't normally see this).
3. Create two _rvp SRV records in the DNS: one for **humandata.se** and one for taurnet.com; both of these records point to the same IM router server.
4. Enable IM for each Windows 2000 user account, pointing to the same virtual IM server.

When a user from either of these two companies starts their IM client, they can log on using their own IM domain name, for example **james@taurnet.com**. The IM client will query the DNS zone taurnet.com for an _rvp SRV; the DNS server will return the hostname **im.humandata.se** and the port number 80. The IM client will then connect to this IM routing server, which will refer the client to the user's real IM home server.

Installing the IM Server

Installing the IM server is easy; it only takes about five minutes and the system requirements are very low. The installation procedure of an IM system in an existing Exchange 2000 organization usually involves these steps:

1. Configure the DNS. This was described in the previous section.
2. Install the IM servers (both the home servers and IM routing servers).
3. Enable IM for the users.

Before we start the actual installation of the IM servers, we must look at the hardware and software requirements.

Hardware and Software Requirements for the IM Server

The hardware necessary to install an IM server in a production environment is very minimal. The actual disk space used by the IM server programs is about 1MB in size; the size of the node database will be small, usually less than 1GB even for a large number of users, since it contains presence status and subscriptions, but no messages. The node database is protected by its own transaction log files, along with two reserved log files each 5MB in size, and a checkpoint file. For highest resilience, you should place the transaction log files on a disk other than the node database. There is really no special requirement regarding memory size, unless you have a very large number of IM users. In other words, an IM server that supports up to 500 IM users doesn't have any extra requirements at all; if you can run Exchange 2000 on this computer, you will also be able to run IM.

Hardware Requirements for the IM Server

The hardware required for installing an IM server is listed below. As usual regarding such values, this is not the recommended hardware configuration for a production environment:

- Pentium 200MHz or greater CPU
- 64MB of memory
- 2GB of disk space; preferably using the NTFS file system for better security
- CD-ROM drive, network card, mouse, keyboard, and a VGA monitor

For large IM installations, you may need to configure one or more dedicated IM servers. When Microsoft tested the IM server for internal use, they found that two IM servers configured with the following hardware could handle up to 15,000 IM users without any problem:

- Four 500MHz Pentium III processors in each server
- 512MB of memory
- 32GB of disk space distributed on one mirrored disk for transaction log files, and one RAID5 disk system

Software Requirements for the IM Server

The software requirements for an IM server are also modest; the IM server must be installed on an Exchange 2000 server running Windows 2000 and IIS 5. There is no difference in how we install a home server and routing server; they only differ in how they are configured. The following software components must exist before an IM server can be installed:

- MS Internet Information Server 5
- The NNTP stack
- The SMTP stack
- A Dynamic DNS server
- Exchange 2000 Server (any version)
- Exchange Messaging and Collaboration
- Exchange System Manager

Permissions Needed to Install the IM Server

To install an IM server, you will need to be an Exchange administrator with administrative permissions in this Administrative Group, as well as a member of the Domain Administrator group. You may also need to configure any firewall or proxy servers to make the IM system work with external clients.

The Installation Procedure

As mentioned before, this is a quick procedure that will take about five minutes to complete. Two components must be installed and configured:

- The IM server software
- The Virtual IM Server object

Installing the IM Server Software

We start by installing the IM server software:

1. Mount the Exchange 2000 Server CD (Enterprise or Standard edition).
2. Start the installation program for Exchange 2000; on the Welcome page, click *Next* to continue.

3. On the Component Selection page, set the Action to Change for the Microsoft Exchange 2000; then change Action to Install for the Microsoft Exchange Instant Messaging Service.

   Select where to install the system files; default is \Program Files\Exchsrvr. Note that you need at least 1MB of free disk space on this disk. Click *Next* to continue.

4. On the Administrative Group page (visible only when you have more than one AG), select the Administrative Group that this IM server will belong to. Click *Next* to continue.

5. On the Licensing Agreement page, select I Agree That... (if you do!); then click *Next* to continue.

6. On the Component Summary page, check that the selected options are correct; if so, click *Next* to start installing files; if not, click Back to correct the error.

7. The Component Progress page will now be displayed; you can follow the installation and see the current status. On the next page, click Finish to complete this IM server installation.

This concludes the software installation; the next step is to configure the virtual IM server.

Creating a Virtual IM Server

Before we can start using the IM server, we must also create a virtual IM server. Note that this server will run as an ISAPI application under the IIS 5; there will not be any separate service for the IM server. Each virtual IM server that is created must be hosted by its own virtual Web server.

Follow these steps to create the virtual IM server object:

1. Start the ESM tool; navigate to the Protocols folder under the server on which you installed the IM software. You will find a new protocol called Instant Messaging (RVP).

2. Right-click the RVP protocol, then select New|Instant Messaging Virtual Server; this will start the IM Virtual Server Wizard.

3. On the Welcome page, click *Next* to continue.

4. On the Enter Display Name page, enter a name for this virtual IM server. This name will later be used when enabling IM clients. Click *Next* to continue.

5. On the Choose IIS Web Site page, select the IIS that will host this IM server; unless you have more than one IIS server, it will be the Default Web Site. Click *Next* to continue.

6. On the Domain Name page, enter the fully qualified domain name for this IM server—for example, im.taurnet.com (assuming you have created such an A record in the DNS for this host). You cannot change the port number; it will be 80. Click *Next* to continue.

7. The Instant Messaging Home Server page is used to define if this will be an IM home server or an IM routing server. If you set the Allow This Server To Host Users Accounts checkbox, it will be a home server. Click *Next* to continue.
8. On the final page, click *Finish* to complete the creation of this virtual IM server.

At this stage, we have installed the IM software and we have configured one virtual IM server; small- and medium-sized organizations will probably install only one IM home server. Those organizations that are satisfied with one such IM home server are now ready to install IM clients and enable users for Instant Messaging. However, if your organization needs more than one IM server, you must repeat the steps above for each server.

Creating and Managing the IM Server

After installing the IM server and creating the virtual IM server, several new objects are created in the Exchange 2000 object tree. This section describes each and every one of them, and how to configure them. The new objects are:

- *Instant Messaging Settings*—Under the Global Settings folder.
- *Instant Messaging (RVP)*—Under the Protocols folder for the server.
- *The new Virtual IM Server object*—Under the RVP folder.

Configuring the Instant Messaging Settings

The Instant Messaging Settings object can be found under Global Settings in the Exchange object tree. It is used for configuring the firewall topology used in the Instant Messaging environment. Follow these steps to configure this object:

1. Start the ESM tool and expand the Global Settings folder.
2. Right-click Instant Messaging Settings and select Properties.
3. The General page has no settings you need to change.
4. On the Firewall Topology page (see Figure 17.5), define what IP address range is on the inside of your firewall; for example, setting the address range192.168.15.0 to 192.168.15.255 will define a complete IP class C net. This configuration is often used when an IM router server is placed on the Demilitarized Zone (DMZ) segment (see Figure 17.6).

   When an IM router server receives a message from a client on the local network, it refers the message to the destination. However, if the message is received from a client outside the local network, then the router server acts as a proxy for this external client. The result is that internal IM home servers are hidden from external clients. The IP address range defined on this page will help the Firewall Topology Module in the routing server differentiate between local and external addresses.

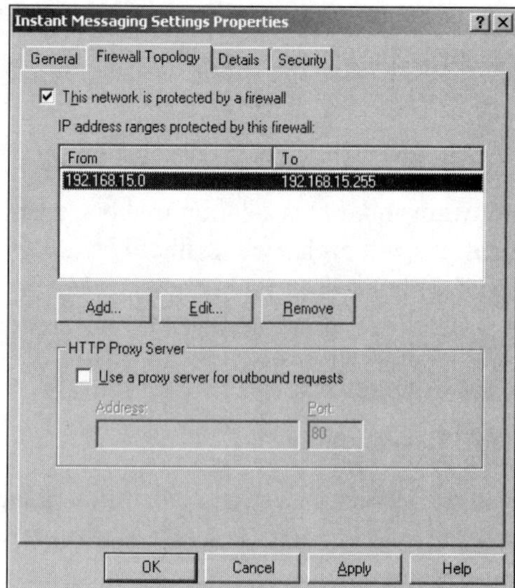

Figure 17.5
The Firewall Topology page for Instant Messaging.

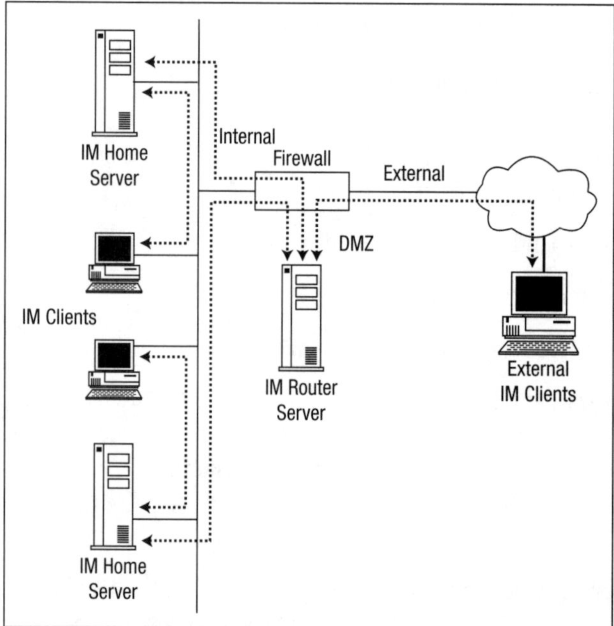

Figure 17.6
Example of an IM network using a DMZ segment with an IM routing server.

By default, all outgoing IM requests go directly to the destination computer. If these requests must pass an HTTP proxy server, you must set the Use A Proxy Server For Outbound Requests checkbox; then enter the IP address to this proxy server and select which port to use (usually port 80).

5. On the Details page, you will find the creation date and the last modification date. You can also add your own administrative notes for this object.
6. On the Security page, you can control which users will have administrative access to this object. By default, the Exchange administrator who has been granted access to the Exchange organization object will have full access by inheritance.

Configuring the RVP Object

This object is used primarily for configuring where to store the node database and its transaction log files for the IM home server; follow these steps to configure this object:

1. Start the ESM tool and expand the Protocols folder for the server hosting IM.
2. Right-click RVP and select Properties.
3. On the General page, use the Browse buttons to modify the directory for the node database, and the transaction log files, respectively. Note: This can't be done from a workstation running ESM; this must be performed directly on the IM server.
4. On the Details page, you will find the creation date and the last modification date. You can also add your own administrative notes for this object.
5. On the Security page, you can control which users have administrative access to this object. By default, the Exchange administrator who has been granted access to the Exchange organization object will have full access.

Configuring Virtual IM Servers

Every IM home server or IM routing server is really a virtual IM server. You can only have one such virtual IM server per virtual Web server, such as the Default Web Server. If you need to configure more than one virtual IM server on a single computer, you must create new virtual Web servers.

The properties for an IM routing server are identical to the IM home server; you cannot really change any of these settings, except the name of the virtual server. There are three property pages for these virtual servers: General, Details, and Security. The last two are identical to the RVP object regarding its content and purpose. The only interesting information is on the General page:

- The DNS name of the physical IM server this virtual server is connected to.
- The name of the virtual Web server hosting this virtual IM server.
- The type of IM server—a home server or a routing server.

If you need to modify these settings, you must actually delete the faulty object and create a new virtual IM server. Note that any IM client that was configured to use this particular virtual server will have to be reconfigured using the AD Users and Computers tool.

IM Logging

When troubleshooting or checking performance of Instant Messaging, protocol logging can provide you with valuable information. Since IM is a Web application, it will be controlled at the Web site level, and Web logging is enabled by default. However, some extended properties that are interesting for IM aren't selected by default; you should open the logging settings for the Web server and make sure these extended properties are selected (the names within parentheses are the names for this attribute in the log file):

- *User name (cs-username)*—The name of the user that accessed the server.
- *Service name (s-sitename)*—The Internet service that was running on the client.
- *Server name (s-computername)*—The name of the server on which the log entry was generated.
- *Method (cs-method)*—The action or IM command the client was trying to perform, such as SUBSCRIBE or PROPFIND.
- *URI Query (cs-uri-query)*—The query the client was trying to perform—for example, the search strings for which the client was seeking a match. If there was no query, this line will be empty.

As always, when the IIS generates log files the time given for every event in this log file will be based on Greenwich Mean Time (GMT), even if you have configured the Exchange server to use a local time zone. This depends on the HTTP logging feature in the IIS server that always uses GMT; since IM is an ISAPI application under the IIS, it will also use this time base.

Configuring IM Logging

To configure logging for the IM and the Web server, follow these steps:

1. Open the Internet Information Services Manager (ISM) tool.
2. Open the properties for the Default Web Site (the site hosting the IM service).
3. Switch to the Web Site page. In the bottom pane, you will see the logging settings. Make sure that logging is enabled and that the active log format is W3C Extended Log File Format; then click the Properties button.
4. On the General Properties page, note where the log files will be stored. Default is *%WindDir*\System32\LogFiles\W3SVC1\exyymmdd.log, where *%WinDir* is the root directory for the Windows 2000 system files (usually the directory WinNT); note that one log file, such as ex010612.log, will be generated every day.
5. Switch to the Extended Properties tab; make sure the properties mentioned above are selected. Be careful not to change any other settings, because this could affect other applications that are dependent on this Web logging. When ready, click *OK* to close this Extended Properties dialog box.
6. Click *OK* to close the properties for this Web site.

Importing the Log File into MS Excel

This log file is best viewed in MS Excel (or any similar spreadsheet application). When you open this log file, Excel will activate its Import Wizard, which will guide you through the import and conversion of this text file; follow these steps to import the log file:

1. Open MS Excel.
2. Select the File|Open menu, and open the log file; this will start the Import Wizard.
3. At step one of the Import Wizard, make the following changes, then click *Next* to continue:
   - Set the Original data type = Delimited
   - Start import at row = 4
4. In the Delimiters pane, set Space and remove all other delimiters; then click Finish to import the file.
5. We must do a few more things: right-click on cell A1 (#Fields), and select Delete. On the next dialog box, select Shift Cells Left, and click *OK*. This will make the header columns and the data columns match.
6. Optional: Every time the World Wide Web Publishing Service is restarted, the four headlines you skipped in Step 3 above will be written again; you should remove them to make this log file easier to read.

Creating and Managing IM Users

All Windows 2000 security principal users can be enabled for Instant Messaging; they don't even have to have an email account. However, contacts can't use IM since they cannot log on to this Windows 2000 domain. Activating IM for a user is easy; just enable the IM feature and configure which virtual IM server they will use.

Enabling IM for Users

You can IM-enable a single user or a large group of users simultaneously. Using the AD Users and Computers tool, use the standard Windows selection commands with the Shift and Ctrl keys to select the group of users. If by mistake you happen to select any Contacts or other objects that can't be IM-enabled with this group of users, they will simply ignore this enabling operation; all users will still be enabled as normal.

Follow these steps to enable Instant Messaging for a selected user:

1. Start the Active Directory Users and Computers tool.
2. Right-click the user and select Exchange Tasks; this will start the Exchange Task Wizard.
3. On the Available Tasks page, select Enable Instant Messaging and click *Next*.

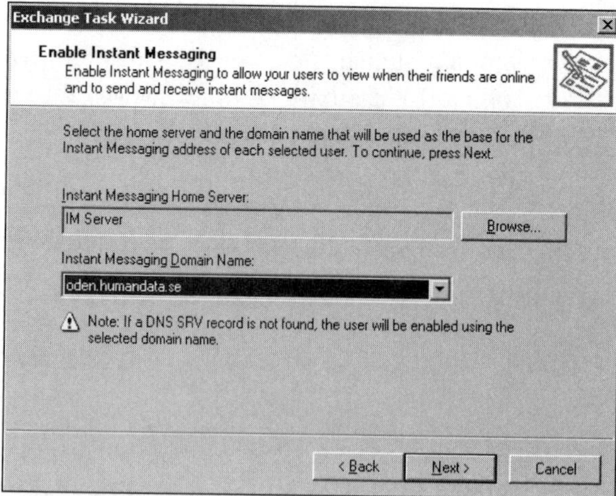

Figure 17.7
The Enable Instant Messaging page.

4. On the Enable Instant Messaging page (see Figure 17.7), click the Browse button and select the virtual IM home server for this client. You must also select which IM domain name this server belongs to; select the domain from the pull-down menu. This IM domain name was defined when you created the virtual IM server in the ESM tool earlier; open the properties for that virtual server and look in the DNS Name field. Click *Next* to continue.

5. The Task In Progress window will quickly pass, and next is the completion page; click Finish to finish enabling IM for this user.

Universal Resource Locators Used by the IM Client

In Step 4 above, you specified the IM home server and the IM domain name; this will create two HTTP Universal Resource Locators (URLs) for each user in their AD properties:

- A URL to the IM home server
- A URL to the IM domain

These URLs will be used internally by the client to find the home server and the routing server (if you only have one single IM home server and no routing server, both of these URLs will point to this server). The reason why the IM client uses URLs is that the RVP protocol is an extension of the HTTP1.1 and Web-DAV protocol, so the system will use standard HTTP URLs to find Instant Messaging resources. Also, individual IM users are identified by URLs internally; for example, my URL looks like this: **http://im.humandata.se/instmsg/aliases/goran**. However, the users will never have to see any of these URLs; all of this is hidden behind the user's IM address, which will be identical to the SMTP address if the system is correctly configured regarding DNS and _rvp SRV resource records, as described earlier in this chapter.

Managing IM Users

There is not really much to manage regarding IM settings for a user; the only thing the administrator will do with an existing IM user is to modify their IM settings or disable their IM feature.

Let's start with disabling an IM feature for an active IM user. This is done by using the AD Users and Computers tool; you actually have two ways of disabling this feature:

- Open the user's properties; on the Exchange Features tab, click Disable.
- Right-click the user; select Exchange Tasks, then select Disable Instant Messaging.

If you need to change the home server for an IM client, here's what to do: Right-click the user (or group of users), select Exchange Tasks, then select Change Instant Messaging Home Server. Another way of doing the same thing would be to first disable the IM feature and then enable it again, this time entering a new home server.

Configuring Privacy for an IM User

Some IM users, such as the CEO and upper management, sometimes want to restrict which users can see their presence status and send IM messages to them. This privacy setting can be centrally managed by the Exchange administrator by following these steps:

1. Start the AD Users and Computers tool.
2. Right-click this IM user and select Properties.
3. Switch to the Privacy tab (see Figure 17.8). The default setting is to allow everyone access to this IM user. Select the option Allow Access Only From These Servers And Users, and select the users and/or IM servers who should be given access.
4. Click *OK* to close this dialog box, and *OK* again to close the properties for this user.

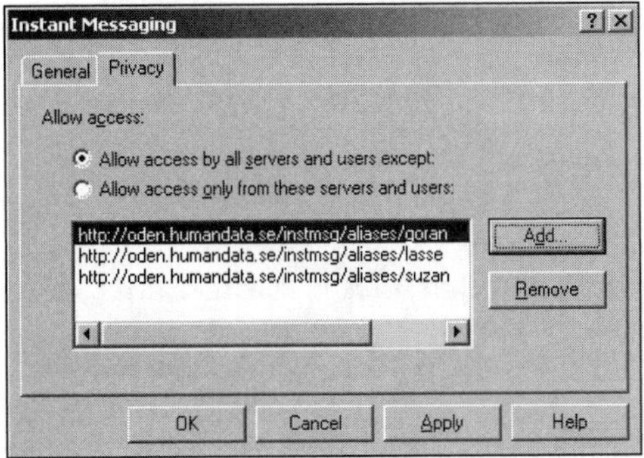

Figure 17.8
Configuring privacy for an IM user.

Installing and Managing the IM Client

In order to use Instant Messaging, the user must install an IM client. Since Microsoft has two IM systems that work completely differently from one another (i.e., one in Exchange 2000 and another in MSN), they also have two different IM clients. However, a new client works with both types of IM systems—the MSM Messenger Service. Described here are all three IM clients that Microsoft offers today:

- *MSN IM Client*—This version can communicate only with the MSN IM system. You can download it from the MSM Web site: **messenger.msn.com**.
- *MS Exchange IM Client*—This client can communicate only with the Exchange 2000 IM system. Version 2.2 of this client is included on the Exchange 2000 CD-ROM in the directory INSTMSG\I386\CLIENT\<*language*>. There are 26 different language versions of this client.
- *MSN Messenger Service*—This client can communicate both with the Exchange 2000 IM system and with the MSN IM system. Version 3.5 of this client can be downloaded from the following Web site: **www.microsoft.com/exchange/downloads/2000/IMclient.asp**. This is the recommended IM client of these three because it has the most features.

Note: *All of these three IM client versions have the same file name: mmsetup.exe; make sure you install the right version!*

Installation Requirements for the IM Client

This is a thin client that doesn't require any particular resources, since it's not storing any information besides the free disk space of about 2.5MB required for the IM program itself. You can install the MSN IM client on any of these operating systems:

- *Windows 95*—Requires that Windows Socket version 2 is installed
- *Windows 98*—All versions
- *Windows NT*—All versions
- *Windows 2000*—All versions
- *Windows XP*—All versions

The client will by default be installed in the \Program Files\Messenger directory on the local hard disk.

Windows XP and Instant Messaging

Windows XP includes the MSN version of the IM client; however, it may not be able to work. The simplest way of fixing this is to install an older IM client, such as MSM Messenger Server IM client or the MS Exchange IM client. But then you may encounter a new problem: you can't install the Exchange IM client since its files are older than the IM files in XP! The only way to solve this is to delete the original MSN IM client in XP before installing the Exchange IM client, by following these steps:

1. Make sure the MSN IM client is not running (it should not even appear in the system tray). Start the file explorer.
2. Go to the directory \Program Files\Messenger.
3. Right-click this folder and select Rename; enter the new name, **MSN-Old**.
4. Run the Exchange 2000 IM client setup.exe program.
5. When the installation of the IM client is finished, and you have tested it to make sure it works properly, you can delete the MSN-Old directory since you no longer need it.

A bonus effect is that this Exchange IM client can also be used for communicating with MSN IM systems. If you are using both types of IM systems, you may want to log on to the Exchange IM system first; do so by starting the new MSN Messenger client, selecting the Tools|Options menu, and switching to the Accounts tab. In the Sign In With This Account First pane, select Exchange Account. Then click *OK* to save and close this object.

Local Registry Settings for the IM Client

All personal settings for the IM client will be stored in the Registry database. For example, when a user adds a contact to be monitored regarding presence status, these contacts are stored in the following location in the Registry:

```
HKEY_CURRENT_USER\Software\Microsoft\Exchange\Messenger\Profiles\
  <URL_to_User>\Contacts
```

If this network client is configured for roaming profiles, then the user's personal registry settings will be copied to the Windows 2000 server every time the user logs out from the network. Next time they log on, even on another computer, their personal registry settings will be downloaded. The consequence of this is that roaming profiles will make these IM contacts follow the user, even if they log on from another computer.

Registry Settings for Policies

The IM client can be configured to follow a particular policy, such as "only log on to Exchange IM," or "remove the commercial banners." This is done by modifying the Registry database, as described in Table 17.1.

Warning! *Be very careful when changing values in the Registry database unless you know exactly what you are doing. Changing the wrong value could make parts or the whole computer unusable! Change these settings at your own risk.*

Table 17.1 Setting policies for the IM client.

Value Name	Data Type	Value	Description
DisableCrossPromo	Binary	0=No (default); 1=Yes	Set this value to prohibit the commercial banner ads that appear in the lower part of the IM client. If this value is set to 1, only the MSN logo will appear. Note: This setting will work only if the ExchangeConn value below is set to 2!
DisableUpdates	Binary	0=No (default); 1=Yes	Set this value to control whether the automatic update notice send by the MSN Messenger Service should be disabled or not. The administrator may not want the users to upgrade every time a new version becomes available.
ExchangeConn	Binary	0=Normal (default), 1=Exchange is primary, 2=Exchange only	This will control what IM service the client will be able to contact. *Normal* means that both MSN and Exchange can be contacted.
IMWarning	String	Text	Use this value to enter a warning message that the user will see when starting up the client. The default message is to warn the user not to give out credit card numbers or passwords over IM sessions. If this string is a single space character, there will be no messages.
DefaultNTLMDomain	String	Text	Use this setting to define the default domain when the user logs on with NTLM authentication.

To set any of the values described in Table 17.1 use Regedit.exe, and navigate to the following Registry key:

```
HKEY_CURRENT_USER\Software\Microsoft\MessengerService\Policies
```

Note that the Policies key must be created manually, and none of the values in Table 17.1 exists from the beginning; you must also create them manually. After changing these settings, the IM client must be restarted.

Configuring the MSN Messaging Service Client

This client is the one that can be used for both Exchange 2000 IM and MSN IM; it has a number of configurations, besides the Registry settings described in the previous section. All these settings must be conducted directly on the IM client; you cannot change any of these values from the server or any other central point.

Features of the MSN Messaging Service Client

Following is a short description of all menus and features available for the MSN Messaging Service client:

- The File menu has the following features:
  - *Sign in/Sign Out*—From the IM home server.
  - *My Status*—Is used to set the user's presence status; select between Online, Busy, Be Right Back, Away, On The Phone, Out To Lunch, and Appear Offline.
  - *Add Contact*—Is used to subscribe to another IM user's presence status.
  - *Delete Contact*—Is used to remove any subscriptions.
  - *View Profile*—Is not used for Exchange IM.
  - *Properties*—Will display the user's IM address and current status.
  - *Send A File*—Allows you to send a file to any online IM user.
  - *Open Received Files*—Will open a window with all previously received files; they will by default be stored under the user's profile in a directory named Messenger Service Received Files.
  - *Close*—Is used to close, but not exit, the IM client; the user will still be logged on.

Note: *Instead of manually entering the IM address for the contact you want to add, you can use the IM Superman utility and select names from the global address list. This tool can be found on the Exchange 2000 Resource Kit, along with information on how to use it.*

- The View menu allows you to hide or display different parts of the client and has the following components:
  - *Toolbar*—The quick buttons for Add, Send, Call, or Page another user.
  - *Search bar*—This displays the general Web search feature on MSN.
  - *Status bar*—Displays your current presence status.
- Use the Tools menu to send messages, initiate voice calls, send mail, etc. Here are the options:
  - *Send an Instant Message*—You can send an IM to other online users.
  - *Send a Message to a Mobile Device*—Requires that mobile communication is set up for this client.
  - *Call*—Initiate a voice call over the network to another user; requires that both parties have a multimedia computer.
  - *Send an Invitation*—To start a Netmeeting session with another user.
  - *Send Mail*—Will start up MS Outlook and prepare for sending an email.
  - *MSN Home*—Will start a browser and connect to the MSN Web site.

- *My E-mail Inbox*—Will activate MS Outlook and display the Inbox folder.
- *My Alerts*—Display recently received alerts, such as logon alerts and new messages.
- *Audio Tuning Wizard*—Will adjust the volume for your speaker and microphone.
- *Options*—Configure a number of options; see the upcoming section, "Configuring Options for the IM Client."

- From the Help menu, use Help Topics to display and search for help about this client and all its features. Select About MSN Messenger Service to see the version number of this client, and copyright notes.

Configuring Options for the IM Client

A surprisingly large number of options exist for this thin client; however, many of them aren't active when using this client with Exchange 2000 IM. Follow these steps to configure all options available for this IM client in the Exchange environment:

1. Open the client, and select the Tools|Options menu.
2. Most of these settings on the Personal page are not used in an Exchange environment, except the options in the My Message Text pane, which you should set as follows:
   - Click the Edit Font option to define the font, size, and style for this user. The recipient of messages from this user will see exactly the same font as the sender.
   - Set the Show Graphics (Emoticons) In Instant Messages option to replace "smileys," such as :-), with ☺.
3. None of the settings on the Phone page can be activated when using the Exchange 2000 IM server.
4. The options on the Preference page (see Figure 17.9) are all active when using the Exchange IM. Set the options as follows:

   On the General pane:

   - *Run this program when Windows starts*—(Default: set); controls if IM will automatically start when you start this computer.
   - *Allow this program to run in the background*—(Default: set); controls if this IM client will continue to run even if another process, such as MS Word, becomes the foreground process.
   - *Show me as "Away" when I'm inactive for X minutes*—(Default: 5); use this setting to define how long the computer must be inactive (i.e., no mouse or keyboard activities) before the presence status changes to Away.

   On the Alerts pane:

   - *Display alerts near the taskbar when contacts come online*—(Default: set); controls if a small pop-up window will be displayed next to the taskbar above the IM icon every

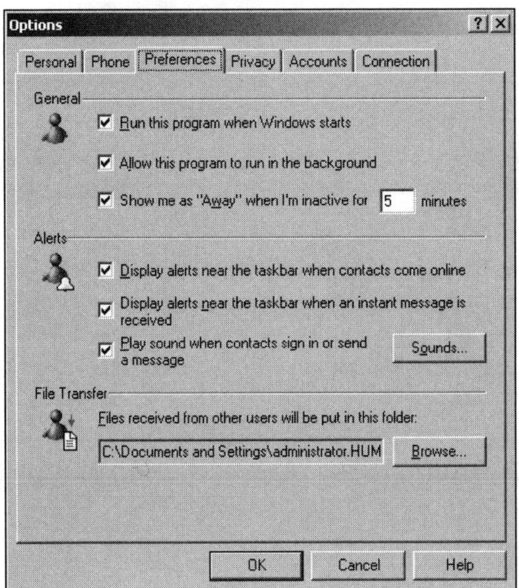

Figure 17.9
The Preference page in the Options dialog window.

time a contact gets online. If you subscribe on many contacts, this feature may be annoying, since you have the status in your IM client anyway.

- *Display alerts near the taskbar when an instant message is received*—(Default: set); this message is self-explanatory.
- *Play sound when contacts sign in or send a message*—(Default: set). Also self-explanatory; to change the sound, click the Sounds button, then scroll down the list of Sound Events for the headline MSN Messenger Service. You can select different sounds for different events, such as new messages or contacts online.

On the File Transfer pane, click the Browse button to select where incoming files will be stored. Default is the Messenger Service Received Files directory located under the user's profile settings—for example, C:\Documents and Settings\Goran\My Documents.

5. Use the Privacy page (see Figure 17.10) to determine what other users can see and do with your information:

   - *My Allow List*—These users can see your presence status and send you messages. Note that there's a group here called All Other Users; this means that all users are allowed. This list consists of the contacts that you added previously.
   - *My Block List*—These users cannot see your presence status or send you messages. You may remember the Privacy tab for the user object in AD Users and Computers; with these two lists, users can define the same thing locally: By blocking the group All Other Users, only the users on the My Allow List will be allowed to send messages and check your status.

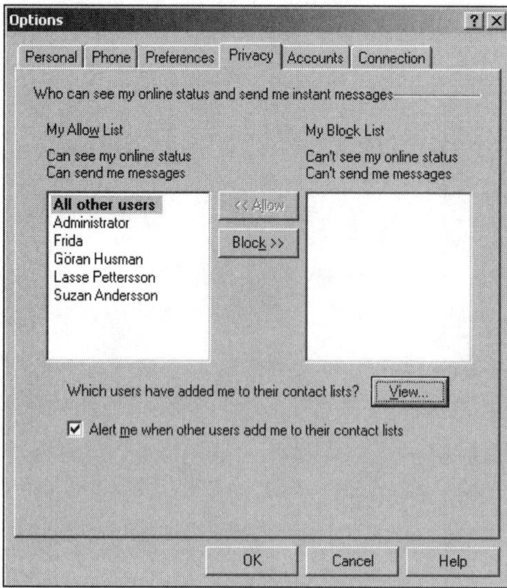

Figure 17.10
The Privacy page in the Options dialog window.

Click the View button to see which other users have added you to their contact list; this information is stored in the IM home server.

Set the checkbox if you want to be alerted whenever someone adds you to their contact list (default set).

6. The Accounts page is used to control access to the Exchange IM account:
   - *Sign in with this account first*—Lets you control what IM service you want to log on to first, Exchange IM or MNS IM. Default is the Exchange IM account.
   - *Exchange Account pane*—Lets you set the sign-in name; click the Advanced button to define how to contact Exchange IM servers outside your organization; see the upcoming section, "Connecting External IM Clients," for more information.
   - *Passport Account*—Used when this IM client also connects to the MSN IM system; if this is the case, you enter your Passport sign-in name and password here.
7. The Connection Preference page lets you define any proxy server settings; if this IM client is connecting to an internal Exchange IM server, you will probably not use these settings. However, if you connect to an Exchange IM server externally, you may pass a proxy server; if so, set the I Use A Proxy Server checkbox and enter the values needed to pass this proxy. These values will be given to you by the administrator for the proxy server.
8. When ready, click *OK* to close this Options dialog box.

Connecting External IM Clients

Connection problems seldom occur when accessing Exchange 2000 IM servers from clients located on the internal network. However, when allowing clients from outside the network firewall, you might need to configure some more settings. To understand what is needed, we must first repeat how the connection works between the client and the IM server; see Figure 17.11.

As you can see from Figure 17.11, the client will always send on TCP port 80, but the server will send its information to the client over a randomly selected TCP port greater than 1023. This works nicely in these two scenarios:

- When the IM client and IM server are on the internal network, such as IM client 1 in Figure 17.11.
- When an external IM client connects to the IM server through the local firewall, such as IM client 2 in Figure 17.11.

The reason it works without any problem with external IM clients is that the firewall labeled FW-1 accepts incoming traffic on port 80, the standard HTTP port. When the server sends information, it will be on a port over 1023; usually firewalls are configured to accept outgoing communications on any port, including those over 1023.

But how about IM client 3 in Figure 17.11? It will most probably fail because this client is protected by its own firewall (FW-2) that will most likely not accept incoming traffic on any port over 1023. The result will be that this client can log on, send messages to other IM users, and display its presence status, but it will not be able to receive any mes-sages or status information, since its own firewall doesn't accept traffic on this port.

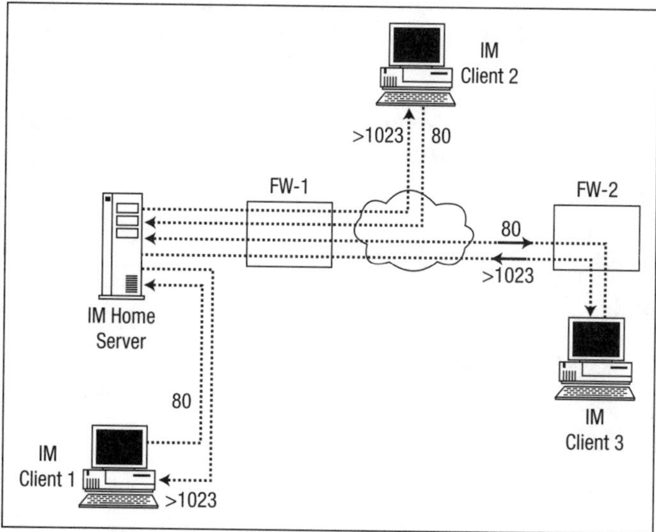

Figure 17.11
Communication between the IM client and IM server.

So how can you solve this? You can do it two ways:

- *Virtual Private Network*—Set up a VPN connection between IM client 3 and your internal network; this will allow any ports to be used, not only for the IM client but for all types of connections, such as Outlook over RCP/MAPI. The drawback is that we must configure a server in our local network to accept VPN connections (using the Windows 2000 RRAS service), and to configure the client to use VPN. It will also result in a slight decrease in performance.
- *Use a particular TCP port*—If you know what TCP port the server will use, you could configure FW-2 to accept incoming traffic on this port. To make it safer, you could configure the firewall to accept incoming traffic on this port, but only from the IP number of the sending IM server.

The question is how to make the server use a particular TCP port. The client randomly chooses this port during the logon procedure. By default the client will select any available port over 1023; however, you can configure the client to select a port within an interval. Select Tools|Options, switch to the Accounts tab, and click the Advanced button (see Figure 17.12).

In Figure 17.12, you can see that I have configured this IM client to use TCP port 1155. Now we need to configure the firewall to accept incoming traffic on this port too. But it's not always this easy; the challenge is that we must configure our IM client to use a TCP port that we *know* is available. If by mistake we select a port that is already in use by another program on this client, then our IM client still can't receive any messages. That is why you can set up a port interval instead of a single port. For example, if you set a port interval between 1150 and 1159, you will have a much greater chance that one of these ports will be free for use. But then we also must configure our firewall to accept incoming traffic on all ports between 1150 and 1159, which can be hard to convince a firewall administrator to accept.

***Note:** This advanced port configuration will only work with Exchange 2000 Service Pack 1 and the Exchange 2000-aware IM client MSN Messenger Service 3.5 or later; see more information in the README.TXT file for SP1.*

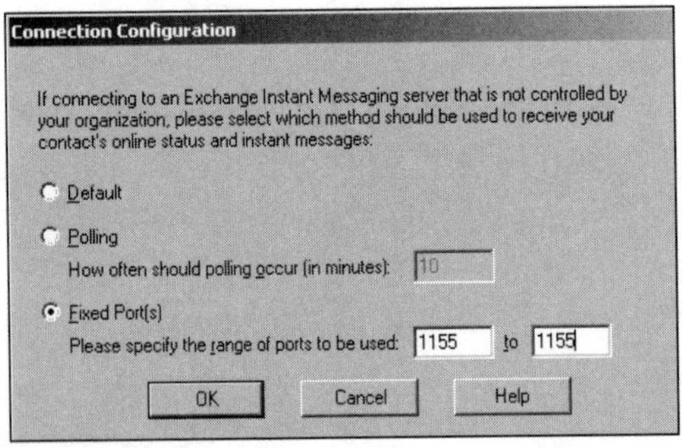

Figure 17.12
The Advanced settings for Exchange accounts.

Troubleshooting Instant Messaging

In this final section, we will discuss how to troubleshoot Instant Messaging. There are some things we must remember when analyzing IM problems; this is an Exchange 2000 add-on that needs access to the Active Directory and DNS server to work. It's also important to remember that the IM system runs as virtual servers within the Internet Information Server (IIS) as an ISAPI application package named InstMsg; if the World Wide Web service stops, the virtual IM server will also stop.

Using NSLookup

You can use NSLookup to check the settings of the RVP resource record; remember, if this _rvp SRV doesn't exist, all IM users will have to use an IM address of the type **user@im.domain.tld**, instead of **user@domain.tld**, which many users will be confused by, since they don't distinguish between the SMTP address or the IM address. Follow these steps to use NSLookup for checking the _rvp SRV record:

1. Open a Command prompt; type **NSLookup**.
2. Make sure this NSLookup is looking in the right DNS server (by default the DNS configured for this client will be used); otherwise, use the Server *<dns_server>* command.
3. Set the query type to Any by this command: **set q=any** and press Enter.
4. Type **_rvp._tcp.<domain_name>** and press Enter.
5. This will give you all the information about the _rvp resource record for the given domain.

For example, to find the _rvp information for the **humandata.se** domain in the Dynamic DNS server **oden.humandata.se**, this is what we would need to enter:

```
C:\>nslookup
Default Server:  oden.humandata.se
Address:  192.168.15.10

> set q=any
> _rvp._tcp.humandata.se
Server:  oden.humandata.se
Address:  192.168.15.10

_rvp._tcp.humandata.se  SRV service location:
          priority       = 0
          weight         = 0
          port           = 80
          svr hostname   = im.humandata.se
im.humandata.se        internet address = 192.168.15.10
>
```

From this listing, we can see that an _rvp record does indeed exist, and that it points to the IM server **im.humandata.se**; any communication to this IM server is supposed to use TCP port 80. Since we only have one IM server, we don't use the priority or weight values. If any of this information is incorrect, open the DNS management tool and correct this value. A common problem is that the svr hostname points to the wrong server. Note that this must be an IM server, a routing server (if such a server exists), or a home server (if there is only one single home server for this IM domain).

Common Errors in IM Installations

Here are some common errors regarding Instant Messaging, with suggestions on what to do and how to solve them:

No Contact between the Client and the Server

- Test to ping the IP address of the IM server (home server or routing server, depending on how your IM system is designed). If this works, try to ping the server again, this time with the FQDN name.
- Make sure the World Wide Web Publishing Service is started.
- It can also depend on a proxy setting in Internet Explorer. Open the Tools|Internet Options menu, switch to the Connections tab, click LAN Settings, and then click Advanced; add the FQDN name of the IM server to the Exceptions dialog box.

Can't Log On to the IM Server

- Check that the user is IM enabled.
- Make sure the user connects to the right IM server.
- Make sure the correct username, password, and/or IM address is given. Remember that without the_rvp resource record in the DNS, the user's IM addresses will be similar to **@im.domain.com**.
- Another reason may be that the user's IM address has more than 20 characters; the 20-character limit exists to make this IM server backward compatible with pre-Windows 2000 servers.

Must Log On with Full IM Domain Name

- If the user tries to log on using the address format **user@domain.tld**, but it doesn't work, make sure the _rvp resource record is correctly configured in the DNS.
- If it works for Windows 2000 clients, but not pre-Windows 2000 clients, such as Windows 9X and Windows NT, they must install the AD client add-on to their clients. You can find this add-on for NT 4 systems at **www.Microsoft.com/ntserver/nts/downloads/other/adsi25/x86.asp**; for Windows 95/98 clients, you will find it on the Windows 2000 CD-ROM in the \Clients\Win9x\Dsclient.exe file.

Clients Can Send but Not Receive Messages

- Check if a firewall is prohibiting inbound messages to the client; refer back to Figure 17.11. If this firewall doesn't allow incoming traffic on this TCP port, no messages will ever pass from the server to the client.
- This can also be the result of a proxy server between the clients and the server; this will also result in an error message written into the HTTP log file. Look for error code 500 in the sc-status field, together with cs-method Notify. If you find this line, you can see in the cs-uri-stem column which user had this problem. When using proxy servers between IM clients and servers, you must configure the RVP protocol to work with this proxy; see the Firewall Topology settings in the section "Configuring the Instant Messaging Settings" that appeared earlier in this chapter.
- If the client has been assigned a new dynamic IP address from its DHCP server without restarting the IM client, then the server will send all messages and notifications to the old IP address.

The Client Gets Disconnected When Changing Its Status

- This can happen if the number of IM client sessions is more than the server can handle; in this case, the server will drop those IM client sessions that it fails to update, instead of giving incorrect information to the client. This is by design.

A Disconnected User Will Still Appear to Be Online

- This will happen if an IM user becomes unexpectedly disconnected from the network, instead of logging out from the server. The IM home server expects the client to send a status notification continuously within a 20-minute interval; if this doesn't happen (as is the case if the user gets disconnected), the server will show the latest status for up to 20 minutes, then it will show this user as offline.

Besides these tips, make sure to check the Microsoft Knowledge Base for more troubleshooting tips regarding Instant Messaging; you will find the Knowledge Base at **search.support.Microsoft.com/kb**. A logical flowchart to help you troubleshoot the most common problems regarding IM appears in Decision Tree 17.1.

Disaster Recovery of a Home Server

If the IM server has crashed and you have lost all your data, you can perform a disaster recovery to restore this server by following these steps:

1. Use the ESM tool on another computer and delete the Virtual IM Server object from the crashed server; make sure to delete the right object if you have more than one virtual IM server!
2. Delete the user's reference to this crashed IM server. If you have another home server active, you can move the users to that server like this: When you delete this virtual

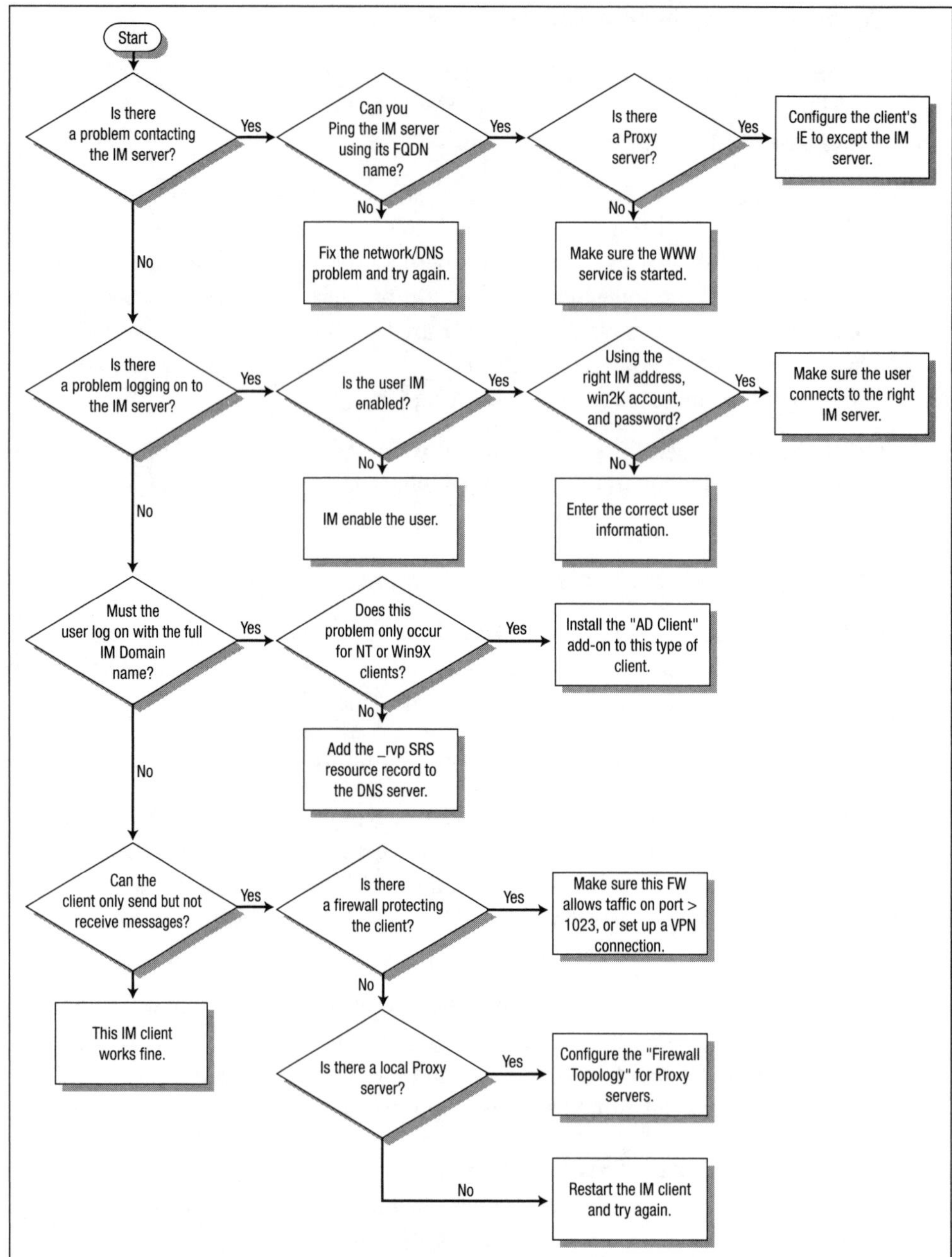

Decision Tree 17.1
Troubleshooting common IM problems.

IM server object, a dialog box displays, enabling you to move all IM users to another IM server. If you don't have an extra server, you must instead disable IM for all users; see Figure 17.13.

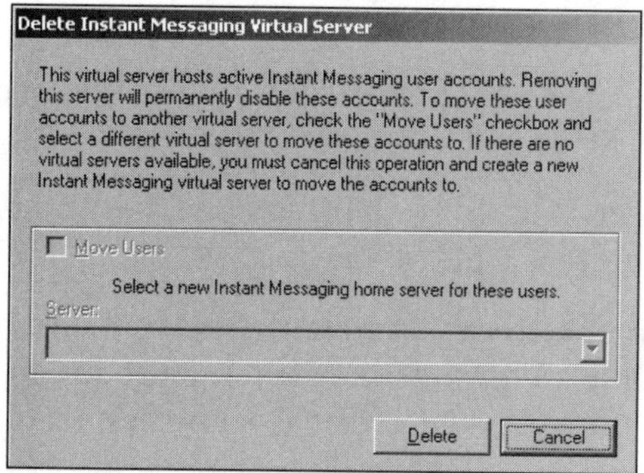

Figure 17.13
Move all users before deleting an IM server.

3. Rebuild the crashed server by installing Windows 2000 Server and adding the latest service pack; install Exchange 2000 using the /disasterrecovery switch and add the latest service pack. Restore the Exchange databases from a backup. Rebuild all Web sites previously located on this server.
4. Re-create the Instant Messaging server, including the virtual IM server object.
5. If the users in Step 2 were moved to another IM server, move them back to the reconstructed server again, using the same method. If they were IM disabled, then IM enable them again.

Summary

This is a list of the more important features and keywords mentioned in this chapter. Use it as a reminder and to make sure you have understood the most important things:

- Instant Messaging (IM) is a new method for realtime conversation between a small number of people, usually only two.
- IM's special feature is presence status: you can see if your contacts are online or not.
- IM allows you to send messages to your contacts; these messages are not stored.
- IM also allows you to send files between the contacts.
- Its greatest advantage compared to chat systems is presence monitoring; you don't have to connect to a chat room to see if a particular person is available or not.
- Whenever one of your contacts (a.k.a. buddies) changes his or her status, you are notified—for example, if they log on or go to lunch.
- The first really popular IM system was ICQ, developed by the Israeli company Mirablis in November 1996.
- Another even more popular IM system was introduced by America Online (AOL); also, Yahoo! has a very popular IM system.

- The transport protocol for all types of IM systems is TCP/IP.
- All IM systems so far have developed their own IM protocol; this protocol describes how to send commands such as Subscribe, Notify, and Message.
- Microsoft's IM protocol is named Rendezvous (RVP); this is based on the Web-DAV protocol, which in turn is an extension of the HTTP version 1.1 protocol.
- RFC 2889, released in February 2000, suggests an IM protocol standard called Instant Messaging and Presence Protocol (IMPP). A new Internet draft is under development that suggests extensions to this RFC; the expectation is that all IM systems will convert to this IM standard later.
- Standard presence settings are: Online, Appear Offline, Busy, Be Right Back, Away, On The Phone, and Out To Lunch. The user can select among any of these settings.
- The IM architecture is built on the following modules: the IM client, the IM home server, and the IM routing server; together they construct an IM domain.
- The IM client always connects to a particular IM home server; this server keeps track of the status for this client, and routes messages to other clients.
- The IM home server is responsible for hosting a number of IM users; one home server can host up to 15,000 users. The server receives and sends messages, notifications, and status between clients and to IM routing servers.
- The IM routing server does not host any users; its primary responsibility is to accept messages and notifications from clients and home servers, and pass them on to the destination home server. Up to 50,000 users can be handled by one routing server.
- Clients never send messages directly between themselves; messages are always sent over a home server.
- If you have two or more home servers, you should set up a routing server that will pass the information between these home servers; the routing server will also make it possible to have a common name space, such as **@im.humandata.se**, although there are several servers.
- The IM server consists of three modules: the Firewall Topology Module (FTM), the Locator Module, and the Server Application Layer. A home server also has a node database.
- The FTM keeps track of which clients and servers are on the internal network (in relation to the firewall). Messages from external networks are received by the routing server that will proxy the traffic between the external computer and the internal server.
- The node database is a JET engine ESE-database with transaction logs (using circular logging); these files are stored in \Exchsrvr\IMData.
- All IM server modules run as ISAPI Web applications under the control of IIS 5.

- Add an _rvp SRV resource record to the DNS server to make it possible for the users to have the same SMTP address as their IM address.
- Add an A record (or an Alias record) with the name IM for your IM server—for example, **im.humandata.se**.
- If you host multiple companies with different domain names on the same home server, you must create one _rvp SRV record for each of these domains.
- Installation is easy; it doesn't require any special hardware except disk space for the node database and a working Exchange 2000 server plus a Dynamic DNS.
- Installation is done in three steps: a) install the IM server software, b) create the Virtual IM Server object, and c) enable IM for the users.
- You can have only one Virtual IM Server per Web site; however, you can create multiple Web sites on the same physical server, each hosting its own virtual IM server.
- The ESM tool has a new object under the Global Settings folder called Instant Messaging Settings; use this to define the Firewall Topology.
- If you have a DMZ segmented firewall topology, you can install one IM routing server on this DMZ. This will simplify communication with external IM servers and clients.
- Logging of IM messages is achieved by the usual Web logging feature; however, you will need to add some extended properties for more IM information.
- Import the log files into MS Excel; it makes them easier to read and analyze.
- Enable IM for users with the AD Users and Computers tool; you can select a whole group or even an entire organizational unit (OU).
- Communication between clients and servers is based on HTTP; this is why the internal address format is HTTP Universal Resource Locators (URLs).
- Microsoft has three different IM clients; two of them can be used in an Exchange 2000 IM environment: the MS Exchange IM client and the MSM Messenger Services client.
- Use the MSM Messenger Services client; it allows communication with both Exchange IM and MSN IM.
- You can change Registry settings in the client to avoid commercial banners and other features.
- The MSM Messenger Services client has a lot of configuration settings and is rich in features; take some time to understand how it works.
- Use NSLookup to check the _rvp SRV record settings in the DNS.
- Use the troubleshooting tips provided in this chapter to help you solve common problems.
- If the IM server crashes, you must follow the disaster recovery procedure described in the troubleshooting section of this chapter.

Chapter 18

Exchange 2000 Conferencing Server

In Chapter 16, we saw how the MS Chat server features public or private chat rooms where members can hold discussions by sending text messages or files to one another. In Chapter 17, we saw how Instant Messaging provides another type of realtime communication that makes it possible to see the presence status of other IM users. Both of these systems are very good within their areas, i.e., to share information in realtime. However, they don't come close to replacing a real live meeting, not even an ISDN-based video conference, since they are limited to sending messages and files. This makes them a poor choice for an online meeting that requires more, such as the ability to share applications like PowerPoint or Excel, or distribute video and voice information to a number of people.

NetMeeting

Microsoft has an application that allows information sharing, including applications, video, and audio in realtime—their NetMeeting client, which has actually been around for several years. NetMeeting allows any number of people to set up a private communication session with the following features:

- *Video and audio conferencing*—Use a Web camera and a microphone to communicate with the other user.
- *Whiteboard*—Lets all invited members see and use the same whiteboard; use it to draw graphics and write text.
- *Chat*—Lets all members chat with one other.
- *File transfer*—Send and receive one or more files in the background during the meeting.
- *Program sharing*—Share any application, such as Excel, with all members. They can see what you are doing in this program; you can also hand control over to any other member.
- *Remote desktop sharing*—Share your whole computer! The other members can see what you are doing, and you can hand control over to any other member. Perfect when supporting remote users.

NetMeeting does have a few drawbacks that make it inappropriate to use as a replacement for normal in-real-life (IRL) meetings; this application is mainly designed for one-on-one conversations, although you can set up a session for more than two people. The drawbacks to NetMeeting are:

- *Video and audio*—Only two people can use the realtime video and audio features in a NetMeeting session: the user that started the session plus the first invited member that uses video and audio. However, all members can share the other features of NetMeeting.
- *Communication*—The user that initiates the NetMeeting session is also its host and central connection point; all shared information passes through this computer and out to the other members. This places a heavy burden on this computer and on the network connection.
- *Inefficient sharing*—When any type of information is shared, the central computer (i.e., the one that started the NetMeeting session) has to send the same information to all the members; for example, when sharing the whiteboard in a NetMeeting session with four members, the central computer must send out the same information three times—one for each member besides itself.
- *Not integrated*—NetMeeting is a standalone product; it's not integrated in Outlook or any other messaging client.
- *No management tools*—The user that starts the session is its manager; you cannot manage NetMeeting sessions from a central point.

Exchange 2000 Conferencing Server

To overcome the drawbacks of NetMeeting and other similar personal conferencing products, Microsoft developed the new Exchange 2000 Conferencing Server (ECS). First, let me tell you what it's not:

- It's not a special Exchange 2000 Server version
- It's not a standalone product
- It's not a set of new client and management tools

In fact, when Microsoft developed ECS, it wanted it to be an integrated module in an existing Exchange 2000 organization, utilizing familiar management tools and clients. The objectives for ECS were that it be:

- *Server-based*—Make it possible to set up online conferences that are controlled and administrated on a server, instead of the peer-to-peer design used in NetMeeting.
- *Integrated*—Integrate it into the existing Outlook clients; make it possible to use clients like Internet Explorer and NetMeeting; make it integrated in Exchange 2000 server.
- *Extensible*—Use existing collaboration protocols, such as T.120 and TAPI 3, while still making it possible to extend with future protocols and service providers.

So what is the Microsoft Conferencing Server? It's an add-on to Exchange 2000 that lets the Exchange administrator manage and control online conferences on a server. The users can use their ordinary Outlook clients to schedule and join conferences; they then use a Web browser, such as Internet Explorer, to participate in these conferences. This product does not replace all existing realtime collaboration applications; you should view it as a complement to be used in certain situations. It's not cheap, and it requires that you have an existing Exchange 2000 organization; but used correctly, it can save your organization a lot of money compared to normal IRL conferences.

Examples of Realtime Conferences

Maybe the best way of understanding how and when to use the ECS is by providing some examples. In the following sections, you will see how NetMeeting compares to Exchange 2000 Conferencing Server when used in two types of realtime conferences.

Example 1: Weekly Meeting Using NetMeeting

In this example, we have a department with two managers, Suzan and Magnus. They have a meeting every week, during which they discuss the current status of their secret project, Zero Gravity. They are located in separate cities, which makes it hard to meet in real life, so they have decided to try NetMeeting for online conferences instead. To assist them, they have a secretary named Jenny. During these meetings, they need to share a mathematical application, as well as some files, besides the usual conversation. If possible, they would like to use voice and audio to make it easier and faster to discuss matters.

Jenny has been given the responsibility of organizing these online meetings. This company doesn't have its own mail system—instead, they all run POP3 clients connected to an ISP, which makes it possible for them to exchange messages using the Internet.

Jenny's first task is to find a suitable time every week when both Suzan and Magnus can participate in these weekly meetings. After some email conversation, they have agreed to meet online every Monday at 9 A.M.

A few minutes before the meeting begins, Jenny starts her NetMeeting client; this will make her the administrator, or host, of this NetMeeting session. She must now find the IP addresses for Suzan and Magnus, to invite them to the meeting. If she knows their IP addresses, she can use them now; if not, she could connect to an Internet Locator Service (ILS) where Suzan and Magnus have registered their NetMeeting clients and invite them using that service. Regardless of how Jenny invites them, both Magnus and Suzan must have their own NetMeeting clients active, waiting for Jenny to invite them.

Jenny starts by inviting Magnus; this makes it possible for Jenny and Magnus to send video and audio by using their Web cameras and multimedia equipment. Next, Jenny invites Suzan; Suzan will not be able to use or view any video or listen to audio signals, since she is not the first invited person. Now we have a situation where two people, Jenny and Magnus, can communicate using video and audio, whereas Suzan has only the chat feature of NetMeeting for communicating with the other two.

During the meeting, Magnus uses the chat feature to talk with Suzan, and he explains his new idea on how to reverse the spin of electrons to achieve zero gravity; he also makes some drawings on the shared whiteboard and shows his calculations in his mathematical application. This takes about 45 minutes, and during this time Jenny can't do anything else with her computer, since it is the host for this NetMeeting session. After that, the meeting is finished for the week; next week at 9 A.M. they will have another meeting.

Example 2: Weekly Meeting Using Exchange 2000 Conferencing Server

Two months have passed since Jenny, Suzan, and Magnus started their NetMeeting sessions. The IT department finally realized that this company needed a messaging system, and implemented Exchange 2000 and Windows 2000. All users also got MS Outlook 2002 installed. The IT department also installed the Exchange 2000 Conferencing Server and created three virtual conference rooms, named VCR-1, VCR-2, and VCR-3; this last virtual conference room is restricted to the Windows 2000 security group "ZG" only, of which Suzan, Magnus, and Jenny are members.

It's only a few days before the next meeting, and Suzan requests to move the meeting to Tuesday. This is an excellent opportunity for Jenny to test the new system and see if it makes life easier for her as the meeting administrator. She starts her Outlook 2002 client and looks at the calendar for next Tuesday. She clicks New Appointment, switches over to view the Attendees Availability tab, and clicks Invite Others to invite Suzan and Magnus as Required, and VCR-3 as a Resource, to this meeting. Jenny manually selects a time that is available for all, or clicks AutoPick to let Outlook search for the first available time; then she sends this meeting request. Immediately she receives a confirmation that VCR-3 is now booked, and the remaining confirmations from Suzan and Magnus show up during the day.

At the designated time of the meeting, all participants, including Jenny, receive a meeting reminder. It contains a button labeled Join Conference; when they click this button, their Web browsers connect them to the conference.

Comparing NetMeeting and Exchange 2000 Conferencing Server

Let's compare the two ways of conducting these meetings. Table 18.1 lists the major differences. As you can see from this table, NetMeeting is not really suitable for meetings with more than two people; but for just two participants, NetMeeting is the perfect choice, since you don't have to schedule any connections. Just invite the other user and start sharing whatever you need.

Since ECS uses standard Web Universal Resource Locators (URLs) to indicate the location of the conference server and invite participants to the conference, it's even possible to invite another attendee while the actual conference is taking place; for example, by using Instant Messaging: If they are online, just send them an invitation with the URL. When they click it, they will be connected to the conference, using their Web browser.

Table 18.1 Comparing NetMeeting and ECS.

Feature	NetMeeting	Exchange 2000 Conferencing Server
Scheduling the meeting	Without any central calendar, Jenny has to use email or the phone to find a suitable time.	Using Exchange 2000 and Outlook, it's easy to find a time for this meeting. In service pack 1 for the Conferencing Server is also a new feature called Web Scheduler that allows Web clients to schedule a meeting.
Invitation	Jenny has to manually invite the attendees, and they must have their NetMeeting available, waiting for her to invite them.	The invitation is similar to any other meeting request in Outlook; shortly before the meeting starts, they get a reminder with a button that will take them to the conference; their Web browser starts automatically.
Hosting	Jenny's computer hosts the meeting; if her computer fails, the entire NetMeeting conference will be disrupted.	The server running the ECS is responsible for the conference. Jenny can even shut down her computer without anything happening.
Network load	Since Jenny's computer is the host, it will receive and send out all types of messages to the recipients; if you have four recipients, the host will send the same message four times.	ECS is clever enough to use the IP technique called Multicast, which broadcasts the information one time, regardless of how many recipients there are; this results in an enormously lesser network load, compared to NetMeeting traffic.
Video and audio	Only the host and the first participant can use video and audio.	All participants can use video and audio.
Client	NetMeeting is a bit complicated to use.	ECS uses a Web browser for the basic conference feature; however, it's possible to use NetMeeting as well.
Suitable for large meetings	No, this would generate too much bandwidth and only two participants could use video and audio.	Yes, ECS is perfect for larger conferences, even with video and audio presentations.

Conferencing Server Overview

In this section, we will discuss the architecture of ECS and how the modules communicate. Let's first look at the two types of realtime conferencing features that Exchange 2000 Conferencing Server offers:

- *Video conference*—Allows users to share video and audio.
- *Data conference*—Chat and share applications, a whiteboard, and files.

An active conference can be one of these types, or it can be both. This is something the administrator configures when he or she creates these virtual conference rooms; these rooms are also known as *conference resources*. These resources are stored in the Active

Directory as normal mailbox-enabled user objects. However, you don't create these resources with the AD Users and Computers tool, as you would with normal users; they are created by the Conferencing Manager, as the ECS management module is called.

The video and data conference services are handled by special components, called Conference Technology Providers (CTPs). The video module is called the Video Conferencing Provider, and the data module is called the Data Conferencing Provider. When a user connects to a video conference with his Web browser, he will be connected to a Web site that is controlled by the Conference Management Service (CMS). This CMS is really what controls all online conferencing services; it is a Windows 2000 service named Microsoft Exchange Conferencing, which is an application called xconfmgr.exe.

When you set up ECS for an online conference, these are the steps that take place:

1. Install ECS on an Exchange 2000 server; this installs the CMS service, which in turn creates a Web application called Conferencing in the Default Web Site.
2. The administrator uses the Conferencing Manager to create a virtual conference room (i.e. a conference resource), with a username, such as VCR-3, and a password.
3. When creating this conference resource, the administrator must decide if this will be a data conference, a video conference, or both, by adding CTP modules to this resource.
4. When this information is stored, a new mailbox-enabled user object will be created in the AD; this is our virtual conference room. It will be listed in the global address list, like any other user.

At this moment, we have a virtual conference room, ready to be used for online conferences. Following are the general steps that take place when our user Suzan sets up a scheduled conference and later joins it:

5. Suzan uses her Outlook client and creates a standard meeting invitation for all participants. However, she must also invite the virtual conference room; in our example, it's VCR-3, so she selects this name from the global address list and adds it as a Resource for this meeting.
6. Suzan then sends this meeting invitation; immediately she receives a reply from VCR-3, accepting this invitation. During the next few hours, she also gets the replies from the other attendees.
7. Shortly before the meeting starts, all attendees receive a reminder by their Outlook. It contains a button for joining the conference, which they click. Their Web browser then starts, and connects to a URL pointing to **http://<host_name>/Conferencing/** followed by a number of seemingly random numbers. The user can now participate in this meeting.

When Suzan's message arrived to the VCR-3 mailbox, this virtual conferencing room notified the CMS module, telling it to prepare for an online conference at a given time, of a certain type (such as video), and with a certain number of people. This sets up the resources necessary on the IIS Conferencing application for performing this conference. When the participants join the conference, or disconnect, this is also handled by the CMS.

Bandwidth and Conferencing Server

Realtime conferencing systems like ECS require a certain amount of bandwidth to make the experience pleasant; if it's too low or of bad quality, you will end up with lots of drop-outs and losses that make it hard to follow the conference. This is the reason that an Exchange Conferencing Server always belongs to a given Windows 2000 site; this site will be referred to as the *conferencing site*. You may recall from Chapter 5 that such a site is a collection of Windows 2000 servers that enjoy a reasonably high bandwidth. What is reasonable depends on how large your organization is: With thousands of users, you may need 10Mbps or maybe even more, whereas a small organization may be fine with 64Kbps. A Windows 2000 site consists of one or more IP-subnets. In existing networks of today, you will most often find that a Windows 2000 site corresponds to the local network for a geographic site; for example, a company with offices in two cities usually has one Windows 2000 site per city, connected over a WAN connection.

Video Conferences

The exact amount of free bandwidth needed for ECS is hard to predict; it depends on many different parameters. For example, a video conference requires much more bandwidth than a data conference. The amount of data sent when using video depends on two things:

- *Size*—A smaller picture generates less data than a large picture. ECS allows two picture sizes—Common Intermediate Format (CIF) 352×288, and Quarter CIF (QCIF) 176×144 pixels.
- *Compression*—All types of multimedia data are compressed before being sent; different compression algorithms allow varying degrees of compression.

The CIF/QCIF format allows up to 30 frames per second to be displayed and is developed for sending video images over network connections, including 28.8Kbps modem connections. Two standards are supported in ECS for this format: H.261 and H.263. The first, H.261, is used when you have at least 64Kbps of available bandwidth, and H.263 is the best protocol for slow connections, down to 28.8Kbps. If you will always use ECS over a local network, you should select H.261.

It would be too much load on the network if one would send video and audio signals in their raw format; to overcome this all this type of data is compressed. The compression algorithms handle both *co*mpression and *de*compression (CODEC) of both video and audio signals, and are often called *codec algorithms*. A codec will take the data (i.e., the picture or the audio signal) and compress this to a fraction of the original size; the price for this is quality—the higher the compression, the lower the quality. However, some algorithms can compress the picture while still keeping the quality within acceptable limits. The codec standard for video conferencing on the Internet is called H.323, and ECS is compliant with this protocol. But there is one problem with the H.323 protocol—it allows only one picture to be displayed; for example, if we have three participants using H.323 clients in an ECS video conference, only one of the pictures will be visible to the others (the one speaking).

However, in Windows 2000, there is a new version of Microsoft's and Intel's proprietary protocol Telephony Application Programming Interface: TAPI 3. It offers even higher quality and compression compared to the H.323 standard. If you use Windows 2000 Professional or Server to connect to an ECS video conference, it will use TAPI 3 instead of H.323. This will not only result in better pictures, it will make it possible to view all participants' pictures simultaneously! This is the reason that TAPI 3 is used as the default for ECS video conferences.

So how about all pre-Windows 2000 computers? They can still use the H.323 protocol, but they will be limited to viewing the current speaker's picture only, and the quality is a bit lower too. To allow H.323 clients to participate in ECS conferences, an H.323 Conference Bridge module in ECS will operate as a gateway between these non-TAPI compliant clients and the Conference Management Service. One H.323 Bridge can handle at least 40 simultaneous connections; if you need more, you could expand the hardware on the ECS server with more memory and CPUs, or you could install an extra H.323 Bridge on another Windows 2000 server. That will load-balance the H.323 client connections.

The audio signal also has its own coded algorithms; ECS supports two of the most common standards: GSM 6.10 and G.711. The first, GSM 6.10, is suitable for slow network links, typical for dial-up connections. The other codec, G.711, gives you better audio quality, but it also demands higher bandwidth.

Data Conferences

This type of conference requires much less bandwidth, since much less data is transferred every second. The protocol used on the Internet for data conferences is called T.120; this standard protocol offers the following services:

- *Realtime data sharing*—T.120 ensures that many participants can send and receive data in realtime. It has an error-correction feature that ensures that the information transferred is correct.
- *Multipoint data conferencing*—This protocol supports a variety of common topologies, such as cascaded, star, and daisy chain connection. This makes it possible to build distributed ECS topologies with T.120 Multipoint Control Units (MCUs).

Exchange Conferencing Server uses T.120 as the default protocol for all data conferences. The T.120 MCU is a small program that accepts data to be sent, and passes it on to the other party, whether it be a conference client or an ECS module. In ECS, the T.120 MCU is implemented in the Data Conferencing Provider; even using the minimum hardware configuration for an Exchange 2000 Conferencing Server, it will be able to handle 500 data conference users simultaneously.

Bandwidth, More Bandwidth!

As you have understood from the previous sections, bandwidth is something you can't get too much of, especially when you are running online video conferences. Just to give you a rough idea of what we are talking about, I will give you some estimates of the data transferred in these situations:

- *QCIF video*—This 176×144 pixel size format consumes about 80 to 130Kbps per user; for example, 10 users consume about 1 megabit/second.
- *CIF video*—This 352×288 format consumes up to four times the QCIF format; for example, 10 users consume up to 4Mbps.
- *G.711 audio*—When people talk, it consumes up to 70Kbps per user.
- *GSM 6.10 audio*—This codec is much more effective; it consumes about 20Kbps per user, but the quality is a bit lower than with G.711.

The message is clear, I hope: Make sure you have the available bandwidth before implementing MS Exchange Conferencing Server for larger groups of users in your organization! Start by creating just a few virtual conference rooms, maybe one data conference and one video conference. Make sure the video conference is limited to a maximum of 10 people; then monitor your network and see how it's affected.

Multicast Communications

One thing that differentiates ECM's video conferences from NetMeeting is the use of IP Multicast. This is a smart technique that makes it possible to send out data to a large group of recipients, without flooding the network. To understand it, you must first understand how normal IP traffic works: When a server wants to send the same information to multiple recipient clients, it must send the information once for each recipient. The reason is that they all have different IP numbers, so the data will only be accepted by the computer with the same IP number as the data packets have in their header. This is how the NetMeeting client distributes video and audio signals; as you can see, this is not a good idea if the number of recipients is more than just two or three.

This problem of distributing data to a large group of computers has been known for a long time, and the solution is IP Multicast. This method works like this: All recipients join a special IP Multicast group that is given a specific IP address; the server then sends out information to this particular IP address, instead of the recipient's individual IP address. It works the same as broadcasting on the network; however, it can also pass routers to other IP segments, making it possible to distribute this data to remote recipient clients.

The prerequisite is that the computers and the networking equipment, such as routers and firewalls, understand IP Multicast; if not, this will not work. Windows 2000 is multicast enabled when IP Multicast is used on local network segments. However, to make the Windows 2000 server understand how to send IP Multicast messages over routers, you must install Multicast Address Dynamic Client Allocation Protocol (MADCAP); you will find more information about it in Windows 2000 Server Online Help, in the IP Multicast section. Once you have installed MADCAP, you must also configure the Video Conferencing Provider module to use IP Multicast.

***Tip:** To check if the routers and other network equipment in your network understand IP Multicasts, you can use these Windows 2000 utilities: MCAST, MRINFO, and ROUTEMON.*

The Conferencing Site

The first installed ECS in a Windows 2000 site will become the active host server for this conferencing site; this server will have the Conference Management Service installed, listed as the Windows 2000 service: Microsoft Exchange Conferencing. If necessary, you can install more than one ECS, but only one of them can be active at a time; if the active server fails, you can then choose to activate another ECS. The active host will be responsible for all tasks regarding conferencing, such as reservations and client requests. If you have two Windows 2000 sites with one ECS each, the clients will be connected to the closest ECS, thus load balancing the conferencing service. If you configure only one ECS, all clients will be connected to that server, regardless of what Windows 2000 site they belong to.

One single server running the Conference Management Service can maintain from thousands to hundreds of thousands of users on a Windows 2000 site; it all depends on the available network bandwidth, the hardware configuration of the server, and the number of simultaneous conferences. Besides local clients accessing the ECS, external clients can also connect, coming from outside the company firewall; however, both the firewall connection and the ECS modules must first be configured properly, . It is easy to configure the ECS for external clients joining data conferences, but video conferences are harder, due to the way TCP/UDP ports are used by the clients. We will talk more about this later in this chapter.

Installing the Conferencing Server

So far we have covered a lot of theoretical, but necessary, background stuff; now it's time to install the conferencing server. First we will look at the hardware and software requirements, then we will walk through an installation and look at each configuration setting.

Requirements for the Conferencing Server

The hardware requirements vary depending on how many conference users you will allow simultaneously, and the number of video conferences. The codec algorithms are resource hungry and will increase the load on the CPU and virtual memory. The *minimum* hardware requirements are:

- 133MHz Pentium processor, or equivalent
- 128MB of RAM

- 250MB of free disk space (a complete ECS installation takes about 18MB).
- A network card, keyboard, VGA monitor, and mouse.

But as always, this is far from a hardware configuration that would be suitable in a production environment. If you will also have Exchange 2000 Server on this computer, you should increase these values! A more realistic configuration that would allow up to 500 simultaneous conference users would be something like this:

- 400MHz Pentium III, or better.
- 256MB of RAM.
- 1GB of free disk space.

The software requirements for the conferencing server are these, assuming you will install a complete ECS:

- Windows 2000 Server, or Windows 2000 Advanced Server.
- Service Pack 1 or later for Windows 2000.
- Exchange 2000 Server or Exchange 2000 Enterprise Server. Note that Exchange must not necessarily be installed on the same computer as ECS; it will be enough if you have one Exchange 2000 server in the same Windows 2000 domain as the conferencing server. It will actually work with Exchange 5.5 also, although not all security features will be available.
- Service Pack 1 or later for Exchange 2000 Server (or SP 4 for Exchange 5.5).
- Service Pack 1 or later for Exchange 2000 Conferencing Server (adds several new features).
- Internet Information Server (IIS 5) for the server hosting the conference access Web pages.
- Active Directory.
- DNS.

If necessary, you can install the MMC-based Conference Manager administrative tool on your workstation; you will then use the same setup program as for the complete ECS, but instead you select to do a Custom Setup and then select the Conferencing Manager only. With this custom setup, it's also possible to install only the T.120 MCU/H.323 Conference Bridge module on a Windows 2000 server, in order to create multiple T.120 MCU and/or H.323 bridges for load balancing. The four modules that can be installed separately are:

- *Conferencing Management Service*—The core module in ECS requires 7.6MB of free disk space.
- *T.120 MCU/H.323 Conference Bridge*—The modules for data conferencing (T.120) and allowing pre-Windows 2000 clients to connect (H.323); requires 1.1MB of free disk space.

- *Conferencing Access Web Pages*—The ASP and Web files used for allowing Web browsers to join and participate in a conference; requires 5.9MB free disk space.
- *Conferencing Manager*—The MMC-based administrative tool for ECS; requires 2MB of free disk space.

Requirements for the Conferencing Clients

In order to participate in an online conference, the clients also need to have some minimum requirements. We start with the hardware requirements necessary to take full advantage of the features offered by Exchange Conferencing Server:

- *Windows 95 clients*—Minimum 90MHz Intel CPU with 16MB of RAM and a VGA monitor; my recommendation is 350MHz CPU with 96MB, or better.
- *Windows NT clients*—Minimum 90MHz Intel CPU with 24MB of RAM; my recommendation is 350MHz CPU with 128MB, or better.
- *Windows 2000 Professional*—Minimum 133MHz Intel CPU with 32MB of RAM; my recommendation is 350MHz CPU with 128MB, or better.
- *Video monitor*—The minimum requirement is a VGA; my recommendation is a 17-inch monitor with at least 800×600 and 16-bit color resolution.
- *Multimedia equipment*—Sound card with microphone and speakers. Don't buy the cheapest around if you are serious about online conferencing! A headset with integrated microphone is excellent for online video conferencing.
- *Video camera*—Most Web cameras will do for normal use; my recommendation is to buy a well-known color camera that has the drivers now and in the upcoming releases of Windows XP. If you select a USB-connected camera, you don't have to struggle with video capture cards. However, for the best quality, you should install a separate video-capture card and a high-quality video camera.

The software required for a client that wants to use all the features of ECS is simple: make sure to use Windows 2000 (any version) or better! Only these clients will have support for TAPI 3 and IP Multicast, which make it possible to view multiple video pictures simultaneously. However, you can also run pre-Windows 2000 computers, but beware that you will not be able to see more than one video at a time, and it will be slower and lower quality. (Yes, you should show this to your boss and tell him it's high time to upgrade all those old Windows 9x computers.) Besides the operating system, these clients will also need the following applications:

- *MS Outlook 200X*—Needed to take full advantage of the booking features of online conferences.
- *NetMeeting 3.01*—Or later; necessary to connect Windows 9X, NT 4, and ME clients to an ECS online conference. You can download the latest version of NetMeeting from this Web page: **www.microsoft.com/windows/netmeeting**. Note that all Windows 2000

computers and later versions have NetMeeting 3.01 already installed (Start|Programs|Accessories|Communications); however, check to see if there is a newer release for Windows 2000 clients.

- *Internet Explorer 5.x*—Or later; in fact, all Web browsers that support download of ActiveX controls and have support for frames and JavaScripts must be enabled. This will be the primary conference client for users with Windows 2000; I recommend that you go for IE 5.5 or later. Pre-Windows 2000 clients will use their NetMeeting client to view video and the Web browser for the other features.

Instead of the NetMeeting client, a user can also use any T.120-compliant client for data conferences and any H.323-compliant client for video/audio conferences; but again, this will prohibit these clients from seeing more than one video picture at a time! As you can see, there is not really any choice. If your organization really wants to use online conferences, you need to upgrade all those clients to Windows 2000; so do it! I would be very surprised if you don't like it.

Installing a Complete Conferencing Server

Okay, we have the necessary hardware and software in place; now let's install the ECS. Select the server that will be your main conferencing server; remember, it doesn't have to be an Exchange 2000 server, but there must be at least one such server in this domain. Follow these steps to install Exchange 2000 Conferencing Server:

1. Mount the CD-ROM with the ECS software—it will automatically start the launch wizard for ECS; otherwise select Start|Run|D:\Launch.exe (assuming D: is your CD-ROM drive).

2. Click Exchange Conferencing Server; this will start the Installation Wizard. Click *Next* to continue.

3. On the License Agreement page, select I Accept if you accept the license agreement and then click *Next*.

4. On the Product Identification page, enter your 25-digit product ID; you will probably find it on the back of the CD case. Then click *Next* to continue.

5. On the Setup Type page, you can select if you want to install the complete ECS package or just a few of the modules. If you select Custom, you will see an extra page (see Figure 18.1) from which you can select which modules to install. You can also select where these files will be installed. By default, these files will be installed in the directory \Program Files\Microsoft Exchange Conferencing Server. When ready, select *Next*.

6. On the Administrative Group page, select which administrative group in Exchange 2000 will administrate the Conferencing Management Service. Note that this page will only be displayed if you have more than one AG. Click *Next* to continue.

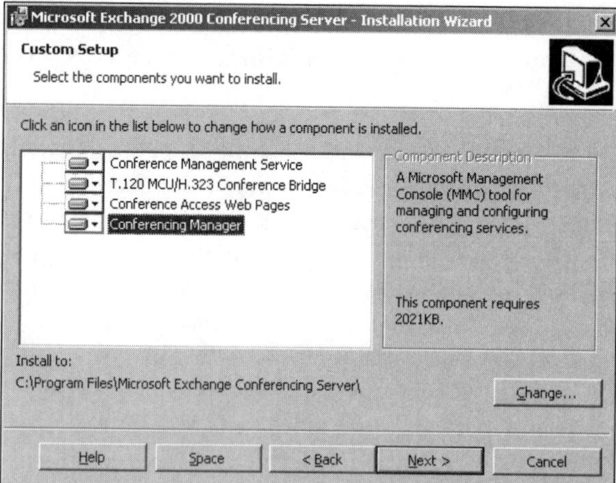

Figure 18.1
The Custom Setup page for ECS.

7. On the Ready To Install The Program page, click *Next* to start the installation. Now the files will be copied to the server, and ECS will be installed. This will only take a few minutes.
8. When the installation is done, click *Finish* to complete this ECS installation.

After the Installation

The installation of ECS is fast and simple; you don't have to restart any services. But let's look at the new services we got with this installation. Open the Windows 2000 services by selecting Start|Program|Administrative Tools|Services. Look for a service named Microsoft Exchange Conferencing. It should have started automatically. If you open its properties (see Figure 18.2), you will find that its executable file name is xconfmgr.exe, and that it is stored in the new directory Program Files\Microsoft Exchange Conferencing Server\. (Microsoft has really started to take advantage of the possibilities with long file and directory names, hasn't it?)

If we look at the Dependencies tab, we will see that it's not dependent on any Exchange 2000 service. This means that Exchange Conferencing Server isn't dependent on a local Exchange 2000 Server installation; this is the reason why you can install ECS on any Windows 2000 server that is a member of a domain where at least one Exchange 2000 server is installed.

Besides the conferencing services, you will also find two other new services, if you have done a complete installation: the Microsoft Exchange H.323 Bridge service and the Microsoft Exchange T.120 MCU service. These two services are obviously the H.323 Bridge and T.120 MCU modules, which can also be installed separately on any Windows 2000 server, if necessary.

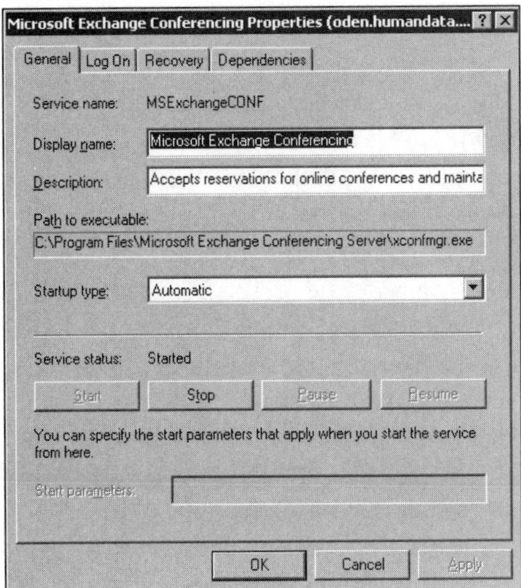

Figure 18.2
The new Microsoft Exchange Conferencing service.

Check the Event Log file to see if there are any warnings or errors related to this installation; if so, take proper action to solve the problem. Usually this is a very simple installation that doesn't have any problems or hiccups; however, things that can disturb the installation are:

- *Permissions*—Not enough properties for installing the ECS software. You must be an administrator with membership in at least Domain Admins and the Administrators group; and you must be a Full Exchange Administrator to create the Conferencing Calendar Mailbox when you start the Conferencing Manager program and connect to the new conferencing site the first time.
- *IIS 5*—The Web server must be working properly before you can install the Conference Active Web Page.
- *Active Directory*—This server must have contact with an AD controller.

If any problems occur during the installation of ECS, make sure to fix the problem, restart your server just to make sure it's in a known state, and rerun the installation again.

Installation of Conferencing Clients

This part is simple; if you have Windows 2000 clients (any version), you don't have to do anything, since these computers already have the necessary versions of NetMeeting and Internet Explorer (IE). However, you should make sure to run the latest versions of these programs; Internet Explorer in particular has several upgrades and security fixes that are important to implement. Check the home page for IE for the latest information: **www.microsoft.com/windows/ie**.

ActiveX Controls for the Conferencing Client

The first time a user connects to an online video conference using Internet Explorer 5.x (or any other ActiveX-compliant Web client), it will download two ActiveX controls needed to present the video and audio information. This is a quick download and the ActiveX controls will automatically be installed; the user doesn't have to restart anything. However, clients that don't have direct access to the Internet cannot install these ActiveX controls. The best solution in this case is to install these files before the user starts Internet Explorer. These two files, Xipcctl.cab and Xcliacc.cab, can be found on the ECS server in the directory: \Program Files\Microsoft Exchange Conferencing Server\Conferencing. Before you can use them, they must be unpacked; follow these steps to do this:

1. Open a Command prompt window on the ECS server and change the current directory by typing **cd \Program Files\Microsoft Exchange Conference Server\Conferencing**.
2. Next, expand the two .cab files to the \Temp directory by typing:

   expand -F:* Xipcctl.cab \temp

   expand -F:* Xcliacc.cab \temp
3. Now we have four new files in this \Temp directory:
   - xcliacc.inf
   - xcliacc_x86.dll
   - xipcctl.inf
   - xipcctl_x86.dll

   Make sure these files are reachable for the clients by copying them to a shared folder. In this example, we copy them to a shared folder named ActiveX on our server Oden.
4. Go to the computer where you want these files installed; open a command prompt window and type:

   regsvr32 \\oden\Active-x\xipcctl_x86.dll (Click *OK* on the dialog box.)

   regsvr32 \\oden\Active-x\xcliacc_x86.dll (Click *OK* on the dialog box.)

Configuring Outlook 2000 for Online Conferences

When using Outlook 2000 for booking resources, you should configure it to display a new button in the meeting request; normally this button is hidden since it will only confuse users who don't run online conferences. Without this button, the user joins a conference one of the following ways:

- *Clicking the URL*—When you sent this meeting request, you received an acceptance message from the virtual conferencing room; the URL to this particular conference is listed in this mail. However, only the meeting organizer receives this URL; therefore, this organizer must send a copy of this URL to all participants before the meeting starts and inform them that they can join the conference by clicking this URL.

- *Browsing the conference list*—All conferences are listed on a particular Web page; you can inform all participants to browse this list and click on the conference to join. The URL to this page is **www.humandata.se/conferencing**; once there, attendees would select Attend A Conference Now (see Figure 18.3).

There is actually an easier way; by enabling Outlook 2000 for online Exchange conferences, you and your participants will see a new button called Join Conference that will appear on the meeting reminder dialog box (see Figure 18.4). It will also activate several other online features (see Figure 18.5), such as the Online Exchange Conference. This new option will display the following two settings on the meeting invitation:

- *External Attendees*—Can be allowed or denied access; if you allow external users, you can also set a password they must know to join this conference.

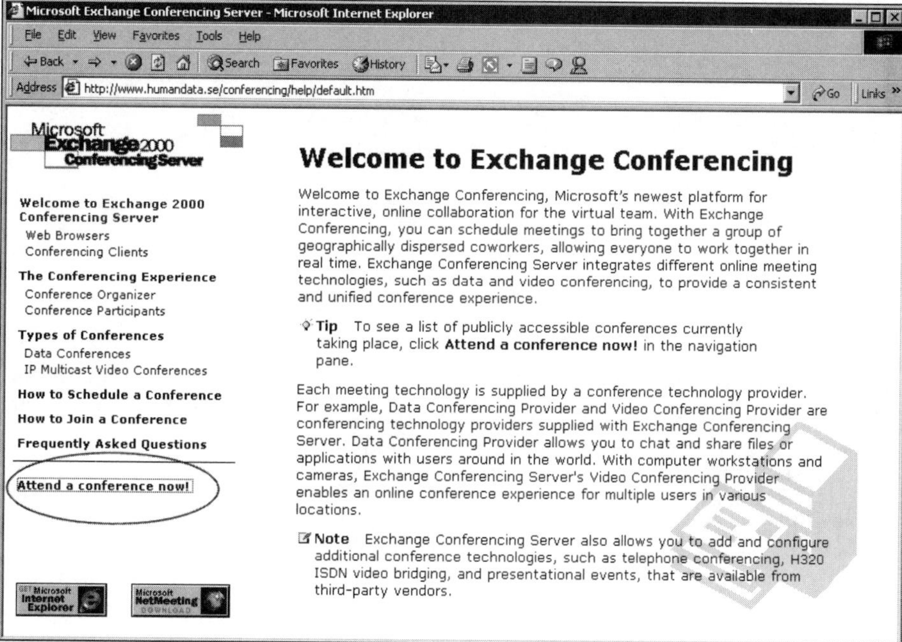

Figure 18.3
The Exchange Conferencing home page.

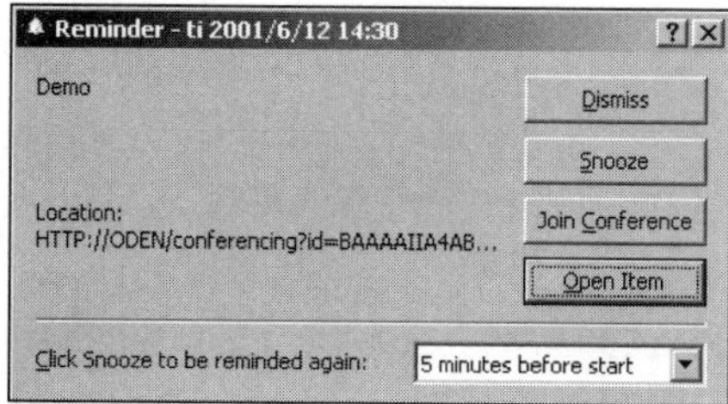

Figure 18.4
The new Join Conference button.

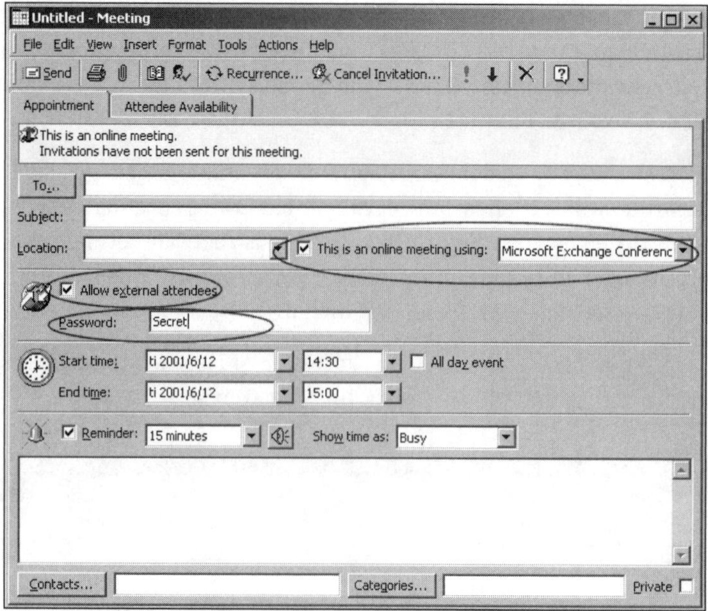

Figure 18.5
The new options available for Exchange online conferences.

- *Password*—The password necessary for joining the conference.

To add these online options to an Outlook 2000 client, you edit the Registry; since this must be done on all Outlook 2000 clients, you could create a Registry file that will add this new Registry key automatically. Start by creating a standard text file like this one (use Notepad or some similar text editor; not MS Word):

```
REGEDIT4
[HKEY_CURRENT_USER\Software\Microsoft\Office\9.0\Outlook\ExchangeConferencing]
```

Save this in a file with the file type .REG—for example OnlineOptions.reg. Test it first to make sure it works, then send it to all Outlook 2000 users; instruct them to save this file to their local disk, then double-click it to add the new Registry key to their computer. Note that they cannot start this file from a command prompt; it must be done from Windows Explorer or a similar program.

***Note:** The user will not be able to start OnlineOptions.reg directly from within Outlook if they have applied the Service Release 1 (SR1) or later for Outlook and Office 2000! This SR1 prohibits dangerous files, such as .reg, from executing directly within Outlook, in order to avoid email-distributed viruses and Trojan horses.*

Another way to distribute this Registry modification is by logon scripts or Windows 2000 user policies and System Management Service (SMS).

Preparing Windows 9X, ME, and NT 4 Clients

As mentioned before, these clients don't have support for the TAPI 3 protocol; this means that they can only see their own video picture plus one other participant's (click the name in the list of participants to see a particular person's video). These clients will not even be able to do this, unless they have version NetMeeting 3.01 or later installed. Download it from **www.microsoft.com/windows/netmeeting**. That will make these types of clients prepared for video conferencing.

However, the H.323 provider will be disabled by default for all video conferences; this will prohibit pre-Windows 2000 clients from joining the conference, although they may have the latest NetMeeting client installed. You may remember that the H.323 protocol was used generally on the Internet for video conferencing, but Microsoft has chosen to implement its proprietary TAPI 3 protocol for Exchange video conferencing. That is why we have to manually activate the H.323 bridge that will work as a gateway between H.323 clients and our TAPI 3 server. Exactly how this is done is described in the next section, in Step 13.

Configuring the Conferencing Server

Now that the server is installed, and our clients prepared, let's look at all the configuration settings for Exchange Conferencing Server. In this section, you will find detailed descriptions of the conferencing objects and their property pages; you will also find some recommendations on how to configure these objects for low-bandwidth situations as well as high-bandwidth situations.

Configuring the Conference Objects

In this example, we will look at the settings for a new ECS server and give you tips on what to configure and why. Follow these steps for a "walkabout" in this new and exciting territory:

1. Start the Conferencing Manager (CM) by selecting Start|Programs|Microsoft Exchange| Conferencing Manager. (On the actual ECM server, you will also see this MMC snap-in added to the ordinary ESM tool.)

2. In the CM, you will see a Console Root folder, and under that the Exchange Conferencing folder. The CM tool is used to manage and configure one conferencing site at a time; you may remember that you can have one ECS per Windows 2000 site. So the first thing we must do is to declare what conferencing site we want to manage: Right-click the Exchange Conferencing folder and select Manage; then select the conference site to manage. The default is Default-First-Site-Name. Then click *OK*.

3. Since this is the first time we're opening this conferencing site, you will be asked if you want to create a Conferencing Calendar Mailbox; click Yes to do so. If you answer no, you will be able to do this later; however, this will also mean that this Exchange conferencing server is disabled until you create this mailbox.

The Conferencing Mailbox is the managing mailbox that will store all scheduled conferences for this conferencing site, regardless of what virtual conference room has been booked. After this mailbox is created, you can create an Outlook profile and start an Outlook session as this user; this is necessary if you want to clean out old meetings, or make any changes in its configuration. A tip is to add your own mailbox account as a delegate with full permission to the calendar, which makes it possible for you to manage this conferencing mailbox from your own client. If you also right-click the Outlook Today object for the conferencing mailbox, then select Properties|Permission and add your mailbox name with Read permissions or higher, you will be able to add this mailbox to your Outlook profile. To do this, log on with your own Outlook profile, select the Tools|Services menu, and select Properties for the Exchange Server. Then switch to the Advanced page, click Add, and type in the name of the conferencing mailbox. Then click *OK* three times until you have closed all property pages. If you now look at your folder list (menu: View|Folder List), you will see your own mailbox and the Conferencing Calendar Mailbox displayed. If you want, you can drag the Calendar folder from that mailbox to your own Outlook Shortcuts for easy access to this folder; rename this calendar so you can distinguish it from your own calendar folder.

4. The first property page you will see when creating the new Conferencing Calendar Mailbox will look like Figure 18.6. Fill it in like this:

   - *Display Name*—Add the name that this mailbox will have in the global address list and wherever this object is presented. Use your company's name standard, if any, but make sure it's clear that this is a special mailbox that people should not send messages to. You can also hide this special mailbox from the address lists the same

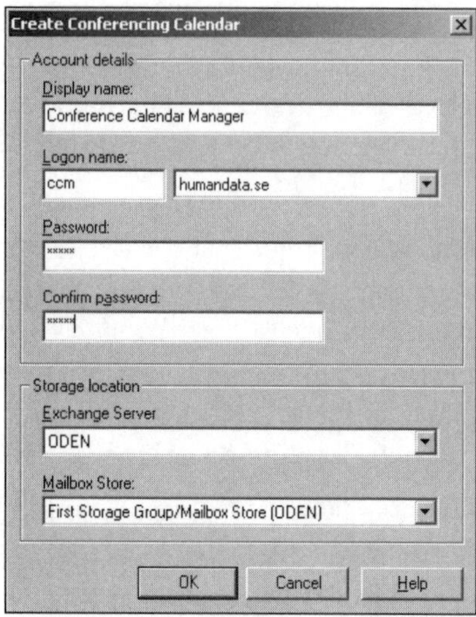

Figure 18.6
Creating the new Conferencing Calendar Mailbox.

way that you hide a normal mailbox: Open the properties for this mailbox, and switch to the tab Exchange Advanced. However, you will not find this mailbox among the normal user accounts in AD Users and Computers. First, make sure you have selected View|Advanced Features; then look in the container named Microsoft Exchange System Objects\Conferencing, and there it is.

- *Logon Name*—Add the Windows 2000 user account name for this new object. Make sure it will be created in the right domain, and add the password for this account.
- *Storage Location*—Select the Exchange 2000 server this mailbox will belong to, and its mailbox store. When ready, click *OK* to continue.

5. The second and last property page for the Conference Calendar Mailbox account will look like Figure 18.7: It will summarize the previous settings and give you a chance to correct any errors. It's possible to create more than one conference calendar mailbox, but normally you don't do this. When you are sure everything is correct, click Close to create this mailbox.
6. You will now see a new folder named Default-First-Site-Name Conferencing Site. If you expand it, you will find two new folders (see Figure 18.8):
   - *Data Conferencing Provider*—This is the T.120 MCU that makes data conferencing possible.
   - *Video Conferencing Provider*—This is the TAPI 3 video and audio provider that makes video conferencing possible. This provider will also host the H.323 bridge to allow pre-Windows 2000 clients to join video conferences.

   These two providers are also known as Conference Technology Providers (CTPs) and are installed by default with ECS. Note that this is an open architecture that will allow third-party vendors to add their own CTP.

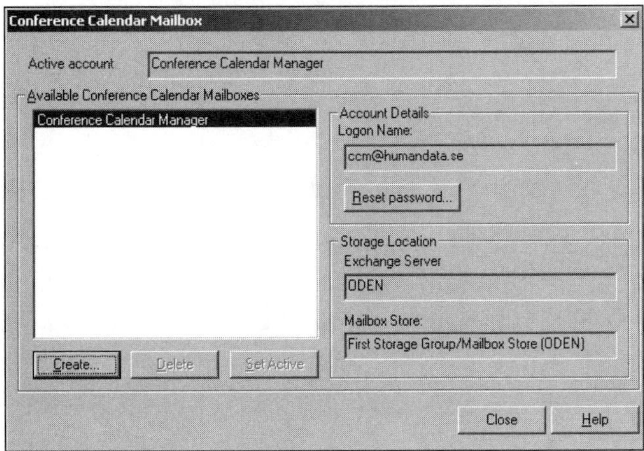

Figure 18.7
The summary page for the new calendar mailbox.

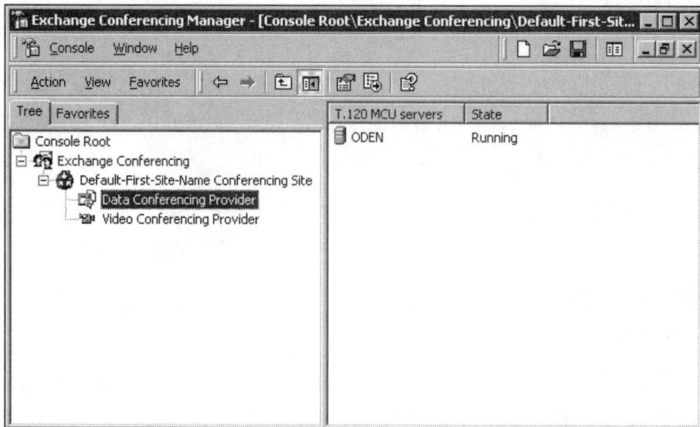

Figure 18.8
The default conferencing site and the two CTPs.

7. Right-click the Data Conferencing Provider and select Properties (see Figure 18.9). The General page will let you define the maximum total number of simultaneous data conference connections for this conferencing site, regardless of how many T.120 MCUs are installed; the default is 500 allocated client connections. If you increase this number, the network load will also increase (under the assumption that the actual number of connections will also increase). Note that the limit of 500 connections is compared to the configured number of users each conference can hold. For example, assume that you set a limit of 100 users; there are four virtual data conference rooms: A (50 users), B (25 users), C (20 users), and D (10 users). Now Anna reserves an A-room

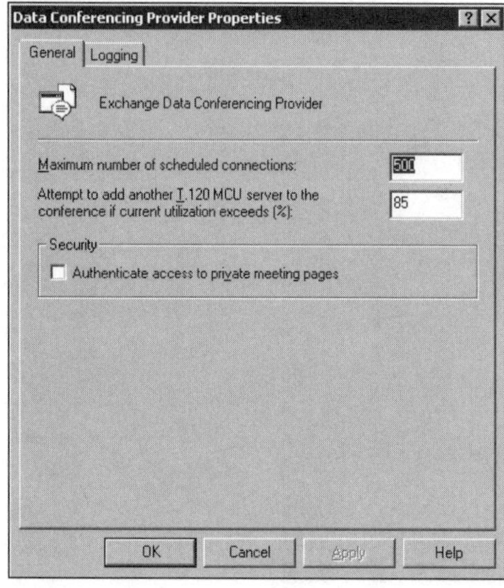

Figure 18.9
The General page for the Data Conferencing Provider.

conference, and Alex reserves a B-room conference. This will be a total of 75 allocated connections. If Marina now tries to reserve an A-room conference, she will be denied, since that would be 125 users total; the best Marina can do is to reserve a B-room with 25 users, or wait until Anna's conference is over.

The Attempt To Add Another T.120 MCU Server To The Conference If Current Utilization Exceeds (%) option is used to set a threshold on when to add another T.120 MCU to this conference for load balancing. This assumes that more than one T.120 MCU is installed. To install an extra MCU on another Windows 2000 server, do a custom setup of ECS. The default threshold is 85 percent. All new client connections that occur after this threshold is reached will be handled by this new MCU. A tip is to set a lower threshold value if the server hosting the MCU is also used for other CPU-intensive services, such as an Exchange 2000 mailbox server; this will avoid the load placed by the conferencing service decreasing the performance of the Exchange server. The default value 85 percent assumes that this server is a dedicated conferencing server.

The Security pane with the option Authenticate Access To Private Meeting Pages provides extended security through the Windows 2000 Kerberos authentication protocols. If this option is set, then all users joining a secure data conference must authenticate before joining the conference by entering their Windows 2000 user logon credentials. This will reduce the risk that someone sneaks into another person's room and joins a conference in the other person's name.

8. The Logging page for the Data Conferencing Provider (see Figure 18.10) is used to select what activities to log. The default setting is to log when the conference starts

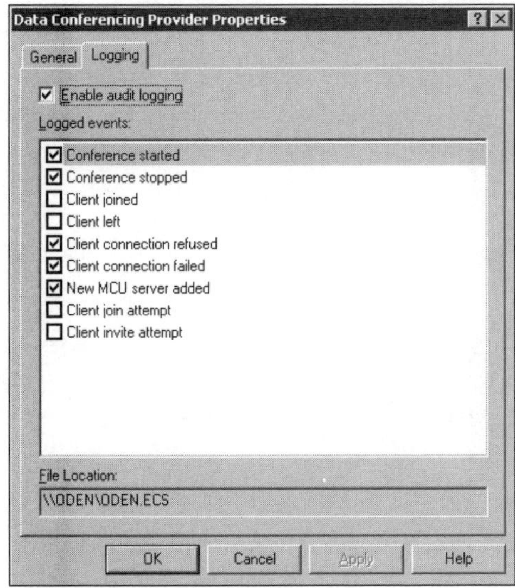

Figure 18.10
The Logging page for the Data Conference Provider.

and stops, and whether any client connections failed or were refused. You can also select to log when clients join and leave the conference, and whether a client has attempted to join or invite others. If you want to stop all logging, clear Enable Audit Logging at the top of the page.

At the bottom of this page is the name of the log file and the directory it's stored in: \\Oden\Oden.ECS. This is a shared folder on the ECS server (Oden in this example) that was created during the setup of ECS; this folder points to the directory \Program Files\Microsoft Exchange Conferencing Server\ODEN.ECS. All log files will be named DCSyyyymmdd.log, where DCS stands for Data Conferencing Service. A new log file will be created each day; after seven days, the log file will automatically be removed. This log file is easiest to understand if it is imported into MS Excel; the file has 22 comma-separated fields with lots of information about the conference sessions; see the section "Log Files in ECS," later in this chapter.

In the help file for this page, there is a description on how to change the log directory; however, this information is incorrect. The only way to change the directories for the log files (both for this data conference provider and all other ECS loggings) is to modify the directory this share points to—for example, using Windows Explorer and reconfiguring this share to point to another directory. When this is done, the ECS service must be restarted. Click *OK* when ready.

9. Let's take a look at the other CTP; right-click the Video Conferencing Provider and select Properties (see Figure 18.11). This object contains only one property page, the

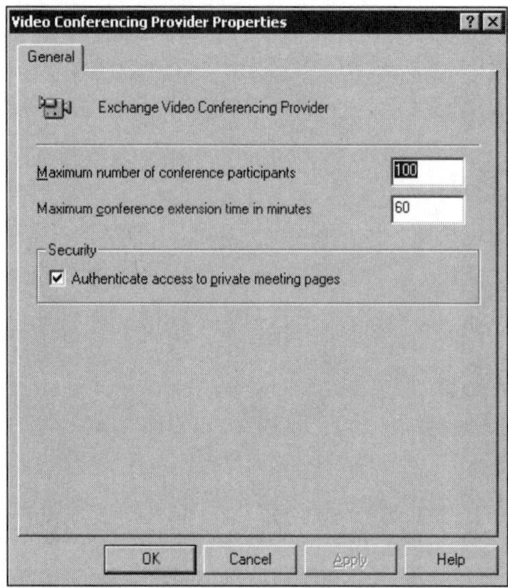

Figure 18.11
The General page for the Video Conferencing Provider.

General page. It is similar to the data conferencing provider object, in the sense that you use it to set a limit on the available connections:

- The maximum Number Of Conference Participants is default set to 100; this means that up to 100 video client sessions can be allocated at one time. Again, this is not the actual number of connected clients—this value calculates the number of connections listed in each virtual conference room; the same example as in Step 4 can be applied here too.
- The Maximum Conference Extension Time In Minutes is default 60; this means that any video conference will be able to continue for 60 more minutes after the scheduled meeting has ended. This makes it possible to gracefully close the video conference without an abrupt ending, in case someone has to say some final words.
- The Security pane contains the same option as for the data conference provider in Step 4. Use this option if you want to force all users to log on before joining the conference.
- There is no Log page for the Video Conference Provider. Click *OK* to close this property window.

10. Finally, let's look at the conferencing site itself; right-click Default-First-Site-Name Conferencing Site and select Properties. It will take us to the General page. You will find two settings there:

    - *Active Conferencing Host Server*—This is the home server for the ECS. Click Modify to set another ECS server as the active conferencing host; before you can do this, you must first install another ECS in this conferencing site. Remember, if you have more than one ECS in one site, only one of them can be active at a time.
    - *Site conference calendar mailbox*—This is the mailbox you created in Step 3. If you need to modify it, click Modify; however, it is highly unlikely that you will ever want to do this.

11. On the Conference Settings page (see Figure 18.12), you can control the URL and some other conference settings. Access URL For User Connections will be the base URL for the IIS 5 that will host the conference access Web page. By default, this page is based on the ECS server name. You can also install these access Web pages on another IIS server; then this field must be changed to use this new server name instead. If this conferencing server will be accessed from the Internet, you should change the server name to a complete FQDN name—for example, **http://oden.humadata.se/conferencing**.

    By default, clients will be able to join the conference 20 minutes before it actually starts; but when a conference time is out, there is no extended time. This can be changed if you want to give the conference a more graceful finish, such as five

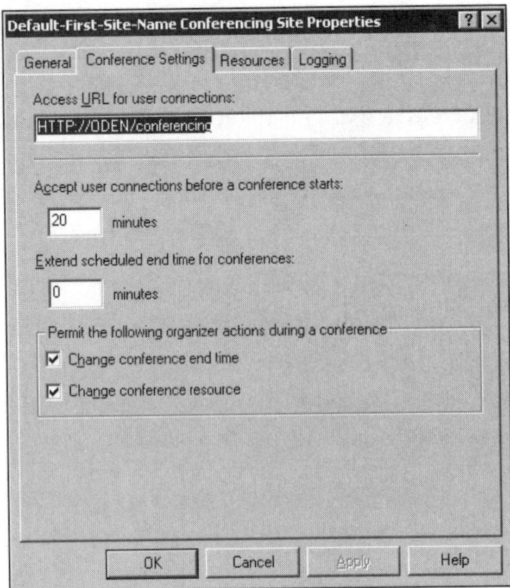

Figure 18.12
The Conference Settings page.

minutes of extra time. To compensate for this, you can decrease the time for joining the conference from 20 to 10 or 15 minutes. Note that these settings are global—they will affect all online conferences on this ECS server.

At the bottom of this page, you can control whether a conference organizer (i.e., the person that initiated the meeting) can extend the time for the conference in case more time than anticipated is needed; the organizer can also change the conference resource, i.e., he or she can change to another virtual conference room, if necessary. Both of these two options are set by default.

12. On the Resources page (see Figure 18.13), you will find all the virtual conference rooms created for this conferencing site; they are also known as conference resources. The first time you use this page, it will be empty. In Figure 18.13, you can see an example with three virtual conference rooms. Click the Add button to create your first resource; this will take you to a new dialog window.

    The New Resource Mailbox window is exactly the same window as you saw when creating the Conference Calendar Mailbox earlier (refer back to Figure 18.6), and you enter the same types of values. However, this time you create a virtual conference room; this room is the resource that your Outlook clients will use when booking a conference resource. Take some time and plan the name standard here. Since all resources have a limited number of participants, it would be practical to see this limit directly in the name. Then you also have three combinations of conference services: video only, data only, and both video and data. This is also very handy if you can see

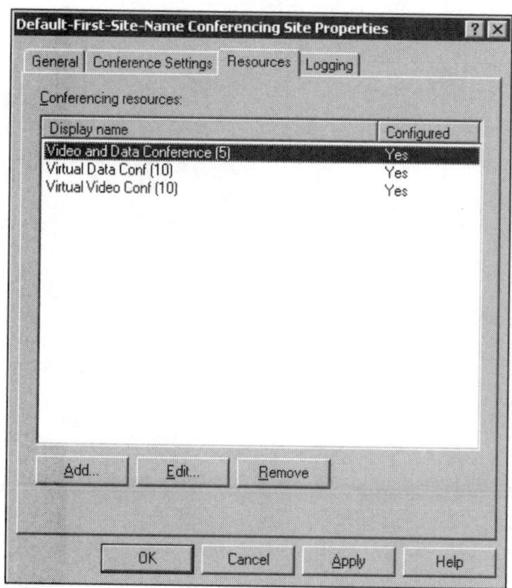

Figure 18.13
The Resources page.

this directly by looking at the resource name. A good name standard for resources could look something like this:

- *#Conference Video (10)*—For a video conference resource with up to 10 people.
- *#Conference Data (50)*—For a data conference resource with up to 50 people.
- *#Conference Video and Data (25)*—For a combined video and data conference with up to 25 people.

You get the idea, I hope. The initial hash sign (#) is just there to group all such conference resources together in the address list; you can use whatever character you want, but just make sure they will be listed together. Remember, these virtual conference rooms will be listed in the global address list!

13. When you are ready with this first page, click *OK* to continue. This will take you to the next page, where you will add the Conference Technology Providers (CTPs) for this virtual conference room. As mentioned before, you have two CTPs that come with ECS: the Data Conference Provider and the Video Conference Provider. You must add at least one CTP here, or your virtual conference room will not work. If you have created a resource called #Conference Vide (10) on the previous page, then you should add the Video CTP here, of course. Click Add and select the proper CTP now, then click *OK*; this will display the property page for this video CTP (see Figure 18.14). Fill in this page like this:

    - *Limit number of meeting participants*—Set the maximum number of clients for this resource here; for example, for the #Conference Video (10), we should enter 10 here.

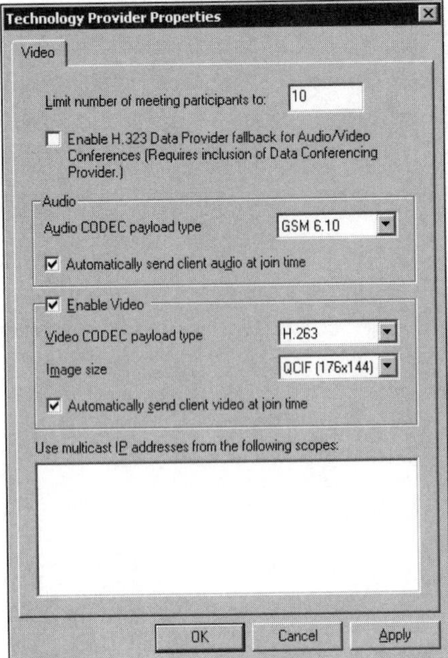

Figure 18.14
Configuring a video CTP resource.

- *Enable H.232 Data Provider*—Fill in this switch box if some of your users have pre-Windows 2000 clients; without this setting, they cannot join this conference since their NetMeeting client only supports H.323 and not TAPI 3. However, note that if you do set this switch, you will no longer be able to configure any other video codec settings below on this page. Don't set this switch unless you must; if you do, you should indicate this H.323 support in the resource name, such as #Conference Video/Bridge (8) or something similar.
- *Audio CODEC payload type*—Select between G.711 (better quality, but requires more bandwidth) and GSM 6.10 (default; lower quality, but works over 28.8Kbps lines, such as modem connections). See also the section "Video Conferences," earlier in this chapter.
- *Automatically send client audio at join time*—Controls whether the client computer will get audio signal by default when connecting to the conference; this is default set.
- *Enable Video*—Controls whether video signals are enabled or not during the conference; sometimes you may only need, or want, audio signal—for example, in a situation with very low bandwidth.
- *Video CODEC payload type*—Select between H.261 (better quality, but requires at least 64Kbps) and H.263 (default; lower quality, but works over 28.8Kbps lines); see also the previous section, "Video Conferences."

- *Image size*—Select between CIF (352×288 pixels) and QCIF (176×144; the default setting, since it requires about 25 percent of the bandwidth that CIF requires).
- *Automatically send client video at join time*—Controls whether the client computer will see video by default when connecting to the conference; this is default set.

The Use Multicast IP Addresses From The Following Scopes field will be empty until you have configured MADCAP on the Windows 2000 domain; see also the previous section "Multicast Communications."

Click *OK* when you are done; this will take you back to the previous window.

14. If you want, you can now add more than one CTP to the same virtual conference room; for example, if your conference room has a name such as #Conference Video and Data (25), you should add both CTPs listed here. When adding a data CTP, you will also get a property page to configure, but this one is much simpler than the video CTP. You actually have only one value to enter—the maximum number of accepted client connections for this data resource. The default is 10. You should indicate this number in the name for this virtual data conference room, such as #Conference Data (10).
15. Finally, we have only one property page left in our Default-First-Site-Name Conferencing Site object: the Logging page. This page is very similar to the logging page described in Step 8; however, it logs the activities of the Conference Management Service (the main conference module, if you remember). You can enable or disable this logging with the Enable Audit Logging checkbox in the top of this window. Down at the bottom is the directory where the log files will be kept; this will be the same place as for the log files generated from the Data Conferencing Provider. The names of these log files follow this format: CMSyyyymmdd.log. One log file is created per day, and after seven days the log files are removed automatically; if you need to save these log files, make sure to move or copy them first.

    This concludes the walkabout of the Default-First-Site-Name Conferencing Site object; click *OK* to save and close all your settings. By the way, you don't have to first click Apply and then OK; only novice administrators do this. The Apply button is there if you want to save some settings but still have the object in question open.

Recommendation for Conference Resources

The most important thing to remember is that online conferences, especially video conferences, generate a lot of network traffic. If you are uncertain about how this will affect your current production environment, I suggest that you start with a limited number of virtual conference rooms, each configured for just a small number of participants. As a rule of thumb, you should calculate that one video conference generates 10 times more network traffic than a data conference with the same number of participants. Before you allow these online conferences, you should have a good idea about your current network load, so start sampling the use of bandwidth some weeks before you deploy ECS. When people start using these conference resources, make sure to monitor the network load carefully. Compare the load with the previous results; this will give you a good estimate of how online conferences affect your production environment.

If you have clients connecting over slow network connections, such as 28.8Kbps lines, or a number of clients sharing a low bandwidth link, such as 64Kbps, you should configure the resources to use the most effective codec algorithms:

- *Video conferences*—Use this type of conference resource rarely; configure it to use QCIF video with GSM 6.10 audio compression. Avoid pre-Windows 2000 clients if possible, since they require the H.323 Bridge module. If you have more than one Windows 2000 site, set up MADCAP and configure IP Multicast.
- *Data conference*—This is the preferred conference type of these two. You don't have much to configure for this type of conference, except to keep the number of participants down to a minimum.

For network scenarios where all clients and servers enjoy 10Mbps or higher, and all computers are running Windows 2000 or later, you could set these configurations to achieve the best quality:

- *Video conference*—Don't allow more participants than necessary; configure the video resources to use CIF for larger and better pictures, and G.711 for best audio quality. Don't allow H.323 bridging. Configure MADCAP if you have more than one site.
- *Data conference*—Set the number of allowed participants according to your organization's need; don't allow more than necessary.

Use Decision Tree 18.1 to guide you in configuring these virtual conference room resources.

Log Files in ECS

The log files that ECS can generate from different modules can give you a lot of information that indicate the use of this conferencing server and its resources. If you use this information regularly, you will be able to estimate whether a new MCU is needed or if some virtual conference rooms are never used, and so on. As described in the previous sections, two objects generate log information:

- *Data Conferencing Provider*—These files are named DCSyyymmdd.log (see Step 8).
- *Conference Management Service*—These files are named CMSyyymmdd.log (see Step 15).

If you open these log files with a spreadsheet program, such as MS Excel, it will be much easier to read them. But then comes the next problem—interpreting the different values. By looking into the online help system in Conferencing Manager, you will (after some searching) find several references to these columns and their meanings. Search for the keyword Log; this will match topics such as:

- *Client Connected*—All fields logged when a client connects.

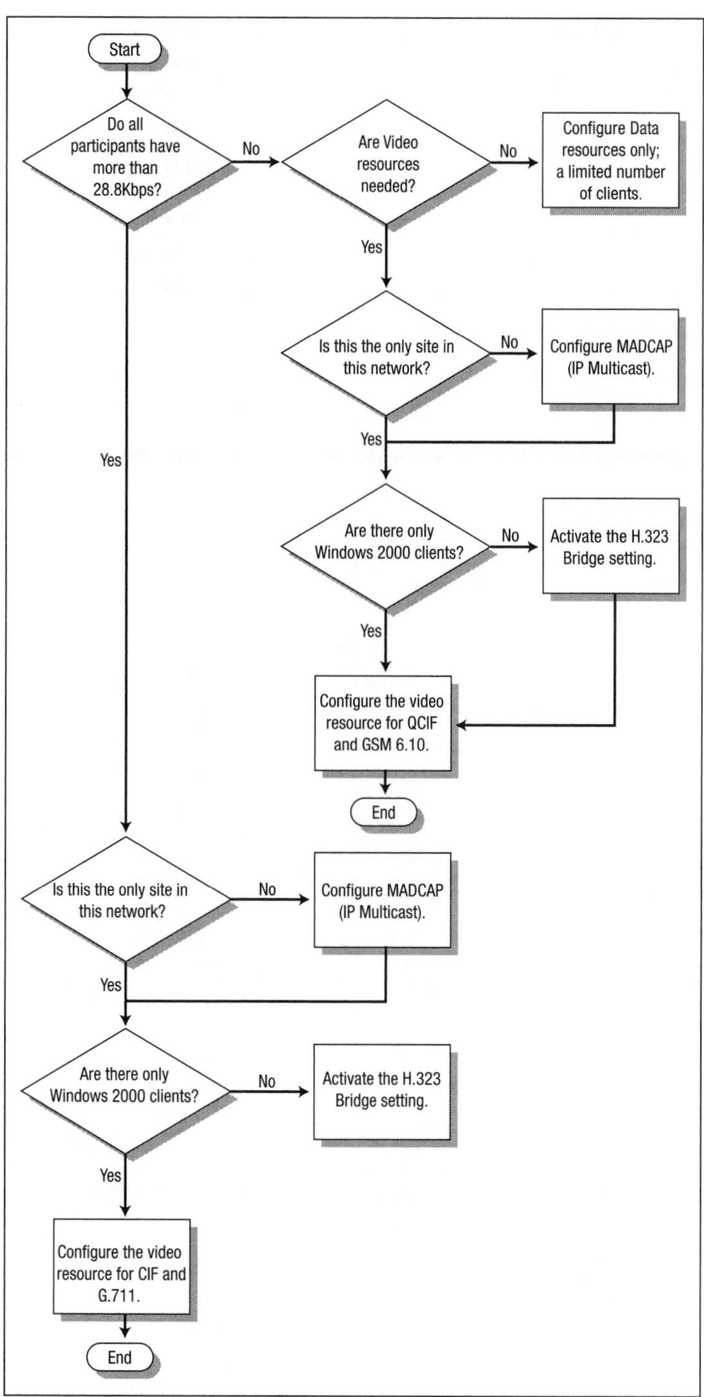

Decision Tree 18.1
Selecting the best configuration for conference resources.

- *Client Connection Denied*—All fields logged when a client was denied access.
- *Conference Started*—All fields logged when the conference started.
- *Conference Stopped*—All fields logged when the conference stopped.

There are 19 different events in total that may be logged. However, the information about the order of these log values is not correct, and some columns don't exist; probably this was changed before Exchange 2000 Conferencing Server was released to the market, but for some reason the help files weren't updated. The correct order of fields in the log files is listed in Table 18.2; note that not all fields are used for all types of events.

Figure 18.15 shows an example of a log file; notice that I have added the header manually. The space on this page doesn't allow for more columns than the first but at least you can get a general idea of how it looks.

Table 18.2 The correct order of fields in the log files.

Field Number	Field Name	Description
1	Event ID	A numerical identifier
2	Message text	A description of the event, such as "Conference started"
3	Event modifier	Complementing description of the "Message Text"
4	Date	The date when the event took place
5	Time	The time when the event took place
6	Conference ID	A numeric conference identifier
7	Meeting ID	A numeric meeting identifier
8	Conference home server	The hostname for the conference server
9	Conference subject	The subject line in the conference invitation
10	Client IP address	The IP address for the client involved in this event
11	Resource mailbox	The O/R address of the virtual conference room
12	Client's computer name	The FQDN name of the client involved in this event
13	Conference organizer's mailbox	The SMTP name of the organizer
14	Number of clients	The number of clients invited to this conference
15	Time (ms)	Time in ms to perform the event described in field 3
16	Private/Public conference	Private=0, Public=1
17	Encrypted communication	Encrypted=0, not encrypted=1
18	Top-node T.120 MCU name	The name of the server hosting the top-node MCU
19	Number of T.120 MCU	The number of the MCU in this conference
20	MCU server name	The name of the server hosting the MCU
21	Remote MCU	The name of the remote MCU
22	Duration	The length of this conference, in minutes

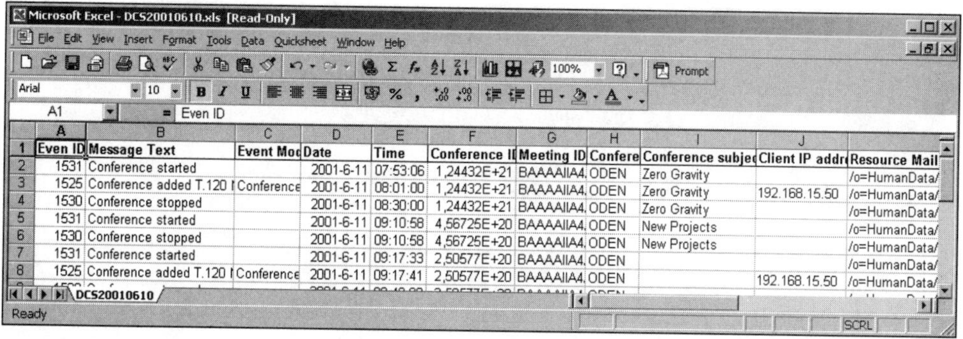

Figure 18.15
Example of a conference log file.

Using Conferencing Server

In this section, I will demonstrate how to work with the Exchange Conferencing Server and its different clients. We assume that we have installed ECS on the server Oden, and that we have Outlook 2000, Outlook ME, and Outlook Web Access clients. We have three virtual conference rooms called Virtual Data Conf (10), Virtual Video Conf (10), and Video and Data Conference (5). The number in parentheses indicates the maximum number of clients for each resource.

How to Book an Online Conference

We start with booking a conference meeting using an Outlook 2000 client that has been configured for Exchange Conferencing with the Registry setting described in the section titled "Configuring Outlook 2000 for Online Conferences." In this example, Anna will book a one-hour data conference meeting by following these steps:

1. Open the Outlook 2000 client and switch to the calendar.
2. Anna selects to create a Meeting Request; she enters the time for the conference and the subject for this invitation. She also adds some extra text in the note field. She sets the This Is An Online Meeting Using checkbox and selects Microsoft Exchange Conference.
3. Next she opens the Attendee Availability tab. Anna wants Göran and Suzan to participate in this meeting, so she enters their names in the All Attendees field. She can directly see their Free/Busy time and see that there is no time conflict.
4. Anna clicks Invite Others, locates the resource named Virtual Data Conf (10), and adds this as a resource to this meeting. Then she clicks OK.
5. The invitation is now ready (see Figure 18.16). Anna clicks Send.
6. Immediately a dialog box appears that confirms that the booking of this resource has been successful; she will also get a confirmation from the Virtual Data Conf (10)

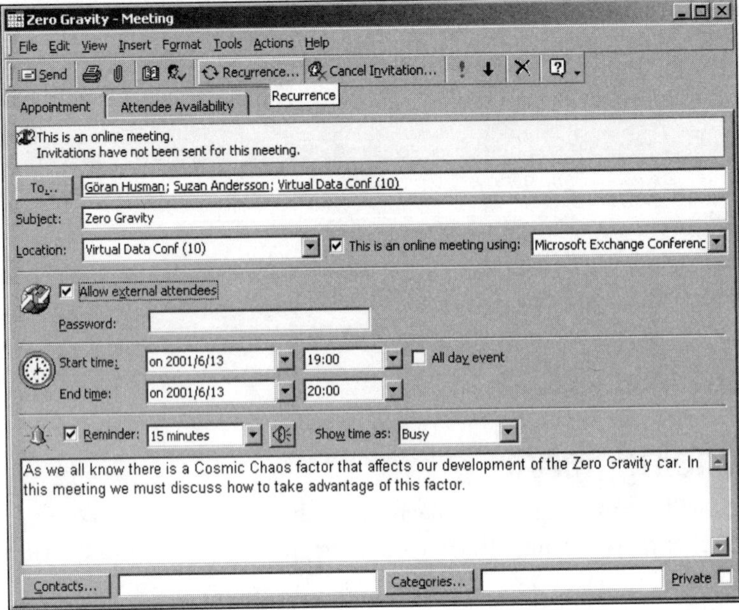

Figure 18.16
The conference meeting invitation.

resource, with a URL to the Web site where the conference will take place. The invitation to Göran and Suzan will contain the same URL.

During the next few hours, Anna receives confirmations from Göran and Suzan. Everything is now ready for the online data conference to start. If Anna had another client instead of Outlook 2000, such as Outlook 97 or Outlook Web Access, she would have done the same thing, except that she would not have seen the This Is An Online Meeting Using option.

Joining an Online Conference

A few minutes before the data conference actually starts, Göran and Suzan receive reminders about this online meeting. If they also have Outlook 2000 that is conference enabled, they will see an extra button saying Join Conference. Or they can click the URL in the invitation received from Anna. A third method would be to open the conference home page; it's usually the server hostname plus the virtual directory named Conferencing—for example, **http://oden.humandata.se/conferencing**. Whatever method is used, it will join the user's Web browser to the conference; the picture would look something similar to Figure 18.17.

In the right pane of this window, you can see the tool buttons. This is a short description of them:

- *Share an application*—With this button, a user can share any active program on his or her computer with all the other participants of this meeting. It's also possible to let any

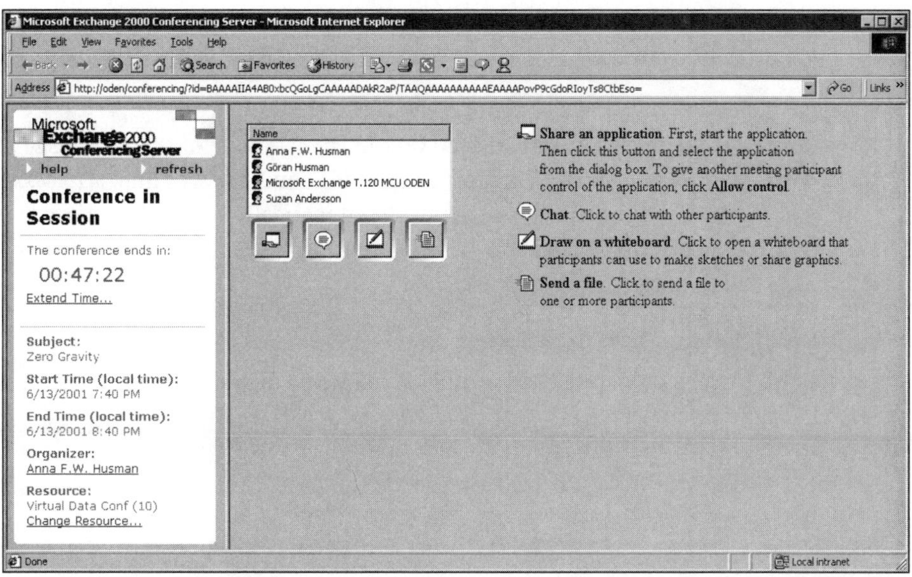

Figure 18.17
Example of a data conference.

other user take control of this application, and work with it as if this user was sitting in front of the remote computer. This is a very powerful feature, perfect for demonstrations, support cases, or just simply to collaborate. For example, assume that Anna has a draft document on her MS Word application; instead of sending it out, she shares it with the others. Suzan then requests control, which Anna grants her, and Suzan can directly make modifications to this document, again which everyone else can see. However, only one person at a time can have control.

- *Chat*—This is a traditional text chat feature. You can't paste any images into this chat, and you don't need to; you have the whiteboard feature for that. You can have a public chat (everyone will see your text), or you can have a private chat with a participant. This is a nice feature when you want to send a private question or comment to one particular participant but you don't want everyone else to see it. After the chat has ended, you have an opportunity to save the complete chat conversation.
- *Whiteboard*—This is like a shared Paintbrush application, but all participants can see and work with it simultaneously. If they all select a different color, it will be much easier to see who has done what.
- *Send a file*—This feature makes it possible to send any file to all participants or to a particular person.

All of these features are well-known to NetMeeting users; in fact, this Web application utilizes the users' local NetMeeting clients to perform these features. This is also very clear if you look at the list of participants; these names are taken from the NetMeeting user profile. For example, if you borrow a computer for joining a conference, and log on to Windows 2000 with your own user account, it will still be the name listed that is defined in NetMeeting!

The organizer of the meeting has a special link in the left pane of this Web page that the others don't have: Extend Time. This can be used to request more time, if necessary. If the time following this meeting is free, you will automatically be granted this extension, assuming that the extension is enabled on the Conference Settings tab for the Default-First-Site-Name Conferencing Site object.

Joining a Video and Data Conference

You can also invite a conference resource that allows a video conference, or even both a video and data conference. You join these conferences exactly the same way as described in the previous steps, but the layout of the conference Web page will be different. For example, in Figure 18.18, you can see what a video and data conference looks like when a

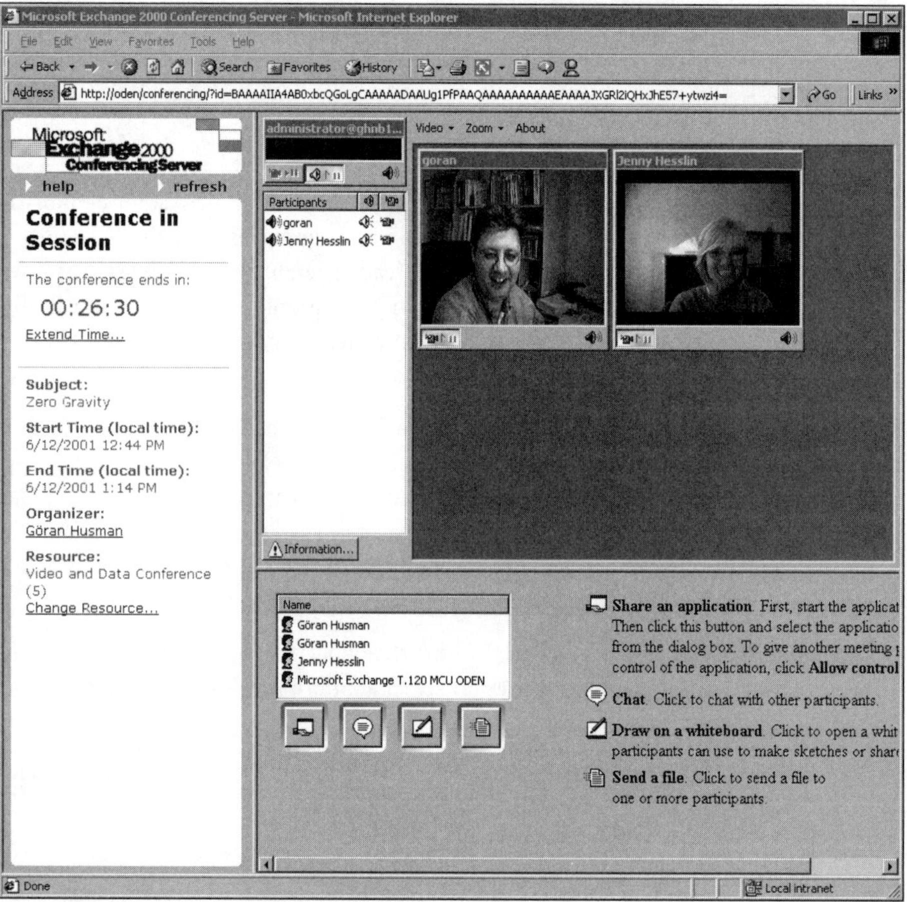

Figure 18.18
A data and video conference on a Windows 2000 client.

participant is running a Windows 2000 client. In this example, we have only two participants and we can see both video pictures; however, if there had been more video clients, we would also see their video pictures here. Notice also that the data conferencing features, such as chat and whiteboard, are available at the bottom of this picture.

If any of the participants uses a non-Windows 2000 client, such as Windows ME or Windows 98, they will not be able to see more than two pictures, regardless of how many participants there are (see Figure 18.19). The reason is that pre-Windows 2000 clients don't support TAPI 3.

Joining a Conference from the Internet

It is also possible to join a conference from outside the firewall, such as Internet clients. But a few things have to be prepared for this to work. First, let me tell you the bad news—don't expect to use video conferences over firewall connections! For this to work, the firewall must be configured to allow all incoming ports over 1023; not many security administrators accept that. An alternative is to place a conference server on the Demilitarized Zone (DMZ) segment, and configure the firewall between the internal network and the DMZ to accept all incoming ports over 1023 from this particular server. The firewall must also accept all ports over 1023 from the Internet clients to this conference server on 18

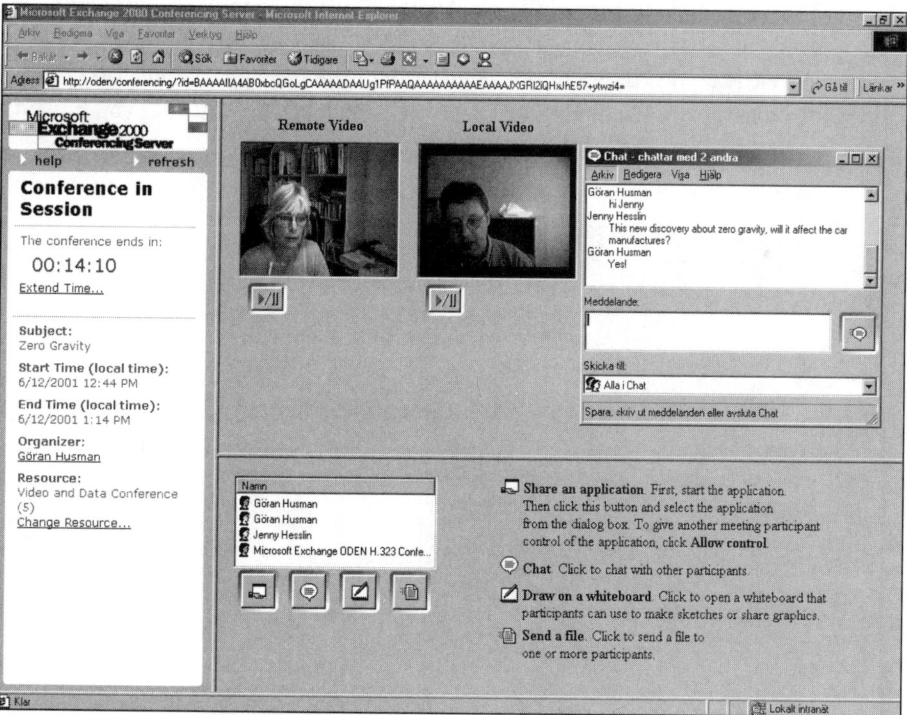

Figure 18.19
A data and video conference on a pre-Windows 2000 client.

the DMZ; however, this is a solution that at least some security administrators can accept. A third solution is to set up a Virtual Private Network (VPN) connection from the client to the internal network; then all ports will be available, regardless of where this client may be situated.

The problem with clients that connect over firewalls is the port they use. Data conference clients and video and audio conference clients use different ports:

- *Data conference*—This resource will use the T.120 MCU communication; T.120 uses TCP port 1503 from client to server. Make sure to open this port for incoming traffic to allow data conferencing.
- *Video and audio conference*—This resource uses two ports, first TCP 1720 for video (H.323), and then TCP 1731 for audio. However, these ports are used only for establishing a connection between the server and the client; after this, a dynamic TCP port randomly selected over 1023 is used. For more information about these ports, see TechNet article Q158623: How to Establish NetMeeting Connections through a Firewall.

Okay, so you have decided to stick with data conferencing only for Internet clients. What else do you have to do? There is one more thing. The URL that invited participants assumes local clients only. You can see this on the URL; it will begin with something like "http://oden/conferencing/id=ABAdb…" Clearly it will be hard to find this server Oden from a client over the Internet. It doesn't help if the client adds an entry to his or her own local host's file either, since that will only solve half of the problem. When this client actually finds the conferencing Web page, it will not see anything. This is what you must do:

1. Open the Conferencing Manager.

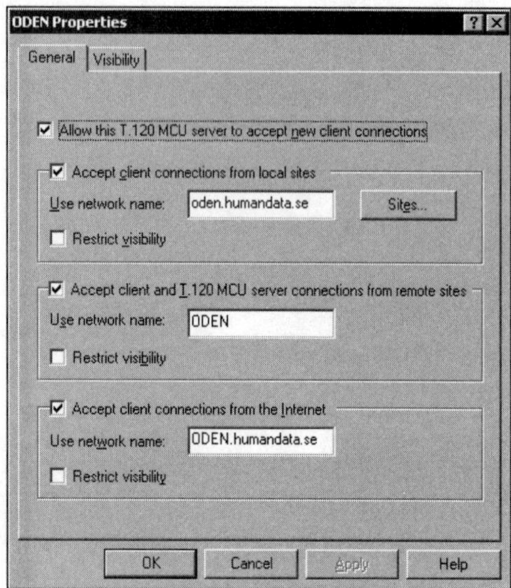

Figure 18.20
The General page for the ECM server.

2. Right-click on Exchange Conferencing and select Managing; then select the Windows 2000 site where your ECS is installed. Here we assume it's the Default First-Site-Name Conferencing site.
3. Click the Data Conferencing Provider folder; you will see the server name of the ECS in the right pane.
4. Right-click that server name and select Properties.
5. On the General page (see Figure 18.20), set the Accept Client Connections From The Internet option and enter an FQDN name to the ECS server. You can also decide to restrict the visibility for Internet clients, if needed; if so, set this checkbox, switch to the Visibility tab, and add the IP address for the clients who are allowed to see and join the conference.

Summary

This is a list of the more important features and keywords mentioned in this chapter. Use it as a reminder and to make sure you have understood the most important things:

- NetMeeting is an application for online conferencing; it has support for video, audio, chat, whiteboard, sending files, and sharing applications.
- NetMeeting can display video pictures from only one person other than the user himself; however, the other features can be shared with a number of users.
- Since the client who initiates the NetMeeting session will also be the conferencing host, all communication between the participants will pass through this computer.
- All information in a NetMeeting session is sent separately to each participant; this greatly increases the network load, especially for video meetings.
- Exchange 2000 Conferencing Server (ECS) takes the responsibility of hosting online conferences; this unloads the burden from the clients.
- ECS has all the features that NetMeeting has, but is much more effective regarding network traffic; you can also set up any number of simultaneous conferences.
- A user can join multiple conferences at the same time; this is not possible with a NetMeeting conference.
- ECS allows a meeting organizer to schedule a conference; ECS will take care of the initial negotiations when connecting clients.
- ECS allows the users to use a Web browser for participating in a conference.
- ECS allows by default two types of conferences: video (with audio) and data conferences.
- A video conference lets all participants use a Web camera to display video pictures of themselves to everyone else; it also allows everyone to talk using their microphone. This feature is very similar to an ISDN video conference.

- A data conference allows the user to share chat, a whiteboard, an application, and to send files to each other—identical to the features of NetMeeting.
- The video and data modules in ECM are known as Conference Technology Providers (CTPs). Besides the two that come with ECM, any third-party vendors can add their own.
- An ECS always belongs to a Windows 2000 site; this is known as the conferencing site.
- Online conferences are bandwidth intensive, especially video conferences.
- Video and audio signals must be compressed before you can transfer them; this is done by Coder/Decoder (codec), which consists of mathematical algorithms.
- ECS allows the administrator to configure the video CTP for Common Intermediate Format (CIF) with 352×288 pixels, or Quarter CIF (QCIF) with 176×144 pixels.
- Video codecs are: H.261 (high quality and high bandwidth) and H.263 (lower quality but acceptable for 28.8Kbps connections).
- Audio codecs are: GSM 6.10 (medium quality, low bandwidth) and G.711 (high quality and high bandwidth).
- ECS uses Microsoft's and Intel's Telephony Application Programming Interface (TAPI) version 3.
- Only Windows 2000 clients and servers have support for TAPI 3.
- Normal Internet video conference format is H.323; TAPI 3 is more effective.
- Pre-Windows 2000 clients, such as Windows 9x, ME, and NT 4, only have support for H.323.
- To allow H.323 clients to join ECS conferences, a H.323 bridge must be activated; by default it's not activated.
- Data conferences use T.120 Multipoint Control Units (MCUs) that control this type of network traffic.
- QCIF uses 80 to 120Kbps per user; CIF uses up to four times that much.
- G.711 uses 70Kbps per user; GSM 6.10 uses 20Kbps per user.
- Multicast Address Dynamic Client Allocation Protocol (MADCAP) must be configured in Windows 2000 if IP Multicast is to be used between sites.
- IP Multicast allows broadcast of video and audio signals, instead of sending the information one time per user; this will reduce the network load to a fraction.
- The Conferencing Manager (CM) is the management tool for ECM; it's an MMC snap-in that can be installed separately on any Windows 2000 computer.

- Hardware and software requirements for installing an ECS server are surprisingly modest; however, be prepared that if you accept thousands of users, you will need a separate server without Exchange 2000 or similar programs.
- The client must be Windows 2000 or later in order to take full advantage of all the features that ECS can offer for video conferences.
- Pre-Windows 2000 clients must download NetMeeting 3.01 or later before they can join an ECS conference.
- The first time the Web client connects to the conference, two ActiveX components are downloaded and installed. They can also be preinstalled.
- Windows 2000 clients must add a Registry key to activate all hidden features for Exchange Conferencing.
- The information about log files is not completely correct in the Help Files; see Table 18.1 for more information.
- Before an online conference can start, you must create virtual conference rooms; they are also known as conference resources.
- You can create a virtual data conference room, a virtual video conference room, or a virtual conference room that has both video and data capacity.
- Each virtual conference room has a limit on how many simultaneous clients it will access; when you create such a room, don't allow more users than necessary.
- Use a name standard for the virtual conference rooms that makes it easy for the user to understand what services it offers and how many users it will allow.
- All virtual conference rooms are listed in the global address list; when you invite people to an online conference meeting, you also invite the virtual conference room as a resource.
- To join a conference, a user can a) click the Join Conference button on the reminder dialog box, b) click the URL received in the invitation, or c) connect their Web browser to the conferencing home page.
- Joining clients from the Internet can be tricky, especially to video conferences. However, data conferences are a bit easier; open the TCP port 1503 on the firewall and configure the ECS server to accept calls from the Internet.
- To allow external clients to video conferences, you could a) open all ports over 1023, b) set up the ECS server on the DMZ segment, or c) connect the client over a VPN tunnel.

Chapter 19

Exchange 2000 and .NET

This chapter discusses Microsoft's new vision of the Internet and how to make the infor-mation in it more easily available to both users and applications. The basic idea Microsoft has is very interesting and attractive, although it might take some time for the average user to understand what Microsoft has in mind. This new vision is called *.NET* (pronounced dot net), and started as a new project during the summer of 2000. It will affect almost every product that Microsoft develops and will take at least two years to complete. The effect that .NET will have on Exchange 2000 is very slight, which is why so little about Exchange 2000 server appears in this chapter; however, this could change as new systems like HailStorm enter the arena. To help you understand what .NET is, I will use several examples of some common problems, and describe how .NET could be used to solve them.

The Problem with Information on the Internet

In this section, I've described three common types of problems with finding the right information; we will refer to these examples later on.

Example 1: Looking for Calendar Information

You are planning a meeting sometime next week with two important customers. How can you find a time that is acceptable for all three participants? You would probably use the phone, or email, or both, to communicate with them and after a day or two, you finally find a time slot that is available for everyone.

Wouldn't it be nice if you could check these two customers' free/busy calendar information directly from Outlook, even though they belong to completely different network systems, and maybe even use a mail system other than Exchange?

Example 2: Looking for a Nearby Garage

The same day this meeting is supposed to take place, your car breaks down on your way to the office. Luckily, you have plenty of time before the meeting starts, so you call for help. However, this is an unfamiliar area of the city; you don't know if there are any repair shops nearby that are authorized to work on your car. What do you do? You call the dealer where you bought the car and ask them for advice; they give you a phone number of a shop, but when you call the number, they don't have time to help you. You call the dealer again, and hopefully this time you get a phone number to a garage that can help you.

Instead of calling the dealer, imagine that you could use a magic wireless device and search for all the repair shops located within two miles of your current position. You could not only get the company names, but you could also find out their opening times, prices, and other relevant information.

Example 3: Looking for Consulting Partners

You actually made it to the meeting, and it was a good meeting, too. However, now you need to find an email consulting company that can assist you in this new project with these two customers; this company must have certain qualifications and areas of expertise. So how can you find this company? You probably wait until you have arrived back at the office again, and then you start asking your colleagues for tips and searching the Internet. You end up finding 253 companies that offer email consulting services; which one do you select? You need to connect to each consulting company that looks promising. (What is promising? A nice business name, or the fact that they are located near your office?) A week later, you have extracted information from the 10 most promising consulting companies and constructed a nice Excel spreadsheet for easy comparison. You show it to your boss, and she says no! You must check at least five more consulting companies. This will take you another week to do. Now your customers start calling you and asking when you're starting the project that you so boldly promised them you'd have up and running within a week. Wouldn't it be nice if you had an application that not only could look up the interesting Web sites for you, but also extract exactly the information you need and present it directly in a spreadsheet?

Analyzing the Problem

All three of these examples have one thing in common—you are looking for information, information that you need fast, right now. This is an everyday life situation for knowledge workers, right? This is what we get paid for! Or is it? I don't think our employers would agree; they don't like to pay us money for searching the Internet for information that we need to do our job—they think that we should know everything already (a bit unrealistic, yes; but that's the advantage to being a boss). But still this is often how work is done today.

So what's the problem, really? I would say that it is to find exactly the information you need, not other types of information that may be just remotely related. Take the situation where you scan the Internet for information, for example using AltaVista, Yahoo!, or similar search engines. The problem is not just to find a match, but to find exactly the right match. And the information you find using AltaVista will not necessarily be the same as you would find using Yahoo! So to be sure, you have to search using several search engines. Or you could purchase smart search applications such as Copernic (**www.copernic.com**) that help you search a number of search engines (see Figure 19.1). They help you find more information, but you still have to analyze each match to see if it's what you are looking for.

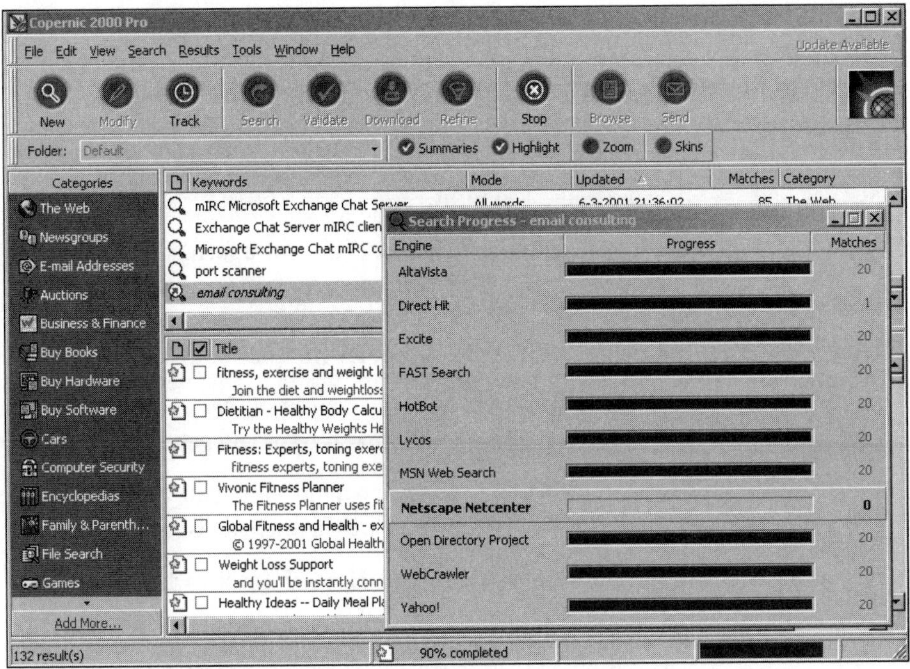

Figure 19.1
Smart Internet search applications.

Even when you have found the right Web site, you still have to search the site for the exact information you need. If you need to compare information found in these different Web sites, you have to manually copy the information to an Excel spreadsheet. This takes time, it's error prone, and it's just plain boring.

For example, assume we found fifteen Web sites that match the consulting profile we are look-ing for in Example 3; now the real labor starts. You have to read the documents on all fifteen Web sites to find the information you are looking for, such as a) if they are an email consulting company that Microsoft recommends, b) their hourly rate, and c) their geographical location.

What We Want

The old rock group Queen has a song in which they sing "We want it all, and we want it now!" This summarizes fairly well what we want, but it's not completely accurate. We want instant access to all the information we are interested in. But this is not what we get when we search the Internet today. Instead, we get what the Web designers of the Web sites anticipated that we are interested in. For example, assume you want to look up a phone number to a company; you connect to their Web site, and on their Contact Us page you find their phone number, address, fax number, and so on. Wouldn't it be perfect if we could just ask this Web site for the phone number and it returned that, and only that?

XML in Springfield

Let's assume that the Internet God and Homer Simpson meet in Springfield one sunny day, and Homer starts asking questions about the Internet:

Homer:	Why do you get me all this information when I search the Internet?
Internet God:	Because you asked for it.
Homer:	But I only wanted a tiny piece of all that information!
Internet God:	Sorry, you get it all, or you get nothing.
Homer:	But this is the Internet world, for Internet God's sake. Can't you fix it?
Internet God:	Well, since Web sites basically consist of files, and your Web client is designed to read those files, that is what you get.
Homer:	I have an idea! Can't you design a model that all Web sites will use to store their data? I mean, you are the Internet God, aren't you?
Internet God:	What have you been drinking, Homer? Exactly what do you mean?
Homer:	I mean that all the data on a Web server is stored in a structure that makes it possible to request just one piece of data, not all.
Internet God:	Like a tree structure, you mean?
Homer:	Yeah! For example, if I want the phone number, I look under the branch Contact Information.
Internet God:	Okay, I see. But how would you know what this tree structure looks like? I mean, a Web site for **Amazon.com** looks very different from NASA's Web site.
Homer:	I know! We let each Web site create their own tree. If we can download this tree to our client, or at least traverse it, we can find what we're looking for.
Internet God:	Clever boy, Homer. But then we must also have a common language for working with this tree structure. Wait, I know, let's call it XML! That sounds kind of high tech, don't you think?
Homer:	Absolutely! All software nerds will love this. Then let's call this tree structure the *XML schema*; that's cool.
Internet God:	Sure! Now, go eat some donuts, Homer. I've got work to do. Bye.

A Truer XML Story

Okay, so maybe the development of the Extensible Markup Language (XML) and its schema structure didn't exactly happen the way I've described here, but the purpose of XML is fairly correctly described. XML is a subset of the Standard Generalized Markup Language (SGML), which was released in 1986 as an ISO standard for describing structured documents regarding content and format. With SGML, it was possible to create a complex document in one word processor, and import it with all attributes preserved in another. When the World Wide Web Consortium (W3C) released version 1 of XML in October 2000, it was based on the same idea: to make it possible to share information between different programs. However, XML focuses on Web documents, making it possible for a Web client to understand every individual piece of information in an XML document received from a Web server.

If all Web servers had XML schemas that described what data they contained, it would be fairly easy for the Web client to extract just the information you are interested in. It's important to understand that the schema for one Web site can, and most likely will, look very different from the schema in another Web site; in fact, different documents on the same Web site may have different XML schemas. So what we have here is a language (XML) to describe the structure of Web documents, and a tree structure that makes it possible to understand what type of information exists on this Web document (the XML schema).

You may wonder what the difference is between XML and Hypertext Markup Language (HTML). The important difference is that HTML is a language with a fixed set of tags—for example, **<H1>** always means a first-level heading. However, XML doesn't have any prefixed tags; the producer of the document is free to invent any tags he or she wants. And this is why we need XML schema, to get a description of the tags used in the XML document. This will give us the following possibilities:

- *Format*—The client can download an XML document and adjust the format to the capability of our browser; for example, an Internet Explorer 5 in Windows 2000 has very different capabilities than a Wireless Application Protocol (WAP) mobile phone.
- *Single items*—The Web client can look for a particular type of data in this document, and ignore the rest.

How XML Solves Some of Our Problems

Do you remember the three examples at the beginning of this chapter? Let's see how XML and its schema can be used to solve at least some of the problems listed there.

XML and Example 1

In this example, the problem was to find information about customers' free and busy time slots. All the information we needed was stored in the customers' calendar systems. This is usually not information that is provided publicly on a Web server, so XML cannot help us with this. We must find another solution to this; more about this later.

XML and Example 2

Here the problem is to find the addresses and phone numbers of nearby garages that are authorized to fix our car. This is information that you can find on the Internet. If these garages have XML-based Web sites, we can use a Web client with XML capabilities to search for these garages, and once we've found them, we can use the XML schema to look up their tags for geographical location, working hours, and phone number. This is a great improvement over a traditional search process.

But in this example, we don't have a PC connected to the Internet; all we have is our mobile phone. If it has support for WAP, we could browse, although it's very time-consuming to search the Internet with this type of device. Another question is how our Web client will know what type of data we are looking for (i.e., the phone number and address); clearly this is not something you can define in an ordinary search in AltaVista. The conclusion is that a search of this type is technically possible to do, but we need to have much more sophisticated Web clients.

XML and Example 3

The problem in this example is similar to Example 2: to find a number of Web sites that match certain search criteria, and when found, to extract just some of the information, such as the company name, address, area of expertise, and hourly rates. We would also like to get all this data directly presented in a spreadsheet. Again, XML and its schema make it possible to create this type of advanced search tool, but no such tools are publicly available today.

Conclusions

With XML and its schema, we have come a long way forward to the scenario where a Web client application can extract single data items from a Web server, instead of presenting the complete document to the user. We must not forget that XML is a very new standard, and it will take some time before Web designers and programmers learn how to use it, both for presenting data with a Web server and for retrieving data with a Web client.

XML is just a language; it is not a communication service. Microsoft and Userland Software have developed a protocol for communicating between two applications over the Internet. This is known as Simple Object Access Protocol (SOAP), and it has been proposed to the Internet Engineering Task Force (IETF) as a standard. SOAP utilizes HTTP, which in turn uses TCP/IP for the physical transportation of data.

One important feature of XML, SOAP, and HTTP is that they're software and vendor independent. You could use them between an Apache Web server and a Unix server and Internet Explorer on a Macintosh computer, on a Compaq iPAQ personal digital assistant (PDA), or even on a smart mobile phone; it doesn't have to be a Microsoft product.

It is clear that XML is the fundamental building block needed for transferring data between all types of applications over the Internet; but it's just a start. We also need smart applications and smart devices. And this journey has just begun. This is what Microsoft's .NET strategy is about—to make all their applications XML aware, in order to be able to send out data to other applications requesting them, or retrieve data from other XML-based sources on the Internet.

Microsoft's .NET Strategy

The journey that Microsoft has started can now simply be described as a shift to distributed computing, instead of the centric server-based concept we all use today. This is actually not a new idea; Oracle's CEO Larry Ellison and Sun Microsystems's CEO Scott McNealy tried around 1997 to introduce the concept of *software-as-a-service* during the age of network computer hype. But they failed, mostly because they could not deliver anything substantial on this concept, and their vision was more of centralized-only resources. However, Microsoft followed these discussions very closely and saw not only the strength in this concept, but also why Oracle and Sun failed to implement it. This was probably the birth of the .NET strategy at Microsoft.

One of the most important prerequisites for distributed computing is a fast connection to the Internet. In 1997, only a few companies actually had a leased line to the Internet, and even fewer had a line faster than 256Kbps. Today we are getting close to a situation where it is possible for most companies in industrialized countries to get fast Internet connections at acceptable prices. Another prerequisite is computer power; following Moore's Law, which states that computer power doubles every 18 months and prices are halved, enough users now have access to the computer power needed for distributed computing and are connected to the Internet.

A number of applications on the Internet already use this distributed computing concept, such as chat clients, NetMeeting, and Napster. However, they are all very focused on one single task, or at least on a very narrow area; they also have their special communication protocols that sometimes even make it impossible to use other vendors' products, such as the different IRC implementations found in the established chat networks. In Microsoft's .NET vision, all of its applications use distributed computing over XML and SOAP, making it possible to communicate with any other vendor that follows the same communication standard.

The Influence of .NET

Microsoft has already spent billions of dollars in research and development related to .NET and distributed computing, and more investments will be made. Microsoft expects the following results from all this research:

- *Development platform*—A new platform for software development that is Internet centric, using XML and SOAP for communicating with other programs.
- *Smart devices*—The development of more advanced and intelligent applications in any type of device, such as mobile phones, personal digital assistants, car computers, TV sets—everything that will be able to communicate with other programs over the Internet one way or the other.
- *User agents*—Intelligent applications that learn what you are interested in and keep you updated in these areas. This type of agent is also smart enough to search the Internet for other sources of this information.
- *Smart applications*—All Windows applications, such as MS Exchange 2000 and MS SQL 2000, will allow clients to retrieve information that they have been granted access to, even from an external Internet client.

.NET as an Internet Platform

Before it's possible to build this marvelous world, programmers must have the means and tools for implementing .NET and XML in their applications. Microsoft is not only enhancing all its products to be .NET compliant, it is also creating a rich set of software development tools and utilities that will help guide the programmer in this new world.

On the outside, .NET may look like one single system, but on the inside it's actually two new and different programming models:

- *Web service*—This is basically what we talked about in our examples so far in this chapter. With the new Web service programming model, applications will expose their data and services to other programs, using HTTP, XML, and SOAP. For example, Exchange 2000 can share the user's free/busy calendar information with authorized Internet users.
- *System programming*—The .NET will also consist of a new Microsoft proprietary system programming model. This new model will slowly replace the current Component Object Model (COM) and the traditional Windows application programming interface (API).

Microsoft has also developed an enhanced version of the traditional Windows programming language C++ that will simplify developing .NET applications. This new version is labeled C# (pronounced C sharp).

The .NET Experience

Microsoft has a new slogan it calls the ".NET Experience." This focuses on how the users will experience the new .NET environment. It will be a dramatically more personal, integrated computing experience using connected XML Web services with their personal smart devices. The experience can be divided into three levels:

- *Personal and integrated experience*—With the new .NET-enabled personal smart devices, every user can view exactly what they are interested in; this could be information collected from multiple XML Web services.
- *Connected XML Web services*—Every user creates an interest profile that describes what type of information they like to view and what information they allow the Web servers to get access to. For example, you may not want a server to see your email address or phone number.
- *Interaction with smart devices*—A user experiences .NET through their personal smart devices. These smart devices are .NET-enabled appliances, such as personal computers, personal digital assistants, and smart mobile phones that run software that makes them more intelligent in their interaction with the users, the network, the information, and other services and devices.

To give you an idea of what a .NET experience is, we'll let Homer Simpson once again meet the Internet God at the shopping mall in Springfield:

Internet God: Hello, Homer. How are you today?

Homer: Hi! I'm okay, but I have really had a hard day; Mr. Burns fired me again.

Internet God:	I'm sorry to hear that; Mr. Burns is a tough man. But I have been thinking of what we discussed the last time.
Homer:	You mean XML and schema? What about it?
Internet God:	Well, I have developed a completely new system of products, based on the XML and what you can do with it.
Homer:	(eating a doughnut): Sorry, can you say that again?
Internet God:	I said, I invented .NET!
Homer:	What kind of strange name is that? .NET! How can it help me?
Internet God:	Here, test this new smart mobile phone; just press your thumb against its window so it will know it's you, then ask it whatever you like.
Homer:	(after cleaning his thumb, and managing to get authenticated): Okay, so what's the deal here? I don't understand. It says Calendar; okay, let's check the calendar. Cool! It's my personal calendar here! How did it get into this device?
Internet God:	You authenticated yourself, remember? And since it's a smart device, it called your Exchange 2000 server and downloaded your personal data. If you change anything, this will be replicated back to the Exchange server.
Homer:	Incredible! How did it know which Exchange server I use?
Internet God:	Since I'm the Internet God, I have entered this information in your phone. But for average users, they could use a smart card or some similar device that stores all their personal information, and enter this card into the phone.
Homer:	Okay, here's a search tool. Let's see. Find me all the bars within 500 yards from where I'm standing. Cool! It found three bars! Sorry, Internet God, got to go now; see you later!

Smart Tags in .NET

If you're running Office XP, you already have some of the .NET experience features implemented. The feature I will describe here is called *smart tags*—they make it possible for small .NET software agents to scan your text for interesting words. For example, assume that you type *New York* in a document; with this new smart tag, you could directly right-click that city and find out its current weather, or a city map, or something that is related to the city.

Another example of the use of smart tags is flight number recognition. Let's assume that you are writing a document about an upcoming flight trip; when you type the flight number, a smart tag will immediately recognize it. Click the special icon that appears above this flight number and you will see a list of options—for example, a browser opens that gives you full information about this flight, such as departure and arrival times, which terminal to go to, and even the type of aircraft.

Both of these smart tag features require you to install smart tags from third-party vendors (see Step 4 below to see how you do this). You can also test the built-in smart tags that Word and Excel have; for example, type the name of a person and this will be recognized by a standard smart tag that offers you options to send mail to this person, schedule a meeting, and so on; see Figure 19.2.

To activate smart tags in Windows XP and other Office XP products, follow these steps:

1. Open Windows XP.
2. Click the menu Tools|AutoCorrect Options.
3. On the Smart Tags tab (see Figure 19.3), select what Recognizers you want to activate. Note that by default, Person Names, Addresses, and Telephone Numbers will be disabled; make sure to enable them before you try this.
4. You can also download new free or trial versions of third-party vendors of smart tags by clicking the More Smart Tags button. This will open a browser to the Office XP home page, where you can list a number of these smart tags.

Note that some of these smart tags you can download are using macros with expired software certificates; this will make the default security settings of Office XP to disable these macros and therefore this particular smart tag. If you still want to run these smart tags, you must change the security setting of your Office XP to a Medium level; I leave it up to you if you think it's worth the risk of doing so or not. To change the security level, follow these steps:

1. Open the menu Tools|Macro|Security.

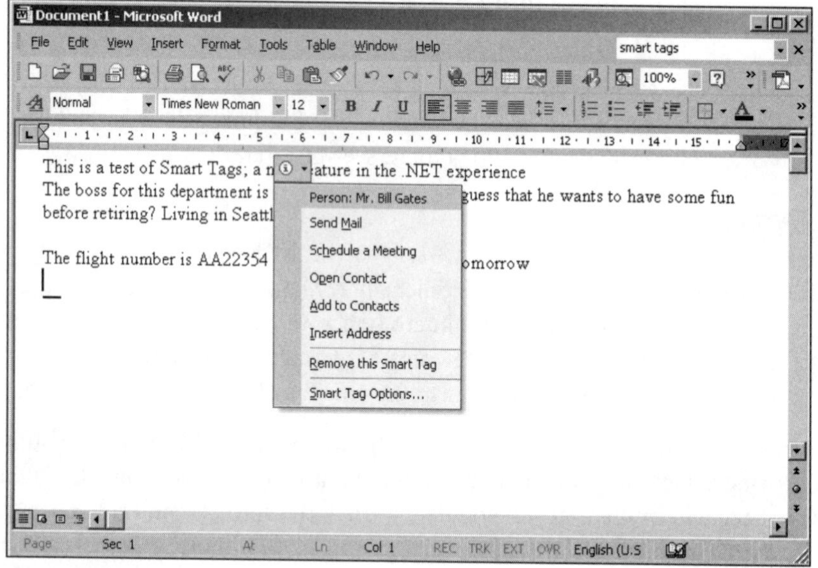

Figure 19.2
An example of smart tags in the .NET experience.

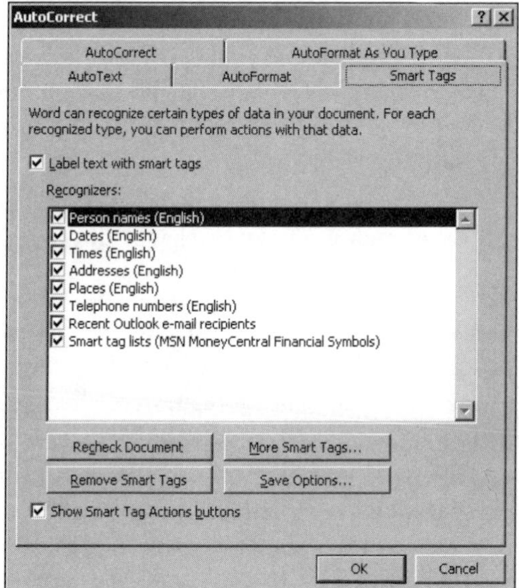

Figure 19.3
The Smart Tags tab for Office XP.

2. Select Medium to be able to choose if you want to run macros or not; the default is High security level, which will prohibit all macros except those signed by trusted sources (see that tab) from being executed; see Figure 19.4.

Sharing Distributed Data

Even this is not new; we have seen several systems that allow data to be distributed over the network. We'll begin with a very early example, a file system. Everyone expects their

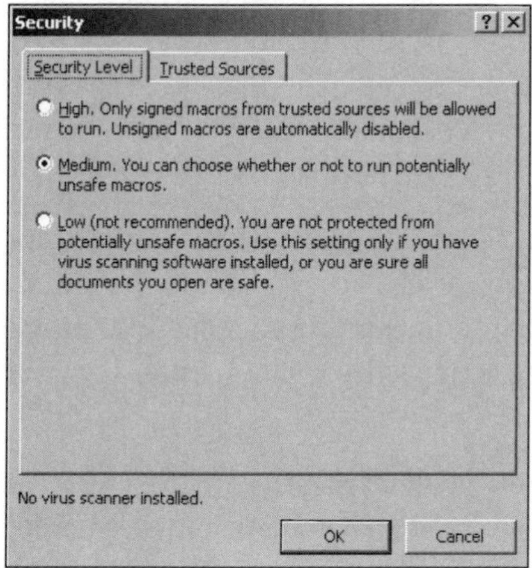

Figure 19.4
Changing the security level in Office XP.

client to be able to use shared disk resources on a network server, regardless of whether they use Windows, Unix, or Novell. Another example is the clipboard; in Windows, it has been possible for many years to share whatever you have on your clipboard with other users on the same network. A third example is Object Linking and Embedding (OLE) documents, such as when an MS Word document includes part of an Excel spreadsheet. This spreadsheet doesn't need to be a local file; it can also be stored on the network. If you select the spreadsheet part of the Word document, Excel menus and features will automatically be displayed instead of Word menus.

These examples have one thing in common—the user utilizes the different features and data objects in other applications. Compare this to how we work with a Web browser; we connect to a Web server, and it sends us the Web document we requested. Then we point to another link, and a new Web document replaces the first. You could say that it's the Web server that's in charge here, not the user. You can't look at multiple Web sites at the same time, unless you use more than one browser. This is one of the fundamental objectives Microsoft has with .NET and XML: to put the user back in charge again. Look at the three examples at the beginning of this chapter; the users have to accept whatever information is in the Web document they are looking at. This is a limitation of the HTML standard; our Web browser works basically as an old IBM 3270 terminal. True, with dynamic HTML and ActiveX components, a Web client can do surprisingly advanced things; just look at the Outlook Web Access 2000 client. However, with XML, it's possible to send data between two applications, not just between a Web client and Web server. And if we are smart when we develop those applications, we will return the control back to the users.

Example of a .NET Application

Here is a simple example of how a .NET application can work, using XML and SOAP as the communication method between two server applications. Assume that you have a small shop that sells spare motorcycle parts. To keep track of these spare parts, you have an inventory program that you update manually when you sell parts and buy new supplies. You also have an accounting system, but it's not connected to the inventory, so you have to enter the same information whenever you sell or buy something. If you are getting short of some parts, you must call the supplier and order some more. All of this is manual work, and all information is entered at least twice.

Now imagine that your inventory program and accounting system both understand XML and use it for transferring data; the next time you sell a part, you update the inventory program, which in turn sends this information to the accounting system. This not only saves you time, but it also reduces the risk of typing errors since you only enter the information once.

Now assume that your suppliers also have XML-compliant ordering systems—then it would be possible to extend your inventory program to send an automatic purchase order whenever the number of spare parts falls below a certain limit. Maybe the supplier's accounting system could even send the invoice by XML to your accounting program; as you can see, the possibilities are almost endless.

Security in the .NET World

Yes, I can hear you screaming: What about security? And you are right; if we are able to view more information wherever we are, and whatever device we use, how can we protect our privacy? The security problem could be divided into two parts:

- *Authentication*—How can we be assured that only the authenticated user will be able to work with this information?
- *Transport security*—How can we trust that no one can eavesdrop on our communications?

Authentication in the .NET World

In our current world, we protect our data with passwords, and the fact that our data isn't all stored in one place. For example, if you managed to crack the password used in my company network, you would be able to access all the information in that environment. However, you would not see mail conversations in my Hotmail accounts, and you wouldn't be able to check my Internet bank account because that data is stored in another server environment.

But if Microsoft succeeds in their .NET attempt, we will be able to access all our information using a smart device and the .NET experience, regardless of where this data is stored. So in fact we are more vulnerable in this brave new world. This means that we need far better authentication methods than just a single password. To be honest, this has not been completely solved yet. One suggestion is that we all get a personal smart card, maybe complemented with a biosensor, such as a fingerprint scanner. This smart card would also contain all the information about ourselves, such as name, social security number, birth date, gender, and so on. With this information, your smart device will be able to log on to any Web service in the world and authenticate without any assistance from you.

This automatic logon process is a necessary feature if the smart device should be able to collect information from many different sources; this would not be possible if you had to enter a password for each of these Web services. Microsoft has the first version of this logon feature running on its MSN Web site—the *Microsoft Passport* service. However, this passport service today uses a password instead of smart cards; the reason for this is twofold: 1) Not many people have smart cards today, and 2) Computers don't come with built-in support for devices like smart cards yet. These problems are related and will be fixed over time.

Secure Transport with .NET

The other security problem that we must solve is to protect the data that is transferred over the network and to wireless devices. This is still an open question. We have discussed a number of security options in this book, but maybe the final solution will be a combination of them all? Since the .NET experience is about Web-based network traffic, we must be aware that all transport of data is by default unprotected. We have at least two very promising methods:

- *SSL*—We can use standard Secure Socket Layer (SSL) encryption.
- *IPSec*—This is encrypted IP traffic.

Both of these methods protect the complete session with a Web service, both the logon procedure and all subsequent data transfers. However, there will probably be only one method in the future, and I would guess that it's going to be IPSec.

No More Shrink-Wrapped Applications?

One of the great debates about the .NET vision is whether it's a new way of distributing software applications. If you read the press or talk with people in the computer business, you may hear that .NET will make standard shrink-wrapped packages like Word, Excel, and other Microsoft applications go away. Instead, you will use a browser that connects to a .NET server offering Word and Excel services. In a way, that's true—you can do that with the features that .NET offers. But Microsoft would be stupid if it abandoned traditional software distribution and bet the entire company on this new software-as-a-service-only feature, and Microsoft isn't stupid. My personal belief is that .NET will not change the traditional way of deploying standard software applications such as Word and Excel in the corporate environment; companies need control over their own environments, both for management and security reasons. They don't want to rely on an Internet connection for all their clients; imagine what would happen if General Electric suddenly lost contact with the Internet. It's easy to see why organizations would be reluctant to depend solely on distributed computing. Just look at the number of companies that have jumped on the previous bandwagon of thin clients; although distributed computing offers a lot of benefits compared to the traditional client/server environment there are only a few companies that actually are using this computer model today, even though they enjoy the luxury of accessing local servers over a 100Mbps network, instead of an Internet connection to an application service provider (ASP) or similar supplier of software services.

However, when we talk about all those upcoming smart devices that Microsoft expects will show up within a year or two, then it's a different thing. It's not smart to implement large and complex applications such as Word on a smart mobile phone or similar device. You'd be better off using an XML-compliant Web client that has the intelligence to connect to servers on the Internet, using the distributed computing model. So we will probably have two types of access to these applications during the next few years—both locally installed and remotely accessed over the Internet. What will happen then is another question; if we assume that millions of users will have constant high-speed access to the Internet, both with leased-lines and wireless, then it will technically be possible to use a browser for all types of services, from word processing to game playing to viewing video. However, people usually prefer to own things instead of rent them. There have been many attempts in all markets to make people pay for individual uses, but as long as buying still exists as a choice, then people tend to buy.

Don't forget that .NET is much more than just distributed computing. It includes XML enabling of all products, which makes information available to other applications on any type of computer or operating system; the XML Web services, which makes it possible to utilize one particular service out of many on a server product; and the Web enabling of almost every application that Microsoft has. All these features will make it possible to achieve a new level of freedom, including:

- *Location*—You can access your information on any Internet-connected computer.
- *Device*—You can access your information with the new wireless smart devices.
- *Information*—You can access information that is stored on many different servers, regardless of what type of computer, operating system, or computer language is used.
- *Interoperability*—Information can be transferred between heterogeneous systems, such as a Microsoft SQL database and an SAP accounting system.

Exchange 2000 and .NET

So what does .NET have to do with Exchange 2000? Well, as a part of the .NET strategy, all Microsoft applications will be XML aware; or, in this case, the data stored in Exchange 2000 stores can be exposed to Internet clients that know how to use XML. In Microsoft's view, these XML clients will use .NET-compliant applications for maximum utilization of the Exchange server.

Exchange 2000 and a .NET Client

Today, all data in Exchange 2000 can be utilized many different ways, and with many different protocols—for example, MAPI, POP3, IMAP4, and NNTP clients and Web clients using Outlook Web Access—but this is only for your personal use. If you want to check the calendar of another user in the same Exchange organization, you can, as long as you have been granted access by the owner of the calendar. But what if you want to view the free/busy calendar information for a user that belongs to another organization? This is a little tricky, but not impossible. You can publish parts of your free/busy information to a Free/Busy Web Service; this can be a Web server on your local intranet, or it could be a public Web server, such as MSN Free/Busy Web Service.

But with a .NET-compliant Exchange 2000 server, you will be able to let external clients look directly into your free/busy information without having to first publish this to a public Web server. Of course, these external clients must authenticate before accessing this data; you don't want just anyone to see your free/busy information.

Remember the first example in this chapter? We need to be able to access calendar information of users outside our own organization. This problem will cease to exist the day these users are running .NET-enabled mail servers, because then our .NET-enabled Outlook clients will be able to send a request directly to their .NET servers and ask for their free/busy schedule; we wouldn't need to call these external users and ask them to read their calendars, we would be able to do it ourselves.

The Web Store

Microsoft describes the database in a .NET-enabled Microsoft server as a *Web Store*; for example, all the stores in an Exchange 2000 server are referred to as the Web Store. Does that ring a bell? Yes, that's right, you've heard this before. We discussed the Web Store many times in this book when we referred to the M: drive that our Exchange Installable File System (ExIFS) created for us. And this Web Store can communicate using XML over HTTP, since it's under the control of the Internet Information Server (IIS). This is the reason that we can use Outlook Web Access clients. In a way, you could say that OWA 2000, with its XML support, is the first step in a .NET application, but that's not completely true since the OWA application can be used with one Web Store only.

Let's look at the .NET-enabled server products Microsoft offers today:

- *Exchange 2000 Server*—Our beloved mail server.
- *SQL Server 2000*—The SQL database server.
- *BizTalk Server 2000*—Translates and transfers data between applications.
- *Internet Security and Acceleration Server*—A firewall and proxy server.
- *Application Center 2000*—Application management and fault-tolerance.
- *Commerce Server 2000*—Web server analysis and scalability.
- *Host Integration Server 2000*—Translates and transfers data to mainframe systems.
- *Mobile Information 2001*—Allows mobile devices to access .NET resources.
- *SharePoint Portal Server 2001*—Web-based document sharing and workflow.

If you look at these products and imagine they all have a Web Store, similar to what Exchange 2000 offers us, can you see that we are now entering a new era in communication where interoperability and accessibility will reach new highs never possible before? Our .NET clients can easily present today's calendar, the number of available items in your inventory database, and statistics from your commercial Web server, all in one single screen. Regardless of the type of smart device you have, if you change devices, the data will follow you, adapting to the features available in each device. Now that will open up a new world of information access. You, the user, will be served data that's interesting to you, in realtime.

XML Web Services

When the .NET vision was introduced during the summer of 2000, Microsoft also described .NET servers as Web Stores. However, this term wasn't really so descriptive since there was more to this .NET than just exposing data; an XML client can also use these .NET servers to perform specific services exposed by these servers. Now Microsoft likes to talk about XML Web services, of which the Web Store is a subcomponent. This is a new way of looking at servers, compared to the traditional way, in which Exchange was a mail server and SQL was a database server.

For a comparison, take a look at the Windows 2000 operating system itself. It has lots of different features, such as a file system, a graphic system, and a printing system. If an application needs to open a file, it will send a request to the file system; if the application needs to print a file, it will contact the printing system. But we still look at all these features as one system that we call Windows 2000.

Now assume we have an application that needs to find out how many samples we have of a particular item in our inventory database; once we know how many items are available, we need to compare this with the number of hits on the Web site where we sell this particular item. Is the demand high or low? Should we order more items? If so, then our application needs access to the mail system. That involves at least three servers: Exchange 2000, SQL 2000, and Commerce 2000. What XML Web services are all about is that our application should be able to look at all these servers and services as if they were part of a larger system, the .NET system.

One way of looking at XML Web services is to think of them as a universal language. It's important to understand that .NET is not a closed system; Microsoft's .NET-enabled servers will be able to communicate with all other XML applications on the Internet, regardless of what operating system or programming language they use. A very attractive feature of Microsoft's XML Web services is that they allow other XML applications to not only transfer data, but also to invoke capabilities on applications without regard to how these applications were built.

Smart Devices

We have discussed *smart devices* several times now, and mentioned intelligent mobile phones and personal digital assistants as examples. All of these devices can be used to access the inbox and calendars of the user's Exchange 2000 mailbox. But what is it about these devices that make them so smart? Here's what they do:

- *User Smart*—This device will know your preferences. It will use the .NET or the HailStorm account (see the next section) to find out your identity, profile, and personal data. It is also smart about your presence—whether you are logged on, where you are, what type of device you are using, and so on. It will also control any notifications that the .NET (or HailStorm) server might want to send to you.
- *Network Smart*—This device will automatically adjust the information transferred, based on the network bandwidth and the type of Internet connection. It will know whether you are online or offline, and when you are shifting in between.
- *Information Smart*—This device will allow you to access, analyze, and act on data anywhere, anytime. It will get you the information you need, when you need it.
- *Environment Smart*—This device will detect other devices on the network and announce their presence. This will make it possible to understand and utilize other services, if necessary.

- *Service Smart*—This device will collect and present information for this user in the optimal format for this type of device; it can also convert the format of the information, including converting text to speech in mobile phones, or handwriting to text on Tablet PCs and similar devices.

Examples of Smart Devices

Besides the traditional personal computers and notebooks, a number of new and exciting smart devices will be entering the market around 2002 and 2003. Microsoft is also developing some of these devices, which include:

- *Stinger*—The next generation of smart mobile phone.
- *Xbox*—The game console with Internet connections.
- *Pocket PC*—A new generation that is .Net enabled will be released during 2002.
- *Tablet PC*—A personal computer in the form of a book, one inch thick.

The Future of .NET

We Exchange professionals must understand that Exchange is no longer a separate messaging server; it's now part of a much larger system, the .NET. One of the new Microsoft projects that will utilize the .NET-enabled Exchange 2000 server and its XML Web services has the code name *HailStorm*. Previously we talked about the possibility of giving the user control over his or her personal data. HailStorm is the first attempt at actually achieving this.

HailStorm

On March 19, 2001, Bill Gates announced the project HailStorm. This project was designed by Mark Lucovsky, in an attempt to make users' experience of the Internet simpler and more intelligent. No longer should a user have to search for interesting data, or log on every time they access a Web server that requires authentication; data that is interesting will automatically be presented to the user, and a single-logon process will be possible, regardless of what Web server you are contacting. At least, that's the idea.

Even before the computer era began in the 1940s, people had dreamt about an assistant, secretary, or butler who would keep track of important events and information. Whenever something happens that you should be aware of, you would be notified immediately.

This is the ultimate goal for the HailStorm project; but Microsoft calls these programs *agents*. Such an agent will learn what's important to you; for example, if you book a flight, you would probably be interested to know if it has been delayed. Or if you collect Frank Zappa albums, you would probably like to know when a new album is released. Of course, standard features like mail, calendars, and contacts must be available to you at all times. The agent you run on your client will be an XML application, probably a Web browser similar to the MSN Explorer if you are running a personal computer, or a simpler application, maybe even just a script, if you are using a smart mobile phone or a pager.

End-User Experience

HailStorm is all about Web-user experience, not about corporate users accessing local servers on the intranet. HailStorm also allows you to create groups of users; these groups could have special settings that are applied to the individual user. For example, a user who is ordering goods from a Web site may not be able to place orders over a given price limit; or the user may only be allowed to see information on a Web server that this group of users is allowed to see, according to company policies.

Note that nothing in HailStorm controls how organizations run their internal Exchange 2000 servers, or any other internal .NET-enabled server. This is important to remember when discussing HailStorm, especially regarding the subscription fee we suggest in the upcoming section "Making Money on the Internet." However, Microsoft has vaguely suggested that a new project that focuses on organizations' internal network structure might follow HailStorm, but no information is available about that at present.

The average end user often perceives different programs as confusing and hard to understand; for example, each Web server has its own search feature, or authentication procedure, and entering a phone number in the mobile phone is done in a different way from entering a phone number in Outlook contacts. What is worse, the information in one system cannot always be transferred to another system; for example, the phone number in a Palm Pilot can't be transferred to a mobile phone. The reason for all these problems is that each device and program is very often an isolated island. This is also true about Web sites; the information you have entered in Amazon.com can't be copied directly into Hotmail.com—you have to enter the information in each system manually.

HailStorm is Microsoft's attempt to remedy all this. For example, instead of having to log on to every Web server that requires authentication, you can log on once to the Microsoft Passport system, using Kerberos authentication. Then whenever you access a Web server that requires you to authenticate, your client will provide the Web server with a Kerberos ticket, without the user having to do anything. The user will experience this as having instant access to the secure parts of the Web server.

Before this single-logon procedure in HailStorm works, a few prerequisites must be fulfilled:

- *Account*—Each user must create a Microsoft Passport account. This account contains the user's name, address, phone numbers, etc.
- *Web server*—The Web server needs to be HailStorm compliant to use the Passport account for authentication.
- *Client*—The client application must be XML-based.

Each user's preferences and pointers to personal data are stored on a central HailStorm server. That makes it possible to log on to the server, using Microsoft Passport, and still be able to see all your personal information, regardless of what type of .NET device you're using. When you log on, it will also update your presence status, exactly like it does in

Instant Messaging. In fact, presence status is a very important part of this automatic HailStorm world; for example, if you have booked a flight to see your mother, and this flight is delayed, HailStorm can notify your mother, if she is a HailStorm user who happens to be online. How does HailStorm know whom to send this notification to? Simple—when you booked the flight in your calendar, you also invited your mother.

Note that no data is stored on the HailStorm server; your personal preferences and pointers to the .NET servers actually store that data. These servers could be an Exchange 2000 server and a third-party Web server that, for example, send you the latest information about your bank account.

User Privacy

One of the biggest drawbacks with using the Internet is the information we spread around. Do you have any idea how many times you enter information about yourself when using Web servers? It doesn't have to be credit card numbers—it can be innocent information such as your email address. This information can later be used to send you unsolicited commercial messages. The privacy issue has generated an intensive debate, especially in Europe. Currently, Web servers legally own any information they collect about their visitors and are free to do whatever they want with it.

The HailStorm project will change that completely. Now all information will be stored on the Microsoft Passport server instead of individual Web servers. Microsoft has legally agreed not to give away any of this information. The Web servers that participate in the HailStorm system must also follow this rule to be a member; any information that the Web server retrieves during a transaction, such as when the user accesses any of its services, must be deleted when the user logs off. However, if the user wants to allow the Web server to store any personal information locally, they can. The user can also set a limited lifetime for such data storage, if necessary.

The consequence is that personal data about a user is now owned by the user, not by the Web server. The user will have full control of what data a Web server can view, and how long the Web server is allowed to keep that data.

HailStorm Architecture

A user will never see any of the internal workings of HailStorm components; they will just enjoy the simple experience of browsing the Internet. However, for software developers, there will be a lot of new features to understand and learn how to take advantage of. HailStorm is built on .NET-enabled applications, which use XML to describe the data, and SOAP for transferring these XML packets between these applications. Each application, device, or service in this system is called a *HailStorm endpoint*.

The developer can use any type of programming language, operating system, or computer to develop HailStorm applications. All HailStorm services are XML Web services; no Microsoft runtime or tool is required to call them. Of course, Microsoft's development tool Visual Studio .NET will have full support to create HailStorm applications as easily as possible, but it's important to understand that you don't need this tool; it's perfectly okay to use Linux development tools if this is more appropriate.

HailStorm offers a set of core services for the user, such as a calendar, location, and profile information. Any application that uses HailStorm can use this information, saving the user from entering this information more than once. The initial set of HailStorm services includes:

- *myAddress*—The electronic and geographic address for an identity
- *myProfile*—Name, nickname, special dates, picture
- *myContacts*—Electronic relationships and address book
- *myLocation*—Electronic and geographical location and rendezvous
- *myNotification*—Notification subscription, management, and routing
- *myInbox*—Inbox items like email and voice mail, including existing mail systems such as MS Exchange 2000
- *myCalendar*—Time and task management
- *myDocuments*—Document storage for this user
- *myApplicationSettings*—Settings for the user's applications
- *myFavoriteWebSites*—Favorite URLs and other Web identifiers
- *myWallet*—Records of receipts, payment instruments (such as credit cards), coupons, and other transaction records
- *myDevice*—Settings for devices, including their capabilities
- *myServices*—The services provided for a user
- *myUsage*—Usage report for the services above

HailStorm is designed to work with all types of XML-enabled devices. It looks and feels like a dynamic, partitioned, schematized XML store. It is accessed via XML message interfaces (XMIs), where service interfaces are exposed as standard SOAP messages. All authentication is based on Kerberos; the user owns their own data and controls which Web servers can access this data, and for what purpose. The new version of Windows XP will have support for HailStorm built into the operating system, thus making all server applications running on Windows XP, such as Exchange 2000, HailStorm compliant.

Making Money on the Internet

Nothing in life is free, as the old saying goes. However, most Internet Web servers are free, but it's sometimes very hard, even for experienced users, to find the correct information. HailStorm will change that; it will be easy to find information—the user will be notified about important events automatically, and this information will follow the user regardless of what smart device he or she uses. Did you think this would be free? Think again. Natu-rally, the driving force behind convincing third-party Web sites to participate in Microsoft's HailStorm project is money. The HailStorm user will pay a subscription fee to be a member, both to Microsoft and to the owner of the Web sites the user accesses. Exactly how much this fee will be is unknown today, but it must be modest if Microsoft wants large number of users to accept HailStorm.

Many have tried to make money out of the Internet, but most have failed. If Microsoft actually manages to make HailStorm a success, then it will probably change the way the Internet is used. Don't expect that Microsoft will be the only one to play this game; Oracle, HP, and Sun Microsystems all have the same idea. When listening to what the computer industry says about HailStorm, you'll hear many critical voices talking about the unfair advantage Microsoft will have in the emerging market for online services. Many users dislike the idea of paying money for something they can (almost) do for free today; however, for the average user, HailStorm might really make a difference in the way they use the Internet, although old Internet nerds like myself may have a hard time understanding why it's necessary. Let's face it, the Internet has changed—it will never be what it was 10 years ago; something has to be done to make it really user friendly. Maybe HailStorm is the solution, or perhaps some other similar product; only time will tell.

Again, the Internet God is walking the earth like an ordinary man when he meets Lisa, another member of the Simpson family:

Lisa:	Hi, Internet God! Great to see you!
Internet God:	Good day, dear Lisa. How are you today?
Lisa:	Great, thanks! My father told me he met you, and first I didn't believe him, but then he showed me the smart mobile phone you gave him.
Internet God:	Yes, it was only fair, since he gave me this divine idea of .NET. In fact, I have continued to develop this concept. I now have a new project I call HailStorm.
Lisa:	Is this a reminder of what will happen to all mortal souls if we don't join this project?
Internet God:	Well, I will answer that question another time. The HailStorm project aims to make the Internet so user friendly that even your father can use it.
Lisa:	Oh! That must be hard. Then you must get a lot of interesting Web sites to join this project?
Internet God:	Yes, that is correct.
Lisa:	I guess there is only one way of making them join: money!
Internet God:	You are clever, Lisa. That's right.
Lisa:	And this money must come from the users, right?

Internet God:	Right again!
Lisa:	Then you'd better make this system really good, or no one will pay for it.
Internet God:	Trust me, it will be a superb system: Your personal data will follow you on whatever device you have; I call them Divine Devices. If something happens on the Internet that's interesting to you, you'll be notified.
Lisa:	Sounds great! But change the name to Smart Devices instead; it sounds better.
Internet God:	Smart Devices? Okay, I agree, I will call them that. Got to go now. Bye, Lisa.
Lisa:	Goodbye, Internet God.

Summary

This is a list of the more important features and keywords mentioned in this chapter. Use it as a reminder and to make sure you have understood the most important things:

- The Internet is hard to use for the average user; every Web site is an isolated island, and each has its own set of rules and authentication procedures.
- The Internet is built for communication between a user and a Web server; it's not for communication between two applications.
- If you want to compare information from multiple servers, for example to compare the price of a car from different dealers, you must manually enter the values into a spreadsheet document.
- The user can't select what information to receive from a Web site; it will always be a complete Web document or nothing.
- Extensible Markup Language (XML) was released as a standard in October 2000; it's used to describe the content of a structured Web document.
- XML is a subset of Standard Generalized Markup Language (SGML), which is used to describe the content of any structured document. However, SGML is too complex for Web purposes; XML better suits the needs of the Internet.
- Hypertext Markup Language (HTML) is also used to describe Web documents; the difference between HTML and XML is that the former has a fixed set of tags, whereas the latter doesn't. XML allows the developer to set his or her own tags.
- The XML structure is described in an XML schema; such a schema is a treelike hierarchical structure that describes the tags and attributes.
- With XML, two heterogeneous applications can exchange data—for example, an inventory database and an accounting system; it could be two applications on the same computer, or on separate computers connected over the Internet.

- XML is a language, not a communication protocol.
- Simple Object Access Protocol (SOAP) is often used to send XML information between servers on the Internet.
- SOAP uses HTTP, which in turn uses TCP/IP for the actual transport on the network.
- .NET is Microsoft's strategy for XML enabling all its applications, from server applications to office applications. It was announced during the summer of 2000.
- With .NET, applications can send and receive XML-formatted documents to any other XML application, regardless of its programming language or operating system.
- The *.NET experience* is a phrase that Microsoft uses to describe the new and much richer user experience achieved with this new technology.
- Microsoft has released a new version of the programming language C called C# (pronounced C sharp); this version has support for .NET applications.
- Smart Tags is a new .NET feature that recognizes words as names, cities, flight numbers, and so on. If you click a recognized word, it will offer you a number of services; for example, you can check a flight number to see if there are any delays.
- Smart tags are implemented in Office XP; you must enable them using Tools|Options. You can download a number of new smart tags from the Internet.
- Security is built into the core of the .NET system. There are two aspects to security: authentication of users, and transport security. .NET only cares about authentication; you have to use IPSec or SSL to secure the transport.
- Exchange 2000 is .NET enabled. Its Web store can expose its data through XML.
- At least nine server products from Microsoft are .NET enabled.
- *XML Web service* is another new phrase from Microsoft; it means that a server can both expose its data through XML and allow external XML clients to utilize its services.
- Smart devices are Internet-connected devices that know who you are, where you are, and what you want. It adjusts data to its own capabilities and also in respect to the available bandwidth.
- Examples of Microsoft's upcoming smart devices include Stinger, Xbox, the next version of Pocket PC, and Tablet PC.
- HailStorm is Microsoft's first realization of .NET features. Its goal is to make the user experience easy, fun, and interesting, using smart devices and personal computers.
- A HailStorm client connects to a HailStorm server; authentication is done against a Microsoft Passport Server, using Kerberos.
- A HailStorm user can access all HailStorm-compliant Web sites without having to log on separately to each one.

- HailStorm lets the user take control over his or her personal data; no Web site will be able to utilize any parts of the user's information, such as email address or phone number, unless the user agrees to that.
- A HailStorm Endpoint is a smart device, a HailStorm-compliant Web site, or any HailStorm application.
- HailStorm users must pay a subscription fee to access some or all of its features.

Index

A

B

C

D

E

F

G

H

I

J

K

L

M

N

O

P

Q

R

S

T

U

X

Z

What's on the CD-ROM

The **Exchange 2000 Server On Site**'s companion CD-ROM contains elements specifically selected to enhance the usefulness of this book, including:

- *Exchange Central*—30-day Trial Version. The Danish software house Add-On Products has specialized in developing cutting edge collaboration tools for the Outlook platform. By creating calendars for resources and giving flexible and friendly screen set-ups, Add-On Products have devised some intuitive solutions, giving detailed access and overview to whoever needs it. Exchange Central is the calendar collaboration tool for enterprises of all sizes. Including front-end receptionist tools for seeing everyone and back-end planner/scheduling and statistic tools for teams, project groups and managers.
- *Archive of the Requests for Comment Referenced in this Book*—You can read the full background information articles sited in the text.
- *Sample Worksheets*—Ready to use for your real-world installation projects.

System Requirements

Software:

- Your operating system must be Windows 2000 or XP Professional.
- You must be running Exchange 2000 Server for Exchange Central.
- Excel 98/2000 is needed to view/edit the worksheets included on the CD-ROM. (The software is not provided on this CD-ROM.)
- An HTML-compatible Web browser is needed to view the Request for Comments included on the CD-ROM.

Hardware:

- An Intel (or equivalent) Pentium 100MHz processor is the minimum platform required; an Intel (or equivalent) Pentium 133MHz processor is recommended.
- 32MB of RAM is the minimum requirement. For example: 32MB of RAM is the minimum requirement.